INFORMING AND EDUCATING ANTI-FRAUD PROFESSIONALS WORLDWIDE

FRAUD EXAMINERS MANUAL

VOLUME II

2005 US EDITION

©1990-2005 by the Association of Certified Fraud Examiners, Inc.

The original purchaser of this volume is authorized to reproduce in any form or by any means up to 50 pages contained in this work for nonprofit, educational, or private use. Such reproduction requires no further permission from the Authors or Publisher and/or payment of any permission fee as long as proper credit is given.

Except as specified above, no portion of this work may be reproduced or transmitted in any form or by any means electronic or mechanical, including photocopying, recording, or by any information storage and retrieval system without the written permission of the Association.

ISBN 1-889277-11-8

Association of Certified Fraud Examiners

The Gregor Building
716 West Avenue
Austin, Texas 78701
(800) 245-3321
(512) 478-9000
www.cfenet.com

DISCLAIMER

Every effort has been made to ensure that the contents of this publication are accurate and free from error. However, it is possible that errors exist, both typographical and in content. Therefore, the information provided herein should be used only as a guide and not as the only source of reference.

The author, advisors, and publishers shall have neither liability nor responsibility to any person or entity with respect to any loss, damage, or injury caused or alleged to be caused directly or indirectly by any information contained in or omitted from this publication.

Printed in the United States of America

Section 2
Legal Elements of Fraud

LAW

TABLE OF CONTENTS

OVERVIEW OF THE UNITED STATES LEGAL SYSTEM
Constitutional, Statutory, and Common Law 2.101
Substantive and Procedural Law 2.102
The Court System 2.103
    Jurisdiction and Venue 2.104
    State and Federal Court Systems 2.104
        State Courts 2.104
        Federal Courts 2.105
Civil and Criminal Actions for Fraud 2.109

THE LAW RELATED FRAUD
Definition of Fraud 2.201
Principal Types of Fraud 2.201
    Misrepresentation of Material Facts 2.201
    Concealment of Material Facts 2.203
    Bribery 2.204
    Illegal Gratuity 2.205
    Commercial Bribery 2.205
    Extortion 2.206
    Conflict of Interest 2.206
    Theft of Money and Property 2.207
        Embezzlement 2.207
        Larceny 2.207
    Theft of Trade Secrets 2.208
        Remedies 2.209
    Breach of Fiduciary Duty 2.209
        Duty of Loyalty 2.209
        Duty of Care 2.210
Federal Legislation Related to Fraud 2.211
    The Sarbanes-Oxley Act (Public Law 107-204) 2.211
        Public Company Accounting Oversight Board 2.212
        Certification Obligations for CEOs and CFOs 2.214
        New Standards for Audit Committee Independence 2.217
        New Standards for Auditor Independence 2.218
        Enhanced Financial Disclosure Requirements 2.220
        Protections for Corporate Whistleblowers under Sarbanes-Oxley 2.221
        Enhanced Penalties for White-Collar Crime 2.223
    Mail Fraud and Wire Fraud 2.226
        Mail Fraud (18 U.S.C. § 1341) 2.226
        Wire Fraud (18 U.S. C. § 1343) 2.227

LAW

THE LAW RELATED FRAUD (CONT.)

"Honest Services" Fraud (18 U.S.C. § 1346) 2.227
Interstate Transportation of Stolen Property (18 U.S.C. § 2314) 2.229
Racketeer Influenced and Corrupt Organizations (RICO) 2.229
    18 U.S.C. § 1962. Prohibited Activities 2.230
    18 U.S.C. § 1963. Criminal Penalties 2.231
    18 U.S.C. § 1964. Civil Remedies 2.231
False Claims and Statements 2.232
    18 U.S.C. § 1001. Statements or Entries Generally 2.233
    18 U.S.C. § 1002. Possession of False Papers to Defraud United States 2.233
    18 U.S.C. § 1003. Demands Against the United States 2.234
    18 U.S.C. § 1005. Bank Entries, Reports and Transactions 2.234
    18 U.S.C. § 1014. Loan and Credit Applications Generally 2.235
    Crop Insurance 2.235
    Conspiracy (18 U.S.C. § 286) 2.236
    False, Fictitious, or Fraudulent Claims (18 U.S.C. § 287) 2.236
    Major Fraud Against the United States (18 U.S.C. § 1031) 2.236
    Civil False Claims Act (18 U.S.C. § 3729, et seq.) 2.237
    Program Fraud Civil Remedies (Public Law 99-509) 2.238
    Civil Monetary Penalty Law (42 U.S.C. § 1320a-7a) 2.238
Insurance Fraud Prevention Act (18 U.S.C. § 1033) 2.239
Federal Corruption Statutes (18 U.S.C. § 201, et seq.) 2.239
    Bribery of Public Officials and Witnesses (18 U.S.C. § 201) 2.239
    Anti-Kickback Act of 1986 (18 U.S.C. §§ 51-58) 2.243
    The Foreign Corrupt Practices Act 2.243
    Theft or Bribery Concerning Programs Receiving Federal Funds 2.246
Federal Securities Laws (The 1933 and 1934 Acts) 2.247
    Sarbanes-Oxley 2.248
Tax Evasion, False Returns, and Failure to File 2.249
Bankruptcy Fraud (18 U.S.C. § 151, et. seq.) 2.249
Statutes Relating to Financial Institutions 2.249
    18 U.S.C. § 1344. Bank Fraud 2.250
    18 U.S.C. § 1345. Injunctions Against Fraud 2.250
    Fraud by Bank Personnel and Receivers 2.251
    Financial Institutions Reform, Recovery and Enforcement Act 2.252
    Financial Institution Anti-Fraud Enforcement Act of 1990 .... 2.252
    Continuing Financial Crime Enterprise Statute (18 U.S.C. § 225) 2.252
    Participation in the Affairs of a Financial Institution
        by a Convicted Felon (12 U.S.C. § 1829) 2.252
    Fraudulent Use of Credit Cards (15 U.S.C. §§ 1644) 2.253
    The Electronic Funds Transfer Act (15 U.S.C. § 1693N(B)) 2.253
Laws Relating to Health Care Fraud 2.254

LAW

THE LAW RELATED FRAUD (CONT.)

Health Care Fraud (18 U.S.C. § 1347)	2.254
Theft or Embezzlement In Connection with Health Care (18 U.S.C. § 669)	2.255
False Statements Relating to Health Care Matters (18 U.S.C. § 1035)	2.255
Obstruction of Criminal Investigations of Health Care Offenses	2.255
Identity Theft	2.255
Fraud and Related Activity in Connection with Identification Documents and Information (18 U.S.C. § 1028)	2.256
The Anti-Phishing Act of 2004	2.257
Aggravated Identity Theft (Title 18, U.S. Code, § 1028A)	2.258
Telemarketing Fraud	2.258
Computers and Access Devices	2.259
Fraud and Related Activity in Connection with Access Devices	2.259
Fraud in Connection with Computers	2.259
Prosecuting Computer Related Frauds	2.265
Internet Crime	2.269
Identifying and Protecting Trade Secrets	2.270
The Uniform Trade Secrets Act	2.271
Economic Espionage Act of 1996 (18 U.S.C. §§ 1831-1839)	2.272
Economic Espionage (18 U.S.C. § 1831)	2.274
Theft of Trade Secrets (18 U.S.C. § 1832)	2.275
Exceptions to Prohibitions (18 U.S.C. § 1833)	2.276
Criminal Forfeiture (18 U.S.C. § 1834)	2.277
Orders to Preserve Confidentiality (18 U.S.C. § 1835)	2.277
Civil Proceedings to Enjoin Violations (18 U.S.C. § 1836)	2.277
Applicability to Conduct Outside the United States (18 U.S.C. § 1837)	2.277
Construction with Other Laws (18 U.S.C. § 1838)	2.278
Definitions (18 U.S.C. § 1839)	2.278
Money Laundering	2.278
Laundering of Monetary Instruments (18 U.S.C. § 1956)	2.279
Engaging in Monetary Transactions in Property Derived from Specified Unlawful Activity (18 U.S.C. § 1957)	2.280
Conspiracy and Aiding and Abetting	2.280
Conspiracy (18 U.S.C. § 371)	2.280
Aiding and Abetting (18 U.S.C. § 2)	2.281
Obstruction of Justice	2.281
Destruction, Alteration, or Falsification of Records in Federal Investigations and Bankruptcy (18 U.S.C. § 1519)	2.282
Destruction of Corporate Audit Records (18 U.S.C. § 1520)	2.282
Obstruction of Federal Audit (18 U.S.C. § 1516)	2.283
Obstructing Examination of Financial Institution (18 U.S.C. § 1517)	2.284
Perjury	2.284

LAW

THE LAW RELATED FRAUD (CONT.)

Fines Under Title 18	2.284
Sentence of Fine (18 U.S.C. § 3571)	2.284
Imposition of a Sentence of Fine and Related Matters (18 U.S.C. § 3572)	2.285
Qui Tam Suits and the False Claims Act	2.288
Filing an Action	2.288
Who Can Bring a Qui Tam Action	2.289
Protections for Whistleblowers	2.290
Federal "Whistleblower" Statutes	2.290
Civil Liability for Reports of Securities Fraud	2.290
Criminal Sanctions for Reports to Law Enforcement	2.291
Other Important Federal Whistleblower Laws	2.291
Civil Service Reform Act (5 U.S.C § 2302)	2.292
Fair Labor Standards Act (FLSA) (29 U.S.C. § 215-16)	2.292
Occupational Safety and Health Act (OSHA) (29 U.S.C. § 660(c))	2.292
Employee Retirement Income Security Act (ERISA), (29 U.S.C. § 1132, 1140)	2.292
Title VII, Equal Employment Opportunities (42 U.S.C. § 2000e-3)	2.292
Age Discrimination in Employment Act (ADEA) (29 U.S.C. § 623(d))	2.293
Civil Rights Claims (42 U.S.C. § 1983)	2.293
National Labor Relations Act (NLRA) (29 U.S.C. § 158)	2.293
Federal Whistleblower Statute for Employees of Defense Contractors	2.293
Federal Deposit Insurance Act; Financial Institution Reform, Recovery, and Enforcement Act of 1989 (12 U.S.C. § 1831j)	2.293
State Statutes	2.294

INDIVIDUAL RIGHTS DURING EXAMINATION

Employee's Duty to Cooperate	2.301
Employee's Rights During the Investigation	2.301
Contractual Rights	2.301
Whistleblowers	2.301
Employee's Constitutional Rights	2.302
Interviews	2.303
Employee's Right Against Self-Incrimination	2.303
Nature of the Right	2.303
Miranda Warnings	2.303
Public Employers	2.304
Presence of Corporate Attorney	2.304
Employee's Right to Counsel	2.304
Applicability	2.304
Employee's Right to Due Process	2.305
State Constitutions	2.305
Federal Statutes	2.305

LAW

INDIVIDUAL RIGHTS DURING EXAMINATION (CONT.)

National Labor Relations Act	2.305
Nondiscrimination Statutes	2.308
Fair Labor Standards	2.308
Common Law Protection in Connection with Interviews	2.308
Invasion of Privacy: Intrusion into Seclusion	2.308
Invasion of Privacy: Public Disclosure of Private Facts	2.308
Outrageous Conduct: Intentional Infliction of Emotional Distress	2.308
Defamation	2.308
Good Faith and Fair Dealing	2.309
Breach of Implied Contract	2.309
False Imprisonment	2.309
Searches and Surveillance	2.310
Employee's Right to Privacy	2.310
U.S. Constitution: Fourth Amendment	2.310
Reasonableness	2.311
Exceptions to the Fourth Amendment Warrant Requirement	2.312
Workplace Searches by Government Employers	2.312
Searches Incident to Arrest	2.315
Searches of Motor Vehicles	2.315
Consent Searches	2.316
Evidence in "Plain View"	2.316
Border, Customs, and Prison Searches	2.316
Surveillance	2.317
Monitoring Employee Phone Calls	2.317
Monitoring Employees' E-Mail and Voice Mail	2.320
Video Surveillance of Employees	2.321
Searching an Employee's Mail	2.321
Effect of Violation of Employee's Rights	2.321
Civil Liability for Damages (42 U.S.C. § 1983)	2.322
State Constitutions and Statutes	2.322
Surreptitious Recording	2.322
Federal and State Nondiscrimination Statutes	2.323
Common Law Protections in Connection with Searches and Surveillance	2.323
Invasion of Privacy: Intrusion into Seclusion	2.323
Invasion of Privacy: Public Disclosure of Private Facts	2.324
Outrageous Conduct: Intentional Infliction of Emotional Distress	2.324
Defamation	2.324
Good Faith and Fair Dealing	2.325
Breach of Implied Contract	2.325
False Imprisonment	2.325
Trespass	2.325
Polygraph Examinations	2.325

LAW

INDIVIDUAL RIGHTS DURING EXAMINATION (CONT.)

Employee Polygraph Protection Act	2.325
Reasonable Suspicion	2.326
Other Federal Statutes	2.326
State Statutes	2.326
Common Law Liability From Polygraph Exams	2.326
Outrageous Conduct	2.326
Invasion of Privacy	2.326
Wrongful Discharge	2.326
Obtaining Information About Employees	2.327
Federal Statutes	2.327
Privacy Act of 1974	2.327
Fair Credit Reporting Act	2.327
Gramm-Leach-Bliley Act	2.328
Health Insurance Portability and Accountability Act	2.329
Discharging a Suspected Wrongdoer	2.330
Good Cause	2.330
Negligent Discharge	2.331
Breach of Implied Contract	2.331
Breach of the Duty of Good Faith and Fair Dealing	2.331
Discharge in Violation of Public Policy	2.331

CRIMINAL PROSECTUTION FOR FRAUD

Basic Principles of Criminal Law	2.401
Fourth Amendment	2.401
Fifth Amendment	2.401
Sixth Amendment	2.401
Fourteenth Amendment	2.402
Arrest and Interrogation	2.402
Interrogation of Suspects	2.402
The Charging Process	2.404
The Grand Jury	2.404
Immunity	2.405
Indictment and Information	2.406
Arraignment	2.406
Prosecutorial Discretion and Plea Bargains	2.407
The Burden of Proof in Criminal Trials	2.408
Pre-trial Motions in Criminal Court	2.409
Motion to Dismiss	2.410
Discovery	2.411
Discovery Under Rule 16	2.411
The Jencks Act (18 U.S.C. § 3500)	2.413

LAW

CRIMINAL PROSECTUTION FOR FRAUD (CONT.)

Exculpatory Information (Brady Material)	2.413
Disclosures by the Defendant	2.413
The Trial Process	2.413
Jury Selection	2.414
Opening Statements	2.414
Presenting Evidence	2.414
Common Legal Issues in Fraud Cases	2.416
Legal Defenses	2.416
Closing Arguments	2.418
Jury Deliberations	2.419
Sentencing	2.419
Sentencing Guidelines	2.420
Sentencing of Organizations	2.420
Setting the Amount of the Fine	2.421
Effective Program to Detect and Prevent Violations of Law	2.422
Due Diligence	2.422
Appeal	2.423

THE CIVIL JUSTICE SYSTEM

Civil Litigation	2.501
Beginning the Civil Action	2.501
The Discovery Stage	2.502
Pre-Trial Motions in Civil Court	2.504
Counterclaims and Cross-Claims	2.506
Alternative Dispute Resolution	2.506
Mediation	2.506
Arbitration	2.507
Trial of a Civil Case	2.507
Fidelity Bond Claims	2.509

BASIC PRINCIPLES OF EVIDENCE

Definition of Evidence	2.601
Three Types of Evidence	2.601
Direct Versus Circumstantial Evidence	2.602
Relevance	2.603
Special Problems Concerning Some Types of Circumstantial Evidence	2.604
Character Evidence	2.604
Exception to the Character Rule	2.604
Opinion	2.605
Exceptions to the Opinion Rule	2.605
Exhibits	2.606

LAW

BASIC PRINCIPLES OF EVIDENCE (CONT.)

Laying the Foundation for Typical Exhibits	2.606
Diagrams	2.606
Correspondence	2.607
Business Records	2.607
Computer Records	2.608
Photographs	2.608
General Points	2.608
The "Best Evidence" Rule	2.609
Chain of Custody	2.609
Hearsay	2.610
Exceptions to the Hearsay Rule	2.610
The Truth of the Statement is Not at Issue	2.610
Admissions	2.611
Statement Against Interest	2.611
Business and Government Records	2.612
Absence of an Entry in Business Records	2.612
Recorded Recollections	2.612
Former Testimony	2.613
Present Sense Impressions	2.613
Then Existing Mental, Emotional, or Physical Condition	2.613
Statements to Medical Personnel	2.613
Printed Matter, Learned Treatises, Refresher Writings	2.614
Other Exceptions	2.614
Excluding Illegally Seized Evidence	2.614
Impeachment	2.615
Privileges	2.615
Attorney-Client Privilege	2.616
The Attorney Work Product Doctrine	2.617
Self Evaluation Privilege	2.618
Marital Privilege	2.619
Law Enforcement Privilege to Withhold the Identity of an Informant	2.619
Expert Witness Testimony	2.619
Disclosure Requirements under the Federal Rules of Civil Procedure	2.621

TESTIFYING AS AN EXPERT WITNESS

Introduction	2.701
Pre-Trial Preparation	2.703
Conflicts of Interest	2.703
Preparing a Report	2.704
Discoverability of Expert's Reports	2.705
The Consulting Expert Exception	2.706

LAW

TESTIFYING AS AN EXPERT WITNESS (CONT.)

Keeping Good Files	2.707
Qualifying as an Expert Witness	2.707
Qualifications	2.708
Testimony	2.709
Daubert Factors	2.709
Preparing to Testify	2.710
Appearance	2.711
Do's and Don'ts	2.711
Direct Examination	2.713
Cross-Examination	2.715
Myopic Vision	2.717
Safety	2.717
Contradiction	2.717
New Information	2.718
Support Opposing Side's Theory	2.718
Bias	2.718
Confrontation	2.718
Sounding Board	2.718
Fees	2.719
Terms of Engagement	2.719
Discrediting the Witness	2.719
Expressing an Opinion on Guilt	2.719
Summary	2.720

FEDERAL RULES OF CIVIL PROCEDURE

I. SCOPE OF RULES—ONE FORM OF ACTION	2.801
Rule 1. Scope and Purpose of Rules	2.801
Rule 2. One Form of Action	2.801
II. COMMENCEMENT OF ACTION; SERVICE OF PROCESS, PLEADINGS, MOTIONS AND ORDERS	2.801
Rule 3. Commencement of Action	2.801
Rule 4. Summons	2.801
Rule 4.1. Service of Other Process	2.805
Rule 5. Service and Filing of Pleadings and Other Papers	2.806
Rule 6. Time	2.807
III. PLEADINGS AND MOTIONS	2.808
Rule 7. Pleadings Allowed; Form of Motions	2.808
Rule 7.1. Disclosure Statement	2.808
Rule 8. General Rules of Pleading	2.808
Rule 9. Pleading Special Matters	2.809
Rule 10. Form of Pleadings	2.810

LAW

FEDERAL RULES OF CIVIL PROCEDURE (CONT.)

Rule 11. Signing of Pleadings, Motions, and Other Papers;
   Representations to Court; Sanctions 2.810
Rule 12. Defenses and Objections—When and How Presented—By Pleading or
   Motion—Motion for Judgment on the Pleadings 2.812
Rule 13. Counterclaim and Cross-Claim 2.814
Rule 14. Third-Party Practice 2.814
Rule 15. Amended and Supplemental Pleadings 2.815
Rule 16. Pre-trial Conferences; Scheduling; Management 2.816

IV. PARTIES 2.818
Rule 17. Parties Plaintiff and Defendant; Capacity 2.818
Rule 18. Joinder of Claims and Remedies 2.819
Rule 19. Joinder of Persons Needed for Just Adjudication 2.819
Rule 20. Permissive Joinder of Parties 2.820
Rule 21. Misjoinder and Non-Joinder of Parties 2.820
Rule 22. Interpleader 2.820
Rule 23. Class Actions 2.820
Rule 23.1. Derivative Actions by Shareholders 2.823
Rule 23.2. Actions Relating to Unincorporated Associations 2.824
Rule 24. Intervention 2.824
Rule 25. Substitution of Parties 2.825

V. DEPOSITIONS AND DISCOVERY 2.825
Rule 26. General Provisions Governing Discovery; Duty of Disclosure 2.825
Rule 27. Depositions Before Action or Pending Appeal 2.831
Rule 28. Persons Before Whom Depositions May Be Taken 2.832
Rule 29. Stipulations Regarding Discovery Procedure 2.833
Rule 30. Depositions Upon Oral Examination 2.833
Rule 31. Depositions Upon Written Questions 2.836
Rule 32. Use of Depositions in Court Proceedings 2.837
Rule 33. Interrogatories to Parties 2.840
Rule 34. Production of Documents and Things and Entry Upon Land
   for Inspection and Other Purposes 2.841
Rule 35. Physical and Mental Examinations of Persons 2.842
Rule 36. Requests for Admission 2.843
Rule 37. Failure to Make or Cooperate in Discovery: Sanctions 2.844

VI. TRIALS 2.846
Rule 38. Jury Trial of Right 2.846
Rule 39. Trial by Jury or by the Court 2.847
Rule 40. Assignment of Cases for Trial 2.847
Rule 41. Dismissal of Actions 2.847
Rule 42. Consolidation; Separate Trials 2.848
Rule 43. Taking of Testimony 2.848
Rule 44. Proof of Official Record 2.849

LAW

FEDERAL RULES OF CIVIL PROCEDURE (CONT.)

Rule 44.1. Determination of Foreign Law 2.849
Rule 45. Subpoena 2.849
Rule 46. Exceptions Unnecessary 2.852
Rule 47. Selection of Jurors 2.852
Rule 48. Number of Jurors—Participation in Verdict 2.852
Rule 49. Special Verdicts and Interrogatories 2.852
Rule 50. Judgment as a Matter of Law in Jury Trials; Alternative Motion
    for New Trial; Conditional Rulings 2.853
Rule 51(c). 2.854
Rule 52. Findings by the Court; Judgment on Partial Findings 2.855
Rule 53. Masters 2.855

VII. JUDGMENT 2.857

Rule 54. Judgments; Costs 2.857
Rule 55. Default 2.858
Rule 56. Summary Judgment 2.859
Rule 57. Declaratory Judgments 2.860
Rule 58. Entry of Judgment 2.860
Rule 59. New Trials; Amendment of Judgments 2.861
Rule 60. Relief From Judgment or Order 2.861
Rule 61. Harmless Error 2.862
Rule 62. Stay of Proceedings to Enforce a Judgment 2.862
Rule 63. Inability of a Judge to Proceed 2.863

VIII. PROVISIONAL AND FINAL REMEDIES 2.863

Rule 64. Seizure of Person or Property 2.863
Rule 65. Injunctions 2.864
Rule 65.1. Security: Proceedings Against Sureties 2.865
Rule 66. Receivers Appointed by Federal Courts 2.865
Rule 67. Deposit in Court 2.865
Rule 68. Offer of Judgment 2.866
Rule 69. Execution 2.866
Rule 70. Judgment for Specific Acts; Vesting Title 2.866
Rule 71. Process in Behalf of and Against Persons Not Parties 2.867

IX. SPECIAL PROCEEDINGS 2.867

Rule 71A. Condemnation of Property 2.867
Rule 72. Magistrate Judges; Pre-trial Orders 2.870
Rule 73. Magistrate Judges; Trial by Consent and Appeal Options 2.871
[Rules 74, 75, and 76 abrogated by Order of the Supreme Court, April 11, 1997] 2.871

X. DISTRICT COURTS AND CLERKS 2.871

Rule 77. District Courts and Clerks 2.871
Rule 78. Motion Day 2.872
Rule 79. Books and Records Kept by the Clerk and Entries Therein 2.872
Rule 80. Stenographer; Stenographic Report or Transcript as Evidence 2.873

LAW

FEDERAL RULES OF CIVIL PROCEDURE (CONT.)
XI. GENERAL PROVISIONS.. 2.873
    Rule 81. Applicability in General... 2.873
    Rule 82. Jurisdiction and Venue Unaffected 2.875
    Rule 83. Rules By District Courts; Judge's Directives... 2.875
    Rule 84. Forms 2.875
    Rule 85. Title 2.875
    Rule 86. Effective Date... 2.875

FEDERAL RULES OF CRIMINAL PROCEDURE
I. SCOPE, PURPOSE, AND CONSTRUCTION 2.901
    Rule 1. Scope.. 2.901
    Rule 2. Purpose and Construction 2.901
II. PRELIMINARY PROCEEDINGS... 2.901
    Rule 3. The Complaint... 2.901
    Rule 4. Arrest Warrant or Summons upon Complaint 2.901
    Rule 5. Initial Appearance 2.902
    Rule 5.1. Preliminary Hearing... 2.903
III. THE GRAND JURY, THE INDICTMENT AND THE INFORMATION 2.904
    Rule 6. The Grand Jury 2.904
    Rule 7. The Indictment and the Information 2.907
    Rule 8. Joinder of Offenses or Defendants 2.908
    Rule 9. Arrest Warrant or Summons Upon Indictment or Information................ 2.908
IV. ARRAIGNMENT AND PREPARATION FOR TRIAL.. 2.909
    Rule 10. Arraignment... 2.909
    Rule 11. Pleas 2.909
    Rule 12. Pleadings and Pre-trial Motions 2.911
    Rule 12.1. Notice of an Alibi Defense... 2.912
    Rule 12.2. Notice of an Insanity Defense; Mental Examination............................. 2.913
    Rule 12.3 Notice of a Public Authority Defense 2.914
    Rule 13. Joint Trial of Separate Cases... 2.915
    Rule 14. Relief from Prejudicial Joinder... 2.916
    Rule 15. Depositions 2.916
    Rule 16. Discovery and Inspection 2.917
    Rule 17. Subpoena 2.919
    Rule 17.1. Pre-trial Conference... 2.920
V. VENUE.. 2.920
    Rule 18. Place of Prosecution and Trial 2.920
    Rule 20. Transfer for Plea and Sentence 2.921
    Rule 21. Transfer for Trial... 2.921
    Rule 22. (Transferred) 2.922
VI. TRIAL.. 2.922

LAW

FEDERAL RULES OF CRIMINAL PROCEDURE (CONT.)

Rule 23. Jury or Non-Jury Trial	2.922
Rule 24. Trial Jurors	2.922
Rule 25. Judge's Disability	2.923
Rule 26. Taking Testimony	2.923
Rule 26.1. Foreign Law Determination	2.923
Rule 26.2. Producing a Witness's Statement	2.923
Rule 26.3. Mistrial	2.924
Rule 27. Proving an Official Record	2.924
Rule 28. Interpreters	2.924
Rule 29. Motion for Judgment of Acquittal	2.925
Rule 29.1. Closing Argument	2.925
Rule 30. Jury Instructions	2.925
Rule 31. Verdict	2.926

VII. POST-CONVICTION PROCEDURES ... 2.926

Rule 32. Sentence and Judgment	2.926
Rule 32.1. Revoking or Modifying Probation or Supervised Release	2.929
Rule 32.2. Criminal Forfeiture	2.931
Rule 33. New Trial	2.932
Rule 34. Arrest of Judgment	2.933
Rule 35. Correcting or Reducing a Sentence	2.933
Rule 36. Clerical Error	2.933
Rule 37. [Reserved]	2.934
Rule 38. Staying a Sentence or a Disability	2.934
Rule 39. [Reserved]	2.934

TITLE VIII. SUPPLEMENTARY AND SPECIAL PROCEEDINGS ... 2.935

Rule 40. Arrest for Failure to Appear in Another District	2.935
Rule 41. Search and Seizure	2.935
Rule 42. Criminal Contempt	2.937

IX. GENERAL PROVISIONS ... 2.938

Rule 43. Defendant's Presence	2.938
Rule 44. Right to and Appointment of Counsel	2.938
Rule 45. Computing and Extending Time	2.939
Rule 47. Motions and Supporting Affidavits	2.941
Rule 48. Dismissal	2.941
Rule 49. Serving and Filing of Papers	2.941
Rule 50. Prompt Disposition	2.942
Rule 51. Preserving Claimed Error	2.942
Rule 52. Harmless and Plain Error	2.942
Rule 53. Courtroom Photographing and Broadcasting Prohibited	2.942
Rule 54. [Transferred] (all of Rule 54 was moved to Rule 1)	2.942
Rule 55. Records	2.942
Rule 56. When Court Is Open	2.942

LAW

FEDERAL RULES OF CRIMINAL PROCEDURE (CONT.)
Rule 57. District Court Rules 2.943
Rule 58. Petty Offenses and Other Misdemeanors 2.943
Rule 60. Title 2.946

FEDERAL RULES OF EVIDENCE
ARTICLE I. GENERAL PROVISIONS 2.1001
    Rule 101. Scope 2.1001
    Rule 102. Purpose and Construction 2.1001
    Rule 103. Rulings on Evidence 2.1001
    Rule 104. Preliminary Questions 2.1001
    Rule 105. Limited Admissibility 2.1002
    Rule 106. Remainder of or Related Writings or Recorded Statements 2.1002
ARTICLE II. JUDICIAL NOTICE 2.1002
    Rule 201. Judicial Notice of Adjudicative Facts 2.1002
ARTICLE III. PRESUMPTIONS IN CIVIL ACTIONS AND PROCEEDINGS 2.1003
    Rule 301. Presumptions in General in Civil Actions and Proceedings 2.1003
    Rule 302. Applicability of State Law in Civil Actions and Proceedings 2.1003
ARTICLE IV. RELEVANCY AND ITS LIMITS 2.1003
    Rule 401. Definition of "Relevant Evidence" 2.1003
    Rule 402. Relevant Evidence Generally Admissible;
    Irrelevant Evidence Inadmissible 2.1003
    Rule 403. Exclusion of Relevant Evidence on Grounds of Prejudice,
    Confusion, or Waste of Time 2.1003
    Rule 404. Character Evidence not Admissible to Prove Conduct;
    Exceptions; Other Crimes 2.1003
    Rule 405. Methods of Proving Character 2.1004
    Rule 406. Habit; Routine Practice 2.1004
    Rule 407. Subsequent Remedial Measures 2.1004
    Rule 408. Compromise and Offers to Compromise 2.1004
    Rule 409. Payment of Medical and Similar Expenses 2.1005
    Rule 410. Inadmissibility of Pleas, Plea Discussions, and Related Statements 2.1005
    Rule 411. Liability Insurance 2.1005
    Rule 412. Sex Offense Cases; Relevance of Alleged Victim's Past
    Sexual Behavior or Alleged Sexual Predisposition 2.1005
    Rule 413. Evidence of Similar Crimes in Sexual Assault Cases 2.1006
    Rule 414. Evidence of Similar Crimes in Child Molestation Cases 2.1007
    Rule 415. Evidence of Similar Acts in Civil Cases Concerning Sexual
    Assault or Child Molestation 2.1007
ARTICLE V. PRIVILEGES 2.1008
    Rule 501. General Rule 2.1008
ARTICLE VI. WITNESSES 2.1008

LAW

FEDERAL RULES OF EVIDENCE (CONT.)

- Rule 601. General Rule of Competency 2.1008
- Rule 602. Lack of Personal Knowledge 2.1008
- Rule 603. Oath or Affirmation 2.1008
- Rule 604. Interpreters 2.1008
- Rule 605. Competency of Judge as Witness 2.1008
- Rule 606. Competency of Juror as Witness 2.1008
- Rule 607. Who May Impeach 2.1009
- Rule 608. Evidence of Character and Conduct of Witness 2.1009
- Rule 609. Impeachment by Evidence of Conviction of Crime 2.1009
- Rule 610. Religious Beliefs or Opinions 2.1010
- Rule 611. Mode and Order of Interrogation and Presentation 2.1010
- Rule 612. Writing Used to Refresh Memory 2.1010
- Rule 613. Prior Statements of Witnesses 2.1011
- Rule 614. Calling and Interrogation of Witnesses by Court 2.1011
- Rule 615. Exclusion of Witnesses 2.1011

ARTICLE VII. OPINIONS AND EXPERT TESTIMONY 2.1011
- Rule 701. Opinion Testimony by Lay Witnesses 2.1011
- Rule 702. Testimony by Experts 2.1012
- Rule 703. Bases of Opinion Testimony by Experts 2.1012
- Rule 704. Opinion on ultimate issue 2.1012
- Rule 705. Disclosure of Facts or Data Underlying Expert Opinion 2.1012
- Rule 706. Court Appointed Experts 2.1012

ARTICLE VIII. HEARSAY 2.1013
- Rule 801. Definitions 2.1013
- Rule 802. Hearsay Rule 2.1013
- Rule 803. Hearsay Exceptions; Availability of Declarant Immaterial 2.1014
- Rule 804. Hearsay Exceptions; Declarant Unavailable 2.1016
- Rule 805. Hearsay within Hearsay 2.1017
- Rule 806. Attacking and Supporting Credibility of Declarant 2.1017
- Rule 807. Residual Exception 2.1017

ARTICLE IX. AUTHENTICATION AND IDENTIFICATION 2.1018
- Rule 901. Requirement of Authentication or Identification 2.1018
- Rule 902. Self-Authentication 2.1018
- Rule 903. Subscribing Witness' Testimony Unnecessary 2.1020

ARTICLE X. CONTENTS OF WRITINGS, RECORDINGS, AND PHOTOGRAPHS 2.1020
- Rule 1001. Definitions 2.1020
- Rule 1002. Requirement of Original 2.1021
- Rule 1003. Admissibility of Duplicates 2.1021
- Rule 1004. Admissibility of other Evidence of Contents 2.1021
- Rule 1005. Public Records 2.1021
- Rule 1006. Summaries 2.1021

LAW

FEDERAL RULES OF EVIDENCE (CONT.)
    Rule 1007. Testimony or Written Admission of Party 2.1021
    Rule 1008. Functions of Court and Jury 2.1022
ARTICLE XI. MISCELLANEOUS RULES 2.1022
    Rule 1101. Applicability of Rules 2.1022
    Rule 1102. Amendments 2.1023
    Rule 1103. Title 2.1023

OVERVIEW OF THE UNITED STATES LEGAL SYSTEM

Constitutional, Statutory, and Common Law

The material below introduces the fraud examiner to the basic concepts of the law. Legal issues related to fraud often are complex and their interpretation might require the assistance of an experienced attorney. The Certified Fraud Examiner always should consult with counsel if legal questions arise during a fraud examination.

The U.S. Constitution and its accompanying amendments are the foundation of our legal system. The Constitution defines and limits the powers of the various branches of the government and guarantees basic rights to all citizens—rights such as equal protection under the law, due process, and the right to be free from unreasonable searches and seizures.

The Constitution is the supreme law of the land. The legislature may not properly pass, the executive branch enforce, nor the judiciary uphold, any law or action that violates its provisions.

Constitutional rights that are of particular importance to Certified Fraud Examiners include those found in the Fourth, Fifth and Sixth Amendments. The Fourth Amendment guarantees the right of all citizens to be free from unreasonable searches and seizures. This means that the government may not seize any records in a criminal case unless there exist reasonable grounds—"probable cause"—to believe that the records would constitute evidence of a crime, and that a suspect may not be arrested unless there is probable cause to believe that he committed an offense. The Fifth Amendment guarantees subjects of a criminal investigation the right to refuse to answer questions or to provide certain personal information that might be incriminating. The Sixth Amendment affords subjects in a criminal investigation the right to counsel, the right to confront (cross-examine) the witnesses against them and the right to a speedy trial.

The two sources of substantive law are *statutes* passed by the federal or state legislatures (and regulations passed by administrative bodies) and the *common law*. The common law consists of the usages and customs of a society as interpreted by the judiciary; it often is referred to as "judge-made" law. Criminal law is statutory, while civil actions can be based on either statutory or common law.

Criminal fraud statutes often contain provisions that do not have any obvious connection to basic principles of right and wrong. For example, a violation of the federal Mail Fraud statute can be charged only if the wrongdoers placed or received a letter in the U.S. mail, regardless of how serious the underlying fraud might be. Similarly, defendants are liable under the Racketeering Influenced and Corrupt Organizations (RICO) statute only if they engage "in a pattern of racketeering activity" through "an enterprise" that is engaged in interstate commerce, while violations of the federal Money Laundering statute occur only if the defendants have engaged in "specified unlawful activity" and have thereafter conducted a "prohibited financial transaction." Certified Fraud Examiners preparing criminal cases must be familiar with the specific technical elements of the applicable statutes, and must carefully review the evidence to make certain that all essential elements of proof are met.

Civil cases prosecuted under the common law usually contain fewer technical elements and incorporate traditional principles of fairness and morality. For example, a plaintiff may file a common law claim for fraud by alleging simply that the defendant misrepresented important facts upon which the plaintiff relied, resulting in loss to the plaintiff.

The common law is based not on statutes passed by the legislatures but upon "precedent" established by previously decided cases stretching back hundreds of years in U.S. and English courts. The decision in an individual case binds judges in later cases of a similar nature, until or unless the rule of law established is overturned by a higher court or the legislature. There are an increasing number of civil statutes in the fraud area, including the federal Civil RICO and Civil False Claims statutes.

Substantive and Procedural Law

The largest categorical dividing line is between substantive law and procedural law. *Substantive law* is comprised of the basic laws of rights and duties (contract law, tort law, criminal law, etc.) as opposed to *procedural law* which involves rules governing pleadings, evidence, jurisdiction, etc.

If someone says an act is "against the law," they mean substantive law. This includes statutes and ordinances at every level; common law, or case law, from all the various courts; and state and federal constitutions.

Procedural law sets out the rules of the legal system, the procedures to be followed in hearing a grievance—this means deadlines, filing requirements, steps to follow in bringing a claim, rules of evidence, and so on. Substantive law sets the terms of any dispute; procedural law dictates *how* a legal dispute is handled.

In federal courts, procedures are governed by the Federal Rules of Civil Procedure and the Federal Rules of Criminal Procedure. (A complete copy of the text of the Federal Rules of Civil Procedure, the Federal Rules of Criminal Procedure, and the Federal Rules of Evidence are included in the Appendix.)

There are special procedural laws governing appeals courts and evidence. *Federal Rules of Appellate Procedure* is collected in the *United States Code* (following title 28); individual courts of appeal may supplement the general rules with their own publications. These are listed under the name of the court (e.g., *Appeals to the Fifth Circuit Manual*).

The *Federal Rules of Evidence* cover what counts as evidence, the conditions of its admissibility in court, and the methods which authorities must use in acquiring and processing evidence. These rules are collected in the *United States Code* (appendix, title 28) and the *Federal Rules of Evidence Service*.

Each state (and some counties) publishes their own procedural rules. Most follow the general outline of the federal rules, but they can be vastly different, so don't be fooled. If you have a specific question about a procedural or evidentiary rule at the state or county level, consult a copy of the rules for the particular jurisdiction, or better yet your attorney.

The Court System

Civil and criminal cases will be filed in either state or federal court. The power to hear a case and render a judgment is strictly limited to a court's jurisdiction that is defined both by geographic boundaries and by the specific powers granted it by the legislature. This reflects the basic constitutional principle of separation of powers: the legislature, elected popularly, enacts the laws; the executive (*e.g.*, state or federal prosecutors) enforces them (with a great deal of discretion); and the judiciary interprets and applies them.

Jurisdiction and Venue

Courts are defined by their jurisdiction and venue. *Jurisdiction* refers to the court's function, the type of cases it is designed to hear. A probate court, for instance, only has jurisdiction to hear cases related to wills and other probate matters. Lower trial courts (such as a justice of the peace court) may only have jurisdiction to hear matters under a certain dollar amount, *e.g.*, cases with less than $5,000 in controversy.

Venue refers to the geographical area covered by the court. A trial court in Dallas County, Texas, for example, can only hear cases which have some connection with either parties or events that occurred in that county. Venue is technically an element of the court's jurisdiction. This issue may be important in deciding where to file charges or claims.

Determining the proper court requires a two-part test. (1) Does the court hear cases of the type in question? Claiming $500,000 in damages, the plaintiff needs a court that hears civil complaints of that magnitude. (2) Does the claim arise within the court's venue? If the claim for damages is against the Missouri office of a company headquartered in Nebraska, determining the proper venue is essential. If you file the claim in North Dakota, the court will have no jurisdiction to hear the case.

State and Federal Court Systems

The U.S. justice system uses separate but interlocking organizations of courts. State courts can decide nearly every type of case, limited only by the U.S. Constitution, their own state constitutions, and state law. Citizens will have most of their legal dealings with the state and local courts situated throughout the country. Most fraud cases will be tried at this level. Probate cases, marital disputes, and real estate suits are heard by state courts.

Federal courts are principally located in larger cities, and hold limited jurisdictions. They hear only those cases over which the Constitution or federal law gives them authority. Generally speaking, this means those cases involving parties from different states or cases involving federal law.

State Courts

Most states use a three- or four-tier system.
- *Lower courts* try misdemeanors and preliminaries for felony cases, and civil disputes below a certain dollar amount (*e.g.*, $10,000 or less).

- *Higher-level trial courts* (sometimes called *Superior* courts) try felony cases, and civil disputes above a certain amount (*e.g.*, $10,000 or more).
- *Appellate courts* review trial court decisions.
- Superior appellate courts, or Supreme courts, review lower appellate court decisions.

Many states have different systems—at the trial court and appellate court levels—for trying civil and criminal cases. Local and state criminal courts might have limited jurisdiction; for example, some courts only handle traffic violations and minor offenses. Some jurisdictions include a small-claims civil court to hear cases involving no more than $2,000 to $3,000.

Federal Courts

The federal system uses a three-tier model.
- *U.S. District Courts* conduct trials on criminal charges and civil complaints under federal law.
- *Courts of Appeal*, including the *Court of Military Appeals*, reviews trial court decisions.
- *The U.S. Supreme Court* reviews lower court decisions. It is sometimes called the court of last resort.

Each federal district has a chief prosecutor, a political appointee, known as the *United States Attorney*, and a staff of prosecutors, known as *Assistant United States Attorneys*. Almost all cases are prosecuted by assistants. Criminal cases at the state and local level are prosecuted by the District Attorney's office or the Attorney General's office.

The federal system also includes specialized courts. These are:
- *Bankruptcy Court*—handles matters involving the U.S. Bankruptcy Code
- *Tax Court*—deals with tax law violations
- *Court of Federal Claims*—jurisdiction over complaints filed against the federal government and its agencies
- *Court of Veterans Appeals*—hears veterans' benefits cases
- *Court of International Trade*—covers business cases of international jurisdiction

FEDERAL COURT SYSTEM

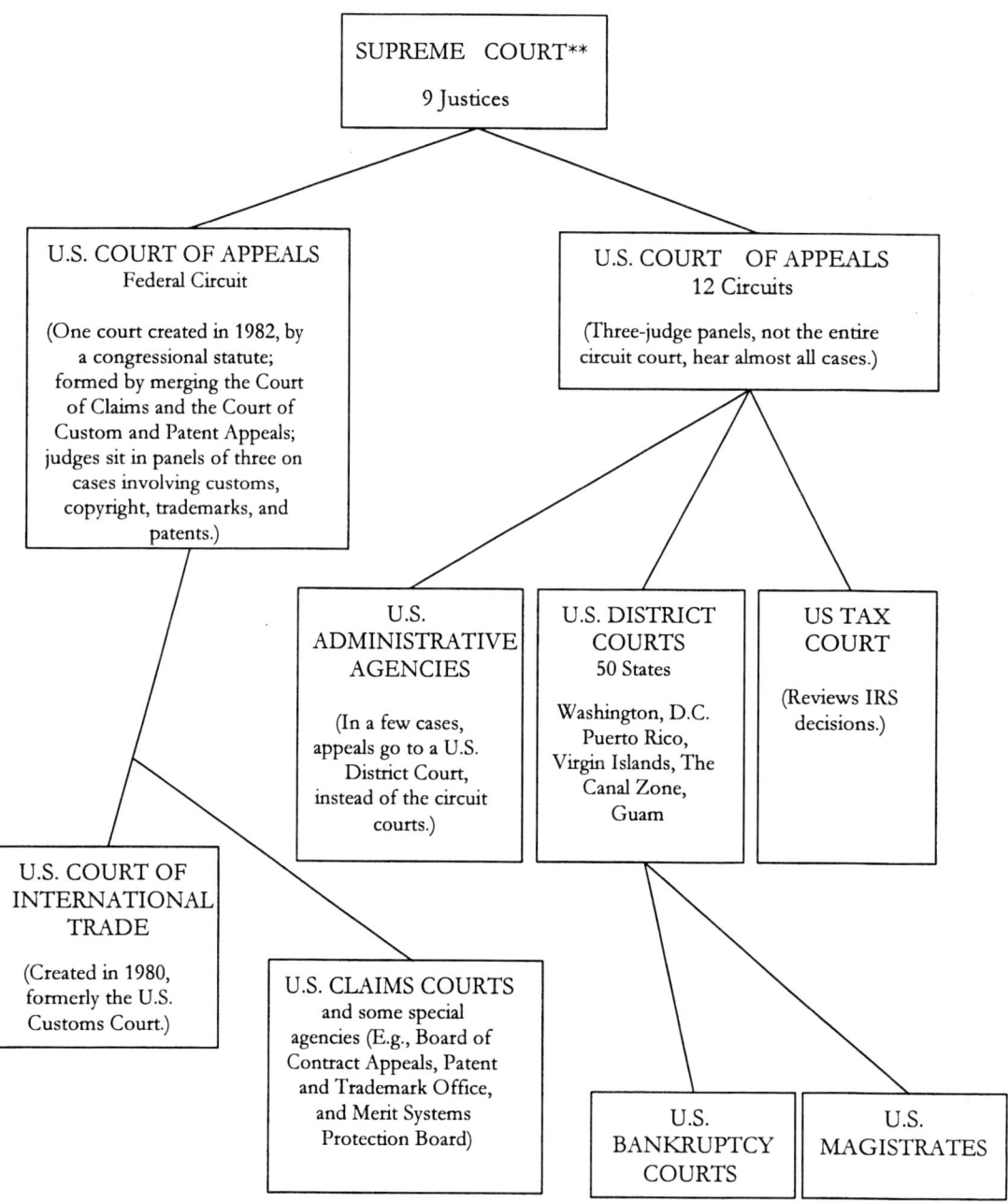

*Although federal administration agencies are not part of the federal judiciary, they are included here because appeals from their decisions go to the federal courts.
**Appeals from the highest state court also may be heard by the U.S. Supreme Court.

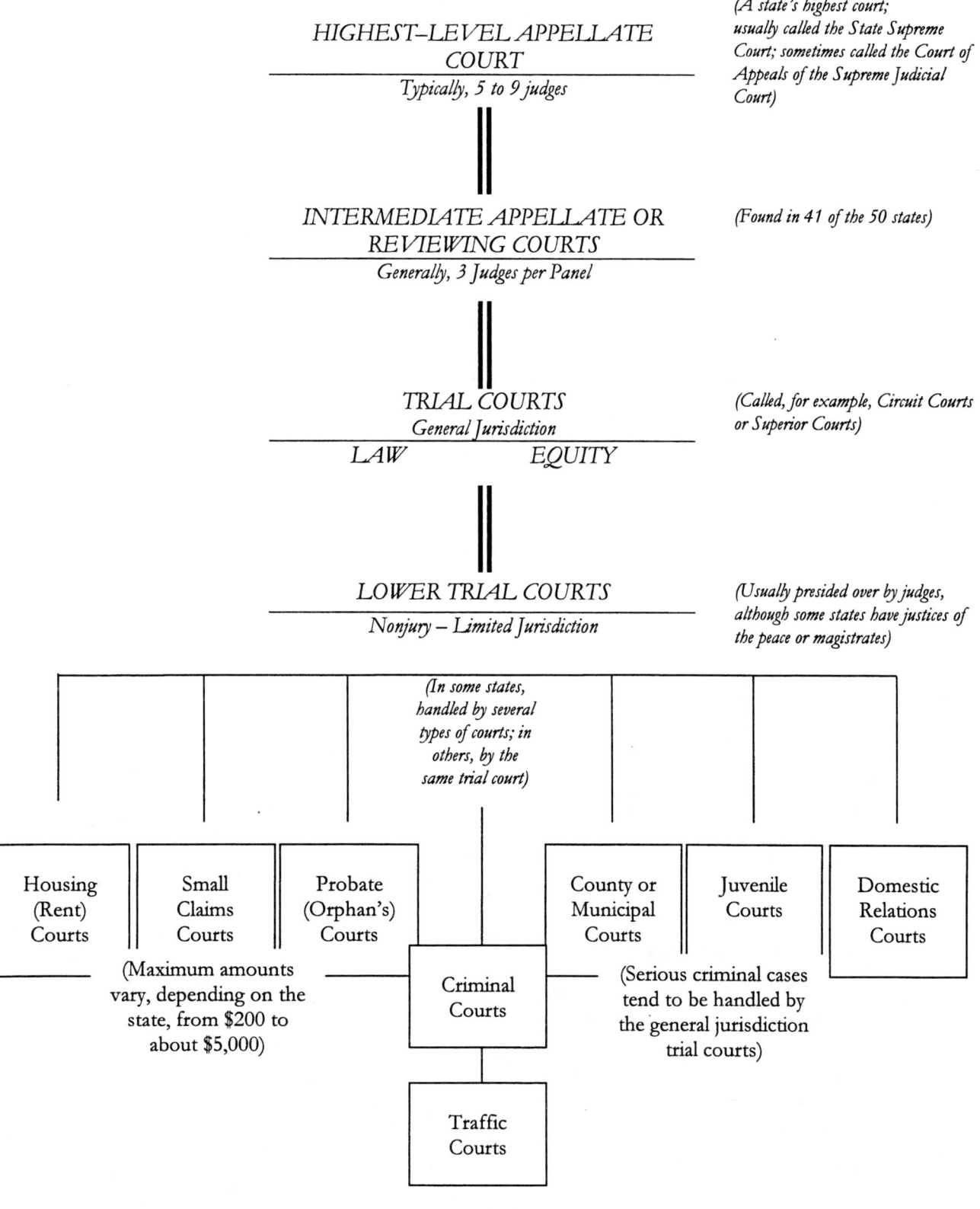

In the trial court, the jury finds the facts. The judge applies the law, rules on evidence, and generally moderates the proceeding to ensure a fair trial. If a jury is waived by the defendant and government, the judge decides both the facts and the law. In a criminal case, the prosecution must prove its case beyond a reasonable doubt; in a civil case, the burden of proof usually is a preponderance of the evidence, a lower standard.

Appeals involve questions of law, or questions involving both law and fact. Most questions of law are decided by *precedent*, that is, prior court decisions of equal or higher authority that have considered similar cases. Obviously, however, disputes exist over what precedent should prevail, with both sides attempting to persuade the court to interpret existing law in a manner favorable to its client.

Because of the Fifth Amendment's double jeopardy provisions, only a convicted defendant in a criminal case can appeal a verdict. The government cannot appeal an acquittal on the merits. If a statute authorizes the prosecution to appeal, such an appeal is constitutional only if the appellate court can decide the appeal without subjecting the defendant to a second trial. The prosecution may, however, appeal adverse pre-trial rulings on the admissibility of evidence and certain other matters that can terminate a prosecution temporarily (but do not result in a decision on the merits in favor of the defendant). Either party in a civil case may appeal a judgment.

An appellate court will not reverse a conviction unless it finds error that affected the "substantial rights" of a party; "harmless error," supposedly not affecting the jury's decision, is tolerated. Defendants are said to be entitled to a fair trial—not a perfect one. If the appellate court reverses, it usually will order a new trial, but also may direct dismissal of the case.

Appeals from decisions of the U.S. District Courts are heard in the *U.S. Court of Appeals* for the "Circuit" which covers a particular geographic area. The United States is divided into 11 judicial circuits, plus the District of Columbia. The U.S. Supreme Court is the highest appellate court in the federal system, and also may hear certain appeals from state courts, particularly on constitutional grounds.

In the federal system, an appeal to the U.S. Supreme Court is accomplished by applying for a *Writ of Certiorari*. Relatively few appeals—"writs"—are granted. The Supreme Court usually hears only those cases that present an important question of constitutional law, or that may be used to resolve a "split" or disagreement on a point of law among the circuits, or that have considerable significance to the judicial system, beyond the interest of the litigants. If the Supreme Court "denies Cert.," the lower court decision stands and the appeal process ends, unless the defendant can find some collateral ground, such as alleged constitutional errors in state court proceedings, to attack the judgment. As death penalty challenges illustrate, appeals on such points, often brought by people in custody under "Habeas Corpus" proceedings, can, in extreme cases, consume a decade or more.

The various state and federal courts operate in separate spheres, confined by their own jurisdictional limitations. State courts are "inferior" to federal courts only in the sense that they are subject to Constitutional and "federal question" limitations. Without these factors, a federal court will not interfere in state court proceedings. A single act might violate both state and federal law, and actions may be brought in separate courts for both violations without violating the double jeopardy protection, although one jurisdiction usually will abstain if the other has already prosecuted.

Civil and Criminal Actions for Fraud

Fraud may be prosecuted criminally or civilly, or both, in sequence or simultaneously. There are a number of differences between criminal and civil actions with which the Certified Fraud Examiner should be familiar. The following is a brief description of some of the differences between civil and criminal actions. More information about each action is contained in the chapters on Criminal Prosecutions and the Civil Justice System.

Criminal actions for fraud are brought by the government acting through the prosecutor's office. The prosecutor has almost unbridled discretion in such matters as to whether or not to bring a criminal case, what charges to file, who to charge and who not to charge, and whether to try the case or to negotiate a plea bargain. Civil actions may be brought by private individuals or organizations, usually without the involvement or permission of the government or court.

Criminal cases are investigated by law enforcement agencies, at times with the assistance of the prosecutor's office and the grand jury. The *grand jury* is an investigative body that is empowered to issue subpoenas for testimony and documents to determine whether a violation of the law has occurred. Law enforcement agencies and the prosecution therefore can subpoena evidence before charges are filed to determine whether an offense has occurred. In civil actions for fraud brought by private parties, however, there generally is no opportunity to compel the production of testimony or other evidence until a complaint is filed.

Criminal investigations and prosecutions for fraud are subject to constitutional limitations, such as those in the Fourth, Fifth and Sixth Amendments, and other procedural rules to protect the rights of the defendant, including the requirement to give *Miranda* warnings. In general, these requirements have limited applicability to civil actions. Violations of constitutional rights in a criminal case can result in the "suppression" or exclusion of any evidence or statement obtained by such means, or in some instances, in dismissal of the indictment.

The burden of proof in a criminal case is always *beyond a reasonable doubt*. In civil cases the burden of proof is lower, usually a *preponderance of the evidence*. Criminal cases are punished by outcomes such as imprisonment, fine, order of restitution, probation, and community service. Civil cases, if successful, result in an award of damages or in some instances the entry of an order or injunction that compels the losing party to take remedial action or to avoid future illegal acts.

Criminal and civil actions for fraud may proceed simultaneously even though such "parallel proceedings" present a dilemma for the defendant. For example, a defendant lawfully may assert his Fifth Amendment right against self-incrimination to avoid answering questions or producing certain documents in the criminal investigation. But he may not do so in the corresponding civil case without suffering the possibility of sanctions that can include the dismissal of affirmative defenses or the striking of testimony. For example, if a defendant takes the stand in a civil case and testifies on his own behalf, he cannot later invoke the Fifth Amendment and refuse to answer questions concerning the same subject matter on cross-examination. If he does, the judge may order that his testimony on direct examination be stricken from the record.

Generally, courts have not been sympathetic to the defendant's dilemma, and have allowed civil discovery to proceed even though criminal charges are pending. In some instances, the court or the parties by agreement may seal the civil record. In rare cases the court may order that the civil case be stayed pending resolution of the criminal case. Normally, however, the court will allow the cases to proceed simultaneously despite the substantial prejudice to the defendant. In parallel civil and criminal cases in which the government is a party, the criminal process, including the use of grand jury subpoenas, may not be used to obtain evidence solely for a civil case.

Criminal and civil actions for fraud may be brought in federal or state court. Federal courts have jurisdiction over federal criminal or civil statutes and certain common law claims that usually involve parties who are residents of different states and controversies where $75,000 or more is at issue. State courts have jurisdiction over state statutes and most common law civil claims.

THE LAW RELATED TO FRAUD

Definition of Fraud

Black's Law Dictionary defines fraud as:

... all multifarious means which human ingenuity can devise, and which are resorted to by one individual to get an advantage over another by false suggestions or suppression of the truth. It includes all surprise, trick, cunning or dissembling, and any unfair way by which another is cheated.

Put more succinctly, fraud includes any intentional or deliberate act to deprive another of property or money by guile, deception or other unfair means.

The principal categories of fraud (or *white-collar crime*) are:
- Misrepresentation of material facts
- Concealment of material facts
- Bribery
- Conflicts of interest
- Theft of money or property
- Theft of trade secrets or intellectual property
- Breach of fiduciary duty
- Statutory offenses

Principal Types of Fraud

Misrepresentation of Material Facts

This is the offense most often thought of when the term fraud is used. Misrepresentation cases can be prosecuted criminally or civilly under a variety of statutes, such as false statements, false claims, mail and wire fraud, or they might be the basis for common law claims. The gist of the offense is the deliberate making of false statements to induce the intended victim to part with money or property.

The specific elements of proof of misrepresentation vary somewhat according to the jurisdiction, and whether the case is prosecuted as a criminal or civil action. The elements normally include:

- A material false statement
- Knowledge of its falsity
- Reliance on the false statement by the victim
- Damages suffered.

In a civil case, it also might be necessary to prove that the victim relied upon the false statements and actually suffered a loss. These elements of proof might not be necessary in a criminal prosecution. Also, in some statutes, materiality is assumed and need not be proved.

In most instances, only false representations of "presently existing facts" may be prosecuted. Opinions, speculative statements about future events, even if made with the intent to mislead, may not be the basis for a fraud case. A used car salesman, for example, who assures the naive customer that the 20-year-old car that was towed to the lot will give him "years of driving pleasure," probably cannot be prosecuted for fraud. If the other elements are present, the salesman could be prosecuted, however, if he tells the customer that the car has been driven only 15,000 miles when he knows that it has gone 150,000 miles.

The rule limiting fraud cases to misrepresentations of existing facts often is applied to bar fraud claims in contract disputes. A party to a contract who promises to perform certain services by a particular date in the future but who fails to do so generally may not be prosecuted for fraud unless the plaintiff can demonstrate that the defendant had the intent not to perform the promised services when the contract was made. Of course, the other party may file an action for breach of contract.

The rule precluding fraud actions based on false "opinions" is subject to certain exceptions, principally cases involving opinions provided by professional advisers, such as Certified Public Accountants.

For example, an independent auditor may be liable for misrepresentation if he:
- Certifies that a financial statement fairly presents the financial condition of the company when the auditor knows it does not,
- Falsely states that the audit was conducted in accordance with generally accepted auditing standards, or
- Deliberately distorts the audit results.

Normally, only material false statements may serve as the basis for a fraud case. Materiality usually refers to statements sufficiently important or relevant to the defendant to influence the defendant's decision. For example, a claim that a company enjoyed a 50 percent growth in profits would probably be material to a prospective investor, whereas a statement that the company was considering moving its headquarters from New York City to Chicago might not be. The materiality of allegedly false statements often is a central issue in security fraud cases.

In all fraud cases, the prosecution or plaintiff must prove that a false statement was intentional and part of a deliberate scheme to defraud. Under the law, there is no such thing as an accidental or negligent fraud. In some instances, particularly those involving civil actions for fraud and securities cases, the intent requirement is met if the prosecution or plaintiff is able to show that the false statements were made *recklessly*; that is, with complete disregard for truth or falsity.

Although a misrepresentation fraud case may not be based on negligent or accidental misrepresentations, in some instances a civil action may be filed for negligent misrepresentation. This action is appropriate if a defendant suffered a loss as a result of the carelessness or negligence of another party upon which the defendant was entitled to rely. Examples would be negligent false statements to a prospective purchaser regarding the value of a closely held company's stock or the accuracy of its financial statements.

Concealment of Material Facts

An action for fraud may be based on the concealment of material facts, but only if the defendant had a duty in the circumstances to disclose. The essential elements of fraud based on failure to disclose material facts are:

- That the defendant had knowledge
- Of a material fact
- That the defendant had a duty to disclose
- And failed to do so
- With the intent to mislead or deceive the other party.

The duty to disclose usually depends on the relationship between the parties. Those people who occupy a special relationship of trust, such as the officers or directors of a corporation, an attorney, accountant, trustee, stockbroker or other agent, may be found to have a duty to fully and completely disclose material facts to the parties who rely upon them. Statutes might expand the duty to disclose to areas in which traditionally there was no such duty, such as to the sellers of personal or real property, or the purchasers or sellers of securities.

Proof that the concealed fact was material probably is the most important element in a concealment case; there can be no liability if the withheld information would not have affected the other party. In addition to fraudulent concealment, a defendant might also be liable for negligent failure to discover and disclose material facts. An accountant, for example, might be liable for failure to discover or report material facts in a financial statement or audit. Of course, as with negligent misrepresentation, the penalties are less severe for negligence than fraudulent misrepresentation, and there is no criminal liability.

Bribery

Bribery includes official bribery, which refers to the corruption of a public official, and commercial bribery, which refers to the corruption of a private individual to gain a commercial or business advantage. The elements of official bribery vary by jurisdiction, but generally are:

- Giving or receiving
- A thing of value
- To influence
- An official act

The *thing of value* is not limited to cash or money. Courts have held that such things as lavish gifts and entertainment, payment of travel and lodging expenses, payment of credit card bills, "loans," promises of future employment, and interests in businesses, can be bribes if they were given or received with the intent to influence or be influenced. Some state statutes might distinguish between felonies or misdemeanors according to the amount of illegal payment.

Proof of corrupt influence often involves demonstration that the person receiving the bribe favored the bribe-payer in some improper or unusual way, such as by providing preferential treatment, bending or breaking the rules, taking extraordinary steps to assist the bribe-payer, or allowing the bribe-payer to defraud the agency or company. It is not necessary, however, that the prosecution or plaintiff demonstrate that the bribe-taker acted improperly; a bribe might be paid to induce an official to perform an act that otherwise would be legal, or an act that the official might have performed without a bribe. Bribery schemes involving these circumstances, however, are difficult to prove and lack appeal for prosecution.

Illegal Gratuity

An is a lesser included offense of official bribery. The elements of an illegal gratuity are:
- Giving or receiving
- A thing of value
- For or because of
- An official act.

An illegal gratuity charge does not require proof of intent to influence. The statute prohibits a public official from accepting any payment of money or other thing of value other than his lawful compensation. In practice, the statute often is applied when relatively small payments, such as gifts or entertainment, are used to attempt to influence a public official.

Commercial Bribery

Commercial bribery may be prosecuted either as a criminal act or by a civil action. About half of the states in the U.S. have criminal statutes that prohibit commercial bribery. If a state does not have a commercial bribery statute, such schemes usually can be prosecuted under criminal fraud statutes on the theory that the payment of a commercial bribe defrauds the business owner of the right to an employee's unbiased and loyal services.

There is no federal statute prohibiting commercial bribery. However, such offenses may be prosecuted at the federal level as mail or wire fraud, or RICO or other violations. The elements of commercial bribery vary by jurisdiction, but typically include:
- Giving or receiving
- A thing of value
- To influence
- A business decision
- Without the knowledge or consent of the principal

The fifth element is included on the theory that a private business owner is not defrauded if the owner knows of or allows employees to accept gifts, favors or other payments from vendors or other business contacts.

Most state commercial bribery statutes are misdemeanors punishable by a jail term of not more than one year. Commercial bribery is a felony in Colorado, Kansas, Texas, Arizona (if the value of the bribe payment is $100 or more) and New Hampshire (if the value of the bribe is $500 or more). The New York commercial bribery law is a typical statute that makes it a misdemeanor to give or receive (or to offer or solicit) "any benefit" without the consent of the employer, with the intent of influencing the employee's business conduct. The Louisiana, Michigan, and New Jersey commercial bribery statutes confer immunity on the party to the scheme who first agrees to testify against the other party in a criminal proceeding.

Businesses injured by commercial bribery schemes may sue for treble damages and attorneys' fees under the Civil RICO statute (Title 18, U.S. Code, Section 1964) and the Clayton Act (Title 15, U.S. Code, Section 13(c)), and for compensatory and punitive damages for common law fraud, conflict of interest, and breach of fiduciary duty. Civil actions may be brought even if commercial bribery is not a crime in a jurisdiction.

Extortion

An extortion case is often the flip side of a bribery case. *Extortion* is defined as the obtaining of property from another with the other party's "consent" having been induced by wrongful use of actual or threatened force or fear. Fear might include the apprehension of possible economic damage or loss. A demand for a bribe or kickback also might constitute extortion.

In most states and the federal system, extortion is not a defense to bribery. That is, a person who makes a bribe payment upon demand of the recipient still is culpable for bribery. In New York, however, extortion may be a defense in certain circumstances.

Conflict of Interest

Statutes in every state and the federal system (as well as common law decisions in all jurisdictions) prohibit people from engaging in conduct which involves a *conflict of interest*. A conflict of interest may be prosecuted civilly or criminally. The criminal statutes vary widely and include prohibitions on public officers from accepting employment with government contractors or lobbying government agencies during specified time periods.

Elements of a typical civil claim for conflict of interest include:
- An agent taking an interest in a transaction
- That is actually or potentially adverse to the principal
- Without full and timely disclosure to and approval by the principal.

An agent includes any person who, under the law, owes a duty of loyalty to another, including officers, directors, and employees of a corporation, public officials, trustees, brokers, independent contractors, attorneys, and accountants. People who do not occupy positions of trust with another party, such as arms-length commercial parties, do not owe a duty of loyalty to each other and therefore are not subject to conflict of interest restrictions.

The defendant in a civil conflict of interest case must repay any losses that the conflict caused and must "disgorge" any profits he earned as a result of the conflict even if there was no actual loss to the principal. The "disloyal" party also might be required to forfeit all compensation received during the period of disloyalty. The victim of a conflict of interest also may void any contracts entered into on its behalf that were the result of or influenced by the conflict.

Theft of Money and Property

Theft is a term often used to describe a wide variety of fraudulent conduct. Many state statutes describe misrepresentation fraud as *theft by deception* or *larceny by trick*. As used here, the term theft is limited to embezzlement, larceny, and misappropriation of trade secrets and proprietary information.

Embezzlement

Embezzlement is the fraudulent appropriation of money or property by a person to whom it has been lawfully entrusted (or to whom lawful possession was given). Embezzlement involves a breach of trust, although it is not necessary to show a fiduciary relationship between the parties. The elements of embezzlement are generally:
- The defendant took or converted
- Without the knowledge or consent of the owner
- Money or property of another
- That was entrusted to the defendant (defendant had lawful possession of the property)

Larceny

Larceny is defined as the unlawful taking of money or property of another with the intent to convert or to deprive the owner. In larceny, unlike embezzlement, the defendant never has lawful possession of the property but may have mere custody of it (e.g., a cashier has custody, not possession, of money in a register). The elements of larceny typically include:
- Unlawful taking or carrying away
- Money or property of another
- Without the consent of the owner
- With the intent to permanently deprive the owner of its use or possession.

Theft of Trade Secrets

Theft or misappropriation of trade secrets may be prosecuted under a variety of federal and state statutes and the common law. *Trade secret* includes not only secret formulas and processes, but more mundane proprietary information, such as customer and price lists, sales figures, business plans, or any other confidential information that has a value to the business and would be potentially harmful if disclosed.

The elements of a typical theft of trade secret claim are:
- That a party possessed information of value to the business
- That was treated confidentially
- That the defendant took or used by breach of an agreement, confidential relationship, or other improper means.

It is critical that the information being sought to be protected was treated confidentially, although absolute secrecy is not required; it is sufficient if the information was "substantially" undisclosed. Limited disclosure to people with a need to know or pursuant to confidentiality agreements will not void the secret. Methods of demonstrating that information was intended to be kept confidential include a written policy describing the information as proprietary or secret; strict limitations on distribution of the information; and physically securing the information to prevent unauthorized access and use.

The owners of the information also should enforce restrictive agreements and act promptly to remedy any inadvertent disclosures. Failure to do so might be construed as a waiver of confidentiality and make it impossible to prevent future use or disclosures.

The most typical defense is that the information was developed independently. If the aggrieved party demonstrates that the information came to the defendant as the result of or during a confidential relationship, the burden of proof shifts to the defendant to demonstrate independent discovery. The defendant also might defend a misappropriation claim by showing that the information was not in fact a secret, that the third party's use was authorized, or that the trade secret or proprietary information had been abandoned by the owner.

Remedies

CIVIL ACTION

An aggrieved party may file a civil action for damages or request an injunction under a variety of federal and state statutes. Civil damages include reimbursement for actual losses caused by the defendant such as lost profits, reimbursement of development expenses and overhead costs, and the cost of efforts to protect the secret or recover damages, as well as for reduction in the value of business. Damages also can be measured by the defendant's profits, which may be ordered paid to the plaintiff. Punitive damages and attorney's fees also may be awarded.

INJUNCTIONS

In addition to or in lieu of money damages, the plaintiff in a civil action for theft of trade secrets also may obtain an injunction prohibiting further use of the information. To obtain an injunction, the plaintiff must demonstrate that:

- It is the proper owner of the trade secret
- An unauthorized person has taken or used the trade secret
- There is a high probability of improper disclosure
- The plaintiff will suffer irreparable injury (meaning that the plaintiff could not be adequately compensated by money damages), and
- The plaintiff probably will win the case.

Injunctions are difficult to obtain, however. Injunctions have been issued in numerous trade secret cases to prevent the use of stolen information, to prohibit an employee in possession of a trade secret from accepting employment with a competitor, or to order the wrongdoer to return the misappropriated information. The injunction usually prohibits use of the trade secret only for that period it would have been required for its legitimate independent development.

Breach of Fiduciary Duty

People in a position of trust or *fiduciary relationship*, such as officers, directors, high-level employees of a corporation or business, agents and brokers, owe certain duties imposed by law to their principals or employers. The principal fiduciary duties are loyalty and care.

Duty of Loyalty

The *duty of loyalty* requires that the employee/agent act solely in the best interest of the employer/principal, free of any self-dealing, conflicts of interest, or other abuse of the principal for personal advantage. Thus, corporate directors, officers, and employees are barred from using corporate property or assets for their personal pursuits, or taking corporate opportunities for themselves. More traditional fraudulent conduct, such as embezzlements, thefts, acceptance of kickbacks, and conflicts of interest also violate the duty of loyalty, and may be prosecuted as such in addition to or instead of the underlying offense.

A breach of duty of loyalty is easier to prove than fraud. The plaintiff does not need to prove criminal or fraudulent intent or the other elements of fraud. To prevail, the plaintiff must show only that the defendant occupied a position of trust or fiduciary relationship as described above and that the defendant breached that duty to benefit personally.

A *breach of fiduciary duty* claim is a civil action. The plaintiff may receive damages for lost profits and recover profits that the disloyal employee earned—in some instances, even the salary paid to the employee or agent during the period of disloyalty. The plaintiff may recover profits earned by the disloyal agent even if the principal did not suffer an actual loss. The plaintiff also may void any contracts entered into on its behalf that were the result of or were influenced by the employee's or agent's disloyalty.

Duty of Care

A corporate officer, director, or high-level employee, as well as other people in a fiduciary relationship, must conduct business affairs prudently with the skill and attention normally exercised by people in similar positions. Fiduciaries who act carelessly or recklessly are responsible for any resulting loss to the corporate shareholders or other principals. Damages may be recovered in a civil action for negligence, mismanagement, or waste of corporate assets.

People in a fiduciary relationship, however, are not guarantors against all business reverses or errors in judgment. The *Business Judgment Rule* protects corporate officers and directors from liability for judgments that were made in good faith (e.g., free of self-dealings or conflicts) and that appeared to be prudent based on the then-known circumstances.

Corporate officers breach their duty of loyalty if they accept kickbacks, engage in a conflict of interest, or otherwise are disloyal. Corporate officers who carelessly fail to prevent such conduct, or fail to enforce controls, or to pursue recovery of losses might breach their duty of care. Corporate defendants in such cases might raise the Business Judgment Rule in defense by showing that they had no reasonable grounds to suspect such conduct or that the cost of prevention or recovery was too high compared to the anticipated returns.

Federal Legislation Related to Fraud

Under our federal system, the prosecution of most white-collar crimes, such as embezzlement, larceny, and false pretenses, is left to the states. Prosecution under the criminal fraud statutes in the U.S. Code requires a federal jurisdictional basis, such as an effect on interstate commerce or mail uses. The U.S. laws often are used to prosecute the larger and more serious crimes primarily because of the generally superior resources of federal law enforcement agencies and their nationwide jurisdiction.

All federal criminal laws are the product of statutes. Statutes vary widely from a statute that prohibits unauthorized use of the "Smoky the Bear" emblem to the criminal provisions of the anti-trust laws. The most important of the hundreds of federal laws, rules, and regulations are listed below.

The Sarbanes-Oxley Act (Public Law 107-204)

On July 30, 2002, President Bush signed into law the Sarbanes-Oxley Act. This law, which was triggered in large part by several corporate accounting scandals that occurred in 2001 and 2002, significantly changes the laws of corporate governance and the rules and regulations under which accounting firms must operate. The Sarbanes-Oxley Act was designed to restore investor confidence in capital markets and help eliminate financial statement fraud in publicly traded companies while at the same time significantly increasing the penalties for corporate accounting fraud. The most significant changes brought on by the Act include:

- The creation of the Public Company Accounting Oversight Board
- Requirements for senior financial officers to certify SEC filings
- New standards for audit committee independence
- New standards for auditor independence
- Enhanced financial disclosure requirements
- New protections for corporate whistleblowers
- Enhanced penalties for white-collar crime

Public Company Accounting Oversight Board

Sarbanes-Oxley § 101 establishes the Public Company Accounting Oversight Board, whose purpose is:

[T]o oversee the audit of public companies that are subject to the securities laws, and related matters, in order to protect the interests of investors and further the public interest in the preparation of informative, accurate, and independent audit reports for companies the securities of which are sold to, and held by and for, public investors.

In short, the Board is charged with overseeing public company audits, setting audit standards, and investigating acts of noncompliance by auditors or audit firms. The Board is to be appointed and overseen by the Securities and Exchange Commission. It is to be made up of five persons, two who are or have been CPAs and three who have never been CPAs. The Act lists the Board's duties, which include:

- Registering public accounting firms that audit publicly traded companies
- Establishing or adopting auditing, quality control, ethics, independence and other standards relating to audits of publicly traded companies
- Inspecting registered public accounting firms
- Investigating registered public accounting firms and their employees, conducting disciplinary hearings, and imposing sanctions where justified
- Performing such other duties as are necessary to promote high professional standards among registered accounting firms, to improve the quality of audit services offered by those firms, and to protect investors
- Enforcing compliance with the Sarbanes-Oxley Act, the rules of the Board, professional standards, and securities laws relating to public company audits

REGISTRATION WITH THE BOARD

Beginning no later than October 23, 2003, public accounting firms must be registered with the Public Company Accounting Oversight Board in order to legally prepare or issue an audit report on a publicly traded company. In order to become registered, accounting firms must disclose, among other things, the names of all public companies they audited in the preceding year, the names of all public companies they expect to audit in the current year, and the annual fees they received from each of their public audit clients for audit, accounting, and non-audit services.

AUDITING, QUALITY CONTROL, AND INDEPENDENCE STANDARDS AND RULES

Sarbanes-Oxley Section 103 of the Act requires the Board to establish standards for auditing, quality control, ethics, independence and other issues relating to audits of publicly traded companies. Although the Act places the responsibility on the Board to establish audit standards, it also sets forth certain rules which the Board is required to include in those auditing standards. These rules include the following:

- Audit work papers must be maintained for at least seven years
- Auditing firms must include a concurring or second partner review and approval of audit reports, and concurring approval in the issuance of the audit report by a qualified person other than the person in charge of the audit
- All audit reports must describe the scope of testing of the company's internal control structure and must present the auditor's findings from the testing, including an evaluation of whether the internal control structure is acceptable and a description of material weaknesses in internal controls and any material noncompliance with controls.

Since the enactment of this Act, the Public Company Accounting Oversight Board (PCAOB), in conjunction with the Security Exchange Commission (SEC) has promulgated several rules requiring compliance with additional auditing standards. Because these rules are extensive and ever-changing, auditors should periodically review the SEC's website for updates and new rules at http://sec.gov/rules/final.shtml.

INSPECTIONS OF REGISTERED PUBLIC ACCOUNTING FIRMS

The Act also authorizes the Board to conduct regular inspections of public accounting firms to assess their degree of compliance with laws, rules, and professional standards regarding audits. Inspections are to be conducted once a year for firms that regularly audit more than 100 public companies and at least once every three years for firms that regularly audit 100 or fewer public companies.

INVESTIGATIONS AND DISCIPLINARY PROCEEDINGS

The Board has the authority to investigate registered public accounting firms (or their employees) for potential violations of the Sarbanes-Oxley Act, professional standards, any rules established by the Board, or any securities laws relating to the preparation and issuance of audit reports. During an investigation, the Board has the power to compel testimony and document production.

The Board has the power to issue sanctions for violations or for non-cooperation with an investigation. Sanctions can include temporary or permanent suspension of a firm's registration with the Board (which would mean that firm could no longer legally audit publicly traded companies), temporary or permanent suspension of a person's right to be associated with a registered public accounting firm, prohibition from auditing public companies, and civil monetary penalties of up to $750,000 for an individual, up to $15,000,000 for a firm.

Certification Obligations for CEOs and CFOs

One of the most significant changes affected by the Sarbanes-Oxley Act is the requirement that the Chief Executive Officer and the Chief Financial Officer of public companies personally certify annual and quarterly SEC filings. These certifications essentially require CEOs and CFOs to take responsibility for their companies' financial statements and prevent them from delegating this responsibility to their subordinates and then claiming ignorance when fraud is uncovered in the financial statements.

There are two types of officer certifications mandated by Sarbanes-Oxley: criminal certifications, which are set forth in Sarbanes-Oxley Section 906 and codified at 18 U.S.C. § 1350, and civil certifications, which are set forth in Sarbanes-Oxley Section 302.

CRIMINAL CERTIFICATIONS (SARBANES-OXLEY § 906)

Periodic filings with the SEC must be accompanied by a statement, signed by the CEO and CFO, which certifies that the report fully complies with the SEC's periodic reporting requirements and that the information in the report fairly presents, in all material respects, the financial condition and results of operation of the company.

These certifications are known as "criminal certifications" because the act imposes criminal penalties on officers who violate the certification requirements.

- Corporate officers who *knowingly* violate the certification requirements are subject to fines of up to $1,000,000 and up to 10 years imprisonment, or both.
- Corporate officers who *willfully* violate the certification requirements are subject to fines of up to $5,000,000 and up to 20 years imprisonment, or both.

FAILURE OF CORPORATE OFFICERS TO CERTIFY FINANCIAL REPORTS (18 U.S.C. § 1350)

(a) CERTIFICATION OF PERIODIC FINANCIAL REPORTS— Each periodic report containing financial statements filed by an issuer with the Securities Exchange

Commission pursuant to section 13(a) or 15(d) of the Securities Exchange Act of 1934 (15 U.S.C. 78m (a) or 78o (d)) shall be accompanied by a written statement by the chief executive officer and chief financial officer (or equivalent thereof) of the issuer.

(b) CONTENT— The statement required under subsection (a) shall certify that the periodic report containing the financial statements fully complies with the requirements of section 13(a) or 15(d) of the Securities Exchange Act pf 1934 (15 U.S.C. 78m or 78o (d)) and that information contained in the periodic report fairly presents, in all material respects, the financial condition and results of operations of the issuer.

(c) CRIMINAL PENALTIES- Whoever—

(1) certifies any statement as set forth in subsections (a) and (b) of this section knowing that the periodic report accompanying the statement does not comport with all the requirements set forth in this section shall be fined not more than $1,000,000 or imprisoned not more than 10 years, or both; or

(2) willfully certifies any statement as set forth in subsections (a) and (b) of this section knowing that the periodic report accompanying the statement does not comport with all the requirements set forth in this section shall be fined not more than $5,000,000, or imprisoned not more than 20 years, or both.

CIVIL CERTIFICATIONS (SARBANES-OXLEY § 302)

Sarbanes-Oxley Section 302 requires the CEO and CFO to personally certify the following in their reports:

- They have personally reviewed the report;
- Based on their knowledge, the report does not contain any material misstatement that would render the financials misleading;
- Based on their knowledge the financial information in the report fairly presents in all material respects the financial condition, results of operations, and cash flow of the company;
- They are responsible for designing, maintaining, and evaluating the company's internal controls, they have evaluated the controls within 90 days prior to the report, and they have presented their conclusions about the effectiveness of those controls in the report
- They have disclosed to the auditors and the audit committee any material weaknesses in the controls and any fraud, whether material or not, that involves management or other employees who have a significant role in the company's internal controls; and

- They have indicated in their report whether there have been significant changes in the company's internal controls since the filing of the last report.

Note that in items 2 and 3 the CEO and CFO are not required to certify that the financials are accurate or that there is no misstatement. They are simply required to certify that *to their knowledge* the financials are accurate and not misleading. However, this does not mean that senior financial officers can simply plead ignorance about their companies' SEC filings in order to avoid liability. The term "fairly presents" in item 3 is a broader standard than what is required by GAAP. In certifying that their SEC filings meet this standard, the CEO and CFO essentially must certify that the company: (1) has selected appropriate accounting policies to ensure the material accuracy of the reports; (2) has properly applied those accounting standards; and (3) has disclosed financial information that reflects the underlying transactions and events of the company. Furthermore, the other new certification rules (see 1, and 4-6 above) mandate that CEOs and CFOs take an active role in their companies' public reporting, and in the design and maintenance of internal controls.

It is significant that in item 4, the CEO and CFO not only have to certify that they are responsible for their companies' internal controls, but also that they have evaluated the controls *within 90 days prior to their quarterly or annual report*. Essentially, this new certification requirement mandates that companies actively and continually re-evaluate their control structures to prevent fraud.

In conjunction with the Sarbanes-Oxley §302 certification requirements on the responsibility of the CEO and CFO for internal controls, Sarbanes-Oxley §404 requires all annual reports to contain an internal control report that: (1) states management's responsibility for establishing and maintaining an adequate internal control structure and procedures for financial reporting; and (2) contains an assessment of the effectiveness of the internal control structure and procedures of the company for financial reporting.

Item 5 requires the CEO and CFO to certify that they have disclosed to their auditors and their audit committee any material weaknesses in the company's internal controls, and also any fraud, *whether material or not,* that involves management or other key employees. Obviously, this is a very broad reporting standard that goes beyond the "material" standard contemplated in SAS 99 (see the discussion of SAS 99 in the chapter on "Management's and Auditors' Responsibilities" in the Financial Transaction section of the Manual). The CEO and CFO now must report to their auditors and audit committee *any fraud* committed by a manager. This places a greater burden on the CEO and CFO to take part in anti-fraud efforts and to be aware of fraudulent activity within their companies in order to meet this certification requirement.

Item 6 is significant because periodic SEC filings must now include statements detailing significant changes to the internal controls of publicly traded companies.

New Standards for Audit Committee Independence
AUDIT COMMITTEE RESPONSIBILITIES

Sarbanes-Oxley Section 301 of the Act requires that the audit committee for each publicly traded company shall be directly responsible for appointing, compensating, and overseeing the work of the company's outside auditors. The act also mandates that the auditors must report directly to the audit committee—not management—and makes it the responsibility of the audit committee to resolve disputes between management and the auditors. Sarbanes-Oxley Section 301 also requires that the audit committee must have the authority and funding to hire independent counsel and any other advisors it deems necessary to carry out its duties.

COMPOSITION OF THE AUDIT COMMITTEE

The Sarbanes-Oxley Act mandates that each member of a company's audit committee must be a member of its board of directors, and must otherwise be "independent." The term "independent" means that the audit committee member can only receive compensation from the company for his or her service on the board of directors, the audit committee, or another committee of the board of directors. They cannot be paid by the company for any other consulting or advisory work.

FINANCIAL EXPERT

Sarbanes-Oxley Section 407 of the Act requires every public company to disclose in its periodic reports to the SEC whether or not the audit committee has at least one member who is a "financial expert," and if not to explain the reasons why. The Act defines a "financial expert" as a person who, through education and experience as a public accountant or auditor, or a CFO, comptroller, chief financial officer or a similar position: (1) has an understanding of generally accepted accounting principles and financial statements; (2) has experience in preparing or auditing financial statements of comparable companies and the application of such principles in accounting for estimates, accruals, and reserves; (3) has experience with internal controls; and (4) has an understanding of audit committee functions.

ESTABLISHING A WHISTLEBLOWING STRUCTURE

The Act makes it the responsibility of the audit committee to establish procedures (e.g., a hotline) for receiving and dealing with complaints and anonymous employee tips regarding irregularities in the company's accounting methods, internal controls, or auditing matters.

New Standards for Auditor Independence
RESTRICTIONS ON NON-AUDIT ACTIVITY

Perhaps the greatest concern arising out of the public accounting scandals of 2001 and 2002 was the fear that public accounting firms that received multimillion-dollar consulting fees from their public company clients could not maintain an appropriate level of objectivity in conducting audits for those clients. In order to address this concern, Congress established a list of activities that public accounting firms are now prohibited from performing on behalf of their audit clients (Sarbanes-Oxley § 201). The prohibited services include:

- Bookkeeping services
- Financial information systems design and implementation
- Appraisal or valuation services, fairness opinions, or contribution-in-kind reports
- Actuarial services
- Internal audit outsource services
- Management functions or human resources
- Broker or dealer, investment adviser, or investment banking services
- Legal services and expert services unrelated to the audit
- Any other service that the Public Company Accounting Oversight Board proscribes

There are certain other non-audit services – most notably tax services – that are not expressly prohibited by Sarbanes-Oxley. However, in order for a public accounting firm to perform these services on behalf of an audit client, that service must be approved in advance by the client's audit committee, which must be disclosed in the client's periodic SEC reports. Furthermore, regarding non-audit services, the SEC prevents accounts from providing audit clients with expert opinions and services, as well as legal representation for advocating the audit client's litigation, regulatory, or administrative interests.

MANDATORY AUDIT PARTNER ROTATION

Sarbanes-Oxley Section 204 requires public accounting firms to rotate the lead audit partner or the partner responsible for reviewing the audit every five years.

NEW CONFLICT OF INTEREST PROVISIONS

Another provision of Sarbanes-Oxley aimed at improving auditor independence is Sarbanes-Oxley § 206, which seeks to limit conflicts or potential conflicts that arise when auditors cross over to work for their former clients. The Act now makes it unlawful for a public accounting firm to audit a company if, within the prior year, the client's CEO, CFO, controller, or chief accounting officer worked for the accounting firm and participated in the company's audit.

AUDITOR REPORTS TO AUDIT COMMITTEES

Sarbanes-Oxley Section 301 requires that auditors report directly to the audit committee, and Sarbanes-Oxley § 204 makes certain requirements as to the contents of those reports. In order to help ensure that the audit committee is aware of questionable accounting policies or treatments that were used in the preparation of the company's financial statements, Sarbanes-Oxley § 204 states that auditors must make a timely report (before any report is filed with the Commission pursuant to the federal securities laws) of the following to the audit committee:

- All critical accounting policies and policies used
- Alternative GAAP methods that were discussed with management, the ramifications of the use of those alternative treatments, and the treatment preferred by the auditors
- Any other material written communications between the auditors and management.

AUDITORS' ATTESTATION TO INTERNAL CONTROLS

As was stated previously, Sarbanes-Oxley § 404 of the Act requires every annual report to contain an internal control report which states that the company's management is responsible for internal controls and which also assesses the effectiveness of the internal control structures. Sarbanes-Oxley Section 404 requires the company's external auditors to attest to and issue a report on management's assessment of internal controls.

IMPROPER INFLUENCE ON AUDITS

The Act also makes it unlawful for any officer or director of a public company to take any action to fraudulently influence, coerce, manipulate, or mislead an auditor in the performance of an audit of the company's financial statements. This is yet another attempt by Congress to ensure the independence and objectivity of audits in order to prevent accounting fraud and strengthen investor confidence in the reliability of public company financial statements.

Enhanced Financial Disclosure Requirements

OFF-BALANCE SHEET TRANSACTIONS

The Sarbanes-Oxley Act directed the SEC to issue rules which require the disclosure of all material off-balance sheet transactions by publicly traded companies. The rules require disclosure of "all material off-balance sheet transactions, arrangements, obligations (including contingent obligations), and other relationships the company may have with unconsolidated entities or persons that may have a material current or future effect on the company's financial condition, changes in financial condition, liquidity, capital expenditures, capital resources, or significant components of revenues or expenses." These disclosures are required in all annual and quarterly SEC reports.

PRO FORMA FINANCIAL INFORMATION

Sarbanes-Oxley Section 401 also directed the SEC to issue new rules on pro forma financial statements. These rules require that pro forma financials must not contain any untrue statements or omissions that would make them misleading and require that the pro forma financials be reconciled to GAAP. These rules apply to all pro forma financial statements that are filed with the SEC or that are included in any public disclosure or press release.

PROHIBITIONS ON PERSONAL LOANS TO EXECUTIVES

Effective immediately, Sarbanes-Oxley § 402 makes it illegal for public companies to make personal loans or otherwise extend credit, either directly or indirectly, to or for any director or executive officer. There is an exception that applies to consumer lenders if the loans are consumer loans of the type the company normally makes to the public, and on the same terms.

RESTRICTIONS ON INSIDER TRADING

Sarbanes-Oxley Section 403 establishes new disclosure requirements for stock transactions by directors and officers of public companies, or by persons who own more than 10 percent of a publicly traded company's stock. SEC rules further specify content and timing requirements of blackout period notices that must be provided to directors and officers. Reports of changes in beneficial ownership by these persons must now be filed with the SEC by the end of the second business day following the transaction.

Under Sarbanes-Oxley § 306, directors and officers are also prohibited from trading in the company's securities during any pension fund blackout periods. This restriction only applies to securities that were acquired as a result of their employment or service to the company. A blackout period is defined as any period of more than three consecutive business days in which at least 50% of the participants in the company's retirement plan are restricted from trading in the company's securities. If a director or officer violates this provision, he or she can be forced to disgorge to the company all profits received from the sale of securities during the blackout period.

CODES OF ETHICS FOR SENIOR FINANCIAL OFFICERS

Pursuant to Sarbanes-Oxley § 406, the SEC must establish rules that require public companies to disclose whether they have adopted a code of ethics for their senior financial officers, and if not, to explain the reasons why. The new rules will also require immediate public disclosure any time there is a change of the code of ethics or a waiver of the code of ethics for a senior financial officer.

ENHANCED REVIEW OF PERIODIC FILINGS

Sarbanes-Oxley Section 408 now requires the SEC to make regular and systematic reviews of disclosures made by public companies in their periodic reports to the SEC. Reviews of a company's disclosures, including its financial statements, must be made at least once every three years. Prior to this enactment, reviews were typically minimal and tended to coincide with registered offerings.

REAL TIME DISCLOSURES

Under Sarbanes-Oxley § 409, public companies must publicly disclose information concerning material changes in their financial condition or operations. These disclosures must be "in plain English" and must be made "on a rapid and current basis."

Protections for Corporate Whistleblowers under Sarbanes-Oxley

The Sarbanes-Oxley Act establishes broad new protections for corporate whistleblowers. There are two sections of the Act that address whistleblower protections: Section 806 deals with civil protections and Sarbanes-Oxley Section 1107 establishes criminal liability for those who retaliate against whistleblowers. Additionally, the first ruling applying the whistleblower protections under Sarbanes-Oxley was rendered in January 2004 by an Administrative Law Judge. The Court in *Welch v. Cardinal Bankshares, Corp.* applied the Act's equitable remedy for wrongful termination and ordered employment reinstatement of the Plaintiff after finding that the Plaintiff's employer fired him in retaliation for reporting potential accounting misconduct within his company (*Welsh v. Cardinal Bankshares, Corp.*, No. 2003-SOX-15 (Dep't Labor, Jan. 28, 2004)).

CIVIL LIABILITY WHISTLEBLOWER PROTECTION
Sarbanes-Oxley Section, which is codified at 18 U.S.C § 1514A, creates civil liability for companies that retaliate against whistleblowers. It should be noted that this provision does not provide universal whistleblower protection; it only protects employees of publicly traded companies. Sarbanes-Oxley § 806 makes it unlawful to fire, demote, suspend, threaten, harass, or in any other manner discriminate against an employee for providing information or aiding in an investigation of securities fraud. In order to trigger Sarbanes-Oxley § 806 protections, the employee must report the suspected misconduct to a federal regulatory or law enforcement agency, a member of Congress or a committee of Congress, or a supervisor. Employees are also protected against retaliation for filing, testifying in, participating in, or otherwise assisting in a proceeding filed or about to be filed relating to an alleged violation of securities laws or SEC rules.

The whistleblower protections apply even if the company is ultimately found not to have committed securities fraud. As long as the employee reasonably believes she is reporting conduct that constitutes a violation of various federal securities laws, then she is protected. The protections not only cover retaliatory acts by the company, but also by any officer, employee, contractor, subcontractor, or agent of the company.

If a public company is found to have violated Sarbanes-Oxley § 806, the Act provides for an award of compensatory damages sufficient to "make the employee whole." Penalties include reinstatement; back pay with interest; and compensation for special damages including litigation costs, expert witness fees, and attorneys' fees.

CRIMINAL SANCTION WHISTLEBLOWER PROTECTION
Sarbanes-Oxley Section 1107 —codified at 18 U.S.C. § 1513—makes it a crime to knowingly, with the intent to retaliate, take any harmful action against a person for providing truthful information relating to the commission or possible commission of any Federal offense. This protection is only triggered when information is provided to a law enforcement officer, it does not apply to reports made to supervisors or to members of Congress, as is the case under Sarbanes-Oxley § 806.

Additionally, the Act codified three new criminal offenses to Title 18 of the CFR. First, it is a criminal offense to alter, destroy, mutilate, conceal, cover-up, or falsify any record or document "with the intent to impede, obstruct, or influence" a federal investigation or bankruptcy proceeding, carrying a maximum sentence of 20 years imprisonment (18 U.S.C. § 1519). Secondly, all auditing accountants of securities issuers must "maintain all audit or review workpapers for a period of 5 years." Where there is a knowing and willful violation of this offense, a sentence of up to 10 years may be imposed (18 U.S.C. § 1520). Finally, the Act made codified an additional securities fraud offence that can carry a maximum sentence of 25 years' imprisonment (18 U.S.C. § 1348).

In general, the coverage of Sarbanes-Oxley § 1107 is much broader than the civil liability whistleblower protections of Sarbanes-Oxley § 806. While the Sarbanes-Oxley § 806 protections apply only to employees of publicly traded companies, Sarbanes-Oxley § 1107's criminal whistleblower protections cover all individuals (and organizations) regardless of where they work. Also, Sarbanes-Oxley § 806 only applies to violations of securities laws or SEC rules and regulations. Sarbanes-Oxley § 1107, on the other hand, protects individuals who provide truthful information about the commission or possible commission of *any Federal offense*.

Violations of Sarbanes-Oxley § 1107 can be punished by fines of up to $250,000 and up to 10 years in prison for individuals. Corporations that violate the act can be fined up to $500,000.

RETALIATING AGAINST A WITNESS, VICTIM, OR AN INFORMANT (18 U.S.C. § 1513)

* * *

(e) Whoever knowingly, with the intent to retaliate, takes any action harmful to any person, including interference with the lawful employment or livelihood of any person, for providing to a law enforcement officer any truthful information relating to the commission or possible commission of any Federal offense, shall be fined under this title or imprisoned not more than 10 years, or both.

Enhanced Penalties for White-Collar Crime

As part of Congress' general effort to deter corporate accounting fraud and other forms of white-collar crime, the Sarbanes-Oxley Act also enhances the criminal penalties for a number of white-collar offenses.

ATTEMPT AND CONSPIRACY

The Act amends the fraud provisions of the United States Code (Chapter 63) to make "attempt" and "conspiracy to commit" offenses subject to the same penalties as the offense itself. This applies to mail fraud, wire fraud, securities fraud, bank fraud, and health care fraud.

ATTEMPT AND CONSPIRACY (18 U.S.C. § 1349)

Any person who attempts or conspires to commit any offense under this chapter [U.S. Code Chapter 63] *shall be subject to the same penalties as those prescribed for the offense, the commission of which was the object of the attempt or conspiracy.*

MAIL FRAUD AND WIRE FRAUD

Sarbanes-Oxley amends the mail fraud and wire fraud statutes (18 U.S.C §§ 1341, 1343), increasing the maximum jail term from five to 20 years.

SECURITIES FRAUD

Sarbanes-Oxley Section 807 of the Act makes securities fraud a crime under 18 U.S.C § 1348, providing for fines up to $250,000 and up to 25 years in prison. The text of the statute is set forth later in this chapter under the section on Securities Laws.

DOCUMENT DESTRUCTION

Sarbanes-Oxley Section 802 makes destroying evidence to obstruct an investigation or any other matter within the jurisdiction of any U.S. department illegal and punishable by a fine of up to $250,000 and up to 20 years in prison.

Sarbanes-Oxley Section 802 also specifically requires that accountants who perform audits on publicly traded companies must maintain all audit or review work papers for a period of five years. Violations of this rule may be punished by fines up to $250,000 and up to 10 years in jail for individuals, or fines up to $500,000 for corporations. (Although Sarbanes-Oxley § 802 only requires work papers to be maintained for five years, keep in mind that under Sarbanes-Oxley § 103, the Public Company Accounting Oversight Board is directed to set standards that require public accounting firms to maintain audit work papers for *seven* years. Accounting firms should design their document retention policies accordingly.)

Sarbanes-Oxley Section 1102 of the Act amends § 1512 of the U.S. Code to make it a criminal offense to corruptly alter, destroy, mutilate or conceal a record or document with the intent to impair its integrity or use in an official proceeding, or to otherwise obstruct, influence, or impede any official proceeding or attempt to do so. Violations of this section are punishable by fines up to $250,000 and imprisonment for up to 20 years.

FREEZING OF ASSETS

During an investigation of possible securities violations by a publicly traded company or any of its officers, directors, partners, agents, controlling persons, or employees, the SEC can petition a federal court to issue a 45-day freeze on "extraordinary payments" to any of the foregoing persons. If granted, the payments will be placed in an interest-bearing escrow account while the investigation commences. This provision was enacted to prevent corporate assets from being improperly distributed while an investigation is underway.

BANKRUPTCY LOOPHOLES

Sarbanes-Oxley Section 803 amends the bankruptcy code so that judgments, settlements, damages, fines, penalties, restitution payments, disgorgement payments, etc., resulting from violations of Federal securities laws are non-dischargeable. This was intended to prevent corporate wrongdoers from sheltering their assets under bankruptcy protection.

DISGORGEMENT OF BONUSES

One of the most unique aspects of the Sarbanes-Oxley Act is § 304, which states that if a publicly traded company is required to prepare an accounting restatement due to the company's material noncompliance, as a result of "misconduct," with any financial reporting requirement under securities laws, then the CEO and CFO must reimburse the company for:
- Any bonus or other incentive-based or equity-based compensation received during the 12 months after the initial filing of the report that requires restating; and
- Any profits realized from the sale of the company's securities during the same 12-month period.

While the Act requires the CEO and CFO to disgorge their bonuses if the company's financial statements have to be restated because of "misconduct," it makes no mention of *whose* misconduct triggers this provision. There is certainly nothing in the text of Sarbanes-Oxley § 304 that limits the disgorgement provision to instances of misconduct by the CEO and CFO. Presumably, then, the CEO and CFO could be required to disgorge their bonuses and profits from the sale of company stock even if they had no knowledge of and took no part in the misconduct that made the restatement necessary.

Mail Fraud and Wire Fraud

The mail fraud statute is the workhorse of federal white-collar prosecutions. It has been used against virtually all types of commercial fraud, public corruption, and security law violations. The statute provides:

Mail Fraud (18 U.S.C. § 1341)

Whoever, having devised or intending to devise any scheme or artifice to defraud, or for obtaining money or property by means of false or fraudulent pretenses, representations, or promises, or to sell, dispose of, loan, exchange, alter, give away, distribute, supply, or furnish or procure for unlawful use any counterfeit or spurious coin, obligation, security, or other article, or anything represented to be or intimated or held out to be such counterfeit or spurious article, for the purpose of executing such scheme or artifice or attempting so to do, places in any post office or authorized depository for mail matter, any matter or thing whatever to be sent or delivered by the Postal Service, deposits or causes to be deposited any matter or thing whatever to be sent or delivered by an private or commercial interstate carrier, or takes or receive, any such matter or thing, or knowingly causes to be delivered by mail according to the direction thereon, or at the place at which it is directed to be delivered by the person to whom it is addressed, any such matter or thing, shall be fined under this title or imprisoned not more than twenty years, or both. If the violation affects a financial institution, such person shall be fined not more than $1,000,000 or imprisoned not more than 30 years, or both.

The gist of the offense is the use of the mails; without it, no matter how large or serious the fraud, there is no federal jurisdiction under this statute. The mailing does not itself need to contain the false and fraudulent representations, as long as it is an integral part of the scheme. What is integral or incidental depends on the facts of each case; generally a mailing that helps advance the scheme in any significant way will be considered sufficient.

Frauds and swindles are not defined in the mail fraud statute or elsewhere in the U.S. Code. Most of the cases treat any intentional scheme to deceive and deprive another of a tangible property right as being within the statute.

It is not necessary that the fraudulent scheme succeed or that the victim suffer a loss for the statute to apply. It also is not necessary that the predicate mailing travel in interstate commerce; any use of the U.S. postal system provides sufficient grounds for federal jurisdiction.

Wire Fraud (18 U.S.C. § 1343)

Whoever, having devised or intending to devise any scheme or artifice to defraud, or for obtaining money or property by means of false or fraudulent pretenses, representations, or promises, transmits or causes to be transmitted by means of wire, radio, or television communication in interstate or foreign commerce, any writings, signs, signals, pictures, or sounds for the purpose of executing such scheme or artifice, shall be fined under this title or imprisoned not more than twenty years, or both. If the violation affects a financial institution, such person shall be fined not more than $1,000,000 or imprisoned not more than 30 years, or both.

The wire fraud statute often is used in tandem with mail fraud counts in federal prosecutions. Unlike mail fraud, however, the wire fraud statute requires an interstate or foreign communication for a violation.

"Honest Services" Fraud (18 U.S.C. § 1346)

Under Title 18, U.S. Code, Section 1346, the mail fraud and the wire fraud statutes may be used to prosecute official corruption, along with the bribery laws, under the theory that the payment or receipt of bribes deprived the public of its right to honest and unbiased services of public servants.

18 U.S.C. § 1346 provides, "the term 'scheme or artifice to defraud' [which is the term used in the mail and wire fraud statutes among others] includes a scheme or artifice to deprive another of the intangible right of honest services."

This statute generally is referred to as the "honest services" fraud statute. The statute arose from the legal principle that the employer-employee relationship creates certain duties and responsibilities owed by an employee to an employer. Employees are prohibited from using this special relationship to the detriment of their employer. Doing so is generally a civil wrong such as breach of fiduciary duty.

However, the trend over the last decade has been for federal prosecutors to redress such wrongs in the criminal context. Congress assisted these efforts by enacting section 1346. This section was meant to be a powerful weapon for the government in that it removed the prosecution's burden of establishing a fraud victim's deprivation of money or property. So long as the prosecutor can establish that the employee breached a duty to provide "honest services" to the victim, a *prima facie* case for mail or wire fraud exists.

Unfortunately, however, how the statute is supposed to be applied has become a vexing problem for the courts. When the statute was passed, prosecutors begin using it in all types of corruption cases. However, several recent court decisions have sought to limit the cases in which the statute can be applied. In the case of *U.S. v. Sawyer*, 85 F.3d 713 (1st Cir. 1996), the U.S. Court of Appeals for the First Circuit reversed the defendant's conviction for mail fraud under 18 U.S.C. § 1346. Mr. Sawyer was a lobbyist for an insurance company. Over the course of several years, Sawyer spent thousands of dollars entertaining Massachusetts legislators with lavish meals and golf outings. Sawyer was convicted of mail fraud on the theory that he deprived the Massachusetts citizenry of the honest services of these state legislators.

The court reversed the mail fraud conviction concluding that the giving of gifts and gratuities did not per se deprive the public of the "honest services" of its legislators. The court said that the payment or receipt of such gratuities did not, and were not intended to affect the honesty and integrity of the public officials' services. The evidence presented at trial was that Sawyer only wanted to gain access to the legislators. There was no evidence that the gifts were intended to coax the officials into doing anything dishonest. In other words, there was no fraudulent intent on the part of Sawyer. The court stated that to prove intent to commit honest services fraud, the jury had to find that Sawyer intended to influence or otherwise improperly affect the officials' performance of their duties.

The case illustrates that there is an unsettled issue regarding when honest services fraud is prosecutable under the mail and wire fraud statutes. It appears that one of the major elements that must be present is actual intent — that the employee take some action adverse to his employer. Most cases that have been prosecuted under Section 1346 have involved public employees; however, the statute can apply in a private employment context as well. However, courts are reluctant to allow a conviction unless there is identifiable harm resulting from the defendant's conduct.

In the case of *U.S. v. Jain*, 93 F.3d 436 (8th Cir. 1996), a psychologist was convicted in a Medicare kickback scheme. Although he was convicted of accepting payments from a psychiatric hospital for referring patients there, the Court of Appeals reversed his conviction for honest services fraud. The court stated, "Where there is no tangible harm to the victim of a private scheme, it is hard to discern what intangible 'rights' have been violated." In fact, the government conceded that there was no evidence of harm to any of the doctor's patients.

As the court stated in the *Jain* case, "the essence of a scheme to defraud is intent to harm the victim." Accordingly, the honest services fraud theory should be reserved for those cases in which either the perpetrator acted with the intent to corrupt the employee, or in cases where there was actual harm caused by the defendant's actions.

Interstate Transportation of Stolen Property (18 U.S.C. § 2314)
The pertinent part of this statute provides:

> *Whoever transports, transmits, or transfers in interstate or foreign commerce any goods, wares, merchandise, securities or money, of the value of $5,000 or more, knowing the same to have been stolen, converted or taken by fraud; or*

> *Whoever, having devised or intending to devise any scheme or artifice to defraud, or for obtaining money or property by means of false or fraudulent pretenses, representations, or promises transports or causes to be transported, or induces any person or persons to travel in, or to be transported in interstate or foreign commerce in the execution or concealment of a scheme or artifice to defraud that person or those persons of money or property having a value of $5,000 or more; or ...*

> *Shall be fined under this title or imprisoned not more than 10 years, or both.*

18 U.S.C. § 2314, popularly known as "ITSP," is often used in fraud prosecutions in conjunction with mail or wire fraud counts, or to provide federal jurisdiction in their absence, when proceeds of a value of $5,000 or more obtained by fraud are transported across state lines. The statute also is violated if a defendant induces the victim to travel in interstate commerce as part of the scheme to defraud. Individual transportation of money or other items valued at less than $5,000 as part of the same scheme may be aggregated to meet the value requirement.

Racketeer Influenced and Corrupt Organizations (RICO) (18, U.S.C. § 1961, et. seq.)
RICO is probably the best-known and most controversial federal statute in use today. Originally enacted in 1970 to fight organized crime's infiltration of legitimate business, its powerful criminal and civil provisions have come to be used in a wide range of fraud cases. The statute outlaws the investment of ill-gotten gains in another business enterprise; the acquisition of an interest in an enterprise through certain illegal acts; and the conduct of the affairs of an enterprise through such acts. Criminal penalties include stiff fines and prison

terms as well as the forfeiture of all illegal proceeds or interests. Civil remedies include treble damages, attorney fees, dissolution of the offending enterprise, and other penalties.

The complex statute provides in its pertinent part:

18 U.S.C. § 1962. Prohibited Activities

(a) It shall be unlawful for any person who has received any income derived, directly or indirectly, from a pattern of racketeering activity or through collection of an unlawful debt in which such person has participated as a principal within the meaning of Section 2, Title 18, United States Code, to use or invest, directly or indirectly, any part of such income, or the proceeds of such income, in acquisition of any interest in, or the establishment or operation of, any enterprise which is engaged in, or the activities of which affect, interstate or foreign commerce. A purchase of securities on the open market for purposes of investment, and without the intention of controlling or participating in the control of the issuer, or of assisting another to do so, shall not be unlawful under this subsection if the securities of the issuer held by the purchaser, the members of his immediate family, and his or their accomplices in any pattern or racketeering activity or the collection of an unlawful debt after such purchase do not amount in aggregate to one percent of the outstanding securities of any one class, and do not confer, either in law or in fact, the power to elect one or more directors of the issuer.

(b) It shall be unlawful for any person through a pattern of racketeering activity or through collection of an unlawful debt to acquire or maintain, directly or indirectly, any interest in or control of any enterprise which is engaged in, or the activities of which affect, interstate or foreign commerce.

(c) It shall be unlawful for any person employed by or associated with any enterprise engaged in, or the activities of which affect, interstate or foreign commerce, to conduct or participate, directly or indirectly, in the conduct of such enterprise's affairs through a pattern of racketeering activity or collection of unlawful debt.

(d) It shall be unlawful for any person to conspire to violate any of the provisions of subsection (a), (b), or (c) of this section.

18 U.S.C. § 1963. Criminal Penalties

(a) Whoever violates any provision of Section 1962 of this chapter shall be fined under this title or imprisoned not more than 20 years (or for life if the violation is based on racketeering activity for which the maximum penalty includes life imprisonment), or both, and shall forfeit to the United States, irrespective of any provision of State law—

(1) any interest the person has acquired or maintained in violation of Section 1962;

(2) any—

    (A) interest in;

    (B) security of;

    (C) claim against; or

    (D) property or contractual right of any kind affording a source of influence over;

any enterprise which the person established, operated, controlled, conducted, or participated in the conduct of, in violation of section 1962; and

(3) any property constituting, or derived from, any proceeds which the person obtained directly or indirectly, from racketeering activity or unlawful debt collection in violation of section 1962.

* * *

18 U.S.C. § 1964. Civil Remedies

(a) The district courts of the United States shall have jurisdiction to prevent and restrain violations of Section 1962 of this chapter by issuing appropriate orders, including, but not limited to: ordering any person to divest himself of any interest, direct or indirect, in any enterprise; imposing reasonable restrictions on the future activities or investments of any person, including, but not limited to, prohibiting any person from engaging in the same type of endeavor as the enterprise engaged in, the activities of which affect interstate or foreign commerce; or ordering dissolution or reorganization of any enterprise, making due provision for the rights of innocent persons.

(b) The Attorney General may institute proceedings under this section. Pending final determination thereof, the court may at any time enter such restraining orders or prohibitions, or take such other actions, including the acceptance of satisfactory performance bonds, as it shall deem proper.

(c) Any person injured in his business or property by reason of a violation of Section 1962 of this chapter may sue therefor in any appropriate United States district court and shall *recover threefold the damages he sustains and the cost of the suit, including a reasonable attorney's fee.*

(d) A final judgment or decree rendered in favor of the United States in any criminal proceeding brought by the United States under this chapter shall estop the defendant from denying the essential allegations of the criminal offense in any subsequent civil proceeding brought by the United States.

18 U.S.C. § 1962(c) is probably the most commonly used offense. The elements of a 1962(c) offense are:

- The defendant was associated with an "enterprise" as defined in the statute, which can be a business, union, a group of individuals "associated in fact;" or even a single individual.
- The enterprise was engaged in or affected interstate commerce.
- The defendant conducted the affairs of the enterprise through a "pattern of racketeering activity," that is, two or more illegal acts, enumerated in the statute as predicate violations, such as mail and wire fraud or ITSP violations.

The most controversial aspect of RICO is its civil provisions. Civil actions may be brought by the government or any private party injured in his business or property. Critics complain that private party suits have been used to reach "deep pocket" defendants, such as accounting firms, who cannot be characterized as "racketeers;" and to coerce unwarranted settlements from blameless defendants fearful of possible treble damage judgments. Supporters contend that a plaintiff cannot recover unless there is proof of fraud or other criminal acts—whoever the defendant—making the stigma of being alleged a racketeer and the award of treble damages justified.

False Claims and Statements

18 U.S.C. § 47 contains a number of related provisions that punish false or fraudulent statements, orally or in writing, made to various federal agencies and departments. The principal statute is 18 U.S.C. § 1001 that prohibits such statements generally and overlaps with many of the more specific laws, such as 18 U.S.C. § 1014, that apply to false statements made on certain loan and credit applications.

18 U.S.C. § 1001 most often is used to prosecute false statements to law enforcement or regulatory officials, not made under oath, in the course of an official investigation, or on an

application for such things as federal employment, credit, and visa applications. The statute—a felony—also may be used in lieu of the misdemeanor provisions of the IRS Code for filing false documents with tax returns. (See the Financial Transactions Section for additional information on tax fraud.)

The false statement statutes of greatest importance to the fraud examiner follow.

18 U.S.C. § 1001. Statements or Entries Generally
(a) Except as otherwise provided in this section, whoever, in any matter within the jurisdiction of the executive, legislative, or judicial branch of the Government of the United States, knowingly and willfully—
- *(1) falsifies, conceals or covers up by any trick, scheme, or device a material fact;*
- *(2) makes any false, fictitious or fraudulent statements or representations;*
- *(3) makes or uses any false writing or document knowing the same to contain any false, fictitious or fraudulent statement or entry;*

shall be fined under this title or imprisoned not more than five years, or both.

(b) Subsection (a) does not apply to a party to a judicial proceeding, or that party's counsel, for statements, representations, writings or documents submitted by such party or counsel to a judge or magistrate in that proceeding.

(c) With respect to any matter within the jurisdiction of the legislative branch, subsection (a) shall apply only to —
- *(1) administrative matters, including a claim for payment, a matter related to the procurement of property or services, personnel or employment practices, or support services, or a document required by law, rule, or regulation to be submitted to the Congress or any office or officer within the legislative branch; or*
- *(2) any investigation or review, conducted pursuant to the authority of any committee, subcommittee, commission or office of the Congress, consistent with the applicable rules of the House or Senate.*

18 U.S.C. § 1002. Possession of False Papers to Defraud United States
Whoever, knowingly and with intent to defraud the United States, or any agency thereof, possesses any false, altered, forged, or counterfeited writing or document for the purpose of enabling another to obtain from the United States, or from any agency, officer or agent thereof,

any sum of money, shall be fined under this title or imprisoned not more than five years, or both.

18 U.S.C. § 1003. Demands Against the United States

Whoever knowingly and fraudulently demands or endeavors to obtain any share or sum in the public stocks of the United States, or to have any part thereof transferred, assigned, sold, or conveyed, or to have any annuity, dividend, pension, wages, gratuity, or other debt due from the United States, or any part thereof, received, or paid by virtue of any false, forged, or counterfeited power of attorney, authority, or instrument, shall be fined under this title or imprisoned not more than five years, or both; but if the sum or value so obtained or attempted to be obtained does not exceed $100, he shall be fined under this title or imprisoned not more than one year, or both.

18 U.S.C. § 1005. Bank Entries, Reports and Transactions

Whoever, being an officer, director, agent or employee of any Federal Reserve Bank, member bank, depository institution holding company, national bank, insured bank, branch or agency of a foreign bank, or organization operating under section 25 or section 25(a) of the Federal Reserve Act without authority from the directors of such bank, branch, agency, or organization or company, issues or puts in circulation any notes of such bank, branch, agency, or organization or company; or

Whoever, without such authority, makes, draws, issues, puts forth, or assigns any certificate of deposit, draft, order, bill of exchange, acceptance, note, debenture, bond, or other obligation, or mortgage, judgment or decree; or

Whoever makes any false entry in any book, report, or statement of such bank, company, branch, agency, or organization with intent to injure or defraud such bank, company, branch, agency, or organization, or any other company, body politic or corporate, or any individual person, or to deceive any officer of such bank, company, branch, agency, or organization, or the Comptroller of the Currency, or the Federal Deposit Insurance Corporation, or any agent or examiner appointed to examine the affairs of such bank, company, branch, agency, or organization or the Board of Governors of the Federal Reserve System;

Whoever with intent to defraud the United States or any agency thereof, or any financial institution referred to in this section, participates or shares in or receives (directly or indirectly) any money, profit, property, or benefits through any transaction, loan, commission, contract, or any other act of any such financial institution—

Shall be fined not more than $1,000,000 or imprisoned not more than thirty years, or both.

18 U.S.C. § 1014. Loan and Credit Applications Generally; Renewals and Discounts; Crop Insurance

Whoever knowingly makes any false statement or report, or willfully overvalues any land, property or security, for the purpose of influencing in any way the action of the Farm Credit Administration, Federal Crop Insurance Corporation or a company the Corporation reinsures, the Secretary of Agriculture acting through the Farmers' Home Administration, the Rural Development Administration, any Farm Credit Bank, production credit association, agriculture credit association, bank for cooperatives, or any division, officer, or employee thereof, or of any regional agricultural credit corporation established pursuant to law, or of the National Agricultural Credit Corporation, a Federal Land Bank, a Federal Land Bank association, a Federal Reserve Bank, a small business investment company, a Federal credit union, an insured State-chartered credit union, any institution the accounts of which are insured by the Federal Deposit Insurance Corporation, the Office of Thrift Supervision, any Federal home loan bank, the Federal Housing Finance Board, the Federal Deposit Insurance Corporation, the Resolution Trust Corporation, the Farm Credit System Insurance Corporation, National Credit Union Administration Board, a branch or agency of a foreign bank (as such terms are defined in paragraphs (1) and (3) of section 1(b) of the International Banking Act of 1978), or an organization operating under section 25 or section 25(a) of the Federal Reserve Act, upon any application, advance, discount, purchase, purchase agreement, repurchase agreement, commitment, or loan, or any change or extension of any of the same, by renewal, deferment of action or otherwise, or the acceptance, release, or substitution of security therefor, shall be fined not more than $1,000,000 or imprisoned not more than thirty years, or both. The term "State-chartered credit union" includes a credit union chartered under the laws of a state of the United States, the District of Columbia, or any commonwealth, territory, or possession of the United States.

A statement is *false* for the purposes of 18 U.S.C. § 1001 if it was known to be untrue when it was made, and is *fraudulent* if it was known to be untrue and was made with the intent to deceive a government agency. For a violation to occur the agency need not actually have been deceived nor must the agency have in fact relied upon the false statement. The statement must have been capable, however, of influencing the agency involved.

The elements of a typical 18 U.S.C. § 1001 violation are set forth below:
- The defendant made a false statement (or used a false document)
- That was material
- Regarding a matter within the jurisdiction of any agency of the United States
- With knowledge of its falsity
- Knowingly and willfully (or with reckless disregard for truth or falsity).

18 U.S.C. § 1005 makes it unlawful, among other things, for any officer, director, agent, or employee of a federally insured or chartered bank to make any false entries on the books of such institution with the intent to injure or defraud the bank or third parties, or to deceive any bank officer, examiners, or government agency. Section 1014 prohibits false statements or reports upon any credit application or related document submitted to a federally insured bank or credit institution for the purpose of influencing such organization's action in any way. As with 18 U.S.C. § 1001, the false statements must be willful, but it need not have been relied upon or actually deceived the agency for a violation to occur.

Conspiracy (18 U.S.C. § 286)

Whoever enters into any agreement, combination, or conspiracy to defraud the United States, or any department or agency thereof, by obtaining or aiding to obtain the payment or allowance of any false or fraudulent claim, shall be fined under this title or imprisoned not more than ten years or both.

False, Fictitious, or Fraudulent Claims (18 U.S.C. § 287)

Whoever makes or presents to any person or officer in the civil, military, or naval service of the United States, or any department or agency thereof, any claim upon or against the United States, or any department or agency thereof, knowing such claim to be false, fictitious, or fraudulent shall imprisoned not more than five years and subject to a fine in the amount provided in this title

Major Fraud Against the United States (18 U.S.C. § 1031)

This statute drastically increases the penalties for fraud upon the United States involving procurement contracts of $1 million or more. The act provides, in its pertinent parts:

(a) Whoever knowingly executes, or attempts to execute, any scheme or artifice with the intent
    (1) to defraud the United States; or

(2) to obtain money or property by means of false or fraudulent pretenses, representations, or promises...

In any procurement of property or services as a prime contractor with the United States or as a subcontractor or supplier on a contract in which there is a prime contract with the United States, if the value of the contract, subcontract, or any constituent part thereof, for such property or services of $1,000,000 or more shall, subject to the application of subsection (c) of this section, be fined not more than $1,000,000, or imprisoned not more than 10 years, or both.

Other provisions of the statute allow for penalties of up to $10 million in fines or twice the amount of the gross loss or gain involved in the offense. The statute contains a special seven-year statute of limitations compared to the normal five-year statute applicable to federal crimes.

The statute also contains a *whistleblower* protection clause that provides that any individual who is discharged, demoted, harassed, or otherwise mistreated as a result of the individual's cooperation in the prosecution of offenses under this section may obtain reinstatement, two times the amount of back-pay due, and other damages, including litigation costs and attorney's fees.

Another provision authorizes the Attorney General to pay up to $250,000 in certain circumstances for information regarding possible prosecutions under this section. This and the "whistleblower" provisions do not apply to people who participated in the offense.

Civil False Claims Act (18 U.S.C. § 3729, et seq.)

The False Claims Act provides in part that a person who commits the following acts is liable to the Government for treble damages it sustains and a civil penalty of $5,000 to $10,000 per false claim:

- Knowingly presents or cause to be presented a false or fraudulent claim for payment or approval [§ 3729 (a) (1)]
- Knowingly makes, uses or causes to be made or used, a false record or statement to get a false or fraudulent claim paid or approved [§ 3729 (a) (2)]
- Conspires to defraud the Government by getting a false or fraudulent claim allowed or paid [§ 3729 (a) (3)]

- Knowingly makes use, or causes to be made or used a false record or statement to conceal, avoid, or decrease an obligation to pay or transmit money or property to the government [§ 3729 (a) (7)]

Knowing and knowingly are defined as the person having actual knowledge of the information; acts in deliberate ignorance of the truth or falsity of the information, or acts in reckless disregard of the truth or falsity of the information. No proof of specific intent to defraud is required.

A claim is defined as any request or demand, whether under a contract or otherwise, for money or property which is made to a contractor, grantee, or other recipient if the U.S. Government provides any portion of the money or property which is requested or demanded, or if the government will reimburse such contractor, grantee, or other recipient for any portion of the money or property which is requested or demanded.

The statute also allows a private person to bring a civil action for a violation of 18 U.S.C. § 3729 for the person and for the government. If the government joins the case, the Justice Department has primary responsibility, but the plaintiff continues to be a party to the action. The plaintiff will be entitled to at least 15% but no more than 25% of the recovery to the U.S. Treasury. If the government does not join the case, the plaintiff might still file action on the case. The plaintiff is then entitled to between 25 and 30 % of the recovery. The plaintiff is also entitled to reasonable attorney fees.

Program Fraud Civil Remedies (Public Law 99-509)

Provides for agency administrative adjudication of false claims that are less than $150,000 and for which the agency has approval to prosecute from the Department of Justice. The purpose of the fraud civil remedy is to provide the agency with the ability to prosecute those cases which would otherwise not be prosecuted in the courts because of the cost of a civil court action.

Civil Monetary Penalty Law (42 U.S.C. § 1320a-7a)

The Civil Monetary Penalty Law (CMPL) was passed to impose administrative sanctions against providers who defraud any federally funded program by filing false claims or other improper billing practices. Any person (including an organization, agency, or other entity, but excluding a beneficiary) that presents or causes to be presented a claim for a medical or other item or service that the person knows or should know the claim is false or fraudulent is subject to a civil monetary penalty.

The recent health care amendments revised the law to include higher penalties. Now, the penalty is not more than $10,000 (formerly $2,000) per line item or service and an assessment of not more than three times (formerly twice) the amount claimed. In addition, the person may be excluded from participation in government programs.

Some examples of false claims and statements include:
- Falsified contractor qualifications
- False certifications or assurances
- False records or invoices
- Invoices from nonexistent companies
- Claims made in duplicate or altered invoices
- Billing for fictitious employees
- Billing for goods and services not provided
- Inflated costs or substitution of cheaper goods.

Other examples of false claims and statements might include false statements about employees, fictitious transactions, and falsified documents.

Insurance Fraud Prevention Act (18 U.S.C. § 1033)

18 U.S. C. § 1033 criminalizes certain actions by people who are "engaged in the business of insurance." The statute makes it a crime to provide false statements or reports to any insurance regulatory agency. It also prohibits false statements of any kind made to anyone regarding the financial condition or solvency of an insurance company. Section 1033 also criminalizes the embezzlement or misappropriation of any money, funds, premiums, or other property related to the insurance business.

Federal Corruption Statutes (18 U.S.C. § 201, et seq.)

Chapter 11 of 18 U.S.C. § 201 has 19 separate criminal provisions that define and prohibit a wide variety of conflicts of interest and other corrupt and unethical conduct involving public officials. The statutes of particular interest to fraud examiners follow.

Bribery of Public Officials and Witnesses (18 U.S.C. § 201)

(a) For the purpose of this section –

(1) The term "public official" means Member of Congress, Delegate, or Resident Commissioner, either before or after such official has qualified, or an officer or employee or person acting for on behalf of the United States or any department, agency or branch of Government thereof, including the District of Columbia, in any official function, under or by authority of any such department, agency, or branch of Government, or a juror;

(2) The term "person who has been selected to be a public official" means any person who has been nominated or appointed to be a public official, or has been officially informed that such person will be soon nominated or appointed; and

(3) The term "official act" means any decision or action on any question, matter, cause, suit, proceeding or controversy, which may at any time be pending, or which may by law be brought before any public official, in such official's official capacity, or in such official's place of trust or profit.

(b) Whoever —
(1) directly or indirectly, corruptly gives, offers or promises anything of value to any public official or person who has been selected to be a public official, or offers or promises any public official or any person who has been selected to be a public official to give anything of value to any other person or entity, with intent —
  (A) to influence any official act; or
  (B) to influence such public official or person who has been selected to be a public official to commit or aid in committing, or collude in, or allow, any fraud, or make opportunity for the commission of any fraud, on the United States; or
  (C) to induce such public official or such person who has been selected to be a public official to do or omit to do any act in violation of the lawful duty of such official or person;

(2) being a public official or person selected to be a public official, directly or indirectly, corruptly demands, seeks, receives, accepts, or agrees to receive or accept anything of value personally or for any other person or entity, in return for:
  (A) being influenced in the performance of any official act;
  (B) being influenced to commit or aid in committing, or to collude in, or allow, any fraud, or make opportunity for the commission of any fraud, on the United States; or
  (C) being induced to do or omit to do any act in violation of the official duty of such official or person;

(3) *directly or indirectly, corruptly gives, offers, or promises anything of value to any person, or offers or promises such person to give anything of value to any other person or entity, with intent to influence the testimony under oath or affirmation of such first-mentioned person as a witness upon a trial, hearing, or other proceeding, before any court, any committee of either House or both Houses of Congress, or any agency, commission, or officer authorized by the laws of the United States to hear evidence or take testimony, or with intent to influence such person to absent himself therefrom;*

(4) *directly or indirectly, corruptly demands, seeks, receives, accepts or agrees to receive or accept anything of value personally or for any other person or entity in return for being influenced in testimony under oath or affirmation as a witness upon any such trial, hearing, or other proceeding, or in return for absenting himself therefrom;*

Shall be fined under this title, or not more than three times the monetary equivalent of the thing of value, whichever is greater, or imprisoned for not more than fifteen years, or both, and may be disqualified from holding any office of honor, trust, or profit under the United States.

(c) Whoever —

  (1) otherwise than as provided by law for the proper discharge of official duty—

   (A) directly or indirectly gives, offers or promises anything of value to any public official, former public official, or person selected to be a public official, for or because of any official act performed or to be performed by such public official, former public official, or person selected to be a public official; or

   (B) being a public official, former public official, or person selected to be a public official, otherwise than as provided by law for the proper discharge of official duty, directly or indirectly demands, seeks, receives, accepts, or because of any official act performed or to be performed by such official or person;

  (2) directly or indirectly, gives, offers, or promises anything of value to any person, for or because of the testimony under oath or affirmation given or to be given by such person as a witness upon a trial, hearing, or other proceeding, before any court, any committee of either House or both Houses of Congress, or any agency, commission, or officer authorized by the laws of the United States to hear evidence or take testimony, or for or because of such person's absence therefrom;

  (3) directly or indirectly, demands, seeks, receives, accepts, or agrees to receive or accept anything of value personally for or because of the testimony under oath or affirmation given or to be given by such person as a witness upon any such trial, hearing, or other proceeding, or for or because of such person's absence therefrom —

Shall be fined under this title or imprisoned for not more than two years, or both.

(d) Paragraphs (3) and (4) of subsection (b) and paragraphs (2) and (3) of subsection (c) shall not be construed to prohibit the payment or receipt of witness fees provided by law, or the payment, by the party upon whose behalf a witness is called and receipt by a witness, of the reasonable cost of travel and subsistence incurred and the reasonable value of time lost in attendance at any such trial, hearing, or proceeding, or in the case of expert witnesses, a reasonable fee for time spent in the preparation of such opinion, and in appearing and testifying.

(e) The offenses and penalties prescribed in this section are separate from and in addition to those prescribed in Sections 1503, 1504, and 1505 of this title.

18 U.S.C. § 201 is the principal federal anti-corruption statute, and applies to virtually any U.S. official, juror, or witness. The section contains two separate offenses: Section 201(b), Bribery, prohibits, in general:

- Giving or receiving
- Anything of value
- With the intent to influence
- An official act.

Section 201(c), Illegal Gratuity offense, outlaws:

- Giving or receiving
- Anything of value
- For or because of
- An official act.

The illegal gratuity statute is a lesser included offense of bribery. As stated, a *bribe* is a payment made with the purpose of influencing (changing) official conduct; a *gratuity* is a payment made to reward or compensate an official for performing duties he lawfully is required to perform. Bribery is punishable by up to 15 years imprisonment, fine, and disqualification from holding public office, while illegal gratuity carries only a maximum two-year term, fine, or both.

18 U.S.C. §§ 212 and 213 forbid the giving of a loan or gratuity "to any examiner or assistant examiner who examines or has authority to examine such bank, branch, agency, organization, corporation, association or institution…" The only reported case construing

these statutes held that the prosecution need not prove that the loan or gratuity was given or received with a corrupt or wrongful intent. The strict application of the statute has been justified by the public's need for disinterested bank examiners.

18 U.S.C. § 215 bars the corrupt giving or receiving of anything of value to influence the action of an employee or agent of a federally connected financial institution. The statute is aimed primarily at reducing corrupt influence in loan-making. Unlike Sections 212 and 213 above, a specific intent to influence or be influenced through the illegal payment must be proven to obtain a conviction. A payment made after a loan has been approved and disbursed may be in violation of the law if it is part of a prearranged plan or agreement.

Anti-Kickback Act of 1986 (18 U.S.C. §§ 51-58)

The act outlaws the giving or receiving of anything of value for the purpose of improperly obtaining or receiving favorable treatment in connection with U.S. government contracts. Willful violations can be punished by a fine, or up to 10 years in prison, or both. Civil penalties up to twice the amount of the kickback also may be assessed. The United States also may offset the amount of any kickback against the amount owed on the prime contract.

41 U.S.C. § 57 requires that the prime contractor have in place in its operations reasonable procedures to prevent and detect kickbacks. If a contractor has reasonable grounds to believe that there has been a violation, the contractor is required to report the possible violation. The contractor also is required to cooperate fully with any federal agency investigation.

According to the congressional notes following the statute, "reasonable procedures to detect and prevent kickbacks" include:
- Educational programs for employees and subcontractors
- Policy manuals
- Special procurement and audit procedures
- Ethics policies
- Applicant screening
- Reporting procedures.

The Foreign Corrupt Practices Act (15 U.S.C. §§ 78dd-1, 78dd-2, 78dd-3, 78m)

The Foreign Corrupt Practices Act (FCPA) was originally enacted in 1977 to prohibit certain publicly held companies from making corrupt payments to foreign officials or political organizations. Other amendments to the Act make it illegal for any U.S. citizen to make such payments. The statute was the result of disclosures from the Watergate investigations of corporate *grease payments* to foreigners to obtain business overseas.

The FCPA criminalizes the bribery of a foreign public official in order to obtain or retain business, and it requires publicly traded companies to keep accurate books and records and adopt internal controls to prevent diversion of assets or other improper use of corporate funds.

Since the FCPA was enacted, there have been a number of international initiatives to strengthen anti-bribery laws around the world. One of the most significant is the work of the Organization for Economic Cooperation and Development (OECD). The OECD has 30 member-countries including many of the world's largest economic powers, such as the U.S., Canada, Germany, France, Japan, Italy, Mexico, Spain, Australia, and the U.K. In response to the articles drafted by the OECD, the member countries have, or are in the process of, drafting new, tougher transnational bribery laws.

ANTI-BRIBERY PROVISIONS

In November of 1998, President Clinton signed the International Anti-Bribery and Fair Competition Act (Public Law 105-366) which expanded the FCPA. As amended, the FCPA prohibits:

- The use of mails or other instrumentality of interstate commerce "corruptly" in furtherance of:
  - A payment of – or an offer, promise, or authorization to pay – money or anything of value to
- Any of the following:
  - A "foreign official,"
  - Any foreign political party or official, or a candidate for office, or
  - Any person (such as an agent partner or intermediary) while "knowing" that the payment will passed on to one of the above
- For the purposes of:
  - Influencing any act or decision of such person or party
  - Inducing such official to do or omit to do any act in violation of the lawful duty of that official, or
  - Inducing such foreign official to use his influence with a foreign government to affect or influence any act or decision of the government

- In order to obtain, retain, or direct business to any person.

The FCPA applies to non-U.S. persons acting within the United States as well as U.S. persons acting outside the United States. It also applies to publicly traded companies as well as any other business with its principal place of business located in the U.S.

RECORDKEEPING PROVISIONS (PUBLIC LAW 105-366)

In addition to outlawing bribery payments, the FCPA also contains separate books and records provisions that require certain public companies to:

(a) *make and keep books, records, and accounts, which, in reasonable detail, accurately and fairly reflect the transactions and dispositions of the assets of the issuer; and*

(b) *devise and maintain a system of internal accounting controls sufficient to provide reasonable assurance that —*

  (i) *transactions are executed in accordance with management's general or specific authorization;*

  (ii) *transactions are recorded as necessary (I) to permit preparation of financial statements in conformity with generally accepted accounting principles or any other criteria applicable to such statements, and (II) to maintain accountability for assets;*

  (iii) *access to assets is permitted only in accordance with management's general or specific authorization; and*

  (iv) *the recorded accountability for assets is compared with the existing assets at reasonable intervals and appropriate action is taken with respect to any differences.*

SEC Regulations enforcing these provisions specifically require that:

17 C.F.R. 240.13(B)(2)-1:

No person shall, directly or indirectly, falsify or cause to be falsified, any book, record or account subject to Section 13(b)(2)(A) of the Securities Exchange Act.

17 C.F.R. 240.13(B)(2)-2:

No director or officer of an issuer shall, directly or indirectly,

(a) make or cause to be made a materially false or misleading statement, or

(b) omit to state, or cause another person to omit "to state, any material fact necessary in order to make statements made, in light of the circumstances under which such statements were made, not misleading to an accountant in connection with (1) any audit or examination of

> *the financial statements of the issuer required to be made pursuant to this subpart or (2) the preparation or filing of any document or report required to be filed with the Commission pursuant to this subpart or otherwise."*

The statute and regulations effectively give the SEC supervisory authority over the financial management and reporting functions of publicly held corporations. The SEC has interpreted its powers under the FCPA broadly, announcing that "it is important that issuers ... review their accounting procedures, systems of internal accounting controls and business practices in order that they may take any actions necessary to comply with the requirements [of] the Act."

15 U.S.C. § 78ff provides that willful violations of the statute may be punished by corporate fines of up to $2,500,000 and prison terms not to exceed ten years. Fines for individuals can be as much as $1 million and 10 years' imprisonment, or both. Administrative and civil relief also is available.

Theft or Bribery Concerning Programs Receiving Federal Funds (18 U.S.C. § 666)

Under this statute, a person can be convicted of a federal offense if he or she commits fraud or theft against a company which receives federal funds. The victim of the theft or bribe must be (1) an organization and (2) must receive benefits in excess of $10,000 within any one-year period under a federal program involving a grant, contract, subsidy, loan, guarantee, insurance, or other form of federal assistance.

In determining whether the organization receives more than $10,000 in benefits, you do not include any of the following: salaries, wages, fees, or other compensation paid, or expenses paid or reimbursed in the usual course of business.

Additionally, the following conditions also must be met:
- The accused must be an agent of an organization (as defined above), a state or local government, or Indian tribal government
- Who embezzled, stole, or otherwise obtained by fraud
- Property valued at $5,000 or more, and
- The property is owned, or is under the care or custody, of the organization or agency

The statute also prohibits the offering or acceptance (or agreement to offer or accept) bribes in relation to any transactions involving an organization or agency if the transaction is valued at $5,000 or more.

Federal Securities Laws (The 1933 and 1934 Acts)

As a result of several high profile corporate scandals in 2001 and 2002, Congress passed the Sarbanes-Oxley Act, which was discussed previously in this chapter. In addition to the numerous reporting and certification requirements for financial statements, the Act also created a new criminal statute relating to securities fraud (18 U.S.C. § 1348) set forth below. In addition to this new statute, there are also numerous other federal statutes which prohibit false statements and other fraudulent activity in connection with securities transactions. The most commonly used are Section 17(a) of the Securities Act of 1933 (popularly known as the *1933 Act*), and Rule 10(b)5, promulgated under the Securities Exchange Act of 1934 (the *1934 Act*). Both contain civil and administrative remedies (such as the power to initiate actions to enjoin further violations) enforced by the Securities and Exchange Commission as well as criminal sanctions enforced by the Department of Justice. Whether a particular violation is prosecuted civilly or criminally depends in large measure on the degree of willfulness that can be proved.

Section 17(a) of the 1933 Act makes it unlawful to employ fraudulent devices or misrepresentations in connection with the offer or sale of securities through jurisdictional facilities (e.g., the U.S. mails), whereas Rule 10(b)5 prohibits the same conduct "in connection" with the "purchase or sale" of any security by "any person." Because Rule 10(b)5 has the broadest reach—including insider trading—it is the most often used. The Rule, found in 17 C.F.R. § 240.10b-5, specifically provides:

> *It shall be unlawful for any person, directly or indirectly, by the use of any means or instrumentality of interstate commerce, or of the mails or of any facility of any national securities exchange,*
>
> *(a) To employ any device, scheme, or artifice to defraud,*
>
> *(b) To make any untrue statement of a material fact or to omit to state a material fact necessary in order to make the statements made, in the light of the circumstances under which they were made, not misleading, or*

> *(c) To engage in any act, practice, or course of business which operates or would operate as a fraud or deceit upon any person, in connection with the purchase or sale of any security.*

Specific intent to defraud is an essential element of a violation of Section 17(a) and Rule 10(b)5. However, *intent to defraud* is defined more broadly in securities regulations than in other areas of common-law fraud, and includes reckless statements, as well as the knowing circulation of half truths and false opinions or predictions that elsewhere might be considered non actionable *puffing*.

Good faith is always a defense to a Section 17(a) or Rule 10(b)-5 fraud action. However, intent can be—and usually is—proved by circumstantial evidence, as in any fraud case. Violations of other indirect anti-fraud provisions of the federal securities laws (such as certain registrations and disclosure requirements) do not require a showing of fraudulent intent.

To allow action, a false statement must be material. The test for materiality is whether there is a substantial likelihood under all the circumstances that a reasonable investor would have considered the misstated or omitted facts significant in deciding whether to invest. Materiality is most often expressed in dollar terms or in terms of its effect on financial statements, but it also might relate to serious questions of management's integrity regardless of the dollar amount involved.

SEC civil actions often are settled by *consent decrees* where the party agrees to stop the offending practice without admitting or denying he engaged in it in the first place. Violations of such decrees may be punishable as contempt with jail terms or fines.

Sarbanes-Oxley

The Sarbanes-Oxley Act passed in June 2002 made a number of important changes to securities law. Sarbanes-Oxley is discussed in more detail earlier in this chapter; however, one of the most significant changes was the addition of a new criminal offense:

SECURITIES FRAUD (18 U.S.C. § 1348)
> *Whoever knowingly executes, or attempts to execute, a scheme or artifice—*
> *(1) to defraud any person in connection with any security of an issuer with a class of securities registered under section 12 of the Securities Exchange Act of 1934 (15*

> U.S.C. 78l) or that is required to file reports under section 15(d) of the Securities Exchange Act of 1934 (15 U.S.C. 78o(d)); or
>
> (2) to obtain, by means of false or fraudulent pretenses, representations, or promises, any money or property in connection with the purchase or sale of any security of an issuer with a class of securities registered under section 12 of the Securities Exchange Act of 1934 (15 U.S.C. 78l) or that is required to file reports under section 15(d) of the Securities Exchange Act of 1934 (15 U.S.C. 78o(d));
>
> shall be fined under this title, or imprisoned not more than 25 years, or both.

Since the statute is new, it may be some time before the reach and impact of this new legislation is understood, but it does offer another weapon in the prosecutor's arsenal.

Tax Evasion, False Returns, and Failure to File
(26 U.S.C. §§ 7201, 7203, 7206[1], et. seq.)

Fraud and corruption prosecutions might include tax evasion, false returns, or failure to file counts if—as is often the case—the recipient of illegal payments has not reported them as income or the payer has attempted to conceal and deduct them as a legitimate business expense.

Bankruptcy Fraud (18 U.S.C. § 151, et. seq.)

Two related but somewhat different types of criminal conduct fall under the general heading of bankruptcy fraud. The first is the *planned bankruptcy* or *bustout* scheme where the wrongdoer sells off for cash, usually below cost, inventory obtained on credit (often through false or inflated financial statements) and then absconds with the proceeds. Formal bankruptcy proceedings often are not initiated and the crime may be prosecuted under general fraud statutes, such as mail or wire fraud.

The second type of bankruptcy offense involves misconduct by a person or entity actually involved or contemplating being involved in a formal bankruptcy proceeding. The federal criminal laws that regulate bankruptcy proceedings are set out in the Financial Transactions Section.

Statutes Relating to Financial Institutions

18 U.S.C. § 1344 is the broadest of all bank fraud statutes. It punishes those obtaining assets owned or controlled by a bank by false or fraudulent pretenses, representations, or promises. It covers both insiders and all other persons, even if not affiliated with the bank. It also

applies to check kiting and to offshore frauds (extraterritorial reach). Bank fraud is a predicate offense under RICO (Racketeer Influenced Corrupt Organization Statute). Penalties for bank fraud include a fine up to $1,000,000 and/or imprisonment of up to 30 years. The bank fraud statute and the related 18 U.S.C. § 1345 that provides for civil actions by the government to enjoin fraudulent activity are set out below.

18 U.S.C. § 1344. Bank Fraud

(a) Whoever knowingly executes, or attempts to execute, a scheme or artifice —

    (1) to defraud a financial institution; or

    (2) to obtain any of the moneys, funds, credits, assets, securities, or other property owned by or under the custody or control of, a financial institution, by means of false or fraudulent pretenses, representations, or promises, shall be fined not more than $1,000,000, or imprisoned not more than thirty years, or both.

18 U.S.C. § 1345. Injunctions Against Fraud

(a)

    (1) If a person is

        (A) violating or about to violate this chapter or section 287, 371 (in so far as such violation involves a conspiracy to defraud the United States or any agency thereof), or 1001 of this title; or

        (B) committing or about to commit a banking law violation (as defined in section 3322(d) of this title),

        (C) committing or about to commit a Federal health care offense

the Attorney General may commence a civil action in any Federal court to enjoin such violation.

    (2) If a person is alienating or disposing of property, or intends to alienate or dispose of property, obtained as a result of a banking law violation (as defined in section 3322(d) of this title) or property which is traceable to such violation, the Attorney General may commence a civil action in Federal court

        (A) to enjoin such alienation or disposition of property; or

        (B) for restraining order to

            (i) prohibit any person from withdrawing, transferring, removing, dissipating, or disposing of any such property or property of equivalent value; and

            (ii) appoint a temporary receiver to administer such restraining order.

> *(3) A permanent or temporary injunction or restraining order shall be granted without bond.*
>
> *(b) The court shall proceed as soon as practicable to the hearing and determination of such an action, and may, at any time before final determination, enter such a restraining order or prohibition, or take such other action, as is warranted to prevent a continuing and substantial injury to the United States or to any person or class of persons for whose protection this action is brought. A proceeding under this section is governed by the Federal Rules of Civil Procedure, except that, if an indictment has been returned against the respondent, discovery is governed by the Federal Rules of Criminal Procedure.*

As in the mail and wire fraud statutes, the terms *scheme* and *artifice to defraud* include any misrepresentations or other conduct intended to deceive others in order to obtain something of value. The prosecution must prove only an attempt to execute the scheme and need not show actual loss, or that the victim institution was deceived, or that the defendant personally benefited from the scheme.

Fraud by Bank Personnel and Receivers

18 U.S.C. § 1006 makes it a crime for "officers, agents, or employees" of financial institutions to defraud financial institutions or the U.S. government by making false entries or withdrawing or transferring funds without authorization. The penalties are severe — up to 30 years in prison and/or a fine of up to $1,000,000.

18 U.S.C. § 1032 makes it a crime for a conservator or receiver of a financial institution to conceal or impede the recovery of funds or property.

18 U.S.C. §§ 656 and 657 are the principal federal bank embezzlement statutes. The essential elements of a typical Section 656 violation are:
- The defendant was an officer, director, agent, or employee of
- A federally insured bank
- Who willfully
- Embezzled, abstracted, purloined, or willfully misapplied funds of the bank
- With the intent to injure or defraud the bank.

The terms *abstract*, *purloin* and *misapply* as used in the statute are largely repetitive and in normal usage mean to take or to convert bank funds for one's own use or the use of a third-party for improper purposes without the bank's knowledge or consent. Section 657 prohibits the embezzlement of funds from designated federally connected lending, credit, and insurance organizations. The basic elements of a violation are the same as those in Section 656.

Financial Institutions Reform, Recovery and Enforcement Act (FIRREA) (12 U.S.C. § 1811, et seq.)

This legislation greatly strengthens the prosecutorial arm against insiders and outsiders. The law's provisions are applicable to any institution-affiliated party, which includes (but is not limited to) directors, officers, employees and controlling shareholders. Institution-affiliated parties can include attorneys, accountants and appraisers.

FIRREA provides for enhanced penalties for convictions of several bank-related statutes. Civil penalties range from to $1,000,000 per day or a total of $5 million for continuing violations, or the amount of wrongful gain or loss.

Financial Institution Anti-Fraud Enforcement Act of 1990 (12 U.S.C. § 4201, et seq.)

This statute sets out procedures for rewarding private parties for reporting violations and providing information concerning the recovery of assets. The statute also allows for the hiring of private counsel to investigate and prosecute civil claims.

Continuing Financial Crime Enterprise Statute (18 U.S.C. § 225)

Also known as the "S&L Kingpin" statute, the law provides for fines of up to $20 million for organizational defendants and fines of up to $10 million and up to life imprisonment for individual defendants receiving $5,000,000 or more during a 24-month period from a criminal enterprise. A "criminal enterprise" is defined as a series of enumerated crimes related to financial institutions.

Participation in the Affairs of a Financial Institution by a Convicted Felon (12 U.S.C. § 1829)

This statute bars people with banking crime convictions from participating in the conduct of the affairs of a financial institution, with certain exceptions. A knowing violation might result in fines of up to $1,000,000 per day and imprisonment of up to five years.

Fraudulent Use of Credit Cards (15 U.S.C. §§ 1644)

This statute provides penalties for the use of counterfeit, fictitious, altered, forged, lost, stolen, or fraudulently obtained credit cards. A violator can be fined up to $10,000 and/or imprisoned for up to 10 years.

The Electronic Funds Transfer Act (15 U.S.C. § 1693N(B))

This Act provides, in part, that whoever:

> *(1) knowingly, in a transaction affecting interstate or foreign commerce, uses or attempts or conspires to use any counterfeit, fictitious, altered, forged, lost, stolen, or fraudulently obtained debit instrument to obtain money, goods, services, or anything else of value, which within any one-year period has a value aggregating $1,000 or more; or*
>
> *(2) with unlawful or fraudulent intent, transports or attempts or conspires to transport in interstate or foreign commerce a counterfeit, fictitious, altered, forged, lost, stolen, or fraudulently obtained debit instrument knowing the same to be counterfeit, fictitious, altered, forged, lost, stolen or fraudulently obtained: or*
>
> *(3) with unlawful or fraudulent intent, uses any instrumentality of interstate or foreign commerce to sell or transport a counterfeit, fictitious, altered, forged, lost, stolen, or fraudulently obtained debit instrument knowing the same to be counterfeit, fictitious, altered, forged, lost, stolen, or fraudulently obtained, or*
>
> *(4) knowingly receives, conceals, uses or transports money, goods, services, or anything else of value (except tickets for interstate or foreign transportation) which (A) within any one-year period has a value aggregating $1,000 or more, (B) has moved in or is part of, or which constitutes interstate or foreign commerce, and (C) has been obtained with a counterfeit, fictitious, altered, forged, lost, stolen, or fraudulently obtained debit instrument; or*
>
> *(5) knowingly receives, conceals, uses, sells or transports in interstate or foreign commerce one or more tickets for interstate or foreign transportation, which (A) within any one-year period have a value aggregating $500 or more, and (B) have been purchased or obtained with one or more counterfeit, fictitious, altered, forged, lost, stolen, or fraudulently obtained debit instrument; or*
>
> *(6) in a transaction affecting interstate or foreign commerce, furnishes money, property, services, or anything else of value, which within any one-year period has a value aggregating $1,000 or more, through the use of any counterfeit, fictitious, altered, forged, lost, stolen, or fraudulently obtained debit instrument knowing the same to be counterfeit, fictitious, altered, forged, lost, stolen, or fraudulently obtained.*

shall be fined not more than $10,000 or imprisoned not more than ten years, or both.

As used in this section, the term *debit instrument* means a card, code, or other device, other than a check, draft, or similar paper instrument, by the use of which a person may initiate an electronic fund transfer.

Laws Relating to Health Care Fraud

Numerous criminal and civil federal and state laws are available in the prosecution of health care fraud. In addition, regulatory agencies are also available for licensure action.

As part of the *Health Insurance Portability and Accountability Act of 1996*, Congress made a number of changes to the federal criminal code. The Act established several new criminal statutes related specifically to health care fraud. The new statutes are:
- Health Care Fraud
- Theft of Embezzlement In Connection with Heath Care
- False Statements Relating to Health Care Matters
- Obstruction of Criminal Investigations of Health Care Offenses

The term "health care benefit program" as used in these statutes is defined to mean "any public or private plan or contract, affecting commerce, under which any medical benefit, item, or service is provided to any individual, and includes any individual or entity who is providing a medical benefit, item, or service for which payment may be made under the plan or contract."

The Act also provides that a judge may order a person convicted of a federal health care offense to forfeit any property that can be traced from the proceeds received from the offense.

Health Care Fraud (18 U.S.C. § 1347)

Whoever knowingly and willfully executes, or attempts to execute, a scheme or artifice—
(1) to defraud any health care benefit program; or
(2) to obtain, by means of false or fraudulent pretenses, representations, or promises, any of the money or property owned by, or under the custody or control of, any health care benefit program,

in connection with the delivery of or payment for health care benefits, items, or services, shall be fined under this title or imprisoned not more than 10 years or both. If the violation results in serious bodily injury (as defined in section 1365 of this title), such person shall be fined under this title or imprisoned not more than 20 years or both; and if the violation results in death, such person shall be fined under this title, or imprisoned for any term of years or for life, or both.

Theft or Embezzlement In Connection with Health Care (18 U.S.C. § 669)

Whoever knowingly and willfully embezzles, steals, or otherwise without authority converts to the use of any person other than the rightful owner, or intentionally misapplies any of the moneys, funds, securities, premiums, credits, property, or other assets of a health care benefit program, shall be fined under this title or imprisoned not more than 10 years, or both; but if the value of such property does not exceed the sum of $100 the defendant shall be fined under this title or imprisoned not more than one year, or both.

False Statements Relating to Health Care Matters (18 U.S.C. § 1035)

Whoever, in any matter involving a health care benefit program, knowingly and willfully—(1) falsifies, conceals, or covers up by any trick, scheme, or device a material fact; or (2) makes any materially false, fictitious, or fraudulent statements or representations, or makes or uses any materially false writing or document knowing the same to contain any materially false, fictitious, or fraudulent statement or entry, in connection with the delivery of or payment for health care benefits, items, or services, shall be fined under this title or imprisoned not more than 5 years, or both.

Obstruction of Criminal Investigations of Health Care Offenses (18 U.S.C. § 1518)

(a) Whoever willfully prevents, obstructs, misleads, delays or attempts to prevent, obstruct, mislead, or delay the communication of information or records relating to a violation of a Federal health care offense to a criminal investigator shall be fined under this title or imprisoned not more than 5 years, or both.

(b) As used in this section the term "criminal investigator" means any individual duly authorized by a department, agency, or armed force of the United States to conduct or engage in investigations for prosecutions for violations of health care offenses.

Identity Theft

In 1998, Congress passed the Identity Theft and Assumption Deterrence Act (18 U.S.C. § 1028). The Act makes identity theft a federal crime with penalties up to 15 years imprisonment and a maximum fine of $250,000. This legislation enables the Secret Service, the Federal Bureau of Investigation, and other law enforcement agencies to combat this crime. It allows for the identity theft victim to seek restitution if there is a conviction. It also establishes the Federal Trade Commission as a central agency to act as a clearinghouse for complaints (against credit reporting agencies and credit grantors), referrals, and resources for assistance for victims of identity theft. Selected provisions of the Act are included below.

Fraud and Related Activity in Connection with Identification Documents and Information (18 U.S.C. § 1028)

(a) *Whoever, in a circumstance described in subsection (c) of this section --*

(1) *knowingly and without lawful authority produces an identification document, authentication feature, or a false identification document;*

(2) *knowingly transfers an identification document, authentication feature, or a false identification document knowing that such document was stolen or produced without lawful authority;*

(3) *knowingly possesses with intent to use unlawfully or transfer unlawfully five or more identification documents (other than those issued lawfully for the use of the possessor), authentication features, or false identification documents;*

(4) *knowingly possesses an identification document (other than one issued lawfully for the use of the possessor), authentication feature, or a false identification document or feature, with the intent such document be used to defraud the United States;*

(5) *knowingly produces, transfers, or possesses a document-making implement or authentication feature with the intent such document-making implement or authentication feature will be used in the production of a false identification document or another document-making implement or authentication feature which will be so used;*

(6) *knowingly possess an identification document or authentication feature that is or appears to be an identification document or authentication feature of the United States which is stolen or produced without lawful authority knowing that such document or feature was stolen or produced without such authority;*

(7) *knowingly transfers, possesses, or uses, without lawful authority, a means of identification of another person with the intent to commit, or to aid or abet, or in connection with, any unlawful activity that constitutes a violation of Federal law or that constitutes a felony under any applicable State or local law; or*

(8) *knowingly traffics in false authentication features for use in false identification documents, document-making implements, or means of identification;*

shall be punished as provided in subsection (b) of this statute.

* * *

(c) The circumstance referred to in subsection (a) of this section is that --
- *(1) the identification document or false identification document is or appears to be issued by or under the authority of the United States or the document-making implement is designed or suited for making such an identification document or false identification document;*
- *(2) the offense is an offense under subsection (a)(4) of this section; or*
- *(3) either --*
  - *(A) the production, transfer, possession, or use prohibited by this section is in or affects interstate or foreign commerce, including transfer of a document by electronic means; or*
  - *(B) the means of identification, identification documents, false identification document, or document-making implement is transported in the mail in the course of the production, transfer, possession, or use prohibited by this section.*

* * *

The Anti-Phishing Act of 2004 (Senate Bill 2636, 108th Congress, 2003-2004)

In July 2004, Senator Leahy introduced a bill known as "The Anti-Phishing Act of 2004." The bill has been referred to a committee on the judiciary for review, and will not likely become law, if at all, for a year or more to come. Nonetheless, the bill is the first serious attempt to criminalize internet fraud before it happens.

Phishing generally occurs when an internet user receives an official-looking email that appears to have been sent by a legitimate business or organization, such as a bank, credit-card company, or government agency. The message informs the user of the need to update or validate important account information by clicking on a link. The link then sends the user to a website that looks strikingly similar to the business or organization mentioned in the e-mail. When the user inputs personal or confidential information, such is targeted to be used for identity theft or fraud.

According to the Anti-Phishing Working Group's (APWG) Phishing Attack Trends Report, there were 1422 phishing scams in the month of June 2004. More than a quarter of these scams involving a phony "Citibank" website. Estimated financial loss as a result of phishing appears to be in the billions and rising.

The proposal criminalizes, in pertinent part, anyone who:

> (a) ... *knowingly, with the intent to carry on any activity which would be a Federal or State crime of fraud or identity theft--*
>
> *(1) creates or procures the creation of a website or domain name that represents itself as a legitimate online business, without the authority or approval of the registered owner of the actual website or domain name of the legitimate online business; and*
>
> *(2) uses that website or domain name to induce, request, ask, or solicit any person to transmit, submit, or provide any means of identification to another...*

Aggravated Identity Theft (Title 18, U.S. Code, § 1028A)

In August 2004, Congress passed the Identity Theft Penalty Enhancement Act (18 U.S.C. § 1028A). This new Act provides that where one "knowingly transfers, possesses, or uses, without lawful authority, a means of identification of another" during and in relation to any felony violation of/or relating to fraud, embezzlement, false statements, and the like, an additional term of imprisonment of 2 years will be imposed on the individual.

Telemarketing Fraud

18 U.S.C. §§ 2325-2327 outlaw telemarketing fraud. For purposes of this statute, "telemarketing" is defined as:

> *[A] plan, program, promotion or campaign that is conducted to induce –*
>
> *(A) purchases of goods or services; or*
>
> *(B) participation in a contest or sweepstakes,*
>
> *by use of 1 or more interstate telephone calls initiated either by a person who is conducting the plan, program, promotion, or campaign or by a prospective purchaser or contest or sweepstakes participant...*

The definition contains an exclusion for the solicitation of sales through direct mail catalogs when the calls are initiated by the customer.

The statute does not specifically outlaw telemarketing fraud. Instead, the statute provides enhanced penalties for persons convicted of identity fraud, fraud in connection with access devices, mail fraud, or wire fraud if that offense was committed in connection with the conduct of "telemarketing." If a person is convicted of one of the listed offense through the use of telemarketing, then the statute provides that up to five years shall be added to the person's sentence. It also provides that if the victims were over the age of 55, then the person shall be sentenced to up to 10 additional years. 18 U.S.C. § 2327 directs the judge to order mandatory restitution in all cases. The courts are also allowed to seize any property used to commit the crime, as well as any proceeds of the crime.

Computers and Access Devices
Fraud and Related Activity in Connection with Access Devices (18 U.S.C. § 1029)

This statute provides penalties for trafficking in counterfeit access devices. A counterfeit access device is defined to mean any fictitious, altered, or forged card, plate, code, account number, or other means of account access that can be used, alone or in conjunction with another access device, to obtain money, goods or services. Penalties include fines of up to $100,000 or twice the value obtained by the offense and/or imprisonment for not more than 20 years.

Fraud in Connection with Computers

Computer crime is a new and somewhat amorphous term referring both to cases in which a computer is the instrument of a crime and those in which it is the object. As the instrument, for example, a computer might be used to direct calls in a scheme to sell shares in a nonexistent gold mine or might be used to steal funds from a bank account. As the object of a crime, the information contained in a computer might be stolen or destroyed. (The Financial Transactions Section contains further information on computer crime.)

Most computer crimes are prosecuted under traditional fraud, theft, and embezzlement statutes. 18 U.S.C. § 1030 makes certain computer-related activity a specific federal offense. The lengthy statute provides:

FRAUD AND RELATED ACTIVITY IN CONNECTION WITH COMPUTERS (18 U.S.C. § 1030)

> *(a) Whoever —*
>> *(1) having knowingly accessed a computer without authorization or exceeding authorized access, and by means of such conduct obtains information that has been determined by the United States Government pursuant to an Executive order or statute to require protection against unauthorized disclosure for reasons of national defense or foreign relations, or any restricted data, as defined in*

paragraph y. of section 11 of the Atomic Energy Act of 1954, with reason to believe that such information so obtained could be used to the injury of the United States, or to the advantage of any foreign nation willfully communicates, delivers, transmits, or causes to be communicated, delivered, or transmitted, or attempts to communicate, deliver, transmit or cause to be communicated, delivered, or transmitted the same to any person not entitled to receive it, or willfully retains the same and fails to deliver it to the officer or employee of the United States entitled to receive it;

(2) intentionally accesses a computer without authorization or exceeds authorized access, and thereby obtains—

(A) information contained in a financial record of a financial institution or of a card issuer as defined in Section 1602(n) of Title 15, or contained in a file of a consumer reporting agency on a consumer, as such terms are defined in the Fair Credit Reporting Act (15 U.S.C. 1681 et. seq.);

(B) information from any department or agency of the United States; or

(C) information from any protected computer if the conduct involved interstate or foreign communication;

(3) intentionally, without authorization to access any nonpublic computer of a department or agency of the United States, accesses such a computer of that department or agency that is exclusively for the use of the Government of the United States or, in the case of a computer not exclusively for such use, is used by or for the Government of the United States and such conduct affects the use by or for of the Government of the United States;

(4) knowingly and with intent to defraud, accesses a protected computer without authorization, or exceeds authorized access, and by means of such conduct furthers the intended fraud and obtains anything of value, unless the object of the fraud and the thing obtained consists only of the use of the computer and the value of such use is not more than $5,000 in any one-year period.

(5)(A)(i) knowingly causes the transmission of a program, information, code or command, and as a result of such conduct, intentionally causes damage without authorization to a protected computer;

(ii) intentionally access a protected computer without authorization, and as a result of such conduct, recklessly causes damage; or

(ii) intentionally access a protected computer without authorization, and as a result of such conduct, causes damage; or

(B) by conduct described in clause (i), (ii), or (iii) of subparagraph (A), caused (or, in the case of an attempted offense, would, if completed, have caused)—

(i) loss to 1 or more persons during any 1-year period (and, for purposes of an investigation, prosecution, or other proceeding brought by the United States only, loss resulting from a related course of conduct affecting 1 or more other protected computers) aggregating at least $5,000 in value;

(ii) the modification or impairment, or potential modification or impairment, of the medical examination, diagnosis, treatment, or care of 1 or more individuals;

(iii) physical injury to any person;

(iv) a threat to public health or safety; or

(v) damage affecting a computer system used by or for a government entity in furtherance of the administration of justice, national defense, or national security.

(6) knowingly and with intent to defraud traffics (as defined in Section 1029) in any password or similar information through which a computer may be accessed without authorization, if—

(A) such trafficking affects interstate or foreign commerce; or

(B) such computer is used by or for the Government of the United States;

(7) with intent to extort from any person any money or other thing of value, transmits in interstate commerce any communication containing any communication containing any threat to cause damage to a protected computer;

shall be punished as provided in subsection (c) of this section.

(b) Whoever attempts to commit an offense under subsection (a) of this section shall be punished as provided in subsection (c).

(c) The punishment for an offense under subsection (a) or (b) of this section is

(1) (A) a fine under this title or imprisonment for not more than ten years, or both, in the case of an offense under subsection (a)(1) of this section which does not occur after a conviction for another offense under this section, or an attempt to commit an offense punishable under this subparagraph; and (B) a fine under this title or imprisonment for not more than twenty years, or both, in the case of an offense under subsection (a)(1) of this section which occurs after a conviction for another offense under this section, or an attempt to commit an offense punishable under this subparagraph; and

(2) (A) except as provided in subparagraph (B), a fine under this title or imprisonment for not more than one year, or both, in the case of an offense under subsection (a)(2), (a)(3), (a)(5)(A)(iii) or (a)(6) of this section which does not occur after a conviction for another offense under this section, or an attempt to commit an offense punishable under this subparagraph;

(B) a fine under this title or imprisonment for not more than 5 years, or both, in the case of an offense under subsection (a)(2) or an attempt to commit an offense punishable under this subparagraph if —

(i) the offense was committed for purposes of commercial advantage or private financial gain;

(ii) the offense was committed in furtherance of any criminal or tortious act in violation of the Constitution or laws of the United States or of any State; or

(iii) the value of the information obtained exceeds $5,000;

(C) a fine under this title or imprisonment for not more than ten years, or both, in the case of an offense under subsection (a)(2), (a)(3) or (a)(6) of this section which occurs after a conviction for another offense under this section, or an attempt to commit an offense punishable under this subparagraph;

(3) (A) a fine under this title or imprisonment for not more than five years, or both, in the case of an offense under subsection (a)(4), or (a)(7) of this section which does not occur after a conviction for another offense under this section, or an attempt to commit an offense punishable under this subparagraph; and

(B) a fine under this title or imprisonment for not more than ten years, or both, in the case of an offense under subsection (a)(4), (a)(5)(A)(iii), or (a)(7) of this section which occurs after a conviction for another offense under this section, or an attempt to commit an offense punishable under this subparagraph; and

(4)(A) a fine under this title, imprisonment for not more than 10 years, or both, in the case of an offense under subsection (a)(5)(A)(i), or an attempt to commit an offense punishable under that subsection;

(B) a fine under this title, imprisonment for not more than 5 years, or both, in the case of an offense under subsection (a)(5)(A)(ii), or an attempt to commit an offense punishable under that subsection;

(C) a fine under this title, imprisonment for not more than 20 years, or both, in the case of an offense under subsection (a)(5)(A)(i) or (a)(5)(A)(ii), or an attempt to commit an offense punishable under either subsection, that occurs after a conviction for another offense under this section.

(d) The United States Secret Service shall, in addition to any other agency having such authority, have the authority to investigate offenses under subsections (a)(2)(A), (a)(2)(B), (a)(3), (a)(4), (a)(5), and (a)(6) of this section. Such authority of the United States Secret Service shall be exercised in accordance with an agreement which shall be entered into by the Secretary of the Treasury and the Attorney General.

(e) As used in this section
- *(1) the term "computer" means an electronic, magnetic, optical, electro-chemical, or other high speed data processing device performing logical, arithmetic, or storage functions, and includes any data storage facility or communications facility directly related to or operating in conjunction with such device, but such term does not include an automated typewriter or typesetter, a portable hand-held calculator, or other similar device;*
- *(2) the term "protected computer" means a computer*
  - *(A) exclusively for the use of a financial institution or the United States Government, or, in the case of a computer not exclusively for such use, used by or for a financial institution or the United States Government and the conduct constituting the offense affects that use by or for the financial institution or the Government; or*
  - *(B) which is used in interstate or foreign commerce or communications, including a computer located outside the United States that is used in a manner that affects interstate or foreign commerce of the United States;*
- *(3) the term "State" includes the District of Columbia, the Commonwealth of Puerto Rico, and any other commonwealth, possession or territory of the United States;*
- *(4) the term "financial institution" means*
  - *(A) an institution with deposits insured by the Federal Deposit Insurance Corporation;*
  - *(B) the Federal Reserve or a member of the Federal Reserve including any Federal Reserve Bank;*
  - *(C) a credit union with accounts insured by the National Credit Union Administration;*
  - *(D) a member of the Federal home loan bank system and any home loan bank;*
  - *(E) any institution of the Farm Credit System under the Farm Credit Act of 1971;*

(F) a broker/dealer registered with the Securities and Exchange Commission pursuant to section 15 of the Securities Exchange Act of 1934;

(G) the Securities Investor Protection Corporation;

(H) a branch or agency of a foreign bank (as such terms are defined in paragraphs (1) and (3) of section 1(b) of the International Banking Act of 1978); and

(I) an organization operating under section 25 or section 25(a) of the Federal Reserve Act.

(5) the term "financial record" means information derived from any record held by a financial institution pertaining to a customer's relationship with the financial institution;

(6) the term "exceeds authorized access" means to access a computer with authorization and to use such access to obtain or alter information in the computer that the accesser is not entitled so to obtain or alter;

(7) the term "department of the United States" means the legislative or judicial branch of the Government or one of the executive departments enumerated in section 101 of title 5;

(8) the term "damage" means any impairment to the integrity or availability of data, a program, a system, or information

(9) the term "government entity" includes the Government of the United States, any State or political subdivision of the United States, any foreign country, and any state, province, municipality, or other political subdivision of a foreign country;

(10) the term "conviction" shall include a conviction under the law of any State for a crime punishable by imprisonment for more than 1 year, an element of which is unauthorized access, or exceeding authorized access, to a computer;

(11) the term "loss" means any reasonable cost to any victim, including the cost of responding to an offense, conducting a damage assessment, and restoring the data, program, system, or information to its condition prior to the offense, and any revenue lost, cost incurred, or other consequential damages incurred because of interruption of service; and

(12) the term "person" means any individual, firm, corporation, educational institution, financial institution, governmental entity, or legal or other entity.

(f) This section does not prohibit any lawfully authorized investigative, protective, or intelligence activity of a law enforcement agency of the United States, a State, or a political subdivision of a State, or of an intelligence agency of the United States.

(g) Any person who suffers damage or loss by reason of a violation of the section may maintain a civil action against the violator to obtain compensatory damages and injunctive relief or other equitable relief. A civil action for a violation of this section may be brought only if the conduct involves 1 of the factors set forth in clause (i), (ii), (iii), (iv), or (v) of subsection (a)(5)(B). Damages for a violation involving only conduct described in subsection (a)(5)(B)(i) are limited to economic damages. No action may be brought under this subsection unless such action is begun within 2 years of the date of the act complained of or the date of the discovery of the damage. No action may be brought under this subsection for the negligent design or manufacture of computer hardware, computer software, or firmware.

(h) The Attorney General and the Secretary of the Treasury shall report to the Congress annually, during the first 3 years following the date of the enactment of this subsection, concerning investigations and prosecutions under section 1030(a)(5) of title 18, United States Code.

In brief, 18 U.S.C. § 1030 punishes any intentional, unauthorized access to a "protected computer" for the purpose of:
- Obtaining restricted data regarding national security
- Obtaining confidential financial information
- Using a computer which is intended for use by the U. S. government
- Committing a fraud
- Damaging or destroying information contained in the computer.

Prosecuting Computer Related Frauds

Federal and state legislatures are moving quickly to make criminal all manner of computer fraud and abuses, such as hardware theft and destruction, misappropriation of software, unauthorized accessing of computers and data communications facilities to steal data or money or to cause mischief.

PROTECTED COMPUTER

Title 18 U.S. Code, § 1030(a)(4) provides that a crime is committed if a person:

> [K]nowingly and with intent to defraud, accesses a protected computer without authorization, or exceeds authorized access, and by means of such conduct furthers the intended fraud and obtains anything of value, unless the object of the fraud and the thing obtained consists only of the use of the computer and the value of such use is not more than $5,000 in any 1-year period.

A *protected computer*, under this section, includes:
- A computer which is used exclusively by a financial institution or the U.S. Government
- Any computer the use of which affects a computer used by a financial institution or the federal government
- A computer that is used in interstate or foreign commerce or communication, including a computer located outside the United States that is used in a manner that affects interstate or foreign commerce of the United States.

The elements of the crime seem to include unauthorized access (or exceeding one's authority), an intent to defraud, and obtaining anything of value. Software as a thing of value would seem to be included. Certainly money is.

COMPUTER USED IN INTERSTATE OR FOREIGN COMMERCE OR COMMUNICATION

18 U.S.C. § 1030 includes computers used in interstate or foreign commerce or communication. Subsection (a)(5) also includes computers located outside the United States if the computer is used in a manner that affects U.S. commerce.

A person commits a violation if he or she uses such a computer to knowingly transmit anything that causes damage to a protected computer. The conduct need not be intentional. A violation occurs if the person accesses a protected computer without authorization and causes damage as a result. The penalty for violations of Sections 1030 includes fines and up to twenty years of imprisonment.

CIVIL REMEDIES

Subsection (g) provides a civil remedy for any person who suffers damage as a result of a violation of Section 1030. In the case of *Shurgard Storage v. Safeguard Self Storage*, 119 F. Supp. 2d 1121 (W.D. Wash. 2000), a U.S. District Court held that the Computer Fraud and Abuse Act could be used against an employee who, without permission, copied information from his employer's computer and sent it by e-mail to a company that he later went to work for. This allows private companies to go after not only hackers, but anyone who steals information from a computer system. It also gives companies another cause of action in the event of trade secret theft, in addition to the Economic Espionage Act discussed later in this chapter.

Additionally, as a result of the USA Patriot Act passed in 2001, the definition of "loss" was broadly amended to include "any reasonable cost to the victim" and includes costs associated with responding to an incident, conducting damage assessments, and restoring systems to their original condition as well as any lost revenue or other consequential damages.

STATE LAWS

At the state level, statutes that might be of use in prosecuting computer crimes would include the penal code violations of larceny (in its many forms), false pretenses, forgery, fraud, embezzlement, vandalism, property destruction, malicious mischief, proprietary information, theft, commercial bribery, and extortion. But most states now expressly provide penalties for crimes perpetrated by use of computers or perpetrated against computers.

At last check, 48 states had either amended their current statutes or enacted new legislation. Vermont and West Virginia had not. The first state to respond to computer crime was Florida whose legislation went into effect on August 1, 1978. Twenty-five states have enacted specific computer crime statutes and 23 states have amended their criminal statutes. Some states use separate codes and some states use categories such as "crimes against property."

COMPUTER CRIME ACT - SPECIFIC STATE STATUTES

Alabama (1985): Ala. Code 13A-8-101

Arkansas (1987): Ark. Stat. sec 5-41-102, 5-41-106

Colorado (1979): Colo. Rev. Stat. Ann. sec 18-5.5-101

Connecticut (1984): Conn. Gen. Stat. Ann. sec. 53a-250

Delaware (1984): Del. Code tit. 11, sec. 931 to 939

Florida (1978): Fla. Stat. Ann. sec. 815.01

Georgia (1981): GA. Code Ann. sec 16-9-90 & sec 16-14-3

Hawaii (1984): Haw. Rev. Stat. 708-890

Idaho (1984): Idaho Code sec. 18-2201

Illinois (1979): Ill Stat. Ann. ch. 38, sec. 16D-1, 16D-7

Iowa (1984): Iowa Code Ann. sec. 716A

Louisiana (1984): La. Rev. Stat. 14:73.1 through 5

Michigan (1979): Mich. Comp. Laws Ann. sec 752.791

Mississippi (1985): Miss Code Ann.. sec. 97-45-1

New Jersey (1984): NJ Rev. Stat. sec. 2A:38A-1 & 2C:20-23 & 52:17B-193

New York (1986): NY Penal Law Art. 156

North Carolina (1979): NC Gen Sat. 14-453

Oklahoma (1984): Okla Stat Ann. tit. 21, sec. 1952-1956

Rhode Island (1979): RI Gen Laws sec. 11-52-1

South Carolina (1984): SC Code sec. 16-16-10

Tennessee (1983): Tenn. Code Ann. sec. 39-3-1401

Texas (1985): Tex. Penal Code sec. 33.01-33.05

Utah (1979): Utah Code Ann. sec. 76-6-701

Virginia (1984): VA Code Ann. sec. 18.2-152.1

Wyoming (1982): Wyo. Stat. sec 6-3-501 through 504

AMENDED STATES' CRIMINAL STATUTES:

Alaska (1984): Als. Stat. sec. 11.46.200(a); 11.46.740; 11.81.900(b)(44)

Arizona (1978): Ariz. Rev. Stat. sec 13-2301E, 13-2316

California (1979): Cal. Penal Code sec. 502

Indiana (1986): IC 35-43-1-4, IC 35-43-2-3

Kansas (1985): Kans. Stat. sec. 21-3755

Kentucky (1984): Ky. Rev. Stat. sec. 434.840

Maine (1975): Me. Rev. Stat. Ann. tit. 17-A sec. 357(1964)

Maryland (1984): Md. Ann. Code Art. 27, sec. 14.6

Massachusetts (1983): Mass. Gen. Laws Ann. ch. 266, sec. 30(2)

Minnesota (1982): Minn. Stat. Ann. sec. 609.87

Missouri (1982): Mo. Ann. stat. sec. 569.093

Montana (1981): Mont. Code Ann. 45-6-310

Nebraska (1985): Neb. Rev. Stat. sec. 28-1343

Nevada (1983): Nev. Rev. Stat. sec. 205-473

New Hampshire (1985): N.H. Rev. Stat. sec. 638:16

New Mexico (1979): Computer Crimes Act of 1979. N.M. Stat. Ann sec. 30-16A-1

North Dakota (1983): ND Cent. Code sec. 12.1-06.1-08

Ohio (1986): Ohio Rev. Code Ann. sec. 2901.01 and 2913.01

Oregon (1985): Or. Rev. Stat. 164.377

Pennsylvania (1983): PA. Stat. Ann. titl. 18, sec. 3933

South Dakota (1982): SD Codified Laws Ann. sec. 43-43B-1

Washington (1984): Wash. Rev. Code Ann. sec. 943.70

Wisconsin (1981): Wisc. Stat. sec. 943.70

Internet Crime

At the current time, there are no federal laws aimed specifically at fraud or other illegal activities conducted over the Internet. However, many of the existing laws can be used to prosecute Internet fraud as well as more traditional fraud schemes. The table below summarizes how existing laws apply to common crimes perpetrated over the Internet:

Types of Unlawful Conduct	Examples of Potentially Applicable Federal Laws
Internet Fraud	15 U.S.C. §§ 45, 52 (unfair or deceptive acts or practices; false advertisements) 15 U.S.C. § 1644 (credit card fraud) 18 U.S.C. §§ 1028, 1029, 1030 (fraud in connection with identification documents and information; fraud in connection with access devices; and fraud in connection with computers) 18 U.S.C. § 1341 et seq. (mail, wire, and bank fraud) 18 U.S.C. § 1345 (injunctions against fraud) 18 U.S.C. § 1956, 1957 (money laundering)
Online Child Pornography, Child Luring, and Related Activities	18 U.S.C. § 2251 et seq. (sexual exploitation and other abuse of children) 18 U.S.C. § 2421 et seq. (transportation for illegal sexual activity)
Internet Sale of Prescription Drugs and Controlled Substances	15 U.S.C. § 45 et seq. (unfair or deceptive acts or practices; false advertisements) 18 U.S.C. § 545 (smuggling goods into the United States) 18 U.S.C. § 1341 et seq. (mail, wire, and bank fraud; injunctions against fraud) 21 U.S.C. § 301 et seq. (Federal Food, Drug, and Cosmetic Act) 21 U.S.C. §§ 822, 829, 841, 863, 951-971 (Drug Abuse Prevention and Control)
Internet Sale of Firearms	18 U.S.C. § 921 et seq. (firearms)
Internet Gambling	15 U.S.C. § 3001 et seq. (Interstate Horseracing Act) 18 U.S.C. § 1084 (transmission of wagering information) 18 U.S.C. §§ 1301 et seq. (lotteries) 18 U.S.C. § 1952 (interstate and foreign travel or transportation in aid of racketeering enterprises) 18 U.S.C. § 1953 (interstate transportation of wagering paraphernalia) 18 U.S.C. § 1955 (prohibition of illegal gambling businesses) 28 U.S.C. §§ 3701-3704 (professional and amateur sports protection)
Internet Sale of Alcohol	18 U.S.C. § 1261 et seq. (liquor traffic)

	27 U.S.C. §§ 122, 204 (shipments into states for possession or sale in violation of state law)
Online Securities Fraud	15 U.S.C. § 77e, 77j, 77q, 77x, 78i, 78j, 78l, 78o, 78ff (securities fraud)
Software Piracy and Intellectual Property Theft	17 U.S.C. § 506 (criminal copyright infringement) 17 U.S.C. § 1201 et seq. (copyright protection and management systems) 18 U.S.C. § 545 (smuggling goods into the United States) 18 U.S.C. §§ 1341, 1343 (frauds and swindles) 18 U.S.C. § 1831 et seq. (protection of trade secrets) 18 U.S.C. §§ 2318-2320 (trafficking in counterfeit labels for phonorecords, copies of computer programs or computer program documentation or packaging, and copies of motion pictures or other audio visual works)

Identifying and Protecting Trade Secrets

Protection against economic and corporate espionage involves implementing and increasing controls, as well as establishing defenses to trade secret intrusion. Trade secrets include but are not limited to, customer lists, vendor contracts, blueprints and construction plans, bidding systems, computer programs, test data, pricing information, recipes, marketing plans, manufacturing processes, and business forms. Essentially, any idea or information that gives its owner an advantage over its competitors can be classified as a trade secret, so long as it generally meets the two criteria set forth below.

To qualify as a trade secret, information must generally meet two criteria. First, it must actually be a "secret." In other words, a company cannot sue an employee or competitor for releasing the information that was already well known and readily available. Second, organizations are required to take reasonable steps to protect their trade secrets from disclosure. Trade secret protection for a piece of information will not exist where the information has been publicly disclosed or where the organization that owns the secret has not taken adequate steps to protect it from disclosure.

Organizations and individuals can maintain legal protection over trade secrets by taking reasonable steps to keep all proprietary information secret. It is imperative that plans are developed to reasonably guard trade secrets from disclosure. The use of nondisclosure and non-competition agreements can provide employers with legal recourse against those who misappropriate proprietary information.

Nondisclosure agreements typically stipulate that all trade secrets, and other proprietary or confidential information shall be kept confidential without disclosure to anyone. These agreements should be signed at the outset and termination of employment. Non-competition agreements generally forbid a current employee from working for competing companies within a certain period of time from termination. Many state courts void such agreements as against "public policy" because they limit future employment of a person. Those states that do allow non-competition agreements require the agreement to be part of an otherwise valid employment agreement. However, where an employee is hired "at will," non-competition agreements are unenforceable.

The Uniform Trade Secrets Act

The Uniform Trade Secrets Act (UTSA) was promulgated by the National Conference of Commissioners on Uniform State Laws in 1979. The UTSA is not a federal law, but several states have adopted versions of it in an effort to protect trade secrets. The UTSA protects against the theft of "formulas, patterns, compilations, programs, devices, methods, techniques, and processes" of information.

Companies attempting to show that a competitor has misappropriated a trade secret under the UTSA must satisfy a two-pronged test:
- It must be demonstrated that the company owned a "trade secret"; and
- The company must prove that the defendant used the trade secret in breach of "an agreement, a confidential relationship or duty, or as a result of discovery by improper means.

In order for information to qualify as a trade secret under the UTSA, the owner of the information must show that:
- The information derived independent economic value from its secrecy, and
- Efforts must have been taken to keep the information secret. The UTSA does not require the trade secret to have been used in business.

The information does not have to derive actual independent value from its secrecy; it is enough if there is potential economic value as a result of the information being kept secret. Thus, for plans or innovations that have not yet been put into effect by a company, the UTSA would still provide protection. The second prong of the definition once again mandates that organizations take reasonable steps to guard their secrets. If information is not treated as a secret by its owner, the organization cannot later seek protection under the UTSA.

The UTSA defines a "misappropriation" of a trade secret as:

- The acquisition of a trade secret of another by a person who knows or has reason to know that the trade secret was acquired by improper means; or
- Disclosure or use of a trade secret of another without express or implied consent by a person who used improper means to acquire knowledge of the trade secret or at the time of disclosure or use, knew or had reason to know that it was a protected trade secret.

The term "improper means" includes such things as theft, bribery, misrepresentation, breach of a duty to maintain secrecy, or espionage through electronic or other means. Note that the UTSA not only proscribes the stealing of a trade secret, but also the use of that trade secret by those who know it was stolen, whether they participated in the theft or not.

The UTSA is not a federal law; instead it was adopted only in various versions by individual states. As a result, the UTSA has fallen prey to certain difficulties. First, the fact that the UTSA was adopted in different versions by different states creates inconsistencies in the interpretation of its provisions. Second, the UTSA is not a criminal statute. The lack of criminal sanctions for violations of the UTSA takes some of the teeth out of its attempts to deter the theft of trade secrets. These are problems that Congress sought to rectify with the passage of the Economic Espionage Act.

Economic Espionage Act of 1996 (18 U.S.C. §§ 1831-1839)

The Economic Espionage Act of 1996 now makes the theft of trade secrets a federal criminal offense. The Department of Justice now has sweeping authority to prosecute trade secret theft whether it is in the United States, via the Internet, or outside the United States.

18 U.S.C. § 1832 makes it a federal criminal act for any person to convert a trade secret to his own benefit or the benefit of others intending or knowing that the offense will injure any owner of the trade secret. The conversion of a trade secret is defined broadly to cover every conceivable act of trade secret misappropriation including theft, appropriation without authorization, concealment, fraud artifice, deception, copying without authorization, duplication, sketches, drawings, photographs, downloads, uploads, alterations, destruction, photocopies, transmissions, deliveries, mail, communications, or other transfers or conveyances of such trade secrets without authorization.

The Act also makes it a federal criminal offense to receive, buy or possess the trade secret information of another person knowing the same to have been stolen, appropriated, obtained or converted without the trade secret owner's authorization.

The term "trade secret" means all forms and types of financial, business, scientific, technical, economic, or engineering information, including patterns, plans, compilations, program devices, formulas, designs, prototypes, methods, techniques, processes, procedures, programs or codes, whether tangible or intangible, and whether or how stored, compiled, or memorialized physically, electronically, graphically, photographically, or in writing if (A) the owner thereof has taken reasonable measures to keep such information secret; and (B) the information derives independent economic value, actual or potential, from not being generally known to, and not being readily ascertainable through proper means by the public.

A violation 18 U.S.C. § 1832 can result in stiff criminal penalties. A person who commits an offense in violation of Section 1832 can be fined and imprisoned up to 10 years. A corporation or other organization can be fined up to $5 million. If the trade secret theft benefits a foreign government, instrumentality, or agent, the penalties are even greater.

18 U.S.C. § 1831 provides that a person can be imprisoned up to 15 years and fined up to $500,000 if the offense is committed "intending or knowing" that the offense will "benefit a foreign government, foreign instrumentality or foreign agent." A corporation or other organization can be fined up to $10 million. A "foreign instrumentality" is defined under the Act to mean any agency, bureau, ministry, component, institution, association, or any legal, commercial or business organization, corporation, firm or entity that is substantially owned, controlled, sponsored, commanded, managed, or dominated by a foreign government. In turn, the term "foreign agent" is defined by the Act to mean any officers, employee, proxy servant, delegate, or representative of a foreign government.

Both "attempts to" commit Section 1831-1832 offenses and "conspiracies" to commit Section 1831-1832 offenses are proscribed by the Act. The same penalties apply to these offenses with increased penalties if the trade secret misappropriation benefits a foreign government, foreign instrumentality or a foreign agent.

Under the Act, there also is criminal forfeiture to the United States of (1) any property constituting or derived from the proceeds of violations of the Act, and (2) the forfeiture of any property used or intended to be used, in any manner or part, to commit or facilitate a violation of the Act. The criminal forfeiture provisions will now enable Federal prosecutors to dismantle entire Internet networks and seek criminal forfeiture of all the computers, printers and other devices used to commit or facilitate the offenses proscribed by the Act.

The Act also authorizes the Attorney General, Deputy Attorney General, or Assistant Attorney General in the Criminal Division of the Justice Department to apply for a federal court order authorizing or approving the interception of wire or oral communications by the FBI or other federal agencies having responsibility for the investigation of the offense. These are the same investigative tools available in other federal criminal prosecutions.

The Act also applies to offenses committed outside the United States if (1) the offender is a citizen or permanent resident alien of the United States, (2) if the corporation or other organization was incorporated or organized in the United States, or (3) an act in furtherance of the offense was committed in the United States. These extraterritorial provisions in the Act will provide the Justice Department with broad authority to prosecute the international theft of trade secrets and will prevent the willful evasion of liability for trade secret misappropriation by using the Internet or other means to transfer the trade secret information outside the United States.

The Attorney General also is authorized to commence civil actions to obtain injunctive relief to protect the trade secret owner from any violations or further violations of the Act. There is no requirement in the Act that criminal indictments be issued first. Therefore, the Justice Department may commence civil actions for injunctive relief at any stage of the investigation. In any prosecution or other proceeding under the Act, the Court is required to issue protective orders and to take such other action as be necessary to preserve the confidentiality of the trade secrets consistent with the Federal Rules of Criminal and Civil Procedure.

Economic Espionage (18 U.S.C. § 1831)

(a) *In General* - *Whoever, intending or knowing that the offense will benefit any foreign government, foreign instrumentality, or foreign agent, knowingly –*

(1) *steals, or without authorization appropriates, takes, carries away, or conceals, or by fraud, artifice, or deception obtains a trade secret;*

(2) *without authorization copies, duplicates, sketches, draws, photographs, downloads, uploads, alters, destroys, photocopies, replicates, transmits, delivers, sends, mails, communicates, or conveys a trade secret,*

(3) *receives, buys, or possesses a trade secret, knowing the same to have been stolen or appropriated, obtained, or converted without authorization,*

(4) *attempts to commit any offense described in any of paragraphs (1) through (3), or*

> *(5) conspires with one or more other persons to commit any offense described in any of paragraphs (1) through (3), and one or more of such persons do any act to effect the object of the conspiracy, shall, except as provided in subsection (b), be fined not more than $500,000 or imprisoned not more than 15 years, or both.*
>
> *(b) <u>Organizations</u> - Any organization that commits any offense described in subsection (a) shall be fined not more than $ 10,000,000.*

18 U.S.C. § 1831 of the Economic Espionage Act is targeted at economic espionage conducted by or on behalf of foreign governments or instrumentalities. In addition to the three general elements of an espionage case that were discussed above (1) the defendant stole, or with or without the authorization of the owner, obtained, destroyed or conveyed information; (2) the defendant knew the information was proprietary; and (3) the information was in fact a trade secret), there is a fourth element that the government must prove to successfully prosecute under §1831. The government must show that the defendant intended or knew that the offense would benefit a foreign government, foreign instrumentality, or foreign agent. Attempts and conspiracies to commit these offenses are also punishable under §1831.

The maximum punishment under §1831 is 15 years imprisonment and a fine of $500,000. If the offense is committed by an organization, the maximum fine $10,000,000.

Theft of Trade Secrets (18 U.S.C. § 1832)

> *(a) Whoever, with intent to convert a trade secret, that is related to or included in a product that is produced for or placed in interstate or foreign commerce, to the economic benefit of anyone other than the owner thereof, and intending or knowing that the offense will injure any owner of that trade secret, knowingly –*
>
>> *(1) steals, or without authorization appropriates, takes, carries away, or conceals, or by fraud, artifice, or deception obtains such information;*
>>
>> *(2) without authorization copies, duplicates, sketches, draws, photographs, downloads, uploads, alters, destroys, photocopies, replicates, transmits, delivers, sends, mails, communicates, or conveys such information;*
>>
>> *(3) receives, buys, or possesses such information, knowing the same to have been stolen or appropriated, obtained, or converted without authorization;*
>>
>> *(4) attempts to commit any offense described in paragraphs (1) through (3); or*

> *(5) conspires with one or more other persons to commit any offense described in paragraphs (1) through (3), and one or more of such persons do any act to effect the object of the conspiracy, shall, except as provided in subsection (b), be fined under this title or imprisoned not more than ten years, or both.*
>
> *(b) Any organization that commits any offense described in subsection (a) shall be fined not more than $5,000,000.*

18 U.S.C. § 1832 is concerned with conventional commercial theft and misappropriation of trade secrets. It principally covers domestic crimes. In addition to three standard elements of espionage, a 18 U.S.C. § 1832 action requires the government to prove the three following elements:

- That the accused intended to convert the trade secret to the economic benefit of someone other than the rightful owner;
- That the accused intended to injure the owner of the trade secret; and
- That the trade secret was related to or included in a product that is produced for or placed in interstate or foreign commerce.

As evidenced by the additional elements, the requirements for prosecution under §1832 are somewhat stricter than under §1831. For example, §1832 requires that the defendant have intended for someone to gain by the misappropriation, whereas §1831 prosecutions can succeed even when the benefits of a theft are non-economic.

The maximum punishments for an offense under §1832 are 10 years imprisonment, a fine, or both. If the offense is committed by an organization, the fine can run as high as $5,000,000. Attempts and conspiracies to commit the domestic theft of trade secrets are also punishable under §1832.

Exceptions to Prohibitions (18 U.S.C. § 1833)

> *This chapter does not prohibit —*
>
> *(1) any otherwise lawful activity conducted by a governmental entity of the United States, a State, or a political subdivision of a State; or*
>
> *(2) the reporting of a suspected violation of law to any governmental entity of the United States, a State, or a political subdivision of a State, if such entity has lawful authority with respect to that violation.*

Criminal Forfeiture (18 U.S.C. § 1834)

(a) The court, in imposing sentence on a person for a violation of this chapter, shall order, in addition to any other sentence imposed, that the person forfeit to the United States —

(1) any property constituting or derived from, any proceeds the person obtained, directly or indirectly, as the result of such violation; and

(2) any of the person's or organization's property used, or intended to be used, in any manner or part, to commit or facilitate the commission of such violation, if the court in its discretion so determines, taking into consideration the nature, scope, and proportionality of the use of the property in the offense.

(b) Property subject to forfeiture under this section, any seizure and disposition thereof, and any administrative or judicial proceeding in relation thereto, shall be governed by section 413 of the Comprehensive Drug Abuse Prevention and Control Act of 1970 (21 U.S.C. 853), except for subsections (d) and 0) of such section, which shall not apply to forfeitures under this section.

Orders to Preserve Confidentiality (18 U.S.C. § 1835)

In any prosecution or other proceeding under this chapter, the court shall enter such orders and take such other action as may be necessary and appropriate to preserve the confidentiality of trade secrets, consistent with the requirements of the Federal Rules of Criminal and Civil Procedure, the Federal Rules of Evidence, and all other applicable laws. An interlocutory appeal by the United States shall lie from a decision or order of a district court authorizing or directing the disclosure of any trade secret.

Civil Proceedings to Enjoin Violations (18 U.S.C. § 1836)

(a) The Attorney General may, in a civil action, obtain appropriate injunctive relief against any violation of this section.

(b) The district courts of the United States shall have exclusive original jurisdiction of civil actions under this subsection.

Applicability to Conduct Outside the United States (18 U.S.C. § 1837)

This chapter also applies to conduct occurring outside the United States if

(1) the offender is a natural person who is a citizen or permanent resident alien of the United States, or an organization organized under the laws of the United States or a State or political subdivision thereof —, or

(2) an act in furtherance of the offense was committed in the United States.

Construction with Other Laws (18 U.S.C. § 1838)

This chapter shall not be construed to preempt or displace any other remedies, whether civil or criminal, provided by United States Federal, State, commonwealth, possession, or territory law for the misappropriation of a trade secret, or to affect the otherwise lawful disclosure of information by any Government employees under section 552 of title 5 (commonly known as the Freedom of Information Act).

Definitions (18 U.S.C. § 1839)

As used in this chapter

(1) the term "foreign instrumentality" means any agency, bureau, ministry, component, institution, association, or any legal, commercial, or business organization, corporation, firm, or entity that is substantially owned, controlled, sponsored, commanded, managed, or dominated by a foreign government:

(2) the term "foreign agent" means any officer, employee, proxy, servant, delegate, or representative of a foreign government:

(3) the term "trade secret" means all forms and types of financial, business, scientific, technical, economic, or engineering information, including patterns, plans, compilations, program devices, formulas, designs, prototypes, methods, techniques, processes, procedures, programs, or codes, whether tangible or intangible, and whether or how stored, compiled, or memorialized physically, electronically, graphically, photographically, or in writing if

(A) the owner thereof has taken reasonable measures to keep such information secret; and

(B) the information derives independent economic value, actual or potential, from not being general known to, and not being readily ascertainable through proper means by the public, and

(4) the term "owner," with respect to a trade secret, means the person or entity in whom or in which rightful legal or equitable title to or license in, the trade secret is reposed.

Money Laundering

A complex statute forbids *money laundering* in connection with a large number of enumerated federal crimes, including but not limited to narcotics trafficking. Pertinent parts of the statute include:

Laundering of Monetary Instruments (18 U.S.C. § 1956)

(a)(1) Whoever, knowing that the property involved in a financial transaction represents the proceeds of some form of unlawful activity, conducts or attempts to conduct such a financial transaction which in fact involves the proceeds of specified unlawful activity

(A)

(i) with the intent to promote the carrying on of specified unlawful activity; or

(ii) with intent to engage in conduct constituting a violation of Section 7201 or 7206 of the Internal Revenue Code of 1986; or

(B) knowing that the transaction is designed in whole or in part —

(i) to conceal or disguise the nature, the location, the source, the ownership, or the control of the proceeds of specified unlawful activity; or

(ii) to avoid a transaction reporting requirement under State or Federal law, [commits an offense].

(2) Whoever transports, transmits, or transfers, or attempts to transport, transmit, or transfer a monetary instrument or funds from a place in the United States to or through a place outside the United States or to a place in United States from or through a place outside the United States —

(A) with the intent to promote the carrying on of specified unlawful activity; or

(B) knowing that the monetary instrument or funds involved in the transportation, transmission, or transfer represent the proceeds of some form of unlawful activity and knowing that such transportation, transmission, or transfer is designed in whole or in part —

(i) to conceal or disguise the nature, the location, the source, the ownership, or the control of the proceeds of specified unlawful activity; or

(ii) to avoid a transaction reporting requirement under State or Federal law, [commits an offense].

(3) Whoever, with the intent —

(A) to promote the carrying on of specified unlawful activity;

(B) to conceal or disguise the nature, location, source, ownership, or control of property believed to be the proceeds of specified unlawful activity; or

(C) to avoid a transaction reporting requirement under State or Federal law,

conducts or attempts to conduct a financial transaction involving property represented by a law enforcement officer to be the proceeds of specified unlawful activity, or property used to conduct or facilitate specified unlawful activity [commits an offense].

The statute provides for fines of up to $500,000 or twice the value of the property involved in the transaction, whichever is greater, or imprisonment for not more than 20 years, or both. The statute also provides for a civil penalty of not more than the greater of the value of the property, funds, or monetary instruments involved in the transaction, or $10,000.

The statute includes extensive definitions of the technical terms referred to. "Specified unlawful activity" includes narcotics-related transactions, transactions related to bankruptcy fraud, bribery, false statements, embezzlement, mail or wire fraud, bank fraud, environmental violations, health care offenses, and a number of other crimes. Additionally, the USA Patriot Act of 2001 added terrorism activities, bribery of public officials, smuggling, and export control violations to the list of unlawful activities.

Assets acquired as a result of violations of the money laundering statutes are subject to forfeiture by the government.

Engaging in Monetary Transactions in Property Derived from Specified Unlawful Activity (18 U.S.C. § 1957)

This statute prohibits any person from depositing, withdrawing, transferring, or exchanging more than $10,000 in funds derived from criminal activity. Violations are punished by fines, up to 10 years imprisonment, and forfeiture of illegally obtained gains.

Conspiracy and Aiding and Abetting

The principal federal conspiracy statute provides:

Conspiracy (18 U.S.C. § 371)

> *If two or more persons conspire either to commit any offense against the United States, or to defraud the United States, or any agency thereof in any manner or for any purpose, and one or more of such persons do any act to effect the object of the conspiracy, each shall be fined under this title or imprisoned not more than five years, or both.*

> *If, however, the offense, the commission of which is the object of the conspiracy, is a misdemeanor only, the punishment for such conspiracy shall not exceed the maximum punishment provided for such misdemeanor.*

The essential elements of this extremely important statute are:
- That the conspiracy was willfully formed.

- That the accused willfully became a member of it.
- That at least one of the conspirators knowingly committed at least one overt act in furtherance of the conspiracy.

The gist of the offense is a combination or agreement of two or more people to accomplish an unlawful purpose by lawful means or a lawful purpose by unlawful means. The purpose of the conspiracy need not be accomplished for a violation to occur; however, at least one of the co-conspirators must have carried out at least one *overt act* in furtherance of the conspiracy. The overt act need not be criminal and could be as innocuous as making a phone call or writing a letter.

Conspiracy counts are favored by prosecutors because they provide evidentiary and pleading advantages. If a conspiracy is shown, the acts and statements of one co-conspirator may be admitted into evidence against all, and each co-conspirator may be convicted for the underlying substantive offense (e.g., destroying government property) committed by any one of its members. A corporation cannot conspire with one of its own employees to commit an offense because the employee and employer are legally viewed as one. However, a corporation can conspire with other business entities or third parties to violate the statute.

Aiding and Abetting (18 U.S.C. § 2)
The aiding and abetting statute provides:

> *(a) Whoever commits an offense against the United States or aids, abets, counsels, commands, induces or procures its commission, is punishable as a principal.*

> *(b) Whoever willfully causes an act to be done which if directly performed by him or another would be an offense against the United States, is punishable as a principal.*

Under this fundamental tenet of criminal law, anyone who induces another to commit an offense, or who aids in its commission may himself be charged and convicted of the underlying offense and subject to its penalties.

Obstruction of Justice
The Obstruction of Justice statutes punish efforts to impede or obstruct the investigation or trial of other substantive offenses. Prosecutors usually are pleased to discover such violations because they add a more sinister flavor to what might be colorless white-collar charges and

help to prove underlying criminal intent. In many instances, these charges draw the stiffest penalties.

There are several *obstruction* statutes in the federal code (see 18 U.S.C. § 1503, et. seq.) that punish, among other things, the attempted or actual destruction of evidence, tampering with or threatening witnesses, jurors or other court personnel.

With respect to fraud examinations, however, two of the most significant criminal statutes were instituted as part of the Sarbanes-Oxley Act of 2002:

Destruction, Alteration, or Falsification of Records in Federal Investigations and Bankruptcy (18 U.S.C. § 1519)

Whoever knowingly alters, destroys, mutilates, conceals, covers up, falsifies, or makes a false entry in any record, document, or tangible object with the intent to impede, obstruct, or influence the investigation or proper administration of any matter within the jurisdiction of any department or agency of the United States or any case filed under title 11, or in relation to or contemplation of any such matter or case, shall be fined under this title, imprisoned not more than 20 years, or both.

Destruction of Corporate Audit Records (18 U.S.C. § 1520)

(a)

(1) *Any accountant who conducts an audit of an issuer of securities to which section 10A(a) of the Securities Exchange Act of 1934 (15 U.S.C. 78j-1(a)) applies, shall maintain all audit or review workpapers for a period of 5 years from the end of the fiscal period in which the audit or review was concluded.*

(2) *The Securities and Exchange Commission shall promulgate, within 180 days, after adequate notice and an opportunity for comment, such rules and regulations, as are reasonably necessary, relating to the retention of relevant records such as workpapers, documents that form the basis of an audit or review, memoranda, correspondence, communications, other documents, and records (including electronic records) which are created, sent, or received in connection with an audit or review and contain conclusions, opinions, analyses, or financial data relating to such an audit or review, which is conducted by any accountant who conducts an audit of an issuer of securities to which section 10A(a) of the Securities Exchange Act of 1934 (15 U.S.C. 78j-1(a)) applies. The Commission may, from time to time, amend or supplement the rules and regulations that it is required to promulgate under this section, after*

> *adequate notice and an opportunity for comment, in order to ensure that such rules and regulations adequately comport with the purposes of this section.*
>
> *(b) Whoever knowingly and willfully violates subsection (a)(1), or any rule or regulation promulgated by the Securities and Exchange Commission under subsection (a)(2), shall be fined under this title, imprisoned not more than 10 years, or both.*
>
> *(c) Nothing in this section shall be deemed to diminish or relieve any person of any other duty or obligation imposed by Federal or State law or regulation to maintain, or refrain from destroying, any document.*

Sarbanes-Oxley also amended § 1512 of the U.S. Code to make it a criminal offense to corruptly alter, destroy, mutilate or conceal a record or document with the intent to impair its integrity or use in an official proceeding, or to otherwise obstruct, influence, or impede any official proceeding or attempt to do so. Violations of this section are punishable by fines up to $250,000 and imprisonment for up to 20 years.

Other important statutes relating to obstruction of justice include:

Obstruction of Federal Audit (18 U.S.C. § 1516)

This statute, originally passed in 1988, makes it a felony to obstruct a federal auditor in the performance of his official duties. The full statute reads:

> *(a) Whoever, with intent to deceive or defraud the United States, endeavors to influence, obstruct, or impede a Federal auditor in the performance of official duties relating to a person receiving in excess of $100,000, directly or indirectly, from the United States in any 1 year period under a contract or subcontract, or relating to any property that is security for a mortgage note that is insured, guaranteed, acquired, or held by the Secretary of Housing and Urban Development pursuant to any Act administered by the Secretary, or relating to any property that is security for a loan that is made or guaranteed under title V of the Housing Act of 1949, shall be fined under this title, or imprisoned not more than 5 years, or both.*
>
> *(b) For purposes of this section-*

(1) the term "Federal auditor" means any person employed on a full- or part-time or contractual basis to perform an audit or a quality assurance inspection for or on behalf of the United States; and

(2) the term "in any 1 year period" has the meaning given to the term "in any one-year period" in section 666.

Obstructing Examination of Financial Institution (18 U.S.C. § 1517)

A similar statute, passed in 1990, makes it a felony to obstruct the examination of a financial institution.

Whoever corruptly obstructs or attempts to obstruct any examination of a financial institution by an agency of the United States with jurisdiction to conduct an examination of such financial institution shall be fined under this title, imprisoned not more than 5 years, or both.

Perjury

Perjury (18 U.S.C. §§ 1621 and 1623) is an intentional false statement given under oath on a material point. Under a related federal statute, 18 U.S.C. § 1623, the government may allege and prove perjury if the defendant makes two irreconcilable contradictory statements without proving which is true and which is false. False and fraudulent statements—orally or in writing—made to a government agency on a material matter also may be punished as a felony under a variety of statutes even if not given under oath.

Fines Under Title 18

Several sections of Title 18 were amended to eliminate a specified maximum fine in the section setting forth the offense. Instead, these criminal statutes usually provide that the offender may "be fined under this title." Unless a section sets forth another amount, the sections below should be used to determine the maximum sentence available.

Sentence of Fine (18 U.S.C. § 3571)

(a) In general. — A defendant who has been found guilty of an offense may be sentenced to pay a fine.

(b) Fines for individuals. — Except as provided in subsection (e) of this section, an individual who has been found guilty of an offense may be fined not more than the greatest of —
(1) the amount specified in the law setting forth the offense;

(2) the applicable amount under subsection (d) of this section;

(3) for a felony, not more than $250,000;

(4) for a misdemeanor resulting in death, not more than $250,000;

(5) for a Class A misdemeanor that does not result in death, not more than $100,000;

(6) for a Class B or C misdemeanor that does not result in death, not more than $5,000; or

(7) for an infraction, not more than $5,000.

(c) Fines for organizations. — Except as provided in subsection (e) of this section, an organization that has been found guilty of an offense may be fined not more than the greatest of —

(1) the amount specified in the law setting forth the offense;

(2) the applicable amount under subsection (d) of this section;

(3) for a felony, not more than $500,000;

(4) for a misdemeanor resulting in death, not more than $500,000;

(5) for a Class A misdemeanor that does not result in death, not more than $200,000;

(6) for a Class B or C misdemeanor that does not result in death, not more than $10,000; and

(7) for an infraction, not more than $10,000.

(d) Alternative fine based on gain or loss. — If any person derives pecuniary gain from the offense, or if the offense results in pecuniary loss to a person other than the defendant, the defendant may be fined not more than the greater of twice the gross gain or twice the gross loss, unless imposition of a fine under this subsection would unduly complicate or prolong the sentencing process.

(e) Special rule for lower fine specified in substantive provision. — If a law setting forth an offense specifies no fine or a fine that is lower than the fine otherwise applicable under this section and such law, by specific reference, exempts the offense from the applicability of the fine otherwise applicable under this section, the defendant may not be fined more than the amount specified in the law setting forth the offense.

Imposition of a Sentence of Fine and Related Matters (18 U.S.C. § 3572)

(a) Factors to be considered. — In determining whether to impose a fine, and the amount, time for payment, and method of payment of a fine, the court shall consider, in addition to the factors set forth in section 3553(a) —

(1) the defendant's income, earning capacity, and financial resources;

(2) the burden that the fine will impose upon the defendant, any person who is financially dependent on the defendant, or any other person (including a government) that would be responsible for the welfare of any person financially dependent on the defendant, relative to the burden that alternative punishments would impose;

(3) any pecuniary loss inflicted upon others as a result of the offense;

(4) whether restitution is ordered or made and the amount of such restitution;

(5) the need to deprive the defendant of illegally obtained gains from the offense;

(6) the expected costs to the government of any imprisonment, supervised release, or probation component of the sentence;

(7) whether the defendant can pass on to consumers or other persons the expense of the fine; and

(8) if the defendant is an organization, the size of the organization and any measure taken by the organization to discipline any officer, director, employee, or agent of the organization responsible for the offense and to prevent a recurrence of such an offense.

(b) Fine not to impair ability to make restitution. — If, as a result of a conviction, the defendant has the obligation to make restitution to a victim of the offense, the court shall impose a fine or other monetary penalty only to the extent that such fine or penalty will not impair the ability of the defendant to make restitution.

(c) Effect of finality of judgment. Notwithstanding the fact that a sentence to pay a fine can subsequently be—

(1) modified or remitted under section 3573;

(2) corrected under <u>rule 35 of the Federal Rules of Criminal Procedure</u> and section 3742; or

(3) appealed and modified under section 3742;

a judgment that includes such a sentence is a final judgment for all other purposes

(d) Time, method of payment, and related items

(1) A person sentenced to pay a fine or other monetary penalty, including restitution, shall make such payment immediately, unless, in the interest of justice, the court provides for payment on a date certain or in installments. If the court provides for payment in installments, the installments shall be in equal monthly payments over the period provided by the court, unless the court establishes another schedule.

(2) *If the judgment, or, in the case of a restitution order, the order, permits other than immediate payment, the length of time over which scheduled payments will be made shall be set by the court, but shall be the shortest time in which full payment can reasonably be made.*

(3) *A judgment for a fine which permits payments in installments shall include a requirement that the defendant will notify the court of any material change in the defendant's economic circumstances that might affect the defendant's ability to pay the fine. Upon receipt of such notice the court may, on its own motion or the motion of any party, adjust the payment schedule, or require immediate payment in full, as the interests of justice require.*

(e) *Alternative sentence precluded.* At the time a defendant is sentenced to pay a fine, the court may not impose an alternative sentence to be carried out if the fine is not paid.

(f) *Responsibility for payment of monetary obligation relating to organization.* If a sentence includes a fine, special assessment, restitution or other monetary obligation (including interest) with respect to an organization, each individual authorized to make disbursements for the organization has a duty to pay the obligation from assets of the organization. If such an obligation is imposed on a director, officer, shareholder, employee, or agent of an organization, payments may not be made, directly or indirectly, from assets of the organization, unless the court finds that such payment is expressly permissible under applicable State law.

(g) *Security for stayed fine.* If a sentence imposing a fine is stayed, the court shall, absent exceptional circumstances (as determined by the court)-
  (1) *require the defendant to deposit, in the registry of the district court, any amount of the fine that is due;*
  (2) *require the defendant to provide a bond or other security to ensure payment of the fine; or*
  (3) *restrain the defendant from transferring or dissipating assets.*

(h) *Delinquency.* A fine or payment of restitution is delinquent if a payment is more than 30 days late.

(i) *Default.* A fine or payment of restitution is in default if a payment is delinquent for more than 90 days. Notwithstanding any installment schedule, when a fine or payment of restitution is in *default, the entire amount of the fine or restitution is due within 30 days after notification of the default, subject to the provisions of section 3613A.*

Qui Tam Suits and the False Claims Act

A *qui tam* suit is one in which a private individual sues on behalf of the government to recover damages for criminal or fraudulent actions committed against the government. It is a civil not a criminal suit. Most qui tam actions are brought under the False Claims Act, 31 U.S.C § 3729 et seq. This statute provides, in part, that anyone who commits the following acts is liable to the government for three times the amount of damages it sustains plus a civil penalty of $5,000 to $10,000 per false claim:

- Knowingly presents or causes to be presented a false or fraudulent claim for payment or approval [§ 3729 (a) (1)]
- Knowingly makes, uses or causes to be made or used, a false record or statement to get a false or fraudulent claim paid or approved [§ 3729 (a) (2)]
- Conspires to defraud the government by getting a false or fraudulent claim allowed or paid [§ 3729 (a) (3)]
- Making or delivering a document certifying receipt of property to be used by the government without completely knowing that the information on the receipt is true [§ 3729 (a) (5)]
- Knowingly makes, uses, or causes to be made or used a false record or statement to conceal, avoid, or decrease an obligation to pay or transmit money or property to the government [§ 3729 (a) (7)]

Most qui tam actions seek to recover damages and statutory penalties for false claims made to the government by government contractors such as defense contractors and health care providers.

In February 2000, the U.S. Department of Justice announced that more than $3 billion has been recovered as a result of qui tam cases filed since the law was amended in 1986. Almost half of that amount was recovered in the last two and a half years.

Filing an Action

If an individual has knowledge that a false claim was submitted to the government, the individual should first retain an attorney. The attorney will then draft a complaint and a disclosure statement. The whistleblower can file the complaint and the disclosure statement under seal in U.S. District Court and copies are served upon the Department of Justice. After the filing of the complaint, the Justice Department has 60 days to investigate the allegations and determine whether it will join the lawsuit. If the department decides not to participate in the lawsuit, the individual has the right to continue to pursue the claim on behalf of the United States. If the department does not participate, the whistleblower will receive a higher portion of any recovery received.

If the Justice Department elects to join the lawsuit, it has the primary responsibility for prosecuting the case and can limit the whistleblower's participation in the action. If the qui tam action is successful, the employee's share of the recovery will range from a minimum of 15 percent to a maximum of 30 percent depending on the extent of the whistleblower's investigation and participation of the action. The judge normally determines the percentage.

Who Can Bring a Qui Tam Action

The False Claims Act provides that any "person" can file a qui tam action as long as they have direct and independent knowledge of the fraud and such knowledge was not obtained from a "public disclosure." The definition of "person" includes not only individuals, but also businesses and state or local government entities. The most common plaintiffs in qui tam actions are employees of government contractors, health care employees, and employees of local, state, or federal government.

The U.S. Supreme Court reaffirmed this definition in an opinion handed down May 22, 2000. In the case of *Vermont Agency of Natural Resources v. U.S. ex rel. Stevens*, 120 S.Ct. 1858, the court resolved a conflict among some of the courts of appeal by stating firmly that private citizens do have the right to sue under the False Claims Act. However, the Court also held that states and state agencies are not subject to liability under the False Claims Act. Therefore, if a state or state agency submits false claims to the federal government, they cannot be sued by a private individual under the provisions of the False Claims Act. The Court did not address the issue of whether the U.S. government could file suit against a state under the FCA.

At the present time, a controversy still exists over whether federal employees can file qui tam actions under the False Claims Act when knowledge of the fraud was obtained through their official duties. At least two federal circuit courts that have addressed the issue have concluded that employees who are required and paid by the government to disclose fraud cannot bring qui tam actions since their knowledge of fraud was not obtained independently.

Thus, federal employees may be prohibited from filing qui tam actions, particularly if detecting fraud is part of their job duties.

Protections for Whistleblowers

Many whistleblowers are employees of the government contractor on which they are blowing the whistle. Obviously, employees might be reluctant to report their employer to the government for fear of retaliation. To address this concern, Congress provided substantial protections to whistleblowers. Title 31, U.S.C., Section 3730(h) prohibits an employer from taking any adverse action (including discharge, demotion or harassment) against an employee "because of lawful acts done by the employee on behalf of the employee or others in furtherance of an action under this section, including the investigation or initiation of, testimony for, or assistance in an action filed or to be filed under this section."

If an employer takes adverse action against the employee, the employee can seek relief against the employer including reinstatement at the same seniority status, an award of two times the employee's back pay plus interest, and any other special damages required to make the employee whole. The employee also can receive reimbursement for all the costs of the litigation, including attorneys' fees.

Although these provisions provide necessary and justifiable protection for employees, in some cases they have the unintended effect of preventing an employer from firing or taking any other action against a whistleblower, even if there is adequate cause. Employers often are unwilling to implement any negative employment decision (no matter how justifiable) against a whistleblower for fear that the employee will add a claim of retaliation to the suit.

Federal "Whistleblower" Statutes

Although the Sarbanes-Oxley Act, passed in 2002, is primarily an accounting reform statute, most people do not realize that it made some extremely significant changes to the whistleblower laws.

Civil Liability for Reports of Securities Fraud

Sarbanes-Oxley § 806 creates 18 U.S.C. § 1514A, a statute that creates civil liability for companies that retaliate against whistleblowers. It should be noted that this provision does not provide universal whistleblower protection; it only protects employees of *publicly traded* companies. 18 U.S.C. § 1514A makes it unlawful to fire, demote, suspend, threaten, harass, or in any other manner discriminate against an employee for providing information or aiding in an investigation of securities fraud. However, the statue requires that the employee must report the suspected misconduct to a federal regulatory or law enforcement agency, a member of Congress or a committee of Congress, or a supervisor. Employees are also protected against retaliation for filing, testifying in, participating in, or otherwise assisting in a proceeding filed or about to be filed relating to an alleged violation of securities laws or SEC rules.

The whistleblower protections apply even if the company is ultimately found not to have committed securities fraud. As long as the employee reasonably believes she is reporting conduct that constitutes a violation of various federal securities laws, then she is protected. The protections not only cover retaliatory acts by the company, but also by any officer, employee, contractor, subcontractor, or agent of the company.

If a public company is found to have violated 18 U.S.C. § 1514A, the Act provides for an award of compensatory damages sufficient to "make the employee whole." Penalties include reinstatement; back pay with interest; and compensation for special damages including litigation costs, expert witness fees, and attorneys' fees.

Criminal Sanctions for Reports to Law Enforcement

Sarbanes-Oxley § 1107 also amended 18 U.S.C. § 1513 to make it a crime to knowingly, with the intent to retaliate, take any harmful action against a person for providing truthful information relating to the commission or possible commission of *any* federal offense, not just securities fraud. This protection is only triggered, however, when information is provided to a law enforcement officer.

Violations of 18 U.S.C. § 1513 can be punished by fines of up to $250,000 and up to 10 years in prison for individuals. Corporations that violate the act can be fined up to $500,000.

Other Important Federal Whistleblower Laws

Besides the False Claims Act, and the two new protections added by Sarbanes-Oxley, there are also a number of other statutes that have protections for whistleblowers. Such statutes include the following:

Civil Service Reform Act (5 U.S.C § 2302).

This comprehensive act prohibits retaliation against federal whistleblowers. An employee filing a complaint under Section 2302 must be covered by the act or the form of retaliation used must be set out in the act. If an employee is unable to meet one of these criteria, the employee may be able to maintain a tort claim under the First Amendment. The act prevents a federal agency from taking any adverse "personnel action" against a civil servant who has reported wrongdoing by the agency.

Fair Labor Standards Act (FLSA) (29 U.S.C. § 215-16).

The act sets minimum wage, overtime pay, equal pay, recordkeeping and child labor standards for employees covered by the act and not exempt from specific provisions. The FLSA contains provisions that prohibit employers from retaliating against employees who report violations.

Occupational Safety and Health Act (OSHA) (29 U.S.C. § 660(c)).

OSHA regulations protect employees who raise complaints about the health and safety of their workplace. Employees who believe they have been retaliated against must file a complaint with the local OSHA office within 30 days after such violation occurs. The Secretary of Labor investigates OSHA complaints. If a violation is found, the secretary sues on behalf of the injured employee.

Employee Retirement Income Security Act (ERISA), (29 U.S.C. § 1132, 1140).

It is unlawful for an employer to retaliate against an employee who participates in an ERISA retirement benefit plan or who gives information or testifies regarding any inquiry or proceeding relating to this act or the Welfare & Pension Plans Disclosure Act. Employee complaints under ERISA should be filed in a federal district court. A copy of the complaint should be served on the Secretary of Labor and the Secretary of the Treasury.

Title VII, Equal Employment Opportunities (42 U.S.C. § 2000e-3).

Title VII prevents employment discrimination based on race, color, religion, sex or national origin and protects both public- and private- sector employees. There is a whistleblower provision that bars retaliation against employees who oppose any practice made an unlawful employment practice under the act or who charge, testify, assist or participate in any manner in the investigation, proceeding or hearing of complaints made under the act.

Age Discrimination in Employment Act (ADEA) (29 U.S.C. § 623(d)).

The ADEA protects public and private-sector employees from age discrimination. It is unlawful for an employer to discharge or discriminate against an employee who has reported a violation of the act by the employer.

Civil Rights Claims (42 U.S.C. § 1983).

Where state action is involved, a whistleblower may be able to bring a claim under Section 1983, which prohibits any person from violating under "color of law" the civil rights of another person.

National Labor Relations Act (NLRA) (29 U.S.C. § 158).

Employees who report violations by their employers of the NLRA are given protection from discharge or discrimination. A complaint should be filed with the regional director of the National Labor Relations Board for the region in which the violation occurred.

Federal Whistleblower Statute for Employees of Defense Contractors (10 U.S.C. § 2409).

An employee of a contractor may not be discharged, demoted or discriminated against for reporting violations of law related to a contract awarded by the head of certain federal agencies (i.e., Department of Defense, Department of the Army, etc.). A person may submit a complaint to the Inspector General of the agency.

Federal Deposit Insurance Act; Financial Institution Reform, Recovery, and Enforcement Act of 1989 (12 U.S.C. § 1831j).

Employees of depository institutions and banking agencies are protected from discharge or discriminatory actions with respect to compensation, terms, conditions or privileges of employment if the employee reports: (1) a possible violation of any law or regulation; (2) gross mismanagement; (3) gross waste of funds; (4) abuse of authority; or (5) a substantial or specific danger to public health.

There are also a number of statutes which provide protections to employees who expose violations of environmental laws. The provisions of these acts are substantially similar. They include the Solid Waste Disposal Act, the Water Pollution Control Act, the Toxic Substances Control Act, the Safe Water Drinking Act, and the Clean Air Act.

State Statutes

Every state has some form of legislation protecting whistleblowers. Many are very specific as to the manner with which a report must be filed, as well as the particular agencies that must receive the report. A particular state also may require that the first report made by an employee be directed to the employer under the notion that the employer be given an opportunity to correct the circumstances that give rise to a potential violation.

INDIVIDUAL RIGHTS DURING EXAMINATIONS

People suspected of fraud have certain rights. Below are some of the common legal issues involved in fraud examinations and investigations.

Employee's Duty to Cooperate

A duty to cooperate exits in every employer/employee relationship. Some states have statutes defining the scope of this duty. For instance, California Labor Code Section 2856 states that an employee "shall substantially comply with all directions of his employer concerning the service on which he is engaged" unless compliance is impossible, unlawful, or would impose unreasonable burdens on the employee. Accordingly, employees have a duty to cooperate during an internal investigation as long as what is requested from them is reasonable. An interview should be considered reasonable if the interview addresses matters within the scope of the employee's actions or duties.

Employee's Rights During the Investigation

While the employee has a duty to cooperate, the employee has certain other rights which further define the scope of that duty.

Contractual Rights

If the employee is a member of a union, the union contract or collective bargaining agreement might contain certain restrictions on the company's investigatory procedures. For instance, the company might be required to notify the union before the interview, and the employee may have the right to have a union representative present. (See *NLRB v. Weingarten, Inc.*, 420 U.S. 251 [1975]). Other employees might have a written employment agreement which might contain provisions concerning the employee's rights during an investigation.

Whistleblowers

Federal law and many state laws provide protection to employees who report improper or illegal acts to government authorities. Most of these laws protect the employee from any adverse employment action or retaliatory action from the employer.

Employee's Constitutional Rights

The Fourth Amendment to the U.S. Constitution prohibits unreasonable searches and seizures. The Fifth Amendment provides that a person cannot be compelled to give information which might incriminate him. The Sixth Amendment provides that a person has the right to an attorney and to confront the witnesses against him.

The general rule is that the U.S. Constitution does not limit the powers of private employers in conducting a corporate investigation. However, that rule is subject to several limitations, and, although a private employer usually cannot be sued for a violation of the Fourth, Fifth, or Sixth Amendments, these provisions still have important implications for the fraud investigator.

PRIVATE ACTION VS. STATE ACTION

In order for an employee to sue an employer for the violation of a constitutional right, there must be some form of "state action" involved. State action is involved during any investigation by a state or federal entity, including investigations of their own employees.

There are no bright-line rules regarding when an investigation can be considered to involve state action. However, the following examples could be considered to involve state action:

- Investigations conducted by a private company but at the suggestion of the state or federal authorities
- Investigations begun by a private company that later are taken over by or expanded by state or federal authorities
- Joint investigations with or aided by state or federal authorities
- Investigations conducted by a private company that are required by state or federal law
- Searches or interrogations conducted by outside investigators who are off-duty state, local or federal authorities

INVESTIGATION BY A PRIVATE COMPANY PURSUANT TO A FEDERAL STATUTE

If an investigation is conducted by a private company in accordance with federal laws, an issue is raised as to whether the corporation's internal investigation could be considered state action.

For example in the case of *Skinner v. Railway Labor Executives Ass'n,* 489 U.S. 602 (1989), the U.S. Supreme Court found that a private railroad acted as an agent for the government when it complied with the provisions of the Federal Railroad Administration Act in administering drug tests to its employees. Under the regulation at issue, the railroad was required by law to conduct the test and the Federal Railroad Administration was authorized to receive the test results.

If a company is conducting an investigation pursuant to such federal laws as the Securities Exchange Act of 1934 or the Foreign Corrupt Practices Act of 1977, the company should be aware of the possible implications of state action. Therefore, before any adverse action is taken against an employee, legal advice should be obtained.

Interviews

Employee's Right Against Self-Incrimination

Fifth Amendment: No person shall be held to answer for a capital, or otherwise infamous crime, unless on a presentment or indictment of a grand jury, except in cases arising in the land or naval forces, or in the militia, when in actual service in time of war and public danger; nor shall any person be subject for the same offense to be twice put in jeopardy of life or limb; nor shall be compelled in any criminal case to be a witness against himself, nor be deprived of life, liberty, or property, without due process of law; nor shall private property be taken for public use without just compensation.

Nature of the Right

An employee has the ability to assert his or her right against self-incrimination during an investigation by either a public or private entity. However, an employee might be subject to dismissal by a private company if he or she fails to cooperate in an investigation.

Miranda Warnings

Generally both private and public employers might interview employees in noncustodial settings without giving Miranda warnings. "Custodial setting" refers to questioning initiated by law enforcement officers after a person has been taken into custody, or otherwise deprived of his freedom or action in any significant way.

In subsequent civil proceedings an adverse inference might be drawn from silence in response to questioning.

Public Employers

The Fifth Amendment right against self-incrimination cannot be infringed upon by public employers. Public entities cannot force employees to choose between their Fifth Amendment right to silence and their jobs.

Presence of Corporate Attorney

Although Miranda warnings might not be required, if a corporate attorney is present during the interview, it is good policy to inform the employee of several things before the interview begins. Counsel should inform the employee of the following:

- Counsel represents the company, not the employee
- The purpose of the interview is to obtain information to provide legal advice to the company
- Information provided by the employee initially will be treated as confidential, but the company ultimately will determine whether to disclose the information to law enforcement agencies
- The employee is expected to answer the questions fully and truthfully

The employee should not discuss the interview with anyone (either inside or outside the company) except his or her attorney.

Depending on the circumstances, the attorney might also wish to advise the employee that he or she is free to retain an attorney. Factors to include in determining whether to give such advice include the degree of evidence of the employee's culpability, whether the evidence is such to draw a conclusion concerning a violation of the law, the likelihood of criminal prosecution if the results of the investigation are disclosed, the existence of a conflict of interest between the employee and the company, and state ethical codes.

Employee's Right to Counsel

<u>Sixth Amendment</u>: In all criminal prosecutions, the accused shall enjoy the right . . . to be confronted with Witnesses against him; to have compulsory process for obtaining witnesses in his favor, and to have the Assistance of Counsel for his defense.

Applicability

If no state action is involved, a private employer can interview an employee without the presence of his attorney. However, the employee, an individual, always has the right to consult an attorney, but there is typically no legal obligation to consult the employee's lawyer prior to the interview or allow the employee's lawyer to sit in during an interview.

Employee's Right to Due Process

Fourteenth Amendment: All persons born or naturalized in the United States, and subject to the jurisdiction thereof, are citizens of the United States and of the State wherein they reside. No State shall make or enforce any law which shall abridge the privileges and immunities of citizens of the United States; nor shall any State deprive any person of life, liberty, or property without due process of law; nor deny to any person within its jurisdiction the equal protection of the laws...

The constitutional right to due process usually is not applicable to employees of private companies. State or federal employers might be required to provide the wrongdoing employee with the following:
- Written notice of the charges
- Adequate opportunity to rebut any charges brought prior to any disciplinary action being taken, which might include the right to call witnesses and the right to be represented by an attorney.

Private employers might also wish to employ the above procedures to avoid a possible civil suit by the employee.

State Constitutions

Many states have constitutional provisions concerning self-incrimination, right to counsel, and due process. The law of your particular state should be examined closely. In some instances, state constitutions provide broader protections than the U.S. Constitution.

Federal Statutes

National Labor Relations Act

The National Labor Relations Act prohibits any form of interrogation by employers that interferes with the rights of the employee to organize, bargain, or otherwise engage in concerted activities for the purpose of bargaining or other mutual aid or protection. An employer might not question an employee about any of these protected activities, either his own or that of other employees.

NEW RULES REGARDING NON-UNION REPRESENTATION DURING INTERVIEWS

In June 2004, the National Labor Relations Board (NLRB) overruled a controversial decision regarding the rights of non-union employees to have a "representative" present during interviews, and reinstated the former 1975 ruling that non-union employees are not entitled to representation during investigatory interviews (*IBM Corp.*, 341 NLRB No. 148 (2004)). The NLRB reasoned that allowing co-workers to sit in as representatives during investigatory interviews would compromise the requisite confidentiality, sensitivity, and thoroughness of the interview. Accordingly, non-union employers no longer have a legal obligation to accept an employee's request for such representation.

UNION EMPLOYEES

Since 1975 and the U.S. Supreme Court decision of *NLRB v. Weingarten*, 420 U.S. 251 (1975), union employees have had the right to union representation during an investigatory interview, provided that the employee "reasonably believes" the interview "might result in disciplinary action." This right derived from the National Labor Relations Act, which provides that employees have the right "to act in concert for mutual aid and protection." In the years since *Weingarten*, this right has only been applied in cases where the employee under investigation was covered by a collective bargaining agreement.

FORMER LAW: NON-UNION EMPLOYEES

In the case of *Epilepsy Foundation of Northeast Ohio* (331 NLRB No. 92; decided July 10, 2000), the NLRB extended the so-called *Weingarten* rights to *non-union* employees. The case involved two workers who were fired from the Epilepsy Foundation. Prior to their discharge, the two employees wrote a memo critical of their supervisor. Later, the Executive Director requested to meet with one of the employees and the supervisor. The employee requested to meet with the Executive Director alone, but the request was denied. The employee then asked if the co-author of the memo could be present at the meeting. This request was also denied. When the employee still expressed apprehension about the meeting, he was told to go home, and he was fired the next day for insubordination.

The NLRB ruled that discharging the employee for refusing to attend the meeting violated the National Labor Relations Act. A majority of the Board felt that the rights set forth in *Weingarten* should apply equally in circumstances where employees are not represented by a union. They reasoned that the right to have a co-worker present at an investigatory interview "greatly enhances the employees' opportunities to act in concert to address the concern that the employer does not initiate or continue a practice of imposing punishment unjustly."

NEW RULES: NON-UNION EMPLOYEES

A representative may be present where the employer allows for such.

No longer must an employer allow a representative to be present where an employee specifically requests representation. However, an employer is not precluded from allowing the employee to have representation upon request.

Employers can always decide not to conduct an interview.

Although employers are never required to conduct an interview, refusing to do so may cause problems of its own. If the company administers disciplinary action without first hearing the employee's side of the story, then the company may be handing the employee a lawsuit for wrongful discharge or a discrimination claim. As a general rule, it is difficult to defend a termination action if the employer did not at least listen to the employee's version of events prior to taking action.

Where the employer allows for employee representation, the employer need not "bargain with" the employee's representative.

Presumably the ruling in *Weingarten* will continue to control this issue. In *Weingarten*, the Supreme Court stated that the representative's role is to assist the employee, and he "may do so by attempting to clarify facts or suggest other employees who may have knowledge of them." The Court made it clear that the employer may insist on hearing the subject's version of events, and the representative is not allowed to direct the subject not to answer a question or to tell the subject to answer questions only once. Therefore, the employer is allowed to conduct the interview without interference by the representative.

Employees do not have a right to be represented at an interview by a private attorney.

Under *Epilepsy*, where an employer failed to comply with the rules requiring representation upon employee request, it could have been subjected to an administrative cease-and-desist order and/or reinstatement of the employee with back pay. However, due to the overturning of *Epilepsy* and reinstatement of *Weingarten*, these penalties will probably not apply unless the non-union employer agrees to allow employee representation.

If an employee requests any type of representation at an interview, you should immediately consult your legal counsel. You should also consult counsel to review your existing policies and procedures to ensure that you are aware of the legal duties, ramifications, and remedies surrounding employee representation.

Nondiscrimination Statutes

Included in the Civil Rights Acts of 1866 and 1871, Title VII of the Civil Rights Act of 1964, and the Age Discrimination in Employment Act of 1970, is the prohibition of singling out employees for interviews based on their race, national origin, religion, sex, or age.

Fair Labor Standards

The Fair Labor Standards require an employer to pay an employee for time spent in an interview.

Common Law Protection in Connection with Interviews

Invasion of Privacy: Intrusion into Seclusion

Questioning employees about activities not related to job performance might constitute an invasion of privacy.

Invasion of Privacy: Public Disclosure of Private Facts

Occurs if employer gives unreasonable publicity to true, but private, information about an employee. For instance, disclosing information obtained in an interview to individuals not involved in the investigation.

Outrageous Conduct: Intentional Infliction of Emotional Distress

Questioning alone, even coupled with accusations and raised voices, probably will not give rise to such a claim.

Defamation

A claim of defamation might arise in the context of an interview as a result of unfounded accusations or statements made by the interviewer, where someone in addition to the employee and the interviewer is present.

A qualified privilege might exist as to statements where the people to whom the statements are published are among those who have an interest in the matter and thus have a right to know. The privilege might be lost if the defamatory statements are communicated with "malice." This usually means that the person communicating the statements knew they were false or made them without regard to whether they were false.

Some courts have held that there can be no defamation arising from an employer's inquiries of its employees concerning their possible involvement in a violation of company policy. The employer might even have duty to investigate, arising from its duty to protect its business, its employees and the public from wrongdoing employees.

Good Faith and Fair Dealing

Several states recognize a duty on the part of employers to deal with their employees fairly and in good faith. This duty might include abiding by all provisions in an employee handbook, *e.g.*, it might contain a provision that interviews will be conducted in a professional manner and only concerning job related matters.

Breach of Implied Contract

Many states now recognize an implied contract between employers and employees arising out of employee handbooks.

False Imprisonment

False imprisonment is restraint by one person of the physical liberty of another without consent or legal justification. A claim of false imprisonment might be made if an employee is detained in any way during a search either of the employee or of the employee's desk, locker, etc. Generally an employer is entitled to question an employee at work about a violation of company policy without incurring liability as long as the employee submits to the questioning voluntarily; that is, not as a result of threats or force. However, the length, nature, and manner of the interview will determine whether liability arises.

False imprisonment factors include:
- Size and nature of the room where an interview takes place (small, windowless, not easily accessible is a negative)
- Lighting in room—soft vs. severe
- Requiring the employee's presence or continued presence by any amount of force, including holding the employee's arm to escort him
- Violent behavior of any kind during the interview, including yelling, pounding on desk, kicking furniture or walls

- Refusing to allow the employee to leave the room, such as by pushing the employee into a chair, locking the door
- The number of people involved in the interview

Searches and Surveillance

Employee's Right to Privacy

In most cases, an employer might investigate its workplace for wrongdoing by means of workplace searches and surveillance of workplace areas or employees. However, there might be constitutional or common law limitations.

U.S. Constitution: Fourth Amendment

The right of the people to be secure in their persons, houses, papers, and effects, against unreasonable searches and seizures, shall not be violated, and no warrants shall issue, but upon probable cause, supported by oath or affirmation, and particularly describing the place to be searched, and the persons or things to be seized.

The Fourth Amendment contains these three broad dictates:
- "Unreasonable" searches and seizures are forbidden.
- All warrants for a search or arrest must be supported by "probable cause," under oath.
- All warrants must "particularly" describe the place to be searched or the person or things to be seized.

In *Katz v. United States*, 389 U.S. 347 (1967), the Supreme Court held that the Fourth Amendment "protects people, not places" (meaning that its provisions extend beyond the property line of the citizen), that the amendment applies wherever there is a "reasonable expectation of privacy," and that a search without a warrant is *"per se* unreasonable," absent exigent circumstances. Thus, the police normally need to obtain a warrant not only to search a house, but also to intercept calls from a public telephone booth, or inspect the contents of a safe deposit box, or to otherwise intrude into matters which the courts would reasonably consider to be private.

In *Johnson v. United States*, 333 U.S. 10 (1948), the Supreme Court ruled that all warrants must be issued by a judge or magistrate (the latter a federal judicial officer empowered to hear misdemeanor cases), explaining that "the point of the Fourth Amendment ... is not that it denies law enforcement the support of the usual inferences which reasonable men draw from evidence. Its protection consists in requiring that those inferences be drawn by a neutral and detached magistrate instead of being judged by the officer engaged in the often competitive enterprise of ferreting out crime."

The "probable cause" requirement of the Fourth Amendment is the central restraint on the power of the police to arrest or search. It has been defined as referring to those facts and circumstances sufficient to cause a person of reasonable caution to believe that a crime has been committed and that the accused committed it. It requires more than mere suspicion or hunch, but less than virtual certainty. "Reasonable grounds to believe" is probably as good a definition as any.

The particularity requirement was intended to prevent "general searches," an abuse that outraged the constitutional draftsmen. In today's terms, the clause would prohibit a search warrant in a white-collar investigation or a subpoena that commanded the production of all the defendant's books and records whether or not relevant to the investigation or trial.

Under the *exclusionary rule* in effect in all federal and state courts, evidence seized in violation of the Fourth Amendment will be suppressed; that is, it may not be used against the accused, with limited exceptions. An unlawful search and seizure, however, does not preclude prosecution or invalidate a subsequent conviction based on other evidence. A person whose Fourth Amendment rights have been violated, whether or not a defendant in a criminal case, may sue for damages through a private civil rights action. For more information on the applicability of the Fourth Amendment to investigations conducted by non-government personnel, please refer to the material on Employees' Constitutional Rights discussed earlier in this chapter.

Reasonableness

Whether it is reasonable to conduct a search and whether the search was conducted in a reasonable manner is determined by the totality of the circumstances. A reasonable search is one carried out pursuant to a search warrant issued upon a showing of probable cause. The determination of reasonableness depends on the individual's reasonable expectation of privacy and the degree of intrusiveness of the search compared to the interest advanced by it. This requirement affects both the need for a warrant and the scope of the search that might be conducted. Even if a warrant is technically required, a search might be conducted without one by law enforcement where probable cause exists to believe a crime has been committed and the circumstances require an immediate search.

> EXAMPLE
> *Where an employee has an office, a desk, wastebasket, locker, or other area assigned exclusively to him, there is more likely to be a reasonable expectation of privacy. Additional evidence of expectation could be a locked door or protection of confidential records. As the intrusion becomes greater, so must the justification of intrusion be greater.*

Exceptions to the Fourth Amendment Warrant Requirement

There are a number of recognized exceptions to the warrant requirement, principally:

- Workplace searches by government employers
- Searches incident to arrest
- Searches of motor vehicles
- Exigent or emergency circumstances, to prevent the destruction of evidence, or while in "hot pursuit" of a suspect
- When the search is conducted pursuant to a valid, voluntary consent
- When the evidence is in "plain view"
- Border, customs, and prison searches

Workplace Searches by Government Employers

Public employers are not generally required to obtain a warrant when they conduct searches for investigations of workplace misconduct. In *O'Connor v. Ortega*, 480 U.S. 709 (1987), the Supreme Court held that requiring warrants for all forms of public workplace searches would be unworkable and would impose intolerable burdens on public employers. Therefore, the Court ruled that workplace searches should be held to a lower standard.

In reaching this decision, the Court stated that when public employers conduct a workplace investigation, their interest is substantially different from the normal interests of law enforcement. The goal of public employers is to ensure that their offices run efficiently, not to enforce the law. Requiring these employers to obtain a warrant for every workplace search would impede the effective administration of the government's work. The Court also found that while public employees have some legitimate privacy interests in the workplace, these interests are less than in other places, such as their homes. Government offices are provided to public employees for the purpose of doing government work, and employees can avoid exposing truly personal belongings at work by simply leaving them at home. Thus, by balancing the strong government interest in maintaining an efficient workplace against the diminished privacy interests of government employees, the court justified the use of a lower standard for workplace searches by government employers. Instead of a warrant requirement based on probable cause, government employers are generally held to a standard of *reasonableness under all the circumstances.*

THE REASONABLENESS STANDARD
Workplace searches by government employers are subject to the reasonableness standard in two circumstances:
- For non-investigatory, work-related purposes, which are wholly unrelated to illegal conduct (such as retrieving a file from someone's desk); and
- For investigations of work-related misconduct.

When a public employer conducts an investigation of work-related misconduct, and when that investigation necessitates a search of an employee's workspace, the employer is not generally required to obtain a warrant to perform the search, nor is the employer required to make a showing of probable cause that the suspect has committed a crime. This does not mean, however, that there are no restrictions on the employer's ability to conduct the search; it still must meet the test for "reasonableness under all the circumstances."

There is a two-part test to determine if a workplace search is reasonable:
The search must be justified at its inception; and
The search must be conducted in a way that is *reasonably related in scope* to the circumstances which justified the interference in the first place.

A search is justified at its inception if there are reasonable grounds for suspecting that the search will turn up evidence that the employee is guilty of work-related misconduct, or if the search is necessary for a non-investigatory purpose such as to retrieve a file. A search is not justified at its inception simply because an employer thinks that the suspect might be engaged in workplace misconduct. The employer must be able to demonstrate a reasonable, clear suspicion, based on factual information, that the area to be searched contains evidence of misconduct.

The second part of the test requires that the search be reasonable in scope. The fact that a search is justified at its inception does not give the employer *carte blanche* authority to intrude upon the suspect's privacy in all areas. The search must be no broader than is necessary to serve the organization's legitimate, work-related purposes.

REASONABLE EXPECTATIONS OF PRIVACY

The Fourth Amendment only applies to workplace searches by government employers where an employee has a reasonable expectation of privacy. Thus, in order to determine if a workplace search will violate an employee's Fourth Amendment rights, an employer must first determine if the employee has a reasonable expectation of privacy in the area to be searched. There is no bright-line rule for determining whether an employee has a reasonable privacy expectation in a particular area. Such a privacy interest can exist for a desk drawer, a file cabinet, a locker, or even an entire office, depending on the circumstances. The issue is whether a reasonable person would expect the area to be free from intrusion. The employee does not have to have an ownership interest in the area to have a reasonable expectation of privacy in the area. Thus, even though a public employer may own the office where an employee works, that employee can still have a privacy interest in the office that prohibits the employer from conducting a search.

The key factor to consider is whether the employee has *exclusive control* over the area in question. If so, this tends to show that the employee has a reasonable expectation of privacy in that area. For instance, assume that an employee has a file cabinet in his office; that he is the only person who uses that file cabinet; that the cabinet has a lock on it; that the employee is the only person with a key; and that the cabinet remains locked when the employee is not using it. These facts indicate that the employee has exclusive control over the contents of the file cabinet, and thus has a reasonable expectation of privacy in its contents. In other words, based on the circumstances, the employee would be justified in believing that others cannot and will not enter the file cabinet without his consent. The employee in this scenario has a constitutionally protected privacy interest in the contents of the file cabinet. A search of this file cabinet by the public employer would have to comport with the *reasonableness* standard as discussed above.

On the other hand, if the file cabinet does not have a lock, if several employees store and retrieve files from that cabinet, and if it is generally understood that they can do so without the employee's consent, then the employee cannot reasonably expect that the contents of the file cabinet will be private. In this case, the employee would not have a reasonable expectation of privacy in the file cabinet, and therefore a search of that file cabinet would not violate the employees' Fourth Amendment rights.

Reasonable privacy expectations can also attach to communications. Employees might reasonably expect personal phone conversations or e-mail messages to be private and free from monitoring. In terms of surveillance, employees are likely to have reasonable privacy expectations in bathrooms, changing rooms and other personal areas within the workplace. Obviously, there are a lot of factors that go into determining whether an employee has a reasonable expectation of privacy. Before conducting a search or surveillance, employers should consult legal counsel to make sure they are not intruding upon an employee's privacy interests.

Searches Incident to Arrest

Police officers may search without a warrant the person of the accused and the area within his immediate control incident to arrest in order to protect themselves and to prevent the destruction of evidence. For the search to be valid the arrest must be valid, i.e., based on probable cause, and not merely a pretext to justify a search. If the arrest is unlawful when made, it cannot be justified by the fruits of the subsequent search, and all evidence obtained must be suppressed.

Searches of Motor Vehicles

An automobile, airplane, or vessel may be searched without a warrant if there is probable cause to believe it contains contraband or other evidence of a crime. This is because of the mobility of the vehicles (hence the risk that evidence may be lost or destroyed while a warrant is being obtained) and the lower expectation of privacy associated with vehicles. If there is probable cause to believe that the vehicle contains contraband, the police are also permitted to remove the vehicle from the scene to a stationhouse in order to conduct a search without obtaining a warrant. Furthermore, the police also may conduct warrantless "inventory" searches of impounded vehicles to secure and protect the owner's personal property, and they may seize contraband or other evidence discovered as a result.

It may also be permissible for law enforcement to make warrantless searches of containers and luggage found within a vehicle. This applies if the police have probable cause to believe there is contraband in the containers, or if they have probable cause to believe there is contraband in the car, and that contraband could be hidden in the containers.

The motor vehicle exception to the warrant requirement does not extend to passengers in the car. However, once a passenger has been arrested, the police are permitted to make a warrantless search of the suspect and the area within his or her control pursuant to the exception for searches incident to arrest, as discussed above.

Consent Searches

Individuals are always free to waive their Fourth Amendment rights. If a suspect consents to a search by police, this eliminates the need for a warrant. However, the courts will closely scrutinize any such "consent" to make sure it was truly voluntary, particularly when it leads to the seizure of incriminating evidence. Consents obtained by deceit, bribery, or misrepresentations are generally held to be involuntary and invalid. (However, when an undercover police officer conceals his identity and as a result an individual allows the officer to enter an area, this amounts to consent, even though the person did not know permission was being granted to a police officer.) Consent *might not* be voluntary if it requires a choice between exercising Constitutional rights and continued employment. There is also no requirement that suspects be informed of their right to refuse consent.

Consent may be implied in circumstances where the individual can choose between entering an area and submitting to a search, or not entering, as when one enters a secured courthouse or boards an airplane or crosses an international border. Consent may be given by third parties to searches of property over which the third parties have authority, such as a co-tenant in a leased apartment.

Evidence in "Plain View"

Evidence in "plain view" of an officer who has a right to be in a position to observe it also may be seized without a warrant. This situation usually occurs when contraband or evidence of another crime is inadvertently discovered during a search or arrest for another offense. The discovery must be truly inadvertent; however, if discovery of the evidence is anticipated and no other exception applies, a warrant must first be obtained.

Border, Customs, and Prison Searches

Border and customs searches are a long-standing exception to the Fourth Amendment and may be conducted without probable cause or a warrant. Searches of prison cells and the monitoring of inmates' telephone conversations also may be conducted without a warrant or probable cause because of security concerns and the absence of a realistic expectation of privacy in prison.

Surveillance

An employer, in certain circumstances, can use monitoring and surveillance methods to uncover employee wrongdoing. Various federal and state laws govern the availability and methods of surveillance techniques. Because of the complexity of these laws, and the differing interpretations of them by state and federal courts, counsel should always be consulted beforehand. For example, if an employer monitors employees' phone calls without following the proper legal procedure, the employer might violate federal or state wiretap laws. The employer might also expose itself to substantial legal liability for invasion of privacy.

To lower the expectation of privacy and to preserve the right to search any and all areas, the employer should adopt a written policy which provides that in order to maintain the security of its operations, the company might gain access to and search all work areas and personal belongings, including desks, file drawers, lockers, briefcases, handbags, pockets, and personal effects. Include in the policy that workplace areas are subject to surveillance and that business phone calls might be monitored. And, as discussed below, the policy also should state that the employer can monitor all electronic communications, such as e-mail, as well as monitor what sites are visited over the Internet.

Monitoring Employee Phone Calls

Interceptions of electronic communications are covered by the Electronic Communications Privacy Act of 1986 (ECPA), 18 U.S.C. §2510, et. seq. Both public and private employers are subject to this statute. In addition to the ECPA, a company's right to monitor employee phone calls is also limited by employees' constitutional and common law privacy rights, as discussed above.

Federal law prohibits all *interception* of wire, oral, or electronic communications except those by:
- The operator of a switchboard or a common carrier as necessary incident to the rendition of service or for the protection of the rights or property of the carrier
- An employee or agent of the Federal Communication Commission in the normal course of employment and in the discharge of statutory duties
- A party to a communication or a person to whom a party has given prior consent to the interception
- A person acting under the Foreign Intelligence Surveillance Act of 1978
- Law enforcement officials with a warrant

- A person using an extension telephone (with limitations)

In general, the ECPA makes it a federal crime for an individual to intentionally or willfully intercept, access, disclose, or use another's oral, or electronic communication. Although interception is generally forbidden, there are three statutory exceptions that permit employers to lawfully monitor phone calls in certain cases. They are:
- The Ordinary Course of Business Exception
- The Provider Exception
- The Consent Exception

ORDINARY COURSE OF BUSINESS EXCEPTION

In order to maintain a claim under the ECPA, the employee must establish that the violator used an "electronic device" (as that term is defined by statute) to intercept the communication. But the ECPA's definition of "electronic device" specifically excludes devices that are used by an employer in the "ordinary course of business." Therefore, employers are permitted to monitor their employees' phone calls as long as the monitoring is done for a legitimate business purpose.

This exception would apply, for instance, where the employer routinely monitors phone communications for purposes of quality control (e.g., monitoring the phone calls of operators, telemarketers, customer service personnel, etc.). It may also apply where there is a legitimate business purpose for the monitoring, such as preventing business losses or employee misconduct. Keep in mind, however, that there must be a specific, legitimate business purpose for the interception. Blanket monitoring probably will be found to violate the act. In *Sanders v. Robert Bosch*, 38 F.3d 736 (4th Cir. 1994), an employer who used a "voice logger" to record all telephone conversations on certain company lines did not fall within the ordinary course of business exception because the employer was unable to state a legitimate business purpose for the interceptions.

Even if a company has a legitimate business purpose for monitoring a phone call, the method used to intercept and monitor the call must be no more intrusive than necessary to achieve the purpose. In *Deal v. Spears*, 980 F.2d 1153 (8th Cir. 1992), an employer who tape-recorded and listened to all calls, including personal calls, was found to have violated the statute even though the employer had legitimate suspicions of theft. Once it becomes apparent that a communication is personal and not otherwise unauthorized, the employer must immediately stop listening to the call. Overly broad efforts to monitor employee calls may give rise to a claim for invasion of privacy.

THE PROVIDER EXCEPTION

The provider exception allows communications system (telephone company) employees to intercept electronic communications in the normal course of business. Providers can monitor phone calls when it is necessary to maintain and protect the system, run quality control checks, or to protect the service against theft or harassment.

CONSENT EXCEPTION

The ECPA allows an entity to intercept an electronic communication if that entity is a party to the communication, or if one of the parties to the communication has given prior consent to the interception. This exception does not apply if the communication is intercepted for the purpose of committing a crime.

In order for an employer to monitor an employee under this exception, the employee must expressly consent to the monitoring. Generally, employers must obtain written consent, such as where an employer presents a written policy explaining that phone calls may be monitored, and employees sign the policy. It is important to point out that a notification that employees *might* be monitored (as opposed to being notified that the phone calls or e-mail *will* be monitored) may be insufficient to qualify for the consent exception. In the case of *Deal v. Spears,* discussed previously, a notification to an employee that her phone calls might be monitored was not enough to find that the employee consented to the recording of her phone calls. Even when an employee consents to monitoring, this does not give the employer unlimited access to the employee's communications. Monitoring still should be conducted only for legitimate business purposes and should be no more broad than necessary.

PEN REGISTERS

Pen registers are devices that can detect the telephone number from which an incoming call has been made. Title 18, Section 3121, of the United States Code generally prohibits the installation of pen registers without a court order. However, there are a number of exceptions under which employers can use pen registers to track their employees' phone activity:
- Phone service providers can use pen registers to protect users (employers) from abuse of service or unlawful use of service.

- Phone service providers can use a pen register to record the fact that a phone call was initiated or completed in order to protect users of the service (employers) from fraudulent, unlawful or abusive use of the service.
- Phone service providers can use a pen register where consent of the user of the service has been obtained.

Monitoring Employees' E-Mail and Voice Mail

There are two major sections of the ECPA: Title I deals with *interception* of electronic communications, and would apply to such actions as the contemporaneous monitoring of employee phone calls. Title II, on the other hand, deals with unlawful *access to stored communications*. Title II will generally govern the employer's right to access employees' e-mail and voice mail.

Title II generally prohibits third parties from accessing stored communications. There are, however, two key exceptions. The *service provider exception* exempts providers of electronic communications services from the restrictions of Title II. In other words, if a message is stored on an e-mail or voice mail system that the company provides, then the employer can access those messages as it sees fit without violating the ECPA. Note, however, that this exception does not allow the employer to access messages stored with an outside provider such as AOL.

Title II also contains a *consent exception*, which permits access of stored messages if such access is authorized by the intended recipient of the communication. This means that employers will be free to access employee e-mail and voice mail (including messages stored with outside providers) as long as the employees have given their consent. This exception provides the safest haven for employers who with to monitor their employees' stored messages. In order to make sure the consent exception will apply, companies should obtain express written consent from all employees for such monitoring as a condition of employment.

In addition to the ECPA, employers must also be aware of employees' constitutional and common law privacy rights in the contents of their e-mail. As was discussed above, it is a good idea for all employers to establish a written policy which notifies employees that their stored messages are the property of the employer, and that they are subject to monitoring by the employer at any time.

Also keep in mind that, as with other forms of searches and surveillance, the courts will not look kindly on overly broad monitoring of stored communications. Employers should only access their employees' stored voice mail or e-mail when there is a legitimate business purpose for doing so, and the access should be no more intrusive than necessary to achieve the purpose.

Video Surveillance of Employees

In some scenarios, investigators may consider the use of video surveillance equipment as part of an internal investigation. In general, video surveillance is not permissible in areas where employees have a legitimate expectation of privacy. For instance, an employer is not allowed to install video cameras in a restroom or dressing room unless there are special circumstances to justify this intrusion on employees' privacy. On the other hand, an employer is much more likely to be allowed to use video surveillance in open areas such as around cash registers or in public hallways. These areas are open to the public and an employee could not reasonably expect privacy there. It is advisable to provide written notice to employees, in advance of any surveillance, informing them that their activities are subject to monitoring. Again, the scope of the surveillance should be no greater than necessary to fulfill the employer's legitimate business purposes.

If video surveillance is accompanied by audio recording, then this type of surveillance would be covered by Title I of the Electronic Communications Privacy Act, which prohibits the interception of wire, electronic, or *oral communication* except in limited circumstances. However, the ECPA does not cover silent video monitoring. The question in this type of surveillance is whether the surveillance violates the employee's constitutional or common law privacy rights.

Searching an Employee's Mail

An employer may not conduct searches of an employee's mail before it's been delivered. Under federal law, any person who takes a letter, postcard, or package from the mail before it's been delivered to the person to whom it was directed, with design to obstruct the correspondence, faces up to five years imprisonment, a fine, or both. See 18 U.S.C. § 1702. However, once the mail has been delivered, then ordinary rules regarding searches apply.

Effect of Violation of Employee's Rights

Illegally seized evidence will be excluded in criminal proceedings. A public employer cannot use illegally seized evidence to discipline an employee. There is no Fourth Amendment prohibition against a private employer using illegally seized evidence to discipline an employee; however, the employer might be exposing itself to litigation for invasion of privacy, trespass, or other common law causes of action described below.

Civil Liability for Damages (42 U.S.C. § 1983)

For public employers there might be a qualified immunity from liability if they act in good faith on the basis of unsettled law. Consent to search can be voluntary, involuntary, or "informed." Consent is *not* voluntary if it requires a choice between Constitutional rights. Consent *might not* be voluntary if it requires a choice between exercising Constitutional rights and continued employment. Courts are split on this issue. (Published "search" policy as a barrier to expectation of privacy is used to diminish or eliminate the expectation altogether.)

State Constitutions and Statutes

Most states have enacted constitutional provisions similar to the Fourth Amendment, and many of the same issues arise under the state constitutions as under the federal Constitution. In most states, standards similar to those applied under the federal Constitution apply. Most states have enacted laws governing an employee's right to privacy in the workplace. Many states have enacted statutes that restrict surveillance, including wiretapping or electronic surveillance, cameras, pen registers, two-way mirrors, or surveillance in particular areas, such as locker rooms, lounges, and rest areas.

Surreptitious Recording

All but thirteen states allow you to record a conversation to which you are a party without informing the other parties to the conversation that you are recording it. Federal wiretap statutes also permit one-party consent of telephone conversations in most circumstances (employees being the most notable exception; see the material on the Electronic Communication Privacy Act discussed previously in this chapter).

The thirty-seven states that allow such recordings are generally referred to as "one-party" states. The District of Columbia is also a "one-party" jurisdiction. The other thirteen states are incorrectly referred to as "two-party" states. Be aware, however, that this is a misnomer because consent of *all* parties to the conversation is required. Currently, the following states require the consent of all parties to a conversation in most circumstances:
- California
- Connecticut
- Delaware

- Florida
- Illinois
- Maryland
- Massachusetts
- Michigan
- Montana
- Nevada
- New Hampshire
- Oregon
- Pennsylvania
- Washington

However, there are variations among states regarding the details of such recordings and their admissibility in court. Before you record a conversation, make sure you consult an attorney or check the laws for your jurisdiction.

Additionally, there are a number of different laws regarding videotaping. At least fifteen states have outlawed the use of hidden cameras in private places. But in some states there is no prohibition on videotaping anyone as long as there is no audio recording. Due to privacy concerns, a number of states have proposed legislation to outlaw surreptitious videotaping in certain circumstances. Since this area of the law is changing constantly, make sure you check the law in your jurisdiction.

Federal and State Nondiscrimination Statutes

Nondiscrimination statutes such as the federal Civil Rights Acts of 1866 and 1871, Title VII of the Civil Rights Act of 1964, and the Age Discrimination in Employment Act of 1970, as well as similar state statutes, protect employees from being singled out for searches on the basis of such characteristics as race, national origin, sex, religion, and age. These laws also protect employees against disparate discipline assessed as a result of a search.

Common Law Protections in Connection with Searches and Surveillance

Invasion of Privacy: Intrusion into Seclusion

Where there is an expectation of privacy on the part of the employee, a search without cause might give rise to a claim of invasion of privacy. The mere gathering of information is not a tort; however, the gathering of confidential information where the intrusion is unreasonable might be a tort. There is no invasion of privacy if the information is open to public view or has been disclosed to others.

An employer can eliminate the potential for claim of invasion of privacy by publishing and following a "search" policy. Also the following measures can be taken:
- Having a written policy regarding searches, surveillance, and telephone monitoring
- Retaining a key to all desks, lockers, etc.
- Requiring employees to provide keys to all personal locks
- Obtaining consent to search

Invasion of Privacy: Public Disclosure of Private Facts
Giving unreasonable publicity to true, but private, information about an employee can give rise to a claim for invasion of privacy. The need to communicate information about the employee must be balanced against the intrusion into the employee's privacy.

Outrageous Conduct: Intentional Infliction of Emotional Distress
The tort of intentional infliction of emotional distress has three basic elements:
The defendant's conduct must have been so outrageous that it goes beyond all possible bounds of decency, and is to be regarded as atrocious and utterly intolerable in a civilized community

The defendant's must have acted with the intent of causing severe emotional distress, or with reckless disregard of whether it would cause severe emotional distress
The plaintiff must have suffered *severe* distress

This is significant particularly to private employers whose searches might not be subject to the Fourth Amendment or similar state constitutional provisions. Both damages for pain and suffering and punitive damages might be awarded.

Defamation
The four elements of defamation are:
- A false statement of fact
- Tending to subject the person to whom it referred to ill will or disrepute
- Published to one or more persons
- Made without privilege

By making a request to an employee to allow a search, a claim of defamation might arise, in that it might suggest that the employee is engaged in wrongdoing.

Good Faith and Fair Dealing
Several states recognize a duty on the part of employers to deal with their employees fairly and in good faith. This duty might include abiding by all company policies and provisions in an employee handbook, including those relating to searches (e.g., how and when they can be conducted) and expectations of privacy on the part of employees.

Breach of Implied Contract
Many states now recognize an implied contract between employers and employees arising out of employee handbooks. An employer with an employee handbook containing provisions relating to searches and/or employee expectations of privacy might find itself contractually bound by those provisions and in breach of contract if the provisions aren't followed to the letter.

False Imprisonment
False imprisonment is the restraint by one person of the physical liberty of another without consent or legal justification. A claim of false imprisonment might be made if an employee is detained in any way during a search, either of the employee himself or of the employee's desk, locker, etc.

Trespass
Trespass is the unauthorized, intentional or negligent entry upon the property of others. A claim of trespass might arise from a search of an employee's locker. It is particularly applicable to surveillance at an employee's home.

Polygraph Examinations

Employee Polygraph Protection Act
The Employee Polygraph Protection Act prohibits the use of polygraphs by most private employers unless the employer is engaged in an ongoing investigation involving economic loss or injury to the employer in the employer's business and has a reasonable suspicion that the employee is involved in the incident.

Reasonable Suspicion

"Reasonable suspicion" is an observable, articulated basis in fact. It is most similar to predication. Private employers cannot use polygraphs to screen applicants for employment. Employers cannot discharge an employee for refusing to take an exam. This act does not protect government employees.

Other Federal Statutes

Other statutes do not address the use of polygraphs directly, but nonetheless might give rise to liability if a polygraph test is administered in a discriminatory fashion (e.g., based on race, sex, or some other prohibited factor), or used to ferret out union sympathies in connection with a union organizing campaign.

State Statutes

Several states have enacted laws addressing the use of polygraph examinations and some are more restrictive than the federal statute. Courts have recognized claims arising from unlawful administration of polygraph exams, and wrongful discharge for refusal to take an exam after having been accused of fraud.

Common Law Liability From Polygraph Exams

Outrageous Conduct

Most courts have found that the circumstances surrounding the giving of a polygraph exam do not in and of themselves rise to the level of outrageous conduct.

Invasion of Privacy

In some states, courts have defined polygraph tests as invasions of privacy. Questions directly related to job performance or the incident under investigation generally are held *not* to be invasions of privacy. Control questions might be an invasion of privacy, though circumstances might warrant the intrusion. Check with counsel.

Wrongful Discharge

The refusal to take a polygraph exam as a basis for discharge is allowable in some states, but is considered wrongful discharge in violation of public policy in others.

Obtaining Information About Employees

Federal Statutes
Privacy Act of 1974
The Privacy Act of 1974 restricts information about individuals, both employees and non-employees, that might be gathered by *government agencies*. An agency might maintain records about a person containing information that is relevant and necessary to accomplish a purpose of the agency. This information might include a person's education, finances, medical history, criminal history, employment history, and identifying information (fingerprint, voice print, or photograph). The employee might have access to the information unless it is investigatory material compiled for law enforcement purposes, statistical records, or material compiled solely for determining suitability, eligibility, or qualification for federal service or promotion.

Fair Credit Reporting Act
The Fair and Accurate Credit Transactions Act of 2003 amended the Fair Credit Reporting Act (FCRA) to exempt certain reports involving employee misconduct investigations.

Previously, employers were required to provide notice and obtain express written consent before obtaining a "consumer report." A "consumer report" was defined to include virtually any information obtained about an employee through any third party.

As a result of these new amendments, an employer who uses a third party to conduct a workplace investigation no longer has to obtain the prior consent of an employee **if** the investigation involves suspected:
- Misconduct;
- Violation of law or regulations; or
- Violation of any pre-existing policy of the employer.

In order to qualify for this exception, the report from the third party must not be communicated to anyone other than the employer, an agent of the employer, or the government.

However, if "adverse action" is taken against the employee based on the results of the investigation, the FCRA still requires that the employer to provide the employee with a summary of the report. "Adverse action" is broadly defined as any employment decision that adversely affects the employee. The summary must "contain the nature and substance of the communication upon which the adverse action is based." It does not, however, have to identify the individuals interviewed or the sources of the information.

Gramm-Leach-Bliley Act

The Gramm-Leach-Bliley Act (GLB) was passed in 1999 and final rules implementing the Act became final in 2001. GLB was originally enacted to allow banks and other companies to offer previously forbidden services such as insurance and securities brokerage services. Congress was worried that these new "super banks" would share customers' financial data to affiliates and other companies to hawk their new products. Therefore, Congress added a provision requiring "financial intuitions" to tell customers about its privacy policy, to notify them of private information the institution intends to share, and to give customers the chance to block such information-sharing.

To implement the new law, Congress ordered regulators to define "financial institution" in the broadest possible terms. Thus, "financial institutions" include not just banks, but also insurance companies, accountants, tax preparation and real estate settlement services, and investment advisors. The text of the rule can be found at 16 C.F.R. Part 313. Additional information about the rule can be found at the Federal Trade Commission's website: www.ftc.gov.

The problem for fraud examiners and investigators is that the privacy rules implemented as part of the GLB have been interpreted to prevent the selling of credit header information. Under the FTC's interpretation of the rule, credit header information cannot be sold except for the very limited purposes allowed under the Fair Credit Reporting Act. The agency reached this decision by concluding that such basic personal information, such as names and addresses, is "financial" information, and, therefore, must be protected by under the GLB Act. Unfortunately, this prevents credit bureaus from selling credit header information (including names, addresses, phone numbers, and Social Security numbers) to private investigators, direct marketers, or other information brokers.

The credit bureaus challenged the FTC's rule in court. However, in May 2001, the U.S. District Court for Washington D.C. upheld the agency's interpretation. The credit bureaus have appealed that decision. Unless the decision is overturned, it appears that it will be more difficult for fraud examiners and investigators to obtain personal information about potential suspects or witnesses.

GLB also made it a criminal offense to engage in "pretexting." Some individuals used pretexting as a means to gather financial information about a subject. Pretexters would contact a financial institution and pretend to be the customer or someone else authorized to obtain financial information and basically trick the financial institution into providing information about the subject.

15 U.S.C. § 6821 (added by GLB) makes it an offense to:
- Use false, fictitious or fraudulent statements or documents to get customer information from a financial institution or directly from a customer of a financial institution;
- Use forged, counterfeit, lost, or stolen documents to get customer information from a financial institution or directly from a customer of a financial institution; or
- Ask another person to get someone else's customer information using false, fictitious or fraudulent statements or using false, fictitious or fraudulent documents or forged, counterfeit, lost, or stolen documents.

Violators can, under certain circumstances, be fined and/or imprisoned up to 10 years.

Health Insurance Portability and Accountability Act (Public Law 104-191, Partially Codified in 45 CFR§§ 160, 164)

The Health Insurance Portability and Accountability Act (HIPPA) instituted several new privacy rules. While most of the rules do not directly affect investigations, fraud examiners should be aware of the rules because they may have an impact on the type of information that can be legally gathered on employees.

The HIPPA privacy rules place restrictions on the availability and use of "protected health information." The definition of this term is extremely broad and covers any information relating to an individual's past, present, or future physical or mental health, payment for services, or health care operations.

If information about the health of an individual, or payments for services, becomes an issue during an investigation, you should immediately contact the human resources department. The HR department should have information about whether the entity is subject to the HIPPA rules and can assist you in compliance with those rules.

The most important thing to note is that if the HIPPA rules apply, you are restricted as to the type of health information you can access without specific written authorization. You should never contact the health care provider, the health plan administrator, or a medical billing services for copies of employee records without first consulting the employer's legal counsel or the HR department.

Discharging a Suspected Wrongdoer

Many employers, when confronted with a possible wrongdoer or an employee who refuses to cooperate in the investigation, immediately want to fire the employee. Whether the employee can or should be discharged depends on the facts of the case and the law in the employer's state. Public employers are governed by stricter standards. Constitutional and statutory laws govern the investigation and termination of public employees. For example, a public employee cannot be terminated for exercising his Fifth Amendment right against self-incrimination.

In some states, absent an employment contract, employment is considered "at will." This means that the employer or the employee can sever their relationship at any time for any reason. In other states, however, employers cannot terminate an employee (even an "at will" employee) if the termination is in violation of a fundamental public policy or statute. Before discharging an employee, it is best to document in the employee's file that the employer has "good cause" to terminate employment.

Good Cause

Although there is no exact definition of "good cause," there are several questions that the company should ask before terminating an employee:

- Did the employee know that the conduct would be subject to discipline?
- Was the rule the employee violated reasonably related to the safe, efficient, or orderly operation of the business?
- Did the company investigate to discover whether the employee violated the rule?
- Did the company conduct a fair and objective investigation?
- Did the company obtain significant evidence of a violation?
- Was the decision nondiscriminatory?
- Was the discipline related to the seriousness of the offense and the prior record of the employee?

If the company feels that discharge of the employee is likely, it should make sure that the employee's actions and the company's actions are well-documented and placed in the employee's personnel file.

Negligent Discharge

At least one state has recognized the right of an employee to sue for the employer's failure to properly investigate charges against the employee before discharging him. Most of the courts that have addressed this issue have refused to recognize the claim.

Breach of Implied Contract

Many states now recognize an implied contract between employers and employees arising out of employee handbooks. Handbook provisions might limit the right to discharge for "just cause," and the issue might be whether the employer has enough evidence of wrongdoing to constitute "just cause."

Breach of the Duty of Good Faith and Fair Dealing

A few states recognize a duty on the part of the employer to deal with its employees fairly and in good faith. Documenting that the employer had good cause to terminate the employee should defeat this claim.

Discharge in Violation of Public Policy

Some states recognize a pubic policy exception to "at will" employment. The employee must prove that his conduct is favored by a relevant public policy and that the employer retaliated against him for engaging in this "protected" activity. Again, the company will need to show that it had good cause to fire the employee and that it was not retaliating against the employee because of the protected conduct.

For example, if an employee is fired because he supported a particular political candidate in the last election, a court or jury might find that his termination is in violation of the general public policy allowing people to vote for whomever they please. However, if the employee was conducting fund-raising activities on company time, the company would likely have good cause to terminate the employee and such termination would not be in retaliation of the employee's support of a particular candidate.

CRIMINAL PROSECUTIONS FOR FRAUD

Basic Principles of Criminal Law

A defendant in a federal or state court is presumed innocent, has the right to remain silent, to confront accusers, to be advised by counsel, to have a speedy trial in front of peers, as well as other protections. Under our system, the government bears the burden of proving the accused guilty beyond a reasonable doubt, and is expected to observe the rights of the defendant scrupulously. The principal guarantees of individual rights are the Fourth, Fifth, and Sixth amendments. These are applied to the states under the "due process" clause of the Fourteenth Amendment. The procedures described in this chapter primarily refer to federal rules. Individual state procedures might differ.

Fourth Amendment

The Fourth Amendment provides that the right of people to be:

... secure in their persons, houses, papers, and effects, against unreasonable searches and seizure, shall not be violated, and no warrants shall issue, but upon probable cause, supported by oath or affirmation, and particularly describing the place to be searched, and the persons or things to be seized.

Fifth Amendment

No person shall be held to answer for a capital, or otherwise infamous crime, unless on a presentment of indictment of a Grand Jury, except in cases arising in the land or naval forces, or in the Militia, when in actual service in time of War or public danger; nor shall any person be subject for the same offense to be twice put in jeopardy of life or limb; nor shall he be compelled in any criminal case to be a witness against himself, nor be deprived of life, liberty, or property, without due process of law; nor shall private property be taken for public use, without just compensation.

Sixth Amendment

In all criminal prosecutions, the accused shall enjoy the right to speedy and public trial, by an impartial jury of the State and district wherein the crime shall have been committed, which district shall have been previously ascertained by law, and to be informed of the nature and cause of the accusation; to be confronted with the witnesses against him; to have compulsory process for obtaining witnesses in his favor; and to have the assistance of counsel for his defense.

Fourteenth Amendment

Section 1. All persons born or naturalized in the United States, and subject to the jurisdiction thereof, are citizens of the United States and of the State wherein they reside. No State shall make or enforce any law which shall abridge the privileges or immunities of citizens of the United States; nor shall any State deprive any person of life, liberty, or property without due process of law; nor deny to any person within its jurisdiction the equal protection of the laws.

Arrest and Interrogation

A police officer or private citizen may arrest in public without a warrant for a felony committed in his presence. An arrest occurs whenever a reasonable person would feel not free to leave.

The Supreme Court has declined to require a warrant preliminary to any arrest because of the "intolerable burdens" such a rule would create for legitimate law enforcement. The Court has held, however, that a warrant normally is required before a person may be arrested in his own home and that a person arrested without a warrant is entitled to prompt judicial determination of probable cause before that person can be detained for any extended period.

Not all police stops are arrests requiring probable cause. In *Terry v. Ohio*, 392 U.S. 1 (1968), the Supreme Court held that the police may briefly detain and question a person for investigative purposes if there are specific "articulable" reasons to do so. A valid stop may yield evidence to effect an arrest. If the police arrest or detain unlawfully, any statements or evidence obtained as a result will be suppressed. The suspect may still be prosecuted, however, if other untainted evidence of wrongdoing exists.

Interrogation of Suspects

The Fifth Amendment provides that no person "shall ... be compelled in any criminal case to be a witness against himself ... " The Fifth Amendment applies only:

- To compelled "testimonial statements": nontestimonial conduct, such as compelling a suspect to appear in a line-up, give handwriting samples, or submit to blood or alcohol tests, is not barred by the Fifth Amendment.
- To individuals. Business entities, including sole proprietorships and other organizations, do not have a Fifth Amendment privilege.

The Fifth Amendment protects an individual's personal papers that are not voluntarily prepared, including tax returns, if incriminating. Documents such as appointment books, correspondence and other records that the subject prepared without government compulsion are not covered by the Amendment and must be produced.

To ensure that every citizen has the opportunity to exercise this fundamental right, the Supreme Court ruled in the landmark case of *Miranda v. Arizona*, 348 U.S. 436 (1966), that the police must give the following warnings before interrogating any suspect held in custody:
- That the suspect has the right to remain silent
- That any statements can be used against him at trial
- That the suspect has a right to the assistance of an attorney
- That an attorney will be appointed to represent the suspect if he cannot afford to retain one.

Once a suspect asserts the right to remain silent, all questioning must cease until counsel is provided. If the defendant thereafter decides to make a statement, the government must show that it was the result of a voluntary, knowing waiver of his rights.

Miranda warnings are required only if the suspect is (1) interrogated (2) while held *in custody*, (3) by *public* authorities. Certain exceptions to the warning requirement apply, such as when immediate questioning is necessary to ensure public safety. The warnings generally are not required when a person is being questioned by private parties.

Apart from the Miranda requirements, a confession also must be voluntary, not coerced by physical or psychological means. Some inducement is permissible, however, such as informing the suspect that a confession might result in more lenient treatment. Using deceit and trickery to extract a confession, such as telling the suspect that an accomplice had confessed when in fact he had not, is treated differently by different courts, some permitting such confessions, others not. No confession will be admitted if the circumstances under which it was obtained render it unreliable.

For more information on the applicability of the Fifth Amendment to investigations conducted by non-government personnel, please refer to the "Individual Rights" chapter.

The Charging Process

A person under arrest must be brought before a magistrate without "unnecessary delay." At this time, the arresting officer must swear to a complaint, establishing probable cause, if the arrest was without a warrant. The defendant will then be advised of the nature of the complaint, of the right to retain counsel or to appointed counsel, and of the general circumstances under which pre-trial release may be obtained.

The Eighth Amendment prohibits "excessive bail." The Supreme Court has recently held that the amendment does not absolutely require pre-trial release, only that if bail is appropriate, it be set no higher than necessary to assure the defendant's presence at trial. Bail may be denied and the defendant held in custody if the judge decides release would pose a serious threat to the safety of the community or to a particular individual, or that no amount of bail or particular conditions of release would prevent the defendant from fleeing.

At the initial appearance, a defendant who has not yet been indicted also is informed of his right to a preliminary examination. This is a formal, adversary hearing, before a judge, at which the defendant may be represented by counsel and can cross-examine witnesses. The purpose of the hearing is to determine whether there is probable cause to hold the defendant for further proceedings, not to establish guilt or innocence. Because of its limited purpose, hearsay and even illegally obtained evidence can be admissible. Motions to suppress must be made to the trial court.

If the magistrate determines at the preliminary examination that there is no probable cause, the complaint will be dismissed and the defendant released. The government may, however, institute a subsequent prosecution for the same offense, presumably with better evidence. Preliminary examinations often are used by defense counsel as an opportunity to get free "discovery" of the details of the prosecution's case. For this reason, some prosecutors prefer to obtain a grand jury indictment. An indictment is held to satisfy the probable cause requirements of the Fifth Amendment, and precludes the need for the preliminary examination.

The Grand Jury

The grand jury consists of 16 to 23 people sworn as jurors who meet in secret deliberation usually in biweekly or monthly sessions to hear witnesses and other evidence presented by prosecutors and to vote on indictments. An indictment or *true bill* must be agreed upon by at least 12 jurors voting without the prosecutor present.

The hearing is a non-adversarial proceeding. The accused has no right to be informed of its deliberations, to know the evidence against him, or to confront the accusers. The accused also has no absolute right to appear before it, and if he does, may not be accompanied by counsel. The accused may, however, periodically leave the grand jury to consult with the attorney.

These severe limitations on the rights of the accused are thought by some to be justified on the grounds that they are necessary to investigate criminal activity effectively, that the grand jury has only the power to accuse, not to convict the defendant. The defendant, if indicted, has full constitutional protections at trial. The grand jury's power has been severely criticized by many legal and public interest groups. Abuse of its processes can do severe damage to innocent parties, particularly public figures to whom an indictment alone can be devastating. For this reason, defense counsel in major white-collar cases now often begin their defense at the grand jury stage to try to convince prosecutors not to indict—rather than waiting—as was traditionally the case, until an indictment is returned.

The grand jury has the right to subpoena witnesses and documents, and refusals to appear or produce may be punishable as contempt, with fines or jail terms until the subpoena is complied with, or the grand jury term expires. A witness or target of the grand jury retains the Fifth Amendment right against self-incrimination.

A grand jury may be used to obtain evidence of possible violations of the criminal law, and its process may not be used as a ruse to obtain evidence for parallel civil actions. A common example of such parallel proceedings would be investigation of possible anti-trust violations. The grand jury may, however, with the appropriate court order, make evidence available to the proper government authorities for a civil proceeding, as long as the primary purpose of its inquiry was to enforce the criminal laws. Access by private parties through court orders to grand jury evidence for use in private civil proceedings is unlikely to be granted because of secrecy requirements, unless substantial need is demonstrated.

Immunity

In the course of a grand jury investigation or a criminal trial the prosecution may apply for a court order compelling testimony from a witness under a grant of immunity. Because immunized testimony cannot be used against the witness in any criminal proceeding, such an order does not violate the Fifth Amendment right against self-incrimination.

Although it is legally permissible to prosecute an immunized witness on the basis of other testimony and evidence, as a matter of practice this is seldom done because of policy considerations and the difficulty of demonstrating—as the law requires—that the subsequent prosecution was not in any way based on the compelled testimony.

A decision to immunize a witness is solely within the discretion of the prosecution. If the application meets statutory requirements, the court must grant the order. If the immunized witness refuses to testify—out of fear of reprisal or for any other reason—the witness will be found in contempt and jailed until he agrees to testify or the grand jury term expires. The witness can then be summoned before a new grand jury and the process repeated indefinitely or until a judge decides that there is no possibility that further incarceration will induce cooperation.

An *immunity order* protects the witness only from prosecution from past crimes about which testimony is compelled; other, undiscovered crimes are not covered, nor is the witness immune from prosecution for perjury based on the immunized testimony. Such testimony also may be used against the witness in a civil proceeding.

Indictment and Information

In the federal system, all offenses punishable by death must be charged by indictment; all felonies (generally crimes punishable by imprisonment for a year or more) must be prosecuted by indictment, unless the defendant waives the requirement, in which case the prosecution may proceed by the filing of an "Information." An *information* is a charge signed only by the prosecutor without the involvement of the grand jury. A misdemeanor may be charged by either an indictment or information.

Arraignment

A defendant named in an indictment, if not already in custody, may be arrested on a warrant. Or, more often in white-collar crime cases, is summoned to appear before a magistrate at a stated time and place to be arraigned. The arraignment must take place in open court, and consists of reading of the indictment or information to the defendant and calling on him to plead. The defendant may plead guilty, not guilty, or nolo contendere. A plea of *nolo contendere* means the defendant does not contest the charges, without formally admitting or denying them. A defendant may plead nolo only with the consent of the court. If accepted, a nolo plea is the same as a plea of guilty for purposes of punishment, but cannot be used as a formal admission of guilt. This makes it a favored plea for corporate defendants facing subsequent civil litigation.

Before the court will accept a guilty plea, it must follow procedures to ensure that the plea is voluntary and accurate; that is, that there is a "factual basis" for the plea. This usually means that the defendant must admit to committing acts that satisfy each element of the offense. In some circumstances, however, a defendant may be allowed to enter an *Alford* plea (named after the Supreme Court case that upheld the practice) under which he pleads guilty, although continuing to assert innocence. Such a plea may be made to obtain the benefits of a plea agreement and to avoid potentially more dire consequences, such as the death penalty, if the defendant is convicted after trial. Before the Court accepts an *Alford* plea, it must satisfy itself that there is strong evidence of guilt and that the defendant understands the consequences. A plea of not guilty sets in motion the adjudicative process described below.

Prosecutorial Discretion and Plea Bargains

Whether criminal cases are actually brought to trial might depend on *prosecutorial discretion*, meaning that the decision to prosecute is left to the discretion of the appropriate jurisdictional authority. Prosecutors exercising this discretion consider issues like the potential for deterrence, the strength of the available evidence, and the resources (time, labor, money) incurred by going to trial. The question is partly about the chances for a guilty verdict, but also about the cost and demands of achieving that verdict. According to federal statistics, about 84 percent of the people arrested are prosecuted; 62 percent of these are convicted, and 34 percent are incarcerated. Cases can be handled through plea bargains or cooperative agreements in exchange for assistance, so it's difficult to say, statistically, how "successful" prosecutorial efforts have been. But when public officials take a case to court, they're generally armed and ready—of those cases that do go to trial, more than 90 percent end in conviction.

High-level crimes, especially those involving public figures, may require special approval for being tried or declined, from the U.S. Department of Justice for example. White-collar crime is sometimes prosecuted on the basis of *declination guidelines* that set out dollar amounts below which cases are not accepted. A prosecutor's office might decide, for example, that securities frauds of less than $500,000 will not be brought to trial. Because of the immense effort required to prosecute many fraudulent acts, prosecutors have to weigh the cost and exertion of going to court versus the amount available for recovery. Accordingly, many businesses are turning to civil actions to redress fraud. As the criminal courts become more and more jammed, companies can often speed up the process by filing their own civil action. Although the perpetrator cannot be given jail time as a result of a purely civil action, he can be ordered to pay back the ill-gotten funds.

Prosecuting attorneys also have the power to settle charges with a *plea bargain* arrangement, avoiding the expenditures of time and effort involved at trial. About 90 percent of criminal defendants never go to trial, opting instead for a deal. Critics have charged that the plea privilege is abused by cynical prosecutors, and leads to dangerous offenders being released quickly and without retribution.

The U.S. Supreme Court disagrees. A majority decision in 1971 declared that the plea bargain is a "highly desirable" part of the justice system because it "leads to prompt and largely final disposition" in most cases; it "avoids much of the corrosive impact of enforced idleness" suffered by defendants who aren't released on bail; it reduces the chances that an accused person will commit a crime while free on bail; and it "enhances whatever may be the rehabilitative prospects" of the guilty by "shortening the time between charge and disposition" [*Santabello* v. *New York*, 404 U.S. 257, 261 (1971)].

Plea bargains also can be a boon to offenders. Some are released from any prosecution whatsoever, and others receive lesser charges. In a study of white-collar criminals, more than 42 percent of cooperating defendants were charged with just one violation of the law, while only 30 percent of non-cooperating defendants were so lucky.

Once charges are filed against them, white-collar defendants are more likely to insist on a trial than other offenders. On average, considering all federal indictments, only about 10 percent of those accused plead not guilty and proceed to trial. But more than 18 percent of defendants in white-collar cases (nearly double the average) insist on their trial. People accused of securities fraud are especially likely to demand their day in court, with well over half of these defendants pleading not guilty.

The Burden of Proof in Criminal Trials

In criminal cases, the verdict must be based on assurance *beyond a reasonable doubt*. The civil trial requires only a "preponderance of the evidence" to support a decision, but criminal trials are tougher. Plainly put, the law instructs jurors and judges hearing criminal cases to be as sure as they possibly can that the defendant committed the acts as charged. In purely philosophical terms, there might always be room for doubt ("Well, did he really…?"). Fraud charges can be especially hard to prove because the evidence is by its nature overwhelmingly circumstantial, *i.e.* composed of documents and their interpretation versus the testimony of eyewitnesses. But arch skepticism is hardly practical in making necessary legal decisions. Deciding "beyond a reasonable doubt" entails making the most assured judgment possible based on the evidence as presented. The appeals process recognizes that more than one examination of the charge(s) might be necessary to ensure an accurate, fair-minded verdict.

The prosecution, as most people remember from high school civics, is responsible for proving the charges against the defendant. The Constitution guarantees that the accused is *presumed innocent* until the prosecution shows otherwise.

Pre-trial Motions in Criminal Court

Criminal trials, like civil proceedings, often begin with pre-trial motions. Some of these are the same regardless of the type of court (civil or criminal). For example, both criminal and civil defendants can make *motions in limine* to exclude certain evidence, can ask that the charge or complaint be made more definite and certain, or can request a postponement of the trial date. Other motions are particular to the criminal process.

Some pre-trial motions typically used in criminal trials are listed below:
- *Motion for Severance.* Sometimes defendants in a large case are tried at the same trial. This motion asks that the defendants be tried separately, or at least that this particular defendant's trial be conducted separately.
- *Motion to Suppress Evidence.* Argues that evidence was improperly obtained, is impertinent or unduly prejudicial, or violates some other right such as the privilege against self-incrimination. In many cases motions to exclude evidence—decided at a *suppression hearing*, where the judge (without a jury) rules on the propriety of the government's conduct—are more important than the trial itself. If the defense is able to exclude illegally seized narcotics, or a tainted confession, or critical books and records, the prosecution might be forced to dismiss the charges (at least temporarily) for lack of adequate proof. On the other hand, an unsuccessful suppression motion might be followed by renewed interest by the defendant in a plea bargain.
- *Motion for a Change of Venue.* Asks to move the trial to another court because the defendant cannot receive a fair trial due to public prejudice.

Motion to Dismiss
There are several grounds upon which a defendant may request that the indictment be dismissed.
- *Speedy Trial.* The indictment may be dismissed for violations of a defendant's right to speedy trial, when the trial date exceeds a certain amount of time after the charge (usually 70 days). A related basis for the motion is alleging pre-indictment delay, when, for example the prosecution took an excessively long time in bringing the indictment.
- *Selective Prosecution.* When multiple perpetrators are involved in a criminal act, a defendant may claim "selective prosecution," accusing the authorities of targeting some individuals and exonerating others without cause. Defendants also may allege "vindictive prosecution." If, after being exonerated on one charge, a person is charged with another, more serious charge, the individual may claim vindictive prosecution.
- *Double Jeopardy.* The "Double Jeopardy" clause of the Fifth Amendment—which prevents someone from being tried for the same crime twice—may be used to request a dismissal. Dismissal motions also may claim that the indictment is invalid because it's based on tainted evidence, insufficient evidence, or illegally seized evidence.
- *Challenging the Sufficiency of the Indictment.* Rule 7 of the Federal Rules of Criminal Procedure requires the indictment to be a plain, concise, but definite statement of the essential facts constituting the charge(s) against the defendant. As discussed previously, the indictment must, therefore, allege all of the essential elements of the crimes charged, including the requisite criminal intent where required by statute. If the indictment is deficient, then the defense can challenge it. The defense may challenge the indictment if the prosecution failed to plead an essential element of the fraud offense or plead the necessary facts.

   For example, if a defendant is charged with mail fraud, the indictment must specifically describe the details of the fraudulent scheme perpetrated through the use of the mail and must set forth the false representations. (See United States v. Hess, 124 U.S. 483 [1888].) If the indictment fails to do this, the court will dismiss the indictment. However, the victory might be short-lived. Even though the indictment is dismissed, the prosecution usually is free to re-file the indictment.

- *Duplicity.* Rule 8(a) of the Federal Rules of Criminal Procedure requires that each count of an indictment state one and only one offense. A count that charges two or more offenses is duplicitous. Unfortunately, what constitutes a single offense often is hard to determine with white-collar criminal statutes. Single and continuing offenses, committed for several objectives or by multiple means, like mail or wire fraud or conspiracy, may be charged in one count, although they alternatively could be charged as separate and distinct counts. Generally, however, if the separate violations are all a part of the same criminal scheme, they can be alleged in the same count. This is sometimes preferable for the defendant because if all of the violations are alleged in one count, it looks to the jury as if the defendant has committed one fraud rather than 50 separate frauds.

- *Multiplicity* is the opposite of duplicity. Multiplicity occurs when two or more counts charge essentially the same offense, thereby exposing the defendant to cumulative punishment for one offense. It is in essence being charged twice for the same offense, which exposes the defendant to double the punishment.

Discovery

Both the defendant and prosecution have statutory rights to certain pre-trial discovery. The defendant may inspect copies of all relevant statements made by him (or, if a corporation, by its employees) in the custody of the government, a copy of the accused's prior criminal record, and all documents, items, test results and other evidence the government intends to introduce at a trial or that are necessary to the defense. The defendant does not, however, have an absolute right to see copies of prior statements made by a witness against him until such witness testifies at trial. In many cases, however, particularly fraud prosecutions where there is less risk of reprisal or tampering with witnesses, the government may voluntarily produce these statements before trial.

Discovery Under Rule 16

Federal Rule of Criminal Procedure 16 identifies the information that each side must disclose. Generally, the defense is entitled to inspect and copy statements made by the defendant. The defense also may inspect the defendant's prior record, material documents, tangible objects, and examination and test reports.

If, and only if, the defendant requests discovery of documents and objects, or of examination and test reports, the government may seek similar kinds of materials from the defense. Any items that must be disclosed are required to be disclosed "as soon as reasonably possible." The court may regulate the discovery process by entering protective orders or punishing the failure to provide the proper information timely.

The rule allows the defense to obtain statements of the defendant made to third parties, as well as government agents, if the statements were reduced to writing. Therefore, any written statements made by the defendant to the CFE investigating the case, if the statements were turned over to law enforcement or the government, must be produced. However, oral statements made to third parties (*i.e.* nongovernmental agents) generally are protected from discovery.

SUMMARY OF RULE 16 DISCLOSURE REQUIREMENTS

- *Statements of the Defendant* — Upon the defendant's request, the government must disclose any relevant written or recorded statements made by the defendant. This includes written records of any relevant statements made by the defendant to a government agent, either before or after arrest, as well as any recorded testimony of the defendant made before a grand jury which relates to the offense charged.
- *The Defendant's Prior Record* — Upon the defendant's request, the government must furnish a copy of the defendant's prior criminal record, if it exists.
- *Documents and Tangible Objects* — Upon the defendant's request, the government must allow the defendant to inspect and copy or photograph any books, papers, documents, photographs, tangible objects, buildings or places which: (1) are material to the preparation of the defendant's case; (2) are intended for use as evidence at trial by the government; or (3) were obtained from the defendant or belong to the defendant.
- *Reports of Examinations and Tests* — Upon the defendant's request, the government must allow the defendant to inspect and copy any results or reports of physical or mental examinations, scientific tests or experiments which are material to the preparation of the defense or which the government plans to use as evidence at trial.
- *Expert Witnesses* — Upon the defendant's request, the government must provide a written summary of the testimony to be given by its expert witnesses. This summary must include the expert's opinions, the basis of those opinions and the qualifications of the expert.

While the State has a broad duty to disclose evidence in criminal cases, there are limits to what it must turn over to the defense. The defendant does not have a right to the work product of the State, which includes reports, memoranda and other internal documents made by the government attorney in preparing for and prosecuting the case. In addition, the defendant does not have a right to inspect statements made by government witnesses prior to the time the witness actually testifies.

The Jencks Act (18 U.S.C. § 3500)

The Jencks Act permits the defendant to obtain, prior to cross-examination, a government witness' prior statements (or portions thereof) that relate to the subject matter of his testimony on direct examination. However, the statute also protects statements from discovery until after the direct examination has been completed. The statements that must be produced include not only the written statements signed by the witness, but also may include notes or memoranda of government agents or prosecutors which set forth what the witness said during interviews.

Exculpatory Information (Brady Material)

The prosecutor has ethical responsibilities not to use evidence that is false and must correct testimony that he knows is false. In 1963, the Supreme Court (in the case of *Brady v. Maryland*, 373 U.S. 83) expanded the prosecution's duty further. Under *Brady*, the prosecution must disclose all evidence requested by the defendant that is material to guilt or punishment, *i.e.*, evidence that would tend to *exculpate* him or reduce his penalty. The government is expressly forbidden to conceal evidence that would call the charges into question.

Disclosures by the Defendant

Prosecution has similar privileges to learn the substance of the defense's case, the basis for the accused person's not-guilty plea. If the defendant requests disclosure of the prosecution's documents and tangible objects, reports of examinations and tests, and its expert witnesses, then the prosecution is correspondingly entitled to disclosure of these items from the defense. The prosecution is not, of course, entitled to disclosure of the defendant's work product, nor is it entitled to statements made by prospective witnesses to the defendant or his attorneys.

The Trial Process

Under the Sixth Amendment, the accused is entitled to a "speedy and public trial, by an impartial jury, in the State and district wherein the crime [was] committed..." In federal courts, the Speedy Trial Act mandates that the defendant be indicted within 30 days of arrest and tried within 70 days of notice of the charges, excluding delays caused by certain enumerated circumstances. If the time limits are not adhered to, the court may dismiss the case, with or without prejudice, depending on the circumstances.

Jury Selection

The Constitution requires that "the trial of all crimes, except in cases of impeachment, shall be by Jury..." In the federal system, the defendant may waive the right with the consent of the court and prosecution. Petty offenses do not require a trial by jury.

Most criminal cases are tried by a jury of 12 with at least two alternates, but the parties may stipulate to a lesser number. The jury is expected to be impartial. The parties or the court may *voir dire* (ask questions of) the prospective jurors to determine their suitability. Each party may remove any number of prospective jurors for cause, such as admitted bias or prejudice, and each side has a limited number of *peremptory challenges*, depending on the offense charged, under which a party may strike a prospective juror without having to provide a reason. The prosecution may not use its peremptory challenges, however, in a way solely influenced by racial factors. The defendant may also challenge the entire jury pool—called the *venire*—if the selection procedures systematically exclude certain groups, such as minorities, women, or young people. The jury that hears the case (the *petit jury*) is not required to reflect a cross-section of the community or contain individuals of the same race or age as the defendant.

Opening Statements

Once the jury is selected and sworn, and after some introductory remarks by the judge, the actual trial begins with the *opening statement* by the prosecution. In it, the prosecutor usually explains the charges, outlines the evidence he intends to produce, and tells the jury that the prosecution will ask for a verdict of guilty. The prosecutor is not permitted to argue the case at this point; that will be done at the end. The defense counsel then gives an opening statement, although on occasion will wait until the defense case begins.

Presenting Evidence

The prosecution presents its case first, and bears the burden of proving every element of the offense beyond a reasonable doubt. The defense is under no obligation to produce any evidence at any time.

As a general rule, a witness' testimony must be confined to facts within personal knowledge rather than conjecture or opinion. A duly-qualified expert witness, however, may give an opinion if the court determines that it will assist the jury to understand the evidence or to determine a fact in issue. Accountants and fraud examiners may be (and often are) called to testify in fraud cases as lay witnesses or experts, or both. See the chapter on Testifying as an Expert Witness for more information.

The Sixth Amendment guarantees a defendant the right to confront and cross-examine witnesses. This is a principal reason why hearsay evidence generally is excluded. If a judge unduly restricts a defendant's right to probe the prosecution's witnesses' credibility or knowledge of the facts, a conviction may be reversed. Far more defendants probably are in jail, however, because their counsel asked one question too many (and got a devastating answer) than because the judge allowed one too few.

The admission of evidence and objections thereto are ruled on by the trial judge. The rules of evidence are complex but can be summarized as intending to limit the evidence presented to the jury to only matters relevant to the specific charges, and to exclude unreliable or unduly prejudicial evidence. The same piece of evidence, however, may be admissible or inadmissible depending on the specific reason for which it is being offered. For example, evidence of other similar crimes or wrongful acts by the defendant may not be offered by the prosecution merely to show that the defendant is more likely to have committed the crime charged. But the same evidence may be introduced to prove intent, if disputed by the defendant, or to rebut a claim of accident or mistake, or to impeach false testimony by the accused.

At the close of the prosecution's case, the defense usually moves for a judgment of acquittal on the ground that the prosecutions evidence—even if believed—is legally insufficient to convict. If the judge grants the motion, the trial ends and the defendant is acquitted. If the motion is denied, the defendant may elect to present evidence or may rest.

If the defendant elects to testify, he is subject to cross-examination, and the prosecution may impeach the defendant's credibility by showing prior convictions. This usually is a deathblow to the defense and is the reason many defendants do not testify. The judge, however, may exclude such evidence as unduly prejudicial, particularly if the prior crime is remote in time or did not involve dishonesty or false statements.

A defendant is entitled to call character witnesses on his behalf who often have no knowledge of the charges or facts in issue but who are prepared to testify to the defendant's character. Such testimony must be given in the form of the witness' opinion or testimony as to the defendant's general good reputation; testimony as to specific incidents of good conduct is not permitted. This seemingly upside-down rule is justified by the belief that testimony as to specific conduct would prove too confusing and time-consuming. And because any character evidence is circumstantial at best, it is considered permissible to limit the testimony to reputation or opinion. Character witnesses may be asked on cross-examination if they have "heard about" alleged wrongful or dishonest acts by the accused, including a prior conviction.

Common Legal Issues in Fraud Cases

Two general types of legal issues—one substantive, the other procedural—are often encountered in fraud examinations. The substantive issue includes the proving of each element of the offense beyond a reasonable doubt, including the element of intent (if intent, in fact, is an element). The procedural issue includes the right to counsel and the manner in which fraud examiners employed by law enforcement have conducted arrests, searches and seizures, and interrogations. Fraud examiners are most likely to encounter legal problems over such issues as the condition, organization, and sanctity of their work papers and their audit assumptions if the case is based on an accounting hypothesis (net worth method, for example).

Accounting data used as evidence often is challenged as not meeting the hearsay exceptions. The issues are whether the proffered documentary evidence is the "best" evidence and whether secondary evidence is admissible when the best evidence is unavailable. Questions often are raised about the business records exception to the hearsay rule; that is, whether a record was made in the ordinary course of doing business or was made in books of account contemporaneously with a business transaction. Another issue often encountered is the expertness of a fraud examiner called to provide expert testimony (opinion evidence). The expert witness' credentials may be challenged and another expert may be called to question the opinion of the first.

Legal Defenses

A *defense* is an assertion by a defendant in a criminal or civil suit that seeks to explain away guilt or civil liability for damages. The more common defenses include:
- Alibi
- Consent
- De minimis infraction (trivial)
- Duress
- Entrapment

- Ignorance
- Mistake
- Infancy
- Insanity
- Necessity
- Protection of property
- Self-defense
- Public duty
- Legal impossibility, and
- Protection of others.

These also might be questions involving statutes of limitation, proper venue, and proper jurisdiction.

In criminal fraud cases where intent is an element of the crime, defense attorneys may advance a number of "smoke screen" theories to excuse their clients of guilt, i.e., by alleging some inhibiting factor to the formulation of intent. For example, while ignorance of the law might be no excuse, it can persuade a jury, particularly if the crime is complex and financial in nature such as an income tax evasion case where the net worth method of income reconstruction has been utilized. Certain of the computerized embezzlements fit this category too, as does bank fraud, securities fraud, and price-fixing conspiracies. While ignorance of the law might not be an excuse, it sometimes induces pity or sorrow.

Insanity may be used as a defense—and often is—in crimes of violence. Notice of an insanity defense usually must be given before trial. Innocent mistake, advanced age, sickness, and illiteracy may be used to evoke sympathy. And while they may not work as defenses, if they are believed, they may persuade the judge or jury to be lenient in sentencing.

The defenses that cause prosecutors the most headaches are assertions of poor investigative work, i.e., improper arrests, searches, seizures, and interrogations, improper handling and documentation of evidence, privacy invasions, libeling, slandering and defaming the defendant during the investigation. In fraud examinations, sloppy auditing and mishandling of work papers might be alleged.

The increased use of the undercover approach in criminal investigations also has led to the increased assertion of entrapment as a defense; that is, that the peace officer or undercover agent solicited, encouraged, or incited the criminal act. Without that incitement, it is alleged the defendant would not have committed the act.

After the defense rests, the court may permit the prosecution to call rebuttal witnesses and the defense to put on re-rebuttal evidence. At the close of all evidence, the defense may make or renew its motion for a judgment of acquittal. The court may reserve its decision, submit the case to the jury, and decide the motion before or after the jury returns with a verdict. The motion may be made for the first time and granted even after the jury brings in a guilty verdict.

At the close of the evidence, the jury usually is temporarily discharged and the parties meet with the judge to submit proposed jury instructions. These will be read to the jury usually after closing arguments, and will include such matters as the basic elements of the charges, the definition of reasonable doubt, the prosecution's burden, and, if requested by the defense, the warning that no adverse inference may be drawn from the failure of the defendant to testify. Some defense counsel do not request this instruction because they believe it merely reminds the jury of the accused's failure to explain or defend his conduct.

Each side is entitled to instructions on the law supporting its theory of the case if there is any credible evidence in its favor even if there is substantial evidence to the contrary. If a request to instruct is denied, to preserve appeal rights, counsel must state his objection and the grounds therefore before the jury retires. This is an extremely important point for defense counsel as errors in instructions are fertile grounds for reversals on appeal.

Closing Arguments

The prosecution argues first, the defense follows, and the prosecution has the opportunity for final rebuttal. The prosecutor is held to a particularly high standard in closing argument. He may not misstate the evidence, express a personal opinion as to the defendant's guilt or the credibility of witnesses, or otherwise make prejudicial or inflammatory remarks. The prosecutor is expected to stick to the facts and to the reasonable inferences that can be drawn therefrom. In most cases the defense argument focuses on attacking the motives and credibility of the government's witnesses and emphasizes the heavy burden of proof the government bears.

Jury Deliberations

After hearing instructions, the jury retires for its deliberations and selects a foreman. Generally, the verdict must be unanimous. However, in some states, such as Oregon and Louisiana, a jury can return a conviction with only 10 of 12 votes. If the jury is unable to reach a verdict, a mistrial will be declared. The defendant can be retried if the prosecution elects to do so; double jeopardy does not attach unless the defendant is acquitted after the jury is sworn.

If a verdict is reached, it is announced in open court by the foreman or the bailiff. Either party may request that the jury be *polled*, that is, that each juror be asked individually whether he concurred in the verdict. If any juror answers no, the jury must return for further deliberations or may be discharged.

Sentencing

Following a verdict of guilty, a sentence must be imposed without unnecessary delay. Prior to the sentencing hearing a probation officer will prepare a pre-sentence report that will review the defendant's character, background, associates, prior criminal record, and other factors relevant to setting an appropriate sentence. The report will recommend a particular sentence or range of sentence. Recent amendments to the Federal Rules of Criminal Procedure require that the pre-sentence report contain a *victim impact statement*, that is, an assessment of the financial, social, psychological, and medical impact upon, and cost to, the victim of the crime. This information may be used to set the punishment or to support a possible restitution order. The defendant and his counsel are allowed to review all or parts of the probation report except the sentencing recommendation.

At the sentencing hearing the defendant, counsel, and the prosecutor may be heard before sentence is imposed. The court may impose a fine, a term of imprisonment, or both, or place the defendant on probation for a specified period and under certain conditions. The court may order restitution to the victims in addition to a fine or prison term or as a condition of probation. A federal statute provides that a defendant who has been found guilty of fraud may be ordered to give notice to the victims, apparently to protect the public from further fraudulent acts by the defendant and to alert the victims to the possibility of civil recoveries.

Sentences of imprisonment for two or more offenses may be ordered to run consecutively or concurrently, depending on the nature and severity of the offenses and other factors. In federal court, a defendant may be fined up to twice the pecuniary gain realized from the crime, or twice the loss sustained by the victim as an alternative to the statutory amounts.

Sentencing Guidelines

The Sentencing Reform Act of 1984 provided for the development of guidelines for the sentencing of individual and organizational offenders. The individual guidelines became effective in 1987, and the guidelines for organizations in 1991.

Under the guidelines, sentencing determinations are made by cross-referencing the *base offense level* assigned to a particular offense with the "defendant's criminal history category." There are 43 basic offense levels (murder and treason being level 43 offenses) and six criminal history categories. Adjustments may be made up or down in each table based on the particular facts and circumstances of the case. For example, the base offense level for crimes involving fraud or deceit is six, but if the fraud involved a loss of more than $2,000, more than minimal planning, or other aggravating circumstances, the base offense level can be substantially increased. The final applicable offense level is then coordinated with the criminal history category of the defendant (which is computed on a point basis according to the number and type of previous convictions and other factors) to arrive at the final sentencing level. The court may depart from the recommended sentence if unique factors are present but any such departure must be supported by specific reasons.

As an example, a defendant with no prior convictions convicted of fraud involving the loss of $10,000 would be sentenced to a term of four to 10 months, absent unusual circumstances. If the fraud resulted in the loss of $1 million, involved more than minimal planning, and was perpetrated by a defendant who had a previous conviction punishable by more than a year in prison, the recommended term of imprisonment would be 41 to 51 months. Under the Sentencing Act, the defendant will serve substantially the sentence he receives (a small reduction is possible for good behavior); the Sentencing Act abolished parole in federal cases.

Sentencing of Organizations

Corporations and other organizations may be criminally liable for offenses committed by their agents if committed in the scope of the agent's duty and with the intended purpose of benefiting the organization.

Sentencing guidelines for organizations indicate that:

- The court must, whenever practicable, order the organization to remedy any harm caused by the offense.
- If the organization operated primarily for a criminal purpose, the fine should be set sufficiently high to divest the organization of all assets.
- The fine range for any other organization should be based on the seriousness of the offense and the culpability of the organization. Culpability generally will be determined by the steps taken by the organization prior to the offense to prevent and detect criminal conduct, the extent of involvement in or tolerance of the offense by the organization's personnel, and the organization's response after an offense had been committed.

Setting the Amount of the Fine

First, the *base fine* is arrived at by determining the greatest of:

- The amount from the offense level fine table
- The pecuniary gain to the organization from the offense
- The pecuniary loss from the offense caused by the organization, to the extent the loss was caused intentionally, knowingly, or recklessly.

The fine amounts on the base offense level fine table range from $5,000 to $72,500. Next, the court calculates the appropriate multipliers for the base fine level, depending on the particular circumstances. Factors that are considered include:

- Involvement in or tolerance of criminal activity
- History
- Whether the organization violated a judicial order or injunction during the offense
- The existence of an effective program to prevent and detect violations of law
- Any self-reporting, cooperation, and acceptance of responsibility
- Obstruction of justice by the organization.

The culpability score is then converted to a multiplier that generates the recommended fine range. The court will consider a number of additional factors to determine where in the range the actual fine will be imposed. An organization must be ordered to serve a period of probation, if the court finds that:

- It is necessary to secure payment of restitution, to enforce a remedial order, or to ensure completion of community service.
- If a monetary penalty is ordered and has not been paid at the time of sentencing and probation is necessary to ensure payment.

- It is necessary to ensure that changes are made to reduce the likelihood of crime.
- It is necessary to accomplish Sentencing Act purposes.
- If the defendant organization sentence does not include a fine.

The length of probation may not exceed five years. In addition, the court has discretion to order the defendant organization to publicize its conviction and the nature of the offense. The court also may order the organization to make periodic reports to the court or the probation department and subject itself to unannounced examinations of its books and records. Finally, the court may order the organization to develop and submit for court approval an effective compliance program.

Effective Program to Detect and Prevent Violations of Law

The guidelines provide credit in the calculation of a fine if the organization has in place an effective program to detect and prevent violations of law. The Act defines such a program as one that is reasonably designed, implemented, and enforced so that it generally will be effective in preventing and detecting criminal conduct. The organization must use *due diligence* in seeking to prevent and detect criminal conduct by its employees.

See the chapter on "Fraud Prevention Programs" in the Criminology section for more information about developing a corporate compliance policy.

Due Diligence

The organization must take at least seven minimum steps to meet the requirement of due diligence:

- Implement policies defining standards and procedures to be followed by the organization's agents and employees.
- Assign specific high-level personnel ultimate responsibility to ensure compliance.
- Use due care not to delegate significant discretionary authority to people whom the organization knows or should have known had a propensity to engage in illegal activities.
- Communicate standards and procedures to all agents and employees and require participation in training programs.
- Take reasonable steps to achieve compliance, e.g., by the use of monitoring and auditing systems, and by having and publicizing a reporting system where employees can refer criminal conduct without fear of retribution (hot line or ombudsman program).
- Consistently enforce standards through appropriate discipline ranging from reprimand to dismissal.

- After detection of an offense, the organization must take all reasonable steps to appropriately respond to the offense and to prevent further similar offenses, including modifying its program and appropriate discipline for the individuals responsible for the offense and for those who failed to detect it.

Appeal

The defendant is advised of his right to appeal at the sentencing hearing. A notice of appeal must be filed within 10 days or, absent a showing of excusable neglect, the right is lost.

Generally, an appeal may be made only for errors of law to which the defendant made timely objection at trial or in pre-trial proceedings. The failure to object is said to waive any claims of error. A timely objection theoretically would permit the trial judge to correct the error at the time, eliminating the delay and expense of an appeal and possible new trial. Very serious errors, however, that are plain on the record and affect substantial rights of the defendant may be raised on an appeal without the necessity for an earlier timely objection.

An appellate court will reverse a conviction only if it finds error that denied the defendant a fair trial. Essentially, an appellate court will not reverse a conviction unless it finds error which affected the "substantial rights" of the defendant; "harmless error," not affecting the jury's decision, is tolerated.

THE CIVIL JUSTICE SYSTEM

In this part we will review the legal aspects of actions by private parties—including fraud examiners, auditors, accountants, security personnel, private investigators, and attorneys—to investigate and recover losses due to fraud. Many of these cases will end up in the civil justice system.

Civil Litigation

Civil actions to recover damages for fraud or to enjoin further fraudulent activity can be filed by private plaintiffs in state or federal courts. Most common-law fraud actions, usually styled *misrepresentation* claims, are filed in state courts. Suits involving parties from different states and involving more than $75,000 in controversy (known as *diversity* cases), or actions brought on the basis of federal statutes, such as the civil RICO provisions, can be brought in federal court. Federal court generally is preferred by plaintiffs in larger cases because of the easier access to witnesses and documents located in different states which the federal rules provide. The procedures described below are largely drawn from the federal rules.

Beginning the Civil Action

A civil action begins with the filing of a complaint in the appropriate court, usually in the jurisdiction in which the defendant or the plaintiff resides, or where the claim arose.

The federal rules provide that the complaint should be a "short and plain statement" showing the court's jurisdiction to hear the case (e.g., in federal court, that there is diversity of citizenship and more than $75,000 in issue), the grounds for relief, and a demand for judgment. Rule 9(b) of the Federal Rules of Civil Procedure requires that the facts entitling the plaintiff to relief be stated with "particularity." Thus, whereas a plaintiff in a negligence case might get into court by merely alleging—without any details or supporting evidence—that the defendant operated his automobile in a negligent manner at such and such a place and time, a fraud plaintiff must plead the alleged fraud in detail: the actual misrepresentations that were made, to whom, how they were false, and so on, depending on the type of fraud claim.

The 9(b) requirement often creates a "Catch-22" for fraud plaintiffs. A company, for example, might have good grounds to believe that it is the victim of a kickback fraud, but might need access to the discovery system (subpoenas for documents and witnesses, etc.) to prove the illegal payments. In such circumstances, particularly where the specific information needed is within the sole control of the defendant, the court might relax the 9(b) requirement somewhat.

The complaint and a summons must be served on the defendant according to the rules. The summons advises the defendant that he has a certain time to answer (usually 20 days) or suffer a default. A corporation may be served through any officer, managing agent, or other agent authorized by law to received process. Process may be served on a defendant outside the state where the court sits if the defendant has significant contacts within the state, such as a corporation conducting business there.

A defendant may file an answer to the complaint, denying liability, add counterclaims against the plaintiff, or file motions to dismiss the action based on grounds such as failure to state a claim, expiration of the statute of limitations, and improper service. In major litigation these procedural challenges might consume a year or more and result in six-figure legal fees before the case reaches the merits of the issue.

The Discovery Stage

If the legal hurdles are overcome, the case enters the discovery stage. *Discovery* refers to the formal process whereby the parties collect evidence and learn the details of the opposing case. Under federal rules, either party may take discovery regarding any matter, not privileged, that is relevant to the subject matter of the action, or that might lead to admissible evidence. The principal means of discovery are oral depositions, written interrogatories, and requests to produce documents.

Depositions are probably the most popular and useful form of discovery. A deposition is sworn testimony given by a party or witness upon questioning by counsel for one of the parties before trial and outside of court, usually in a lawyer's office. Opposing counsel and a stenographer, who administers the oath and transcribes the testimony, also are present. Deposition testimony may be used to obtain evidence about the party's own or the opponent's case, or to preserve testimony for trial. In the federal system, a witness outside the subpoena power of the court can be deposed in the area he resides and the transcript read to the jury at trial. If the deposing attorney wishes to inspect or refer during the proceedings to certain documents in the witness' possession, these can be demanded by a *subpoena duces tecum*, a legal order for the witness to produce the documents for reference during the deposition.

Unless otherwise specified, statements made during a deposition can be produced as evidence during the trial. According to federal guidelines, "examination and cross-examination of witnesses may proceed as permitted at the trial... ." The deponent or counsel can object to particular questions, as in a trial. At a deposition, the person must answer the question, even when counsel enters an official objection; the evidence is "taken subject to the objections" (Federal Rule of Civil Procedure 30). This means the objection is duly noted, and if the depositional evidence is presented at trial, the judge will be asked to rule on the objection before that part of the deposition is read to the jury.

An *interrogatory* is something like a written deposition. Interrogatories are questions that are submitted to an opposing party in a suit. Interrogatories cannot be given to anyone other than a party to a suit. Questions are submitted to the witness in writing. If the receiving party thinks that a question is improper, then he or she may object to the question. If no objection is given, then the party must answer the question in writing. All answers must be sworn to under oath. Interrogatories are less expensive to perform than depositions. Some parties will try to provide as little information as possible but still give a "truthful" answer. However that tactic can backfire—if the answering party does not provide the information requested, that party cannot introduce evidence on those issues at trial and can be sanctioned by the court. Interrogatories are covered under Federal Rule of Civil Procedure 33.

Requests to Produce Documents may be served on opposing parties. Records from third party witnesses or institutions may be obtained by subpoenas that often must be accompanied by deposition notices as well to take testimony to authenticate the documents. Discovery can be an extremely expensive and time-consuming process, often taking years to complete, particularly in complex litigation such as fraud actions. Proposals to reform and streamline the system are constantly advocated, but seldom adopted, in large measure because trial lawyers are unwilling to give up or to limit their opportunities to learn about and look for weaknesses in their opponent's case.

A *request for admission* is designed to assist in stipulating certain facts. Admission helps set what is, and is not, at issue in a suit. The request contains statements which are presented to the opposing party (witnesses and outside parties are not subject to requests for admission). To the declarative, "I, Daisy Miller, have discussed my company's operations with individuals employed by our competition," Daisy replies either "Admitted" or "Denied." She may also "object to the question," if she feels it's inappropriate or impertinent to the proceedings. Or she can decline to answer, since the issue is in dispute (she doesn't deny conversations, just the implication of the question), or because she doesn't have enough information to answer. Requests for admission often are used near the end of the discovery process to narrow the focus of the dispute. Any admissions established become part of the official record and may be produced during the trial.

Requests for admission also are used to authenticate documents. For instance:
- *Exhibit A is a true and correct copy of check No. 3456.*
- *Exhibit A was signed by you.*
- *The signature shown on Exhibit A is your signature.*

Either side of a dispute can request a *physical or mental examination* of a party to the suit. The person's condition must be "in controversy" and shown to be pertinent to the proceedings. The request is made "on motion for good cause" and the examination performed by qualified personnel. It may seem unthinkable that a defendant would plead insanity to a fraud charge, but mental and physical instability can be part of a defendant's argument for mitigating circumstances. The physical or mental health of a defendant also may come into play if the defendant files a counterclaim alleging mental anguish as the result of an improper search, wrongful termination, invasion of privacy, etc.

Pre-Trial Motions in Civil Court

There may be a series of *pre-trial conferences* in which the parties to the suit sit down with the judge. These exchanges are designed to narrow the dispute to as few contested points as possible, and to remove procedural obstacles that could delay a trial. Judges also may encourage parties to settle during this stage.

Some common pre-trial motions are listed below. However, please note that the actual names of the motions vary among jurisdictions:
- *Writ of Attachment.* In some cases, a party may *attach* or secure assets before trial to prevent the defendant from disposing of them while the lawsuit is pending if the party can show that the defendant is likely to dispose of assets. Most courts do not like to issue writs of attachment, and attachment is usually available only in certain types of suit. Ordinarily, judges are very reluctant to deprive a defendant of his property until a determination has been made that he is liable to the plaintiff. Also, if the plaintiff loses the suit, the defendant can sue for damages. In most cases the party requesting attachment will be required to post a bond in the amount of the attached property.

Sequestration is similar to attachment. The difference is that the property is physically delivered to the court for safe-keeping.

- *Motions for Injunctive Relief.* In a fraud case, the defendant is likely to have misappropriated assets. There may be a substantial risk that once a complaint is filed against the defendant, he or she may try to hide or transfer the ill-gotten gains. If the money or assets taken can be located, the plaintiff can ask for a writ of attachment to physically secure the assets. However, there often cases where the money may not be located yet. In these cases the plaintiff or the prosecutor can ask the judge to issue an *injunction*. A *temporary restraining order,* or *TRO,* is sort of an emergency injunction that can be entered without the defendant being present. It is only good for 1-2 days until the defendant can appear before the judge. If a lawsuit between the parties is pending, a judge can issue a *preliminary injunction* which in effect freezes everything until a trial can be held. The injunction will prohibit the defendant from transferring or moving any assets unless first approved by the court.
- *Motion to Dismiss.* Asks a judge to throw out the complaint as legally unsound.
- *Motion to Make More Definite and Certain.* Asks for greater detail and/or specificity in the complaint.
- *Motion in Limine.* Requests the court to prohibit opposing counsel from referring to or offering evidence on matters that are highly prejudicial.
- *Motion to Strike.* Asks that inflammatory, prejudicial or irrelevant material be stricken from the record.
- *Motion for a Continuance.* Asks to postpone a hearing, conference or an upcoming trial. Some courts grant one or two routinely; other districts require justification for each motion for continuance.
- *Motion for Summary Judgment.* Asks a judge to decide the case, without a trial, on the basis of the evidence in the complaint and answer. Judges also may consider *affidavits* or *declarations* (sworn written statements), contracts, or other materials in reaching their summary decision. Either side in a lawsuit can file for summary judgment. The motion is granted unless it can be shown that some of the facts as presented are in dispute.

Once one side files a motion, the other side can object and file an opposing motion. There generally will be a hearing in person before the judge on the motion. Sometimes, a judge reviews the material in each side's motion papers and will issue a *tentative ruling* just before the hearing to indicate which way the opinion is likely to go. This gives each side an idea of how to prepare their arguments for the hearing. At the hearing, each side argues its case to the judge and answers questions from the bench. The judge may announce a decision immediately or take the matter "under submission," making the final ruling later.

Counterclaims and Cross-Claims

Besides the available motions, defendants also can file a *counterclaim* against the plaintiff in a civil action. This does just what the name implies. It levels accusations against the original plaintiff, who is now the defendant of the counterclaim. Popularly known as a "countersuit," the specifics of this claim may be filed as part of the defendant's answer, or as a separate document. The two complaints will be tried concurrently, the final judgment stipulating a decision on each side's petition.

Additionally, a defendant may file a *cross-claim* against one of its co-defendants. A cross-claim is simply an action between co-parties, *i.e.* claims between two defendants or two plaintiffs.

The most common occasion for counterclaims in a fraud case is when an employer sues an ex-employee for fraud. Set forth below are some of the more common counterclaims which may be asserted as a result of an investigation, particularly one involving employees:

- Invasion of Privacy: Intrusion into Seclusion
- Invasion of Privacy: Public Disclosure of Private Facts
- Outrageous Conduct/Intentional Infliction of Emotional Distress
- Defamation
- Good Faith and Fair Dealing
- Breach of Implied Contract
- False Imprisonment
- Trespass

Alternative Dispute Resolution

Another trend in the law is toward allowing or encouraging parties to a civil action to resolve their disputes without the necessity of a trial. Alternative dispute resolution usually involves one of two types of methods: mediation or arbitration.

Mediation

Mediation is the process whereby an impartial third-person assists the parties in reaching a resolution of the dispute. The mediator does not decide who should win, but instead works with the parties to reach a mutually agreeable settlement.

Arbitration

Arbitration is the process whereby the dispute is submitted to an impartial third-person who then decides the outcome of the case, *i.e.* which party should win. The arbitrator acts as a judge or jury would by deciding the case on its merits. An arbitration can be either "binding" or "nonbinding." If the arbitration is binding, then the decision of the arbitrator is final, and the parties cannot later submit their dispute to a judge or jury for determination.

Today, many contracts contain arbitration clauses providing that if a dispute arises between the parties to the contract, both parties agree to submit their claims to binding arbitration rather than filing suit.

Trial of a Civil Case

Trial procedures in civil actions are similar to criminal cases with several notable exceptions. Juries need not consist of 12 people; many civil cases are heard by six jurors. The parties also may stipulate that the verdict need not be unanimous. The burden of proof for the civil plaintiff is lower than for the criminal prosecutor. In most cases, the plaintiff must prove his case by only the *preponderance of the evidence*, meaning that there must be only slightly more evidence in favor than against. The Fifth Amendment privilege against self-incrimination is more limited in civil proceedings; a party still may refuse to answer questions or produce evidence, but if he does, inferences might be drawn and the refusal may be disclosed to the jury. The judge also may enter sanctions against the party refusing to produce evidence up to and including the entry of a judgment against such party.

Various privileges are recognized in civil proceedings, such as the *marital privilege,* preventing one spouse from being compelled to testify against another; the *attorney-client privilege*, prohibiting the disclosure of communications between an attorney and his client for the purpose of rendering legal advice; and the *work product doctrine*, protecting an attorney's notes and certain other materials the attorney prepares in anticipation of litigation. Work undertaken by an accountant, investigator, or fraud examiner at the direction of an attorney also may be protected by the attorney-client privilege and the work product doctrine. See the chapter on "Evidence" for more information.

Civil trials begin with the plaintiff's counsel speaking first. As in criminal trials, the opening is devoted to introducing the parties, stating the nature of the dispute, and outlining the evidence the party expects to produce.

The plaintiff offers evidence first. In many civil trials, the proof consists of the witnesses and counsel reading portions of depositions taken in discovery from witnesses outside the subpoena power of the court. This tends to be particularly uninteresting for the jury, and may be very prejudicial for a party forced to rely on a great deal of such testimony. Answers to written interrogatories by the opposing party also may be read to the jury, which, if extensive, can be even more boring.

Civil parties also may call expert witnesses to give their opinion on matters thought to be too technical for the average juror to understand. Fraud examiners and accountants may be used as experts in commercial cases to compute and testify to damages. As with expert psychiatric testimony in criminal trials, each side usually produces a qualified expert who disagrees categorically with everything the expert for the other side says. Because the jury usually learns through cross-examination that each expert has been paid handsomely for preparation and trial time—and because jurors generally have a difficult time understanding and evaluating expert testimony—such testimony often has little effect on the outcome of the trial.

The same rules of evidence apply in civil and criminal trials with certain exceptions, such as the application of the Fifth Amendment privilege against self-incrimination noted above. Witnesses, except experts, must relate only facts—not opinions—and irrelevant and prejudicial evidence is excluded, as is most hearsay. Both parties may cross-examine and attempt to impeach the other side's witnesses in essentially the same manner as at a criminal trial.

The defendant may make a *motion for judgment as a matter of law* (also referred to as a *motion for a directed verdict*) at the close of the plaintiff's case, on the grounds that even if the plaintiff's evidence is believed, the defendant still is entitled to a judgment as a matter of law. Both sides may make such a motion at the close of all the evidence. If such motions are denied, both sides argue to the jury, the plaintiff first. The plaintiff usually is afforded an opportunity for *final rebuttal*. The jury is then instructed on the law, both as to elements of liability and damages, and then retires for deliberations. Within 10 days of the verdict, the losing party may renew his *motion for judgment as a matter of law* and move for a new trial. In state court practice, the motion for judgment as a matter of law also may be referred to as a *motion for judgment notwithstanding the verdict*, or *motion for judgment n.o.v. (non obstante veredicto)*.

Both sides may appeal from an adverse verdict, either as to liability or damages. As in the criminal system, the appellate court is largely limited to reviewing the legal decision of the trial court rather than the factual determination of the jury. The appeals court may reverse and remand for a new trial on some or all of the issues, may order that a certain portion of the awarded damages be remitted, or may enter final judgment, if legal grounds are clear, in favor of either party.

A plaintiff who obtains a money judgment often must take additional steps to collect it. This might include garnishing the wages of the defendant or levying against his nonexempt assets. In many instances, particularly in fraud litigation, a judgment might go uncollected because the defendant has already squandered or secreted the assets. In the latter circumstances, a plaintiff may conduct *post-judgment discovery*, including a deposition of the defendant, in an attempt to locate assets to satisfy a judgment.

Fidelity Bond Claims

The fidelity bond claim is an often overlooked method of recovery for losses due to internal fraud. A *fidelity bond* is a policy issued by many large insurance companies under which the insured entity is covered against losses caused by the dishonest or fraudulent acts of its employees. Dishonest or fraudulent acts typically are defined as those acts committed with the intent to:

- Cause the insured to sustain a loss.
- Obtain a financial benefit for the employee or for any third party intended by the employee, other than his proper compensation.

As with any other insurance agreement, fidelity policies have deductibles, a limit of liability (often in the millions of dollars), and certain exclusions. To collect, the insured must submit a sworn proof of loss claim within specified time limits, together with supporting evidence of liability and the amount of loss. Proof of loss is entirely the responsibility of the insured; the carrier will not conduct nor assist in the investigation nor will it reimburse investigative or legal costs incurred in making a claim.

Most policies have express subrogation provisions that provide that if the insurance company pays a claim, it acquires the rights of the insured to sue the wrongdoer. Policyholders are prohibited from interfering with these rights in any way at the risk of jeopardizing coverage, such as releasing the wrongdoer from liability. Therefore, no settlement agreements or releases should be executed with a dishonest employee or any confederate unless the insurance company consents.

BASIC PRINCIPLES OF EVIDENCE

Definition of Evidence

Black's Law Dictionary defines evidence as:

Anything perceivable by the five senses, and any proof such as testimony of witnesses, records, documents, facts, data, or tangible objects legally presented at trial to prove a contention and induce a belief in the minds of a jury.

Evidence refers to an intricate rule, developed and refined over hundreds of years, that is designed to ensure that only relevant and probative evidence is admitted in court proceedings, and that irrelevant, unreliable and prejudicial evidence is excluded, so that cases can be fairly and expeditiously decided.

Every aspect of trying a case—from filing the complaint through discovery, into the presentation of witnesses and exhibits—is affected by rules of evidence. This body of law covers not just what counts as evidence, but how that evidence is gathered, handled, and presented.

Evidence in federal courts is governed by the Federal Rules of Evidence. These rules set out what can and can't be introduced during a dispute. In the late 1960s, a U.S. Supreme Court panel began codifying centuries of common law into the Federal Rules of Evidence (FRE). What had previously been a far-flung set of precedents, buried in local jurisdictions and lengthy appeals decisions, was gathered into a singular body of information. Congress passed the Uniform Code of Evidence in 1974 as Public Law No. 93-595. State and local courts often have some specialized rules of evidence, but these rules are themselves based on federal guidelines. The complete text of the Federal Rules of Evidence is contained in the Appendix.

The rules of evidence are complex and counsel should be contacted if an important question of evidence arises. This part focuses on the more important rules and those of greatest interest to Certified Fraud Examiners.

Three Types of Evidence

Evidence is anything perceptible by the five senses which is invoked in the process of arguing a case. Documents, spoken recollections, data of various sorts, and physical objects are all potentially evidence. Evidence is simply anything that relates to the proving or disproving of a fact or consequence. With the known universe available for court inspection, legal authorities have narrowed the field by setting up categories to evaluate evidentiary significance.

Evidence is classified in three different ways: testimonial, real, and demonstrative. *Testimony* refers to the oral statements made by witnesses under oath. *Real evidence* describes physical objects which played a part in the issues being litigated. A canceled check, an invoice, a ledger, letters and documents are real evidence, but the term includes any physical evidence. Therefore, a typewriter or printer in a case involving questioned documents is clearly real evidence; so is a tape recording, since members of the court can experience the sounds firsthand. *Demonstrative* evidence is a tangible item that illustrates some material proposition (*e.g.*, a map, a chart, a summary). It differs from real evidence in that demonstrative evidence was not part of the underlying event; it was created specifically for the trial. Its purpose is to provide a visual aid for the jury. Nonetheless, it is evidence, and can be considered by the jury in reaching a verdict.

Direct Versus Circumstantial Evidence

Admissible evidence may be either direct or circumstantial. *Direct evidence* includes testimony that tends to prove or disprove a fact in issue directly, such as eyewitness testimony or a confession. *Circumstantial evidence* is evidence that tends to prove or disprove facts in issue indirectly, by inference. Many fraud cases are proved entirely by circumstantial evidence, or by a combination of circumstantial and direct evidence, but seldom by direct evidence alone. The most difficult element to prove in many fraud cases —fraudulent intent—is usually proved circumstantially, and necessarily so, because direct proof of the defendant's state of mind, absent a confession or the testimony of a co-conspirator, is impossible.

In a circumstantial case, the court may instruct the jury that the prosecution must exclude all inferences from the facts other than its determination of guilt. Even if no such instruction is given, the Certified Fraud Examiner should apply the same standard in preparing a circumstantial case.

Relevance

The admissibility of evidence depends on a wide variety of factors—and, in large part, on the discretion of the trial judge—but the most important factor is relevance. Rule 401 of the Federal Rules of Evidence defines *relevant evidence* as evidence "having any tendency to make the existence of any fact that is of consequence to determination of the action more probable or less probable than it would be without the evidence." In other words, relevant evidence is evidence that tends to prove or disprove a fact in issue. The facts in issue, of course, vary according to the case, but generally can be said to be those that tend to prove the essential elements of the offense or claim as well as related matters such as motive, opportunity, identity of the parties, and credibility.

Whether a particular piece of evidence is relevant or not depends on what the evidence is offered to prove. An item of evidence might be relevant and admissible if offered to prove one thing, but not relevant and inadmissible if offered to prove something else. For example, under Rule 404(b) of the Federal Rules of Evidence, evidence of other crimes, wrongs, or acts committed by the defendant would not be admissible if offered to prove that the defendant is generally a bad person, and therefore is likely to have committed the crime with which he is charged. But evidence would be admissible if offered to prove motive, intent, identity, absence of mistake, or modus operandi, if such factors are at issue. If evidence of other wrongs or acts is admitted, the judge will instruct the jury that they may consider the evidence only as it relates to the narrow issue for which it was admitted and may not consider it for any other purpose.

That evidence is relevant does not, however, automatically mean that it will be admitted. Under Rule 403 of the Federal Rules of Evidence, relevant evidence still might be excluded if it is unduly prejudicial, threatens to confuse or mislead the jury, or to cause unnecessary delay, waste of time, or is merely cumulative. Relevant evidence also might be excluded if it is subject to certain privileges as noted below. Thus, evidence of drug addiction technically might be relevant to prove motive for embezzlement or fraud, but the judge still might exclude the evidence if he believes that its probative value is outweighed by the danger of prejudice to the defendant. Evidence of other crimes and acts, as discussed above, otherwise relevant, also might be excluded for the same reason.

Special Problems Concerning Some Types of Circumstantial Evidence

Special rules govern certain types of evidence which have been found over the years to be so misleading and prejudicial that they have been categorically excluded. Such evidence is always excluded unless an exception applies.

Character Evidence

In civil and criminal trials there is a strong policy forbidding character evidence (FRE 404). This means testimony or exhibits that purport to establish a "trait of character" or propensity to behave in a particular way. There are some good reasons to leave "character" out of the discussion whenever possible. First, the subjective nature of the description—one person's "gruff" is another viewer's "aggressive."

Besides, character is not an absolute indicator of behavior. That is, it's pretty common to remark how "out of character" somebody's actions were in a given situation. So there's always a chance someone was acting out of character, making the behavioral propensity (if there was one) useless in the legal exchange.

Finally, testimony about character has a reckless potential to be mistakenly founded, misled or concocted. It's always possible to "misjudge" someone, especially if we only know the person in limited circumstances like work or a social club. And it's exceedingly easy to fabricate incidents about character and, for shrewd talkers, to manipulate perceptions of personality. In a fraud case, it must be shown that the defendant committed the act in question. There is too great a danger of prejudicing the jury if you allow testimony about the defendant just being a bad person. Whether he is a bad person or not ought to have no bearing on whether or not he committed the act in question.

Exception to the Character Rule

In civil cases, character evidence is rarely admissible. In criminal cases, there are some instances where character evidence is relevant to the charge at hand. *Character evidence may be admitted in criminal trials* if character is an element of proving the act. For example, if the mental condition or legal competency of the accused is in question, character evidence is allowable. Evidence that the accused has committed other crimes is not generally admissible to prove character, but may be admitted to show something else, such as proof of motive, opportunity or intent to commit an act.

Some of the exceptions for use of character evidence in criminal cases include:
- The motive for the crime
- The ability and means of committing the crime (possession of a weapon, tool, or skill used in the commission of the act)
- The opportunity to commit the crime
- Threats or expressions of ill will by the accused
- Physical evidence at the scene linked to the accused
- The suspect's conduct and comments during arrest
- Attempts to conceal identity
- Attempts to destroy evidence
- Valid confessions

Opinion

Witnesses are only allowed to testify about what they've actually experienced firsthand, and then only their factual observations (FRE 701). In general, witnesses provide a report on what they know, and keep their opinions and conclusions to themselves.

Exceptions to the Opinion Rule

There are ways to get a witness's opinion into the record. For example, an employee at a securities firm blows the whistle on his superiors for a high-level stock fraud. Defense suggests the investigation was an invasion of privacy. Prosecutors are justifying their secret eight-month investigation on the basis of the whistleblower's tip. The prosecution will enter the whistler's "opinion" and his suspicions of fraud to show that the SEC was justified in conducting its investigation. In this case, the opinion is admissible. However, the reason it is allowed in is not to show that management is guilty, but to show what prompted the SEC investigation.

Opinions are admissible if they pass a three-part test:
- Does the witness have direct personal knowledge of the facts to which the opinion pertains?
- Is the opinion of the common, everyday sort, i.e., doesn't involve specialized knowledge or tests?
- Is the opinion NOT part of a legal judgment, reserved for the jury or judge to decide?

Opinions from ordinary witnesses have to be based on personal experience and have some bearing on the *facts* (as opposed to the *judgment*) of the case. This distinction is further refined in situations involving hearsay and personal judgment, discussed below. Expert witnesses are exempt from the opinion rule, since experts are hired to render a professional opinion.

Exhibits

Exhibits are the tangible objects presented as evidence. Therefore, both real evidence and demonstrative evidence are entered into the record as exhibits. This includes documents like contracts, letters, and receipts; plus photographs, X-rays, baseball bats, knives, fountain pens and computer files. In short, *anything that isn't testimony is an exhibit.* Testimony is what people say. Exhibits are the "props."

An exhibit used for purely "illustrative purposes" is a type of *demonstrative evidence*. Demonstrative evidence includes charts, graphs, and summaries that help to simplify complicated evidence for the jury. Such evidence is admissible if the court decides that it presents a fair and balanced summary or picture of the evidence and is not unduly prejudicial.

In complex fraud cases, such evidence is extremely useful, but care should be taken to keep the charts and exhibits simple. The evidence that is summarized must be made available to the other party, and the court may order that the underlying documentation be produced in court.

At the most basic level, the evidence must be established as reliable. If a piece of real evidence can't be authenticated—as to who owned and used the item, for example—the evidence won't be admitted, even if it's plainly relevant. There is a similar sort of "credibility test" for witnesses. If testimony is to become admissible evidence, the witness has to demonstrate that the knowledge being communicated is believable and was gained by personal experience. Below are some of the issues you will encounter in proving to the judge that a particular exhibit is reliable.

Laying the Foundation for Typical Exhibits
Diagrams

A diagram (on paper or some other tangible display) can be admitted as evidence with no more foundation than the assent of a witness: "Is this a fair representation of the suite where you work?" It doesn't have to be true to scale, or particularly detailed. A diagram can be prepared before trial, during trial, or prepped outside the court and finished during questioning. If the witness or the opposition objects to the diagram, further foundation may need to be established. Diagrams can be used in tandem with photos or other representational evidence, or as assistance in demonstrations to the jury.

Correspondence

Letters and faxes require a foundation to establish authorship. Depending on the document and situation, the foundation is laid in one of several ways: (1) the author is present and claims authorship; (2) a witness testifies to seeing the author write the document; (3) with handwritten letters, a witness verifies the author's penmanship; (4) with typed or machine-written documents, the witness verifies the author's signature; (5) a witness testifies that the contents of the document point decisively to the author. These and many other document issues may require the participation of a *questioned documents expert*. These professionals are trained to analyze virtually every aspect of document production, from handwriting to the approximate strength of the letter **A** when struck from a particular manual typewriter.

Business Records

Business records can encompass a broad range of documents, from all sorts of organizations, including corporations, small businesses, nonprofit operations, and community groups. There is a three-part test for establishing the accuracy of business records.

- The document was prepared as a usual part of doing business, *i.e.*, was not prepared specifically for litigation.
- The document was prepared reasonably near the time of the event it describes.
- The organization's way of keeping records is demonstrably reliable.

The requirements for government documents are the same as for other business records. The distinction between government and business records arose because of narrow interpretations of the law that separated nonprofit from for-profit enterprises. Today, most records, regardless of origin, are called business records.

Note: Exhibits such as business records and correspondence are vulnerable to objections as hearsay. The materials can be barred as unreliable out-of-court statements unless a trustworthy foundation can be established. It might be necessary to have a member of the record-keeping or archival staff testify how records are kept and that these particular records were created in the normal course of business.

Computer Records

To be admitted as evidence, *computerized records* need only meet the usual business-records foundation. This supporting material will include information on the computing machine used, any software, and the record-keeping process. A business record, electronic or otherwise, is legal as long as it's kept in the normal course of business. When there are clear routines for compiling information, admitting the record into court will be routine. However, the investigator, as with any piece of evidence, must take steps during the investigation process to preserve the evidence and protect the chain of custody.

Photographs

Photographs can be tricky: they need foundation to establish their fidelity to the object they claim to represent. Generally it's enough to have a witness familiar with the object or space in a photo to corroborate, "Yes, that's the hallway running between our two buildings." The matter gets more complicated when a photo is controversial. This can require technical specifications for proper foundation. In the most famous trial since Sam Shephard, O.J. Simpson's lawyers challenged a photo of the defendant wearing Bruno Mali shoes as "doctored." Both sides introduced experts to discuss whether the photo had been altered, what sort of camera, lens and environmental conditions were involved, etc. The same issues can arise with photos in any trial.

In some unusual situations, a photo may reveal information which no witness can corroborate. There has been at least one instance where the background of a photo showed a stabbing that took place in a crowd. No one, not even the photographer, saw the stabbing at the time. In unusual situations where a photo communicates evidence not substantiated elsewhere, the foundation of the photograph will need more strength—including technical details on the camera, the film, who took the shot, why and where, etc.

The exceptions make photos seem more legally fraught than they are. They usually are admitted with little objection. Photos don't even have to be contemporary with the crime or grievance they pertain to. If a photograph is established as accurate in its portrayal, it can be shot after the original act.

General Points

Either side can enter exhibits into the record, given the proper foundation. Once admitted, the evidence is available for use by either side. It doesn't matter who entered a hammer into evidence; either side can use it during questioning.

It also doesn't matter when exhibits are admitted. They may be introduced into evidence during direct examination: opposing counsel is allowed to inspect the exhibit; the witness confirms the exhibit, which has been marked Exhibit A (or Exhibit 1). (Some courts use letters for exhibits while some court use numbers. Usually the exhibit is identified by which side enters it, *e.g.*, Plaintiff's Exhibit 1.)

When everyone agrees, exhibits can be directly entered into the record, without foundational review, by a simple stipulation. Both parties sign the stipulation form, describing and acknowledging the exhibit.

The "Best Evidence" Rule

Sometimes testimony may be rejected because of the *"best evidence" rule.* This prohibits a party from testifying about the contents of a document without producing the document itself. Also known as the *"original writing" rule*, it requires that when a witness testifies about the contents of a document, at least a fair copy of the original must be available for inspection. If there isn't an original, an authenticatible copy will do. If the document is lost—no original, no copies—the judge will have to be convinced there's good reason to forgo the exhibit and admit the testimony. Fraud examiners can use copies in preparing their case reports, but at trial the original must be produced if it's available. Certified copies of public records should always be obtained.

Chain of Custody

Chain of custody issues, like those discussed regarding experiments above, are a paramount issue in any case, affecting every piece of physical evidence. *Chain of custody* refers to (1) who has had possession of an object, and (2) what they've done with it. This rule is especially pertinent to the discovery process, since discovery is the appropriate stage to be conducting tests and otherwise inspecting evidence. Gaps in the chain of custody (when it's not clear what occurred with a set of records, for example) or outright mishandling (a group of questioned documents wasn't properly sealed, perhaps), can dishevel a case but not wreck it outright.

Courts have found in some cases that even though there have been mistakes in the chain of custody, the mistake affects the "weight" though not the "admissibility" of evidence. That is to say, the evidence will still be allowed into the record, but will be accompanied by a forthright description of any improprieties which have occurred in the chain. The jury and judge are supposed to consider the improprieties when they deliberate, "weighing" the case for guilt or innocence. In fraud cases, the array of physical evidence, all the paper documents, audio and video recordings, and information-processing equipment, such as computers, demands some close monitoring in the chain of custody. This is an area of the law which either side—plaintiff or defendant—can manipulate in order to avoid talking about the evidence itself, rambling instead like a filibustering senator over "who touched what and when and why that means we will not see or discuss the item in question."

Hearsay

FRE 801 defines hearsay as "a statement, other than one made ... at the trial or hearing, offered in evidence to prove the truth of the matter asserted." This sets apart virtually anything said outside the courtroom, or outside an officially designated function of the court like a deposition. Excluding hearsay on one level means witnesses can't say, "He said ... she said." Each person testifies to his or her own experience. This is designed to protect the credibility and condition of testimony, and to preserve each side's right to cross-examine witnesses.

Each witness in the trial will be questioned about personal, firsthand encounters. Unless their statements satisfy one of the exceptions discussed below, witnesses will speak only about things they have experienced themselves. If possible, evidence should be presented in the courtroom so that the jury can determine the weight to give each piece of evidence.

However, the hearsay rule is full of exceptions—ways to get information into the record, even though it's technically hearsay—which accounts for the rule's infamy in courtroom dramas and in real courtrooms. A basic distinction lies with the nature of the statement under consideration. The law is specifically designed to exclude statements which are offered "to prove the truth of the matter asserted" in the statement. So any hearsay statement offered to directly prove the charge is barred. Simply put, a conviction can't rest on a "she-said/he-said" (hearsay) recollection.

Exceptions to the Hearsay Rule

The Truth of the Statement is Not at Issue

The hearsay rule only applies if the statement is being offered to prove the truth of the matter contained in the statement. Therefore, if the statement is offered for some other purpose, it, technically, is not hearsay. Any out-of-court statement can be admitted if it (1) is relevant to some aspect of the proceedings, *and* (2) is not offered for the truth of its contents. Most often such statements are used to show a person's knowledge or state of mind at a particular time. For instance, a witness will be allowed to testify that she heard the defendant say, "I can't stand this company. They owe me big time." The statement cannot be used to prove that the defendant actually stole from the company; however, it can be admitted to show that the defendant's state of mind—that he was disgruntled.

Admissions

Anything spoken or written by a party to a lawsuit can be entered into the record, provided the statement can be corroborated and is relevant. Each side can use its adversary's out-of-court statements as evidence.

For example, during your investigation of the case prior to trial, you interviewed the defendant. During the interview, he tells you that he falsified the invoices. Later he denies making the statement. If you take the stand and tell the jury that the defendant told you he falsified invoices, technically that statement is hearsay. However, since it is an admission, it will be admitted under this exception to the rule.

An admission is not necessarily an outright confession. A witness may testify that a bank officer told her, "I have ways of getting loans approved that no one else knows about." The statement alone doesn't prove loan fraud against the officer, but it does establish, by his own admission, his stated intent to subvert the security controls of the institution.

In cases involving corporations, large groups, or government agencies, any statement made by a member of the organization is potentially an admission. The person who made the statement has to be directly authorized to speak for the organization, or perform a job related to the issue under discussion. An agent employed by Jefferson Realtors who says, "You've been defrauded here" to an aggrieved client has made an admission on behalf of the company. A janitor at Jefferson, however, can't make the same admission because janitorial duties aren't related to the formation of contracts, and chances are the janitor isn't authorized to make corporate declarations. On the other hand, an agent makes contracts on the company's behalf, so the statement is an admission even if the agent isn't the official spokesperson for Jefferson's legal affairs.

Statement Against Interest

A *statement against interest* is a special form of admission in which a prior statement is at odds with the declarant's current claim. In prosecuting a tax evasion charge, prosecutors may present a financial statement used by the defendant to obtain a loan; this is a statement against interest because the document declares a higher net worth than he now claims to have.

Business and Government Records

We commonly think of invoices, receipts and official documents as the final legal word. Technically speaking, though, business and government records are hearsay; they're prepared outside the courtroom. A special exception for these materials makes them admissible if they are provided with a legal foundation.

The admissibility of records rests on two criteria: *have they been prepared during "regularly conducted business activity?"* and *are they verifiably trustworthy?* Materials prepared specifically for trial are not admissible as business records. Anything which casts doubt on the veracity of these documents can bar them. In situations where the charge involves altered documents, the materials are admitted to prove the charge of alteration—not for their truth value—so the hearsay rule doesn't apply.

Computerized records have had no trouble being accepted as evidence. Generally, the hearsay exception for business records applies, *i.e.*, as long as the records have been compiled as a regular facet of doing business, they're admissible.

Absence of an Entry in Business Records

Evidence that a matter is not included in the memoranda or reports kept in the regular course of business may be admissible to prove that a certain event did not occur, if the matter was one about which a memorandum or report regularly was made and preserved, unless the source of information or the circumstances indicate a lack of trustworthiness.

Recorded Recollections

A memorandum or record about a matter concerning which the witness once had knowledge but now has forgotten, and that was made or adopted by the witness when the matter was fresh in memory, and is shown to be accurate, may be admissible. Such memoranda or records also may be shown to a witness who has temporarily forgotten the events in order to refresh the witness' recollection and allow the testimony to be more complete or accurate.

Former Testimony

Testimony given by the declarant at another hearing is admissible if the party against whom the testimony is now offered then had an opportunity and similar motive to examine the witness as in the present trial.

Present Sense Impressions

Courts assume that statements made during or immediately after a significant event are reliable, so present sense impressions are admissible. A witness can report that he first suspected fraud at Securities Plus by noting that his superior said, "Oh my God! This can't be happening!" when he was informed that there would be an audit. Present sense impressions have to reasonably coincide with the event itself.

Some courts are particularly strict about present sense, allowing only those statements which indicate "excited utterances," *i.e.*, things said as part of a startling or otherwise tense situation. This is called the *res gestae* rule. These statements are made spontaneously by a defendant during great emotional strain, perhaps during an arrest or at the scene of an accident.

Then Existing Mental, Emotional, or Physical Condition

Statements which establish the declarant's state of mind and/or body are admissible. Specifically the rule lists "state of mind, emotion, sensation, or physical condition ..., pain, and bodily health" as acceptable subject matter, along with extremely personalized thought processes such as "intent, plan, motive, design, mental feeling ... ." Defense attorneys at a fraud trial sometimes use arguments about what their client *intended*, or the *confusion and stress* the person was suffering. For instance, the defendant was seen shredding documents, he was overheard to say, "They'll never prove anything now." The statement may be admitted to show the defendant's state of mind at the time he was shredding the documents. It also shows that the defendant acted with the intent to destroy the documents. Hearsay statements that help establish this intention are admissible as exceptions.

Statements to Medical Personnel

Anything first communicated during a medical examination is admissible as a hearsay exception. This includes medical history, symptoms, pain, and the general character of the medical condition. These statements don't even have to have been made by the patient. They can involve someone (parent or spouse) accompanying the patient.

Printed Matter, Learned Treatises, Refresher Writings

Written materials that add to the court's knowledge of an issue are excepted from the hearsay rule. This exception often bears on the testimony of expert witnesses who often use published material in their work.

Printed materials which support technical or professional assertions are admissible if they are "generally used and relied upon by the public or by persons in particular occupations." The rule specifically mentions market reports and commercial publications.

Learned treatises are admissible when they bear on testimony, though some courts limit the rule. In these jurisdictions, specialized "treatises, periodicals or pamphlets" can be referenced only during cross-examination. In a world of proliferating, and sometimes contradictory, sources of information, just what counts as a learned treatise and what is a fringe group's manifesto isn't immediately clear.

Writing used to refresh a witness's memory is admissible under special circumstances. Whistler wants to see some notes he wrote two years ago, for example, making sure he's got the numbers right in his testimony. He's allowed to consult the notes and continue with his testimony. There's a lawyerly aspect to this rule—the text of the notes is admissible, too, but only if the *opposing* attorney requests the admission.

Other Exceptions

Miscellaneous exceptions to the hearsay rule include things like *dying declarations* and *ancient documents*. For those instances not specified in any rule, there remains the judge's discretion: anything the judge deems *trustworthy* for the purposes of its presentation is admissible. This is the cornerstone of the rule. Hearsay is excluded in the first place because it supposedly lacks trustworthiness; some things can be excepted from the rule, and admitted as evidence, if they can be established as trustworthy.

Excluding Illegally Seized Evidence

There is an implication that evidence obtained improperly is tainted and unfit. The Fourth Amendment sets out this cornerstone exclusionary rule, barring anything obtained by authorities without proper authorization from the owner or possessor, or through a court-ordered search warrant. Generally, this rule applies only in criminal cases. However, the Fourth Amendment also applies to government employers. Therefore, a public employer cannot use illegally seized evidence to discipline an employee. There is no Fourth Amendment prohibition against a *private* employer using illegally seized evidence to discipline an employee; however, the employer might be exposing itself to litigation for invasion of privacy, trespass, or other common law causes of action, but the evidence may still be admitted in court.

Impeachment

The discussion above concerns the manner in which evidence is introduced at trial, usually during direct examination. There is, of course, another side to testimony: cross-examination. Under the Rules of Evidence and the Sixth Amendment—which guarantees a defendant the right to confront witnesses—the adverse party is entitled to offer evidence to impeach the testimony or credibility of a witness. Impeachment usually is attempted by trying to show that the witness:

- Is influenced by bias or self-interest.
- Made prior inconsistent statements.
- Has been convicted of a felony.
- Has a reputation for untruthfulness.

Under Rule 609, evidence of a prior felony conviction may be admissible if the felony occurred within the last 10 years and the judge finds that the probative value of the evidence outweighs the prejudicial effect on the defendant. Evidence that a witness has been convicted of a crime that involves dishonesty or false statement may be admissible even if the crime is not a felony. Although evidence that a witness has a bad reputation for truthfulness may be admitted to impeach, proof of specific instances of misconduct or untruthfulness is not admissible.

Certified Fraud Examiners should keep in mind that the above methods of impeachment may be used not only on the defendant and defense witnesses but also on witnesses for the prosecution. Inquiries should be made before trial to determine if a prosecution or defense witness is subject to impeachment, and, if so, appropriate steps should be taken.

Privileges

Otherwise relevant evidence may be excluded if its admission would violate a recognized privilege. The most important privileges are as follows:

Attorney-Client Privilege

This privilege precludes disclosure of communications between an attorney and client, but only if the following conditions are met:
- The client retained the attorney
- To provide legal advice
- And thereafter communicated with the attorney on a confidential basis, and
- Has not waived the privilege.

The privilege applies to individuals as well as corporations or other business entities. In the context of an investigation of a company, communications generally will be protected under the attorney-client privilege if the following elements are present:
- The communications were made by corporate employees to counsel
- The communications were made at the direction of corporate superiors in order for the company to obtain legal advice from counsel
- The employees were aware that the communications were being made in order for the company to obtain legal advice
- The information needed was not available from upper management
- The communications concerned matters within the scope of the employees' corporate duties
- The communications were confidential when made and were kept confidential by the company.

A general counsel's participation in an investigation conducted by management does not automatically create an attorney-client privilege. The key element is that the attorney (whether in-house counsel or outside counsel) is conducting the investigation for the purpose of providing legal advice to the company. The privilege generally extends to information gathered by investigators if the investigator is acting at the direction of the attorney.

Special care should be taken to ensure that the attorney-client privilege is not waived inadvertently by giving documents or communicating information to anyone outside the investigation team, including members of law enforcement. If information gathered during an investigation is shared with law enforcement, then the privilege may be waived not only as to the information given, but also to any other information relating to the same subject matter. This is known as "horizontal" waiver. Some courts have held that waiver of the privilege as to one document implies waiver as to all documents concerning the same subject matter.

If a fraud examiner feels that a case should be referred for criminal prosecution, the examiner should consult with the attorney before providing any information to government or law enforcement authorities. For example, if an investigator submits a copy of his report to the prosecutor who initiates criminal proceedings based on the findings in the report, the criminal defendant may be able to require the investigator to provide all the documents he or she used in writing the report. In such an instance, the investigator may be considered to have waived the privilege. Likewise, if law enforcement requests the results of an investigation or information gathered during an investigation, the attorney should be consulted before turning over the information. Some courts have held that the privilege is not waived if a company is subpoenaed to produce the information.

The attorney-client privilege prevents disclosure of the communications—the letters, memos or contents of telephone calls—between the attorney and client, not of the underlying facts or documentary evidence in the case. A client may not refuse to produce documents or other relevant evidence merely because such evidence was previously given to the attorney.

Similarly, the attorney-client privilege does not prevent disclosure of communications that relate to business rather than legal advice. Corporate counsel often are consulted and give advice on matters related to the conduct of the business rather than to legal issues. Such communications would be discoverable.

Finally, the attorney-client privilege may not be asserted if the communication involved the attempted or actual commission of a present crime or fraud. The attorney does not have to be a participant in the fraud for the waiver to apply.

The Attorney Work Product Doctrine

Under Rule 26(b)(3) of the Federal Rules of Civil Procedure, and under comparable state rules, documents and tangible things which are prepared in anticipation of litigation are protected by the *attorney's work product doctrine or privilege*. The privilege is conditional in part: the opposing party may obtain access to otherwise privileged investigative documents and things through pre-trial discovery if it can show *substantial need* for the protected information and that the information cannot be obtained from another source. But the attorney's mental impressions, opinions, and strategies concerning the litigation are absolutely privileged and cannot be discovered even with a showing of *substantial need*. The privilege extends not only to information and documents prepared by a party or the party's attorneys, but also by the consultants and examiners hired by the attorneys. For instance, communications with and any work or analysis done by an expert with whom the attorney has consulted is privileged as work product, although that privilege will be waived if the expert is called to testify as an expert witness at trial.

The privilege applies only to documents and things *prepared in anticipation of litigation or for trial*. Documents and tangible things prepared in the course of an in-house or other pre-litigation investigation, even if at the direction of an attorney, may not be privileged if they were not prepared *in anticipation of litigation*. Just because there is a possibility of future litigation does not mean that the investigation is in anticipation thereof. Litigation must be actually planned and the work for which protection is sought must have been undertaken for the specific purpose of preparing for that litigation. On the other hand, if the work to be protected was done *in anticipation of litigation*, then it does not matter in most jurisdictions that no lawsuit has been filed yet.

The privilege protects documents and things prepared in anticipation of litigation from compelled disclosure. However, it does not render the facts themselves confidential, privileged, or non-discoverable. Thus, while reports, interview notes, and transcripts might not be discoverable under the privilege, the facts learned may have to be provided in response to properly phrased discovery requests. Similarly, the privilege does not prevent discovery of the identity of witnesses and the existence of interview notes, tapes, or transcripts. The extent to which interview notes and transcripts and other factual reports prepared in anticipation of litigation are actually protected from discovery by a party opponent may vary between jurisdictions and may depend on the facts and circumstances of a given case.

Although the privilege can be waived, the courts do not agree on whether the same rules governing waiver of the attorney-client privilege also apply to the waiver of the work product privilege. Therefore, the examiner should abide by the same rules governing disclosure of materials protected by the attorney-client privilege.

Self Evaluation Privilege

The self-evaluation privilege (also referred to as the self-critical privilege) may provide some protection for the investigative work product. This privilege is based on the need to encourage voluntary internal reviews and compliance programs. It applies if an organization can demonstrate that is attempting to police itself in an area of public interest, and that disclosure of the work product would prejudice such efforts. The privilege is a relatively new concept and is not recognized in all jurisdictions. It is much weaker than the attorney-client and attorney work product privileges.

Marital Privilege

There are two forms of the marital or spousal privilege: (1) the *confidential communications privilege*, enabling either spouse to prevent the other from testifying regarding a communication during marriage between the two that was intended to be in confidence, and (2) the *adversary testimony privilege*, protecting spouses from being compelled to testify against each other while they are married. Usually, the confidential communications privilege continues after the termination of the marriage; the adverse testimony privilege does not. There is no privilege that permits a person not to testify against other family members, although, as a matter of policy, many law enforcement agencies will not compel testimony from immediate family members.

Law Enforcement Privilege to Withhold the Identity of an Informant

Law enforcement agencies may legitimately withhold the identity of an informant unless disclosure is necessary to ensure that the defendant receives a fair trial. In such circumstances, the prosecution has to decide whether to forego prosecution or disclose the identity of the informant. In the private sector, there is no equivalent privilege. Certified Fraud Examiners or others who are investigating on behalf of a private client may be compelled by court order to disclose the identity of an informant or any other witness. This possibility should be disclosed to potential witnesses who may request confidentiality. See the Investigation Section for more information.

There are a number of other privileges that are less likely to be asserted in fraud actions, including the *priest-penitent* and *physician-patient* privileges. A few states have a weak *accountant-client* privilege that allows an accountant to resist production of a client's work papers or documents. No such privilege is recognized in federal court and the state privileges may be overcome by a showing of need or by the service of a subpoena.

Expert Witness Testimony

Under Rule 702 of the Federal Rules of Evidence, a witness qualified as an expert by "knowledge, skill, experience, training or education" may testify in the form of an opinion or otherwise to "scientific, technical or other specialized knowledge" if such testimony will "assist the trier of fact to understand the evidence or to determine the fact in issue." The determination of whether a witness is qualified as an expert or whether expert testimony is needed is left to the discretion of the trial judge. There is no particular educational requirement for expert testimony; a witness with no formal education may be qualified based on training or experience.

Rule 703 says that an expert may testify based on facts that are disclosed at or before the hearing in which the expert testifies. The facts need not themselves be admissible in evidence if they are of "a type reasonably relied upon by experts in a particular field." This rule allows an expert to employ data usually used by experts in the field, though the data itself may not be admissible. An example might be a table of interest rates taken from a Department of Commerce publication.

Substantive exhibits must be authenticated by the testimony of the expert, although he need not prepare the chart as long as the witness supervised its preparation. The expert must be able to verify all calculations personally and must be able to identify all underlying data. If an expert witness is to maintain credibility, the supporting data's reliability should be unimpeachable.

- Government publications usually provide the most acceptable data in court.
- Studies by private organizations usually provide the next best source.

Some data might be considered hearsay; an accountant, for example, as an expert witness may rely on private sources in forming an opinion if such sources normally are relied upon by accountants. If the accountant has been declared an expert witness, he may use any trustworthy data source in forming an opinion.

The determination of whether particular data from which an expert formed his opinion were "of a type reasonably relied upon by experts in the particular field" is left to the discretion of the trial judge. The majority of states require the expert to predicate testimony on firsthand perception, or in the alternative, the expert may draw upon information "admitted in evidence at the hearing" at which he is called to testify.

Federal law recognizes a third source of facts, i.e., information "made known to" the expert before the hearing. The Federal Rule provides that if the facts or data are of a type reasonably relied upon by experts in the particular field in forming opinions, they need not be admissible in evidence.

Disclosure Requirements under the Federal Rules of Civil Procedure

The U. S. Supreme Court amended the Federal Rules of Civil Procedure in 1993 to require automatic disclosure of information by each party. Rule 26(1) provides that the following information must be disclosed without waiting for a request from the other side: (1) each individual who is likely to have knowledge of the events concerning the lawsuit, (2) a copy or description of all documents relevant to the disputed fact issues, (3) a computation of damages, and (4) any relevant insurance agreement.

There also are significant changes in the rules concerning expert witnesses. The amendments to Rule 26 require certain disclosures concerning people who may be used as expert witnesses at trial. The rule applies to experts who have been retained specifically for a given case, and it includes employees of a party if part of the employees' duties involves giving expert testimony. A written report must produced for each expert witness.

The report must be prepared and signed by the witness and must include the following:
- A complete statement of all opinions to be expressed and the basis and reasons for such opinions
- The data or other information considered by the witness in forming the opinion
- Any exhibits to be used as a summary of or in support for the opinions
- The qualifications of the witness, including a list of all publications authored by the witness within the preceding 10 years
- The compensation to be paid for the witness' study and testimony
- A listing of any other case in which the witness has testified as an expert at trial or by deposition within the preceding four years.

Note that the witness must turn over anything used by the witness in forming his or her opinion. If privileged or confidential documents are used by the witness, those documents must be given to the opposing party.

The new rules will require that the identity and report of the expert must be disclosed at least 90 days before trial. The disclosure of an expert whose testimony is intended solely to contradict or rebut another witness' testimony must be disclosed within 30 days after the other witness' disclosure. An individual must supplement the written report or deposition testimony at least 30 days before trial if he becomes aware that previous disclosures might have been materially incomplete or incorrect.

Depositions may be taken of any expert whose opinions may be presented at trial. However, each side is limited to 10 depositions unless permission is granted by the court for additional depositions.

These mandatory disclosure requirements remain controversial. Attorneys and judges cannot agree on whether the requirements add unnecessary expense or whether they promote uniformity and fairness. At least one of those goals, uniformity, has not been realized. Rule 26 provides that the disclosure requirements are mandatory unless a particular district court provides otherwise by order or local rule. Several district courts have elected not to adopt Rule 26 and have written their own local rules in its place. Accordingly, instead of providing a uniform system of disclosing information, the amendments have led to a system of different rules for different districts.

TESTIFYING AS AN EXPERT WITNESS

Introduction

Certified Fraud Examiners, accountants, and auditors often are called upon to provide testimony in criminal and civil prosecutions where their services can be used to support investigations of matters such as financial frauds, embezzlements, misapplication of funds, arson for profit, bankruptcy fraud, improper accounting practices, and tax evasion. They also may be used as defense witnesses or to support the defendant's counsel on matters that involve accounting or audit issues.

Generally, the expert plays an ongoing part with the litigation team. Lawyers often count on the expert to help crystallize the judge and jury's understanding of their case. In his book, *Effective Expert Witnessing*, author Jack V. Matson lists the four main functions of all expert testimony and offers advice on fulfilling each assigned duty:

- *Establish the facts.* You must first develop a strategy to collect and examine the documentation in the case. The discovery process, which is a mechanism for full disclosure of all knowledge pertinent to the case, usually yields a vast amount of paper, which the expert then must sift through to make a preliminary classification of relevance.
- *Interpret the facts.* Tie together cause and effect relationships with the data and the facts for the technical basis of your case. Do not be fooled by correlation that seemingly links cause and effect but holds no theoretical justification.
- *Comment on the opposing expert's facts and opinions.* Develop a good understanding of the opposing experts by reviewing their educational background and experience. Read their publications. Probe for weaknesses that your side might exploit. Oftentimes trials become a battle of the experts. Prepare for the battle with as much intelligence as you can muster. Take apart the opposition's expert report, which represents the other side's best case, piece by piece. Your attorney needs to know the most intimate details about the facts and opinions contained in that report.
- *Define the professional standards in the particular area of your opponent's expertise.* One of the most critically important ways an expert is used in trial is to define the "standard of care" exercised by fellow professionals in the field. Standard of care has been traditionally defined on the basis of judgment normally exercised by professionals in good standing. Additionally, the professional must be informed or aware of current practices and promulgation. Obsolete practices are now considered by the court to be negligent practices. Thus, professionals must exercise reasonable, informed judgment in carrying out their duties. You, as the expert, will be called upon to define the professional

standard and to measure that against the standard of care exercised by the professional(s) on the other side.

Qualifying fraud examiners, accountants, and auditors as technical experts generally is not a difficult task. Questions are posed to them concerning their professional credentials, i.e., education, work experience, licensing or certification, technical training courses, books and journal articles written, offices held in professional associations, awards and commendations received.

Smart defense lawyers generally are not likely to challenge the credentials of experts, assuming they meet at least minimum standards of professional competence. To do so may give these experts an opportunity to highlight fully their professional credentials and perhaps make a greater impression on the jury or judge, thus adding more weight to their testimony.

If called by the prosecution, examiners might testify to their findings, and if called by the defense, they might testify regarding opinions expressed by the prosecution's expert—to create doubt in the jury's mind about the credibility or weight to be given to that expert.

To become a "credible" expert witness, one must be a member in good standing of the profession, and usually be recognized as an authority in that profession or some specialized aspect of practice within it.

An expert witness in the area of accounting must have a thorough knowledge not only of generally accepted accounting principles, but also of current promulgations. The expert's expertise often might involve special knowledge of a specific industry. In this case, the expert should be aware of recent developments and any important issues within that area.

The expert also must be analytical and be able to work with incomplete data. The expert, however, might not always be able to recognize when data is incomplete. As a result, the expert might make assumptions that will then be open for interpretation or attack. If all data have not been made available, then the opposing counsel might be able to offer alternate scenarios that are more plausible under the circumstances, thus discrediting the expert.

The examiner also may be called upon to give an opinion different than that reached by an equally credible expert on the other side. This might be due to different interpretations of the facts of the case. In some instances, given equally plausible alternatives, the case might be decided on whichever side has the most credible expert witness.

Pre-Trial Preparation

Pre-trial preparation remains key to becoming a successful expert witness. And success often depends on full inquiry and thorough investigation. Following the initial complaint and answer, the discovery process usually begins with one side giving the other a set of written questions, called interrogatories. Your assistance may begin by composing the questions or by providing the replies, depending on your side of engagement. Both sides then submit requests to the other for production of records pertinent to the case. A financial expert is often expected to educate a lawyer on the types of documents typically available. Most everything—from a single deposit slip to continuous ATM videotapes to voluminous accounting ledgers—is subject to discovery.

But many times, financial crime experts on the prosecutor's side must scale a mountain of documents or scroll through a heap of computer files to find the core facts that show criminal intent or behavior. The defense may bury the other side in paper to hide or trivialize vital documentation. Because an efficient search saves time and money, successful experts develop an early strategy and tick off a detailed checklist to achieve their goals within a specific time frame.

It often is useful to have a list of all other witnesses, including those for the other side. This is important so that the expert is not surprised by the existence of other experts or reports. Further, one can then determine if it is necessary to be present for the testimony of those witnesses and can obtain the necessary court approval. If another expert will be present, then it becomes incumbent upon the expert witness to examine the alternate reports and to assess whether or not reasonable points are brought up by the other side that might affect the credibility of the expert's report.

Conflicts of Interest

Aside from assessing your qualifications to serve on a particular case, you must quickly determine if any conflicts of interest exist—or even appear to exist—which might preclude your participation. Before engagement, ask for the names of all parties involved. Review the names with your associates as well, requesting full disclosure of any connections, however remote. Prior or ongoing relationships may suggest to others that you could not provide undivided loyalty to the cause and your client. First and foremost, an expert witness should possess the ability to render an impartial opinion—an ability ideally above reproach because it surely will be scrutinized and perhaps challenged by the other side.

Preparing a Report

Obviously, careful consideration should be given to the preparation of an expert report, which documents your findings and opinions for both sides. It puts your reputation on the line. A well-written report that lays out a strong case might even prompt an early settlement. On the other hand, it also lets the opposition see the strengths and weaknesses of your case and better prepares them for your deposition and trial testimony.

Keep the following six tips in mind when preparing an expert report:
- Be brief.
- Avoid ambiguity or inexact language.
- Avoid generalizations; be specific.
- Add charts or graphs where appropriate.
- Reference your work.
- Meticulously check the report for accuracy and neatness.

An important problem in the preparation of reports and accounting summaries arises from the delegation of tasks to subordinates. If the person giving evidence has not had direct knowledge or has not examined the specific documents or prepared the summaries, the expert might be trapped under the hearsay rule. If tasks are delegated, it is important that the review process entail comparison of all original work documentation.

It also is important to know the effect of other assumptions on the conclusion or opinion reached in the report. It often is possible to trap an expert into giving alternate opinions based upon assumptions that had not been considered. Generally, working papers and schedules supporting the report should not show contradictory conclusions as they may be produced in court. This is not to advocate that working papers should be deleted or amended subsequent to preparation; rather, it is a caution that these papers should be prepared with the precept that they could ultimately be submitted to the court and, as such, should take an appropriate form at the time of preparation.

Once they accept a case, many experts immediately start assembling a *narrative* version of the events. This detailed summary of the facts of the case serves as the raw material for rendering an official opinion. It's important that the text be written with care and professionalism—as the discussion below outlines, the text may (and probably will) have to be produced during discovery. Additionally, a well-written narrative helps the attorney in preparing and executing the case at trial.

Discoverability of Expert's Reports
Caution is the by-word for expert witnesses at every step of the legal drama. According to discovery rules governing expert testimony, everything the expert says or writes about the case after being hired is subject to discovery by opposing counsel. That means everything: narrative versions of the case, comments to the press or law enforcement, hypothetical reconstructions, even notes can be demanded and used by the opposing party. A shrewd attorney can use an expert's notebook—which contains "dry runs" at an opinion and other purely deliberative information—to call the witness's testimony into question. The only exception, as discussed below, is when the expert is hired by the attorney purely on a consulting basis.

Because all "data or other information considered by the witness in forming the opinions" is admissible in court, experts should never destroy drafts, notes, recordings, or any other form of documentation used to form the expert's opinion (Federal Rules of Civil Procedure, Rule 26(a)).

In legalese, an expert witness has no *privilege*. The principle of privilege exists to protect certain core societal relationships (attorney-client, husband-wife), but the expert witness' relationship with clients is not among those protected. If the expert's opinions will be presented in court, everything related to the expert's opinion is discoverable.

Rule 26(a) of the Federal Rules of Civil Procedure requires both sides to provide information about their expert witnesses. Although the court or the parties may agree to eliminate or modify these requirements, attorneys generally are required to disclose the following information:
- A list of expert witnesses who are expected to testify at trial
- A complete statement of all opinions to be expressed and the bases and reasons for them
- A list of all data or other information considered by the expert in forming his opinion

- All exhibits prepared in summary or support of the opinions
- A description of the witness' qualifications including a list of all publications written by the witness in the last 10 years
- The compensation to be paid for the study and testimony
- A list of any other cases in which the witness testified as an expert at trial or by deposition within the preceding four years

In a case of purloined bond certificates, for example, the defense naturally wants to know who the prosecution's expert is (a Mr. Thompson). They also want to know what Mr. Thompson plans to say regarding the case. (He's going to show that the bonds weren't purloined, or stolen, at all; they were replaced with fakes, while the originals were used in a botched investment scam. He'll include in his testimony an analysis of the fakes compared with a legitimate bond. Thompson, a Minnesota CFE, has traced the actual bonds to a Minneapolis financials firm.)

In fact, anything an expert carries into a deposition is subject to discovery. Attorneys have been known to request a search of someone's attaché case in order to get at important materials. This sharp edge of discovery is why experts insist on being deposed away from their own workplace; if they didn't, their entire files would be subject to discovery.

The Consulting Expert Exception

There's an exception of course: experts may consult on the attorney's *work product*, i.e., materials the attorney prepares as background for a case. While performing background work, the expert is said to be working as an *associate* of the attorney, so the exchange is protected—they are two professionals conferring. However, once the expert is hired as a *witness*, and begins entering opinions as part of the attorney's case, there is no privilege for any contribution the expert makes. The distinction is something like this: when acting as "witnesses," experts are bringing official information to the court, and so must disclose any contact with the case; when experts act as "consultants" or "associates" for attorneys or law enforcement, they are only assisting the attorney, and do not have to disclose their involvement in the case.

There is, of course, one trap for the unwary. The rule is that if an expert will testify at trial, everything he does regarding the case must be turned over to the other side. If an expert works only as a consultant to the attorney, then his work product is not discoverable. However, if a *testifying* expert reviews the work of a *consultant* expert, then the work of the consultant expert will be discoverable. Just remember this, if you are hired to testify at trial, ANYTHING you used to form your opinion will be subject to review by the opposing party. This includes notes from other experts, documents received from the plaintiff or defendant, and any documents or notes from the attorney. Be sure to consultant with the attorney before you review anything. If the attorney has not given the document to you, then ask before you read. Otherwise, you may inadvertently destroy the confidentiality or privilege of the material.

Keeping Good Files

The best way to protect the confidentiality of information is to keep good files. Dan Poynter reports that experts routinely "reduce their files to useful reports only" once they've been officially engaged as a witness for trial.[1] No one is recommending that files be *sanitized*, Poynter adds, just *updated*. The difference may be subject to abuse, but it's simple: any materials which serve as the basis for an expert's opinion must be in the file. Notes, documents or tests that serve as background, or that represent unfruitful lines of investigation don't have to be included, and probably shouldn't be. The attorney trying the case doesn't want an expert having to answer about dead ends or exploratory jaunts; a shrewd cross-examiner can turn a hastily scribbled hypothetical into "reasonable doubt," just enough to avert a conviction. So, in the best case scenario, an expert presents to the court an opinion and its basis; nothing more, nothing less.

Qualifying as an Expert Witness

Just what constitutes expert status? Generally, the term refers to someone whose education and professional credentials establish their knowledge of a particular set of practices. As with exhibits, counsel must lay a foundation for the expert's testimony. This means showing that by formal education, advanced study, and/or experience, the witness is sufficiently knowledgeable on the subject at hand. The foundation may be established during the pre-trial stage, or during direct examination.

Unfortunately, at least in federal court, it appears that it is becoming increasingly difficult to testify in federal courts as an expert and to understand the standards and rules to qualify as an expert.

---

[1] Poynter, Dan. *The Expert Witness Handbook.* Santa Barbara: Para Publishing, 1997: p. 82.

In the case of *Kumho Tire Co. v. Carmichael*, (Case No. 97-1709, decided March 23, 1999), the U.S. Supreme Court told trial judges they must block experts from offering their opinions in court unless their testimony meets a rigorous standard of reliability. In the previous case of *Daubert v. Merrell Dow Pharmaceuticals*, 509 U.S. 579 (1993), the Supreme Court had stated that judges should act as "gatekeepers" and keep out scientific testimony that is not based on the methods of science. In *Kumho Tire*, the Supreme Court stated that the judge's gate keeping function applies not just in cases dealing with scientific evidence, but in any case involving testimony based on "technical" and "other specialized knowledge." This means that expert testimony given by Certified Fraud Examiners or accountants must be judged against the standards set forth by the Supreme Court in the *Daubert* case. These standards are discussed in more detail below.

Before allowing an expert to testify before the jury, the judge must make two determinations:
- Is the person qualified as an expert witness?
- Will the expertise of the witness assist the jury in understanding the evidence or determining a fact at issue?

Qualifications

The evaluation process mainly centers around the candidate's formal education and work experience—whether that includes 30 years in law enforcement or 10 years in a large accounting firm. But credentials also cover the candidate's:
- Awards and honors
- Licensing or certification
- Technical training
- Published books and journal articles
- Positions in professional associations, societies, and organizations

The important thing to remember is that a person can be qualified as an expert based on either special training or experience. A person does not have to be a CFE in order to testify as an expert on fraud detection techniques if that person has sufficient practical experience in those techniques. The importance of the CFE designation is that it is a recognition of the special skills you have demonstrated to become a CFE.

It is most helpful to have prior experience as an expert with litigation or criminal matters. This is primarily as a result of what is learned during the experience of testifying. Further, it often is of assistance to have been accepted as an expert in other matters, thereby easing current acceptance. A danger exists, however, of appearing to be a "professional witness."

The counsel introducing the witness often will read the expert's qualifications or ask specific questions to establish the witness' credentials. Although the expert's qualifications are not often contested, it does happen. Over and above being accepted by both parties, the expert witness most importantly must be accepted by the court.

Testimony

The second question the judge must answer focuses on what opinions the expert will actually testify to in court. The testimony must by such that it will assist the jury, and based on the decisions of the Supreme Court in *Daubert* and *Kumho Tire*, the judge must also ensure that the conclusions are based on scientific principles or some generally accepted test of reliability. A hunch, even though based on years of practical experience, will not suffice.

Daubert Factors

The Court listed four factors to be considered:
- Whether the theory or technique relied upon by the expert can be or has been tested.
- Whether it has been subjected to peer review and publication.
- Whether it enjoys general acceptance within the relevant scientific community.
- Whether the technique has a high error rate.

In response to these cases, Rule 702 of the Federal Rules of Evidence was modified to specifically include the standards set forth by the Supreme Court in *Daubert* and *Kumho Tire*. Rule 702 now reads:

If scientific, technical, or other specialized knowledge will assist the trier of fact to understand the evidence or to determine a fact in issue, a witness qualified as an expert by knowledge, skill, experience, training, or education, may testify thereto in the form of an opinion or otherwise, if (1) the testimony is based upon sufficient facts or data, (2) the testimony is the product of reliable principles and methods, and (3) the witness has applied the principles and methods reliably to the facts of the case.

Accordingly, CFEs should be sure to fully cover the rationale for their assumptions and determine whether the assumptions are supported by the facts presented during discovery. Assumptions that are contrary to the evidence may be ruled as implausible, thus causing the judge to exclude the expert's report.

When preparing your report or testimony, keep in mind the factors set forth above. Make sure that you document the conclusions you reached, how you reached those conclusions, what evidence you based the conclusions on, and what professional techniques or knowledge were used. It would also be a good idea to keep a list of professional books or journals that advocate or sanction whatever principles were used in drawing your conclusions.

Preparing to Testify

The majority of cases filed will not go to trial. They will be resolved either through a settlement agreement or a plea bargain. Therefore, most experts' experience in testifying comes by having their deposition taken. A deposition serves as a powerful discovery device that may be used to compel anyone associated with the case to give oral testimony under oath. Although you cannot decline to testify, an expert may be allowed to specify a convenient time and place.

Sometimes the party requesting the deposition pays the opposing expert's fee—which consists of the time spent giving the deposition, at your standard hourly rate or in half-day or full-day increments, plus travel time. This usually occurs in federal court. Most state courts require each side to pay the expenses of the expert's they hire. An expert charges his client for the time spent preparing for deposition and for testifying.

In addition to the required court reporter, the proceeding may be recorded by a camera or a voice recorder. A judge is not present during this question-and-answer session.
For skilled investigators, deposition provides a golden opportunity to hear the other side's case aloud. The opposition may set ulterior goals as well, including:
- To learn new information or confirm existing facts
- To appraise the expert's ability as a witness
- To lock the expert into a hard-to-defend position
- To create a written record for future impeachment

Before testifying at a deposition or at trial, the expert should ensure that required graphic displays are ready and available, that all important discussions with the lawyer have been held, and that the expert has a complete understanding of the report and other relevant issues. The expert should ensure that he has agreement with counsel as to the sequence of evidence and the strategy for presenting it. It often is useful to have a "dry run" at the direct testimony, with all the questions posed by the counsel to the expert, to avoid surprises during trial.

At pre-testimony meetings, it is appropriate to discuss the qualifications of the witness again to ensure that they are current, to discuss the strengths and weaknesses of the case, and to discuss and agree as to what parts of the expert's reports, if any, are to be entered as exhibits.

Appearance

The appearance of the expert witness often lends itself to an assessment of the credibility of that witness. It is recommended that the witness be well-groomed and neatly dressed. In the witness box, the witness should maintain a poised, alert appearance, stand firmly, and be ready to take the oath. It is important to keep control of one's hands, to avoid fidgeting, and to maintain eye contact with the questioner. As the judge will be taking notes, the witness should speak slowly to ensure that the judge does not fall behind. The voice should be strong and directed to the questioner. The witness should enunciate clearly.

Do's and Don'ts

There are other considerations in making an expert a credible witness. Some tips are:
- Dress conservatively.
- Exude an alert and confident attitude.
- Tell the truth.
- Maintain eye contact with the inquisitor as much as possible.
- Ask that a long or imprecise question be rephrased or broken into smaller components.
- Take a breath before answering each question in a slow and deliberate manner.
- Explain complex concepts in a lay person's terms.
- Be friendly and polite to all parties present.
- Correct any misstatements as soon as detected.
- Speak clearly and audibly.
- Refrain from using professional jargon.
- Use simple rather than complex terms to describe findings and opinions.
- Answer the specific questions—don't go off on tangents or volunteer more than the question requires.
- Don't verbally fence with the attorney.
- Don't try to be humorous or hip.
- Look directly at the question poser.

- Maintain a professional demeanor—don't smile gratuitously at the judge, jury, or the lawyers.
- Be calm and deliberate in responding to questions—think before you speak.
- Wear conservative business attire.
- Use graphs, charts, and other visual aids if they help to clarify a point.
- Don't read from notes if you can avoid it. (The opposition lawyer will probably demand to see such notes if you do, and you will then look like you rehearsed your testimony—and did so rather badly).
- If you have documents to introduce, have them organized so that you can quickly retrieve them when asked to do so.
- Don't "hem and haw" or stammer. Recover your composure when a tough or complex question is posed.
- Ask for a repetition of the question or clarification if you don't fully comprehend it.
- If you don't know the answer, say so. Don't guess.
- In cross-examination, don't respond too quickly. Counsel for your side might wish to interpose an objection to the question.
- If the judge or jury member elects to ask a question, respond to it by looking their way.
- Don't stare off into space, at the floor, or at the ceiling.
- Be friendly and polite to all sides.
- Don't raise your voice in anger if the opponent's lawyer tries to bait you.
- Be honest. Don't invent. Don't inflate. Don't be evasive.

Several things should be avoided. These range from drinking five cups of coffee immediately prior to testimony, chewing bubble gum while giving evidence, to small physical mannerisms that might affect your appearance. These physical mannerisms, which might be as simple as rubbing one's hands together continually, looking down at one's hands, fidgeting on the stand, or jingling coins in a pocket, could become irritating to the judge and jury.

Similar to trial proceedings, the opposition commonly drills an expert about his credentials, his methodology, and his conclusions pertaining to the case. Unlike trial, the expert quite often answers tersely, giving only a straight "yes" or "no." For inquiries that require more, you should respond directly and precisely and refrain from volunteering any information. It is not your duty to educate the other side at deposition. You may ask for a recess or a break if needed.

Pour over the written transcription of your deposition afterward to ensure accuracy, immediately correcting any omissions or errors, whether made by you or the stenographer. Notify your lawyer if your opinion has changed since deposition. If you are present at the deposition of the opposing expert, you may be asked to summarize your impressions afterward and note any gray areas that call for further lines of inquiry.

Direct Examination

Experts are hired for their opinions, so they aren't subject to the usual restrictions about statements of judgment. Besides this, experts have other leeway not given to ordinary witnesses. They may rely on documents or exchanges which would otherwise be inadmissible as hearsay. This allows them to use articles, academic papers, professional texts and consultations in rendering their opinion of the case. These materials are admissible as long as they were used by the expert in developing his opinion.

Experts are commonly asked to answer *narrative questions*, which is all but forbidden to lay witnesses. Fraud cases, with their divergent paths of activity and intrigue, can require complex summarizing in order for the facts to make any sense. The average group of jurors has never considered how someone could manipulate store inventories to drive up the company's stock price, then make millions on the phony surge. The expert witness in cases like this often will begin testimony by recounting the narrative background of a case, the tests and experiments that were performed during the investigation, and a summary of the findings based on professional expertise.

Expert witnesses also are allowed to demonstrate their findings by using *hypotheticals*: fictional situations, analogous to the act in question, which clarify and highlight particular aspects of the dispute. The hypothetical has to be constructed exquisitely. Appeals courts have been adamant that the facts of the case being tried have to be reflected directly in the hypothetical situation; there must be no exaggeration or obscuring in the presentation.

Experts sometimes use specialized materials in reaching and communicating their opinions. Professional publications and sources of information that normally are used in the course of business may be produced as part of the trial. Federal rules require only that the source be "generally used and relied on" by people in that field.

Finally, experts may use special exhibits to demonstrate facts about the case or some aspect of their opinion. These exhibits may include charts, diagrams, annotated documents or photos. If the exhibit is offered to prove a fact, it must satisfy the rules applicable to any other piece of evidence in the case. In demonstrating a professional opinion, the role of the exhibit must be clear, and its applicability to the present case justified if necessary.

The purpose of direct examination is to enable counsel for the side you represent to draw out the evidence to prove the case. Most likely, this will be only a reiteration of what previously has been discussed with your counsel outside the courtroom. It is still very important, however, to refresh your memory beforehand by reference to anything you may have read, written, or given in evidence on the case.

Direct examination is the most organized aspect of the trial; it is the stage in which the expert's credibility must be established with the judge or jury. According to the concept of the primary memory, people remember best what they hear first and last. This often is a useful idea to employ in giving or structuring evidence. Another noteworthy point is that the jurors often have limited attention spans in a long trial; thus, it is often useful to use a "grab/give/conclude" method of presenting evidence.

To a witness, the interpretation of questions and the ability to listen are crucial skills. Even though the witness might already have gone through a mock direct examination, it is critical that each question be carefully evaluated again—the witness should reflect upon the questions asked and not anticipate them (they might have been changed, anyway, since the time of rehearsal).

The answers to all questions should be clear and concise and, where complex terms are used, they should be clarified. Use of notes should be limited as much as possible in order to maintain eye contact.

Schedules, if any, should be described accurately and succinctly in lay person's terms. Schedules are, by their nature, concise documents and should be described in that manner. If opinions are given, they should be stated with conviction.

Certain standards for Certified Fraud Examiners are found in the Code of Professional Ethics (please see the Criminology and Ethics Section). Specifically, Certified Fraud Examiners are prohibited from expressing opinions as to guilt or innocence of any person or party. This is not to say that the expert witness cannot testify to the badges or hallmarks or characteristics of fraud found in the case. It also does not mean that the Certified Fraud Examiner cannot testify that, based on the evidence, he believes that the accused may have committed the offense. But the ultimate guilt or innocence of any person or party is the sole responsibility of the judge and jury. The Certified Fraud Examiner typically will not be permitted to testify to the ultimate fact questions.

Cross-Examination

Cross-examination is truly the highlight of the adversary court system. It is geared to allow counsel to either clarify or to make points at the witness' expense. It generally is the most difficult part of the trial process for any witness. Anything can turn up that might refute or embarrass the witness. The witness' credibility is constantly called into question.

The goals of the opposing counsel during cross-examination are threefold. The first goal is to diminish the importance of the expert testimony just presented. The second goal is to have the expert testify in support of the opposing position by providing a series of assumptions. The third goal is to attack the opinion itself or to show the inadequacies in the expert's opinion, thereby discrediting the opinion, the report, and the witness.

The opposing counsel can attack or question anything that has been said or entered into court. This includes notes, working papers, affidavits, will-says, reports, and preliminary trial or discovery transcripts. Often, cross-examination creates an atmosphere of confrontation and contradiction.

The witness must not take attacks or attempts to discredit personally. There are many ways to discredit an expert witness. Throughout the process, it is important for the witness to maintain pride and professional integrity. An adage to remember is that "even mud can be worn well."

Opposing counsel wants to reduce or limit the impact of the witness' evidence—it is natural to feel a certain amount of apprehension, and this might do a great deal to keep the witness alert. The jury often watches the judge and therefore the expert often can take a clue as to the tempo and reaction of the jury and the judge to the evidence being presented. Slight changes in style and presentation could be made accordingly.

The opposing counsel usually has a plan of cross-examination in mind and an expert witness should be able to anticipate this direction to prevent falling into a trap. A danger to this, of course, is that the witness will spend as much time planning ahead as answering the questions, and might not be giving appropriate attention to the immediate questions. Further, in attempting to anticipate, the witness might misunderstand the question.

Generally, it is a rule of thumb that free information should not be given away or volunteered. During the answer, it often might be extremely difficult to avoid getting trapped in various assumptions, "what if" scenarios, and generalities presented by counsel during cross-examination. If this occurs, retrench by asking for a question to be rephrased in smaller components.

It is critical never to underestimate the expertise of the opposing counsel. Often, opposing counsel will be underplaying their understanding of the issues to lull the expert into a sense of security. This can lead the expert into a difficult situation. Opposing counsel's golden rule is to cross-examine only if it would benefit the case. In asking questions of the witness, opposing counsel generally will ask either short questions in plain words or will ask leading questions. Usually counsel knows the answers to the questions.

The opposing counsel generally will evaluate answers and then take a specific approach that furthers the argument. Generally, the witness will not be allowed to explain or elaborate on the question as that would allow the witness to alter the thrust of a carefully orchestrated cross-examination. Opposing counsel continually is questioning or evaluating how the last question and answer could be used against the witness.

Opposing counsel often will prepare by reading all earlier testimony and publications of the witness. The opposing counsel also might speak to other lawyers as to the witness' capabilities in court if they have had experience with the witness. If weaknesses are discovered, the questioning probably will be directed to that area.

Opposing counsel also might attempt to take psychological control of a witness by:
- Using physical presence to intimidate
- Nonstop eye contact
- Challenging space of the witness
- Asking questions at a fast pace to confuse witness
- Not allowing the expert to explain or deviate from the exact question.

Physical domination often is used by opposing counsel. Opposing counsel will quickly discover the response pattern of the expert and might take an aggressive stance to lead the expert to the point where he is unsure.

The following strategic methods could be employed to discredit a witness or to diminish the importance of his testimony. These methods could be used singly or in conjunction with one another and are not an all-encompassing list. A good counsel in cross-examination will quickly discover the witness' weak areas and employ any possible techniques to achieve his goal.

Myopic Vision

Myopic vision entails getting the expert to admit to a great amount of time being spent in the investigation of a matter, then selecting an area to highlight about which the expert is unsure or has not done much work. This area might not be central to the issues in the case, but it must be relevant to the conclusions reached. Then, the opposing counsel will make a large issue of it and prove that the expert's vision is myopic in that the work was limited in extent or scope and, as such, substandard. At the same time, the matter of fees could be drawn in to show that large sums were expended to have this "obviously incomplete" work done.

Safety

This approach often is taken by not attacking the expert and hence lulling him into a feeling of false security. Then, opposing counsel might find a small hole that quickly can be enlarged. This approach often is characterized by being friendly and conciliatory, by which the jury is made sympathetic to the cause of the opposing counsel. Opposing counsel also might attempt to achieve a certain amount of association with the witness that will make the witness want to help the opposing counsel to bring out information. Doing so may result in the witness giving information that otherwise would not have been given. With this additional information, it might be possible to find a chink or hole in the evidence and open it further.

Contradiction

Opposing counsel might use leading questions to force the witness into a hard or contradictory position. Alternately, counsel can establish the credibility in court of a potentially contradicting document or quote from other articles written by experts in the field. If these documents or articles are in contradiction to the expert, then an admission can be obtained from the expert as to that contradiction. If a contradiction exits, the expert might be drawn into an argument as to who is the most appropriate or experienced person. Instances have also occurred where the witness has contradicted himself or his own article written several years prior merely because of his lack of memory or confusion due to the attack.

New Information

Opposing counsel may introduce new information that the expert might not be aware of. This normally is done to introduce confusion in the witness' mind in the hope that the witness might contradict himself or develop a series of alternate scenarios, given the new information to show that the existing report and opinions are no longer of value.

Support Opposing Side's Theory

This approach recognizes an expert's qualifications and evidence. The same information used by the expert is then interpreted by opposing counsel in a different fashion to support an alternate theory. By getting the expert to agree to the alternate interpretation of the facts and the alternate theory, the opposing counsel, in effect, has made the expert a witness for the other side. This technique is useful to obtain concessions from the witness that would damage his conclusions and, ultimately, his credibility.

Bias

This method draws the expert's counsel and the expert together to show possible collusion as to the evidence being presented and hence to demonstrate bias. This can be shown if the opposing counsel can determine that the expert's counsel had instructed the witness as to what to say or by limiting the expert's scope and hence his conclusions. This approach also can focus on the question of whether or not the expert was told by his client what to do and look for. With this approach, opposing counsel might attempt to show that the expert overlooked important documentation in an effort to assist his client.

Confrontation

This method involves the use of a confrontation of wills to put the witness into a situation where he might lose emotional control and show anger. Once a witness has exploded, credibility normally disappears.

Sounding Board

This method uses the witness as a sounding board to reacquaint the jury with the favorable aspects (to opposing counsel) of the case. This technique often uses the "is it not true?" and "would you agree with me?" approach. Constant nonstop agreement is useful to browbeat the expert. In the eyes of the judge and jury, agreement with various questions raised by the opposing counsel also might be assumed to be a general concurrence with the position of opposing counsel.

Fees

This method attacks the witness on the basis of taking an inordinate amount of time for the result given. Further, the attack might indicate a lack of complete work and might be correlated to the fee charged. This method often is related to "bias" and "myopic vision." It might be suggested that the witness and his opinion are, in fact, biased. This technique often builds to a conclusion in which the opposing counsel arrives that the work was superficial and unprofessional, yet that a great deal of money was received by the expert for this and other areas of service to the client. The inference is that the testimony was purchased or that the expert was paid to overlook facts contradictory to the conclusions reached.

Terms of Engagement

This technique normally is employed by obtaining the original engagement letter and examining the terms of engagement. Opposing counsel can then show that the expert intended to look only at various items in support of his client and glossed over alternative theories, generally to the detriment of the opposition. As such, the witness could be portrayed as partial.

Discrediting the Witness

Discrediting the witness is based upon the concept of proving that the expert is unworthy to be a credible witness instructor to the court. This often can be accomplished by showing that the expert is currently or has previously been grossly biased, prejudiced, corrupt, convicted of criminal activities, shown to engage in immoral activities, made inconsistent statements, acquired a reputation for a lack of veracity, and/or exaggerated his qualifications. Discrediting also could consist of looking at the quality of the expert's educational background to reveal any other unusual activities that might bias the witness or exclude him from the court as an expert.

Expressing an Opinion on Guilt

Article Five of the Association of Certified Fraud Examiners Code of Professional Ethics states:

A fraud examiner, in conducting examinations, will obtain evidence or other documentation to establish a reasonable basis for any opinion rendered. No opinion shall be expressed regarding the guilt or innocence of any person or party.

The rule that prohibits opinions regarding the guilt or innocence of any person or party is a rule of prudence. Clearly, it is prudent for a Certified Fraud Examiner to refrain from usurping the role of jury. In a courtroom, no good attorney would ask a Certified Fraud Examiner for such a conclusion, and no alert judge would allow such testimony.

The fraud examiner's job is to present the evidence in his report. Such evidence might constitute a convincing case pointing to the guilt or innocence of a person. But a clear line should be drawn between a report that essentially says "Here is the evidence" and one that steps over the line and says "He is the guilty (innocent) person." Nevertheless, there is a fine line between recommending action—forwarding the evidence to a law enforcement agency or filing a complaint or lawsuit—and giving an opinion on guilt or innocence. Certified Fraud Examiners might make such recommendations because they think the evidence is strong enough to support a case. They might even have a conclusion about whether the suspect committed a crime. The rule does not prohibit the Certified Fraud Examiner, under the proper circumstances, from accusing the person under investigation. However, the ultimate decision of whether a person is "guilty" or "innocent" is for a jury to determine. The CFE is free to report the facts and the conclusions that can be drawn from those facts, but the decision as to whether or not a person is guilty of a crime is a decision for the judge or jury.

Summary

Harold A. Feder in his book, *Succeeding As an Expert Witness*, suggests keeping the following in mind while you are working on a particular case:

- Keep an open mind
- Do not approach a case with predetermined conclusions as to causation, culpability, fault, or damage
- Remember that attorneys and clients come to you with facts which might be slanted, either accidentally or purposefully
- Carefully follow your own well-established investigative steps; develop forms, procedures, and processes which will ensure that you do not overlook evidence

While preparing to testify or present evidence, remember the following:
- Prepare your material completely
- Know your material thoroughly
- Plan your testimony in advance
- Be alert
- Listen carefully.
- Carefully consider each answer, and pause before answering
- Be honest and avoid bias
- Clarify—use simple words
- Keep your cool
- Maintain professional pride and integrity throughout

One of the best things you can do is to stay current about new developments in your field. It takes a concerted effort to stay on top of changes and advances in any industry, as well as the latest forensic investigation methods. To be a successful expert witness in any area of accounting, for instance, you must have a thorough knowledge not only of generally accepted accounting principles, but also current promulgation. For cases involving credit card fraud, you must have a basic understanding of your nation's electronic banking system. While active practice in your field of expertise—in other words, experience—remains your single most valuable source of knowledge, other sources abound.

Actions which maintain and improve your current credentials and make you a better expert witness include:
- Pursuing continuing education and training opportunities
- Reading trade journals and publications
- Joining and participating in professional societies and associations
- Teaching, lecturing, and holding seminars
- Attending specialized seminars and workshops
- Writing for trade journals and publications
- Taking advanced computer courses

You can practice your oral delivery skills, and hence improve your credibility, by actively pursuing public speaking engagements and opportunities. To feel more comfortable on the legal stage, you may wish to visit your local courtroom to observe another financial expert giving testimony in similar cases. Cable television, especially local government shows and the

Court-TV channel, likewise offers a chance to see other experts in action in a variety of situations.

The remainder of the Law Section contains the complete Rules of Federal Criminal and Civil Procedures, as well as the Federal Rules of Evidence.

LAW APPENDIX

FEDERAL RULES OF CIVIL PROCEDURE

As Amended to March 27, 2003

I. SCOPE OF RULES—ONE FORM OF ACTION

Rule 1. Scope and Purpose of Rules

These rules govern the procedure in the United States district courts in all suits of a civil nature whether cognizable as cases at law or in equity or in admiralty, with the exceptions stated in Rule 81. They shall be construed and administered to secure the just, speedy, and inexpensive determination of every action.

Rule 2. One Form of Action

There shall be one form of action to be known as "civil action."

II. COMMENCEMENT OF ACTION; SERVICE OF PROCESS, PLEADINGS, MOTIONS AND ORDERS

Rule 3. Commencement of Action

A civil action is commenced by filing a complaint with the court.

Rule 4. Summons

(a) Form. The summons shall be signed by the clerk, bear the seal of the court, identify the court and the parties, be directed to the defendant, and state the name and address of the plaintiff's attorney, or, if unrepresented, of the plaintiff. It shall also state the time within which the defendant must appear and defend, and notify the defendant that failure to do so will result in a judgment by default against the defendant for the relief demanded in the complaint. The court may allow a summons to be amended.

(b) Issuance. Upon or after filing the complaint, the plaintiff may present a summons to the clerk for signature and seal. If the summons is in proper form, the clerk shall sign, seal, and issue it to the plaintiff for service on the defendant. A summons, or a copy of the summons if addressed to multiple defendants, shall be issued for each defendant to be served.

(c) Service with Complaint; by Whom Made.

(1) A summons shall be served together with a copy of the complaint. The plaintiff is responsible for service of a summons and complaint within the time allowed under subdivision (m) and shall furnish the person effecting service with the necessary copies of the summons and complaint.

(2) Service may be effected by any person who is not a party and who is at least 18 years of age. At the request of the plaintiff, however, the court may direct that service be effected by a United States marshal, deputy United States marshal, or other person or officer specially appointed by the court for that purpose. Such an appointment must be made when the plaintiff is authorized to proceed in forma pauperis pursuant to 28 U.S.C. §1915 or is authorized to proceed as a seaman under 28 U.S.C. § 1916.

(d) Waiver of Service; Duty to Save Costs of Service; Request to Waive.

(1) A defendant who waives service of a summons does not thereby waive any objection to the venue or to the jurisdiction of the court over the person of the defendant.

(2) An individual, corporation, or association that is subject to service under subdivision (e), (f), or (h) and that receives notice of an action in the manner provided in this paragraph has a duty to avoid unnecessary costs of serving the summons. To avoid costs, the plaintiff may notify such a defendant of the commencement of the action and request that the defendant waive service of a summons. The notice and request

(A) shall be in writing and shall be addressed directly to the defendant, if an individual, or else to an officer or managing or general agent (or other agent authorized by appointment or law to receive service of process) of a defendant subject to service under subdivision (h);

(B) shall be dispatched through first-class mail or other reliable means;

(C) shall be accompanied by a copy of the complaint and shall identify the court in which it has been filed;

(D) shall inform the defendant, by means of a text prescribed in an official form promulgated pursuant to Rule 84, of the consequences of compliance and of a failure to comply with the request;

(E) shall set forth the date on which the request is sent;

(F) shall allow the defendant a reasonable time to return the waiver, which shall be at least 30 days from the date on which the request is sent, or 60 days from that date if the defendant is addressed outside any judicial district of the United States; and

(G) shall provide the defendant with an extra copy of the notice and request, as well as a prepaid means of compliance in writing.

If a defendant located within the United States fails to comply with a request for waiver made by a plaintiff located within the United States, the court shall impose the costs subsequently incurred in effecting service on the defendant unless good cause for the failure be shown.

(3) A defendant that, before being served with process, timely returns a waiver so requested is not required to serve an answer to the complaint until 60 days after the date on which the request for waiver of service was sent, or 90 days after that date if the defendant was addressed outside any judicial district of the United States.

(4) When the plaintiff files a waiver of service with the court, the action shall proceed, except as provided in paragraph (3), as if a summons and complaint had been served at the time of filing the waiver, and no proof of service shall be required.

(5) The costs to be imposed on a defendant under paragraph (2) for failure to comply with a request to waive service of a summons shall include the costs subsequently incurred in effecting service under subdivision (e), (f), or (h), together with the costs, including a reasonable attorney's fee, of any motion required to collect the costs of service.

(e) Service Upon Individuals Within a Judicial District of the United States. Unless otherwise provided by federal law, service upon an individual from whom a waiver has not been obtained and filed, other than an infant or an incompetent person, may be effected in any judicial district of the United States:

(1) pursuant to the law of the state in which the district court is located, or in which service is effected, for the service of a summons upon the defendant in an action brought in the courts of general jurisdiction of the State; or

(2) by delivering a copy of the summons and of the complaint to the individual personally or by leaving copies thereof at the individual's dwelling house or usual place of abode with some person of suitable age and discretion then residing therein or by delivering a copy of the summons and of the complaint to an agent authorized by appointment or by law to receive service of process.

(f) Service Upon Individuals in a Foreign Country. Unless otherwise provided by federal law, service upon an individual from whom a waiver has not been obtained and filed, other than an infant or an incompetent person, may be effected in a place not within any judicial district of the United States:

(1) by any internationally agreed means reasonably calculated to give notice, such as those means authorized by the Hague Convention on the Service Abroad of Judicial and Extrajudicial Documents; or

(2) if there is no internationally agreed means of service or the applicable international agreement allows other means of service, provided that service is reasonably calculated to give notice:

(A) in the manner prescribed by the law of the foreign country for service in that country in an action in any of its courts of general jurisdiction; or

(B) as directed by the foreign authority in response to a letter rogatory or letter of request; or

(C) unless prohibited by the law of the foreign country, by

(i) delivery to the individual personally of a copy of the summons and the complaint; or

(ii) any form of mail requiring a signed receipt, to be addressed and dispatched by the clerk of the court to the party to be served; or

(3) by other means not prohibited by international agreement as may be directed by the court.

(g) Service Upon Infants and Incompetent Persons. Service upon an infant or an incompetent person in a judicial district of the United States shall be effected in the manner prescribed by the law of the state in which the service is made for the service of summons or other like process upon any such defendant in an action brought in the courts of general jurisdiction of that state. Service upon an infant or an incompetent person in a place not within any judicial district of the United States shall be effected in the manner prescribed by paragraph (2)(A) or (2)(B) of subdivision (f) or by such means as the court may direct.

(h) Service Upon Corporations and Associations. Unless otherwise provided by federal law, service upon a domestic or foreign corporation or upon a partnership or other unincorporated association that is subject to suit under a common name, and from which a waiver of service has not been obtained and filed, shall be effected:

(1) in a judicial district of the United States in the manner prescribed for individuals by subdivision (e)(1), or by delivering a copy of the summons and of the complaint to an officer, a managing or general agent, or to any other agent authorized by appointment or by law to receive service of process and, if the agent is one authorized by statute to receive service and the statute so requires, by also mailing a copy to the defendant, or

(2) in a place not within any judicial district of the United States in any manner prescribed for individuals by subdivision (f) except personal delivery as provided in paragraph (2)(C)(i) thereof.

(i) Serving the United States, Its Agencies, Corporations, Officers, or Employees.

(1) Service upon the United States shall be effected

(A) by delivering a copy of the summons and of the complaint to the United States attorney for the district in which the action is brought or to an assistant United States attorney or clerical employee designated by the United States attorney in a writing filed with the clerk of the court or by sending a copy of the summons and of the complaint by registered or certified mail addressed to the civil process clerk at the office of the United States attorney and

(B) by also sending a copy of the summons and of the complaint by registered or certified mail to the Attorney General of the United States at Washington, District of Columbia, and

(C) in any action attacking the validity of an order of an officer or agency of the United States not made a party, by also sending a copy of the summons and of the complaint by registered or certified mail to the officer or agency.

(2) (A) Service on an agency or corporation of the United States, or an officer or employee of the United States sued only in an official capacity, is effected by serving the United States in the manner prescribed by Rule 4(i)(1) and by also sending a copy of the summons and complaint by registered or certified mail to the officer, employee, agency, or corporation.

(B) Service on an officer or employee of the United States sued in an individual capacity for acts or omissions occurring in connection with the performance of duties on behalf of the United States - whether or not the officer or employee is sued also in an official capacity - is effected by serving the United States in the manner prescribed by Rule 4(i)(1) and by serving the officer or employee in the manner prescribed by Rule 4 (e), (f), or (g).

(3) The court shall allow a reasonable time to serve process under Rule 4(i) for the purpose of curing the failure to serve:

(A) all persons required to be served in an action governed by Rule 4(i)(2)(A), if the plaintiff has served either the United States attorney or the Attorney General of the United States, or

(B) the United States in an action governed by Rule 4(i)(2)(B), if the plaintiff has served an officer or employee of the United States sued in an individual capacity.

(j) Service Upon Foreign, State, or Local Governments.

(1) Service upon a foreign state or a political subdivision, agency, or instrumentality thereof shall be effected pursuant to 28 U.S.C. § 1608.

(2) Service upon a state, municipal corporation, or other governmental organization subject to suit shall be effected by delivering a copy of the summons and of the complaint to its chief executive officer or by serving the summons and complaint in the manner prescribed by the law of that state for the service of summons or other like process upon any such defendant.

(k) Territorial Limits of Effective Service.

(1) Service of a summons or filing a waiver of service is effective to establish jurisdiction over the person of a defendant

(A) who could be subjected to the jurisdiction of a court of general jurisdiction in the state in which the district court is located, or

(B) who is a party joined under Rule 14 or Rule 19 and is served at a place within a judicial district of the United States and not more than 100 miles from the place from which the summons issues, or

(C) who is subject to the federal interpleader jurisdiction under 28 U.S.C. § 1335, or

(D) when authorized by a statute of the United States.

(2) If the exercise of jurisdiction is consistent with the Constitution and laws of the United States, serving a summons or filing a waiver of service is also effective, with respect to claims arising under federal law, to establish personal jurisdiction over the person of any defendant who is not subject to the jurisdiction of the courts of general jurisdiction of any state.

(l) Proof of Service. If service is not waived, the person effecting service shall make proof thereof to the court. If service is made by a person other than a United States marshal or deputy United States marshal, the person shall make affidavit thereof. Proof of service in a place not within any judicial district of the United States shall, if effected under paragraph (1) of subdivision (f), be made pursuant to the applicable treaty or convention, and shall, if effected under paragraph (2) or (3) thereof, include a receipt signed by the addressee or other evidence of delivery to the addressee satisfactory to the court. Failure to make proof of service does not affect the validity of the service. The court may allow proof of service to be amended.

(m) Time Limit for Service. If service of the summons and complaint is not made upon a defendant within 120 days after the filing of the complaint, the court, upon motion or on its own initiative after notice to the plaintiff, shall dismiss the action without prejudice as to that defendant or direct that service be effected within a specified time; provided that if the plaintiff shows good cause for the failure, the court shall extend the time for service for an appropriate period. This subdivision does not apply to service in a foreign country pursuant to subdivision (f) or (j)(1).

(n) Seizure of Property; Service of Summons Not Feasible.

(1) If a statute of the United States so provides, the court may assert jurisdiction over property. Notice to claimants of the property shall then be sent in the manner provided by the statute or by service of a summons under this rule.

(2) Upon a showing that personal jurisdiction over a defendant cannot, in the district where the action is brought, be obtained with reasonable efforts by service of summons in any manner authorized by this rule, the court may assert jurisdiction over any of the defendant's assets found within the district by seizing the assets under the circumstances and in the manner provided by the law of the state in which the district court is located.

Rule 4.1. Service of Other Process

(a) Generally. Process other than a summons as provided in Rule 4 or subpoena as provided in Rule 45 shall be served by a United States marshal, a deputy United States marshal, or a person specially appointed for that purpose, who shall make proof of service as provided in Rule 4(l). The process may be served anywhere within the territorial limits of the state in which the district court is located, and, when authorized by a statute of the United States, beyond the territorial limits of that state.

(b) Enforcement of Orders: Commitment for Civil Contempt. An order of civil commitment of a person held to be in contempt of a decree or injunction issued to enforce the laws of the United States may be served and enforced in any district. Other orders in civil contempt proceedings shall be served in the state in which the court issuing the order to be enforced is located or elsewhere within the United States if not more than 100 miles from the place at which the order to be enforced was issued.

Rule 5. Service and Filing of Pleadings and Other Papers

(a) Service: When Required. Except as otherwise provided in these rules, every order required by its terms to be served, every pleading subsequent to the original complaint unless the court otherwise orders because of numerous defendants, every paper relating to discovery required to be served upon a party unless the court otherwise orders, every written motion other than one which may be heard ex parte, and every written notice, appearance, demand, offer of judgment, designation of record on appeal, and similar paper shall be served upon each of the parties. No service need be made on parties in default for failure to appear except that pleadings asserting new or additional claims for relief against them shall be served upon them in the manner provided for service of summons in Rule 4.

In an action begun by seizure of property, in which no person need be or is named as defendant, any service required to be made prior to the filing of an answer, claim, or appearance shall be made upon the person having custody or possession of the property at the time of its seizure.

(b) Same: How Made. Whenever under these rules service is required or permitted to be made upon a party represented by an attorney the service shall be made upon the attorney unless service upon the party is ordered by the court. Service upon the attorney or upon a party shall be made by delivering a copy to the attorney or party or by mailing it to the attorney or party at the attorney's or party's last known address or, if no address is known, by leaving it with the clerk of the court. Delivery of a copy within this rule means: handing it to the attorney or to the party; or leaving it at the attorney's or party's office with a clerk or other person in charge thereof; or, if there is no one in charge, leaving it in a conspicuous place therein; or, if the office is closed or the person to be served has no office, leaving it at the person's dwelling house or usual place of abode with some person of suitable age and discretion then residing therein. Service by mail is complete upon mailing.

(c) Same: Numerous Defendants. In any action in which there are unusually large numbers of defendants, the court, upon motion or of its own initiative, may order that service of the pleadings of the defendants and replies thereto need not be made as between the defendants and that any cross-claim, counterclaim, or matter constituting an avoidance or affirmative defense contained therein shall be deemed to be denied or avoided by all other parties and that the filing of any such pleading and service thereof upon the plaintiff constitutes due notice of it to the parties. A copy of every such order shall be served upon the parties in such manner and form as the court directs.

(d) Filing; Certificate of Service. All papers after the complaint required to be served upon a party, together with a certificate of service, must be filed with the court within a reasonable time after service, but disclosures under Rule 26(a)(1) or (2) and the following discovery requests and responses must not be filed until they are used in the proceeding or the court orders filing: (i) depositions, (ii) interrogatories, (iii) requests for documents or to permit entry upon land, and (iv) requests for admission.

(e) Filing with the Court Defined. The filing of papers with the court as required by these rules shall be made by filing them with the clerk of the court, except that the judge may permit the papers to be filed with the judge, in which event the judge shall note thereon the filing date and forthwith transmit them to the office of the clerk. A court may by local rule permit papers to be filed, signed, or verified by electronic means that are consistent with standards, if any, that the Judicial Conference of the United States establishes. A paper filed by electronic means in compliance with a local rule constitutes a written paper for the purpose of applying these rules. The clerk shall not refuse to accept for filing any paper presented for that purpose solely because it is not presented in proper form as required by these rules or any local rules or practices.

Rule 6. Time

(a) Computation. In computing any period of time prescribed or allowed by these rules, by the local rules of any district court, by order of court, or by any applicable statute, the day of the act, event, or default from which the designated period of time begins to run shall not be included. The last day of the period so computed shall be included, unless it is a Saturday, a Sunday, or a legal holiday, or, when the act to be done is the filing of a paper in court, a day on which weather or other conditions have made the office of the clerk of the district court inaccessible, in which event the period runs until the end of the next day which is not one of the aforementioned days. When the period of time prescribed or allowed is less than 11 days, intermediate, Saturdays, Sundays, and legal holidays shall be excluded in the computation. As used in this rule and in Rule 77(c), "legal holiday" includes New Year's Day, Birthday of Martin Luther King, Jr., Washington's Birthday, Memorial Day, Independence Day, Labor Day, Columbus Day, Veterans Day, Thanksgiving Day, Christmas Day, and any other day appointed as a holiday by the President or the Congress of the United States, or by the state in which the district court is held.

(b) Enlargement. When by these rules or by a notice given thereunder or by order of court an act is required or allowed to be done at or within a specified time, the court for cause shown may at any time in its discretion (1) with or without motion or notice order the period enlarged if request therefor is made before the expiration of the period originally prescribed or as extended by a previous order, or (2) upon motion made after the expiration of the specified period permit the act to be done where the failure to act was the result of excusable neglect; but it may not extend the time for taking any action under Rules 50(b) and (c)(2), 52(b), 59(b), (d) and (e), and 60(b), except to the extent and under the conditions stated in them.

(c) [Rescinded. Feb. 28, 1966, eff. July 1, 1966.]

(d) For Motions—Affidavits. A written motion, other than one which may be heard ex parte, and notice of the hearing thereof shall be served not later than 5 days before the time specified for the hearing, unless a different period is fixed by these rules or by order of the court. Such an order may for cause shown be made on ex parte application. When a motion is supported by affidavit, the affidavit shall be served with the motion; and, except as otherwise provided in Rule 59(c), opposing affidavits may be served not later than one day before the hearing, unless the court permits them to be served at some other time.

(e) Additional Time After Service by Mail. Whenever a party has the right or is required to do some act or take some proceedings within a prescribed period after the service of a notice or other paper upon the party and the notice or paper is served upon the party by mail, three days shall be added to the prescribed period.

III. PLEADINGS AND MOTIONS

Rule 7. Pleadings Allowed; Form of Motions

(a) **Pleadings.** There shall be a complaint and an answer; a reply to a counterclaim denominated as such; an answer to a cross-claim, if the answer contains a cross-claim; a third-party complaint, if a person who was not an original party is summoned under the provisions of Rule 14; and a third-party answer, if a third-party complaint is served. No other pleading shall be allowed, except that the court may order a reply to an answer or a third-party answer.

(b) **Motions and Other Papers.**

(1) An application to the court for an order shall be by motion which, unless made during a hearing or trial, shall be made in writing, shall state with particularity the grounds therefor, and shall set forth the relief or order sought. The requirement of writing is fulfilled if the motion is stated in a written notice of the hearing of the motion.

(2) The rules applicable to captions and other matters of form of pleadings apply to all motions and other papers provided for by these rules.

(3) All motions shall be signed in accordance with Rule 11.

(c) **Demurrers, Pleas, Etc., Abolished.** Demurrers, pleas, and exceptions for insufficiency of a pleading shall not be used.

Rule 7.1. Disclosure Statement
(a) **Who Must File: Nongovernmental Corporate Party.**
A nongovernmental corporate party to an action or proceeding in a district court must file two copies of a statement that identifies any parent corporation and any publicly held corporation that owns 10% or more of its stock or states that there is no such corporation.
(b) **Time for Filing; Supplemental Filing.**
A party must:
(1) file the Rule 7.1(a) statement with its first appearance, pleading, petition, motion, response, or other request addressed to the court, and
(2) promptly file a supplemental statement upon any change in the information that the statement requires.

Rule 8. General Rules of Pleading

(a) **Claims for Relief.** A pleading which sets forth a claim for relief, whether an original claim, counterclaim, cross-claim, or third-party claim, shall contain (1) a short and plain statement of the grounds upon which the court's jurisdiction depends, unless the court already has jurisdiction and the claim needs no new grounds of jurisdiction to support it, (2) a short and plain statement of the claim showing that the pleader is entitled to relief, and (3) a demand for judgment for the relief the pleader seeks. Relief in the alternative or of several different types may be demanded.

(b) **Defenses; Form of Denials.** A party shall state in short and plain terms the party's defenses to each claim asserted and shall admit or deny the averments upon which the adverse party relies. If a party is without knowledge or information sufficient to form a belief as to the truth of an averment, the party shall so state and this has the effect of a denial. Denials shall fairly meet the substance of the averments denied. When a pleader intends in good faith to deny only a part or a qualification of an averment, the pleader shall specify so much of it as is true and material and shall deny only the remainder. Unless the pleader intends in good faith to controvert all the averments of the preceding pleading, the pleader may make denials as specific denials of designated averments or paragraphs or may generally deny all the averments except such designated averments or paragraphs as the pleader expressly admits; but, when the pleader does so intend to controvert all its averments, including averments of the grounds upon which the court's jurisdiction depends, the pleader may do so by general denial subject to the obligations set forth in Rule 11.

(c) **Affirmative Defenses.** In pleading to a preceding pleading, a party shall set forth affirmatively accord and satisfaction, arbitration and award, assumption of risk, contributory negligence, discharge in bankruptcy, duress, estoppel, failure of consideration, fraud, illegality, injury by fellow servant, laches, license, payment, release, res judicata, statute of frauds, statute of limitations, waiver, and any other matter constituting an avoidance or affirmative defense. When a party has mistakenly designated a defense as a counterclaim or a counterclaim as a defense, the court on terms, if justice so requires, shall treat the pleading as if there had been a proper designation.

(d) **Effect of Failure to Deny.** Averments in a pleading to which a responsive pleading is required, other than those as to the amount of damage, are admitted when not denied in the responsive pleading. Averments in a pleading to which no responsive pleading is required or permitted shall be taken as denied or avoided.

(e) **Pleading to be Concise and Direct; Consistency.**

(1) Each averment of a pleading shall be simple, concise, and direct. No technical forms of pleading or motions are required.

(2) A party may set forth two or more statements of a claim or defense alternately or hypothetically, either in one count or defense or in separate counts or defenses. When two or more statements are made in the alternative and one of them if made independently would be sufficient, the pleading is not made insufficient by the insufficiency of one or more of the alternative statements. A party may also state as many separate claims or defenses as the party has regardless of consistency and whether based on legal, equitable, or maritime grounds. All statements shall be made subject to the obligations set forth in Rule 11.

(f) **Construction of Pleadings.** All pleadings shall be so construed as to do substantial justice.

Rule 9. Pleading Special Matters

(a) **Capacity.** It is not necessary to aver the capacity of a party to sue or be sued or the authority of a party to sue or be sued in a representative capacity or the legal existence of an organized association of persons that is made a party, except to the extent required to show the jurisdiction of the court. When a party desires to raise an issue as to the legal existence of any party or the capacity of any party to sue or be sued or the authority of a party to sue or be sued in a representative capacity, the party desiring to raise the issue shall do so by specific negative averment, which shall include such supporting particulars as are peculiarly within the pleader's knowledge.

(b) **Fraud, Mistake, Condition of the Mind.** In all averments of fraud or mistake, the circumstances constituting fraud or mistake shall be stated with particularity. Malice, intent, knowledge, and other condition of mind of a person may be averred generally.

(c) **Conditions Precedent.** In pleading the performance or occurrence of conditions precedent, it is sufficient to aver generally that all conditions precedent have been performed or have occurred. A denial of performance or occurrence shall be made specifically and with particularity.

(d) **Official Document or Act.** In pleading an official document or official act it is sufficient to aver that the document was issued or the act done in compliance with law.

(e) **Judgment.** In pleading a judgment or decision of a domestic or foreign court, judicial or quasi-judicial tribunal, or of a board or officer, it is sufficient to aver the judgment or decision without setting forth matter showing jurisdiction to render it.

(f) **Time and Place.** For the purpose of testing the sufficiency of a pleading, averments of time and place are material and shall be considered like all other averments of material matter.

(g) **Special Damage.** When items of special damage are claimed, they shall be specifically stated.

(h) **Admiralty and Maritime Claims.** A pleading or count setting forth a claim for relief within the admiralty and maritime jurisdiction that is also within the jurisdiction of the district court on some other ground may contain a statement identifying the claim as an admiralty or maritime claim for the purposes of Rules 14(c), 38(e), 82, and the Supple-mental Rules for Certain Admiralty and Maritime Claims. If the claim is cognizable only in admiralty, it is an admiralty or maritime claim for those purposes whether so identified or not. The amendment of a pleading to add or withdraw an identifying statement is governed by the principles of Rule 15. A case that includes an admiralty or maritime claim within this subdivision is an admiralty case within 28 U.S.C. § 1292(a)(3).

Rule 10. Form of Pleadings

(a) **Caption; Names of Parties.** Every pleading shall contain a caption setting forth the name of the court, the title of the action, the file number, and a designation as in Rule 7(a). In the complaint the title of the action shall include the names of all the parties, but in other pleadings it is sufficient to state the name of the first party on each side with an appropriate indication of other parties.

(b) **Paragraphs; Separate Statements.** All averments of claim or defense shall be made in numbered paragraphs, the contents of each of which shall be limited as far as practicable to a statement of a single set of circumstances; and a paragraph may be referred to by number in all succeeding pleadings. Each claim founded upon a separate transaction or occurrence and each defense other than denials shall be stated in a separate count or defense whenever a separation facilitates the clear presentation of the matters set forth.

(c) **Adoption by Reference; Exhibits.** Statements in a pleading may be adopted by reference in a different part of the same pleading or in another pleading or in any motion. A copy of any written instrument which is an exhibit to a pleading is a part thereof for all purposes.

Rule 11. Signing of Pleadings, Motions, and Other Papers; Representations to Court; Sanctions

(a) **Signature.** Every pleading, written motion, and other paper shall be signed by at least one attorney of record in the attorney's individual name, or, if the party is not represented by an attorney, shall be signed by the party. Each paper shall state the signer's
address and telephone number, if any. Except when otherwise specifically provided by rule or statute, pleadings need not be verified or accompanied by affidavit. An unsigned paper shall

be stricken unless omission of the signature is corrected promptly after being called to the attention of the attorney or party.

(b) Representations to Court. By presenting to the court (whether by signing, filing, submitting, or later advocating) a pleading, written motion, or other paper, an attorney or unrepresented party is certifying that to the best of the person's knowledge, information, and belief, formed after an inquiry reasonable under the circumstances, —

(1) it is not being presented for any improper purpose, such as to harass or to cause unnecessary delay or needless increase in the cost of litigation;

(2) the claims, defenses, and other legal contentions therein are warranted by existing law or by a non-frivolous argument for the extension, modification, or reversal of existing law or the establishment of new law;

(3) the allegations and other factual contentions have evidentiary support or, if specifically so identified, are likely to have evidentiary support after a reasonable opportunity for further investigation or discovery; and

(4) the denials of factual contentions are warranted on the evidence or, if specifically so identified, are reasonably based on a lack of information or belief.

(c) Sanctions. If, after notice and a reasonable opportunity to respond, the court determines that subdivision (b) has been violated, the court may, subject to the conditions stated below, impose an appropriate sanction upon the attorneys, law firms, or parties that have violated subdivision (b) or are responsible for the violation.

(1) How Initiated.

(A) By Motion. A motion for sanctions under this rule shall be made separately from other motions or requests and shall describe the specific conduct alleged to violate subdivision (b). It shall be served as provided in Rule 5, but shall not be filed with or presented to the court unless, within 21 days after service of the motion (or such other period as the court may prescribe), the challenged paper, claim, defense, contention, allegation, or denial is not withdrawn or appropriately corrected. If warranted, the court may award to the party prevailing on the motion the reasonable expenses and attorney's fees incurred in presenting or opposing the motion. Absent exceptional circumstances, a law firm shall be held jointly responsible for violations committed by its partners, associates, and employees.

(B) On Court's Initiative. On its own initiative, the court may enter an order describing the specific conduct that appears to violate subdivision (b) and directing an attorney, law firm, or party to show cause why it has not violated subdivision (b) with respect thereto.

(2) Nature of Sanction; Limitations. A sanction imposed for violation of this rule shall be limited to what is sufficient to deter repetition of such conduct or comparable conduct by others similarly situated. Subject to the limitations in subparagraphs (A) and (B), the sanction may consist of, or include, directives of a non-monetary nature, an order to pay a penalty into court, or, if imposed on motion and warranted for effective deterrence, an order directing payment to the movant of some or all of the reasonable attorneys' fees and other expenses incurred as a direct result of the violation.

(A) Monetary sanctions may not be awarded against a represented party for a violation of subdivision (b)(2).

(B) Monetary sanctions may not be awarded on the court's initiative unless the court issues its order to show cause before a voluntary dismissal or settlement of the claims made by or against the party which is, or whose attorneys are, to be sanctioned.

(3) Order. When imposing sanctions, the court shall describe the conduct determined to constitute a violation of this rule and explain the basis for the sanction imposed.

(d) Inapplicability to Discovery. Subdivisions (a) through (c) of this rule do not apply to disclosures and discovery requests, responses, objections, and motions that are subject to the provisions of Rules 26 through 37.

Rule 12. Defenses and Objections—When and How Presented—By Pleading or Motion—Motion for Judgment on the Pleadings

(a) When Presented.

(1) Unless a different time is prescribed in a statute of the United States, a defendant shall serve an answer

(A) within 20 days after being served with the summons and complaint, or

(B) if service of the summons has been timely waived on request under Rule 4(d), within 60 days after the date when the request for waiver was sent, or within 90 days after that date if the defendant was addressed outside any judicial district of the United States.

(2) A party served with a pleading stating a cross-claim against that party shall serve an answer thereto within 20 days after being served. The plaintiff shall serve a reply to a counterclaim in the answer within 20 days after service of the answer, or, if a reply is ordered by the court, within 20 days after service of the order, unless the order otherwise directs.

(3) (A) The United States, an agency of the United States, or an officer or employee of the United States sued in an official capacity, shall serve an answer to the complaint or cross-claim - or a reply to a counterclaim - within 60 days after the United States attorney is served with the pleading asserting the claim.

(B) An officer or employee of the United States sued in an individual capacity for acts or omissions occurring in connection with the performance of duties on behalf of the United States shall serve an answer to the complaint or cross-claim - or a reply to a counterclaim - within 60 days after service on the officer or employee, or service on the United States attorney, whichever is later.

(4) Unless a different time is fixed by court order, the service of a motion permitted under this rule alters these periods of time as follows:

(A) if the court denies the motion or postpones its disposition until the trial on the merits, the responsive pleading shall be served within 10 days after notice of the court's action; or

(B) if the court grants a motion for a more definite statement, the responsive pleading shall be served within 10 days after the service of the more definite statement.

(b) How Presented. Every defense, in law or fact, to a claim for relief in any pleading, whether a claim, counterclaim, cross-claim, or third-party claim, shall be asserted in the responsive pleading thereto if one is required, except that the following defenses may at the option of the pleader be made by motion: (1) lack of jurisdiction over the subject matter, (2) lack of jurisdiction over the person, (3) improper venue, (4) insufficiency of process, (5) insufficiency of service of process, (6) failure to state a claim upon which relief can be granted, (7) failure to join a party under Rule 19. A motion making any of these defenses shall be made before pleading if a further pleading is permitted. No defense or objection is waived by being joined with one or more other defenses or objections in a responsive pleading or motion. If a pleading sets forth a claim for relief to which the adverse party is
not required to serve a responsive pleading, the adverse party may assert at the trial any defense in law or fact to that claim for relief. If, on a motion asserting the defense numbered (6) to dismiss for failure of the pleading to state a claim upon which relief can be granted, matters outside the pleading are presented to and not excluded by the court, the motion shall

be treated as one for summary judgment and disposed of as provided in Rule 56, and all parties shall be given reasonable opportunity to present all material made pertinent to such a motion by Rule 56.

(c) Motion for Judgment on the Pleadings. After the pleadings are closed but within such time as not to delay the trial, any party may move for judgment on the pleadings. If, on a motion for judgment on the pleadings, matters outside the pleadings are presented to and not excluded by the court, the motion shall be treated as one for summary judgment and disposed of as provided in Rule 56, and all parties shall be given reasonable opportunity to present all material made pertinent to such a motion by Rule 56.

(d) Preliminary Hearings. The defenses specifically enumerated (1)-(7) in subdivision (b) of this rule, whether made in a pleading or by motion, and the motion for judgment mentioned in subdivision (c) of this rule shall be heard and determined before trial on application of any party, unless the court orders that the hearing and determination thereof be deferred until the trial.

(e) Motion for More Definite Statement. If a pleading to which a responsive pleading is permitted is so vague or ambiguous that a party cannot reasonably be required to frame a responsive pleading, the party may move for a more definite statement before interposing a responsive pleading. The motion shall point out the defects complained of and the details desired. If the motion is granted and the order of the court is not obeyed within 10 days after notice of the order or within such other time as the court may fix, the court may strike the pleading to which the motion was directed or make such order as it deems just.

(f) Motion to Strike. Upon motion made by a party before responding to a pleading or, if no responsive pleading is permitted by these rules, upon motion made by a party within 20 days after the service of the pleading upon the party or upon the court's own initiative at any time, the court may order stricken from any pleading any insufficient
defense or any redundant, immaterial, impertinent, or scandalous matter.

(g) Consolidation of Defenses in Motion. A party who makes a motion under this rule may join with it any other motions herein provided for and then available to the party. If a party makes a motion under this rule but omits therefrom any defense or objection then available to the party which this rule permits to be raised by motion, the party shall not thereafter make a motion based on the defense or objection so omitted, except a motion as provided in subdivision (h)(2) hereof on any of the grounds there stated.

(h) Waiver or Preservation of Certain Defenses.

(1) A defense of lack of jurisdiction over the person, improper venue, insufficiency of process, or insufficiency of service of process is waived (A) if omitted from a motion in the circumstances described in subdivision (g), or (B) if it is neither made by motion under this rule nor included in a responsive pleading or an amendment thereof permitted by Rule 15(a) to be made as a matter of course.

(2) A defense of failure to state a claim upon which relief can be granted, a defense of failure to join a party indispensable under Rule 19, and an objection of failure to state a legal defense to a claim may be made in any pleading permitted or ordered under Rule 7(a), or by motion for judgment on the pleadings, or at the trial on the merits.

(3) Whenever it appears by suggestion of the parties or otherwise that the court lacks jurisdiction of the subject matter, the court shall dismiss the action.

Rule 13. Counterclaim and Cross-Claim

(a) **Compulsory Counterclaims.** A pleading shall state as a counterclaim any claim which at the time of serving the pleading the pleader has against any opposing party, if it arises out of the transaction or occurrence that is the subject matter of the opposing party's claim and does not require for its adjudication the presence of third parties of whom the court cannot acquire jurisdiction. But the pleader need not state the claim if (1) at the time the action was commenced the claim was the subject of another pending action, or (2) the opposing party brought suit upon the claim by attachment or other process by which the court did not acquire jurisdiction to render a personal judgment on that claim, and the pleader is not stating any counterclaim under this Rule 13.

(b) **Permissive Counterclaims.** A pleading may state as a counterclaim any claim against an opposing party not arising out of the transaction or occurrence that is the subject matter of the opposing party's claim.

(c) **Counterclaim Exceeding Opposing Claim.** A counterclaim may or may not diminish or defeat the recovery sought by the opposing party. It may claim relief exceeding in amount or different in kind from that sought in the pleading of the opposing party.

(d) **Counterclaim Against the United States.** These rules shall not be construed to enlarge beyond the limits now fixed by law the right to assert counterclaims or to claim credits against the United States or an officer or agency thereof.

(e) **Counterclaim Maturing or Acquired After Pleading.** A claim which either matured or was acquired by the pleader after serving a pleading may, with the permission of the court, be presented as a counterclaim by supplemental pleading.

(f) **Omitted Counterclaim.** When a pleader fails to set up a counterclaim through oversight, inadvertence, or excusable neglect, or when justice requires, the pleader may by leave of court set up the counterclaim by amendment.

(g) **Cross-Claim Against Co-Party.** A pleading may state as a cross-claim any claim by one party against a co-party arising out of the transaction or occurrence that is the subject matter either of the original action or of a counterclaim therein or relating to any property that is the subject matter of the original action. Such cross-claim may include a claim that the party against whom it is asserted is or may be liable to the cross-claimant for all or part of a claim asserted in the action against the cross-claimant.

(h) **Joinder of Additional Parties.** Persons other than those made parties to the original action may be made parties to a counterclaim or cross-claim in accordance with the provisions of Rules 19 and 20.

(i) Separate Trials; Separate Judgments. If the court orders separate trials as provided in Rule 42(b), judgment on a counterclaim or cross-claim may be rendered in accordance with the terms of Rule 54(b) when the court has jurisdiction so to do, even if the claims of the opposing party have been dismissed or otherwise disposed of.

Rule 14. Third-Party Practice

(a) **When Defendant May Bring in Third Party.** At any time after commencement of the action a defending party, as a third-party plaintiff, may cause a summons and complaint to be served upon a person not a party to the action who is or may be liable to the third-party plaintiff for all or part of the plaintiff's claim against the third-party plaintiff. The third-party plaintiff need not obtain leave to make the service if the third-party plaintiff files the third-party complaint not later than 10 days after serving the original answer. Otherwise the third-party plaintiff must obtain leave on motion upon notice to all parties to the action. The person served with the summons and third-party complaint, hereinafter called the third-party defendant, shall make any defenses to the third-party plaintiff's claim as provided in Rule 12 and any counterclaims against the third-party plaintiff and cross-claims against other third-party defendants as provided in Rule 13. The third-party defendant may assert against the plaintiff any defenses which the third-party plaintiff has to the plaintiff's claim. The third-party defendant may also assert any claim against the plaintiff arising out of the transaction or occurrence that is the subject matter of the plaintiff's claim against the third-party plaintiff. The plaintiff may assert any claim against the third-party defendant arising out of the transaction or occurrence that is the subject matter of the plaintiff's claim against the third-party plaintiff, and the third-party defendant thereupon shall assert any defenses as provided in Rule 12 and any counterclaims and cross-claims as provided in Rule 13. Any party may move to strike the third-party claim, or for its severance or separate trial. A third-party defendant may proceed under this rule against any person not a party to the action who is or may be liable to the third-party defendant for all or part of the claim made in the action against the third-party defendant. The third-party complaint, if within the admiralty and maritime jurisdiction, may be in rem against a vessel, cargo, or other property subject to admiralty or maritime process in rem, in which case references in this rule to the summons include the warrant of arrest, and references to the third-party plaintiff or defendant include, where appropriate, a person who asserts a right under Supplemental Rule C(6)(b)(i) in the property arrested.

(b) **When Plaintiff May Bring in Third Party.** When a counterclaim is asserted against a plaintiff, the plaintiff may cause a third party to be brought in under circumstances which under this rule would entitle a defendant to do so.

(c) **Admiralty and Maritime Claims.** When a plaintiff asserts an admiralty or maritime claim within the meaning of Rule 9(h), the defendant or person who asserts a right under Supplemental Rule C(6)(b)(i), as a third-party plaintiff, may bring in a third-party defendant who may be wholly or partly liable, either to the plaintiff or to the third-party plaintiff, by way of remedy over, contribution, or otherwise on account of the same transaction, occurrence, or series of transactions or occurrences. In such a case the third-party plaintiff may also demand judgment against the third-party defendant in favor of the plaintiff, in which event the third-party defendant shall make any defenses to the claim of the plaintiff as well as to that of the third-party plaintiff in the manner provided in Rule 12 and the action shall proceed as if the plaintiff had commenced it against the third-party defendant as well as the third-party plaintiff.

Rule 15. Amended and Supplemental Pleadings

(a) **Amendments.** A party may amend the party's pleading once as a matter of course at any time before a responsive pleading is served or, if the pleading is one to which no responsive pleading is permitted and the action has not been placed upon the trial calendar, the party may so amend it at any time within 20 days after it is served. Otherwise a party may amend the party's pleading only by leave of court or by written consent of the adverse party; and leave shall be freely given when justice so requires. A party shall plead in response to an amended pleading within the time remaining for response to the original pleading or within 10 days after service of the amended pleading, whichever period may be the longer, unless the court otherwise orders.

(b) **Amendments to Conform to the Evidence.** When issues not raised by the pleadings are tried by express or implied consent of the parties, they shall be treated in all respects as if they had been raised in the pleadings. Such amendment of the pleadings as may be necessary

to cause them to conform to the evidence and to raise these issues may be made upon motion of any party at any time, even after judgment; but failure so to
amend does not affect the result of the trial of these issues. If evidence is objected to at the trial on the ground that it is not within the issues made by the pleadings, the court may allow the pleadings to be amended and shall do so freely when the presentation of the merits of the action will be subserved thereby and the objecting party fails to satisfy the court that the admission of such evidence would prejudice the party in maintaining the party's action or defense upon the merits. The court may grant a continuance to enable the
objecting party to meet such evidence.

(c) **Relation Back of Amendments.** An Amendment of a pleading relates back to the date of the original pleading when

(1) relation back is permitted by the law that provides the statute of limitations applicable to the action, or

(2) the claim or defense asserted in the amended pleading arose out of the conduct, transaction, or occurrence set forth or attempted to be set forth in the original pleading, or

(3) the amendment changes the party or the naming of the party against whom a claim is asserted if the foregoing provision (2) is satisfied and, within the period provided by Rule 4(m) for service of the summons and complaint, the party to be brought in by amendment (A) has received such notice of the institution of the action that the party will
not be prejudiced in maintaining a defense on the merits, and (B) knew or should have known that, but for a mistake concerning the identity of the proper party, the action would have been brought against the party.

The delivery or mailing of process to the United States Attorney, or United States Attorney's designee, or the Attorney General of the United States, or an agency or officer who would have been a proper defendant if named, satisfies the requirement of subparagraphs (A) and (B) of this paragraph (3) with respect to the United States or any agency or officer thereof to be brought into the action as a defendant.

(d) **Supplemental Pleadings.** Upon motion of a party the court may, upon reasonable notice and upon such terms as are just, permit the party to serve a supplemental pleading setting forth transactions or occurrences or events which have happened since the date of the pleading sought to be supplemented. Permission may be granted even though the
original pleading is defective in its statement of a claim for relief or defense. If the court deems it advisable that the adverse party plead to the supplemental pleading, it shall so order, specifying the time therefor.

Rule 16. Pre-trial Conferences; Scheduling; Management

(a) **Pre-trial Conferences; Objectives.** In any action, the court may in its discretion direct the attorneys for the parties and any unrepresented parties to appear before it for a conference or conferences before trial for such purposes as

(1) expediting the disposition of the action;

(2) establishing early and continuing control so that the case will not be protracted because of lack of management;

(3) discouraging wasteful pre-trial activities;

(4) improving the quality of the trial through more thorough preparation, and;

(5) facilitating the settlement of the case.

(b) Scheduling and Planning. Except in categories of actions exempted by district court rule as inappropriate, the district judge, or a magistrate judge when authorized by district court rule, shall, after receiving the report from the parties under Rule 26(f) or after consulting with the attorneys for the parties and any unrepresented parties by a scheduling conference, telephone, mail, or other suitable means, enter a scheduling order that limits the time

(1) to join other parties and to amend the pleadings;
(2) to file motions; and
(3) to complete discovery.

The scheduling order may also include

(4) modifications of the times for disclosures under Rules 26(a) and 26(e)(1) and of the extent of discovery to be permitted;
(5) the date or dates for conferences before trial, a final pre-trial conference, and trial; and
(6) any other matters appropriate in the circumstances of the case.

The order shall issue as soon as practicable but in any event within 90 days after the appearance of a defendant and within 120 days after the complaint has been served on a defendant. A schedule shall not be modified except upon a showing of good cause and by leave of the district judge or, when authorized by local rule, by a magistrate judge.

(c) Subjects for Consideration at Pre-trial Conferences. At any conference under this rule consideration may be given, and the court may take appropriate action, with respect to

(1) the formulation and simplification of the issues, including the elimination of frivolous claims or defenses;
(2) the necessity or desirability of amendments to the pleadings;
(3) the possibility of obtaining admissions of fact and of documents which will avoid unnecessary proof, stipulations regarding the authenticity of documents, and advance rulings from the court on the admissibility of evidence;
(4) the avoidance of unnecessary proof and of cumulative evidence, and limitations or restrictions on the use of testimony under Rule 702 of the Federal Rules of Evidence;
(5) the appropriateness and timing of summary adjudication under Rule 56;
(6) the control and scheduling of discovery, including orders affecting disclosures and discovery pursuant to Rule 26 and Rules 29 through 37;
(7) the identification of witnesses and documents, the need and schedule for filing and exchanging pre-trial briefs, and the date or dates for further conferences and for trial;
(8) the advisability of referring matters to a magistrate judge or master;
(9) settlement and the use of special procedures to assist in resolving the dispute when authorized by statute or local rule;
(10) the form and substance of the pre-trial order;
(11) the disposition of pending motions;
(12) the need for adopting special procedures for managing potentially difficult or protracted actions that may involve complex issues, multiple parties, difficult legal questions, or unusual proof problems;
(13) an order for a separate trial pursuant to Rule 42(b) with respect to a claim, counter-claim, cross-claim, or third-party claim, or with respect to any particular issue in the case;
(14) an order directing a party or parties to present evidence early in the trial with respect to a manageable issue that could, on the evidence, be the basis for a judgment as a matter of law under Rule 50(a) or a judgment on partial findings under Rule 52(c);
(15) an order establishing a reasonable limit on the time allowed for presenting evidence; and

(16) such other matters as may facilitate the just, speedy, and inexpensive disposition of the action.

At least one of the attorneys for each party participating in any conference before trial shall have authority to enter into stipulations and to make admissions regarding all matters that the participants may reasonably anticipate may be discussed. If appropriate, the court may require that a party or its representative be present or reasonably available by telephone in order to consider possible settlement of the dispute.

(d) Final Pre-trial Conference. Any final pre-trial conference shall be held as close to the time of trial as reasonable under the circumstances. The participants at any such conference shall formulate a plan for trial, including a program for facilitating the admission of evidence. The conference shall be attended by at least one of the attorneys who will conduct the trial for each of the parties and by any unrepresented parties.

(e) Pre-trial Orders. After any conference held pursuant to this rule, an order shall be entered reciting the action taken. This order shall control the subsequent course of the action unless modified by a subsequent order. The order following a final pre-trial conference shall be modified only to prevent manifest injustice.

(f) Sanctions. If a party or party's attorney fails to obey a scheduling or pre-trial order, or if no appearance is made on behalf of a party at a scheduling or pre-trial conference, or if a party or party's attorney is substantially unprepared to participate in the conference, or if a party or party's attorney fails to participate in good faith, the judge, upon motion or the judge's own initiative, may make such orders with regard thereto as are just, and among others any of the orders provided in Rule 37(b)(2)(B), (C), (D). In lieu of or in addition to any other sanction, the judge shall require the party or the attorney representing the party or both to pay the reasonable expenses incurred because of any noncompliance with this rule, including attorney's fees, unless the judge finds that the noncompliance was substantially justified or that other circumstances make an award of expenses unjust.

IV. PARTIES

Rule 17. Parties Plaintiff and Defendant; Capacity

(a) Real Party In Interest. Every action shall be prosecuted in the name of the real party in interest. An executor, administrator, guardian, bailee, trustee of an express trust, a party with whom or in whose name a contract has been made for the benefit of another, or a party authorized by statute may sue in that person's own name without joining the party for whose benefit the action is brought; and when a statute of the United States so provides, an action for the use or benefit of another shall be brought in the name of the United States. No action shall be dismissed on the ground that it is not prosecuted in the name of the real party in interest until a reasonable time has been allowed after objection for ratification of commencement of the action by, or joinder or substitution of, the real party in interest; and such ratification, joinder, or substitution shall have the same effect as if the action had been commenced in the name of the real party in interest.

(b) Capacity to Sue or be Sued. The capacity of an individual, other than one acting in a representative capacity, to sue or be sued shall be determined by the law of the individual's domicile. The capacity of a corporation to sue or be sued shall be determined by the law under which it was organized. In all other cases capacity to sue or be sued shall be determined by the law of the state in which the district court is held, except (1) that a partnership or other unincorporated association, which has no such capacity by the law of such state, may sue or be sued in its common name for the purpose of enforcing for or against it a substantive right existing under the Constitution or laws of the United States, and (2) that the capacity of a receiver appointed by a court of the United States to sue or be sued in a court of the United States is governed by Title 28, U.S.C.754 and 959(a).

(c) Infants or Incompetent Persons. Whenever an infant or incompetent person has a representative, such as a general guardian, committee, conservator, or other like fiduciary, the representative may sue or defend on behalf of the infant or incompetent person. An infant or incompetent person who does not have a duly appointed representative may sue by next friend or by a guardian ad litem. The court shall appoint a guardian ad litem for an infant or incompetent person not otherwise represented in an action or shall make such other order as it deems proper for the protection of the infant or incompetent person.

Rule 18. Joinder of Claims and Remedies

(a) Joinder of Claims. A party asserting a claim to relief as an original claim, counterclaim, cross-claim, or third-party claim, may join, either as independent or as alternate claims, as many claims, legal, equitable, or maritime, as the party has against an opposing party.

(b) Joinder of Remedies; Fraudulent Conveyances. Whenever a claim is one heretofore cognizable only after another claim has been prosecuted to a conclusion, the two claims may be joined in a single action; but the court shall grant relief in that action only in accordance with the relative substantive rights of the parties. In particular, a plaintiff may state a claim for money and a claim to have set aside a conveyance fraudulent as to that plaintiff, without first having obtained a judgment establishing the claim for money.

Rule 19. Joinder of Persons Needed for Just Adjudication

(a) Persons to be Joined if Feasible. A person who is subject to service of process and whose joinder will not deprive the court of jurisdiction over the subject matter of the action shall be joined as a party in the action if (1) in the person's absence complete relief cannot be accorded among those already parties, or (2) the person claims an interest relating to the subject of the action and is so situated that the disposition of the action in the person's absence may (i) as a practical matter impair or impede the person's ability to protect that interest or (ii) leave any of the persons already parties subject to a substantial risk of incurring double, multiple, or otherwise inconsistent obligations by reason of the claimed interest. If the person has not been so joined, the court shall order that the person be made a party. If the person should join as a plaintiff but refuses to do so, the person may be made a defendant, or, in a proper case, an involuntary plaintiff. If the joined party objects to venue and joinder of that party would render the venue of the action improper, that party shall be dismissed from the action.

(b) Determination by Court Whenever Joinder not Feasible. If a person as described in subdivision (a)(1)-(2) hereof cannot be made a party, the court shall determine whether in equity and good conscience the action should proceed among the parties before it, or should be dismissed, the absent person being thus regarded as indispensable. The factors to be considered by the court include: first, to what extent a judgment rendered in the person's absence might be prejudicial to the person or those already parties; second, the extent to which, by protective provisions in the judgment, by the shaping of relief, or other measures, the prejudice can be lessened or avoided; third, whether a judgment rendered in the person's absence will be adequate; fourth, whether the plaintiff will have an adequate remedy if the action is dismissed for non-joinder.

(c) Pleading Reasons for Nonjoinder. A pleading asserting a claim for relief shall state the names, if known to the pleader, of any persons as described in subdivision (a)(1)-(2) hereof who are not joined, and the reasons why they are not joined.

(d) Exception of Class Actions. This rule is subject to the provisions of Rule 23.

Rule 20. Permissive Joinder of Parties
(a) Permissive Joinder. All persons may join in one action as plaintiffs if they assert any right to relief jointly, severally, or in the alternative in respect of or arising out of the same transaction, occurrence, or series of transactions or occurrences and if any question of law or fact common to all these persons will arise in the action. All persons (and any vessel, cargo or other property subject to admiralty process in rem) may be joined in one action as defendants if there is asserted against them jointly, severally, or in the alternative, any right to relief in respect of or arising out of the same transaction, occurrence, or series of transactions or occurrences and if any question of law or fact common to all defendants will arise in the action. A plaintiff or defendant need not be interested in obtaining or defending against all the relief demanded. Judgment may be given for one or more of the plaintiffs according to their respective rights to relief, and against one or more defendants according to their respective liabilities.

(b) Separate Trials. The court may make such orders as will prevent a party from being embarrassed, delayed, or put to expense by the inclusion of a party against whom the party asserts no claim and who asserts no claim against the party, and may order separate trials or make other orders to prevent delay or prejudice.

Rule 21. Misjoinder and Non-Joinder of Parties
Misjoinder of parties is not ground for dismissal of an action. Parties may be dropped or added by order of the court on motion of any party or of its own initiative at any stage of the action and on such terms as are just. Any claim against a party may be severed and proceeded with separately.

Rule 22. Interpleader
(1) Persons having claims against the plaintiff may be joined as defendants and required to interplead when their claims are such that the plaintiff is or may be exposed to double or multiple liability. It is not ground for objection to the joinder that the claims of the several claimants or the titles on which their claims depend do not have a common origin or are not identical but are adverse to and independent of one another, or that the plaintiff avers that the plaintiff is not liable in whole or in part to any or all of the claimants defendant exposed to similar liability may obtain such interpleader by way of cross-claim or counterclaim. The provisions of this rule supplement and do not in any way limit the joinder of parties permitted in Rule 20.

(2) The remedy herein provided is in addition to and in no way supersedes or limits the remedy provided by Title 28, U.S.C.1335, 1397, and 2361.Actions under those provisions shall be conducted in accordance with these rules.

Rule 23. Class Actions
(a) Prerequisites to a Class Action. One or more members of a class may sue or be sued as representative parties on behalf of all only if (1) the class is so numerous that joinder of all members is impracticable, (2) there are questions of law or fact common to the class, (3) the claims or defenses of the representative parties are typical of the claims or defenses of the

class, and (4) the representative parties will fairly and adequately protect the interests of the class.

(b) Class Actions Maintainable. An action may be maintained as a class action if the prerequisites of subdivision (a) are satisfied, and in addition:

(1) the prosecution of separate actions by or against individual members of the class would create a risk of:

(A) inconsistent or varying adjudications with respect to individual members of the class which would establish incompatible standards of conduct for the party opposing the class, or

(B) adjudications with respect to individual members of the class which would as a practical matter be dispositive of the interests of the other members not parties to the adjudications or substantially impair or impede their ability to protect their interests; or

(2) the party opposing the class has acted or refused to act on grounds generally applicable to the class, thereby making appropriate final injunctive relief or corresponding declaratory relief with respect to the class as a whole; or

(3) the court finds that the questions of law or fact common to the members of the class predominate over any questions affecting only individual members, and that a class action is superior to other available methods for the fair and efficient adjudication of the controversy. The matters pertinent to the findings include:(A) the interest of members of the class in individually controlling the prosecution or defense of separate actions; (B) the extent and nature of any litigation concerning the controversy already commenced by or against members of the class; (C) the desirability or undesirability of concentrating the litigation of the claims in the particular forum; (D) the difficulties likely to be encountered in the management of a class action.

(c) Determining by Order Whether to Certify a Class Action; Appointing Class Counsel; Notice and Membership in a Class; Judgment; Multiple Classes and Subclasses.

(1)

(A) When a person sues or is sued as a representative of a class, the court must—at an early practicable time—determine by order whether to certify the action as a class action.

(B) An order certifying a class action must define the class and the class claims, issues, or defenses, and must appoint class counsel under Rule 23(g).

(C) An order under Rule 23©(1) may be altered or amended before final judgment.

(2)

(A) For any class to be certified under Rule 23(b)(1) or (2), the court may direct appropriate notice to the class.

(B) For any class certified under Rule 23(b)(3), the court must direct the class members the best notice practicable under the circumstances, including individual notice to all members who can be identified through reasonable effort. The notice must concisely and clearly state in plain, easily understood language:

- the nature of the action,
- the definition of the class certified,
- the class claim, issues, or defenses,
- that a class member may enter an appearance through counsel if the member so desires,
- that the court will exclude from the class any member who requests exclusion, stating when and how members may elect to be excluded, and
- the binding effect of a class judgment on class members under Rule 23(c)(3).

(3) The judgment in an action maintained as a class action under subdivision (b)(1) or (b)(2), whether or not favorable to the class, shall include and describe those whom the court finds to be members of the class. The judgment in an action maintained as a class action under subdivision (b)(3), whether or not favorable to the class, shall include and specify or describe those to whom the notice provided in subdivision (c)(2) was directed, and who have not requested exclusion, and whom the court finds to be members of the class.

(4) When appropriate (A) an action may be brought or maintained as a class action with respect to particular issues, or (B) a class may be divided into subclasses and each subclass treated as a class, and the provisions of this rule shall then be construed and applied accordingly.

(d) Orders in Conduct of Actions. In the conduct of actions to which this rule applies, the court may make appropriate orders: (1) determining the course of proceedings or prescribing measures to prevent undue repetition or complication in the presentation of evidence or argument; (2) requiring, for the protection of the members of the class or otherwise for the fair conduct of the action, that notice be given in such manner as the court may direct to some or all of the members of any step in the action or of the proposed extent of the judgment, or of the opportunity of members to signify whether they consider the representation fair and adequate, to intervene and present claims or defenses, or otherwise to come into the action; (3) imposing conditions on the representative parties or on intervenors; (4) requiring that the pleadings be amended to eliminate therefrom allegations as to representation of absent persons, and that the action proceed accordingly; (5) dealing with similar procedural matters. The orders may be combined with an order under Rule 16, and may be altered or amended as may be desirable from time to time.

(e) Settlement, Voluntary Dismissal, or Compromise.

(1)

(A) The court must approve any settlement, voluntary dismissal, or compromise of the claims, issues, or defenses of a certified class.

(B) The court must direct notice in a reasonable manner to all class members who would be bound by a proposed settlement, voluntary dismissal, or compromise.

(C) The court may approve a settlement, voluntary dismissal, or compromise that would bind class members only after a hearing and on finding that the settlement, voluntary dismissal, or compromise is fair, reasonable, and adequate.

(2) The parties seeking approval of a settlement, voluntary dismissal, or compromise under Rule 23(e)(1) must file a statement identifying any agreement made in connection with the proposed settlement, voluntary dismissal, or compromise.

(3) In an action previously certified as a class action under Rule 23(b)(3), the court may refuse to approve a settlement unless it affords a new opportunity to request exclusion to individual class members who had an earlier opportunity to request exclusion but did not do so.

(4)

(A) Any class member may object to a proposed settlement, voluntary dismissal, or compromise that requires court approval under Rule 23(e)(1)(A).

(B) An objection made under Rule 23(e)(4)(A) may be withdrawn only with the court's approval.

(f) Appeals. A court of appeals may in its discretion permit an appeal from an order of a district court granting or denying class action certification under this rule if application is made to it within ten days after entry of the order. An appeal does not stay proceedings in the district court unless the district judge or the court of appeals so orders.

(g) Class Counsel.
(1) Appointing Class Counsel.
(A) Unless a statute provides otherwise, a court that certifies a class must appoint class counsel.
(B) An attorney appointed to serve as class counsel must fairly and adequately represent the interests of the class.
(C) In appointing class counsel, the court
   (i) must consider:
   - the work counsel has done in identifying or investigating potential claims in the action,
   - counsel's experience in handling class actions, other complex litigation, and claims of the type asserted in the action,
   - counsel's knowledge of the applicable law, and
   - the resources counsel will commit to representing the class;

   (ii) may consider any other matter pertinent to counsel's ability to fairly and adequately represent the interests of the class;
   (iii) may direct potential class counsel to provide information on any subject pertinent to the appointment and to propose terms for attorney fees and nontaxable costs; and
   (iv) may make further orders in connection with the appointment.

(2) Appointment Procedure.
(A) The court may designate interim counsel to act on behalf of the putative class before determining whether to certify the action as a class action.
(B) When there is one applicant for appointment as class counsel, the court may appoint that applicant only if the applicant is adequate under Rule 23(g)(1)(B) and (C). If more than one adequate applicant seeks appointment as class counsel, the court must appoint the applicant best able to represent the interests of the class.
(C) The order appointing class counsel may include provisions about the award of attorney fees or nontaxable costs under Rule 23(h).

(h) Attorney Fees Award. In an action certified as a class action, the court may award reasonable attorney fees and nontaxable costs authorized by law or by agreement of the parties as follows:

(1) Motion for Award of Attorney Fees. A claim for an award of attorney fees and nontaxable costs must be made by motion under Rule 54(d)(2), subject to the provisions of this subdivision, at a time set by the court. Notice of the motion must be served on all parties and, for motions by class counsel, directed to class members in a reasonable manner.

(2) Objections to Motion. A class member, or a party from whom payment is sought, may object to the motion.

(3) Hearing and Findings. The court may hold a hearing and must find the facts and state its conclusions of law on the motion under Rule 52(a).

(4) Reference to Special Master or Magistrate Judge. The court may refer issues related to the amount of the award to a special master or to a magistrate judge as provided in Rule 54(d)(2)(D).

Rule 23.1. Derivative Actions by Shareholders

In a derivative action brought by one or more shareholders or members to enforce a right of a corporation or of an unincorporated association, the corporation or association having failed to enforce a right which may properly be asserted by it, the complaint shall be verified and shall allege (1) that the plaintiff was a shareholder or member at the time of the transaction of which the plaintiff complains or that the plaintiff's share or membership thereafter devolved on the plaintiff by operation of law, and (2) that the action is not a collusive one to confer jurisdiction on a court of the United States which it would not otherwise have. The complaint shall also allege with particularity the efforts, if any, made by the plaintiff to obtain the action the plaintiff desires from the directors or comparable authority and, if necessary, from the shareholders or members, and the reasons for the plaintiff's failure to obtain the action or for not making the effort. The derivative action may not be maintained if it appears that the plaintiff does not fairly and adequately represent the interests of the shareholders or members similarly situated in enforcing the right of the corporation or association. The action shall not be dismissed or compromised without the approval of the court, and notice of the proposed dismissal or compromise shall be given to shareholders or members in such manner as the court directs.

Rule 23.2. Actions Relating to Unincorporated Associations

An action brought by or against the members of an unincorporated association as a class by naming certain members as representative parties may be maintained only if it appears that the representative parties will fairly and adequately protect the interests of the association and its members. In the conduct of the action the court may make appropriate orders corresponding with those described in Rule 23(d), and the procedure for dismissal or compromise of the action shall correspond with that provided in Rule 23(e).

Rule 24. Intervention

(a) Intervention of Right. Upon timely application anyone shall be permitted to intervene in an action:(1) when a statute of the United States confers an unconditional right to intervene; or (2) when the applicant claims an interest relating to the property or trans-action which is the subject of the action and the applicant is so situated that the disposition of the action may as a practical matter impair or impede the applicant's ability to protect that interest, unless the applicant's interest is adequately represented by existing parties.

(b) Permissive Intervention. Upon timely application anyone may be permitted to intervene in an action:(1) when a statute of the United States confers a conditional right to intervene; or (2) when an applicant's claim or defense and the main action have a question of law or fact in common. When a party to an action relies for ground of claim or defense upon any statute or executive order administered by a federal or state governmental officer or agency or upon any regulation, order, requirement or agreement issued or made pursuant to the statute or executive order, the officer or agency upon timely application may be permitted to intervene in the action. In exercising its discretion the court shall consider whether the intervention will unduly delay or prejudice the adjudication of the rights of the original parties.

(c) Procedure. A person desiring to intervene shall serve a motion to intervene upon the parties as provided in Rule 5. The motion shall state the grounds therefor and shall be accompanied by a pleading setting forth the claim or defense for which intervention is sought. The same procedure shall be followed when a statute of the United States gives a right to intervene. When the constitutionality of an act of Congress affecting the public interest is drawn in question in any action in which the United States or an officer, agency, or employee thereof is not a party, the court shall notify the Attorney General of the United States as provided in Title 28, U.S.C. § 2403. When the constitutionality of any statute of a State affecting the public interest is drawn in question in any action in which that State or any agency, officer, or employee thereof is not a party, the court shall notify the attorney general of the State as provided in Title 28, U.S.C. § 2403. A party challenging the constitutionality of legislation should call the attention of the court to its consequential duty, but failure to do so is not a waiver of any constitutional right otherwise timely asserted.

Rule 25. Substitution of Parties
(a) Death.

(1) If a party dies and the claim is not thereby extinguished, the court may order substitution of the proper parties. The motion for substitution may be made by any party or by the successors or representatives of the deceased party and, together with the notice of hearing, shall be served on the parties as provided in Rule 5 and upon persons not parties in the manner provided in Rule 4 for the service of a summons, and may be served in any judicial district. Unless the motion for substitution is made not later than 90 days after the death is suggested upon the record by service of a statement of the fact of the death as provided herein for the service of the motion, the action shall be dismissed as to the deceased party.

(2) In the event of the death of one or more of the plaintiffs or of one or more of the defendants in an action in which the right sought to be enforced survives only to the surviving plaintiffs or only against the surviving defendants, the action does not abate. The death shall be suggested upon the record and the action shall proceed in favor of or against the surviving parties.

(b) Incompetency. If a party becomes incompetent, the court upon motion served as provided in subdivision (a) of this rule may allow the action to be continued by or against the party's representative.

(c) Transfer of Interest. In case of any transfer of interest, the action may be continued by or against the original party, unless the court upon motion directs the person to whom the interest is transferred to be substituted in the action or joined with the original party. Service of the motion shall be made as provided in subdivision (a) of this rule.

(d) Public Officers; Death or Separation from Office.

(1) When a public officer is a party to an action in his official capacity and during its pendency dies, resigns, or otherwise ceases to hold office, the action does not abate and the officer's successor is automatically substituted as a party. Proceedings following the substitution shall be in the name of the substituted party, but any misnomer not affecting the substantial rights of the parties shall be disregarded. An order of substitution may be entered at any time, but the omission to enter such an order shall not affect the substitution.

(2) A public officer who sues or is sued in an official capacity may be described as a party by the officer's official title rather than by name; but the court may require the officer's name to be added.

V. DEPOSITIONS AND DISCOVERY

Rule 26. General Provisions Governing Discovery; Duty of Disclosure
(a) Required Disclosures; Methods to Discover Additional Matter.

(1) Initial Disclosures. Except in categories of proceedings specified in Rule 26(a)(1)(E), or to the extent otherwise stipulated or directed by order, a party must, without awaiting a discovery request, provide to other parties:

(A) the name and, if known, the address and telephone number of each individual likely to have discoverable information that the disclosing party may use to support its claims or defenses, unless solely for impeachment, identifying the subjects of the information;

(B) a copy of, or a description by category and location of, all documents, data compilations, and tangible things that are in the possession, custody, or control of the party and that the disclosing party may use to support its claims or defenses, unless solely for impeachment;

(C) a computation of any category of damages claimed by the disclosing party, making available for inspection and copying as under Rule 34 the documents or other evidentiary material, not privileged or protected from disclosure, on which such computation is based, including materials bearing on the nature and extent of injuries suffered; and

(D) for inspection and copying as under Rule 34 any insurance agreement under which any person carrying on an insurance business may be liable to satisfy part or all of a judgment which may be entered in the action or to indemnify or reimburse for payments made to satisfy the judgment.

(E) The following categories of proceedings are exempt from initial disclosure under Rule 26(a)(1) :

(i) an action for review on an administrative record;

(ii) a petition for habeas corpus or other proceeding to challenge a criminal conviction or sentence;

(iii) an action brought without counsel by a person in custody of the United States, a state, or a state subdivision;

(iv) an action to enforce or quash an administrative summons or subpoena;

(v) an action by the United States to recover benefit payments;

(vi) an action by the United States to collect on a student loan guaranteed by the United States;

(vii) a proceeding ancillary to proceedings in other courts; and

(viii) an action to enforce an arbitration award.

These disclosures must be made at or within 14 days after the Rule 26(f) conference unless a different time is set by stipulation or court order, or unless a party objects during the conference that initial disclosures are not appropriate in the circumstances of the action and states the objection in the Rule 26(f) discovery plan. In ruling on the objection, the court must determine what disclosures - if any - are to be made, and set the time for disclosure. Any party first served or otherwise joined after the Rule 26(f) conference must make these disclosures within 30 days after being served or joined unless a different time is set by stipulation or court order. A party must make its initial disclosures based on the information then reasonably available to it and is not excused from making its disclosures because it has not fully completed its investigation of the case or because it challenges the sufficiency of another party's disclosures or because another party has not made its disclosures.

(2) Disclosure of Expert Testimony.

(A) In addition to the disclosures required by paragraph (1), a party shall disclose to other parties the identity of any person who may be used at trial to present evidence under Rules 702, 703, or 705 of the Federal Rules of Evidence.

(B) Except as otherwise stipulated or directed by the court, this disclosure shall, with respect to a witness who is retained or specially employed to provide expert testimony in the case or whose duties as an employee of the party regularly involve giving expert testimony, be accompanied by a written report prepared and signed by the witness. The report shall contain a complete statement of all opinions to be expressed and the basis and reasons therefor; the data or other information considered by the witness in forming the opinions; any exhibits to be used as a summary of or support for the opinions; the qualifications of the witness, including a list of all publications authored by the witness within the preceding ten years; the compensation to be paid for the study and testimony; and a listing of any other cases in which the witness has testified as an expert at trial or by deposition within the preceding four years.

(C) These disclosures shall be made at the times and in the sequence directed by the court. In the absence of other directions from the court or stipulation by the parties, the disclosures shall be made at least 90 days before the trial date or the date the case is to be ready for trial or, if the evidence is intended solely to contradict or rebut evidence on the same subject matter identified by another party under paragraph (2)(B), within 30 days after the disclosure made by the other party. The parties shall supplement these disclosures when required under subdivision (e)(1).

(3) **Pre-trial Disclosures.** In addition to the disclosures required by Rule 26(a)(1) and (2), a party must provide to other parties and promptly file with the court the following information regarding the evidence that it may present at trial other than solely for impeachment:

(A) the name and, if not previously provided, the address and telephone number of each witness, separately identifying those whom the party expects to present and those whom the party may call if the need arises;

(B) the designation of those witnesses whose testimony is expected to be presented by means of a deposition and, if not taken stenographically, a transcript of the pertinent portions of the deposition testimony; and

(C) an appropriate identification of each document or other exhibit, including summaries of other evidence, separately identifying those which the party expects to offer and those which the party may offer if the need arises.

Unless otherwise directed by the court, these disclosures must be made at least 30 days before trial. Within 14 days thereafter, unless a different time is specified by the court, a party may serve and promptly file a list disclosing (i) any objections to the use under Rule 32(a) of a deposition designated by another party under Rule 26(a)(3)(B), and (ii) any objection, together with the grounds therefor, that may be made to the admissibility of materials identified under Rule 26(a)(3)(C). Objections not so disclosed, other than objections under Rules 402 and 403 of the Federal Rules of Evidence, are waived unless excused by the court for good cause.

(4) **Form of Disclosures; Filing.** Unless the court orders otherwise, all disclosures under Rules 26(a)(1) through (3) must be made in writing, signed, and served.

(5) **Methods to Discover Additional Matter.** Parties may obtain discovery by one or more of the following methods: depositions upon oral examination or written questions; written interrogatories; production of documents or things or permission to enter upon land or other property under Rule 34 or 45(a)(1)(C), for inspection and other purposes; physical and mental examinations; and requests for admission.

(b) Discovery Scope and Limits. Unless otherwise limited by order of the court in accordance with these rules, the scope of discovery is as follows:

(1) **In General.** Parties may obtain discovery regarding any matter, not privileged, that is relevant to the claim or defense of any party, including the existence, description, nature, custody, condition, and location of any books, documents, or other tangible things and the identity and location of persons having knowledge of any discoverable matter. For good cause, the court may order discovery of any matter relevant to the subject matter involved in the action. Relevant information need not be admissible at the trial if the discovery appears

reasonably calculated to lead to the discovery of admissible evidence. All discovery is subject to the limitations imposed by Rule 26(b)(2)(i), (ii), and (iii).

(2) Limitations. By order, the court may alter the limits in these rules on the number of depositions and interrogatories or the length of depositions under Rule 30 . By order or local rule, the court may also limit the number of requests under Rule 36 . The frequency or extent of use of the discovery methods otherwise permitted under these rules and by any local rule shall be limited by the court if it determines that: (i) the discovery sought is unreasonably cumulative or duplicative, or is obtainable from some other source that is more convenient, less burdensome, or less expensive; (ii) the party seeking discovery has had ample opportunity by discovery in the action to obtain the information sought; or (iii) the burden or expense of the proposed discovery outweighs its likely benefit, taking into account the needs of the case, the amount in controversy, the parties' resources, the importance of the issues at stake in the litigation, and the importance of the proposed discovery in resolving the issues. The court may act upon its own initiative after reasonable notice or pursuant to a motion under Rule 26(c) .

(3) Trial Preparation: Materials. Subject to the provisions of subdivision (b)(4) of this rule, a party may obtain discovery of documents and tangible things otherwise discoverable under subdivision (b)(1) of this rule and prepared in anticipation of litigation or for trial by or for another party or by or for that other party's representative (including the other party's attorney, consultant, surety, indemnitor, insurer, or agent) only upon a showing that the party seeking discovery has substantial need of the materials in the preparation of the party's case and that the party is unable without undue hardship to obtain the substantial equivalent of the materials by other means. In ordering discovery of such materials when the required showing has been made, the court shall protect against disclosure of the mental impressions, conclusions, opinions, or legal theories of an attorney or other representative of a party concerning the litigation.

A party may obtain without the required showing a statement concerning the action or its subject matter previously made by that party. Upon request, a person not a party may obtain without the required showing a statement concerning the action or its subject matter previously made by that person. If the request is refused, the person may move for a court order. The provisions of Rule 37(a)(4) apply to the award of expenses incurred in relation to the motion. For purposes of this paragraph, a statement previously made is (A) a written statement signed or otherwise adopted or approved by the person making it, or (B) a stenographic, mechanical, electrical, or other recording, or a transcription thereof, which is a substantially verbatim recital of an oral statement by the person making it and contemporaneously recorded.

(4) Trial Preparation: Experts.

(A) A party may depose any person who has been identified as an expert whose opinions may be presented at trial. If a report from the expert is required under subdivision (a)(2)(B), the deposition shall not be conducted until after the report is provided.

(B) A party may, through interrogatories or by deposition, discover facts known or opinions held by an expert who has been retained or specially employed by another party in anticipation of litigation or preparation for trial and who is not expected to be called as a witness at trial only as provided in Rule 35(b) or upon a showing of exceptional circumstances under which it is impracticable for the party seeking discovery to obtain facts or opinions on the same subject by other means.

(C) Unless manifest injustice would result, (i) the court shall require that the party seeking discovery pay the expert a reasonable fee for time spent in responding to discovery under this subdivision; and (ii) with respect to discovery obtained under subdivision (b)(4)(B) of this rule the court shall require the party seeking discovery to pay the other party a fair portion of the fees and expenses reasonably incurred by the latter party in obtaining facts and opinions from the expert.

(5) Claims of Privilege or Protection of Trial Preparation Materials. When a party withholds information otherwise discoverable under these rules by claiming that it is privileged or subject to protection as trial preparation material, the party shall make the claim expressly and shall describe the nature of the documents, communications, or things not produced or disclosed in a manner that, without revealing information itself privileged or protected, will enable other parties to assess the applicability of the privilege or protection.

(c) Protective Orders. Upon motion by a party or by the person from whom discovery is sought, accompanied by a certification that the movant has in good faith conferred or attempted to confer with other affected parties in an effort to resolve the dispute without court action, and for good cause shown, the court in which the action is pending or alternatively, on matters relating to a deposition, the court in the district where the deposition is to be taken may make any order which justice requires to protect a party or person from annoyance, embarrassment, oppression, or undue burden or expense, including one or more of the following:

(1) that the disclosure or discovery not be had:

(2) that the disclosure or discovery may be had only on specified terms and conditions, including a designation of the time or place;

(3) that the discovery may be had only by a method of discovery other than that selected by the party seeking discovery;

(4) that certain matters not be inquired into, or that the scope of the disclosure or discovery be limited to certain matters;

(5) that discovery be conducted with no one present except persons designated by the court;

(6) that a deposition, after being sealed, be opened only by order of the court;

(7) that a trade secret or other confidential research, development, or commercial information not be revealed or be revealed only in a designated way; and

(8) that the parties simultaneously file specified documents or information enclosed in sealed envelopes to be opened as directed by the court.

If the motion for a protective order is denied in whole or in part, the court may, on such terms and conditions as are just, order that any party or other person provide or permit discovery. The provisions of Rule 37(a)(4) apply to the award of expenses incurred in relation to the motion.

(d) Timing and Sequence of Discovery. Except in categories of proceedings exempted from initial disclosure under Rule 26(a)(1)(E), or when authorized under these rules or by order or agreement of the parties, a party may not seek discovery from any source before the parties have conferred as required by Rule 26(f). Unless the court upon motion, for the convenience of parties and witnesses and in the interests of justice, orders otherwise, methods of discovery may be used in any sequence, and the fact that a party is conducting discovery, whether by deposition or otherwise, does not operate to delay any other party's discovery.

(e) Supplementation of Disclosures and Responses. A party who has made a disclosure under subdivision (a) or responded to a request for discovery with a disclosure or response is under a duty to supplement or correct the disclosure or response to include information thereafter acquired if ordered by the court or in the following circumstances:

(1) A party is under a duty to supplement at appropriate intervals its disclosures under subdivision (a) if the party learns that in some material respect the information disclosed is incomplete or incorrect and if the additional or corrective information has not otherwise been made known to the other parties during the discovery process or in writing. With respect to testimony of an expert from whom a report is required under subdivision (a)(2)(B) the duty extends both to information contained in the report and to information provided through a deposition of the expert, and any additions or other changes to this
information shall be disclosed by the time the party's disclosures under Rule 26(a)(3) are due.

(2) A party is under a duty seasonably to amend a prior response to an interrogatory, request for production, or request for admission if the party learns that the response is in some material respect incomplete or incorrect and if the additional or corrective information has not otherwise been made known to the other parties during the discovery
process or in writing.

(f) Conference of Parties; Planning for Discovery.
Except in categories of proceedings exempted from initial disclosure under Rule 26(a)(1)(E) or when otherwise ordered, the parties must, as soon as practicable and in any event at least 21 days before a scheduling conference is held or a scheduling order is due under Rule 16(b), confer to consider the nature and basis of their claims and defenses and the possibilities for a prompt settlement or resolution of the case, to make or arrange for the disclosures required by Rule 26(a)(1), and to develop a proposed discovery plan that indicates the parties' views and proposals concerning:

(1) what changes should be made in the timing, form, or requirement for disclosures under Rule 26(a), including a statement as to when disclosures under Rule 26(a)(1) were made or will be made;

(2) the subjects on which discovery may be needed, when discovery should be completed, and whether discovery should be conducted in phases or be limited to or focused upon particular issues;

(3) what changes should be made in the limitations on discovery imposed under these rules or by local rule, and what other limitations should be imposed; and

(4) any other orders that should be entered by the court under Rule 26(c) or under Rule 16(b) and (c).

The attorneys of record and all unrepresented parties that have appeared in the case are jointly responsible for arranging the conference, for attempting in good faith to agree on the proposed discovery plan, and for submitting to the court within 14 days after the conference a written report outlining the plan. A court may order that the parties or attorneys attend the conference in person. If necessary to comply with its expedited schedule for Rule 16(b) conferences, a court may by local rule (i) require that the conference between the parties occur fewer than 21 days before the scheduling conference is held or a scheduling order is due under Rule 16(b), and (ii) require that the written report outlining the discovery plan be filed fewer than 14 days after the conference between the parties, or excuse the parties from submitting a written report and permit them to report orally on their discovery plan at the Rule 16(b) conference.

(g) Signing of Disclosures, Discovery Requests, Responses, and Objections.
(1) Every disclosure made pursuant to subdivision (a)(1) or subdivision (a)(3) shall be signed by at least one attorney of record in the attorney's individual name, whose address shall be stated. An unrepresented party shall sign the disclosure and state the party's

address. The signature of the attorney or party constitutes a certification that to the best of the signer's knowledge, information, and belief, formed after a reasonable inquiry, the disclosure is complete and correct as of the time it is made.

(2) Every discovery request, response, or objection made by a party represented by an attorney shall be signed by at least one attorney of record in the attorney's individual name, whose address shall be stated. An unrepresented party shall sign the request, response, or objection and state the party's address. The signature of the attorney or party constitutes a certification that to the best of the signer's knowledge, information, and belief, formed after a reasonable inquiry, the request, response, or objection is:

(A) consistent with these rules and warranted by existing law or a good faith argument for the extension, modification, or reversal of existing law;

(B) not interposed for any improper purpose, such as to harass or to cause unnecessary delay or needless increase in the cost of litigation; and

(C) not unreasonable or unduly burdensome or expensive, given the needs of the case, the discovery already had in the case, the amount in controversy, and the importance of the issues at stake in the litigation.

If a request, response, or objection is not signed, it shall be stricken unless it is signed promptly after the omission is called to the attention of the party making the request, response, or objection, and a party shall not be obligated to take any action with respect to it until it is signed.

(3) If without substantial justification a certification is made in violation of the rule, the court, upon motion or upon its own initiative, shall impose upon the person who made the certification, the party on whose behalf the disclosure, request, response, or objection is made, or both, an appropriate sanction, which may include an order to pay the amount of the reasonable expenses incurred because of the violation, including a reasonable attorney's fee.

Rule 27. Depositions Before Action or Pending Appeal

(a) Before Action.

(1) Petition. A person who desires to perpetuate testimony regarding any matter that may be cognizable in any court of the United States may file a verified petition in the United States district court in the district of the residence of any expected adverse party. The petition shall be entitled in the name of the petitioner and shall show: 1, that the petitioner expects to be a party to an action cognizable in a court of the United States but is presently unable to bring it or cause it to be brought, 2, the subject matter of the expected action and the petitioner's interest therein, 3, the facts which the petitioner desires to establish by the proposed testimony and the reasons for desiring to perpetuate it, 4, the names or a description of the persons the petitioner expects will be adverse parties and their addresses so far as known, and 5, the names and addresses of the persons to be examined and the substance of the testimony which the petitioner expects to elicit from each, and shall ask for an order authorizing the petitioner to take the depositions of the persons to be examined named in the petition, for the purpose of perpetuating their testimony.

(2) Notice and Service. The petitioner shall thereafter serve a notice upon each person named in the petition as an expected adverse party, together with a copy of the petition, stating that the petitioner will apply to the court, at a time and place named therein, for the order described in the petition. At least 20 days before the date of hearing the notice shall be served either within or without the district or state in the manner provided in Rule 4(d) for service of summons; but if such service cannot with due diligence be made upon any expected

adverse party named in the petition, the court may make such order as is just for service by publication or otherwise, and shall appoint, for persons not served in the manner provided in Rule 4(d), an attorney who shall represent them, and, in case they are not otherwise represented, shall cross-examine the deponent. If any expected adverse party is a minor or incompetent the provisions of Rule 17(c) apply.

(3) Order and Examination. If the court is satisfied that the perpetuation of the testimony may prevent a failure or delay of justice, it shall make an order designating or describing the persons whose depositions may be taken and specifying the subject matter of the examination and whether the depositions shall be taken upon oral examination or written interrogatories. The depositions may then be taken in accordance with these rules; and the court may make orders of the character provided for by Rules 34 and 35. For the purpose of applying these rules to depositions for perpetuating testimony, each reference therein to the court in which the action is pending shall be deemed to refer to the court in which the petition for such deposition was filed.

(4) Use of Deposition. If a deposition to perpetuate testimony is taken under these rules or if, although not so taken, it would be admissible in evidence in the courts of the state in which it is taken, it may be used in any action involving the same subject matter subsequently brought in a United States district court, in accordance with the provisions of Rule 32(a).

(b) Pending Appeal. If an appeal has been taken from a judgment of a district court or before the taking of an appeal if the time therefor has not expired, the district court in which the judgment was rendered may allow the taking of the depositions of witnesses to perpetuate their testimony for use in the event of further proceedings in the district court. In such case the party who desires to perpetuate the testimony may make a motion in the district court for leave to take the depositions, upon the same notice and service thereof as if the action was pending in the district court. The motion shall show (1) the names and addresses of persons to be examined and the substance of the testimony which the party expects to elicit from each; (2) the reasons for perpetuating their testimony. If the court finds that the perpetuation of the testimony is proper to avoid a failure or delay of justice, it may make an order allowing the depositions to be taken and may make orders of the character provided for by Rules 34 and 35, and thereupon the depositions may be taken and used in the same manner and under the same conditions as are prescribed in these rules for depositions taken in actions pending in the district court.

(c) Perpetuation by Action. This rule does not limit the power of a court to entertain an action to perpetuate testimony.

Rule 28. Persons Before Whom Depositions May Be Taken

(a) Within the United States. Within the United States or within a territory or insular possession subject to the jurisdiction of the United States, depositions shall be taken before an officer authorized to administer oaths by the laws of the United States or of the place where the examination is held, or before a person appointed by the court in which the action is pending. A person so appointed has power to administer oaths and take testimony. The term officer as used in Rules 30, 31 and 32 includes a person appointed by the court or designated by the parties under Rule 29.

(b) In Foreign Countries. Depositions may be taken in a foreign country (1) pursuant to any applicable treaty or convention, or (2) pursuant to a letter of request (whether or not captioned a letter rogatory), or (3) on notice before a person authorized to administer oaths in the place where the examination is held, either by the law thereof or by the law of the United States, or (4) before a person commissioned by the court, and a person so commissioned shall have the power by virtue of the commission to administer any necessary oath and take testimony. A commission or a letter of request shall be issued on application and notice and on terms that are just and appropriate. It is not requisite to the issuance of a commission or a letter of request that the taking of the deposition in any other manner is impracticable or inconvenient; and both a commission and a letter of request may be issued in proper cases. A notice or commission may designate the person before whom the deposition is to be taken either by name or descriptive title. A letter of request may be addressed "To the Appropriate Authority in [here name the country]." When a letter of request or any other device is used pursuant to any applicable treaty or convention, it shall be captioned in the form prescribed by that treaty or convention. Evidence obtained in response to a letter of request need not be excluded merely because it is not a verbatim transcript, because the testimony was not taken under oath, or because of any similar departure from the requirements for depositions taken within the United States under these rules.

(c) Disqualification for Interest. No deposition shall be taken before a person who is a relative or employee or attorney or counsel of any of the parties, or is a relative or employee of such attorney or counsel, or is financially interested in the action.

Rule 29. Stipulations Regarding Discovery Procedure

Unless otherwise directed by the court, the parties may by written stipulation (1) provide that depositions may be taken before any person, at any time or place, upon any notice, and in any manner and when so taken may be used like other depositions, and (2) modify other procedures governing or limitations placed upon discovery, except that stipulations extending the time provided in Rules 33, 34, and 36 for responses to discovery, for hearing of a motion, or for trial, be made only with the approval of the court.

Rule 30. Depositions Upon Oral Examination

(a) When Depositions May Be Taken; When Leave Required.

(1) A party may take the testimony of any person, including a party, by deposition upon oral examination without leave of court except as provided in paragraph (2). The attendance of witnesses may be compelled by subpoena as provided in Rule 45.

(2) A party must obtain leave of court, which shall be granted to the extent consistent with the principles stated in Rule 26(b)(2), if the person to be examined is confined in prison or if, without the written stipulation of the parties.

(A) a proposed deposition would result in more than ten depositions being taken under this rule or Rule 31 by the plaintiffs, or by the defendants, or by third-party defendants;

(B) the person to be examined already has been deposed in the case; or

(C) a party seeks to take a deposition before the time specified in Rule 26(d) unless the notice contains a certification, with supporting facts, that the person to be examined is expected to leave the United States and be unavailable for examination in this country unless deposed before that time.

(b) Notice of Examination: General Requirements; Method of Recording; Production of Documents and Things; Deposition of Organization; Deposition by Telephone.

(1) A party desiring to take the deposition of any person upon oral examination shall give reasonable notice in writing to every other party to the action. The notice shall state the time and place for taking the deposition and the name and address of each person to be examined, if known, and, if the name is not known, a general description sufficient to identify the person or the particular class or group to which the person belongs. If a subpoena duces tecum is to be served on the person to be examined, the designation of the materials to be produced as set forth in the subpoena shall be attached to, or included in, the notice.

(2) The party taking the deposition shall state in the notice the method by which the testimony shall be recorded. Unless the court orders otherwise, it may be recorded by sound, sound-and-visual, or stenographic means, and the party taking the deposition shall bear the cost of the recording. Any party may arrange for a transcription to be made from the recording of a deposition taken by non-stenographic means.

(3) With prior notice to the deponent and other parties, any party may designate another method to record the deponent's testimony in addition to the method specified by the person taking the deposition. The additional record or transcript shall be made at that party's expense unless the court otherwise orders.

(4) Unless otherwise agreed by the parties, a deposition shall be conducted before an officer appointed or designated under Rule 28 and shall begin with a statement on the record by the officer that includes (A) the officer's name and business address; (B) the date, time, and place of the deposition; (C) the name of the deponent; (D) the administration of the oath or affirmation to the deponent; and (E) an identification of all persons present. If the deposition is recorded other than stenographically, the officer shall repeat items (A) through (C) at the beginning of each unit of recorded tape or other recording medium. The appearance or demeanor of deponents or attorneys shall not be distorted through camera or sound-recording techniques. At the end of the deposition, the officer shall state on the record that the deposition is complete and shall set forth any stipulations made by counsel concerning the custody of the transcript or recording and the exhibits, or concerning other pertinent matters.

(5) The notice to a party deponent may be accompanied by a request made in compliance with Rule 34 for the production of documents and tangible things at the taking of the deposition. The procedure of Rule 34 shall apply to the request.

(6) A party may in the party's notice and in a subpoena name as the deponent a public or private corporation or a partnership or association or governmental agency and describe with reasonable particularity the matters on which examination is requested. In that event, the organization so named shall designate one or more officers, directors, or managing agents, or other persons who consent to testify on its behalf, and may set forth, for each person designated, the matters on which the person will testify. A subpoena shall advise a non-party organization of its duty to make such a designation. The persons so designated shall testify as to matters known or reasonably available to the organization. This subdivision (b)(6) does not preclude taking a deposition by any other procedure authorized in these rules.

(7) The parties may stipulate in writing or the court may upon motion order that a deposition be taken by telephone or other remote electronic means. For the purposes of this rule and Rules 28(a), 37(a)(1), and 37(b)(1) a deposition taken by such means is taken in the district and at the place where the deponent is to answer questions.

(c) **Examination and Cross-Examination; Record of Examination; Oath; Objections.** Examination and cross-examination of witnesses may proceed as permitted at the trial under the provisions of the Federal Rules of Evidence except Rules 103 and 615.

The officer before whom the deposition is to be taken shall put the witness on oath or affirmation and shall personally, or by someone acting under the officer's direction and in the officer's presence, record the testimony of the witness. The testimony shall be taken stenographically or recorded by any other method authorized by subdivision (b)(2) of this rule. All objections made at the time of the examination to the qualifications of the officer taking the deposition, to the manner of taking it, to the evidence presented, to the conduct of any party, or to any other aspect of the proceedings shall be noted by the officer upon the record of the deposition; but the examination shall proceed, with the testimony being taken subject to the objections. In lieu of participating in the oral examination, parties may serve written questions in a sealed envelope on the party taking the deposition and the party taking the deposition shall transmit them to the officer, who shall propound them to the witness and record the answers verbatim.

(d) **Schedule and Duration; Motion to Terminate or Limit Examination.**

(1) Any objection during a deposition must be stated concisely and in a non-argumentative and non-suggestive manner. A person may instruct a deponent not to answer only when necessary to preserve a privilege, to enforce a limitation directed by the court, or to present a motion under Rule 30(d)(4).

(2) Unless otherwise authorized by the court or stipulated by the parties, a deposition is limited to one day of seven hours. The court must allow additional time consistent with Rule 26(b)(2) if needed for a fair examination of the deponent or if the deponent or another person, or other circumstance, impedes or delays the examination.

(3) If the court finds that any impediment, delay, or other conduct has frustrated the fair examination of the deponent, it may impose upon the persons responsible an appropriate sanction, including the reasonable costs and attorney's fees incurred by any parties as a result thereof.

(4) At any time during a deposition, on motion of a party or of the deponent and upon a showing that the examination is being conducted in bad faith or in such manner as unreasonably to annoy, embarrass, or oppress the deponent or party, the court in which the action is pending or the court in the district where the deposition is being taken may order the officer conducting the examination to cease forthwith from taking the deposition, or may limit the scope and manner of the taking of the deposition as provided in Rule 26(c). If the order made terminates the examination, it may be resumed thereafter only upon the order of the court in which the action is pending. Upon demand of the objecting party or deponent, the taking of the deposition must be suspended for the time necessary to make a motion for an order. The provisions of Rule 37(a)(4) apply to the award of expenses incurred in relation to the motion.

(e) **Review by Witness; Changes; Signing**. If requested by the deponent or a party before completion of the deposition, the deponent shall have 30 days after being notified by the officer that the transcript or recording is available in which to review the transcript or recording and, if there are changes in form or substance, to sign a statement reciting such changes and the reasons given by the deponent for making them. The officer shall indicate in the certificate prescribed by subdivision (f)(1) whether any review was requested and, if so, shall append any changes made by the deponent during the period allowed.

(f) **Certification and Filing by Officer; Exhibits; Copies; Notice of Filing.**

(1) The officer must certify that the witness was duly sworn by the officer and that the deposition is a true record of the testimony given by the witness. This certificate must be in writing and accompany the record of the deposition. Unless otherwise ordered by the court, the officer must securely seal the deposition in an envelope or package indorsed with the title

of the action and marked "Deposition of [here insert name of witness]" and must promptly send it to the attorney who arranged for the transcript or recording, who must store it under conditions that will protect it against loss, destruction, tampering, or deterioration. Documents and things produced for inspection during the examination of the witness must, upon the request of a party, be marked for identification and annexed to the deposition and may be inspected and copied by any party, except that if the person producing the materials desires to retain them the person may (A) offer copies to be marked for identification and annexed to the deposition and to serve thereafter as originals if the person affords to all parties fair opportunity to verify the copies by comparison with the originals, or (B) offer the originals to be marked for identification, after giving to each party an opportunity to inspect and copy them, in which event the materials may then be used in the same manner as if annexed to the deposition. Any party may move for an order that the original be annexed to and returned with the deposition to the court, pending final disposition of the case.

(2) Unless otherwise ordered by the court or agreed by the parties, the officer shall retain stenographic notes of any deposition taken stenographically or a copy of the recording of any deposition taken by another method. Upon payment of reasonable charges therefor, the officer shall furnish a copy of the transcript or other recording of the deposition to any party or to the deponent.

(3) The party taking the deposition shall give prompt notice of its filing to all other parties.

(g) Failure to Attend or to Serve Subpoena; Expenses.

(1) If the party giving the notice of the taking of a deposition fails to attend and proceed therewith and another party attends in person or by attorney pursuant to the notice, the court may order the party giving the notice to pay to such other party the reasonable expenses incurred by that party and that party's attorney in attending, including reasonable attorney's fees.

(2) If the party giving the notice of the taking of a deposition of a witness fails to serve a subpoena upon the witness and the witness because of such failure does not attend, and if another party attends in person or by attorney because that party expects the deposition of that witness to be taken, the court may order the party giving the notice to pay to such other party the reasonable expenses incurred by that party and that party's attorney in attending, including reasonable attorney's fees.

Rule 31. Depositions Upon Written Questions
(a) Serving Questions; Notice.

(1) A party may take the testimony of any person, including a party, by deposition upon written questions without leave of court except as provided in paragraph (2). The attendance of witnesses may be compelled by the use of subpoena as provided in Rule 45.

(2) A party must obtain leave of court, which shall be granted to the extent consistent with the principles stated in Rule 26(b)(2), if the person to be examined is confined in prison or if, without the written stipulation of the parties.

(A) a proposed deposition would result in more than ten depositions being taken under this rule or Rule 30 by the plaintiffs, or by the defendants, or by third-party defendants;

(B) the person to be examined has already been deposed in the case; or

(C) a party seeks to take a deposition before the time specified in Rule 26(d).

(3) A party desiring to take a deposition upon written questions shall serve them upon every other party with a notice stating (1) the name and address of the person who is to

answer them, if known, and if the name is not known, a general description sufficient to identify the person or the particular class or group to which the person belongs, and (2) the name or descriptive title and address of the officer before whom the deposition is to be taken. A deposition upon written questions may be taken of a public or private corporation or a partnership or association or governmental agency in accordance with the provisions of Rule 30(b)(6).

(4) Within 14 days after the notice and written questions are served, a party may serve cross questions upon all other parties. Within 7 days after being served with cross questions, a party may serve redirect questions upon all other parties. Within 7 days after being served with redirect questions, a party may serve recross questions upon all other parties. The court may for cause shown enlarge or shorten the time.

(b) **Officer to Take Responses and Prepare Record.** A copy of the notice and copies of all questions served shall be delivered by the party taking the deposition to the officer designated in the notice, who shall proceed promptly, in the manner provided by Rule 30(c), (e), and (f), to take the testimony of the witness in response to the questions and to prepare, certify, and file or mail the deposition, attaching thereto the copy of the notice and the questions received by the officer.

(c) **Notice of Filing.** When the deposition is filed the party taking it shall promptly give notice thereof to all other parties.

Rule 32. Use of Depositions in Court Proceedings.

(a) **Use of Depositions.** At the trial or upon the hearing of a motion or an interlocutory proceeding, any part or all of a deposition, so far as admissible under the rules of evidence applied as though the witness were then present and testifying, may be used against any party who was present or represented at the taking of the deposition or who had reasonable notice thereof, in accordance with any of the following provisions:

(1) Any deposition may be used by any party for the purpose of contradicting or impeaching the testimony of deponent as a witness, or for any other purpose permitted by the Federal Rules of Evidence.

(2) The deposition of a party or of anyone who at the time of taking the deposition was an officer, director, or managing agent, or a person designated under Rule 30(b)(6) or 31(a) to testify on behalf of a public or private corporation, partnership or association or governmental agency which is a party may be used by an adverse party for any purpose.

(3) The deposition of a witness, whether or not a party, may be used by any party for any purpose if the court finds:

(A) that the witness is dead; or

(B) that the witness is at a greater distance than 100 miles from the place of trial or hearing, or is out of the United States, unless it appears that the absence of the witness was procured by the party offering the deposition; or

(C) that the witness is unable to attend or testify because of age, illness, infirmity, or imprisonment; or

(D) that the party offering the deposition has been unable to procure the attendance of the witness by subpoena; or

(E) upon application and notice, that such exceptional circumstances exist as to make it desirable, in the interest of justice and with due regard to the importance of presenting the testimony of witnesses orally in open court, to allow the deposition to be used.

A deposition taken without leave of court pursuant to a notice under Rule 30(a)(2)(C) shall not be used against a party who demonstrates that, when served with the notice, it was unable through the exercise of diligence to obtain counsel to represent it at the taking of the deposition; nor shall a deposition be used against a party who, having received less than 11 days notice of a deposition, has promptly upon receiving such notice filed a motion for a protective order under Rule 26(c)(2) requesting that the deposition not be held or be held at a different time or place and such motion is pending at the time the deposition is held.

(4) If only part of a deposition is offered in evidence by a party, an adverse party may require the offeror to introduce any other part which ought in fairness to be considered with the part introduced, and any party may introduce any other parts.

Substitution of parties pursuant to Rule 25 does not affect the right to use depositions previously taken; and, when an action has been brought in any court of the United States or of any State and another action involving the same subject matter is afterward brought between the same parties or their representatives or successors in interest, all depositions lawfully taken and duly filed in the former action may be used in the latter as if originally taken therefor. A deposition previously taken may also be used as permitted by the Federal Rules of Evidence.

(b) Objections to Admissibility. Subject to the provisions of Rule 28(b) and subdivision (d)(3) of this rule, objection may be made at the trial or hearing to receiving in evidence any deposition or part thereof for any reason which would require the exclusion of the evidence if the witness were then present and testifying.

(c) Form of Presentation. Except as otherwise directed by the court, a party offering deposition testimony pursuant to this rule may offer it in stenographic or non-stenographic form, but, if in non-stenographic form, the party shall also provide the court with a transcript of the portions so offered. On request of any party in a case tried before a jury, deposition testimony offered other than for impeachment purposes shall be presented in non-stenographic form, if available, unless the court for good cause orders otherwise.

(d) Effect of Errors and Irregularities in Depositions.

(1) As to Notice. All errors and irregularities in the notice for taking a deposition are waived unless written objection is promptly served upon the party giving the notice.

(2) As to Disqualification of Officer. Objection to taking a deposition because of disqualification of the officer before whom it is to be taken is waived unless made before the taking of the deposition begins or as soon thereafter as the disqualification becomes known or could be discovered with reasonable diligence.

(3) As to Taking of Deposition.

(A) Objections to the competency of a witness or to the competency, relevancy, or materiality of testimony are not waived by failure to make them before or during the taking of the deposition, unless the ground of the objection is one which might have been obviated or removed if presented at that time.

(B) Errors and irregularities occurring at the oral examination in the manner of taking the deposition, in the form of the questions or answers, in the oath or affirmation, or in the conduct of parties, and errors of any kind which might be obviated, removed, or cured if promptly presented, are waived unless seasonable objection thereto is made at the taking of the deposition.

(C) Objections to the form of written questions submitted under Rule 31 are waived unless served in writing upon the party propounding them within the time allowed for serving the succeeding cross or other questions and within 5 days after service of the last questions authorized.

(4) As to Completion and Return of Deposition. Errors and irregularities in the manner in which the testimony is transcribed or the deposition is prepared, signed, certified, sealed, indorsed, transmitted, filed, or otherwise dealt with by the officer under Rules 30 and 31 are waived unless a motion to suppress the deposition or some part thereof is made with reasonable promptness after such defect is, or with due diligence might have been, ascertained.

At the trial or upon the hearing of a motion or an interlocutory proceeding, any part or all of a deposition, so far as admissible under the rules of evidence applied as though the witness were then present and testifying, may be used against any party who was present or represented at the taking of the deposition or who had reasonable notice thereof, in accordance with any of the following provisions:

(1) Any deposition may be used by any party for the purpose of contradicting or impeaching the testimony of deponent as a witness, or for any other purpose permitted by the Federal Rules of Evidence.

(2) The deposition of a party or of anyone who at the time of taking the deposition was an officer, director, or managing agent, or a person designated under Rule 30(b)(6) or 31(a) to testify on behalf of a public or private corporation, partnership or association or governmental agency which is a party may be used by an adverse party for any purpose.

(3) The deposition of a witness, whether or not a party, may be used by any party for any purpose if the court finds:

(A) that the witness is dead; or

(B) that the witness is at a greater distance than 100 miles from the place of trial or hearing, or is out of the United States, unless it appears that the absence of the witness was procured by the party offering the deposition; or

(C) that the witness is unable to attend or testify because of age, illness, infirmity, or imprisonment; or

(D) that the party offering the deposition has been unable to procure the attendance of the witness by subpoena; or

(E) upon application and notice, that such exceptional circumstances exist as to make it desirable, in the interest of justice and with due regard to the importance of presenting the testimony of witnesses orally in open court, to allow the deposition to be used.

A deposition taken without leave of court pursuant to a notice under Rule 30(a)(2)(C) shall not be used against a party who demonstrates that, when served with the notice, it was unable through the exercise of diligence to obtain counsel to represent it at the taking of the deposition; nor shall a deposition be used against a party who, having received less than 11 days notice of a deposition, has promptly upon receiving such notice filed a motion for a protective order under Rule 26(c)(2) requesting that the deposition not be held or be held at a different time or place and such motion is pending at the time the deposition is held.

(4) If only part of a deposition is offered in evidence by a party, an adverse party may require the offeror to introduce any other part which ought in fairness to be considered with the part introduced, and any party may introduce any other parts.

Substitution of parties pursuant to Rule 25 does not affect the right to use depositions previously taken; and, when an action has been brought in any court of the United States or of any State and another action involving the same subject matter is afterward brought between the same parties or their representatives or successors in interest, all depositions lawfully taken and duly filed in the former action may be used in the latter as if originally taken therefor. A deposition previously taken may also be used as permitted by the Federal Rules of Evidence.

(b) Objections to Admissibility. Subject to the provisions of Rule 28(b) and subdivision (d)(3) of this rule, objection may be made at the trial or hearing to receiving in evidence any deposition or part thereof for any reason which would require the exclusion of the evidence if the witness were then present and testifying.

(c) Form of Presentation. Except as otherwise directed by the court, a party offering deposition testimony pursuant to this rule may offer it in stenographic or non-stenographic form, but, if in non-stenographic form, the party shall also provide the court with a transcript of the portions so offered. On request of any party in a case tried before a jury, deposition testimony offered other than for impeachment purposes shall be presented in non-stenographic form, if available, unless the court for good cause orders otherwise.

(d) Effect of Errors and Irregularities in Depositions.

(1) As to Notice. All errors and irregularities in the notice for taking a deposition are waived unless written objection is promptly served upon the party giving the notice.

(2) As to Disqualification of Officer. Objection to taking a deposition because of disqualification of the officer before whom it is to be taken is waived unless made before the taking of the deposition begins or as soon thereafter as the disqualification becomes known or could be discovered with reasonable diligence.

(3) As to Taking of Deposition.

(A) Objections to the competency of a witness or to the competency, relevancy, or materiality of testimony are not waived by failure to make them before or during the taking of the deposition, unless the ground of the objection is one which might have been obviated or removed if presented at that time.

(B) Errors and irregularities occurring at the oral examination in the manner of taking the deposition, in the form of the questions or answers, in the oath or affirmation, or in the conduct of parties, and errors of any kind which might be obviated, removed, or cured if promptly presented, are waived unless seasonable objection thereto is made at the taking of the deposition.

(C) Objections to the form of written questions submitted under Rule 31 are waived unless served in writing upon the party propounding them within the time allowed for serving the succeeding cross or other questions and within 5 days after service of the last questions authorized.

(4) As to Completion and Return of Deposition. Errors and irregularities in the manner in which the testimony is transcribed or the deposition is prepared, signed, certified, sealed, indorsed, transmitted, filed, or otherwise dealt with by the officer under Rules 30 and 31 are waived unless a motion to suppress the deposition or some part thereof is made with reasonable promptness after such defect is, or with due diligence might have been, ascertained.

Rule 33. Interrogatories to Parties

(a) Availability. Without leave of court or written stipulation, any party may serve upon any other party written interrogatories, not exceeding 25 in number including all discrete subparts, to be answered by the party served or, if the party served is a public or private corporation or a partnership or association or governmental agency, by any officer or agent, who shall furnish such information as is available to the party. Leave to serve additional interrogatories shall be granted to the extent consistent with the principles of Rule 26(b)(2). Without leave of court or written stipulation, interrogatories may not be served before the time specified in Rule 26(d).

(b) Answers and Objections.

(1) Each interrogatory shall be answered separately and fully in writing under oath, unless it is objected to, in which event the objecting party shall state the reasons for objection and shall answer to the extent the interrogatory is not objectionable.

(2) The answers are to be signed by the person making them, and the objections signed by the attorney making them.

(3) The party upon whom the interrogatories have been served shall serve a copy of the answers, and objections if any, within 30 days after the service of the interrogatories. A shorter or longer time may be directed by the court or, in the absence of such an order, agreed to in writing by the parties subject to Rule 29.

(4) All grounds for an objection to an interrogatory shall be stated with specificity. Any ground not stated in a timely objection is waived unless the party's failure to object is excused by the court for good cause shown.

(5) The party submitting the interrogatories may move for an order under Rule 37(a) with respect to any objection to or other failure to answer an interrogatory.

(c) Scope; Use at Trial. Interrogatories may relate to any matters which can be inquired into under Rule 26(b)(1), and the answers may be used to the extent permitted by the rules of evidence.

An interrogatory otherwise proper is not necessarily objectionable merely because an answer to the interrogatory involves an opinion or contention that relates to fact or the application of law to fact, but the court may order that such an interrogatory need not be answered until after designated discovery has been completed or until a pre-trial conference or other later time.

(d) Option to Produce Business Records. Where the answer to an interrogatory may be derived or ascertained from the business records of the party upon whom the interrogatory has been served or from an examination, audit or inspection of such business records, including a compilation, abstract or summary thereof and the burden of deriving or ascertaining the answer is substantially the same for the party serving the interrogatory as for the party served, it is a sufficient answer to such interrogatory to specify the records from which the answer may be derived or ascertained and to afford to the party serving the interrogatory reasonable opportunity to examine, audit or inspect such records and to make copies, compilations, abstracts or summaries. A specification shall be in sufficient detail to permit the interrogating party to locate and to identify, as readily as can the party served, the records from which the answer may be ascertained.

Rule 34. Production of Documents and Things and Entry Upon Land for Inspection and Other Purposes

(a) Scope. Any party may serve on any other party a request (1) to produce and permit the party making the request, or someone acting on the requestor's behalf, to inspect and copy, any designated documents (including writings, drawings, graphs, charts, photo-graphs, phonorecords, and other data compilations from which information can be obtained, translated, if necessary, by the respondent through detection devices into reasonably usable form), or to inspect and copy, test, or sample any tangible things which constitute or contain matters within the scope of Rule 26(b) and which are in the possession, custody or control of the party upon whom the request is served; or (2) to permit entry upon designated land or other property in the possession or control of the party upon whom the request is served for the purpose of inspection and measuring, surveying, photographing, testing, or sampling the property or any designated object or operation thereon, within the scope of Rule 26(b).

(b) Procedure. The request shall set forth, either by individual item or by category, the items to be inspected, and describe each with reasonable particularity. The request shall specify a reasonable time, place, and manner of making the inspection and performing the related acts. Without leave of court or written stipulation, a request may not be served before the time specified in Rule 26(d).

The party upon whom the request is served shall serve a written response within 30 days after the service of the request. A shorter or longer time may be directed by the court or, in the absence of such an order, agreed to in writing by the parties, subject to Rule 29. The response shall state, with respect to each item or category, that inspection and related activities will be permitted as requested, unless the request is objected to, in which event the reasons for the objection shall be stated. If objection is made to part of an item or category, the part shall be specified and inspection permitted of the remaining parts. The party submitting the request may move for an order under Rule 37(a) with respect to any objection to or other failure to respond to the request or any part thereof, or any failure to permit inspection as requested.

A party who produces documents for inspection shall produce them as they are kept in the usual course of business or shall organize and label them to correspond with the categories in the request.

(c) Persons Not Parties. A person not a party to the action may be compelled to produce documents and things or to submit to an inspection as provided in Rule 45.

Rule 35. Physical and Mental Examinations of Persons

(a) Order for Examination. When the mental or physical condition (including the blood group) of a party or of a person in the custody or under the legal control of a party, is in controversy, the court in which the action is pending may order the party to submit to a physical or mental examination by a suitably licensed or certified examiner or to produce for examination the person in the party's custody or legal control. The order may be made only on motion for good cause shown and upon notice to the person to be examined and to all parties and shall specify the time, place, manner, conditions, and scope of the examination and the person or persons by whom it is to be made.

(b) Report of Examiner.

(1) If requested by the party against whom an order is made under Rule 35(a) or the person examined, the party causing the examination to be made shall deliver to the requesting party a copy of the detailed written report of the examiner setting out the examiner's findings, including results of all tests made, diagnoses and conclusions, together with like reports of all earlier examinations of the same condition. After delivery the party causing the examination shall be entitled upon request to receive from the party against whom the order is made a like report of any examination, previously or thereafter made, of the same condition, unless, in the case of a report of examination of a person not a party, the party shows that the party is unable to obtain it. The court on motion may make an order against a party requiring delivery of a report on such terms as are just, and if an examiner fails or refuses to make a report the court may exclude the examiner's testimony if offered at trial.

(2) By requesting and obtaining a report of the examination so ordered or by taking the deposition of the examiner, the party examined waives any privilege the party may have in that action or any other involving the same controversy, regarding the testimony of every other person who has examined or may thereafter examine the party in respect of the same mental or physical condition.

(3) This subdivision applies to examinations made by agreement of the parties, unless the agreement expressly provides otherwise. This subdivision does not preclude discovery of a report of an examiner or the taking of a deposition of the examiner in accordance with the provisions of any other rule.

Rule 36. Requests for Admission

(a) Request for Admission. A party may serve upon any other party a written request for the admission, for purposes of the pending action only, of the truth of any matters within the scope of Rule 26(b)(1) set forth in the request that relate to statements or opinions of fact or of the application of law to fact, including the genuineness of any documents described in the request. Copies of documents shall be served with the request unless they have been or are otherwise furnished or made available for inspection and copying. Without leave of court or written stipulation, requests for admission may not be served before the time specified in Rule 26(d).

Each matter of which an admission is requested shall be separately set forth. The matter is admitted unless, within 30 days after service of the request, or within such shorter or longer time as the court may allow or as the parties may agree to in writing, subject to Rule 29, the party to whom the request is directed serves upon the party requesting the admission a written answer or objection addressed to the matter, signed by the party or by the party's attorney. If objection is made, the reasons therefor shall be stated. The answer shall specifically deny the matter or set forth in detail the reasons why the answering party cannot truthfully admit or deny the matter. A denial shall fairly meet the substance of the requested admission, and when good faith requires that a party qualify an answer or deny only a part of the matter of which an admission is requested, the party shall specify so much of it as is true and qualify or deny the remainder. An answering party may not give lack of information or knowledge as a reason for failure to admit or deny unless the party states that the party has made reasonable inquiry and that the information known or readily obtainable by the party is insufficient to enable the party to admit or deny. A party who considers that a matter of which an admission has been requested presents a genuine issue for trial may not, on that ground alone, object to the request; the party may, subject to the provisions of Rule 37(c), deny the matter or set forth reasons why the party cannot admit or deny it.

The party who has requested the admissions may move to determine the sufficiency of the answers or objections. Unless the court determines that an objection is justified, it shall order that an answer be served. If the court determines that an answer does not comply with the requirements of this rule, it may order either that the matter is admitted or that an amended answer be served. The court may, in lieu of these orders, determine that final disposition of the request be made at a pre-trial conference or at a designated time prior to trial. The provisions of Rule 37(a)(4) apply to the award of expenses incurred in relation to the motion.

(b) Effect of Admission. Any matter admitted under this rule is conclusively established unless the court on motion permits withdrawal or amendment of the admission. Subject to the provision of Rule 16 governing amendment of a pre-trial order, the court may permit withdrawal or amendment when the presentation of the merits of the action will be subserved thereby and the party who obtained the admission fails to satisfy the court that withdrawal or amendment will prejudice that party in maintaining the action or defense on the merits. Any admission made by a party under this rule is for the purpose of the pending action only and is not an admission for any other purpose nor may it be used against the party in any other proceeding.

Rule 37. Failure to Make or Cooperate in Discovery: Sanctions

(a) Motion For Order Compelling Disclosure or Discovery. A party, upon reasonable notice to other parties and all persons affected thereby, may apply for an order compelling disclosure or discovery as follows:

(1) Appropriate Court. An application for an order to a party shall be made to the court in which the action is pending. An application for an order to a person who is not a party shall be made to the court in the district where the discovery is being, or is to be, taken.

(2) Motion.

(A) If a party fails to make a disclosure required by Rule 26(a), any other party may move to compel disclosure and for appropriate sanctions. The motion must include a certification that the movant has in good faith conferred or attempted to confer with the party not making the disclosure in an effort to secure the disclosure without court action.

(B) If a deponent fails to answer a question propounded or submitted under Rules 30 or 31, or a corporation or other entity fails to make a designation under Rule 30(b)(6) or 31(a), or a party fails to answer an interrogatory submitted under Rule 33, or if a party, in response to a request for inspection submitted under Rule 34, fails to respond that inspection will be permitted as requested or fails to permit inspection as requested, the discovering party may move for an order compelling an answer, or a designation, or an order compelling inspection in accordance with the request. The motion must include a certification that the movant has in good faith conferred or attempted to confer with the person or party failing to make the discovery in an effort to secure the information or material without court action. When taking a deposition on oral examination, the proponent of the question may complete or adjourn the examination before applying for an order.

(3) Evasive or Incomplete Disclosure, Answer, or Response. For purposes of this subdivision an evasive or incomplete disclosure, answer, or response is to be treated as a failure to disclose, answer, or respond.

(4) Expenses and Sanctions.

(A) If the motion is granted or if the disclosure or requested discovery is provided after the motion was filed, the court shall, after affording an opportunity to be heard, require the party or deponent whose conduct necessitated the motion or the party or attorney advising such conduct or both of them to pay to the moving party the reasonable expenses incurred in making the motion, including attorney's fees, unless the court finds that the motion was filed without the movant's first making a good faith effort to obtain the disclosure or discovery without court action, or that the opposing party's nondisclosure, response, or objection was substantially justified, or that other circumstances make an award of expenses unjust.

(B) If the motion is denied, the court may enter any protective order authorized under Rule 26(c) and shall, after affording an opportunity to be heard, require the moving party or the attorney filing the motion or both of them to pay to the party or deponent who opposed the motion the reasonable expenses incurred in opposing the motion, including attorney's fees, unless the court finds that the making of the motion was substantially justified or that other circumstances make an award of expenses unjust.

(C) If the motion is granted in part and denied in part, the court may enter any protective order authorized under Rule 26(c) and may, after affording an opportunity to be heard, apportion the reasonable expenses incurred in relation to the motion among the parties and persons in a just manner.

(b) Failure to Comply with Order.

(1) Sanctions by Court in District Where Deposition is Taken. If a deponent fails to be sworn or to answer a question after being directed to do so by the court in the district in which the deposition is being taken, the failure may be considered a contempt of that court.

(2) Sanctions by Court in Which Action is Pending. If a party or an officer, director, or managing agent of a party or a person designated under Rule 30(b)(6) or 31(a) to testify on behalf of a party fails to obey an order to provide or permit discovery, including an order made under subdivision (a) of this rule or Rule 35, or if a party fails to obey an order entered under Rule 26(f), the court in which the action is pending may make such orders in regard to the failure as are just, and among others the following:

(A) An order that the matters regarding which the order was made or any other designated facts shall be taken to be established for the purposes of the action in accordance with the claim of the party obtaining the order;

(B) An order refusing to allow the disobedient party to support or oppose designated claims or defenses, or prohibiting that party from introducing designated matters in evidence;

(C) An order striking out pleadings or parts thereof, or staying further proceedings until the order is obeyed, or dismissing the action or proceeding or any part thereof, or rendering a judgment by default against the disobedient party;

(D) In lieu of any of the foregoing orders or in addition thereto, an order treating as a contempt of court the failure to obey any orders except an order to submit to a physical or mental examination;

(E) Where a party has failed to comply with an order under Rule 35(a) requiring that party to produce another for examination, such orders as are listed in paragraphs (A), (B), and (C) of this subdivision, unless the party failing to comply shows that that party is unable to produce such person for examination.

In lieu of any of the foregoing orders or in addition thereto, the court shall require the party failing to obey the order or the attorney advising that party or both to pay the reasonable expenses, including attorney's fees, caused by the failure, unless the court finds that the failure was substantially justified or that other circumstances make an award of expenses unjust.

(c) Failure to Disclose; False or Misleading Disclosure; Refusal to Admit.

(1) A party that without substantial justification fails to disclose information required by Rule 26(a) or 26(e)(1), or to amend a prior response to discovery as required by Rule 26(e)(2), is not, unless such failure is harmless, permitted to use as evidence at a trial, at a hearing, or on a motion any witness or information not so disclosed. In addition to or in lieu of this sanction, the court, on motion and after affording an opportunity to be heard, may impose other appropriate sanctions. In addition to requiring payment of reasonable expenses, including attorney's fees, caused by the failure, these sanctions may include any of the actions authorized under Rule 37(b)(2)(A), (B), and (C) and may include informing the jury of the failure to make the disclosure.

(2) If a party fails to admit the genuineness of any document or the truth of any matter as requested under Rule 36, and if the party requesting the admissions thereafter proves the genuineness of the document or the truth of the matter, the requesting party may apply to the court for an order requiring the other party to pay the reasonable expenses incurred in making that proof, including reasonable attorney's fees. The court shall make the order unless it finds that (A) the request was held objectionable pursuant to Rule 36(a), or (B) the admission sought was of no substantial importance, or (C) the party failing to admit had reasonable ground to believe that the party might prevail on the matter, or (D) there was other good reason for the failure to admit.

(d) Failure of Party to Attend at Own Deposition or Serve Answers to Interrogatories or Respond to Request for Inspection. [Effective Dec. 1, 1993.] If a party or an officer, director, or managing agent of a party or a person designated under Rule 30(b)(6) or 31(a) to testify on behalf of a party fails (1) to appear before the officer who is to take the deposition, after being served with a proper notice, or (2) to serve answers or objections to interrogatories submitted under Rule 33, after proper service of the interrogatories, or (3) to serve a written response to a request for inspection submitted under Rule 34, after proper service of the request, the court in which the action is pending on motion may make such orders in regard to the failure as are just, and among others it may take any action authorized under subparagraphs (A), (B), and (C) of subdivision (b)(2) of this rule. Any motion specifying a failure under clause (2) or (3) of this subdivision shall include a certification that the movant has in good faith conferred or attempted to confer with the party failing to answer or respond in an effort to obtain such answer or response without court action. In lieu of any order or in addition thereto, the court shall require the party failing to act or the attorney advising that party or both to pay the reasonable expenses, including attorney's fees, caused by the failure unless the court finds that the failure was substantially justified or that other circumstances make an award of expenses unjust.

The failure to act described in this subdivision may not be excused on the ground that the discovery sought is objectionable unless the party failing to act has a pending motion for a protective order as provided by Rule 26(c).

(e) [Abrogated]

(f) [Repealed. Pub.L. 96-481, Title II, ☐ 205(a), Oct. 21, 1980, 94 Stat. 2330.]

(g) Failure to Participate in the Framing of a Discovery Plan. If a party or a party's attorney fails to participate in good faith in the development and submission of a proposed discovery plan as required by Rule 26(f), the court may, after opportunity for hearing, require such party or attorney to pay to any other party the reasonable expenses, including attorney's fees, caused by the failure.

VI. TRIALS

Rule 38. Jury Trial of Right

(a) Right Preserved. The right of trial by jury as declared by the Seventh Amendment to the Constitution or as given by a statute of the United States shall be preserved to the parties inviolate.

(b) Demand. Any party may demand a trial by jury of any issue triable of right by a jury by (1) serving upon the other parties a demand therefor in writing at any time after the commencement of the action and not later than 10 days after the service of the last pleading directed to such issue, and (2) filing the demand as required by Rule 5(d). Such demand may be indorsed upon a pleading of the party.

(c) Same: Specification of Issues. In the demand a party may specify the issues which the party wishes so tried; otherwise the party shall be deemed to have demanded trial by jury for all the issues so triable. If the party has demanded trial by jury for only some of the issues, any other party within 10 days after service of the demand or such lesser time as the court may order, may serve a demand for trial by jury of any other or all of the issues of fact in the action.

(d) **Waiver.** The failure of a party to serve and file a demand as required by this rule constitutes a waiver by the party of trial by jury. A demand for trial by jury made as herein provided may not be withdrawn without the consent of the parties.

(e) **Admiralty and Maritime Claims.** These rules shall not be construed to create a right to trial by jury of the issues in an admiralty or maritime claim within the meaning of Rule 9(h).

Rule 39. Trial by Jury or by the Court

(a) **By Jury.** When trial by jury has been demanded as provided in Rule 38, the action shall be designated upon the docket as a jury action. The trial of all issues so demanded shall be by jury, unless (1) the parties or their attorneys of record, by written stipulation filed with the court or by an oral stipulation made in open court and entered in the record, consent to trial by the court sitting without a jury or (2) the court upon motion or of its own initiative finds that a right of trial by jury of some or all of those issues does not exist under the Constitution or statutes of the United States.

(b) **By the Court.** Issues not demanded for trial by jury as provided in Rule 38 shall be tried by the court; but, notwithstanding the failure of a party to demand a jury in an action in which such a demand might have been made of right, the court in its discretion upon motion may order a trial by a jury of any or all issues.

(c) **Advisory Jury and Trial by Consent.** In all actions not triable of right by a jury the court upon motion or of its own initiative may try any issue with an advisory jury or, except in actions against the United States when a statute of the United States provides for trial without a jury, the court, with the consent of both parties, may order a trial with a jury whose verdict has the same effect as if trial by jury had been a matter of right.

Rule 40. Assignment of Cases for Trial

The district courts shall provide by rule for the placing of actions upon the trial calendar (1) without request of the parties or (2) upon request of a party and notice to the other parties or (3) in such other manner as the courts deem expedient. Precedence shall be given to actions entitled thereto by any statute of the United States.

Rule 41. Dismissal of Actions

(a) **Voluntary Dismissal: Effect Thereof.**

(1) By Plaintiff; by Stipulation. Subject to the provisions of Rule 23(e), of Rule 66, and of any statute of the United States, an action may be dismissed by the plaintiff without order of court (i) by filing a notice of dismissal at any time before service by the adverse party of an answer or of a motion for summary judgment, whichever first occurs, or (ii) by filing a stipulation of dismissal signed by all parties who have appeared in the action. Unless otherwise stated in the notice of dismissal or stipulation, the dismissal is without prejudice, except that a notice of dismissal operates as an adjudication upon the merits when filed by a plaintiff who has once dismissed in any court of the United States or of any state an action based on or including the same claim.

(2) By Order of Court. Except as provided in paragraph (1) of this subdivision of this rule, an action shall not be dismissed at the plaintiff's instance save upon order of the court and upon such terms and conditions as the court deems proper. If a counterclaim has been pleaded by a defendant prior to the service upon the defendant of the plaintiff's motion to

dismiss, the action shall not be dismissed against the defendant's objection unless the counterclaim can remain pending for independent adjudication by the court. Unless otherwise specified in the order, a dismissal under this paragraph is without prejudice.

(b) Involuntary Dismissal: Effect Thereof. For failure of the plaintiff to prosecute or to comply with these rules or any order of court, a defendant may move for dismissal of an action or of any claim against the defendant. Unless the court in its order for dismissal otherwise specifies, a dismissal under this subdivision and any dismissal not provided for in this rule, other than a dismissal for lack of jurisdiction, for improper venue, or for failure to join a party under Rule 19, operates as an adjudication upon the merits.

(c) Dismissal of Counterclaim, Cross-Claim, or Third-Party Claim. The provisions of this rule apply to the dismissal of any counterclaim, cross-claim, or third-party claim. A voluntary dismissal by the claimant alone pursuant to paragraph (1) of subdivision (a) of this rule shall be made before a responsive pleading is served or, if there is none, before the introduction of evidence at the trial or hearing.

(d) Costs of Previously Dismissed Action. If a plaintiff who has once dismissed an action in any court commences an action based upon or including the same claim against the same defendant, the court may make such order for the payment of costs of the action previously dismissed as it may deem proper and may stay the proceedings in the action until the plaintiff has complied with the order.

Rule 42. Consolidation; Separate Trials

(a) Consolidation. When actions involving a common question of law or fact are pending before the court, it may order a joint hearing or trial of any or all the matters in issue in the actions; it may order all the actions consolidated; and it may make such orders concerning proceedings therein as may tend to avoid unnecessary costs or delay.

(b) Separate Trials. The court, in furtherance of convenience or to avoid prejudice, or when separate trials will be conducive to expedition and economy, may order a separate trial of any claim, cross-claim, counterclaim, or third-party claim, or of any separate issue or of any number of claims, cross-claims, counterclaims, third-party claims, or issues, always preserving inviolate the right of trial by jury as declared by the Seventh Amendment to the Constitution or as given by a statute of the United States.

Rule 43. Taking of Testimony

(a) Form. In every trial, the testimony of witnesses shall be taken in open court, unless a federal law, these rules, the Federal Rules of Evidence, or other rules adopted by the Supreme Court provide otherwise. The court may, for good cause shown in compelling circumstances and upon appropriate safeguards, permit presentation of testimony in open court by contemporaneous transmission from a different location.

(b), (c) [Abrogated]

(d) Affirmation in Lieu of Oath. Whenever under these rules an oath is required to be taken, a solemn affirmation may be accepted in lieu thereof.

(e) Evidence on Motions. When a motion is based on facts not appearing of record the court may hear the matter on affidavits presented by the respective parties, but the court may direct that the matter be heard wholly or partly on oral testimony or deposition.

(f) Interpreters. The court may appoint an interpreter of its own selection and may fix the interpreter's reasonable compensation. The compensation shall be paid out of funds provided by law or by one or more of the parties as the court may direct, and may be taxed ultimately as costs, in the discretion of the court.

Rule 44. Proof of Official Record
(a) Authentication.

(1) Domestic. An official record kept within the United States, or any state, district, or commonwealth, or within a territory subject to the administrative or judicial jurisdiction of the United States, or an entry therein, when admissible for any purpose, may be evidenced by an official publication thereof or by a copy attested by the officer having the legal custody of the record, or by the officer's deputy, and accompanied by a certificate that such officer has the custody. The certificate may be made by a judge of a court of record of the district or political subdivision in which the record is kept, authenticated by the seal of the court, or may be made by any public officer having a seal of office and having official duties in the district or political subdivision in which the record is kept, authenticated by the seal of the officer's office. (2) Foreign. A foreign official record, or an entry therein, when admissible for any purpose, may be evidenced by an official publication thereof; or a copy thereof, attested by a person authorized to make the attestation, and accompanied by a final certification as to the genuineness of the signature and official position (i) of the attesting person, or (ii) of any foreign official whose certificate of genuineness of signature and official position relates to the attestation or is in a chain of certificates of genuineness of signature and official position relating to the attestation. A final certification may be made by a secretary of embassy or legation, consul general, vice consul, or consular agent of the United States, or a diplomatic or consular official of the foreign country assigned or accredited to the United States. If reasonable opportunity has been given to all parties to investigate the authenticity and accuracy of the documents, the court may, for good cause shown, (i) admit an attested copy without final certification or (ii) permit the foreign official record to be evidenced by an attested summary with or without a final certification. The final certification is unnecessary if the record and the attestation are certified as provided in a treaty or convention to which the United States and the foreign country in which the official record is located are parties.

(b) Lack of Record. A written statement that after diligent search no record or entry of a specified tenor is found to exist in the records designated by the statement, authenticated as provided in subdivision (a) (1) of this rule in the case of a domestic record, or complying with the requirements of subdivision (a) (2) of this rule for a summary in the case of a foreign record, is admissible as evidence that the records contain no such record or entry.

(c) Other Proof. This rule does not prevent the proof of official records or of entry or lack of entry therein by any other method authorized by law.

Rule 44.1. Determination of Foreign Law

A party who intends to raise an issue concerning the law of a foreign country shall give notice by pleadings or other reasonable written notice. The court, in determining foreign law, may consider any relevant material or source, including testimony, whether or not submitted by a party or admissible under the Federal Rules of Evidence. The court's determination shall be treated as a ruling on a question of law.

Rule 45. Subpoena
(a) Form; Issuance.
(1) Every subpoena shall

(A) state the name of the court from which it is issued; and

(B) state the title of the action, the name of the court in which it is pending, and its civil action number; and

(C) command each person to whom it is directed to attend and give testimony or to produce and permit inspection and copying of designated books, documents or tangible things in the possession, custody or control of that person, or to permit inspection of premises, at a time and place therein specified; and

(D) set forth the text of subdivisions (c) and (d) of this rule. A command to produce evidence or to permit inspection may be joined with a command to appear at trial or hearing or at deposition, or may be issued separately.

(2) A subpoena commanding attendance at a trial or hearing shall issue from the court for the district in which the hearing or trial is to be held. A subpoena for attendance at a deposition shall issue from the court for the district designated by the notice of deposition as the district in which the deposition is to be taken. If separate from a subpoena commanding the attendance of a person, a subpoena for production or inspection shall issue from the court for the district in which the production or inspection is to be made.

(3) The clerk shall issue a subpoena, signed but otherwise in blank, to a party requesting it, who shall complete it before service. An attorney as officer of the court may also issue and sign a subpoena on behalf of

(A) a court in which the attorney is authorized to practice; or

(B) a court for a district in which a deposition or production is compelled by the subpoena, if the deposition or production pertains to an action pending in a court in which the attorney is authorized to practice.

(b) Service

(1) A subpoena may be served by any person who is not a party and is not less than 18 years of age. Service of a subpoena upon a person named therein shall be made by delivering a copy thereof to such person and, if the person's attendance is commanded, by tendering to that person the fees for one day's attendance and the mileage allowed by law. When the subpoena is issued on behalf of the United States or an officer or agency thereof, fees and mileage need not be tendered. Prior notice of any commanded production of documents and things or inspection of premises before trial shall be served on each party in the manner prescribed by Rule 5(b).

(2) Subject to the provisions of clause (ii) of subparagraph (c)(3)(A) of this rule, a subpoena may be served at any place within the district of the court by which it is issued, or at any place without the district that is within 100 miles of the place of the deposition, hearing, trial, production, or inspection specified in the subpoena or at any place within the state where a state statute or rule of court permits service of a subpoena issued by a state court of general jurisdiction sitting in the place of the deposition, hearing, trial, production, or inspection specified in the subpoena. When a statute of the United States provides therefor, the court upon proper application and cause shown may authorize the service of a subpoena at any other place. A subpoena directed to a witness in a foreign country who is a national or resident of the United States shall issue under the circumstances and in the manner and be served as provided in Title 28, U.S.C. § 1783.

(3) Proof of service when necessary shall be made by filing with the clerk of the court by which the subpoena is issued a statement of the date and manner of service and of the names of the persons served, certified by the person who made the service.

(c) Protection of Persons Subject to Subpoenas.

(1) A party or an attorney responsible for the issuance and service of a subpoena shall take reasonable steps to avoid imposing undue burden or expense on a person subject to that subpoena. The court on behalf of which the subpoena was issued shall enforce this duty and impose upon the party or attorney in breach of this duty an appropriate sanction, which may include, but is not limited to, lost earnings and a reasonable attorney's fee.

(2)(A) A person commanded to produce and permit inspection and copying of designated books, papers, documents or tangible things, or inspection of premises need not appear in person at the place of production or inspection unless commanded to appear for deposition, hearing or trial.

(B) Subject to paragraph (d)(2) of this rule, a person commanded to produce and permit inspection and copying may, within 14 days after service of the subpoena or before the time specified for compliance if such time is less than 14 days after service, serve upon the party or attorney designated in the subpoena written objection to inspection or copying of any or all of the designated materials or of the premises. If objection is made, the party serving the subpoena shall not be entitled to inspect and copy the materials or inspect the premises except pursuant to an order of the court by which the subpoena was issued. If objection has been made, the party serving the subpoena may, upon notice to the person commanded to produce, move at any time for an order to compel the production. Such an order to compel production shall protect any person who is not a party or an officer of a party from significant expense resulting from the inspection and copying commanded.

(3)(A) On timely motion, the court by which a subpoena was issued shall quash or modify the subpoena if it (i) fails to allow reasonable time for compliance; (ii) requires a person who is not a party or an officer of a party to travel to a place more than 100 miles from the place where that person resides, is employed or regularly transacts business in person, except that, subject to the provisions of clause (c)(3)(B)(iii) of this rule, such a person may in order to attend trial be commanded to travel from any such place within the state in which the trial is held, or (iii) requires disclosure of privileged or other protected matter and no exception or waiver applies, or (iv) subjects a person to undue burden.

(B) If a subpoena (i) requires disclosure of a trade secret or other confidential research, development, or commercial information, or (ii) requires disclosure of an unretained expert's opinion or information not describing specific events or occurrences in dispute and resulting from the expert's study made not at the request of any party, or (iii) requires a person who is not a party or an officer of a party to incur substantial expense to travel more than 100 miles to attend trial, the court may, to protect a person subject to or affected by the subpoena, quash or modify the subpoena or, if the party in whose behalf the subpoena is issued shows a substantial need for the testimony or material that cannot be otherwise met without undue hardship and assures that the person to whom the subpoena is addressed will be reasonably compensated, the court may order appearance or production only upon specified conditions.

(d) Duties in Responding to Subpoena.

(1) A person responding to a subpoena to produce documents shall produce them as they are kept in the usual course of business or shall organize and label them to correspond with the categories in the demand.

(2) When information subject to a subpoena is withheld on a claim that it is privileged or subject to protection as trial preparation materials, the claim shall be made expressly and shall be supported by a description of the nature of the documents, communications, or things not produced that is sufficient to enable the demanding party to contest the claim.

(e) Contempt. Failure by any person without adequate excuse to obey a subpoena served upon that person may be deemed a contempt of the court from which the subpoena issued. An adequate cause for failure to obey exists when a subpoena purports to require a non-party to attend or produce at a place not within the limits provided by clause (ii) of subparagraph (c)(3)(A).

Rule 46. Exceptions Unnecessary

Formal exceptions to rulings or orders of the court are unnecessary; but for all purposes for which an exception has heretofore been necessary it is sufficient that a party, at the time the ruling or order of the court is made or sought, makes known to the court the action which the party desires the court to take or the party's objection to the action of the court and the grounds therefor; and, if a party has no opportunity to object to a ruling or order at the time it is made, the absence of an objection does not thereafter prejudice the party.

Rule 47. Selection of Jurors

(a) Examination of Jurors. The court may permit the parties or their attorneys to conduct the examination of prospective jurors or may itself conduct the examination. In the latter event, the court shall permit the parties or their attorneys to supplement the examination by such further inquiry as it deems proper or shall itself submit to the prospective jurors such additional questions of the parties or their attorneys as it deems proper.

(b) Peremptory Challenges. The court shall allow the number of peremptory challenges provided by 28 U.S.C. § 1870.

(c) Excuse. The court may for good cause excuse a juror from service during trial or deliberation.

Rule 48. Number of Jurors—Participation in Verdict

The court shall seat a jury of not fewer than six and not more than twelve members and all jurors shall participate in the verdict unless excused from service by the court pursuant to Rule 47(c).Unless the parties otherwise stipulate, (1) the verdict shall be unanimous and (2) no verdict shall be taken from a jury reduced in size to fewer than six members.

Rule 49. Special Verdicts and Interrogatories

(a) Special Verdicts. The court may require a jury to return only a special verdict in the form of a special written finding upon each issue of fact. In that event the court may submit to the jury written questions susceptible of categorical or other brief answer or may submit written forms of the several special findings which might properly be made under the pleadings and evidence; or it may use such other method of submitting the issues and requiring the written findings thereon as it deems most appropriate. The court shall give to the jury such explanation and instruction concerning the matter thus submitted as may be necessary to enable the jury to make its findings upon each issue. If in so doing the court omits any issue of fact raised by the pleadings or by the evidence, each party waives the right to a trial by jury of the issue so omitted unless before the jury retires the party demands its submission to the jury. As to an issue omitted without such demand the court may make a finding; or, if it fails to do so, it shall be deemed to have made a finding in accord with the judgment on the special verdict.

(b) General Verdict Accompanied by Answer to Interrogatories. The court may submit to the jury, together with appropriate forms for a general verdict, written interrogatories upon one or more issues of fact the decision of which is necessary to a verdict. The court shall give such explanation or instruction as may be necessary to enable the jury both to make answers to the interrogatories and to render a general verdict, and the court shall direct the jury both to make written answers and to render a general verdict. When the general verdict and the answers are harmonious, the appropriate judgment upon the verdict and answers shall be entered pursuant to Rule 58. When the answers are consistent with each other but one or more is inconsistent with the general verdict, judgment may be entered pursuant to Rule 58 in accordance with the answers, notwithstanding the general verdict, or the court may return the jury for further consideration of its answers and verdict or may order a new trial. When the answers are inconsistent with each other and one or more is likewise inconsistent with the general verdict, judgment shall not be entered, but the court shall return the jury for further consideration of its answers and verdict or shall order a new trial.

Rule 50. Judgment as a Matter of Law in Jury Trials; Alternative Motion for New Trial; Conditional Rulings

(a) Judgment as a Matter of Law.

(1) If during a trial by jury a party has been fully heard on an issue and there is no legally sufficient evidentiary basis for a reasonable jury to find for that party on that issue, the court may determine the issue against that party and may grant a motion for judgment as a matter of law against that party with respect to a claim or defense that cannot under the controlling law be maintained or defeated without a favorable finding on that issue.

(2) Motions for judgment as a matter of law may be made at any time before submission of the case to the jury. Such a motion shall specify the judgment sought and the law and the facts on which the moving party is entitled to the judgment.

(b) Renewing Motion for Judgment After Trial; Alternative Motion for New Trial. If, for any reason, the court does not grant a motion for judgment as a matter of law made at the close of all the evidence, the court is considered to have submitted the action to the jury subject to the court's later deciding the legal questions raised by the motion. The movant may renew its request for judgment as a matter of law by filing a motion no later than 10 days after entry of judgmentXand may alternatively request a new trial or join a motion for a new trial under Rule 59. In ruling on a renewed motion, the court may:

(1) if a verdict was returned:
   (A) allow the judgment to stand
   (B) order a new trial, or
   (C) direct entry of judgment as a matter of law; or

(2) if no verdict was returned:
   (A) order a new trial, or
   (B) direct entry of judgment as a matter of law.

(c) Granting Renewed Motion for Judgment as a Matter of Law; Conditional Rulings; New Trial Motion.

(1) If the renewed motion for judgment as a matter of law is granted, the court shall also rule on the motion for a new trial, if any, by determining whether it should be granted if the judgment is thereafter vacated or reversed, and shall specify the grounds for granting or denying the motion for the new trial. If the motion for a new trial is thus conditionally granted, the order thereon does not affect the finality of the judgment. In case the motion for a new trial has been conditionally granted and the judgment is reversed on appeal, the new trial shall proceed unless the appellate court has otherwise ordered. In case the motion for a new trial has been conditionally denied, the appellee on appeal may assert error in that denial; and if the judgment is reversed on appeal, subsequent proceedings shall be in accordance with the order of the appellate court.

(2) Any motion for a new trial under Rule 59 by a party against whom judgment as a matter of law is rendered shall be filed no later than 10 days after entry of the judgment.

(d) Same: Denial of Motion for Judgment as a Matter of Law. If the motion for judgment as a matter of law is denied, the party who prevailed on that motion may, as appellee, assert grounds entitling the party to a new trial in the event the appellate court concludes that the trial court erred in denying the motion for judgment. If the appellate court reverses the judgment, nothing in this rule precludes it from determining that the appellee is entitled to a new trial, or from directing the trial court to determine whether a new trial shall be granted.

Rule 51. Instructions to Jury; Objections; Preserving a Claim of Error
(a) Requests.
(1) A party may, at the close of the evidence or at an earlier reasonable time that the court directs, file and furnish to every other party written requests that the court instruct the jury on the law as set forth in the requests.
(2) After the close of the evidence, a party may:
(A) file requests for instructions on issues that could not reasonably have been anticipated at an earlier time for requests set under Rule 51(a)(1), and
(B) with the court's permission file untimely requests for instructions on any issue.
(b) Instructions. The court:
(1) must inform the parties of its proposed instructions and proposed action on the requests before instructing the jury and before final jury arguments;
(2) must give the parties an opportunity to object on the record and out of the jury's hearing to the proposed instructions and actions on requests before the instructions and arguments are delivered; and
(3) may instruct the jury at any time after trial begins and before the jury is discharged.
(c) Objections.
(1) A party who objects to an instruction or the failure to give an instruction must do so on the record, stating distinctly the matter objected to and the grounds of the objection.
(2) An objection is timely if:
(A) a party that has been informed of an instruction or action on a request before the jury is instructed and before final jury arguments, as provided by Rule 51(b)(1), objects at the opportunity for objection required by Rule 51(b)(2); or
(B) a party that has not been informed of an instruction or action on a request before the time for objection provided under Rule 51(b)(2) objects promptly after learning that the instruction or request will be, or has been, given or refused.
(d) Assigning Error; Plain Error.
(1) A party may assign as error:
(A) an error in an instruction actually given if that party made a proper objection under Rule 51(c), or
(B) a failure to give an instruction if that party made a proper request under Rule 51(a), and--unless the court made a definitive ruling on the record rejecting the request--also made a proper objection under Rule 51(c).
(2) A court may consider a plain error in the instructions affecting substantial rights that has not been preserved as required by Rule 51(d)(1)(A) or (B).

Rule 52. Findings by the Court; Judgment on Partial Findings

(a) **Effect.** In all actions tried upon the facts without a jury or with an advisory jury, the court shall find the facts specially and state separately its conclusions of law thereon, and judgment shall be entered pursuant to Rule 58; and in granting or refusing interlocutory injunctions the court shall similarly set forth the findings of fact and conclusions of law which constitute the grounds of its action. Requests for findings are not necessary for purposes of review. Findings of fact, whether based on oral or documentary evidence, shall not be set aside unless clearly erroneous, and due regard shall be given to the opportunity of the trial court to judge of the credibility of the witnesses. The findings of a master, to the extent that the court adopts them, shall be considered as the findings of the court. It will be sufficient if the findings of fact and conclusions of law are stated orally and recorded in open court following the close of the evidence or appear in an opinion or memorandum of decision filed by the court. Findings of fact and conclusions of law are unnecessary on decisions of motions under Rule 12 or 56 or any other motion except as provided in subdivision (c) of this rule.

(b) **Amendment.** Upon motion of a party made not later than 10 days after entry of judgment the court may amend its findings or make additional findings and may amend the judgment accordingly. The motion may be made with a motion for a new trial pursuant to Rule 59. When findings of fact are made in actions tried by the court without a jury, the question of the sufficiency of the evidence to support the findings may thereafter be raised whether or not the party raising the question has made in the district court an objection to such findings or has made a motion to amend them or a motion for judgment.

(c) **Judgment on Partial Findings.** If during a trial without a jury a party has been fully heard on an issue and the court finds against the party on that issue, the court may enter judgment as a matter of law against that party with respect to a claim or defense that cannot under the controlling law be maintained or defeated without a favorable finding on that issue, or the court may decline to render any judgment until the close of all the evidence. Such a judgment shall be supported by findings of fact and conclusions of law as required by subdivision (a) of this rule.

Rule 53. Masters

(a) **Appointment.**

(1) Unless a statute provides otherwise, a court may appoint a master only to:

(A) perform duties consented to by the parties;

(B) hold trial proceedings and make or recommend findings of fact on issues to be decided by the court without a jury if appointment is warranted by

   (i) some exceptional condition, or

   (ii) the need to perform an accounting or resolve a difficult computation of damages; or

(C) address pretrial and post-trial matters that cannot be addressed effectively and timely by an available district judge or magistrate judge of the district.

(2) A master must not have a relationship to the parties, counsel, action, or court that would require disqualification of a judge under 28 U.S.C. § 455 unless the parties consent with the court's approval to appointment of a particular person after disclosure of any potential grounds for disqualification.

(3) In appointing a master, the court must consider the fairness of imposing the likely expenses on the parties and must protect against unreasonable expense or delay.

(b) **Order Appointing Master.**

(1) Notice. The court must give the parties notice and an opportunity to be heard before appointing a master. A party may suggest candidates for appointment.

(2) Contents. The order appointing a master must direct the master to proceed with all reasonable diligence and must state:

(A) the master's duties, including any investigation or enforcement duties, and any limits on the master's authority under Rule 53(c);

(B) the circumstances--if any--in which the master may communicate ex parte with the court or a party;

(C) the nature of the materials to be preserved and filed as the record of the master's activities;

(D) the time limits, method of filing the record, other procedures, and standards for reviewing the master's orders, findings, and recommendations; and

(E) the basis, terms, and procedure for fixing the master's compensation under Rule 53(h).

(3) Entry of Order. The court may enter the order appointing a master only after the master has filed an affidavit disclosing whether there is any ground for disqualification under 28 U.S.C. § 455 and, if a ground for disqualification is disclosed, after the parties have consented with the court's approval to waive the disqualification.

(4) Amendment. The order appointing a master may be amended at any time after notice to the parties, and an opportunity to be heard.

(c) Master's Authority. Unless the appointing order expressly directs otherwise, a master has authority to regulate all proceedings and take all appropriate measures to perform fairly and efficiently the assigned duties. The master may by order impose upon a party any non-contempt sanction provided by Rule 37 or 45, and may recommend a contempt sanction against a party and sanctions against a nonparty.

(d) Evidentiary Hearings. Unless the appointing order expressly directs otherwise, a master conducting an evidentiary hearing may exercise the power of the appointing court to compel, take, and record evidence.

(e) Master's Orders. A master who makes an order must file the order and promptly serve a copy on each party. The clerk must enter the order on the docket.

(f) Master's Reports. A master must report to the court as required by the order of appointment. The master must file the report and promptly serve a copy of the report on each party unless the court directs otherwise.

(g) Action on Master's Order, Report, or Recommendations.

(1) Action. In acting on a master's order, report, or recommendations, the court must afford an opportunity to be heard and may receive evidence, and may: adopt or affirm; modify; wholly or partly reject or reverse; or resubmit to the master with instructions.

(2) Time To Object or Move. A party may file objections to--or a motion to adopt or modify--the master's order, report, or recommendations no later than 20 days from the time the master's order, report, or recommendations are served, unless the court sets a different time.

(3) Fact Findings. The court must decide de novo all objections to findings of fact made or recommended by a master unless the parties stipulate with the court's consent that:

(A) the master's findings will be reviewed for clear error, or

(B) the findings of a master appointed under Rule 53(a)(1)(A) or (C) will be final.

(4) Legal Conclusions. The court must decide de novo all objections to conclusions of law made or recommended by a master.

(5) Procedural Matters. Unless the order of appointment establishes a different standard of review, the court may set aside a master's ruling on a procedural matter only for an abuse of discretion.

(h) Compensation.

(1) Fixing Compensation. The court must fix the master's compensation before or after judgment on the basis and terms stated in the order of appointment, but the court may set a new basis and terms after notice and an opportunity to be heard.

(2) Payment. The compensation fixed under Rule 53(h)(1) must be paid either:

(A) by a party or parties; or

(B) from a fund or subject matter of the action within the court's control.

(3) Allocation. The court must allocate payment of the master's compensation among the parties after considering the nature and amount of the controversy, the means of the parties, and the extent to which any party is more responsible than other parties for the reference to a master. An interim allocation may be amended to reflect a decision on the merits.

(i) Appointment of Magistrate Judge. A magistrate judge is subject to this rule only when the order referring a matter to the magistrate judge expressly provides that the reference is made under this rule.

VII. JUDGMENT

Rule 54. Judgments; Costs

(a) Definition; Form. "Judgment" as used in these rules includes a decree and any order from which an appeal lies. A judgment shall not contain a recital of pleadings, the report of a master, or the record of prior proceedings.

(b) Judgment Upon Multiple Claims or Involving Multiple Parties. When more than one claim for relief is presented in an action, whether as a claim, counterclaim, cross-claim, or third-party claim, or when multiple parties are involved, the court may direct the entry of a final judgment as to one or more but fewer than all of the claims or parties only upon an express determination that there is no just reason for delay and upon an express direction for the entry of judgment. In the absence of such determination and direction, any order or other form of decision, however designated, which adjudicates fewer than all the claims or the rights and liabilities of fewer than all the parties shall not terminate the action as to any of the claims or parties, and the order or other form of decision is subject to revision at any time before the entry of judgment adjudicating all the claims and the rights and liabilities of all the parties.

(c) Demand for Judgment. A judgment by default shall not be different in kind from or exceed in amount that prayed for in the demand for judgment. Except as to a party against whom a judgment is entered by default, every final judgment shall grant the relief to which the party in whose favor it is rendered is entitled, even if the party has not demanded such relief in the party's pleadings.

(d) Costs; Attorneys' Fees.

(1) Costs Other than Attorneys' Fees. Except when express provision therefor is made either in a statute of the United States or in these rules, costs other than attorneys' fees shall be allowed as of course to the prevailing party unless the court otherwise directs; but costs against the United States, its officers, and agencies shall be imposed only to the extent permitted by law. Such costs may be taxed by the clerk on one day's notice. On motion served within 5 days thereafter, the action of the clerk may be reviewed by the court.

(2) Attorneys' Fees.

(A) Claims for attorneys' fees and related nontaxable expenses shall be made by motion unless the substantive law governing the action provides for the recovery of such fees as an element of damages to be proved at trial.

(B) Unless otherwise provided by statute or order of the court, the motion must be filed no later than 14 days after entry of judgment; must specify the judgment and the statute, rule, or other grounds entitling the moving party to the award; and must state the amount or provide a fair estimate of the amount sought. If directed by the court, the motion shall also disclose the terms of any agreement with respect to fees to be paid for the services for which claim is made.

(C) On request of a party or class member, the court shall afford an opportunity for adversary submissions with respect to the motion in accordance with Rule 43(e) or Rule 78. The court may determine issues of liability for fees before receiving submissions bearing on issues of evaluation of services for which liability is imposed by the court. The court shall find the facts and state its conclusions of law as provided in Rule 52(a).

(D) By local rule the court may establish special procedures by which issues relating to such fees may be resolved without extensive evidentiary hearings. In addition, the court may refer issues relating to the value of services to a special master under Rule 53 without regard to the provisions of Rule 53(a)(1) and may refer a motion for attorneys' fees to a magistrate judge under Rule 72(b) as if it were a dispositive pretrial matter.

(E) The provisions of subparagraphs (A) through (D) do not apply to claims for fees and expenses as sanctions for violations of these rules or under 28 U.S.C. § 1927.

Rule 55. Default

(a) **Entry.** When a party against whom a judgment for affirmative relief is sought has failed to plead or otherwise defend as provided by these rules and that fact is made to appear by affidavit or otherwise, the clerk shall enter the party's default.

(b) **Judgment.** Judgment by default may be entered as follows:

(1) By the Clerk. When the plaintiff's claim against a defendant is for a sum certain or for a sum which can by computation be made certain, the clerk upon request of the plaintiff and upon affidavit of the amount due shall enter judgment for that amount and costs against the defendant, if the defendant has been defaulted for failure to appear and if he is not an infant or incompetent person.

(2) By the Court. In all other cases the party entitled to a judgment by default shall apply to the court therefor; but no judgment by default shall be entered against an infant or incompetent person unless represented in the action by a general guardian, committee, conservator, or other such representative who has appeared therein. If the party against whom judgment by default is sought has appeared in the action, the party (or, if appearing by representative, the party's representative) shall be served with written notice of the application for judgment at least 3 days prior to the hearing on such application. If, in order to enable the court to enter judgment or to carry it into effect, it is necessary to take an account or to determine the amount of damages or to establish the truth of any averment by evidence or to make an investigation of any other matter, the court may conduct such hearings or order such references as it deems necessary and proper and shall accord a right of trial by jury to the parties when and as required by any statute of the United States.

(c) **Setting Aside Default.** For good cause shown the court may set aside an entry of default and, if a judgment by default has been entered, may likewise set it aside in accordance with Rule 60(b).

(d) **Plaintiffs, Counterclaimants, Cross-Claimants.** The provisions of this rule apply whether the party entitled to the judgment by default is a plaintiff, a third-party plaintiff, or a party who has pleaded a cross-claim or counterclaim. In all cases a judgment by default is subject to the limitations of Rule 54(c).

(e) Judgment Against the United States. No judgment by default shall be entered against the United States or an officer or agency thereof unless the claimant establishes a claim or right to relief by evidence satisfactory to the court.

Rule 56. Summary Judgment

(a) For Claimant. A party seeking to recover upon a claim, counterclaim, or cross-claim or to obtain a declaratory judgment may, at any time after the expiration of 20 days from the commencement of the action or after service of a motion for summary judgment by the adverse party, move with or without supporting affidavits for a summary judgment in the party's favor upon all or any part thereof.

(b) For Defending Party. A party against whom a claim, counterclaim, or cross-claim is asserted or a declaratory judgment is sought may, at any time, move with or without supporting affidavits for a summary judgment in the party's favor as to all or any part thereof.

(c) Motion and Proceedings Thereon. The motion shall be served at least 10 days before the time fixed for the hearing. The adverse party prior to the day of hearing may serve opposing affidavits. The judgment sought shall be rendered forthwith if the pleadings, depositions, answers to interrogatories, and admissions on file, together with the affidavits, if any, show that there is no genuine issue as to any material fact and that the moving party is entitled to a judgment as a matter of law. A summary judgment, interlocutory in character, may be rendered on the issue of liability alone although there is a genuine issue as to the amount of damages.

(d) Case Not Fully Adjudicated on Motion. If on motion under this rule judgment is not rendered upon the whole case or for all the relief asked and a trial is necessary, the court at the hearing of the motion, by examining the pleadings and the evidence before it and by interrogating counsel, shall if practicable ascertain what material facts exist without substantial controversy and what material facts are actually and in good faith controverted. It shall thereupon make an order specifying the facts that appear without substantial controversy, including the extent to which the amount of damages or other relief is not in controversy, and directing such further proceedings in the action as are just. Upon the trial of the action the facts so specified shall be deemed established, and the trial shall be conducted accordingly.

(e) Form of Affidavits; Further Testimony; Defense Required. Supporting and opposing affidavits shall be made on personal knowledge, shall set forth such facts as would be admissible in evidence, and shall show affirmatively that the affiant is competent to testify to the matters stated therein. Sworn or certified copies of all papers or parts thereof referred to in an affidavit shall be attached thereto or served therewith. The court may permit affidavits to be supplemented or opposed by depositions, answers to interrogatories, or further affidavits. When a motion for summary judgment is made and supported as provided in this rule, an adverse party may not rest upon the mere allegations or denials of the adverse party's pleading, but the adverse party's response, by affidavits or as otherwise provided in this rule, must set forth specific facts showing that there is a genuine issue for trial. If the adverse party does not so respond, summary judgment, if appropriate, shall be entered against the adverse party.

(f) When Affidavits are Unavailable. Should it appear from the affidavits of a party opposing the motion that the party cannot for reasons stated present by affidavit facts essential to justify the party's opposition, the court may refuse the application for judgment or may order a continuance to permit affidavits to be obtained or depositions to be taken or discovery to be had or may make such other order as is just.

(g) Affidavits Made in Bad Faith. Should it appear to the satisfaction of the court at any time that any of the affidavits presented pursuant to this rule are presented in bad faith or solely for the purpose of delay, the court shall forthwith order the party employing them to pay to the other party the amount of the reasonable expenses which the filing of the affidavits caused the other party to incur, including reasonable attorney's fees, and any offending party or attorney may be adjudged guilty of contempt.

Rule 57. Declaratory Judgments

The procedure for obtaining a declaratory judgment pursuant to Title 28 U.S.C. § 2201, shall be in accordance with these rules, and the right to trial by jury may be demanded under the circumstances and in the manner provided in Rules 38 and 39. The existence of another adequate remedy does not preclude a judgment for declaratory relief in cases where it is appropriate. The court may order a speedy hearing of an action for a declaratory judgment and may advance it on the calendar.

Rule 58. Entry of Judgment
(a) Separate Document.
  (1) Every judgment and amended judgment must be set forth on a separate document, but a separate document is not required for an order disposing of a motion:
   (A) for judgment under Rule 50(b);
   (B) to amend or make additional findings of fact under Rule 52(b);
   (C) for attorney fees under Rule 54;
   (D) for a new trial, or to alter or amend the judgment, under Rule 59; or
   (E) for relief under Rule 60.
  (2) Subject to Rule 54(b):
   (A) unless the court orders otherwise, the clerk must, without awaiting the court's direction, promptly prepare, sign, and enter the judgment when:
    (i) the jury returns a general verdict,
    (ii) the court awards only costs or a sum certain, or
    (iii) the court denies all relief;
   (B) the court must promptly approve the form of the judgment, which the clerk must promptly enter, when:
    (i) the jury returns a special verdict or a general verdict accompanied by interrogatories, or
    (ii) the court grants other relief not described in Rule 58(a)(2).

(b) Time of Entry.
Judgment is entered for purposes of these rules:
  (1) if Rule 58(a)(1) does not require a separate document, when it is entered in the civil docket under Rule 79(a), and
  (2) if Rule 58(a)(1) requires a separate document, when it is entered in the civil docket under Rule 79(a) and when the earlier of these events occurs:
   (A) when it is set forth on a separate document, or
   (B) when 150 days have run from entry in the civil docket under Rule 79(a).

(c) Cost or Fee Awards.

(1) Entry of judgment may not be delayed, nor the time for appeal extended, in order to tax costs or award fees, except as provided in Rule 58(c)(2).

(2) When a timely motion for attorney fees is made under Rule 54(d)(2), the court may act before a notice of appeal has been filed and has become effective to order that the motion have the same effect under Federal Rule of Appellate Procedure 4(a)(4) as a timely motion under Rule 59.

(d) Request for Entry.

A party may request that judgment be set forth on a separate document as required by Rule 58(a)(1).

Rule 59. New Trials; Amendment of Judgments

(a) Grounds. A new trial may be granted to all or any of the parties and on all or part of the issues (1) in an action in which there has been a trial by jury, for any of the reasons for which new trials have heretofore been granted in actions at law in the courts of the United States; and (2) in an action tried without a jury for any of the reasons for which rehearings have heretofore been granted in suits in equity in the courts of the United States. On a motion for a new trial in an action tried without a jury, the court may open the judgment if one has been entered, take additional testimony, amend findings of fact and conclusions of law or make new findings and conclusions, and direct the entry of a new judgment.

(b) Time for Motion. Any motion for a new trial shall be filed no later than 10 days after entry of the judgment.

(c) Time for Serving Affidavits. When a motion for new trial is based on affidavits, they shall be filed with the motion. The opposing party has 10 days after service to file opposing affidavits, but that period may be extended for up to 20 days, either by the court for good cause or by the parties' written stipulation. The court may permit reply affidavits.

(d) On Court's Initiative; Notice; Specifying Grounds. No later than 10 days after entry of judgment the court, on its own, may order a new trial for any reason that would justify granting one on a party's motion. After giving the parties notice and an opportunity to be heard, the court may grant a timely motion for a new trial for a reason not stated in the motion. When granting a new trial on its own initiative or for a reason not stated in a motion, the court shall specify the grounds in its order.

(e) Motion to Alter or Amend Judgment. Any motion to alter or amend a judgment shall be filed no later than 10 days after entry of the judgment.

Rule 60. Relief From Judgment or Order

(a) Clerical Mistakes. Clerical mistakes in judgments, orders or other parts of the record and errors therein arising from oversight or omission may be corrected by the court at any time of its own initiative or on the motion of any party and after such notice, if any, as the court orders. During the pendency of an appeal, such mistakes may be so corrected before the appeal is docketed in the appellate court, and thereafter while the appeal is pending may be so corrected with leave of the appellate court.

(b) Mistakes; Inadvertence; Excusable Neglect; Newly Discovered Evidence; Fraud, etc. On motion and upon such terms as are just, the court may relieve a party or a party's legal representative from a final judgment, order, or proceeding for the following reasons: (1) mistake, inadvertence, surprise, or excusable neglect; (2) newly discovered evidence which by due diligence could not have been discovered in time to move for a new trial under Rule 59(b); (3) fraud (whether heretofore denominated intrinsic or extrinsic), misrepresentation, or other misconduct of an adverse party; (4) the judgment is void; (5) the judgment has been satisfied, released, or discharged, or a prior judgment upon which it is based has been reversed or otherwise vacated, or it is no longer equitable that the judgment should have prospective application; or (6) any other reason justifying relief from the operation of the judgment. The motion shall be made within a reasonable time, and for reasons (1), (2), and (3) not more than one year after the judgment, order, or proceeding was entered or taken. A motion under this subdivision (b) does not affect the finality of a judgment or suspend its operation. This rule does not limit the power of a court to entertain an independent action to relieve a party from a judgment, order, or proceeding, or to grant relief to a defendant not actually personally notified as provided in Title 28, U.S.C., § 1655, or to set aside a judgment for fraud upon the court. Writs of coram nobis, coram vobis, audita querela, and bills of review and bills in the nature of a bill of review, are abolished, and the procedure for obtaining any relief from a judgment shall be by motion as prescribed in these rules or by an independent action.

Rule 61. Harmless Error

No error in either the admission or the exclusion of evidence and no error or defect in any ruling or order or in anything done or omitted by the court or by any of the parties is ground for granting a new trial or for setting aside a verdict or for vacating, modifying or otherwise disturbing a judgment or order, unless refusal to take such action appears to the court inconsistent with substantial justice. The court at every stage of the proceeding must disregard any error or defect in the proceeding which does not affect the substantial rights of the parties.

Rule 62. Stay of Proceedings to Enforce a Judgment

(a) **Automatic Stay; Exceptions—Injunctions, Receiverships, and Patent Accountings.** Except as stated herein, no execution shall issue upon a judgment nor shall proceedings be taken for its enforcement until the expiration of 10 days after its entry. Unless otherwise ordered by the court, an interlocutory or final judgment in an action for an injunction or in a receivership action, or a judgment or order directing an accounting in an action for infringement of letters patent, shall not be stayed during the period after its entry and until an appeal is taken or during the pendency of an appeal. The provisions of subdivision (c) of this rule govern the suspending, modifying, restoring, or granting of an injunction during the pendency of an appeal.

(b) **Stay on Motion for New Trial or for Judgment.** In its discretion and on such conditions for the security of the adverse party as are proper, the court may stay the execution of or any proceedings to enforce a judgment pending the disposition of a motion for a new trial or to alter or amend a judgment made pursuant to Rule 59, or of a motion for relief from a judgment or order made pursuant to Rule 60, or of a motion for judgment in accordance with a motion for a directed verdict made pursuant to Rule 50, or of a motion for amendment to the findings or for additional findings made pursuant to Rule 52(b).

(c) **Injunction Pending Appeal.** When an appeal is taken from an interlocutory or final judgment granting, dissolving, or denying an injunction, the court in its discretion may suspend, modify, restore, or grant an injunction during the pendency of the appeal upon such terms as to bond or otherwise as it considers proper for the security of the rights of the adverse party. If the judgment appealed from is rendered by a district court of three judges specially constituted pursuant to a statute of the United States, no such order shall be made except (1) by such court sitting in open court or (2) by the assent of all the judges of such court evidenced by their signatures to the order.

(d) Stay Upon Appeal. When an appeal is taken the appellant by giving a supersedeas bond may obtain a stay subject to the exceptions contained in subdivision (a) of this rule. The bond may be given at or after the time of filing the notice of appeal or of procuring the order allowing the appeal, as the case may be. The stay is effective when the supersedeas bond is approved by the court.

(e) Stay in Favor of the United States or Agency Thereof. When an appeal is taken by the United States or an officer or agency thereof or by direction of any department of the Government of the United States and the operation or enforcement of the judgment is stayed, no bond, obligation, or other security shall be required from the appellant.

(f) Stay According to State Law. In any state in which a judgment is a lien upon the property of the judgment debtor and in which the judgment debtor is entitled to a stay of execution, a judgment debtor is entitled, in the district court held therein, to such stay as would be accorded the judgment debtor had the action been maintained in the courts of that state.

(g) Power of Appellate Court Not Limited. The provisions in this rule do not limit any power of an appellate court or of a judge or justice thereof to stay proceedings during the pendency of an appeal or to suspend, modify, restore, or grant an injunction during the pendency of an appeal or to make any order appropriate to preserve the status quo or the effectiveness of the judgment subsequently to be entered.

(h) Stay of Judgment as to Multiple Claims or Multiple Parties. When a court has ordered a final judgment under the conditions stated in Rule 54(b), the court may stay enforcement of that judgment until the entering of a subsequent judgment or judgments and may prescribe such conditions as are necessary to secure the benefit thereof to the party in whose favor the judgment is entered.

Rule 63. Inability of a Judge to Proceed

If a trial or hearing has been commenced and the judge is unable to proceed, any other judge may proceed with it upon certifying familiarity with the record and determining that the proceedings in the case may be completed without prejudice to the parties. In a hearing or trial without a jury, the successor judge shall at the request of a party recall any witness whose testimony is material and disputed and who is available to testify again without undue burden. The successor judge may also recall any other witness.

VIII. PROVISIONAL AND FINAL REMEDIES

Rule 64. Seizure of Person or Property

At the commencement of and during the course of an action, all remedies providing for seizure of person or property for the purpose of securing satisfaction of the judgment ultimately to be entered in the action are available under the circumstances and in the manner provided by the law of the state in which the district court is held, existing at the time the remedy is sought, subject to the following qualifications: (1) any existing statute of the United States governs to the extent to which it is applicable; (2) the action in which any of the foregoing remedies is used shall be commenced and prosecuted or, if removed from a state court, shall be prosecuted after removal, pursuant to these rules. The remedies thus available include arrest, attachment, garnishment,, sequestration, and other corresponding or equivalent remedies, however designated and regardless of whether by state procedure the remedy is ancillary to an action or must be obtained by an independent action.

Rule 65. Injunctions
   (a) Preliminary Injunction.
   (1) Notice. No preliminary injunction shall be issued without notice to the adverse party.
   (2) Consolidation of Hearing With Trial on Merits. Before or after the commencement of the hearing of an application for a preliminary injunction, the court may order the trial of the action on the merits to be advanced and consolidated with the hearing of the application. Even when this consolidation is not ordered, any evidence received upon an application for a preliminary injunction which would be admissible upon the trial on the merits becomes part of the record on the trial and need not be repeated upon the trial. This subdivision (a)(2) shall be so construed and applied as to save to the parties any rights they may have to trial by jury.
   (b) Temporary Restraining Order; Notice; Hearing; Duration. A temporary restraining order may be granted without written or oral notice to the adverse party or that party's attorney only if (1) it clearly appears from specific facts shown by affidavit or by the verified complaint that immediate and irreparable injury, loss, or damage will result to the applicant before the adverse party or that party's attorney can be heard in opposition, and (2) the applicant's attorney certifies to the court in writing the efforts, if any, which have been made to give the notice and the reasons supporting the claim that notice should not be required. Every temporary restraining order granted without notice shall be endorsed with the date and hour of issuance; shall be filed forthwith in the clerk's office and entered of record; shall define the injury and state why it is irreparable and why the order was granted without notice; and shall expire by its terms within such time after entry, not to exceed 10 days, as the court fixes, unless within the time so fixed the order, for good cause shown, is extended for a like period or unless the party against whom the order is directed consents that it may be extended for a longer period. The reasons for the extension shall be entered of record. In case a temporary restraining order is granted without notice, the motion for a preliminary injunction shall be set down for hearing at the earliest possible time and takes precedence of all matters except older matters of the same character; and when the motion comes on for hearing the party who obtained the temporary restraining order shall proceed with the application for a preliminary injunction and, if the party does not do so, the court shall dissolve the temporary restraining order. On 2 days' notice to the party who obtained the temporary restraining order without notice or on such shorter notice to that party as the court may prescribe, the adverse party may appear and move its dissolution or modification and in that event the court shall proceed to hear and determine such motion as expeditiously as the ends of justice require.
   (c) Security. No restraining order or preliminary injunction shall issue except upon the giving of security by the applicant, in such sum as the court deems proper, for the payment of such costs and damages as may be incurred or suffered by any party who is found to have been wrongfully enjoined or restrained. No such security shall be required of the United States or of an officer or agency thereof. The provisions of Rule 65.1 apply to a surety upon a bond or undertaking under this rule.

(d) Form and Scope of Injunction or Restraining Order. Every order granting an injunction and every restraining order shall set forth the reasons for its issuance; shall be specific in terms; shall describe in reasonable detail, and not by reference to the complaint or other document, the act or acts sought to be restrained; and is binding only upon the parties to the action, their officers, agents, servants, employees, and attorneys, and upon those persons in active concert or participation with them who receive actual notice of the order by personal service or otherwise.

(e) Employer and Employee; Interpleader; Constitutional Cases. These rules do not modify any statute of the United States relating to temporary restraining orders and preliminary injunctions in actions affecting employer and employee; or the provisions of Title 28, U.S.C., § 2361, relating to preliminary injunctions in actions of interpleader or in the nature of interpleader; or Title 28, U.S.C., § 2284, relating to actions required by Act of Congress to be heard and determined by a district court of three judges.

Rule 65.1. Security: Proceedings Against Sureties

Whenever these rules, including the Supplemental Rules for Certain Admiralty and Maritime Claims, require or permit the giving of security by a party, and security is given in the form of a bond or stipulation or other undertaking with one or more sureties, each surety submits to the jurisdiction of the court and irrevocably appoints the clerk of the court as the surety's agent upon whom any papers affecting the surety's liability on the bond or undertaking may be served. The surety's liability may be enforced on motion without the necessity of an independent action. The motion and such notice of the motion as the court prescribes may be served on the clerk of the court, who shall forthwith mail copies to the sureties if their addresses are known.

Rule 66. Receivers Appointed by Federal Courts

An action wherein a receiver has been appointed shall not be dismissed except by order of the court. The practice in the administration of estates by receivers or by other similar officers appointed by the court shall be in accordance with the practice heretofore followed in the courts of the United States or as provided in rules promulgated by the district courts. In all other respects the action in which the appointment of a receiver is sought or which is brought by or against a receiver is governed by these rules.

Rule 67. Deposit in Court

In an action in which any part of the relief sought is a judgment for a sum of money or the disposition of a sum of money or the disposition of any other thing capable of delivery, a party, upon notice to every other party, and by leave of court, may deposit with the court all or any part of such sum or thing, whether or not that party claims all or any part of the sum or thing. The party making the deposit shall serve the order permitting deposit on the clerk of the court. Money paid into court under this rule shall be deposited and withdrawn in accordance with the provisions of Title 28 U.S.C. §§ 2041, and 2042; the Act of June 26, 1934, c. 756,23, as amended (48 Stat. 1236, 58 Stat. 845), U.S.C. Title 31 §725v; or any like statute. The fund shall be deposited in an interest bearing account or invested in an interest bearing instrument approved by the court.

Rule 68. Offer of Judgment

At any time more than 10 days before the trial begins, a party defending against a claim may serve upon the adverse party an offer to allow judgment to be taken against the defending party for the money or property or to the effect specified in the offer, with costs then accrued. If within 10 days after the service of the offer the adverse party serves written notice that the offer is accepted, either party may then file the offer and notice of acceptance together with proof of service thereof and thereupon the clerk shall enter judgment. An offer not accepted shall be deemed withdrawn and evidence thereof is not admissible except in a proceeding to determine costs. If the judgment finally obtained by the offeree is not more favorable than the offer, the offeree must pay the costs incurred after the making of the offer. The fact that an offer is made but not accepted does not preclude a subsequent offer. When the liability of one party to another has been determined by verdict or order or judgment, but the amount or extent of the liability remains to be determined by further proceedings, the party adjudged liable may make an offer of judgment, which shall have the same effect as an offer made before trial if it is served within a reasonable time not less than 10 days prior to the commencement of hearings to determine the amount or extent of liability.

Rule 69. Execution

(a) In General. Process to enforce a judgment for the payment of money shall be a writ of execution, unless the court directs otherwise. The procedure on execution, in proceedings supplementary to and in aid of a judgment, and in proceedings on and in aid of execution shall be in accordance with the practice and procedure of the state in which the district court is held, existing at the time the remedy is sought, except that any statute of the United States governs to the extent that it is applicable. In aid of the judgment or execution, the judgment creditor or a successor in interest when that interest appears of record, may obtain discovery from any person, including the judgment debtor, in the manner provided in these rules or in the manner provided by the practice of the state in which the district court is held.

(b) Against Certain Public Officers. When a judgment has been entered against a collector or other officer of revenue under the circumstances stated in Title 28, U.S.C., § 2006, or against an officer of Congress in an action mentioned in the Act of March 3, 1875, ch. 130, § 8 (18 Stat. 401), U.S.C., Title 2, § 118, and when the court has given the certificate of probable cause for the officer's act as provided in those statutes, execution shall not issue against the officer or the officer's property but the final judgment shall be satisfied as provided in such statutes.

Rule 70. Judgment for Specific Acts; Vesting Title

If a judgment directs a party to execute a conveyance of land or to deliver deeds or other documents or to perform any other specific act and the party fails to comply within the time specified, the court may direct the act to be done at the cost of the disobedient party by some other person appointed by the court and the act when so done has like effect as if done by the party. On application of the party entitled to performance, the clerk shall issue a writ of attachment or sequestration against the property of the disobedient party to compel obedience to the judgment. The court may also in proper cases adjudge the party in contempt. If real or personal property is within the district, the court in lieu of directing a conveyance thereof may enter a judgment divesting the title of any party and vesting it in others and such judgment has the effect of a conveyance executed in due form of law. When any order or judgment is for the delivery of possession, the party in whose favor it is entered is entitled to a writ of execution or assistance upon application to the clerk.

Rule 71. Process in Behalf of and Against Persons Not Parties

When an order is made in favor of a person who is not a party to the action, that person may enforce obedience to the order by the same process as if a party; and, when obedience to an order may be lawfully enforced against a person who is not a party, that person is liable to the same process for enforcing obedience to the order as if a party.

IX. SPECIAL PROCEEDINGS

Rule 71A. Condemnation of Property

(a) **Applicability of Other Rules**. The Rules of Civil Procedure for the United States District Courts govern the procedure for the condemnation of real and personal property under the power of eminent domain, except as otherwise provided in this rule.

(b) **Joinder of Properties**. The plaintiff may join in the same action one or more separate pieces of property, whether in the same or different ownership and whether or not sought for the same use.

(c) **Complaint**.

(1) Caption. The complaint shall contain a caption as provided in Rule 10(a), except that the plaintiff shall name as defendants the property, designated generally by kind, quantity, and location, and at least one of the owners of some part of or interest in the property.

(2) Contents. The complaint shall contain a short and plain statement of the authority for the taking, the use for which the property is to be taken, a description of the property sufficient for its identification, the interests to be acquired, and as to each separate piece of property a designation of the defendants who have been joined as owners thereof or of some interest therein. Upon the commencement of the action, the plaintiff need join as defendants only the persons having or claiming an interest in the property whose names are then known, but prior to any hearing involving the compensation to be paid for a piece of property, the plaintiff shall add as defendants all persons having or claiming an interest in that property whose names can be ascertained by a reasonably diligent search of the records, considering the character and value of the property involved and the interests to be acquired, and also those whose names have otherwise been learned. All others may be made defendants under the designation "Unknown Owners." Process shall be served as provided in subdivision (d) of this rule upon all defendants, whether named as defendants at the time of the commencement of the action or subsequently added, and a defendant may answer as provided in subdivision (e) of this rule. The court meanwhile may order such distribution of a deposit as the facts warrant.

(3) Filing. In addition to filing the complaint with the court, the plaintiff shall furnish to the clerk at least one copy thereof for the use of the defendants and additional copies at the request of the clerk or of a defendant.

(d) **Process**.

(1) Notice; Delivery. Upon the filing of the complaint the plaintiff shall forthwith deliver to the clerk joint or several notices directed to the defendants named or designated in the complaint. Additional notices directed to defendants subsequently added shall be so delivered.

The delivery of the notice and its service have the same effect as the delivery and service of the summons under Rule 4.

(2) Same; Form. Each notice shall state the court, the title of the action, the name of the defendant to whom it is directed, that the action is to condemn property, a description of the defendant's property sufficient for its identification, the interest to be taken, the authority for the taking, the uses for which the property is to be taken, that the defendant may serve upon the plaintiff's attorney an answer within 20 days after service of the notice, and that the failure so to serve an answer constitutes a consent to the taking and to the authority of the court to proceed to hear the action and to fix the compensation. The notice shall conclude with the name of the plaintiff's attorney and an address within the district in which action is brought where the attorney may be served. The notice need contain a description of no other property than that to be taken from the defendants to whom it is directed.

(3) Service of Notice.

(A) Personal Service. Personal service of the notice (but without copies of the complaint) shall be made in accordance with Rule 4 upon a defendant whose residence is known and who resides within the United States or a territory subject to the administrative or judicial jurisdiction of the United States.

(B) Service by Publication. Upon the filing of a certificate of the plaintiff's attorney stating that the attorney believes a defendant cannot be personally served, because after diligent inquiry within the state in which the complaint if filed the defendant's place of residence cannot be ascertained by the plaintiff or, if ascertained, that it is beyond the territorial limits of personal service as provided in this rule, service of the notice shall be made on this defendant by publication in a newspaper published in the county where the property is located, or if there is no such newspaper, then in a newspaper having a general circulation where the property is located, once a week for not less than three successive weeks. Prior to the last publication, a copy of the notice shall also be mailed to a defendant who cannot be personally served as provided in this rule but whose place of residence is then known. Unknown owners may be served by publication in like manner by a notice addressed to "Unknown Owners."

Service by publication is complete upon the date of the last publication. Proof of publication and mailing shall be made by certificate of the plaintiff's attorney, to which shall be attached a printed copy of the published notice with the name and dates of the newspaper marked thereon.

(4) Return; Amendment. Proof of service of the notice shall be made and amendment of the notice or proof of its service allowed in the manner provided for the return and amendment of the summons under Rule 4.

(e) **Appearance or answer**. If a defendant has no objection or defense to the taking of the defendant's property, the defendant may serve a notice of appearance designating the property in which the defendant claims to be interested. Thereafter, the defendant shall receive notice of all proceedings affecting it. If a defendant has any objection or defense to the taking of the property, the defendant shall serve an answer within 20 days after the service of notice upon the defendant. The answer shall identify the property in which the defendant claims to have an interest, state the nature and extent of the interest claimed, and state all the defendant's objections and defenses to the taking of the property. A defendant waives all defenses and objections not so presented, but at the trial of the issue of just compensation, whether or not the defendant has previously appeared or answered, the defendant may present evidence as to the amount of the compensation to be paid for the property, and the defendant may share in the distribution of the award. No other pleading or motion asserting any additional defense or objection shall be allowed.

(f) Amendment of Pleadings. Without leave of court, the plaintiff may amend the complaint at any time before the trial of the issue of compensation and as many times as desired, but no amendment shall be made which will result in a dismissal forbidden by subdivision (i) of this rule. The plaintiff need not serve a copy of an amendment, but shall serve notice of the filing, as provided in Rule 5(b), upon any party affected thereby who has appeared and, in the manner provided in subdivision (d) of this rule, upon any party affected thereby who has not appeared. The plaintiff shall furnish to the clerk of the court for the use of the defendants at least one copy of each amendment, and he shall furnish additional copies on the request of the clerk or of a defendant. Within the time allowed by subdivision (e) of this rule a defendant may serve an answer to the amended pleading, in the form and manner and with the same effect as there provided.

(g) Substitution of Parties. If a defendant dies or becomes incompetent or transfers an interest after the defendant's joinder, the court may order substitution of the proper party upon motion and notice of hearing. If the motion and notice of hearing are to be served upon a person not already a party, service shall be made as provided in subdivision (d)(3) of this rule.

(h) Trial. If the action involves the exercise of the power of eminent domain under the law of the United States, any tribunal specially constituted by an Act of Congress governing the case for the trial of the issue of just compensation shall be the tribunal for the determination of that issue; but if there is no such specially constituted tribunal any party may have a trial by jury of the issue of just compensation by filing a demand therefor within the time allowed for answer or within such further time as the court may fix, unless the court in its discretion orders that, because of the character, location, or quantity of the property to be condemned, or for other reasons in the interest of justice, the issue of compensation shall be determined by a commission of three persons appointed by it.

In the event that a commission is appointed the court may direct that not more than two additional persons serve as alternate commissioners to hear the case and replace commissioners who, prior to the time when a decision is filed, are found by the court to be unable or disqualified to perform their duties. An alternate who does not replace a regular commissioner shall be discharged after the commission renders its final decision. Before appointing the members of the commission and alternates the court shall advise the parties of the identity and qualifications of each prospective commissioner and alternate and may permit the parties to examine each such designee. The parties shall not be permitted or required by the court to suggest nominees. Each party shall have the right to object for valid cause to the appointment of any person as a commissioner or alternate. If a commission is appointed it shall have the authority of a master provided in Rule 53(c) and proceedings before it shall be governed by the provisions of Rule 53(d). Its action and report shall be determined by a majority and its findings and report shall have the effect, and be dealt with by the court in accordance with the practice, prescribed in Rule 53(e), (f), and (g). Trial of all issues shall otherwise be by the court.

(i) Dismissal of Action.

(1) As of Right. If no hearing has begun to determine the compensation to be paid for a piece of property and the plaintiff has not acquired the title or a lesser interest in or taken possession, the plaintiff may dismiss the action as to that property, without an order of the court, by filing a notice of dismissal setting forth a brief description of the property as to which the action is dismissed.

(2) By Stipulation. Before the entry of any judgment vesting the plaintiff with title or a lesser interest in or possession of property, the action may be dismissed in whole or in part, without an order of the court, as to any property by filing a stipulation of dismissal by the plaintiff and the defendant affected thereby; and, if the parties so stipulate, the court may vacate any judgment that has been entered.

(3) By Order of the Court. At any time before compensation for a piece of property has been determined and paid and after motion and hearing, the court may dismiss the action as to that property, except that it shall not dismiss the action as to any part of the property of which the plaintiff has taken possession or in which the plaintiff has taken title or a lesser interest, but shall award just compensation for the possession, title or lesser interest so taken. The court at any time may drop a defendant unnecessarily or improperly joined.

(4) Effect. Except as otherwise provided in the notice, or stipulation of dismissal, or order of the court, any dismissal is without prejudice.

(j) **Deposit and its Distribution**. The plaintiff shall deposit with the court any money required by law as a condition to the exercise of the power of eminent domain; and, although not so required, may make a deposit when permitted by statute. In such cases the court and attorneys shall expedite the proceedings for the distribution of the money so deposited and for the ascertainment and payment of just compensation. If the compensation finally awarded to any defendant exceeds the amount which has been paid to that defendant on distribution of the deposit, the court shall enter judgment against the plaintiff and in favor of that defendant for the deficiency. If the compensation finally awarded to any defendant is less than the amount which has been paid to that defendant, the court shall enter judgment against that defendant and in favor of the plaintiff for the overpayment.

(k) **Condemnation Under a State's Power of Eminent** Domain. The practice as herein prescribed governs in actions involving the exercise of the power of eminent domain under the law of a state, provided that if the state law makes provision for trial of any issue by jury, or for trial of the issue of compensation or both, that provision shall be followed.

(l) **Costs**. Costs are not subject to Rule 54(d).

Rule 72. Magistrate Judges; Pre-trial Orders

(a) **Nondispositive Matters.** A magistrate judge to whom a pre-trial matter not dispositive of a claim or defense of a party is referred to hear and determine shall promptly conduct such proceedings as are required and when appropriate enter into the record a written order setting forth the disposition of the matter. Within 10 days after being served with a copy of the magistrate judge's order, a party may serve and file objections to the order; a party may not thereafter assign as error a defect in the magistrate judge's order to which objection was not timely made. The district judge to whom the case is assigned shall consider such objections and shall modify or set aside any portion of the magistrate judge's order found to be clearly erroneous or contrary to law.

(b) **Dispositive Motions and Prisoner Petitions.** A magistrate judge assigned without consent of the parties to hear a pre-trial matter dispositive of a claim or defense of a party or a prisoner petition challenging the conditions of confinement shall promptly conduct such proceedings as are required. A record shall be made of all evidentiary proceedings before the magistrate judge, and a record may be made of such other proceedings as the magistrate judge deems necessary. The magistrate judge shall enter into the record a recommendation for disposition of the matter, including proposed findings of fact when appropriate. The clerk shall forthwith mail copies to all parties.

A party objecting to the recommended disposition of the matter shall promptly arrange for the transcription of the record, or portions of it as all parties may agree upon or the magistrate judge deems sufficient, unless the district judge otherwise directs. Within 10 days after being served with a copy of the recommended disposition, a party may serve and file specific, written objections to the proposed findings and recommendations. A party may respond to another party's objections within 10 days after being served with a copy thereof. The district judge to whom the case is assigned shall make a de novo determination upon the record, or after additional evidence, of any portion of the magistrate judge's disposition to which specific written objection has been made in accordance with this rule. The district judge may accept, reject, or modify the recommended decision, receive further evidence, or recommit the matter to the magistrate judge with instructions.

Rule 73. Magistrate Judges; Trial by Consent and Appeal Options

(a) **Powers; Procedure.** When specially designated to exercise such jurisdiction by local rule or order of the district court and when all parties consent thereto, a magistrate judge may exercise the authority provided by Title 28, U.S.C. § 636(c) and may conduct any or all proceedings, including a jury or non-jury trial, in a civil case. A record of the proceedings shall be made in accordance with the requirements of Title 28, U.S.C. § 636(c)(5).

(b) **Consent.** When a magistrate judge has been designated to exercise civil trial jurisdiction, the clerk shall give written notice to the parties of their opportunity to consent to the exercise by a magistrate judge of civil jurisdiction over the case, as authorized by Title 28, U.S.C. § 636(c). If, within the period specified by local rule, the parties agree to a magistrate judge's exercise of such authority, they shall execute and file a joint form of consent or separate forms of consent setting forth such election.

A district judge, magistrate judge, or other court official may again advise the parties of the availability of the magistrate judge, but, in so doing, shall also advise the parties that they are free to withhold consent without adverse substantive consequences. A district judge or magistrate judge shall not be informed of a party's response to the clerk's notification, unless all parties have consented to the referral of the matter to a magistrate judge.

The district judge, for good cause shown on the judge's own initiative, or under extraordinary circumstances shown by a party, may vacate a reference of a civil matter to a magistrate judge under this subdivision.

(c) **Appeal.** In accordance with Title 28, U.S.C. § 636(c)(3), appeal from a judgment entered upon direction of a magistrate judge in proceedings under this rule will lie to the court of appeals as it would from a judgment of the district court.

[Rules 74, 75, and 76 abrogated by Order of the Supreme Court, April 11, 1997]

X. DISTRICT COURTS AND CLERKS

Rule 77. District Courts and Clerks

(a) **District Courts Always Open.** The district courts shall be deemed always open for the purpose of filing any pleading or other proper paper, of issuing and returning mesne and final process, and of making and directing all interlocutory motions, orders, and rules.

(b) **Trials and Hearings; Orders in Chambers.** All trials upon the merits shall be conducted in open court and so far as convenient in a regular court room. All other acts or proceedings may be done or conducted by a judge in chambers, without the attendance of the clerk or other court officials and at any place either within or without the district; but no hearing, other than one ex parte, shall be conducted outside the district without the consent of all parties affected thereby.

(c) Clerk's Office and Orders by Clerk. The clerk's office with the clerk or a deputy in attendance shall be open during business hours on all days except Saturdays, Sundays, and legal holidays, but a district court may provide by local rule or order that its clerk's office shall be open for specified hours on Saturdays or particular legal holidays other than New Year's Day, Birthday of Martin Luther King, Jr., Washington's Birthday, Memorial Day, Independence Day, Labor Day, Columbus Day, Veterans Day, Thanksgiving Day, and Christmas Day. All motions and applications in the clerk's office for issuing mesne process, for issuing final process to enforce and execute judgments, for entering defaults or judgments by default, and for other proceedings which do not require allowance or order of the court are grantable of course by the clerk; but the clerk's action may be suspended or altered or rescinded by the court upon cause shown.

(d) Notice of Orders or Judgments. Immediately upon the entry of an order or judgment the clerk shall serve a notice of the entry by mail in the manner provided for in Rule 5 upon each party who is not in default for failure to appear, and shall make a note in the docket of the mailing. Any party may in addition serve a notice of such entry in the manner provided in Rule 5 for the service of papers. Lack of notice of the entry by the clerk does not affect the time to appeal or relieve or authorize the court to relieve a party for failure to appeal within the time allowed, except as permitted in Rule 4(a) of the Federal Rules of Appellate Procedure.

Rule 78. Motion Day

Unless local conditions make it impracticable, each district court shall establish regular times and places, at intervals sufficiently frequent for the prompt dispatch of business, at which motions requiring notice and hearing may be heard and disposed of; but the judge at any time or place and on such notice, if any, as the judge considers reasonable may make orders for the advancement, conduct, and hearing of actions.

To expedite its business, the court may make provision by rule or order for the submission and determination of motions without oral hearing upon brief written statements of reasons in support and opposition.

Rule 79. Books and Records Kept by the Clerk and Entries Therein

(a) Civil Docket. The clerk shall keep a book known as "civil docket" of such form and style as may be prescribed by the Director of the Administrative Office of the United States Courts with the approval of the Judicial Conference of the United States, and shall enter therein each civil action to which these rules are made applicable. Actions shall be assigned consecutive file numbers. The file number of each action shall be noted on the folio of the docket whereon the first entry of the action is made. All papers filed with the clerk, all process issued and returns made thereon, all appearances, orders, verdicts, and judgments shall be entered chronologically in the civil docket on the folio assigned to the action and shall be marked with its file number. These entries shall be brief but shall show the nature of each paper filed or writ issued and the substance of each order or judgment of the court and of the returns showing execution of process. The entry of an order or judgment shall show the date the entry is made. When in an action trial by jury has been properly demanded or ordered the clerk shall enter the word "jury" on the folio assigned to that action.

(b) Civil Judgments and Orders. The clerk shall keep, in such form and manner as the Director of the Administrative Office of the United States Courts with the approval of the Judicial Conference of the United States may prescribe, a correct copy of every final judgment or appealable order, or order affecting title to or lien upon real or personal property, and any other order which the court may direct to be kept.

(c) Indices; Calendars. Suitable indices of the civil docket and of every civil judgment and order referred to in subdivision (b) of this rule shall be kept by the clerk under the direction of the court. There shall be prepared under the direction of the court calendars of all actions ready for trial, which shall distinguish "jury actions" from "court actions."

(d) Other Books and Records of the Clerk. The clerk shall also keep such other books and records as may be required from time to time by the Director of the Administrative Office of the United States Court with the approval of the Judicial Conference of the United States.

Rule 80. Stenographer; Stenographic Report or Transcript as Evidence
(a), (b) [Abrogated]
(c) Stenographic Report or Transcript as Evidence. Whenever the testimony of a witness at a trial or hearing which was stenographically reported is admissible in evidence at a later trial, it may be proved by the transcript thereof duly certified by the person who reported the testimony.

XI. GENERAL PROVISIONS

Rule 81. Applicability in General
(a) To What Proceedings Applicable.
(1) These rules do not apply to prize proceedings in admiralty governed by Title 10, U.S.C. §§7651-7681. They do not apply to proceedings in bankruptcy or proceedings in copyright under Title 17, U.S.C., except in so far as they may be made applicable thereto by rules promulgated by Supreme Court of the United States. They do not apply to mental health proceedings in the United States District Court for the District of Columbia.

(2) These rules are applicable to proceedings for admission to citizenship, habeas corpus, and quo warranto, to the extent that the practice in such proceedings is not set forth in statutes of the United States, the Rules Governing Section 2254 Cases, or the Rules Governing Section 2255 Proceedings, and has heretofore conformed to the practice in civil actions.

(3) In proceedings under Title 9, U.S.C., relating to arbitration, or under the Act of May 20, 1926, ch. 347, § 9 (44 Stat. 585), U.S.C., Title 45, §159, relating to boards of arbitration of railway labor disputes, these rules apply only to the extent that matters of procedure are not provided for in those statutes. These rules apply to proceedings to compel the giving of testimony or production of documents in accordance with a subpoena issued by an officer or agency of the United States under any statute of the United States except as otherwise provided by statute or by rules of the district court or by order of the court in the proceedings.

(4) These rules do not alter the method prescribed by the Act of February 18, 1922, c. 57, § 2 (42 Stat. 388), U.S.C., Title 7, § 292; or by the Act of June 10, 1930, c. 436, § 7 (46 Stat. 534), as amended, U.S.C., Title 7, § 499g(c), for instituting proceedings in the United States district courts to review orders of the Secretary of Agriculture; or prescribed by the Act of

June 25, 1934, c. 742, § 2 (48 Stat. 1214), U.S.C., Title 15, §522, for instituting proceedings to review orders of the Secretary of the Interior; or prescribed by the Act of February 22, 1935, c. 18, § 5 (49 Stat. 31), U.S.C., Title 15, §715d(c), as extended, for instituting proceedings to review orders of petroleum control boards; but the conduct of such proceedings in the district courts shall be made to conform to these rules so far as applicable.

(5) These rules do not alter the practice in the United States district courts prescribed in the Act of July 5, 1935, c. 372, §§ 9 and 10 (49 Stat. 453), as amended, U.S.C., Title 29, §§ 159 and 160, for beginning and conducting proceedings to enforce orders of the National Labor Relations Board; and in respects not covered by those statutes, the practice in the district courts shall conform to these rules so far as applicable.

(6) These rules apply to proceedings for enforcement or review of compensation orders under the Longshoremen's and Harbor Workers' Compensation Act, Act of March 4, 1927, c. 509, §§ 18, 21 (44 Stat. 1434, 1436), as amended, U.S.C., Title 33, §§ 918, 921, except to the extent that matters of procedure are provided for in that Act. The provisions for service by publication and for answer in proceedings to cancel certificates of citizenship under the Act of June 27, 1952, c. 477, Title III, c. 2, § 340 (66 Stat. 260), U.S.C., Title 8, § 1451, remain in effect.

(7) [Abrogated]

(b) Scire Facias and Mandamus. The writs of scire facias and mandamus are abolished. Relief heretofore available by mandamus or scire facias may be obtained by appropriate action or by appropriate motion under the practice prescribed in these rules.

(c) Removed Actions. These rules apply to civil actions removed to the United States district courts from the state courts and govern procedure after removal. Repleading is not necessary unless the court so orders. In a removed action in which the defendant has not answered, the defendant shall answer or present the other defenses or objections available under these rules within 20 days after the receipt through service or otherwise of a copy of the initial pleading setting forth the claim for relief upon which the action or proceeding is based, or within 20 days after the service of summons upon such initial pleading, then filed, or within 5 days after the filing of the petition for removal, whichever period is longest. If at the time of removal all necessary pleadings have been served, a party entitled to trial by jury under Rule 38 shall be accorded it, if the party's demand therefor is served within 10 days after the petition for removal is filed if the party is the petitioner, or if not the petitioner within 10 days after service on the party of the notice of filing the petition party who, prior to removal, has made an express demand for trial by jury in accordance with state law, need not make a demand after removal. If state law applicable in the court from which the case is removed does not require the parties to make express demands in order to claim trial by jury, they need not make demands after removal unless the court directs that they do so within a specified time if they desire to claim trial by jury. The court may make this direction on its own motion and shall do so as a matter of course at the request of any party. The failure of a party to make demand as directed constitutes a waiver by that party of trial by jury.

(d) [Abrogated]

(e) Law Applicable. Whenever in these rules the law of the state in which the district court is held is made applicable, the law applied in the District of Columbia governs proceedings in the United States District Court for the District of Columbia. When the word "state" is used, it includes, if appropriate, the District of Columbia. When the term "statute of the United States" is used, it includes, so far as concerns proceedings in the United States District Court for the District of Columbia, any Act of Congress locally applicable to and in force in the District of Columbia. When the law of a state is referred to, the word "law" includes the statutes of that state and the state judicial decisions construing them.

(f) References to Officer of the United States. Under any rule in which reference is made to an officer or agency of the United States, the term "officer" includes a district director of internal revenue, a former district director or collector of internal revenue, or the personal representative of a deceased district director or collector of internal revenue.

Rule 82. Jurisdiction and Venue Unaffected

These rules shall not be construed to extend or limit the jurisdiction of the United States district courts or the venue of actions therein. An admiralty or maritime claim within the meaning of Rule 9(h) shall not be treated as a civil action for the purposes of Title 28, U.S.C. §§ 1391-93.

Rule 83. Rules By District Courts; Judge's Directives

(a) Local Rules

(1) Each district court, acting by a majority of its district judges, may, after giving appropriate public notice and an opportunity for comment, make and amend rules governing its practice. A local rule shall be consistent withXbut not duplicative ofXActs of Congress and rules adopted under 28 U.S.C. §§ 2072 AND 2075, and shall conform to any uniform numbering system prescribed by the Judicial Conference of the United States. A local rule takes effect on the date specified by the district court and remains in effect unless amended by the court or abrogated by the judicial council of the circuit. Copies of rules and amendments shall, upon their promulgation, be furnished to the judicial council and the Administrative Office of the United States Courts and be made available to the public.

(2) A local rule imposing a requirement of form shall not be enforced in a manner that causes a party to lose rights because of a non-willful failure to comply with the requirement.

(b) Procedures When There Is No Controlling Law A judge may regulate practice in any manner consistent with federal law, rules adopted under 28 U.S.C. §§ 2072 and 2075, and local rules of the district. No sanction or other disadvantage may be imposed for noncompliance with any requirement not in federal law, federal rules, or the local district rules unless the alleged violator has been furnished in the particular case with actual notice of the requirement.

Rule 84. Forms

The forms contained in the Appendix of Forms are sufficient under the rules and are intended to indicate the simplicity and brevity of statement which the rules contemplate.

Rule 85. Title

These rules may be known and cited as the Federal Rules of Civil Procedure.

Rule 86. Effective Date

(a) Effective Date of Original Rules. These rules will take effect on the day which is 3 months subsequent to the adjournment of the second regular session of the 75th Congress, but if that day is prior to September 1, 1938, then these rules will take effect on September 1, 1938. They govern all proceedings in actions brought after they take effect and also all further proceedings in actions then pending, except to the extent that in the opinion of the court their application in a particular action pending when the rules take effect would not be feasible or would work injustice, in which event the former procedure applies.

(b) Effective Date of Amendments. The amendments adopted by the Supreme Court on December 27, 1946, and transmitted to the Attorney General on January 2, 1947, shall take effect on the day which is three months subsequent to the adjournment of the first regular session of the 80th Congress, but, if that day is prior to September 1, 1947, then these amendments shall take effect on September 1, 1947. They govern all proceedings in actions brought after they take effect and also all further proceedings in actions then pending, except to the extent that in the opinion of the court their application in a particular action pending when the amendments take effect would not be feasible or would work injustice, in which event the former procedure applies.

(c) Effective Date of Amendments. The amendments adopted by the Supreme Court on December 29, 1948, and transmitted to the Attorney General on December 31, 1948, shall take effect on the day following the adjournment of the first regular session of the 81st Congress.

(d) Effective Date of Amendments. The amendments adopted by the Supreme Court on April 17, 1961, and transmitted to the Congress on April 18, 1961, shall take effect on July 19, 1961. They govern all proceedings in actions brought after they take effect and also all further proceedings in actions then pending, except to the extent that in the opinion of the court their application in a particular action pending when the amendments take effect would not be feasible or would work injustice, in which event the former procedure applies.

(e) Effective Date of Amendments. The amendments adopted by the Supreme Court on January 21, 1963, and transmitted to the Congress on January 21, 1963, shall take effect on July 1, 1963. They govern all proceedings in actions brought after they take effect and also all further proceedings in actions then pending, except to the extent that in the opinion of the court their application in a particular action pending when the amendments take effect would not be feasible or would work injustice, in which event the former procedure applies.

FEDERAL RULES OF CRIMINAL PROCEDURE

As Amended to December 1, 2004

I. SCOPE, PURPOSE, AND CONSTRUCTION

Rule 1. Scope

These rules govern the procedure in all criminal proceedings in the courts of the United States, as provided in Rule 54(a); and, whenever specifically provided in one of the rules, to preliminary, supplementary, and special proceedings before United States magistrate judges and at proceedings before state and local judicial officers.

Rule 2. Purpose and Construction

These rules are intended to provide for the just determination of every criminal proceeding. They shall be construed to secure simplicity in procedure, fairness in administration and the elimination of unjustifiable expense and delay.

II. PRELIMINARY PROCEEDINGS

Rule 3. The Complaint

The complaint is a written statement of the essential facts constituting the offense charged. It must be made under oath before a magistrate judge or, if none is reasonably available, before a state or local judicial officer.

Rule 4. Arrest Warrant or Summons upon Complaint

(a) **Issuance**. If it appears from the complaint, or from an affidavit or affidavits filed with the complaint, that there is probable cause to believe that an offense has been committed and that the defendant has committed it, a warrant for the arrest of the defendant shall issue to any officer authorized by law to execute it. Upon the request of the attorney for the government a summons instead of a warrant shall issue. More than one warrant or summons may issue on the same complaint. If a defendant fails to appear in response to the summons, a warrant shall issue.

(b) **Form.**

(1) *Warrant*. The warrant shall be signed by the magistrate judge and shall contain the name of the defendant or, if the defendant's name is unknown, any name or description by which the defendant can be identified with reasonable certainty. It shall describe the offense charged in the complaint. It shall command that the defendant be arrested and brought before the nearest available magistrate judge.

(2) *Summons*. The summons should be in the same form as the warrant except that it shall summon the defendant to appear before a magistrate at a stated time and place.

(c) **Execution or Service; and Return.**

(1) *By Whom*. The warrant shall be executed by a marshal or by some other officer authorized by law. The summons may be served by any person authorized to serve a summons in a civil action.

(2) **Location.** The warrant may be executed or the summons may be served at any place within the jurisdiction of the United States or anywhere else a federal statute authorizes an arrest.

(3) **Manner.** The warrant shall be executed by the arrest of the defendant. The officer need not have the warrant at the time of the arrest but upon request shall show the warrant to the defendant as soon as possible. If the officer does not have the warrant at the time of the arrest, the officer shall then inform the defendant of the offense charged and of the fact that a warrant has been issued. The summons shall be served upon a defendant by delivering a copy to the defendant personally, or by leaving it at the defendant's dwelling house or usual place of abode with some person of suitable age and discretion then residing therein and by mailing a copy of the summons to the defendant's last known address. A summons is served on an organization by delivering a copy to an officer, to a managing or general agent or to another agent appointed or legally authorized to receive service of process. A copy must also be mailed to the organization's last known address within the district or to its principal place of business elsewhere in the United States.

(4) **Return.** The officer executing a warrant shall make return thereof to the magistrate judge or other officer before whom the defendant is brought pursuant to Rule 5. At the request of the attorney for the government any unexecuted warrant shall be returned to and canceled by the magistrate judge by whom it was issued or, if none is reasonably available, by a state or local judicial officer. On or before the return day the person to whom a summons was delivered for service shall make return thereof to the magistrate judge before whom the summons is returnable. At the request of the attorney for the government made at any time while the complaint is pending, a warrant returned unexecuted and not canceled or a summons returned unserved or a duplicate thereof may be delivered by the magistrate judge to the marshal or other authorized person for execution or service.

Rule 5. Initial Appearance
  (a) **In General.**
  (1) **Appearance Upon an Arrest.** Except as otherwise provided in this rule, an officer making an arrest within or outside the United States, under a warrant issued upon a complaint or any person making an arrest without a warrant shall take the arrested person without unnecessary delay before the nearest available federal magistrate judge or, if a federal magistrate judge is not reasonably available, before a state or local judicial officer authorized by 18 U.S.C. § 3041. If a person arrested without a warrant is brought before a magistrate judge, a complaint, satisfying the probable cause requirements of Rule 4(a), shall be promptly filed. When a person, arrested with or without a warrant or given a summons, appears initially before the magistrate judge, the magistrate judge shall proceed in accordance with the applicable subdivisions of this rule.

  (2) **Exceptions.** An officer making an arrest under a warrant issued upon a complaint charging solely a violation of 18 U.S.C. § 1073 need not comply with this rule if the person arrested is transferred without unnecessary delay to the custody of appropriate state or local authorities in the district of arrest and an attorney for the government moves promptly, in the district in which the warrant was issued, to dismiss the complaint. If a defendant is arrested for violating probation or supervised release, Rule 32.1 applies. If a defendant is arrested for failing to appear in another district, Rule 40 applies.

  (3) **Appearance Upon a Summons.** When a defendant appears in response to a summons under Rule 4, a magistrate judge must proceed under Rule 5(d) or (e), as applicable.

(b) Arrest Without a Warrant. If a defendant is arrested without a warrant, a complaint meeting Rule 4(a)'s requirement of probable cause must be promptly filed in the district where the offense was allegedly committed.

(c) Place of Initial Appearance; Transfer to Another District.

(1) Arrest in the District Where the Offense Was Allegedly Committed. If the defendant is arrested in the district where the offense was allegedly committed:

(A) the initial appearance must be in that district; and

(B) if a magistrate judge is not reasonably available, the initial appearance may be before a state or local judicial officer.

(2) Arrest in a District Other Than Where the Offense Was Allegedly Committed. If the defendant was arrested in a district other than where the offense was allegedly committed, the initial appearance must be in the district of arrest or in an adjacent district. If the appearance can occur more promptly there or the offense was allegedly committed there, the initial appearance will occur on the day of arrest.

(3) Procedures in a District Other Than Where the Offense Was Allegedly Committed. If the initial appearance occurs in a district other than where the offense was allegedly committed, the following procedures apply: the magistrate judge must inform the defendant about the provisions of Rule 20; if the defendant was arrested without a warrant, the district court where the offense was allegedly committed must first issue a warrant before the magistrate judge transfers the defendant to that district; the magistrate judge must conduct a preliminary hearing if required by Rule 5.1 or Rule 58(b)(2)(G); the magistrate judge must transfer the defendant to the district where the offense was allegedly committed if the government produces the warrant, a certified copy of the warrant, a facsimile of either, or other appropriate form of either; and when a defendant is transferred and discharged, the clerk must promptly transmit the papers and any bail to the clerk in the district where the offense was allegedly committed.

(d) Procedure in a Felony Case.

(1) Advice. If the defendant is charged with a felony, the judge must inform the defendant of the complaint against the defendant, and any affidavit filed with it; the defendant's right to retain counsel or to request that counsel be appointed if the defendant cannot obtain counsel; the circumstances, if any, under which the defendant may secure pre-trial release; any right to a preliminary hearing, and the defendant's right not to make a statement, and that any statement made may be used against the defendant.

(2) Consulting with Counsel. The judge must allow the defendant reasonable opportunity to consult with counsel.

(3) Detention or Release. The judge must detain or release the defendant as provided by statute or these rules.

(4) Plea. A defendant may be asked to plead only under Rule 10.

(e) Procedure in a Misdemeanor Case. If the defendant is charged with a misdemeanor only, the judge must inform the defendant in accordance with Rule 58 (b)(2).

(f) Video Teleconferencing. Video teleconferencing may be used to conduct an appearance under this rule if the defendant consents.

Rule 5.1. Preliminary Hearing

(a) In General. If a defendant is charged with an offense other than a petty offense, a magistrate judge must conduct a preliminary hearing unless: the defendant waives the hearing; the defendant is indicted; the government files an information under Rule 7(b) charging the defendant with a felony; the government files an information charging the defendant with a misdemeanor or the defendant is charged with a misdemeanor and consents to trial before a magistrate judge.

(b) Selecting a District. A defendant arrested in a district other than where the offense was allegedly committed may elect to have the preliminary hearing conducted in the district where the prosecution is pending.

(c) Scheduling. The magistrate judge must hold the preliminary hearing within a reasonable time, but no later than 10 days after the initial appearance if the defendant is in custody and no later than 20 days if not in custody.

(d) Extending the Time. With the defendant's consent and upon a showing of good cause – taking into account the public interest in the prompt disposition of criminal cases – a magistrate judge may extend the time limits in Rule 5.1(c) on or more times. If the defendant does not consent, the magistrate judge may extend the time limits only on a showing that extraordinary circumstances exist and justice requires the delay.

(e) Hearing and Finding. At the preliminary hearing, the defendant may cross-examine adverse witnesses and may introduce evidence but may not object to evidence on the ground that it was unlawfully acquired. If the magistrate judge finds probable cause to believe an offense has been committed and the defendant committed it, the magistrate judge must promptly require the defendant to appear for further proceedings.

(f) Discharging the Defendant. If the magistrate judge finds no probable cause to believe an offense has been committed or the defendant committed it, the magistrate judge must dismiss the complaint and discharge the defendant. A discharge does not preclude the government from later prosecuting the defendant for the same offense.

(g) Recording the Proceedings. The preliminary hearing must be recorded by a court reporter or by a suitable recording device. A recording of the proceeding may be made available to any party upon request. A copy of the recording and a transcript may be provided to any party upon request and upon any payment required by applicable Judicial Conference regulations.

(h) Producing a Statement.

(1) In General. Rule 26.2(a)-(d) and (f) applies at any hearing under this rule, unless the magistrate judge for good cause rules otherwise in a particular case.

(2) Sanctions for Not Producing a Statement. If a party disobeys a Rule 26.2 order to deliver a statement to the moving party, the magistrate judge must not consider the testimony of a witness whose statement is withheld.

III. THE GRAND JURY, THE INDICTMENT AND THE INFORMATION

Rule 6. The Grand Jury

(a) Summoning a Grand Jury.

(1) In General. When the public interest so requires, the court must order that one or more grand juries be summoned. A grand jury must have 16 to 23 members, and the court must order that enough legally qualified persons be summoned to meet this requirement.

(2) Alternate Jurors. When a grand jury is selected, the court may also select alternate jurors. Alternate jurors must have the same qualifications and be selected in the same manner as any other juror. Alternate jurors replace jurors in the same sequence in which the alternates were selected. An alternate juror who replaces a juror is subject to the same challenges, takes the same oath, and has the same authority as the other jurors.

(b) Objections to Grand Jury and to Grand Jurors.

(1) Challenges. The attorney for the government or a defendant who has been held to answer in the district court may challenge the array of jurors on the ground that the grand jury was not selected, drawn or summoned in accordance with law, and may challenge an individual juror on the ground that the juror is not legally qualified.

(2) Motion to Dismiss an Indictment. A party may move to dismiss the indictment based on an objection to the grand jury or on an individual juror's lack of legal qualification, unless the court has previously ruled on the same objection under Rule 6(b)(1). The motion to dismiss is governed by 28 U.S.C. sec. 1867(e). The court must not dismiss the indictment on the ground that a grand juror was not legally qualified if the record shows that at least 12 qualified jurors concurred in the indictment.

(c) Foreperson and Deputy Foreperson. The court shall appoint one of the jurors to be foreperson and another to be deputy foreperson. The foreperson shall have power to administer oaths and affirmations and shall sign all indictments. The foreperson or another juror designated by the foreperson shall keep record of the number of jurors concurring in the finding of every indictment and shall file the record with the clerk of the court, but the record shall not be made public except on order of the court. During the absence of the foreperson, the deputy foreperson shall act as foreperson.

(d) Who May Be Present.

(1) While the Grand Jury is in Session. Attorneys for the government, the witness under examination, interpreters when needed and, for the purpose of taking the evidence, a stenographer or operator of a recording device may be present while the grand jury is in session.

(2) During Deliberations and Voting. No person other than the jurors, and any interpreter necessary to assist a juror who is hearing or speech impaired, may be present while the grand jury is deliberating or voting.

(e) Recording and Disclosure of Proceedings.

(1) Recording of Proceedings. All proceedings, except when the grand jury is deliberating or voting, shall be recorded stenographically or by an electronic recording device. An unintentional failure of any recording to reproduce all or any portion of a proceeding shall not affect the validity of the prosecution. The recording or reporter's notes or any transcript prepared therefrom shall remain in the custody or control of the attorney for the government unless otherwise ordered by the court in a particular case.

(2) General Rule of Secrecy. No obligation of secrecy may be imposed on any person except in accordance with Rule 6(e) (2)(B). Unless these rules provide otherwise, the following persons must not disclose a matter occurring before the grand jury: a grand juror, an interpreter, a stenographer, an operator of a recording device, a typist who transcribes recorded testimony, an attorney for the government, or any person to whom disclosure is made under Rule 6(e)(3)(A)(ii) or (iii).

(3) Exceptions.

(A) Disclosure otherwise prohibited by this rule of matters occurring before the grand jury, other than its deliberations and the vote of any grand juror, may be made to-

   (i) an attorney for the government for use in the performance of such attorney's duty;

   (ii) any government personnel (including personnel of a state or subdivision of a state) as are deemed necessary by an attorney for the government to assist an attorney for the government in the performance of such attorney's duty to enforce federal criminal law.

(iii) a person authorized by 18 USC sec. 3322.

(B) Any person to whom matters are disclosed under Rule 6(e) (3)(A)(ii) of this paragraph shall not utilize that grand jury material for any purpose other than assisting the attorney for the government in the performance of such attorney's duty to enforce federal criminal law. An attorney for the government shall promptly provide the district court, before which was impaneled the grand jury whose material has been so disclosed, with the names of the persons to whom such disclosure has been made, and shall certify that the attorney has advised such persons of their obligation of secrecy under this rule.

(C) An attorney for the government may disclose any grand-jury matter.

(D) An attorney for the government may disclose any grand-jury matter involving foreign intelligence, counterintelligence (as defined in 50 U.S.C. sec. 401a), or foreign intelligence information (as defined in Rule 6(e)(3)(D)(iii)) to any federal law enforcement, intelligence, protective, immigration, national defense, or national security official to assist the official receiving the information in the performance of that official's duties. (i) Any federal official who receives information under Rule 6(e)(3)(D) may use the information only as necessary in the conduct of that person's official duties subject to any limitations on the unauthorized disclosure of such information. (ii) Within a reasonable time after disclosure is made under Rule 6(e)(3)(D), an attorney for the government must file, under seal, a notice with the court in the district where the grand jury convened stating that such information was disclosed and the departments, agencies, or entities to which the disclosure was made.

(iii) As used in Rule 6(e)(3)(D), the term "foreign intelligence information" means:
  (a) information, whether or not it concerns a United States person, that relates to the ability of the United States to protect against actual or potential attack or other grave hostile acts of a foreign power or its agent; sabotage or international terrorism by a foreign power or its agent; or clandestine intelligence activities by an intelligence service or network of a foreign power or by its agent; or
  (b) information, whether or not it concerns a United States person, with respect to a foreign power or foreign territory that relates to the national defense or the security of the United States; or the conduct of the foreign affairs of the United States.

(E) The court may authorize disclosure--at a time, in a manner, and subject to any other conditions that it directs--of a grand-jury matter: (i) preliminarily to or in connection with a judicial proceeding; (ii) at the request of a defendant who shows that a ground may exist to dismiss the indictment because of a matter that occurred before the grand jury; (iii) at the request of the government if it shows that the matter may disclose a violation of state or Indian tribal criminal law, as long as the disclosure is to an appropriate state, state subdivision, or Indian tribal official for the purpose of enforcing that law; or (iv) at the request of the government if it shows that the matter may disclose a violation of military criminal law under the Uniform Code of Military Justice, as long as the disclosure is to an appropriate military official for the purpose of enforcing that law.

(F) A petition to disclose a grand-jury matter under Rule 6(e)(3)(E)(i) must be filed in the district where the grand jury convened. Unless the hearing is ex parte--as it may be when the government is the petitioner--the petitioner must serve the petition on, and the court must afford a reasonable opportunity to appear and be heard to:
  (i) an attorney for the government;
  (ii) the parties to the judicial proceeding; and
  (iii) any other person whom the court may designate.

(G) If the petition to disclose arises out of a judicial proceeding in another district, the petitioned court must transfer the petition to the other court unless the petitioned court can reasonably determine whether disclosure is proper. If the petitioned court decides to transfer, it must send to the transferee court the material sought to be disclosed, if feasible, and a written evaluation of the need for continued grand jury secrecy. The transferee court must afford those persons identified in Rule 6(e)(3)(F) a reasonable opportunity to appear and be heard.

(4) Sealed Indictments. The federal magistrate judge to whom an indictment is returned may direct that the indictment be kept secret until the defendant is in custody or has been released pending trial. Thereupon the clerk shall seal the indictment and no person shall disclose the return of the indictment except when necessary for the issuance and execution of a warrant or summons.

(5) Closed Hearing. Subject to any right to an open hearing in contempt proceedings, the court shall order a hearing on matters affecting a grand jury proceeding to be closed to the extent necessary to prevent disclosure of matters occurring before a grand jury.

(6) Sealed Records. Records, orders and subpoenas relating to grand jury proceedings shall be kept under seal to the extent and for such time as is necessary to prevent disclosure of matters occurring before a grand jury.

(7) Contempt. A knowing violation of Rule 6 may be punished as a contempt of court.

(f) Indictment and Return. An indictment may be found only upon the concurrence of 12 or more jurors. The indictment shall be returned by the grand jury to a federal magistrate judge in open court. If a complaint or information is pending against the defendant and 12 jurors do not concur in finding an indictment, the foreperson shall so report to a federal magistrate judge in writing forthwith.

(g) Discharging the Grand Jury. A grand jury shall serve until discharged by the court, but no grand jury may serve more than 18 months unless the court extends the service of the grand jury for a period of six months or less upon a determination that such extension is in the public interest.

(h) Excusing a Juror. At any time for cause shown the court may excuse a juror either temporarily or permanently, and in the latter event the court may impanel another person in place of the juror excused.

(i) "Indian Tribe" Defined. "Indian Tribe" means an Indian tribe recognized by the Secretary of the Interior on a list published in the Federal Register under 25 USC sec. 479a-1.

Rule 7. The Indictment and the Information

(a) When Used.

(1) Felony. An offense (other than criminal contempt) must be prosecuted by an indictment if it is punishable:

(A) by death; or

(B) by imprisonment for more than one year.

(2) Misdemeanor. An offense punishable by imprisonment for one year or less may be prosecuted in accordance with Rule 58(b)(1).

(b) Waiving Indictment. An offense punishable by imprisonment for more than one year may be prosecuted by information if the defendant--in open court and after being advised of the nature of the charge and of the defendant's rights--waives prosecution by indictment.

(c) Nature and Contents.

(1) In General. The indictment or information must be a plain, concise, and definite written statement of the essential facts constituting the offense charged and must be signed by an attorney for the government. It need not contain a formal introduction or conclusion. A count may incorporate by reference an allegation made in another count. A count may allege that the means by which the defendant committed the offense are unknown or that the defendant committed it by one or more specified means. For each count, the indictment or information must give the official or customary citation of the statute, rule, regulation, or other provision of law that the defendant is alleged to have violated. For purposes of an indictment referred to in section 3282 of title 18, United States Code, for which the identity of the defendant is unknown, it shall be sufficient for the indictment to describe the defendant as an individual whose name is unknown, but who has a particular DNA profile, as that term is defined in that section 3282.

(2) Criminal Forfeiture. No judgment of forfeiture may be entered in a criminal proceeding unless the indictment or the information provides notice that the defendant has an interest in property that is subject to forfeiture in accordance with the applicable statute.

(3) Citation Error. Unless the defendant was misled and thereby prejudiced, neither an error in a citation nor a citation's omission is a ground to dismiss the indictment or information or to reverse a conviction.

(d) Surplusage. Upon the defendant's motion, the court may strike surplusage from the indictment or information.

(e) Amending an Information. Unless an additional or different offense is charged or a substantial right of the defendant is prejudiced, the court may permit an information to be amended at any time before the verdict or finding.

(f) Bill of Particulars. The court may direct the government to file a bill of particulars. The defendant may move for a bill of particulars before or within 10 days after arraignment or at a later time if the court permits. The government may amend a bill of particulars subject to such conditions as justice requires.

Rule 8. Joinder of Offenses or Defendants

(a) Joinder of Offenses. Two or more offenses may be charged in the same indictment or information in a separate count for each offense if the offenses charged, whether felonies or misdemeanors or both, are of the same or similar character or are based on the same act or transaction or on two or more acts or transactions connected together or constituting parts of a common scheme or plan.

(b) Joinder of Defendants. Two or more defendants may be charged in the same indictment or information if they are alleged to have participated in the same act or transaction or in the same series of acts or transactions constituting an offense or offenses. Such defendants may be charged in one or more counts together or separately and all of the defendants need not be charged in each count.

Rule 9. Arrest Warrant or Summons Upon Indictment or Information

(a) Issuance. The court must issue a warrant – or at the government's request, a summons – for each defendant named in an indictment or named in an information if one or more affidavits accompanying the information establish probable cause to believe that an offense has been committed and that the defendant committed it. The court may issue more than one warrant or summons for the same defendant. If a defendant fails to appear in response to a summons, the court may, and upon request of an attorney for the government must, issue a warrant. The court must issue the arrest warrant to an officer authorized to execute it or the summons to a person authorized to serve it.

(b) Form.

(1) Warrant. The form of the warrant shall be as provided in Rule 4(b)(1) except that it shall be signed by the clerk, it shall describe the offense charged in the indictment or information.

(2) Summons. The summons shall be in the same form as the warrant except that it shall summon the defendant to appear before a magistrate judge at a stated time and place.

(c) Execution or Service; Return; Initial Appearance.

(1) Execution or Service. The warrant must be executed or the summons served as provided in Rule 4(c)(1), (2) and (3).

(2) Return. A warrant or summons must be returned in accordance with Rule 4(c)(4).

(3) Initial Appearance. When an arrested or summoned defendant first appears before the court, the judge must proceed under Rule 5.

IV. ARRAIGNMENT AND PREPARATION FOR TRIAL

Rule 10. Arraignment

(a) **In General.** Arraignment shall be conducted in open court and shall consist of reading the indictment or information to the defendant or stating to the defendant the substance of the charge and calling on the defendant to plead thereto. The defendant shall be given a copy of the indictment or information before being called upon to plead.

(b) **Waiving Appearance.** A defendant need not be present for the arraignment if the defendant has been charged by indictment or misdemeanor information; the defendant, in a written waiver signed by both the defendant and defense counsel, has waived appearance and has affirmed that the defendant received a copy of the indictment or information and that the plea is not guilty; and the court accepts the waiver.

(c) **Video Teleconferencing.** Video teleconferencing may be used to arraign a defendant if the defendant consents.

Rule 11. Pleas

(a) **Entering a Plea.**

(1) In General. A defendant may plead not guilty, guilty, or nolo contendere. If a defendant refuses to plead, or if a defendant is an organization, as defined in 18 U.S.C. §18, fails to appear, the court shall enter a plea of not guilty.

(2) Conditional Plea. With the approval of the court and the consent of the government, a defendant may enter a conditional plea of guilty or nolo contendere, reserving in writing the right, on appeal from the judgment, to review of the adverse determination of any specified pre-trial motion. A defendant who prevails on appeal shall be allowed to withdraw the plea.

(3) Nolo Contendere. A defendant may plead nolo contendere only with the consent of the court. Such a plea shall be accepted by the court only after due consideration of the views of the parties and the interest of the public in the effective administration of justice.

(4) Failure to Enter a Plea. If a defendant refuses to enter a plea or if a defendant organization fails to appear, the court must enter a plea of not guilty.

(b) Considering and Accepting a Guilty or Nolo Contendere Plea.
(1) Advising and Questioning the Defendant.
Before accepting a plea of guilty or nolo contendere, the defendant may be placed under oath, the court must address the defendant personally in open court and inform the defendant of, and determine that the defendant understands, the following:

(A) the government's right, in a prosecution for perjury or false statement, to use against the defendant any statement that the defendant gives under oath;

(B) the right to plead not guilty, or having already so pleaded, to persist in that plea;

(C) the right to a jury trial;

(D) the right to be represented by counsel--and if necessary have the court appoint counsel--at trial and at every other stage of the proceeding;

(E) the right at trial to confront and cross-examine adverse witnesses, to be protected from compelled self-incrimination, to testify and present evidence, and to compel the attendance of witnesses;

(F) the defendant's waiver of these trial rights if the court accepts a plea of guilty or nolo contendere;

(G) the nature of each charge to which the defendant is pleading;

(H) any maximum possible penalty, including imprisonment, fine, and term of supervised release;

(I) any mandatory minimum penalty;

(J) any applicable forfeiture;

(K) the court's authority to order restitution;

(L) the court's obligation to impose a special assessment;

(M) the court's obligation to apply the Sentencing Guidelines, and the court's discretion to depart from those guidelines under some circumstances; and

(N) the terms of any plea-agreement provision waiving the right to appeal or to collaterally attack the sentence.

(2) Ensuring That a Plea is Voluntary. Before accepting a plea of guilty or nolo contendere, the court must address the defendant personally in open court and determine that the plea is voluntary and did not result from force, threats, or promises (other than promises in a plea agreement).

(3) Determining the Factual Basis for a Plea. Before entering judgment on a guilty plea, the court must determine that there is a factual basis for the plea.

(c) Plea Agreement Procedure.

(1) In General. The attorney for the government and the attorney for the defendant or the defendant when acting pro se may agree that, upon the defendant's entering of a plea of guilty or nolo contendere to a charged offense, or to a lesser or related offense, the attorney for the government will:

(A) not bring, or move to dismiss other charges; or

(B) recommend, or agree not to oppose the defendant's request for a particular sentence or sentencing range, or that a particular provision of the Sentencing Guidelines, or policy statement, or sentencing factor is or is not applicable to the case. Any such recommendation or request is not binding on the court; or

(C) agree that a specific sentence or sentencing range is the appropriate disposition of the case, or that a particular provision of the Sentencing Guidelines, or policy statement or sentencing factor is or is not applicable to the case. Such a plea agreement is binding on the court once it is accepted by the court.

The court shall not participate in any discussions between parties concerning any such plea agreement.

  (2) Disclosure of a Plea Agreement. The parties must disclose the plea agreement in open court when the plea is offered, unless the court for good cause allows the parties to disclose the plea agreement in camera.

  (3) Judicial Consideration of a Plea Agreement. (A) To the extent the plea agreement is of the type specified in Rule 11(c)(1)(A) or (C), the court may accept the agreement, reject it, or defer a decision until the court has reviewed the presentence report. (B) To the extent the plea agreement is of the type specified in Rule 11(c)(1)(B), the court must advise the defendant that the defendant has no right to withdraw the plea if the court does not follow the recommendation or request.

  (4) Accepting a Plea Agreement. If the court accepts the plea agreement, it must inform the defendant that to the extent the plea agreement is of the type specified in Rule 11(c)(1)(A) or (C), the agreed disposition will be included in the judgment.

  (5) Rejecting a Plea Agreement. If the court rejects a plea agreement containing provisions of the type specified in Rule 11(c)(1)(A) or (C), the court must do the following on the record and in open court (or, for good cause, in camera):) inform the parties that the court rejects the plea agreement; advise the defendant personally that the court is not required to follow the plea agreement and give the defendant the opportunity to withdraw the plea; and advise the defendant personally that if the plea is not withdrawn, the court may dispose of the case less favorably toward the defendant than the plea agreement contemplated.

  (d) Withdrawing a Guilty or Nolo Contendere Plea. A defendant may withdraw a plea of guilty or nolo contendere:

> (1) before the court accepts the plea, for any reason or no reason; or
> (2) after the court accepts the plea, but before it imposes sentence if:
> (A) the court rejects a plea agreement under Rule 11(c)(5); or

(B) the defendant can show a fair and just reason for requesting the withdrawal.

  (e) Finality of a Guilty or Nolo Contendere Plea. After the court imposes sentence, the defendant may not withdraw a plea of guilty or nolo contendere, and the plea may be set aside only on direct appeal or collateral attack.

  (f) Admissibility or Inadmissibility of a Plea, Plea Discussions, and Related Statements. The admissibility or inadmissibility of a plea, a plea discussion, and any related statement is governed by Federal Rule of Evidence 410.

  (g) Recording the Proceedings. The proceedings during which the defendant enters a plea must be recorded by a court reporter or by a suitable recording device. If there is a guilty plea or a nolo contendere plea, the record must include the inquiries and advice to the defendant required under Rule 11(b) and (c).

  (h) Harmless Error. A variance from the requirements of this rule is harmless error if it does not affect substantial rights.

Rule 12. Pleadings and Pre-trial Motions

  (a) Pleadings. Pleadings in criminal proceedings shall be the indictment and the information, and the pleas of not guilty, guilty and nolo contendere.

  (b) Pre-trial Motions.

  (1) In General. Rule 47 applies to a pre-trial motion.

(2) Motions That May Be Made Before Trial. A party may raise by pre-trial motion any defense, objection, or request that the court can determine without a trial of the general issue.

(3) Motions That Must Be Made Before Trial. The following must be raised before trial:

(A) a motion alleging a defect in instituting the prosecution;

(B) a motion alleging a defect in the indictment or information--but at any time while the case is pending, the court may hear a claim that the indictment or information fails to invoke the court's jurisdiction or to state an offense;

(C) a motion to suppress evidence;

(D) a Rule 14 motion to sever charges or defendants; and

(E) a Rule 16 motion for discovery.

(4) Notice of the Government's Intent to Use Evidence.

(A) At the Discretion of the Government. At the arraignment or as soon thereafter as is practicable, the government may give notice to the defendant of its intention to use specified evidence at trial in order to afford the defendant an opportunity to raise objections to such evidence prior to trial under Rule 12(b)(3)(C).

(B) At the Request of the Defendant. At the arraignment or as soon thereafter as is practicable the defendant may, in order to afford an opportunity to move to suppress evidence under Rule 12 (b)(3)(C), request notice of the government's intention to use (in its evidence-in-chief at trial) any evidence which the defendant may be entitled to discover under Rule 16 subject to any relevant limitations prescribed in Rule 16.

(c) Motion Deadline. The court may, at the arraignment or as soon afterward as practicable, set a deadline for the parties to make pre-trial motions and may also schedule a motion hearing.

(d) Ruling on Motion. A motion made before trial shall be determined before trial unless the court, for good cause, orders that it be deferred for determination at the trial of the general issue or until after verdict, but no such determination shall be deferred if a party's right to appeal is adversely affected. Where factual issues are involved in deter-mining a motion, the court shall state its essential findings on the record.

(e) Waiver of a Defense, Objection or Request. A party waives any Rule 12(b)(3) defense, objection, or request not raised by the deadline the court sets under Rule 12(c) or by any extension the court provides. For good cause, the court may grant relief from the waiver.

(f) Recording the Proceedings. All proceedings at a motion hearing, including any findings of fact and conclusions of law made orally by the court, must be recorded by a court reporter or a suitable recording device.

(g) Defendant's Continued Custody or Release Status. If the court grants a motion to dismiss based on a defect in instituting the prosecution, in the indictment, or in the information, it may order the defendant to be released or detained under 18 U.S.C. sec. 3142 for a specified time until a new indictment or information is filed. This rule does not affect any federal statutory period of limitations.

(h) Producing Statements at a Suppression Hearing. Rule 26.2 applies at a suppression hearing under Rule 12(b)(3)(C). At a suppression hearing, a law enforcement officer is considered a government witness.

Rule 12.1. Notice of an Alibi Defense

(a) Government's Request for Notice and Defendant's Response.

(1) Government's Request. An attorney for the government may request in writing that the defendant notify an attorney for the government of any intended alibi defense. The request must state the time, date, and place of the alleged offense.

(2) Defendant's Response. Within 10 days after the request, or at some other time the court sets, the defendant must serve written notice on an attorney for the government of any intended alibi defense. The defendant's notice must state:

(A) each specific place where the defendant claims to have been at the time of the alleged offense; and

(B) the name, address, and telephone number of each alibi witness on whom the defendant intends to rely.

(b) Disclosing Government Witnesses.

(1) Disclosure. If the defendant serves a Rule 12.1(a)(2) notice, an attorney for the government must disclose in writing to the defendant or the defendant's attorney:

(A) the name, address, and telephone number of each witness the government intends to rely on to establish the defendant's presence at the scene of the alleged offense; and

(B) each government rebuttal witness to the defendant's alibi defense.

(1)(2) Time to Disclose. Unless the court directs otherwise, an attorney for the government must give its Rule 12.1(b)(1) disclosure within 10 days after the defendant serves notice of an intended alibi defense under Rule 12.1(a)(2), but no later than 10 days before trial.

(c) Continuing Duty to Disclose. Both an attorney for the government and the defendant must promptly disclose in writing to the other party the name, address, and telephone number of each additional witness if:

(1) the disclosing party learns of the witness before or during trial; and

(2) the witness should have been disclosed under Rule 12.1(a) or (b) if the disclosing party had known of the witness earlier.

(d) Exceptions. For good cause shown, the court may grant an exception to any of the requirements of Rule 12.1 (a)-(c).

(e) Failure to Comply. Upon the failure of either party to comply with the requirements of this rule, the court may exclude the testimony of any undisclosed witness offered by such party as to the defendant's absence from or presence at, the scene of the alleged offense. This rule shall not limit the right of the defendant to testify.

(f) Inadmissibility of Withdrawn Intention. Evidence of an intention to rely on an alibi defense, later withdrawn, or of a statement made in connection with that intention, is not, in any civil or criminal proceeding, admissible against the person who gave notice of the intention.

Rule 12.2. Notice of an Insanity Defense; Mental Examination

(a) Notice of an Insanity Defense. If a defendant intends to rely upon the defense of insanity at the time of the alleged offense, the defendant shall, within the time provided for the filing of pre-trial motions or at such later time as the court may direct, notify the attorney for the government in writing of such intention and file a copy of such notice with the clerk. If there is a failure to comply with the requirements of this subdivision, insanity may not be raised as a defense. The court may, for good cause, allow late filing of the notice or grant additional time to the parties to prepare for trial or make such other order as may be appropriate.

(b) Notice of Expert Evidence of a Mental Condition. If a defendant intends to introduce expert testimony relating to a mental disease or defect or any other mental condition of the defendant bearing on either (1) the issue of guilt or (2) the issue of punishment in a capital case, the defendant must--within the time provided for filing a pre-trial motion or at any later time the court sets--notify an attorney for the government in writing of this intention and file a copy of the notice with the clerk. The court may, for good cause, allow the defendant to file the notice late, grant the parties additional trial-preparation time, or make other appropriate orders.

(c) Mental Examination

(1) Authority to Order an Examination; Procedures.

(A) The court may order the defendant to submit to a competency examination under 18 U.S.C. sec. 4241.

(B) If the defendant provides notice under Rule 12.2(a), the court must, upon the government's motion, order the defendant to be examined under 18 U.S.C. sec. 4242. If the defendant provides notice under Rule 12.2(b) the court may, upon the government's motion, order the defendant to be examined under procedures ordered by the court.

(2) Disclosing Results and Reports of Capital Sentencing Examination.

The results and reports of any examination conducted solely under Rule 12.2(c)(1) after notice under Rule 12.2(b)(2) must be sealed and must not be disclosed to any attorney for the government or the defendant unless the defendant is found guilty of one or more capital crimes and the defendant confirms an intent to offer during sentencing proceedings expert evidence on mental condition.

(3) Disclosing Results and Reports of the Defendant's Expert Examination. After disclosure under Rule 12.2(c)(2) of the results and reports of the government's examination, the defendant must disclose to the government the results and reports of any examination on mental condition conducted by the defendant's expert about which the defendant intends to introduce expert evidence.

(4) Inadmissibility of a Defendant's Statements. No statement made by a defendant in the course of any examination conducted under this rule (whether conducted with or without the defendant's consent), no testimony by the expert based on the statement, and no other fruits of the statement may be admitted into evidence against the defendant in any criminal proceeding except on an issue regarding mental condition on which the defendant:

(A) has introduced evidence of incompetency or evidence requiring notice under Rule 12.2(a) or (b)(1), or

(B) has introduced expert evidence in a capital sentencing proceeding requiring notice under Rule 12.2(b)(2).

(d) Failure to Comply. If there is a failure to give notice when required under Rule 12.2(b) or does not submit to an examination when ordered under Rule 12.2(c), the court may exclude any expert evidence from the defendant on the issue of the defendant's mental disease, mental defect, or any other mental condition bearing on the defendant's guilt or the issue of punishment in a capital case.

(e) Inadmissibility of Withdrawn Intention. Evidence of an intention as to which notice was given under Rule 12.2(a) or (b), later withdrawn, is not, in any civil or criminal proceeding, admissible against the person who gave notice of the intention.

Rule 12.3 Notice of a Public Authority Defense

(a) Notice of the Defense and Disclosure of Witnesses.

(1) Notice in General. If a defendant intends to assert a defense of actual or believed exercise of public authority on behalf of a law enforcement agency or federal intelligence agency at the time of the alleged offense, the defendant must so notify an attorney for the government in writing and must file a copy of the notice with the clerk within the time provided for filing a pre-trial motion, or at any later time the court sets. The notice filed with the clerk must be under seal if the notice identifies a federal intelligence agency as the source of public authority.

(2) **Contents of Notice.** The notice must contain the following information:
(A) the law enforcement agency or federal intelligence agency involved;
(B) the agency member on whose behalf the defendant claims to have acted; and
(C) the time during which the defendant claims to have acted with public authority.

(3) **Response to the Notice.** An attorney for the government must serve a written response on the defendant or the defendant's attorney within 10 days after receiving the defendant's notice, but no later than 20 days before trial. The response must admit or deny that the defendant exercised the public authority identified in the defendant's notice.

(4) **Disclosing Witnesses.**
(A) Government's Request. An attorney for the government may request in writing that the defendant disclose the name, address, and telephone number of each witness the defendant intends to rely on to establish a public-authority defense. An attorney for the government may serve the request when the government serves its response to the defendant's notice under Rule 12.3(a)(3), or later, but must serve the request no later than 20 days before trial.

(B) Defendant's Response. Within 7 days after receiving the government's request, the defendant must serve on an attorney for the government a written statement of the name, address, and telephone number of each witness.

(C) Government's Reply. Within 7 days after receiving the defendant's statement, an attorney for the government must serve on the defendant or the defendant's attorney a written statement of the name, address, and telephone number of each witness the government intends to rely on to oppose the defendant's public-authority defense.

(5) **Additional Time.** The court may, for good cause, allow a party additional time to comply with this rule.

(b) Continuing Duty to Disclose. Both an attorney for the government and the defendant must promptly disclose in writing to the other party the name, address, and telephone number of any additional witness if:
(1) the disclosing party learns of the witness before or during trial; and
(2) the witness should have been disclosed under Rule 12.3(a)(4) if the disclosing party had known of the witness earlier.

(c) Failure to Comply. If a party fails to comply with this rule, the court may exclude the testimony of any undisclosed witness regarding the public-authority defense. This rule does not limit the defendant's right to testify.

(d) Protective Procedures Unaffected. This rule does not limit the court's authority to issue appropriate protective orders or to order that any filings be under seal.

(e) Inadmissibility of Withdrawn Intention. Evidence of an intention as to which notice was given under Rule 12.3(a), later withdrawn, is not, in any civil or criminal proceeding, admissible against the person who gave notice of the intention.

Rule 13. Joint Trial of Separate Cases

The court may order that separate cases be tried together as though brought in a single indictment or information if all offenses and all defendants could have been joined in a single indictment or information.

Rule 14. Relief from Prejudicial Joinder

(a) Relief. If the joinder of offenses or defendants in an indictment, an information, or a consolidation for trial appears to prejudice a defendant or the government, the court may order separate trials of counts, sever the defendants' trials, or provide any other relief that justice requires.

(b) Defendant's Statements. Before ruling on a defendant's motion to sever, the court may order an attorney for the government to deliver to the court for in camera inspection any defendant's statement that the government intends to use as evidence.

Rule 15. Depositions

(a) When Taken.

(1) In General. . A party may move that a prospective witness be deposed in order to preserve testimony for trial. The court may grant the motion because of exceptional circumstances and in the interest of justice. If the court orders the deposition to be taken, it may also require the deponent to produce at the deposition any designated material that is not privileged, including any book, paper, document, record, recording, or data.

(2) Detained Material Witness. A witness who is detained under 18 U.S.C. sec. 3144 may request to be deposed by filing a written motion and giving notice to the parties. The court may then order that the deposition be taken and may discharge the witness after the witness has signed under oath the deposition transcript.

(b) Notice.

(1) In General. A party seeking to take a deposition must give every other party reasonable written notice of the deposition's date and location. The notice must state the name and address of each deponent. If requested by a party receiving the notice, the court may, for good cause, change the deposition's date or location.

(2) To the Custodial Officer. A party seeking to take the deposition must also notify the officer who has custody of the defendant of the scheduled date and location.

(c) Defendant's Presence.

(1) Defendant in Custody. The officer who has custody of the defendant must produce the defendant at the deposition and keep the defendant in the witness's presence during the examination, unless the defendant:

(A) waives in writing the right to be present; or

(B) persists in disruptive conduct justifying exclusion after being warned by the court that disruptive conduct will result in the defendant's exclusion.

(2) Defendant Not in Custody. A defendant who is not in custody has the right upon request to be present at the deposition, subject to any conditions imposed by the court. If the government tenders the defendant's expenses as provided in Rule 15(d) but the defendant still fails to appear, the defendant--absent good cause--waives both the right to appear and any objection to the taking and use of the deposition based on that right.

(d) Expenses If the deposition was requested by the government, the court may--or if the defendant is unable to bear the deposition expenses, the court must--order the government to pay:

(1) any reasonable travel and subsistence expenses of the defendant and the defendant's attorney to attend the deposition; and

(2) the costs of the deposition transcript.

(e) Manner of Taking. Unless these rules or a court order provides otherwise, a deposition must be taken and filed in the same manner as a deposition in a civil action, except that:

(1) A defendant may not be deposed without that defendant's consent.

(2) The scope and manner of the deposition examination and cross-examination must be the same as would be allowed during trial.

(3) The government must provide to the defendant or the defendant's attorney, for use at the deposition, any statement of the deponent in the government's possession to which the defendant would be entitled at trial.

(f) Use of Evidence. A party may use all or part of a deposition as provided by the Federal Rules of Evidence.

(g) Objections. A party objecting to deposition testimony or evidence must state the grounds for the objection during the deposition.

(h) Deposition by Agreement Permitted. The parties may by agreement take and use a deposition with the court's consent.

Rule 16. Discovery and Inspection
(a) Governmental Disclosure
(1) Information Subject to Disclosure.

(A) *Defendant's Oral Statement.* Upon a defendant's request, the government must disclose to the defendant the substance of any relevant oral statement made by the defendant, before or after arrest, in response to interrogation by a person the defendant knew was a government agent if the government intends to use the statement at trial.

(B) *Defendant's Written or Recorded Statement.* Upon a defendant's request, the government must disclose to the defendant, and make available for inspection, copying, or photographing, all of the following:

(i) any relevant written or recorded statement by the defendant if: the statement is within the government's possession, custody, or control; and the attorney for the government knows – or through due diligence could know – that the statement exists.

(ii) the portion of any written record containing the substance of any relevant oral statement made before or after arrest if the defendant made the statement in response to interrogation by a person the defendant knew was a government agent; and

(iii) the defendant's recorded testimony before a grand jury relating to the charged offense.

(C) Organizational Defendant. Upon a defendant's request, if the defendant is an organization, the government must disclose to the defendant any statement described in Rule 16(a)(1)(A) and (B) if the government contends that the person making the statement:

(i) was legally able to bind the defendant regarding the subject of the statement because of that person's position as the defendant's director, officer, employee, or agent; or

(ii) was personally involved in the alleged conduct constituting the offense and was legally able to bind the defendant regarding that conduct because of that person's position as the defendant's director, officer, employee, or agent.

(D) *Defendant's Prior Record.* Upon a defendant's request, the government must furnish the defendant with a copy of the defendant's prior criminal record that is within the government's possession, custody, or control if the attorney for the government knows – or through due diligence could know – that the record exists.

(E) *Documents and Objects.* Upon a defendant's request, the government must permit the defendant to inspect and to copy or photograph books, papers, documents, data, photographs, tangible objects, buildings or places, or copies or portions of any of these items, if the item is within the government's possession, custody, or control and:

(i) the item is material to preparing the defense;

(ii) the government intends to use the item in its case-in-chief at trial; or

(iii) the item was obtained from or belongs to the defendant.

(F) *Reports of Examinations and Tests.* Upon a defendant's request, the government must permit a defendant to inspect and to copy or photograph the results or reports of any physical or mental examination and of any scientific test or experiment if:

(i) the item is within the government's possession, custody, or control;

(ii) the attorney for the government knows--or through due diligence could know--that the item exists; and

(iii) the item is material to preparing the defense or the government intends to use the item in its case-in-chief at trial.

(G) *Expert Witnesses.* At the defendant's request, the government must give to the defendant a written summary of any testimony that the government intends to use under Rules 702, 703, or 705 of the Federal Rules of Evidence during its case-in-chief at trial. If the government requests discovery under subdivision (b)(1)(C)(ii) and the defendant complies, the government must, at the defendant's request, give to the defendant a written summary of testimony that the government intends to use under Rules 702, 703, or 705 of the Federal Rules of Evidence as evidence at trial on the issue of the defendant's mental condition. The summary provided under this subparagraph must describe the witness's opinions, the bases and reasons for those opinions, and the witness's qualifications.

(2) Information Not Subject to Disclosure. Except as Rule 16(a)(1) provides otherwise, this rule does not authorize the discovery or inspection of reports, memoranda, or other internal government documents made by an attorney for the government or other government agent in connection with investigating or prosecuting the case. Nor does this rule authorize the discovery or inspection of statements made by prospective government witnesses except as provided in 18 U.S.C. § 3500.

(3) Grand Jury Transcripts. This rule does not apply to the discovery or inspection of a grand jury's recorded proceedings, except as provided in Rules 6, 12(h), 16(a)(1), and 26.2.

(b) Defendant's Disclosure.

(1) Information Subject to Disclosure.

(A) Documents and Objects. If a defendant requests disclosure under Rule 16(a)(1)(E) and the government complies, then the defendant must permit the government, upon request, to inspect and to copy or photograph books, papers, documents, data, photographs, tangible objects, buildings or places, or copies or portions of any of these items if: (i) the item is within the defendant's possession, custody, or control; and (ii) the defendant intends to use the item in the defendant's case-in-chief at trial.

(B) Reports of Examinations and Tests. If a defendant requests disclosure under Rule 16(a)(1)(F) and the government complies, the defendant must permit the government, upon request, to inspect and to copy of photograph upon compliance with such request by the government, the defendant, on request of the government, shall permit the government to inspect and copy or photograph any results or reports of physical or mental examinations and of scientific tests or experiments made in connection with the particular case, or copies thereof, within the possession or control of the defendant, which the defendant intends to introduce as evidence in chief at the trial or which were prepared by a witness whom the defendant intends to call at the trial when the results or reports relate to that witness' testimony.

(C) Expert Witnesses. Under the following circumstances, the defendant shall, at the government's request, disclose to the government a written summary of testimony that the defendant intends to use under Rules 702, 703, or 705 of the Federal Rules of Evidence as evidence at trial: (i) if the defendant requests disclosure under subdivision (a)(1)(E) of this rule and the government complies, or (ii) if the defendant has given notice under Rule 12.2(b) of an intent to present expert testimony on the defendant's mental condition. This summary shall describe the witnesses' opinions, the bases and reasons for those opinions, and the witnesses' qualifications.

(2) **Information Not Subject to Disclosure.** Except as to scientific or medical reports, Rule 16(b)(1) does not authorize the discovery or inspection of reports, memoranda, or other internal defense documents made by the defendant, or the defendant's attorneys or agents in connection with the investigation or defense of the case, or of statements made by the defendant, or by government or defense witnesses, or by prospective government or defense witnesses, to the defendant, the defendant's agents or attorneys.

(c) **Continuing Duty to Disclose.** A party who discovers additional evidence or material before or during trial must promptly disclose its existence to the other party or the court if:

(1) the evidence or material is subject to discovery or inspection under this rule; and

(2) the other party previously requested, or the court ordered, its production.

(d) **Regulation of Discovery.**

(1) **Protective and Modifying Orders.** At any time the court may, for good cause, deny, restrict, or defer discovery or inspection, or grant other appropriate relief. The court may permit a party to show good cause by a written statement that the court will inspect ex parte. If relief is granted, the court must preserve the entire text of the party's statement under seal.

(2) **Failure to Comply.** If a party fails to comply with this rule, the court may order: that party to permit the discovery or inspection; specify its time, place, and manner, and prescribe other just terms and conditions; grant a continuance; prohibit that party from introducing the undisclosed evidence; or enter any other order that is just under the circumstances.

Rule 17. Subpoena

(a) **Content.** A subpoena must state the court's name and the title of the proceeding, include the seal of the court, and command the witness to attend and testify at the time and place the subpoena specifies. The clerk must issue a blank subpoena--signed and sealed--to the party requesting it, and that party must fill in the blanks before the subpoena is served.

(b) **Defendants Unable to Pay.** Upon a defendant's ex parte application, the court must order that a subpoena be issued for a named witness if the defendant shows an inability to pay the witness's fees and the necessity of the witness's presence for an adequate defense. If the court orders a subpoena to be issued, the process costs and witness fees will be paid in the same manner as those paid for witnesses the government subpoenas.

(c) **Producing Documents and Objects.**

(1) **In General.** A subpoena may order the witness to produce any books, papers, documents, data, or other objects the subpoena designates. The court may direct the witness to produce the designated items in court before trial or before they are to be offered in evidence. When the items arrive, the court may permit the parties and their attorneys to inspect all or part of them.

(2) Quashing or Modifying the Subpoena. On motion made promptly, the court may quash or modify the subpoena if compliance would be unreasonable or oppressive.

(d) Service. A subpoena may be served by the marshal, by a deputy marshal or by any other person who is not a party and who is not less than 18 years of age. Service of a subpoena shall be made by delivering a copy thereof to the person named and by tendering to that person the fee for 1 day's attendance and the mileage allowed by law. Fees and mileage need not be tendered to the witness upon service of a subpoena issued in behalf of the United States or an officer or agency thereof.

(e) Place of Service.

(1) In United States. A subpoena requiring the attendance of a witness at a hearing or trial may be served at any place within the United States.

(2) In a Foreign Country If the witness is in a foreign country, 28 U.S.C. Sec. 1783 governs the subpoena's service.

(f) Issuing a Deposition Subpoena.

(1) Issuance. An order to take a deposition authorizes the issuance by the clerk of the court for the district in which the deposition is to be taken of subpoenas for the persons named or described therein.

(2) Place. After considering the convenience of the witness and the parties, the court may order – and the subpoena may require – the witness to appear anywhere the court designates.

(g) Contempt. The court (other than a magistrate judge) may hold in contempt a witness who, without adequate excuse, disobeys a subpoena issued by a federal court in that district. A magistrate judge may hold in contempt a witness who, without adequate excuse, disobeys a subpoena issued by that magistrate judge as provided in 28 U.S.C. Sec. 636(e).

(h) Information Not Subject to Subpoena. Statements made by witnesses or prospective witnesses may not be subpoenaed from the government or the defendant under this rule, but shall be subject to production only in accordance with the provisions of Rule 26.2.

Rule 17.1. Pre-trial Conference

At any time after the filing of the indictment or information the court upon motion of any party or upon its own motion may order one or more conferences to consider such matters as will promote a fair and expeditious trial. At the conclusion of a conference the court shall prepare and file a memorandum of the matters agreed upon. No admissions made by the defendant or the defendant's attorney at the conference shall be used against the defendant unless the admissions are reduced to writing and signed by the defendant and the defendant's attorney. This rule shall not be invoked in the case of a defendant who is not represented by counsel.

V. VENUE

Rule 18. Place of Prosecution and Trial

Except as otherwise permitted by statute or by these rules, the prosecution shall be had in a district in which the offense was committed. The court shall fix the place of trial within the district with due regard to the convenience of the defendant and the witnesses and the prompt administration of justice.

Rule 19. [Reserved]

Rule 20. Transfer for Plea and Sentence

(a) Consent to Transfer. A prosecution may be transferred from the district where the indictment or information is pending, or from which a warrant on a complaint has been issued, to the district where the defendant is arrested, held, or present if:

(1) the defendant states in writing a wish to plead guilty or nolo contendere and to waive trial in the district where the indictment, information, or complaint is pending, consents in writing to the court's disposing of the case in the transferee district, and files the statement in the transferee district; and

(2) the United States attorneys in both districts approve the transfer in writing.

(b) Clerk's Duties. After receiving the defendant's statement and the required approvals, the clerk where the indictment, information, or complaint is pending must send the file, or a certified copy, to the clerk in the transferee district.

(c) Effect of a Not Guilty Plea. If after the proceeding has been transferred pursuant to Rule 20(a) the defendant pleads not guilty, the clerk shall return the papers to the court in which the prosecution was commenced, and the proceeding shall be restored to the docket of that court. The defendant's statement that the defendant wishes to plead guilty or nolo contendere shall not be used against that defendant.

(d) Juveniles.

(1) Consent to Transfer. A juvenile, as defined in 18 U.S.C. Sec. 5031, may be proceeded against as a juvenile delinquent in the district where the juvenile is arrested, held, or present if:

(A) the alleged offense that occurred in the other district is not punishable by death or life imprisonment;

(B) an attorney has advised the juvenile;

(C) the court has informed the juvenile of the juvenile's rights--including the right to be returned to the district where the offense allegedly occurred--and the consequences of waiving those rights;

(D) the juvenile, after receiving the court's information about rights, consents in writing to be proceeded against in the transferee district, and files the consent in the transferee district;

(E) the United States attorneys for both districts approve the transfer in writing; and

(F) the transferee court approves the transfer.

(2) Clerk's Duties. After receiving the juvenile's written consent and the required approvals, the clerk where the indictment, information, or complaint is pending or where the alleged offense occurred must send the file, or a certified copy, to the clerk in the transferee district.

Rule 21. Transfer for Trial

(a) For Prejudice. Upon the defendant's motion, the court must transfer the proceeding against that defendant to another district if the court is satisfied that so great a prejudice against the defendant exists in the transferring district that the defendant cannot obtain a fair and impartial trial there.

(b) For Convenience. Upon the defendant's motion, the court may transfer the proceeding, or one or more counts, against that defendant to another district for the convenience of the parties and witnesses and in the interest of justice.

(c) Proceedings on Transfer. When the court orders a transfer, the clerk must send to the transferee district the file, or a certified copy, and any bail taken. The prosecution will then continue in the transferee district.

Rule 22. (Transferred)

VI. TRIAL

Rule 23. Jury or Non-Jury Trial

(a) **Jury Trial.** If the defendant is entitled to a jury trial, the trial must be by jury unless: the defendant waives a jury trial in writing; the government consents; and the court approves.

(b) **Jury Size.** (1) *In General.* A jury consists of 12 persons unless this rule provides otherwise.

(2) *Stipulation for a Smaller Jury.* At any time before the verdict, the parties may, with the court's approval, stipulate in writing that:

(A) the jury may consist of fewer than 12 persons; or

(B) a jury of fewer than 12 persons may return a verdict if the court finds it necessary to excuse a juror for good cause after the trial begins.

(3) *Court Order for a Jury of 11.* After the jury has retired to deliberate, the court may permit a jury of 11 persons to return a verdict, even without a stipulation by the parties, if the court finds good cause to excuse a juror.

(c) **Non-Jury Trial.** In a case tried without a jury, the court must find the defendant guilty or not guilty. If a party requests before the finding of guilty or not guilty, the court must state findings of fact in open court or in written decision or opinion.

Rule 24. Trial Jurors

(a) **Examination.**

(1) **In General.** The court may examine prospective jurors or may permit the attorneys for the parties to do so.

(2) **Court Examinations.** If the court examines the jurors, it must permit the attorneys for the parties to: ask further questions that the court considers proper; or submit further questions that the court may ask if it considers them proper.

(b) **Peremptory Challenges.** Each side is entitled to the number of peremptory challenges to prospective jurors specified below. The court may allow additional peremptory challenges to multiple defendants, and may allow the defendants to exercise those challenges separately or jointly.

(1) *Capital Case.* Each side has 20 peremptory challenges when the government seeks the death penalty.

(2) *Other Felony Case.* The government has 6 peremptory challenges and the defendant or defendants jointly have 10 peremptory challenges when the defendant is charged with a crime punishable by imprisonment of more than one year.

(3) *Misdemeanor Case.* Each side has peremptory challenges when the defendant is charged with a crime punishable by fine, imprisonment of one year or less, or both.

(c) **Alternate Jurors.**

(1) **In General.** The court may impanel up to 6 alternate jurors to replace any jurors who are unable to perform or who are disqualified from performing their duties.

(2) **Procedure.** (A) Alternate jurors must have the same qualifications and be selected and sworn in the same manner as any other juror. (B) Alternate jurors replace jurors in the same sequence in which the alternates were selected. An alternate juror who replaces a juror has the same authority as the other jurors.

(3) Retaining Alternate Jurors. The court may retain alternate jurors after the jury retires to deliberate. The court must ensure that a retained alternate does not discuss the case with anyone until that alternate replaces a juror or is discharged. If an alternate replaces a juror after deliberations have begun, the court must instruct the jury to begin its deliberations anew.

(4) Peremptory Challenges. Each side is entitled to the number of additional peremptory challenges to prospective alternate jurors specified below. These additional challenges may be used only to remove alternate jurors.

(A) *One or Two Alternates.* One additional peremptory challenge is permitted when one or two alternates are impaneled.

(B) *Three or Four Alternates.* Two additional peremptory challenges are permitted when three or four alternates are impaneled.

(C) *Five or Six Alternates.* Three additional peremptory challenges are permitted when five or six alternates are impaneled.

Rule 25. Judge's Disability

(a) During Trial. If by reason of death, sickness or other disability the judge before whom a jury trial has commenced is unable to proceed with the trial, any other judge regularly sitting in or assigned to the court, upon certifying familiarity with the record of the trial, may proceed with and finish the trial.

(b) After Verdict or Finding of Guilt.

(1) In General. After a verdict or finding of guilty, any judge regularly sitting in or assigned to a court may complete the court's duties if the judge who presided at trial cannot perform those duties because of absence, death, sickness, or other disability.

(2) Granting a New Trial. The successor judge may grant a new trial if satisfied that:

(A) a judge other than the one who presided at the trial cannot perform the post-trial duties; or

(B) a new trial is necessary for some other reason.

Rule 26. Taking Testimony

In every trial the testimony of witnesses must be taken in open court, unless otherwise provided by a statute or by rules adopted under 28 U.S.C. Sec. 2072-2077.

Rule 26.1. Foreign Law Determination

A party intending to raise an issue of foreign law must provide the court and all parties with reasonable written notice. Issues of foreign law are questions of law, but in deciding such issues a court may consider any relevant material or source – including testimony – without regard to the Federal Rules of Evidence.

Rule 26.2. Producing a Witness's Statement

(a) Motion to Produce. After a witness other than the defendant has testified on direct examination, the court, on motion of a party who did not call the witness, shall order the attorney for the government or the defendant and the defendant's attorney, as the case may be, to produce, for the examination and use of the moving party, any statement of the witness that is in their possession and that relates to the subject matter concerning which the witness has testified.

(b) Producing the Entire Statement. If the entire statement relates to the subject matter of the witness's testimony, the court must order that the statement be delivered to the moving party.

(c) Producing a Redacted Statement. If the party who called the witness claims that the statement contains information that is privileged or does not relate to the subject matter of the witness's testimony, the court must inspect the statement in camera. After excising any privileged or unrelated portions, the court must order delivery of the redacted statement to the moving party. If the defendant objects to an excision, the court must preserve the entire statement with the excised portion indicated, under seal, as part of the record.

(d) Recess to Examine a Statement. The court may recess the proceedings to allow time for a party to examine the statement and prepare for its use.

(e) Sanction for Failure to Produce or Deliver a Statement. If the party who called the witness disobeys an order to produce or deliver a statement, the court must strike the witness's testimony from the record. If an attorney for the government disobeys the order, the court must declare a mistrial if justice so requires.

(f) "Statement" Defined. As used in this rule, a "statement" of a witness means:

(1) a written statement made by the witness that is signed or otherwise adopted or approved by the witness;

(2) a substantially verbatim, contemporaneously recorded recital of the witness's oral statement that is contained in any recording or any transcription of a recording; or

(3) a statement, however taken or recorded, or a transcription thereof, made by the witness to a grand jury.

(g) Scope. This rule applies at trial, at a suppression hearing conducted under Rule 12, and to the extent specified in the following rules:

(1) in Rule 5.1(h) (preliminary hearing);

(2) in Rule 32(i)(2) (sentencing);

(3) in Rule 32(1)(e) (hearing to revoke or modify probation or supervised release);

(4) in Rule 46(j) (detention hearing); and

(5) in Rule 8 of the Rules of Governing Proceedings under 28 U.S.C. Sec. 2255..

Rule 26.3. Mistrial

Before ordering a mistrial, the court shall provide an opportunity for the government and for each defendant to comment on the propriety of the order, including whether each party consents or objects to a mistrial, and to suggest any alternatives.

Rule 27. Proving an Official Record

An official record or an entry therein or the lack of such a record or entry may be proved in the same manner as in civil actions.

Rule 28. Interpreters

The court may appoint an interpreter of its own selection and may fix the reasonable compensation of such interpreter. Such compensation shall be paid out of funds provided by law or by the government, as the court may direct.

Rule 29. Motion for Judgment of Acquittal

(a) Motion Before Submission to Jury. After the government closes its evidence or after the close of all the evidence, the court on the defendant's motion must enter a judgment of acquittal of any offense for which the evidence is insufficient to sustain a conviction. The court may on its own consider whether the evidence is insufficient to sustain a conviction. If the court denies a motion for a judgment of acquittal at the close of the government's evidence, the defendant may offer evidence without having reserved the right to do so.

(b) Reserving Decision. The court may reserve decision on a motion for judgment of acquittal, proceed with the trial (where the motion is made before the close of all the evidence), submit the case to the jury and decide the motion either before the jury returns a verdict or after it returns a verdict of guilty or is discharged without having returned a verdict. If the court reserves decision, it must decide the motion on the basis of the evidence at the time the ruling was reserved.

(c) Motion After Discharge of Jury.

(1) Time of Motion. A defendant may move for a judgment of acquittal, or renew such a motion, within 7 days after a guilty verdict or after the court discharges the jury, whichever is later, or within any other time the court sets during the 7-day period.

(2) Ruling on the Motion. If the jury has returned a guilty verdict, the court may set aside the verdict and enter an acquittal. If the jury has failed to return a verdict, the court may enter a judgment of acquittal.

(3) No Prior Motion Required. A defendant is not required to move for a judgment of acquittal before the court submits the case to the jury as a prerequisite for making such a motion after jury discharge.

(d) Conditional Ruling on a Motion for a New Trial.

(1) Motion for a New Trial. If the court enters a judgment of acquittal after a guilty verdict, the court must also conditionally determine whether any motion for a new trial should be granted if the judgment of acquittal is later vacated or reversed. The court must specify the reasons for that determination.

(2) Finality. The court's order conditionally granting a motion for a new trial does not affect the finality of the judgment of acquittal.

(3) Appeal.

(A) Grant of a Motion of New Trial. If the court conditionally grants a motion for a new trial and an appellate court later reverses the judgment of acquittal, the trial court must proceed with the new trial unless the appellate court orders otherwise.

(B) *Denial of a Motion for a New Trial.* If the court conditionally denies a motion for a new trial, an appellee may assert that the denial was erroneous. If the appellate court later reverses the judgment of acquittal, the trial court must proceed as the appellate court directs.

Rule 29.1. Closing Argument

Closing arguments proceed in the following order:

(1) the government argues;
(2) the defense argues; and
(3) the government rebuts.

Rule 30. Jury Instructions

(a) In General. Any party may request in writing that the court instruct the jury on the law as specified in the request. The request must be made at the close of the evidence or at any earlier time that the court reasonably sets. When the request is made, the requesting party must furnish a copy to every other party.

(b) **Ruling on a Request.** The court must inform the parties before closing arguments how it intends to rule on the requested instructions.

(c) **Time for Giving Instructions.** The court may instruct the jury before or after the arguments are completed, or at both times.

(d) **Objections to Instructions.** A party who objects to any portion of the instructions or to a failure to give a requested instruction must inform the court of the specific objection and the grounds for the objection before the jury retires to deliberate. An opportunity must be given to object out of the jury's hearing and, on request, out of the jury's presence. Failure to object in accordance with this rule precludes appellate review, except as permitted under Rule 52(b).

Rule 31. Verdict

(a) **Return.** The verdict shall be unanimous. It shall be returned by the jury to the judge in open court.

(b) **Partial Verdicts, Mistrial, and Retrial.**

(1) **Multiple Defendants.** If there are two or more defendants, the jury at any time during its deliberations may return a verdict or verdicts with respect to a defendant or defendants as to whom it has agreed.

(2) **Multiple Counts.** If the jury cannot agree on all counts as to any defendant, the jury may return a verdict on those counts on which it has agreed.

(3) **Mistrial and Retrial.** If the jury cannot agree on a verdict on one or more counts, the court may declare a mistrial on those counts. The government may retry any defendant on any count on which the jury could not agree.

(c) **Lesser Offense or Attempt.** A defendant may be found guilty of any of the following:

(1) an offense necessarily included in the offense charged;

(2) an attempt to commit the offense charged; or

(3) an attempt to commit an offense necessarily included in the offense charged, if the attempt is an offense in its own right.

(d) **Jury Poll.** After a verdict is returned but before the jury is discharged, the court shall, on a party's request, or may on its own motion, poll the jurors individually. If the poll reveals a lack of unanimity, the court may direct the jury to deliberate further or may declare a mistrial and discharge the jury.

(e) **Criminal Forfeiture.** (Abrogated April 17, 2000; Eff. Dec. 1, 2000)

VII. POST-CONVICTION PROCEDURES

Rule 32. Sentence and Judgment

(a) **Definitions.** The following definitions apply under this rule:

(1) "Crime of violence or sexual abuse" means:

(A) a crime that involves the use, attempted use, or threatened use of physical force against another's person or property; or

(B) a crime under 18 U.S.C. sec. 2241-2248 or sec. 2251-2257.

(2) "Victim" means an individual against whom the defendant committed an offense for which the court will impose sentence.

(b) Time of Sentencing.

(1) In General. The court must impose sentence without unnecessary delay.

(2) Changing Time Limits. The court may, for good cause, change any time limits prescribed in this rule.

(c) Presentence Investigation.

(1) Required Investigation.

(A) In General. The probation officer must conduct a presentence investigation and submit a report to the court before it imposes sentence unless:

(i) 18 U.S.C. sec. 3593(c) or another statute requires otherwise; or

(ii) the court finds that the information in the record enables it to meaningfully exercise its sentencing authority under 18 U.S.C. sec. 3553, and the court explains its finding on the record.

(B) *Restitution.* If the law requires restitution, the probation officer must conduct an investigation and submit a report that contains sufficient information for the court to order restitution.

(2) Interviewing the Defendant. The probation officer who interviews a defendant as part of a presentence investigation must, on request, give the defendant's attorney notice and a reasonable opportunity to attend the interview.

(d) Presentence Report.

(1) Applying the Sentencing Guidelines. The presentence report must:

(A) identify all applicable guidelines and policy statements of the Sentencing Commission;

(B) calculate the defendant's offense level and criminal history category;

(C) state the resulting sentencing range and kinds of sentences available;

(D) identify any factor relevant to:

(i) the appropriate kind of sentence, or

(ii) the appropriate sentence within the applicable sentencing range; and

(E) identify any basis for departing from the applicable sentencing range.

(2) Additional Information. The presentence report must also contain the following information:

(A) the defendant's history and characteristics, including:

(i) any prior criminal record;

(ii) the defendant's financial condition; and

(iii) any circumstances affecting the defendant's behavior that may be helpful in imposing sentence or in correctional treatment;

(B) verified information, stated in a non-argumentative style, that assesses the financial, social, psychological, and medical impact on any individual against whom the offense has been committed;

(C) when appropriate, the nature and extent of non-prison programs and resources available to the defendant;

(D) when the law provides for restitution, information sufficient for a restitution order;

(E) if the court orders a study under 18 U.S.C. sec. 3552(b), any resulting report and recommendation; and

(F) any other information that the court requires.

(3) Exclusions. The presentence report must exclude the following:

(A) any diagnoses that, if disclosed, might seriously disrupt a rehabilitation program;

(B) any sources of information obtained upon a promise of confidentiality; and

(C) any other information that, if disclosed, might result in physical or other harm to the defendant or others.

(e) Disclosing the Report and Recommendation.

(1) Time to Disclose. Unless the defendant has consented in writing, the probation officer must not submit a presentence report to the court or disclose its contents to anyone until the defendant has pleaded guilty or nolo contendere, or has been found guilty.

(2) Minimum Required Notice. The probation officer must give the presentence report to the defendant, the defendant's attorney, and an attorney for the government at least 35 days before sentencing unless the defendant waives this minimum period.

(3) Sentence Recommendation. By local rule or by order in a case, the court may direct the probation officer not to disclose to anyone other than the court the officer's recommendation on the sentence.

(f) Objecting to the Report.

(1) Time to Object. Within 14 days after receiving the presentence report, the parties must state in writing any objections, including objections to material information, sentencing guideline ranges, and policy statements contained in or omitted from the report.

(2) Serving Objections. An objecting party must provide a copy of its objections to the opposing party and to the probation officer.

(3) Action on Objections. After receiving objections, the probation officer may meet with the parties to discuss the objections. The probation officer may then investigate further and revise the presentence report as appropriate.

(g) Submitting the Report. At least 7 days before sentencing, the probation officer must submit to the court and to the parties the presentence report and an addendum containing any unresolved objections, the grounds for those objections, and the probation officer's comments on them.

(h) Notice of Possible Departure From Sentencing Guidelines. Before the court may depart from the applicable sentencing range on a ground not identified for departure either in the presentence report or in a party's prehearing submission, the court must give the parties reasonable notice that it is contemplating such a departure. The notice must specify any ground on which the court is contemplating a departure.

(i) Sentencing.

(1) In General. At sentencing, the court:

(A) must verify that the defendant and the defendant's attorney have read and discussed the presentence report and any addendum to the report;

(B) must give to the defendant and an attorney for the government a written summary of-- or summarize in camera--any information excluded from the presentence report under Rule 32(d)(3) on which the court will rely in sentencing, and give them a reasonable opportunity to comment on that information;

(C) must allow the parties' attorneys to comment on the probation officer's determinations and other matters relating to an appropriate sentence; and

(D) may, for good cause, allow a party to make a new objection at any time before sentence is imposed.

(2) Introducing Evidence; Producing a Statement. The court may permit the parties to introduce evidence on the objections. If a witness testifies at sentencing, Rule 26.2(a)-(d) and (f) applies. If a party fails to comply with a Rule 26.2 order to produce a witness's statement, the court must not consider that witness's testimony.

(3) Court Determinations. At sentencing, the court:

(A) may accept any undisputed portion of the presentence report as a finding of fact;

(B) must--for any disputed portion of the presentence report or other controverted matter--rule on the dispute or determine that a ruling is unnecessary either because the matter will not affect sentencing, or because the court will not consider the matter in sentencing; and

(C) must append a copy of the court's determinations under this rule to any copy of the presentence report made available to the Bureau of Prisons.

(4) Opportunity to Speak.

(A) By a Party. Before imposing sentence, the court must:

(i) provide the defendant's attorney an opportunity to speak on the defendant's behalf;

(ii) address the defendant personally in order to permit the defendant to speak or present any information to mitigate the sentence; and

(iii) provide an attorney for the government an opportunity to speak equivalent to that of the defendant's attorney.

(B) By a Victim. Before imposing sentence, the court must address any victim of a crime of violence or sexual abuse who is present at sentencing and must permit the victim to speak or submit any information about the sentence. Whether or not the victim is present, a victim's right to address the court may be exercised by the following persons if present:

(i) a parent or legal guardian, if the victim is younger than 18 years or is incompetent; or

(ii) one or more family members or relatives the court designates, if the victim is deceased or incapacitated.

(C) In Camera Proceedings. Upon a party's motion and for good cause, the court may hear in camera any statement made under Rule 32(i)(4).

(j) Defendant's Right to Appeal.

(1) Advice of a Right to Appeal.

(A) Appealing a Conviction. If the defendant pleaded not guilty and was convicted, after sentencing the court must advise the defendant of the right to appeal the conviction.

(B) Appealing a Sentence. After sentencing--regardless of the defendant's plea--the court must advise the defendant of any right to appeal the sentence.

(C) Appeal Costs. The court must advise a defendant who is unable to pay appeal costs of the right to ask for permission to appeal in forma pauperis.

(2) Clerk's Filing of Notice. If the defendant so requests, the clerk must immediately prepare and file a notice of appeal on the defendant's behalf.

(k) Judgment.

(1) In General. In the judgment of conviction, the court must set forth the plea, the jury verdict or the court's findings, the adjudication, and the sentence. If the defendant is found not guilty or is otherwise entitled to be discharged, the court must so order. The judge must sign the judgment, and the clerk must enter it.

(2) Criminal Forfeiture. Forfeiture procedures are governed by Rule 32.2.

Rule 32.1. Revoking or Modifying Probation or Supervised Release

(a) Initial Appearance.

(1) Person In Custody. A person held in custody for violating probation or supervised release must be taken without unnecessary delay before a magistrate judge.

(A) If the person is held in custody in the district where an alleged violation occurred, the initial appearance must be in that district.

(B) If the person is held in custody in a district other than where an alleged violation occurred, the initial appearance must be in that district, or in an adjacent district if the appearance can occur more promptly there.

(2) Upon a Summons. When a person appears in response to a summons for violating probation or supervised release, a magistrate judge must proceed under this rule.

(3) Advice. The judge must inform the person of the following:

(A) the alleged violation of probation or supervised release;

(B) the person's right to retain counsel or to request that counsel be appointed if the person cannot obtain counsel; and

(C) the person's right, if held in custody, to a preliminary hearing under Rule 32.1(b)(1).

(4) Appearance in the District With Jurisdiction. If the person is arrested or appears in the district that has jurisdiction to conduct a revocation hearing – either originally or by transfer of jurisdiction – the court must proceed under Rule 32.1(b)-(e).

(5) Appearance in a District Lacking Jurisdiction. If the person is arrested or appears in a district that does not have jurisdiction to conduct a revocation hearing, the magistrate judge must:

(A) if the alleged violation occurred in the district of arrest, conduct a preliminary hearing under Rule 32.1(b) and either:

(i) transfer the person to the district that has jurisdiction, if the judge finds probable cause to believe that a violation occurred; or

(ii) dismiss the proceedings and so notify the court that has jurisdiction, if the judge finds no probable cause to believe that a violation occurred; or

(B) if the alleged violation did not occur in the district of arrest, transfer the person to the district that has jurisdiction if:

(i) the government produces certified copies of the judgment, warrant, and warrant application; and

(ii) the judge finds that the person is the same person named in the warrant.

(6) Release or Detention. The magistrate judge may release or detain the person under 18 U.S.C. sec. 3143(a) pending further proceedings. The burden of establishing that the person will not flee or pose a danger to any other person or to the community rests with the person.

(b) Revocation.

(1) Preliminary Hearing.

(A) In General. If a person is in custody for violating a condition of probation or supervised release, a magistrate judge must promptly conduct a hearing to determine whether there is probable cause to believe that a violation occurred. The person may waive the hearing.

(B) Requirements. The hearing must be recorded by a court reporter or by a suitable recording device. The judge must give the person:

(i) notice of the hearing and its purpose, the alleged violation, and the person's right to retain counsel or to request that counsel be appointed if the person cannot obtain counsel;

(ii) an opportunity to appear at the hearing and present evidence; and

(iii) upon request, an opportunity to question any adverse witness, unless the judge determines that the interest of justice does not require the witness to appear.

(C) Referral. If the judge finds probable cause, the judge must conduct a revocation hearing. If the judge does not find probable cause, the judge must dismiss the proceeding.

(c) Modification.

(1) In General. Before modifying the conditions of probation or supervised release, the court must hold a hearing, at which the person has the right to counsel.

(2) Exceptions. A hearing is not required if:

(A) the person waives the hearing; or

(B) the relief sought is favorable to the person and does not extend the term of probation or of supervised release; and

(C) an attorney for the government has received notice of the relief sought, has had a reasonable opportunity to object, and has not done so.

(d) Disposition of the Case. The court's disposition of the case is governed by 18 U.S.C. sec. 3563 and sec. 3565 (probation) and sec. 3583 (supervised release).

(e) Producing a Statement. Rule 26.2(a)-(d) and (f) applies at a hearing under this rule. If a party fails to comply with a Rule 26.2 order to produce a witness's statement, the court must not consider that witness's testimony.

Rule 32.2. Criminal Forfeiture

(a) Notice to the Defendant. A court shall not enter a judgment of forfeiture in a criminal proceeding unless the indictment or information contains notice to the defendant that the government will seek the forfeiture of property as part of any sentence in accordance with the applicable statute.

(b) Entering a Preliminary Order of Forfeiture.

(1) In General. As soon as practicable after a verdict or finding of guilty, or after a plea of guilty or nolo contendere is accepted, on any count in an indictment or information regarding which criminal forfeiture is sought, the court must determine what property is subject to forfeiture under the applicable statute. If the government seeks forfeiture of specific property, the court must determine whether the government has established the requisite nexus between the property and the offense. If the government seeks a personal money judgment, the court must determine the amount of money that the defendant will be ordered to pay. The court's determination may be based on evidence already in the record, including any written plea agreement or, if the forfeiture is contested, on evidence or information presented by the parties at a hearing after the verdict or finding of guilt.

(2) Preliminary Order. If the court finds that property is subject to forfeiture, it must promptly enter a preliminary order of forfeiture setting forth the amount of any money judgment or directing the forfeiture of specific property without regard to any third party's interest in all or part of it. Determining whether a third party has such an interest must be deferred until any third party files a claim in an ancillary proceeding under Rule 32.2(c).

(3) Seizing Property. The entry of a preliminary order of forfeiture authorizes the Attorney General (or a designee) to seize the specific property subject to forfeiture; to conduct any discovery the court considers proper in identifying, locating, or disposing of the property; and to commence proceedings that comply with any statutes governing third-party rights. At sentencing—or at any time before sentencing if the defendant consents—the order of forfeiture becomes final as to the defendant and shall be made a part of the sentence and included in the judgment. The court may include in the order of forfeiture conditions reasonably necessary to preserve the property's value pending any appeal.

(4) Jury Determination. Upon a party's request in a case in which a jury returns a verdict of guilty, the jury shall determine whether the government has established the requisite nexus between the property and the offense committed by the defendant.

(c) Ancillary Proceeding; Entering a Final Order of Forfeiture.

(1) In General. If, as prescribed by statute, a third party files a petition asserting an interest in the property to be forfeited, the court shall conduct an ancillary proceeding but no ancillary proceeding is required to the extent that the forfeiture consists of a money judgment.

(A) In the ancillary proceeding, the court may, on motion, dismiss the petition for lack of standing, for failure to state a claim, or for any other lawful reason. For the purposes of the motion, the facts set forth in the petition are assumed to be true.

(B) After disposing of any motion filed under Rule 32.2(c)(1)(A) and before conducting a hearing on the petition, the court may permit the parties to conduct discovery in accordance with the Federal Rules of Civil Procedure if the court determines that discovery in necessary or desirable to resolve factual issues. When discovery ends, a party may move for summary judgment under Rule 56 of the Federal Rules of Civil Procedure.

(2) Entering a Final Order. When the ancillary proceeding ends, the court shall enter a final order of forfeiture by amending the preliminary order as necessary to account for any third-party rights. If no third party files a timely claim, the preliminary order becomes the final order of forfeiture, if the court finds that the defendant (or any combination of defendants convicted in the case) had an interest in the property that is forfeitable under the applicable statute. The defendant may not object to the entry of the final order of forfeiture on the ground that the property belongs, in whole or in part, to a codefendant or third party, nor may a third party object to the final order on the ground that the third party had an interest in the property.

(3) Multiple Petitions. If multiple third-party petitions are filed in the same case, an order dismissing or granting one petition is not appealable until rulings are made on all petitions, unless the court determines that there is no just reason for delay.

(4) An ancillary proceeding is not part of sentencing. An ancillary proceeding is not part of sentencing.

(d) Stay Pending Appeal. If a defendant appeals from a conviction or order of forfeiture, the court may stay the order of forfeiture on terms appropriate to ensure that the property remains available pending appellate review. A stay does not delay the ancillary proceeding or the determination of a third party's rights or interests. If the court rules in favor of any third party while an appeal is pending, the court may amend the order of forfeiture but shall not transfer any property interest to a third party until the decision on appeal becomes final, unless the defendant consents in writing or on the record.

(e) Subsequently Located Property: Substitute Property

(1) In General. On the government's motion, the court may at any time enter an order of forfeiture or amend an existing order of forfeiture to include property that:

(A) is subject to forfeiture under an existing order of forfeiture but was located and identified after that order was entered; or

(B) is substitute property that qualifies for forfeiture under an applicable statute.

(2) Procedure. If the government shows that the property is subject to forfeiture under Rule 32.2(e)(1), the court shall:

(A) enter an order forfeiting that property, or amend an existing preliminary or final order to include it; and

(B) if a third party files a petition claiming an interest in the property, conduct an ancillary proceeding under Rule 32.2(c).

(3) Jury Trial Limited. There is no right to trial by jury under Rule 32.2(e).

Rule 33. New Trial

(a) Defendant's Motion. Upon the defendant's motion, the court may vacate any judgment and grant a new trial if the interest of justice so requires. If the case was tried without a jury, the court may take additional testimony and enter a new judgment.

(b) Time to File.

(1) Newly Discovered Evidence. Any motion for a new trial grounded on newly discovered evidence must be filed within 3 years after the verdict or finding of guilty. If an appeal is pending, the court may not grant a motion for a new trial until the appellate court remands the case.

(2) Other Grounds. Any motion for a new trial grounded on any reason other than newly discovered evidence must be filed within 7 days after the verdict or finding of guilty, or within such further time as the court sets during the 7-day period.

Rule 34. Arrest of Judgment

(a) In General. Upon the defendant's motion or on its own, the court must arrest judgment if:

(1) the indictment or information does not charge an offense; or

(2) the court does not have jurisdiction of the charged offense.

(b) Time to File. The defendant must move to arrest judgment within 7 days after the court accepts a verdict or finding of guilty, or after a plea of guilty or nolo contendere, or within such further time as the court sets during the 7-day period.

Rule 35. Correcting or Reducing a Sentence

(a) Correcting Clear Error. Within 7 days after sentencing, the court may correct a sentence that resulted from arithmetical, technical, or other clear error.

(b) Reducing a Sentence for Substantial Assistance.

(1) In General. Upon the government's motion made within one year of sentencing, the court may reduce a sentence if:

(A) the defendant, after sentencing, provided substantial assistance in investigating or prosecuting another person; and

(B) reducing the sentence accords with the Sentencing Commission's guidelines and policy statements.

(2) Later Motion. Upon the government's motion made more than one year after sentencing, the court may reduce a sentence if the defendant's substantial assistance involved:

(A) information not known to the defendant until one year or more after sentencing;

(B) information provided by the defendant to the government within one year of sentencing, but which did not become useful to the government until more than one year after sentencing; or

(C) information the usefulness of which could not reasonably have been anticipated by the defendant until more than one year after sentencing and which was promptly provided to the government after its usefulness was reasonably apparent to the defendant.

(3) Evaluating Substantial Assistance. In evaluating whether the defendant has provided substantial assistance, the court may consider the defendant's presentence assistance.

(4) Below Statutory Minimum. When acting under Rule 35(b), the court may reduce the sentence to a level below the minimum sentence established by statute.

Rule 36. Clerical Error

After giving any notice it considers appropriate, the court may at any time correct a clerical error in a judgment, order, or other part of the record, or correct an error in the record arising from oversight or omission.

Rule 37. [Reserved]

Rule 38. Staying a Sentence or a Disability

(a) **Death Sentence.** A sentence of death shall be stayed if an appeal is taken from the conviction or sentence.

(b) **Imprisonment.**

(1) **Stay Granted.** If the defendant is released pending appeal, the court must stay a sentence of imprisonment.

(2) **Stay Denied; Place of Confinement.** If the defendant is not released pending appeal, the court may recommend to the Attorney General that the defendant be confined near the place of the trial or appeal for a period reasonably necessary to permit the defendant to assist in preparing the appeal.

(c) **Fine.** If the defendant appeals, the district court, or the court of appeals under Federal Rule of Appellate Procedure 8, may stay a sentence to pay a fine or a fine and costs. The court may stay the sentence on any terms considered appropriate and may require the defendant to:

(1) deposit all or part of the fine and costs into the district court's registry pending appeal;

(2) post a bond to pay the fine and costs; or

(3) submit to an examination concerning the defendant's assets and, if appropriate, order the defendant to refrain from dissipating assets.

(d) **Probation.** If the defendant appeals, the court may stay a sentence of probation. The court must set the terms of any stay.

(e) **Restitution and Notice to Victims.**

(1) **In General.** If the defendant appeals, the district court, or the court of appeals under Federal Rule of Appellate Procedure 8, may stay--on any terms considered appropriate--any sentence providing for restitution under 18 U.S.C. sec. 3556 or notice under 18 U.S.C. sec. 3555.

(2) **Ensuring Compliance.** The court may issue any order reasonably necessary to ensure compliance with a restitution order or a notice order after disposition of an appeal, including:

(A) a restraining order;

(B) an injunction;

(C) an order requiring the defendant to deposit all or part of any monetary restitution into the district court's registry; or

(D) an order requiring the defendant to post a bond.

(f) **Forfeiture.** A stay of a forfeiture order is governed by Rule 32.2(d).

(g) **Disability.** If the defendant's conviction or sentence creates a civil or employment disability under federal law, the district court, or the court of appeals under Federal Rule of Appellate Procedure 8, may stay the disability pending appeal on any terms considered appropriate. The court may issue any order reasonably necessary to protect the interest represented by the disability pending appeal, including a restraining order or an injunction.

Rule 39. [Reserved]

TITLE VIII. SUPPLEMENTARY AND SPECIAL PROCEEDINGS

Rule 40. Arrest for Failure to Appear in Another District

(a) In General. If a person is arrested under a warrant issued in another district for failing to appear--as required by the terms of that person's release under 18 U.S.C. sec. 3141-3156 or by a subpoena--the person must be taken without unnecessary delay before a magistrate judge in the district of the arrest.

(b) Proceedings. The judge must proceed under Rule 5(c)(3) as applicable.

(c) Release or Detention Order. The judge may modify any previous release or detention order issued in another district, but must state in writing the reasons for doing so.

Rule 41. Search and Seizure

(a) Scope and Definitions.

(1) Scope. This rule does not modify any statute regulating search or seizure, or the issuance and execution of a search warrant in special circumstances.

(2) Definitions. The following definitions apply under this rule:

(A) "Property" includes documents, books, papers, any other tangible objects, and information.

(B) "Daytime" means the hours between 6:00 a.m. and 10:00 p.m. according to local time.

(C) "Federal law enforcement officer" means a government agent (other than an attorney for the government) who is engaged in enforcing the criminal laws and is within any category of officers authorized by the Attorney General to request a search warrant.

(b) Authority to Issue a Warrant. At the request of a federal law enforcement officer or an attorney for the government:

(1) a magistrate judge with authority in the district – or if none is reasonably available, a judge of a state court of record in the district – has authority to issue a warrant to search for and seize a person or property located within the district;

(2) a magistrate judge with authority in the district has authority to issue a warrant for a person or property outside the district if the person or property is located within the district when the warrant is issued but might move or be moved outside the district before the warrant is executed; and

(3) a magistrate judge – in an investigation of domestic terrorism or international terrorism (as defined in 18 U.S.C. sec. 2331) – having authority in any district in which activities related to the terrorism may have occurred, may issue a warrant for a person or property within or outside that district.

(c) Persons or Property Subject to Search or Seizure. A warrant may be issued for any of the following:

(1) evidence of a crime;

(2) contraband, fruits of crime, or other items illegally possessed;

(3) property designed for use, intended for use, or used in committing a crime; or

(4) a person to be arrested or a person who is unlawfully restrained.

(d) Obtaining a Warrant.

(1) Probable Cause. After receiving an affidavit or other information, a magistrate judge or a judge of a state court of record must issue the warrant if there is probable cause to search for and seize a person or property under Rule 41(c).

(2) Requesting a Warrant in the Presence of a Judge.

(A) Warrant on an Affidavit. When a federal law enforcement officer or an attorney for the government presents an affidavit in support of a warrant, the judge may require the affiant to appear personally and may examine under oath the affiant and any witness the affiant produces.

(B) Warrant on Sworn Testimony. The judge may wholly or partially dispense with a written affidavit and base a warrant on sworn testimony if doing so is reasonable under the circumstances.

(C) Recording Testimony. Testimony taken in support of a warrant must be recorded by a court reporter or by a suitable recording device, and the judge must file the transcript or recording with the clerk, along with any affidavit.

(3) Requesting a Warrant by Telephonic or Other Means.

(A) In General. A magistrate judge may issue a warrant based on information communicated by telephone or other appropriate means, including facsimile transmission.

(B) Recording Testimony. Upon learning that an applicant is requesting a warrant, a magistrate judge must:

(i) place under oath the applicant and any person on whose testimony the application is based; and

(ii) make a verbatim record of the conversation with a suitable recording device, if available, or by a court reporter, or in writing.

(C) Certifying Testimony. The magistrate judge must have any recording or court reporter's notes transcribed, certify the transcription's accuracy, and file a copy of the record and the transcription with the clerk. Any written verbatim record must be signed by the magistrate judge and filed with the clerk.

(D) Suppression Limited. Absent a finding of bad faith, evidence obtained from a warrant issued under Rule 41(d)(3)(A) is not subject to suppression on the ground that issuing the warrant in that manner was unreasonable under the circumstances.

(e) Issuing the Warrant.

(1) In General. The magistrate judge or a judge of a state court of record must issue the warrant to an officer authorized to execute it.

(2) Contents of the Warrant. The warrant must identify the person or property to be searched, identify any person or property to be seized, and designate the magistrate judge to whom it must be returned. The warrant must command the officer to: (A) execute the warrant within a specified time no longer than 10 days; (B) execute the warrant during the daytime, unless the judge for good cause expressly authorizes execution at another time; and (C) return the warrant to the magistrate judge designated in the warrant.

(3) Warrant by Telephonic or Other Means. If a magistrate judge decides to proceed under Rule 41(d)(3)(A), the following additional procedures apply: (A) *Preparing a Proposed Duplicate Original Warrant.* The applicant must prepare a "proposed duplicate original warrant" and must read or otherwise transmit the contents of that document verbatim to the magistrate judge. (B) *Preparing an Original Warrant.* The magistrate judge must enter the contents of the proposed duplicate original warrant into an original warrant. (C) *Modifications.* The magistrate judge may direct the applicant to modify the proposed duplicate original warrant. In that case, the judge must also modify the original warrant. (D) *Signing the Original Warrant and the Duplicate Original Warrant.* Upon determining to issue the warrant, the magistrate judge must immediately sign the original warrant, enter on its face the exact time it is issued, and direct the applicant to sign the judge's name on the duplicate original warrant.

(f) Executing and Returning the Warrant.

(1) Noting the Time. The officer executing the warrant must enter on its face the exact date and time it is executed.

(2) Inventory. An officer present during the execution of the warrant must prepare and verify an inventory of any property seized. The officer must do so in the presence of another officer and the person from whom, or from whose premises, the property was taken. If either one is not present, the officer must prepare and verify the inventory in the presence of at least one other credible person.

(3) Receipt. The officer executing the warrant must:

(A) give a copy of the warrant and a receipt for the property taken to the person from whom, or from whose premises, the property was taken; or

(B) leave a copy of the warrant and receipt at the place where the officer took the property.

(4) Return. The officer executing the warrant must promptly return it--together with a copy of the inventory--to the magistrate judge designated on the warrant. The judge must, on request, give a copy of the inventory to the person from whom, or from whose premises, the property was taken and to the applicant for the warrant.

(g) Motion to Return Property. A person aggrieved by an unlawful search and seizure of property or by the deprivation of property may move for the property's return. The motion must be filed in the district where the property was seized. The court must receive evidence on any factual issue necessary to decide the motion. If it grants the motion, the court must return the property to the movant, but may impose reasonable conditions to protect access to the property and its use in later proceedings.

(h) Motion to Suppress. A defendant may move to suppress evidence in the court where the trial will occur, as Rule 12 provides.

(i) Forwarding Papers to the Clerk. The magistrate judge to whom the warrant is returned must attach to the warrant a copy of the return, of the inventory, and of all other related papers and must deliver them to the clerk in the district where the property was seized.

Rule 42. Criminal Contempt

(a) Disposition After Notice. Any person who commits criminal contempt may be punished for that contempt after prosecution on notice.

(1) Notice. The court must give the person notice in open court, in an order to show cause, or in an arrest order. The notice must:

(A) state the time and place of the trial;

(B) allow the defendant a reasonable time to prepare a defense; and

(C) state the essential facts constituting the charged criminal contempt and describe it as such.

(2) Appointing a Prosecutor. The court must request that the contempt be prosecuted by an attorney for the government, unless the interest of justice requires the appointment of another attorney. If the government declines the request, the court must appoint another attorney to prosecute the contempt.

(3) Trial and Disposition. A person being prosecuted for criminal contempt is entitled to a jury trial in any case in which federal law so provides and must be released or detained as Rule 46 provides. If the criminal contempt involves disrespect toward or criticism of a judge, that judge is disqualified from presiding at the contempt trial or hearing unless the defendant consents. Upon a finding or verdict of guilty, the court must impose the punishment.

(b) Summary Disposition. Notwithstanding any other provision of these rules, the court (other than a magistrate judge) may summarily punish a person who commits criminal contempt in its presence if the judge saw or heard the contemptuous conduct and so certifies; a magistrate judge may summarily punish a person as provided in 28 U.S.C. sec. 636(e). The contempt order must recite the facts, be signed by the judge, and be filed with the clerk.

IX. GENERAL PROVISIONS

Rule 43. Defendant's Presence

(a) When Required. Unless this rule, Rule 5, or Rule 10 provides otherwise, the defendant must be present at:

(1) the initial appearance, the initial arraignment, and the plea;

(2) every trial stage, including jury empanelment and the return of the verdict; and

(3) sentencing.

(b) When Not Required. A defendant need not be present under any of the following circumstances:

(1) Organizational Defendant. The defendant is an organization represented by counsel who is present.

(2) Misdemeanor Offense. The offense is punishable by fine or by imprisonment for not more than one year, or both, and with the defendant's written consent, the court permits arraignment, plea, trial, and sentencing to occur in the defendant's absence.

(3) Conference or Hearing on a Legal Question. The proceeding involves only a conference or hearing on a question of law.

(4) Sentence Correction. The proceeding involves the correction or reduction of sentence under Rule 35 or 18 U.S.C. sec. 3582(c).

(c) Waiving Continued Presence.

(1) In General. A defendant who was initially present at trial, or who had pleaded guilty or nolo contendere, waives the right to be present under the following circumstances:

(A) when the defendant is voluntarily absent after the trial has begun, regardless of whether the court informed the defendant of an obligation to remain during trial;

(B) in a non-capital case, when the defendant is voluntarily absent during sentencing; or

(C) when the court warns the defendant that it will remove the defendant from the courtroom for disruptive behavior, but the defendant persists in conduct that justifies removal from the courtroom.

(2) Waiver's Effect. If the defendant waives the right to be present, the trial may proceed to completion, including the verdict's return and sentencing, during the defendant's absence.

Rule 44. Right to and Appointment of Counsel

(a) Right to Appointed Counsel. A defendant who is unable to obtain counsel is entitled to have counsel appointed to represent the defendant at every stage of the proceeding from initial appearance through appeal, unless the defendant waives this right.

(b) Appointment Procedure. Federal law and local court rules govern the procedure for implementing the right to counsel.

(c) Inquiry Into Joint Representation.

(1) Joint Representation. Joint representation occurs when:

(A) two or more defendants have been charged jointly under Rule 8(b) or have been joined for trial under Rule 13; and

(B) the defendants are represented by the same counsel, or counsel who are associated in law practice.

(2) Court's Responsibilities in Cases of Joint Representation. The court must promptly inquire about the propriety of joint representation and must personally advise each defendant of the right to the effective assistance of counsel, including separate representation. Unless there is good cause to believe that no conflict of interest is likely to arise, the court must take appropriate measures to protect each defendant's right to counsel.

Rule 45. Computing and Extending Time

(a) Computing Time. The following rules apply in computing any period of time specified in these rules, any local rule, or any court order:

(1) Day of the Event Excluded. Exclude the day of the act, event, or default that begins the period.

(2) Exclusion from Brief Periods. Exclude intermediate Saturdays, Sundays, and legal holidays when the period is less than 11 days.

(3) Last Day. Include the last day of the period unless it is a Saturday, Sunday, legal holiday, or day on which weather or other conditions make the clerk's office inaccessible. When the last day is excluded, the period runs until the end of the next day that is not a Saturday, Sunday, legal holiday, or day when the clerk's office is inaccessible.

(4) "Legal Holiday" Defined. As used in this rule, "legal holiday" means:

(A) the day set aside by statute for observing:

(i) New Year's Day;

(ii) Martin Luther King, Jr.'s Birthday;

(iii) Washington's Birthday;

(iv) Memorial Day;

(v) Independence Day;

(vi) Labor Day;

(vii) Columbus Day;

(viii) Veterans' Day;

(ix) Thanksgiving Day;

(x) Christmas Day; and

(B) any other day declared a holiday by the President, the Congress, or the state where the district court is held.

(b) Extending Time.

(1) In General. When an act must or may be done within a specified period, the court on its own may extend the time, or for good cause may do so on a party's motion made:

(A) before the originally prescribed or previously extended time expires; or

(B) after the time expires if the party failed to act because of excusable neglect.

(2) Exceptions. The court may not extend the time to take any action under Rules 29, 33, 34, and 35, except as stated in those rules.

(c) Additional Time After Service. When these rules permit or require a party to act within a specified period after a notice or a paper has been served on that party, 3 days are added to the period if service occurs in the manner provided under Federal Rule of Civil Procedure 5(b)(2)(B), (C), or (D).

Rule 46. Release from Custody; Supervising Detention

(a) **Before Trial.** The provisions of 18 U.S.C. sec. 3142 and 3144 govern pre-trial release.

(b) **During Trial.** A person released before trial continues on release during trial under the same terms and conditions. But the court may order different terms and conditions or terminate the release if necessary to ensure that the person will be present during trial or that the person's conduct will not obstruct the orderly and expeditious progress of the trial.

(c) **Pending Sentencing or Appeal.** The provisions of 18 U.S.C. sec. 3143 govern release pending sentencing or appeal. The burden of establishing that the defendant will not flee or pose a danger to any other person or to the community rests with the defendant.

(d) **Pending Hearing on a Violation of Probation or Supervised Release.** Rule 32.1(a)(6) governs release pending a hearing on a violation of probation or supervised release.

(e) **Surety.** The court must not approve a bond unless any surety appears to be qualified. Every surety, except a legally approved corporate surety, must demonstrate by affidavit that its assets are adequate. The court may require the affidavit to describe the following:

(1) the property that the surety proposes to use as security;

(2) any encumbrance on that property;

(3) the number and amount of any other undischarged bonds and bail undertakings the surety has issued; and

(4) any other liability of the surety.

(f) **Bail Forfeiture.**

(1) **Declaration.** The court must declare the bail forfeited if a condition of the bond is breached.

(2) **Setting Aside.** The court may set aside in whole or in part a bail forfeiture upon any condition the court may impose if:

(A) the surety later surrenders into custody the person released on the surety's appearance bond; or

(B) it appears that justice does not require bail forfeiture.

(3) **Enforcement.**

(A) Default Judgment and Execution. If it does not set aside a bail forfeiture, the court must, upon the government's motion, enter a default judgment.

(B) Jurisdiction and Service. By entering into a bond, each surety submits to the district court's jurisdiction and irrevocably appoints the district clerk as its agent to receive service of any filings affecting its liability.

(C) Motion to Enforce. The court may, upon the government's motion, enforce the surety's liability without an independent action. The government must serve any motion, and notice as the court prescribes, on the district clerk. If so served, the clerk must promptly mail a copy to the surety at its last known address.

(4) **Remission.** After entering a judgment under Rule 46(f)(3), the court may remit in whole or in part the judgment under the same conditions specified in Rule 46(f)(2).

(g) **Exoneration.** The court must exonerate the surety and release any bail when a bond condition has been satisfied or when the court has set aside or remitted the forfeiture. The court must exonerate a surety who deposits cash in the amount of the bond or timely surrenders the defendant into custody.

(h) **Supervising Detention Pending Trial.**

(1) In General. To eliminate unnecessary detention, the court must supervise the detention within the district of any defendants awaiting trial and of any persons held as material witnesses.

(2) Reports. An attorney for the government must report biweekly to the court, listing each material witness held in custody for more than 10 days pending indictment, arraignment, or trial. For each material witness listed in the report, an attorney for the government must state why the witness should not be released with or without a deposition being taken under Rule 15(a).

(i) **Forfeiture of Property.** The court may dispose of a charged offense by ordering the forfeiture of 18 U.S.C. sec. 3142(c)(1)(B)(xi) property under 18 U.S.C. sec. 3146(d), if a fine in the amount of the property's value would be an appropriate sentence for the charged offense.

(j) **Producing a Statement.**

(1) In General. Rule 26.2(a)-(d) and (f) applies at a detention hearing under 18 U.S.C. sec. 3142, unless the court for good cause rules otherwise.

(2) Sanctions for Not Producing a Statement. If a party disobeys a Rule 26.2 order to produce a witness's statement, the court must not consider that witness's testimony at the detention hearing.

Rule 47. Motions and Supporting Affidavits

(a) **In General.** A party applying to the court for an order must do so by motion.

(b) **Form and Content of a Motion.** A motion--except when made during a trial or hearing--must be in writing, unless the court permits the party to make the motion by other means. A motion must state the grounds on which it is based and the relief or order sought. A motion may be supported by affidavit.

(c) **Timing of a Motion.** A party must serve a written motion--other than one that the court may hear ex parte--and any hearing notice at least 5 days before the hearing date, unless a rule or court order sets a different period. For good cause, the court may set a different period upon ex parte application.

(d) **Affidavit Supporting a Motion.** The moving party must serve any supporting affidavit with the motion. A responding party must serve any opposing affidavit at least one day before the hearing, unless the court permits later service.

Rule 48. Dismissal

(a) **By the Government.** The government may, with leave of court, dismiss an indictment, information, or complaint. The government may not dismiss the prosecution during trial without the defendant's consent.

(b) **By the Court.** The court may dismiss an indictment, information, or complaint if unnecessary delay occurs in:

(1) presenting a charge to a grand jury;

(2) filing an information against a defendant; or

(3) bringing a defendant to trial.

Rule 49. Serving and Filing of Papers

(a) **When Required.** A party must serve on every other party any written motion (other than one to be heard ex parte), written notice, designation of the record on appeal, or similar paper.

(b) **How Made.** Service must be made in the manner provided for a civil action. When these rules or a court order requires or permits service on a party represented by an attorney, service must be made on the attorney instead of the party, unless the court orders otherwise.

(c) Notice of a Court Order. When the court issues an order on any post-arraignment motion, the clerk must provide notice in a manner provided for in a civil action. Except as Federal Rule of Appellate Procedure 4(b) provides otherwise, the clerk's failure to give notice does not affect the time to appeal, or relieve--or authorize the court to relieve--a party's failure to appeal within the allowed time.

(d) Filing. A party must file with the court a copy of any paper the party is required to serve. A paper must be filed in a manner provided for in a civil action.

Rule 50. Prompt Disposition

Scheduling preference must be given to criminal proceedings as far as practicable.

Rule 51. Preserving Claimed Error

(a) Exceptions Unnecessary. Exceptions to rulings or orders of the court are unnecessary.

(b) Preserving a Claim of Error. A party may preserve a claim of error by informing the court--when the court ruling or order is made or sought--of the action the party wishes the court to take, or the party's objection to the court's action and the grounds for that objection. If a party does not have an opportunity to object to a ruling or order, the absence of an objection does not later prejudice that party. A ruling or order that admits or excludes evidence is governed by Federal Rule of Evidence 103.

Rule 52. Harmless and Plain Error

(a) Harmless Error. Any error, defect, irregularity or variance which does not affect substantial rights must be disregarded.

(b) Plain Error. A plain error that affects substantial rights may be considered even though it was not brought to the court's attention.

Rule 53. Courtroom Photographing and Broadcasting Prohibited

Except as otherwise provided by a statute or these rules, the court must not permit the taking of photographs in the courtroom during judicial proceedings or the broadcasting of judicial proceedings from the courtroom.

Rule 54. [Transferred] (all of Rule 54 was moved to Rule 1)

Rule 55. Records

The clerk of the district court must keep records of criminal proceedings in the form prescribed by the Director of the Administrative Office of the United States Courts. The clerk must enter in the records every court order or judgment and the date of entry.

Rule 56. When Court Is Open

(a) In General. A district court is considered always open for any filing, and for issuing and returning process, making a motion, or entering an order.

(b) Office Hours. The clerk's office--with the clerk or a deputy in attendance--must be open during business hours on all days except Saturdays, Sundays, and legal holidays.

(c) **Special Hours.** A court may provide by local rule or order that its clerk's office will be open for specified hours on Saturdays or legal holidays other than those set aside by statute for observing New Year's Day, Martin Luther King, Jr.'s Birthday, Washington's Birthday, Memorial Day, Independence Day, Labor Day, Columbus Day, Veterans' Day, Thanksgiving Day, and Christmas Day.

Rule 57. District Court Rules

(a) **In General.**

(1) **Adopting Local Rules.** Each district court acting by a majority of its district judges may, after giving appropriate public notice and an opportunity to comment, make and amend rules governing its practice. A local rule must be consistent with--but not duplicative of-- federal statutes and rules adopted under 28 U.S.C. sec. 2072 and must conform to any uniform numbering system prescribed by the Judicial Conference of the United States.

(2) **Limiting Enforcement.** A local rule imposing a requirement of form must not be enforced in a manner that causes a party to lose rights because of an unintentional failure to comply with the requirement.

(b) **Procedure When There Is No Controlling Law.** A judge may regulate practice in any manner consistent with federal law, these rules, and the local rules of the district. No sanction or other disadvantage may be imposed for noncompliance with any requirement not in federal law, federal rules, or the local district rules unless the alleged violator was furnished with actual notice of the requirement before the noncompliance.

(c) **Effective Date and Notice.** A local rule adopted under this rule takes effect on the date specified by the district court and remains in effect unless amended by the district court or abrogated by the judicial council of the circuit in which the district is located. Copies of local rules and their amendments, when promulgated, must be furnished to the judicial council and the Administrative Office of the United States Courts and must be made available to the public.

Rule 58. Petty Offenses and Other Misdemeanors

(a) **Scope.**

(1) **In General.** These rules apply in petty offense and other misdemeanor cases and on appeal to a district judge in a case tried by a magistrate judge, unless this rule provides otherwise.

(2) **Petty Offense Case without Imprisonment.** In a case involving a petty offense for which no sentence of imprisonment will be imposed, the court may follow any provision of these rules that is not inconsistent with this rule and that the court considers appropriate.

(3) **Definition.** As used in this rule, the term "petty offense for which no sentence of imprisonment will be imposed" means a petty offense for which the court determines that, in the event of conviction, no sentence of imprisonment will be imposed.

(b) **Pre-trial Procedures.**

(1) **Charging Document.** The trial of a misdemeanor may proceed on an indictment, information, or complaint or, in the case of a petty offense, on a citation or violation notice.

(2) **Initial Appearance.** At the defendant's initial appearance on a petty offense or other misdemeanor charge, the magistrate judge must inform the defendant of the following:

(A) the charge, and the minimum and maximum penalties, including imprisonment, fines, any special assessment under 18 U.S.C. sec. 3013, and restitution under 18 U.S.C. sec. 3556;

(B) the right to retain counsel;

(C) the right to request the appointment of counsel if the defendant is unable to retain counsel--unless the charge is a petty offense for which the appointment of counsel is not required;

(D) the defendant's right not to make a statement, and that any statement made may be used against the defendant;

(E) the right to trial, judgment, and sentencing before a district judge--unless:

(i) the charge is a petty offense; or

(ii) the defendant consents to trial, judgment, and sentencing before a magistrate judge;

(F) the right to a jury trial before either a magistrate judge or a district judge--unless the charge is a petty offense; and

(G) if the defendant is held in custody and charged with a misdemeanor other than a petty offense, the right to a preliminary hearing under Rule 5.1, and the general circumstances, if any, under which the defendant may secure pre-trial release.

(3) Arraignment.

(A) Plea Before a Magistrate Judge. A magistrate judge may take the defendant's plea in a petty offense case. In every other misdemeanor case, a magistrate judge may take the plea only if the defendant consents either in writing or on the record to be tried before a magistrate judge and specifically waives trial before a district judge. The defendant may plead not guilty, guilty, or (with the consent of the magistrate judge) nolo contendere.

(B) Failure to Consent. Except in a petty offense case, the magistrate judge must order a defendant who does not consent to trial before a magistrate judge to appear before a district judge for further proceedings.

(c) Additional Procedures in Certain Petty Offense Cases. The following procedures also apply in a case involving a petty offense for which no sentence of imprisonment will be imposed:

(1) Guilty or Nolo Contendere Plea. The court must not accept a guilty or nolo contendere plea unless satisfied that the defendant understands the nature of the charge and the maximum possible penalty.

(2) Waiving Venue.

(A) Conditions of Waiving Venue. If a defendant is arrested, held, or present in a district different from the one where the indictment, information, complaint, citation, or violation notice is pending, the defendant may state in writing a desire to plead guilty or nolo contendere; to waive venue and trial in the district where the proceeding is pending; and to consent to the court's disposing of the case in the district where the defendant was arrested, is held, or is present.

(B) Effect of Waiving Venue. Unless the defendant later pleads not guilty, the prosecution will proceed in the district where the defendant was arrested, is held, or is present. The district clerk must notify the clerk in the original district of the defendant's waiver of venue. The defendant's statement of a desire to plead guilty or nolo contendere is not admissible against the defendant.

(3) Sentencing. The court must give the defendant an opportunity to be heard in mitigation and then proceed immediately to sentencing. The court may, however, postpone sentencing to allow the probation service to investigate or to permit either party to submit additional information.

(4) Notice of a Right to Appeal. After imposing sentence in a case tried on a not-guilty plea, the court must advise the defendant of a right to appeal the conviction and of any right to appeal the sentence. If the defendant was convicted on a plea of guilty or nolo contendere, the court must advise the defendant of any right to appeal the sentence.

(d) Paying a Fixed Sum in Lieu of Appearance.

(1) In General. If the court has a local rule governing forfeiture of collateral, the court may accept a fixed-sum payment in lieu of the defendant's appearance and end the case, but the fixed sum may not exceed the maximum fine allowed by law.

(2) Notice to Appear. If the defendant fails to pay a fixed sum, request a hearing, or appear in response to a citation or violation notice, the district clerk or a magistrate judge may issue a notice for the defendant to appear before the court on a date certain. The notice may give the defendant an additional opportunity to pay a fixed sum in lieu of appearance. The district clerk must serve the notice on the defendant by mailing a copy to the defendant's last known address.

(3) Summons or Warrant. Upon an indictment, or upon a showing by one of the other charging documents specified in Rule 58(b)(1) of probable cause to believe that an offense has been committed and that the defendant has committed it, the court may issue an arrest warrant or, if no warrant is requested by an attorney for the government, a summons. The showing of probable cause must be made under oath or under penalty of perjury, but the affiant need not appear before the court. If the defendant fails to appear before the court in response to a summons, the court may summarily issue a warrant for the defendant's arrest.

(e) Recording the Proceedings. The court must record any proceedings under this rule by using a court reporter or a suitable recording device.

(f) New Trial. Rule 33 applies to a motion for a new trial.

(g) Appeal.

(1) From a District Judge's Order or Judgment. The Federal Rules of Appellate Procedure govern an appeal from a district judge's order or a judgment of conviction or sentence.

(2) From a Magistrate Judge's Order or Judgment.

(A) Interlocutory Appeal. Either party may appeal an order of a magistrate judge to a district judge within 10 days of its entry if a district judge's order could similarly be appealed. The party appealing must file a notice with the clerk specifying the order being appealed and must serve a copy on the adverse party.

(B) Appeal from a Conviction or Sentence. A defendant may appeal a magistrate judge's judgment of conviction or sentence to a district judge within 10 days of its entry. To appeal, the defendant must file a notice with the clerk specifying the judgment being appealed and must serve a copy on an attorney for the government.

(C) Record. The record consists of the original papers and exhibits in the case; any transcript, tape, or other recording of the proceedings; and a certified copy of the docket entries. For purposes of the appeal, a copy of the record of the proceedings must be made available to a defendant who establishes by affidavit an inability to pay or give security for the record. The Director of the Administrative Office of the United States Courts must pay for those copies.

(D) Scope of Appeal. The defendant is not entitled to a trial de novo by a district judge. The scope of the appeal is the same as in an appeal to the court of appeals from a judgment entered by a district judge.

(3) Stay of Execution and Release Pending Appeal. Rule 38 applies to a stay of a judgment of conviction or sentence. The court may release the defendant pending appeal under the law relating to release pending appeal from a district court to a court of appeals.

Rule 59. [Deleted]

Rule 60. Title

These rules may be known and cited as the Federal Rules of Criminal Procedure.

FEDERAL RULES OF EVIDENCE FOR UNITED STATES COURTS AND MAGISTRATES

As amended to December 1, 2003

ARTICLE I. GENERAL PROVISIONS

Rule 101. Scope

These rules govern proceedings in the courts of the United States and before the United States bankruptcy judges and United States magistrate judges, to the extent and with the exceptions stated in rule 1101.

Rule 102. Purpose and Construction

These rules shall be construed to secure fairness in administration, elimination of unjustifiable expense and delay, and promotion of growth and development of the law of evidence to the end that the truth may be ascertained and proceedings justly determined.

Rule 103. Rulings on Evidence

(a) Effect of erroneous ruling. Error may not be predicated upon a ruling which admits or excludes evidence unless a substantial right of the party is affected, and:

(1) Objection. In case the ruling is one admitting evidence, a timely objection or motion to strike appears of record, stating the specific ground of objection, if the specific ground was not apparent from the context; or

(2) Offer of proof. In case the ruling is one excluding evidence, the substance of the evidence was made known to the court by offer or was apparent from the context within which questions were asked.

Once the court makes a definitive ruling on the record, admitting or excluding evidence, either at or before trial, a party need not renew an objection or offer of proof to preserve a claim of error for appeal.

(b) Record of offer and ruling. The court may add any other or further statement which shows the character of the evidence, the form in which it was offered, the objection made, and the ruling thereon. It may direct the making of an offer in question and answer form.

(c) Hearing of jury. In jury cases, proceedings shall be conducted, to the extent practicable, so as to prevent inadmissible evidence from being suggested to the jury by any means, such as making statements or offers of proof or asking questions in the hearing of the jury.

(d) Plain error. Nothing in this rule precludes taking notice of plain errors affecting substantial rights although they were not brought to the attention of the court.

Rule 104. Preliminary Questions

(a) Questions of admissibility generally. Preliminary questions concerning the qualification of a person to be a witness, the existence of a privilege, or the admissibility of evidence shall be determined by the court, subject to the provisions of subdivision (b). In making its determination it is not bound by the rules of evidence except those with respect to privileges.

(b) Relevancy conditioned on fact. When the relevancy of evidence depends upon the fulfillment of a condition of fact, the court shall admit it upon, or subject to, the introduction of evidence sufficient to support a finding of the fulfillment of the condition.

(c) Hearing of jury. Hearings on the admissibility of confessions shall in all cases be conducted out of the hearing of the jury. Hearings on other preliminary matters shall be so conducted when the interests of justice require, or when an accused is a witness and so requests.

(d) Testimony by accused. The accused does not, by testifying upon a preliminary matter, become subject to cross-examination as to other issues in the case.

(e) Weight and credibility. This rule does not limit the right of a party to introduce before the jury evidence relevant to weight or credibility.

Rule 105. Limited Admissibility

When evidence which is admissible as to one party or for one purpose but not admissible as to another party or for another purpose is admitted, the court, upon request, shall restrict the evidence to its proper scope and instruct the jury accordingly.

Rule 106. Remainder of or Related Writings or Recorded Statements

When a writing or recorded statement or part thereof is introduced by a party, an adverse party may require the introduction at that time of any other part or any other writing or recorded statement which ought in fairness to be considered contemporaneously with it.

ARTICLE II. JUDICIAL NOTICE

Rule 201. Judicial Notice of Adjudicative Facts

(a) Scope of rule. This rule governs only judicial notice of adjudicative facts.

(b) Kinds of facts. A judicially noticed fact must be one not subject to reasonable dispute in that it is either (1) generally known within the territorial jurisdiction of the trial court or (2) capable of accurate and ready determination by resort to sources whose accuracy cannot reasonably be questioned.

(c) When discretionary. A court may take judicial notice, whether requested or not.

(d) When mandatory. A court shall take judicial notice if requested by a party and supplied with the necessary information.

(e) Opportunity to be heard. A party is entitled upon timely request to an opportunity to be heard as to the propriety of taking judicial notice and the tenor of the matter noticed. In the absence of prior notification, the request may be made after judicial notice has been taken.

(f) Time of taking notice. Judicial notice may be taken at any stage of the proceeding.

(g) Instructing jury. In a civil action or proceeding, the court shall instruct the jury to accept as conclusive any fact judicially noticed. In a criminal case, the court shall instruct the jury that it may, but is not required to, accept as conclusive any fact judicially noticed.

ARTICLE III. PRESUMPTIONS IN CIVIL ACTIONS AND PROCEEDINGS

Rule 301. Presumptions in General in Civil Actions and Proceedings

In all civil actions and proceedings not otherwise provided for by Act of Congress or by these rules, a presumption imposes on the party against whom it is directed the burden of going forward with evidence to rebut or meet the presumption, but does not shift to such party the burden of proof in the sense of the risk of non persuasion, which remains throughout the trial upon the party on whom it was originally cast.

Rule 302. Applicability of State Law in Civil Actions and Proceedings

In civil actions and proceedings, the effect of a presumption respecting a fact which is an element of a claim or defense as to which State law supplies the rule of decision is determined in accordance with State law.

ARTICLE IV. RELEVANCY AND ITS LIMITS

Rule 401. Definition of "Relevant Evidence"

"Relevant evidence" means evidence having any tendency to make the existence of any fact that is of consequence to the determination of the action more probable or less probable than it would be without the evidence.

Rule 402. Relevant Evidence Generally Admissible; Irrelevant Evidence Inadmissible

All relevant evidence is admissible, except as otherwise provided by the Constitution of the United States, by Act of Congress, by these rules, or by other rules prescribed by the Supreme Court pursuant to statutory authority. Evidence which is not relevant is not admissible.

Rule 403. Exclusion of Relevant Evidence on Grounds of Prejudice, Confusion, or Waste of Time

Although relevant, evidence may be excluded if its probative value is substantially outweighed by the danger of unfair prejudice, confusion of the issues, or misleading the jury, or by considerations of undue delay, waste of time, or needless presentation of cumulative evidence.

Rule 404. Character Evidence not Admissible to Prove Conduct; Exceptions; Other Crimes

(a) Character evidence generally. Evidence of a person's character or a trait of character is not admissible for the purpose of proving action in conformity therewith on a particular occasion, except:

(1) Character of accused. Evidence of a pertinent trait of character offered by an accused, or by the prosecution to rebut the same, or if evidence of a trait of character of the alleged victim of the crime is offered by an accused and admitted under Rule 404(a)(2), evidence of the same trait of character of the accused offered by the prosecution;

(2) Character of victim. Evidence of a pertinent trait of character of the alleged victim of the crime offered by an accused, or by the prosecution to rebut the same, or evidence of a

character trait of peacefulness of the alleged victim offered by the prosecution in a homicide case to rebut evidence that the alleged victim was the first aggressor;

(3) **Character of witness.** Evidence of the character of a witness, as provided in rules 607, 608, and 609.

(b) Other crimes, wrongs, or acts. Evidence of other crimes, wrongs, or acts is not admissible to prove the character of a person in order to show action in conformity therewith. It may, however, be admissible for other purposes, such as proof of motive, opportunity, intent, preparation, plan, knowledge, identity, or absence of mistake or accident, provided that upon request by the accused, the prosecution in a criminal case shall provide reasonable notice in advance of trial, or during trial if the court excuses pre-trial notice on good cause shown, of the general nature of any such evidence it intends to introduce at trial.

Rule 405. Methods of Proving Character

(a) Reputation or opinion. In all cases in which evidence of character or a trait of character of a person is admissible, proof may be made by testimony as to reputation or by testimony in the form of an opinion. On cross-examination, inquiry is allowable into relevant specific instances of conduct.

(b) Specific instances of conduct. In cases in which character or a trait of character of a person is an essential element of a charge, claim, or defense, proof may also be made of specific instances of that person's conduct.

Rule 406. Habit; Routine Practice

Evidence of the habit of a person or of the routine practice of an organization, whether corroborated or not and regardless of the presence of eyewitnesses, is relevant to prove that the conduct of the person or organization on a particular occasion was in conformity with the habit or routine practice.

Rule 407. Subsequent Remedial Measures

When, after an injury or harm allegedly caused by an event, measures are taken that, if taken previously, would have made the injury or harm less likely to occur, evidence of the subsequent measures is not admissible to prove negligence, culpable conduct, a defect in a product, a defect in a product's design, or a need for a warning or instruction. This rule does not require the exclusion of evidence of subsequent measures when offered for another purpose, such as proving ownership, control, or feasibility of precautionary measures, if controverted, or impeachment.

Rule 408. Compromise and Offers to Compromise

Evidence of (1) furnishing or offering or promising to furnish, or (2) accepting or offering or promising to accept, a valuable consideration in compromising or attempting to compromise a claim which was disputed as to either validity or amount, is not admissible to prove liability for or invalidity of the claim or its amount. Evidence of conduct or statements made in compromise negotiations is likewise not admissible. This rule does not require the exclusion of any evidence otherwise discoverable merely because it is presented in the course of compromise negotiations. This rule also does not require exclusion when the evidence is offered for another purpose, such as proving bias or prejudice of a witness, negating a contention of undue delay, or proving an effort to obstruct a criminal investigation or prosecution.

Rule 409. Payment of Medical and Similar Expenses

Evidence of furnishing or offering or promising to pay medical, hospital, or similar expenses occasioned by an injury is not admissible to prove liability for the injury.

Rule 410. Inadmissibility of Pleas, Plea Discussions, and Related Statements

Except as otherwise provided in this rule, evidence of the following is not, in any civil or criminal proceeding, admissible against the defendant who made the plea or was a participant in the plea discussions:

(1) a plea of guilty which was later withdrawn;
(2) a plea of nolo contendere;
(3) any statement made in the course of any proceedings under Rule 11 of the Federal Rules of Criminal Procedure or comparable state procedure regarding either of the foregoing pleas; or
(4) any statement made in the course of plea discussions with an attorney for the prosecuting authority which do not result in a plea of guilty or which result in a plea of guilty later withdrawn.

However, such a statement is inadmissible (i) in any proceeding wherein another statement made in the course of the same plea or plea discussions has been introduced and the statement ought in fairness be considered contemporaneously with it, or (ii) in a criminal proceeding for perjury or false statement if the statement was made by the defendant under oath, on the record and in the presence of counsel.

Rule 411. Liability Insurance

Evidence that a person was or was not insured against liability is not admissible upon the issue whether the person acted negligently or otherwise wrongfully. This rule does not require the exclusion of evidence of insurance against liability when offered for another purpose, such as proof of agency, ownership, or control, or bias or prejudice of a witness.

Rule 412. Sex Offense Cases; Relevance of Alleged Victim's Past Sexual Behavior or Alleged Sexual Predisposition

(a) **Evidence generally inadmissible.** The following evidence is not admissible in any civil or criminal proceeding involving alleged sexual misconduct except as provided in subdivisions (b) and (c):

(1) Evidence offered to prove that any alleged victim engaged in other sexual behavior.
(2) Evidence offered to prove any alleged victim's sexual predisposition.

(b) **Exceptions.**
(1) In a criminal case, the following evidence is admissible, if otherwise admissible under these rules:
    (A) evidence of specific instances of sexual behavior by the alleged victim offered to prove that a person other than the accused was the source of semen, injury or other physical evidence;

(B) evidence of specific instances of sexual behavior by the alleged victim with respect to the person accused of the sexual misconduct offered by the accused to prove consent or by the prosecution; and
(C) evidence the exclusion of which would violate the constitutional rights of the defendant.
(2) In a civil case, evidence offered to prove the sexual behavior or sexual predisposition of any alleged victim is admissible if it is otherwise admissible under these rules and its probative value substantially outweighs the danger of harm to any victim and of unfair prejudice to any party. Evidence of an alleged victim's reputation is admissible only if it has been placed in controversy by the alleged victim.

(c) Procedure to determine admissibility.
(1) A party intending to offer evidence under subdivision (b) must X
   (A) file a written motion at least 14 days before trial specifically describing the evidence and stating the purpose for which it is offered unless the court, for good cause requires a different time for filing or permits filing during trial; and
   (B) serve the motion on all parties and notify the alleged victim or, when appropriate, the alleged victim's guardian or representative.
(2) Before admitting evidence under this rule the court must conduct a hearing in camera and afford the victim and parties a right to attend and be heard. The motion, related papers, and the record of the hearing must be sealed and remain under seal unless the court orders otherwise.

Rule 413. Evidence of Similar Crimes in Sexual Assault Cases

(a) In a criminal case in which the defendant is accused of an offense of sexual assault, evidence of the defendant's commission of another offense or offenses of sexual assault is admissible, and may be considered for its bearing on any matter to which it is relevant.
(b) In a case in which the Government intends to offer evidence under this rule, the attorney for the Government shall disclose the evidence to the defendant, including statements of witnesses or a summary of the substance of any testimony that is expected to be offered, at least fifteen days before the scheduled date of trial or at such later time as the court may allow for good cause.
(c) This rule shall not be construed to limit the admission or consideration of evidence under any other rule.
(d) For purposes of this rule and Rule 415, "offense of sexual assault" means a crime under Federal law or the law of a State (as defined in section 513 of title 18, United States Code) that involvedX
   (1) any conduct proscribed by chapter 109A of title 18, United States Code;
   (2) contact, without consent, between any part of the defendant's body or an object and the genitals or anus of another person;
   (3) contact, without consent, between the genitals or anus of the defendant and any part of another person's body;
   (4) deriving sexual pleasure or gratification from the infliction of death, bodily injury, or physical pain on another person; or
   (5) an attempt or conspiracy to engage in conduct described in paragraphs (1)X(4).

Rule 414. Evidence of Similar Crimes in Child Molestation Cases

(a) In a criminal case in which the defendant is accused of an offense of child molestation, evidence of the defendant's commission of another offense or offenses of child molestation is admissible, and may be considered for its bearing on any matter to which it is relevant.

(b) In a case in which the Government intends to offer evidence under this rule, the attorney for the Government shall disclose the evidence to the defendant, including statements of witnesses or a summary of the substance of any testimony that is expected to be offered, at least fifteen days before the scheduled date of trial or at such later time as the court may allow for good cause.

(c) This rule shall not be construed to limit the admission or consideration of evidence under any other rule.

(d) For purposes of this rule and Rule 415, "child" means a person below the age of fourteen, and "offense of child molestation" means a crime under Federal law or the law of a State (as defined in section 513 of title 18, United States Code) that involvedX

    (1) any conduct proscribed by chapter 109A of title 18, United States Code, that was committed in relation to a child;

    (2) any conduct proscribed by chapter 110 of title 18, United States Code;

    (3) contact between any part of the defendant's body or an object and the genitals or anus of a child;

    (4) contact between the genitals or anus of the defendant and any part of the body of a child;

    (5) deriving sexual pleasure or gratification from the infliction of death, bodily injury, or physical pain on a child; or

    (6) an attempt or conspiracy to engage in conduct described in paragraphs (1)X(5).

Rule 415. Evidence of Similar Acts in Civil Cases Concerning Sexual Assault or Child Molestation

(a) In a civil case in which a claim for damages or other relief is predicated on a party's alleged commission of conduct constituting an offense of sexual assault or child molestation, evidence of that party's commission of another offense or offenses of sexual assault or child molestation is admissible and may be considered as provided in Rule 413 and Rule 414 of these rules.

(b) A party who intends to offer evidence under this Rule shall disclose the evidence to the party against whom it will be offered, including statement of witnesses or a summary of the substance of any testimony that is expected to be offered, at least fifteen days before the scheduled date of trial or at such later time as the court may allow for good cause.

(c) This rule shall not be construed to limit the admission or consideration of evidence under any other rule.

ARTICLE V. PRIVILEGES

Rule 501. General Rule
Except as otherwise required by the Constitution of the United States or provided by Act of Congress or in rules prescribed by the Supreme Court pursuant to statutory authority, the privilege of a witness, person, government, State, or political subdivision thereof shall be governed by the principles of the common law as they may be interpreted by the courts of the United States in the light of reason and experience. However, in civil actions and proceedings, with respect to an element of a claim or defense as to which State law supplies the rule of decision, the privilege of a witness, person, government, State, or political subdivision thereof shall be determined in accordance with State law.

ARTICLE VI. WITNESSES

Rule 601. General Rule of Competency
Every person is competent to be a witness except as otherwise provided in these rules. However, in civil actions and proceedings, with respect to an element of a claim or defense as to which State law supplies the rule of decision, the competency of a witness shall be determined in accordance with State law.

Rule 602. Lack of Personal Knowledge
A witness may not testify to a matter unless evidence is introduced sufficient to support a finding that the witness has personal knowledge of the matter. Evidence to prove personal knowledge may, but need not, consist of the witness' own testimony. This rule is subject to the provisions of Rule 703, relating to opinion testimony by expert witnesses.

Rule 603. Oath or Affirmation
Before testifying, every witness shall be required to declare that the witness will testify truthfully, by oath or affirmation administered in a form calculated to awaken the witness' conscience and impress the witness' mind with the duty to do so.

Rule 604. Interpreters
An interpreter is subject to the provisions of these rules relating to qualification as an expert and the administration of an oath or affirmation to make a true translation.

Rule 605. Competency of Judge as Witness
The judge presiding at the trial may not testify in that trial as a witness. No objection need be made in order to preserve the point.

Rule 606. Competency of Juror as Witness
(a) **At the trial.** A member of the jury may not testify as a witness before that jury in the trial of the case in which the juror is sitting. If the juror is called so to testify, the opposing party shall be afforded an opportunity to object out of the presence of the jury.

(b) **Inquiry into validity of verdict or indictment.** Upon an inquiry into the validity of a verdict or indictment, a juror may not testify as to any matter or statement occurring during the course of the jury's deliberations or to the effect of anything upon that or any other juror's mind or emotions as influencing the juror to assent to or dissent from the verdict or indictment or concerning the juror's mental processes in connection therewith, except that a juror may testify on the question whether extraneous prejudicial information was improperly brought to the jury's attention or whether any outside influence was improperly brought to bear upon any juror. Nor may a juror's affidavit or evidence of any statement by the juror concerning a matter about which the juror would be precluded from testifying be received for these purposes.

Rule 607. Who May Impeach

The credibility of a witness may be attacked by any party, including the party calling the witness.

Rule 608. Evidence of Character and Conduct of Witness

(a) Opinion and reputation evidence of character. The credibility of a witness may be attacked or supported by evidence in the form of opinion or reputation, but subject to these limitations: (1) the evidence may refer only to character for truthfulness or untruthfulness, and (2) evidence of truthful character is admissible only after the character of the witness for truthfulness has been attacked by opinion or reputation evidence or otherwise.

(b) Specific instances of conduct. Specific instances of conduct. Specific instances of the conduct of a witness, for the purpose of attacking or supporting the witness' character for truthfulness, other than conviction of crime as provided in rule 609, may not be proved by extrinsic evidence. They may, however, in the discretion of the court, if probative of truthfulness or untruthfulness, be inquired into on cross-examination of the witness (1) concerning the witness' character for truthfulness or untruthfulness, or (2) concerning the character for truthfulness or untruthfulness of another witness as to which character the witness being cross-examined has testified.

The giving of testimony, whether by an accused or by any other witness, does not operate as a waiver of the accused's or the witness' privilege against self-incrimination when examined with respect to matters that relate only to character for truthfulness.

Rule 609. Impeachment by Evidence of Conviction of Crime

(a) General rule. For the purpose of attacking the credibility of a witness,

(1) evidence that a witness other than an accused has been convicted of a crime shall be admitted, subject to Rule 403, if the crime was punishable by death or imprisonment in excess of one year under the law under which the witness was convicted, and evidence that an accused has been convicted of such a crime shall be admitted if the court determines that the probative value of admitting this evidence outweighs its prejudicial effect to the accused; and

(2) evidence that any witness has been convicted of a crime shall be admitted if it involved dishonesty or false statement, regardless of the punishment.

(b) Time limit. Evidence of a conviction under this rule is not admissible if a period of more than ten years has elapsed since the date of the conviction or of the release of the witness from the confinement imposed for that conviction, whichever is the later date, unless the court determines, in the interests of justice, that the probative value of the conviction supported by specific facts and circumstances substantially outweighs its prejudicial effect. However, evidence of a conviction more than 10 years old as calculated herein, is not admissible unless the proponent gives to the adverse party sufficient advance written notice of intent to use such evidence to provide the adverse party with a fair opportunity to contest the use of such evidence.

(c) Effect of pardon, annulment, or certificate of rehabilitation. Evidence of a conviction is not admissible under this rule if (1) the conviction has been the subject of a pardon, annulment, certificate of rehabilitation, or other equivalent procedure based on a finding of the rehabilitation of the person convicted, and that person has not been convicted of a subsequent crime which was punishable by death or imprisonment in excess of one year, or (2) the conviction has been the subject of a pardon, annulment, or other equivalent procedure based on a finding of innocence.

(d) Juvenile adjudications. Evidence of juvenile adjudications is generally not admissible under this rule. The court may, however, in a criminal case allow evidence of a juvenile adjudication of a witness other than the accused if conviction of the offense would be admissible to attack the credibility of an adult and the court is satisfied that admission in evidence is necessary for a fair determination of the issue of guilt or innocence.

(e) Pendency of appeal. The pendency of an appeal therefrom does not render evidence of a conviction inadmissible. Evidence of the pendency of an appeal is admissible.

Rule 610. Religious Beliefs or Opinions

Evidence of the beliefs or opinions of a witness on matters of religion is not admissible for the purpose of showing that by reason of their nature the witness' credibility is impaired or enhanced.

Rule 611. Mode and Order of Interrogation and Presentation

(a) Control by court. The court shall exercise reasonable control over the mode and order of interrogating witnesses and presenting evidence so as to (1) make the interrogation and presentation effective for the ascertainment of the truth, (2) avoid needless consumption of time, and (3) protect witnesses from harassment or undue embarrassment.

(b) Scope of cross-examination. Cross-examination should be limited to the subject matter of the direct examination and matters affecting the credibility of the witness. The court may, in the exercise of discretion, permit inquiry into additional matters as if on direct examination.

(c) Leading questions. Leading questions should not be used on the direct examination of a witness except as may be necessary to develop the witness' testimony. Ordinarily leading questions should be permitted on cross-examination. When a party calls a hostile witness, an adverse party, or a witness identified with an adverse party, interrogation may be by leading questions.

Rule 612. Writing Used to Refresh Memory

Except as otherwise provided in criminal proceedings by section 3500 of Title 18, United States Code, if a witness uses a writing to refresh memory for the purpose of testifying, either—

(1) while testifying, or

(2) before testifying, if the court in its discretion determines it is necessary in the interests of justice, an adverse party is entitled to have the writing produced at the hearing, to inspect it, to cross-examine the witness thereon, and to introduce in evidence those portions which relate to the testimony of the witness. If it is claimed that the writing contains matters not related to the subject matter of the testimony the court shall examine the writing in camera, excise any portions not so related, and order delivery of the remainder to the party entitled thereto. Any portion withheld over objections shall be preserved and made available to the appellate court in the event of an appeal. If a writing is not produced or delivered pursuant to order under this rule, the court shall make any order justice requires, except that in criminal cases when the prosecution elects not to comply, the order shall be one striking the testimony or, if the court in its discretion determines that the interests of justice so require, declaring a mistrial.

Rule 613. Prior Statements of Witnesses

(a) **Examining witness concerning prior statement.** In examining a witness concerning a prior statement made by the witness, whether written or not, the statement need not be shown nor its contents disclosed to the witness at that time, but on request the same shall be shown or disclosed to opposing counsel.

(b) **Extrinsic evidence of prior inconsistent statement of witness.** Extrinsic evidence of a prior inconsistent statement by a witness is not admissible unless the witness is afforded an opportunity to explain or deny the same and the opposite party is afforded an opportunity to interrogate the witness thereon, or the interests of justice otherwise require. This provision does not apply to admissions of a party-opponent as defined in Rule 801(d)(2).

Rule 614. Calling and Interrogation of Witnesses by Court

(a) **Calling by court.** The court may, on its own motion or at the suggestion of a party, call witnesses, and all parties are entitled to cross-examine witnesses thus called.

(b) **Interrogation by court.** The court may interrogate witnesses, whether called by itself or by a party.

(c) **Objections.** Objections to the calling of witnesses by the court or to interrogation by it may be made at the time or at the next available opportunity when the jury is not present.

Rule 615. Exclusion of Witnesses

At the request of a party the court shall order witnesses excluded so that they cannot hear the testimony of other witnesses, and it may make the order of its own motion. This rule does not authorize exclusion of (1) a party who is a natural person, or (2) an officer or employee of a party which is not a natural person designated as its representative by its attorney, or (3) a person whose presence is shown by a party to be essential to the presentation of the party's cause, or (4) a person authorized by statute to be present.

ARTICLE VII. OPINIONS AND EXPERT TESTIMONY

Rule 701. Opinion Testimony by Lay Witnesses

If the witness is not testifying as an expert, the witness' testimony in the form of opinions or inferences is limited to those opinions or inferences which are (a) rationally based on the perception of the witness, (b) helpful to a clear understanding of the witness' testimony or the determination of a fact in issue, and (c) not based on scientific, technical, or other specialized knowledge within the scope of Rule 702.

Rule 702. Testimony by Experts

If scientific, technical, or other specialized knowledge will assist the trier of fact to understand the evidence or to determine a fact in issue, a witness qualified as an expert by knowledge, skill, experience, training, or education, may testify thereto in the form of an opinion or otherwise, if (1) the testimony is based upon sufficient facts or data, (2) the testimony is the product of reliable principles and methods, and (3) the witness has applied the principles and methods reliably to the facts of the case.

Rule 703. Bases of Opinion Testimony by Experts

The facts or data in the particular case upon which an expert bases an opinion or inference may be those perceived by or made known to the expert at or before the hearing. If of a type reasonably relied upon by experts in the particular field in forming opinions or inferences upon the subject, the facts or data need not be admissible in evidence in order for the opinion or inference to be admitted. Facts or data that are otherwise inadmissible shall not be disclosed to the jury by the proponent of the opinion or inference unless the court determines that their probative value in assisting the jury to evaluate the expert's opinion substantially outweighs their prejudicial effect.

Rule 704. Opinion on ultimate issue

(a) Except as provided in subdivision (b), testimony in the form of an opinion or inference otherwise admissible is not objectionable because it embraces an ultimate issue to be decided by the trier of fact.

(b) No expert witness testifying with respect to the mental state or condition of a defendant in a criminal case may state an opinion or inference as to whether the defendant did or did not have the mental state or condition constituting an element of the crime charged or of a defense thereto. Such ultimate issues are matters for the trier of fact alone.

Rule 705. Disclosure of Facts or Data Underlying Expert Opinion

The expert may testify in terms of opinion or inference and give reasons therefor without first testifying to the underlying facts or data, unless the court requires otherwise. The expert may in any event be required to disclose the underlying facts or data on cross-examination.

Rule 706. Court Appointed Experts

(a) Appointment. The court may on its own motion or on the motion of any party enter an order to show cause why expert witnesses should not be appointed, and may request the parties to submit nominations. The court may appoint any expert witnesses agreed upon by the parties, and may appoint expert witnesses of its own selection. An expert witness shall not be appointed by the court unless the witness consents to act. A witness so appointed shall be informed of the witness' duties by the court in writing, a copy of which shall be filed with the clerk, or at a conference in which the parties shall have opportunity to participate. A witness so appointed shall advise the parties of the witness' findings, if any; the witness' deposition may be taken by any party; and the witness may be called to testify by the court or any party. The witness shall be subject to cross-examination by each party, including a party calling the witness.

(b) Compensation. Expert witnesses so appointed are entitled to reasonable compensation in whatever sum the court may allow. The compensation thus fixed is payable from funds which may be provided by law in criminal cases and civil actions and proceedings involving just compensation under the fifth amendment. In other civil actions and proceedings the compensation shall be paid by the parties in such proportion and at such time as the court directs, and thereafter charged in like manner as other costs.

(c) Disclosure of appointment. In the exercise of its discretion, the court may authorize disclosure to the jury of the fact that the court appointed the expert witness.

(d) Parties' experts of own selection. Nothing in this rule limits the parties in calling expert witnesses of their own selection.

ARTICLE VIII. HEARSAY

Rule 801. Definitions

The following definitions apply under this article:

(a) Statement. A "statement" is (1) an oral or written assertion or (2) nonverbal conduct of a person, if it is intended by the person as an assertion.

(b) Declarant. A "declarant" is a person who makes a statement.

(c) Hearsay. "Hearsay" is a statement, other than one made by the declarant while testifying at the trial or hearing, offered in evidence to prove the truth of the matter asserted.

(d) Statements which are not hearsay. A statement is not hearsay if

(1) Prior statement by witness. The declarant testifies at the trial or hearing and is subject to cross-examination concerning the statement, and the statement is (A) inconsistent with the declarant's testimony, and was given under oath subject to the penalty of perjury at a trial, hearing, or other proceeding, or in a deposition, or (B) consistent with the declarant's testimony and is offered to rebut an express or implied charge against the declarant of recent fabrication or improper influence or motive, or (C) one of identification of a person made after perceiving the person; or

(2) Admission by party-opponent. The statement is offered against a party and is (A) the party's own statement, in either an individual or a representative capacity or (B) a statement of which the party has manifested an adoption or belief in its truth, or (C) a statement by a person authorized by the party to make a statement concerning the subject, or (D) a statement by the party's agent or servant concerning a matter within the scope of the agency or employment, made during the existence of the relationship, or (E) a statement by a coconspirator of a party during the course and in furtherance of the conspiracy. The contents of the statement shall be considered but are not alone sufficient to establish the declarant's authority under subdivision (C), the agency or employment relationship and scope thereof under subdivision (D), or the existence of the conspiracy and the participation therein of the declarant and the party against whom the statement is offered under subdivision (E).

Rule 802. Hearsay Rule

Hearsay is not admissible except as provided by these rules or by other rules prescribed by the Supreme Court pursuant to statutory authority or by Act of Congress.

Rule 803. Hearsay Exceptions; Availability of Declarant Immaterial

The following are not excluded by the hearsay rule, even though the declarant is available as a witness:

(1) Present sense impression. A statement describing or explaining an event or condition made while the declarant was perceiving the event or condition, or immediately thereafter.

(2) Excited utterance. A statement relating to a startling event or condition made while the declarant was under the stress of excitement caused by the event or condition. **(3) Then existing mental, emotional, or physical condition.** A statement of the declarant's then existing state of mind, emotion, sensation, or physical condition (such as intent, plan, motive, design, mental feeling, pain, and bodily health), but not including a statement of memory or belief to prove the fact remembered or believed unless it relates to the execution, revocation, identification, or terms of declarant's will.

(4) Statements for purposes of medical diagnosis or treatment. Statements made for purposes of medical diagnosis or treatment and describing medical history, or past or present symptoms, pain, or sensations, or the inception or general character of the cause or external source thereof insofar as reasonably pertinent to diagnosis or treatment.

(5) Recorded recollection. A memorandum or record concerning a matter about which a witness once had knowledge but now has insufficient recollection to enable the witness to testify fully and accurately, shown to have been made or adopted by the witness when the matter was fresh in the witness' memory and to reflect that knowledge correctly. If admitted, the memorandum or record may be read into evidence but may not itself be received as an exhibit unless offered by an adverse party.

(6) Records of regularly conducted activity. A memorandum, report, record, or data compilation, in any form, of acts, events, conditions, opinions, or diagnoses, made at or near the time by, or from information transmitted by, a person with knowledge, if kept in the course of a regularly conducted business activity, and if it was the regular practice of that business activity to make the memorandum, report, record, or data compilation, all as shown by the testimony of the custodian or other qualified witness, or by certification that complies with Rule 902(11), Rule 902(12), or a statute permitting certification, unless the source of information or the method or circumstances of preparation indicate lack of trustworthiness. The term "business" as used in this paragraph includes business, institution, association, profession, occupation, and calling of every kind, whether or not conducted for profit.

(7) Absence of entry in records kept in accordance with the provisions of paragraph (6). Evidence that a matter is not included in the memoranda reports, records, or data compilations, in any form, kept in accordance with the provisions of paragraph (6), to prove the nonoccurrence or nonexistence of the matter, if the matter was of a kind of which a memorandum, report, record, or data compilation was regularly made and preserved, unless the sources of information or other circumstances indicate lack of trustworthiness.

(8) Public records and reports. Records, reports, statements, or data compilations, in any form, of public offices or agencies, setting forth (A) the activities of the office or agency, or (B) matters observed pursuant to duty imposed by law as to which matters there was a duty to report, excluding, however, in criminal cases matters observed by police officers and other law enforcement personnel, or (C) in civil actions and proceedings and against the Government in criminal cases, factual findings resulting from an investigation made pursuant to authority granted by law, unless the sources of information or other circumstances indicate lack of trustworthiness.

(9) Records of vital statistics. Records or data compilations, in any form, of births, fetal deaths, deaths, or marriages, if the report thereof was made to a public office pursuant to requirements of law.

(10) Absence of public record or entry. To prove the absence of a record, report, statement, or data compilation, in any form, or the nonoccurrence or nonexistence of a matter of which a record, report, statement, or data compilation, in any form, was regularly made and preserved by a public office or agency, evidence in the form of a certification in accordance with Rule 902, or testimony, that diligent search failed to disclose the record, report, statement, or data compilation, or entry.

(11) Records of religious organizations. Statements of births, marriages, divorces, deaths, legitimacy, ancestry, relationship by blood or marriage, or other similar facts of personal or family history, contained in a regularly kept record of a religious organization.

(12) Marriage, baptismal, and similar certificates. Statements of fact contained in a certificate that the maker performed a marriage or other ceremony or administered a sacrament, made by a clergyman, public official, or other person authorized by the rules or practices of a religious organization or by law to perform the act certified, and purporting to have been issued at the time of the act or within a reasonable time thereafter.

(13) Family records. Statements of fact concerning personal or family history contained in family Bibles, genealogies, charts, engravings on rings, inscriptions on family portraits, engravings on urns, crypts, or tombstones, or the like.

(14) Records of documents affecting an interest in property. The record of a document purporting to establish or affect an interest in property, as proof of the content of the original recorded document and its execution and delivery by each person by whom it purports to have been executed, if the record is a record of a public office and an applicable statute authorizes the recording of documents of that kind in that office.

(15) Statements in documents affecting an interest in property. A statement contained in a document purporting to establish or affect an interest in property if the matter stated was relevant to the purpose of the document, unless dealings with the property since the document was made have been inconsistent with the truth of the statement or the purport of the document.

(16) Statements in ancient documents. Statements in a document in existence 20 years or more the authenticity of which is established.

(17) Market reports, commercial publications. Market quotations, tabulations, lists, directories, or other published compilations, generally used and relied upon by the public or by persons in particular occupations.

(18) Learned treatises. To the extent called to the attention of an expert witness upon cross-examination or relied upon by the expert witness in direct examination, statements contained in published treatises, periodicals, or pamphlets on a subject of history, medicine, or other science or art, established as a reliable authority by the testimony or admission of the witness or by other expert testimony or by judicial notice. If admitted, the statements may be read into evidence but may not be received as exhibits.

(19) Reputation concerning personal or family history. Reputation among members of a person's family by blood, adoption, or marriage, or among a person's associates, or in the community, concerning a person's birth, adoption, marriage, divorce, death, legitimacy, relationship by blood, adoption, or marriage, ancestry, or other similar fact of personal or family history.

(20) Reputation concerning boundaries or general history. Reputation in a community, arising before the controversy, as to boundaries of or customs affecting lands in the community, and reputation as to events of general history important to the community or State or nation in which located.

(21) Reputation as to character. Reputation of a person's character among associates or in the community.

(22) Judgment of previous conviction. Evidence of a final judgment, entered after a trial or upon a plea of guilty (but not upon a plea of nolo contendere), adjudging a person guilty of a crime punishable by death or imprisonment in excess of one year, to prove any fact essential to sustain the judgment, but not including, when offered by the Government in a criminal prosecution for purposes other than impeachment, judgments against persons other than the accused. The pendency of an appeal may be shown but does not affect admissibility.

(23) Judgment as to personal, family or general history, or boundaries. Judgments as proof of matters of personal, family or general history, or boundaries, essential to the judgment, if the same would be provable by evidence of reputation.

(24) Other exceptions. A statement not specifically covered by any of the foregoing exceptions but having equivalent circumstantial guarantees of trustworthiness, if the court determines that (A) the statement is offered as evidence of a material fact; (B) the statement is more probative on the point for which it is offered than any other evidence which the proponent can procure through reasonable efforts; and (C) the general purposes of these rules and the interests of justice will best be served by admission of the statement into evidence. However, a statement may not be admitted under this exception unless the proponent of it makes known to the adverse party sufficiently in advance of the trial or hearing to provide the adverse party with a fair opportunity to prepare to meet it, the proponent's intention to offer the statement and the particulars of it, including the name and address of the declarant.

Rule 804. Hearsay Exceptions; Declarant Unavailable

(a) Definition of unavailability. "Unavailability as a witness" includes situations in which the declarant

(1) is exempted by ruling of the court on the ground of privilege from testifying concerning the subject matter of the declarant's statement; or

(2) persists in refusing to testify concerning the subject matter of the declarant's statement despite an order of the court to do so; or

(3) testifies to a lack of memory of the subject matter of the declarant's statement; or

(4) is unable to be present or to testify at the hearing because of death or then existing physical or mental illness or infirmity; or

(5) is absent from the hearing and the proponent of a statement has been unable to procure the declarant's attendance (or in the case of a hearsay exception under subdivision (b)(2), (3), or (4), the declarant's attendance or testimony) by process or other reasonable means.

A declarant is not unavailable as a witness if exemption, refusal, claim of lack of memory, inability, or absence is due to the procurement or wrongdoing of the proponent of a statement for the purpose of preventing the witness from attending or testifying.

(b) Hearsay exceptions. The following are not excluded by the hearsay rule if the declarant is unavailable as a witness:

(1) Former testimony. Testimony given as a witness at another hearing of the same or a different proceeding, or in a deposition taken in compliance with law in the course of the same or another proceeding, if the party against whom the testimony is now offered, or, in a civil action or proceeding, a predecessor in interest, had an opportunity and similar motive to develop the testimony by direct, cross, or redirect examination.

(2) Statement under belief of impending death. In a prosecution for homicide or in a civil action or proceeding, a statement made by a declarant while believing that the declarant's death was imminent, concerning the cause or circumstances of what the declarant believed to be impending death.

(3) Statement against interest. A statement which was at the time of its making so far contrary to the declarant's pecuniary or proprietary interest, or so far tended to subject the declarant to civil or criminal liability, or to render invalid a claim by the declarant against another, that a reasonable person in the declarant's position would not have made the statement unless believing it to be true. A statement tending to expose the declarant to criminal liability and offered to exculpate the accused is not admissible unless corroborating circumstances clearly indicate the trustworthiness of the statement.

(4) Statement of personal or family history. (A) A statement concerning the declarant's own birth, adoption, marriage, divorce, legitimacy, relationship by blood, adoption, or marriage, ancestry, or other similar fact of personal or family history, even though declarant had no means of acquiring personal knowledge of the matter stated; or (B) a statement concerning the foregoing matters, and death also, of another person, if the declarant was related to the other by blood, adoption, or marriage or was so intimately associated with the other's family as to be likely to have accurate information concerning the matter declared.

(5) [Transferred to Rule 807]

(6) Forfeiture by wrongdoing. A statement offered against a party that has engaged or acquiesced in wrongdoing that was intended to, and did, procure the unavailability of the declarant as a witness.

Rule 805. Hearsay within Hearsay

Hearsay included within hearsay is not excluded under the hearsay rule if each part of the combined statements conforms with an exception to the hearsay rule provided in these rules.

Rule 806. Attacking and Supporting Credibility of Declarant

When a hearsay statement, or a statement defined in Rule 801(d)(2), (C), (D), or (E), has been admitted in evidence, the credibility of the declarant may be attacked, and if attacked may be supported, by any evidence which would be admissible for those purposes if declarant had testified as a witness. Evidence of a statement or conduct by the declarant at any time, inconsistent with the declarant's hearsay statement, is not subject to any requirement that the declarant may have been afforded an opportunity to deny or explain. If the party against whom a hearsay statement has been admitted calls the declarant as a witness, the party is entitled to examine the declarant on the statement as if under cross-examination.

Rule 807. Residual Exception

A statement not specifically covered by Rule 803 or 804 but having equivalent circumstantial guarantees of trustworthiness, is not excluded by the hearsay rule, if the court determines that (A) the statement is offered as evidence of a material fact; (B) the statement is more probative on the point for which it is offered than any other evidence which the proponent can procure through reasonable efforts; and (C) the general purposes of these rules and the interests of justice will best be served by admission of the statement into evidence. However, a statement may not be admitted under this exception unless the proponent of it makes known to the adverse party sufficiently in advance of the trial or hearing to provide the adverse party with a fair opportunity to prepare to meet it, the proponent's intention to offer the statement and the particulars of it, including the name and address of the declarant.

ARTICLE IX. AUTHENTICATION AND IDENTIFICATION

Rule 901. Requirement of Authentication or Identification

  (a) General provision. The requirement of authentication or identification as a condition precedent to admissibility is satisfied by evidence sufficient to support a finding that the matter in question is what its proponent claims.

  (b) Illustrations. By way of illustration only, and not by way of limitation, the following are examples of authentication or identification conforming with the requirements of this rule:

  (1) Testimony of witness with knowledge. Testimony that a matter is what it is claimed to be.

  (2) Non-expert opinion on handwriting. Non expert opinion as to the genuineness of handwriting, based upon familiarity not acquired for purposes of the litigation.

  (3) Comparison by trier or expert witness. Comparison by the trier of fact or by expert witnesses with specimens which have been authenticated.

  (4) Distinctive characteristics and the like. Appearance, contents, substance, internal patterns, or other distinctive characteristics, taken in conjunction with circumstances.

  (5) Voice identification. Identification of a voice, whether heard firsthand or through mechanical or electronic transmission or recording, by opinion based upon hearing the voice at any time under circumstances connecting it with the alleged speaker.

  (6) Telephone conversations. Telephone conversations, by evidence that a call was made to the number assigned at the time by the telephone company to a particular person or business, if (A) in the case of a person, circumstances, including self-identification, show the person answering to be the one called, or (B) in the case of a business, the call was made to a place of business and the conversation related to business reasonably transacted over the telephone.

  (7) Public records or reports. Evidence that a writing authorized by law to be recorded or filed and in fact recorded or filed in a public office, or a purported public record, report, statement, or data compilation, in any form, is from the public office where items of this nature are kept.

  (8) Ancient documents or data compilation. Evidence that a document or data compilation, in any form, (A) is in such condition as to create no suspicion concerning its authenticity, (B) was in a place where it, if authentic, would likely be, and (C) has been in existence 20 years or more at the time it is offered.

  (9) Process or system. Evidence describing a process or system used to produce a result and showing that the process or system produces an accurate result.

  (10) Methods provided by statute or rule. Any method of authentication or identification provided by Act of Congress or by other rules prescribed by the Supreme Court pursuant to statutory authority.

Rule 902. Self-Authentication

  Extrinsic evidence of authenticity as a condition precedent to admissibility is not required with respect to the following:

(1) Domestic public documents under seal. A document bearing a seal purporting to be that of the United States, or of any State, district, Commonwealth, territory, or insular possession thereof, or the Panama Canal Zone, or the Trust Territory of the Pacific Islands, or of a political subdivision, department, officer, or agency thereof, and a signature purporting to be an attestation or execution.

(2) Domestic public documents not under seal. A document purporting to bear the signature in the official capacity of an officer or employee of any entity included in paragraph (1) hereof, having no seal, if a public officer having a seal and having official duties in the district or political subdivision of the officer or employee certifies under seal that the signer has the official capacity and that the signature is genuine.

(3) Foreign public documents. A document purporting to be executed or attested in an official capacity by a person authorized by the laws of a foreign country to make the execution or attestation, and accompanied by a final certification as to the genuineness of the signature and official position (A) of the executing or attesting person, or (B) of any foreign official whose certificate of genuineness of signature and official position relates to the execution or attestation or is in a chain of certificates of genuineness of signature and official position relating to the execution or attestation. A final certification may be made by a secretary of an embassy or legation, consul general, consul, vice consul, or consular agent of the United States, or a diplomatic or consular official of the foreign country assigned or accredited to the United States. If reasonable opportunity has been given to all parties to investigate the authenticity and accuracy of official documents, the court may, for good cause shown, order that they be treated as presumptively authentic without final certification or permit them to be evidenced by an attested summary with or without final certification.

(4) Certified copies of public records. A copy of an official record or report or entry therein, or of a document authorized by law to be recorded or filed and actually recorded or filed in a public office, including data compilations in any form, certified as correct by the custodian or other person authorized to make the certification, by certificate complying with paragraph (1), (2), or (3) of this rule or complying with any Act of Congress or rule prescribed by the Supreme Court pursuant to statutory authority.

(5) Official publications. Books, pamphlets, or other publications purporting to be issued by public authority.

(6) Newspapers and periodicals. Printed materials purporting to be newspapers or periodicals.

(7) Trade inscriptions and the like. Inscriptions, signs, tags, or labels purporting to have been affixed in the course of business and indicating ownership, control, or origin.

(8) Acknowledged documents. Documents accompanied by a certificate of acknowledgment executed in the manner provided by law by a notary public or other officer authorized by law to take acknowledgments.

(9) Commercial paper and related documents. Commercial paper, signatures thereon, and documents relating thereto to the extent provided by general commercial law.

(10) Presumptions under Acts of Congress. Any signature, document, or other matter declared by Act of Congress to be presumptively or prima facie genuine or authentic.

(11) Certified Domestic Records of Regularly Conducted Activity. The original or a duplicate of a domestic record of regularly conducted activity that would be admissible under Rule 803(6) if accompanied by a written declaration of its custodian or other qualified person, in a manner complying with any Act of Congress or rule prescribed by the Supreme Court pursuant to statutory authority, certifying that the record –

(A) was made at or near the time of the occurrence of the matters set forth by, of from information transmitted by, a person with knowledge of those matters;

(B) was kept in the ordinary course of the regularly conducted activity; and

(C) was made by the regularly conducted activity as a regular practice.

A party intending to offer a record into evidence under this paragraph must provide written notice of that intention to all adverse parties, and must make the record and declaration available for inspection sufficiently in advance of their offer into evidence to provide an adverse party with a fair opportunity to challenge them.

(12) Certified Foreign Records of Regularly Conducted Activity. In a civil case, the original or a duplicate of a foreign record of regularly conducted activity that would be admissible under Rule 803(6) if accompanied by a written declaration by its custodian or other qualified person certifying that the record –

(A) was made at or near the time of the occurrence of the matters set forth by, of from information transmitted by, a person with knowledge of those matters;

(B) was kept in the ordinary course of the regularly conducted activity; and

(C) was made by the regularly conducted activity as a regular practice.

The declaration must be signed in a manner that, if falsely made, would subject the maker to criminal penalties under the laws of the country where the declaration was signed. A party intending to offer a record into evidence under this paragraph must provide written notice of that intention to all adverse parties, and must make the record and declaration available for inspection sufficiently in advance of their offer into evidence to provide an adverse party with a fair opportunity to challenge them.

Rule 903. Subscribing Witness' Testimony Unnecessary

The testimony of a subscribing witness is not necessary to authenticate a writing unless required by the laws of the jurisdiction whose laws govern the validity of the writing.

ARTICLE X. CONTENTS OF WRITINGS, RECORDINGS, AND PHOTOGRAPHS

Rule 1001. Definitions

For purposes of this article the following definitions are applicable:

(1) Writings and recordings. "Writings" and "recordings" consist of letters, words, or numbers, or their equivalent, set down by handwriting, typewriting, printing, photostating, photographing, magnetic impulse, mechanical or electronic recording, or other form of data compilation.

(2) Photographs. "Photographs" include still photographs, X-ray films, video tapes, and motion pictures.

(3) Original. An "original" of a writing or recording is the writing or recording itself or any counterpart intended to have the same effect by a person executing or issuing it. An "original" of a photograph includes the negative or any print therefrom. If data are stored in a computer or similar device, any printout or other output readable by sight, shown to reflect the data accurately, is an "original."

(4) Duplicate. A "duplicate" is a counterpart produced by the same impression as the original, or from the same matrix, or by means of photography, including enlargements and miniatures, or by mechanical or electronic rerecording, or by chemical reproduction, or by other equivalent techniques which accurately reproduces the original.

Rule 1002. Requirement of Original

To prove the content of a writing, recording, or photograph, the original writing, recording, or photograph is required, except as otherwise provided in these rules or by Act of Congress.

Rule 1003. Admissibility of Duplicates

A duplicate is admissible to the same extent as an original unless (1) a genuine question is raised as to the authenticity of the original or (2) in the circumstances it would be unfair to admit the duplicate in lieu of the original.

Rule 1004. Admissibility of other Evidence of Contents

The original is not required, and other evidence of the contents of a writing, recording, or photograph is admissible if

(1) Originals lost or destroyed. All originals are lost or have been destroyed, unless the proponent lost or destroyed them in bad faith; or

(2) Original not obtainable. No original can be obtained by any available judicial process or procedure; or

(3) Original in possession of opponent. At a time when an original was under the control of the party against whom offered, that party was put on notice, by the pleadings or otherwise, that the contents would be a subject of proof at the hearing, and that party does not produce the original at the hearing; or

(4) Collateral matters. The writing, recording, or photograph is not closely related to a controlling issue.

Rule 1005. Public Records

The contents of an official record, or of a document authorized to be recorded or filed and actually recorded or filed, including data compilations in any form, if otherwise admissible, may be proved by copy, certified as correct in accordance with Rule 902 or testified to be correct by a witness who has compared it with the original. If a copy which complies with the foregoing cannot be obtained by the exercise of reasonable diligence, then other evidence of the contents may be given.

Rule 1006. Summaries

The contents of voluminous writings, recordings, or photographs which cannot conveniently be examined in court may be presented in the form of a chart, summary, or calculation. The originals, or duplicates, shall be made available for examination or copying, or both, by other parties at reasonable time and place. The court may order that they be produced in court.

Rule 1007. Testimony or Written Admission of Party

Contents of writings, recordings, or photographs may be proved by the testimony or deposition of the party against whom offered or by that party's written admission, without accounting for the non production of the original.

Rule 1008. Functions of Court and Jury

When the admissibility of other evidence of contents of writings, recordings, or photographs under these rules depends upon the fulfillment of a condition of fact, the question whether the condition has been fulfilled is ordinarily for the court to determine in accordance with the provisions of Rule 104. However, when an issue is raised (a) whether the asserted writing ever existed, or (b) whether another writing, recording, or photograph produced at the trial is the original, or (c) whether other evidence of contents correctly reflects the contents, the issue is for the trier of fact to determine as in the case of other issues of fact.

ARTICLE XI. MISCELLANEOUS RULES

Rule 1101. Applicability of Rules

(a) Courts and judges. These rules apply to the United States district courts, the District Court of Guam, the District Court of the Virgin Islands, the District Court for the Northern Mariana Islands, the United States courts of appeals, the United States Claims Court, and to United States bankruptcy judges and United States magistrate judges, in the actions, cases, and proceedings and to the extent hereinafter set forth. The terms "judge" and "court" in these rules include United States bankruptcy judges and United States magistrate judges.

(b) Proceedings generally. These rules apply generally to civil actions and proceedings, including admiralty and maritime cases, to criminal cases and proceedings, to contempt proceedings except those in which the court may act summarily, and to proceedings and cases under Title 11, United States Code.

(c) Rule of privilege. The rule with respect to privileges applies at all stages of all actions, cases, and proceedings.

(d) Rules inapplicable. The rules (other than with respect to privileges) do not apply in the following situations:

(1) Preliminary questions of fact. The determination of questions of fact preliminary to admissibility of evidence when the issue is to be determined by the court under Rule 104.

(2) Grand jury. Proceedings before grand juries.

(3) Miscellaneous proceedings. Proceedings for extradition or rendition; preliminary examinations in criminal cases; sentencing, or granting or revoking probation; issuance of warrants for arrest, criminal summonses, and search warrants; and proceedings with respect to release on bail or otherwise.

(e) Rules applicable in part. In the following proceedings these rules apply to the extent that matters of evidence are not provided for in the statutes which govern procedure therein or in other rules prescribed by the Supreme Court pursuant to statutory authority: the trial of misdemeanors or other petty offenses before the United States magistrate judges; review of agency actions when the facts are subject to trial de novo under section 706(2)(F) of Title 5, United States Code; review of orders of the Secretary of Agriculture under section 2 of the Act entitled "An Act to authorize association of producers of agricultural products" approved February 18, 1922 (7 U.S.C. § 292), and under sections 6 and 7(c) of the Perishable Agricultural Commodities Act, 1930 (7 U.S.C. §§ 499f, 499g(c)); naturalization and revocation of naturalization under sections 310-318 of the Immigration and Nationality Act (8 U.S.C. §§ 1421-1429); prize proceedings in admiralty under sections 7651-7681 of Title 10, United States

Code; review of orders of the Secretary of the Interior under section 2 of the Act entitled "An Act authorizing associations of producers of aquatic products" approved June 25, 1934 (15 U.S.C. § 522); review of orders of petroleum control boards under section 5 of the Act entitled "An Act to regulate interstate and foreign commerce in petroleum and its products by prohibiting the shipment in such commerce of petroleum and its products produced in violation of State law, and for other purposes," approved February 22, 1935 (15 U.S.C. § 715d); actions for fines, penalties, or forfeitures under part V of Title IV of the Tariff Act of 1930 (19 U.S.C. §§ 1581-1624), or under the Anti-Smuggling Act (19 U.S.C. §§ 1701-1711); criminal libel for condemnation, exclusion of imports, or other proceedings under the Federal Food, Drug, and Cosmetic Act (21 U.S.C. §§ 301-392); disputes between seamen under sections 4079, 4080, and 4081 of the Revised Statutes (22 U.S.C. §§ 256-258); habeas corpus under sections 2241-2254 of Title 28, United States Code; motions to vacate, set aside or correct sentence under section 2255 of Title 28, United States Code; actions for penalties for refusal to transport destitute seamen under section 4578 of the Revised Statutes (46 U.S.C. § 679); actions against the United States under the Act entitled "An Act authorizing suits against the United States in admiralty for damage caused by and salvage service rendered to public vessels belonging to the United States, and for other purposes," approved March 3, 1925 (46 U.S.C. §§ 781-790), as implemented by section 7730 of Title 10, United States Code.

Rule 1102. Amendments

Amendments to the Federal Rules of Evidence may be made as provided in section 2072 of Title 28 of the United States Code.

Rule 1103. Title

These rules may be known and cited as the Federal Rules of Evidence.

Section 3
Fraud Investigation

INVESTIGATION

TABLE OF CONTENTS

ANALYZING DOCUMENTS

Chain of Custody	3.101
Obtaining Documentary Evidence	3.102
Types of Evidence	3.103
Organization of Evidence	3.103
Chronologies	3.103
To-Do Lists	3.104
Examining Fraudulent Documents	3.104
Early Consultation with an Expert Can Prove Valuable	3.105
Types of Forensic Document Examinations	3.105
Handling Documents as Physical Evidence	3.106
Preserving for Fingerprint Examinations	3.106
Charred or Partially Burned Documents	3.107
Recognizing Phony Documents	3.107
Identifying Writings	3.108
Class Characteristics	3.108
"Copy-book" Styles	3.109
"Copycat" Styles	3.109
Natural Variations, Disguise, and Distortions	3.109
Variation	3.109
Disguise	3.109
Distortions	3.110
Forgeries	3.110
The Document Expert's Findings	3.111
Non-Identification	3.111
Identification	3.111
Inconclusive	3.111
How to Obtain Handwriting Samples	3.112
Undictated Writing Samples	3.112
Dictated Writing Samples	3.113
Obtaining Dictated Handwriting Samples by Court Order	3.113
Preparation for Taking Dictated Handwriting Samples	3.113
Directions for Obtaining Dictated Handwriting Samples	3.113
Typewriters and Computer Printers	3.114
Typewriter Ribbons Could Be Evidence	3.114
Avoid Taking Unnecessary Samples	3.115
Taking Typewriter Samples	3.115
Photocopies	3.116
Identifying the Source of a Photocopy	3.116
Permanent "Trash Marks"	3.116

2005 Fraud Examiners Manual

INVESTIGATION

ANALYZING DOCUMENTS (CONT.)

Transient "Trash Marks"	3.117
Taking Photocopier Samples	3.117
"Dating" a Document	3.118
The "Alibi" Document	3.118
The "Long Lost" Will	3.118
Valuable Historical and Collectible Documents	3.118
Anachronisms in Documentary Materials	3.118
Indented Writings	3.119
Developing Indented Writings	3.120
Counterfeit Printed Documents	3.120
Counterfeiting Methods	3.120
Detecting Counterfeits	3.121
Fingerprints	3.121
Fingerprints on Paper or Other Absorbent Porous Surfaces	3.122
Fingerprints on Hard, Non-Porous Surfaces	3.122
Fingerprint Comparison Standards	3.123
Sources for Expert Document Examinations	3.123
Law Enforcement Laboratories	3.123
Forensic Document Experts in Private Practice	3.124
Graphologists (Graphoanalysts)	3.124

INTERVIEW THEORY AND APPLICATION

Preparation	3.201
Characteristics of a Good Interview	3.201
Characteristics of a Good Interviewer	3.202
Question Typology	3.202
Introductory Questions	3.203
Informational Questions	3.203
Closing Questions	3.203
Assessment Questions	3.203
Admission-Seeking Questions	3.203
Legal Elements of Interviewing	3.204
Legal Authority to Conduct Interviews	3.204
Use of Deception in Interviews	3.204
Frazier vs. Cupp	3.204
Elements of Conversations	3.204
Expression	3.204
Persuasion	3.205
Therapy	3.205
Ritual	3.205
Information Exchange	3.205

INVESTIGATION

INTERVIEW THEORY AND APPLICATION (CONT.)

Inhibitors of Communication 3.206
    Competing Demands for Time 3.206
    Ego Threat 3.206
        Repression 3.206
        Disapproval 3.206
        Loss of Status 3.207
    Etiquette 3.207
    Trauma 3.207
    Forgetting 3.207
    Chronological Confusion 3.208
    Inferential Confusion 3.208
    Unconscious Behavior 3.208

Facilitators of Communication 3.208
    Fulfilling Expectations 3.209
    Recognition 3.209
    Altruistic Appeals 3.209
    Sympathetic Understanding 3.209
    New Experience 3.210
    Catharsis 3.210
    Need for Meaning 3.210
    Extrinsic Rewards 3.210

Introductory Questions 3.211
    Provide the Introduction 3.211
    Establish Rapport 3.211
    Establish the Interview Theme 3.211
    Observe Reactions 3.212
    Theme Development 3.212
    Methodology 3.213
        Physical Contact 3.213
        Establish the Purpose of Interview 3.214
        Don't Interview More than One Person 3.214
        Privacy 3.214
        Ask Nonsensitive Questions 3.214
        Get a Commitment for Assistance 3.215
        Establish Transitional Statement 3.216
        Seek Continuous Agreement 3.217
        Do Not Invade Body Space 3.217

Informational Questions 3.217
    Open Questions 3.218
    Closed Questions 3.218
    Leading Questions 3.218

INVESTIGATION

INTERVIEW THEORY AND APPLICATION (CONT.)

Double-Negative Questions 3.219
Complex Questions 3.219
Attitude Questions 3.219
Question Sequences 3.220
Controlled Answer Techniques 3.220
Free Narratives 3.221
Informational Question Techniques 3.221
Note-Taking 3.222
    Maintain Eye Contact 3.222
    Opinions 3.222
    Writing Down Questions 3.222
    Documenting Results 3.223
Observing Interview Reactions 3.223
    Proxemics 3.223
    Chronemics 3.223
    Kinetics 3.224
    Paralinguistics 3.224
Theme Development 3.224
Methodology 3.225
    Begin with Background Questions 3.225
    Observe Verbal and Nonverbal Behavior 3.226
    Ask Nonleading (Open) Questions 3.226
    Approach Sensitive Questions Carefully 3.227
Dealing with Resistance 3.227
    "I'm Too Busy" 3.227
    "I Don't Know Anything About It" 3.228
    "I Don't Remember" 3.228
    "What Do You Mean by That?" 3.229
Difficult People 3.229
    Don't React 3.229
    Disarm the Person 3.229
    Change Tactics 3.229
    Make it Easy to Say "Yes" 3.229
    Make it Hard to Say "No" 3.230
Volatile Interviews 3.230
    Physical Symptoms 3.230
    Other Considerations 3.231
    Overcoming Objections 3.232
Assessment Questions 3.233
    Norming or Calibrating 3.233
    Physiology of Deception 3.233

INVESTIGATION

INTERVIEW THEORY AND APPLICATION (CONT.)

Verbal Clues	3.234
Nonverbal Clues	3.237
Methodology	3.238
Closing Questions	3.242
Admission-Seeking Questions	3.245
Purpose of Questions	3.246
Preparation	3.246
Interview Room	3.246
Presence of Outsiders	3.246
Miranda Warnings	3.247
Theme Development	3.247
Steps in the Admission-Seeking Interview	3.248
Direct Accusation	3.248
Observe Reaction	3.249
Repeat Accusation	3.249
Interrupt Denials	3.249
Delays	3.250
Interruptions	3.251
Reasoning	3.251
Establish Rationalization	3.251
Unfair Treatment	3.252
Inadequate Recognition	3.252
Financial Problems	3.253
Aberration of Conduct	3.253
Family Problems	3.254
Accuser's Actions	3.254
Stress, Drugs, and Alcohol	3.255
Revenge	3.255
Depersonalizing the Victim	3.255
Minor Moral Infraction	3.256
Altruism	3.256
Genuine Need	3.257
Diffuse Alibis	3.257
Display Physical Evidence	3.257
Discuss Witnesses	3.258
Discuss Deceptions	3.259
Present Alternative	3.259
Benchmark Admission	3.260
Reinforce Rationalization	3.261
Verbal Confession	3.261
Motive for Offense	3.264

INVESTIGATION

INTERVIEW THEORY AND APPLICATION (CONT.)

Others Involved	3.265
Physical Evidence	3.265
Specifics of Each Offense	3.267
Kinesic Interview and Interrogation	3.268
Self-Initiated Verbal Statements	3.269
Prompted Verbal Responses	3.269
Structured Questions	3.270
Nonverbal Behavior/Body Language	3.270
Criteria-Based Statement Analysis	3.271
Parts of Speech	3.272
Pronouns	3.272
Possessive Pronouns	3.273
Verbs	3.273
Balance of the Statement	3.274
General Characteristics	3.274
Specific Content	3.275
Peculiarities of Content	3.275
The Cognitive Interview Technique	3.276
The Narrative Phase	3.277
Reconstruct the Circumstances of the Event	3.278
Instruct the Eyewitness to Report Everything and Be Complete	3.278
Recall the Events in Different Orders	3.278
Change Perspective	3.279
Specific Items of Information	3.279
Physical Appearance	3.279
Names	3.279
Number	3.280
Speech Characteristics	3.280
Conversation	3.280

COVERT EXAMINATIONS

Covert Examinations	3.301
Establishing an Identity	3.302
Objectives	3.303
Problems in Covert Operations	3.304
Entrapment	3.305
Surveillance	3.305
Methods of Surveillance	3.306
Preparation	3.306
Electronic Equipment	3.306
Basic Precautions	3.307

INVESTIGATION

COVERT EXAMINATIONS (CONT.)

Techniques of Foot Surveillance	3.307
One-Person Surveillance	3.307
Two-Person Surveillance	3.307
Three-Person Surveillance	3.308
Other Techniques	3.308
Techniques of Vehicle Surveillance	3.309
General	3.309
One-Vehicle Surveillance	3.309
Two-Vehicle Surveillance	3.310
Fixed Surveillance	3.310
Satellite Surveillance	3.310
Night Surveillance Equipment	3.311
Sources and Informants	3.311
Types of Informants	3.312
Basic Lead Informants	3.312
Participant Informants	3.312
Covert Informants	3.312
The Accomplice/Witness	3.313
Objectives of Source and Informant Information	3.313
Recruitment of Sources and Informants	3.314
Motives of Sources and Informants	3.315
Sources	3.315
Informants	3.315
Legal Considerations	3.316
Reporting Contacts	3.317
Promises of Confidentiality	3.318
Use of Operatives	3.319
Sources for Satellite Imagery and Related Materials	3.319
Satellite and Civil Liberties	3.320

SOURCES OF INFORMATION

Rules Governing Public Record Information	3.401
Freedom of Information Act (FOIA)	3.401
Fair Credit Reporting Act (FCRA)	3.402
Gramm-Leach-Bliley Act	3.403
Privacy Act of 1974	3.405
Right to Financial Privacy Act	3.405
Postal Privacy Act of 1993	3.405
Americans with Disabilities Act (ADA)	3.405
Driver's Privacy Protection Act	3.406
Health Insurance Portability and Accountability Act	3.406

INVESTIGATION

SOURCES OF INFORMATION (CONT.)

City Government	3.407
Building Inspector	3.407
Health Department	3.407
Personnel Department	3.407
Public Schools	3.407
Regulatory Agencies	3.408
Tax Assessor/Collector	3.408
Utility Company Records	3.408
County Government	3.409
Coroner	3.409
Court Clerk	3.409
Personnel Department	3.411
Public Schools	3.411
Registrar of Voters	3.411
Recorder	3.411
Regulatory Agencies	3.412
Welfare Commission	3.412
State Government	3.413
Business Filings Division	3.413
Fictitious Business Names/DBA	3.413
Uniform Commercial Code Filings	3.414
Employee/Labor Department	3.414
State Tax Department	3.414
Professional Associations and Licensing Boards	3.415
Other State Regulatory Agencies	3.416
Federal Government	3.417
Inspectors General	3.417
Commodity Futures Trading Commission	3.419
Department of Agriculture (USDA)	3.419
Department of Commerce	3.420
Social Security Administration	3.420
Department of Defense (DOD)	3.422
Department of Education	3.422
Department of Housing and Urban Development (HUD)	3.422
Department of Justice	3.423
Department of Labor	3.423
Department of State	3.423
Department of the Treasury	3.424
Department of Veterans Affairs (VA)	3.425
Drug Enforcement Agency	3.425
Federal Aviation Administration (FAA)	3.425

INVESTIGATION

SOURCES OF INFORMATION (CONT.)

Federal Bureau of Investigation	3.425
Federal Communications Commission (FCC)	3.425
Federal Energy Regulatory Commission	3.425
Federal Maritime Commission	3.426
General Services Administration (GSA)	3.426
Interstate Commerce Commission (ICC)	3.426
National Aeronautics and Space Administration (NASA)	3.426
National Archives and Records Administration	3.426
National Railroad Passenger Corporation (Amtrak)	3.427
Nuclear Regulatory Commission (NRC)	3.427
Resolution Trust Corporation (RTC)	3.428
Securities and Exchange Commission (SEC)	3.428
Small Business Administration (SBA)	3.429
Bureau of Public Debt	3.430
Federal Highway Administration	3.430
U.S. Citizenship and Immigration Services	3.430
U.S. Coast Guard	3.430
U.S. General Accounting Office	3.430
U.S. Postal Service	3.430
Federal Procurement Data System	3.431
FedWorld Information Network	3.431
Commercial Sources	3.431
Better Business Bureau	3.431
Chamber of Commerce	3.431
Abstract and Title Companies	3.432
Bonding Companies	3.432
Credit Card Records	3.432
Stockbrokers	3.432
Western Union	3.432
Car Fax	3.432
International Air Transport Association	3.432
International Foundation for Art Research	3.433
National Association of Insurance Commissioners	3.433
Phonefiche	3.433
Select Phone	3.433
Credit Records	3.433
Types of Retail Information	3.434
Information Available from Credit Bureaus	3.434
Commercial Databases and Research Reference Services	3.435
Type of Information Available	3.435
On-Line Information Vendors	3.436

INVESTIGATION

SOURCES OF INFORMATION (CONT.)

Directories	3.436
American Medical Association Directory	3.437
America's Corporate Families and International Affiliates	3.437
Best Insurance Reports	3.437
Wilson Biological and Agricultural Index	3.437
CD-ROMs in Print	3.438
City Directories	3.438
Congressional Directory	3.438
Directories in Print	3.438
Directory of Companies Filing Annual Reports With the SEC	3.439
Directory of Corporate Affiliations—Who Owns Whom	3.439
Dow Jones-Irwin Business and Investment Almanac	3.439
D&B's Million Dollar Directory	3.439
Encyclopedia of Business Information Sources	3.439
Federal Database Finder	3.439
Gale's Encyclopedia of Associations	3.439
Gale Guide to Internet Databases	3.440
Guide to American Directories	3.440
Index Medicus	3.440
Index to Legal Periodicals	3.440
Insurance Reporting Services	3.440
Lloyd's Register of Classed Yachts and Register of American Yachts	3.440
Lloyd's Register of Shipping and B. Lloyd's Weekly Register	3.440
Lloyd's Voyage Record and Shipping Index	3.440
List of Shipowners	3.441
Register of International Shipowning Groups	3.441
Register of Offshore Units, Submersibles and Underwater Systems	3.441
Weekly List of Alterations to the Register of Ships	3.441
Magazines for Libraries	3.441
Martindale-Hubbell Law Directory	3.442
Moody's	3.442
Moody's Bank and Finance Manual	3.442
Moody's Bank and Finance News Reports	3.442
National Auto Theft Bureau	3.442
The National Directory of Law Enforcement Administrators	3.442
National Trade and Professional Associations of the United States	3.443
The New York Times Index	3.443
Phonedisc USA	3.443
Public Affairs Information Service	3.443
Reader's Guide to Periodical Literature	3.443

INVESTIGATION

SOURCES OF INFORMATION (CONT.)

Predicasts Funk and Scott Index, United States 3.443
    Standard & Poor's Corporation Records 3.443
Standard & Poor's Register of Corporations, Directors and Executives 3.444
Who's Who Series 3.444
Associations Yellow Book 3.444
Corporate Yellow Book 3.444
Encyclopedia of Associations 3.445
Federal Organization Charts 3.445
Federal Regional Yellow Book 3.445
Financial Yellow Book 3.445
Foreign Representatives in the U.S. Yellow Book 3.445
Gale Directory of Databases 3.446
Gale Directory of Publications and Broadcast Media 3.446
Government Affairs Yellow Book 3.446
Judicial Yellow Book 3.446
Law Firms Yellow Book 3.447
Municipal Yellow Book 3.447
News Media Yellow Book 3.447
State Yellow Book 3.447
Thomson Bank Directory (replaces the Rand McNally Bankers Directory) 3.447
Banks and Financial Institutions 3.448
    Federal Regulatory Agencies 3.449
        Export-Import Bank of the United States 3.449
        Farm Credit Administration 3.449
        Federal Deposit Insurance Corporation (FDIC) 3.449
        Federal Housing Finance Board 3.450
        Federal Reserve System 3.450
        National Credit Union Administration 3.451
        Office of the Comptroller of the Currency 3.451
Investigative and Law Enforcement Information Centers and Databases 3.451
    Canadian Interface 3.451
    Central Index System (CIS) 3.451
    Consular Lookout and Support System (CLASS) 3.452
    Defense Clearance and Investigations Index (DCII) 3.452
    El Paso Intelligence Center (EPIC) 3.452
    Financial Crimes Enforcement Network (FinCEN) 3.453
    Interagency Border Inspection System (IBIS) 3.454
    International Chamber of Commerce Commercial Crime Bureau 3.454
    International Criminal Police Organization 3.454
    International Criminal Police Organization Case Tracking System (ICTS) 3.455

INVESTIGATION

SOURCES OF INFORMATION (CONT.)

Interstate Identification Index (III)	3.455
Joint Maritime Information Element (JMIE)	3.456
Law Enforcement Support Center (LESC)	3.456
List of Parties Excluded From Federal Procurement and Nonprocurement Programs	3.456
National Tracing Center (NTC)	3.456
National White-Collar Crime Center	3.457
Narcotics and Dangerous Drugs Information System (NADDIS)	3.457
National Alien Information Lookout System (NAILS)	3.457
National Crime Information Center (NCIC)	3.457
National Law Enforcement Telecommunications System (NLETS)	3.458
Nonimmigrant Information Systems (NIIS)	3.459
Operational Activities Special Information System (OASIS)	3.459
Regional Information Sharing System (RISS)	3.459
SENTRY	3.460
South Pacific Islands Criminal Intelligence Network (SPICIN)	3.461
Treasury Enforcement Communications Systems (TECS)	3.461
United Nations Crime and Justice Information Network (UNCJIN)	3.462
Washington Area Law Enforcement System (WALES)	3.462
World Criminal Justice Library Network (WCJLN)	3.462

ACCESSING INFORMATION ON-LINE

Accessing Information Through Computer Databases	3.501
Limitations of Databases	3.502
Commercial On-Line Services	3.502
Using an On-Line Service to Find Information	3.503
How to Locate People Using On-Line Records	3.503
Types of Searches	3.504
Obtaining Financial Information and Locating Assets	3.505
Searches for "Hard Assets"	3.505
Searches for Asset Potential	3.506
Finding Legal Records	3.506
On-Site Court Searches	3.506
Index/Broad Coverage Searches	3.507
Conducting Background Checks	3.507
Due Diligence	3.508
Employment Background	3.508
Records Service Companies	3.509
ChoicePoint (www.choicepoint.net)	3.510
CDB Infotek (www.choicepointon-line.com/cdb)	3.510
IRSC (www.irsc.com)	3.510

INVESTIGATION

ACCESSING INFORMATION ON-LINE (CONT.)

    Database Technologies On-line, or DBT On-line (www.dbton-line.com) 3.510
    USDatalink (www.usdatalink.com) 3.511
    infoUSA.com (www.infousa.com) 3.511
    Security Software Solutions (www.ssn-locate.com) 3.511
    Diligenz (www.diligenz.com) 3.511
    KnowX (www.knowx.com) 3.511
    Dialog Information Retrieval Service (www.dialog.com) 3.512
    D&B (formerly Dun & Bradstreet) (www.dnb.com) 3.512
    LexisNexis (www.lexisnexis.com) 3.512
    Experian (www.experian.com) 3.512
    DCS Information Systems (www.dcs-amerifind.com/) 3.513
    G.A. Public Records Services (www.gaprs.com) 3.513
  Newspaper/Media Databases 3.513
    Factiva (www.factiva.com) 3.513
    LexisNexis (www.LexisNexis.com) 3.514
    Electric Library (www.elibrary.com) 3.514
    Data Times (http// www.umi.com/proquest/) 3.514
    Other News Database Services 3.514
The Internet 3.514
  Search Engines 3.515
    Google (www.google.com) 3.515
    Yahoo! (www.yahoo.com) 3.515
    HotBot (www.hotbot.com) 3.515
    Excite (www.excite.com) 3.516
    Lycos (www.lycos.com) 3.516
    Ask Jeeves (www.askjeeves.com) 3.516
    AltaVista (www.altavista.com) 3.516
    Google Groups (www.groups.google.com) 3.516
  Directories 3.517
    Yahoo! (www.yahoo.com) 3.517
    WWW virtual library (www.w3.org/vl/) 3.517
    Internet Public Library (www.ipl.org) 3.517
  Metasearch Engines 3.518
    Metacrawler (www.metacrawler.com) 3.518
    Dogpile (www.dogpile.com) 3.518
    Northern Light (www.northernlight.com) 3.518
A Guide to Successful Searching 3.518
  Running Searches 3.518
  Boolean Operators 3.518
Websites Table 3.520

INVESTIGATION

DATA ANALYSIS AND REPORTING TOOLS

Data Analysis Software Functions 3.601
    Sorting 3.601
        Record Selection 3.602
        Joining Files 3.603
        Multi-File Processing 3.603
        Correlation Analysis 3.604
        Verifying Multiples of a Number 3.604
        Compliance Verification 3.604
        Duplicate Searches 3.605
        Vertical Ratio Analysis 3.605
        Horizontal Ratio Analysis 3.605
        Date Functions 3.606
        Graphing 3.607
    Examples of Data Analysis Functions 3.607
        General Ledger Analysis 3.607
        Accounts Receivable 3.608
        Sales Analysis 3.608
        Accounts Payable 3.608
        Asset Management 3.608
        Cash Disbursement 3.609
        Payroll 3.609
        Purchasing 3.609
    Data Analysis Checklist 3.609
    Evaluating Data Analysis Software 3.610
    Evaluating Data Mining Consultants 3.610
Data Analysis Software 3.611
    ACL for Windows 3.611
        ACL Practical Examples 3.616
    ActiveData for Excel 3.623
        Fraud Detection Techniques for Accounts Payable 3.624
        Fraud Detection Techniques for the General Ledger 3.627
        Fraud Detection Techniques for Revenue 3.629
    AutoAudit 3.630
        Risk Assessment 3.631
    SNAP! Reporter 3.631
    DataWatch Corporation's Monarch for Windows 3.631
        Monarch Capabilities, 1: Financial Analysis and Risk Assessment 3.633
        Monarch Capabilities, 2: Date Tests 3.633
    DATAS® for ACL, IDEA, and Excel 3.634
    IDEA for Windows 3.636

INVESTIGATION

DATA ANALYSIS AND REPORTING TOOLS (CONT.)

Computer Forensic Tools	3.636
EnCase	3.636
Reporting and Case Management Software	3.638
i2 Analyst's Notebook	3.639
Link Analysis	3.639
Network Analysis	3.640
Time Line Analysis	3.641
Transaction Pattern	3.641
Database Visualization	3.642
CaseMap by CaseSoft	3.642
NetMap by Alta Analytics	3.645
MAGNUM Case Management Software	3.646
WATSON and POWERCASE, from XANALYS	3.646
Other Fraud-Related Software	3.648
ComputerCOP P3 and ComputerCOP Forensic	3.648
CyberCop Software	3.648
Fraud Prevention SmartSystem	3.648
Infoglide Software Corporation	3.648
Promisemark, Inc.	3.648
Search Software America	3.648
Syfact, The Corporate Intelligence Management System	3.649
The Case File	3.649
Wizsoft, Inc.	3.649

TRACING ILLICIT TRANSACTIONS

Comprehensive Guidelines for Information to be Collected in Financial Interviews	3.701
Identification	3.701
Birth	3.701
Address During Pertinent Years	3.701
Occupation	3.701
General Background	3.702
Financial Institutions (Business and Personal)	3.702
Sources of Income	3.703
Net Income and Expenditures	3.703
Liabilities	3.703
Expenditures	3.704
Business Operations	3.704
Books and Records	3.704
Business Receipts	3.705
Direct Methods of Tracing Financial Transactions	3.705
Banks	3.705

INVESTIGATION

TRACING ILLICIT TRANSACTIONS (CONT.)

Types of Banks	3.706
Internal Bookkeeping Procedures	3.706
Retention of Records	3.706
Types of Bank Records	3.707
Signature Cards	3.707
Negotiated Checks	3.708
Deposit Tickets	3.713
Wire Transfers	3.715
Intrabank Transfers	3.715
Savings Accounts	3.715
Certificates of Deposit (CDs)	3.715
Bank Ledgers and Bank Statements	3.715
Bank Ledger Cards—Manual System	3.716
Bank Statements—Computerized System	3.716
Savings Account Statement	3.716
Cashier's Checks	3.716
Bank Drafts	3.717
Traveler's Checks	3.717
Bank Money Orders	3.717
Certified Checks	3.718
Loans	3.718
Mortgage Loan Files	3.719
Check Credit Loans	3.719
Credit Cards	3.720
Bank Collection Department Records	3.720
Safe-Deposit Boxes	3.720
Bank Secrecy Act Documents	3.721
Stock Brokerage Records	3.721
Tax Returns and Related Documents	3.722
Indirect Methods of Tracing Financial Transactions	3.722
Elements of Financial Examination Techniques	3.723
The Environment	3.723
The Accounting System	3.724
Various Detection Techniques	3.724
Statistical Sampling	3.724
Net Worth Methods	3.727
The Financial/Behavioral Profile	3.729
The Behavioral Profile	3.732
Net Worth Analysis	3.733
Locating Hidden Assets	3.740
Common Asset Hiding Techniques	3.740

INVESTIGATION

TRACING ILLICIT TRANSACTIONS (CONT.)

Transfer to Family Members or Parties Under Their Control	3.740
Children's or Family Trust	3.740
Home Mortgage Pay-Down	3.740
Insurance Policies	3.741
Prepaid Credit Cards	3.741
Savings Bond Purchases	3.741
Cashier's Checks and Traveler's Checks	3.741
Computer Databases	3.742
Locating Assets Through Subpoenas	3.742
Locating Assets Offshore	3.742
Office of International Affairs	3.744
Letter Rogatory	3.745
Mutual Legal Assistance Treaties (MLATs)	3.746
Public Records	3.746

REPORTING STANDARDS

Preparation	3.801
Accuracy of Reports	3.801
Clarity	3.802
Impartiality and Relevance	3.802
Timeliness	3.802
Reporting Mistakes	3.803
Conclusions and Opinions	3.803
Opinions	3.803
Evidence	3.803
Copy Documents	3.803
Safeguarding and Maintaining Documents	3.803
Effective Note-taking	3.804
Organization of Information	3.805
Chronological	3.805
By Transaction	3.805
Analyzing the Reader	3.805
Company Insiders	3.806
Attorneys	3.806
Defendants and Witnesses	3.806
Press	3.806
Juries	3.806
Outlining	3.807
Step One	3.807
Step Two	3.807
Step Three	3.807

INVESTIGATION

REPORTING STANDARDS (CONT.)

Style	3.808
Voice	3.808
Person	3.808
Point of View	3.809
Constructing Clear Sentences	3.809
Rambling Sentences	3.809
Run-on Sentences	3.810
Omitted Verbs	3.810
Omitted Subjects	3.810
Unnecessary Compound Sentences	3.810
Misplaced Modifiers	3.811
Paragraph Structure	3.811
Report Structure	3.811
Memoranda	3.812
Cover Page or Letter	3.812
Exhibits	3.813
Forms	3.813
Consent to Search	3.813
Receipt for Property	3.813
Telephone Recording Consent	3.814
Advice of Rights	3.814
Consent to Record	3.814
Customer Consent and Authorization for Access to Financial Records	3.814
Evidence Control Log	3.814
Signed Statements	3.815
Voluntariness of Confessions	3.815
Intent	3.815
Approximate Dates of Offense	3.816
Approximate Amounts of Losses	3.816
Approximate Number of Instances	3.816
Willingness to Cooperate	3.816
Excuse Clause	3.816
Confessor Reads Statement	3.817
Truthfulness of Statement	3.817
Key Points in Signed Statements	3.817
Visual Aids	3.818
Link Network Diagrams	3.818
Matrices	3.819
Time Flow Diagrams	3.820
Summaries of Witnesses' Statements	3.821
Engagement Contracts	3.822

INVESTIGATION

REPORTING STANDARDS (CONT.)
Elements of the Engagement Contract 3.822
    The Long Form 3.823
    The Short Form 3.823
    Terms 3.823
    Close 3.823
    Opinions 3.824

APPENDIX

FRAUD EXAMINATION CHECKLIST
Fraud Examination Checklist 3.901

SAMPLE REPORT
Bailey Books, Incorporated 3.1001

FORMS
Consent to Search 3.1101
Telephone Recording Consent 3.1103
Consent to Record 3.1104
Customer Consent and Authorization for Access to Financial Records 3.1105
Evidence Control Log 3.1106

ENGAGEMENT CONTRACTS AND OPINION LETTERS
Engagement Letters
    Fraud Policy Review Proposal 3.1201
    Fraud Examination Proposal 3.1202
    Fraud Policy Review Opinion 3.1203
Fraud Examination Opinion Letters
    Evidence Does Not Support Allegation 3.1205
    Evidence Supports Allegation 3.1206
    Inconclusive Evidence 3.1207

ANALYZING DOCUMENTS

The fraud examiner usually will obtain a great deal of documentary evidence. It is critical that the examiner understand the relevance of this evidence, and how it should be preserved and presented. Always keep in mind that documents can either help or hurt a case, depending on which ones are presented and how they are presented. The goal is to make certain that all relevant documents are included, and all irrelevant documents eliminated. Many examiners pay too much attention to documents. It is easy to get bogged down in detail when examining records and to lose sight of a simple fact: documents do not make cases, witnesses make cases. The documents make or break the witness. So-called "paper cases" often confuse and bore a jury.

Basic procedures in handling evidence are required for it to be accepted by the court. Proof must be provided that the evidence is relevant and material. Evidence submitted must be properly identified, and it must be established that the proper chain of custody was maintained.

The relevance of documents cannot be determined easily early in a case. For that reason, it is recommended that all possible relevant documents be obtained. If they are not needed, they can always be returned. Here are a few general rules regarding the collection of documents:
- Obtain original documents where feasible. Make working copies for review, and keep the originals segregated.
- Do not touch originals any more than necessary; they might later have to undergo forensic analysis.
- Maintain a good filing system for the documents. This is especially critical where large numbers of documents are obtained. Losing a key document is an unpardonable sin, and can mortally damage the case. Documents can be stamped sequentially for easy reference.

Chain of Custody

From the moment evidence is received, its *chain of custody* must be maintained for it to be accepted by the court. This means that a record must be made when the item is received or when it leaves the care, custody, or control of the fraud examiner. This is best handled by a memorandum of interview with the custodian of the records when the evidence is received. The memorandum should state:

- What items were received
- When they were received
- From whom they were received
- Where they are maintained

If the item is later turned over to someone else, a record of this should be made—preferably in memorandum form. All evidence received should be uniquely marked so that it can be identified later. The preferable way is to initial and date the item; however, this can pose problems in the case of original business records furnished voluntarily. For them, a small tick mark or other nondescript identifier can be used. If it is not practical to mark the original document, it should be placed in a sealed envelope, which should then be initialed and dated.

Obtaining Documentary Evidence

Where both parties agree, it is always possible to obtain evidence by consent. This is the preferred method. The consent can be oral or written. In the cases of information obtained from possible adverse witnesses, or the target of the examination, it is recommended that the consent be in writing. Sample forms are contained in the Appendix to the Report Writing Chapter. However, in many cases, the investigator will not wish to alert the suspect to his intentions, and other routes must be taken.

Where the evidence is owned and in the control of the party that requests the investigation, for instance in desk drawers in the office, then the investigator is usually able to obtain the documents as required.

Where evidence is held by other parties, or in uncontrolled locations, specific legal action is required before attempting to obtain it. This usually takes the form of a subpoena or other order from the court to produce the documents and records (including electronic records). Other forms of court orders can be used to obtain witness evidence and statements.

Under no circumstances should the investigator attempt to obtain documents by other means, as this can lead to charges of theft, trespass, and other sanctions. Further details are provided in the Law Section of this *Manual*.

Types of Evidence

Evidence generally is either direct or circumstantial. *Direct evidence* shows prima facie the facts at issue. What constitutes direct evidence depends on the factors involved. In the case of possible kickbacks by Linda Reed Collins, for example, direct evidence might be a check from the vendor to her.

Circumstantial evidence is that which indirectly shows culpability. In the case of a kickback allegation against Collins, cash deposits of unknown origin deposited to her account around the time of the suspect transaction could be considered circumstantial evidence.

Organization of Evidence

Keeping track of the amount of paper generated is one of the biggest problems in fraud cases. It is essential that documents obtained be properly organized early on in an examination, and that they be continuously reorganized as the case progresses. Remember, it is usually difficult to ascertain the relevance of the evidence early in the case. Good organization in complex cases includes the following:

- Segregating documents by either witness or transaction. Chronological organization is the least preferred method.
- Making a "key document" file for easy access to the most relevant documents. Periodically review the key document files. Move the less important documents to back-up files and keep only the most relevant paper in the main files.
- Establishing a database early on in the case of a large amount of information. This database can be kept manually or computerized and accessed by keywords or Bates Stamp Number. The database should include, at a minimum, the date of the document, the individual from whom the document was obtained, date obtained, a brief description, and the subject to whom the document pertains.

Chronologies

A chronology of events should be commenced early in the case. The purpose is to establish the chain of events leading to the proof. The chronology might or might not be made a part of the formal report; at a minimum, it can be used for analysis of the case and placed in a working paper binder. Keep the chronology brief and include only information necessary to prove the case. By making the chronology too detailed, you defeat its purpose. The chronology should be revised as necessary, adding new information and deleting the irrelevant.

To-Do Lists

Another indispensable aid is the "to-do" list. The list, which must be updated frequently, should be kept in a stenographer's pad or other permanent ring binder to allow a cumulative record. In a very complex case, the list can be broken into long- and short-term objectives: that which must be done eventually, (e.g., prove elements of a particular count), and that which should be done tomorrow, (e.g., conduct an interview or draft a subpoena). However organized, some such sort of list must be kept, as important points otherwise will be forgotten in the lengthy case. A sample checklist is included in the chapter on Report Writing.

Examining Fraudulent Documents

Statements by witnesses make up most of a fraud case. However, forged, altered, fabricated, and other suspicious documents are regularly encountered in fraud matters. Most business, legal, or financial transactions will produce a substantial amount of paper including contracts, agreements, wills, order forms, invoices, statements, etc. These documents can be evidence in establishing that a fraud was committed, in determining the nature and scope of the fraud, and in identifying the parties responsible.

The fraud examiner is not expected to be a document expert. He should, however, be aware of ways to spot phony documents and have a knowledge of the capabilities and limitations of forensic examinations. Expert forensic examinations conducted as a part of a fraud investigation can contribute to its success in several ways:

- Expert examination results can assist in developing and proving the fraud theory; who did what and when did they do it.
- Expert examination results can corroborate or refute statements by witnesses or fraud suspects.
- Having the results of expert examinations beforehand can provide significant leverage for the examiner during his interviews with fraud suspects, even resulting in admissions of guilt when they are confronted with the factual evidence.
- Forensic handwriting examinations and comparisons can result in the positive identification of the writer or signer of a document. Since writing is a conscious act, the identification might serve to prove that a particular act is intentional or willful. Proof of intent is usually necessary to prosecute a wrongdoer successfully.

Early Consultation with an Expert Can Prove Valuable

An expert's assistance can be of value early in an investigation, not just in preparation for a trial. Fraud examiners should consider consulting with experts early in their investigation or inquiry if they suspect that significant documents are phony, have been forged, altered, or otherwise manipulated. Many times the scope of an investigation can be narrowed or directed by eliminating multiple suspects through handwriting examinations. The expert's findings might solidify the fraud examiner's theories of how the fraud was committed, or they can prevent wasted effort by proving theories incorrect at an earlier stage. See the end of this section for more information about finding help in document examinations.

Types of Forensic Document Examinations

There are many different types of forensic document examinations. However, most examinations (more than 95% of all U.S. Federal Bureau of Investigation Laboratory document examinations, for example) concern signatures, handwriting, hand printing, or documents created by a typewriter or word processor. Additionally, issues concerning photocopies and determining when a document was prepared frequently arise. Fraud examiners should be aware that many different types of forensic examinations are possible, but that the following forensic examinations could be of particular value when a fraud involves documents:

- Detection of forged signatures
- Identification of the writers of signatures, handwriting, and hand printing
- Detecting altered documents
- Detecting and restoring erasures and eradications
- Determining when a document was or was not prepared
- Detecting counterfeited documents and examining printed documents
- Detecting and restoring faint indented writings
- Comparisons of paper and inks
- Determining whether two sheets of paper came from the same tablet or pad of paper
- Examinations of paper folds and sequence of folds
- Comparisons of torn or cut paper edges
- Restoration of charred and partially burned documents
- Identifying the machine that made a photocopy and whether two copies were made on the same machine
- Examinations of facsimile (fax) copies
- Identifying the source of, or alterations to, notary seals, wax seals and cachets

- Detecting the opening and resealing of sealed documents and examining adhesives
- Detecting inserted text in typewritten, printed, or handwritten documents
- Determining the sequence of handwritten text, signatures, and typewriting
- Identifying rubber stamp impressions
- Identifying mechanical check-writer and numbering device impressions

Handling Documents as Physical Evidence

A document can be a piece of physical evidence and not just a source of information. As a piece of evidence it should be handled carefully and stored properly in a sealed, initialed, and dated paper folder or envelope to avoid damage or contamination. If necessary, make a working copy and preserve the original document for submission to a forensic document examiner. Most forensic examinations will require the original document, not a copy of it, since most photocopies do not reproduce original writings, typewriting, or other features with sufficient clarity or detail to allow adequate examination.

When initialing a document for future identification, do it in a non-critical area and use a different type of writing instrument than was used for the questioned writings on the document. The examiner should never write or make markings on the original document other than his unobtrusive initials for identification. Do not add new folds, staple it, place paper clips on it, crumple it, or do anything else which would affect or change it from its original condition. If stored in an envelope, be careful not to write on the envelope and cause indentations on the original document inside. Photocopies and laser-printed documents should always be stored in paper folders or envelopes, not transparent plastic envelopes, which can result in the copies sticking to the plastic and destroying some features of the document.

Preserving for Fingerprint Examinations

If fingerprint examinations are anticipated use gloves to handle the documents. (Be careful if tweezers are used since they can leave indentations which might obscure faint indented writings or the identifiable indentations which are sometimes left by photocopy and fax machines.) If you or other known persons have inadvertently handled the documents with bare hands, the names of all such persons should be provided to the fingerprint specialist. It might be necessary to provide him with sets of inked fingerprints of these persons for elimination purposes. (See the later section on "Fingerprints" for additional information.)

Charred or Partially Burned Documents

These documents might contain valuable evidence if restored by experts, but they are very fragile and should be handled with extreme care. For proper preservation and storage, trained experts might use special polyester film sheets and envelopes which are not readily available to the fraud examiner. The examiner can best preserve such evidence for submission to the forensic expert by using a sturdy crush-proof container into which he places layers of cotton (available in rolls at fabric and sewing materials shops). Carefully slide a sheet of paper or thin cardboard under the burned fragments, lift them and place them on the layers of cotton, then remove the paper used for lifting. Gently place additional layers of cotton over the fragments until the container is filled. Do not compress the cotton. Seal the container, initial and date it, add an identifying contents label or exhibit number, and clearly write or stamp "Fragile" on the container.

Recognizing Phony Documents

Forensic document examiners apply scientific methods and use a variety of technical instruments in conducting examinations and comparisons of documents. Individual minute characteristics in handwriting and typewriting are examined and compared with genuine comparison standards. Detailed analyses are made of document features for proof of changes or modifications. Instruments used include sensitive measuring devices, low-power magnifying glasses, several types of microscopes, ultraviolet and infrared lighting, optical filters, micro and macro photography, computerized image enhancement systems, sensitive instruments to detect faint indented writings, and numerous others. Various chemical analyses are also conducted.

Although not expected to be a documents expert, an observant fraud examiner might be able to recognize some features of documents which could alert him to their fraudulent nature:

- *Signature forgeries* might be recognized by irregularities noticeable in the written letters and/or by their differences in size from a genuine signature. A side-by-side comparison with a genuine signature might reveal the differences. However, remember that advanced age, poor health, temporary injury, and the use of drugs and alcohol can result in similar characteristics and might mislead the examiner. Genuine comparison samples should be obtained and a forensic document examiner consulted to make an expert determination. (See the later section on "How to Obtain Handwriting Samples.")
- *Substituted pages* in multiple-page documents such as contracts, wills, etc. can often be spotted by holding each page in front of a bright light. Differences in the whiteness,

density, thickness, opacity, and paper fiber patterns of the substituted sheets might be apparent.
- Some *ink differences, alterations, erasures,* and *obliterations* are also revealed by holding the paper in front of a bright light or holding a light over the writings at different angles and observing differences in the color and reflectivity of the inks or disturbances to the paper surface.
- *Counterfeited printed documents* such as checks, stock and bond certificates, business forms and stationery, birth certificates, drivers' licenses and other identification documents, etc. are sometimes readily disclosed by side-by-side comparisons with corresponding genuine documents. Be alert for the use of incorrect or different versions or form revisions of the documents. For forensic examinations it will be necessary to obtain and furnish genuine comparison samples of the printed documents to the document examiner. (See the later section on "Counterfeit Printed Documents.")
- *Suspicious indented writings* might be revealed by reducing the light in the room and holding a bright beam of light (a narrow beam flashlight or small high-intensity lamp will do the job) low and parallel to the page surface. (See the later section on "Indented Writings.")

Identifying Writings

The development of a person's handwriting usually begins at an early age as part of his formal education. So-called "copy-book" styles are taught and the students are instructed through exercises to emulate as nearly as possible those letter formations. However, from the very beginning the students' writing skills vary considerably due to their differing physical and mental capabilities. These differences between individuals increase with age, physical development and the acquisition of skills, differing aesthetic values, differences in education, and differences in the personal and professional usage of writing. As a result, each person's writings contain a unique and identifiable combination of acquired individual personal characteristics and shared "class" characteristics. Forensic document examiners are trained and experienced in examining and comparing writings and assessing this combination of individual and class characteristics in making expert determinations of identity or non-identity.

Class Characteristics

Fraud examiners should not be misled in developing suspects by mistaking class characteristics in writings that seem to look "alike" as evidence of identity. The writings of some persons might share superficial similarities in appearance and style and seem to be alike to the layman when, in fact, they are very different. Forensic document examiners can correct this mistake.

"Copy-book" Styles

Some of a writer's letter shapes, handwriting style, and other characteristics might be shared by other writers because they were taught the same original copy-book system. In the United States, different states and different school districts within the states teach several different copy-book systems. (See Fig.1) Internationally, different systems are also taught, i.e., Russian, French, German, et. al. (See Fig.2) Remnants of the system taught might be retained by the writers. (See Fig.3) As an example, second-language writings of persons taught in a Cyrillic (Russian) alphabet style will be influenced by those letter styles and might contain some similarities. As another example, the hand printing and numeral styles taught to draftsmen, architects, and engineers might result in apparent similarities in the hand printing of persons trained in those professions.

"Copycat" Styles

Some writers, especially adolescents, the young, and the easily influenced, might adopt the general handwriting style or some individual letter designs of a respected teacher or parent, or one shared by their peers. An example is the exaggerated rounded letter forms and circular "i" dots and periods that form the so-called "bubble writings" of some adolescent females. This style is usually abandoned as the person matures. (See Fig.4)

Natural Variations, Disguise, and Distortions

Variation

No one signs his signature or writes *exactly* the same way twice since writing is a human act of coordinated mental and muscular activity, not the precise, repetitive action of a machine. However, each writer has his own fairly specific range of natural variation. Several examples of writing are necessary for a forensic document examiner to establish if a questioned writing is, or is not, within the range of natural variation of a particular writer. If fraud examiners find two signatures that are exactly alike, then at least one is a forgery, probably a tracing. (See the later section on "Forgeries.")

Disguise

Disguise is the conscious, intentional, effort by a person to change or conceal his normal writings. Disguise is attempted in an effort to prepare writings that can later be disclaimed or that the writer hopes will be anonymous and cannot be traced to the source. The success of an attempt to disguise writings depends upon the writer's skill and knowledge of writings. Most attempts at disguise involve one or more of the following: change in slant, change in size, change in shapes of capital (upper-case) letters, changes in the shapes and sizes of loops in letters which contain them, use of bizarre letter designs, or block (squared) hand printing. Only rarely is the opposite, non-writing hand used. Fraud examiners should be aware that it is possible to successfully disguise writings to the point where they cannot be positively identified, even by experts. This is especially true when only a limited amount of writings are involved.

Distortions

Distortions are unintentional changes to a person's writings which are beyond his range of natural variation. Distortion can be caused by temporary impairment due to illness, injury to the writing hand or arm, substance abuse, extreme physical weakness, etc., by an unusual writing environment, irregular or unusual writing surface, unfamiliar writing materials, etc., or might be permanent due to extreme age and feebleness. Fraud examiners should be aware that distortions in writings can on occasion be so severe that positive identifications of a person's writings might not be possible, even by experts.

Forgeries

A forgery is defined as any writing prepared with the intent to deceive or defraud. Most forgeries are signatures. Forgery can be done by *simulation,* by *tracing,* or by *freehand preparation.* (See Figs.5a - 5d)

SIMULATED AND TRACED FORGERIES

A simulated or traced forgery is a writing, usually a signature, prepared by carefully copying or tracing a model example of another person's writings. Although identifiable as a forgery, a simulated or traced signature forgery often does not contain enough normal handwriting characteristics of the forger to permit expert identification.

Remember, no one writes his signature *exactly* the same way twice. If two signatures look exactly alike, try superimposing the signature areas of the two documents by holding them in front of a bright light. If they precisely match then one, or both, are traced forgeries. Be aware that in some instances it might be possible to locate the original document bearing the genuine signature which was traced. This regularly occurs in employee fraud and embezzlement cases in banks and other financial institutions where the account holder's signature card on file served as the source for the tracing. If the forged signature(s) precisely superimposes over the genuine signature, then it is also likely that faint indentations might be present in the signature area of the original genuine document. Also, ink traces from the genuine signature might be transferred to the reverse side of the traced signature(s). Latent fingerprint treatment of the original source document might reveal the fingerprints of the suspect.

FREEHAND FORGERIES

A writing, usually a signature, prepared by a writer signing the name of another person without knowing what the real person's signature looks like. The writers of freehand forgeries usually can be identified by experts.

"AUTOFORGERIES"

The true-name signature of a person, prepared by him in a distorted or disguised fashion in order to later deny it and disclaim it as genuine. This attempt at fraud has occurred in falsely reported traveler's check theft cases, in cases involving disputed home mortgage and other loan documents, credit card frauds, and others.

The Document Expert's Findings

A forensic document examiner *cannot* determine with accuracy the writer's age, sex, race, which writing hand was used, physical or mental condition, personality, or character from handwriting examinations. There are three basic outcomes from forensic handwriting comparisons:

Non-Identification

The suspected person did not write the signature or other writings on the questioned document.

Identification

The suspected person did write the signature or other writings on the questioned document.

Inconclusive

No definite determinations were possible as to whether the suspected person did or did not write the signature or other writings on the questioned document. This outcome is often the result of insufficient or inadequate handwriting samples of the suspect or when a photocopy rather that the original document is submitted to the expert for examinations.

Though inconclusive, some writings might contain sufficient characteristics in common to indicate possible identity, or sufficient differences to indicate that the suspected person might not have prepared the writings. The expert might suggest additional leads for the fraud examiner which could resolve the inconclusive results of the comparisons.

How to Obtain Handwriting Samples

Positive results from forensic handwriting examinations and comparisons often depend upon how well the fraud examiner has assembled adequate handwriting and signature samples of the suspects for submission to the forensic expert. The samples must be comparable to the writings on the evidence documents. Hand printing cannot be compared with handwriting. Capital letters cannot be compared with small letters. The samples must contain the same letters and combinations of letters whether undictated or dictated. For example: "John" cannot be compared with "Susan," "hot" with "cold," "black" with "white," or "July" with "September."

Undictated Writing Samples

Try to obtain samples of a suspect's or victim's signature or other writings which were not prepared by him specifically for comparison purposes, but which can be authenticated. Courts will accept as authentic comparison documents any writings which were witnessed by others. Also acceptable are documents which were created "in the normal course of business," such as canceled checks; signed or written documents in employee personnel records; applications for employment, licenses, or home utilities installations; and many others. The fraud examiner should use personal experiences and knowledge of the suspect's routine activities in locating sources for these types of samples.

When the evidence documents include suspected forged signatures, several genuine samples of the forgery victim's signature should be obtained for submission to the expert. If possible, include any documents bearing genuine signatures of the victim's that the suspect might have had access to and which might have served as a model for tracing or simulation.

Undictated writing samples should:
- Be as contemporaneous as possible to the date of the preparation of the evidence documents; i.e. if the questioned writings were prepared in the 1970s, writings recently prepared by a suspect might not be adequate for comparisons. However, except for

infirmity or extreme age, the writings of most adults usually do not change much except over long periods of time
- Consist of the same signature or words containing many of the same letters and combinations of letters as the questioned writings on the evidence documents
- Consist of the same type of writings as on the evidence documents, i.e. hand printed or handwritten, capital letters or small letters or a combination of both
- Consist, if possible, of the same kinds of writings; i.e. a person's informal writings, such as hastily prepared signatures on credit card charge forms, might be very different from more formal writings, such as a signature on a contract or other legal document

Dictated Writing Samples

Try to obtain samples of a suspect's or victim's signature or writings specifically for comparison purposes, either voluntarily or by obtaining a legal order.

Obtaining Dictated Handwriting Samples by Court Order

When obtaining a legal order for samples, the investigator and/or attorney should ensure that the order specifies that the samples should be provided in the writer's normal manner and in sufficient quantity, text, and form, at the interviewer's discretion, to permit a determination of identity or non-identity. A court order with these specifications will permit an inference of guilt, or might allow pursuit of contempt of court charges if the suspect refuses to comply or attempts to prevent identification by intentionally disguising his writings, limiting the amount of writings, or failing to follow the interviewer's instructions and dictations.

Preparation for Taking Dictated Handwriting Samples

Since expert handwriting identifications can truly prove the case, adequate pre-interview preparation by the fraud examiner is essential. At the time of the interview session to obtain dictated writing samples the investigator should have all of the proper writing materials and should have the original or copies of the evidence documents to serve as a guide for dictating the sample text. Do not rush through the interview. Take as much time as necessary. Take short comfort breaks if the suspect tires. Do not allow the suspect to see the evidence documents either before or during the taking of the samples.

Directions for Obtaining Dictated Handwriting Samples

Dictated writing samples should be obtained by using the same types of materials as the evidence document: writing instrument (ball-point pen, fountain pen, pencil, etc.), paper (lined, unlined, size of sheet), or forms (check forms, business forms, etc.). For purposes of the samples, an investigator can use a genuine form of the same or similar kind, make many photocopies of it, and have the samples prepared on the blank copies.

To help the suspect relax, begin by having him write miscellaneous innocuous text such as his name, the date, and a statement as to the voluntary nature of the samples being prepared. This statement will also assist later in getting the samples admitted in court.

Patiently dictate to the suspect the same text or text containing the same letters and combinations of letters of the same type (hand printed, handwritten, capital, or small letters) as the questioned writings on the evidence document. Do not assist the suspect in the spelling of words, punctuation, grammar, paragraphs, etc.

Obtain one sample at a time on separate sheets or forms with each sheet or form being removed from the sight of the suspect after completion and before the next is prepared. To ensure that the suspect's range of normal variation is displayed, several samples of each text should be obtained.

Be alert for any attempts to disguise normal writings, e.g., exaggerated slant, very rapid writing or very slow and awkward writing, unusually large or small writing, or bizarre letter formations. (See the later section on "Natural Variation, Disguise and Distortion.")

Typewriters and Computer Printers

Typewriting prepared on traditional typebar/segment-shift typewriters, both manual and electric, can often be positively identified by experts from mechanical defects unique to each machine. Typewritten texts prepared on later model typewriters equipped with interchangeable daisy wheel, ball, or basket type elements are difficult, if not impossible to identify. Computerized dot matrix, ink jet, thermal transfer, or laser (electrostatic) printers are rarely identifiable. Usually, the only expert determinations concerning these typewriters and printers are that the same typeface design and size (font), letter spacing, and print process were used.

Typewriter Ribbons Could Be Evidence

Old-style fabric typewriter ribbons rarely are of any value in determining whether a particular typewriter was used to prepare a questioned document. Fortunately for investigators, most modern manual and electric typewriters, regardless of whether typebar or single element, are equipped with single-use ribbons. If it is suspected that an evidence document was recently prepared on such a machine, removal and examination of the ribbon might reveal the text of the document. Expert examination of the ribbon might positively prove that the typewriter and ribbon were used to produce the document.

Avoid Taking Unnecessary Samples

Fraud examiners do not have to be experts in order to make preliminary elimination of some suspect typewriters and narrow down the number of typewriters they might have to take samples from. Although there are hundreds of different fonts in use on computer printers, traditional manual and some electronic typewriters might be eliminated by differences in their typeface designs.

Although fonts might appear to be very similar, the observant fraud examiner can differentiate between them by concentrating on those letters and numerals which most often differ (See Fig.6). Note first whether the letter styles on the evidence document and the typewriter are *serif* (the letters have small horizontal or vertical bars at the beginning and ending lines of the letters) or *non-serif* (no small bars). If they differ, then the typewriter is not the one used. Next, look at the shapes of the letters and numerals. Pay particular attention to the small letters f, g, r, t, and w, and the numerals 2, 3, 4, and 5. If any of those differ in shape, then the typewriter is not the one used.

Taking Typewriter Samples

Always remove, retain, and preserve the original ribbon first, before taking any samples. Place it in a sealed envelope and initial it for later identification. After removing and preserving the original ribbon, replace it with a new one and type the samples in the same text as the questioned document. Repeat portions of the questioned text several times. After taking samples with a ribbon, shift the ribbon adjustment to the "stencil" position.

Insert a sheet of carbon paper on top of a sheet of paper and type directly onto the carbon paper, using it as a "ribbon" to make typed text on the sheet of paper. Again, type the questioned text several times. As each specimen is made, record the brand name, model, and serial number of the typewriter used and initial and date each sheet. Place the ribbon and specimens in a plastic or heavy envelope and submit them to the expert along with the questioned evidence documents in separate envelopes.

Photocopies

Increasingly, photocopies are retained as "original" records of documents (particularly in outgoing correspondence files) and can become the only evidence of a document because the original document cannot be located, or, in some cases, cannot be released, such as in the case of official public records

Fraud examiners and other investigators sometimes submit a copy of a document for examination because they do not wish to part with the original. As a result, the document examiner will probably not be able to determine features and reach conclusions that could have been made from the original document. When at all possible, the fraud examiner should obtain the original document for the document examiner and should not submit a copy.

Identifying the Source of a Photocopy

Photocopies can be the actual original evidence in the case of:

- Anonymous letters
- Unauthorized "leaks" of information in the form of copies of letters, memoranda, files, and other records
- Copies made to conceal forgeries or to insert or manipulate text
- Spurious "disinformation" dissemination of phony official documents

Locating the source of a copy can be crucial in some investigations. It is sometimes possible to determine what kind of copier was used to produce the copy in question. Some types of machines leave minute markings, indentations, and other features on the copy which will assist the expert in determining the brand and model of the machine used. It is also possible to identify the particular machine used by examining the pattern of unique and identifiable "trash marks" (specks, spots, streaks, edge markings, etc.) it leaves on copies and comparing them with copies from a known machine. The fraud examiner should be aware, however, that some of these markings have permanence while others are transient and temporary.

Permanent "Trash Marks"

These uniquely identifiable markings on copies are usually caused by accidental deep scratches and imperfections in the copier's glass surface or document cover, in the printing element surface, or other permanent machine parts which are not readily replaced or changed during servicing of the machine. These marks can be reproduced on copies for years until the machine is repaired or the part replaced.

Transient "Trash Marks"

These uniquely identifiable markings on copies are usually caused by dirt, smudges, or small bits of foreign matter on or in machine surfaces which will appear only until the machine is cleaned or serviced. These markings prove not only that a particular machine was used to produce the copy, but that documents which share the same transient trash marks might have been produced at approximately the same time. This is one of several ways to determine when a document was prepared.

Taking Photocopier Samples

First, without placing any document in the machine, make six "blank" copies. As the machine produces each "copy," remove it, turn it over and on the reverse side initial and number each copy *in the same sequence* they were produced by the machine. (These copies will reproduce all "trash marks" made by the machine, including the entire document cover, glass surface, and internal printing element surface. Six sample copies are needed since different models of machines have varying printing element surface sizes, usually ranging in size from one to three sheet impressions before repeating on the same area of the surface.)

Second, place a ruler or other calibrated measuring device on the glass document surface, close the cover, and make six copies. (These copies will permit a determination of the standard amount of reduction or enlargement the machine makes when in the "actual size" or 1 to 1 mode.) If the machine requires that a document be fed into it, rather than having a glass document surface, use any sample document available as an "original" and include that sample document along with the copies of it. On the reverse of each copy, initial and number the copies in the same sequence they were produced by the machine, as outlined in the first step.

Third, place a sample document containing both typewritten and handwritten text on the glass document surface in the standard position, close the document cover, and again print six copies, initialing and numbering as previously directed. Also include the sample document with the copy samples.

Place all of the sample copies and sample documents into a large sturdy paper or card-board envelope or folder (do not use a plastic envelope) on which you have previously noted the make, model, and location of the machine. Initial, date, and seal the envelope and submit it to the document examiner along with the questioned evidence documents.

"Dating" a Document

Is the document genuine, or a back-dated fabrication? This question sometimes arises during fraud inquiries, and the answer can be determined through scientific examinations of the document by forensic experts. The fraud examiner should be alert for this type of fraud and have some knowledge of what can be done, as well as an awareness of the limitations.

The "Alibi" Document

These documents suddenly appear "from out of nowhere" and often late in the course of an investigation, inquiry, or trial. They are always favorable to the suspect and refute previously developed information or evidence which is damaging to the suspect. Many prove to be fabricated.

The "Long Lost" Will

The sudden appearance of a new will that post-dates and supersedes all other wills sometimes is all too common. Amazingly, it often leaves large portions of the estate to the person who found it, and only a photocopy can be located. Many prove to have been fabricated using the "cut and paste" method. Although not involving photocopies, the much publicized fabricated and forged "Mormon Will" of Howard Hughes in the mid-1970s is a prime example.

Valuable Historical and Collectible Documents

The production of phony historical and collectible documents, artworks, and antiques has been a lucrative field for fraud artists for hundreds of years and continues to the present. Recent major frauds involving losses of millions of dollars have involved such diverse phony documents as the fake "Hitler Diaries," counterfeited rare baseball cards, forged autographs of historical figures and celebrities, fake old treaties with Native American tribes, newly discovered handwritten "rough drafts" of the U.S. Declaration of Independence, Lincoln's Gettysburg Address and other famous historical documents, several counterfeited and forged "Mormon" documents, counterfeited "first edition" books and many others.

Anachronisms in Documentary Materials

Exposure of fraudulent historical documents often relies upon the combined skills of investigators, historical experts, scientific laboratories, and forensic document examiners. Accurate handwriting comparisons are rarely possible in the absence of adequate contemporaneous genuine writings of the purported author. Instead, examinations are made of the materials used to produce the documents such as paper, ink, printing, adhesives and seals, bindings, and covers. Detection of back-dated contemporary documents usually relies upon diligent investigation and the techniques of the forensic document examiner.

When adequate handwriting or signature samples are available, expert comparisons can expose the forgery. Otherwise, in order to disprove the purported date of the document, analyses of the materials might prove that they did not exist at the time the document was supposedly prepared. Expert examinations of contemporary documentary materials include:

- Ink analyses and comparisons with a library of ink standards maintained by the U.S. Secret Service Laboratory in Washington, D.C. to determine the kind of ink and when it was first manufactured.
- Examinations of typewriting and comparisons with collections of typewriter reference standards maintained by forensic laboratories to determine the kind of typewriter that was used and when the typewriter was first manufactured.
- Examinations of paper, especially watermarked paper, and searches of reference materials to determine who manufactured the paper and when it was first produced.
- Examinations of photocopies and fax copies and comparisons with reference standards to determine what kind of machine was used and when those machines were first produced.
- Comparisons of questioned photocopies with photocopies known to have been produced on a particular machine on a particular date can prove or disprove the date of the questioned copy.

Fraud examiners should note that there are currently no methods for accurately determining how long ink, typewriting, or photocopier/printer toner have been on paper.

Indented Writings

Fraud examiners should be alert for the presence of incriminating indented writings, or the absence of logical indentations, both of which can be valuable in proving fraud. In some situations documents are routinely kept in multiple-page sets such as in some legal forms, multiple-copy invoices, in notebooks, tablets and pads, on clipboards, etc. In these situations the writings on one sheet should correspond to indentations on the following sheet. The absence of corresponding indented writings on the following sheet, or the presence of indented writings on one sheet which do not correspond with the text of the writings on the preceding sheet, could provide proof that pages have been removed and substituted.

Developing Indented Writings

Never attempt to develop indented writings by shading or scratching on the surface of a sheet of paper with a pencil. This will reveal deep indentations, but it will not reveal the faint ones and will permanently prevent expert examinations from developing them. Other types of technical examinations might also be prevented by this defacing of the document.

Some indented writings can be visualized by taking the document to an area with subdued overhead lighting, placing the document on a flat surface, and shining a bright beam of light such as a small-beam flashlight or small high-intensity lamp across the paper surface at a low oblique angle or parallel to the surface. Since shadows in the indentations will only show at right angles to the beam of light, it will be necessary to move the light around in several positions and note the changing shadows as they form the text of the indentations.

Document experts use special lighting and photographic techniques and sensitive instruments such as the electrostatic detection apparatus (ESDA) to detect and permanently record extremely faint indented writings which cannot be visualized by the oblique lighting method.

Counterfeit Printed Documents

Most documents which have monetary value such as currency, bank checks, traveler's checks, money orders, bearer bonds, postage stamps, gift certificates, lottery tickets, etc., have all been counterfeited at one time or another. Other documents often counterfeited include identity documents such as passports, birth certificates, drivers' licenses, and government and commercial employee identity cards. Others include commercial product labels, business stationery and forms, business logos, motor vehicle titles and registration forms, and safety inspection stickers. Despite most preventive measures, if a document has some value it can be, and probably has been, counterfeited. Counterfeiting has become big business, especially in some third-world countries, where the latest developments in printing technology are being used to produce large quantities of high quality counterfeit documents and "knock-off" phony products in violation of international copyright and trademark laws.

Counterfeiting Methods

The days of old-style counterfeiters, who were skilled artisans carefully and skillfully etching counterfeit printing plates, are over. Today most counterfeit documents are prepared by various photo-reproduction processes such as the photo-offset printing process (lithography) and flexography, which uses rubberized printing "plates." These processes begin with the photographic reproduction of a model genuine document. The photographic negatives are then carefully retouched to remove the filled in text, serial numbers, etc. which appeared on the genuine document. Printing plates are then made from the retouched negatives and counterfeit copies are printed from the plates.

Rapidly advancing technology now allows larcenous novices with no commercial printing experience to use sophisticated computerized scanners, computer graphics software, multicolor computer printers, and full-color photocopy machines to produce relatively high-quality counterfeit documents.

Detecting Counterfeits

Many counterfeits can be detected by making a side-by-side comparison with a corresponding genuine document. Be alert for different versions or form revisions. Look for subtle differences in ink colors and brilliance, different types of paper substrate, the use of different typestyles and type sizes (fonts), and evidence of the retouching which was done to remove the text which had been filled in on the genuine model document used in the reproduction. The retouching will be most evident in areas where the text, serial numbers, etc., especially if printed in black ink, are superimposed on a background design.

When furnished with genuine documents for comparisons with suspected counterfeits, forensic document examiners can also make expert differentiations between the printing processes, ink formulations, and paper substrates used. In some instances it has been possible for the experts to reconstruct portions of the filled in text or serial numbers which appeared on the model genuine document, but were removed in the retouching process. In this fashion the specific original document used by the counterfeiter can sometimes be determined. By tracing the history of its ownership and who had possession of it, the counterfeiter can be located and identified. Treatment of the original model genuine document for latent fingerprints might positively identify the counterfeiter and other persons who handled the genuine document.

Fingerprints

Latent (non-visible) prints are left on surfaces by the body oils, salts, and amino acids clinging to or exuded by friction ridges in the skin on fingers, palms of the hands, and soles of the feet and are unique personal identifiers. Latent prints might also be deposited on surfaces by hands, fingers, and bare feet through the transfer of materials such as oils and greases. Patent (visible) prints are sometimes deposited on surfaces by hands, fingers and bare feet through the transfer of materials such as blood, paint, soot, and soil.

Latent prints absorbed into protected porous surfaces such as paper in files or pages in books have been known to survive for decades and still be identifiable after chemical development. However, latent fingerprints on hard, non-porous surfaces can be destroyed or deteriorate rapidly if handled, not protected from the environment, or exposed to high temperatures, humidity, or water.

Fraud examiners should wear protective gloves or carefully use tweezers when handling latent fingerprint evidence to avoid smudging and contamination. Tweezers should not be used on documents if indented writing or photocopier examinations are planned.

Fingerprints on Paper or Other Absorbent Porous Surfaces

Fraud examiners should never try to develop latent fingerprints which have been absorbed into paper or other porous materials by dusting with fingerprint powder or any other means.

Such efforts not only will be unsuccessful, but will prevent additional examinations. Preserve the evidence by placing the item into a plastic bag or cellophane protector. Label the container with the examiner's initials, the date, and an identifying exhibit number. Experts will use various methods on these materials, including iodine fuming, brushing or spraying silver nitrate solutions and ninhydrin spray, which actually react with the body chemicals and other substances in the latent print which have soaked into the absorbent surface. Some of these methods will permanently discolor a document.

Fingerprints on Hard, Non-Porous Surfaces

Items with hard, non-porous surfaces such as plastic, metal, and glass objects can be dusted for the presence of latent fingerprints left on their surfaces. Special fingerprint dusting powders and lifting materials are available from law enforcement suppliers. The dry powdered toner used in some photocopy machines has also been used successfully for fingerprint dusting.

After dusting the surface and locating a suspected print or partial print, blow or gently brush off the excess powder. Remove the developed print with adhesive lifting tape and place the tape on an index card which contrasts in color with the dusting powder used. Mark the card with initials, the date, an identifying exhibit number, and where the print was found.

Some latent prints on non-porous surfaces might not be developed by the dusting method. If possible, rather than dusting the item the fraud examiner should retain it, place it in a protective container, initial, date, and label the container with an identifying exhibit number and submit it to a fingerprint expert for processing. Rather than dusting, fingerprint experts might use cyanoacrylate ("super-glue") fuming or a laser to successfully develop and photograph the latent prints on some materials, such as black plastic bags.

Fingerprint Comparison Standards
The fingerprints of millions of persons are maintained in repositories of fingerprint cards maintained by law enforcement agencies throughout the world. These cards contain the inked fingerprints of persons who have been arrested, served in military services, applied for employment at various levels of government, and persons who have volunteered their fingerprints to assist in personal identification in the event of their deaths. Many of these fingerprint databases have been computerized and are linked by networks. However, millions of persons do not fit in any of these categories and have never been fingerprinted.

If a suspect has never been fingerprinted or refuses to voluntarily furnish inked print samples, it might be necessary for the fraud examiner to obtain a legal court order directing the suspect to furnish inked prints for identification purposes. Even though the evidence items might have been handled by several persons, they might still bear latent prints of the guilty party. If the items have been inadvertently handled by other known persons, including the fraud examiner, then inked prints of all of those persons should also be obtained and submitted to the fingerprint expert along with the evidence items and the inked prints of suspects.

Sources for Expert Document Examinations

Law Enforcement Laboratories
In cases where criminal prosecutions are likely, there are excellent forensic laboratories available through law enforcement agencies at the local, state, and national levels of the criminal justice system.

Forensic Document Experts in Private Practice

When an expert's services are needed, a fraud examiner can identify and locate fully qualified and court certified expert forensic document examiners available in a particular geographical area by contacting the following organizations:

American Board of Forensic Document Examiners
7887 San Felipe, Suite 122
Houston, Texas 77063
(713) 784-9537

American Academy of Forensic Sciences
410 North 21st Street
Colorado Springs, Colorado 80904-2798
(719) 836-1100

Graphologists (Graphoanalysts)

Graphology (graphoanalysis) has been described as a pseudoscience in which its practitioners have the purported ability to determine a person's character, moral traits (honesty/dishonesty, etc.), personality, and mental state based upon an analysis of that person's handwriting. Graphology is often erroneously confused with forensic document examinations, especially by the media. Fraud examiners should be aware that some of those practicing graphological analyses might have little academic scientific training. They might be self-taught or graduates of a correspondence course. Since a conclusive accuracy level has not been established for those examinations, expert testimony by graphologists is often rejected by the courts. Fraud examiners should be cautious in relying on handwriting identifications made by some of these "handwriting experts."

Figure 1: Copybook Styles Taught in U.S. Schools

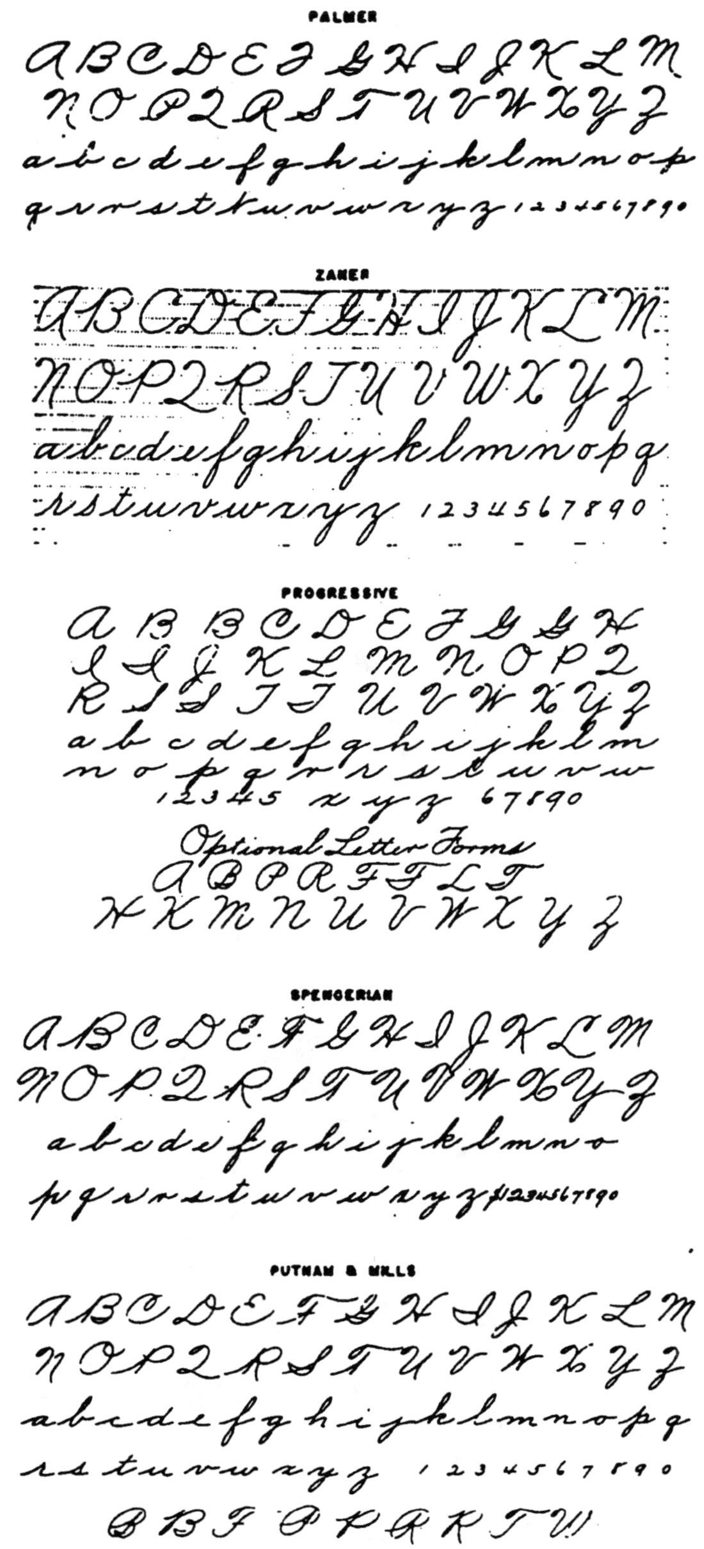

Figure 2: Cursive Styles Taught in Some European Schools

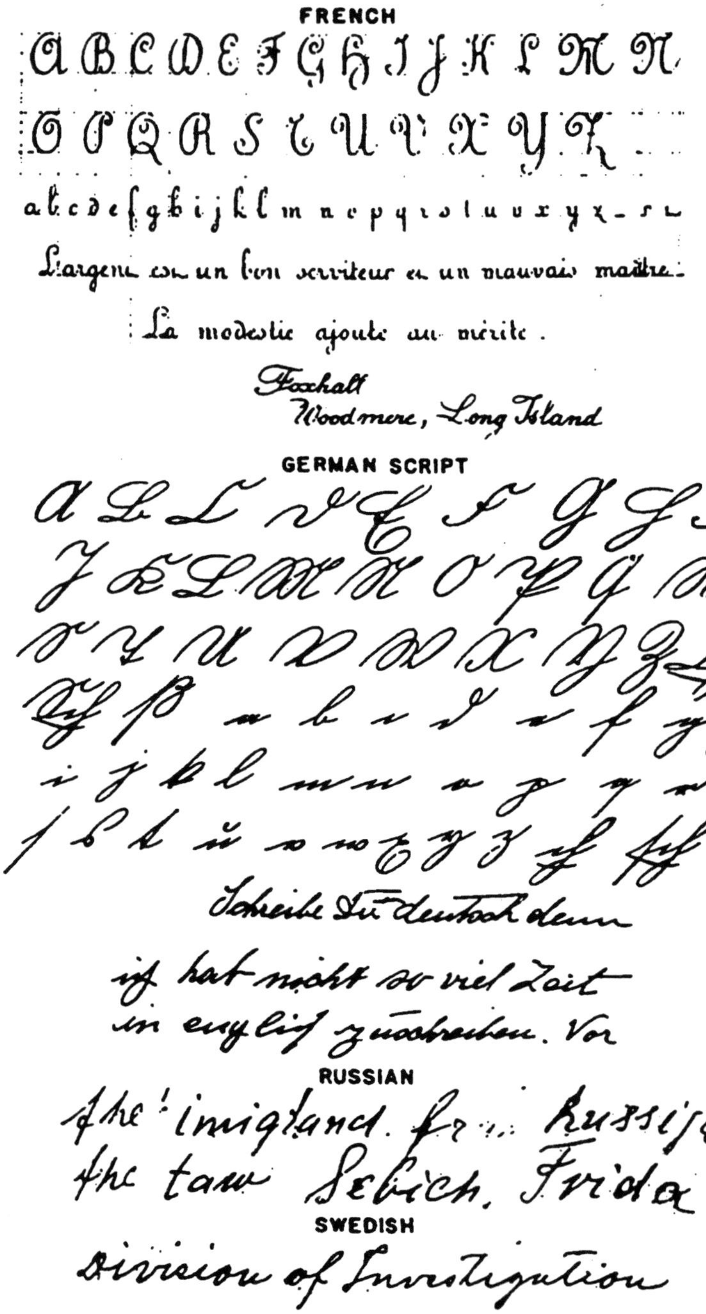

Figure 3: Writings Retaining Influence of German Style

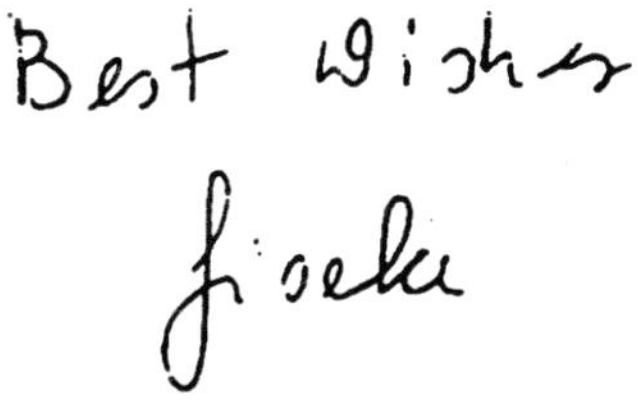

Best Wishes
Gisela

Figure 4: Teenage "Bubble Writings"

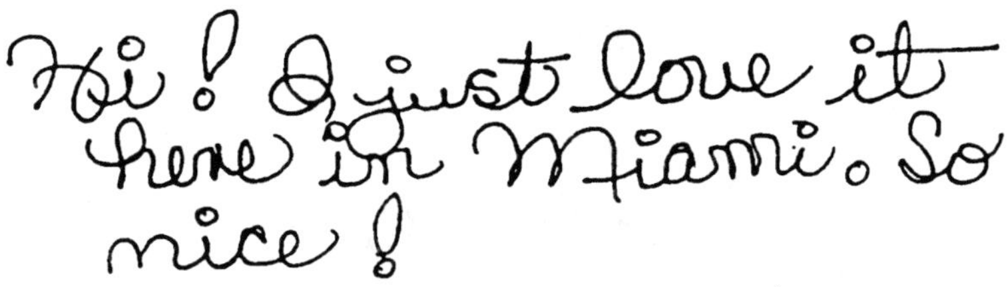

Hi! I just love it here in Miami. So nice!

Figure 5a: Genuine Signature

Figure 5b: Traced Forgery

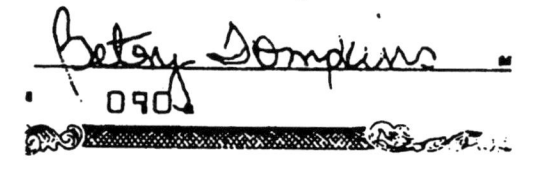

Figure 5c: Simulated Firgery

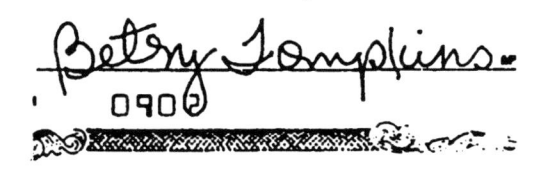

Figure 5d: Freehand Forgery

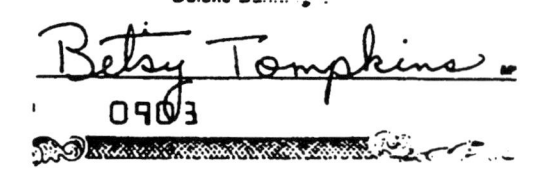

Figure 6: Sample Typestyle Designs (Fonts)

ABCDEFGHIJKLMNOPQRSTUVWXYZ abcdefghijklmnopqrstuvwxyz 1234567890

ABCDEFGHIJKLMNOPQRSTUVWXYZ abcdefghijklmnopqrstuvwxyz 1234567890

ABCDEFGHIJKLMNOPQRSTUVWXYZ abcdefghijklmnopqrstuvwxyz 1234567890

ABCDEFGHIJKLMNOPQRSTUVWXYZ ABCDEFGHIJKLMNOPQRSTUVWXYZ 1234567890

ABCDEFGHIJKLMNOPQRSTUVWXYZ abcdefghijklmnopqrstuvwxyz 1234567890

ABCDEFGHIJKLMNOPQRSTUVWXYZ abcdefghijklmnopqrstuvwxyz 1234567890

ABCDEFGHIJKLMNOPQRSTUVWXYZ abcdefghijklmnopqrstuvwxyz 1234567890

ABCDEFGHIJKLMNOPQRSTUVWXYZ abcdefghijklmnopqrstuvwxyz 1234567890

ABCDEFGHIJKLMNOPQRSTUVWXYZ abcdefghijklmnopqrstuvwxyz 1234567890

ABCDEFGHIJKLMNOPQRSTUVWXYZ abcdefghijklmnopqrstuvwxyz 1234567890

ABCDEFGHIJKLMNOPQRSTUVWXYZ abcdefghijklmnopqrstuvwxyz 1234567890

ABCDEFGHIJKLMNOPQRSTUVWXYZ abcdefghijklmnopqrstuvwxyz 1234567890

INTERVIEW THEORY AND APPLICATION

An *interview* is a question-and-answer session designed to elicit information. It differs from an ordinary conversation in that the interview is structured, not free-form, and is designed for a purpose. An interview might consist of only one question or a series of questions.

Preparation

Before embarking on an interview, the examiner should review the case file to ensure that it does not contain important information that has been overlooked. In addition, the examiner should review the case file to learn what information is known to the witness. The hypothesis should be reviewed to make sure it reflects the obtained documents.

The examiner should consider what type of information can be supplied by each of the potential witnesses. Generally, the most vulnerable witness should be interviewed after the more reluctant witnesses. This will provide the examiner a broader base of information that can be used to formulate later questions. However, the timing of interviews is at the discretion of the examination team.

Characteristics of a Good Interview

Good interviews share common characteristics. The interview should be of sufficient length and depth to uncover relevant facts. Most interviewers tend to get too little, rather than too much, information.

A good interview includes all pertinent information and excludes irrelevant information. From the outset, it should be determined what information is relevant, and that information should be sought. Extraneous or useless facts tend to complicate the gathering and analysis of the information unnecessarily.

The interview should be conducted as closely as possible to the event in question. With the passage of time, memories of potential witnesses and respondents become faulty, and critical details can be lost or forgotten. A good interview is *objective* in scope. It should be aimed at gathering information in a fair and impartial manner.

Characteristics of a Good Interviewer

All good interviewers share certain characteristics. Above all, they are "people persons," and are talented at human interaction. Successful interviewers are the type of people with whom others are willing to share information. The good interviewer does not interrupt the respondent with unnecessary questions. During the interview, much pertinent information results from volunteered information, as opposed to responses to a specific question. The good interviewer displays interest in his subject and in what is being said.

The respondent must understand that the interviewer is attempting to obtain only the relevant facts and is not "out to get" someone. This can best be done by phrasing questions in a nonaccusatory manner. Little is accomplished when the interviewer is formal, ostentatious, or attempts to impress the respondent with his authority. Information gathering is best accomplished by approaching the interview in an informal and low-key fashion.

If the respondent perceives that the interviewer is biased, or is attempting to confirm foregone conclusions, the respondent will be less likely to cooperate. Accordingly, the interviewer should make every effort to demonstrate a lack of bias.

Professionalism in the interview often involves a state of mind and a commitment to excellence. The interviewer should be on time, be professionally attired, and be fair in all dealings with the respondent. It is absolutely vital that the interviewer not appear to be a threat. If people perceive that they are the target of an inquiry, they will be less likely to cooperate.

Question Typology

The interviewer can ask five general types of questions: introductory, informational, assessment, closing, and admission-seeking. In routine interview situations, where the object is to gather information from neutral or corroborative witnesses, only three of the five types will normally be asked: introductory, informational, and closing questions. If the interviewer has reasonable cause to believe the respondent is not being truthful, assessment questions can be asked. Finally, if the interviewer decides with reasonable cause that the respondent is responsible for misdeeds, admission-seeking questions can be posed.

Introductory Questions

Introductory questions are used by the interviewer for two primary purposes: to provide an introduction, and to get the respondent to verbally agree to cooperate in the interview. This is done in a step-by-step procedure in which the interviewer briefly states the purpose for the contact, then poses a question designed to get the respondent to agree to talk further.

Informational Questions

Once the proper format for the interview is set, the interviewer then turns to the fact-gathering portion. There are essentially three types of questions that can be asked: open, closed, and leading. These question types are discussed in more detail below. Each type is used in a logical sequence to maximize the development of information. If the interviewer has reason to believe that the respondent is being untruthful, then assessment questions can be posed. Otherwise, the interview is brought to a logical close.

Closing Questions

In routine interviews, certain questions are asked at closing for the purposes of reconfirming the facts, obtaining previously undiscovered information, seeking new evidence, and maintaining goodwill.

Assessment Questions

If the interviewer has reason to believe the respondent is being deceptive, certain types of hypothetical, nonaccusatory questions can be posed. By observing the verbal and non-verbal responses of the respondent to these questions, the interviewer can assess the respondent's credibility with some degree of accuracy. That assessment will form the basis of the interviewer's decision about whether to pose admission-seeking questions to obtain a legal admission of wrongdoing.

Admission-Seeking Questions

Admission-seeking interviews are reserved specifically for individuals whose culpability is reasonably certain. Admission-seeking questions are posed in an exact order designed to: (1) clear an innocent person or (2) encourage the culpable person to confess. These questions must not violate the rights and privileges of the person being interviewed.

Legal Elements of Interviewing

Legal Authority to Conduct Interviews

In most instances, legal authority is not required to interview people or to inquire into matters. The federal constitution gives any citizen the authority to inquire into virtually any subject area, as long as the rights of individuals are not transgressed in the process. Generally, no license is required to conduct interviews; however, if the interviewer represents himself as an investigator, some states require a license.

Use of Deception in Interviews

Surprisingly, the use of deception to gain information can sometimes be employed legally. The theory is that information can be obtained by nearly any means, with the exception of force or threats. The interviewer, however, might not employ any deception likely to cause an innocent person to confess. The use of deception is not justified regarding promises of leniency, promises of confidentiality, or to obtain a monetary or business advantage.

Frazier vs. Cupp

The U. S. Supreme Court (394 U.S. 731) ruled that deception was not unlawful in this particular case. The police untruthfully told Subject A that Subject B had confessed to a crime and implicated Subject A. The court ruled that the deception alone was insufficient to invalidate the interview process.

Elements of Conversations

Since an interview is essentially a structured conversation, it is helpful to understand the basic elements of communications. Whenever two or more human beings are conversing, several types of communication occur—either one at a time or in combination.

Expression

A common function of conversation is self-expression. One or more of the conversationalists might need to express ideas, feelings, attitudes, or moods. The illusion of an audience is central to a personal expression. The urge for spontaneous expression can be a vital asset in interviewing, and it should be encouraged in the respondent. It can be directed by the interviewer toward information-gathering objectives, but the interviewer should not give way to the urge for personal self-expression.

INFORMING
AND EDUCATING
ANTI-FRAUD
PROFESSIONALS
WORLDWIDE

FRAUD EXAMINERS MANUAL

VOLUME III

2005 US EDITION

©1990-2005 by the Association of Certified Fraud Examiners, Inc.

The original purchaser of this volume is authorized to reproduce in any form or by any means up to 50 pages contained in this work for nonprofit, educational, or private use. Such reproduction requires no further permission from the Authors or Publisher and/or payment of any permission fee as long as proper credit is given.

Except as specified above, no portion of this work may be reproduced or transmitted in any form or by any means electronic or mechanical, including photocopying, recording, or by any information storage and retrieval system without the written permission of the Association.

ISBN 1-889277-11-8

ACFE

Association of Certified Fraud Examiners

The Gregor Building
716 West Avenue
Austin, Texas 78701
(800) 245-3321
(512) 478-9000
www.cfenet.com

DISCLAIMER

Every effort has been made to ensure that the contents of this publication are accurate and free from error. However, it is possible that errors exist, both typographical and in content. Therefore, the information provided herein should be used only as a guide and not as the only source of reference.

The author, advisors, and publishers shall have neither liability nor responsibility to any person or entity with respect to any loss, damage, or injury caused or alleged to be caused directly or indirectly by any information contained in or omitted from this publication.

Printed in the United States of America

Inhaltsübersicht

Volume 1 3

Section 1 : Financial Transactions an Fraud Schemes 3

Part 1 Occupational Frauds 3

1. Accounting Concepts / Responsibilities 3
   - 1.1 Accounting Concepts 3
   - 1.2 Managment's and Auditors' Responsibilities 3
2. Fraud and Misappropriation 3
   - 2.1 Financial Statement Fraud 3
   - 2.2 Asset Misappropriation: Cash Theft 3
   - 2.3 Asset Misappropriation: Fraudulent Disbursements 3
   - 2.4 Asset Misappropriation: Inventory and Other Assets 3
3. Others 3
   - 3.1 Bribery and Corruption 3
   - 3.2 Intellectual Property 3

Part 2 Other Frauds 3

1. Financial *(first)* and Insurance 3
   - 1.1 Financial Institution Fraud 3
   - 1.2 Check and Credit Card Fraud 3
   - 1.3 Insurance Fraud 3
2. Health Care Fraud 3
3. Bankruptcy Fraud 3
4. Tax Fraud 3
5. Financial *(second)* 3
   - 5.1 Securities Fraud 3
   - 5.2 Money Laundering 3
6. Consumer Fraud 3
7. Computer an Internet Fraud 3
8. Public Sector Fraud 3
9. Contract and Producement Fraud 3

Volume 2 4

Section 2 : Law 4

Part 1 : Law 4

1. Overview of the United States Legal System 4
2. The Law related to Fraud 4
3. Rights and Prosecution 4
   - 3.1 Individual Rights during Examinations 4
   - 3.2 Criminal Prosecutions for Fraud 4
   - 3.3 The Civil Justice System 4
4. Examination and Testyfying 4
   - 4.1 Basic Principles of Evidence 4
   - 4.2 Testifying as an Expert Witness 4

Part 2 : Appendix *(Federal Rules of ...)* 4

1. Civil Procedure 4
2. Criminal Procedure 4
3. Evidence 4

Volume 3

Section 3 : Investigation
Part 1 : Investigation
1. Analyzing and Interviewing
1.1 Analyzing Documents
1.2 Interview Theory and Application
2. Getting Information
2.1 Covert Operations
2.2 Sources Of Information
2.3 Accessing Information On-Line
3. Analyzing and Reporting
3.1 Data Analysis and Reporting Tools
3.2 Tracing Illicit Transactions
3.3 Reporting Standards
Part 2 : Appendix
1. Fraud Examination Checklist
2. Sample Reports
3. Forms
4. Engagement Contracts and Opinion Letters

Section 4 : Criminology and Ethics
1. Introductions to Criminology / Understanding Human Behavior
2. Theories of Crime Causation
2.1 White-Colar Crime
2.2 Organizational Crime
2.3 Occupational Crime
3. Preventing and Punishment
3.1 Fraud Preventing Programs
3.2 Punishment and the Criminal Justice System
4. Ethical and professional Standards
4.1 Ethics for Fraud Examiners
4.2 ACFE Code of Ethics
4.3 ACFE Code of Professional Standards

One of the most common errors made by novice interviewers is to yield to the temptation to impress the respondent with their knowledge of the subject of the interview. In doing so, interviewers run the risk of making the respondent feel threatened, with the resultant tendency for respondents to guard responses rather than express their feelings frankly. Experienced interviewers will have the discipline to control their own responses.

Persuasion

The concepts of persuasion and expression differ in that persuasion essentially is aimed at convincing the other person. There are times when persuasion can be used effectively in the interview. This is mostly through convincing the person of the legitimacy of the interview.

Therapy

Making people feel good about themselves often is a function of conversation. In an ordinary conversation with a friend, a person often expresses ideas and feelings to remove emotional tension. This release is called *catharsis*, and is encouraged, for example, in psychiatric interviews. There are many times when the information sought in an interview is closely related to the respondent's inner conflicts and tensions. For example, in the area of fraud, a person embezzling money from the company will typically feel guilty. A skillful interviewer will know the therapeutic implication of such a feeling when attempting to develop information.

Ritual

Some aspects of conversation are ritualistic, that is, they merely are a form of verbal behavior that has no real significance other than to provide security in interpersonal relations. Examples include "Good Morning!" and "How are you today?" In interviewing, we must learn to detect ritualistic answers by the respondent, and avoid giving them ourselves. The interviewer must be aware of the danger of engaging in ritualistic conversation and then confusing the results with valid information.

Information Exchange

Information exchange is the central purpose of the interview. The word *exchange* reminds us that the flow of information in an interview goes both ways. Too frequently, interviewers become so concerned with the information they wish to obtain that they do not properly exchange information with the respondent. Although details of what the interviewer says should be carefully measured, don't be "cagey." This tactic rarely works. Two basic problems occur in the exchange of information. One, the information sought by the interviewer is not of equal importance to the respondent. Second, there is often a communication barrier between people of diverse backgrounds. These barriers are common between people who don't know one another.

Inhibitors of Communication

To be an effective interviewer, one must understand that certain matters inhibit communication, while others facilitate it. It is the interviewer's task to minimize inhibitors and maximize facilitators. An *inhibitor* is any social-psychological barrier that impedes the flow of relevant information by making the respondent unable or unwilling to provide the information to the interviewer. Eight inhibitors to communication are listed below. The first four tend to make the respondent unwilling; the last four make the respondent unable to give the information, even though willing.

Competing Demands for Time

The respondent might hesitate to begin an interview because of other time demands. The subject does not necessarily place a negative value on being interviewed, but weighs the value of being interviewed against doing something else. The successful interviewer must convince the respondent that the interview is a good use of time.

Ego Threat

The respondent in some cases might withhold information because of a perceived threat to his self-esteem. There are three broad categories of ego threats: repression, disapproval, and loss of status.

Repression

The strongest ego threat is repression. Respondents might not only refuse to admit information to the interviewer; they might also refuse to admit the information inwardly. They are being honest when answering that they do not know; or that they have forgotten. Embezzlers, for example, might repress memory of the act because it does not conform to their moral code.

Disapproval

A less intense but more common effect of ego threat is found when respondents possess information but are hesitant to admit it because they anticipate disapproval from the interviewer. If respondents are made to feel that the interviewer will not condemn them, they might welcome the opportunity to divulge information. A generally accepting and sympathetic attitude toward the respondent goes far toward eliciting candid responses.

Loss of Status

Sometimes respondents fear losing status if the information provided becomes public. This can sometimes be overcome by the interviewer's assurance that the information will be handled confidentially.

Etiquette

The etiquette barrier operates when an answer to the interviewer's question contains information perceived by the respondent as inappropriate. Answering candidly would be considered in poor taste or evidence of a lack of proper etiquette. For example, there are certain things that men do not discuss in front of women and vice versa, things that students do not tell teachers, things that doctors do not tell patients. The desire to avoid embarrassing, shocking, or threatening answers is distinct from the fear of exposing oneself. Often, the negative effects of the etiquette barrier might be forestalled by selecting the appropriate interviewer and setting for the interview.

Trauma

Trauma denotes an acutely unpleasant feeling associated with crisis experiences. The unpleasant feeling often is brought to the surface when the respondent is reporting the experience. Trauma is common when talking to victims, and usually can be overcome by sensitive handling of the issue.

Forgetting

A frequent inhibitor to communication is the respondent's inability to recall certain types of information. This is not a problem if the objectives of the interview deal only with current attitudes, beliefs, or expectations. The natural fading of the memory over time makes it easier for the ego-defense system to reconstruct one's own image of the past by omission, addition, or distortion.

The memory problem is a much more frequent obstacle than is generally expected by interviewers. Even some of the most simple and obvious facts cannot be elicited because of the respondent's memory problems. There are three factors which contribute to recollection of an event.

First, the vividness of the person's recall is related to the event's original emotional impact, its meaningfulness at the time, and the degree to which the person's ego is involved. A second factor is the amount of time that has elapsed since the event. Third is the nature of the interview situation, including the interviewer's techniques and tactics.

Knowledge of these factors will help the interviewer anticipate where the problems might occur. And there are certain techniques, discussed later, that will help the interviewer overcome many of these memory problems.

Chronological Confusion

Chronological confusion is commonly encountered in interviews seeking case history information. This term refers to the respondent's tendency to confuse the order of experiences. This can occur in two ways: two or more events might be correctly recalled, but the respondent is unsure of the sequence. Or only one event might be recalled, and it is incorrectly assumed to have been true at an earlier point.

Inferential Confusion

This term denotes confusion and inaccuracies resulting from errors of inference. These errors generally fall into two categories: induction or deduction. *Induction* is when the respondent is asked to convert concrete experiences into a higher level of generalization. *Deduction* is where the respondent is asked to give concrete examples of certain categories of experience.

Unconscious Behavior

Often the interview objectives call for information about a person's unconscious behavior. There are three types of unconscious behavior. The first type is *custom* or *habit*. Next is *circular reaction*, which is the immediate, unwitting response of one person to the subliminal, nonverbal clues of another, which arises under special circumstances. The third type of unconscious behavior occurs under an *acute emotional crisis* where the behavior does not follow a habitual pattern and where it does not result from a reaction to others.

Facilitators of Communication

Facilitators of communication are those social-psychological forces that make conversations, including interviews, easier to accomplish. These facilitators require a basic understanding of what motivates people.

Fulfilling Expectations

One of the important forces in social interaction is the tendency for one person to communicate, verbally or nonverbally, his expectations to the other person. The second person then tends to respond, consciously or unconsciously, to those expectations. This might be viewed as one manifestation of the more general human tendency to conform to the group and to the anticipations of higher-status people. It is in this conformity to group norms that security is sought.

In the interview setting, the interviewer communicates expectations to the respondent. The interviewer should be able to transmit both a general expectation of cooperation, as well as a more specific expectation that the respondent will answer the questions truthfully. The interviewer must clearly distinguish between asking for information and expecting it. The former is mainly verbal communication, while the latter is accomplished through nonverbal behavior. The interviewer who expects the respondent to cooperate likely will be more successful than one who only asks questions.

Recognition

All human beings need the recognition and the esteem of others. Social interaction often depends upon an exchange of social goods. People will "perform" in exchange for recognition and other social rewards. The need for recognition can be fulfilled by attention from people outside the individual's social circle. The skillful and insightful interviewer takes advantage of every opportunity to give the respondent *sincere* recognition.

Altruistic Appeals

There seems to be a need for humans to identify with some higher value or cause beyond immediate self-interest. This might sometimes take the form of identification with the objectives of some larger group. Altruistic deeds usually increase self-esteem whether or not the deeds have been made public. This distinguishes altruism from publicity. Altruism is of major importance in motivating many respondents. Interviewers who understand the respondent's value system can use strategy and techniques that appeal to altruism.

Sympathetic Understanding

Human beings need the sympathetic response of others. They like to share their joys, fears, successes, and failures. This need for understanding differs from the need for recognition that requires success and increased status. Interviewers who reflect a sympathetic attitude and who know how to direct that attitude toward the objectives of the interview will find their percentages of success much higher than those who do not.

New Experience

People welcome new experiences. Although variety might not be the only spice of life, escape from the dreary routine is sought by everyone. Sometimes the respondent is motivated by curiosity regarding the interviewer. Interviewers should consider this when deciding what to say about themselves. One must not assume that just because an interview is a new experience that it will satisfy the respondent's needs. Aspects of the respondent's perception of the new experience can be ego-threatening. The respondent might be anxious about the impression left with the interviewer. This apprehensiveness often can be detected by the interviewer at the beginning of the contact. Once these fears are dispelled, the respondent frequently finds the interview a new and interesting experience.

Catharsis

Catharsis is the process by which a person obtains a release from unpleasant emotional tensions by talking about the source of these tensions. We often feel better by talking about something that upsets us. Although we all are familiar with the frequent necessity for catharsis in ourselves, we do not always perceive the same need in others. The need for sympathetic understanding and the need for catharsis are related, but they are not the same thing. The interviewer who does not have time to listen to what he considers inconsequential egocentric talk, often will not find the respondent ready to share important consequences.

Need for Meaning

Another general trait common to people is the need for meaning. Every society has a set of assumptions, values, explanations, and myths lending order to the society. The concept of need for meaning is related to cognitive dissonance. There is a psychological tension set up when an individual becomes aware of incongruence of facts, assumptions, and interpretations. This tension is painful and its reduction is rewarding to the individual. In cases where the interview topic deals directly with the sources disturbing a person's system of meaning, there is a strong motivation for the respondent to talk it through, if he is convinced of the interviewer's interest.

Extrinsic Rewards

This term refers to rewards motivating the respondent other than those gained directly from being involved in the interview. These extrinsic rewards are helpful insofar as the respondent sees the interview as a means to an end. Many forms of extrinsic rewards can come into play in the interview situation, including money, job advancement, and retention of privileges. What is extrinsic to the interviewer might not be so to the respondent. A sensitive interviewer will be able to recognize what extrinsic rewards the respondent receives, if any, from being interviewed.

Introductory Questions

One of the most difficult aspects of an interview is getting started. Indeed, the introduction might be the hardest part. The interviewer and the respondent, in many instances, have not met before. The interviewer has a tall order: meet the person, state a reason for the interview, establish necessary rapport, and get the information. The introduction is accomplished through questions as opposed to statements. The questions allow the interviewer to assess feedback from the respondent. This is an important aspect of the introduction. If the respondent is reluctant to be interviewed, that fact will come out through the introductory questions. Introductory questions are designed to meet the four objectives below.

Provide the Introduction

Obviously, the interviewer must introduce himself before the interview commences. The interviewer should generally indicate his name and company, avoiding titles. This is not always the case, but the more informal the interview, generally the more relaxed the respondent.

Establish Rapport

Webster's defines *rapport* as a "relation marked by harmony, conformity, accord, or affinity." In other words, there must be some common ground established before questioning begins. This is usually accomplished by the interviewer spending a few minutes with the respondent in "small talk." This aspect, however, should not be overdone. Most people are aware that the interviewer is there for a meaningful purpose and not to chit-chat.

Establish the Interview Theme

The interviewer must state the purpose of the interview in some way prior to the commencement of serious questioning. Otherwise, the respondent might be confused, threatened, or overly cautious. Stating the purpose of the interview is known as establishing the "interview theme."

Observe Reactions

The interviewer must be skilled in interpreting the respondent's reactions to questions. Social scientists say that more than half the communication between individuals is nonspoken. The interviewer must, therefore, observe systematically, though in a nondescript manner, the various responses the respondent gives during the course of the conversation.

This is done by first posing nonsensitive questions while establishing rapport. During this phase, the interviewer attempts to find some common ground to "connect" with the respondent. After the interviewer establishes some rapport through normal conversation, the respondent's reactions are observed. This will serve as a baseline for observing behavior when more sensitive questions are asked. If the respondent's verbal and nonverbal behavior are inconsistent from one type of question to another, the interviewer will attempt to determine why.

Theme Development

The interview theme might be related only indirectly to the actual purpose of the interview. The goal of the theme is to get the respondent to "buy in" to assisting in the interview. Generally, the most effective interview theme is that help is being sought. Nearly all human beings get satisfaction from helping others.

In most interviews, the interviewer should approach the respondent so that person is made to feel important in helping out. During this phase of the interview, the respondent must not feel threatened in any way. An effective approach is the "Columbo-style," (although perhaps not in such a crumpled way) in which at least two thoughts go through the mind of Columbo's subjects: (1) he is no threat to me and (2) he really needs my help.

In the following examples, the interviewer is introducing himself to a fellow employee.

EXAMPLE

WRONG

Interviewer:

"Ms. De La Garza, I am Loren Bridges, a Certified Fraud Examiner with Bailey Books' fraud examination unit. I am investigating a case of suspected fraud, and you might know something about it. How long have you worked here at the company?"

RIGHT

Interviewer:

"Ms. De La Garza, I am Loren Bridges. I work here at the company. Have we met before?"

Respondent:

"I don't think so."

Interviewer:

"I am working on an assignment and I need your help. Do you have a few minutes I can spend with you?"

Methodology

Respondents must perceive that they have something in common with the interviewer, and should feel good about the situation. This is best accomplished when respondents perceive the interviewer as being open and friendly. The following techniques promote this perception.

Physical Contact

Make physical contact with the person being interviewed by shaking hands. Making physical contact helps break down psychological barriers to communication. The interviewer is cautioned from invading the respondent's personal space, however, as this might make the person uncomfortable.

The interviewer uses body language to create the impression of trust during the interview by gesturing openly with the arms, clasping hands together, and leaning forward in a manner to indicate interest. Rapport can be established through verbal techniques by using soft words, agreeing with the respondent, and avoiding negative terms.

When contacting a respondent for the first time, the interviewer must identify himself. This is best accomplished by stating your name. Unless a specific reason exists, the interviewer should generally omit a title. The less formality in general, the better. In some instances, stating a title cannot be avoided. In those cases, the title used should not conjure up emotion or possible fear in the mind of the respondent.

Establish the Purpose of Interview

The purpose of the interview must be established. Obviously, when the interviewer makes official contact with a respondent, some reason must be given. The reason or purpose of the interview should be general and not specific. The specific interview purpose will be related to the respondent later. The stated purpose for the interview should be one that is logical for the respondent to accept and easy for the interviewer to explain. Normally, the more general, the better.

EXAMPLE

Interviewer:

"I am working on a matter and I need your help."

OR

"I am doing a review of procedures here at the company."

OR

"I am developing some information on our purchasing procedures."

Don't Interview More than One Person

One of the basic rules is to question only one person at a time. The testimony of one respondent will invariably influence the testimony of another. There are few hard and fast rules, but this is one of them.

Privacy

Another basic rule is to conduct interviews under conditions of privacy. The interview is best conducted out of the sight and sound of friends, relatives, or fellow employees. People are very reluctant to furnish information within the hearing of others.

Ask Nonsensitive Questions

Sensitive questions should be scrupulously avoided until well into the interview. And then such questions should be asked only after careful deliberation and planning. During the introductory phase, emotive words of all types generally should be avoided. Such words normally put people on the defensive, and they are less reluctant to answer and to cooperate.

EXAMPLE

Instead of	*Use*
Investigation	*Inquiry*
Audit	*Review*
Interview	*Ask a few questions*
Embezzle/steal/theft	*Shortage or paperwork problems*

Get a Commitment for Assistance

Failure to get a commitment from the respondent to assist is one of the common mistakes made even by experienced interviewers. This is a critical step in setting the tone for the interview. A commitment of assistance requires positive action on the part of the person being interviewed. Remaining silent or simply nodding the head generally is not sufficient.

The interviewer should ask for the commitment before the interview commences, and should encourage the respondent to voice that "yes" aloud. If the interviewer encounters silence the first time, the question should be repeated in a slightly different way until the respondent verbalizes commitment. In the Linda Reed Collins case, Bridges, the Certified Fraud Examiner, introduces himself to Mary Rodriguez De La Garza, who works in the purchasing department of Bailey Books Incorporated.

EXAMPLE

Interviewer:
"Ms. De La Garza, I'm Loren Bridges. I'm doing a review of our purchasing function. Do you have a few minutes?"

Respondent:
"Yes."

Interviewer:
"I am gathering some information on certain company procedures. Maybe you can help me?"

Respondent:
No response.

Interviewer:

"Could I get you to help me, if you can?"

Respondent:

"Yes. What's this about?"

Establish Transitional Statement

At this point, the interviewer has gotten a commitment for assistance, and must describe in more detail the purpose of the interview. This is done with the transitional statement used to provide a legitimate basis for the inquiry, and to explain to respondents how they fit into the inquiry. This usually is done by means of a broad description. When interviewing employees in the same company, most of them already presume the legitimacy of your request for assistance. After describing the basic nature of the inquiry with the transitional statement, the interviewer should seek a second commitment for assistance.

EXAMPLE

Interviewer:

"It's pretty routine, really. I'm gathering some information about the purchasing function and how it is supposed to work. It would be helpful to me if I could start by asking you to basically tell me about your job. O.K.?"

When interviewing strangers, the interviewer might have to describe with more particularity how the respondent's assistance is needed. This can be accomplished by one or more of the methods illustrated below, where the interviewer is talking to an outside vendor.

EXAMPLE

Interviewer:

"It's pretty routine, really. As I say, I work for Bailey Books and I've been assigned a project to gather some information about some of our procedures. And because you work for one of our vendors, I thought it might be helpful to talk to you. Okay?"

OR

"It's pretty routine, really. I have been asked by the company to gather information on some of our procedures. I thought you might be able to help by answering a few questions. Okay?"

OR

"It's pretty routine, really. I have been asked by the company to gather some information, and they suggested I might contact you. Okay?"

Seek Continuous Agreement

Throughout the interview process—from the introduction to the close—the interviewer should attempt to phrase questions so that they can be answered "yes." It is easier for people to reply in the affirmative than the negative.

EXAMPLE

Interviewer:

"Okay?"

"Can you help me?"

"That's okay, isn't it?"

Do Not Invade Body Space

During the introductory part of the interview, the interviewer generally should remain at a distance of four to six feet. Do not invade the personal zone (closer than about three feet) as it might make the respondent uncomfortable.

Informational Questions

Informational questions are nonconfrontational, nonthreatening, and are asked for information-gathering purposes. The great majority of the interviewer's questions fall into this category. Types of questions include:

- Conducting an interview to gain an understanding of accounting control systems
- Interviews concerning documents
- Gathering information regarding business operations or systems
- Pre-employment interviews

Informational questions seek to elicit unbiased factual information. The interviewer will be alert to inconsistency in facts or behavior. Informational questions—as well as others—fall into several general categories: open, closed, leading, double-negative, complex, and attitude.

Open Questions

Open questions are those worded in a way which makes it difficult to answer "yes" or "no." Nor is the answer dependent on the question. The typical open question calls for a monologue response, and it can be answered in several different ways. During the information phase of the interview, the interviewer should endeavor to ask primarily open questions. This is to stimulate conversation. Some of the best open questions are subtle commands.

EXAMPLE

Interviewer:

"Please tell me about your job."

"Please tell me about the operation of your department."

"What do you think about this problem?"

"Please describe the procedures to me."

Closed Questions

Closed questions are those which require a precise answer: usually "yes" or "no." Closed questions also deal with specifics, such as amounts, dates, and times. As far as possible, closed questions should be avoided in the informational part of the interview. They are used extensively in closing questions.

EXAMPLE

Interviewer:

"Do you work here?"

"What day of the week did it happen?"

Leading Questions

Leading questions contain the answer as a part of the question. Most commonly, they are used to confirm facts already known. Although leading questions usually are discouraged in court proceedings, they can be used effectively in interview situations.

EXAMPLE

Interviewer:

"So there have been no changes in the operation since last year?"

"Are you still employed by the Bailey Books Corporation?"

"You got promoted, right?"

"Don't you get your income from various sources?"

Double-Negative Questions

Questions or statements containing double-negatives are confusing and often suggest an answer opposite to the correct one. They should not be used.

EXAMPLE

Interviewer:

"Didn't you suspect that something wasn't right?"

Complex Questions

Complex questions and statements are too complicated to be easily understood, cover more than one subject or topic, require more than one answer, and/or require a complicated answer. They should be avoided.

EXAMPLE

Interviewer:

"What are your duties here, and how long have you been employed?"

Attitude Questions

The attitude of the interviewer can be conveyed by the structure of the question or statement, and by the manner in which the question is asked. When the interviewer wishes to establish a friendly mood, these questions can be employed.

EXAMPLE

Interviewer:

"How are you doing this morning, Ms. De La Garza?"

"Do you like sports?"

It is always a good idea, however, to ask a question for which you know beforehand that the answer will be "yes."

Question Sequences

As a general rule, questioning should proceed from the general to the specific; that is, it is best to seek general information before seeking details. A variation is to "reach backward" with the questions, by beginning with known information and working toward unknown areas. An efficient method of doing this is to recount the known information and then frame the next question as a logical continuation of the facts previously related.

It is common, especially in accounting and fraud-related matters, for figures or numbers to be critical. Unfortunately, some witnesses are unable to recall specific amounts. The interviewer can jog the memory of the respondent by comparing unknown items with items of known quantity.

EXAMPLE

Interviewer:

"Was the amount of money involved more than last year's figure?"

Controlled Answer Techniques

Controlled answer techniques or statements might be used to stimulate a desired answer or impression. These techniques direct the interview toward a specific point. For example, it might be possible to get a person to admit knowledge of a matter by phrasing the question like this, *"I understand you were present when the internal controls were developed, so would you please describe how they were constructed?"* This phrasing provides a stronger incentive for the respondent to admit knowledge than does: *"Were you present when the internal controls were developed?"*

To stimulate the person to agree to talk, or to provide information, you might use an example such as, *"Because you are not involved in this matter, I am sure you would not mind discussing it with me."* This provides a stronger incentive to cooperate than: *"Do you have any objections to telling me what you know?"* Avoid negative construction, such as, *"I don't guess you would mind answering a few questions?"*

Free Narratives

The *free narrative* is an orderly, continuous account of an event or incident, given with or without prompting. It is used to get a quick resumé of what is known about a matter. Be sure to designate specifically the occurrence that you wish to discuss.

Sometimes the respondent must be controlled to prevent unnecessary digression. Otherwise, use a minimum of interruptions, and do not stop the narrative without good reason. The respondent sometimes will provide valuable clues when talking about things that are only partially related to the matter under inquiry.

Informational Question Techniques

Below are suggestions to improve the quality of the interview during the information-gathering phase.

- Begin by asking questions that are not likely to cause the respondent to become defensive or hostile.
- Ask the questions in a manner that will develop the facts in the order of their occurrence, or in some other systematic order.
- Ask only one question at a time, and frame the question so that only one answer is required.
- Ask straightforward and frank questions; generally avoid shrewd approaches.
- Give the respondent ample time to answer; do not rush.
- Try to help the respondent remember, but do not suggest answers; and be careful not to imply any particular answer by facial expressions, gestures, methods of asking questions, or types of questions asked.
- Repeat or rephrase questions, if necessary, to get the desired facts.
- Be sure you understand the answers, and if they are not perfectly clear, have the respondent interpret them at that time instead of saving this for later.
- Give the respondent an opportunity to qualify his answers.
- Separate facts from inferences.
- Have the respondent give comparisons by percentages, fractions, estimates of time and distance, and other such comparisons to ascertain accuracy.
- Get all of the facts; almost every respondent can give you information beyond what was initially provided.
- After the respondent has given a narrative account, ask questions about every item that has been discussed.

- Upon conclusion of the direct questioning, ask the respondent to summarize the information given; then summarize the facts, and have the respondent verify that these conclusions are correct.

Note-Taking

The interviewer frequently will need to take notes during the interview. Start each interview on a separate sheet of paper. This procedure can be especially helpful should documents from a particular interview be subpoenaed. Do not try to write down all the information you are given during an interview, only the pertinent facts. Taking too many notes will make the interview process cumbersome and might inhibit the respondent. If a quote is particularly relevant, try to write it down verbatim. Enclose all direct quotes in quotation marks.

Do not slow down the interview process for note-taking. Instead, jot down key words or phrases, then go back over the details at the end of the interview. In general, it is better to err on the side of taking too few notes rather than too many.

Maintain Eye Contact

Maintain eye contact with the respondent as much as possible during note-taking. Just as eye contact personalizes all human communication, it creates a more comfortable environment and facilitates the flow of information during the interview process.

Opinions

Avoid making notes regarding your overall opinions or impressions of a witness. Such notes can cause you problems with your credibility if they are later produced in court. Be careful not to show excitement when note-taking. During interviews of targets and adverse witnesses, take notes in a manner that does not indicate the significance of the information; that is, never allow note-taking to "telegraph" your emotions.

Writing Down Questions

Whenever possible, do not write down a list of interview questions. Let the interview flow freely. Inadvertently allowing the respondent to read a written list of questions can provide an opportunity to fabricate an answer. Certainly, writing down key points the interviewer wants to discuss might be appropriate.

Documenting Results

Expound the notes from the results of questioning as soon as possible after concluding the interview—preferably immediately afterward. If this procedure is followed, the examiner will not have to take copious notes during the interview. Law enforcement officials generally are required to maintain notes. In the private sector, the notes can usually be destroyed once a memorandum has been prepared summarizing the interview. (See the Law Section for more information.)

Observing Interview Reactions

The interviewer must be knowledgeable about the behavior of individuals during the interview situation. Most nonverbal clues to behavior fall within one of the following categories: proxemics, chronemics, kinetics, or paralinguistics.

Proxemics

Proxemic communication is the use of interpersonal space to convey meaning. The relationship between the interviewer and respondent is both a cause and effect of proxemic behavior. If the distance between the interviewer and the respondent is greater, there is more of a tendency for them to watch each other's eyes for clues to meaning.

It is important to position the respondent's chair and the interviewer's chair at an acceptable distance. The correct conversational distance varies from one culture to another. In the Middle East, the distance is quite short; in Latin America, equals of the same sex carry on a conversation at a much closer distance than in North America. Often, as the subject matter of the interview changes, the interviewer can note the changes in the proxemic behavior of the respondent. If the person is free to back away, he might do so when the topic becomes unpleasant or sensitive.

Chronemics

Chronemic communication refers to the use of time in interpersonal relationships to convey meaning, attitudes, and desires. If the respondent is late in keeping an appointment, for example, this might convey a lack of interest in or avoidance of the interview.

The most important chronemic technique used by interviewers is in the timing of questions. The interviewer can control the length of pauses and the rate of his speech. This is called *pacing*. The interviewer can also control the length of time after the respondent has finished a sentence before another question is posed. This is called the *silent probe*.

Pacing is one of the principal nonverbal methods of setting an appropriate mood. The tense interviewer often communicates anxiety by a rapid-fire rate of speech which in turn might increase anxiety in the respondent. To establish the more thoughtful, deliberative mood usually needed to stimulate free association, the interviewer must take the initiative in setting a more relaxed, deliberate pace.

Kinetics

Kinetic communication involves the use of body movement to convey meaning. Even though posture, hands, and feet all communicate, interviewers tend to focus attention on the face and are more accurate in their judgments of others if they can see facial movements and expressions. When the interviewer concentrates on facial expressions, the primary interest is eye contact. Eye contact primarily communicates the desire to make or avoid communication. A person who feels shame normally will drop the eyes to avoid the glance of another. This is not only to avoid seeing disapproval, but to conceal personal shame and confusion.

Paralinguistics

Paralinguistic communication involves the use of volume, pitch, and voice quality to convey meaning. One of the basic differences between written and verbal communication is that oral speech gives the full range of nonverbal accompaniment. For example, a "no" answer might not really mean no; it depends on the way in which the "no" is said.

The interviewer must learn to listen and observe changes in the nonverbal accompaniment and whether the verbal and nonverbal are harmoniously reinforcing or tend to give conflicting signals, as in cases where the respondent is trying to deceive the interviewer. Ten emotions have been studied by social scientists: anger, fear, happiness, jealousy, love, nervousness, pride, sadness, satisfaction, and sympathy. Some emotions, like anger and nervousness, can be more reliably identified than the others.

Theme Development

All questions should be nonaccusatory. Nothing closes up the lines of communication in an interview like an accusatory question. Interviewers are cautioned to formulate their questions in a way that will not bring about a strong emotional reaction from the respondent.

Move from nonsensitive to sensitive. If the respondent starts to become uncomfortable with the questioning, the interviewer should move into a different area and approach the sensitive question later from a different vantage point.

Some people will not volunteer information; they must be asked. The interviewer must not be reluctant to ask sensitive questions after the proper basis has been established. If the interviewer poses the question with confidence and with the attitude that an answer is expected, the respondent will be much more likely to furnish the requested information. If the interviewer is apologetic or lacks confidence in the question, the respondent is much less likely to answer.

Methodology

Once the introduction has been completed, the interviewer needs a transition into the body of the interview. This usually is accomplished by asking people an easy question about themselves or their duties.

EXAMPLE

Interviewer:

"As I said, I am informally gathering information about Bailey's operations. I don't know if you can really help me. Can you give me an idea of what you do here?"

Begin with Background Questions

Assuming the respondent does not have a problem answering the transitional question, the interviewer should then ask a series of easy, open questions designed to get the respondent to talk about himself.

EXAMPLE

Interviewer:

"What is your exact title?"

"What do your responsibilities involve?"

"How long have you been assigned here?"

"What do you like best about your job?"

"What do you like least about your job?"

"What would you eventually like to do for the company?"

"Overall, how do you like your current job?"

Observe Verbal and Nonverbal Behavior

During the period when the respondent is talking about himself, the interviewer should discreetly observe verbal and nonverbal behavior.

Ask Nonleading (Open) Questions

Open questioning techniques are used almost exclusively in the informational phase of the interview. The questions must be inquisitory and not accusatory. Remember, the most effective question is constructed as a subtle command.

EXAMPLE

Interviewer:
"Please tell me about _____."

"Please tell me about your current job procedures."

"Please tell me what paperwork you are responsible for."

"Please explain the chain of command in your department."

"Please tell me what procedures are in effect to prevent errors in the paperwork."

"Please explain what you understand to be the system of checks and balances (or internal controls) in your department."

"Please explain where you see areas that need to be improved in the system of checks and balances in your department."

Once the respondent has answered open questions, the interviewer can go back and review the facts in greater detail. If the answers are inconsistent, try to clarify them. But the interviewer should not challenge the honesty or integrity of the respondent at this point.

Approach Sensitive Questions Carefully

Words such as "routine questions" can be used to play down the significance of the inquiry. It is important for information-gathering purposes that the interviewer not react excessively to the respondent's statements. The interviewer should not express shock, disgust, or similar emotions during the interview. Following are examples of ways to discuss fraud within a company. The questions are posed in a hypothetical way to avoid being accusatory.

EXAMPLE

Interviewer:

"Part of my job is to prevent and uncover waste, fraud, and abuse. You understand that, don't you?"

"Please tell me where you think the company is wasting assets or money."

"Where do you think the company is vulnerable to someone here abusing their position?"

Dealing with Resistance

There is always the possibility that the respondent will refuse a request for interview. When the respondent and the interviewer have no connection, studies show that as many as 65 percent of the respondents will refuse an interview if contacted first by telephone. In contrast, one study concluded that only a third of the respondents will be reluctant to be interviewed when contacted in person. The more unpleasant the topic, the more likely the respondent is to refuse.

With inexperienced interviewers, there is a danger that the interviewer will perceive resistance when there is none. As a result, the interviewer might become defensive. It is incumbent upon the interviewer to overcome such feelings to complete the interview. Following are specific examples of the types of resistance that will be encountered and how to try to overcome them.

"I'm Too Busy"

When the interviewer contacts the respondent without a previous appointment, there is a possibility that the respondent will be too busy at the moment to cooperate. "I'm too busy" also is used as an excuse for the real source of the person's resistance which might be lethargy, ego threat, or dislike of talking to strangers. These situations can be diffused by the interviewer stressing that:

- The interview will be short
- The interviewer is already there
- The project is important
- The interview will not be difficult
- The interviewer needs help

"I Don't Know Anything About It"

The interviewer will sometimes get this response immediately after stating the purpose of the interview. This resistance is typically diffused by accepting the statement, and then returning with a question. For example, if a person says, "I don't know anything," a typical response would be:

EXAMPLE

Interviewer:

"I see. What do your duties involve, then?"

OR

"Well, that was one of the things I wanted to find out. Do you know about internal controls, then?"

"I Don't Remember"

Usually, this is not an expression of resistance. Instead, it is an expression of modesty, tentativeness, or caution. One of the best ways to respond is to simply remain silent while the person is deliberating. He is saying, in effect, "Give me a moment to think." If this is not successful, the best way to counter is to pose an alternate, narrower question. As with other symptoms of resistance, the resistance is accepted and diffused, and an alternate question is posed.

EXAMPLE

Interviewer:

"Mr. McGuire, I understand you might not remember the entire transaction. Do you remember if it was more than $10,000?"

OR

"It's okay if you don't remember the details. Do you remember how it made you react at the time?"

"What Do You Mean by That?"

When the respondent asks this question, it might represent a symptom of mild resistance with which the respondent is attempting to shift the attention from himself to the interviewer. It also might be a way for the respondent to stall for time while deliberating. Or it could be that the respondent is not sure what the interviewer's question means. The interviewer should typically react to such a question by treating it as a mere request for clarification. The interviewer should not become defensive; to do so generally will escalate the resistance.

Difficult People

The interviewer invariably will encounter a few difficult people. There are five common-sense steps to take with such people.

Don't React

Sometimes a respondent will insist on giving the interviewer a "hard time" for no apparent reason. Though, in reality, there can be a multitude of reasons why the person refuses to cooperate. There are three natural reactions for the interviewer verbally assailed by the respondent: to strike back, to give in, or to terminate the interview. None of these tactics is satisfactory, as none leads to a productive interview. Instead, the interviewer should consciously ensure that he does not react to anger with hostility.

Disarm the Person

A common mistake is to try to reason with an unreceptive person. You must disarm the hostile person. The best tactic is surprise. If the person is stonewalling, he expects the interviewer to apply pressure; if attacking, the person expects the interviewer to resist. To disarm the person, listen, acknowledge the point, and agree wherever you can.

Change Tactics

In some situations, changing tactics to reduce hostility might be the only viable option. This means casting what the respondent says in a form that directs attention back to the problem and to the interests of both sides. This normally means asking the respondent what he would do to solve the problem.

Make it Easy to Say "Yes"

In trying to negotiate with difficult people, the usual tactic is for the interviewer to make a statement and attempt to get the respondent to agree with it. A better choice is to agree with one of the respondent's statements and go from there. It is better to break statements into smaller ones that would be difficult to disagree with. This helps the difficult person save face.

Make it Hard to Say "No"

One way of making it difficult to say "no" is by asking reality-based (what-if) questions. These types of questions are used to get the respondent to think of the consequences of not agreeing.

EXAMPLE

Interviewer:

"What do you think will happen if we don't agree?"

"What do you think I will have to do from here?"

"What will you do?"

Volatile Interviews

A *volatile interview* is one that has the potential to bring about strong emotional reactions in the respondent. Typical volatile interviews involve close friends and relatives of a miscreant, co-conspirators, and similar individuals.

The personality characteristics of those involved in the volatile interview vary. The types listed represent the most common personality characteristics associated with volatile interviews. Some individuals, by nature, are resentful of authority figures, such as fraud examiners and law enforcement officers.

Friends, relatives, and romantic interests of a target often make for a difficult interview. They perceive that the examiner is "out to get" someone close to them.

Physical Symptoms

In volatile interviews, the individual typically reacts, rather than thinks; and frequently the individual is openly hostile to the interviewer. Individuals under high emotion frequently have a dry mouth, and tend to lick their lips and swallow more frequently than normal. Throat clearing also is an audible sign of emotion. Restlessness is observed by fidgets, shifts in a chair, and foot-tapping. People under emotional stress frequently perspire more than normal.

Under stress, a person's complexion frequently changes. People might look red or flushed, or might appear to be pale. During stress, the heart beats more frequently, and a keen observer can see the carotid artery actually pulsate. The carotid artery is the large artery on each side of the neck.

If an individual in a normal situation maintains eye contact, he might be under stress when eye contact is avoided. It is important to realize that symptoms are not present in all emotional situations.

Other Considerations

There should be two interviewers involved in potentially volatile situations. This procedure provides psychological strength for the interviewers. Additionally, the second person can serve as a witness in the event the interview turns bad.

Surprise should be employed in any interview that is considered potentially volatile. In many instances, the potentially volatile respondent is unaware that he is going to be questioned, and will therefore be off guard. If the interview is not conducted by surprise, the interviewer runs the risk of the respondent not showing up, showing up with a witness, or being present with counsel.

In a potentially volatile interview, the order of questions should be out of sequence. This is to keep the volatile respondent from knowing exactly the nature of the inquiry, and where it is leading. Although the interviewer will endeavor to obtain information regarding who, what, why, when, where, and how, the order of the questioning will vary from that of other interviews. This technique is especially important in situations where the respondent might be attempting to protect himself.

The hypothetical question generally is considered to be less threatening, and is, therefore, ideally suited for the potentially volatile interview. For example, if you are interviewing Smith regarding Jones, rather than saying, *"Did Mr. Jones do it?"* ask, *"Is there any reason why Mr. Jones would have done it?"*

Overcoming Objections

Volatile witnesses voice numerous objections to being interviewed. Some of the most common objections (along with a suggested response) are listed below.

EXAMPLE

Respondent:

"*I don't want to be involved.*"

Interviewer:

Answer this question by pointing out that you would not be there, asking questions, if the respondent were not involved. Point out that you are saving the respondent trouble by discussing the matter "informally" (Do not say "off the record").

Respondent:

"*Why should I talk to you?*"

Interviewer:

Answer that you are trying to clear up a problem, and that the respondent's assistance is important.

Respondent:

"*You can't prove that!*"

Interviewer:

Tell the person that you are not trying to prove or disprove; you are simply gathering information.

Respondent:

"*You can't make me talk!*"

Interviewer:

Tell the person that you are not attempting to make him do anything; you are trying to resolve a problem, and would deeply appreciate help.

Assessment Questions

Assessment questions seek to establish the credibility of the respondent. They are used only when the interviewer considers previous statements by the respondent to be inconsistent because of possible deception.

Once the respondent has answered all questions about the event, and the interviewer has reason to believe the respondent is being deceptive, a theme must be established to justify additional questions. This theme can ordinarily be put forth by saying, *"I have a few additional questions."* Do not indicate in any way that these questions are for a different purpose than seeking information.

Norming or Calibrating

Norming or *calibrating* is the process of observing behavior before critical questions are asked, as opposed to doing so during questioning. Norming should be a routine part of all interviews. People with truthful attitudes will answer questions one way; those with untruthful attitudes generally will answer them differently. Assessment questions ask for agreement to matters that are against the principles of most honest people. In other words, dishonest people are likely to agree with many of the statements, while honest people won't. Assessment questions are designed primarily to get a verbal or nonverbal reaction from the respondent. The interviewer will then carefully assess that reaction. Suggestions for observing the verbal and physical behavior of the respondent include:

- Use your senses of touch, sight, and hearing to establish a norm
- Do not stare or call attention to the person's behavior symptoms
- Be aware of the respondent's entire body
- Observe the timing and consistency of behavior
- Note clusters of behaviors

On the basis of the respondent's reaction to the assessment questions, the interviewer then considers all the verbal and nonverbal responses together (not in isolation) to decide whether to proceed to the admission-seeking phase of the interview. No one behavior should be isolated or a conclusion drawn from it. They should be considered together.

Physiology of Deception

It is said that everyone lies and does so for one of two reasons: to receive rewards or to avoid punishment. In most people, lying produces stress. The human body will attempt to relieve this stress (even in practiced liars) through verbal and nonverbal clues.

Conclusions concerning behavior must be tempered by a number of factors. The physical environment in which the interview is conducted can affect behavior. If the respondent is comfortable, fewer behavior quirks might be exhibited. The more intelligent the respondent, the more reliable verbal and nonverbal clues will be. If the respondent is biased toward the interviewer, or vice versa, this will affect behavior.

People who are mentally unstable, or are under the influence of drugs, will be unsuitable to interview. Behavior symptoms of juveniles generally are unreliable. Racial, ethnic, and economic factors should be carefully noted. Some cultures, for example, discourage looking directly at someone. Other cultures use certain body language that might be misinterpreted. Because professional pathological liars often are familiar with interview techniques, they are less likely to furnish observable behavioral clues.

Verbal Clues
CHANGES IN SPEECH PATTERNS
Deceptive people often speed up or slow down their speech, or speak louder. There might be a change in the voice pitch; as a person becomes tense, the vocal chords constrict. Deceptive people also have a tendency to cough or clear their throats during times of deception.

REPETITION OF THE QUESTION
Liars frequently will repeat the interviewer's question to gain more time to think of what to say. The deceptive individual will say, *"What was that again?"* or use similar language.

COMMENTS REGARDING INTERVIEW
Deceptive people often will complain about the physical environment of the interview room, such as, *"It's cold in here."* They also will sometimes ask how much longer the interview will take.

SELECTIVE MEMORY
In some cases, the deceptive person will have a fine memory for insignificant events, but when it comes to the important facts, *"just can't seem to remember."*

MAKING EXCUSES

Dishonest people frequently will make excuses about things that look bad for them, such as, *"I'm always nervous; don't pay any attention to that."*

OATHS

On frequent occasions, dishonest people will add what they believe to be credibility to their lies by use of emphasis. Expressions such as *"I swear to God,"* or *"Honestly,"* or *"Frankly,"* or *"To tell the truth,"* are frequently used.

CHARACTER TESTIMONY

A liar often will request that the interviewer, *"Check with my wife,"* or *"Talk to my minister."* This is frequently done to add credibility to the false statement.

ANSWERING WITH A QUESTION

Rather than deny the allegations outright, the liar might frequently answer with a question such as, *"Why would I do something like that?"* As a variation, the deceptive person sometimes will question the interview procedure by asking, *"Why are you picking on me?"*

OVERUSE OF RESPECT

Some deceptive people will go out of their way to be respectful and friendly. When accused of wrongdoing, it is unnatural for a person to react in a friendly and respectful manner.

EXAMPLE

Respondent:

"I'm sorry, sir, I know you're just doing your job. But I didn't do it."

INCREASING WEAKER DENIALS

When an honest person is accused of something he did not do, that person is likely to become angry or forceful in making the denial. The more the person is accused, the more forceful the denial becomes. The dishonest person, on the other hand, is likely to make a weak denial. Upon repeated accusations, the dishonest person's denials become weaker, to the point that the person becomes silent.

FAILURE TO DENY

Dishonest people are more likely than honest people to deny an event specifically. An honest person might offer a simple and clear *"no"* while the dishonest person will qualify the denial: *"No, I did not steal $43,500 from the Company on June 27."* Other qualified denial phrases include, *"To the best of my memory,"* and *"As far as I recall,"* or similar language.

AVOIDANCE OF EMOTIVE WORDS

A liar often will avoid emotionally provocative terms such as "steal," "lie," and "crime." Instead, the dishonest person frequently prefers "soft" words such as "borrow," and "it" (referring to the deed in question).

REFUSAL TO IMPLICATE OTHER SUSPECTS

Both the honest respondent and the liar will have a natural reluctance to name others involved in misdeeds. However, the liar frequently will refuse to implicate possible suspects, no matter how much pressure is applied by the interviewer. This is because the culpable person does not want the circle of suspicion to be narrowed.

TOLERANT ATTITUDES

Dishonest people typically have tolerant attitudes toward miscreant conduct. The interviewer in an internal theft case might ask, *"What should happen to this person when he is caught?"* The honest person usually will say, *"They should be fired/prosecuted."* The dishonest individual, on the other hand, is much more likely to reply, *"How should I know?"* or, *"Maybe he is a good employee who got into problems. Perhaps they should be given a second chance."*

RELUCTANCE TO TERMINATE INTERVIEW

Dishonest people generally will be more reluctant than honest ones to terminate the interview. The dishonest individual wants to convince the interviewer that he is not responsible, so that the investigation will not continue. The honest person, on the other hand, generally has no such reluctance.

FEIGNED UNCONCERN

The dishonest person often will try to appear casual and unconcerned and frequently will adopt an unnatural slouching posture, and might react to questions with nervous or false laughter or feeble attempts at humor. The honest person, on the other hand, typically will be very concerned about being suspected of wrongdoing, and will treat the interviewer's questions seriously.

Nonverbal Clues

FULL BODY MOTIONS

When asked sensitive or emotive questions, the dishonest person typically will change his posture completely—as if moving away from the interviewer. The honest person frequently will lean forward toward the interviewer when questions are serious.

ANATOMICAL PHYSICAL RESPONSES

Anatomical physical responses are those involuntary reactions by the body to fright such as increased heart rate, shallow or labored breathing, or excessive perspiration. These reactions are typical of dishonest people accused of wrongdoing.

ILLUSTRATORS

Illustrators are the motions made primarily with the hands to demonstrate points when talking. During nonthreatening questions, the illustrators might be done at one rate. During threatening questions, the use of illustrators might increase or decrease.

HANDS OVER THE MOUTH

Frequently, dishonest people will cover the mouth with the hand or fingers during deception. This reaction goes back to childhood, when many children cover their mouths when telling a lie. It is done subconsciously to conceal the statement.

MANIPULATORS

Manipulators are those motions such as picking lint from clothing, playing with objects such as pencils, or holding one's hands while talking. Manipulators are displacement activities, to reduce nervousness.

FLEEING POSITIONS

During the interview, dishonest people often will posture themselves in a "fleeing position." While the head and trunk might be facing the interviewer, the feet and lower portion of the body might be pointing toward the door in an unconscious effort to flee from the interviewer.

CROSSING THE ARMS

Crossing one's arms over the middle zones of the body is a classic defensive reaction to difficult or uncomfortable questions. A variation is crossing the feet under the chair and locking them. These crossing motions occur mostly when being deceptive.

REACTION TO EVIDENCE

While trying to be outwardly concerned, the guilty person will have a keen interest in implicating evidence. The dishonest person often will look at documents presented by the interviewer, attempt to be casual about observing them, and then shove them away, as wanting nothing to do with the evidence.

Most actions that are designed to interrupt the flow of speech are stress-related. Examples include:
- Closing the mouth tightly
- Pursing lips
- Covering the mouth with the hand
- Lip and tongue biting
- Licking the lips
- Chewing on objects

Genuine smiles usually involve the whole mouth; false ones are confined to the upper half. People involved in deception tend to smirk rather than to smile.

CROSSING

The body or legs might be crossed to reduce stress. When the hands are crossing the body, it is a defensive gesture, to protect the "soft underbelly."

Methodology

The following assessment questions can be asked. Note that the questions go logically from the least to the most sensitive. In most examples, the question's basis is explained before the question is asked. The initial questions seek agreement.

The following questions assume the examiner has some reason to believe the respondent, a company employee, has knowledge of a suspected fraud.

EXAMPLE

Interviewer:

"The company is particularly concerned about fraud and abuse. There are some new laws in effect that will cost the company millions if abuses go on and we don't try to find them. Do you know which law I am talking about?"

EXPLANATION

Most individuals will not know about the laws concerning corporate sentencing guidelines, and will, therefore, answer "no." The purpose of this question is to get the respondent to understand the serious nature of fraud and abuse.

EXAMPLE

Interviewer:

"Congress recently passed a law last year that can levy fines of more than $200 million against companies that don't try to clean their own houses. $200 million is a lot of money, so you can understand why the company's concerned, can't you?"

EXPLANATION

The majority of people will say "yes" to this question. In the event of a "no" answer, the interviewer should explain the issue fully and, thereafter, attempt to get the respondent's agreement. If that agreement is not forthcoming, the interviewer should assess why not.

EXAMPLE

Interviewer:

"Of course, they are not talking about a loyal employee who gets in a bind. They're talking more about senior management. Have you ever read in the newspapers about what kind of people engage in company misdeeds?"

EXPLANATION

Most people read the newspapers and are at least generally familiar with the problem of fraud and abuse. Agreement by the respondent is expected to this question.

EXAMPLE

Interviewer:

"Most of them aren't criminals at all. A lot of times, they're just trying to save their jobs or just trying to get by because the company is so cheap that they won't pay people what they are worth. Do you know what I mean?"

EXPLANATION

Although the honest person and the dishonest person will both probably answer "yes" to this question, the honest individual is less likely to accept the premise that these people are not wrongdoers. Many honest people might reply, *"Yes, I understand, but that doesn't justify stealing."*

EXAMPLE

Interviewer:

"Why do you think someone around here might be justified in taking company property?"

EXPLANATION

Because fraud perpetrators frequently justify their acts, the dishonest individual is more likely than the honest person to attempt a justification, such as, *"Everyone does it,"* or *"The company should treat people better if they don't want them to steal."* The honest person, on the other hand, is much more likely to say, *"There is no justification for stealing from the company. It is dishonest."*

EXAMPLE

Interviewer:

"How do you think we should deal with someone who got in a bind and did something wrong in the eyes of the company?"

EXPLANATION

Similar to other questions in this series, the honest person wants to "throw the book" at the miscreant; the culpable individual typically will say,

"How should I know? It's not up to me," or, *"If they were a good employee, maybe we should give them another chance."*

EXAMPLE

Interviewer:

"Do you think someone in your department might have taken something from the company because they thought they were justified?"

EXPLANATION

Most people—honest or dishonest—will answer "no" to this question. However, the culpable person more likely will say "yes" without elaborating. The honest person, if answering "yes," will most likely provide details.

EXAMPLE

Interviewer:

"Have you ever felt yourself—even though you didn't go through with it—justified in taking advantage of your position?"

EXPLANATION

Again, most people, both honest and dishonest, will answer this question "no." However, the dishonest person is more likely to acknowledge having at least "thought" of doing it.

EXAMPLE

Interviewer:

"Who in your department do you feel would think they were justified in doing something against the company?"

EXPLANATION

The dishonest person will not likely furnish an answer to this question, saying instead that, *"I guess anyone could have a justification if they wanted to."* The honest individual, on the other hand, is more likely to name names—albeit reluctantly.

EXAMPLE

Interviewer:

"Do you believe that most people will tell their manager if they believed a colleague was doing something wrong, like committing fraud against the company?"

EXPLANATION

The honest person has more of a sense of integrity, and is much more likely to report a misdeed. The dishonest person, on the other hand, is more likely to say "no." When pressed for an explanation, this person typically will say, *"No, nothing would be done about it, and they wouldn't believe me anyhow."*

EXAMPLE

Interviewer:

"Is there any reason why someone who works with you would say they thought you might feel justified in doing something wrong?"

EXPLANATION

This is a hypothetical question designed to place the thought in the mind of a wrongdoer that someone has named him as a suspect. The honest person typically will say "no." The dishonest person is more likely to try to explain by saying something like, *"I know there are people around here that don't like me."*

EXAMPLE

Interviewer:

"What would concern you most if you did something wrong and it was found out?"

EXPLANATION

The dishonest person is likely to say something like, *"I wouldn't want to go to jail."* The honest person, on the other hand, might reject the notion by saying, *"I'm not concerned at all, because I haven't done anything."* If the honest person does explain, it usually will be along the lines of disappointing friends or family; the dishonest person is more likely to mention punitive measures.

TYPICAL ATTITUDES DISPLAYED BY RESPONDENTS	
Truthful	**Untruthful**
Calm	Impatient
Relaxed	Tense
Cooperative	Defensive
Concerned	Outwardly unconcerned
Sincere	Overly friendly, polite
Inflexible	Defeated
Cordial	Surly

Closing Questions

Closing the interview on a positive note is a must in informational interviews. The closing serves several purposes. First, it is not unusual for the interviewer to have misunderstood or misinterpreted statements of the respondent. Therefore, the interviewer should go over key facts to make certain they have been comprehended. The closing questions phase also seeks to obtain facts previously unknown. It provides the respondent further opportunity to say whatever they want about the matter at hand.

If appropriate, the interviewer can ask if there are other documents or witnesses that would be helpful to the case. Do not promise confidentiality; instead, say, *"I'll keep your name as quiet as possible."* Finally, the interviewer wants to leave the discussion on a positive note.

People being interviewed often do not volunteer additional information regarding other witnesses or evidence. The theme, therefore, is to provide the respondent an opportunity to furnish further relevant facts or opinions. At the conclusion, attempt to determine which facts provided by the respondent are the most relevant. Do not attempt to go over all the information a second time.

EXAMPLE

Interviewer:
"Ms. De La Garza, I want to make sure I have my information straight. Let me take a minute and summarize what we've discussed."

Go over each of the key facts in summary form. The questions should be closed, so that the witness can respond either "yes" or "no."

EXAMPLE

Interviewer:
"You have known Linda Reed Collins eight years, correct?"

"You knew Collins had some financial problems, is that right?"

"You suspected—but didn't know for sure—that Collins might have had an improper relationship with one of our vendors. Is that correct?"

On absolutely vital facts provided by the respondent, add *"Are you sure?"*

EXAMPLE

Interviewer:
"Ms. De La Garza, are you sure you suspected Ms. Collins falsified invoices?"

To obtain additional facts, ask the respondent if there is something else they would like to say. This gives the correct impression that the interviewer is interested in all relevant information, regardless of which side it favors. Try to actively involve the respondent in helping solve the case—"*If you were trying to resolve this issue, what would you do?*"

EXAMPLE

Interviewer:

"*Ms. De La Garza, there might be someone else I should talk to. Are there documents available that relate to this that we haven't already discussed? If I keep your name as quiet as possible, are there any suggestions you can give me about who else I might talk to about this?*"

OR

"*Are there any other documents or evidence I might look for?*"

OR

"*If you were in my shoes, what would you do next?*"

Ask respondents if they have been treated fairly. It is especially helpful to ask this when the respondent has not been cooperative, or at the conclusion of an admission-seeking interview. The interviewer generally should ask the question as if it were perfunctory.

EXAMPLE

Interviewer:

"*Ms. De La Garza, this is just a standard question. Do you feel that I have treated you fairly in this interview?*"

Ask if the respondent has anything else to say. This gives the respondent one final time to make any statement. Also ask if the interviewer can call with any additional questions. It leaves the door open to additional cooperation.

Leave the respondent a business card or a telephone number. Invite the respondent to call about anything else relevant. In some cases, the interviewer should attempt to obtain a commitment that the respondent will not discuss the matter. This step is not recommended with adverse or hostile respondents.

EXAMPLE

Interviewer:

"In these kinds of situations, innocent people can have their reputation hurt because of rumor and innuendo. We don't want that to happen and neither do you. Therefore, I'd like your cooperation. Can I count on you not to discuss this until all the facts are out?"

Shake hands with respondents, and thank them for their time and information.

EXAMPLE

Interviewer:

"Ms. De La Garza, I know you have given your time and effort to help me. I appreciate it. Good-bye."

Admission-Seeking Questions

The interviewer should ask accusatory or admission-seeking questions only when there is a reasonable probability that the respondent has committed the act in question. An assessment of culpability might be based on verbal and nonverbal responses to interview questions, as well as documents, physical evidence, and other interviews.

A transitional theme is necessary when proceeding from assessment-seeking questions to admission-seeking questions. Part of the purpose of this theme is to create in the mind of the miscreant that he has been caught. Under the ideal circumstance, the interviewer will leave the room for just a few minutes, saying this is to "check on something." If the interviewer has incriminating documents, copies can be placed inside a file folder and brought back to the interview. If no documents exist, it might be appropriate to fill a file folder with blank paper.

EXAMPLE

When the interviewer returns to the room, the file folder is placed on the desk, and the interviewer asks, "Is there something that you would like to tell me about_____?"

OR

"Is there any reason why someone would say that you _____?"

Hand the documents to the respondent and ask for "comments." Do not introduce the evidence or explain it. In about 20 percent of the cases, the miscreant will admit to incriminating conduct. If not, proceed. Once the interviewer is reasonably convinced of guilt, it might be appropriate to confront the respondent. Admission-seeking questions have at least three purposes.

Purpose of Questions

The first purpose of admission-seeking questions is to distinguish innocent people from guilty. A culpable individual frequently will confess during the admission-seeking phase of an interview, while an innocent person will not do so unless threats or coercion are used. In some instances, the only way to differentiate the culpable from the innocent is to seek an admission of guilt.

The second purpose is to obtain a valid confession. Confessions, under the law, must be voluntarily obtained. The importance of a valid and binding confession to wrongdoing cannot be overstated. Finally, the confessor should be asked to sign a written statement acknowledging the facts. Although oral confessions are legally as binding as written ones, the written statement has greater credibility. It also discourages miscreants from later attempting to recant.

Preparation

The interview should be scheduled when the interviewer can control the situation. It normally should not be conducted on the accused's turf, and is best conducted by surprise.

Interview Room

The location should establish a sense of privacy. The door should be closed but not locked, and there should be no physical barriers preventing the target from leaving. This is to avoid allegations of "custodial interrogation."

Distractions should be kept to a minimum. Ideally, there should be no photographs, windows, or other objects in the room. Chairs should be placed about six feet apart, and the accused should not be permitted to sit behind a desk. This is to prohibit a psychological barrier for the accused to "hide behind." Notes, if taken during the interview, should be done in a way that does not reveal their significance.

Presence of Outsiders

It is usually not necessary to inform the subject that he should have counsel present. Of course, this right cannot be denied if the subject wishes to have an attorney present. If counsel is present, you should have an understanding that he will be an observer only; attorneys should not ask questions or object. Other than the subject and two examiners, no other observers usually should be permitted in the admission-seeking interview. If the accused is in a union, a union representative (or a union attorney) might have the right to attend. However, this might present legal problems in "broadcasting" the allegation to a third-party. It is very difficult to obtain a confession with witnesses present. The examiner should therefore consider whether the case can be proven without the admission-seeking interview. (Please refer to the Law Section of the *Manual* for more information.)

Miranda Warnings

As a general rule, private employees conducting an internal investigation are not required to give Miranda warnings; however, there are exceptions to the rule. (See the "Individual Rights" section for more information.)

Theme Development

People rarely confess voluntarily. People will confess to matters when they perceive that the benefits of confession outweigh the penalties. A good interviewer, through the application of sophisticated techniques, will be able to convince the respondent that the confession is in his best interest.

People generally will not confess if they believe that there is doubt in the mind of the accuser as to their guilt. The interviewer must convey absolute confidence in the admission-seeking—even if not fully convinced. The interviewer must make the accusation in the form of a statement of fact. Accusatory questions do not ask:

"Did you do it?"

They ask:

"Why did you do it?"

An innocent person generally will not accept the question's premise. People confessing need adequate time to come to terms with their guilt; obtaining admissions and confessions takes patience. Therefore, admission-seeking interviews should be done only when there is sufficient privacy and time is not a factor. The interviewer must not express disgust, outrage, or moral condemnation about the confessor's actions. To do so goes against the basic logic of obtaining confessions, which can be summed up as *maximize sympathy and minimize the perception of moral wrongdoing.*

The interviewer must offer a morally acceptable reason for the confessor's behavior. The interviewer cannot convey to the accused that he is a "bad person." Guilty people will almost never confess under such conditions. The interviewer must be firm, but must project compassion, understanding, and sympathy to obtain a confession. The interviewer must attempt to keep the confessor from voicing a denial. Once the accused denies the act, overcoming that position will be very difficult.

It is generally legal to accuse innocent people of misdeeds they did not commit as long as the:

- Accuser has reasonable suspicion or predication to believe the accused has committed an offense.
- Accusation is made under conditions of privacy.
- Accuser does not take any action likely to make an innocent person confess.
- Accusation is conducted under reasonable conditions.

Steps in the Admission-Seeking Interview
Direct Accusation

The accusation should not be made in the form of a question, but a statement. Emotive words such as "steal," "fraud," and "crime" should be avoided during the accusatory process. The accusation should be phrased so that the accused is psychologically "trapped," with no way out.

EXAMPLE

WRONG:

"We have reason to believe that you ..."

OR

"We think (suspect) you might have ..."

RIGHT:

"Our investigation has clearly established that you:
- *made a false entry (avoid "fraud")*
- *took company assets without permission (avoid using "theft," "embezzlement," or "stealing")*
- *took money from a vendor (avoid "bribe" or "kickback")*

* *have not told the complete truth (avoid "lie" or "fraud")*

OR

"We have been conducting an investigation into _____, and you are clearly the only person we have not been able to eliminate as being responsible."

Observe Reaction

When accused of wrongdoing, the typical guilty person will react with silence. If the accused does deny culpability, those denials usually will be weak. In some cases, the accused will almost mumble the denial. It is common for the culpable individual to avoid outright denials. Rather, that person will give reasons why he could not have committed the act in question. The innocent person sometimes will react with genuine shock at being accused. It is not at all unusual for an innocent person, wrongfully accused, to react with anger. As opposed to the guilty person, the innocent person will strongly deny carrying out the act or acts in question.

Repeat Accusation

If the accused does not strenuously object after the accusation is made, it should be repeated with the same degree of conviction and strength.

EXAMPLE

Interviewer:

"As I said, Linda, our examination has concluded that you are the responsible person. It is not so much a question of what you did, but why you did it."

Interrupt Denials

Both the truthful and untruthful person normally will object to the accusation and attempt denial. It is very important in instances where the examiner is convinced of the individual's guilt that the denial be interrupted. An innocent person is unlikely to allow the interviewer to prevail in stopping the denial.

It becomes extremely difficult for the accused to change a denial once it is uttered. If the person denies the accusation and later admits it, he is admitting to lying. This is very hard to do; the interviewer's job is to make this task easier. Several techniques can stop or interrupt denials. A guilty person more than an innocent one is likely to stop short of an outright denial ("I didn't do it."), and more apt to furnish the interviewer with explanations as to why he is not the responsible party.

EXAMPLE

Respondent:

"I wasn't even there the day that entry was made."

OR

"It could have been anybody."

OR

"I don't know what you're talking about."

It is important to emphasize that both the innocent and culpable will make an outright denial if forced to do so. Accordingly, the interviewer should not solicit a denial at this stage of the admission-seeking interview.

EXAMPLE

WRONG

Interviewer:

"Did you do this?"

OR

"Are you the responsible person?"

RIGHT

Interviewer:

"Why did you do this?"

Delays

One of the most effective techniques to stop or interrupt the denial is through a delaying tactic. The interviewer should not argue with the accused, but rather attempt to delay the outright denial.

EXAMPLE

Interviewer:

"Linda, I hear what you are saying, but let me finish first. Then you can talk."

The innocent person usually will not "hold on" or let the interviewer continue to develop the theme.

Interruptions

Occasionally, it might be necessary to interrupt the accused's attempted denial repeatedly. Because this stage is crucial, the interviewer should be prepared to increase the tone of the interruptions to the point when he is prepared to say: *"Linda, if you keep interrupting, I am going to have to terminate this conversation."* The guilty individual will find this threatening, since he wants to know the extent of incriminating evidence in the interviewer's possession.

Reasoning

If the above techniques are unsuccessful, the interviewer might attempt to reason with the accused, and employ some of the tactics normally used for diffusing alibis (see below). The accused is presented with evidence implicating him. The interviewer normally should not disclose all the facts of the case, but rather small portions here and there.

EXAMPLE

Interviewer:

"I know what you say, Linda, but that doesn't square with these invoices here in front of me. Look at the invoice in the amount of $102,136. The facts clearly show you are responsible."
(Do not ask the accused to explain the evidence at this point.)

OR

"Linda, I have talked to many people before I sat down here with you. I am not asking you if you're responsible; I know you are. This is your opportunity to tell your side to someone who can understand." (Do not disclose the identity or number of the witnesses who have been interviewed.)

Establish Rationalization

Once the accusation has been made, repeated, and denials are stopped, it is time for the interviewer to establish a morally acceptable rationalization that will allow the accused to square the misdeed with his conscience. It is not necessary that this theme be related to the underlying causes of the misconduct. It is common and acceptable for the accused to explain away the moral consequences of the action by seizing onto any plausible explanation other than being a "bad person."

If the accused does not seem to relate to one theme, the interviewer should go on to another until one seems to fit. Thereafter, that theme should be developed fully. Note that the theme development explains away the moral—but not the legal—consequences of the misdeed. The interviewer is cautioned not to make any statements that would lead the accused to believe he will be excused from legal liability by cooperating.

The questions posed in the examples, rather than being confrontational, constantly seek agreement from the accused. The interviewer must strike a balance between being in control of the interview and still appearing compassionate and understanding. Again, no matter what conduct the accused has supposedly committed, the interviewer should not express shock, outrage, or condemnation.

Unfair Treatment

Probably the most common explanation for criminal activity in general, and internal fraud in particular, is in the accused's attempt to achieve equity. Studies have shown that counter-productive employee behavior—including stealing—is motivated primarily by job dissatisfaction. Employees and others feel that "striking back" is important to their self-esteem. The sensitive interviewer can capitalize on these feelings by suggesting to the accused that he is a victim.

EXAMPLE

Interviewer:

"Linda, I feel like I know what makes you tick. And I know it isn't like you to do something like this without a reason. You have worked hard here to get a good reputation. I don't think the company has paid you what you're really worth. And that's the way you feel too, isn't it?"

OR

"Linda, I've seen situations like this before. And I think the company brought this on themselves. If you had been fairly treated, this wouldn't have happened, don't you agree?"

Inadequate Recognition

Some employees might feel that their efforts have gone completely without notice by the company. As with similar themes, the interviewer should be empathetic.

EXAMPLE

Interviewer:

"Linda, I have found out a few things about you. It looks to me that you have given a lot more to this company than they have recognized. Isn't that right, Linda?"

Financial Problems

Internal criminals, especially executives and upper management, frequently engage in fraud to conceal their true financial condition—either personal or business. Here are examples of how to develop a theme involving financial problems as a motive. In the following example, E.J. is an executive of a company and is suspected of fraud.

EXAMPLE

Interviewer:

"E. J., I was astonished to find out some of your investments have taken such a beating. I don't know how you managed to keep everything afloat as well as you did. You just did this to stay alive financially, didn't you, E. J.?"

OR

"E.J., I have found out what you've been paid around here, and frankly I was surprised. I thought it might be a lot more. No wonder you had to get involved in this. You pretty much needed to do this to survive, didn't you?"

Aberration of Conduct

Many miscreants believe their conduct constitutes an aberration in their lives, and that it is not representative of their true character. The interviewer might establish this theme by the following examples:

EXAMPLE

Interviewer:

"Linda, I know this is totally out of character for you. I know that this would never have happened if something wasn't going on in your life. Isn't that right, Linda?"

OR

"E. J., you've worked hard all your life to get a good reputation. I feel you wouldn't normally have done something like this; it just doesn't fit unless you felt like you were forced into it. You felt forced to do this, didn't you, E.J.?"

Family Problems

Some people commit fraud because of family problems—financial woes caused by divorce, an unfaithful spouse, or demanding children. Men especially—who have been socially conditioned to tie their masculinity to earning power—might hold the notion that wealth connotes family respect. For their part, women have been found to commit white-collar crime in the name of their responsibility to the needs of their husbands and children. The skillful interviewer can convert this motive to his advantage by one of the following approaches:

EXAMPLE

Interviewer:

"Linda, I know you have had some family problems. I know your recent divorce has been difficult for you. And I know how it is when these problems occur. You would have never done this if it hadn't been for family problems, isn't that right, Linda?"

OR

"E.J., someone in your position and with your ethics just doesn't do things like this without a reason. And I think that reason has to do with trying to make the best possible life for your family. I know it would be difficult for me to admit to my family that we're not as well off as we were last year. And that's why you did this, isn't it, E.J.?"

Accuser's Actions

Don't disclose the accuser's identity if it is not already known. But in cases where the accuser's identity is known to the accused, it can be helpful to blame the accuser for the problem. The accuser can be a colleague, manager, auditor, fraud examiner, or any similar person. Or, the problem can be blamed on the company.

EXAMPLE

Interviewer:

"Linda, you know what these auditors are like. They are hired to turn over every stone. I wonder how they would look if we put them under a microscope? Compared to other things that are going on, what you've done isn't that bad. Right, Linda?"

OR

"E. J., I really blame a large part of this on the company. If some of the things that went on around this company were known, it would make what you've done seem pretty small in comparison, wouldn't it, E.J.?"

Stress, Drugs, and Alcohol

Employees sometimes will turn to drugs or alcohol to reduce stress. In some instances, the stress itself will lead to aberrant behavior in a few individuals. A rationalization established by the interviewer could be similar to the following:

EXAMPLE

Interviewer:

"Linda, I know what you've done isn't really you. Inside, you have been in a lot of turmoil. A lot of people drink too much when they have problems. I have been through periods like that myself. And when things build up inside, it sometimes makes all of us do something we shouldn't. That's what happened here, isn't it, Linda?"

OR

"E. J., you're one of the most respected men in this company. I know you have been under tremendous pressure to succeed. Too much pressure, really. There is only so much any of us can take. That's behind what has happened here, isn't it, E.J.?"

Revenge

Similar to other themes, revenge can be effectively developed as a motive. In this technique, the interviewer attempts to blame the offense on the accused's feeling that he must "get back" at someone or something.

EXAMPLE

Interviewer:

"Linda, what has happened is out of character for you. I think you were trying to get back at your supervisor for the time he passed you over for a raise. I would probably feel the same. That's what happened, isn't it, Linda?"

OR

"E. J., everyone around here knows that the board has not supported you in your efforts to turn around this company. I would understand if you said to yourself, 'I'll show them.' Is that what happened, E.J.?"

Depersonalizing the Victim

In cases involving employee theft, an effective technique is to depersonalize the victim. The accused is better able to cope with the moral dilemma of his actions if the victim is a faceless corporation or agency.

EXAMPLE

Interviewer:

"Linda, it isn't like you took something from a friend or neighbor. I can see how you could say, 'Well, this would be okay to do as long as it was against the company, and not my co-workers.' Is that right, Linda?"

OR

"E.J., it's not like what you've done has really hurt one person. Maybe you thought of it this way: 'At most, I've cost each shareholder a few cents.' Is that the way it was, E.J.?"

Minor Moral Infraction

The interviewer in many cases can reduce the accused's perception of the moral seriousness of the matter. This is not to be confused with the legal seriousness. Fraud examiners and interviewers should be careful to avoid making statements that could be construed as relieving legal responsibility. For example, the examiner should not state: *"It is not a big deal, legally. It's just a technical violation."* Instead, the interviewer should play down the moral side. One effective way is through comparisons, such as those illustrated below:

EXAMPLE

Interviewer:

"Linda, this problem we have doesn't mean you're 'Jack the Ripper.' When you compare what you've done to things other people do, this situation seems pretty insignificant, doesn't it?"

OR

"E.J., everything is relative. What you've done doesn't even come close to some of the other things that have happened. You're not Ivan Boesky, right E.J.?"

OR

"I could see myself in your place. I probably would have done the same thing, wouldn't I?"

Altruism

In many cases, the moral seriousness of the matter can be reduced by claiming the action was for the benefit of others. This especially is true if the accused views himself as a caring person.

EXAMPLE

Interviewer:

"Linda, I know you didn't do this for yourself. I have looked into this matter carefully, and I think you did this to help your husband, didn't you?"

OR

"E.J., you have a big responsibility in this company. A lot of people depend on you for their jobs. I just know you did this because you thought you were doing the right thing for the company, didn't you?"

Genuine Need

In a very small number of cases, fraud is predicated by genuine need. For example, the accused might be paying for the medical care of sick parents or a child. Or some other financial disaster might have befallen the miscreant. In those cases, the following techniques might be effective:

EXAMPLE

Interviewer:

"Linda, I don't know many people who have had so many bad things happen all at once. I can see where you thought this was pretty much a matter of life or death, right, Linda?"

OR

"E.J., you're like everyone else: you have to put food on the table. But in your position, it is very difficult to ask for help. You genuinely needed to do this to survive, didn't you, E.J.?"

Diffuse Alibis

Even if the accused is presented with an appropriate rationalization, it is likely that he will continue to want to deny culpability. When the interviewer is successful in stopping denials, the accused normally will then turn to various reasons why he could not have committed the act in question. The purpose of this stage is to convince the accused of the weight of the evidence against him. Miscreants usually have a keen interest in material that tends to implicate them. Alibis generally can be diffused using one of the methods listed below.

Display Physical Evidence

It is common for most guilty people to overestimate the amount of physical evidence. The interviewer wants to try and reinforce this notion in the way the evidence is laid out to the accused. The physical evidence—usually documents in fraud matters—generally should be displayed one piece at a time, in reverse order of importance. In this way, the full extent of the evidence is not immediately known by the accused. When the accused no longer denies culpability, the interviewer should stop displaying evidence.

Each time a document or piece of evidence is laid out to the accused, its significance should be noted by the interviewer. During this phase, the accused is still trying to come to grips with being caught. The interviewer should, therefore, expect that the accused will attempt to lie his way out of the situation. Like denials, the interviewer should stop the alibis and other falsehoods before they are fully articulated.

Once the alibis are diffused, the interviewer should return to the theme being developed. Following is an example of this technique where Linda Reed Collins set up a fictitious company and embezzled money by approving payments from her employer to a shell corporation.

EXAMPLE

Respondent:

"I couldn't have done this. I am not responsible for paying invoices."

Interviewer:

"Here is one of the invoices in question (display document). We have never received the merchandise." (Don't mention whether or not you have talked to the accounts payable department or whether you have subjected the invoice to any document analysis.)

"Look, Linda, it is useless for you to try to deny the truth. We have lots of evidence. Let's just try to work this out, but you've got to help me, O.K.?" (Don't accuse the person of lying—this just prolongs the process.)

Discuss Witnesses

Another technique for diffusing alibis is to discuss the testimony of witnesses. The objective is to give enough information about what other people would say without providing too much. Ideally, the interviewer's statement will create the impression in the mind of the accused that many people are in a position to contradict his story.

The interviewer is again cautioned about furnishing enough information to the accused so that he can identify the witnesses. This might place the witness in a difficult position, and the accused could contact the witness in an effort to influence testimony. The accused could take reprisals against potential witnesses, though this is rare.

EXAMPLE

Respondent:

"I couldn't possibly have done this. It would require the approval of a supervisor."

Interviewer:

"In normal situations it would. The problem is that your statement doesn't hold up. There are several people who will tell a completely different story. I can understand how you would want me to believe that. But you're only worsening the situation by making these statements. If you will help me on this, you'll also be helping yourself. Understand?"

Discuss Deceptions

The final technique is to discuss the accused's deceptions. The purpose is to appeal to the accused's logic, not to scold or degrade. This technique is sometimes the only one available if physical evidence is lacking. As with other interview situations, the word "lying" should be avoided.

EXAMPLE

Respondent:

"There is no way I could have done this. I didn't have the opportunity."

Interviewer:

"Linda, here is the situation: you know what you've done, and so do I. I can understand it is difficult for you to admit. But if all the facts have to be presented, everyone will reach the same inescapable conclusion: you are responsible. If you continue to deny what you've done, you'll just make the situation worse. You understand that, don't you?"

Present Alternative

After the accused's alibis have been diffused, he normally will become quiet and withdrawn. Some people in this situation might cry. (If so, be comforting. Do not discourage the accused from showing emotion.) In this stage the accused is deliberating whether or not to confess. The interviewer at this point should present an alternative question to the accused. The alternative question forces the accused to make one of two choices. One alternative allows the accused a morally acceptable reason for the misdeed; the other paints the accused in a negative light. Regardless of which answer the accused chooses, he is acknowledging guilt.

EXAMPLE

Interviewer:

"Linda, did you plan this deliberately, or did it just happen?"

OR

"Linda, did you just want extra money, or did you do this because you had financial problems?"

OR

"Linda, did you just get greedy, or did you do this because of the way the company has treated you?"

Benchmark Admission

Either way the accused answers the alternative question—either yes or no—he has made a culpable statement, or *benchmark admission*. Once the benchmark admission is made, the miscreant has made a subconscious decision to confess. The questions above are structured so that the negative alternative is presented first, followed by the positive alternative. In this way, the accused only has to nod or say "yes" for the benchmark admission to be made. The accused also commonly will answer in the negative.

EXAMPLE

Respondent:

"I didn't do it deliberately."

OR

"I didn't do it just because I wanted extra money."

OR

"No, I'm not just greedy."

In the cases where the accused answers the alternative question in the negative, the interviewer should press further for a positive admission.

EXAMPLE

Interviewer:

"Then it just happened on the spur of the moment?"

OR

"Then you did it to take care of your financial problems?"

OR

"Then you did it because of the way you've been treated here?"

Should the accused still not respond to the alternative question with the benchmark admission, the interviewer should repeat the questions or variations thereof until the benchmark admission is made. It is important for the interviewer to get a response which is tantamount to a commitment to confess. Because only a commitment is sought at this point, the questions for the benchmark admission should be constructed as leading questions, so they can be answered "yes" or "no," rather than requiring any sort of explanation. That will come later.

Reinforce Rationalization

Once the benchmark admission is made, the interviewer should reinforce the confessor's decision. Then the interviewer should make the transition into the verbal confession, where the details of the offense are obtained. Reinforcing the rationalization developed earlier will help the confessor feel comfortable, believing that the interviewer does not look down on him.

EXAMPLE

Interviewer:

"Linda, I am glad to hear that you had a good reason to do this. That reinforces what I thought all along—that you were caught up in extraordinary circumstances. When was the first time you did it?"

Verbal Confession

The transition to the verbal confession is made when the accused furnishes the first detailed information about the offense. Thereafter, it is the interviewer's job to probe gently for additional details—preferably including those that would be known only to the miscreant. As with any interview, there are three general approaches to obtaining the verbal confession: chronologically, by transaction, or by event. The approach to be taken should be governed by the circumstances of the case.

During the admission-seeking interview, it is best to first confirm the general details of the offense. For example, the interviewer will want the accused's estimates of the amounts involved, other parties to the offense, and the location of physical evidence. After these basic facts are confirmed, the interviewer can then return to the specifics, in chronological order. It is imperative that the interviewer obtain an early admission that the accused knew the conduct in question was wrong. This confirms the essential element of intent.

Because of the nature of the psychology of confessions, most confessors will lie about one or more aspects of the offense, even though confirming overall guilt. When this happens during the verbal confession, the interviewer should make a mental note of the discrepancy and proceed as if the falsehood had been accepted as truthful.

Such discrepancies should be saved until all other relevant facts are provided by the accused. If the discrepancies are material to the offense, then the interviewer should either resolve them at the end of the verbal confession or wait and correct them in the written confession. If not material, such information can be omitted altogether from the written confession. The following items of information should be obtained during the verbal confession:

THE ACCUSED KNEW THE CONDUCT WAS WRONG

Intent is required in all matters involving fraud. Not only must the confessor have committed the act, he must have intended to commit it. This information can be developed as illustrated in this example.

EXAMPLE

Interviewer:

"Linda, now that you have decided to help yourself, I can help you, too. I need to ask you some questions to get this cleared up. As I understand it, you did this, and you knew it was wrong, but you didn't really mean to hurt the company, is that right?"

(Note that the question is phrased so that the confessor acknowledges intent, but "didn't mean to hurt" anyone. Make sure the question is not phrased so that the confessor falsely says that he "didn't mean to do it.")

FACTS KNOWN ONLY TO CONFESSOR

Once the intent question is solved, the questioning turns to those facts known only to the confessor. These facts include—at a minimum—the accused's estimates of the number of instances of wrongful conduct as well as the total amount of money involved. The questions should not be phrased so that the confessor can answer "yes" or "no."

ESTIMATE OF NUMBER OF INSTANCES/AMOUNTS

In fraud matters especially, it is common for the accused to underestimate the amount of funds involved as well as the number of instances. This is probably because of a natural tendency of the human mind to block out unpleasant matters. Take the figures with a grain of salt. If the accused's response is "I don't know," start high with the amounts and gradually come down.

EXAMPLE

Interviewer:

"Linda, how many times do you think this happened?"

Respondent:

"I don't have any idea."

Interviewer:

"Was it as many as 100 times?"

Respondent:

"No way!"

Interviewer:

"How about 75 times?"

Respondent:

"That's still too high. Probably not more than two or three times."

Interviewer:

"Are you pretty sure, Linda?" (If the accused's estimates are too low, gently get her to acknowledge a higher figure. But do not challenge the accused by calling her a liar.)

Respondent:

"Maybe three times, but certainly not more than that."

Motive for Offense

Motive is an important element of establishing the offense. The motive might be the same as the theme the interviewer developed earlier—or it might not. The most common response is "*I don't know.*" The interviewer should probe for additional information, but if it is not forthcoming, then attribute the motive to the theme developed earlier. The motive should be established along the lines below.

EXAMPLE

Interviewer:

"*Linda, we have discussed what might have led you to do this. But I need to hear it in your words. Why do you think you did this?*"

WHEN OFFENSE COMMENCED

The interviewer will want to know the approximate date and time that the offense started. This usually is developed by a question similar to the following:

EXAMPLE

Interviewer:

"*Linda, I am sure you remember the first time this happened.*"

Respondent:

"*Yes.*"

Interviewer:

"*Tell me about it.*"

Respondent:

"*Around the middle of January of last year.*"

Interviewer:

"*Linda, I admire you for having the courage to talk about this. You're doing the right thing. Tell me in detail about the first time.*"

WHEN/IF OFFENSE WAS TERMINATED

In fraud matters, especially internal fraud, the offenses usually are continuous. That is, the miscreant seldom stops before he is discovered. If appropriate, the interviewer should seek the date the offense terminated. The question typically is phrased as follows:

EXAMPLE

Interviewer:

"Linda, when was the last time you did this?"

Others Involved

Most frauds are solo ventures—committed without the aid of an accomplice. Rather than ask if anyone else was "involved," phrase the question something like this:

EXAMPLE

Interviewer:

"Linda, who else knew about this besides you?"

By asking who else "knew," the interviewer is in effect not only asking for the names of possible conspirators, but also about others who might have known what was going on but failed to report it. This question should be leading, not *"did someone else know?"* but rather *"who else knew?"*

Physical Evidence

Physical evidence—regardless of how limited it might be—should be obtained from the confessor. In many instances, illicit income from fraud is deposited directly in the bank accounts of the perpetrator. The interviewer typically will want to ask the confessor to surrender his banking records voluntarily for review. It is recommended that: (1) either a separate written authorization or (2) language be added to the confession noting the voluntary surrender of banking information. The first method generally is preferable.

If there are other relevant records that can be obtained only with the confessor's consent, permission to review those should be sought during the oral confession. In some instances, it might be advisable to delay this step until the written confession is obtained. The request for physical evidence from the confessor can be set up like this:

EXAMPLE

Interviewer:

"*Linda, as a part of wrapping up the details, I will be needing your banking records (or other physical evidence). You understand that, don't you?*"

Respondent:

"*No, I don't.*"

Interviewer:

"*Well, I just need to document the facts and clear up any remaining questions. You have decided to tell the complete story, including your side of it. I just want to make sure the facts are accurate and fair to you. We want to make sure you're not blamed for something someone else did. And I want to report that you cooperated fully and wanted to do the right thing, okay?*" (Avoid the use of the word "evidence" or references to higher tribunals, e.g., "courts" or "prosecutors.")

Respondent:

"*Okay.*"

Interviewer:

"*Where do you keep your bank accounts?* (If the interviewer knows of at least one bank where the confessor does business, the question should be phrased: *Linda, where do you do business besides Florida Marine National Bank?*)"

Respondent:

"*Just Florida Marine.*"

Interviewer:

"*I'll need to get your okay to get them from the bank if we need them. Where do you keep the original records?*" (Do not ask the accused's permission to look at the records, rather tell her the records are needed. Let the accused object if she has a problem with it.)

DISPOSITION OF PROCEEDS

If it has not come out earlier, the interviewer should find out in general what happened to any illicit income derived from the misdeeds. It is typical for the money to have been used for frivolous or ostentatious purposes. It is important, however, that the confessor sees his actions in a more positive light; the interviewer should avoid comments or questions relating to "high living."

EXAMPLE

Interviewer:

"*Linda, what happened to the money?*" (Let the accused explain; do not suggest an answer unless the confessor does not respond.)

LOCATION OF ASSETS

In appropriate situations, the interviewer will want to find out if there are residual assets that the confessor can use to reduce losses. Rather than ask the accused "*is there anything left?*" the question should be phrased as "*what's left?*"

EXAMPLE

Interviewer:

"*Linda, what do you have left from all of this?*"

Respondent:

"*Not much. I used most of the money to cover my husband's bills and financial problems. A little money and a boat that is paid for is all I have.*"

Interviewer:

"*Well, whatever it is, this whole thing will look a lot better if you volunteered to return what you could, don't you agree?*" (Remember do not specifically promise the confessor leniency; it typically will invalidate the confession.)

Specifics of Each Offense

Once the major hurdles are overcome, the interviewer should then return to the specifics of each offense. Generally, this should simply start with the first instance and work through chronologically in a logical fashion.

Because these questions are information-seeking, they should be open phrased so that the answer is independent of the question. It is best to seek the independent recollections of the confessor first before displaying physical evidence. If the confessor cannot independently recall, documents can be used to refresh his recollection. It generally is best to resolve all issues on each instance before proceeding to the next. In determining the specifics of the offense, the interviewer usually should ask:

- Who has knowledge of this transaction?
- What does this document mean?
- When did this transaction occur?
- Where did the proceeds of the transaction go?
- Why was the transaction done?
- How was the transaction covered up?

Interviewing is a difficult act, seldom mastered without considerable practice. The preceding techniques, when properly employed, can immeasurably aid in developing truthful, reliable, and legally valid information.

Kinesic Interview and Interrogation

The kinesic interview or interrogation is a method that has become more popular among the law enforcement community in recent years. This type of interview is different than traditional interview methods, because the interviewer is not necessarily looking for a confession from the interview subject. Instead of searching for information from the subject, the interviewer is attempting to assess whether the subject is telling the truth.

In the book *The Kinesic Interview Technique*, authors Frederick C. Link and D. Glen Foster define the kinesic interview technique as:

"[An interview technique] used for gaining information from an individual who is not willingly or intentionally disclosing it."

Link and Foster believe that the kinesic interview technique is based entirely on the concept of stress — an event or circumstance that forces an individual's mind or body out of psychological equilibrium. When stress occurs, humans, as any other living creature, have an emotional reaction. Link and Foster refer to this as the "fight or flight syndrome," in which we either run from a stressful situation or brace to face it. Either way, they hypothesize, our animalistic tendencies dictate that we must react to stress. When this concept is applied to the interview situation, the kinesic interview technique is applied to attempt to read the interview subject's reaction to stress.

This method relies, in a broad sense, on the interviewer's ability to observe the interview subject for signs or symptoms of deceit. The kinesic interview is conducted not just to observe what the subject says, but also how the subject says it; the subject's gestures, posturing, facial expressions, and voice inflection are just a few of the traits that an investigator looks at. This style of interviewing assumes that when most human beings lie or are deceitful to others, they will reveal this deceit through their "body language."

These reactions are generally subconscious; in most cases, the interviewee does not even realize that he or she is acting noticeably different. The actions or signs that an interviewer is looking for are called *meaningful behavior*- activities that may suggest that an interviewee is under stress.

Link and Foster identify three distinct categories into which meaningful behavior can be divided:
- Self-initiated verbal statements which the interviewee initiates without prompting.
- Prompted verbal responses or statements made by the interviewee in response to structured questions asked by the interviewer.
- Nonverbal behavior or body language which includes body positioning movements, lack of movement, and observable physiological changes.

Self-Initiated Verbal Statements

These responses from interviewees are made without any prompting by the interviewer. Examples of these statements include changes in speech pattern, overly respectful or friendly words directed at the interviewer, or indirect answers and statements. The subject's speech speed will tend to increase, or the subject will hesitate or stammer frequently before giving any responses. These verbal clues are a subconscious attempt by the interviewee to dodge the line of questioning or suppress the guilty feelings the subject feels.

Generally, a dishonest person is much more likely to give more self-initiated verbal signs than a person who is telling the truth.

Prompted Verbal Responses

Prompted verbal responses can be important tools for an interrogator to differentiate an honest person from a deceitful one. By utilizing a series of structured questions, we can generally get a very good indication of how truthful the subject is. These should be woven into a casual conversation so that the subject is not aware of the significance of the questions. The structured questions must not appear to be interrogational in manner.

Structured Questions

The fraud examiner has several loaded question types to utilize in the kinesic interview which may shed light on the guilt or innocence of the interview subject.

- Punishment Question- The interviewer will casually discuss the punishment of the crime's perpetrator with the subject, asking, for example, *"What do you think should happen to the criminal?"* When posed with this sort of question, generally the innocent person, having nothing invested in the crime, will answer that the criminal should be severely punished, saying something like, *"Lock him up and throw away the key."* The interview subject who is guilty of the crime, on the other hand, will generally answer that the criminal should be treated fairly, saying for example, *"The person who stole that money is very sick and probably needs mental help."* In essence, the guilty person is more likely to answer *"Don't hurt me."*

- Physical Evidence Question- This type of question is meant to jar the suspect into making a mistake. The interviewer will suggest that there is a piece of evidence that might link the interviewee to a crime, asking, *"Is there any reason that your fingerprints might have been found near the crime scene?"* This question does not assert that there is any evidence. The innocent person, knowing that he or she had nothing to do with the crime, will simply answer "No," unconcerned about the possible evidence. The guilty party will often become concerned with this possible evidence and attempt to cover for this evidence with another lie.

- Crime Existence Question- A variation on this question would be *"Do you think that this crime was even committed?"* To the guilty party, this question represents a possible way out, and that person is likely to say "no," while the innocent person will likely answer "yes."

Nonverbal Behavior/Body Language

The evaluation of an interview subject's body language can provide the fraud examiner with numerous insights into the subject's true intentions. Quite often, while an interviewee says one thing, his body language tells an entirely different story. The first step in this process is to evaluate the "normal" body language of the subject. While we will discuss some general tendencies which suggest that a subject is being less than truthful, the interviewer must first evaluate the subject's natural tendencies. Many people use their hands often when they speak, while others do not.

For most people, the head is the most expressive portion of the body. Several facial traits or expressions can be read by the interviewer, among them:

- Eyes- The single most important nonverbal sign that an interviewer must look for and recognize are breaks in eye contact by the subject. The subject might close his eyes, cover his eyes, or turn or lower his head. Any of these breaks in eye contact during the interview can suggest a subject's deceit.
- Eyebrow movement- When a subject display's disbelief or concern during an interview, it is often a false or deceptive reaction to the interviewer's questioning.
- Touching the face- Many subjects, when under stress, resort to repeatedly touching the tip of the nose or rubbing the chins. This is often a nervous reaction to a threatening situation.
- Blushing- A person whose face or cheeks become red is generally experiencing increased blood pressure, indicating pressure or stress.
- Adam's Apple- The subject's larynx will quite often move up and down when he is concerned or nervous.
- Carotid Arteries- Often the veins in a person's neck will become exposed when that person becomes nervous.

In addition, many interviewees will attempt to cover or defend themselves through body language by crossing their arms or their legs. This is generally a defensive posture.

Several factors should be considered when applying these techniques:

- No single behavior, by itself, proves anything.
- Behaviors must be relatively consistent when the stimuli are repeated.
- The interviewer must establish what is normal or "baseline" behavior for each subject and then look for changes from the baseline. These observed changes in the subject's baseline behavior are diagnosed in "clusters" and not individually.
- Behaviors must be timely.
- Observing and interpreting behaviors is hard work.
- The subjects are watching us while we are watching them.
- Kinesic interviewing is not as reliable with some groups as with the general population.

Criteria-Based Statement Analysis

When collecting witness accounts or interviews concerning a particular fraud case, fraud examiners must continually assess how honest the interviewee has been. Criteria-based statement analysis can be utilized as a tool to uncover just how truthful a subject has been after the interview is complete. This technique is different than a kinesic interview in that the fraud examiner is not analyzing the body language or nonverbal clues a subject has given, but instead the language used by the subject.

Statement analysis is based on the notion that when humans speak, whether intentionally or unconsciously, we specifically select the language we use. In general, the verbal clues that a subject offers while speaking are just as prominent as any nonverbal tip-offs. The tense that an interviewee uses is often the indication that the interviewee knows more than he or she is letting on.

For instance, in the Susan Smith case in 1996, Smith claimed that a carjacker forced her out of her car and took the car with her two children in the back seat. When the children's father spoke of the missing toddlers, he spoke of them in present tense; when Smith mentioned their names, investigators noticed that she continually referred to the boys in the past tense, indicating that she knew them to be deceased. Upon interrogation, Smith confessed to driving the car into a lake, killing her children.

Parts of Speech

The main items of interest to the fraud examiner during a statement analysis are the particular words that the subject utilizes. Breaking down the subject's sentences carefully may reveal many undetected tendencies of the subject's speech.

Pronouns

When describing an incident or situation, a truthful subject will most likely use the pronoun "I." If the subject is guilty of an offense or involved in some fashion, that person will attempt to distance himself from the situation by removing the "I" from his statement. Often, the "I" will be replaced by "we," as though the subject had little involvement in or was not responsible for the situation.

EXAMPLE

"I went to the grocery store with my girlfriend, but I didn't steal any of the items."

"We went to the grocery store, but we didn't steal anything."

The subject's reasoning, subconsciously, is to remove himself as far away from the situation as possible. By swapping "we" for "I" in the sentences, the perpetrator hopes to deflect attention or blame.

In a situation in which the subject uses "we" constantly, the subject is tipping the interviewer that the subject has some sort of relationship with another party in the situation. If, for example, the subject continually uses impersonal pronouns, such as "my girlfriend and I" rather than "we," this indicates a lack of personal involvement with the subject's girlfriend. Fraud examiners can utilize this pronoun use to determine whether the interviewee is involved in a fraudulent situation with other employees.

Possessive Pronouns

When an interviewee is giving bogus testimony concerning an event, he will often drop the possessive pronoun to shift the blame to an exterior force.

EXAMPLE

"I got on my register at 10:30. I was working at my register when I was called away by my supervisor. When I returned to the register, the register was open and the cash was gone."

In this statement, the subject referred to the register as "my register" up until the controversial act took place. At that point, "my register" becomes "the register," indicating that the subject no longer wants to be associated with a corrupted register. This pronoun switch indicates that the subject is being less than truthful.

Verbs

Verbs are very important pieces of the statement analysis puzzle, because the tense that is used by the interviewee will shed light on whether the incident has been recalled or improvised. Because the subject should be recalling events from the past, the verb tense used to recount the story should be past also.

EXAMPLE

"My wife and I left the house at 7:00, went to dinner and then saw a movie. We returned to the house after the movie was over."

However, the deceptive interviewee will often change the verb tense at precisely the moment at which he or she is no longer recalling, but rather improvising the event.

EXAMPLE

"My wife and I left the house at 7:00, went to dinner and then saw a movie. We return to the house and as we pull up to it, we see shattered glass on the driveway."

Verb tense is also crucial during questioning of a witness concerning the whereabouts of another person, such as in cases of possible kidnapping. If the person interviewed continually refers to the missing person in the past tense, there is a good chance that the missing person has been harmed. Again, the Susan Smith case is a textbook example of how verb tense usage can lead to a confession.

Balance of the Statement

When most interview subjects recount an event, the subject's version will be naturally balanced. The subject will spend a fairly equal amount of time telling what happened before the event, what took place during the event, and what happened during the aftermath. Fraud examiners should look at the sheer amount of time or number of sentences a subject spends on each topic in order to get a rough estimate of how balanced the account is. If any of the portions of the account are woefully short, the subject is almost certainly lying. By performing this type of analyzation, the fraud examiner can also determine what elements are absent from the story in a short amount of time.

In the book *Criteria-Based Statement Analysis*, German psychologists Max Stellar and Guenter Koehnken identify a number of separate criteria that the fraud examiner can take into consideration when attempting to analyze a just completed interview.

General Characteristics

- Logical Structure-The fraud examiner first examines the statement for "plot holes," checking to ensure that the recounting of events is chronologically correct and does not contain contradictions.
- Unstructured Production- The fraud examiner should examine this criterion at the beginning of the interview by allowing the subject to recount the event without influence or questioning. Generally, an honest person will not tell an interviewer exactly what has taken place in complete chronological order, from start to finish. It is much more likely that the initial recounting of events will be told in a scattershot fashion, but that these

facts and details will eventually mesh into a complete version. When an interview subject is able to sit down and initially describe the events that have taken place in complete detail, from beginning to end, it is likely that the story has been rehearsed.
- Quantity of Details- An honest subject is more likely to be able to recall many details within an interview than a dishonest subject. When most subjects fabricate a story, they are unable to bolster the story with very many details.

Specific Content

- Contextual Embedding- This criterion suggests that a truthful subject's statement will be tightly woven with incidental details, such as the subject's daily routine, habits, or family relationships. A deceptive subject is much less likely to associate an event with seemingly insignificant details such as these, choosing to focus only on covering up the major event that is being discussed.
- Descriptions of Interaction- The truthful subject is likely to have some description of the actions and emotions involved with the described incident or people involved in the incident.
- Reproduction of Conversation- Often, the witness will become animated with repeating any conversation that occurred during the particular incident. When this occurs, the subject is generally telling the truth, as it is difficult for a fraudster to create cohesive dialogue on the spot.
- Unexpected Complications During the Incident- Description of incidents which disrupt the event, such as a sudden halt or interruption of the event, indicate that the subject is speaking truthfully.

Peculiarities of Content

- Unusual Details- The appearance of quirky but believable details lends credibility to the subject. Fabricated statements rarely contain these types of descriptions.
- Superfluous Details- A subject who provides details that are not essential or even related to the recalled event are most often speaking truthfully. A deceitful subject is so preoccupied with not telling the truth that he or she will excise this type of information from the story.
- Accurately Reported Details Misunderstood- When a witness describes details that he or she does not understand or comprehend, but the details do make sense to the interviewer, the witness is most often telling the truth.
- Related External Associations- In this criterion, the interviewer looks for points at which the interview subject relates the particular experience with some personal or external

experiences. When the subject makes a relationship between the event and something that has previously occurred in his life, he is very likely being honest.

- Accounts of Subjective Mental State- The subject who fills the interview with descriptions of feelings and emotions throughout the event is very likely being truthful. When a subject cannot provide such feelings during the interview, this suggests that the subject has not thought through his deceptive story very thoroughly.

- Attribution of Perpetrator's Mental State- The honest subject will often recount the perceived mental state of the perpetrator, suggesting what they believe the perpetrator was thinking or feeling at the time of the event.

- Spontaneous Corrections- An interview subject may often correct himself during the course of the interview, making alterations to earlier details or events. When a subject does this, he or she is most often giving truthful testimony. The deceptive subject wants to project as honest a façade as possible and does not want to correct himself, because in the subject's mind this gives the appearance of deceit.

- Admitting Lack of Memory- This criterion works closely with the previous one, in that an honest interviewee will often admit to not remembering certain details. When the interviewee is lying to the interviewer, he or she wants to be as complete as possible in covering the fraudulent tracks.

- Raising Doubts about One's Own Testimony- A deceitful interviewee will almost never raise any concerns about whether the testimony given is absolutely correct. If the subject has concerns that he or she is correct, that subject is probably telling the truth.

- Self-Deprecation- The mention of any self-incriminating or personally unflattering details during the interview suggests that the interviewee is credible. A person who attempts to fabricate a story will not want to paint an unsavory picture of himself.

- Pardoning the Perpetrator- Should the interviewee attempt to excuse the perpetrator or avoid "bashing" the fraudster, the interviewee is likely being honest.

The Cognitive Interview Technique

Police and fraud investigators must often rely on the testimony of witnesses to bring the facts of a case together. The testimony of an important witness can determine the entire outcome of a fraud case, so it is essential that witness' words be as reliable and detailed as possible.

Unfortunately, witnesses are human, and humans are prone to make errors. Fraud investigators must understand that in a time of crisis, or even in a situation in which the witness was simply not paying close attention, the eyewitness can easily miss acute details.

Often witnesses have trouble recalling large portions of events simply because they didn't know at the time that they needed to be looking for specific details. Dr. R. Edward Geiselman and Dr. Ronald P. Fisher write in the National Institute of Justice article *Interviewing Victims and Witnesses of Crime* that "most victims and eyewitnesses…are so occupied with the event that they do not have the time to try to learn or memorize details about a suspect at the time of the crime."

Because of these problems, different techniques for filling out the witnesses' testimony have been developed to assist the investigator. One of the first techniques developed was the use of hypnosis on witnesses. The notion behind this strategy was that an investigator could open the mind of a witness and pick into his/her subconscious for specific details. The merits of this technique are highly debatable and have been hotly contested in courts of law.

But more recently, the cognitive interview technique was developed to serve much the same purpose. This approach has proven far more effective than questionable hypnosis techniques and has been deemed a reliable method in the court of law.

The cognitive interview technique was established, researched, and fine-tuned by Dr. Geiselman, a professor at the University of California, Los Angeles, and other colleagues in the psychiatric profession. Geiselman and others have written numerous articles and governmental documents detailing the extensive research dealing with the interviewing of witnesses.

Geiselman believes that the cognitive interview should be split into two distinct phases: the narrative phase and the specific detail phase. When these phases are used in succession during an interview, it is likely that an investigator will come away from an interview with an excellent witness account of an event. The narrative phase deals more with "what happened" during the event; the specific detail phase works more to track down who was involved with the event and nails down specific details about the suspect.

The Narrative Phase
The first portion of the cognitive interview is the narrative phase, in which the witness tells the "whole story." The investigator first should allow the witness to recount the situation, using several steps to guide the narrative portion. There are four primary steps in the narrative phase of the cognitive interview process:
- Reconstruct the circumstances of the event

- Instruct the eyewitness to report everything and be complete
- Recall the events in different orders
- Change perspectives

Reconstruct the Circumstances of the Event

Geiselman has described this first, important step as the portion of the interview in which the investigator should get the eyewitness to describe the surroundings in which the incident occurred. The investigator should ask the witness to describe everything from the weather, the time of day, and the look and feel of the environment in which the incident took place. What did the people and/or objects in the surroundings look like?

The objective of this step is to get the witness back into the situation, so that he/she will vividly recall the unfolding events. An excellent tool investigators can utilize to accomplish this first step is to ask the eyewitness to remember what sort of emotional state he/she was in at the time of the occurrence.

Instruct the Eyewitness to Report Everything and Be Complete

In this stage, the interviewer should ask the eyewitness to recount every last detail and inform the witness to be as complete as possible. Geiselman says that often a witness will withhold information that he/she is not certain will be relevant to the investigation. He suggests that the investigator instruct the witness not to omit anything when giving testimony to investigators, no matter how trivial the information might seem. The small details that the witness remembers during the interview may not be directly beneficial to the investigation, but they will be important to helping the witness remember the events descriptively and thoroughly.

Recall the Events in Different Orders

Geiselman believes that constructing the event in a different order will allow the witness the freedom to completely recreate the event. When recounting the event in sequential order, the witness may very well forget minute details in an effort to describe what happened next. Another suggestion Geiselman has for the interviewer is to ask the witness to construct the event from the single moment or thing that left the greatest impression on the witness. From there, the interviewer may gain a foothold on the perspective from which the witness experienced the event.

Change Perspective

The final step of the cognitive interview process is to get the witness to alter his/her perspective of the event. The investigator should ask the witness to reconstruct the scenario and assume a different position within the situation. For instance, Geiselman says that a good technique is to ask the witness to pretend to be a different person within the event, and recount the event from that perspective. What was the other person thinking or feeling? This technique may seem a bit odd, but it may allow the witness to consider various elements of the event that he previously had not.

Specific Items of Information

Once the narrative portion of the interview is completed, it is likely that the investigator will still have questions about specific items of information. Geiselman and his contemporaries have developed a system of five techniques to cultivate specific details and items of information from the witness. The five categories are:

- Physical appearance
- Names
- Numbers
- Speech characteristics
- Conversation

Physical Appearance

The investigator can often elicit additional information about the event by asking the witness to describe the suspect. A particularly effective technique is to ask the witness whether the suspect reminded the witness of anyone he/she knows. Often, physical descriptions such as the type of clothing that a suspect was wearing or the particular way a suspect walked or looked will not be presented during the narrative phase of the interview. This additional information, however, can be key to linking a suspect with a specific crime.

Names

Often, the names of the suspect or another person will be spoken during an event, but many times the event proves too traumatic or happens too quickly for a witness to recall. Geiselman says that when a witness does not first remember any names spoken during the event, the investigator may still be able to trigger the memory of the witness. Ask the witness to attempt to recall the first letter of the suspect's name (or any other names spoken) by going through the alphabet one letter at a time.

Number

Once the witness has possibly established the first letter of the suspect's name, the investigator should ask the witness how many syllables or letters were in the name. Establishing whether the name was long or short may effectively jar the witness' memory.

Speech Characteristics

The investigator can also ask the witness what types of speech characteristic the suspect has. Geiselman again suggests asking the witness whether the suspect's speech reminds the witness of anyone else. The interviewer should also determine whether the suspect had any specific accent, an awkward or unusual voice, or used any words repeatedly during the event.

Conversation

The witness should be asked whether anything that the suspect or anyone else said during the event elicited an unusual response. Did the suspect or any other witnesses react in a strange manner to anything that was said?

The extensive research that Dr. Geiselman and his colleagues have done on the cognitive interview technique has shown that the technique improves the recall performance of witnesses when compared to the standard interview techniques. The emphasis is on the witness' recollection of details to give investigators a more complete picture of what actually happened during a specific event.

COVERT EXAMINATIONS

A *covert operation* is designed to obtain evidence by use of agents whose true role is undisclosed to the target. There are two major forms of covert operations: *undercover operations* and *surveillance operations*.

Several distinctions define these types of covert operations. Undercover operations seek to develop evidence directly from people involved in the offense through the use of disguise and deceit. Rather than waiting for the information to come by other routes, there is a conscious decision to seek it out. In contrast, surveillance operations use the skills of observation to determine activity of individuals. The surveillance operation is designed to gather information.

Covert operations require the highest degree of skill and planning. Used in a timely manner with great care, a covert operation can produce results that cannot be achieved in any other way. Used incorrectly or handled badly, covert operations can lead to death, injury, serious financial liability, and embarrassment.

Disguise and deceit in undercover operations are well-recognized by the courts as a legitimate function of public and private law enforcement, provided the undercover operation is based on sufficient probable cause. Covert operations cannot be conducted as "fishing expeditions." Justification for conducting the operation must be legally sound and defensible and must not violate a person's reasonable expectation of privacy.

Prior to an undercover operation, it is essential that the basis for the operation be committed to writing, preferably in memo form (see Report Writing). The memorandum should clearly state:

- The information upon which the covert operation will be based,
- The information that is expected to be gained from the operation,
- The identities of suspects, if any, and
- Operatives under your care, custody, or control.

A fraud examiner is undercover when he officially abandons his identity as an examiner and adopts one designed to obtain information from people who do not realize his true identity. The assumed identity might involve only the adoption of another name or it might require an elaborate cover. The aim should be to avoid being compromised, to minimize danger to the fraud examiner, and to assure ultimate success of the operation.

Information sought might include the location of outlets for stolen goods, subject's methods of operation, detailed personal data on all subjects, and any other relevant information. Information should be developed with care to avoid alerting the targets or their associates. Only those people who need to know should be informed of the undercover investigation.

Establishing an Identity

A cover story must be fabricated to conceal the true identity of the fraud examiner. The story should help the examiner gain the subject's confidence but it should rarely, if ever, be wholly fictitious. The examiner should be from a city with which he is familiar, but not from the home city of the subject. Arrangements should be made to have key people in the fictitious history corroborate the undercover examiner's claims.

Particular attention should be paid to items carried by the undercover examiner such as pocketbooks, watches, rings, tokens, suitcases, ticket stubs, miscellaneous papers, matches, letters, and sums of money. Documents and identity cards should show the appropriate amount of wear and tear. The fraud examiner should be able to explain how each item came into his possession.

There should be a natural contact between the undercover examiner and the subject. The background story should contain elements that will bring the suspect and the examiner together without any contrived effort. A mutual interest in hobbies, sports, and other leisure activities can provide an opportunity for getting acquainted. The examiner should not pose as an authority on a subject unless totally qualified. Many times an examiner's admitted lack of knowledge—but an interest in—a given subject will help make the subject feel important and not threatened.

According to Timothy J. Walsh, the following situations are those in which covert operations have traditionally worked well:

- When there is reliable information about criminal activity or asset losses, but insufficient detail for prevention or apprehension.
- When losses are known to be occurring in an area, but there is no information as to how they are occurring or who is responsible.

- When it is desirable to gather information concerning personal relationships or to identify the contacts made with or by certain people.
- When it is desirable to compare actual practices with supposed or required practices.
- When it is important to obtain information in an indirect manner from people believed to possess it.

Covert operations should be used when there is no other practical way to obtain necessary information.

Objectives

According to Paul O'Connell in an article for *Security Management*[1], one of the first steps in initiating an undercover operation is to identify the objectives of the investigation. The objectives must specifically identify what the operation is designed to discover, such as the identity of the fraudulent worker responsible for a specific crime.

The specific objectives of a covert operation depend on the type of investigation being conducted. The objectives in a surveillance of a warehouse would not be the same as one designed to determine if Collins is receiving a kickback from Nagel. However, all covert operations have similar general objectives:

- *To obtain evidence of a past, current, or future crime.* This evidence usually bears on the culpability of individuals. If an operative in a covert investigation is posing as a thief, for example, actual thieves might confess their involvement to him, unaware that their conversations were being recorded.
- *To identify those engaged in possible illegal activity.* If, for example, cash is missing, a covert investigation or surveillance might disclose who is committing the offense. Thereafter, the covert operation might be discontinued, and the evidence gathered by more traditional means.
- *To recover illegal gains.* If an accounts payable clerk has been stealing to purchase an automobile, locating the car might permit civil litigation to recover it.
- *To identify co-conspirators.* If an employee is in collusion with another employee, a covert operation might lead to the identity of the second individual.
- *To identify the modus operandi.* Again, in the case of missing goods, the identity of the perpetrator might be known or suspected, but the internal control deficiencies

---

[1] O'Connell, E. Paul. "Is a Ruse the Best Route?" *Security Management*. December 1995, p. 26-30.

permitting the theft might be unknown. A covert operation might discover the missing link.

Problems in Covert Operations

In addition to the legal problems a fraud examiner might encounter, a covert operation is the most costly and risky work an examiner can undertake. Such operations consume great amounts of human resources. They should be used only with extreme care, and as a last resort. If the case can be made any other way, the fraud examiner should stay away from covert operations.

There are laws governing surreptitious audio and/or video recordings. In some jurisdictions, it is unlawful to make an audio recording or to listen in on a conversation unless you are a party to that conversation. In other jurisdictions, it is lawful to record any conversation as long as one party to the conversation consents.

Recording conversations with eavesdropping devices (supersensitive microphones that listen from behind closed doors, for example) usually is illegal. People behind closed doors have a reasonable expectation of privacy. Videotaping or photographing someone in a public place is legal, if the person does not have a "reasonable expectation" of privacy in such a place. For instance, a restroom or locker room might be a "public place," but people have a reasonable expectation of privacy that they will not be photographed. If operatives or witnesses are used to record telephone or other conversations, written consent should be obtained. Sample forms used for this purpose can be found in the chapter on Report Writing.

As just mentioned, it is generally not a crime to videotape a person in public if the tape is not to be used for commercial purposes (i.e., you will not be selling the tape). However, if any part of the person's conversation or words are picked up on videotape, then the taping is subject to all of the laws and rules regarding the recording of conversations (i.e., it's as if you were recording the person on the telephone; you may be prohibited from recording the conversation if you are not a party or you do not have the person's consent).

In summary, the laws governing audio and video recordings can be confusing and complex. Please refer to the Law Section and the "Individual Rights" chapter for more information, and be sure and contact a lawyer if you have any doubts.

Entrapment

Entrapment poses the biggest legal problem in covert operations, particularly in undercover operations. It is imperative that the operation be properly predicated. Again, covert operations must not be used for "fishing expeditions."

EXAMPLE

A store owner was concerned because his inventory costs were unusually high in relation to sales. He hired a private investigator who posed as a contract driver who picked up and delivered merchandise from and to the store. The investigator proceeded to offer kickbacks to all employees in the shipping department if they would allow him to leave without signing for the merchandise. One employee took the bait, and was subsequently arrested for theft. The case was thrown out because of entrapment. The courts ruled that there was no reason to believe, simply because of a high cost of sales, that merchandise was being stolen. Furthermore, the investigator had no suspect in mind; he was simply "fishing."

Surveillance

Surveillance is the planned observation of people, places, or objects. It is normally concerned with people. Places and objects observed usually are incidental to the primary interest of gathering information about certain people.

There are two general types of surveillance: mobile and fixed. Mobile surveillance sometimes is referred to as "tailing" or "shadowing," and fixed surveillance as a "stakeout" or "plant." Mobile surveillance can be done on foot or by vehicle and is carried out when people being observed move from location to location. A fixed surveillance is used when a person or activity remains in place, although the observers might move from one vantage point to another in the immediate area.

Surveillance, whether by foot or vehicle, is predominantly an exercise in common sense, skill, tact, and ingenuity on the part of the observer. Carefully planned and properly executed surveillance can be of tremendous value in an investigation; conversely, lack of preparation, poor timing, and unsound surveillance practices can destroy an otherwise good case.

Surveillance can be used to locate residences, businesses, or other places of interest to the investigation, and places where criminal activity is conducted. It also can produce important evidence concerning the scope and nature of a person's activities. Surveillance activities must be carefully recorded. Detailed notes and logs, films and video (often with special lenses and light sources), tape recordings, and use of miniature electronic listening devices must be used appropriately.

Methods of Surveillance

During *loose surveillance*, targets need not be kept under constant observation. The surveillance should be discontinued if the person becomes suspicious. In *close surveillance*, subjects are kept under observation continuously even if they appear to become suspicious.

Circumstances might require a change from a loose to a close surveillance. Pre-planning helps, but the examiner must observe and interpret the act or circumstances to decide what tactic to employ. If the plan calls for loose surveillance until the completion of a specified act, or until a meeting with another person after which the subject is to be put under close surveillance or apprehended, the observer must determine when the specific incident has taken place.

Preparation

The observer's attire should fit in with the area and/or group. Dress should be conservative, unless conservative dress is not appropriate for the area. Attire should not be loud or flashy so that if the subject notes the observer, he will be less likely to form any lasting impression. Minor changes in outer clothing or hand-carried items might alter the overall impression and help to prevent recognition by the subject.

Two or more observers working together need complete agreement about the surveillance techniques and schedule. Discreet signals will help each observer understand any given situation. Planning is essential, but the observers' adaptability and ingenuity are vital. Observers should be chosen both for aptitude and resourcefulness. They must have poise, patience, and endurance. Prior to the surveillance, the observer should prepare and document a cover story that will stand up under scrutiny. This cover story should provide a reasonable excuse for being in the area and for doing what has to be done there.

Electronic Equipment

Use of electronic surveillance equipment should be considered. For surveillance on foot, transmitting and receiving devices easily can be hidden on the person without arousing suspicion. Transmitters can be concealed in packages, briefcases, or on the person. Light-gathering binoculars and/or metascope equipment for night surveillance should be used if necessary. See the Law Section for a description of legal electronic monitoring techniques.

Basic Precautions

An observer should refrain from making abrupt, unnatural moves that could attract attention. Disguises such as false beards are impractical, hard to maintain, and easily detectable. The observer should not look directly into the subject's eyes. Inexperienced observers must overcome the tendency to believe that they have been "made" (identified) because the subject glances at them several times. The geography of the area where surveillance is to take place should be studied carefully. The observer should know the location of cul-de-sacs or dead-end streets or alleys to avoid being trapped or discovered. A suspicious subject might suddenly reverse course, enter a dead-end street, board and suddenly depart from public transportation, or engage in a variety of other evasive actions. The observer can counter these strategies by following approved surveillance techniques.

Techniques of Foot Surveillance

One-Person Surveillance

One-person surveillance is best for a fixed surveillance. If a moving one-person surveillance must be used, the observer should follow the subject on the same side of the street and keep fairly close. Crowd and street conditions will dictate the appropriate distance. When the subject turns a corner in an under-crowded area the observer should continue crossing the intersecting street. By glancing up the street in the subject's direction, the subject's position and actions can be noted.

In a crowded area, surveillance distances might be decreased. Unless the subject is standing just around the corner, surveillance can be continued from the same side of the street. Do not turn a corner immediately behind the subject. When operating across the street from the subject, circumstances will dictate whether to operate forward, to the rear, or abreast of the target. The observer should be abreast of the target when he turns a corner to observe any contact with individuals or entry into a building.

Two-Person Surveillance

In the "A-B" surveillance technique, the observer directly behind the target is known as the "A" observer. "A" follows the target, and "B" follows "A" either on the same side or from across the street. When both observers operate from the same side of the street, and the subject turns a corner, "A" continues in the original direction and crosses the intersecting street. From a vantage point, "A" signals the correct moves to "B." When "B" is operating across the street and the subject turns a corner to the right, "B" will cross the street behind the subject and take up the "A" position. This move should be prearranged. No signals should be necessary. All visual signals should be discreet and consistent with the environment. Should the subject turn to the left and cross the street toward "B," "B" should drop back to avoid meeting the subject. "B" should keep "A" in sight to observe signals indicating his next move.

Three-Person Surveillance

The "A-B-C" technique of surveillance is intended to keep two sides of the subject covered. "A" follows the subject. "B" follows "A" and concentrates on keeping him rather than the subject in sight. The normal position for "B" is behind "A." "C" normally operates across the street from the subject and slightly to his rear, enabling "C" to observe the subject without turning his head. Variations, such as having both "B" and "C" across the street or all three of the observers behind the subject on the same side of the street, might be necessary because of crowded conditions or traffic. In this technique, if the subject turns a corner, "A" continues in the original direction, crosses the intersecting street, and then signals instructions to the other observers from that vantage point. Either "B" or "C" can be given the "A" position and "A" might take up the original "C" position and continue his observation of the subject from across the street.

In another variation of this technique, both "A" and "B" might continue in the original direction and cross the street. "A" signals "C" to take up the "A" position. "B" then recrosses the street and assumes his former "B" position. "A" assumes the "C" position. In the third situation, when "C" notices that the subject is about to turn a corner, "C" signals both "A" and "B" what positions to assume.

Other Techniques

There are other ways to lessen the chance of an observer being "made." First, by either pre-arrangement or signal, the two or more observers can change places with each other. This is commonly referred to as the "leap-frog" method.

Progressive surveillance is used when extreme caution is necessary. With this technique, the subject is followed a certain distance and the surveillance is discontinued and the time noted. The next day another observer picks up the subject at the time and place where the surveillance was previously discontinued, and again follows the subject for a short distance. This continues day after day until the surveillance is completed.

Techniques of Vehicle Surveillance
General
Vehicle surveillance demands additional preparations. A dependable vehicle similar to types commonly found in the area where the surveillance is to take place must be used. This can be a panel truck, automobile, or a large truck or trailer. The license should be of the state and country where the surveillance will take place. If more than one vehicle is to be used, two-way radio or cellular telephone conversation usually is necessary. Consideration should be given to gasoline, water, first aid equipment, and road map requirements.

Whenever possible, combining foot and vehicular surveillance is an advantage. The observers likely will remain more alert. When a subject parks his vehicle and remains in it, an observer on foot can better monitor the subject's actions and those of passersby.

As in foot surveillance, vehicular surveillance requires inconspicuous actions. Observers should generally stay in the same lane as the target to avoid having to make turns from the wrong lane. If the situation allows, observers should change direction, perhaps going around a block in order to break continuity before the suspect becomes suspicious. It is difficult at night to be sure they are following the right vehicle. The target's car can be kept in sight better if it is distinctive. If the opportunity arises, reflective tape can be attached to the rear of the subject's car. The dome light of the observer's car should be disconnected so that the light will not show when a door is opened. Headlights and license plate lights can be wired to allow them to be turned on or off.

One-Vehicle Surveillance
When one vehicle is used, it must remain close enough to allow the observers to monitor the subject's actions, but far enough behind to avoid detection. When a subject's car stops, one observer should follow his actions on foot. The subject normally will not expect to be tailed by a person on foot while he is using his car. When the subject turns a corner, the observers can make one of two possible moves. They can continue in the original direction, cross the intersecting street and make a U-turn; the subject will take little interest in a car turning into the street behind him coming from the opposite direction. An alternative would be to continue in the original direction, cross the intersecting street and continue around the block.

Two-Vehicle Surveillance

This technique uses two vehicles to follow the subject at different distances on the same street, as in the "A-B" method of foot surveillance. This technique can be varied by having one vehicle going in the same direction as the subject on a parallel street while receiving radio-transmitted directions from the observers directly behind the subject. This technique is more flexible because the two vehicles can exchange places from time to time.

Fixed Surveillance

In a fixed surveillance, or stakeout, the subject remains stationary. The observer can move around for closer observation. When one observer is detailed to watch a place with more than one exit, he might have to move about considerably. When preparing for a stakeout, the base of operations should be well planned. It might be a store, apartment, house, automobile, or truck. A thorough—but cautious—area reconnaissance should be conducted. Necessary equipment should be readily available, such as binoculars, electronic investigative aids, cameras, and sound recording devices.

Satellite Surveillance

Although fraud examiners will rarely need it, satellite data are now available. For a relatively small amount, an examiner can buy detailed images from nearly anywhere in the world.

Plant security lends itself to satellite imagery. In addition to providing much of the same information as conventional satellite photographs, multispectral imagery can detect muddy ground, paths taken by people and vehicles, and other information that might help identify potential security problems.

Satellite imagery can be useful in surveillance if it is combined with more traditional types of photographic intelligence. This is especially true for large estates or industrial sites where aerial photography is prohibited. It also can be beneficial in a covert operation.

Satellite imagery can help to determine ways to penetrate a site, develop a map of the grounds, and identify important areas. In addition, satellite imagery can be used to investigate areas that are too remote, expensive, or dangerous to send operatives.

Buying satellite imagery is simple if the latitude and longitude of the target is known. The product ranges from photographic prints of the image to magnetic tapes of geographically corrected data. Prints, not much different from the enlargements from a film processor, usually are the cheapest product. While they don't allow sophisticated enhancement, they only require a magnifying glass to examine.

The next most expensive product is a transparency or a negative. It allows the interpreter to make prints and is convenient for exhibiting with an overhead projector. Stereograms are pairs of images that show the same object from slightly different positions and provide a three-dimensional view when looked at with stereoscopic glasses. They are either available as prints or transparencies. Magnetic tape is the digitized version of the images. A particularly sophisticated analysis of the target is possible with magnetic tape.

Night Surveillance Equipment

Basically, there are two types of night viewing devices: *active* and *passive*. The active type puts out its own light source, an infrared beam, which is visible to the user through the infrared scope that is part of the unit. The advantage of the active type of night viewing device is that the user can see in total darkness. Disadvantages include limited range and the fact that the infrared beam is visible to anyone looking through an infrared scope or through a passive night viewing device.

The passive type of night viewing device electronically amplifies whatever existing light is in the environment, such as moonlight or sky glow. This is why such units sometimes are referred to as "starlight scopes." Night viewing devices have been in use since 1969. Their primary purpose is to allow the observation of events occurring more than one block away at night. Night viewing devices, with adapters, can be attached to the front of cameras to obtain evidence that will stand up in court. Television videotapes, movies, and still photos can all be obtained using night viewing devices.

Sources and Informants

Sources and informants both serve the same purpose—to provide information to help develop a case. However, there are notable differences between confidential sources and confidential informants. The terms should not be used interchangeably.

A *confidential source* furnishes information as a result of occupation or profession and has no culpability in the alleged offense. For example, confidential sources might include barbers, attorneys, accountants, and law enforcement personnel. A *confidential informant* has a direct or indirect involvement in the matter under investigation, and might be culpable. The distinction between the two is their involvement in the offense. Informants can pose treacherous legal issues for the examiner.

Melsheimer suggests that from his experience as federal prosecutor, no piece of evidence is quite as convincing to a jury as a secretly photographed or recorded conversation that an informant can obtain firsthand. This information is generally accepted as a "slam dunk" for a criminal prosecutor, because there is little that a white-collar criminal can dispute when caught in the act of a fraud. For this reason, the use of informants is only likely to increase in the future of fraud investigations.

Types of Informants

In the book *Criminal Investigations*, authors Paul B. Weston and Kenneth M. Wells identify several different types of informants: the basic lead informant, the participant informant, the covert informant, and the accomplice/witness.

Basic Lead Informants

This type of informant supplies information to the police about illicit activities that they have encountered. The reasons that the informant decides to supply this information are varied; some informants simply want to "do their part" to stop an unscrupulous activity, while others are interested in harming the criminals they are informing against. For instance, many informants in the drug, prostitution, or illegal gambling areas are involved in those areas as well and intend to knock off some of their competition. Whatever the reason, these informants' only role in a covert investigation is to supply law enforcement with information.

Participant Informants

The participant informant is directly involved in gathering preliminary evidence in the investigation. The informant in this instance not only supplies an investigation with information, but the informant also is involved in setting up a "sting" operation, initiating contact with the criminal for arrest purposes. A participant informant is just as the title would suggest- a participant in the investigation of fraudulent or criminal activity.

Covert Informants

A covert informant serves the same basic function that any other type of informant does by supplying information to authorities on criminal behavior. The difference in this category is that a covert informant is one who has been "imbedded" in a situation or scenario for a number of years and is called upon only sporadically for tip-offs and leads. These types of informants are often referred to as "moles," because of the nature of their insulated situation as inside sources. Weston and Wells identify two instances in which covert informants are commonly used: in organized crime and hate extremist group investigations, covert informants are often culled to get information about upcoming criminal activities by the groups.

The Accomplice/Witness

The accomplice/witness informant is called upon by investigators quite often to provide information on criminal activity. The distinction in this category is that if the accomplice/witness informant were not feeding information to investigators, he or she would likely be liable to prosecution for the same offense. The accomplice informant is often persuaded to "spill the beans" on a co-conspirator in exchange for leniency in the prosecution phase of the investigation.

Objectives of Source and Informant Information

There are three essential procedures when using sources and informants. The first is to keep the person's identity as confidential as possible. Second, to independently verify the information provided by the source or informant. Third, to develop witness and documentary evidence from independently verified information.

If the confidential source or informant has provided documents, names of potential witnesses, or other evidence, all reasonable steps must be taken to protect the identity of that source. Care should be taken to ensure that questioning of other witnesses is done in a manner that does not reveal its origin. This usually can be accomplished through the phrasing of questions. For example, Mary Rodriguez De La Garza furnished confidential information about Linda Reed Collins. When the examiner confronts Collins, he does not want her to know that he has talked to Ms. De La Garza.

EXAMPLE

WRONG

"*Ms. Collins, someone told me you were taking kickbacks.*"

RIGHT

"*Ms. Collins, I have information indicating you are taking money from a vendor.*"

You have made the confrontation direct, but you have not revealed the origin of your information. If Collins presses to learn how you knew:

Ms. Collins:
"Who did you get that information from?"
Examiner:
"Documents I have from the company's records, plus other inquiries conducted in this matter."

In this example, if need be, the examiner would display the evidence from witnesses and documents that would not reveal the source or informant's identity. The information from the source or informant is basically useless unless the examiner can verify its authenticity and independently corroborate it. Suppose a source furnishes the examiner with copies of accounts payable documents showing that Bailey Books Incorporated's cost of materials has increased by 16 percent since Linda Reed Collins took over the account at the Orion Corporation. This kind of evidence would corroborate the source's story. If a source told the examiner that Collins frequently had drinks with Jim Nagel, the account representative for Orion, the examiner would want to find out some way to verify this report. The third objective when using sources is to develop the witness' information and other evidence so that it makes a cohesive case.

Recruitment of Sources and Informants
Fraud examiners should keep in mind the need to develop sources. Business and financial institution executives, law enforcement and other governmental personnel, medical and educational professionals, and internal and external auditors are good contacts for fraud examiners.

The examiner should endeavor to make contacts in the community well in advance of needing information; this is simply good public relations. If the fraud examiner receives an allegation and needs confidential information, perhaps a source cultivated earlier can assist. Sources need to feel confident that they can share information without being compromised. In theory, the source will never have to testify; he has no firsthand knowledge, his information comes from a witness or document.

The examiner also might meet sources when tracking leads during a specific investigation. He might interview a stockbroker from whom the target purchased stock who does not want his identity revealed. The examiner should not encourage a person to provide confidential information, but rather try to get reports on the record. But if the source's information must be kept confidential, abide by that promise.

Active recruitment of informants generally is not desirable; it might appear untoward to a jury. It is better to encourage an informant to come forward. It is desirable to develop an informant relationship, but this situation must be handled carefully. The examiner must clearly document an adequate predication for informant involvement. The most serious question is the culpability of the informant. There have been cases where the informant is more guilty than the target. The court might rule that the informant's information cannot be introduced.

Motives of Sources and Informants

Sources

In some instances (but not many), the source might want money or other consideration for furnishing information. The examiner should not offer any compensation. It is better to have the source request it. This is to avoid any allegation of misconduct on the part of the examiner for paying for information. Sources have their reasons for informing. It might be the sense of importance that comes from being involved—a chance to play "detective." In other cases, the source might have a grudge against the target. Other reasons include a feeling of moral responsibility to report information. Perhaps more than any other reason, a source will furnish information because he likes and trusts the examiner and wants to help.

Informants

Informants, especially incidental ones, commonly want something in return for their information. They take the attitude that their involvement has personal risk, and they want to be paid for their "trouble." The informant is likely to be predisposed to sell information to the highest bidder.

Many informants—perhaps the majority—are unstable. As often as not, an informant's motivation is to "get" the target, not because of any sense of morality, but because the informant and the target are closely involved. In the case of drug dealing, for example, an informant might furnish information because the target is the competition. In other cases, the informant is motivated by a sense of self-importance. He is a "big man"; people take him seriously.

Probably the most common reason informants supply information is because they are involved in the offense, and by furnishing information on the target (which is commonly false), they can diffuse suspicion from their own activities. In many instances, the examiner initially does not know the truth about the informant.

The fraud examiner must also be aware of the overzealous informant. Melsheimer cautions that most of the recently catalogued cases concerning the abuse of informants were the result of "involved informants who are private citizens, self-motivated to satisfy their law enforcement sponsors at virtually any cost." In an attempt to ingratiate themselves to investigators, the informant will often engage in unscrupulous activities to provide the information they think the investigators are looking for. The fraud examiner must lay out the ground rules for the informant before beginning this type of investigation or risk the embarrassment (and punishment) that a less-than truthful informant can provide

Legal Considerations

As noted, dealing with sources and informants is fraught with legal pitfalls. The examiner should be circumspect in all interactions with sources and informants. The examiner might be able to trust a source—but rarely an informant. Always document contacts with sources and informants in case of problems.

Many jurisdictions guarantee the accused the right to confront his accuser. That is an absolute right of the accused; it is not possible to cross-examine someone who lurks behind a cloak of secrecy. The examiner usually will not be able to testify to what a source or informant told because of the "hearsay" rule. The witness can testify only to what he knows, not what someone else has said.

If a decision is made to pay an informant or source, the payment should be made in cash and a receipt should be secured. If the source will not sign a receipt, do not pay. There have been numerous instances where a receipt was not obtained and the informant subsequently denied receiving funds or challenged the amount. The examiner then has to defend himself without proof; indeed, some investigators have been accused of having embezzled the payments. Payments should only be on a COD basis. The information should be furnished and verified before turning over any money. If not, the examiner might become the victim of a scam.

Entrapment sometimes is raised as a criminal defense. This is especially true when the informant is doing things at the behest of law enforcement. The defense is that the target is innocent, but was unlawfully lured into a crime that he otherwise would not have committed. This can best be overcome by ensuring that the source or informant only gathers information and plays a limited role in the case.

Reporting Contacts

It is recommended that all contacts with informants and sources be reported on a memorandum of interview, although the confidential source's or informant's identity should not be included in the report. Symbols to denote the informant's identity should be used. It is further recommended that sources be preceded with an "S" followed by a unique identifier (i.e., source #1 would be "S-1" source #2 would be "S-2"). The symbol for informants would then be "I-1" and "I-2."

As a general rule, disclosure of the identities of sources and informants should be on a strict need-to-know basis. For that reason, the person's identity should be maintained in a secure file with limited access and cross-indexed by his symbol number. Information should be noted in writing as to: (1) the reliability of the source, if known and (2) whether the person is in a position to furnish relevant information.

EXAMPLE

"A source of unknown reliability, but in a position to furnish relevant information (hereinafter referred to as S-1), advised as follows:"

OR

"An informant of known reliability and in a position to furnish relevant information (hereinafter referred to as I-2) advised as follows:"

The fraud examiner is not in a position to promise leniency to people involved in the commission of a crime or tort. To do so is serious misconduct and a violation of the Certified Fraud Examiner Code of Professional Ethics. Promises of leniency can only come from the prosecutor or the courts. The examiner might truthfully tell the informant that his cooperation will be made known to the authorities, and that people who cooperate generally are treated better.

For reasons previously discussed, it is best not to use sources and informants in ongoing crimes as "double agents." Such action is inherently risky and places the examiner in the position of having to defend the actions of the source or informant, actions that, in most cases, the examiner cannot control. This leaves the case open to attack during legal proceedings. If it appears critical that the source be used as an agent, get the approval of the prosecutor and/or attorney before proceeding.

Promises of Confidentiality

Fraud examiners are not in a position to offer unqualified confidentiality. Therefore, any promises made to an informant or source should be qualified. In the case of an examiner who is employed by a governmental agency, there might be an absolute duty not to hold sources and informants in confidence. In many law enforcement agencies, an investigator might not have informants or sources that are unknown to the agency. Governmental agencies also regularly share information on criminal investigations with prosecutors, including the identity of the source of information. The same regulations and considerations could govern business entities.

EXAMPLE

During the examination of Collins, you contact Roger McGuire, a co-worker of Collins. McGuire will talk to you only in confidence. You know Bailey's policies are to prosecute all criminal offenses. McGuire seems to be the key to making a case against Collins. You believe you can independently verify the allegations McGuire furnishes, but you will not be certain until you talk to him. It might be necessary to call McGuire to testify against Collins in order to make the case.

WRONG

"Mr. McGuire, I promise I will not tell anyone about your talking to me."

RIGHT

"Mr. McGuire, I promise I will not tell Ms. Collins about your talking to me."

The second is a conditional promise; the examiner will not directly tell Collins, but that doesn't mean someone else won't. At some point, informants and sources often become witnesses. Under no circumstances should an examiner promise a source or informant that his identity will not become known.

Use of Operatives

Operatives are subject to greater control than informants. In a typical scenario, a source or informant advises that information exists or that a crime currently is being committed. The informant's motives might or might not be altruistic. For example, a warehouse worker approaches the fraud examiner and says that Collins is stealing inventory. The informant wants money for her assistance in apprehending Collins. The examiner does not know whether the informant is telling the truth or whether she is trying to divert attention from herself.

The informant suggested that she secretly record a conversation with Collins, getting Collins to admit to the theft. If an informant conducts the investigation under the examiner's direction, he then becomes an operative. To demonstrate a worst-case scenario, consider the following example. Without the examiner's knowledge or consent, the informant plants a tape recorder in the break room at the warehouse, and records conversations to which he is not a party. This is a violation of the law regarding interception of communication. Although the recording was made without the examiner's knowledge or consent, the case nonetheless is compromised. The informant might insist that he tape-recorded the conversations at the examiner's request, thereby placing the examiner in the unenviable position of having to defend himself.

Most operatives lack the training to conduct an investigation, and they cannot, in many instances, be trusted. It is vital that operatives be properly monitored and supervised. Obtain background information on the operative to ensure his degree of culpability in the offense, if any. Make certain that the operative clearly understands the objectives of the covert operation, and ensure that he is regularly debriefed before and after critical meetings with the target. Be careful that the operative does not take any action without proper authorization.

Sources for Satellite Imagery and Related Materials
SPOT Image Corporation
Sells imagery from the French SPOT satellite
www.spot.com
(703) 715-3100
14595 Avion Parkway, Suite 500
Chantilly, VA 20151

EROS
Sells aerial photographs, some radar images, and photographs from U.S. space missions
http://edc.usgs.gov/
(800) 252-4547 or (605) 594-6933

U.S. Geological Survey Customer Service
EROS Data Center
47914 252nd Street
Sioux Falls, SD 57198-0001

The Orthoshop
Makes maps and corrects satellite imagery
www.orthoshop.com
(602) 798-1323
1121 W. Grant Road, Suite 401
Tucson, AZ 85705

Satellite and Civil Liberties

In the 1980s, the Supreme Court made several rulings that established the legal basis for satellite surveillance. Some of these key rulings are listed below.

California v. Ciraolo, 106 S.Ct. 1809, 1810 (1986). The court ruled that aerial photographs did not interfere with a person's expectation of privacy.

United States v. Dunn, 55 U.S.L.W. 4251, 4253 (1987). The court held that open areas are not protected by Fourth Amendment rights.

Dow Chemical Company v. United States, 106 S.Ct. 1819 (1986). The court enunciated standards regarding the legality of aerial photography. It expressed concern about satellite surveillance, but did not establish any legal distinction between aerial photography and satellite surveillance.

SOURCES OF INFORMATION

There is a surprising amount of information about both individuals and businesses that can be accessed without a subpoena. For instance, there is an enormous amount of information contained in public records. Public record information can refer either to information *developed* about the public or information *open* to the public. This chapter covers a variety of public information resources for the fraud examiner. Some—principally those maintained by agencies—are available simply for the asking. Others are restricted to law enforcement agencies, while still others can be accessed only by means of court proceedings such as subpoenas. This chapter also includes references to directories and databases which can be accessed with little or no cost to find information on virtually anyone.

The fraud examiner must be certain that information obtained is done so legally. Records from confidential sources generally cannot be introduced as evidence; in criminal cases, illegally obtained documentary evidence falls under the exclusionary rule (see the Law Section). In civil cases, using illegally obtained documentation might give rise to tort actions or other sanctions against the fraud examiner. Following is a list of information available from city, county, state, and federal agencies.

Rules Governing Public Record Information

Freedom of Information Act (FOIA)

The FOIA is the primary Act that governs the availability of governmental records to the general public. The Act sets very specific guidelines on which governmental records are open to the public and which are not. The records which are available are known as "public records," raw records of information which are compiled and maintained by government agencies. The various records are maintained at one of the three government levels: federal, state, or county/local. Although the FOIA is a federal Act, most states have adopted very similar versions of the FOIA to cover the state and local jurisdictions. While these versions are similar to the original FOIA, the individually passed state acts may differ slightly in specific legal areas from state to state.

The FOIA and its individual state counterparts regulate:
- The type of records that a governmental agency may maintain about a person.

- The conditions under which such information may be disclosed to another government agency.
- The circumstances and methods under which an individual may obtain copies of agency records that pertain to him.

Generally speaking, government records about an individual are prohibited from release. The disclosure of these records constitutes an invasion of privacy. A person may obtain copies of his own records by requesting them in writing from the agency that maintains them. Such requests often are denied, in whole or in part, because of numerous exceptions to the disclosure requirements. Some of these exceptions include the pendency of an ongoing investigation or concerns about national security. A person denied access to records may appeal through that agency or through the courts.

Most records are maintained at the county or local level, a fact which can seriously hamper any fraud investigation; it can be very difficult for the fraud examiner to catch up with a fraudster who understands the county filing procedures and chooses to operate in different counties. However, there are records available at different governmental levels.

The FOIA provides for public access to the following information:
- Tax rolls
- Voter registration
- Assumed names
- Real property records
- Divorce/probate suits

Information NOT deemed to be public records under the FOIA are:
- Banking records
- Trust records
- Telephone records
- Passenger lists
- Stock ownership

Fair Credit Reporting Act (FCRA)
The Fair and Accurate Credit Transactions Act of 2003 amended the Fair Credit Reporting Act (FCRA) to exempt certain reports involving employee misconduct investigations.

Previously, employers were required to provide notice and obtain express written consent before obtaining a "consumer report." A "consumer report" was defined to include virtually any information obtained about an employee through any third party.

As a result of these new amendments, an employer who uses a third party to conduct a workplace investigation no longer has to obtain the prior consent of an employee **if** the investigation involves suspected:

- Misconduct;
- Violation of law or regulations; or
- Violation of any pre-existing policy of the employer.

In order to qualify for this exception, the report from the third party must not be communicated to anyone other than the employer, an agent of the employer, or the government.

However, if "adverse action" is taken against the employee based on the results of the investigation, the FCRA still requires that the employer to provide the employee with a summary of the report. "Adverse action" is broadly defined as any employment decision that adversely affects the employee. The summary must "contain the nature and substance of the communication upon which the adverse action is based." It does not, however, have to identify the individuals interviewed or the sources of the information.

Gramm-Leach-Bliley Act

The Gramm-Leach-Bliley Act (GLB) was passed in 1999 and final rules implementing the Act became final in 2001. GLB was originally enacted to allow banks and other companies to offer previously forbidden services such as insurance and securities brokerage services. Congress was worried that these new "super banks" would share customers' financial data to affiliates and other companies to hawk their new products. Therefore, Congress added a provision requiring "financial intuitions" to tell customers about its privacy policy, to notify them of private information the institution intends to share, and to give customers the chance to block such information-sharing.

To implement the new law, Congress ordered regulators to define "financial institution" in the broadest possible terms. Thus, "financial institutions" include not just banks, but also insurance companies, accountants, tax preparation and real estate settlement services, and investment advisors. The text of the rule can be found at 16 C.F.R. Part 313. Additional information about the rule can be found at the Federal Trade Commission's website: www.ftc.gov.

The problem for fraud examiners and investigators is that the privacy rules implemented as part of the GLB have been interpreted to prevent the selling of credit header information. Under the FTC's interpretation of the rule, credit header information cannot be sold except for the very limited purposes allowed under the Fair Credit Reporting Act. The agency reached this decision by concluding that such basic personal information, such as names and addresses, is "financial" information, and, therefore, must be protected by under the GLB Act. Unfortunately, this prevents credit bureaus from selling credit header information (including names, addresses, phone numbers, and Social Security numbers) to private investigators, direct marketers, or other information brokers.

The credit bureaus challenged the FTC's rule in court. However, in May 2001, the U.S. District Court for Washington D.C. upheld the agency's interpretation. The credit bureaus have appealed that decision. Unless the decision is overturned, it appears that it will be more difficult for fraud examiners and investigators to obtain personal information about potential suspects or witnesses.

GLB also made it a criminal offense to engage in "pretexting." Some individuals used pretexting as a means to gather financial information about a subject. Pretexters would contact a financial institution and pretend to be the customer or someone else authorized to obtain financial information and basically trick the financial institution into providing information about the subject.

Section 6821 of Title 15 of the U.S. Code (added by GLB) makes it an offense to:
- Use false, fictitious or fraudulent statements or documents to get customer information from a financial institution or directly from a customer of a financial institution;
- Use forged, counterfeit, lost, or stolen documents to get customer information from a financial institution or directly from a customer of a financial institution; or
- Ask another person to get someone else's customer information using false, fictitious or fraudulent statements or using false, fictitious or fraudulent documents or forged, counterfeit, lost, or stolen documents.

Violators can, under certain circumstances, be fined and/or imprisoned up to 10 years.

Privacy Act of 1974

The *Privacy Act of 1974* restricts information about individuals, both employees and non-employees, that may be gathered by government agencies. An agency may maintain records about a person containing information that is relevant and necessary to accomplish a purpose of the agency. This information may include a person's education, finances, medical history, criminal history, employment history, and identifying information (fingerprint, voice print, or photograph). The person may have access to his information unless it is investigatory material compiled for law enforcement purposes, statistical records, or material compiled solely for determining suitability, eligibility, or qualification for federal service or promotion.

Right to Financial Privacy Act

The *Right to Financial Privacy Act* prohibits financial institutions from disclosing financial information about individual customers to government agencies without:

- The customer's consent
- A court order
- Subpoena
- Search warrant
- Other formal demand, with limited exceptions

Although the statute applies only to demands by government agencies, most banks and other financial institutions also will not release such information to private parties absent legal process, such as a subpoena issued in a civil lawsuit.

Postal Privacy Act of 1993

This law allows the U.S. Postal Service to promulgate its own regulations with regard to public information with the result that public access to forwarding address information ended. Moreover, maintenance of the National Change of Address file also ended.

Americans with Disabilities Act (ADA)

Among other matters, this Act purports to prevent prospective employers from using Workers' Compensation records in denying employment to otherwise qualified job applicants.

Driver's Privacy Protection Act

In 1999, Congress made significant changes to the Driver's Privacy Protection Act of 1994 (18, U.S. Code, Section 2721). The new law bars states from releasing drivers' Social Security numbers, photographs, or certain other information unless they obtain "the express consent" of the person in advance. Before the 1999 amendments, drivers could "opt out" and ask that their information not be released. Under the new law, drivers are under an "opt in" system which requires that they expressly authorize the release of the information. Although the law was challenged in court, the U.S. Supreme Court, in January 2000, upheld the constitutionality of the new amendments.

These amendments make it extremely difficult to obtain almost any up-to-date information from state motor vehicle departments. Such information can only be obtained if the driver has expressly consented to its release. Therefore, companies may wish to consider having employees sign a consent form as early as the employment application stage. For example, the Driver's Privacy Protection Act does not prohibit the use of MVR records for pre-employment screening, but the state can only release the records with the driver's consent.

Health Insurance Portability and Accountability Act

The Health Insurance Portability and Accountability Act (HIPPA) instituted several new privacy rules. While most of the rules do not directly affect investigations, fraud examiners should be aware of the rules because they may have an impact on the type of information that can be legally gathered on employees.

The HIPPA privacy rules place restrictions on the availability and use of "protected health information." The definition of this term is extremely broad and covers any information relating to an individual's past, present, or future physical or mental health, payment for services, or health care operations.

If information about the health of an individual, or payments for services, becomes an issue during an investigation, you should immediately contact the human resources department. The HR department should have information about whether the entity is subject to the HIPPA rules and can assist you in compliance with those rules.

The most important thing to note is that if the HIPPA rules apply, you are restricted as to the type of health information you can access without specific written authorization. You should never contact the health care provider, the health plan administrator, or a medical billing services for copies of employee records without first consulting the employer's legal counsel or the HR department.

City Government

Building Inspector

The following information generally is available through a city building inspector's office:

- Building permits, showing the name of applicant, address of construction, estimated cost, and the name of builder or contractor.
- Blueprints and plans showing construction details often are submitted with applications for building permits.
- Building inspectors' reports, containing information regarding compliance with construction specifications.

Health Department

Most local health or fire departments conduct routine inspections of businesses for health and safety code or fire code violations. These inspectors might have valuable information about the business, its operations, the employees, and the owners.

Death certificates usually can be found at city, county, or state health departments. A death certificate provides the name of the deceased, address, sex, age, race, birthplace, birth date, death place, date and time of death, Social Security number, medical certificate, and coroner's certificate. Additionally, a death certificate generally provides information about the deceased's parents and their occupations.

Personnel Department

The city personnel department maintains personal history statements about city employees and political leaders as well as employment records, efficiency reports, and records of salary liens on city employees.

Public Schools

City school systems maintain teachers' biographies, showing personal data, education, and former employment; and student records, showing biographies (in some school districts), grades, and disciplinary actions.

Regulatory Agencies

Applications for business licenses, contained in the files of city regulatory agencies, often have valuable information on certain types of enterprises. In many cities the following businesses would have to apply for licenses to operate:

- Businesses seeking liquor licenses.
- Professionals, including certified public accountants, dentists, doctors, plumbers, electricians, and optometrists.
- Restaurants, bars, and night clubs (which frequently are inspected by health and fire departments).
- Businesses operating under names other than the owners' names (such businesses must register under assumed names and are included in the city's DBA [doing business as] files).

Tax Assessor/Collector

A city tax assessor's office maintains maps of real property in the city, including a property's dimensions, address, owner, taxable value, and improvements. A city tax collector's office maintains the following information:

- Names and addresses of payers of property taxes, even if the taxes were paid by individuals other than the apparent owners
- Legal descriptions of property
- Amounts of taxes paid on real and personal property
- Delinquency status of taxes
- Names of former property owners

Utility Company Records

Many utility companies are nonprofit corporations or municipalities. Although the recent trend has been to restrict access to utility company records, check with the utility companies in the subject's area to see what, if any, information is available. Utility records might contain the phone number of the customer, even if that number is unlisted. In addition, be sure to check the names of friends or relatives.

County Government

Coroner

A county coroner's register generally contains the name or a description of the deceased; date of inquest, if any; property found on the deceased and its disposition; and the cause of death.

Court Clerk

A great deal of litigation occurs each year and many people might be subject to judicial action either voluntarily or not. Researching civil and criminal suits can provide invaluable information assisting in:
- The location of individuals
- Identifying pending actions
- Uncovering closed cases
- Insight into marital status (family)
- Tracing sources of funds (probate)
- Identifying financial conditions (bankruptcy)
- Litigation history
- Outstanding judgments

Many of the civil suits are readily accessible as a public record, however, criminal and juvenile actions might not be as "open" to review.

Court levels vary by jurisdiction, as do the names of the levels. Different case types are filed at different levels and in different courts. The researcher might be required to check several courts and several levels to uncover the information desired.

A researcher typically will have access to microfiche listings of cases or parties within the individual court system through the clerk's office. Some courts are set up to provide computerized access to this information. Normally, one must be able to provide a case number in order to access the actual court file. The Party Name Index will provide the case number.

A wealth of information is available from reviewing court files. Often, civil or criminal actions might not be readily known and the researcher must be able to identify the jurisdiction, county, or court involved.

Court clerks maintain files on all active and closed lawsuits in their jurisdictions. Information regarding these suits are public record and can be searched by scanning the indexes for subject's name as a plaintiff or defendant.

Based on court issues and the financial nature of the claim, different levels of courts might have jurisdiction of a given case. To determine a full picture of the litigation against a company or individual, you must search each of the following courts:
- County Civil Court
- State District Court (criminal/civil)
- District Court (criminal/civil)
- Bankruptcy Court (federal)
- Probate Court (inheritance)

Subject data fields will contain:
- The complaint for or against the subject (direct and reverse indexes)
- The subject's last known address (either through the lawsuit's pleadings or the court officer's citation and subpoena returns)
- Other personal information on the subject, depending on the type of suit

A divorce suit file frequently contains the subject's financial inventory, submitted at the time of the divorce or separation, as well as the partition of assets to each party in the settlement. Personal injury suits frequently will contain an accident report, injury history, statements of the involved parties, and will reveal the financial settlement of the case. Financial suits will disclose the debtors and creditors and present an outside view of an individual's business history or ability to perform.

The court clerk also maintains criminal court files that might contain information describing the offenses and the counts. These files also might contain the complainant's signature (exemplar); a transcript of the preliminary hearing; the names of the prosecuting and defense attorneys; the probation officer's report, with a background investigation of the defendant; and the subpoenas issued in the case.

Bankruptcy documents usually are located in the federal bankruptcy court for the district where the debtor resided or had his principal place of business. When checking bankruptcy court records, remember to check not only the subject individual or business, but also any related businesses, principals, employees, or relatives.

Personnel Department

A county personnel department maintains information similar to that maintained by a city personnel department.

Public Schools

County public school systems maintain information similar to that found in city public school systems.

Registrar of Voters

In order to vote, one must register in his or her respective precinct by filling out a form detailing the person's name, address, date of birth, signature, and, in some cases, the Social Security number.

Voter registration records routinely are verified by the county and old addresses are deleted as new ones appear.

Recorder

A county recorder's office maintains the following information:
- Documents pertaining to real estate transactions—including deeds, grants, transfers and mortgages of real estate, releases of mortgages, powers of attorney, and leases that have been acknowledged or approved
- Mortgages on personal property
- Marriage license records and applications including information on previous marriages, maiden names, addresses, and dates of birth
- Wills admitted to probate
- Official bonds
- Notices of mechanic's liens
- Transcripts of judgments that are made liens on real estate
- Notices of attachment on real estate
- Papers in connection with bankruptcy
- Certified copies of decrees and judgments of courts of record
- Other documents permitted by law to be recorded, such as the Department of Defense's DOD 214 Forms, recorded by some veterans as evidence of veteran status, particularly in those states where veterans are granted reduced property tax rates

Real property records are extremely important. They are relatively easy to access and contain a vast amount of information. Each real estate transaction will list a deed verifying the transfer of the property. If the individual either buys or sells a house or vacant land, or becomes subject to a state or federal lien, the transaction will be reflected in the county real property indexes. If improvements are made to the property, such as the addition of a new room or the installation of a pool, then a mechanic's lien or other notice might be on file in the county property records.

Real property records generally will include the following:
- Residency and addresses of buyer and seller (referred to respectively as grantor and grantee)
- Price of the property (see tax stamps if listed)
- Mortgage company and amount originally financed
- Real estate ownership
- Who financed the transaction, if applicable
- Title companies involved
- Improvements to the property and the names and addresses of the contractors

Regulatory Agencies

County regulatory agencies maintain information similar to that held by city regulatory agencies. A county tax assessor's office maintains information similar to that held by a city tax assessor's office. A county tax collector's office maintains information similar to that maintained by a city tax collector's office.

Welfare Commission

Files of a county welfare commission are based on information gathered by social workers, psychologists, and physicians. Frequently, the recipient of benefits provides the information, which generally is not verified. Files contain such information as the recipient's address, previous employment, how much the recipient earned, property the recipient or the recipient's relatives might have, the family's attitudes, the state of their health, and criminal records.

State Government

Business Filings Division

Corporations must be registered with the Secretary of State (or state corporation bureau or corporate registry office) in the state where the company does business. These corporate records will include:

- Corporate name
- Ownership information
- Stock value
- Initial shareholders
- Directors and officers
- Registered agent
- Principal office
- Date of incorporation
- Standing/Status

This information will permit the investigator to review a corporate structure, identify the registered agent, and trace incorporation dates. The records often will include limited partnership information as well.

Some states also require foreign corporations (corporations which were incorporated in another state) be registered with the state corporation office if the foreign corporation transacts business in that state. For example, if a corporation chartered in Delaware wishes to transact business in Texas, it must file an Application for Certificate of Authority. The application is filed with the Secretary of State and must include the date of incorporation, the principal office, the address of the registered agent, and the names of the officers and directors.

Fictitious Business Names/DBA

DBA (doing business as) information typically is filed at the county level, though many states require filing with the state. This information will provide insight into the true business venture behind the name. Very similar to corporate filings with the Secretary of State, these records will allow you to trace the corporation's roots or prove ownership in sole proprietorships, partnerships, limited partnerships, joint ventures, and trusts.

Uniform Commercial Code Filings

In order to obtain a perfected security interest in personal property, a lender must file UCC statements with the Secretary of State or with the county level unit.

Banks, finance companies and other lenders will generate records or recorded filings of financial transactions conducted with individuals and businesses, such as purchases of household furniture, appliances, boats and yachts, automobiles, aircraft, and business equipment.

These filings produced as the result of the transactions will identify:
- Debtor or joint debtors
- Current address of the debtors
- Name of the financial lender
- Type of collateral pledged as security
- Date of filing and continuations

UCC filings can disclose when and where a person obtains personal loans, the type of property pledged to the lender to secure the loan, and the current address of the debtor. These documents are great sources for reviewing itemized lists of personal property held by the debtor.

Employee/Labor Department

Some states, under their labor departments, require the filing of periodic lists of employees, revealing their names, Social Security numbers, and salaries. In addition, by examining previous filings, an investigator can locate former employees.

State Tax Department

Some state revenue departments require certain businesses to obtain licenses or permits, such as a sales tax permit. The licenses and the applications are generally public record. If the business is delinquent in the payment of its taxes, the local or state tax investigator or collector might be able to provide "inside" information concerning the business.

Law enforcement officials might be able to gain access to corporate, business, and personal state tax information. These records might unwittingly reveal hidden assets or investments. Loans to or from officers, stockholders, or related entities should be examined closely. Also, mortgages, notes, and bonds shown as liabilities on a corporate return should be investigated. Tax returns might also disclose the identity of the accountant or attorney preparing the return.

Professional Associations and Licensing Boards

Many state and local agencies or bodies maintain records identifying individuals holding special licenses or memberships. These can include:

- Medical practitioners such as doctors, dentists, nurses
- Social workers
- Attorneys
- Certified Public Accountants
- Real estate licensees
- Notaries
- Law enforcement personnel
- Firefighters
- Security guards
- Stockbrokers
- Teachers
- Insurance agents
- Private investigators
- Bail bond agents
- Travel agents
- Barbers, cosmetologists
- Contractors, engineers, electricians, architects

The licenses and applications granted by the state might be public record. Some applications contain no more than a name and address. However, other applications contain lengthy personal information such as previous residential addresses, previous employers, education and training, and financial statements. Some agencies are required to conduct a background investigation before issuance of a license.

Also, the state regulatory or licensing agency might have the authority to suspend or revoke the licenses necessary for the business to operate.

Many professional organizations maintain their own listings of members or licensees. They might be reluctant to provide information beyond the person's name and current standing in the association.

Other State Regulatory Agencies

A state's Bureau of Vital Statistics, where birth certificates generally are filed, is an excellent source of information. Birth certificates can provide a child's name, sex, date of birth, and address of place of birth, as well as the names of the attending physician, midwife, and/or other assistants; the parents' names, ages, address, race, place of birth, and occupations; the mother's maiden name; and the number of siblings. (In some states, birth certificates might be found at the city or county level.)

At the state government level, the following records can be found:
- Auto licenses, auto transfers, and sales of vehicles
- Civil service applications
- Driver's licenses
- Health department records
- Inheritance and gift tax returns
- Name changes
- Occupancy and business licenses
- Parole officer's and probation department's files
- Personal property tax returns
- School and voter registrations
- State income tax returns
- Welfare agency records

The following state departments and agencies might also maintain information valuable to fraud examiners:
- Bureau of Professional and Vocational Standards or Department of Licensing (especially professional associations, partnerships, and corporations)
- Controller/Treasurer
- Department of Agriculture
- Department of Industrial Relations
- Department of Motor Vehicles—maintains information on driver's licenses, vehicle registrations, titling, car dealers, car salespeople, wrecking yards, tow companies, smog inspection facilities, and (in some states) auto repair businesses
- Department of Natural Resources
- Horse Racing Board/Gambling Commission
- Office of the Attorney General
- Secretary of State (Corporations Division)

- State Board of Equalization
- State Police or Highway Patrol
- State Securities Commission
- State Utility Commission

Federal Government

Information about various federal agencies can be obtained by the following reference guides:

- *Chart of the Organizations of the Federal Executive Departments and Agencies*, prepared by the U.S. Senate Committee on Governmental Affairs
- *Congressional Staff Directory and Federal Staff Directory*, prepared annually by Congressional Staff Directory, Ltd., Mount Vernon, Virginia
- *Congressional Directory*, prepared by the U.S. Government Printing Office
- *The United States Government Manual*, prepared by the Office of the Federal Register, National Archives, and Records Administration

Inspectors General

Inspectors general can provide valuable information, especially to official law enforcement personnel, about businesses they have investigated or audited and they are good guides to other information sources in their departments or agencies. Most offices of inspectors general maintain centralized index and case file systems. Congress established inspectors general to combat government fraud, waste, and abuse in federal departments, agencies, and designated the entities listed below.

Federal Entity	Telephone Number
Agency for International Development	(202) 712-1023
Agriculture, Department of	(202) 720-5677
Amtrak	(202) 906-4600
Appalachian Regional Commission	(202) 884-7799
Central Intelligence Agency	(703) 874-2555
Commerce, Department of	(202) 482-4661
Commodity Futures Trading Commission	(202) 418-5110
Consumer Product Safety Commission	(301) 504-7644
Corporation for Public Broadcasting	(202) 879-9600
Defense, Department of	(703) 695-4249

Education, Department of	(202) 205-5400
Energy, Department of	(202) 586-5575
Environmental Protection Agency	(202) 566-2391
Equal Employment Opportunity Commission	(202) 663-4900
Farm Credit Administration	(703) 883-4316
Federal Communications Commission	(202) 418-0476
Federal Election Commission	(202) 694-1015
Federal Emergency Management Agency	(202) 646-3910
Federal Housing Finance Board	(202) 408-2544
Federal Labor Relations Authority	(202) 218-7770
Federal Maritime Commission	(202) 523-5863
Federal Reserve Board	(202) 452-6400
Federal Trade Commission	(202) 326-2800
General Services Administration	(202) 501-0450
Government Printing Office	(202) 512-0039
Health and Human Services, Department of	(202) 619-3148
Housing and Urban Development, Department of	(202) 708-0430
Information Agency, U.S.	(202) 401-7931
Interior, Department of the	(202) 208-5745
International Broadcasting Bureau	(202) 401-7000
International Trade Commission, U.S.	(800) 500-0333
Justice, Department of	(202) 514-3435
Labor, Department of	(202) 523-7296
Legal Services Corporation	(202) 295-1660
Merit Systems Protection Board	(202) 653-7200
National Aeronautics and Space Administration	(202) 358-1220
National Archives and Records Administration	(301) 837-3000
National Credit Union Administration	(703) 518-6350
National Endowment for the Arts	(202) 682-5402
National Endowment for the Humanities	(202) 606-8350
National Labor Relations Board	(202) 273-3891
National Science Foundation	(703) 292-7100
Nuclear Regulatory Commission	(301) 415-5930
Office of Personnel Management	(202) 606-1200
Pension Benefit Guaranty Corporation	(202) 326-4020
Postal Service, U.S.	(202) 268-4267

Railroad Retirement Board	(312) 751-4350
Securities and Exchange Commission	(202) 942-8800
Small Business Administration	(202) 205-6580
State, Department of	(202) 647-9450
Tennessee Valley Authority	(865) 632-3550
Transportation, Department of	(202) 366-1959
Treasury, Department of the	(202) 622-1090
Veterans Affairs, Department of	(202) 565-7702

Commodity Futures Trading Commission

This commission maintains the following information:

- Registration information concerning firms and individuals
- Administrative and injunctive actions filed by the Commission against firms and individuals
- Financial reports filed by Commission registrants
- Customer complaints filed against Commission registrants

The National Futures Association is a self-regulatory organization authorized by the Commodity Exchange Act; it operates under the supervision of the Commission. The NFA is a one-stop information source for all types of registration and disciplinary information regarding firms and individuals in the futures industry. This information includes registration status and employment history; disciplinary actions filed by the NFA, the Commission, and the commodity exchanges; and customer complaints filed under the Commission's Reparations Program. The NFA's Information Center can be called at (800) 621-3570 or, within Illinois, at (312) 781-1410.

Department of Agriculture (USDA)

Some USDA agencies maintain or have access to financial records concerning contracts with the agency; recipients of various benefits, such as food stamps and free or reduced- price school lunch meals; farmland improvements; and federal crop insurance coverage. Various USDA agencies maintain information about gaining access to records concerning the following:

- Meat or poultry companies
- Feedlot owners or operators, livestock brokers, meat packers, or canneries
- Ownership, management, or the operations of—or certain financial data concerning—farms or ranches participating in USDA programs

- Retail grocery stores authorized to accept food stamps
- Rural electric or telephone cooperatives
- Applications for and receipt of loans, loan guarantees, grants, or contracts with or from USDA agencies
- Applications for and indemnities paid by federal crop insurance
- Logging (tree harvesting) companies that remove timber from national forests
- Certain improvements to farm land
- The import or export of agricultural commodities, animals, or plants
- Personnel data on current or former USDA employees

Department of Commerce

The Department of Commerce has information on international trade, social and economic conditions and trends, patents, trademarks, ocean studies, domestic economic development, as well as some information on minority businesses.

Social Security Administration

The Social Security Administration retains original applications for Social Security numbers. Applications list an applicant's name (maiden and married names for women), date of birth, place of birth, sex, race, parents' names, and address at time of application.

If a Social Security number is known, it might lead to helpful information regarding the location where the card was issued. Because many people apply for a Social Security number at a young age, this can help to locate an individual's place of birth. There are nine digits in the Social Security number. With the exception of the 700 series, the first three digits reflect the state of issue. Some states and Puerto Rico have more than one series of numbers. The last six digits are individual identifiers. Here is a listing of the states of issue of the first three digits:

Social Security Number Chart

Initial Numbers	State of Issuance
001-003	New Hampshire
004-007	Maine
008-009	Vermont
010-034	Massachusetts
035-039	Rhode Island
040-049	Connecticut
050-134	New York
135-158	New Jersey

159-211	Pennsylvania
212-220	Maryland
221-222	Delaware
223-231, 691-699*	Virginia
232-236	West Virginia
237-246, 232, 681-690*	North Carolina
247-251, 654-658*	South Carolina
252-260, 667-675*	Georgia
261-267, 589-595, 766-772	Florida
268-302	Ohio
303-317	Indiana
318-361	Illinois
362-386	Michigan
387-399	Wisconsin
400-407	Kentucky
408-415, 756-763*	Tennessee
416-424	Alabama
425-428, 587, 588*, 752-755*	Mississippi
429-432, 676-679*	Arkansas
433-439, 659-665*	Louisiana
440-448	Oklahoma
449-467, 627-645	Texas
468-477	Minnesota
478-485	Iowa
486-500	Missouri
501-502	North Dakota
503-504	South Dakota
505-508	Nebraska
509-515	Kansas
516-517	Montana
518-519	Idaho
520	Wyoming
521-524, 650-653*	Colorado
525, 585, 648, 649*	New Mexico
526-527, 600-601	Arizona
525-529, 646-647	Utah
530, 680*	Nevada
531-539	Washington
540-544	Oregon
545-573, 602-626	California
574	Alaska
575-576, 750-751*	Hawaii
577-579	District of Columbia
580 groups 01-18 (groups 20 above PR)	Virgin Islands
580-584, 596-599	Puerto Rico
586	Guam, American Samoa, Northern Mariana Islands, Philippine Islands

700-728	Railroad employees under the special retirement act**
729-733	Enumeration at Entry

* New areas allocated but not yet issued

** Issuance of these numbers to railroad employees was discontinued July 1, 1963.

Department of Defense (DOD)

Information concerning military pay, dependents, allotments, deposits, and other financial information is maintained by the following:

ARMY
Defense Finance and Accounting Service
Indianapolis Center
Indianapolis, IN 46249-0001

AIR FORCE
Defense Finance and Accounting Service
Denver Center
Lowry Air Force Base
Denver, CO 80279-5000

NAVY
Defense Finance and Accounting Service
Cleveland Center
1240 East Ninth Street
Cleveland, OH 44199-2055

MARINE CORPS
Defense Finance and Accounting Service
Kansas City Center
Kansas City, MO 64197-0001

Department of Education

Financial and earnings statements from parents of students applying for Pell Grants (formerly called Basic Educational Opportunity Grants) are maintained by the Department of Education's Inspector General.

Department of Housing and Urban Development (HUD)

HUD's Compliance Division conducts investigations of alleged HUD violations. This division handles investigations of false statements on credit applications for Federal Housing Administration (FHA) loans, mortgagers' certification of no outstanding obligations, cost certificates, and other areas of fraud. HUD maintains central index files in Washington D.C. containing information regarding HUD programs and participants, including such individuals and businesses as mortgage companies, developers, and borrowers.

Department of Justice

The Department of Justice's U.S. National Central Bureau of the International Criminal Police Organization (USNCB-INTERPOL) has direct contact with law enforcement authorities in more than 155 INTERPOL member countries. The USNCB, therefore, can request information regarding ownership, previous investigations, and any other material legally releasable. The information available is determined by the laws of the countries from which the material is requested.

Department of Labor

The Department of Labor has information about the Federal Employees Compensation Act, the Job Partnership Training Act, the Occupational Safety Health Act, and the Mine Safety Health Act. The Department retains substantial data on businesses that have special work programs affiliated with it.

The Office of Labor-Management Standards (OLMS) administers and enforces most of the provisions of the Labor-Managment Reporting and Disclosure Act of 1959 (LMRDA). The LMRDA has reporting requirements for certain labor organizations, union officers and employees, employers, labor relations consultants, and surety companies. The LMRDA requires covered labor organizations to annually file reports with the OLMS. The information required includes names and titles of officers; rates of dues and fees; loans receivable; other investments; other assets; other liabilities; fixed assets; loans payable; sales of investments and fixed assets; disbursement to officers; disbursement to employees; purchase of investments and fixed assets; benefits; and contributions, gifts, and grants.

In addition, surety companies which issue bonds required by LMRDA or the Employee Retirement Income Security Act of 1974 (ERISA) are required to report premiums received and claims paid.

Department of State

The Department of State maintains data on import and export licenses. The State Department's Bureau of Diplomatic Security has information relating to previous investigations conducted by that office.

Department of the Treasury

The Department of the Treasury includes four statutory inspector general law enforcement agencies.

The Bureau of Alcohol, Tobacco and Firearms (ATF) retains:
- Data on distilleries, wineries, breweries, manufacturers of tobacco products, wholesale and retail dealers of alcoholic beverages, and certain other manufacturers, dealers, and users of alcohol
- Investigative reports of alleged violations under its jurisdiction
- A list of federally licensed firearms manufacturers, importers, and dealers
- A complete list of all federally licensed explosive manufacturers, importers, and dealers

Within the Internal Revenue Service (IRS), the Criminal Investigation Division (CID) conducts investigations of tax fraud relating to income tax, excise tax, currency transaction report violations, and occupational tax violations. The release of taxpayer information to other than IRS personnel requires special procedures. The IRS Inspection Service maintains information on subjects of investigation and their relationships to IRS employees, i.e., threats made against, collusion with, and bribery of IRS employees.

The U.S. Customs Service retains data on businesses that are involved in the import and export area, including lists and records of importers and exporters and lists and records of custom house brokers and truckers. The Office of Investigations looks into alleged violations of import and export practices. The Customs Service also is involved in the National Narcotics Border Interdiction System, and special agents from the Office of Investigations have been participating in the Organized Crime Drug Enforcement Task Force. Customs might provide information relative to businesses that violate the statutes it enforces.

The U.S. Secret Service maintains records on forgers, counterfeiters, and businesses that have contacted the Service concerning forged or counterfeit obligations of the United States, such as Treasury notes. In addition, the Treasurer of the United States can provide copies of canceled checks paid by the U.S. Treasury.

Department of Veterans Affairs (VA)

Records of loans, tuition payments, insurance payments, and nonrestrictive medical data related to disability pensions are maintained at VA regional offices located in several metropolitan areas throughout the country.

Drug Enforcement Agency

The Drug Enforcement Administration (DEA) maintains information on licensed handlers of narcotics and the criminal records of users, pushers, and suppliers of narcotics.

Federal Aviation Administration (FAA)

The FAA maintains records reflecting the chain of ownership of all civil aircraft in the United States. These records include documents about the manufacture, sale, transfer, inspection, and modification of an aircraft, including the bill of sale, sales contract, mortgage, and liens.

The FAA also maintains records on pilots, aircraft mechanics, flight engineers, and other individuals that it certifies for flight safety positions. These records include information on certificates held, medicals, and law enforcement history.

Federal Bureau of Investigation

The Federal Bureau of Investigation (FBI) provides information on criminal records and fingerprints, as well as nonrestricted information pertaining to criminal offenses and subversive activities. It also provides information about wanted, missing, and unidentified people and foreign fugitives. The FBI maintains the Index to State Criminal History Records and Criminal History Records of Federal Offenders.

Federal Communications Commission (FCC)

The FCC licenses all radio operators in the United States. Individuals or corporate bodies applying for authority to construct new broadcast stations or to change existing stations also must file with the FCC. Information contained in the filings includes details on programming, technical aspects of the proposed facilities, ownership, and financial status.

Federal Energy Regulatory Commission

Electric utility and natural gas companies are required to file annual reports with the Federal Energy Regulatory Commission. The reports provide excellent financial pictures of the companies as well as other information, e.g., officers, directors, and stockholders who own more than 10 percent of the company.

Federal Maritime Commission

The Federal Maritime Commission investigates applicants for licenses to engage in oceangoing freight-forwarding activities. Applicants provide information to the Commission covering most aspects of their history, including name, residence, date and place of birth, and citizenship of all corporate officers and directors; names of partnership members of individual proprietors; and names of direct holders of 5 percent or more of company stock.

General Services Administration (GSA)

The GSA has considerable information on architects, engineers, personal property auctioneers, real estate appraisers, construction contractors, sales brokers, and businesses that contract with the GSA. The agency also maintains the "GSA Consolidated List," a computerized roster of suspended and debarred bidders.

Interstate Commerce Commission (ICC)

The ICC requires interstate truck lines and other shippers to file annual reports on their financial activities. The ICC also has information concerning individuals who are or have been officers of transportation firms engaged in interstate commerce. This information includes an officer's employment and financial affiliations. In addition, most ICC safety inspectors are good sources of "reference" information because they have personal knowledge of the supervisory employees of the various carriers in their region.

National Aeronautics and Space Administration (NASA)

More than 85 percent of NASA's multibillion-dollar budget goes to NASA contractors. Files maintained by its Office of Procurement contain information about a firm and its employees. NASA requires that contractors submit the following data with their pro-posals: name and qualifications of the contractor and resumes of the personnel who will be directly assigned to the project. The resumes should include educational background, work experience, length of service with the firm, and projects on which these individuals have worked.

National Archives and Records Administration

The National Archives and Records Administration operates federal records centers throughout the country, including the National Personnel Records Center in St. Louis, MO and the Office of the Federal Register in Washington, D.C. It also is responsible for regional archives and the presidential libraries. The National Personnel Records Center in St. Louis stores the personnel records of former members of the armed forces and former federal civilian employees. Procedures for investigative inquiries into these records are available from the Center. For information, call +1 (314) 263-7201.

The *Federal Register* is the medium for notifying the public of official agency actions; all federal regulations must be published in it. The Office of the Federal Register provides a periodic workshop on the use of the *Federal Register* as an information source. A handbook on the uses of the *Federal Register* also is available. For information, call +1 (202) 523-5240.

National Railroad Passenger Corporation (Amtrak)

Amtrak maintains information on passengers, including reservation histories, methods of payment, and dates of travel; the railroad industry; railroad contractors; subcontractors; vendors; and train routes and schedules.

Nuclear Regulatory Commission (NRC)

The NRC maintains applications and licenses of people and companies that export nuclear material and equipment from the United States. The NRC determines whether proposed exports would be inimical to our defense and security and, for certain exports, whether they come under the terms of an agreement, which establishes the ground rules for nuclear cooperation and trade between the United States and the country of destination.

Office of Foreign Assets Control (OFAC)

The Office of Foreign Assets Control (OFAC) is an office within the Department of the Treasury charged with administering and enforcing U.S. sanction policies against targeted foreign organizations and individuals that sponsor terrorism, and international narcotics traffickers. OFAC maintains a list of individuals, governmental entities, companies, and merchant vessels around the world that are known or suspected to engage in illegal activities. Persons or entities on the list, known as Specially Designated Nationals and Blocked Persons ("SDNs"), include foreign agents, front organizations, terrorists and terrorist organizations, and drug traffickers. The list contains over 5,000 variations on names of individuals, governmental entities, companies, and merchant vessels and is updated on a regular basis.

Resolution Trust Corporation (RTC)

The RTC is a federally chartered corporation created to contain, manage, and resolve failed savings institutions and recover funds through the management and ultimate sale of the institutions' assets. The RTC maintains information on failed savings institutions, including their ownership and officers, identities of loan borrowers, contracts, and previous investigations.

Securities and Exchange Commission (SEC)

The SEC maintains public records of corporations with stocks and securities sold to the public. These records include the following:
- Financial statements
- Identification of officers and directors
- Identification of owners of more than 10 percent of a business' stock
- A description of the registrant's properties and businesses
- A description of the significant provisions of the security to be offered for sale and its relationship to the registrant's other capital securities
- Identification of events of interest to investors
- Identification of accountants and attorneys
- A history of the business

The SEC maintains files on individuals and firms reported to it for violating federal or state securities laws. The information in these files pertains to official actions taken against such people and firms, including denials, refusals, suspensions, and revocations of registrations; injunctions, fraud orders, stop orders, and cease and desist orders; and arrests, indictments, convictions, sentences, and other official actions.

The *Securities and Exchange Commission Summary* also lists the changes in beneficial ownership by officers, directors, and principal stockholders of securities listed and registered on a national securities exchange or of securities of public utility companies and certain closed-end investment companies.

Copies of the documents maintained by the SEC are available at SEC's regional or branch offices in the following cities: Atlanta; Miami; Boston; Chicago; Cleveland; Detroit; St. Louis; Denver; Salt Lake City; Fort Worth; Los Angeles; San Francisco; New York; Seattle; Washington, D.C.; and Philadelphia.

Access to some SEC filings are available through the Internet at www.sec.gov.

Corporate filings include the following:
- *Annual Report of Publicly Traded Company* (Form 10-K)—excerpts or complete report is available via LEXIS or Dialog databases, i.e., Disclosure
- *Quarterly Report of Publicly Traded Company* (Form 10-Q)—same as 10-K
- *Special Events in Publicly Traded Company* (Form 8-K)—transactions resulting in change of controlling interest
- *Registration of Security* (Form 8-A)—prospectus and data relative to the issuer
- *Registration of Security by Successor* (Form 8-B)—name of issuer, relationship to primary registrant/issuer
- *Special Events in Foreign Security* (Form 6-K)—information similar to 10-K and 8-K, except the security is registered under another U.S. law
- *Report of Acquisition of Beneficial Ownership of 5% or More of Capital Stock of Public Company* (Form 13-D)—identity of each person or firm acquiring beneficial ownership of 5 percent or more of capital stock, or identity of each person or firm constituting a group that acquires such beneficial ownership; description of security; agreements or other undertakings by reporting entity; if acquisition results in change of control, background on each person reporting; and sources of funds for acquisition, purpose of acquisition, and relationship of parties

Small Business Administration (SBA)

The SBA guarantees loans made by private lenders and makes direct loans for business construction, expansion, or conversion; for purchase of machinery, equipment, facilities, supplies, or materials; and for working capital. A loan applicant (sole owner, partnership, corporation, or other) must complete SBA forms, providing information about the business and its principals (owners, officers, and directors).

The SBA arranges contracts and guarantees loans for qualified, small, minority-owned businesses. For some of these businesses, the SBA might be the only source for financial and other information about the businesses, their principals, their assets, and other data. Because their stock is not publicly held, these businesses are not subject to public disclosure laws. The SBA also connects small firms owned by socially and economically disadvantaged Americans with contracts set aside by other federal agencies for the purposes of increasing opportunities for small businesses generally.

Bureau of Public Debt

The Bureau of the Public Debt maintains information on purchased and redeemed U.S. saving bonds (registered bonds), marketable securities, and special securities. Information maintained includes the series of bonds involved and the surname, given name, middle name or initial, and address of each person in whose name bonds were purchased.

Federal Highway Administration

FHWA, Office of Motor Carriers, licenses, regulates, inspects, and registers all motor carriers operating in interstate commerce. It keeps records of its inspections of motor carriers and a history of violations of each carrier.

U.S. Citizenship and Immigration Services

Formerly the Immigration and Naturalization Service (INS), the UCIS retains a number of records, including: alien registration records, in effect since August 27, 1940 (from July 1, 1920, to August 27, 1940, each immigrant was given an Immigrant's Identification Card); lists of passengers and crews on vessels from foreign ports; passenger manifests and declarations (ship, date, and point of entry); naturalization records (names of witnesses to naturalization proceedings and acquaintances of the individual); deportation proceedings; and financial statements of aliens and people sponsoring an immigrant entry.

U.S. Coast Guard

The Coast Guard maintains names of merchant mariners on U.S. vessels and investigative records pertaining to them, records relating to maritime drug smuggling, records on criminal investigations, and records on documented U.S. vessels.

U.S. General Accounting Office

GAO's World Wide Web home page provides access to recent GAO audit products and Comptroller General decisions, as well as information on how to order paper copies of both recent and older GAO products. In addition, GAO audit products from fiscal year 1995 forward and recent decisions are available in electronic form at the Government Printing Office's Internet site. GAO products, including those not available on the Internet, may also be ordered by calling (202) 512-6000 or TDD (301) 413-0006.

U.S. Postal Service

The Postal Service maintains the names and addresses of post office box holders. Check with the local post office to learn the identity of the inspector who can furnish the information. Photocopies of postal money orders and requests for copies of postal money orders are made through the local U.S. Postal Inspection Service office, usually by subpoena.

Federal Procurement Data System

With expenditures by the executive branch rising over $200 billion a year, keeping track of who paid what to whom is no small task. The Federal Procurement Data System does just that, however, by summarizing transactions and services negotiated throughout the year. Roughly seventy federal agencies report their contracts and purchases to the FPDS, which catalogs the information for government as well as public use. Contracts agreed upon as long ago as 1978 are searchable. Obviously the best source for federal procurement information, the FPDS website (http://fpds.gsa.gov/) is also fairly explanatory and easy to navigate.

FedWorld Information Network

FedWorld is a one-stop shopping spot for federal government information, including a government locator database, U.S. Customs rulings, Supreme Court decisions, and a foreign news alert service. Their website is www.fedworld.gov.

Commercial Sources

Associations and lobby groups have information about their member firms. Two of the best sources are the Better Business Bureau and a city's Chamber of Commerce.

Better Business Bureau

A number of Better Business Bureaus are located throughout the country. They are sponsored by local businesses and offer a variety of services, including background information on local businesses and organizations. The bureaus generally keep information about criminal rackets and cons and their operators and can provide information about the business reputations of local groups.

Chamber of Commerce

Chambers of Commerce generally have city directories and often keep back issues of the directories. They also have information regarding reputations of businesses and operators in the area.

Abstract and Title Companies

In addition to records of individual transactions, abstract and title companies often publish and distribute papers to attorneys, real estate brokers, insurance companies, and financial institutions. These papers contain information about transfers of property, locations, mortgage amounts, and release of mortgages.

Bonding Companies

An application for a bond contains the applicant's (person or firm) financial statement and data. This essentially is the same information that is required in loan applications (though in greater detail).

Credit Card Records

Information on expenditures can be obtained from firms such as Mastercard, American Express, Diners Club, Discover, and Visa. This information usually requires a subpoena.

Stockbrokers

Stockbrokers maintain information similar to that of banks on many of their clients, especially those who have margin accounts. They maintain records of transactions for all clients.

Western Union

Records for paid money orders are stored in Minneapolis, and contain the original telegram, by purchaser or sender, and bank drafts by Western Union. Western Union retains orders for less than $1,000 for two years and orders of $1,000 or more for six years.

Car Fax

Car Fax is a private service that provides a history of automobiles. It determines whether there is an odometer discrepancy or evidence of prior salvage or title washing. It covers most of the U.S. and contains over 45 million problem records for over 18 million vehicles.

International Air Transport Association

This association has information on all international matters dealing with aviation security, including counterterrorism efforts worldwide. It also monitors and attempts to prevent fraud against airlines, such as ticket fraud.

International Foundation for Art Research

IFAR is a nonprofit organization established in 1969 to help prevent the circulation of forged and misattributed works of art. IFAR offers an Authentication Service to help resolve controversies concerning the authenticity of works of art. IFAR also publishes reports ten times a year with articles on authentication research, art law, theft and recovery, and extensive listing of recently reported stolen and missing art and antiques. The IFAR can be contacted at (212) 391-6234.

National Association of Insurance Commissioners

This association is an organization of insurance regulators from the 50 states, the District of Columbia, and the 4 U.S. territories. It provides a forum for the development of policy when uniformity is appropriate. A state regulator's primary responsibility is to protect the interests of insurance consumers and the association helps regulators fulfill that obligation.

Phonefiche

The Phonefiche *Community Cross-Reference Guide* is divided into three parts—U.S. directories, Canadian directories, and Puerto Rican directories—and each part is subdivided into sections entitled Community Index and Directory Coverage. The guide is both a compendium to Phonefiche and an independent reference tool. It facilitates the use of telephone directories in any format and provides search assistance for directories included in the Phonefiche program.

The guide includes a revised listing of all U.S., Canadian, and Puerto Rican telephone books arranged in alphabetical order by state or province.

Select Phone

This six-disk CD-ROM set provides telephone numbers from millions of residential and commercial listings across the U.S. Searchable elements include name, street, city, state, zip code, area code, telephone number, and standard industrial classification code. Search results can be sorted, printed, or downloaded. Currency is indicated by the month and the year a listing appeared in a printed directory. This set is updated quarterly.

Credit Records

Practically all lines of business have specialized credit reporting associations that can provide credit information on individuals and businesses, including trade information, designation of lenders and creditors, types of businesses, date accounts were opened, terms of payment agreed upon, highest credit, balance owing, and paying habits. Some credit reports also give the name of the bank the subject does business with and the size of the subject's accounts. The three most frequently used sources are Equifax Services, Experian (formerly TRW), and TransUnion. Generally, a subscription is required to obtain information from these sources, and their dissemination is governed by the Fair Credit Reporting Act. New amendments to the Act have placed further restrictions on when a consumer credit report can be used. In many cases, the consumer must be notified or must consent to the use of the report for employment purposes. Please consult the information on the Fair Credit Reporting Act presented previously in this chapter for more information about the legality of using consumer credit reports.

There essentially are two types of credit reporting agencies. The first is known as a *file-based credit reporting agency*, which develops its information from credit files and public records. The other type is known as an *investigative credit reporting agency*, which gathers most of its information through interviews.

Types of Retail Information

Credit bureaus are used primarily by retail organizations, and typically maintain the following information:

- Consumer information, such as address, age, family members, employers, income levels, length of employment, the extent of other obligations, and the like
- Account information, such as payment schedules, items purchased, defaults (if any), and buying habits
- Marketing information, such as customers broken down by age, sex, income levels, and other classifications
- Information on current and former employees

Information Available from Credit Bureaus

Credit bureaus rely on information supplied by organizations granting credit. In a typical situation, the potential creditor calls the credit bureau (or makes an on-line request) for information. The creditor receives details regarding other credit histories of the individual, such as payment schedules and delinquencies.

The credit bureau also gathers public record information such as bankruptcies, judgments, divorces, criminal convictions, and registered chattel mortgages. Information is regularly updated at the request of the consumer or by request of the credit grantor.

Commercial Databases and Research Reference Services

Electronic databases are a rapidly growing source of information. Databases, generally, do not provide any more information than can be accessed from other sources. However, they have two distinct advantages—search speed and constant access.

On-line databases allow the user to retrieve the requested information through a computer system. Generally, there is an initial fee for the necessary software that enables the computer to communicate with the database. Additional charges apply for any information retrieved from the database.

Commercial databases that do not offer on-line capabilities (report services) are more prevalent in the industry and less expensive. They provide the user with information on a one-time basis for a nominal charge. There are no software charges or monthly fees. Therefore, off-line databases are more cost effective for the occasional user.

Type of Information Available

The type of information available from report services include:
- Credit reports
- Driving records
- County and statewide criminal conviction history
- Worker's compensation records
- Education verifications
- Professional license verifications
- Social Security locator
- National address locator
- National telephone identifier
- County and statewide real property records
- Federal criminal and civil record checks
- Consumer public filings
- Military locator
- Name and address of neighbors

- State and county civil records
- Business public filings
- Business credit checks
- Corporate records (by state)
- FAA registrations
- Pleasure craft registrations
- Vehicle registration (by license number or name of person or company)
- National criss-cross service
- Federal bankruptcy course searches
- Grantor and grantee searches
- Abstracts of judgments
- Tax liens

On-Line Information Vendors

There are a number of companies which offer wide access to public records, credit reports, and newspapers and periodicals. Some of the more commonly used sources are:
- ChoicePoint
- CDB Infotek
- IRSC
- Database Technologies On-line (DBT On-line)
- Lexis-Nexis
- USDatalink
- infoUSA.com
- Diligenz
- KnowX
- Dialog Information Retrieval Service

A complete description of these services and other information available through the computer is discussed in the next chapter, "Accessing Information On-Line."

Directories

Directories provide data on national, trade, business, and commercial associations. Some of the more frequently used directories are the following:

American Medical Association Directory

This directory, published by the American Medical Association, lists the following information:

- The presidents and secretaries of all county medical associations
- Doctors—by states and cities in states, year of birth, medical school and year of graduation, year of license, residence and office addresses, specialties, and membership in associated medical organizations
- A name index of all doctors

America's Corporate Families and International Affiliates

This three-volume directory provides complete demographic marketing data on more than 11,000 U.S. corporations and their 76,000 subsidiaries, divisions, and branches. Volume III of this directory covers nearly 3,000 foreign ultimate parent companies and their 11,000 U.S. subsidiaries, and nearly 3,000 U.S. ultimate parent corporations and their 18,000 foreign subsidiaries. Corporate family listings are presented in three useful classifications: alphabetical, geographical, and industrial.

Best Insurance Reports

The annual edition of the *Best Insurance Reports* presents comprehensive statistical reports of the financial position, history, and operating results of legal reserve life insurance companies, fraternal benefit societies, and assessment associations operating in the United States and Canada. The individual report on each institution includes a review of its history, management and operations, investments, operating results, and other statistical compilations.

Wilson Biological and Agricultural Index

This source is a cumulative subject index to English language periodicals. The main body of the index, arranged alphabetically, consists of biological and agricultural subject entries referring to periodical articles. A separate listing of book reviews follows the subject entries.

Indexed subjects include agricultural chemicals, agricultural economics, agricultural engineering, agriculture and agricultural research, animal husbandry, biochemistry, biology, biotechnology, botany, ecology, entomology, environmental science, fishery sciences, food science, forestry, genetics and cytology, horticulture, marine biology and limnology, microbiology, nutrition, physiology, plant pathology, soil science, veterinary medicine, and zoology.

CD-ROMs in Print

This directory, published by Meckler in Westport, CT, contains a list of information available on CD-ROM.

City Directories

City directories usually contain the name, residence, occupation, and sometimes the place of employment of the city's influential people. Such directories generally can be found at public libraries, chambers of commerce, and secondhand book stores.

Congressional Directory

(Superintendent of Documents, Washington, D.C.)

This source contains the following information:
- Biographical sketches of senators, representatives, and federal judges
- Names, office addresses, and office telephone numbers of judicial and executive department personnel, such as members of boards, commissions, bureaus, and committees
- Names of foreign diplomatic and consular officers in the United States, with locations of offices and names of personnel assigned
- Names of U.S. diplomatic and consular officers overseas, with addresses
- Names—and frequently office addresses and telephone numbers—of congressional, judicial, and executive department staff
- Names of officials, addresses, and telephone numbers of District of Columbia agencies and committees and of many international organizations
- Names of members of the press entitled to use the press galleries of the House and/or Senate
- Members of the White House News Photographers' Association and the Radio, Television, and Periodical Press Galleries (in the U.S. Capitol), listed by name and news organization represented, including business address and telephone number

Directories in Print

This publication, published by Gale Research, thoroughly describes and indexes about 14,000 directories of all kinds, including business and industrial directories, professional and scientific rosters, foreign directories, and other lists and guides.

Directory of Companies Filing Annual Reports With the Securities and Exchange Commission Under the Securities Exchange Act of 1934

Published by the SEC and available from the Government Printing Office, this directory helps to determine whether a parent company is public or private.

Directory of Corporate Affiliations—Who Owns Whom

This directory provides information on subsidiaries and associate companies and how they fit into their parent companies. It is published by the National Register Publishing Company.

Dow Jones-Irwin Business and Investment Almanac

Published by Dow Jones-Irwin, this book contains information on stocks, SEC filings, mutual funds, and definitions of important financial terms. It also contains a guide to on-line business databases and a directory of other business sources of information.

D&B's Million Dollar Directory

This directory, published by D&B (formerly Dun & Bradstreet) provides information on industries, utilities, transportation companies, banks, trust companies, mutual and stock insurance companies, as well as wholesalers and retailers whose net worth exceeds $500,000. Information available includes annual sales, corporate officers, locations, phone numbers, type of business, and number of employees.

Encyclopedia of Business Information Sources

Published by Gale Research, this directory contains listings by topic of many reference works in print and on CD-ROM.

Federal Database Finder

Published by Information USA and Gale Research, this guide serves as both a list of government databases and government experts.

Gale's Encyclopedia of Associations

This source lists each chartered public and private association in the United States (and some foreign countries) and provides valuable information about the association's officers and purpose.

Gale Guide to Internet Databases

Published by Gale Research, this book contains a list of government, academic, research, and educational databases and other electronic information available through the Internet.

Guide to American Directories

Published by Todd Publications, this guide lists more than 11,000 directories of individuals, institutions, and business firms.

Index Medicus

This source is a classified index of the world's medical literature. It covers publications in all major languages and includes periodical articles and other analytical material as well as books, pamphlets, and theses.

Index to Legal Periodicals

This source is similar to the *Reader's Guide to Periodical Literature*, but it covers only legal periodicals, bar association, and judicial council reports.

Insurance Reporting Services

These are agencies in business with or subsidized by insurance companies or under-writers. They gather information concerning policyholders. Such information includes loss histories, investigations of losses, and recovery of property.

Lloyd's Register of Classed Yachts and Register of American Yachts

These registers list the names and descriptions of yachts, their classification, the names and addresses of owners, yacht clubs, and flags. (The *Register of American Yachts* includes only U.S. and Canadian yachts 1904-1978.)

Lloyd's Register of Shipping and B. Lloyd's Weekly Register

These registers list all seagoing merchant and passenger ships of the world, as well as each ship's owner, material of construction, rig, tonnage, builder, date built, dimensions, port of registry, and engines. For commercial ships sailing worldwide, the registers also list each ship's registry, flag, and last and next port of call.

Lloyd's Voyage Record and Shipping Index

The monthly voyage record details recent voyage history of over 22,000 vessels in commercial service reporting movements collected continuously by Lloyd's agents. The weekly index reports on the current voyages, latest reported movements, and essential characteristics of approximately 22,000 merchant vessels worldwide. Consists of three sections: World Fleet Details, Market Briefing, and Buyers' Guide.

List of Shipowners

This list includes over 40,000 owners, managers, and managing agents for vessels listed in the Register of Ships. It is published annually in August and includes postal addresses; telephone, telex and telefax numbers; fleet lists; and a geographical index. Subscribers receive ten free updates per year.

Register of International Shipowning Groups

This register is available in three volumes annually (April, August, and December). The register is indexed by ship and company name and lists 20,000 companies operating on ships of at least 1,000 gross tons or more; ownership of 30,000 ships; registered owners, grouped by ship management company; and subsidiaries and associate companies, identified together with owners' representatives.

Register of Offshore Units, Submersibles and Underwater Systems

This register is published annually in September. It contains sections listing mobile drilling rigs, submersibles, underwater systems, work units (ships, barges, and platforms) used for a variety of offshore work, owners, and addresses of offshore support ships with their fleet lists.

Weekly List of Alterations to the Register of Ships

This list is a noncumulative set of amendments—in alphabetical order by ship name—to details published in the Register of Ships. Although the amendments will appear in the ten supplements, the Weekly List is intended for those who need to receive updated information expeditiously.

Magazines for Libraries

Written by Bill and Linda Katz and published by R.R. Bowker, this book lists virtually every magazine (general, technical, and scholarly) that a library might wish to stock. The book also describes the formats in which the magazines are available (CD-ROM, microfiche, etc.).

Martindale-Hubbell Law Directory
This directory, published annually, contains biographical information on most lawyers in private practice in the United States and Canada.

Moody's
Moody's publications are similar to Dun & Bradstreet's. Moody's reports can provide information about firms listed on the New York and American stock exchanges as well as companies listed on regional American exchanges.

Moody's Bank and Finance Manual
This three-volume manual covers the field of finance represented by banks, insurance companies, investment companies, unit investment trusts, and miscellaneous financial enterprises. Also included in the manual are real estate companies and real estate investment trusts.

Moody's Bank and Finance News Reports
These reports are published on Tuesday and Friday of each week and contain material updating *Moody's Bank and Finance Manual*. The reports include—among other information—news items, interim financial statements, personnel changes, new company descriptions, merger proposals, details about new debts and stock issues, security offerings, announcements of new financing, and call notices.

National Auto Theft Bureau
This bureau is maintained by auto insurance companies to reduce auto theft rates through investigation and apprehension. The bureau investigates abandoned and wrecked vehicles, wrecking yards, and junk dealers. It maintains files on professional auto thieves and theft rings. The bureau is national in scope and is connected by teletype (also to Canada). The bureau has an office staff in most state motor vehicle department head-quarters to check ownership and registrations, but has no legal or official police power.

The National Directory of Law Enforcement Administrators
This source lists the following information: names, addresses, telephone numbers, and fax numbers of highway patrols; prosecuting attorneys; and municipal, county, campus, state correctional, federal, military, airport, harbor, and many other related law enforcement agencies.

National Trade and Professional Associations of the United States

This directory lists over 7,500 active national trade and professional associations and labor unions.

The New York Times Index

This source is published semimonthly. It includes an exact reference to date, page, and column of *The New York Times* edition in which articles will be found. It contains cross references to names and related topics. The brief synopses of articles often are sufficient to answer questions.

Phonedisc USA

Produced by InfoUSA, this CD-ROM set contains the phone numbers, names, and addresses of millions of business and residential telephone customers.

Public Affairs Information Service

This source is a subject index to the current literature—books, documents, pamphlets, articles in periodicals, and mimeographed material—in the public affairs field. The source includes selective indexing to more than 1,000 periodicals. It is a particularly useful index for information about political science, government, legislation, economics, and sociology.

Reader's Guide to Periodical Literature

The *Reader's Guide* refers to articles in more than 250 popular magazines. It is published semimonthly; its cumulative index is published every two years. The guide contains a full dictionary cataloging of all articles, i.e., by author, subject, and title where possible. The entries refer to the volume, number of the periodical, starting and inclusive pages of the article, date of publication, and graphic material in the article, such as portraits.

Predicasts Funk and Scott Index, United States

Updated monthly, this directory indexes most periodicals, such as newspapers. Funk and Scott also publishes quarterly the *Index of Corporate Change*, which lists recent business activities, such as mergers and acquisitions.

Standard & Poor's Corporation Records

This is a service provided by Standard and Poor to its subscribers. The reports cover companies that are publicly traded and include their brief history, financial statements, capital structure, lines of business, subsidiaries, and officers and directors.

Standard & Poor's Register of Corporations, Directors and Executives

This three-volume directory lists about 55,000 public and private companies, as well as the names and titles of more than 500,000 officials. Company information includes financial data, Securities Information Center (SIC) numbers, products and services, and the number of employees. The information is similar to that provided by Dun & Bradstreet and Moody's.

Who's Who Series

This series of sources contains information—such as schools attended, fields of study, and degrees; occupational background; and office addresses—submitted by the individual at the request of the publisher. Publications in the series cover occupations ranging from student to surgeon and psychologist. There are regional publications and a *Who Was Who* of deceased people.

Associations Yellow Book

This is a directory of major trade and professional associations. Semiannual editions of the Associations Yellow Book provide current information on chief staff executive turnovers, changes in staff and governing boards, mergers, and name changes. It features: (1) over 41,000 officers, executives, and staff, with titles, affiliations, education, telephone and fax numbers, at more than 1,000 associations with budgets over $2 million; (2) addresses and e-mail addresses and telephone and fax numbers of headquarters and branches, and Internet addresses for headquarters; (3) boards members, with outside affiliations; (4) committees and chairmen, Washington representatives, political action committees, and foundations; (5) publications, including editors; and (6) annual budget, tax status, number of employees, and number of members.

Corporate Yellow Book

This is a directory of the people who manage, direct, and shape the largest public and privately held companies in the United States. It enables subscribers to access corporate leaders, including board members who are taking increased responsibility for corporate decision making. The directory features: (1) over 1,000 leading corporations and over 6,000 subsidiaries and divisions; (2) names and titles of over 51,000 executives, including more than 9,000 corporate board members and their outside affiliations; (3) direct-dial telephone numbers of executives; (4) addresses, telephone and fax numbers, and Internet addresses of corporate headquarters and domestic and foreign subsidiaries and divisions; and (5) contacts for administrative services, such as benefits, corporate contributions, foundations, government affairs, information systems, libraries and information centers, purchasing, real estate and facilities, recruitment, and shareholder relations.

Encyclopedia of Associations

The Encyclopedia of Associations is a comprehensive source of detailed information on over 81,000 nonprofit and membership organizations worldwide. It provides addresses and descriptions of professional societies, trade associations, labor unions, cultural and religious organizations, fan clubs, and other groups of all types. It is published by Gale Research.

Federal Organization Charts

This loose-leaf chart produced by Carroll Publishing Company provides names, addresses, and telephone numbers for staff members in the White House, executive departments, independent agencies, quasi-governmental organizations, and congressional support offices. It has name and key word indexes and is updated monthly. Due to its high cost and time-consuming maintenance, it is mostly available at selected federal government libraries.

Federal Regional Yellow Book

This yellow book describes federal regional offices located outside Washington, D.C. It contains over 37,000 regional directors and administrative staff members of federal departments and agencies. It also has information on administrators and professional staff at federal laboratories, research centers, military installations, and service academies.

Financial Yellow Book

This directory lists names and titles of over 26,000 executives, including over 5,000 board members at over 800 leading financial institutions and over 3,000 subsidiaries. The directory has four indexes—on company, geographical location, individual name, and industry. An Exchanges and Markets section has been added that lists leading exchanges and markets in the U.S.

Foreign Representatives in the U.S. Yellow Book

This directory has sections on corporations, financial institutions, foreign nations, intergovernmental organizations, foreign press, and law firms. It includes officials' titles, addresses, and telephone and fax numbers.

Gale Directory of Databases

This directory provides detailed descriptions of nearly 11,000 publicly available databases accessible through an on-line vendor or batch processor or for purchase. Its scope includes all types of databases in all subject areas. Information under each entry is organized for rapid retrieval via computer. Producer contact information is also included in each entry.

Gale Directory of Publications and Broadcast Media (Formerly Ayer Directory of Publications)

This three-volume annual directory contains information on 50,000 newspapers, magazines, newsletters, and directories published in the U.S. and Canada including nearly 12,000 radio, television, and cable TV stations. Arrangement is alphabetical by location, name, and media type. The information given about each publication includes its address, phone number, frequency of publication, names of editors and publishers, advertising rate, and circulation. Material on electronic media includes programming formats, network affiliations, operating hours, key personnel, advertising rates, and wattage. Indexes of publishers and subjects are included, as are maps showing sites where media originates.

Government Affairs Yellow Book

This yellow book lists corporations, financial institutions, trade and professional associations, 40 labor unions, interest groups including coalitions, public interest groups, consumer advocacy groups, think tanks, and leadership PACs. A section on Federal, State and Municipal Government includes government affairs staff for federal agencies, state governments, and leading cities and counties. The Government Affairs Representatives section lists over 950 lobbying firms, law firms, and public relations firms. It details the issues the lobbyists contest as well as the coalitions they form to advance their legislative agenda. Four indexes are included—on organization, subject, geographical location, and individual name. Biographical data is included on each professional.

Judicial Yellow Book

This directory provides detailed biographical information for state and federal judges and gives information on each judge's staff, including law clerks. It features more than 2,100 judges in the federal court system and more than 1,250 state judges of the highest appellate courts.

Law Firms Yellow Book

This directory has information on 800 of the largest corporate law firms in the U.S. It focuses on the 23,000 administrators and attorneys in these firms, and it is indexed by specialties, law schools, management/administrative personnel, geography, and personnel. It is updated semiannually.

Municipal Yellow Book

This directory provides information on over 33,000 elected and appointed officials in U.S. cities, and authorities, including name, address, and telephone and fax numbers. It contains sections on cities and countries, which feature complex hierarchies of municipal officials. This directory also has listings for local departments, agencies, subdivisions, and branches.

News Media Yellow Book

Over 38,000 reporters, writers, editors, and producers at more than 2,500 national news media organizations are listed in this yellow book. It features nine sections—on newspapers, news services, networks, television stations, radio stations, programs, periodicals, non-U.S. media, and publishers. New features added to this yellow book are contacts for administrative services, biographical appendix, and photographs of leading journalists. This directory is fully updated on a quarterly basis.

State Yellow Book

This directory provides information on who's who in the executive and legislative branches of the 50 state governments, as well as American Samoa, Guam, Puerto Rico, and the Virgin Islands. It has both a subject and personnel index and includes information on government officials, departments, agencies, and legislative committees. Informational profiles of all states and territories are also provided.

Thomson Bank Directory (replaces the Rand McNally Bankers Directory)

This annual directory produced in one volume is a guide to over 13,000 banks worldwide. Entries include the name, address, and telephone number of the bank; type of charter; funds processor; automated clearinghouse; holding company; asset rank; financial figures; balance sheets; officers and directors; branches; subsidiaries; and foreign offices.

Banks and Financial Institutions

On November 12, 1999 the *Financial Services Modernization Act* was signed into law. A portion of this new law deals with the privacy of consumer information held by financial institutions. The Act requires the federal government to adopt regulations requiring financial institutions to ensure the security and confidentiality of customer records and information. The Act also makes it a crime to obtain, disclose, or provide documents under false pretenses pertaining to customer information of a financial institution. This includes not only banks, but also stock brokerage firms, insurance companies, loan companies, credit card issuers, and credit bureaus.

The Act applies not only to those persons who use false pretenses, but also to any third-party requesting the information when it is known or should be known that false pretenses will be used. Certain limited exceptions do apply. Exempted parties include law enforcement agencies and insurance companies conducting related claims investigations. It also exempts state licensed private investigators who are attempting to collect delinquent child support.

Under the new law, fraud examiners should be extremely careful about obtaining financial information from financial institutions. Additionally, if the government is requesting information, it must also comply with the Right to Financial Privacy Act (12 U.S.C. Secs. 3401-3422).

As a general rule of thumb, financial information can be obtained only by subpoena. If you are able to obtain a subpoena, the following information should be requested:

- Central master files of customers (depositors, debtors, and safe deposit box holders) are maintained by the bank. The bank usually requires the customer's consent, a search warrant, or a court order before an authorized bank official can open a safe deposit box.
- Savings account applications can provide handwriting samples and certain personal information about customers, varying from one bank to another. Savings account deposit records reflect date of deposit, amounts of currency and checks, drawee banks of checks, and dates and amounts of withdrawals. In cases of large withdrawals, some banks request a reason for the withdrawal from the customer. The customer is not required to give the information, however, nor can the bank refuse to honor the withdrawal. Some savings and loan associations might demand notice on large withdrawals.
- Applications for checking accounts also provide handwriting samples and certain personal information, varying from one bank to another. Checking account deposit slips

reflect date of deposit, amounts of currency and checks, and drawee banks of checks. These slips also might identify the account holder's financial associates.

Federal Regulatory Agencies

Export-Import Bank of the United States

The Export-Import Bank loans funds to foreign countries and businesses to buy goods from U.S. companies. The borrower can obtain up to 50 percent of the purchase price of the goods being acquired. The selling company must submit to the bank a supplier certificate. Included in this certificate is a required statement regarding commissions paid, especially in a foreign country, to foreign sales "representatives" or "agents."

Farm Credit Administration

The Farm Credit Administration oversees and regulates the two entities within the farm credit system: the Production Credit Association, providing farm operating loans, and the Federal Land Bank, which grants loans to farmers to buy land.

Federal Deposit Insurance Corporation (FDIC)

Federal or state banks or savings associations that apply to be insured by the FDIC must submit an application that covers financial history, financial condition, capital structure, management, future earning prospects, convenience to and needs of the community, and consistency of corporate powers. FDIC insured banks are examined annually by FDIC insured examiners; FDIC savings associations are examined periodically by FDIC examiners.

Each examination includes an appraisal of management, directors, officers, and staff. The reports contain white and pink sheets. The white sheets provide examination findings; a copy is given to the bank's board of directors. The examiner retains the pink sheets containing confidential information, including an alphabetical list of all directors, officers, and principal employees; their titles; and comments on every individual to the extent possible. The examiner also comments on the capabilities of each individual, gives his approximate age, and cites other business affiliations. Additionally, the examiner completes a form on each individual, setting forth his estimated net worth, par value of stock owned, and salary.

Inquiries regarding types of records available to the public (including records available under the Freedom of Information Act) should be directed to the appropriate FDIC regional office or to the Office of the Executive Secretary, which can be called at (202) 898-3811.

Federal Housing Finance Board

The Federal Housing Finance Board is an independent regulatory agency in the executive branch. The Finance Board succeeded the Federal Home Loan Bank Board and is responsible for administering and enforcing the Federal Home Loan Bank Act.

The Finance Board supervises the Federal Home Loan Banks created by the act and issues regulations and orders for carrying out the purposes of the Act. Savings associations that make long-term home mortgage loans are eligible to become members of a Federal Home Loan Bank. The Board implements community-oriented mortgage lending and affordable housing advance programs; prescribes rules and conditions under which banks are authorized to borrow; and issues consolidated Federal Home Loan Bank bonds, notes, or debentures, that are the joint and several obligation of all Federal Home Loan Banks. It requires annual financial audits of each bank, appoints six directors to the board of directors of each bank, conducts the election of the remaining directors, and approves dividends paid by each bank. It ensures that the Federal Home Loan Banks remain adequately capitalized and operate in a sound manner.

The Federal Home Loan Bank System provides a flexible credit reserve for member savings institutions engaged in home mortgage lending. The system includes 12 regional Federal Home Loan Banks that are mixed-ownership government corporations. Each member institution is required to purchase stock and own the capital stock of Federal Home Loan Banks. The banks obtain other lendable funds by issuing consolidated obligations in money and capital markets, through time-and-demand deposits accepted from member institutions, and from other Federal Home Loan Banks. These banks provide loans to their members.

Federal Reserve System

The Federal Reserve System is a valuable source of information on banks that it has chartered. On an annual basis, Reserve System examiners visit and report on chartered banks. Their examination reports contain two parts: the open part, a copy of which is given to the bank, and the confidential part, which is kept by the Reserve System and contains qualifications of management, lists of officers and directors, and background data on the officers.

A bank must file a registration statement for its securities. The registration statement must be followed by an annual report that provides considerable data on the securities issued as well as employment information on all directors and those who own more than 10 percent of any class of the bank's securities. The Reserve System maintains these statements.

National Credit Union Administration

The National Credit Union Administration regulates, insures, and supervises all federal credit unions as well as state chartered credit unions that apply for its insurance.

Office of the Comptroller of the Currency

The Office of the Comptroller of the Currency, which is within the U.S. Department of the Treasury, regulates national banks and maintains information concerning them. National bank examinations are made to determine banks' financial positions and to evaluate bank assets. Bank examiners' reports contain information about bank records, loans, and operations. In view of their purpose and the basis on which they are obtained, reports of national bank examinations, as well as related correspondence and papers, are considered confidential. Requests for these documents should include the subject's name and address, the information desired, the reason it is needed, and the intended use.

Investigative and Law Enforcement Information Centers and Databases

Canadian Interface

The Canadian Interface is a semiautomated link between law enforcement information networks of the United States and Canada. It allows the 50 U.S. states, federal agencies that are members of the National Law Enforcement Telecommunications System (NLETS), and their Canadian counterparts to exchange police information through NLETS, using the INTERPOL National Central Bureaus in Washington and Ottawa as the necessary interface. For further information see "National Law Enforcement Telecommunications System" information available from the Canadian Interface.

Central Index System (CIS)

The CIS is an Immigration and Naturalization Service (INS) system on the location of "A-files." The system contains information on legal immigrants, naturalized citizens, and aliens who have been formally deported or excluded. It also contains information on some aliens who have come to the attention of INS because of an investigation or an application for benefits, but files are not created on all such aliens. Available information usually includes name, date of birth, nationality, and the INS files control office, as well as the date of entry and immigration status. The immigration status should not be considered definitive unless it is confirmed by an INS officer.

Consular Lookout and Support System (CLASS)

CLASS is the successor to the Department of State's Automated Visa Lookout System. CLASS provides information on foreign nationals who might apply for visas to the United States.

Defense Clearance and Investigations Index (DCII)

The DCII is the single, automated central repository that identifies investigations conducted by DOD and personnel security determinations made by DOD adjudicative authorities.

The DCII is an unclassified system and is operated by the Defense Investigative Service. Access is limited to the DOD and other federal agencies with adjudicative, investigative, or counterintelligence missions. Information contained in the DCII is protected under the Privacy Act of 1974.

The DCII database consists of an alphabetical index of personal names and impersonal titles that appear as subjects, co-subjects, victims, or cross-referenced incidental subjects in investigative documents maintained for DOD criminal, counterintelligence fraud, and personnel security investigative activities. In addition, personnel security determinations are filed, by subject, in the DCII.

El Paso Intelligence Center (EPIC)

EPIC's primary mission is to provide to federal law enforcement entities a complete and accurate intelligence picture of worldwide movements of transportable drugs, weapons, and illegal aliens into the United States. It analyzes raw data and provides tactical and operational intelligence to agencies involved in the antidrug effort. EPIC also provides strategic assessments of drug movement and concealment techniques. In addition, EPIC supports state and local law enforcement entities with drug intelligence. All 50 states, Puerto Rico, and the Virgin Islands have signed agreements with it.

EPIC member agencies include the Bureau of Alcohol, Tobacco and Firearms; U.S. Coast Guard; U.S. Customs Service; Department of Defense; Drug Enforcement Administration; Federal Aviation Administration; Federal Bureau of Investigation; Immigration and Naturalization Service; Internal Revenue Service; U.S. Marshals Service; U.S. Secret Service;

and Department of State, Bureau of Diplomatic Service. Member agencies have direct access to all EPIC information, with appropriate safeguards to provide for the protection and the secure communication of highly sensitive or classified information. State and local law enforcement entities have access to EPIC data through a designated group within the respective organization or through a member agency.

Financial Crimes Enforcement Network (FinCEN)
The FinCEN—an organization established by the U.S. Department of the Treasury — collects, analyzes, and disseminates intelligence on financial crimes. Its mission is to provide a governmentwide, multisource intelligence and analytical network to support law enforcement agencies in the detection, investigation, and prosecution of financial crimes. The participating agencies are the Bureau of Alcohol, Tobacco and Firearms; U.S. Customs Service; Drug Enforcement Administration; Federal Bureau of Investigation; Internal Revenue Service; U.S. Marshals Service; Postal Inspection Service; and U.S. Secret Service. The FinCEN is located at 3833 N. Fairfax Drive, Arlington, Virginia 22203. It can be called at (800) SOS-BUCK (767-2825).

The FinCEN's financial database contains information from reports required under the Bank Secrecy Act, including the Currency Transaction Report, Report of International Transportation of Currency or Monetary Instruments, Currency Transaction Report by Casinos, and Reports of Foreign Bank and Financial Accounts. Furthermore, FinCEN has access to data from IRS Form 8300 (Reports of Cash Payments Over $10,000 Received in a Trade or Business).

The FinCEN produces two types of products—tactical support documents and strategic analyses. The tactical support products either provide information and leads on criminal organizations and activities that are under investigation by law enforcement, or proactively identify previously undetected criminal organizations and activities so that investigations can be initiated. The FinCEN's work product can also assist in identifying assets for seizure and forfeiture purposes and supporting ongoing investigations. Its strategic analyses look at financial crimes and money laundering with an emphasis on the future. The FinCEN collects, processes, analyzes, and develops intelligence on emerging trends, patterns, and issues related to the proceeds of illicit activities.

FinCEN uses the majority of its resources to assist agencies in investigations of the financial aspects of illegal narcotics trade. FinCEN then prioritizes investigations of such nonnarcotic crimes as money laundering, Bank Secrecy Act violations, corruption, treason, bankruptcy fraud, financial institution fraud, and government contract fraud. In both the narcotic and nonnarcotic areas, FinCEN concentrates on investigations of national or international criminal organizations.

Interagency Border Inspection System (IBIS)

IBIS was initiated in 1989 to improve border enforcement and to facilitate inspection of individuals applying for admission to the United States at ports of entry and pre-inspection facilities. IBIS is a presidential priority with continuing White House guidance regarding policy, coordination, and control. The Immigration and Naturalization Service; U.S. Customs Service; State Department, Bureau of Consular Affairs; and Department of Agriculture have formed a joint working group to design, implement, and support IBIS. These agencies will provide an integrated computer capability for verifying document authenticity; automating lookout checks by inspectors; and enhancing border security against threats of terrorism, narcotics trafficking, and other violations.

International Chamber of Commerce Commercial Crime Bureau

The ICC established the Commercial Crime Bureau in January 1992. The CCB was formed to act as a focal point for fraud prevention and to encourage cooperation between commerce and law enforcement agencies. The CCB maintains an extensive database on all aspects of commercial fraud. Information about the CCB is available from ICC Commercial Crime Services, Maritime House, 1 Linton Road, Barking, Essex, 1G11 8HG (UK).

International Criminal Police Organization

The International Criminal Police Organization, better known by its radio designation as INTERPOL, is a network of National Central Bureaus in more than 155 member countries that share information with each other to assist law enforcement agencies in the detection and deterrence of international crime. Each Bureau is an agency of the member country's government and serves as the liaison between that country's law enforcement agencies and the INTERPOL network. In the United States, the National Central Bureau (USNCB) is under the direction and control of the Department of Justice.

To support ongoing investigations that require international assistance, INTERPOL provides information on the following:
- Location of suspects/fugitives/witnesses
- International wanted circulars

- Criminal history check
- Terrorism prevention
- Stolen art
- Tracing of weapons and motor vehicles abroad
- License plate, driver license check, and vehicle registration data

Requests are made directly to the U.S. National Central Bureau, Washington, D.C., by calling +1 (202) 272-8383, or by mail to: INTERPOL-USNCB, U.S. Department of Justice, Washington, D.C. 20530.

International Criminal Police Organization Case Tracking System (ICTS)

The International Criminal Police Organization (INTERPOL) Case Tracking Systems (ICTS), located at the U.S. National Central Bureau (USNCB) in Washington, D.C., contains information about people, property, and organizations involved in international criminal activity. The USNCB can determine the history of an international connection in an investigation or the existence of any previous international criminal activity. The USNCB operates to provide international support for U.S. law enforcement.

Sixteen federal and state law enforcement agencies are represented at the USNCB, and all 50 states have established INTERPOL liaison offices. For information about the liaison offices, call the USNCB at (202) 272-8383 or FTS 272-8383. Agencies represented at the USNCB include the following: the Bureau of Alcohol, Tobacco and Firearms; Criminal Division of the U.S. Department of Justice; Department of Agriculture, Office of the Inspector General; Diplomatic Security Service of the U.S. Department of State; Drug Enforcement Administration; Federal Bureau of Investigation; Federal Law Enforcement Training Center; Illinois State Police; Immigration and Naturalization Service; Internal Revenue Service; Naval Investigative Service; Office of the Comptroller of the Currency; U.S. Customs Service; U.S. Marshals Service; U.S. Postal Inspection Service; and U.S. Secret Service.

Interstate Identification Index (III)

The III system contains information on the criminal records of about 11 million people with an FBI record, specifically people born in 1956 or later. The system also contains information on people born prior to 1956 whose first arrest was recorded with the FBI in 1974 or later. It also has selected older records for certain fugitives and repeat offenders. (See "National Crime Information Center.")

Joint Maritime Information Element (JMIE)

The JMIE—a consortium of 15 U.S. government agencies in the law enforcement and intelligence communities—is developing a consolidated maritime database. Consortium members are the Naval Intelligence Command, Military Sealift Command, Drug Enforcement Administration and its El Paso Intelligence Center, Department of State, Executive Office of the President's Office of National Drug Policy, U.S. Customs Service, Central Intelligence Agency, U.S. Coast Guard, Maritime Administration, Department of Energy, Defense Intelligence Agency, Immigration and Naturalization Service, INTERPOL, Bureau of Census, and National Security Agency.

The system provides information on maritime-related law enforcement and national foreign intelligence data to aid members' operational targeting, such as narcotics interdiction, smuggling, sea and defense zone surveillance, border control, petroleum traffic monitoring, and emergency sealift management. Fourteen sites are operational, allowing access to data sources that provide at-sea and in-port location information and characteristics on commercial and private vessels and vessel registration files for Florida, California, Delaware, Puerto Rico, and the Virgin Islands.

Law Enforcement Support Center (LESC)

INS' LESC—located in South Burlington, Vermont—provides information on aliens who have been arrested. The center's staff queries six INS databases in responding to requests from federal, state, and local law enforcement agencies. Direct access to the center is available from the National Law Enforcement Telecommunications System, 24 hours a day, 7 days a week. Because of the sensitive nature of the information provided by LESC, it can only be accessed by agencies authorized to request criminal record information over the National Law Enforcement Telecommunications System.

List of Parties Excluded From Federal Procurement and Nonprocurement Programs

The List is maintained by the General Services Administration for the use of federal programs and activities. Issued monthly, it identifies those parties excluded from receiving (1) federal contracts or certain subcontracts and (2) certain types of federal financial and nonfinancial assistance and benefits.

National Tracing Center (NTC)

NTC, a branch of the Firearms Enforcement Division of ATF, provides 24-hour assistance to ATF field offices and law enforcement agencies worldwide. Using ATF's Firearms

Tracing System, NTC systematically tracks firearms used to commit crimes from their place of manufacture to the place of sale.

National White-Collar Crime Center

The Center is dedicated to supporting law enforcement in the prevention, investigation, and prosecution of economic crimes. The Center has a database system that contains information on individuals and businesses suspected of economic criminal activity, including advance-fee loan schemes, credit card fraud, computer fraud, and securities and investment fraud. It can be contacted at (800) 221-4424 or (804) 323-3563.

Narcotics and Dangerous Drugs Information System (NADDIS)

Inquiries should be limited to narcotics-related cases or files and/or smugglers of funds, other contraband, and aliens. NADDIS is accessible through EPIC.

National Alien Information Lookout System (NAILS)

NAILS is an Immigration and Naturalization Service system. The system provides an index of the names of all individuals who might be denied entry into the United States. Names in NAILS are passed to the Treasury Enforcement Communications System (TECS); therefore, a search of NAILS is not necessary if TECS has been searched.

National Crime Information Center (NCIC)

The NCIC, located at the FBI headquarters in Washington, is a widely used law enforcement computer system. Most major law enforcement agencies have NCIC connections.

The NCIC often is compared to a large file cabinet, with each file having its own label or classification. This cabinet of data contains information concerning the following:

- Stolen, missing, or recovered guns
- Stolen articles (that have a serial number)
- Wanted people (for questioning or arrest)
- Stolen/wanted vehicles (autos, aircraft, motorcycles)
- Stolen license plates
- Stolen, embezzled, or missing securities, stocks, bonds, and currency
- Stolen/wanted boats
- Missing people
- Index to state criminal history records and criminal history records of federal offenders
- Unidentified people

- Foreign fugitives

The NCIC, through the Interstate Identification Index (III), can provide an investigator with a record of a subject's prior major federal offenses, arrests, and dispositions. The III also contains an index to similar information concerning state offenses occurring in those states participating in the III program. Background information also can be obtained from the III record. For example, if a subject's name, date of birth, race, and sex are entered, the investigator would receive the FBI number, full name, height, weight, eye color, hair color, fingerprint classification, alias, total number of arrests, charges, convictions, and dispositions.

National Law Enforcement Telecommunications System (NLETS)
The NLETS is a sophisticated message switching network that links all law enforcement and criminal justice agencies in the United States, Puerto Rico, and, through a computerized link to INTERPOL, Canada. Agencies include state and local law enforcement groups, motor vehicle and licensing departments, and a variety of federal enforcement offices, such as the U.S. Customs Service, Federal Bureau of Investigation, Department of Justice, U.S. Secret Service, U.S. Marshals Service, Naval Investigative Service, Air Force Office of Special Investigations, Department of State, Department of the Army, and the Department of the Interior. The National Auto Theft Bureau also is linked to NLETS.

A great deal of information is available to law enforcement through the network, including:
- Vehicle registrations by license or vehicle identification number
- Driver's license and driver history by name and date of birth, or driver's license number
- Criminal records by name and date of birth, state identification number, or FBI number
- Boat registrations by hull number, registration number, or name
- Snowmobile registrations by registration number, vehicle identification number, or owner's name and date of birth
- Hazardous material file by UN number, which is an internationally recognized code for hazardous material
- Private aircraft tracking data by registration number or date range
- Aircraft registrations by registration number, serial number, or name of registrant
- Directory of participating agencies by originating agency identifier

Through an interface with the Royal Canadian Mounted Police's Canadian Police Information Centre, many files are available, such as:
- Wanted people by name and date of birth

- Stolen vehicles by license number or vehicle identification number
- Stolen articles by serial number
- Stolen guns by serial number
- Stolen securities by serial number, corporation name, issuer, or name of owner
- Stolen boats and motors by license number, hull number, registration number, or name of owner

Users can send free-form messages to other users either individually or via a broadcast message.

Nonimmigrant Information Systems (NIIS)

The NIIS is an Immigration and Naturalization Service system. The system contains information on the arrivals and departures of nonimmigrants or aliens coming to the United States for a temporary stay. Canadians and Mexicans who visit for pleasure are not entered into the system. The NIIS also contains entry and departure data on students. Information can be retrieved by nationality, port of entry, admission class, and date of entry.

Operational Activities Special Information System (OASIS)

OASIS is an Immigration and Naturalization Service (INS) system of information about the activities and associations of individuals known, or suspected, to be involved with the smuggling of aliens into the United States, as well as about immigration fraud and criminal aliens. The system contains information on alien smugglers and smuggling incidents as well as addresses, phone numbers, and vehicles involved in alien smuggling cases.

Regional Information Sharing System (RISS)

The RISS program consists of seven multistate projects that facilitate regional criminal information exchange and provide other related support service to federal, state, and local law enforcement agencies throughout all 50 states.

- *Leviticus*—Includes 35 law enforcement and regulatory agencies. It is a specialized regional enforcement project designed to combat criminal activity within the coal, oil, natural gas, and precious metals industries. Leviticus is located at 7400 Beaufont Springs Drive, Suite 310, Richmond, Virginia 23225, and it can be called at (800) 221-4424 or (804) 323-3563.
- *Middle Atlantic-Great Lakes Organized Crime Law Enforcement Network (MAGLOCLEN)*—It includes 262 law enforcement agencies in Indiana, Michigan, Ohio, Pennsylvania, New York, New Jersey, Delaware, Maryland, and Washington, D.C. In addition, several

Canadian departments are active MAGLOCLEN members. The MAGLOCLEN is located at Mountain View Office Park, 850 Bear Tavern Road, 2nd Floor, Suite 206, West Trenton, New Jersey 08628, and it can be called at (800) 345-1322 or (609) 530-2801.

- *Mid-States Organized Crime Information Center (MOCIC)*—It includes 690 law enforcement agencies in North Dakota, South Dakota, Nebraska, Kansas, Minnesota, Iowa, Missouri, Wisconsin, and Illinois. The MOCIC is located at #4 Corporate Centre, #205, Springfield, Missouri 65804, and it can be called at (800) 798-0110 or at (417) 883-4383.
- *New England State Police Information Network (NESPIN)*—It incorporates 272 law enforcement agencies in Maine, New Hampshire, Vermont, Massachusetts, Connecticut, and Rhode Island. The NESPIN is located at 21 Mazzeo Drive, Suite 201, Randolph, Massachusetts 02368, and it can be called at (800) 343-5682 or (617) 986-6544.
- *Regional Organized Crime Information Center (ROCIC)*—It serves 503 law enforcement agencies in Texas, Oklahoma, Louisiana, Arkansas, Mississippi, Alabama, Tennessee, Kentucky, West Virginia, Virginia, North Carolina, South Carolina, Georgia, and Florida. The ROCIC is located at 545 Marriot Drive, Suite 850, Nashville, Tennessee 37210, and it can be called at (800) 238-7985.
- *Rocky Mountain Information Network (RMIN)*—It has 620 participating agencies in Arizona, New Mexico, Colorado, Utah, Nevada, Idaho, Wyoming, and Montana. The RMIN is located at 3802 N. 53rd Avenue, Suite 301, Phoenix, Arizona 85031, and it can be called at (800) 821- 0640.
- *Western States Information Network (WSIN)*—It provides narcotics intelligence and related services to its 697 member law enforcement agencies in California, Oregon, Washington, Alaska, and Hawaii. The WSIN address is P.O. Box 903198, Sacramento, California 94203-1980, and it can be called at (800) 824-7902 (outside of California) and (800) 952-5258 (in California).

SENTRY

SENTRY is a Federal Bureau of Prisons on-line database. It contains information on all federal prisoners incarcerated since 1980. The information includes physical description, inmate profile, inmate location or release location, numerical identifiers, personal history data, security designation, past and present institution assignments, custody classification, and sentencing information. To obtain information, call the Sacramento Intelligence Unit at (916) 551-1750.

South Pacific Islands Criminal Intelligence Network (SPICIN)

SPICIN is a law enforcement program by the South Pacific Chiefs of Police Organization made up of 21 member countries including American Samoa, Australia, The Commonwealth of Northern Mariana Islands (Saipan), Cook Islands, the Federated States of Micronesia, Fiji, French Polynesia (Tahiti), Guam, Kiribati, the Kingdom of Tonga, Marshall Islands, Nauru, New Caledonia, New Zealand, Niue, Palau, Papua-New Guinea, Solomon Islands, Tuvalu, Vanuatu, and Western Samoa.

The primary purpose of SPICIN is to promote the gathering, recording, and exchanging of information not otherwise available through normal channels. Information made available concerns drug trafficking, mobile criminals, organized/white collar crime, terrorism, the use of the Pacific Island waters and aircraft, and other information of a criminal nature that concerns law enforcement in the Pacific region and elsewhere.

Treasury Enforcement Communications Systems (TECS)

The TECS is a Department of the Treasury system managed by the U.S. Customs Service. It is a system of telecommunications terminals located in law enforcement facilities of the Treasury Department. The terminals are connected to a computer in Newington, Virginia.

The TECS contains lookout information on people and property. It also has access to the National Law Enforcement Telecommunications System (NLETS) and the National Crime Information Center (NCIC).

Participants include the U.S. Customs Service; Bureau of Alcohol, Tobacco and Firearms; Drug Enforcement Administration; Immigration and Naturalization Service; Department of State; U.S. Coast Guard; Federal Bureau of Investigation (NCIC Section); U. S. Marshals Service; Internal Revenue Service; EPIC; INTERPOL (National Central Bureau); and Department of Agriculture.

The TECS works on a soundex-type system. If an inquiry is made regarding a certain name, then all similar sounding names on record are provided to the inquirer. Inquiries on TECS might be made by name alone, even if no identifying number—such as date of birth, FBI number, or Social Security number—is available.

When TECS provides a list of similar sounding names, the subjects' sex, race, and date of birth also are included. The inquirer then can determine which subject, if any, is of interest.

If a name is selected, TECS can provide additional information. That might include, but is not limited to special instructions (such as "armed and dangerous"), full name, race, sex, height, weight, hair color, eye color, date of birth, fugitive (which agency), background information, miscellaneous number (such as FBI), where and by whom a warrant is held, date of offense, alias, case number, and NCIC number.

United Nations Crime and Justice Information Network (UNCJIN)
UNCJIN is funded in part by the U.S. Bureau of Justice Statistics. The goal of UNCJIN is to establish a worldwide network to enhance dissemination and the exchange of information concerning criminal justice and crime prevention issues.

Washington Area Law Enforcement System (WALES)
WALES is one of the state-level law enforcement computer systems and is listed here to illustrate systems available in nearly all states.

WALES is sponsored by Washington, D.C.'s Metropolitan Police Department and is available to state and federal investigators when they are coordinated with the Metropolitan Police Department. WALES operates on a soundex system. Only the subject's name is needed for a query. WALES gathers information only on Washington, D.C., residents. The system also interfaces with NCIC and NLETS, and can provide investigators with information such as on the following:
- Stolen property
- Wanted people
- Filed complaints (lists violations by address)
- Gun registrations
- Court case disposition and status
- Driver's licenses and motor vehicle registrations
- Business licenses
- Traffic accidents

World Criminal Justice Library Network (WCJLN)
WCJLN is working to establish a network to share services and information concerning criminal justice. The group is in the process of developing an international network to disseminate national and international crime statistics and criminal justice profiles.

ACCESSING INFORMATION ON-LINE

Fraud examiners now have a number of on-line investigative resources available through their personal computers. Whether available through the Internet, via CD-ROM, or by using specialized software, public records and printed information such as newspaper and magazine clips are readily accessible through the computer.

Accessing Information Through Computer Databases

As you can see, there is a plethora of public records which can aid the fraud examiner. Not so long ago, a person had to physically travel to the county courthouse or state capital to search for public records. No more. A fraud examiner now has enough information available through different computer sources to conduct entire inquiries without leaving his seat.

On-line public records databases are numerous and varied. Most can be readily accessed from your own computer once you become a subscriber. The costs associated with these databases can be equally varied. There are several computer access options available and an examiner should be prepared to use any and all, separately or in combination. Keep in mind, however, that it may be necessary to spend time examining the actual documents in order to get the whole picture.

Not many counties or states have direct access to their records through a personal computer. Some states have their own on-line access but most do not. A public record database will tell the researcher whether a particular record, or some of the information contained in that record, exists. However, it is important to note that it will not provide a copy of the actual document. For example, you can conduct a property record search to find out that John Doe owns property at 121 Main Street in Peoria, IL, but if you need a copy of the actual deed, it will have to be retrieved from the county clerk's office.

There is a wealth of information now available on the Internet. The Internet is basically a giant network linking thousands of computers and databases throughout the world. A caveat—remember that on-line records companies have to get their information from somewhere. Often it comes directly from the county. But, if the information in the county's records is incorrect, then the report you will receive from the database company will also be incorrect. Therefore, it is important to remember that accessing information on-line is never a full substitute for an examination of the actual public record itself.

Remember, however, that if you access information through an on-line service, you may be subject to the provisions of the Fair Credit Reporting Act as discussed in the previous chapter. Before accessing such information, you should always contact your attorney.

Limitations of Databases

The main limitations of database searches are:

- On-line coverage varies widely from state to state. The fraud examiner should determine whether specific information is available for each investigation.
- Searches are limited in the area they cover. Fortunately for the crook, most of his public record "evidence" is generally filed at the county level. If he is smart enough to know how to conduct transactions outside his normal locality, then he can be tough to track without using multijurisdictional on-line sources. Making sure you are looking in the right county is important. You can be off by one county and miss pertinent land holdings, divorce records, liens, etc.
- All on-line public records are brief abstracts of the original public record.
- The "source" of the information compiled in a vendor's database must be reliable.
- The accuracy and currency of information must be checked.
- The records or publications that have been compiled on an electronic format may not "go back" very far.
- Also, Internet search engines are notoriously erratic in their retrieval.

Commercial On-Line Services

Any public records search should begin with a commercial on-line service. There are several companies that provide varying levels of public record information to subscribers. A description of some of these companies and the records they can provide are discussed later.

These companies provide access to a wide range of information. The information is stored on a central database which a subscriber can access from his or her computer. Some information is actually retrieved in hard copy and mailed or faxed to the subscriber, even though the request was made through the on-line service.

Some companies require a yearly or monthly subscription fee in addition to the fee for each search. Others operate on a "pay as you go" principle which allows you to pay only for the searches you conduct. Therefore, it is important to shop around to get the best deal for your level of usage.

For some practitioners, it may be more economical to enlist the aid of service companies, information brokers, and professional on-line investigators. These companies will conduct research for examiners, typically utilizing on-line services and manual document retrieval from local sources. Although the cost of these services is higher than doing it yourself, it may be the best choice for occasional records searches.

Using an On-Line Service to Find Information

In the past, investigators hot on the heels of an asset-hider or suspect were hamstrung by the available investigative resources. In attempting to uncover unreported income, the investigator was forced to travel to the courthouse for the county in which the suspect conducted business, request the county files available, and take a number. These treks to the middle-of-nowhere were rarely cost-effective and often fruitless in the search for pertinent information.

This has all changed, however, and now maybe the flatfoot's feet won't be so flat. Thanks to the advent of on-line investigative services, such as Lexis-Nexis or Choice Point, inquiries to the far-flung reaches of the U.S. can be conducted from a personal computer. These services have packaged a variety of invaluable investigative sources at very reasonable prices.

Access to these services is accomplished in either one of two ways. Some services allow users to log into the service through an Internet site. Others provide you with software. Access to their database is accomplished by using their software program and a modem to log into their system. Each user has a user ID and password to gain access.

The following is a description of how on-line searches can be used to locate people, locate assets, find legal records, and conduct background checks.

How to Locate People Using On-Line Records

In order to maximize the results of the search, the first step will be to develop a past address in which the subscriber has some confidence. Search activities will begin from that point. Second, the user should recognize the rank order of the more to less powerful searches, which are identified below. Third, it is always important to keep in mind the cost effectiveness of the search activity and avoid ordering on-line searches that give the user information not needed, or in which there is little interest.

It is important to recognize that the search methodology used by most on-line services is "text string matching," which means that all information entered to the right of the data inquiry field will seek an exact match in the database. Typically, you may use truncation techniques (partial or abbreviated entries such as the first initial of the first name) only with first names and business names.

Types of Searches

- *Credit Bureau Header* searches are among the most powerful locator tools. Nearly all persons have been involved in some credit activity either under their true names or an "a/k/a." Where persons are not recorded it may simply be because the individuals are very young or very old. It is appropriate to keep in mind that in the case of common names, it may also be necessary to use the Social Security number or date of birth to differentiate the subject from other persons with the same name. The "headers" offer two search mechanisms that can be thought of as the obverse and reverse sides of a coin. First, you can develop a current address, or address history, and Social Security number(s) associated with the target by using a past address that is generally up to seven years old. Second, once the Social Security number is in hand the "headers" can be searched for matches. Certainly if the examiner has a valid Social Security number available the "header" search can begin at that point since the Social Security number is in effect a national identity number. While the Social Security number is theoretically protected from disclosure by its owner under the Privacy Act, it is practically not possible in modern life to exist on an individual basis without disclosing it within the publicly available records arena.

- *A Current Occupant/New Address* search may be used to identify the true occupant of an address thought to be occupied by the person being sought, to confirm occupancy, to develop a possible forwarding address, or to develop a list of neighbors who may be contacted for information as to the location of the person being sought.

- *Last Name* searches are available for those situations where precise past address information is not available. The searches seem to produce better results if the name is not common. For example, if the examiner is searching for a person of a certain ethnic or cultural background with a name common to that background, and in a geographical area known to be inhabited by individuals of the same cultural or ethnic background, differentiating information will be important. It should also be noted that some of these searches provide neighbors who can be contacted on a pretext basis to aid in location efforts.

- *Bankruptcy Filings, Tax Liens, and Court Judgments* have emerged in recent years as locator tools, because where such records exist on an individual, a valid Social Security number will be identified. These searches have emerged as locator tools owing to the dramatic increase in individual bankruptcy claims. For example, in 1996 over one million new filings were made, which was an all time record.

- *DMV* records were once thought to be good locator tools, but recent restrictions on the use of such data has reduced the effectiveness of such searches. Note the discussion of these searches under Section II, Regulations. Moreover, the update quality of individual state records supplied by state authorities may not be adequate to locating people in a transient, fast-paced society. Still, searches such as *Driver Identification* can be useful on a spot basis.

- In a few states *Voter Registration* records are available, but as with *DMV* records, the update quality of these records may not meet today's people location challenges. However, to the extent that date of birth information is available, such records can serve as an adjunct to other searches. Also note any legal restrictions attached to the use of voter information.

Obtaining Financial Information and Locating Assets

Information to answer the question of whether assets exist, where they exist, and whether such assets are recoverable will generally be found within federal, state, local, and proprietary records. These records can be further divided between those searches useful in identifying "hard" assets, and those designed to illuminate the issue of whether the target of the search has any potential for assets, credit capacity, or credit worthiness.

Searches for "Hard Assets"
- The ownership of real property may be discoverable through the use of *Property* searches, to the extent they are available at the local or county level within individual states.
- The ownership of vehicles can be inferred through the use of the *DMV Vehicle Name Index,* to the extent the records within the controlling state agency reflect vehicles registered to a specific person or organization at a particular address. Conversely, the

ownership of a particular vehicle may be inferred from the *DMV Vehicle Registration* searches.

- The use of the *Assumed Business Name* search may be helpful in identifying a sole proprietorship business in which executable assets are available. The *Sales Tax Registration* available in California and Texas may also be helpful in this area.
- The *Uniform Commercial Code (UCC)* is extraordinary in that it can be useful in a wide variety of business situations. In this case, where a bank lender has secured a loan through some type of chattel as collateral, and has sought to perfect its lien on the chattel through a UCC filing at the state level, it can be fairly assumed that the debtor has a bank account with the secured party. Thus, a bank account asset may be identified as a recoverable asset.
- The ownership of an aircraft can be determined by searching the *Aircraft Ownership* by business name, person name, or wing number.

Searches for Asset Potential

- The question of whether it is realistically possible to recover known assets may be partially answered by searching *Bankruptcy Filings, Tax Liens,* and *Judgments*.
- Again, the versatility of the *UCC* search is seen through the identification of assets that may have been pledged, in whole or in part, to secure a loan.
- Both the *consumer credit reports* and the *business credit reports* search may develop a clearer picture of the target's potential for asset recovery in terms of credit capacity and creditworthiness.

Finding Legal Records

The searches available to find these records can be grouped in three broad categories: on-site court searches, index or broad coverage searches, and public filings.

On-Site Court Searches

These searches are directed by court, by county, or as is the case with federal records, by the District Court for the particular area. Accordingly, the examiner must carefully consider the potential location of court records. Such considerations would include the residence location, the business or employment location, or perhaps even the location of past residency/business/employment. While the information returned will consist of data concerning any type of litigation including civil actions, criminal actions, divorces, judgments, etc., it will not return information concerning litigation that has been sealed by the court or information concerning juvenile offenders.

Note: The coverage for these searches varies according to which service is used. Additionally, each court has varying rules regarding how the search is conducted, hours of availability for public information searches, repository location, or search methods. If the subscriber is interested in a particular type of record, such as a divorce record, it may be necessary to call the company's customer support unit so that the search inquiry can be "tweaked" to meet the subscriber's needs. Types of records available include:

- *Civil Court Federal Records,* including *Bankruptcy Records,* are available for all types of civil litigation conducted in federal court.
- *Criminal Court Federal Records* are available for felony charges.
- *Civil Court State Records* are available based on a division of upper and lower court records; such division being a function of the differences within each state concerning the amounts in controversy.
- *Criminal Court State Records* can be obtained on a ten or seven year search basis, and for either felonies, misdemeanors, or a combination of both.

Index/Broad Coverage Searches

These searches are available to the subscriber for those situations requiring a search strategy broader than the by court/by county method used with on-site court record searches, or which make use of an index giving basic information concerning the existence of court records. Such searches include:

- *Defendant Suits* are available in all states but provide coverage limited to specific counties and courts. The "help" menus should be reviewed carefully to ascertain the scope of the search in individual states.
- *Criminal Convictions-Statewide* searches are available in some jurisdictions. Careful attention is to be paid to the "help" menus for each state describing special release requirements, the number of years available, whether the record is for convictions only, and whether the search encompasses both felonies and misdemeanors.
- *Marriage/Divorce Index* searches are available in some states.

Conducting Background Checks

This type of search activity generally involves two broad areas: discovering what the public records reveal with respect to individuals and businesses with whom the subscriber may wish to do business, and discovering information about prospective employees.

Due Diligence

As business organizations seek to identify vendors, clients, or strategic partners, or to loan or collect money, they frequently conduct public record inquiries focused on other businesses, or individuals who are principals of business organizations. This type of public record inquiry involves such issues as verification of application information, debt burden, adverse financial information, credit capacity or worthiness, business relationships (the so called "family tree"), litigation history, or criminal background. Useful searches include the following:

- *Corporate/Limited Partnership* searches are available in all states to verify information, identify principals and develop other business relationships.
- *Bankruptcy Filings, Tax Liens,* and *Judgments* searches respond to issues of adverse financial information and credit capacity/worthiness.
- *UCC* filings respond to questions of debt burden.
- *Civil Court State Records* and *Civil Court Federal Records* respond to questions concerning litigation history, past business relationships, and the potential for debt burden either as a function of an adverse judgment or as a function of financing expensive litigation.
- *Criminal Court State Records* and *Criminal Court Federal Records* serve to identify the possibility of a criminal background.
- The use of *consumer credit reports* and *business credit reports* helps resolve questions concerning credit capacity and creditworthiness. In addition, the business report is useful in verifying information, understanding business relationships, and developing basic financial information about an organization.
- *OSHA (Occupational Safety and Health Administration)* searches may be useful tools in developing adverse information or verifying information given by a prospective vendor, client, or strategic partner.
- *Aircraft Mechanics, Airmen, Medical License, DEA Controlled Substances* and *Other License* may serve to verify that basic professional and occupational standards are met by a prospective vendor, client, or strategic partner.

Employment Background

Public record and on-line record inquiries in this area have increased significantly over the past few years owing to economic and sociological conditions. Corporate "downsizing" has disaffected an increasing number of workers to the point that it is easier for them to rationalize employee defalcation, fraud, or embezzlement. The same economic phenomenon of downsizing, business pressure to increase productivity, and the friction of modern life have apparently produced an increase in work place violence. Liabilities for employers and businesses have expanded through negligence standards and the *respondeat superior* doctrine for such tortious conduct as vehicle operation, assault, battery, false imprisonment, sexual harassment, and discrimination. Finally, liability potential has inhibited past employers in responding to inquiries from a prospective employer with the result that prospective employers must increasingly rely on public record information. Some of the searches useful in developing background information are listed below:

- *"Header" Searches* are useful in confirming address and Social Security number information.
- *Criminal Court State Records, Criminal Court Federal Records,* and *Criminal Convictions-Statewide* may be used to uncover past criminal problems presaging similar difficulties. Indeed, criminal background checks may be mandated by law. For example, the Clinton Anti-Crime Bill of 1996 apparently permits a felony indictment where an insurance company knowingly hires a convicted felon.
- *Aircraft Mechanics, Airmen, Medical License* and *Other Licenses* are available to ensure that basic job requirements are met in the appropriate circumstance.
- *Consumer credit reports* may be obtained for purposes of employee selection, retention, and promotion.
- Public filings such as *Bankruptcy Filings, Tax Liens,* and *Judgments* may be obtained to identify adverse financial matters that can serve as potential motivators for fraud, defamation, and embezzlement.
- Where a prospective or current employee drives a personally owned vehicle or an employer owned vehicle in furthering the interests of the employer, such activity may expose the employer to liability for damages; therefore, *DMV Driving Records* must be checked.
- Basic information concerning job qualification can be verified through the *Education Verification* and *Employment Verification* searches. Note: These are verification tools only; they are not definitional in terms of discovering past or current employment.
- *Workers' Compensation* searches may *not* be used by an employer in making an adverse decision concerning the hiring of an otherwise qualified applicant.

Records Service Companies

Listed below is some brief information about some of the larger records service companies. You can shop various services to find the one that meets your needs in the most cost-effective manner, and the one that fits your current case. In some instances, it may be necessary to use more than one service to get an accurate and complete profile. These companies get their information from various sources and on various update schedules, so a search in any one database may return different results than a search done elsewhere.

ChoicePoint (www.choicepoint.net)

ChoicePoint's origins lie in providing information to the insurance industry. It has graduated to a broader client base, however, and has expanded its services to include government and business. Its services are divided into various categories ranging from Insurance Information Services, which include credit and claims records, to Consumer Services, such as credential verification. A well-established and publicly traded organization, ChoicePoint has gradually assimilated smaller companies that provide similar services.

CDB Infotek (www.choicepointon-line.com/cdb)

CDB Infotek is a well-rounded, on-line investigative database providing access to records in all 50 states. Now a ChoicePoint subsidiary, CDB's services are still comprehensive, including county, state, and federal public records. Investigators' search possibilities encompass credit header information, motor vehicle and court record searches, business and people locating devices. From this database, a fraud examiner is able to locate any piece of information about a subject pertaining to possible second addresses, business addresses, credit information, and so on. CDB is one of the finest and most user-friendly investigations databases.

IRSC (www.irsc.com)

IRSC bills itself as "the road to information for human resources, corporate security, insurance, private investigation, financial, and legal." Another ChoicePoint company, IRSC is a quality on-line investigative database containing several distinctive features. It offers a full range of credit bureau header information, motor vehicle and bankruptcy court records, property tax records, and voter registration records. IRSC covers a good portion of counties in the U.S., but if the company does not have a county's automated records, they send a researcher directly to the county courthouse to obtain the information. Another bonus of employing IRSC is its easy-to-use software.

Database Technologies On-line, or DBT On-line (www.dbton-line.com)

Yet another ChoicePoint tributary, DBT On-line is *the* source to turn to when trying to locate a person via the Internet. The database is geared toward locating possible second or former addresses of a subject. DBT also has a wide range of hidden asset and credit information in the states of Florida and Texas, as well as a good amount of information in other states.

USDatalink (www.usdatalink.com)

This investigative database cannot retrieve the information for a fraud examiner as quickly as some of the other databases on the market, but US Datalink is the only company that relies entirely on manual searches for its information. US Datalink exclusively sends its researchers to the county courthouse to look up the information that has been requested, as opposed to the electronic and possibly faulty information that other on-line investigative databases use. Therefore, if a fraud examiner has the time to wait for his inquiry, US Datalink might be the most reliable option. The database also has media resources.

infoUSA.com (www.infousa.com)

infoUSA users have access to information on 12 million businesses. Among the facts they can produce are sales volume, corporate linkage, contact names and titles, company history, credit rating code, and any headlines involving the business. The versatility of the searches is one of infoUSA's better features. Searches can be performed according to business size, location, length of time in operation, gender or race of owners, and industry.

Security Software Solutions (www.ssn-locate.com)

This database company specializes in providing information on Social Security number verification, possible mail drop addresses, date of birth, and death records. With this database, an investigator is able to match a Social Security number to a name with Security Software Solutions' Veris SSN Validation Service, which is costly but very accurate.

Diligenz (www.diligenz.com)

Diligenz is a great database for retrieving information about businesses. With its weekly database updates, Diligenz's strength lies in the reliability of its public record information. Diligenz can produce a business's financial statements, records pertaining to corporate status, business credit, and licensing information. UCC filings, bankruptcy, judgments, and corporate good standing searches are just a few of their services.

KnowX (www.knowx.com)

KnowX claims to be the most comprehensive source of public information on the Web and it just might be. It offers easily navigable public records searches in various categories, among them asset searches, adverse filings, and people and business locator tools. One can also verify licenses, conduct background checks, and look up a company's history. KnowX is an altogether user friendly source of information.

Dialog Information Retrieval Service (www.dialog.com)

Dialog now offers more than 400 databases. It contains more than 80 million records, including references and abstracts of published literature, statistical tables, the full text of selected articles, and directory, business, and financial data.

D&B (formerly Dun & Bradstreet) (www.dnb.com)

The variety of information available through D&B (formerly Dun & Bradstreet) is amazing. It is probably one of the most comprehensive and diverse sources available, with facts on 11 million U.S. companies. International business information is searchable as well. D&B is renowned for products like *America's Corporate Families* and *Industry Norms and Key Business Ratios*, both excellent tools. Information can be purchased in CD-ROM form or via their website.

LexisNexis (www.lexisnexis.com)

In one form or another, LexisNexis has been in the information business for nearly 30 years and it shows. It prides itself on being "the company that invented electronic information research" and judging by the wealth of products and services it offers, that claim is not hard to believe. Its search possibilities are conveniently divided into legal, governmental, and business fields. Users have the option of searching by publication as well. Its public records database is extensive yet very well ordered.

Experian (www.experian.com)

Experian provides services on consumer and business credit, direct marketing, and real estate information services. Its National Consumer Data Base is updated 65 times per year with information on more than 90% of U.S. households. The National Business Data Base has facts on 15 million companies in all industries.

Some of the services provided are:
- Property Profile, Recent Home Sales, and Home Portfolio Reports help to estimate a home's value and provide an understanding of a particular neighborhood
- Business Snapshot Reports summarize credit histories—including payment patterns and legal filings—of small businesses or contractors

DCS Information Systems (www.dcs-amerifind.com/)

Founded in 1967, DCS is an established source for investigative information. Its Amerifind is separated into four areas, making searches simple:

- PrimeData provides banking and finance information
- QuickFind is a security and fraud-related information tool
- FraudTracer serves the insurance industry
- CaseMaker is designed for law enforcement and government

G.A. Public Records Services (www.gaprs.com)

G.A. Public Records Services specializes in on-site county level criminal record information. They can usually provide a report within 24 - 72 hours. They have access to records in over 3,100 counties coast to coast, and on any given month will visit over 1,800 different counties. G.A. Public Records Services provides search services for employment screening, corporate due diligence, fraud investigations, private investigations, and tenant screening.

Newspaper/Media Databases

Newspapers, periodicals, and journals can be excellent sources of information in a fraud investigation, particularly when searching for background information on an individual or a business. In a Houston case, a person accused of insider trading was cleared using materials from an on-line database search. Defense attorneys gathered over 300 published comments about the company's financial prospects, and showed that someone following the advice distributed freely in the press would have made *more* money than the accused. (Source: Paul Burnstein's *Computers for Lawyers*.)

Searchable databases containing information from literally hundreds of published sources can usually be accessed for free at most libraries. There are also a number of on-line databases that deal specifically with news and media resources. These databases compile a number of different media resources and allow the user to search for a specific topic, returning articles or transcripts that pertain to the requested subject. Most publications allow users to at least search their archives for free; full text of articles is available, usually for a fee. Using one of the services below allows users to search many publications at once.

Factiva (www.factiva.com)

Formerly Dow Jones' News Retrieval, Factiva is tailored for business and financial news searches, maintaining a catalog of over 9,000 business publications, newspapers, and wire services. Factiva allows users to pay only for the articles downloaded and does not require an annual subscription.

LexisNexis (www.LexisNexis.com)

LexisNexis is a legal and business information database that provides its subscribers with daily newspapers for either a flat fee or a per-use fee. LexisNexis maintains a cavernous database of U.S. and international media sources, including daily newspapers, magazines, and television transcripts. In addition, LexisNexis offers a service in which the user can request immediate information on difficult-to-find topics. LexisNexis will research the topic give the user information on the topic as quickly as possible.

Electric Library (www.elibrary.com)

Although its collection is not as large as either of the previous services, Electric Library is very economical and does carry a large number of articles from major newspaper and magazines. For a yearly fee, users have unlimited access to its database.

Data Times (http// www.umi.com/proquest/)

Proquest is Bell & Howell Information and Learning's (formerly UMI) on-line information service. They boast one of the world's largest collections of information, including summaries of articles from over 8,000 publications, with many in full text, full image format. In 1998, The Library of Congress named Bell & Howell's ongoing dissertation collection the official U.S. offsite repository for dissertations and theses in electronic format.

Other News Database Services
- Ensemble Information Systems (www.ensemble.com)
- Internet Wire (www.interviewwire.com)
- Infosage (www.infosage.com)
- Los Angeles Times-Washington Post News Service (www.newsservice.com)

The Internet

The Internet is not organized by any uniform system, such as the library's Dewey decimal system or the Library of Congress codes to catalog books. Instead, it remains a free-floating, loosely strung gold mine of information, available to those who understand how to use it. Unless you know the exact addresses of the Internet pages you are looking for, learning how to find the information is a must.

An Internet site, or page, is a single Web address, generally introduced by a person or a company to post discussions of a topic or sell a certain line of products. There are a number of websites that will be of use to a fraud examiner listed and discussed at the end of this chapter.

Search Engines

The most basic way to find information is to execute Internet searches on "search engines" and "website directories." Search engines are website tools that allow you to type in keywords describing the subject you are interested in. The search engine will then scour the pages of the Internet and attempt to locate pages that may have pertinent information. So, for instance, in a search for the keyword "fraud," the search engine will likely bring back a number of pages which have some relevant link to fraud (such as the Association of Certified Fraud Examiners' website, located at www.cfenet.com). There are several prominent search engines on the Internet and each reacts in different ways. An extensive list of search engines is provided at the end of the chapter; however, a few of the more popular sites are described below:

Google (www.google.com)
Google is an increasingly popular engine because of its speed and ranking technology. Individual Web pages are ranked by the engine's software according to how often the page is linked to by others, determining the page's "importance" by the number of links and the identity of the linking page. Google is a good way to find targeted information on a particular topic. Much of the techniques commercial services use to push their information to the top of search results is discarded by Google's ranking software.

Yahoo! (www.yahoo.com)
Yahoo is a multifaceted website, containing a first-rate directory (see below), but is also equipped with an excellent search engine. The Yahoo engine acts quite differently than Altavista's fine-toothed comb. Yahoo's filters will return far fewer pages than Altavista, concentrating on ten to twenty pages that will likely be of interest. You should not use Yahoo to find minute, hard-to-find information, but it is a good source for locating information you're sure is out there.

HotBot (www.hotbot.com)
HotBot offers an interesting feature: when the user's search has been run by the engine, the results of the search are ranked by HotBot in order of probability of useful information.

HotBot attempts to combine Yahoo's pinpoint accuracy with Altavista's thorough searches. The engine functions quite a bit like Altavista in that it reads the text of every page, looking for the user's keywords. Hotbot is an excellent tool for finding specific information. Besides its up-to-date index, it provides an easy interface for constructing precise queries.

Excite (www.excite.com)
This engine is good for broad general topics. The service offers a simultaneous search of the Web, news headlines, sports scores, and company information. Results are grouped on a single page. Weeding through the results can sometimes be a chore.

Lycos (www.lycos.com)
Lycos provides advanced search capabilities, including the ability to search for specific media. Its Lycos Pro feature allows users to fine tune searches. Lycos's index of Web pages is smaller than some other services'.

Ask Jeeves (www.askjeeves.com)
This is a good site for beginners and for general queries. The engine leads users through questions to help narrow the search, and also searches six other search sites. (For similar services, see Metasearch Engines, below.) Jeeves's ability to interpret natural language makes it easy to use, though constructing precise queries can be difficult for the same reason.

AltaVista (www.altavista.com)
AltaVista is a detail-oriented search engine. Because it reads through the individual text of every page listed on the Internet, AltaVista is very useful for finding random information. If you are simply "casting your line" to see what information might be available on a topic, this is a good engine to use. However, AltaVista's searches are so thorough, you will encounter every page that contains your keyword(s), ending with as many as 200,000 hits. Successful AltaVista searching requires you to construct your search carefully.

Google Groups (www.groups.google.com)
This search engine (part of Google) scans thousands of postings of Usenet groups. Usenet groups are electronic bulletin boards classified by subject. A search using Google Groups will reveal instances in which the terms you specify appear in a posting on the Internet. You can search by the name or e-mail address of users who have posted to newsgroups, or by subject, keywords, attachments, and so on.

Directories

The road to mining information on the Internet does not always go through search engines. Some of the best investigative tools an examiner has on-line are known as "directories." As the name suggests, directories are specialized websites that collect the names of numerous other related websites, allowing the user to browse through a complete listing of possible sites to visit. Directories contain direct links to pages that have a common interest. There are some all-inclusive directories that cover a plethora of different topics, and there are others that are more focused on particular subjects or disciplines. These include several accounting and auditing directories that fraud examiners may find very useful.

The upside to using directories is that you can logically navigate a search, easing through the different categories until you find what you are looking for. However, directories contain only a portion of the sites and pages available on the Internet, so be forewarned: directories should be used by the fraud examiner in concert with a search engine, not instead of one.

Yahoo! (www.yahoo.com)

Yahoo has a search engine, but it is most useful as a directory. Yahoo has an intricate directory, possibly the most comprehensive and all-inclusive on the Web. The directory is built and maintained by Yahoo employees, with input from users. Yahoo functions much like a pyramid, beginning with several large pools of categories, such as entertainment and government, and allows the user to select more specific options from each. For instance, an examiner could select "education," then "universities," then "university libraries," until finally encountering a direct link to the main library catalog for the University of Texas. By paring down your selections to more and more narrow topics, you can generally find several good websites containing the information you are interested in.

WWW virtual library (www.w3.org/vl/)

The VL is the oldest catalog of the Web, started by Tim Berners-Lee, the creator of the HTML that makes the Web possible. Unlike commercial catalogs, it is run by a loose confederation of volunteers who compile pages of key links for particular areas in which they are expert. This is not the biggest index of the Web but the VL pages are widely praised as guides to particular sections of the Web.

Internet Public Library (www.ipl.org)

Run by librarians, this service indexes Web pages by topic. Also contains an array of guides, such as on-line magazines and newspapers, associations, and tips for conducting research.

Metasearch Engines

Several sites are designed to search several search engines at once. Ask Jeeves, described above, has such an option. Other sites are described below.

Metacrawler (www.metacrawler.com)

Searches seven search engines and aggregates the results. Metacrawler's limited search options make it hard to construct precise queries.

Dogpile (www.dogpile.com)

Dogpile searches up to 13 search engines, over two dozen news services, and sorts the results according to the search engine that found them. It's a good way to evaluate the results obtained through various search engines.

Northern Light (www.northernlight.com)

Northern Light indexes Web pages, and also searches through pay-per-view articles not generally available. Results are sorted into folders under various topic headings.

A Guide to Successful Searching

Running Searches

The Internet is not so much a service as a tool. To tap its rich information sources, you have to learn how to construct proper queries. That is, you have to learn how to ask for what you want. Search engines all have their limitations, but the most serious impediment to locating good information is the user's lack of search skills.

Most searching uses keywords. For instance, hunting for the latest statistics on check fraud, the logical keywords are *check fraud*. But if you typed in those words, the search engine would return numerous sites that have nothing to do with check fraud. By placing both words inside quotation marks ("check fraud") you will get better results. Still, the list of hits will be in the thousands, so you may want to narrow the search using the techniques below.

Boolean Operators

The best way to utilize a search engine is to use two, or possibly three, keywords that best describe the topic. If the words succeed one another, as in the case of "check fraud," then it may be beneficial to use *Boolean operators* to aid one's search. Boolean operators are symbols that help the search engine to better understand exactly what it is searching for. Putting the "+" symbol between "check+fraud," for example, will indicate to the search engine that it is to search only for pages which have the word "fraud" immediately following "check." If you insert the word "and," so that the search reads "check and fraud," the search engine will understand to search for websites and pages that contain both the words "check" and "fraud," but not necessarily right next to each other.

Some of the more common Boolean operator symbols, or connectors, are shown below.

BOOLEAN CONNECTORS

+	Designates words which must appear right next to each other
–	Designates words which should not appear on a Web page
" "	Designates a list of words which must appear together, such as "holy cow"
and	Designates two or more words which must both appear on a page, but not necessarily next to each other
or	Designates two connected words, one of which must appear on a page
not	Designates words which should not appear on the page, much like the minus sign
near	Designates words which appear within a certain number of words of each other

Websites Table

The following is a list of websites grouped by topic which should prove useful to fraud examiners and other anti-fraud professionals:

Search Engines

1Blink	http://www.1blink.com
About.com	http://www.about.com
AltaVista	http://www.altavista.digital.com
C4	http://www.c4.com
Complete Planet	http://www.completeplanet.com
Dogpile	http://www.dogpile.com
Excite	http://www.excite.com
GO.com	http://infoseek.go.com
Google	http://www.google.com
GoTo	http://www.goto.com
HotBot	http://www.hotbot.lycos.com
I Won	http://www.iwon.com
Infomine	http://infomine.ucr.edu/
Internet 101	http://www2.awl.com/cseng/titles/0-201-32553-5/website/html/search_engines.html
Profusion	http://www.profusion.com
Law Crawler — Legal Issues	http://lawcrawler.findlaw.com/
Legal Engine	http://www.legalengine.com
Cop Seek Directory and Police Search Engine	http://www.leolinks.com/
LookSmart	http://www.looksmart.com
Lycos	http://www.lycos.com
Mamma.com	http://www.mamma.com
Metacrawler	http://www.metacrawler.com
Multicrawl	http://www.multicrawl.com
Search Guide	http://www.searchguide.com
Netscape Search	http://search.netscape.com/
Northern Light	http://www.northernlight.com
Overture	http://www.overture.com
ProFusion	http://www.profusion.com
Savvy Search.com	http://www.search.com/
Search Engine Watch	http://www.searchenginewatch.com/
Search Monger	http://www.searchmonger.com/
Search.com	http://search.cnet.com/
Snap	http://nbci.msnbc.com/nbci.asp
Surf Wax	http://www.surfwax.com/
The Big Hub	http://www.thebighub.com/
The Front Page	http://www.thefrontpage.com/search
WebCrawler	http://www.webcrawler.com
Yahoo	http://www.yahoo.com

News Sources

ABC	http://abc.go.com
ABCNews.com	http://abcnews.go.com
APB News — Crime, Justice, Safety	http://www.apbnews.com/
CBS	http://www.cbsnews.cbs.com
CNBC	http://moneycentral.msn.com
CNN Interactive	http://www.cnn.com

CRAYON	http://www.crayon.net
Dialog	http://www.dialogweb.com
Factiva	http://www.factiva.com
Find Articles	http://www.findarticles.com
FOX	http://www.foxnews.com
Investigative Reporters and Editors	http://www.ire.org
Lexis-Nexis	http://www.lexis-nexis.com
MSNBC	http://www.msnbc.msn.com
NBC	http://www.nbc.com
News alert	http://www.newsalert.com
News Central	http://www.All-links.com/newscentral/
News.com	http://www.news.com
Newslink	http://www.newslink.org
Refdesk	http://www.refdesk.com
Reuters	http://www.reuters.com
Salon	http://www.salon.com/
Slate	http://Slate.msn.com/
The Council of State Governments	http://www.statesnews.org/
High Beam Research	http://www.highbeam.com/library/index.asp
Wired News	http://www.wired.com/news

Newspapers

Annapolis Capital	http://www.capitalonline.com
Augusta Chronicle	http://augustachronicle.com/
Baltimore Sun	http://www.baltimoresun.com
Boston Globe	http://www.boston.com/globe
Casper Star-Tribune (WY)	http://www.trib.com
Chattanooga Free Press	http://www.timesfreepress.com
Chicago Sun Times	http://www.suntimes.com/index
Chicago Tribune	http://www.chicagotribune.com/
Christian Science Monitor	http://www.csmonitor.com/
Colorado Springs Gazette-Tele.	http://www.gazette.com
Daily Gazette (NY)	http://www.dailygazette.com
Dallas Morning News	http://www.dallasnews.com
Deseret Morning News (UT)	http://www.deseretnews.com
Detroit Free Press	http://www.freep.com
Evansville Courier (IN)	http://www.courierpress.com
Florida Times Union	http://jacksonville.com/
Fort Worth Star Telegram	http://www.dfw.com
Gainesville Sun	http://www. www.sunone.com
Houston Chronicle	http://www.chron.com
Knoxville News-Sentinel	http://www.knoxnews.com
Los Angeles Times	http://www.latimes.com
Miami Herald	http://www.miami.com
Missoulian (MT)	http://www.missoulian.com
New York Daily News	http://www.nydailynews.com
New York Post	http://www.nypost.com
Newsday	http://www.newsday.com
Norfolk Virginian-Pilot	http://www.pilotonline.com
Orange County Register	http://www.ocregister.com
Orlando Sentinel	http://www.orlandosentinel.com
Raleigh New	http://www.nando.net
Roanoke Times	http://www.roanoke.com

Salt Lake Tribune	http://www.sltrib.com
San Diego Union-Tribune	http://www.uniontrib.com
San Francisco Chronicle	http://www.sfgate.com
The Mercury News	http://www.mercurynews.com/mld/mercurynews/
Seattle Times	http://www.seattletimes.com
Sioux City Journal	http://www.siouxcityjournal.com
Twin Cities Pioneer Press	http://www.twincities.com/mld/twincities
St. Petersburg Times	http://www.sptimes.com
The New York Times on the Web	http://www.nytimes.com
USA Today	http://www.usatoday.com
Wall Street Journal	http://www.wsj.com
Washington Post	http://www.washingtonpost.com/

University Library Sites

Brigham Young University	http://www.lib.byu.edu
Cal State Long Beach University	http://www.csulb.edu/library
Carnegie-Mellon University	http://www.library.cmu.edu
Claremont Colleges	http://voxlibris.claremont.edu
Cornell University	http://campusgw.library.cornell.edu
Drexel University	http://www.library.drexel.edu
Duke University	http://www.lib.duke.edu
Eastern Michigan University	http://www.emich.edu
Georgetown University	http://www.georgetown.edu/home/libraries.html
Harvard University (HOLLIS—Harvard On-line Library Information System)	http://lib.harvard.edu/
Indiana Univ./Purdue Univ.	http://www.ulib.iupui.edu
Iowa State University	http://www.lib.iastate.edu
Johns Hopkins University	http://www.welch.jhu.edu
Kansas State University	http://www.lib.ksu.edu
Louisiana State University	http://www.lsu.edu
Mansfield University	http://www.mnsfld.edu/depts/lib/index.html
Miami (OH) University	http://www.lib.muohio.edu
Middle Tennessee State University	http://www.mtsu.edu/~library
MIT University	http://web.mit.edu
New Mexico State University	http://lib.nmsu.edu
North Carolina State University	http://www.lib.ncsu.edu
Princeton University	http://libweb.princeton.edu
Tulane University	http://www.tulane.edu/~html
University of Arizona	http://www.arizona.edu/home/libraries.shtml
University of Cal-Berkeley	http://www.lib.berkeley.edu
University of Cal-Los Angeles	http://www.library.ucla.edu
University of Cal-Riverside	http://library.ucr.edu
University of Florida	http://web.uflib.ufl.edu
University of Houston	http://info.lib.uh.edu
University of Idaho	http://drseuss.lib.uidaho.edu
University of Iowa	http://www.lib.uiowa.edu/index.html
University of Maine	http://www.maine.edu/lib.html
University of Maryland	http://www.lib.umd.edu
University of Michigan	http://www.lib.umich.edu
University of Minnesota	http://www1.umn.edu
University of New Orleans	http://library.uno.edu
University of North Carolina	http://www.ils.unc.edu/ils/library
University of North Carolina-Charlotte	http://www.library.uncc.edu/

| Investigation | Accessing Information On-Line |

University of Virginia	http://www.lib.virginia.edu/
Vanderbilt University	http://www.library.vanderbilt.edu
Washington University of Washington	http://www.lib.washington.edu

State Government Listings

Alabama	http://www.state.al.us
Alaska	http://www.state.ak.us/
Arizona	http://az.gov
Arkansas	http://www.state.ar.us/
California	http://www.state.ca.us/
Colorado	http://colorado.gov
Connecticut	http://www.state.ct.us/
Delaware	http://delaware.gov
Florida	http://www.state.fl.us/
Georgia	http://www.state.ga.us/
Hawaii	http://www.hawaii.gov/
Idaho	http://www.state.id.us/
Illinois	http://www.state.il.us/
Indiana	http://in.gov/
Iowa	http://www.iowa.gov
Kansas	http://accesskansas.org
Kentucky	http://kentucky.gov
Louisiana	http://www.louisiana.gov
Maine	http://www.state.me.us/
Maryland	http://www.maryland.gov
Massachusetts	http://www.mass.gov/
Michigan	http://www.michigan.gov/
Minnesota	http://www.state.mn.us/
Mississippi	http://www.state.ms.us
Missouri	http://www.state.mo.us/
Montana	http://www.state.mt.us/
Nebraska	http://www.state.ne.us/
Nevada	http://www.silverstate.nv.us/
New Hampshire	http://www.nv.gov
New Jersey	http://www.state.nj.us/
New Mexico	http://www.state.nm.us/
New York	http://www.state.ny.us/
North Carolina	http://www.ncgov.com/
North Dakota	http://www.discovernd.com/government/
Ohio	http://www.ohio.gov
Oklahoma	http://www.oklaosf.state.ok.us/
Oregon	http://www.oregon.gov/
Pennsylvania	http://www.state.pa.us/
Rhode Island	http://www.state.ri.us/
South Carolina	http://www.myscgov.com/
South Dakota	http://www.state.sd.us/
Tennessee	http://www.state.tn.us/
Texas	http://www.state.tx.us/
Utah	http://www.utah.gov/
Vermont	http://vermont.gov
Virginia	http://www.state.va.us/
Washington	http://access.wa.gov/
West Virginia	http://www.state.wv.us/

Accessing Information On-Line Investigation

Wisconsin	http://www.wisconsin.gov/
Wyoming	http://wyoming.gov

Telephone Numbers & Addresses

AT&T AnyWho	http://www.anywho.com
555-1212	http://www.555-1212.com
Big Yellow	http://www.bigyellow.com
Bigbook	http://www.bigbook.com
Bigfoot	http://www.bigfoot.com
Database America People Finder	http://adp.infousa.com
E-mail addresses	http://www.555-1212.com
GTE Superpages	http://www.superpages.com
Homepage Finder	http://www.help4web.net/search/email/ahoy.htm
InfoSpace	http://www.infospace.com
InfoUSA	http://www.infousa.com
Military Locator Service	http://www.militarycity.com
Military Personnel Records	http://www.nara.gov/regional/mpr.html
Naked in Cyberspace	http://www.technosearch.com/naked/directory.htm
Open Market's Commercial Sites	http://www.openmarket.com
PayPhone	http://www.payphone.com
People Search	http://www.peoplesearch.net
Register.com	http://www.register.com
Semaphore Corp	http://www.semaphorecorp.com
Switchboard	http://www.switchboard.com
The PI Mall	http://www.pimall.com/
U.S Web Finder	http://uswebfinder.com/home.cfm
WhoWhere?	http://www.whowhere.lycos.com
Worldpages	http://www.worldpages.com
Yahoo! People Search	http://people.yahoo.com
Zip2 Yellow Pages	http://www.infospace.com

Maps

4Maps.com	http://www.4maps.4anything.com
Excite Travel	http://www.excite.com/
MapBlast	http://www.mapblast.com
MapQuest	http://www.mapquest.com
Maps On Us	http://www.mapsonus.com
Mileage Calculator	http://www.indo.com/distance/

Databases — Public Record Searches

Autotrack	http://www.autotrackxp.com
BRB Publishing	http://www.brbpub.com
ChoicePoint	http://www.choicepoint.net
ChoicePoint: AutotrackXP	http://www.autotrackxp.com
ChoicePoint: CDB Infotek	http://www.choicepointonline.com/cdb/
ChoicePoint: Database Technologies	http://www.dbtonline.com
ChoicePoint: KnowX	http://www.knowx.com
DCS Information Systems	http://www.dnis.com
Dialog	http://www.dialog.com
Diligenz	http://www.diligenz.com
Dun & Bradstreet	http://www.dnb.com
Experian	http://www.experian.com/catalog_us/atoz.html
Fedworld	Http://www.fedworld.gov

G.S. Public Record Services	http://www.gaprs.com
InfoUSA	http://www.infousa.com
Lexis-Nexis	http://www.lexisnexis.com
Loc8fast	http://www.loc8fast.com
Merlin Information Systems	http://www.merlindata.com
Public Interest Registry	http://www.pir.org
Public Data	http://www.publicdata.com
Veris	http://veris.info/
US Datalink	http://www.usdatalink.com
Usgovsearch	http://www.usgovsearch.northernlight.com

Legal Resources

Docusearch	http://www/docusearch.com
Administrative Office of the U.S. Courts	http://www.uscourts.gov
Attorney search	http://lawyers.findlaw.com
California Laws	http://www.leginfo.ca.gov
Court House News	http://www.courtnews.com/
Cyber Securities Laws	http://www.cybersecuritieslaw.com
Divorce Central	http://www.divorcecentral.com
Federal Legislative Information on the Internet	http://thomas.loc.gov/
Find Law	http://www.findlaw.com/
Federal and State Codes and Statutes	www.findlaw.com/casecode
Florida Statutes	http://www.fdle.state.fl.us/statutes/
American Lawyer's Media	http://www.law.com
Law Office.com	http://www.lawyers.findlaw.com
Law on the Web	http://www.law.com/
Lawyers	http://www.lawyers.com/
Legal Ethics	http://www.legalethics.com/index.law
Legal Info Institute of Cornell	http://www.law.cornell.edu/
Legal Research on the Web	http://gsulaw.gsu.edu/metaindex/
Martindale-Hubble	http://www.martindale.com
Comptroller of the Currency/U.S. Department of the Treasury	http://www.occ.treas.gov/
My Counsel	http://www.mycounsel.com
Nolo	http://www.nolo.com
On-line Sunshine – Florida Legislature	http://www.leg.state.fl.us/
Reporters Committee — Freedom of Press	http://www.rcfp.org
Reporters Committee — Taping Conversations	http://www.rcfp.org/taping/index.html
State Court Locator	http://www.courts.net
U.S. Supreme Court Decisions	http://www.fedworld.gov/supcourt/index.htm
U.S. Supreme Court Internet Sites	http://www.ccle.fourh.umn.edu/SupCt.htm
U.S. Supreme Court –Oyez Project -Northwestern University	http://www.oyez.org/oyez/frontpage
University of Chicago Law School	http://www.law.uchicago.edu
University of Mass. Law	http://www.umass.edu/legal
Virtual Law Library	http://www.law.indiana.edu/v-lib
Washington Document Services	http://www.wdsdocs.com
West Legal Directory	http://www.directory.findlaw.com

Government Sites and Criminal Justice Resources

Bureau of Alcohol, Tobacco and Firearms and Explosives(ATF)	http://www.atf.gov/
Bureau of Industry and Security	http://www.bxa.doc.gov/

Center for Criminal Justice Technology	http://www.mitretek.org/business_areas/justice/cjiti/cjiti.html
Central Intelligence Agency	http://www.cia.gov
Class Actions	http://www.classaction.com/
Class Actions	http://securities.stanford.edu/
Class Actions	http://securities.lcsr.com/MW/welcome.html
Federal Citizen Information Center	http://www.pueblo.gsa.gov
County Sheriff's Offices — By State	http://www.corrections.com/links/county.html
Court Websites	http://www.ncsconline.org/d_kis/info_court_web_sites.html
LexisNexis Courtlink	http://www.lexisnexis.com/courtlink/online
Database of Government Websites	http://firstgov.gov
FBI Law Enforcement Bulletin	http://www.fbi.gov/publications/leb/leb.htm
FBI U.S. Department of Homeland Security	http://www.nipc.gov
Fed World File Transfer Protocol and Retrieve Service	http://www.fedworld.gov
Federal Bureau of Investigation Home Page	http://www.fbi.gov/
Federal Bureau of Prisons	http://www.bop.gov/
Federal Election Commission	http://www.fec.gov
Political Moneyline	http://www.tray.com/fecinfo/
Federal Inspectors General	http://www.ignet.gov/
Federal Judicial Center	http://www.fjc.gov/
Federal Register	http://www.archives.gov/index.html
Firstgov	http://www.firstgov.com
Florida Department of Corrections	http://www.dc.state.fl.us/
Florida Department of Law Enforcement	http://www.fdle.state.fl.us/
Florida Department of State	http://www.dos.state.fl.us/
Florida Government Website	http://myflorida.com
GovSpot	http://www.govspot.com
Internal Revenue Service	http://www.irs.gov
Internet Wiretap	http://www.spies.com
Investigators Guide to the Sources of Information (GAO/OSI-97-2)	http://www.gao.gov/special.pubs/soi.htm
Law Enforcement on the Web	http://www.ih2000.net/ira/ira.htm
Library of Congress	http://lcweb.loc.gov
National Address Server	http://www.cedar.buffalo.edu/adserv.html
National Archives and Records Administration	http://www.nara.gov
National Center for State Courts	http://www.ncsconline.org
National Criminal Justice Reference Service	http://www.ncjrs.org
Nonprofit Gateway	http://www.firstgov.gov/business/nonprofit.shtml
Office of Defense Trade Controls	http://www.pmdtc.org/debar059.htm
Police Officers Internet Directory	http://www.officer.com/
Public Access to Electronic Records — PACER	http://pacer.psc.uscourts.gov/
Published List of Recalls	http://www.dot.gov/affairs/nhtsain.htm
Royal Canadian Mounted Police	http://www.rcmp-grc.gc.ca/
SEC Enforcement Actions	http://www.sec.gov/enforce.htm
SEC Enforcement Division	http://www.sec.gov/divisions/enforce.htm
Securities & Exchange Commission	http://www.sec.gov/edgarhp.htm
Selective Service System	http://www.sss.gov
Sex Offenders Registry	http://www.crimetime.com/SPguide.htm
Social Security Death Index Search	http://www.ancestry.com/search/rectype/vital/ssdi/main.htm
SSN Validation Database	http://www.ssa.gov
State and Federal Prisons	http://www.bop.gov
State and Local Government Internet sites	http://www.statelocalgov.net/index.cfm
State Legislatures	http://www.ncsl.org/
Superior Information Services	http://superiorinfo.com

Texas Department of Public Safety — Convictions	http://records.txdps.state.tx.us/
U.S. Commodity Futures Trading Commission	http://www.cftc.gov
U.S. Department of Justice	http://www.usdoj.gov/
U.S. Department of Justice — Computer Crime and Intellectual Property	http://www.cybercrime.gov/
U.S. Federal Agencies	http://www.ignet.gov/
U.S. Federal Communications Commission	http://www.fcc.gov
U.S. Federal Deposit Insurance Corporation	http://www.fdic.gov
U.S. Federal Drug Administration	http://www.fda.gov
U.S. General Services Administration	http://www.gsa.gov
U.S. Federal Register	http://www.nara.gov/fedreg/
U.S. Federal Register — Daily postings	http://www.gpoaccess.gov/fr/index.html
U.S. Federal Trade Commission	http://www.ftc.gov
U.S. General Accounting Office	http://www.gao.gov
U.S. Government Printing Office	http://www.gpoaccess.gov/index.html
U.S. Patent and Trademark Office	http://www.uspto.gov
U.S. Postal Office Zip Code	http://www.usps.gov/ncsc/
U.S. Supreme Court	http://www.supremecourtus.gov
United Nations Crime & Justice Information Network (UNCJIN)	http://www.uncjin.org
Vital Records Database	http://www.vitalrec.com
Voter's Registration	http://www.governmentrecords.com/
White House	http://www.whitehouse.gov

Other Fraud-Related and Websites of Interest

ACFE Albany Chapter	http://www.theiia.org/chapters/index.cfm?cid=87
ACL—Data Analysis Software	http://www.acl.com
Active Most Wanted and Criminal Investigations	http://www.activemostwanted.com
ACUA	http://www.acua.org
AFU and Urban Legends Archive	http://www.snopes.com
Any Birthday	http://www.anybirthday.com
Association of Certified Fraud Examiners	http://www.cfenet.com
Better Business Bureau Web Server Home Page	http://www.bbb.org
Broward County Sheriff's Office	http://www.sheriff.org
Canadian Bankers Association: Consumer Tips	http://www.cba.ca
Check Fraud Tips	http://www.checkfraud.org/
Company Site Locator	http://www.switchboard.com
Company Sleuth	http://www.companysleuth.com
Computer Security Institute	http://www.gocsi.com
Consumer Education	http://www.consumer.gov/
Cop Net: International Law Enforcement	http://www.copnet.org/
Corrections Industry	http://www.corrections.com/
CPA Directory	http://www.cpadirectory.com/index.cfm
Check Fraud	http://www.ckfraud.org
Crimetime Publishing Company	http://www.crimetime.com/online.html
Cyber Space Law Center	http://www.findlaw.com/
Cybercop	http://all.net/cybercop/index.html
Cyberensics	http://www.cyberensics.net/
Dan Moldea	http://www.moldea.com
Administration for Children & Families	http://www.acf.dhhs.gov/
Detecting Deception - Don Rabon	http://www.donrabon.net
Employment Schemes	http://www.usps.gov/websites/depart/inspect/emplmenu.htm
Fraud Bureau	http://www.fraudbureau.com

Fraud Index	http://www.scambusters.org
Fuld & Company's Internet Intelligence Index	http://www.fuld.com
High Technology Crime Investigation Association	http://htcia.org/
Hoover's	http://www.hoovers.com
Identity Theft	http://www.privacyrights.org
Identity Theft	http://www.consumer.gov/idtheft/
Identity Theft Assumption and Deterrence Act	http://www.identitytheft.org/title18.htm
Inspection Service Consumer Fraud	http://www.usps.gov/websites/depart/inspect/consmenu.htm
Internet Anti-Scam	http://www.nerdworld.com/nw1319.html
Internet Center for Corruption Research	http://www.gwdg.de/~uwvw/icr.htm
Internet Chain Letters	http://hoaxbusters.ciac.org
Internet Fraud Complaint Center	http://www.ifccfbi.gov
Inventor Fraud	http://www.inventorfraud.com
Investor Protection Trust	http://www.investorprotection.org
Joscon Network	http://linz1.net/fraud.html
National Criminal Justice Reference Service	http://askncjrs@ncjrs.org/
National Institute for Consumer Education	http://www.nice.emich.edu
Missing Money	http://www.missingmoney.com
Municipal Bond Scandals	http://www.lissack.com
National Charities Information Bureau	http://give.org
National Consumer Complaint Center	http://www.alexanderlaw.com/nccc/
National Cybercrime Training Partnership	http://www.nctp.org/
National Fraud Information Center	http://www.fraud.org
National White Collar Crime Center	http://www.nw3c.org/
Network Solutions — Website operator information	http://www.netsol.com
Nigeria-The 419 Coalition Website	http://home.rica.net/alphae/419coal/
Noble Ventures - Asset Searches	http://www.listcompiler.com/home.html
Offshore Business News & Research	http://offshorebusiness.com
On-line Fraud Info Center	http://www.fraud.org
On-line Scams	http://www.ftc.gov/fte/consumer.htm
Other Consumer Frauds	http://www.usps.com/postalinspectors/fraud
Ponzi Schemes	http://www.crimes-of-persuasion.com
Privacy Headquarters	http://www.complianceheadquarters.com
Privacy Net/Consumer Net	http://www.privacytools.com/
Privacy Rights Clearinghouse	http://www.privacyrights.org/
Prolific Fraud Scams	http://www.cityofevanston.org/departments/police/communitystrategies/prolific_fraud_scams.htm
Scambusters	http://www.scambusters.com/index.html
Scams and Swindles	http://www.swindles.com/
ScamWatch	http://www.scamwatch.com
Security Management On-line	http://www.securitymanagement.com/
SPA Anti-Piracy Home Page	http://www.spa.org/piracy/
SSA Fraud Reporting	http://www.ssa.gov/oig/hotline/guidelines.htm
Taxpayers Against Fraud	http://www.taf.org
TD Bank-Fraud Prevention	http://www.td.com
TruSecure Corporation	http://www.trusecure.com
Urban Legends Reference Pages	http://www.urbanlegends.com
USA Websites	http://www.usawebpages.com/
Virus Bulletin	http://www.virusbtn.com/
Website hoax – F-Secure	http://www.europe.f-secure.com/virus-info/hoax
Website hoax – Kumite	http://www.vmyths.com
Website hoax — Symantec	http://www.symantec.com/avcenter/hoax.html
Whistleblower's Website	http://www.whistleblowers.com
World Bank	http://www.worldbank.org

Health Care/Insurance Fraud

(4)Medical Ethics	http://4medicalethics.4anything.com/
Insurance Association of America	http://www.allianceai.org
AMA Physician Select	http://www.ama-assn.org/aps/amahg.htm
America's Health Insurance PlansPlans	http://aahp.org/
American Bar Association — Medicine & Law Committee	http://www.abanet.org/tips/medicine/links.html#fraud
American Medical Association	http://www.ama-assn.org/
Coalition Against Insurance Fraud	http://www.insurancefraud.org
Computer Based Records Institute	http://www.cpri.org
Corrections Links — Health Care	http://www.corrections.com/healthnetwork/index.aspx
Healthfinder — Health Information Guide	http://www.healthfinder.gov
Departments of Insurance – State Benefit Services Group	http://www.bsg.com/resources/relatedsites/statedept.asp
Ed Hayes — Indexes to medical sites	http://www.edhayes.com/
Excluded Parties List	http://epls.arnet.gov/
Fraud Defense Network	http://www.frauddefense.com
Fraud News	http://www.fraudnews.com
Health Insurance Association of America	http://www.hiaa.org
Health Law Resource	http://www.netreach.net/~wmanning/
Centers for Medicare and Medicaid Services	http://www.cms.hhs.gov
Insurance Fraud Research Register	http://www.ifb.org/ifrrpdf.htm
International Association of Special Investigation Units	http://www.iasiu.com
Medical Economics Magazine	http://www.pdr.net/memag/index.htm
Medical Information Bureau	http://www.mib.com
Medicare Fraud Alerts	http://
Medicare Fraud and Abuse Training — On-line	http://www.cms.hhs.gov/medlearn
National Association of Insurance Commissioners	http://www.naic.org
National Coalition on Health Care	http://www.nchc.org
National Council Against Health Fraud	http://www.ncahf.org/
National Fraud Information Center	http://www.fraud.org
National Health Care Anti-Fraud Association	http://www.nhcaa.org
National Insurance Crime Bureau	http://www.nicb.org
National Medical Reporter — Health Care links	http://medicalreporter.health.org/links.html
National Practitioner Data Bank	http://www.npdb-hipdb.com
Net-Trace Insurance Links	http://www.nettrace.com.au
Office of Inspector General	http://www.hhs.gov/infoquality/OIGinfo2.htm
Office of Investigations	http://www.ssa.gov/oig/investigations/index.htm
PDR — Physician Desk Reference	http://www.pdr.net/
Quackwatch Consumer Health Fraud	http://www.quackwatch.com/
Research America — hot medical links	http://www.researchamerica.org/links/index.html
Seattle University Law Library	http://www.law.seattleu.edu/library
The Health Law Resource	http://www.netreach.net/~wmanning
The HMO Page	http://www.hmopage.org
Ultimate Insurance Links	http://www.ultimateinsurancelinks.com/
University of Florida – College of Medicine – Compliance	http://www.med.ufl.edu/complian
Insurance Quotes.com	http://www.insurancequotes.com
Workers Compensation Information	http://www.comp.state.nc.us/ncic/pages/all50.htm

State Insurance Fraud Divisions (not all Divisions have websites)

Alaska	http://www.dced.state.ak.us/insurance
Arizona	http://www.state.az.us/id/
Arkansas	http://www.arkansas.gov/insurance/fraudinvestigation/insurancefraud_p1.html
California	http://www.insurance.ca.gov/FRD/Frd_main.htm
Colorado	http://www.dora.state.co.us/Insurance
Connecticut	http://www.state.ct.us/cid/
Delaware	http://www.state.de.us/inscom/index.html
Florida	http://www.fldfs.com
Georgia	http://www.InsComm.State.Ga.US/
Hawaii	http://www.state.hi.us/dcca/ins/branches2.html
Idaho	http://www.doi.state.id.us/
Illinois	http://www.state.il.us/ins/default.htm
Indiana	http://www.state.in.us/idoi
Iowa	http://www.iid.state.ia.us/
Kansas	http://www.ksinsurance.org
Kentucky	http://www.doi.state.ky.us/kentucky/
Louisiana	http://www.ldi.state.la.us/
Maine	http://www.state.me.us/pfr/ins/ins_index.htm
Maryland	http://www.mdarchives.state.md.us/msa/mdmanual/25ind/html/47insur.html
Massachusetts	http://www.ifb.org/default_java.htm
Michigan	http://www.michigan.gov/cis/1,1607,7-154-10555---,00.html
Minnesota	http://www.commerce.state.mn.us/
Mississippi	http://www.doi.state.ms.us/
Missouri	http://insurance.state.mo.us/consumer/index.html
Montana	http://sao.state.mt.us/sao/insurance/index.html
Nebraska	http://www.nol.org/home/NDOI/
Nevada	http://www.doi.state.nv.us
New Hampshire	http://www.nh.gov/insurance
New Jersey	http://www.state.nj.us/dobi
New York	http://www.ins.state.ny.us
North Carolina	http://www.ncdoi.com/
North Dakota	http://www.state.nd.us/ndins/
Ohio	http://www.ins.state.oh.us/
Oklahoma	http://www.oid.state.ok.us
Oregon	http://www.cbs.state.or.us/external/ins/index.html
Pennsylvania	http://www.insurance.state.pa.us/ins/site/default.asp
Puerto Rico	http://www.ocs.gobierno.pr
Rhode Island	http://www.dbr.state.ri.us/insurance.html
South Carolina	http://www.doi.state.sc.us
South Dakota	http://www.state.sd.us/insurance/comply.htm
Tennessee	http://www.state.tn.us/consumer/
Texas	http://www.tdi.state.tx.us/consumer/cpportal.html
Utah	http://www.insurance.state.ut.us/
Vermont	http://www.bishca.state.vt.us/
Virginia	http://www.vsp.state.va.us/bciifd.htm
Washington	http://www.insurance.wa.gov
Wisconsin	http://oci.wi.gov/oci_home.htm
Wyoming	http://insurance.state.wy.us/

Telecom Fraud/Security

AT&T Fraud Education	http://www.att.com/fraud/att.html
Bell Atlantic, Verizon	http://newscenter.verizon.com/kit/servicestandard/scams.vtml
Cerebrus Solutions	http://www.cerebrussolutions.com
SBC	http://www.sbc.com/gen/press-room?pid=5526
National Association of Securities Dealers (NASD)	http://www.investor.nasd.com/
Travelassist Magazine — Phone Card Fraud	http://www.travelassist.com/mag/a27.html

Auditing

Columbia University Internal Audit	http://www.columbia.edu/cu/ia
COSO	http://www.coso.org
Government Auditing Standards	http://www.gao.gov/govaud/ybk01.htm
Institute of Internal Auditors	http://www.theiia.org
Internal Auditing World Wide Web	http://www.bitwise.net/iawww
Netsurfer Focus — Computer and Network Security	http://www.netsurf.com/nsf/lib/index.html
UNC Business Manual — Internal Audit Section	http://www.ais.unc.edu/busman/bmhome.html

Investment Resources

Corporate Information	http://www.corporateinformation.com
FreeEDGAR	http://www.freeedgar.com
Thestreet.com	http://www.thestreet.com/
Internet News	http://stocks.internetnews.com
Kiplinger	http://www.kiplinger.com

International Sites
Global Search Engines

Bubl link	http://www.bubl.ac.uk/link/
Euro-seek	http://www.euroseek.net/
Matilda — Mega Search Engine Australia	http://www.aussieseek.com
Search New Zealand	http://www.searchnz.co.nz/
Voila	http://www.voila.com/
WebWombat	http://webwombat.com.au/

Newspapers

Newspaper Society Database	http://www.nsdatabase.co.uk/index.html
This is London	http://www.thisislondon.co.uk
Financial Times	http://news.ft.com
Le Monde	http://www.lemonde.fr
Newspaper Society	http://www.newspapersoc.org.uk
The Daily Telegraph	http://www.telegraph.co.uk
The Guardian Unlimited	http://www.guardian.co.uk or www.newsunlimited.co.uk
The Independent	http://www.independent.co.uk
The Irish Times	http://www.ireland.com
The Scotsman	http://www.Scotsman.com
The Sunday Times Online	http://www.timesonline.co.uk
The Times	http://www.the-times.co.uk
Times Higher Education Supplement	http://www.thes.co.uk

News and Information Services

Association of Investigative Journalists	http://www.aij-uk.com
BBC News	http://www.bbc.co.uk
Canada.com	http://www.canada.com/national
Euronews	http://www.euronews.net/

Future Events News Service	http://www.fensap.com
Parliament of Australia: Hansard (House of Commons Debates	http://www.aph.gov.au/hansard/index.htm
Ireland By Net	http://www.irelandbynet.com
ITN On-line	http://www.itn.co.uk
Microsoft Network News	http://www.msn.com
NewsNow	http://www.newsnow.co.uk
NineMSN	http://ninemsn.com.au/
Sky News	http://www.sky.co.uk/news
The Economist	http://www.economist.co.uk
The Press Association	http://www.pa.press.net
UK Business Park — Media News	http://www.ukbusinesspark.co.uk
Yahoo UK News	http://uk.news.yahoo.com

Libraries

Aberdeen University	http://www.abdn.ac.uk/diss/library
British Library	http://www.bl.uk
Cambridge University	http://www.lib.cam.ac.uk
Edinburgh University	http://www.lib.ed.ac.uk/lib
Exeter University	http://www.ex.ac.uk/library/
Glasgow University	http://www.gla.ac.uk/library
King's College, London	http://www.kcl.ac.uk/depsta/iss/library
Oxford University	http://www.ox.ac.uk/libraries/
Public Libraries	http://www.earl.org.uk
University College, London	http://www.ucl.ac.uk/UCL-info/divisions/library/index.htm
University of Bath	http://www.bath.ac.uk/library
University of East Anglia	http://www.lib.uea.ac.uk

Telephone Numbers

Scoot	http://www.scoot.co.uk
UK Tracker	http://www.angelfire.com/on/touchtone99/tracker.html
Yellow Pages	http://www.yell.co.uk

Maps

MultiMap	http://www.multimap.com/map/places.cgi
Ordnance Survey	http://www.ordsvy.gov.uk
Street Map	http://www.streetmap.co.uk
The RAC	http://www.rac.co.uk
UK On-line	

Legal Resources

Access to Law	http://www.Accesstolaw.org/
Centre for Commercial Law Studies — University of London	http://www.ccls.edu/ccls.html
Consumer Law Center	http://www.hg.org/consume.html
Dundee University Legal Websites Directory	http://www.Dundee.ac.uk/law/resources/index.php
InfoLaw Gateway	http://www.infolaw.co.uk
Law Link: Irish Company Information	http://www.lawlink.ie
The Court Service	http://www.courtservice.gov.uk
The International Centre for Commercial Law	http://www.legal500.com/index.php
The Law Commission	http://www.lawcom.gov.uk
The Law Society	http://www.lawsoc.org.uk

Government Sites and Law Enforcement Sites

Australia — Attorney General's Department	http://law.gov.au/wotl.html
Australia Ministerial Council	http://www.consumer.gov.au/
Australia/New Zealand Consumer Affairs Links	http://www.consumer.act.gov.au/
Australian Courts and Legislation	http://www.nla.gov.au/oz/gov/leg.html
Australian Department of Foreign Affairs and Trade	http://www.dfat.gov.au/
Australian Federal Privacy Commissioner	http://www.privacy.gov.au/
Government Information Centre	http://www.ukonline.gov.uk
Informatin Commissiner's Office	http://www.informationcommissioner.gov.uk
Department of Trade and Industry	http://www.dti.gov.uk
Financial Services Authority	http://www.fsa.gov.uk
Foreign and Commonwealth Office	http://www.fco.gov.uk
HM Treasury	http://www.hm-treasury.gov.uk
UK Police Forces	http://www.police.uk
International Centre for Criminal Law Reform and Criminal Justice Policy	http://www.icclr.law.ubc.ca
Investment Management Regulatory Organisation	http://www.fsa.gov.uk/pubs/additional/index-2002.html
National Criminal Intelligence Service	http://www.ncis.co.uk
New Zealand Consumer Affairs	http://www.consumeraffairs.govt.nz
New Zealand Government On-line	http://www.govt.nz/
New Zealand Police Links	http://www.policeassn.org.nz/links.htm
Organized Crime – Nathanson Centre	http://www.yorku.ca/nathanson
UK Patent Office	http://www.patent.gov.uk
Public Records Office	http://www.pro.gov.uk
Royal Canadian Mounted Police	http://www.rcmp-grc.gc.ca/
The European Commission	http://Europa.eu.int/comm/
The Home Office	http://www.homeoffice.gov.uk
The Securities and Futures Authority	http://www.sfa.org.uk
United Kingdom Parliament	http://www.parliament.uk
Worldwide Embassies and Consulates	http://consulate.travel.com.hk/

Specialized Fraud-Related and Websites of Interest

Association of British Insurers	http://www.insurance.org.uk
Australian Institute of Criminology	http://www.aic.gov.au/
Department for Work and Pensions	http://www.dwp.gov.uk/
Financial Scandals	http://www.ex.ac.uk/~Rdavies/arian/scandals/
Fraud Web	http://www.fraudweb.co.uk
HM Treasury	http://www.hm-treasury.gov.uk/
New Zealand – Scam Watch	http://www.consumeraffairs.govt.nz/scamwatch/index.html
Serious Fraud Office	http://www.sfo.gov.uk
Siemens Fraud Management Guide	http://www.siemenscomms.co.uk/useful_information/telecom_guides/fraud/index.htm
UK Bankruptcy and Insolvency Website	http://www.insolvency.co.uk

International Accounting and Auditing

UK National Audit Office	http://www.nao.gov.uk
Inland Revenue	http://www.inlandrevenue.gov.uk
Insolvency Procedures and Corporate Rescue	http://www.shef.ac.uk/uni/academic/I-M/mgt/research/insolven.html
The Society of Practitioners of Insolvency	http://www.insolvency.co.uk/ip
Institute of Chartered Accountants in England and Wales	http://www.icaew.co.uk
Association of Charted Certified Accountants	http://www.acca.co.uk
Charted Institute of Management Accountants	http://www.cimaglobal.com

Institute of Chartered Accountants in Scotland	http://www.icas.org.uk
Institute of Chartered Accountants in Ireland	http://www.icai.ie
London Society of Chartered Accountants	http://www.lsca.co.uk
London International Financial Futures and Options Exchange	http://www.liffe.com
Netsurfer Focus on Computer and Network Security	http://www.netsurf.com/nsf/v01/01/nsf.01.01.html

DATA ANALYSIS AND REPORTING TOOLS

In the past 10 years, software companies have developed computer programs that enable users to sift through mounds of information. These programs identify current customers, potential customers, and future trends within their respective industries, and can be configured to identify breaks in audit control programs and anomalies in accounting records. Fraud examiners and auditors use data analysis software as the ultimate system of red flags, detecting a fraudulent situation long before previously possible.

Data Analysis Software Functions

Computers can be utilized to scan the database information for several different types of information, creating a red flag system. To perform this, most software packages use a combination of different functions. These functions are:

- Sorting
- Record selection
- Joining files
- Multi-file processing
- Correction analysis
- Verifying multiples of a number
- Compliance verification
- Duplicate searches
- Vertical ratio analysis
- Horizontal ratio analysis
- Date functions

Sorting

To sort means to arrange data in a meaningful order. Sorting is nothing new; most reports you read are sorted in some way. With sorted data, you can quickly pick out what is important. An investigator can ask a program to sort various information, such as alphabetically or numerically. For instance, when searching for a suspected fraudster's name within thousands in a check disbursement file, the software can quickly sort a list of payee names.

Sample Customer Sales Data

Date	Invoice	Customer	Amount
5/4/02	M3158001	J789889	$12,500.00
7/5/02	M5958256	Q189425	$14,580.00
8/9/02	M8897158	T681897	$38,889.00
7/25/01	M1569897	T888971	$87,569.56
12/20/02	M3158001	P123089	$12,500.00
1/8/02	M2098159	W555258	$56,347.23

Data sorted by Invoice

Date	Invoice	Customer	Amount
7/25/01	M1569897	T888971	$87,569.56
1/8/02	M2098159	W555258	$56,347.23
5/4/02	M3158001	J789889	$12,500.00
12/20/02	M3158001	P123089	$12,500.00
7/5/02	M5958256	Q189425	$14,580.00
8/9/02	M8897158	T681897	$38,889.00

Data sorted by Amount

Date	Invoice	Customer	Amount
5/4/02	M3158001	J789889	$12,500.00
12/20/02	M3158001	P123089	$12,500.00
7/5/02	M5958256	Q189425	$14,580.00
8/9/02	M8897158	T681897	$38,889.00
1/8/02	M2098159	W555258	$56,347.23
7/25/01	M1569897	T888971	$87,569.56

Record Selection

Specific record selection is accomplished by a request or query of the computer to find the occurrences of items or records in a field. This type of request will only return instances where the record did occur, effectively reducing large amounts of information into concise lists. Often, additional criteria placed on the record selection or query will reveal a more pertinent list of information. Most data analysis programs include simple FIND macros to help locate specific records.

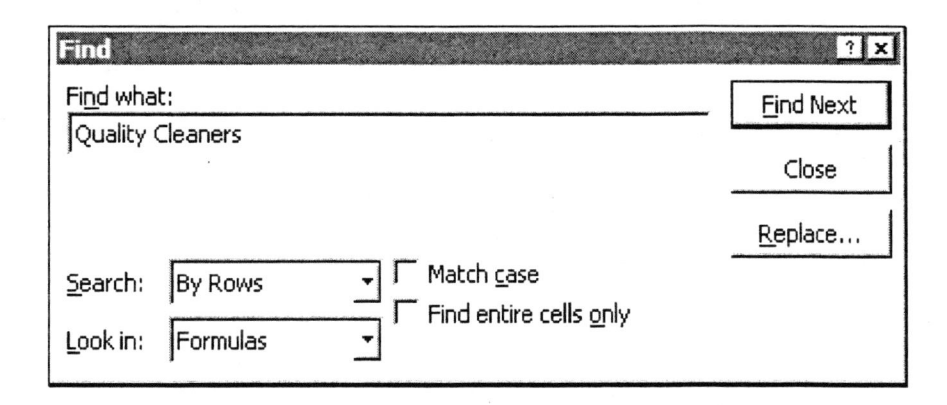

Joining Files

The join function gathers together the specified parts of different data files. Joining files combines fields from two sorted input files into a third file. Join is used to match data in a transaction file with records in a master file, such as matching invoice data in an accounts receivable file to a master cluster. For example, you may need to compare two different files to find differing records between files. The following is an example of how joining two files can easily provide that information.

File 1

Customer	Account	Balance	Last Invoice
Jerry's Cleaners	555221	$12,500	12/30/02
Quality Garments	555658	$9,283	11/15/02
Beverly's Tailoring	554891	$27,588	01/15/02

File 2

Customer	Account	Balance	Last Invoice
Quality Garments	555658	$9,283	11/15/02
McCloud's Fabrics	556897	$10,888	09/24/02
Beverly's Tailoring	554891	$27,588	01/15/02

The *JOINED* exception file

Customer	Account	Balance	Last Invoice
McCloud's Fabrics	556897	$10,888	09/24/02
Jerry's Cleaners	555221	$12,500	12/30/02

Multi-File Processing

Multi-file processing allows you to relate several files by defining relationships between multiple files, without the use of the join command. A common data relationship would be to relate an outstanding invoice master file to an accounts receivable file based on the customer number. The relationship can be further extended to include an invoice detail file based on invoice number. This relationship will allow you to see which customers have outstanding invoices sorted by date.

Correlation Analysis

Using this function, investigators can determine the relationships between different variables in the raw data. Investigators can learn a lot about computer data files by learning the relationship between two variables. For example, we should expect a strong correlation between these independent and dependent variables because a direct relationship exists between the two variables. Hotel costs should increase as the number of days traveled increases. The gallons of paint used should increase as the number of houses built increases. You can probably use many more such relationships.

Independent Variable	Dependent Variable
Number of days traveling	Hotel cost
Quantity of paper produced	Starch consumed
Number of houses built	Paint used

Verifying Multiples of a Number

With this function, an auditor can determine whether regularly dispersed checks, such as reimbursement for mileage, are consistent within the regular rate. For instance, if the mileage checks do not measure up to the 30-cents-per-mile rate, an automatic red flag should go up.

Compliance Verification

This function determines whether company policies are met by employee transactions. If a company limits the amount of its reimbursements, the software can check to see that this limit is being observed. Many times fraud examiners can find early indications of fraud by testing detail data for values above or below specified amounts. For example, when employees are out of town, do they adhere to company policy of spending not more than $30 a day for meals? For starters, we can look at all expense report data and select those where meal expense exceeds $30. With the information returned from this simple query, we have a starting point for suspecting fraud. Even though these variances are small ($2 and $3), the time taken to perform further research with respect to small variances can be well invested. The trail might lead to something big. After further investigation, you might learn the employee did not have supporting documentation to submit because a vendor's sales representative paid for all the meals. If this is the case, you have two fraud suspects, the employee and the employee's boss who approved the report.

Duplicate Searches
Fraud examiners and auditors can perform searches on invoice disbursements numerically to see if any invoices have been paid twice. By cross-checking the invoices with the vendors paid, duplicate billing can be easy to catch.

Vertical Ratio Analysis
Vertical analysis is a technique for analyzing the relationships between the items on an income statement, balance sheet, or statement of cash flows by expressing components as percentages. In the vertical analysis of an income statement, net sales is assigned 100%; on a balance sheet, total assets or liabilities and equity is assigned 100%. All other items are expressed as a percentage of these two numbers.

By performing this function, you can determine whether paid expenditures over a period are reasonable amounts. If one area of company expenses seems abnormally large for a short amount of time, a red flag should immediately be raised.

Horizontal Ratio Analysis
Horizontal analysis is a technique for analyzing the percentage change in individual financial statement items, from one year to the next. The first year in the analysis is considered the base year, and the changes to subsequent years are computed as a percentage of the base year.

This function determines the trends of a company's expenses, inventory, etc. Discrepancies in a company's net profit or a large shift in amount of inventory would suggest that something is not right within the company.

BALANCE SHEET	Vertical Analysis				Horizontal Analysis	
	Year One		Year Two		Change	%Change
Assets						
Current Assets						
Cash	45,000	14%	15,000	4%	(30,000)	-67%
Accts Receivable	150,000	45%	200,000	47%	50,000	33%
Inventory	75,000	23%	150,000	35%	75,000	100%
Fixed Assets (net)	60,000	18%	60,000	14%	-	0%
Total	330,000	100%	425,000	100%	95,000	29%
Acc'ts Payable	95,000	29%	215,000	51%	120,000	126%
Long-term Debt	60,000	18%	60,000	14%	-	0%
Stockholder's Equity						
Common Stock	25,000	8%	25,000	6%	-	0%
Paid-in Capital	75,000	23%	75,000	18%	-	0%
Retained Earnings	75,000	23%	50,000	12%	(25,000)	-33%
Total	330,000	100%	425,000	100%	95,000	29%

INCOME STATEMENT	Vertical Analysis				Horizontal Analysis	
	Year One		Year Two		Change	%Change
Net Sales	250,000	100%	450,000	100%	200,000	80%
Cost of Goods Sold	125,000	50%	300,000	67%	175,000	140%
Gross Margin	125,000	50%	150,000	33%	25,000	20%
Operating Expenses						
Selling Expenses	50,000	20%	75,000	17%	25,000	50%
Administrative Expenses	60,000	24%	100,000	22%	40,000	67%
Net Income	15,000	6%	(25,000)	-6%	(40,000)	-267%

Date Functions

Various software programs allow you to check for differences in dates, such as invoice dates. By verifying that check disbursements are consistent, you can ensure that no suspicious payments were arranged by an employee. Analysis programs will also allow for aging of data. The following is an example of accounts receivable aging.

```
Last Result
3 AGE ON DATE CUTOFF 921231 INTERVAL 0,30,60,90,120,10000 TO SCREEN
Page ...   1                                    08/21/97  10:52:16
Produced with ACL by: Training Version, 48K Limit

    <<< AGE over 0-> 10,000 >>>
    >>> Minimum encountered was 21
    >>> Maximum encountered was 864

DATE                    COUNT    <-- %
      0 ->      29        212    27.46%
     30 ->      59        240    31.09%
     60 ->      89        178    23.06%
     90 ->     119        107    13.86%
    120 -> 10,000          35     4.53%

                          772   100.00%
```

Graphing

Graphs, like pictures, are worth a thousand words. Data analysis programs can provide numerous types of graphs to give fraud examiners a quick glance of the data. For example an inquiry should be made as to why November expenses are $10,000 more than the monthly normal.

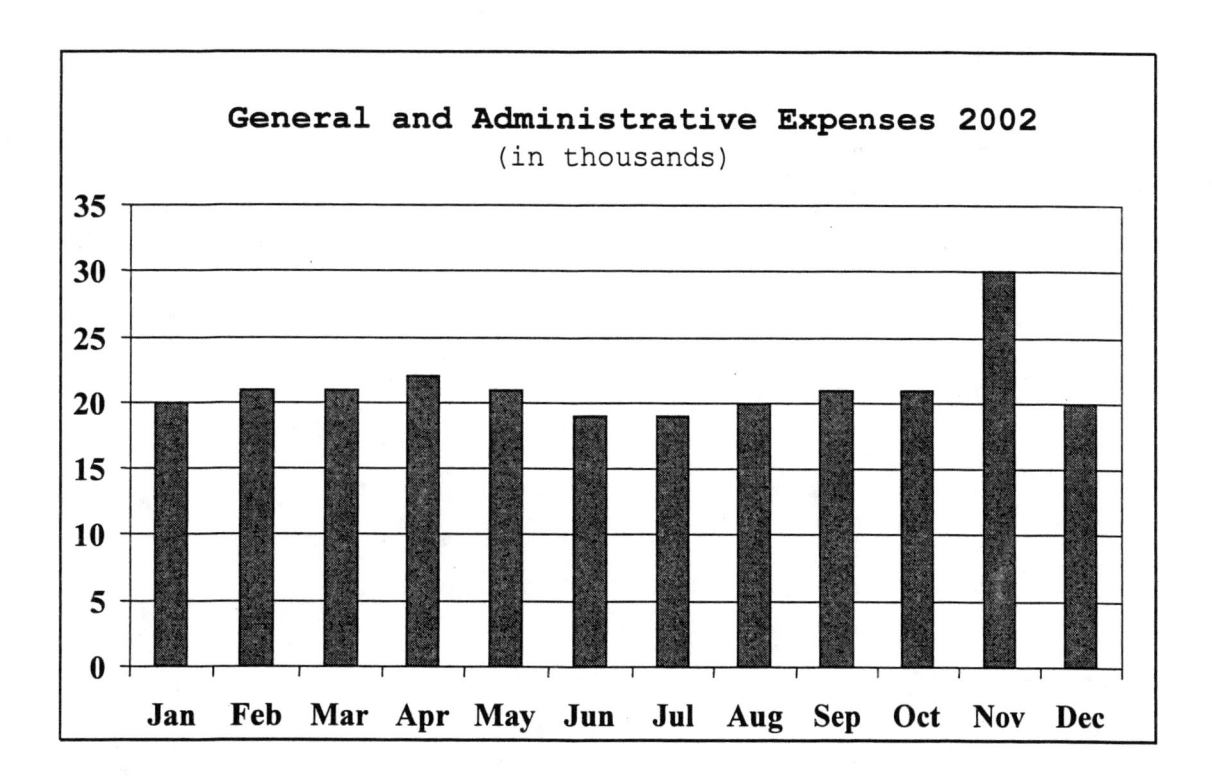

General and Administrative Expenses 2002
(in thousands)

Month	Jan	Feb	Mar	Apr	May	Jun	Jul	Aug	Sep	Oct	Nov	Dec
Amount	20	21	21	22	21	19	19	20	21	21	30	20

Examples of Data Analysis Functions

The following are typical examples of data analysis queries that can be performed by data analysis software:

General Ledger Analysis
- Select specific journal entries for analysis
- Create actual to budget comparison reports
- Analyze and confirm specific ledger accounts for legitimate transaction activity
- Speed account reconciliation through specialized account queries
- Calculate financial ratios
- Calculate percentage comparison ratio between accounts
- Prepare custom reports, cash flow, profit/loss, and asset and liability total reports
- Compare summaries by major account in any order (low-high, high-low)

- Create reports in any format by account, division, department, etc.

Accounts Receivable
- Create a list of customer limit increases and decreases
- Age accounts receivable in various formats
- Identify gaps in sequential forms such as invoices
- Identify duplicate invoices or customer account number entries
- Show specified reports on credits taken by customers
- Report customer summaries by invoice, product, etc.
- Identify customer activity by age, product, etc.
- Compare customer credit limits and current or past balances

Sales Analysis
- Create a report of all system overrides and sales exceptions
- Analyze returns and allowances by store, department, or other areas
- Summarize trends by customer type, products, salesperson, etc.
- Compare ratios of current sales to outstanding receivables or other variables
- Generate reports on a correlation between product demand or supply and sales prices

Accounts Payable
- Audit paid invoices for manual comparison with actual invoices
- Summarize large invoices by amount, vendor, etc.
- Identify debits to expense accounts outside of set default accounts
- Reconcile check registers to disbursements by vendor invoice
- Verify vendor 1099 requirements
- Create vendor detail and summary analysis reports
- Review recurring monthly expenses and compare to posted/paid invoices
- Generate a report on specified vouchers for manual audit or investigation

Asset Management
- Generate depreciation to cost reports
- Compare book and tax depreciation and indicate variances
- Sort asset values by asset type or dollar amount
- Select samples for asset existence verification
- Recalculate expense and reserve amounts using replacement costs

Cash Disbursement
- Summarize cash disbursements by account, bank, department, vendor, etc.
- Verify audit trail for all disbursements by purchase order, vendor, department, etc.
- Generate vendor cash activity summary for analysis
- Identify disbursements by department, supervisor approval, or amount limits

Payroll
- Summarize payroll activity by specific criteria for review
- Identify changes to payroll or employee files
- Compare timecard and payroll rates for possible discrepancies
- Prepare check amount reports for amounts over a certain limit
- Check proper supervisory authorization on payroll disbursements

Purchasing
- Track schedule receipt dates versus actual receipt dates, summary and detail
- Compare vendor performance by summarizing item delivery times and amounts
- Isolate purchase order types for analysis
- Analyze late shipments

Data Analysis Checklist
Following are some key issues to address as you conduct a data analysis.
- Ensure data validity and data integrity. As we move data from one venue to another there is always a concern. One of the concerns is data validity. Is the data valid and pertinent to our investigation? The second concern is integrity. Is the valid data we have selected correct? A simple check or audit of the validity and integrity of the data will be the first step we need to consider.
- Consider data format and structure. This consideration is important when we wish to import/export data with our computer. A date can be formatted into a number of different styles such as mm/dd/yyyy. The structure of the data will also be important along with the extension. A text file will have a .txt extension associated with it. What format is the current data in? What format will our computer require? How do we get the data from here to there if the data formats and structures are different?
- Count the zeros. Perform a preliminary analysis to insure that the key strategic issue you are about to develop is worth the effort before initiating your fraud investigation.
- Consider the spectrum of distinct levels of aggregation at which fraud monitoring is required. Determine the lowest level (transaction level), the highest level (multiparty

criminal conspiracies), and the intervening layers that may be present in your industry and respective data.

- Begin with the end in mind. Stephen Covey in his book, *The Seven Habits of Highly Effective People*, states that beginning with end in mind is good habit to attain. When we develop our fraud intelligence action plan, be certain to consider the end result. One question to ask may be, "Will this algorithm/consultant hold up under the intense scrutiny of a court of law?"

Evaluating Data Analysis Software

In short, there are no silver bullets. But any data analysis software should possess the following minimum requirements:

- Data import/export capabilities. Considering your data format and structure, how easy is data imported/exported?
- Data visualization. How easy is it to move your data from a spreadsheet form into a graphic for analysis and interpretation?
- Look for a suite of tools. Just as there is not one screwdriver for every job, nor is there only one software for your fraud intelligence efforts. Choose the most appropriate set of tools per your data and then select the software that best fits your current and future needs.
- Develop a two-pronged fraud intelligence by computer effort. Utilize commercial software currently on the market and begin collaborative activities with the academics at your local university. There are numerous software packages in various stages of development in academia that are in need of data to test their product. This can prove to be a win-win for both parties. You have the data and they have the prototype software in need of data to test.

Evaluating Data Mining Consultants

When considering the use of a data mining specialist, several qualities should be assessed:

- Innovation – The data mining environment is relatively new. How does the individual stay current? Look for professional associations, publications, and training in your area of investigation.
- Creativity – Can the individual work in a creative environment such as fraud intelligence? Can the individual work unsupervised and be expected to produce results? Since fraud is a moving target—how has a past client platform altered from the original investigation? Why/how did that occur? What were the results?

- Experience – Does the individual have experience in the type of investigation you are planning? Does the individual have experience in the type of software/tools you are planning? Does the individual have experience in the type of data you are planning?

The embodiment of this expertise might take one, two, three or more people. You really need people who understand what it is they are looking for – and what they can do with it once they find it.

Data Analysis Software

There are many types of data analysis software on the market these days, and every year new products and new versions of old products emerge. Because every fraud examination involving data analysis is different, it would be impossible to recommend one software product to serve every purpose. Choosing a data analysis tool is something that the fraud examiner must evaluate on each individual case. A fraud examiner should research applications intensively to decide which package is most appropriate for the current investigation.

Data mining and knowledge discovery software are generally classified into the following categories:

- Public domain/shareware: available free or for a nominal charge through websites, ftp sites, and newsgroups. Some of the more common freeware includes SAOimage, SuperMongo, Tiny Tim, and xv. Many shareware programs, such as WINKS v4.62, allow users a trial period, after which they must pay a fee to reactivate the software. Freeware and shareware programs can be located through Internet search engines and through software download services such as ZD Net.
- Research prototypes/beta versions: free software in the development stages; users are asked to review performance, report malfunctions, etc. An example is KyPlot v2.0 beta 13, from Koichi Yoshioka.
- Commercial applications: general release products, usually with technical support and warranty. The most prominent of these are discussed below.

ACL for Windows

ACL (Version 7.1) is a data analysis, audit, and reporting software package which functions very much like traditional database query programs. Because it is read-only, ACL keeps the original data source completely intact. When the software runs analytical functions, it simply looks at and presents the raw data in different ways, without altering the original data. This gives auditors greater confidence in their findings than they would get from an application that allowed overwriting, inadvertent or otherwise, of the original data.

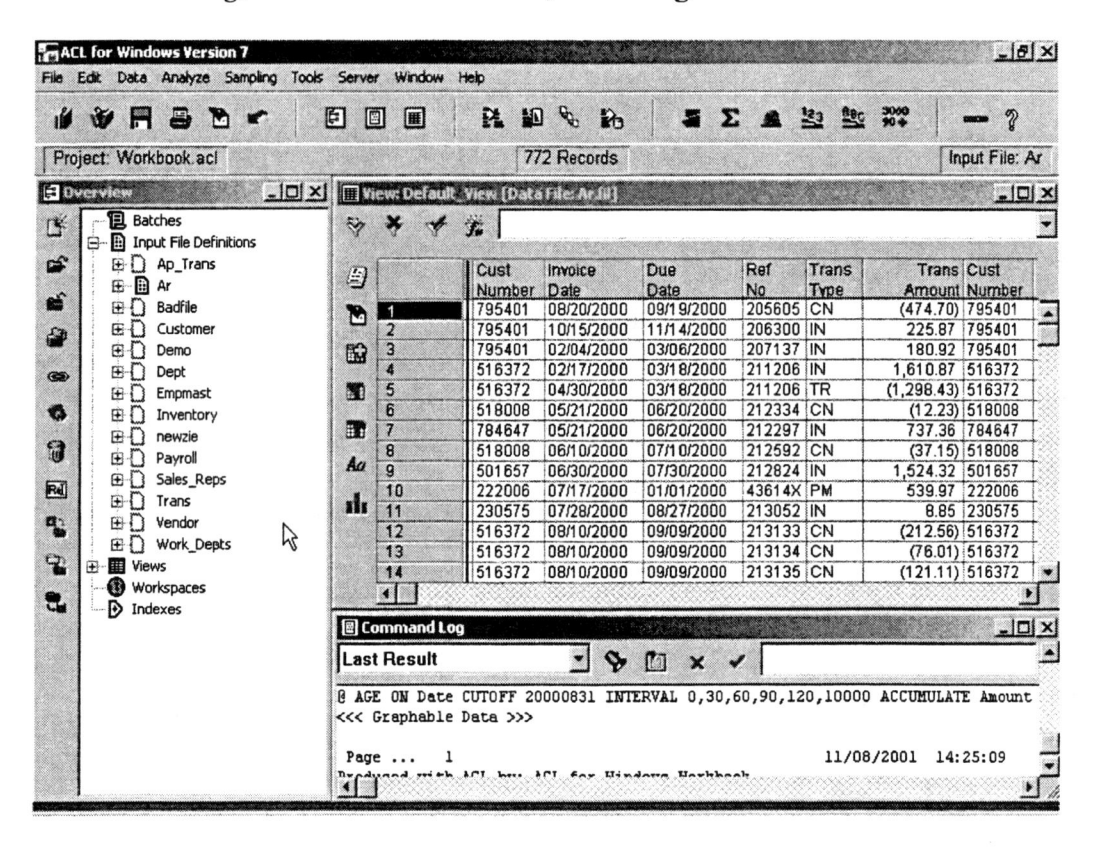

The software's ODBC support links ACL with the client's ODBC-compliant databases. With the appropriate drivers, one can read data from databases such as Btrieve, Clipper, INFORMIX, INGRES, Microsoft Access, Oracle, Paradox, PROGRESS, and Sybase. Excel files are easily imported for use in *ACL for Windows*.

ACL has several features useful to fraud examiners and auditors. The program sorts and summarizes data on multiple levels, so it is possible to sort or summarize a file by any combination of fields at the same time. ACL is also able to locate numerical gaps in sequencing, which can be especially useful when investigating a series of invoices. ACL also has functionality that allows you to apply Benford's Law to large transaction volumes to help you identify possible fraudulent instances. Some of the most common functions used by fraud examiners include:

- Comparing employee and vendor addresses to identify employees who are also posing as vendors;
- Identifying vendors using P.O. Box addresses;

- Identifying missing or fraudulent checks or invoices by analyzing the sequence of all transactions;
- Identifying all vendors with more than one vendor code or more than one mailing address, or multiple vendors sharing the same mailing address;
- Identifying invoices with no purchase order number; and
- Identifying transactions that fall just below financial control or contract limits by stratifying payments by amount.

Inventory Margin Analysis

For a simple demonstration, suppose an officer at Bud's Builders is suspected of inflating profits to cover up for his embezzlement. To find which items have extraordinary profit margins, you would use ACL's Expression Builder to help you analyze the data. In this case you want to find out which items show a profit (MktVal less Value) greater than the item's cost, represented by the "Value" field.

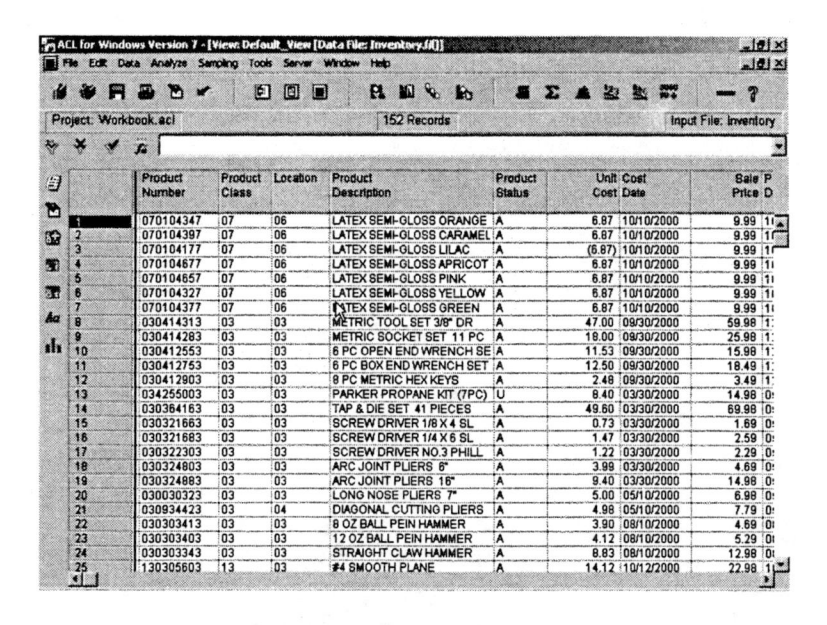

The ACL Expression Builder is an automated dialog that allows you to set the terms of an analysis. To analyze when profit exceeds cost, you:

Click the STATISTICS button in the View window, or pull down the Analyze menu and select "Statistics." The Statistics dialog box appears.

The Statistics dialog box displays the numeric and date fields available for analysis. To get statistics on the cost, highlight Value.

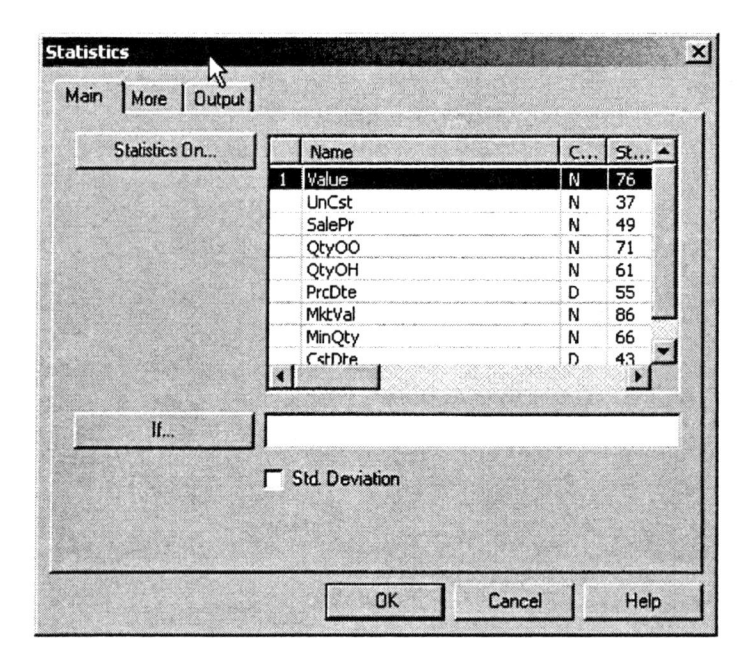

Next, Click the [If] button, in the lower left corner.

The expression builder appears, allowing you to set a condition, or local filter, for the Statistics command.

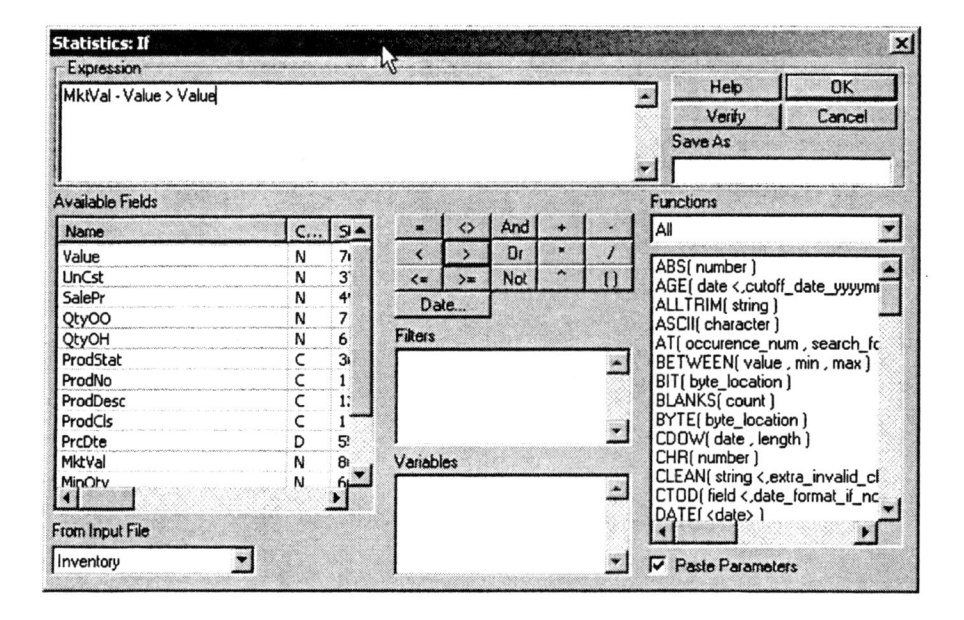

By selecting fields from the "Available Fields" list box, create the following expression: *MktVal - Value > Value* in the Expression text box and click OK. This indicates you only want statistics on records for which the profit exceeds the cost. When you return to the Statistics dialog box, click OK to execute the command.

The results of this command indicate that of 152 product records, 15 records have a profit greater than cost. The results also show that the highest total cost was $5,639.38, the lowest was $10,167.60, and the total cost of the 15 items found was $1,905.75. Immediately, you can recognize that anomalies exist that are worthy of further investigation. From here you would proceed to display the 15 records and explore your hypothesis further.

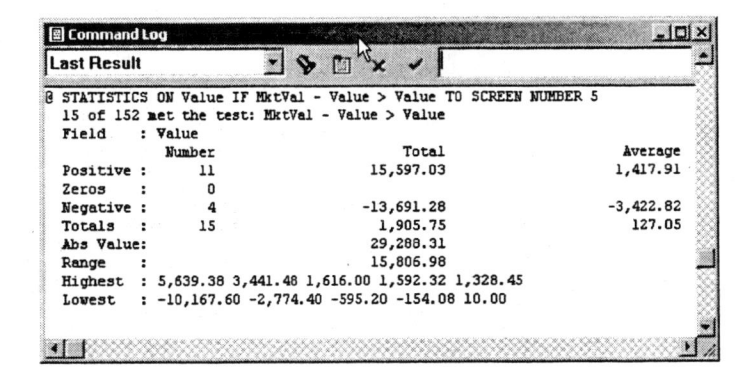

```
Command Log                                           _|□|x|
Last Result                    ▼  ▸ ▣ x ✓ |

@ STATISTICS ON Value IF MktVal - Value > Value TO SCREEN NUMBER 5
  15 of 152 met the test: MktVal - Value > Value
  Field     : Value
              Number              Total            Average
  Positive :    11              15,597.03          1,417.91
  Zeros    :     0
  Negative :     4             -13,691.28         -3,422.82
  Totals   :    15               1,905.75            127.05
  Abs Value:                    29,288.31
  Range    :                    15,806.98
  Highest  : 5,639.38 3,441.48 1,616.00 1,592.32 1,328.45
  Lowest   : -10,167.60 -2,774.40 -595.20 -154.08 10.00
```

Advanced Features

Advanced users can take advantage of ACL features including:

- *Batches*, a series of ACL commands stored in an ACL project. This series of commands can be executed repeatedly and automatically. Any command can be stored in a batch.
- *Dialog builder*, allowing users to custom design a dialog box for variables, files, and selection criteria during an interactive batch.
- *Oversampling* includes the selection order number of randomly sampled items.
- *If Command* applies a condition to an entire file before command execution within a batch.
- *Set Filter command* enables commands after Set Filter to be applied only to the filtered records in a batch.

Display Features

Display options allow users to create many different types of graphs from the Histogram, Stratify, Classify, Age, and Benford commands. These graphs can be saved as bitmap files for import into other software programs and/or your investigation reports.

ACL Practical Examples
AGING DATA

The Age command produces aged summaries of data. Aged summaries can be based on the current data or on data you specify. ACL displays the number of records in each age period in the generated "Count" field as well as the accumulation of any numeric field you select. You can view aged data to find out the age of invoices that have been outstanding since the fiscal year ended or since they were issued. To open a new input file to work with accounts receivable data, do the following:

Double click on the AR input file. ACL opens the accounts receivable transaction file, Ar.fil, and displays the Default View.

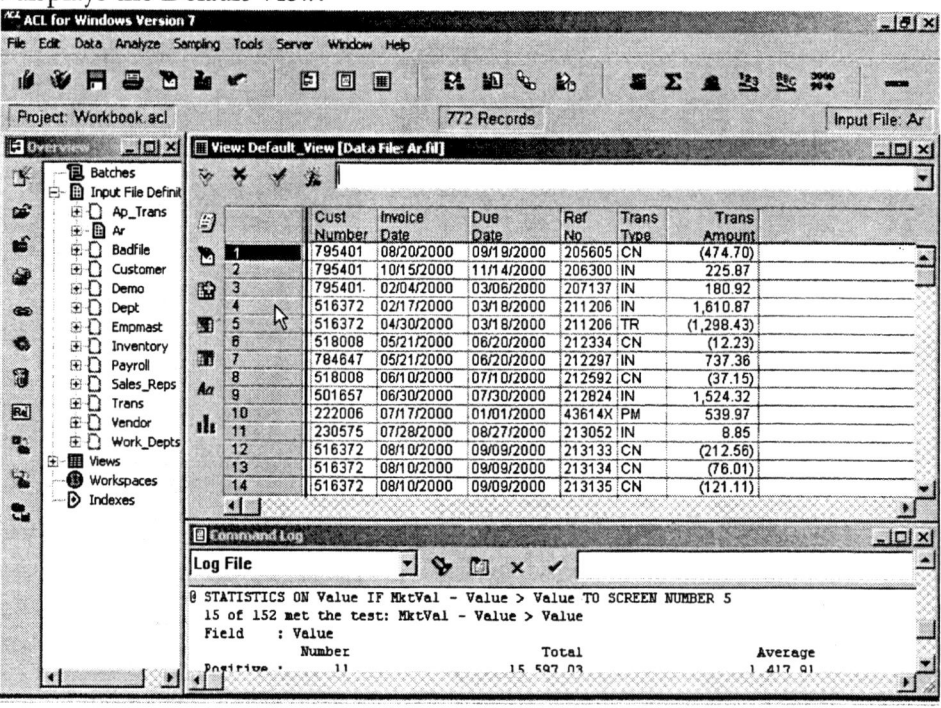

This file contains outstanding amounts owed by customers as of December 31, 2000.
1. Click on the AGE button, or select "Analyze" from the menu bar and choose Age. ACL displays the Age dialog box.
2. Select "Due" from the Age On dropdown menu.
3. In the Cutoff Date text box select December 31, 2000 using the Date Selector.
4. In the Accumulate Fields list box, click on AMOUNT. The Age dialog box now looks like this:

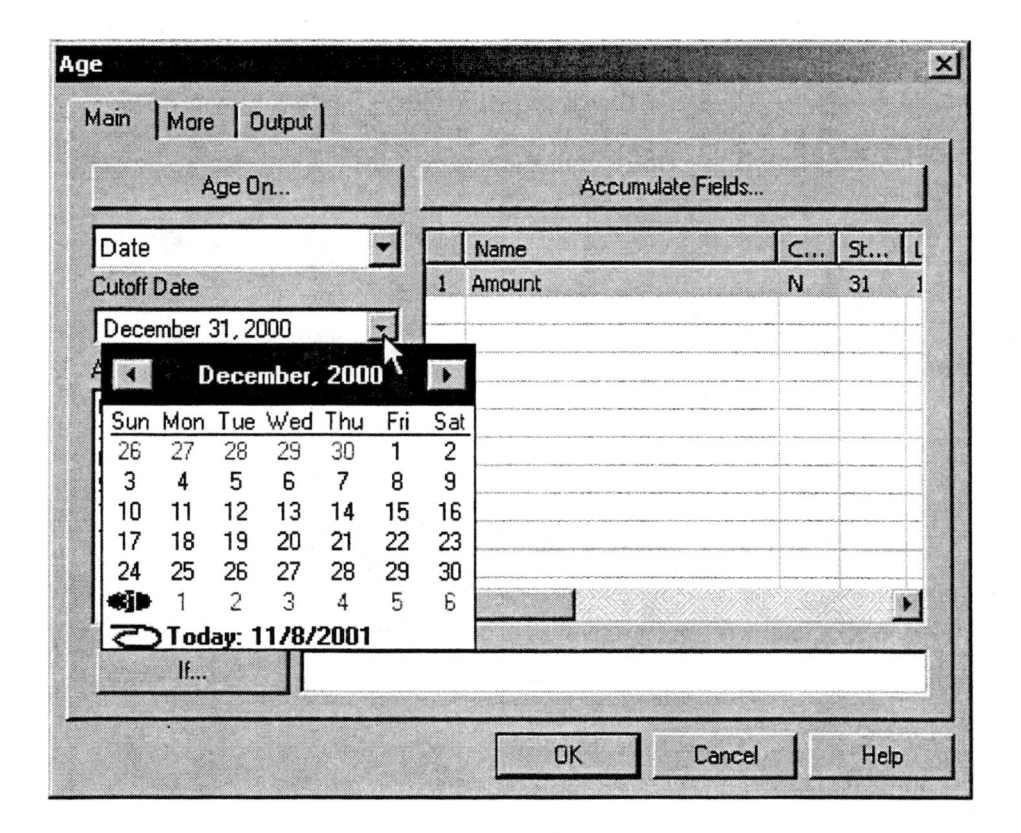

ACL provides the default values of 0, 30, 60, 90, 120, and 10,000 days for aging periods. These numbers indicate the lower bounds of the aging period. The last default period of 10,000 is intended to be large enough to include all overdue amounts.

5. Click OK. ACL displays the result.

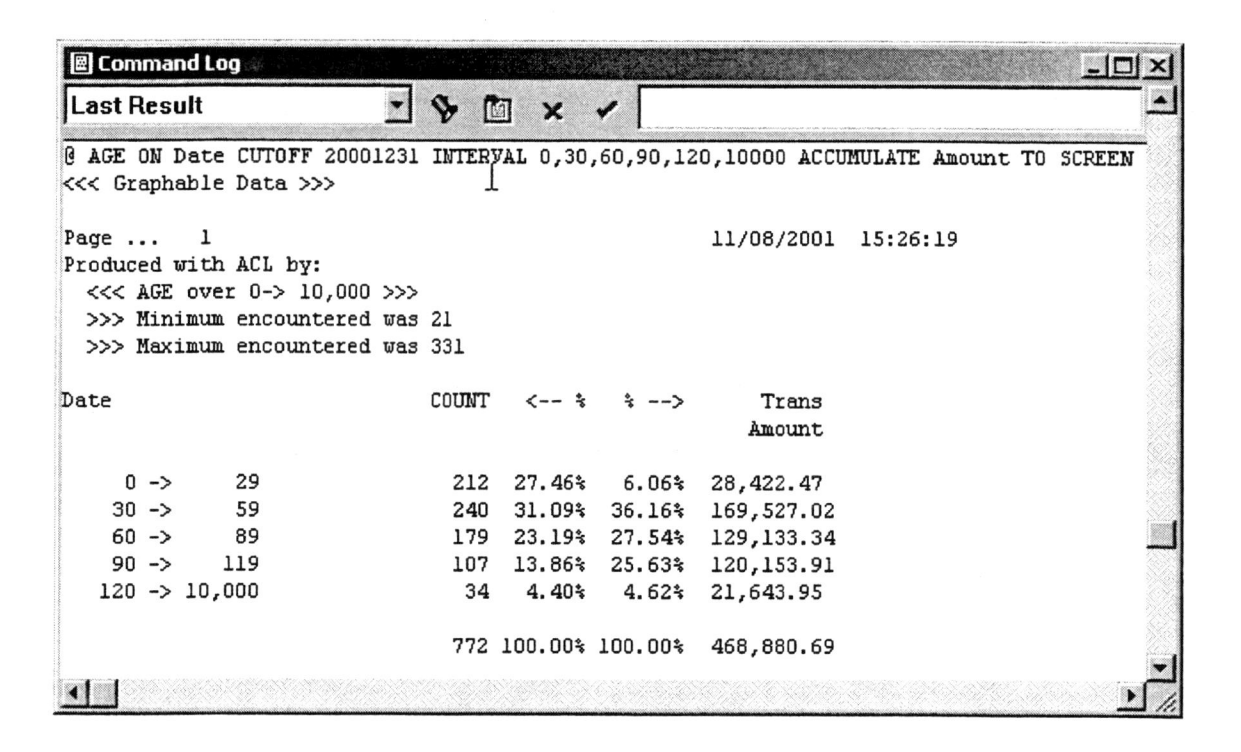

```
@ AGE ON Date CUTOFF 20001231 INTERVAL 0,30,60,90,120,10000 ACCUMULATE Amount TO SCREEN
<<< Graphable Data >>>

Page ...    1                                    11/08/2001   15:26:19
Produced with ACL by:
  <<< AGE over 0-> 10,000 >>>
  >>> Minimum encountered was 21
  >>> Maximum encountered was 331

Date                          COUNT   <-- %    % -->     Trans
                                                         Amount

    0 ->      29                212   27.46%   6.06%    28,422.47
   30 ->      59                240   31.09%  36.16%   169,527.02
   60 ->      89                179   23.19%  27.54%   129,133.34
   90 ->     119                107   13.86%  25.63%   120,153.91
  120 ->  10,000                 34    4.40%   4.62%    21,643.95

                                772  100.00% 100.00%   468,880.69
```

You can see all the aged transactions in the file, grouped according to the default aging periods. ACL shows that $21,643.95 of the outstanding balances is more than 120 days overdue as of the cutoff date. You may want to investigate the long overdue balances further, to get more details on the aged records.

ACL will allow you to Age receivable data, independent of the customer's accounting program. With this command the fraud examiner can determine if there are outstanding balances which warrant investigation, verify internal aging reports for accuracy, and verify account balances.

Extracting Specific Records to Another File

ACL will also allow you to retrieve records with specific ages. The AGE() function calculates the number of days between any two dates you specify. If you do not specify a second date, AGE() uses the current system date. For example, you can use AGE() to compare a receivable transaction date to a year end date in order to determine account ages at year end.

To extract the account number, amount, and invoice date for all items aged more than 180 days as of the fiscal year end of Dec. 31, 1992, do the following:

1. Select "Extract" from the Data dropdown menu.

2. Click on the FIELDS radio button.
3. In the Extract Fields list box, click on NO, then hold down Control and click on AMOUNT and DATE.
4. In the If... text box, type AGE(Date,`20001231`)>180. The first part of the expression tells ACL to use the AGE() function to compare the data in the date field to the date December 31, 2000, stored in yyyymmdd format.
5. Click in the To... box and type AGED. The Extract dialog box now looks like this:

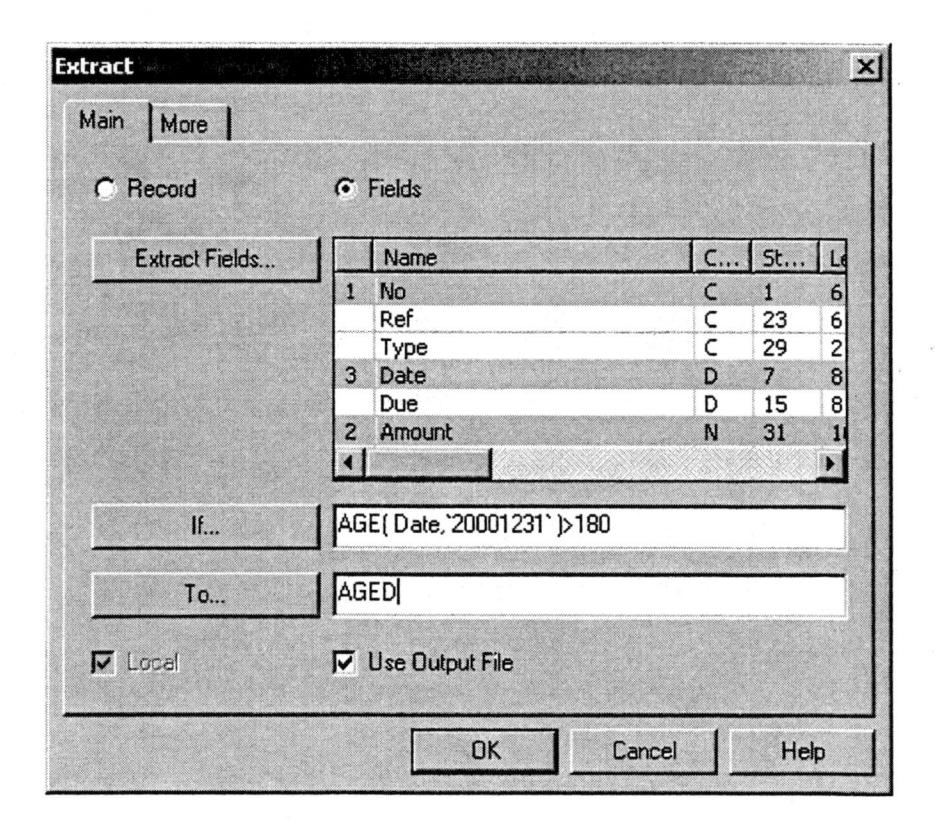

6. Click OK to execute the command. In the Last Result window, ACL tells you that 7 records met the test and that 3 fields were activated.

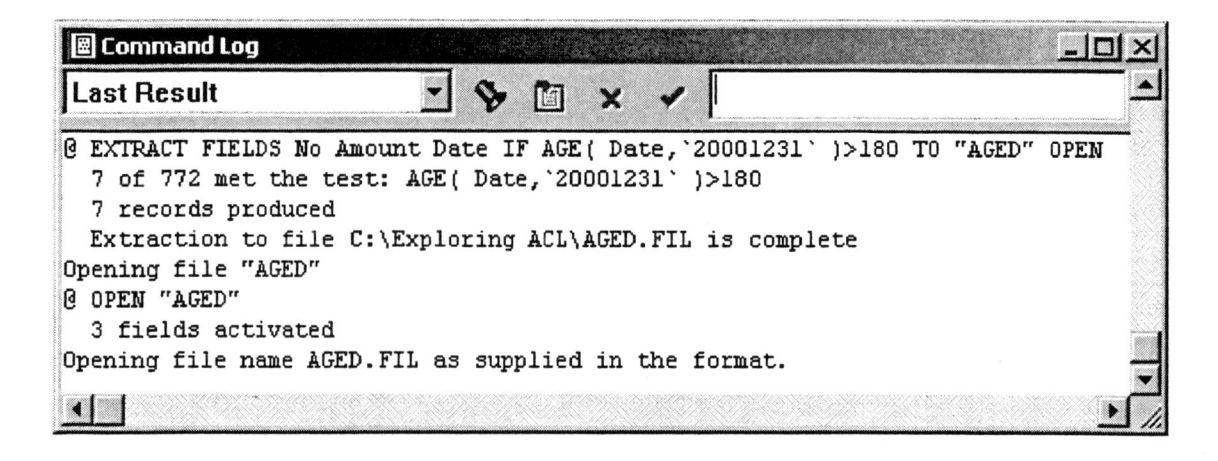

```
Command Log
Last Result
@ EXTRACT FIELDS No Amount Date IF AGE( Date,`20001231` )>180 TO "AGED" OPEN
  7 of 772 met the test: AGE( Date,`20001231` )>180
  7 records produced
  Extraction to file C:\Exploring ACL\AGED.FIL is complete
Opening file "AGED"
@ OPEN "AGED"
  3 fields activated
Opening file name AGED.FIL as supplied in the format.
```

7. ACL automatically opens the file and displays the invoices aged by more than 180 days as of the end of 2000.

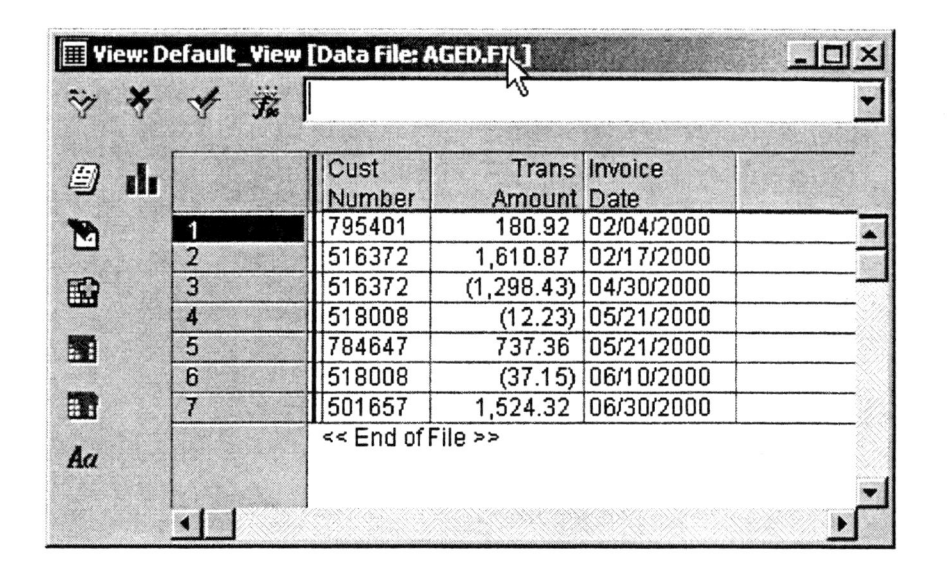

Cust Number	Trans Amount	Invoice Date
795401	180.92	02/04/2000
516372	1,610.87	02/17/2000
516372	(1,298.43)	04/30/2000
518008	(12.23)	05/21/2000
784647	737.36	05/21/2000
518008	(37.15)	06/10/2000
501657	1,524.32	06/30/2000
<< End of File >>		

IDENTIFYING DUPLICATES

Identifying duplicate invoices can help to detect inaccuracies in the Payroll file. To test the file for duplicate employee numbers:

1. Click the Duplicates icon or select it from the "Analyze" menu. ACL displays the Sequence dialog box.
2. In the Sequence On list box, click on EmpNo (for employee number).
3. In the List Fields list box, click on Cheque_No.
4. Hold down Control and click first on Pay_Date and then on WorkDept.
5. Click OK. ACL displays the result.

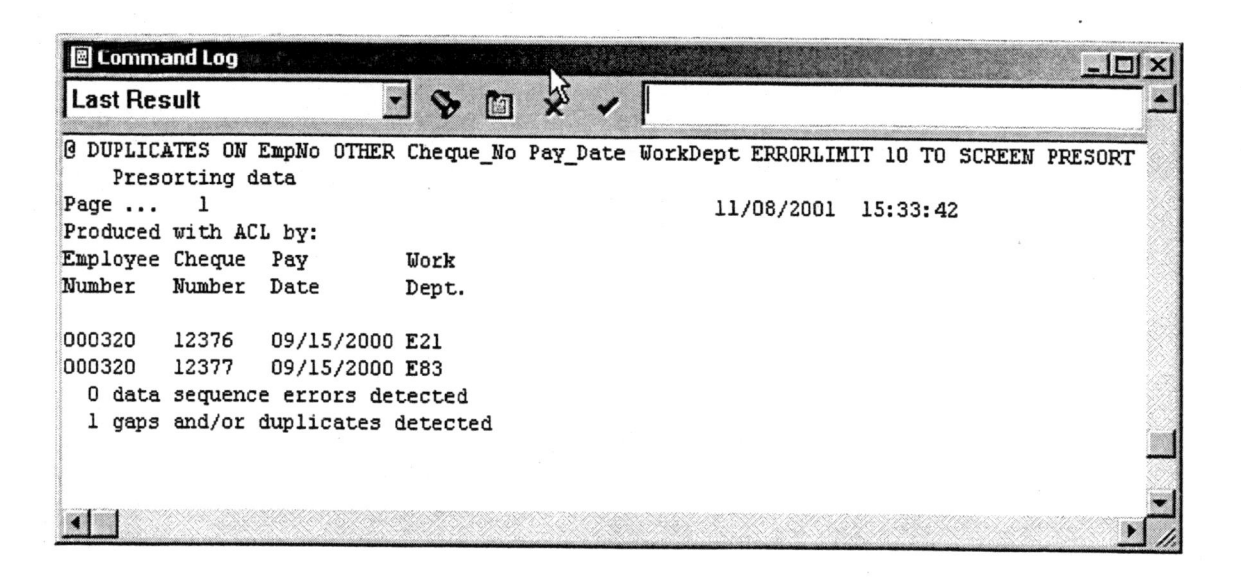

```
┌─ Command Log ──────────────────────────────────────────── _ □ × ┐
│ Last Result        ▼  🔧 📋 ❌ ✓                              │
│ @ DUPLICATES ON EmpNo OTHER Cheque_No Pay_Date WorkDept ERRORLIMIT 10 TO SCREEN PRESORT │
│     Presorting data                                             │
│ Page ...   1                                    11/08/2001  15:33:42 │
│ Produced with ACL by:                                           │
│ Employee  Cheque  Pay         Work                              │
│ Number    Number  Date        Dept.                             │
│                                                                 │
│ 000320    12376   09/15/2000  E21                               │
│ 000320    12377   09/15/2000  E83                               │
│   0 data sequence errors detected                               │
│   1 gaps and/or duplicates detected                             │
└─────────────────────────────────────────────────────────────────┘
```

For each occurrence of an employee number in the file, ACL shows the employee number, the payment date, the check number, and the work department. A blank line would separate each set of multiple occurrences, if there were any. ACL tells you at the end of the result that the file has a total of one multiple occurrence of employee numbers. This employee was issued two checks, each one for a different department. ACL also reports all multiples.

LISTING GAP RANGES

When you test for gaps, you can test for a range of missing items or identify individual missing items. The default is to test for a gap range. This can identify payroll checks that may be missing from the data.

1. Click the Gaps icon. ACL displays the Gaps dialog box.
2. In the Sequence On list box, click on Cheque_No.
3. Click OK. ACL reports that there is one gap in the check number sequence.

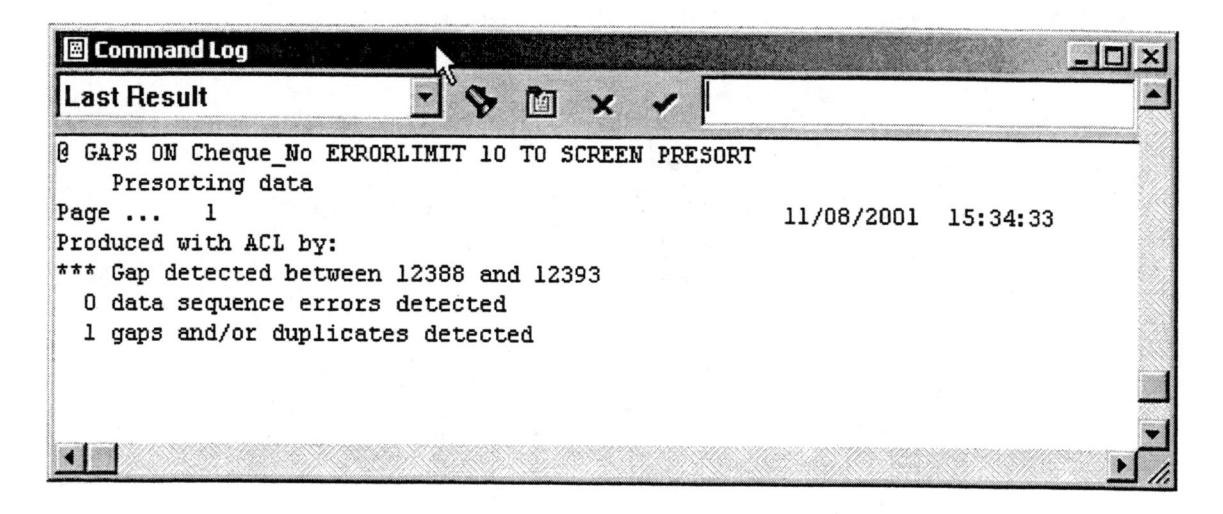

```
┌─ Command Log ──────────────────────────────────────────── _ □ × ┐
│ Last Result        ▼  🔧 📋 × ✓                               │
│ @ GAPS ON Cheque_No ERRORLIMIT 10 TO SCREEN PRESORT             │
│     Presorting data                                             │
│ Page ...   1                                    11/08/2001  15:34:33 │
│ Produced with ACL by:                                           │
│ *** Gap detected between 12388 and 12393                        │
│   0 data sequence errors detected                               │
│   1 gaps and/or duplicates detected                             │
└─────────────────────────────────────────────────────────────────┘
```

ACL lists the invoice numbers on either side of each gap range, so you can see where the gaps exist.

In order to see a list of the missing check numbers, re-run the command only this time select the "List Missing Items" radio button in the command dialog. The output will list all the missing checks.

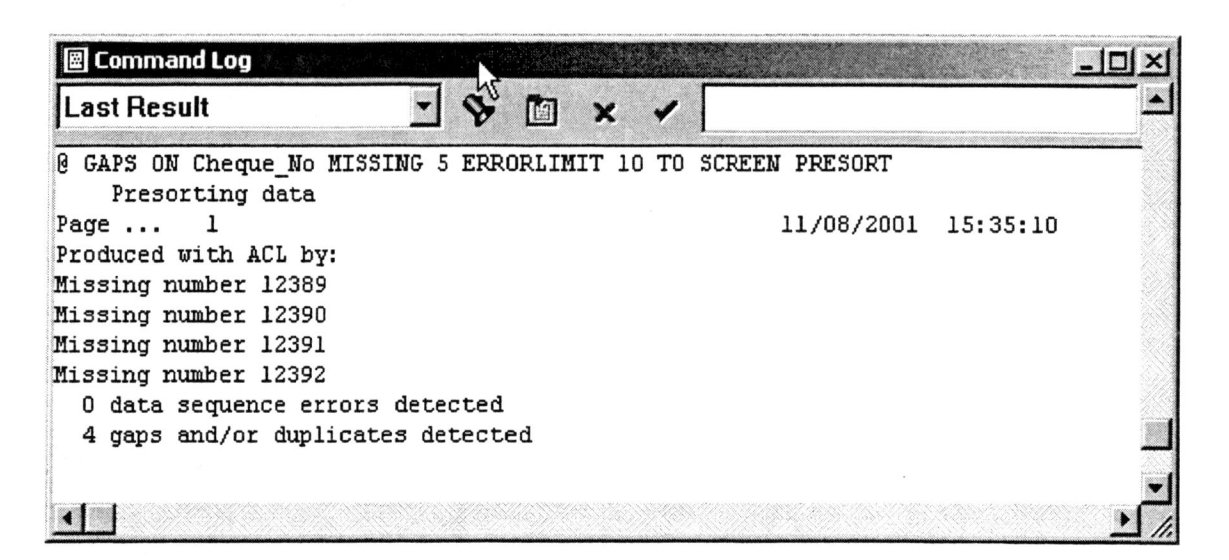

```
Command Log
Last Result
@ GAPS ON Cheque_No MISSING 5 ERRORLIMIT 10 TO SCREEN PRESORT
    Presorting data
Page ...   1                                        11/08/2001   15:35:10
Produced with ACL by:
Missing number 12389
Missing number 12390
Missing number 12391
Missing number 12392
  0 data sequence errors detected
  4 gaps and/or duplicates detected
```

Like other data analysis programs, ACL Software is designed to read data files as well as report files. ACL reads EDBIC - mainframe generic character-set files, as well as ASCII files and unusual field formats (e.g., packed and zoned decimal). It is possible to read complex report files with ACL, and the process is as straightforward as the same procedure in Monarch. Furthermore, ACL performs a number of functions not available in Monarch and other data analysis programs:

- Sequence testing — to gaps and duplicates in a sequence.
- Aging analysis — to easily produce delinquency and obsolesce category reports.
- Stratification analysis — to analyze how many records and to accumulate numeric data that fall into various other categories.
- Statistical sampling — to perform statistical sampling with minimal effort.
- Join and merge capabilities — to join and merge multiple files into one output file using one or more key field(s).
- Relations capabilities — to recreate relational databases or to create logical relationships among more than two files for increased data access.

For more information, you may contact ACL Software at 1550 Alberni Street, Vancouver, B.C., Canada V6G 1A5 or (604) 669-4225, or at www.acl.com.

ActiveData for Excel

ActiveData for Excel is an affordable, easy-to-use tool for advanced data manipulation and analysis within the Excel environment.

Many accountants, auditors, and fraud examiners use Excel for basic data analysis tasks. For example, Excel allows users to sort, subtotal, filter, and merge data. They can create calculated fields, as well as, perform statistical analysis such as regression. For all of the above reasons and more, Microsoft Excel has become an industry standard in managing and analyzing organizational data.

However, Excel has many limitations that do not make it the best tool for fraud detection and other auditing functions. ActiveData for Excel was designed by a group with over 17 years of experience in computer aided audit and fraud detection techniques to overcome these limitations. The table below shows how ActiveData for Excel overcomes these limitations.

Excel Limitation	How Does ActiveData for Excel Compensate For The Limitation?
Does not document the fraud examiners work in easy to access logs for later reference and work paper storage.	ActiveData for Excel provides a log of each processed step (as a comment in cell A1 of the worksheet created via ActiveData for Excel processing). Then, using the *Index Sheets* function, a summary page of all comment fields can easily be created for review; in essence creating an audit log of all work performed with the spreadsheet data.
Has difficulty in performing data analysis and management tests such as relating tables. Although it can be accomplished, it is an onerous task.	ActiveData for Excel provides over 100 data analysis and management features that automate functions some of which may be possible in Excel, albeit extremely difficult from a technical perspective.

Does not have functionality specifically tailored to the fraud examiner. For example, a sample can be calculated in just a couple of clicks with minimal training within specifically designed audit software. In Excel, it can be done, but it does take much effort and guidance.	The over 100 ActiveData for Excel features are tailored to the auditor, accountant and fraud examiner. For example, you can use ActiveData for Excel to find duplicate records in a few clicks (rather than setting up complex formulas within Excel)

The following are some examples of how ActiveData can be used for fraud detection.

Fraud Detection Techniques for Accounts Payable

VENDOR SUMMARY TOTALS PERIOD ONE TO PERIOD TWO COMPARISON

This is a basic analytical report to identify trends in vendor purchase history. A trend analysis should be completed to identify key vendors that have increased or decreased substantially. This can best be assessed using the dollar and percentage variance fields, which can be added as calculated fields in Excel. Based on the changes in the business environment and/or new company projects, a reasonableness assessment should be performed on the vendor changes.

DESCRIPTIVE STATISTICS / BENFORD'S LAW ANALYSIS

The descriptive statistics provides maximum amount, minimum amount, average amount and other high-level statistics. These statistics should be reviewed for reasonableness such as a high value of negative amounts or a maximum amount that looks too high.

Then, a Benford's Law analysis of the first two digits of your data, as well as, a list of all amounts from highest to lowest frequency is provided for review. Benford's Law maintains that certain digits show up more than others. A one will appear as the first non-zero digit roughly 30% of the time; two will be the leading digit 18% of the time; nine will lead off just 4.6% of the time. Zero is most likely to be the second digit, popping in there 12% of the time. It's all very predictable. Benford's Law never fails to work. With it, you can tell if someone fakes data that are derived from other data. It can also identify errors within the data that appear "out of place" given their frequency of appearance.

It is suggested that the Benford's Law analysis first be executed so the most statistical outliers can be reviewed. As a follow up to these tests, a Query Sheet should be used to query outlier activity for additional review.

ABOVE AVERAGE PAYMENTS TO A VENDOR (OVER TWO TIMES THE AVERAGE)

Unusually large payments to a vendor in relation to the average is a sign of error (i.e., key punch error) or fraud (i.e., kickback scheme where vendor is paid additional amounts that are kicked-back to the employee entering the payment into the system).

For vendors with unusual payments above the average, a sample of the "average" payment invoices, as well as, the unusual payment invoice should be reviewed. The reasonableness of the purchase should be assessed based on the documentation reviewed. The auditor should be keenly aware of the potential for a key punch error regarding the unusual payment and/or the possibility of the vendor purposely overcharging the organization.

DUPLICATE PAYMENT TESTING

Duplicate payments to vendors normally represent errors that the computer system was unable to detect. In most systems, a check will be made as to whether the vendor number, invoice number and amount are the same. This test could be run to ensure this basic control is operational and also test for other permutations of duplication. Any results from this test should first be reviewed for trends. For example, rent payments that occur on a monthly basis may appear to be duplicate payments when, in fact they are simply regularly occurring payments. Note also that certain accounting packages allow the issuance of partial payments (i.e. a payment to the same vendor with the same invoice number, and amount). Therefore it is advised that the auditor review whether the system allows such payments and omit them prior to running this application.

Voided checks should also be reviewed as if a payment is made first on a regular check and then on a voided one, only one payment was technically made.

EMPLOYEE TO VENDOR ADDRESS MATCH

This test identifies same/similar fields between the vendor and employee master table in an attempt to identify fraudulent payments to employees. While this test explains how to complete this task for addresses, the same could be done for phone numbers, tax identification numbers, and other personal information.

Once the results are produced, the auditor should scan them to determine if there are any valid address matches between the employee and vendor tables. As a next step, a Query Sheet could be performed of the actual invoices posted to that vendor to determine whether they are fraudulent. Two notes when completing this review are as follows:

- Since this exercise may detect fraud, it may be beneficial to locate the invoices or vendor information independent of the accounts payable department (who may be culpable for creating the false vendor account)
- Since it is common to pay employee travel and entertainment expenses or employee advances this should be the key reason to not consider the payments fraudulent. If possible, the vendor file should be filtered for all employee travel and entertainment vendor accounts prior to running this test.

IDENTIFYING PAYMENTS MADE AFTER PERIOD END FOR VALID LIABILITIES AT PERIOD END

This report works to identify unrecorded liabilities. A common scheme is for an organization to "hold" an invoice by not entering it into the system. Then, after period end, the invoice will be entered into the system thereby evading the expense charge in the year under review.

The invoices identified in this test should be reviewed for reasonableness and materiality. If not material, further test work may not be considered necessary. If material, trends may be identified in the types of invoices or the vendor. The final analysis should include pulling the actual invoices to determine whether they are for services rendered or products received before the period end.

IDENTIFY EXCEEDED PURCHASE ORDERS

This report works to identify authorization issues within an accounts payable process whereby the invoices paid exceed the approved purchase order amount. Aside from assessing the authorized limits, this reports tests the system control that should not allow an invoice to be paid above a pre-determined limit (i.e., normally between 5% and 10%).

This may also highlight frauds:

- Where a valid purchase order is provided to authorize payment yet inflated payments are made to assist the fraudster in some way.
- Where vendors working with an employee create a purchase order with valid unit prices yet inflate those prices when the invoices are sent.

This test may highlight a computer system control issue (that should check for exceeded purchase orders) or may identify numerous overrides to the computer system. These overrides may be within the normal course of business (i.e., purchase order prices were meant to be at the invoice price rate but were entered in error on the purchase order) but also may highlight fraudulent activity. Regardless, the auditor should walk though the entering of a purchase order and associated invoices to understand the system controls. Once understood, the differences presented in this test can be investigated by vouching to purchase order and invoice documentation.

Fraud Detection Techniques for the General Ledger

STRATIFY GENERAL LEDGER DETAIL INFORMATION

Look at the multitude of activities in a general ledger and ask yourself, "How can I survey this data in an extremely quick manner while efficiently planning my audit"? This test should provide the answer by helping the auditor focus on large dollar postings, while helping to assess the administrative burden from maintaining low dollar activity.

The stratification report should be reviewed for:
- Unreasonably large balances where activity could be queried for recalculation and proper classification
- High number of transactions with low accumulated activity for possible consolidation
- Planning detailed testing of the journal entry approval process

JOURNAL ENTRY GAP TESTS

Gaps may signal incomplete data processing or, in the situation of journal entries, possible hidden entries. Usually, a method of documenting these occurrences, along with a review by an independent party, is sufficient to ensure the completeness and accuracy of processing. However, it is rare that a journal entry gap test is performed in the Accounting Department (it is more common in the Accounts Payable area related to the check sequence) so this may be the first time this test is being performed.

Gaps in the journal entry sequence should be reviewed with Accounting Department. The test work should answer the following questions:
- What procedures are in place to document and approve all gaps in the respective sequences?
- How are gaps communicated to management?

IDENTIFY NONSTANDARD JOURNAL ENTRIES MADE IN A TIMEFRAME AFTER YEAR END RELATED TO SPECIFIC ACCOUNTS

Nonstandard journal entries generally are those that are posted manually (rather than through an automated feed from a fixed asset or accounts receivable subledger). Such entries are more prone to error and fraud due mainly to the human error, judgment normally being applied in the support for the entry, and the possibility for management override in authorizing the entry. This is especially true for entries made just after year end (related to the prior year) as these entries are more prone to be adjustments for the fiscal year's annual reporting.

Given the above, the test of these entries should include:
- Reviewing the journal entry and associated supporting documentation
- Ensuring the approvals are appropriate for the size and nature of the journal entry
- Assessing whether Generally Accepted Accounting Principles ("GAAP") are being applied

SUMMARIZE ACTIVITY BY USER ACCOUNT

This test looks for:
- Standard names such as "DEFAULT" or "TEST". These Ids usually have equally simple passwords for a hacker to guess and should generally be avoided. Replacements to these generic user Ids would be specific Ids associated with that person using the system (i.e., RLANZA).
- Unrecognized or terminated employees. This test focuses more on the responsiveness within the MIS function to ensure that, at any point in time, only authorized employees have system access. Such employees can be found by reviewing the list created with this test to an active employee roster.
- Users that have access beyond their level of responsibility. This access may highlight a non-segregation of duties where a person has an opportunity to commit fraud by being able to initiate, authorize, and/or record a transaction.

The resulting report should be reviewed bearing in mind the above considerations. It should be recommended that:
- Default passwords be deleted and replaced with specific Ids
- Employees not on the active employee roster be deleted.

- Users that are posting high activity or may have access to other non-segregated functions be reviewed to assess whether other controls are needed to mitigate the access level being afforded to the individual.

Fraud Detection Techniques for Revenue

MISSING / UNUSUAL CUSTOMER MASTERFILE INFORMATION / MATCH TO PRIOR YEAR FOR CHANGES

This report will identify changes in the customer masterfile (additions and deletions). Given that most systems do not track the changes in the customer masterfile (there is no "Last Maintained on Date" field), this report sometimes is the only means of determining changes in the customer master.

The fraud examiner should review major additions and/or deletions to the customer masterfile. Given that there is a high potential for fraud on newly added customers (i.e., posting false sales invoices to phony customer accounts to inflate period end sales balances), the names and addresses for such customers should be reviewed to those employees having access to enter invoices into the system. This can be done using the accounts payable test also described in this book that matched vendor address to employee address files. Since this exercise may detect fraud, it may be beneficial to locate the invoices or customer files independent of the accounts receivable department (who may be culpable for creating the false customer accounts).

CASH RECEIPT TO OPEN INVOICE MATCHING

This test helps assess the existence and valuation of open invoices at period end based on the cash received subsequent to year end. Therefore, it is one of the most popular tests used by fraud examiners in assessing the existence of period end invoices.

Based on this test, the fraud examiner can easily assess whether open invoices were paid off with cash (and therefore existed at year end) and for those still outstanding, whether they should be further reviewed from the perspective of year end valuation. Most probably, such invoices relate to customers that regularly pay late but could represent new customer payment issues and/or fraudulent sales posted at year end that will never receive cash.

AGE RECEIVABLES, EXTRACT OLDER BALANCES, AND SUMMARIZE BY CUSTOMER

This test mainly recalculates the aging of the invoices in the accounts receivable ledger for review against the company-derived report. Any differences between this calculation and the report used by management may be due to a system error, a poorly designed report, or fraud. As to the fraud aspect, the organization may want to hide the true payment patterns of customers to minimize their bad debt valuation reserve at year end.

The aging report should be reconciled to the organization's accounts receivable aging report. Any differences should be investigated. One approach is to extract a sampling of invoices (see previous test on performing a sample of invoices) within a specific aging group and reconcile to the aging report, on an invoice by invoice basis. This work may identify report errors or an attempt by the organization to hide the true aging of accounts receivable. Focus of test work should be on more current aging categories that may be inflated inappropriately.

The aging report also highlights customer balances, once the invoices are summarized by customer, older than a pre-defined "old" limit. This may be 180 or 270 days after which payment of such invoices is unlikely. Large customer balances could be reviewed with management as to their collectibility and possibly, with the actual customer. This analysis would further support the year end bad debt reserve calculation.

CALCULATE THE DIFFERENCE BETWEEN SHIP AND INVOICE DATES, AS WELL AS, INVOICE DATES WITH NO SHIPMENTS

Untimely invoicing, erroneous and/or fraudulent sales invoices may be detected if invoices are sent without valid shipments. In this case, revenue is potentially being recorded prior to being earned. Further research of these invoices should be done independent of the sales and accounts receivable functions in order to ensure an independent analysis.

For more information about ActiveData for Excel, contact InformationActive, Inc. at (613) 569-4675 or www.informactionactive.com.

AutoAudit

From Paisley Consulting, AutoAudit is a comprehensive, integrated audit automation system. In addition to the workpapers and reporting functionality, AutoAudit has entity level and process level risk assessment, staff scheduling, resource planning, issue tracking, time reporting, expense reporting, quality assurance, department metrics, and an ad hoc reporting module. All of these modules are integrated and data automatically flows from one module into the next. AutoAudit is designed to automate all of the primary processes which occur in an audit department.

Risk Assessment

Although the program automates many parts of any type of audit, of particular interest to fraud examiners is the risk assessment functions. AutoAudit offers an integrated risk assessment module with the option of following either a horizontal methodology (Business Process Risk Assessment) or a vertical methodology (audit universe made up of user defined auditable entities), or allowing the user to utilize both methodologies. Specific risks and processes are identified by the client and the risk factors and weightings can be customized to fit the specific needs of the department and industry. Information about the inherent and residual risks help determine issues during the audit, and the information obtained during fieldwork can be pushed back into the risk assessment to use as the starting point for the next cycle of planning and auditing.

For more information, you may contact Paisley Consulting at www.paisleyconsulting.com.

SNAP! Reporter

Snap! Reporter by Paisley Consulting is a data mining software designed for use with Lotus Notes and Microsoft Excel spreadsheets, and Access databases. Its chief virtue is its ease of use. Most software requires a familiarity with databases and data mining techniques, but anyone with basic spreadsheet skills can produce reports and graphics with Snap! Data retrieval and analysis are automated with one-button functions; some tasks are accomplished by drag-and-drop.

Snap! produces Ganntt Charts and counts occurrences of key words rather than only charting actual numbers. The software also creates stacked non-columnar reports and generates multiple Relationized Data Sets from one originating record — functions not available in other products. Snap! is not as powerful as some other data mining software, but it is easier to use. It is adequate to most tasks, though more complex cases may need a stronger package.

For more information, you may contact Paisley Consulting at www.paisleyconsulting.com.

DataWatch Corporation's Monarch for Windows

Monarch is unique because it transforms electronic editions of reports, generated by other programs, into text files, spreadsheets, or database tables. Data that is retrieved in electronic form from an accounting system, for instance, or downloaded from an on-line source, is then broken down into individual records by Monarch's model. Monarch reads report files produced on any mainframe, midrange, client/server, or PC system. These files are commonly known as print files, spool files, TXT files, formatted ASCII files, PRN files, and SDF files. Monarch can also read DBF files and delimited ASCII files. These records can then be manipulated by programs such as Borland's dBase, Microsoft Access, Paradox, Lotus 123, or Microsoft's Excel.

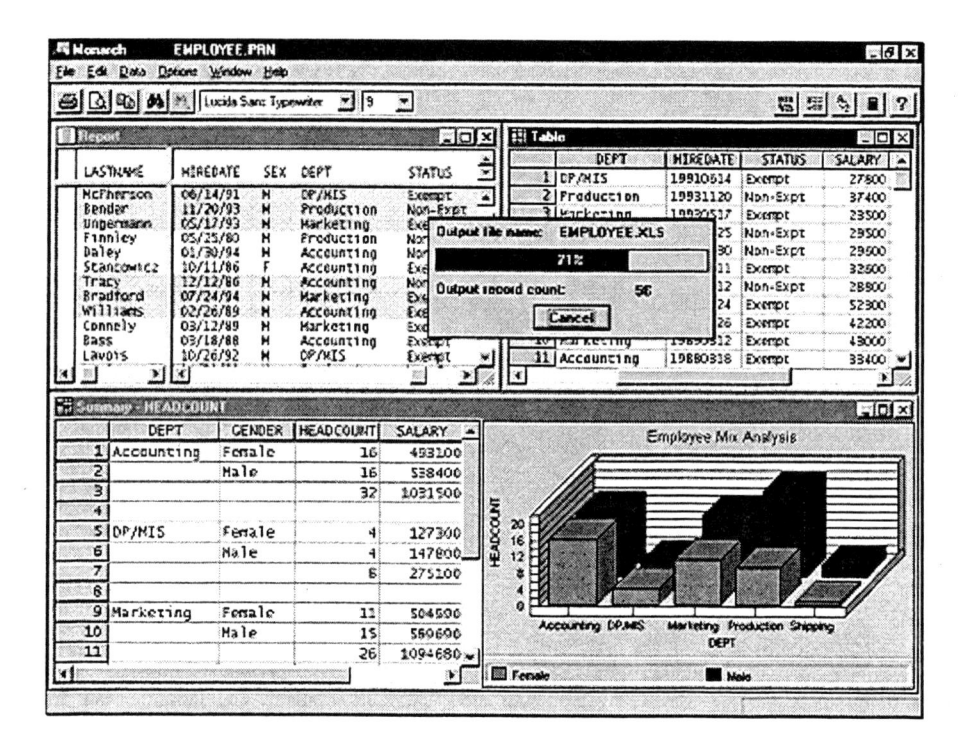

Monarch specializes in reading complex reports in ASCII (plain text) format. Its data mining capabilities are useful for data integrity testing. Monarch can be used by itself or in tandem with other audit software such as ACL. The advantages of using Monarch instead of audit software include:

- Monarch's use of print spools, which are often easier to obtain than database files.
- Monarch uses print spool files whereas audit software uses database files.
- Monarch is less expensive and easier to learn than audit software.

However, investigators will derive maximum benefit using Monarch in conjunction with an audit software tool.

Monarch serves three main functions for investigators:
- Performs automated auditing tests and tests of various program controls.

- Verifies data on management- or external party- report generation accuracy.
- Proactively identifies errors and fraudulent activity.

Monarch Capabilities, 1: Financial Analysis and Risk Assessment

Investigators can use Monarch to perform several functions in a financial analysis or risk assessment:

- Summary window — To summarize information by a different criteria than the report did.
- Sorting data within the Table window — To generate an alphabetically sorted list or to identify the largest or smallest transactions.
- Time series analysis — Monarch can compile information from twelve separate reports into a month-by-month summary, allowing the investigator to identify trends.
- Graphing data within the Summary window — The investigator can graph any information in the Summary window into a pie, area, line, or bar chart quickly to visualize composition, trends, or distribution. This charting is much more straight forward than in spreadsheet programs, such as MS Excel and Lotus 1-2-3.
- Create calculated fields — Custom calculations can be performed on existing data file fields, or new fields, not present in the original data file.

Here a few practical examples of Monarch investigative capabilities. The software allows investigators to:

- View the 20 largest vendors by invoice amount, to compare the amount with their expectations of those amounts.
- Summarize by purchase order number to determine if the sum of all transactions related to that purchase order exceed the amount authorized by the purchase order.
- Measure transaction volume and amount processed by each input clerk to identify unusual activity.
- Compare budget versus actual figures by computing a difference field.
- Chart customer delinquency trends for the past twelve months.

Monarch Capabilities, 2: Date Tests

Monarch handles dates in much the same manner that popular spreadsheets do—it stores them as the number of days from January 1, 1900. In this manner, it can compare dates and use them in mathematical equations, such as subtracting two dates to show the number of days between the two events.

Examples of time-related integrity tests include:
- Delinquency analysis — To prepare delinquency aging category reports (0-30 days, 31 to 60 days, etc.) when these reports do not exist. Or to prepare such a report to verify the accuracy of the computer-generated report delinquency category subtotals.
- Obsolescence analysis — Monarch can compare the date that inventory was acquired to the report date to provide the number of days inventory has been held. This information can be used in an obsolescence aging category report or to filter inventory items which have been held for more than a predetermined number of days.
- Cut-off Analysis — To determine transactions near the financial statement cut-off date, to insure that they were recorded in the proper period. This procedure uses Monarch's filtering capabilities to isolate records with particular transactions dated within certain time periods.

If you need more information about Monarch write to 3 Lewis Road, Boston, MA 02178 or call (617) 489-0230.

DATAS® for ACL, IDEA, and Excel

DATAS uses the Benford's Law mathematical formula to differentiate normal audit patterns from suspect ones.

Some of the features of DATAS® include the following:
The product employs Benford's law of numbers, which allows 100% of a population to be examined using graphs that can be imported into any audit report.

FIRST DIGITS

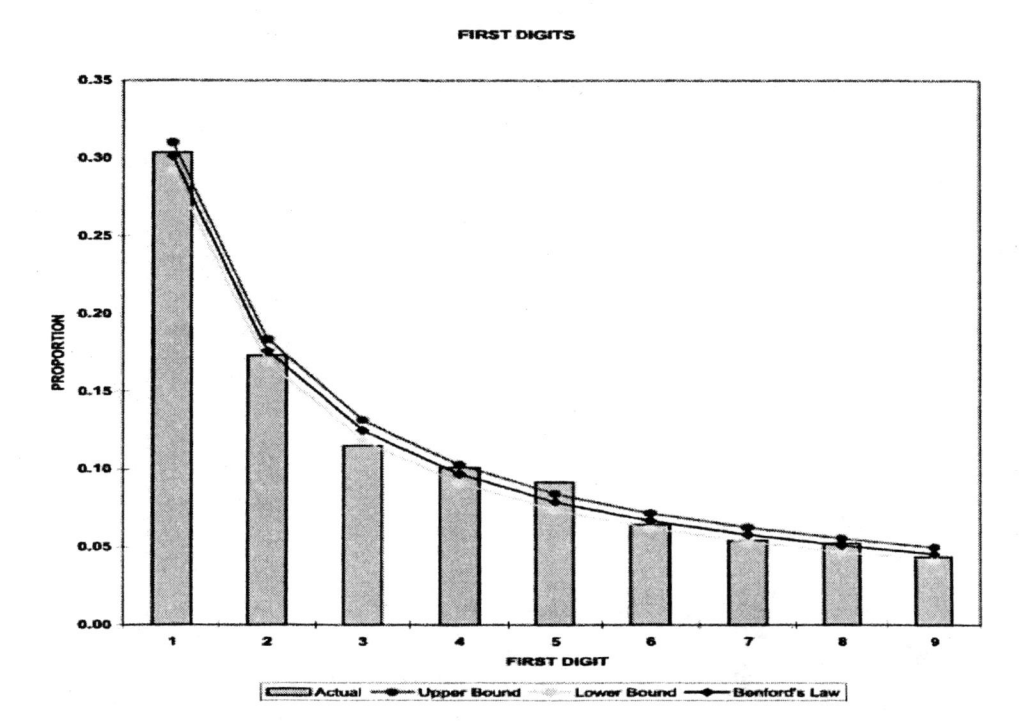

[Chart: Bar chart comparing Actual proportions against Upper Bound, Lower Bound, and Benford's Law across first digits 1-9, with proportion on y-axis ranging from 0.00 to 0.35]

The system looks for fraudulent or irregular activity by pinpointing abnormal use of certain digits. It also checks questionable estimations in the current period or potential fraudulent payments through the use of round number analysis.

Exceptions can be identified by reviewing digit patterns of computer system processing before and after system conversions. Further, entries that are multiples larger or smaller than similar entries can be identified by vendor or general ledger account.

Processing inefficiencies can be identified through a quick summary of abnormal levels of low-dollar transactions. Such inefficiencies could be due to similar payments to vendors or numerous immaterial accounting adjustments that could be consolidated.

DATAS® also contains an excellent duplication detection tester that can run over 10 tests to look for duplication in databases. Audit areas for duplication analysis include payments, inventory, general ledger, and sales registers.
DATAS® can be used with ACL, IDEA, or Excel.

For more information, please see www.digitalanalysison-line.com.

IDEA for Windows

This software provides some functionality previously only available to EDP auditors and systems specialists. It was developed using the latest Windows development techniques and interface design standards. IDEA lets the user make inquiries of data files, perform random unit sampling, and calculate totals and averages. The software will perform specific criteria searches, unusual item queries, and identify gaps or duplicates in sequences. IDEA includes a number of tools to prevent and detect fraud including personal vetting, independent authorization of transactions, and observation of employees. This software considers purchasing, payroll, and banking the most common places for the occurrence of fraud.

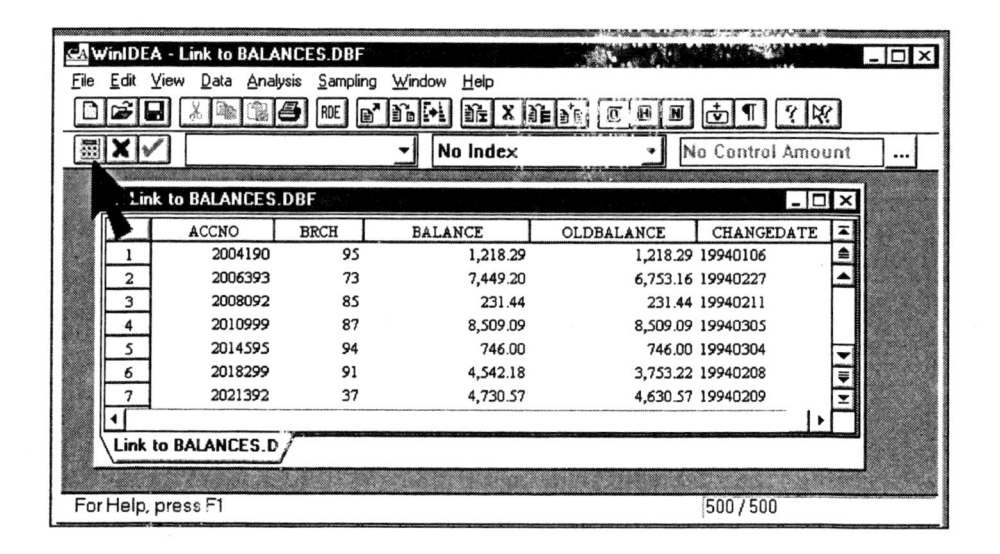

IDEA (*Interactive Data Extraction & Analysis*) is a PC based file interrogation package that allows accountants, auditors, and financial managers to view, sample, and analyze data from any other computerized systems.

For more information about IDEA, you may visit their website at www.caseware-idea.com.

Computer Forensic Tools

EnCase

EnCase is a computer forensics software program developed by Guidance Software. It allows the user to acquire evidence from a computer drive without harming or changing the original files. Once the evidence is acquired, the software can also be used to view and organize the evidence found, as well as generate a final report. In addition to its forensic function, it can also be used for data recovery, systems auditing, data management, backup, and archiving.

The EnCase program can perform the following functions:
- Read any IDE or SCSI hard drive or CD-ROM and save an exact snapshot of the disk to an Evidence File
- Password protect any piece of evidence to control the chain of custody
- View the entire drive image, including hidden and unallocated disk space and partitions and search it for keywords
- View files without changing the file contents or date-time stamps
- Analyze the file and folder structure on all FAT12, FAT16, FAT32, NTFS, HFS, HFS+, CD, EXT2 (Linux), and UFS (UNIX) hard disks and removable media
- Combine any number of evidence files together to create a case. Through a single examination, view, search, filter, and sort every file from every disk and computer in the case and see the results graphically on screen
- Have all evidence, searches, and bookmarks recorded on a typeset report
- Powerful search features including background search, GREP keywords, and automatic Unicode finds
- Analyze and authenticate file signatures to find those that have been renamed to conceal their contents
- Build and use your own Hash library to identify known files
- Built-in picture viewer and gallery view enables rapid isolation and book marking of contraband
- EScript macro language allows automation of complex filtering and recovery tasks
- Easy manipulation and organization of keywords and bookmarks with "drag-n-drop" ease
- Ability to acquire and preview via included network cable
- Built in viewers for registry files, zip files, and DBX (Outlook Express 5) files
- Ability to acquire and preview Palm PDAs
- Ability to acquire and preview both hardware and software RAIDs

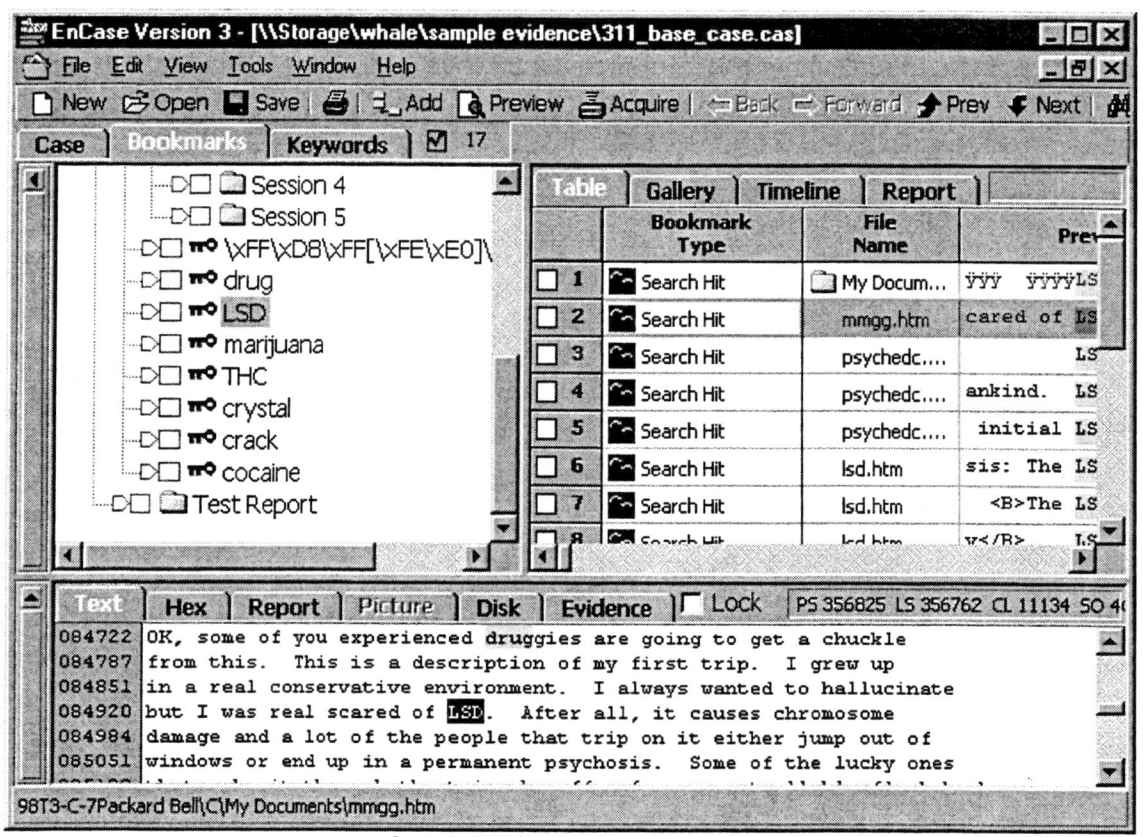

Search hits in the Table view

There are three main components to EnCase: the acquisition of evidence, the analysis of that acquisition, and the reporting of the evidence. The advantage of using a computer forensics program is that the original evidence is not altered at all. The analysis is done completely on the forensically sound duplicate, or clone, of the original media.

For more information about EnCase, you may contact Guidance Software in Pasadena, CA (626-229-9191) or www.EnCase.com.

Reporting and Case Management Software

There are a number of programs that can assist the fraud examiner in managing the data and information gathered. These programs can also be used to create reports, graphs, and charts of a particular case. Some of the most useful of these programs for fraud investigations are discussed below.

i2 Analyst's Notebook

i2 software company offers a professional visualization and analysis tool named Analyst's Notebook. The Analyst's Notebook provides a set of tools for exploring, interpreting, and displaying complex information to help extend problem-solving capability. Some of the analyses are summarized below.

Link Analysis

Link analysis is a technique which reveals the structure and content of a body of information by representing it as a set of interconnected, linked objects (or entities). Analyst's Notebook diagrams depict the associations by linking different entities such as people, vehicles, and organizations, or the flow of commodities, such as money and property.

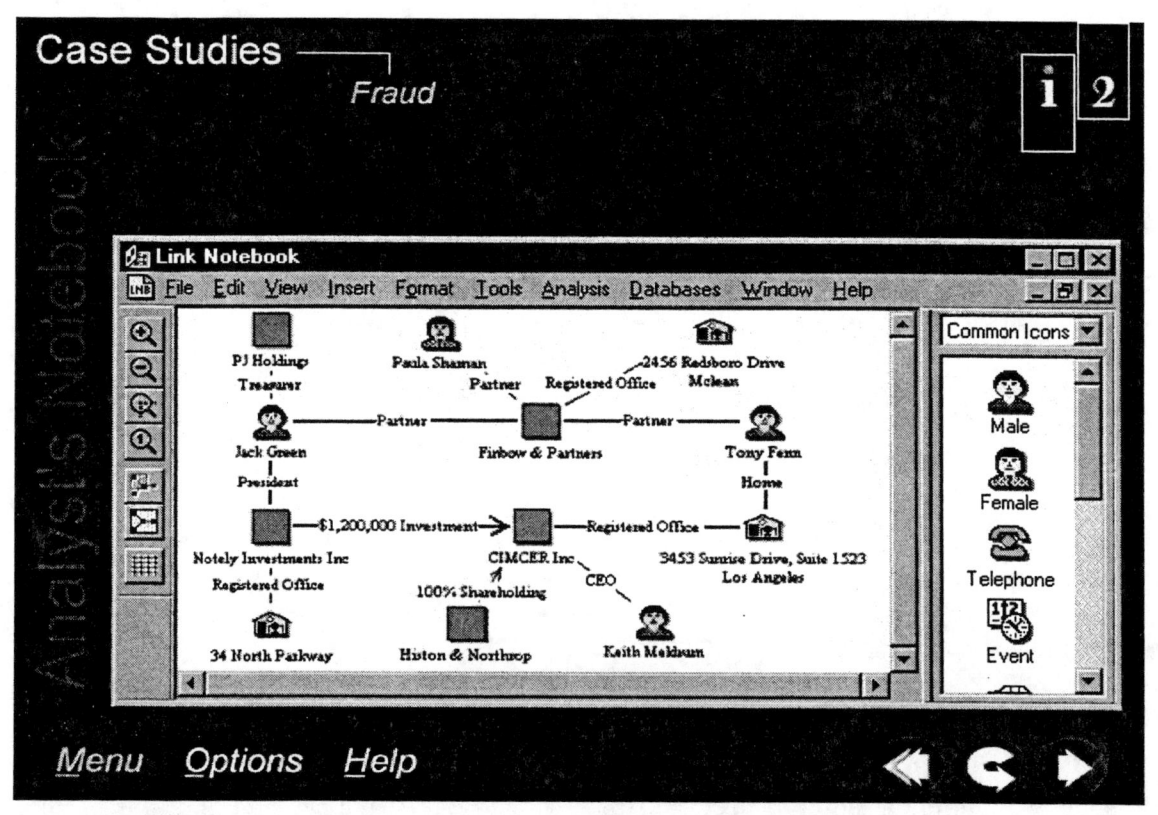

The case example above began with a suspicious investment of $1,200,000 from Notely Investments, Inc. to CIMCER, Inc. The president of Notely Investments is Jack Green. A records search revealed that Jack Green is the treasurer of PJ Holdings and a partner in Finbow & Partners. The other partners are Paula Sherman and Tony Fenn. A records search revealed that Tony Fenn's home address is 3453 Sunrise Drive, Suite 1523 in Los Angeles. The registered office for CIMCER, Inc. is also 3453 Sunrise Drive, Suite 1523.

By displaying this information graphically, it is easy to see that there is a link between Notely Investments and CIMCER, Inc. It also makes it easier for a jury or prosecutor to see the relationships among the parties.

Network Analysis

Network analysis applies the techniques of link analysis to large datasets. The technique is particularly useful in the analysis of telephone transactions, account transfers, and Internet traffic — anything that involves a large number of events or transactions. The process begins by importing the data from a text file or spreadsheet. The program then generates a chart based on the relationships between the items.

In the diagram below, the dark phone icon in the center represents the suspect's phone. The chart clearly shows that 11 calls were made between the suspect's phone and 791-555-2213; 17 calls were made between the suspect's phone and 791-555-1210; and 8 calls were made between the suspect and 791-555-9835. The top line of the chart also shows a connection between two of the other phone numbers. Three calls were made to 791-555-5570 from two of the phone numbers that are also linked to the suspect. This could provide you with information that a previously unknown third-party may be involved in the scheme.

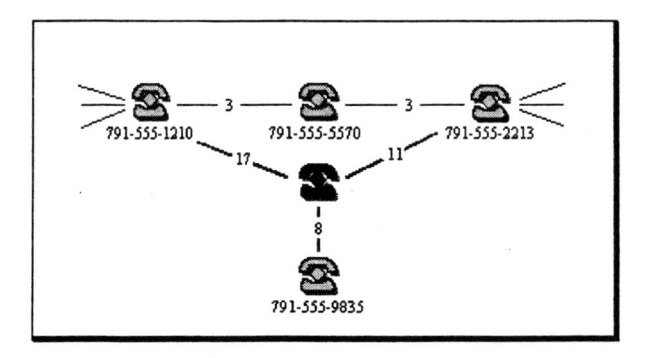

The Link Notebook feature can be used to automatically find groups of highly interconnected entities, known as clusters. The clusters can be copied from the complex chart to an empty one for closer inspection. Similarly, the Find Path command finds the shortest path between two selected entities on a chart. For example, you can select two accounts and the Link Notebook will find the intermediate entities through which money hay have passed between them.

The chart below, for instance, demonstrates a relationship between Cal Jenkins and Tom Homlin. Money was transferred from Jenkins' account to account number 43545-566-564.

Money was transferred from that account to account number 45435-4543-455. Money from that account was then transferred to an account held by Tom Homlin.

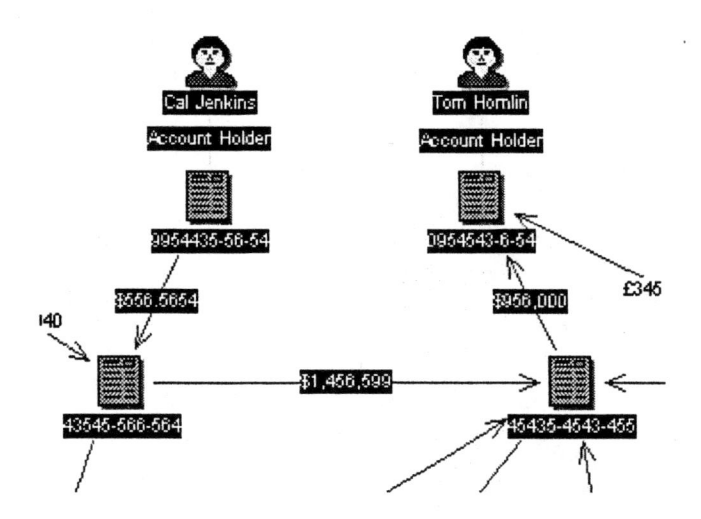

Time Line Analysis

Time line charts reveal how related events unfold chronologically. They are useful for establishing cause and effect between events, for corroborating witness statements and for simulating a likely sequence.

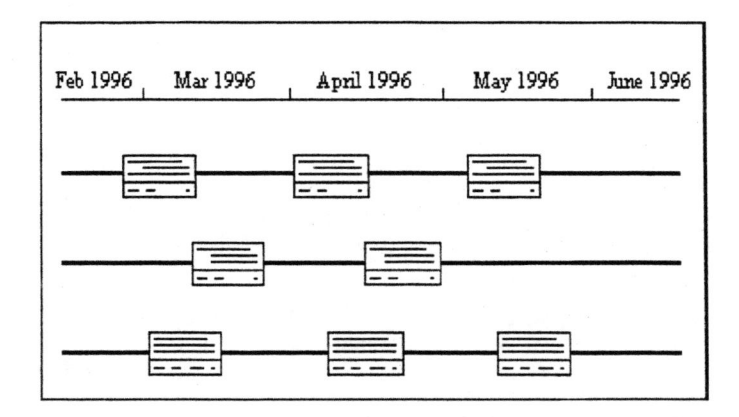

Transaction Pattern

Where the activity between subjects is more significant than the activity of each one taken singly, Analyst's Notebook will generate a transaction pattern analysis chart. These charts find repeated patterns of activity, such as a particular sequence of telephone calls indicating a chain of command, or a pattern of account transfers revealing a mechanism for fraud.

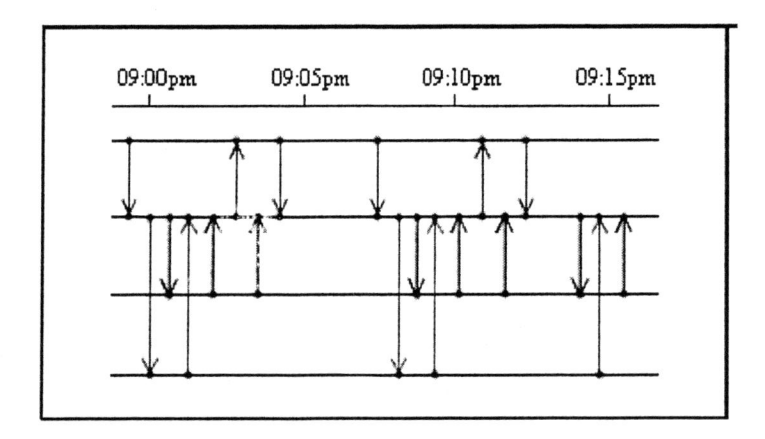

Database Visualization

The Analyst's Notebook will generate charts automatically from a wide variety of computer-based sources such as databases, word processors, and spreadsheets.

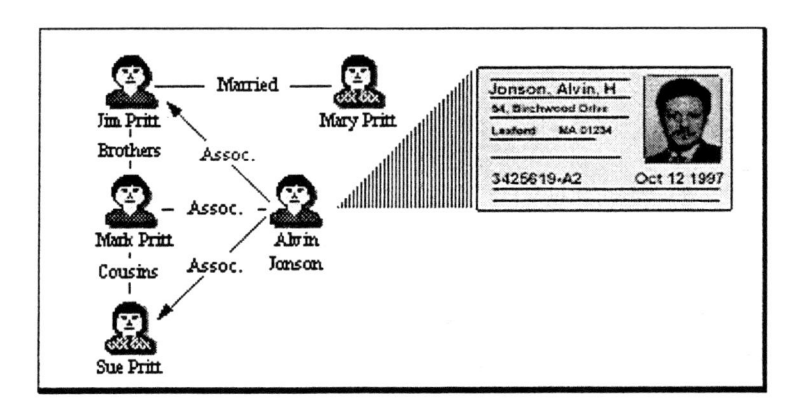

For more information on the Analyst's Notebook, please contact i2 Inc. at 6551 Loisdale Court, Suite 600, Springfield, VA 22150 or call them at (703) 921-0195.

CaseMap by CaseSoft

CaseMap is a database product that you can use to organize information about the facts, the cast of characters, the issues and questions in any investigation.

When you create a CaseMap file, the program automatically sets up a series of spreadsheets used to organize critical case knowledge. This process focuses on creating four analysis reports — a Cast of Characters, a Chronology, an Issue List, and a Question List. These reports provide a framework for organizing and evaluating critical case knowledge. If multiple people are involved in the analysis process, the reports provide a way to divide responsibility and share results.

Facts Spreadsheet

Includes creation of a case Chronology where the investigator can enter facts, dates, and times. You can also include the source of each piece of information. You may also distinguish between disputed and undisputed facts and keep track of the status of each item.

Objects Spreadsheet

Allows you to organize your cast of characters, a list of the individuals and organizations you know to be involved in your case. This report should also catalog key documents and other important pieces of physical evidence.

Issue Spreadsheet

Build an outline of the issues, including both legal claims and critical factual disputes. Your outline can be any number of levels deep. Rather than listing just the top-level issues, consider breaking each claim down to its component parts.

Question Spreadsheet

At the early stages of your investigation, many questions will occur. The Question spreadsheet allows you to filter and sort your open items using various all kinds of criteria. Your CaseMap report includes a column for the question (Question Text) and another column where you can capture notes regarding the answer (Answer Text). Also included is a column (Eval) for evaluating the criticality of each question. Use A (extremely critical), B, C, and D scaling to make your assessment. Other columns available for your Question List are "Assigned To" and "Answer Due Date."

Research Spreadsheets

Organize and explore your knowledge about the precedents and statutes that bear on a case, and include links to actual case law using the Authorities and Extracts spreadsheets.

Use the Authorities spreadsheet to manage top-level information about precedents, statutes, and other types of case research. Use the Extracts spreadsheet to capture details about particular sections of interest excerpted from important case law and statutes.

Linking

The program also provides the ability to link pieces of data in one spreadsheet with the source data or other relevant data in another sheet.

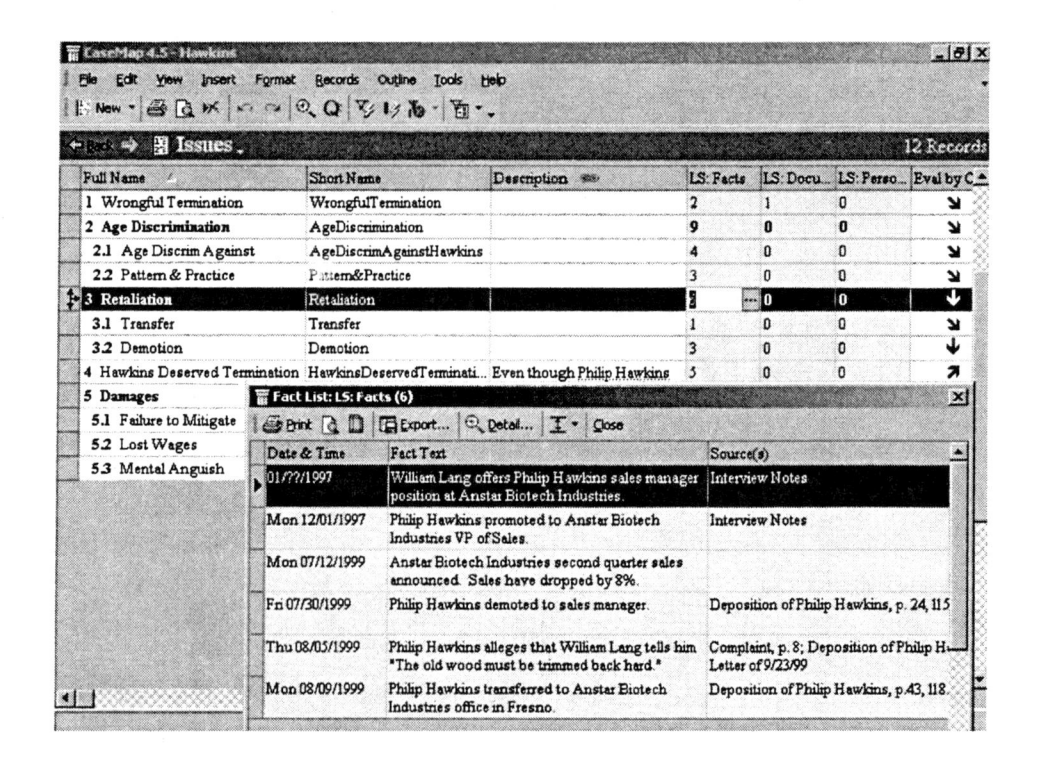

Filtering

Once you organize the information, you can explore it. The most powerful case exploration tool in CaseMap is filtering. A filter operation limits the rows that appear in a spreadsheet and on your printed report to those that meet criteria you specify.

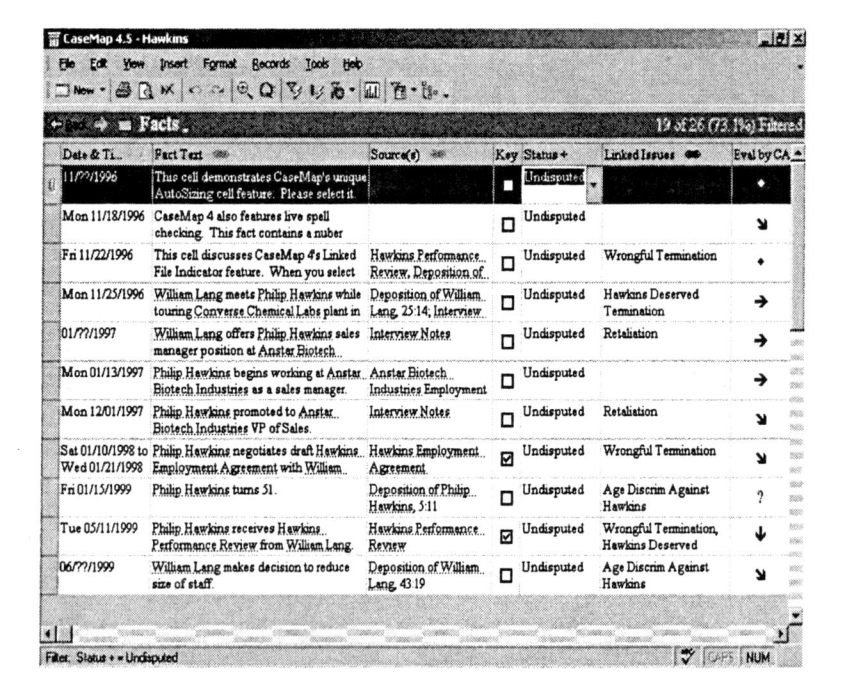

"By Issue" Reports

The "By Issue" Report feature allows the user to display Facts, Documents, Case Law, and other types of case information grouped by the issues to which they are linked. You choose whether this report is sent to MS Word, WordPerfect, or to HTML. Issues are listed in the order that they appear in your issue outline. Below each issue name is a table of the items linked to it.

CaseMap Facts by Issue Report

Case: Hawkins
Created: 6/5/2003 1:54:18 PM

Issue: 1 Wrongful Termination

Date & Time	Fact Text	Source(s)	Key	Status +	Linked Issues	Eval by CA
Tue 05/11/1999	Philip Hawkins receives Hawkins Performance Review from William Lang. Is rated a 1 "Outstanding Performer."	Hawkins Performance Review	Yes	Undisputed	Wrongful Termination, Hawkins Deserved Termination	Heavily Against Us
Fri 11/12/1999	Reduction in force takes place. 55 Anstar Biotech Industries employees are let go including Philip Hawkins.		Yes	Undisputed	Wrongful Termination, Age Discrim Against Hawkins	Heavily Against Us

Issue: 2 Age Discrimination

Date & Time	Fact Text	Source(s)	Key	Status +	Linked Issues	Eval by CA
Sat 01/10/1998 to Wed 01/21/1998	Philip Hawkins negotiates draft Hawkins Employment Agreement with William Lang.	Hawkins Employment Agreement	Yes	Undisputed	Age Discrimination	Against Us
02/??/1998	William Lang tells Philip Hawkins that he has changed his mind regarding the Hawkins Employment Agreement. It is not in force as it was never signed and changes were not	Philip Hawkins, Deposition of William Lang, p. 19, 13.	Yes	Disputed by: Opposition	Age Discrimination	Against Us

Linking With Other Applications

CaseMap contains linking capabilities for use with other software applications, including Adobe Acrobat, TextMap, Summation, Concordance, LiveNote, Binder, Sanction and others.

CaseMap is published by CaseSoft. 5000 Sawgrass Circle, Ponte Vedra Beach, FL 32082; (904) 273-5000. (www.casesoft.com/index.shtml)

NetMap by Alta Analytics

The program reveals patterns, trends, and relationships as it processes massive amounts of data. The data can be graphically modeled and further analyzed. Though originally developed for anti-fraud efforts in the insurance industry, the NetMap suite of products has been adapted for use by law enforcement, banking, network, security, retail, electronic commerce, and data warehousing sectors. Netmap runs on NT and UNIX and requires a server.

NetMap increases a user's analytical range by using a proprietary system of "fuzzy logic" searching technology and algorithmic techniques. Suppose, for example, a database contains entries for Joanna Williams at 1211 Cameron Ln., and for Jo Williams at 1211 Camtown. Perhaps these are two identities for the same person. But a literal search system cannot recognize the connection. IdentiFind, Alta's fuzzy logic technology, is designed to detect similarities between two otherwise very different records.

For more information of NetMap, contact Alta Analytics, 480 Olde Worthington Road, Suite 300, Westerville, OH 43082 or call them at (800) 638-6277. Or, you can visit their website at www.altaanalytics.com.

MAGNUM Case Management Software

MAGNUM assists fraud examines and investigators by helping to automate and process investigation information. After the initial complaint or suspicion, the investigator creates an electronic file in MAGNUM. The investigator can then use the software to document evidence collected, create interview reports and notes, and generate investigative reports. Additionally, investigators can work off-line and then upload the new information back to the central database. MAGNUM can also be used to create management reports that track complaints and investigations.

The software is sold by Paisley Consulting. For more information, you may contact them at www.paisleyconsulting.com.

WATSON and POWERCASE, from XANALYS

Watson allows users to construct database queries in natural, everyday language and displays the results in graphic form. The displays may be link charts, event charts, or transaction charts. Watson also suggests possible investigative paths and allows the user to pose scenarios and analyze possible outcomes. The program is compatible with other database programs, such as Microsoft Access, Oracle, and Sybase.

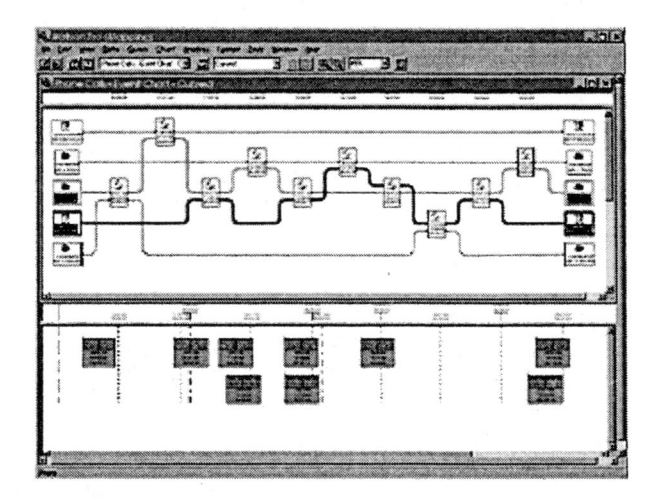

Watson users can customize the attributes of objects represented in charts. For example, in a chart for analyzing credit card fraud, incidents involving *counterfeit cards* can be coded in a different color than those involving *stolen cards*. Then, you can easily zero in on the locations where counterfeit cards have been frequently used and see the impact that counterfeit card use has on the overall incidence of fraud.

Or, in a network of cash transactions, all transactions that involved an automatic teller machine can be instantly identified. In a chart showing the membership of an organization, you can isolate certain relationships, such as those among shareholders and company officers.

PowerCase is a case management system for investigators. PowerCase can organize every aspect of the investigation process, from managing documents and allocating resources, to analyzing evidence and preparing for court. The PowerIndexing feature automatically extracts key information from the text in statements and reports to create a case database.

PowerCase is recommended for use in tandem with Watson, so that Watson's graphic modeling capabilities complement the project management function of PowerCase. PowerCase automatically researches each item in its database to eliminate duplicate entries. PowerCase's matching techniques—including Soundex, Synonym, and Truncated Match—ensure the integrity of data. The auto research function can be applied to transaction data such as telephone call information and cash transactions between bank accounts. It quickly highlights relationships among records. PowerCase can create reports and listings of documents suitable for litigation or other formal presentations. Formats can be customized to support procedures typically encountered at the final stages of the investigation or discovery processes.

For more information on Watson from Global Graphics Software at 95 Sawyer Road, Three University Park, Waltham, MA 02453, or telephone them at (781) 392-1600. Their website is www.globalgraphics.com.

Other Fraud-Related Software

ComputerCOP P3 and ComputerCOP Forensic
Software performs in-depth computer examinations on-site. P3 is designed for Parole, Probation, and Pretrial Officers. Forensic is designed for Law Enforcement and related agencies tasked to perform computer forensics in the field. (www.computercop.com)

CyberCop Software
Software to be used with handheld computers to keep track of investigative cases and references. (www.cybercop-software.com)

Fraud Prevention SmartSystem
Phone fraud prevention software that incorporates all proven anti-fraud technologies into a single system. (www.beckcomputers.com)

Infoglide Software Corporation
Database tool that helps organizations find incidences of fraud, false aliases, and security threat and risk by finding connections between people, places, and/or events. (www.infoglidesoftware.com)

Promisemark, Inc.
A suite of Internet and data-related service products tailored to protect computers, data and identity in an on-line environment. (www.promisemark.com)

Search Software America
Various applications used for SSA's Core Technology that performs search and matching algorithms for any country and language. (www.searchsoftware.com/Products/index.htm)

Syfact, The Corporate Intelligence Management System

Syfact is designed to prevent and combat financial crime used within security departments of financial institutions and insurance companies. (www.syfact.com)

The Case File

A program to assist in major crime case management and case preparation. (www.casefile.com)

Wizsoft, Inc.

Software based on mathematical algorithms for the business sector in the fields of data mining, data auditing, concept-based text search engines, and knowledge management. (www.wizsoft.com)

TRACING ILLICIT TRANSACTIONS

Interviewing in order to obtain financial data involves the systematic questioning of people who have knowledge of the events, the people involved, and the physical evidence surrounding the case. Financial interviewing is not unlike other kinds of interviewing. However, evidence often develops in bits and pieces, that when viewed separately, might appear to lead nowhere. Frustration is common, and tactics and techniques might have to be modified. Diligence, patience, and persistence are essential for successful results. The following is a checklist of general information that can be covered in the financial interview.

Comprehensive Guidelines for Information to be Collected in Financial Interviews

Identification
- Full name
- Alias
- Reason for alias

Birth
- Date and place of birth
- Citizenship
- Father's name; living? (If deceased, when?)
- Mother's name; living? (If deceased, when?)

Address During Pertinent Years
- Resident address; phone number
- Business address; phone number
- Other present or prior address(es)
- Marital status; if married, date and place of marriage
- If divorced; when and where
- Spouse's maiden name
- Spouse's parents; living? (If deceased, when?)
- Children's names and ages; other dependents

Occupation
- Present occupation

- Company name and address
- Present salary
- Length of time employed
- Additional employment
- Prior occupations
- Spouse's occupation

General Background
- Physical health
- Mental health
- Education
- Professional qualifications
- Military service
- Passport, Social Security, and/or Social Insurance numbers (for identification purposes)
- Ever been investigated for financial crimes?
- Ever been arrested?
- Ever filed bankruptcy? If so, who acted as receiver/trustee?
- Hobbies, interests

Financial Institutions (Business and Personal)
- Financial institution accounts
- Safe deposit boxes (request inventory); in whose name; contents; does anyone else have access?
- Credit cards
- Trusts; beneficiary, donor, or trustee
- Mutual funds or other securities owned
- Brokers; currency exchanges used
- Life insurance
- Indirect dealings – e.g., through lawyers or accountants
- Cashier's checks
- Money orders, bank drafts, traveler's checks

Sources of Income

- Salaries, wages, business receipts
- Interest and dividends
- Sale of securities
- Rents and royalties
- Pensions, trusts, annuities, etc.
- Gifts (money, property, etc.)
- Inheritances
- Loans
- Mortgages
- Sales of assets
- Municipal bond interest
- Insurance settlements
- Damages from legal actions
- Any other source of funds, ever

Net Income and Expenditures

- Current cash on hand, including cash in safe deposit boxes, but not cash in bank accounts
- Location of current cash
- Largest amount of cash ever on hand; location
- End-of-year cash
- Notes receivable
- Mortgages receivable
- Life insurance policies
- Automobiles
- Real estate
- Stocks, bonds, and other securities
- Jewelry, furs
- Airplanes, boats
- Any other assets valued

Liabilities

- Payables
- Loans
- Assets purchased by financing

- Mortgages
- Bonds

Expenditures
- Debt reduction
- Insurance premiums
- Interest expense
- Contributions
- Medical
- Travel
- Real estate and other taxes
- Household wages, i.e., babysitter, housekeeper, gardener, etc.
- Casualty losses

Business Operations
- Name and address
- Date organized and nature (corporation, partnership)
- Company or business registration numbers
- Tax identification numbers
- Title and duties
- Reporting arrangements – to and from whom?
- Banking and cash handling arrangements
- Investment; where and when
- Subsidiaries and associates
- Key people

Books and Records
- Nature of accounting system (e.g., cash, accrual)
- Period covered
- Location
- Name of person maintaining and controlling
- Types (journal, ledgers, minute books, canceled checks, bank statements, invoices, cash)
- External auditors

Business Receipts

- Form (eletronic, check, or cash)
- Are all receipts deposited? Where?
- Are business receipts segregated from personal ones?
- Are expenses ever paid with undeposited receipts?
- Arrangements for foreign currency payments
- Trade finance arrangements, letters of credit, etc.

Direct Methods of Tracing Financial Transactions

Banks

Fraud examiners should recognize that in most instances bank records are not readily obtainable. Substantial requirements usually must be met to justify legal process (subpoena, search warrant, and the like), which banks customarily will demand as a condition for disclosure. Preliminary investigation is of the utmost importance to lay the basis for obtaining such records. More information on banking transactions is contained in the Financial Transactions section.

The availability of investigative avenues often determines whether a promising fraud examination will grind to a halt or proceed successfully. Legal advice from a prosecutor or civil counsel should be sought in all such instances. It also should be recognized that bank officials and employees can be questioned by fraud examiners in the same manner as any other potential witnesses and that their responses to proper inquiries might provide important information.

Bank records are perhaps the single most important financial source available to a fraud examiner. In addition to their use as evidence for fraud, a bank's records might provide leads on sources of funds, expenditures, and personal affairs.

The following information can be of value to fraud examiners seeking information from banks concerning pertinent financial transactions of economic crime perpetrators. It is based in part on the operational guidelines issued by the American Bankers Association to all member banks in the United States and on the training guides issued by the U.S. Department of the Treasury.

Types of Banks

Banks are classified primarily by their major services.

- Commercial banks offer businesses and individuals such services as checking accounts, loans, and exchange instruments.
- Savings banks and savings and loan associations handle savings accounts and mortgage loans.
- Trust companies handle property for others under various types of fiduciary accommodations.

Many banks combine all three services. Banks are organized under either state or national banking laws.

The basic bank functions are as follows:
- Receive deposits
- Pay checks
- Transfer funds
- Make loans
- Collect sundry financial instruments
- Hold and administer property for others
- Perform other services, such as safe deposit box rentals

Internal Bookkeeping Procedures

The internal record keeping practices and procedures of banks not only are complex but they constantly are changing because of the growing sophistication of computer technology. Banks are moving steadily toward an electronic funds transfer system that will eliminate the use of checks. Such a system will automatically transfer money from the account of the purchaser to the account of the seller. "Paper trails" will disappear. Detailed familiarity with the intricacies of internal bank operations is not essential, however, for the fraud examiner to obtain the types of information necessary for investigations. What is essential is the knowledge that records of customers' transactions are maintained and retained.

Retention of Records

The provisions of Titles I and II of Public Law 91-508, Financial Record Keeping and Currency and Foreign Transactions Act, make it mandatory to retain records of customers' transactions. U.S. Treasury Regulations, implementing Public Law 91-508, provide in part that an original, microfilm, or other copy or reproduction of most demand deposits (checking account) and savings account records must be retained for five years. The records must include signature cards; statements, ledger cards, or other records disclosing all transactions, that is, deposits and withdrawals; and copies of customers' checks, bank drafts, money orders and cashier's checks drawn on the bank or issued and payable by it.

In addition, banks must retain for a two-year period all records necessary to reconstruct a customer's checking account (the records must include copies of the customer's deposit tickets) or to trace and supply a description of a check deposited to a customer's checking account.

These requirements apply to checks written or deposits made in excess of $100. It should be noted that most banks find it cheaper to microfilm all pertinent records, including the checks and deposits in amounts less than $100, rather than sort their records into two categories. If a transaction is less than $100 and appears to be of particular interest, there is a strong likelihood that the necessary records to identify the transaction are available.

The regulations further provide that both sides of checks, drafts, or money orders must be reproduced unless the reverse side is blank. The regulations also provide that banks must maintain their records so that they can be made available, upon request, within a "reasonable period of time."

Types of Bank Records

Bank records identified and discussed below are limited to those of particular interest to fraud examiners.

Signature Cards

The signature card is the evidence of a contract between the customer and bank. When a depositor opens an account, the bank requires that a signature card be signed. By signing the card, the depositor becomes a party to a contract with the bank under which he accepts all rules and regulations of the bank and authorizes the bank to honor his orders for withdrawing funds. For a corporation or a partnership account, the signature card is accompanied by copies of resolutions of the board of directors or partnership agreements naming the person authorized to draw checks on the accounts.

The signature card is a source of valuable information. Although its form varies, the card usually contains such data as banking connections, and the date and amount of the initial deposit. The initial deposit traced through the bank's records may disclose a source of income. The identification of the person who opened the account might be significant, especially if the depositor used an alias.

Many banks investigate the references given by a new customer. They might also make inquiries of various credit reporting agencies. This information is contained in a correspondence file or a credit file that can contain comments of the person who opened the account and might show information given by the depositor when opening the account.

In banks using ADP (Automatic Data Processing), the signature card also contains an account number assigned to the customer. In tracing information about a subject's transactions with the bank, the account number must be used. If it does not appear on the signature card, it can be located in the bank's cross-reference file. Assigned account numbers are encoded on other documents relating to the depositor by means of a system called MICR (Magnetic Ink Character Recognition). The card also might contain the depositor's Social Security number.

The signature card might define the account as either a regular or a special checking account. The main difference between the two is the service charge made by the bank. The regular checking account is used mostly by businesses and individuals who maintain large average balances. The special checking account is used by individuals who usually have small account balances.

When requesting the signature card, the fraud examiner should determine whether the bank maintains any type of central file. Most large banks have a central file that lists all departments with which a customer has had dealings. If the bank has such a file, the examiner does not need to check with each department to obtain information. The subject might at one time have had a bank account that later was closed. Requests for information from a bank about a subject always should include a reference to both active and closed accounts. Records of closed accounts usually are maintained in a separate file.

Negotiated Checks

Canceled checks written by a subject or received from others provide the fraud examiner with much more than amounts, payees, and endorsees. Of particular interest are checks that have been cashed. All banks use a series of codes or symbols imprinted on the front of a check to show that the check has been "cashed." The specific codes used in various areas can be obtained locally.

A useful technique is to list the information from the subject's checks on a spreadsheet (either manual or electronic). Checks should be listed by number and date on the left with the payee, amount, and purpose, if known, of the check to the right. This will show the subject's routine monthly or annual expenditures that can be useful for computing the comparative net worth. The absence of a check for a recurring payment for a particular month might indicate a cash payment, which in turn would indicate possible undisclosed cash income. Examine the backs of checks payable to cash and note where they were cashed. The depository stamp can identify the bank at which the check was cashed. This information may provide a lead to another bank account.

CHECK 21

"With image exchange, and the emerging fraud detection technology, banks will be able to know if sufficient funds are in the account…whether the customer is who he or she claims to be…and whether the check is legitimate."[2]

In July 2003, Congress issued final regulations regarding the availability of funds and collection of checks. As of October 28, 2004, a new provision of Section 12, Part 229 of the Code of Federal Regulations, known as "Check 21," creates "substitute checks," the new negotiable instruments that become the legal equivalent of paper checks. This provision facilitates the efficient collection and return of checks in electronic form by alleviating the collection requirement that depository banks actually send the original paper checks to collecting banks for payment.

Under Check 21, a depository bank can transfer check information electronically to a collecting bank via a substitute check for presentment. The collecting bank is then required to take presentment of the substitute check so long as it meets all the legal requirements of the original check. Therefore, rather than actually processing and sending an original paper check across cities and states, the depositing bank can now collect the substitute check electronically.

---

[2] Robertson, Bill and Ken Gahre. *White-Collar Crime Fighter.* Vol. 6, No. 1, *Check 21: Blackjack for Check Fraud Fighters?* Ridgefield, CT: White Collar Crime101, LLC., 2004.

A substitute check is a paper reproduction of the original check that states, "This is a legal copy of your check. You can use it the same way you would use the original check." Upon transfer, presentment, or return, a bank warrants that the substitute check submitted is an accurate depiction of the physical check, and that no depository bank, drawee, drawer, or indorser will be asked or required to pay a check that has already been paid. Essentially, this legend on the substitute check informs consumers of their rights to expedited recrediting of an amount charged *if* there is a disputed item and the original or substituted copy is necessary to prove the validity of the charge on the account. Under this new law, the validity of a charge becomes an issue when a consumer is charged twice for a check, the substitute check is illegible, or the original check was not properly copied during the imaging process.

Fraud examiners are concerned that Check 21 will significantly reduce the available physical evidence that is traditionally obtained in check and bank fraud cases because the physical checks will no longer be available. Although it is true that handwriting experts will be unable to verify the authenticity of these new "substitute checks," the majority of check and bank fraud cases no longer use such testimony due to the fact that most forged checks contain the copied and pasted signature of the account holder. Furthermore, Check 21 places the risk of loss associated with substitute checks on the reconverting bank that first transferred, presented, or returned the substitute check. Although the reconverting banks can allocate such loss among themselves, they may remain liable under warranty claim, indemnity, or recrediting claims.

In the upcoming years, we should be experiencing enormous change in the way checks are deposited and collected. With luck, Check 21 may allow for expedited funds availability as well as an efficient means of countering counterfeit and altered checks.

TRACING CHECKS

Tracing checks is facilitated by the use of bank identification symbols. Fraud examiners do not have to understand the internal bookkeeping procedures used by banks. However, the concept of bank identification symbols is of interest. All checks printed for banking institutions contain an ABA transmit number. These numbers represent an identification code developed by the American Bankers Association. The ABA transit number enables a check to be routed to the bank of origin. In the process of routing, a trail is left.

MICR (MAGNETIC INK CHARACTER RECOGNITION)

MICR is a machine language and is a check design standard to which all banks must conform. Numeric information is printed in magnetic ink on the bottom of bank checks and other documents. This coding is electronically scanned by computers that convert the magnetic ink notations into electronic impulses readable by a computer. MICR information is printed in groupings called fields. The first field on the left on bank checks is the Federal Reserve check routing code and the next is the ABA transit number. These numbers also appear in the upper right corner of the check.

The account number field shows the drawer's assigned account number at the bank. When the check is processed through the bank, an additional field is added on the right for the amount of the check. The dollar amount of the check always should equal the encoded MICR amount. These two figures should be compared to make sure that the subject did not alter the returned check. All checks, drafts, and similar items that are not encoded with magnetic ink cannot be cleared through the Federal Reserve system without special handling.

PREFIX NUMBERS OF CITIES IN NUMERICAL ORDER

When the ABA established the city and state prefix numbering system, it did so by the geographical location of the reserve cities in existence at the time. The prefix numbers identify city and state documents. For example, numbers 1 through 49, as seen on the following page, were given to the most populated reserve cities and major banking centers at the time. The rest of the numbers, 50 through 99 were assigned to the states from East to West. The principal numbers 50, 60, 70, 80 and 90 were given to the main collecting financial centers (New York, Pennsylvania, Illinois, Missouri and California). The numbers before and after each principal number were generally designated to nearby states.

PREFIX NUMBERS OF CITIES AND STATES

1-49	Reserve Cities
50-99	States
50-58	Eastern States
59	Alaska, American Samoa, Guam, Hawaii, Puerto Rico and the Virgin Islands
60-69	Southeastern States
70-79	Central States
80-88	Southwestern States
90-99	Western States

RESERVE CITY, MAJOR BANKING CENTER & STATE PREFIX NUMBERS

1 New York, NY	34 Tacoma, WA	68 Virginia
2 Chicago, IL	35 Houston, TX	69 West Virginia
3 Philadelphia, PA	36 St. Joseph, MO	70 Illinois
4 St. Louis, MO	37 Fort Worth, TX	71 Indiana
5 Boston, MA	38 Savannah, GA	72 Iowa
6 Cleveland, OH	39 Oklahoma City, OK	73 Kentucky
7 Baltimore, MD	40 Wichita, KS	74 Michigan
8 Pittsburgh, PA	41 Sioux City, IA	75 Minnesota
9 Detroit, MI	43 Lincoln, NE	76 Nebraska
10 Buffalo, NY	44 Topeka, KS	77 North Dakota
11 San Francisco, CA	45 Dubuque, IA	78 South Dakota
12 Milwaukee, WI	46 Galveston, TX	79 Wisconsin
13 Cincinnati, OH	47 Cedar Rapids, IA	80 Missouri
14 New Orleans, LA	48 Waco, TX	81 Arkansas
15 Washington, DC	49 Muskosgee, OK	82 Colorado
16 Los Angeles, CA	50 New York	83 Kansas
17 Minneapolis, MN	51 Connecticut	84 Louisiana
18 Kansas City, MO	52 Maine	85 Mississippi
19 Seattle, WA	53 Massachusetts	86 Oklahoma
20 Indianapolis, IN	54 New Hampshire	87 Tennessee
21 Louisville, KY	55 New Jersey	88 Texas
22 St. Paul, MN	56 Ohio	89 ---
23 Denver, CO	57 Rhode Island	90 California
24 Portland, OR	58 Vermont	91 Arizona
25 Columbus, OH	59 AL, AS, GU, HI, PR, VI[3]	92 Idaho
26 Memphis, TN	60 Pennsylvania	93 Montana
27 Omaha, NE	61 Alabama	94 Nevada
28 Spokane, WA	62 Delaware	95 New Mexico
29 Albany, NY	63 Florida	96 Oregon
30 San Antonio, TX	64 Georgia	97 Utah
31 Salt Lake City, UT	65 Maryland	98 Washington
32 Dallas, TX	66 North Carolina	99 Wyoming

---

[3] AL: Alaska; AS: American Samoa; GU: Guam; HI: Hawaii; PR: Puerto Rico; VI: Virgin Islands

All banks in an area served by a Federal Reserve bank or branch carry the routing symbol of the Federal Reserve bank or branch. The Federal Reserve routing symbol (FRRS) encompasses the first four digits of the nine-digit routing number. This routing symbol identifies where Federal Reserve bank is located. The first two numbers of the FRRS designate the Federal Reserve District in which the bank is located (as shown below). The 12 Federal Reserve Districts and numbers are as follows:

- 01 - Boston, MA
- 02 - New York, NY
- 03 - Philidelphia, PA
- 04 - Cleveland, OH
- 05 - Richmond, VA
- 06 - Atlanta, GA
- 07 - Chicago, IL
- 08 - St. Louis, MO
- 09 - Minneapolis, MN
- 10 - Kansas City, KS
- 11 - Dallas, TX
- 12 - San Franscisco, CA

The next two numbers designate the specific bank location of the Federal Reserve branch. A thrift institution is designated when 2 is added to the first digit of the FRRS. For example, if there is a thrift institution in the first district (Boston) the designation would be "21." If the thrift institution is in a district that has a double digit, such as San Franscisco, the designation becomes "32." The next four numbers of the routing number sequence are always unique to the financial institution; and the last number of the 9 digit routing number is a digit derived from an algorithmic calculation.

Deposit Tickets

The deposit ticket is the principal source document for crediting the customer's account. Deposits are first recorded on the deposit ticket or slip that usually segregates currency, coins, and checks. The checks are listed separately. In many localities the depositor writes the ABA number or the name of the maker of the check on the deposit ticket. Either of these might help to identify the source of the check. In other localities the bank writes the ABA number on the deposit ticket, and in some banks no identifying data is entered on the deposit ticket. Regardless of the detail contained on a deposit ticket, bank recordkeeping systems allow deposits to be identified and traced to their sources.

In working with deposit tickets, the fraud examiner must remember that sometimes the depositor "splits" the deposit, that is, only part of the checks presented are actually deposited. In these instances, the customer either receives cash or requests that part of the proceeds be applied to a note or interest due the bank. In some instances, it might be important to determine the total amount of cash and checks presented for deposit before deductions. When this is the case, the fraud examiner should inquire from the bank how split deposits are handled.

Deposit items can be broken down into two types: *on-us items* and *clearinghouse items*.

ON-US ITEMS

The bank should be able to trace the source of any *on-us items*. The source might be loan proceeds, certificates of deposit, wire transfers, bank checks, or checks from other deposits at that bank. If the deposit is the proceeds from a loan, obtain and analyze the loan file. Examination of the loan file is discussed later in this section. If the deposit came from a wire transfer, trace the wire transfer to the originating bank to see where the funds for the wire transfer originated. This search could lead to other accounts, other witnesses, co-conspirators, or offshore transactions.

Bank checks (such as cashier's checks and money orders) could be an indication of "smurfing" operations (structured currency transactions). Look for large numbers of cashier's checks in even amounts deposited on a regular basis. Cashier's checks often lead to the discovery of hidden assets. Such checks often are used to distribute the proceeds of loans, the sale of securities, real estate closing proceeds, and similar items.

CLEARINGHOUSE ITEMS

Clearinghouse items include those items which are sent to a local clearinghouse for processing as well as those which are sent to out-of-town banks such as Federal Reserve Banks. Since tracking down these items will involve obtaining records from third-party banks, it might be more time consuming and probably will require legal process.

To determine whether an item is an on-us item or a clearinghouse item, first look to see whether the bank on which the check was drawn is the same as the bank in which it was deposited. If the names are not the same, check the endorsements on the back of the check. If the item has a different bank's endorsement or a Federal Reserve Bank's endorsement, it is a clearinghouse item. The endorsement should contain the name of the processing bank or its transit number.

Wire Transfers

Like any other transactions, banks keep records of the wire transfers performed. The records will identify who sent the wire, where it was sent, the date, and the amount. If the transfer was to a bank in the United States, the bank should have a record of the account number of the account into which the funds were deposited. If the wire was sent offshore, however, tracing the transfer depends on the laws and policies of the country and the receiving institution.

Intrabank Transfers

Other departments within a bank can credit the depositor's account for funds collected, such as the proceeds of loans or items held by the bank for collection. Items held by the bank for collection are not always deposited to the customer's account but sometimes are remitted directly to the customer.

Savings Accounts

These are referred to as time deposits because sometimes they are not as readily available to the customer as deposits to a checking account. Funds in a savings account might be subject to a 30-day notice of withdrawal.

Certificates of Deposit (CDs)

CDs are funds left with a bank for a definite period of time, for example, two years, that draw a higher rate of interest than the ordinary savings account. When these are cashed early, Federal Reserve regulations require a penalty.

Bank Ledgers and Bank Statements

Each bank has a bookkeeping department that maintains customer accounts. The bookkeeping department sorts checks to prepare them for posting; posts checks to customers' accounts; posts deposits and other credits; takes care of special items, such as "stop payments"; and proves and balances general ledger totals for various types of accounts. How this work is performed depends on whether a manual or a computerized system is used. Different types of records are generated by the two systems. However, a customer's account can be reconstructed under either system.

Bank Ledger Cards—Manual System

Ledger cards are the basic records produced by any manual system. They show all checks, deposits, and other transactions affecting customers' accounts. Ledger cards are the customers' monthly statements. The bank keeps the ledger cards and second, or duplicate, copies of the customers' statements. Some banks microfilm these records as well as the checks returned to the depositors with the monthly statements.

Bank Statements—Computerized System

No historical ledger cards are produced in an automated system. In a computerized system, statements are produced periodically (generally monthly) for checking accounts. The bank has either microfilm or duplicates of all statements. It is easier to trace transactions and records with detailed statements showing all transactions. When only summary, or "bobtail," statements are available, all the transactions that make up the statement must be reconstructed.

Savings Account Statement

Under the manual system, most banks use ledger cards similar to those for checking accounts to maintain records of savings accounts. A few banks mail statements to depositors at stated intervals. In a computerized system, the procedure for reconstructing a savings account is similar to that for checking accounts. In some instances, copies of periodic statements are available to expedite the process. If not, the account must be reconstructed item by item.

Exchange instruments are vehicles by which the bank transfers funds. They are cashier's checks, bank drafts, traveler's checks, bank money orders, and certified checks. Bank exchange instruments often are purchased with currency; therefore, they may be good sources of information about a subject's currency transactions.

Cashier's Checks

These checks which are issued by the bank are called treasurer's checks when issued by a trust company. They frequently are an excellent lead to other bank accounts, stock, real property, and other assets. Because they can be held indefinitely, subjects sometimes purchase cashier's checks instead of keeping large amounts of currency on hand. In reconstructing a subject's transactions with cashier's checks, be sure that all checks are accounted for because subjects sometimes exchange previously purchased checks for new ones.

Bank checks such as cashier's checks can be extremely time consuming and expensive to locate unless you know the date and number of the check. However, if the subject has deposited a bank check into his account, or purchased a bank check using a check from his account, then copies of bank checks are much easier to obtain because the subject's account records will reveal the date and number of the bank check.

Bank Drafts

These are checks drawn by the issuing bank on its account with another bank. Often this other account is in the geographical area where the purchaser desires to make a payment. Bank drafts also can be used when a subject does not want to carry a large amount of cash.

Traveler's Checks

These are checks issued in predetermined amounts by the American Express Company and several large U.S. banks. Local banks purchase them from issuing companies of U.S. banks and then sell them to the public. Traveler's checks require two signatures of the purchaser, one when purchased and the other when cashed. Tracing of traveler's checks is done by serial number. The issuing company usually keeps records of traveler's checks sent to it by the selling bank. Traveler's checks do not expire.

The local bank that sold the checks might keep a copy of the sales order that lists the serial numbers. If the numbers are not available, the issuing bank might be able to supply the information if it is known when the checks were purchased. Canceled checks can be obtained from the American Express Company or from other issuing banks. A target can purchase large amounts of traveler's checks from one bank and place them in another to avoid arousing suspicion by depositing cash.

Bank Money Orders

These are similar to cashier's checks but usually are for small amounts. Like cashier's checks, money orders may be resorted to by subjects reluctant to use cash.

Certified Checks

These are customer's checks on which "certified" is written or stamped across the front by the bank. This certification is a guarantee that the bank will pay the amount of the check. Certified checks are liabilities of the bank and, when paid, are kept by the bank. These checks are immediately charged against the customer's account by debit memorandums. Some banks permit customers to retrieve the original checks by surrendering the debit memorandum.

Loans

Loan records can prove important information regarding a subject. In loan records, the collateral that secures them, and the results of (bank) credit investigations, a bank has a wealth of information. When a bank makes a commercial loan to an individual, it requires detailed asset and liability statements from the borrower. The loan file also might include the results of credit inquiries regarding paying habits, loan amounts, and present unpaid balances. A bank credit department generally maintains the following basic records:

- *The credit or loan file*—loan application, financial statement, and general economic history of the customer.
- *The liability ledger*—the customer's liability to the bank both at the present time and past times. These sheets also contain information such as the loan date, note number, amount of the loan, interest rate, due date, and payments.
- *The collateral file*—a complete description of the items pledged as security for loans. Records of such collateral can provide valuable information about a subject's assets.

Indications of unusual loans include loans in odd amounts or loans that were not deposited into the subject's bank account. Loans that show unusual repayments also should be traced. Lump-sum payments and odd-amount payments are unusual. Accelerated payments or large pay downs on the balance might indicate sudden wealth.

Loan records also might reveal collusion between the bank and the subject. For instance, if the records show that a loan repayment is long overdue or the loan has an extended rollover, collusion might exist. Also, loans made in contravention to the bank's normal loan or a loan that appears to be in excess of the individual's ability to repay suggests a "special relationship" between the bank and the subject.

Loan proceeds might be deposited into hidden accounts, or hidden accounts might be used for loan payments. Loans might be secured by hidden assets or co-signed by previously unknown cohorts. Alternatively, the subject might have taken out the loan for someone else. Tracing the ultimate disposition of the proceeds will uncover those leads.

Tracing the disposition of loan proceeds is similar to tracing deposit transactions. The proceeds could have been deposited within the bank into the subject's account or someone else's account, or they might be used to purchase a certificate of deposit. The funds might have been sent to the wire transfer department for transmittal to another bank. More commonly, the proceeds will be given to the customer in the form of a bank check. The bank should be able to trace the check to determine where it was deposited or cashed. The loan proceeds might have been used to finance an asset, the down payment for which came from illegal funds. Tracing the source of loan payments will provide some leads; for instance, the payments might be made from a previously unknown account. Payments made by a third-party might reveal a cohort or a kickback or bribe scheme.

The loan application should contain a financial statement, or its equivalent, on which the subject may identify other accounts and assets. The file might also contain tax returns, credit agency reports, and notes of interviews by the loan officer. The security for the loan, if any, might be a hidden asset.

Mortgage Loan Files
Mortgage loan files often contain the most detailed financial statements submitted by the subject. The loan file should identify the title company which handled the closing, the homeowner's insurance carrier, the closing attorney, and perhaps the real estate broker. The title company files often contain copies of the cashier's checks used for the down payment, which can identify new accounts.

The home owner's insurance policy might contain a rider that lists the home owner's valuable assets, such as jewelry or furs, perhaps with appraisals and purchase receipts. The closing attorney will have many of the same materials found in the title company files. The real estate broker might keep copies of personal checks used for deposits, and provide information about other real estate transactions by the subjects. Don't forget to look for accelerated or lump sum payments on the mortgage balance.

Check Credit Loans
Check credit is another loan service that more and more banks are offering. Under a check credit plan, the bank agrees to extend credit to a customer up to a maximum amount. If the

amount of the check is not in the customer's account, the resulting over-draft is set up as a loan. The bank then bills the customer for the loan. Another plan is a specialized checking account that is used only up to a predetermined amount under a loan agreement; the outstanding balance is treated as an installment loan by the bank. Copies of loan agreements and statements under both plans can be obtained from the bank files.

Credit Cards

Banks are doing increasing business in credit cards. Under bank credit card plans, the cardholder can charge purchases at stores, restaurants, and other places that agree to accept the charges. Under most plans, the cardholder can elect to pay the entire balance in one payment or to pay in installments under arrangements similar to a loan account. The records of importance to the economic crime investigator are the application for a card and the bank's copies of monthly statements sent to the cardholder. In some banks, copies of the individual charges also are available. The monthly statements and the individual charge documents listing the stores where the cardholder has made purchases can furnish valuable leads about the spending habits of the target. Most banks offering credit card plans are affiliated with a national system.

Bank Collection Department Records

The bank's collection department, which normally is involved in collecting amounts due on installment contracts and notes, can be used to collect personal checks (usually in large amounts and with special instructions), thus circumventing the normal record-keeping associated with checking accounts. Such a transaction will not be reflected on the target's regular checking account statements, but will appear in the collection department records. A copy of the check also will be microfilmed.

Safe-Deposit Boxes

Safe-deposit boxes are private vault space rented by banks to customers. Because state laws differ, the nature of the relationship varies between a bank and the safe-deposit box holders. Banks keep no record of safe-deposit box contents and rarely know what the boxes contain. The rental contract records identify the renters, the person or people who have access to the boxes, their signatures, and the dates of the original agreements and later renewals. They also might contain other identifying information, including the name of the initiating bank officer. The officer's name could be significant if the subject (who might have used an alias in renting the box) must be identified.

Records showing access to the boxes vary from bank to bank. They contain the signatures of the people entering the boxes and usually the dates and times of entry. The entry records are filed in box number order. The frequency of entry and the times and dates of entries might be significant and might correspond to the times and dates of deposits or withdrawals from other accounts or to the purchases and sales of securities, property, and in other situations.

Since the bank records will not show the contents of the box, the fraud examiner can request permission to inventory the box with the target present, carefully noting and describing the exact contents (for example, legal description on deeds, numbers of insurance policies, etc.).

Bank Secrecy Act Documents

Under the requirements of the Bank Secrecy Act, banks and other financial institutions are required to file Currency Transaction Reports, Suspicious Activity Reports, and other reports detailing large cash transactions or suspicious activity. (See the chapter on Money Laundering for a complete description of each report.) These reports will reflect the identity, address, and Social Security number of the person making the cash transaction, total amount, and certain other information. Some organizations are exempt from the filing requirement, including certain high volume cash businesses, government agencies, and payroll account holders.

Stock Brokerage Records

Many stock brokerage houses now offer the same type of services as banks: check writing privileges, credit cards, loans (against the value of securities held), as well as their normal securities business. All records pertaining to the subject should be requested; however, make sure that the request specifically includes the following:

- *Application*— when a customer opens an account, he typically will fill out an account application that will contain personal and financial data such as bank accounts.
- *Customer account cards*—this card is kept in the broker's personal files for reference. It will include all transactions conducted for the customer.
- *Signature card*—a signature card should be on file which will show all those authorized to conduct transactions on the account.
- *Securities receipts*—these receipts are issued to a customer when he or she delivers securities to the broker for sale.
- *Cash receipts*—these receipts are issued to a customer when he or she delivers currency to the broker.

- *Confirmation slips*—confirmation slips are issued to a customer to show the type of transaction (buy or sell) and the amount involved in the transaction.
- *Securities delivered receipt*—this receipt is signed by the customer when a securities purchase is delivered to the customer.
- *Brokerage account statement*—this statement usually is issued monthly and provides information on all transactions conducted during the reporting period. It lists all purchases and sales, the name of the security, the number of units, the amount per unit, the total amount of the transaction, the account balance, payments received from the customer, disbursements to the customer, and the securities which are held by the brokerage firm for the customer.

The examiner primarily is interested in the source of funds used to purchase securities or deposited to a cash account. The subject's monthly account statements, which are somewhat more complex than equivalent bank statements, reflect these transactions. They can be interpreted with the help of explanatory material on the statement or with the assistance of an employee of the firm. Receipts for stock purchase and deposit receipts should reflect whether the payment was in currency or check and the ABA code of the bank on which the check was drawn. Brokerage checks issued to the subject from stock sale proceeds also should be examined, as these might be deposited directly to a new account or endorsed over and paid directly to third parties for the purchase of assets.

Tax Returns and Related Documents

Personal tax returns, if available, might provide indirect evidence of illicit payments, such as profits or losses from previously undisclosed business ventures, or interest and dividends on hidden CDs and bank accounts. The returns also might reveal deductions and expenses, such as real estate taxes, that can lead to previously unknown funds or assets. Commercial bribes often are reported as consulting fees or other miscellaneous income. The target's accountant and tax preparer also should be interviewed, and their files and work papers subpoenaed, if possible.

Indirect Methods of Tracing Financial Transactions

A subject's income can be established by the direct or indirect approach. The direct approach, or the specific-items method of proving income, relies upon specific transactions, such as sales or expenses, to determine income. The indirect approach relies upon circumstantial proof of income using such methods as net worth, source and application of funds, and bank deposits.

Almost all individuals and business entities determine income by the specific-items or specific-transactions method. Most entities engaged in legitimate pursuits maintain books and records in which they record transactions as they occur, and their income computations are based upon the total transactions during a given period. In fraud examinations, income usually can be established more readily by the direct approach; for this reason, it should be used whenever possible.

In many fraud schemes, however, a subject's books and records are not made available to the examiner. Therefore, an indirect approach must be taken using the net worth, source and application of funds, or bank deposit methods. Although these methods are circumstantial proof, courts have approved their use in civil and criminal cases on the theory that proof of a subject's unexplained funds or property might establish a prima facie understatement of income.

Elements of Financial Examination Techniques

To examine company books and records for fraud, the fraud examiner must know and understand the environment where the entity operates, the entity's accounting system (the types of schemes indicative to the entity and the controls that are designed to prevent fraud schemes), basic concealment methods, and various detection techniques.

The Environment

It is critical to understand the business (or government) environment where the entity operates. To understand the environment, you must have a firm grasp of the nature of the business, the competition, the market share, the financing structure, the vendors (suppliers), major customers, the methods of receipts (i.e., cash or on account) and disbursements, the procurement methods (i.e., whether goods and services are obtained through a bidding process or not), the general economic climate, and the personnel pool available to the entity. It is through the understanding of the entity as an operating enterprise that you can assess the risks associated with the particular operations. The risks and peculiarities of the entity will help shape the nature of potential fraud schemes which can be perpetrated by the entity's employees.

The Accounting System

Understanding the basic accounting system and its integration with the operations of the business is important. The basic accounting system, including the system of internal controls, is the key element in providing evidence of past, present, and future internal fraud. Internal fraud that is on-book will appear within the entity's financial records. The audit trail might be obscure, but it will exist nonetheless. If the internal fraud is off-book, then other evidence might appear which, with diligent fraud examination techniques, might also be uncovered.

All internal fraud has an impact on the bottom line. However, fraud in small amounts will be harder to detect because of its immaterial amount relative to the financial statements as a whole. If an internal fraud scheme is large enough, it will have an effect on the entity's financial statements.

Various Detection Techniques

Though there are many fraud detection methods, whatever method is employed will usually require the examination of source documents. Many times, these source documents provide the evidence necessary to prove fraud in a court of law. Additionally, in many cases, the source documents will help establish the intent of the fraud offenders.

Individual or groups of documents can be examined in several ways to detect possible fraud. Because most internal fraud is continuous in nature, groups of documents can be analyzed for exceptions and trends. Many times a large population must be sampled to determine, with statistical validity, if documents have been altered. Statistical sampling quantifies the risk of arriving at an incorrect conclusion; it is generally necessary with large populations.

EXAMPLE

Fraud examiners want to examine sales invoices for proper approvals in a company with $2 billion in annual sales. The average sales invoice is $15,000. By selecting a valid statistical sample of sales, the examiners can project the effectiveness of internal controls regarding the approval of the sales invoices, assuming proper interpretation of test results. If deficiencies exist in the controls, then those results should become apparent in the test results.

Statistical Sampling

If an anomaly is found in the financial statements and transactions and further investigation is desired, it might be appropriate to pull a statistical sample. By using statistical sampling, the examiner can look at fewer transactions rather than the entire population.

There are two basic risks associated with statistical sampling: sampling risk and nonsampling risk. *Sampling risk* is the probability that the sample is not representative of the population; *nonsampling risk* is the possibility of making the wrong decision. Nonsampling risk cannot be quantified. However, fraud examiners can control it through adequate planning and supervision of audit engagements.

When using statistical sampling, you must draw a random sample. That is, each member of the population must have an equal chance of being selected. There are two primary types of statistical sampling: attribute and discovery.

SAMPLING FOR ATTRIBUTES

Sampling for attributes is used by auditors or fraud examiners looking for a deviation occurrence rate. (*Deviations, errors,* and *exceptions* are synonyms.) When performing this type of sampling, you are looking for the presence or absence of a defined condition.

EXAMPLE

For each sales invoice in the sample, is there a corresponding shipping order? The answer to the question can only be either "yes" or "no." If the control condition is that each sales invoice is not recorded until there has been a shipping order attached, then any "no" response for a booked sale would represent an error.

DISCOVERY SAMPLING

This is the best type of sampling for auditing for fraud, because it is sampling until one occurrence is found. Discovery sampling deals with the probability of discovering at least one error in a given sample size if the population error is a certain percentage. This type of sampling is directed toward a specific objective, such as:

"If I believe some kind of error or irregularity might exist in the records, what sample size will I have to audit to have assurance of finding at least one example?"

EXAMPLE

Discovery sampling is best used when looking for things such as forged checks, or intercompany sales which have been improperly classified as sales to outsiders.

RANDOM SAMPLES

When using the discovery sampling technique, the selection of samples should be done *randomly*. In order for a sample to be random, each and every member of the population must have an equal opportunity of being selected.

Items in the population can be numbered and selected by reference to a random number table. Or, if the items in the population already have numbers (such as check numbers or invoice numbers) then a random sample can be selected by using a random number generator from a computer software program. In order to select a random sample, (1) identify a number for every item in the population, (2) correspond the random numbers with each item in the population, (3) select the route through the random number table, and (4) select the sample.

Additionally, make sure that you consistently follow the pattern picked for corresponding random numbers to items in the population, and that you document the random number selection process in the event the sample needs rechecking or additional sample items need to be selected for testing. If the sample is selected randomly and the sample is large enough, then the sample should represent the population.

DOCUMENTS

Often, fraud will be concealed in questionable documents. Missing or altered documents are some of the principal indicators of fraud, and such occurrences should be thoroughly investigated. Certain documents are a natural part of the accounting system. However, when a pattern of these documents occurs, or an unusual quantity of these documents are noted, further examination might be warranted.

The common-sense test should be applied to any document that appears to have questionable features under the circumstances, such as amounts too high or too low; odd names, times, places; identical names and addresses. Fraud often can involve questionable journal entries in the records, such as inappropriate charges to expense accounts or inventory. For example, large journal entries in the inventory accounts near year-end might point to a cover-up of inventory theft.

An overabundant number of voids might mean that a fraudster is voiding legitimate sales and pocketing the proceeds. Excessive credit memos also might signal the reversal of legitimate sales and the diversion of cash. Too many late charges might indicate that an account receivable is delinquent because it is a fictitious account and, therefore, will never be paid. Stale items on any reconciliation bear watching. For example, stale outstanding checks could be a concealment for embezzlement losses or diverted cash. Original documents, such as invoices, should be used to authorize transactions because photocopied or duplicate documents can be subject to manipulation and alteration.

Net Worth Methods

Examining for fraud not only involves the examination of the entity's books and records; it might also entail the estimation of the fraud suspect's change in net worth or expenditures. If fraud is suspected, then using either of the net worth methods might help in establishing evidence of a fraud.

The net worth method (or comparative net worth analysis) is used to prove illicit income circumstantially, by showing that a person's assets or expenditures for a given period exceed that which can be accounted for from known or admitted sources of income. The net worth method is a reliable method for estimating a person's ill-gotten gains. The method is used extensively by the Internal Revenue Service, especially in drug and money laundering cases.

The net worth method relies on the familiar balance sheet format readily recognizable in the business world and presents a complete financial picture of a subject. It is based on the theory that increases or decreases in a person's net worth during a period, adjusted for living expenses, allow a determination of income.

Net worth can be defined as the difference between assets and liabilities at a particular point in time. By comparing the subject's net worth at the beginning and end of a period, usually a calendar year, the economic crime investigator can determine the increase or decrease in net worth. Adjustments are then made for living expenses to arrive at income. Income includes receipts derived from all sources. Thus, by subtracting funds from known sources (salary, wages, interest, or dividends, for example), funds from unknown or illegal sources can be calculated.

The courts approved using the net worth method in the leading Supreme Court case of *Holland v. United States*, 348 U.S. 121 (1954), along with the three companion cases, Smith v. United States, 348 U.S. 147 (1954); Friedberg v. United States, 348 142 (1954); and United States v. Calderon, 348 U.S. 160 (1954). These cases outlined broad principles to govern the trial and review of cases based upon the net worth method of proving income.

The net worth method often is used when several of the subject's assets and/or liabilities have changed during the period under examination and when the target's financial records are not available.

An individual's assets, liabilities, and living expenses can be determined from a variety of sources, such as:
- The subject
- Informants or sources
- Real estate records
- Judgment and lien records
- Bankruptcy records
- State motor vehicle records
- Loan applications
- Financial statements
- Accountant's work papers
- Lawsuits and depositions
- Surveillance
- Credit card applications or statements
- Tax returns
- Insurance records
- Child support and divorce records
- Employment applications and salary checks
- Companions or associates
- Canceled checks and deposited items

The question might arise regarding why items that do not change should be included in the net worth statement, particularly since they have no bearing on the final result. The answer is that a net worth statement gives "a complete financial picture" of the subject, and therefore should be as complete as possible so that the target will not be able to contest it on the ground that items were omitted. Additionally, the net worth statement can be the foundation for examination of the subject, and a complete statement will prove extremely valuable at that time.

There are two basic methods of net worth computation: The *asset method* and the *expenditures*, or *sources and applications of funds method*. They are discussed in detail herein.

The *asset method* should be used when the subject has invested illegal funds to accumulate wealth and acquire assets, causing net worth (value of assets over liabilities) to increase from year to year. The *expenditures method* is best used when the subject spends illicit income on consumables (travel, entertainment) that would not cause an increase in net worth.

Begin both methods by assembling the financial profile. Identify all major assets and liabilities, sources of income and major expenses during the relevant period. The increase, if any, in the subject's net worth or the level of expenditures is then compared to the legitimate funds available. Unaccounted funds might be inferred to come from illicit or hidden sources.

The Financial/Behavioral Profile

The first step is to prepare the *Financial/Behavioral Profile* of the suspect. This is essentially a financial statement with certain modifications and additions which shows what the defendant owns, owes, earns, and spends at any given point, or over a period of time. The profile might yield direct evidence of illegal income or hidden assets, or circumstantial evidence thereof, by showing that the suspect's expenditures exceeded known sources of income.

The financial profile will identify most illicit funds which are deposited to accounts or expended in significant amounts. It will not catch relatively small currency transactions, particularly if they were for concealed activities, consumables, or for unusual one-time expenses such as medical bills.

Determine the target's assets, liabilities, income and expenses from the following sources:
- Interviews
- The target
- Associates
- Financial sources (accountant, banker) documents
- Bank account records
- Mortgage and loan files
- Credit card records
- Tax returns
- Public records
- Business filings
- Real estate filings
- Court records

STEP NO. 1

Identify all significant assets held by the suspect. An asset is cash (on hand) or anything else of value that can be converted into cash.

Cash on hand is coin and currency (bills, Federal Reserve notes, "greenbacks") in the subject's possession (on the subject's person, in the subject's residence or other place in a nominee's hands, or in a safe-deposit box). It does not include money in any account with a financial institution. When using the net worth method, the item sometimes most difficult to prove is the cash on hand, which usually is claimed by defendants to be of an amount sufficient to account for all or part of the unknown sources of income. To establish a firm starting net worth, it must be shown that the target had no large cash sums for which he was not given credit. This usually is done by offering evidence that negates the existence of a cash hoard. Such evidence might include:

- Written or oral admissions of the subject concerning net worth (a signed net worth statement or an oral statement as to cash on hand)
- Low earnings in pre-examination years, as shown by records of former employers and/or tax returns filed by subject
- Net worth, as established by books and records of the subject
- Financial statement presented for credit or other purposes at a time before or during the period under examination (banks, loan companies, and bonding companies are some of the better sources from which to obtain this type of document)
- Bankruptcy before examination periods
- Prior indebtedness, compromise of overdue debts, and avoidance of bankruptcy
- Installment buying
- History of low earnings and expenditures, and checks returned for insufficient funds (a financial history covering members of the subject's family also might be helpful)
- Loss of furniture and business because of financial reasons
- Receipt of some type of public assistance

STEP NO. 2

Identify all significant liabilities. A liability is an obligation (debt) arising from an oral or written promise to pay.

STEP NO. 3

Identify all income sources during the relevant time period. Income includes money or other things of value received in exchange for services or goods. Income is never included as an asset. Loan proceeds are not included as income but are treated as an asset, which is offset by a corresponding liability.

STEP NO. 4

Identify all significant expenses incurred during the relevant period. An expense is any payment for consumables, for personal or business reasons, over the relevant time period. Expenses are not included as liabilities.

STEP NO. 5

Analyze the information you have collected by using the following charts:

The Financial Profile

TYPICAL ASSETS		For each significant asset determine:
Residence	Jewelry	-When was it acquired and from whom?
Real Estate	Clothing	- How much did it cost?
Bank accounts	Collectibles	- How was it paid for (currency, check, cashier's check)?
Stocks and bonds	Pensions Home	- What source of funds was used to acquire it?
Automobiles	Furnishings	- What documentation exists for the purchase and where is it?
Insurance	Boats	
Cash on hand		

TYPICAL LIABILITIES	For each significant liability, determine:
Mortgage(s)	-What was the original amount of the liability?
Other loans	-What is the present balance due?
Lines of credit	-When was the liability incurred?
Credit cards	-What was the purpose for the loan or debt?
Installment purchases	-How were the proceeds used and where were they deposited?
Accounts payable	
Taxes and other bills	-What security (collateral), if any, was given for the debt?
Alimony and child support	
	-What documentation exists for the transaction and where is it?
	-Was the debt written off as a bad loan for tax purposes?
	-Who was the creditor or lender?

TYPICAL SOURCES OF FUNDS		For each source of funds, determine:
Salary Gifts Rental income Dividends Interest Sale of assets	Insurance proceeds Commissions and fees Awards Inheritances Disability payments	-What was the total amount during a given period? -What was the source? -How was it paid for (currency, check, other means)? -When were the funds received? -Where was it deposited? -How was it spent? -What documentation exists (e.g., W-2 or 1099 forms) and where is it?

TYPICAL EXPENDITURES		For each major expenditure item, determine:
Rent and mortgage Health costs Interest on loans Credit cards Car payments Travel	Clothing Utilities Food Insurance	-What was the total amount spent? -How was it paid for? -Where were the funds obtained to pay the expense? -What documentation exists and where is it? -When was the payment made?

The Behavioral Profile

The financial profile might give inaccurate or false negative readings unless such activities are identified. This is done through preparation of the Behavioral Profile. The Behavioral Profile might also provide evidence of a possible motive of the crime, such as large debts, as well as additional evidence of illicit funds. For example, if the suspect spent significant amounts of cash, and had no corresponding cash withdrawals from his disclosed bank accounts, or no admitted sources of cash income, he or she *must have* other undisclosed sources of income.

Using the Financial/Behavioral Profile as a guide, request an interview with the suspect. Pin down the suspect's income, assets, and accounts. Otherwise, the subject might invent excuses or prepare false testimony or documentation to account for the alleged unexplained income.

Net Worth Analysis

Any recipient of funds, whether honest or suspect, has only four ways of disposing of income: save it, buy assets, pay off debts, or spend it.

Net worth analysis begins with the completion of a suspect's financial profile. Through identification of the suspect's assets, liabilities, income, and expenses, a net worth statement can be determined. Once completed, changes in the suspect's net worth can be compared to his known income, and differences can be inferred to be from unknown sources.

COMPARATIVE NET WORTH - ASSET METHOD FORMULA

	Assets
−	Liabilities
=	Net Worth
−	prior year's net worth
=	Net Worth increase
+	living expenses
=	Income (or Expenditures)
−	funds from known sources
=	Funds from Unknown Sources

In computing the Comparative Net Worth, these issues should be considered:
- All assets should be valued at cost—not fair market value. Subsequent appreciation or depreciation of assets is ignored.
- The amount of funds available to the subject from legitimate sources should be estimated or computed generously. The amount of the subject's expenditures, particularly hard-to-document living costs, such as food and entertainment, should be estimated conservatively to give the subject the benefit of any doubt. In attempting to estimate personal living expenses, you should consult the U.S. Bureau of Labor Statistics. This agency publishes an annual table that details personal living expenses such as utilities, food, gas, etc.
- Always attempt to interview the subject to identify all alleged sources of funds and to negate defenses that he or she might raise later.

COMPUTING THE COMPARATIVE NET WORTH - ASSET METHOD
- Establish the starting point, generally the year before the target's illegal activities begin. This will be referred to as "Year One" in the following computations.

- Compute the target's net worth at the end of Year One. Identify all assets held by the subject, valued at cost, including assets acquired earlier, and the amount of current liabilities.

The difference between the value of the assets and the liabilities is the target's net worth at Year One, or "Opening Net Worth."

EXAMPLE

Year One:

Assets at Cost		Liabilities	
Residence	$100,00	Mortgage balance	$ 90,000
Stocks & bonds	30,000	Automobile loan	
Automobile	20,000	balance	10,000
TOTAL	$150,000	TOTAL	$100,000

Assets	$150,000
Liabilities	-100,000
Net Worth	$50,000

Compute the target's net worth for year two, using the same method:

EXAMPLE

Year Two:

Assets at Cost		Liabilities	
Residence	$100,000	Mortgage balance	$ 50,000
Stocks & bonds	30,000		
Automobile	20,000	Automobile loan	
C.D.	50,000	balance	0
TOTAL	$200,000	TOTAL	$ 50,000

Assets	$200,000
Liabilities	- 50,000
Net Worth	$150,000

Note that in the example the target's net worth increased by $100,000 during year two. To determine the source of such increase, determine the target's known income, during year two, and subtract known expenses for year two.

EXAMPLE
Year Two:

Income		Expenses	
Salary	$30,000	Mortgage Interest Payments	$20,000
Commissions	20,000	Living Expenses	10,000
TOTAL	$50,000	TOTAL	$ 30,000

The difference between the target's income and expenses equals the increase (or decrease) in net worth from year one to year two which can be attributed to known sources. Here it is $20,000. Subtract the increase in net worth from known sources from the total increase in net worth to determine the amount from unknown sources.

EXAMPLE

Total Increase in Net Worth	$ 100,000
Increase attributed to Known Sources	<20,000>
Dollars From Unknown Sources	$ 80,000

Repeat the above steps for subsequent years as necessary.

EXPENDITURES METHOD

With the expenditures method, a comparison is made between the suspect's known expenditures and known sources of funds during a given period of time. Any excess expenditures must be the result of income from unknown sources. It is closely related to the net worth analysis, accounting variations of the same principle.

EXPENDITURES (COMPARATIVE NET WORTH) FORMULA

	Expenditures (Application of Funds)
−	Known Source of Funds
=	*Funds from Unknown Sources*

Establish the subject's known expenditures for the relevant year. "Expenditures" include the use or application of funds for any purpose, including deposits to bank accounts, purchase of major assets, travel and entertainment expenses, and payment of loan and credit card debts.

Identify all sources of funds available to the subject, including loans and gifts, as well as cash on hand from previous years. The difference between the amount of the subject's expenditures and known income is the amount attributed to unknown sources.

EXAMPLE

Subject	Year One	Year Two
Application of Funds:		
Increase in bank balance	$ 2,000	$10,000
Down payment on residence	——	10,000
Purchase of automobile	10,000	——
Mortgage payments	8,000	20,000
Credit card payments	5,000	10,000
Other expenses	15,000	30,000
TOTAL	**$ 40,000**	**$80,000**
Less: Known Sources of Funds		
Cash on hand	1,000	
Salary	30,000	38,000
Interest earned on savings Account	1,000	2,000
Loan proceeds	8,000	
TOTAL	**$40,000**	**$40,000**
Funds from Unknown or Illegal Sources	**0**	**$40,000**

The following example demonstrates how a net worth analysis assisted prosecutors in their amended complaint against a fraud suspect.

EXAMPLE

R. Peery, age 40, the executive director of a five-state commission planning a low-level radioactive waste dump was charged with two new charges of felony theft. Peery also was charged with one federal count of wire fraud.

Peery was accused of wiring $115,000 to a personal account in Georgia, and prosecutors said they suspected him of taking $600,000. He was also charged with two counts of using commission funds in Nebraska to buy cars, a 1990 BMW valued at $67,000 and a 1991 BMW valued at $92,000.

Peery was paid $52,000 annually. He lived in a house valued at $305,000 and at the time of his arrest had six luxury cars, including Jaguars, Mercedes-Benzes and BMW's.

BANK DEPOSITS METHOD

The bank deposits method is a means to prove unknown sources of funds by indirect or circumstantial evidence. Similar to the other indirect approaches, the bank deposits method computes income by showing what happened to a subject's funds. It is based on the theory that if a subject receives money, only two things can be done with it—it can be deposited or it can be spent. By this method, income is proved through an analysis of bank deposits, cancelled checks, and the subject's currency transactions. Adjustments for nonincome items are made to arrive at income. A basic formula for the bank deposits method is

	Total Deposits to all accounts
−	Transfer and redeposits
=	Net deposits to all accounts
+	Cash expenditures
=	Total receipts from all sources
−	Funds from known sources
=	Funds from unknown or illegal sources

The bank deposits method is recommended as a primary method of proof when most of the subject's income is deposited and the subject's books and records are unavailable, withheld, incomplete, or maintained on a cash basis. Use of the bank deposits method is not limited to these circumstances, however. Even though the target's books and records might appear to be complete and accurate, the method still can be used and there is no requirement to disprove the accuracy of the books and records.

The basic sources of information for the bank deposits computation are interviews, analyses of the books and records, and analyses of the bank accounts. A thorough interview will determine the subject's expenditures by cash and checks, identify all bank accounts, and determine all loans and other receipts.

TOTAL DEPOSITS

Total deposits consist not only of amounts deposited to all bank accounts maintained or controlled by the target but also deposits made to accounts in savings and loan companies, investment trusts, brokerage houses, and credit unions. Total deposits also include the accumulation (increase) of cash on hand. Because some subjects have bank accounts in fictitious names or under special titles, such as "Special Account No. 1," "Trustee Account," or "Trading Account," the investigator should look for this type of account during the investigation. If a subject lists checks on a deposit ticket and deducts an amount paid to him in cash (split deposit), only the net amount of the deposit should be used in computing total deposits.

Additional items that must be included in deposits are property and notes that the subject received in payment for services. The accepted practice is to consider these items as depositories into which funds have been placed for future use.

NET DEPOSITS

All transfers or exchanges between bank accounts as well as funds that are redeposited are nonincome items and are subtracted from total deposits to yield net deposits. Failure to eliminate these items would result in an overstatement of income.

CASH EXPENDITURES

Cash expenditures consist of the total outlay of funds less net bank disbursements. The total outlay of funds includes all payments made by cash or check. There is no need to determine which part was paid by cash and which part by check. Total outlays include but are not limited to:

- Purchase of capital assets to investments (determined from settlement sheets, invoices, statements, and the like)
- Loan repayments (determined from loan ledgers of banks or other creditors)
- Living expenses (can be determined from the same sources presented in the net worth and expenditures sections)
- Purchases, business expenses (less noncash items, such as depreciation), rental expenses, and the like

Net bank disbursements can be determined by the following formula:

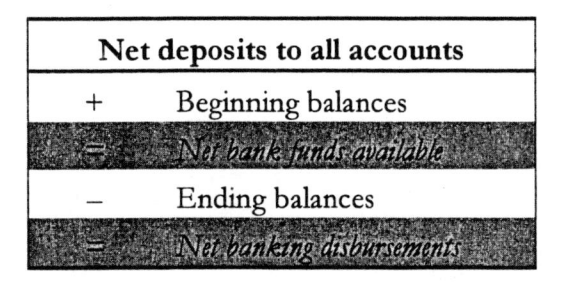

	Net deposits to all accounts
+	Beginning balances
=	Net bank funds available
−	Ending balances
=	Net banking disbursements

Funds from known sources include but are not limited to salaries, business profits, insurance proceeds, gifts received, loans, and inheritances. Funds from known sources are subtracted from total receipts (or income) to arrive at funds from unknown or illegal sources.

REBUTTING DEFENSES TO THE COMPARATIVE NET WORTH ANALYSIS

Circumstantial evidence of excess income often is met with the defense that the extra funds came from cash accumulated earlier or other legitimate sources, such as loans from relatives. To rebut these defenses, the fraud examiner must pin down the amount of cash on hand at the beginning of the relevant period (through, for example, amounts listed on financial statements or claimed in interviews), and do the following:

- Obtain a financial history of the target and spouse, through interviews and other means, showing dates and places of employment, salary and bonuses, and any other related income.
- Determine whether the spouse had any separate source of funds that were used to purchase jointly held assets or deposited in joint accounts. If so, the spouse must be included in the financial profile calculations.
- Claims of a prior substantial cash hoard might be rebutted by showing that the target lived penuriously, borrowed money, made installment purchases, incurred large debts, was delinquent on accounts, had a poor credit rating, or filed for bankruptcy. Claims that cash came from family or other private loans might be rebutted by showing that the alleged lender was incapable of generating the amounts supposedly lent, the absence of any documentation reflecting the source of the alleged loan (no bank account withdrawals), and the absence of other sources of funds available to the lender.

The net worth analysis—if records can be obtained—is a significant tool in documenting ill-gotten gains. With this basis, the following part covers the major schemes used to commit fraud against companies and government agencies.

Locating Hidden Assets

Common Asset Hiding Techniques

In addition to opening hidden bank accounts or purchasing real estate through a "straw" or front, a target might attempt to preserve his assets by transferring them to other parties or to accounts that might escape detection.

Transfer to Family Members or Parties Under Their Control

The most common means of hiding assets, particularly real estate and business interests, is to transfer the asset into the hands of another party that will allow the target to maintain control. In many cases, the target will transfer the asset to the spouse (or another member of the spouse's family), and husbands might make the transfer in his wife's maiden name.

Such transfers can be identified through a search of voter registration, marriage records, and probate in the spouse's maiden name. Transfers to family members can be detected by comparing the target's previous financial statement with the newest one. Those assets appearing on the oldest statement but not appearing on the most recent statement should be examined closely to determine the nature of the transaction, the purchaser's identity, and the consideration for the sale.

Children's or Family Trust

The defendant in a financial case might seek to protect assets by transferring them to a children's or family trust from a personal estate. These assets would then be protected from judgment or bankruptcy proceedings in a court of law. If the transfer was made to defeat creditors, however, it can be set aside by the court.

Home Mortgage Pay-Down

In many cases, subjects seek to hide their assets from seizure by prepaying a significant portion of their home mortgage. This might allow the subject to shelter his assets in a homestead exemption (as allowed in Texas, Florida and other states) that will survive bankruptcy or other claims against them. By documenting the mortgage prepayment, the fraud examiner can often show undisclosed or hidden income from outside sources.

EXAMPLE
A cashier's check for $96,000 was found to have been used as a prepayment to a home mortgage. By obtaining the front and back of the cashier's check, fraud examiners were able to locate another bank account of the defendant.

Insurance Policies

Under the terms of a whole life or universal life insurance policy, the borrower may make additional payments that accrue at a high interest rate and enhance the overall value of the insurance policy.

A sophisticated subject might deposit substantial monies into an existing insurance policy thinking that the fraud examiner will not look beyond the face value of the policy into the equity built up by prepayments. The fraud examiner should, therefore, always examine the financial statement of a target to locate insurance policies and examine the equity in these policies as a potential asset.

Prepaid Credit Cards

Many credit accounts today permit the card holder to prepay their accounts. Many people attempting to hide assets have used the prepayment option to hide cash from creditors. Prepayment of credit card accounts can also be found in Cash Management Accounts (CMAs) offered by stock brokerage firms.

Savings Bond Purchases

Drug dealers and tax evaders often use Savings Bond purchases as a means to conceal their ready cash. In several recent cases, defendants in financial crimes have purchased bonds in their individual names, the name of their spouse (in her maiden name) or in their children's names.

Cashier's Checks and Traveler's Checks

Many criminals purchase cashier's checks and traveler's checks in an attempt to hide their financial dealings and reduce the amount of cash they have to carry. Through the purchase of cashier's checks or traveler's checks in denominations of less than $10,000.00, the criminal can carry negotiable financial instruments that can be exchanged almost any place in the world.

Computer Databases

To begin a computer based investigation, contact the county clerk and court clerk to determine which records are available on microfiche and which records they provide by computer access. Next, determine how much record checking is necessary, which records should be focused on and the location of concentration. Areas of concentration might include microfiche records of voter registration, computer access to court records, and real estate files. Information on computerized databases is located in the chapter on Accessing Information On-Line.

Locating Assets Through Subpoenas

Criminal and some civil fraud examiners will have subpoena power allowing them to obtain nonpublic records, including bank account and loan records, records from accountants and tax preparers (including income tax returns and related documents), mortgage company records, telephone toll records, credit card statements, credit reporting company records, hotel and travel records, telex records, overnight package envelopes, and passports.

Locating Assets Offshore

More sophisticated targets might try to hide their assets offshore, often in tax havens and secrecy jurisdictions. Historically, some of the most popular offshore jurisdictions have been Switzerland, Cayman Islands, Netherlands Antilles, and Panama.

Steps to be taken to locate offshore assets include:
- Review domestic bank account records for wire transfers or other transactions involving off-shore bank accounts.
- Determine whether the subject personally traveled overseas. Overseas travel can often be documented from U.S. Customs records available through FinCEN.
- Attempt to locate the subject's travel agency.

Attempt to identify means employed to move cash off-shore by:
- Use of multiple cashier's checks
- Overnight mail envelopes
- Other methods

After funds have been traced offshore, the next step is to look for transfers back to the United States. A sophisticated target might use a foreign attorney or bank officer as a trustee or front to purchase assets in the United States, or appoint the trustee as manager of a United States business.

Subjects also might obtain access to their assets offshore by using foreign credit cards. Many international institutions now offer MasterCard or VISA accounts. All account records are maintained in the foreign country. Sophisticated subjects might obtain foreign passports (in a fictitious name, if requested). Some countries offer such passports to people who deposit $25,000 in the state run financial institution.

It may difficult to obtain information on foreign banks, but it is not impossible. Dun & Bradstreet publishes several guides with information about businesses in Latin America, Europe, and other regions of the world. The U.S. Department of Commerce has foreign country experts who can direct you to sources of business information on any country in the world.

Also, with the expansion of the Internet as a means of global communication, information on foreign countries and businesses is available through the Internet or through a commercial database or on-line service.

In his book *Competitor Intelligence*, Leonard Fuld provides a useful chapter on locating information on foreign businesses. He suggests the following resources as starting points:
- Securities brokers with expertise in dealing with foreign businesses.
- The International Trade Commission
- International trade shows
- Foreign consulates
- Foreign chambers of commerce
- Foreign magazines and directories

Fuld provides a list of consulates, chambers of commerce, magazines and directories in his book. Fuld suggests checking *Euromoney 500* which contains profiles of the world's top 500 banks or *The Europa Year Book* which provides basic data on banks around the world.

The text of newspapers such as *The New York Times* or *The Washington Post* may be searched for articles on the foreign bank or the foreign country involved. The texts of these and other large newspapers are available through on-line services such as NEXIS or through CD-ROM disk.

If the subject engages in a mail-order or retail business, a simple way to get information about the subject's bank accounts is to send him a check. Ronald L. Mendell in his book *How To Do Financial Asset Investigations* suggests buying a small item from the subject by using a check. When the canceled check is returned, it will provide the name and possibly the account number of the subject's bank. He suggests that if the subject does not engage in mail-order sales, the same goal may be accomplished by sending the subject a small "refund" check.

Office of International Affairs

The U. S. Department of Justice, Office of International Affairs (OIA), in certain circumstances, can offer assistance to U.S. fraud examiners seeking to recover offshore assets.

OIA is responsible for:
- Extradition requests
- Requests for foreign documentary evidence, bank and business records and other official documents
- Interviews and depositions of foreign witnesses
- Assistance to obtain appearance of foreign witnesses in U.S. courts
- Foreign searches and seizures, compelled handwriting exemplars and electronic surveillance.

The OIA uses a number of legal resources to obtain information from foreign countries. Letters Rogatory are formal requests by the courts of one country to the courts of another country. The OIA also uses Mutual Legal Assistance Treaties (MLATs) between the United States and foreign countries that provide for the exchange of information and documents relating to narcotics, money laundering and other financial crimes. Some of the countries currently having treaties in force are Switzerland, Italy, Netherlands, Turkey, Caicos, Canada, Cayman Islands, Bahamas, Anguilla, Montserrat, British Virgin Islands, Argentina, United Kingdom, Jamaica, Republic of Korea, Nigeria, Panama, and Spain. More countries are being added to the list each year. Some foreign governments, such as Switzerland, will provide information to the United States without a specific agreement on mutual assistance.

Another method of obtaining foreign bank or business records is by obtaining a release and consent form from the defendant. Execution of such a waiver can be compelled by order of a U.S. court. This procedure is not universally accepted, particularly in Switzerland, the Channel Islands, the Turks and Caicos Islands, or the Cayman Islands.

Letter Rogatory

The information needed for a Letter Rogatory request is as follows:

- The facts of the case showing at least a reasonable suspicion that the offense under investigation might have been committed
- The names and identifying information of people or entities involved in the matter
- The names and identifying information of witnesses or entities whose names might be on bank records (if accounts are held in other names)
- The names, addresses and other information concerning banks, businesses or bank account numbers
- The offenses being investigated or prosecuted in the United States, to include penalties
- The assistance requested of the foreign country, whether it is documents, testimony, freezing of assets, etc. (If you want a foreign magistrate to question a witness, write out the questions that you want the witness to be asked, even if you ask to be present during the questioning).
- The procedures to be followed (how to authenticate business documents and records for use in U.S. courts).

The procedure for making formal requests by a Letter Rogatory is as follows:

- Call the OIA team handling the relevant part of the world concerning the search for current guidance and assistance
- Draft a Letter Rogatory following an exemplar or other materials provided by the OIA
- Have the OIA representative review and approve the draft
- The prosecutor then will file a motion in federal court for issuance of a Letter Rogatory, together with a memorandum in support and proposed order (submit two copies, one for the clerk and one for the foreign court, to be signed by the judge)
- Judge signs both Letters Rogatory
- File one signed Letter Rogatory with the Clerk of the Court
- Have the court clerk authenticate the second signed Letter Rogatory either via apostille or exemplification certificate
- Have Letter Rogatory translated into proper language
- Send signed Letter Rogatory and translation to OIA for transmission through diplomatic channels to the proper foreign government

- The Minister of Justice in the foreign country normally presents the Letter Rogatory to the appropriate court
- The foreign court determines whether to execute the Letter Rogatory. If determination is favorable, the court then obtains the documents, testimony and other information
- Evidence resulting from execution of the Letter Rogatory is returned through diplomatic channels to the OIA
- The OIA will then forward the information to the prosecutor

Mutual Legal Assistance Treaties (MLATs)

Requests for foreign assistance under MLATs usually are quicker and more efficient. The procedure for making formal requests by MLAT is as follows:

- No U.S. Court involvement is required
- The prosecutor calls OIA for current guidance and will send a draft request to OIA for editing
- When OIA director approves the request, OIA transmits the request to the foreign central or competent authority
- If a translation is required, the requesting agency is responsible for obtaining it
- OIA transmits the translation to the requested country
- The requested country's proper authority determines whether the request meets treaty requirements, and if it does, transmits the request to the appropriate recorder agency for execution
- The executing authority transmits the evidence through the proper authority to the OIA which forwards it to the prosecutor
- Fraud examiner/prosecutor should inspect the evidence for responsiveness and completeness as well as certificates of authenticity of business records (notify the OIA at once of any problems)

Public Records

Of course, a great deal of information which is useful in tracing illicit transactions, particularly real and personal property filings, is a matter of public record. The chapters on "Sources of Information" and "Accessing Information On-Line" should be consulted for more information.

REPORTING STANDARDS

Documenting results is a particularly important function in fraud examinations. In many instances, the written report is the only evidence that the work was performed. Cases can be won or lost on the strength of the written report. It conveys to the litigator all the evidence and provides credence to the fraud examination and to the examiner's work. It forces the examiner to consider his actions during an investigation by requiring that they will be documented. It omits irrelevant information, thereby allowing pertinent facts to stand out. A first-rate written report is based upon a first-rate examination.

Preparation

The fraud examiner must adequately prepare prior to any interview or information-gathering process. Proper preparation entails analyzing what is to be expected as an end product. It also should involve having a good idea of what is to be learned from each witness.

Active listening is an essential function of effective report writing. The fraud examiner must have good listening skills so that the information is properly assimilated, evaluated, and communicated to others. Listening skills are learned. Listening involves perceiving what the respondent is actually communicating. To do so properly, you must set aside any preconceived notions and listen objectively—not only to what is being said—but how it is said and why. The fraud examiner should withhold judgment until the entire message has been heard.

Active listening often involves participating with the respondent during the information-gathering process. Participation conveys interest in the subject and promotes rapport. Participation might require reacting openly to information by verbal and nonverbal responses.

Accuracy of Reports

Each contact an examiner makes during the course of a fraud examination should be recorded on a timely basis in a *memorandum of interview*. Although there is no need to recapitulate testimony word for word, for accuracy's sake the fraud examiner should include all facts of possible relevance.

You should reconfirm dates and supporting information with the respondent. It is important to reconfirm the facts *before* the report is written, not after. Attachments to the report, if any, should be completely described. Inaccuracies and careless errors are inexcusable and can render a report useless.

Clarity

Investigative reports on fraud examinations should convey pertinent information in the clearest possible language. If necessary, quote the respondent directly (provided the quotation does not distort the context). Convey only the facts; do not editorialize or give judgments. Use complex or technical terms in their proper contexts, and, where necessary, explain their meaning. Do not use jargon since the report might be read by people who will not be familiar with esoteric or technical terminology.

Impartiality and Relevance

Report all facts without bias. Everything relevant should be included regardless of which side it favors or what it proves or disproves. At the outset of a fraud examination, the examiner should carefully determine what information will be needed to prove the case and attempt to include only this information. A report should include only those matters that are relevant to the examination. However, almost every investigation yields much information of which the relevance is not immediately known. In such cases, it is best to opt for completeness.

Timeliness

Timeliness of reports is extremely important because it tends to enhance the accuracy of witness testimony. Another aim of timeliness is to preserve the examiner's memory of the interview(s). All interviews should be transcribed as soon as possible after the questioning. Upon completing the examination, the examiner should prepare a final or interim report (whichever is appropriate) as soon as possible.

Reporting Mistakes

Conclusions and Opinions

In a report writing context, conclusions and opinions are similar, but are not identical. *Conclusions* are based upon observations of the evidence, whereas *opinions* call for an interpretation of the facts. The fraud examiner must be very circumspect about drawing conclusions. In most situations, the conclusions from the examination should be self-evident, and should not need to be pointed out in the report. If the conclusions are not obvious, the report might need to be clarified.

Opinions

Avoid stating *opinions* regarding the guilt or innocence of any person or party. The Certified Fraud Examiner Code of Professional Ethics specifically prohibits statements of opinions as to guilt or innocence, as this is the job of the judge or jury (See the Criminology and Ethics Section). Opinions regarding technical matters are permitted if the fraud examiner is qualified as an expert in the matter being considered. For example, a permissible expert opinion might be in regard to the relative adequacy of an entity's internal controls. Another opinion might discuss whether financial transactions conform to generally accepted accounting principles.

Evidence

Strict legal guidelines determine how evidence is handled and its chain of custody. The fraud examiner can avoid evidence maintenance problems by simply documenting—in memorandum form—the receipt or release of all evidence.

Copy Documents

Most fraud case evidence will be in document form. When operating under a lawful court order that compels a custodian to furnish original documents, the examiner should copy those documents (preferably in the presence of the custodian). Then the examiner should furnish the custodian with a receipt describing the documents copied or taken. A sample receipt can be found in the Appendix to Report Writing.

Safeguarding and Maintaining Documents

After obtaining documents, the examiner should secure them for evidence. Be sure that only those people with an absolute need for these documents can gain access to them. For practical purposes, it usually is best to copy all documents. (Original documents usually are not included in reports.) Mark all original documents in a unique manner, preferably by using initials and dates. To avoid defacing originals, use a small but distinctive tick mark or other form of identifier.

When documents are voluntarily furnished, leave the originals in place and work with the copies. If originals are later lost, stolen, or misplaced, the copies normally can be introduced in court under the "best evidence" rule. (See the Law Section.) Don't take shortcuts with evidence, and certainly do not lose or misplace crucial documents. It is inexcusable for a fraud examiner to mishandle evidence; doing so will almost certainly compromise the case.

Effective Note-taking

Note-taking is a demanding and necessary fraud examination skill; good reports are based on good notes. Once the notes have helped the examiner prepare a memorandum of interview, they have fulfilled their essential purpose. However, some jurisdictions require that notes pertaining to criminal matters be retained for evidence.

The most common types of note-taking include manual, stenographic, and electronic. Manual note-taking is the most usual method. Its main advantage is that no extra people are required to be present during the interview. However, manual note-taking can be obtrusive and distracting while questioning.

A stenographer might be present during the interview to take notes (rather than a verbatim transcript). This allows the interviewer to concentrate on the questioning. A potential disadvantage of this method is that the respondent might be inhibited by the presence of another individual.

Electronic note-taking commonly entails tape recording an interview, then summarizing the recording to reflect the most pertinent information. Its main advantages are increased accuracy and information-gathering efficiency. It can be especially helpful in complicated interview situations, or in situations where terminology is defined or explained.

Electronic note-taking has the disadvantage of requiring a duplication of effort. In some instances, an electronic recording device can be inhibiting. In a limited number of situations it might be illegal without the respondent's consent. See the Law Section for more information.

Organization of Information

Because of the amount of information and number of documents that might be collected during a fraud examination, the examiner should plan early and plan well. If circumstances permit, an information database should be established in the early phases of the case. Report information can be presented either in chronological order or by transaction. The options are discussed below.

Chronological

This method presents facts in the order in which they were uncovered. For example, if an anonymous tip predicated the fraud examination, the information received would be presented first in the report. Thereafter, the reader would follow the development of each step as the case progressed.

Information from each witness should be presented in a chronological manner. If interviewing an associate of the target, for example, relay the information in a fashion that begins at the point the associate first met the target, then proceed through the course of pertinent events that lead to the present.

By Transaction

If a multitude of documents support several instances of fraud, this information should be presented by separating individual transactions. For example, in a case of internal fraud involving six different instances of embezzlement, the documents and the related interviews might best be understood if presented as a group. Thereafter, detail the remaining transactions chronologically.

Analyzing the Reader

Keep in mind that the fraud examination report will be read by the general public and the opposition. *Under no circumstances should the examiner prepare a communication with the idea that the information will not be disclosed to adverse third parties.* Write the report with this caveat in mind. A fraud examination should stand on its own. It should adequately answer the classic questions of who, what, why, where, when, and how. If the report is prepared properly, the reader should not have to refer to any other documents to understand the issues. Fraud examination reports most likely will be read by the following individuals:

Company Insiders

Managers and executives probably will review reports of cases involving internal fraud and misdeeds. Because these documents likely will be reviewed by people outside the company as well, they should not address internal control deficiencies, management issues, or other sensitive company considerations. Instead, these matters should be dealt with in a separate letter or other form of communication.

Attorneys

Reports will be read by attorneys from within the organization and without. In reports prepared at the request of counsel, mark each page "privileged and confidential." This procedure will document any privilege claim (discussed below). Understand, however, that marking the report in such a manner will not necessarily ensure that the privilege will be sustained.

Attorneys for the defendant(s) likely will gain access to a report during the discovery phase of civil litigation. These lawyers will scrutinize the report for errors, omissions, and/or misstatements. You should be certain that the report is accurate down to the most seemingly unimportant detail. Defense attorneys will cite the smallest error as evidence that the entire document is inaccurate. In criminal cases, prosecuting attorneys and law enforcement personnel also will review a report. These individuals will look primarily at evidence and witness statements that will best sustain a criminal prosecution.

Defendants and Witnesses

In either civil or criminal litigation, the defendants eventually will see most, if not all, of a report. If the case reaches court, the witnesses one identified and interviewed will be provided with copies of their own statements, if not the entire report.

Press

In some instances, the press might gain access to a report. Report data might be obtained from information disclosed during litigation or, in some instances, from confidential sources. The press is particularly adept at uncovering mistakes and incorrect conclusions drawn by the fraud examiner.

Juries

When the case reaches trial, the jury usually will receive the entire report for review and analysis. Juries normally do not have a background in business and accounting matters, therefore, *the report should be as simple and as easy to understand as possible*. Of all the important individuals who will review the report, the members of the jury will by far be the most important.

Outlining

Outlines of reports and memoranda of interview can be helpful in long or complex fraud examinations. Report outlines can take many forms, depending on the type(s) of information one must relay. Although the following outlining technique is mechanical, it is easy to master and well suited to unraveling the complexities of large and difficult subjects.

Step One

Group naturally related items and write them down on note cards, and then determine whether they are exactly what is needed to meet the demands of the objective, the reader, and the scope of coverage. When they are grouped, arrange them in the proper order and label them with Roman numerals. For example, the major outline could be:

EXAMPLE

    I. First-level head
       A. Second-level head
          1. Third-level head
             a. Fourth-level head
                (1) Fifth-level head

Step Two

Mark each of the note cards with the appropriate Roman numeral and capital letter. Sort the note cards by major and minor headings. Transfer the notes to paper, converting them to complete sentences.

Step Three

Polish the rough outline. Check to ensure that the subordination of minor headings to major headings is logical and sequential. Check for unity. Stay within the established scope of coverage. Resist the temptation to report irrelevant facts. Check the outline for completeness; scan it to see whether more information is needed.

Style

Write each report in a style that is clear, concise, and to the point. Poorly constructed or grammatically incorrect sentences can ruin even an otherwise flawless fraud examination. The purpose for writing a report is to convey information to a reader; therefore, it is the examiner's responsibility to communicate effectively and efficiently. The two cardinal sins of report writing are *vagueness and wordiness*. Common breaches of good basic writing include:

- Improperly placed or ambiguous modifiers (changes sentence context)
- Use of technical jargon, slang, and/or colloquialisms (places the burden to understand upon the reader)
- Use of unnecessary, high-flown verbiage (in an attempt to impress the reader)

Voice

In grammar, *voice* indicates the relation of the subject to the action of the verb. When the verb is in the active voice, the subject acts; when it is in the passive voice, the subject is acted upon.

EXAMPLE

John Doe *wrote* the report. (active)

OR

The report *was written* by John Doe. (passive)

Both of the sentences say the same thing, but each has a different *emphasis*. In the first sentence emphasis is on the subject, *John Doe*, whereas in the second sentence the focus is on the object, *the report*. Notice how much stronger and more forceful the active sentence is. Always use the active voice unless there is good reason to use the passive. Because they are wordy and indirect, passive sentences are harder for the reader to understand.

EXAMPLE

Instances of fraud *are* most likely to be *reported* by co-workers. (passive)

OR

Co-workers *report* most instances of fraud. (active)

Person

Person refers to the form of a personal pronoun that indicates whether the pronoun represents the writer, the person written to, or the person (or thing) written about.

EXAMPLE

I did not find a record of the deposit.

Point of View

Point of view indicates the writer's relation to the information presented, as reflected in the use of person. The writer usually expresses point of view in first-, second-, or third-person personal pronouns. The use of the first person indicates that the writer is a participant or observer ("This happened to me," "I saw that"). The second and third person indicate that the writer is writing about other people ("This happened to her, to them, to it"). When writing a report, one should never use *the writer* to replace *I* in a mistaken attempt to sound formal or dignified.

CHANGE: *The writer* believes that this examination will be completed by the end of June.

TO: *I* believe that this examination will be completed by the end of June.

Constructing Clear Sentences

Sentences that make up a report should be simple and clear. Whenever possible, use uncomplicated sentences to state complex ideas. If readers must cope with a complicated sentence in addition to a complex idea, they are likely to become confused. Common sentence structure mistakes to avoid are discussed below.

Rambling Sentences

Sentences that contain more information than the reader can comfortably absorb are known as *rambling sentences*. The remedy for a rambling sentence is to divide it into two or more sentences. Put the main message of the rambling sentence into the first of the revised sentences.

CHANGE: The payment to which a subcontractor is entitled should be made promptly in order that in the event of a subsequent contractual dispute, the general contractors might not be held in default of contract by virtue of nonpayment.

TO: Pay subcontractors promptly. Then, if a contractual dispute should occur, the general contractor cannot be held in default for nonpayment.

Run-on Sentences

A *run-on sentence* is two or more sentences without punctuation to separate them. Run-on sentences can be corrected by creating two sentences or by joining the two clauses with a semicolon (if they are closely related).

> CHANGE: The new manager instituted several new procedures some were impractical. (run-on sentence)

> TO: The new manager instituted several new procedures. Some were impractical. (period)
>
> OR
>
> TO: The new manager instituted several new procedures; some were impractical. (semicolon)

Omitted Verbs

Do not omit a required verb.

> CHANGE: I never have and probably never will locate the missing file.

> TO: I never have *located* and probably never will locate the missing file.

Omitted Subjects

Do not omit a subject.

> CHANGE: He regarded price fixing as wrong, but until abolished by law, he engaged in it, as did everyone else.

> TO: He regarded price fixing as wrong, but until *it was* abolished by law, he engaged in it, as did everyone else.

Unnecessary Compound Sentences

Avoid compound sentences containing clauses that have little or no logical relationship to one another.

> CHANGE: The ledger contains several examples of altered data entries, *and it usually is stored in the company's safe.*

TO: The ledger contains several examples of altered data entries. It usually is stored in the company's safe.

Misplaced Modifiers

A modifier (a word, a phrase, or a clause) is misplaced when it modifies, or appears to modify, the wrong word or phrase.

CHANGE: I *almost* located all the missing files.

TO: I located *almost* all the missing files.

Possible confusion in sentences of this type can be avoided by placing the modifier immediately before the word it is intended to modify.

CHANGE: All businessmen are *not* talented in mathematics. (The implication is that *no* businessman is talented in mathematics.)

TO: *Not* all businessmen are talented in mathematics.

Paragraph Structure

State a paragraph's main point in its first sentence. Subsequent sentences should support and clarify that main point. For the purposes of report writing, paragraphs should be short. Readers can be daunted by long, complicated paragraphs that contain multiple issues. (Note also that short paragraphs result in more white space on the page, making the document more readable.)

Report Structure

Reporting formats vary widely. Some organizations, especially governmental investigative bodies, use report forms so that case information is provided in a consistent manner.

The basic reporting documents are:
- Memoranda
- Exhibits, documents, or enclosures
- Indexes

- Cover page
- Transmittal letter

The Linda Reed Collins case study report, attached as an appendix, is but one acceptable approach. If the report is distributed outside the organization, it often is necessary to prepare an additional transmittal letter. Original exhibits and evidence—depending on the circumstances—often can be attached separately.

The heart of the report is the memorandum of interview and one memorandum should be prepared for each official contact. Once all the memoranda of interviews are completed, they typically are assembled in chronological order and indexed.

Memoranda

Use memoranda to document all interviews and other pertinent information discovered during the examination. Each memorandum should contain the following information where appropriate:

- Heading
- File number or control number
- Name of person reporting
- Case name or subject
- Subject of memorandum
- Date
- Details of Facts
- Interview was voluntary
- Indicate that one provided one's identity
- The witness was informed of the nature of the inquiry
- Date of inquiry
- How the interview was conducted (in person, by telephone, etc.)
- If the interview was electronically recorded
- Facts learned during inquiry

Cover Page or Letter

A *cover page* summarizes the examination's salient points. The cover page should be direct and succinct, and might or might not include an opinion. If a report is submitted to an outside agency (such as law enforcement or outside counsel), a cover letter should accompany it.

The cover letter should recapitulate information in the report and summarize the principal weaknesses. It is not necessary to list all witnesses, only those most valuable.

Exhibits

As a general rule, copies of exhibits should be included in the report and not attached separately. However, bulky files (including working papers and similar exhibits) might be attached separately and referred to in the body of the report. The chain of custody should be maintained over original documents.

Forms

A complete fraud examination report must document every step of the information-gathering process. Because the orderly and legal presentation of evidence requires the examiner to organize a great deal of information, the examiner should use the forms available to facilitate this task (see Appendix). As a general rule, these forms are kept in the file and not included in the report unless necessary. These forms include the following:

Consent to Search

A *Consent to Search* form documents the fact that a person has been informed of his Constitutional rights, stating that:
- The premises cannot be searched without a search warrant
- The person can refuse to consent to such a search

The signatures on the bottom of the form (subject(s) and witness(es)) indicate that the person is voluntarily giving the examiner written permission to search the premises and to remove whatever papers, documents, or other property he might desire.

Receipt for Property

A *Receipt for Property* form is a multipurpose document used to list items of evidence that have been received, returned, or released. This form includes the following information:
- Date of transfer
- Property owner's name
- Owner's address
- Description of item(s)
- Signature lines ("Received by" and "Received From")

Telephone Recording Consent

A *Telephone Recording Consent* form stipulates where, when, and with whom telephone conversations can be tape recorded. This form states that the subject has granted permission without threats or promises of any kind, and it must be signed by the subject and witnesses. Be cautioned that the form alone does not make the conduct illegal or legal. See the Law Section for information on the interception of communications.

Advice of Rights

An *Advice of Rights* form effectively "Mirandizes" an individual; that is, it informs a person that:

- He might remain silent in the face of questioning
- Whatever the person says can be used against him in a court of law
- If requested an attorney will be appointed for him before questioning
- He might stop answering questions at any time, whether an attorney is present or not.

If Mirandizing is applicable, this form should be signed and witnessed.

Consent to Record

A *Consent to Record* form documents the fact that an individual has given the examiner permission to record specific conversations. This form must be signed and witnessed. It details the:

- Name of the individual
- His address
- Location of the conversation(s)
- Who might record the conversation(s)
- Name of the subject(s) with whom the individual might converse
- Date(s) of the conversation(s)

Customer Consent and Authorization for Access to Financial Records

This form authorizes a financial institution to disclose the customer's own records to the examiner or other specifically listed individuals. It must be signed by the account holder.

Evidence Control Log

In the case of significant items of evidence, it might be advisable to prepare an *evidence control log*, a form that documents:

- Evidence control center location

- Bank safe-deposit box location
- Other evidence location
- Signature(s) of person(s) placing in or removing evidence from Repository
- Reasons why evidence was moved
- File case number
- Time(s) and date(s) authorized individuals entered and departed Evidence Repository

Signed Statements

The verbal confession should be reduced to a short and concise written statement. The interviewer should prepare the statement and present it to the confessor for his signature. The statement should be prepared before the confessor leaves the interview. Rarely should it exceed two or three handwritten pages. The following points should be covered in every signed statement:

Voluntariness of Confessions

The general law of confessions requires that they be completely voluntary. This should be set forth specifically in the first paragraph with the date of the interview.

Intent

There is no such thing as an accidental fraud or crime. Both require as part of the elements of proof the fact that the confessor knew the conduct was wrong and intended to commit the act. This can best be accomplished by using precise language in the statement that clearly describes the act (e.g., *"I wrongfully took assets from the company that weren't mine"* versus *"I borrowed money from the company without telling anyone"*).

As a general rule, strong emotive words, such as "lie" and "steal," should be avoided, as the confessor might balk at signing the statement. Still, the wording must be precise. Following are suggested wordings:

	EXAMPLE
Instead of	*Use*
Lie	*I knew the statement/action was untrue.*
Steal	*wrongfully took the property of _____ for my own benefit.*

Embezzle	*wrongfully took _____'s property, which had been entrusted to me, and used it for my own benefit.*
Fraud	*I knowingly told _____ an untrue statement and he/she/they relied on it.*

Approximate Dates of Offense

Unless the exact dates of the offense are known, the word "approximately" must precede any dates of the offense. If the confessor is unsure about the dates, language to that effect should be included.

Approximate Amounts of Losses

Include the approximate losses, making sure they are labeled as such. It is satisfactory to state a range ("probably not less than $_____ or more than $_____").

Approximate Number of Instances

Ranges also are satisfactory for the number of instances. The number is important because it helps establish intent by showing a repeated pattern of activity.

Willingness to Cooperate

It makes it easier for the confessor when he perceives that the statement includes language portraying him in a more favorable light. The confessor can convert that natural tendency by emphasizing cooperation and willingness to make amends.

EXAMPLE

"I am willing to cooperate in helping undo what I have done. I promise that I will try to repay whatever damages I caused by my actions."

Excuse Clause

The confessor's moral excuse should be mentioned. The interviewer should ensure the excuse clause wording does not diminish legal responsibility.

EXAMPLE

WRONG:

"I didn't mean to do this." (implies lack of intent)

RIGHT:

"I wouldn't have done this if it had not been for pressing financial problems. I didn't mean to hurt anyone."

Confessor Reads Statement

The confessor must acknowledge that he read the statement and he should initial all the pages of the statement. It might be advisable to insert intentional errors in the statement so that the confessor will notice them. The errors are crossed out, the correct information is inserted, and the confessor is asked to initial the changes. Whether this step is advisable depends on the likelihood that the confessor will attempt to retract the statement or claim it was not read.

Truthfulness of Statement

The written statement should state specifically that it is true. This adds weight to it. However, the language also should allow for mistakes.

EXAMPLE

"This statement is true and complete to the best of my current recollection."

Key Points in Signed Statements

There is no legal requirement that a statement must be in the handwriting or wording of the declarant. Because the examiner usually knows how to draft a valid statement, to let a confessor draft the statement generally is not a good idea. A statement's *wording* should be precise.

Declarants should read and sign the statement without undue delay. Do not ask the confessor to sign the statement; instead, say *"Please sign here."* Although there is no legal requirement, it is a good idea to have two people witness the signing of a statement.

There should not be *more than one written statement for each offense.* If facts are inadvertently omitted, they can later be added to the original statement as an addendum. For legal purposes, prepare separate statements for unrelated offenses. This rule applies because the target might be tried more than once—once for each offense. Preserve all notes taken during an interview, especially those concerning a confession. Having access to pertinent notes can aid in a cross-examination regarding the validity of a signed statement. Stenographic notes, if any, also should be preserved. Once a confession is obtained, substantiate it through additional investigation, if necessary.

Visual Aids

Occasionally, the fraud examiner might include visual aids prepared either as part of the report or to be used as exhibits at trial. Visual aids should be kept simple. Several different types of visual aids are discussed below.

Link Network Diagrams

Link networks show the relationships between people, organizations, and events. Different symbols are used to represent different entities: a square can symbolize an organization; a circle, a person; a triangle, an event; and so forth. It doesn't matter which symbols you use as long as you use them consistently. Confirmed connections between entities can be represented by a solid line or enclosure within another symbol. Speculative or presumed relationships can be indicated by broken lines. To achieve its intended purpose, a graphic always should be clear. Don't cross lines if possible.

EXAMPLE

Smith is vice-president of the ABC Corporation and president of the DEF Corporation, a subsidiary of ABC. Jones is general partner in the first and second partnerships. Brown and Green are limited partners in the First Partnership. Brown and Black are limited partners in the Second Partnership. Black is also a general partner in the Third Partnership. Smith also might have an interest in the First Partnership.

LINK NETWORK DIAGRAM

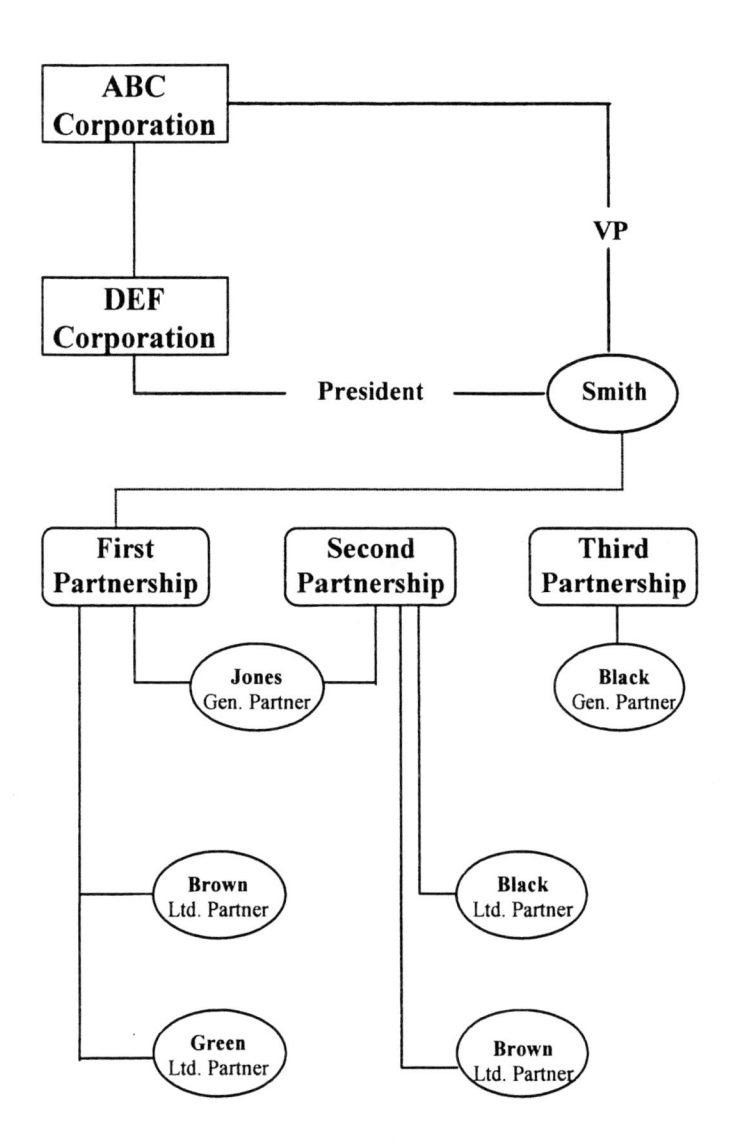

Matrices

A matrix is a grid that shows the relationship (or points of contacts) between a number of entities. Known contacts can be differentiated from presumed contacts by means of a bullet l or a circle m.

A matrix can be used to identify the direction and frequency of telephone traffic between suspect parties.

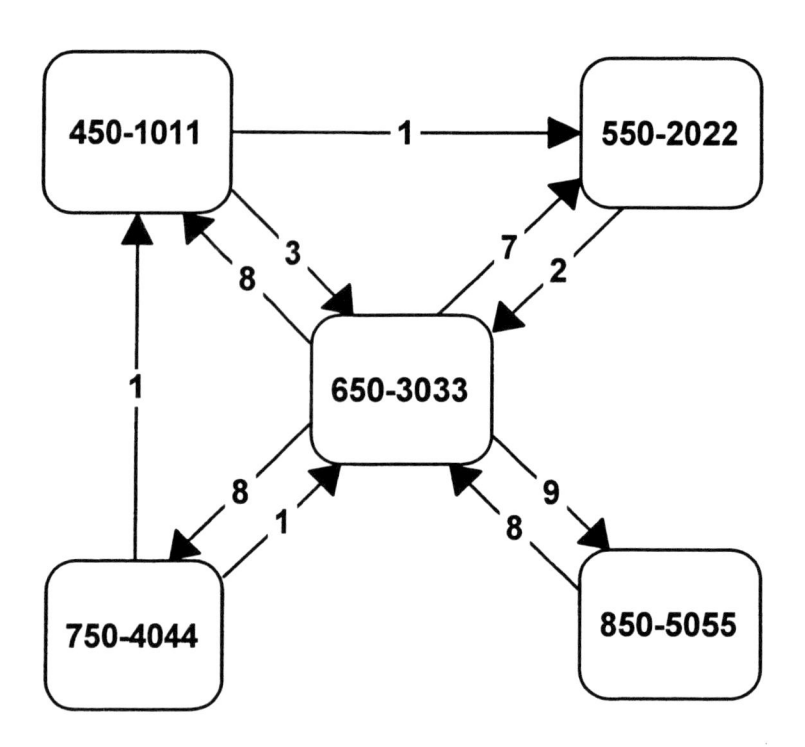

```
        ┌─────────┐                    ┌─────────┐
        │ 450-1011│ ──────── 1 ──────► │ 550-2022│
        └─────────┘                    └─────────┘
           ▲  ▲  ╲  3            7  ╱  ▲
           │  │   ╲ 8            2 ╱   │
           │  │    ▼              ▼    │
           1  │   ┌─────────┐
              │   │ 650-3033│
              │   └─────────┘
              │    ╱  ▲   ▲  ╲
              │  8╱  1│   │8  ╲9
              │  ▼    │   │    ▼
        ┌─────────┐           ┌─────────┐
        │ 750-4044│           │ 850-5055│
        └─────────┘           └─────────┘
```

This information also can be represented in chart form.

	450-1011	550-2022	650-3033	750-4044	850-5055	Total Outgoing Calls
450-1011	X	1	3			4
550-2022		X	2			2
650-3033	8	7	X	8	9	32
750-4044	1		1	X		2
850-5055			8		X	8
Total Incoming Calls	9	8	14	8	9	

Time Flow Diagrams

The following chart shows the relationship of significant events, in the order that they occurred.

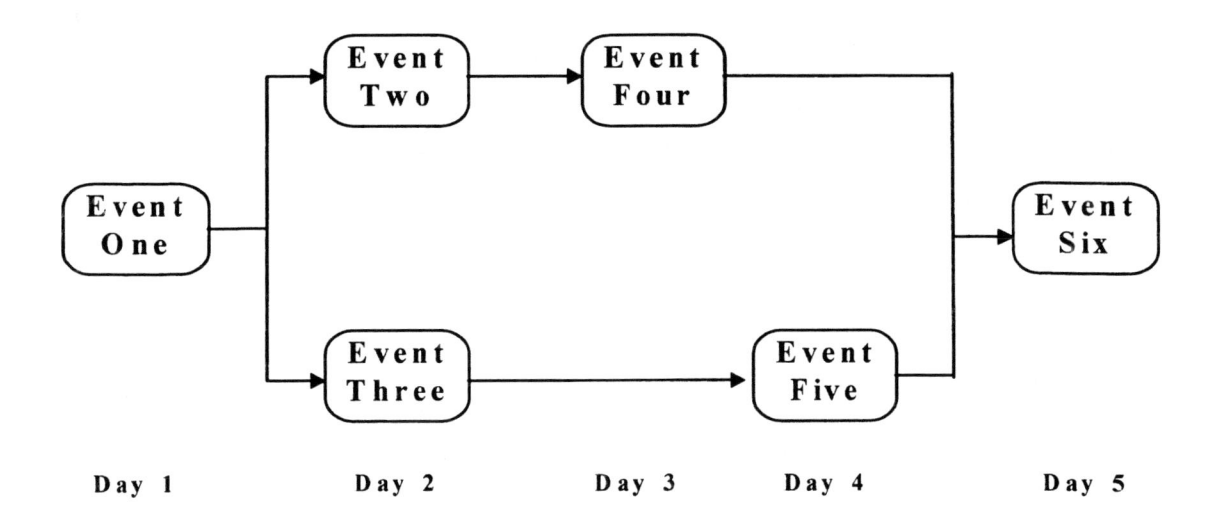

```
          Event            Event
          Two    ───────▶  Four
         ╱                      ╲
        ╱                        ╲
 Event                              Event
 One                                Six
        ╲                        ╱
         ╲                      ╱
          Event            Event
          Three  ───────▶  Five

 Day 1     Day 2     Day 3     Day 4     Day 5
```

Summaries of Witnesses' Statements

Reduce voluminous testimony and witness statements to summary form in order to identify inconsistent statements and to permit quick review. To identify pertinent passages, indicate briefly the topic being covered at a given point, and a synopsis of the statement (see example below).

Summary of Evidence

Linda Reed Collins

Page	Topic	Testimony
5	Collins hired 6/1/XX	Personnel file
5	Collins promoted to Purchaser 11/8/XX	Personnel file
8	Collins and Nagel friends	De la Garza interview
15	Checks to Orion	Robinson interview
30	Indebtedness of Collins	Public records

Keep the synopsis as succinct as possible. Too much detail will impair the summary's utility. The examiner or someone familiar with the facts and issues in the case should prepare the summary, not an assistant who does not know what might or might not be relevant. The summary also can be useful as a basis for a chronology.

An example of a report of a fraud examination is included in the Appendix to Report Writing. The fraud examiner typically also will prepare other written documents including but not limited to engagement contracts and opinion letters.

Engagement Contracts

Certified Fraud Examiners sometimes are hired for specific engagements. The examiner always should prepare an engagement letter so that he and the client have a clear understanding of the objectives of the assignment. If the terms of the engagement are defined in a contract, any later dispute becomes easier to resolve.

According to the Code of Professional Ethics, a Certified Fraud Examiner:
- Will accept only assignments for which there is a reasonable expectation that the work will be completed with professional competence
- Will obtain evidence or other documentation to establish a reasonable basis for any opinion rendered
- Will disclose all material matters discovered during the course of an examination which, if omitted, could cause a distortion of the facts

The engagement letter should be written with these standards in mind. The first question one must answer in preparing a contract is: Who is one's client? Have one been engaged by the plaintiff, the defendant, or their counsel? Often the engagement letter will be addressed to attorneys. This can be either corporate or outside counsel.

There are two primary forms of engagement letters: the long form and the short form. The long form spells out the details of what examination techniques you intend to follow while the short form does not. See the Appendix to Report Writing for examples of each type of engagement contracts.

Elements of the Engagement Contract

Engagement letters have four basic parts: opening, body (long or short), terms, and close. In the opening paragraph state the purpose of the engagement. Be specific as to whether the letter is an engagement or a proposal letter. The body of the letter will follow either the long form or the short form.

The Long Form

The long form is similar to an engagement letter prepared for specific scope examinations performed by auditors. The examiner describes the procedures in detail and limits the scope of an examination to the procedures defined. It is not recommended for use in engagements requiring the investigation of fraud allegations and a concluding opinion on the existence of fraud.

At the onset, the examiner might not know what procedures will be necessary to resolve the allegation. Consequently, it is difficult to describe, with any precision, the anticipated procedures before the examination begins.

The Short Form

The short form engagement letter outlines the general scope of the engagement. For example, it might describe that the services will include an investigation of a fraud allegation received over the hotline, or by an anonymous tip, or an audit anomaly.

The short form also might confirm that the examiner has access to any personnel or documentation deemed necessary to carry out the assignment. This type of engagement letter is best used for work that ultimately will require an opinion on a fraud allegation. Because the examiner will not know the nature of the alleged fraud at the onset, it is best to not limit the examination's scope.

Terms

The terms paragraph includes the fee, either flat rate or hourly, and the method of payment. This is an excellent time to ask for a retainer and to describe the billing procedures. Also address the issue of out-of-pocket expenses. If travel is required, discuss the anticipated cost of travel and the number of trips.

Close

In the closing section, thank the addressee for the opportunity of working with him. Provide a phone number where one can be reached and any special instructions, such as a pager and FAX numbers. Ask the addressee to sign one copy, and return it in the envelope. Don't forget to supply a signature plate for the returned letter and a self-addressed stamped envelope.

Opinions

The Certified Fraud Examiner is often asked for an opinion about the existence of fraud. He might be engaged to perform fraud deterrence services or to resolve a fraud allegation.

In the former instance, the opinion will address the strengths and weaknesses of the client's current fraud deterrence system, and include recommendations to strengthen that system. If specific instances of possible fraudulent conduct are uncovered, those also should be addressed.

In the latter situation, the examiner must be attentive to the Certified Fraud Examiner Code of Professional Ethics, in that

> *... no opinion shall be expressed regarding the guilt or innocence of any person or party.*

In the cases where a fraud examination has been conducted, the examiner has three outcomes: evidence was obtained supporting the allegation of fraud; evidence was gathered which does not support such an allegation; and evidence was inconclusive. In the first instance, the opinion will vary depending on whether or not the perpetrator confessed to the alleged crime. In the second case, the examiner can state that the evidence does not support the fraud charge. The examiner is not able to declare that there was no fraud. In the final case, the examiner can state that the evidence is inconclusive; it neither supports nor refutes the allegation. Examples of opinions appear in the Appendix.

Fraud Examination Checklist

It is often helpful to prepare "To Do" lists, or "Checklists," of the documents to be examined and the potential witness to be interviewed. For reference, a sample checklist is located in the Appendix. It is not intended to cover all aspects of the examination, but rather to provide the examination team assistance in planning the investigation.

INVESTIGATION APPENDIX

APPENDIX A

FRAUD EXAMINATION CHECKLIST

Case Name: _____   Case No.: _____

	YES	NO

1. Fully debriefed all informants and witnesses?

2. Documented the allegation in writing?

3. Identified all possible schemes or indicators of fraud?

4. Developed fraud theory?

5. Notified legal counsel and discussed whether to proceed?

6. Obtained, recorded, and filed all pertinent information and documents in the files?

7. Determined the potential loss?

8. Identified potential witnesses?

9. Determined if error or mistake made?

APPENDIX A

FRAUD EXAMINATION CHECKLIST

Case Name: _____   Case No.: _____

	YES	NO

10. Reviewed internal controls?

11. Developed an investigative plan?

12. Determined the type of evidence needed to pursue?

13. Identified indicators showing intent?

14. Reviewed payroll records and canceled checks?

    – Identified all bank accounts

    – Identified number of exemptions

    – Identified who might be endorsing checks

15. Reviewed personal expense reports?

    – Identified unusually high expenses

    – Identified credit card used

APPENDIX A

FRAUD EXAMINATION CHECKLIST

Case Name: _____ Case No.: _____

	YES	NO

- Identified where suspect entertains clients

- Identified duplicate submissions

16. Performed background/asset check?

    - Driver's License violations

    - Motor Vehicle Registration records

    - Regulatory licenses

    - Vital Statistics

    - Building permits

    - Business filings

        * Fictitious Names Indices

        * Business licenses

        * Corporate records

        * Limited partnerships

        * SEC filings

APPENDIX A

FRAUD EXAMINATION CHECKLIST

Case Name: _____   Case No.: _____

	YES	NO

- County and State records

    * Criminal

    * Civil

    * Domestic

    * Probate

    * Real estate records

- Federal court filings

    * Criminal

    * Civil

    * Bankruptcy

- Consumer credit records

- Business reporting services

17. Determined who should be interviewed?

APPENDIX A

FRAUD EXAMINATION CHECKLIST

Case Name: _____   Case No.: _____

	YES	NO

18. Developed interview approach?

19. Performed Financial Analysis

　— Vertical Analysis

　— Horizontal Analysis

　— Ratio Analysis

　— Rationalizations

　— Industry Analysis

　— Net Worth Analysis

20. Will undercover operation be used?

　— Plan developed

　— Approval received

　— Operation completed

APPENDIX A

FRAUD EXAMINATION CHECKLIST

Case Name: _____ Case No.: _____

	YES	NO

21. Will surveillance be used?

    – Plan developed

    – Personnel set up

    – Surveillance curtailed

22. Developed other informants?

23. Use Mail Covers?

24. Performed Link Analysis?

25. Identified computers that might be linked to investigation?

    – Identify expertise needed

    – Data downloaded

    – Data printed

APPENDIX A

FRAUD EXAMINATION CHECKLIST

Case Name: _____   Case No.: _____

	YES	NO

26. Performed Forensic Analysis?

   — Handwriting

   — Typewriter

   — Reviewed altered documents

   — Ink analysis

   — Document restoration

27. Interviews Conducted?

   — Interviews documented

   — Signed statements received

   — Identified other witnesses to interview

   — Interviewee knows how to get in touch with one

28. Completed documentation and report to management?

APPENDIX A

FRAUD EXAMINATION CHECKLIST

Case Name: _____ Case No.: _____

	YES	NO

29. Notified management?

30. Employee(s) terminated?

   – Received identification badge or deleted from system

   – Notified Security not to allow access to corporate premises

   – Personal belongings identified and arrangements made for employee to collect

31. Report written?

   – Heading

   – Summary

   – Memorandum

   – Pertinent correspondence

   – Documentation of interviews

   – Pertinent evidence included

APPENDIX A

FRAUD EXAMINATION CHECKLIST

Case Name: _____   Case No.: _____

	YES	NO

- Index

- Cover page

- Report approved by supervisor

32. Appointment made with law enforcement agency?

33. Follow-up contact made with investigators?

APPENDIX A

FRAUD EXAMINATION CHECKLIST

Case Name: _____   **Case No.:** _____

Documents To Be Examined	**To Do**	**Date Received**
ACCOUNTING RECORDS		
Balance Sheet		
Income Statement		
Statement of Cash Flows		
Bank Statement		
Expense Account		
Computer Password		
Other: _____		
PERSONNEL RECORDS		
Date of Employment		
Signed Ethics Agreement (Conflict of Interest Statement)		
Current Address		
Prior Addresses		
Spouse's Name		
Maiden Name		
Children's Names		
Prior Employment		
Prior Supervisor		
Insurance Information (Covered Dependents)		
Employee Evaluation (Performance Reviews)		
Garnishments		
Vacation Schedule		
Other: _____		

APPENDIX A

FRAUD EXAMINATION CHECKLIST

Case Name: _____   Case No.: _____

Documents To Be Examined	To Do	Date Received
PERSONAL RECORDS		
Bank Statements		
Tax Returns		
Insurance Policies		
Mortgage Records		
Brokerage Statements		
Credit Card Statements		
Telephone Records		
Other Business Records		
Investments		
Vehicle Information		
Diaries (Calendars)		
PUBLIC RECORDS - PERSONAL		
Civil Filings		
State		
Federal		
Criminal Filings		
State		
Federal		
Property Tax Records		
By Name		
By Address		
Tax Liens		
Financing		
Other:		

2005 Fraud Examiners Manual

APPENDIX A

FRAUD EXAMINATION CHECKLIST

Case Name: _____ **Case No.:** _____

Documents To Be Examined	**To Do**	**Date Received**
Judgments		
Garnishments		
Domestic Relations Records		
Divorce		
Property Settlement		
Financial Statements		
Tax Returns		
Depositions		
Probate Records		
U.S. Bankruptcy Filings		
Financial Statements		
Bank Statements		
Property Ownership		
Education Verification		
University/College		
Professional Licenses		
UCC Filings		
Corporate Records		
• Company Name		
• Individual (Incorporators)		
Assumed Name Index		
Vehicles Owned		

APPENDIX A

FRAUD EXAMINATION CHECKLIST

Case Name: _____ Case No.: _____

Documents To Be Examined	To Do	Date Received

- Lienholder

Boats Owned

- Lienholder

Aircraft Owned

- Lienholder

PUBLIC RECORDS - BUSINESS

Utility Records

UCC Filings

Tax Receipts

- Tax Liens
- Who Actually Pays the Taxes?

Post Office Box Application

Civil Filings

- State
- Federal

Assumed Name Index

Corporate Charter (Bylaws)

Business Credit History

- Dun & Bradstreet
- Better Business Bureau

APPENDIX A

FRAUD EXAMINATION CHECKLIST

Case Name: _____ Case No.: _____

Documents To Be Examined	To Do	Date Received
Other: _____		

APPENDIX A

FRAUD EXAMINATION CHECKLIST

Case Name: _____ Case No.: _____

Neutral Witnesses:

Name	Phone	Date Contacted	Interview Completed	Report Date

APPENDIX A

FRAUD EXAMINATION CHECKLIST

Case Name: _____ **Case No.:** _____

Adverse Witnesses:

Name	Phone	Date Contacted	Interview Completed	Report Date

APPENDIX A

FRAUD EXAMINATION CHECKLIST

Case Name: _____ Case No.: _____

Co-conspirators:

Name	Phone	Date Contacted	Interview Completed	Report Date

APPENDIX A

FRAUD EXAMINATION CHECKLIST

Case Name: _____   **Case No.:** _____

Suspects:

Name	Phone	Date Contacted	Interview Completed	Report Date

Bailey Books Incorporated
6200 Bayshore Drive
St. Augustine, FL 32082

Personal and Confidential

May 23, 2002

Lt. Jason Fishbeck
St. Augustine Police Department
382 Harbor View Circle
St. Augustine, FL 32084

Re: Linda Reed Collins, (File 02-4422)

Dear Lt. Fishbeck:

Attached is my report of a fraud examination dated May 23, 2002, with respect to the above captioned matter.

The report reflects that Collins, a purchasing agent for Bailey Books Inc., furnished a signed statement on May 1, 2002, indicating she had accepted at least $197,773 in commercial bribes and other illicit income in a conspiracy with James R. Nagel, an account representative for Orion Corporation, St. Augustine. Orion is a supplier of paper and related products to Bailey Books.

If proved in judicial proceedings, Collins and Nagel could be in violation of Title 7, Section 323A of the Florida Criminal Code (Commercial Bribery).

It is the policy of Bailey Books to report such matters to the appropriate authorities, and to assist in criminal prosecution. Accordingly, we would be willing to supply assistance, documentation, and expertise to your department in the resolution of this case.

If I might be of assistance, please do not hesitate to call.

Sincerely,

Loren D. Bridges
Certified Fraud Examiner

| Sample Report | Investigation Appendix |

Bailey Books Incorporated
6200 Bayshore Drive
St. Augustine, FL 32082

Personal and Confidential

May 23, 2002

Mr. Hal B. Marlow
Chief Executive Officer
Bailey Books Incorporated
6200 Bayshore Drive
St. Augustine, FL 32082

Re: Linda Reed Collins

Dear Mr. Marlow:

We have conducted a fraud examination concerning a possible misappropriation of assets of Bailey Books Incorporated. This examination was predicated upon an anonymous telephone call alleging improprieties on the part of Linda Reed Collins, Bailey's purchasing manager.

Our examination was conducted in accordance with lawful fraud examination techniques, which include—but are not limited to—examination of books and records, voluntary interviews with appropriate personnel, and other such evidence-gathering procedures as necessary under the circumstances.

During the pendency of this examination, Ms. Collins and her confederate, James R. Nagel of Orion Corporation, voluntarily furnished signed statements indicating that they misappropriated at least $197,773 to their personal benefit.

Based upon the results of our examination and the confessions of Ms. Collins and Mr. Nagel, these actions, if proved in a court of law, could constitute a violation of criminal and/or civil law.

Very truly yours,

Loren D. Bridges
Certified Fraud Examiner

Bailey Books Incorporated

EXECUTIVE SUMMARY

CONFIDENTIAL

Linda Reed Collins has been employed in the purchasing department of Bailey Books since June 1, 1997. She was promoted to Purchasing Manager effective November 8, 1999.

On January 28, 2002, the fraud examination unit at Bailey Books received an anonymous telephone call from an unidentified man who claimed that he was a former supplier to Bailey. The caller alleged certain improprieties in the bidding and procurement process.

Based upon this initial predication, a fraud examination was conducted, which included reviews of relevant records and interviews of appropriate personnel. The fraud examination revealed multiple purchases by Bailey Books from Orion Corporation, the amount of which has increased significantly from 1999 to the present.

Interviews of Bailey personnel indicated that Ms. Collins might have a personal relationship with Mr. Nagel. On May 1, 2002, Nagel and Collins were interviewed. Both furnished voluntary signed statements indicating that they had appropriated at least $197,773 from Bailey by establishing a fictitious vendor to which Bailey checks were directed. The checks purported to be for supplies purchased by Bailey when in fact no supplies or other items were purchased for this amount. Nagel and Collins used the proceeds for their personal benefit.

As reflected by the attached letter dated May 23, 2002, based on all the evidence, Collins and Nagel could be in violation of Florida criminal and/or civil laws.

Loren D. Bridges
Certified Fraud Examiner

Bailey Books Incorporated

INDEX TO REPORT

ITEM	PAGE
Memorandum of Predication	1
Review of Selected Purchases	2
Interview of Mark W. Steinberg	4
Purchasing Guidelines	5
Review of Personnel Files	6
Interview of Roger Donald McGuire	7
Interview of Mary Rodriguez De La Garza	8
Interview of Sara Louise Dawson	10
Conversation with Thomas C. Green, Attorney	11
Meeting with Mark W. Steinberg	12
Interview of Sara Louise Dawson	13
Interview of Becky Robinson	15
Orion Invoice	16
Orion Invoice	17
Interview of Ernie Quincy	18
Review of Checks Payable to Orion	19
David Levey Interview	22
Interview of Mary Rodriguez De La Garza	23
Surveillance Log	24
Interview of Confidential Source	25
Review of County Records	26
Review of State Records	27
Review of Chattel Mortgages	28
Review of Dun & Bradstreet Records	29
Review of Public Records	30
Interview of James R. Nagel	31
Interview of Owen Stetford	32
Interview of James R. Nagel	33
Statement by James R. Nagel	34
Interview of Linda Reed Collins	35
Statement by Linda Reed Collins	36

Bailey Books Incorporated

MEMO OF PREDICATION

TO: FILE (02-4422)
FROM: LOREN D. BRIDGES, CFE
SUBJECT: ANONYMOUS TELEPHONE CALL
DATE: JANUARY 28, 2002

On January 28, 2002, at approximately 10:12 a.m., I received a telephone call from an unidentified man, who said that he had been a long-term supplier to Bailey for sundry office supplies and paper.

The caller—who refused to reveal his identity—said that ever since Linda Reed Collins had taken over as Purchasing Manager, he had been gradually "squeezed out" from doing business with Bailey. The caller declined to furnish additional information.

Based upon the predication supplied above, a fraud examination is being commenced.

(Page 1)

Bailey Books Incorporated

MEMORANDUM

TO: FILE (02-4422)
FROM: LOREN D. BRIDGES, CFE
SUBJECT: REVIEW OF SELECTED PURCHASES FROM 1999-2001
DATE: JANUARY 30, 2002

Attached is a schedule of purchases prepared from individual vendor files. The purchases reflect that Orion Corp. has received an increasing share of the paper business from Bailey over the last several years, but has submitted written bids in only 63 percent of the cases over that period.

(Page 2)

Bailey Books Incorporated

Selected Purchases 1999-2001

Vendor	Items Purchased	Purchaser	1999	2000	2001	Date of Last Bid	% Increase (Decrease) Previous Yr. 2000-2001	% Increase (Decrease) Previous Yr. 1999-2000	% Increase (Decrease) Prev 2 Yrs. 1999-2001
Armour	Books	MRD	$683,409	$702,929	$810,100	12/01/01	15.2%	2.9%	18.5%
Burdick	Sundries	LRC	62,443	70,959	76,722	N/A	8.1%	13.6%	22.9%
Canon	Magazines	MRD	1,404,360	1,957,601	2,361,149	11/03/01	20.6%	39.4%	68.1%
DeBois, Inc.	Paper	LRC	321,644	218,404	121,986	06/08/01	(44.1%)	(32.1%)	(62.1%)
Elton Books	Books	RDM	874,893	781,602	649,188	07/21/01	(16.9%)	(10.7%)	(25.8%)
Fergeson	Books	RDM	921,666	1,021,440	1,567,811	09/08/01	53.5%	10.8%	70.1%
Guyford	Magazines	MRD	2,377,821	2,868,988	3,262,490	10/08/01	13.7%	20.7%	37.2%
Hyman, Inc.	Supplies	LRC	31,640	40,022	46,911	10/22/01	17.2%	26.5%	48.3%
Intertec	Books	RDM	821,904	898,683	959,604	11/18/01	6.8%	9.3%	16.8%
Jerrico	Paper	LRC	486,401	111,923	93,499	08/04/01	(16.5%)	(77.0%)	(80.8%)
Julian-Borg	Magazines	MRD	431,470	589,182	371,920	02/07/01	(36.9%)	36.6%	(13.8%)
King Features	Magazines	MRD	436,820	492,687	504,360	11/18/01	2.4%	12.8%	15.5%
Lycorp	Sundries	LRC	16,280	17,404	21,410	N/A	23.0%	6.9%	31.5%
Medallian	Books	RDM	---	61,227	410,163	12/15/01	569.9%	---	---
Northwood	Books	RDM	861,382	992,121	---	12/07/99	---	15.2%	(100.0%)
Orion Corp.	Paper	LRC	86,904	416,777	803,493	11/02/00	92.8%	379.6%	824.6%
Peterson	Supplies	LRC	114,623	---	---	N/A	---	---	---
Quick	Supplies	LRC	---	96,732	110,441	11/03/01	14.2%	---	---
Robertson	Books	RDM	2,361,912	3,040,319	3,516,811	12/01/01	15.7%	28.7%	48.9%
Steele	Magazines	MRD	621,490	823,707	482,082	11/03/01	(41.5%)	32.5%	(22.4%)
Telecom	Sundries	LRC	81,406	101,193	146,316	N/A	44.6%	24.3%	79.7%
Union Bay	Books	RDM	4,322,639	4,971,682	5,368,114	12/03/01	8.0%	15.0%	24.2%
Victory	Magazines	MRD	123,844	141,909	143,286	06/09/01	1.0%	14.6%	15.7%
Williams	Sundries	LRC	31,629	35,111	42,686	N/A	21.6%	11.0%	35.0%

(Page 3)

Bailey Books Incorporated

MEMORANDUM

TO: FILE (02-4422)
FROM: LOREN D. BRIDGES, CFE
SUBJECT: INTERVIEW OF MARK W. STEINBERG, CPA
CHIEF FINANCIAL OFFICER
DATE: FEBRUARY 1, 2002

Mark W. Steinberg, CPA, Chief Financial Officer of Bailey Books, was interviewed in his office, Room 836, 6200 Bayshore, St. Augustine, FL. The purpose of the meeting was to advise Mr. Steinberg of the proposed fraud examination, to obtain his approval of the proposed plan, and to secure basic information from him on the purchasing function.

Mr. Steinberg was advised of the nature of the anonymous allegations and the result of our initial vendor review. He also was informed of our plan to review personnel files and other internal company documents and to discreetly interview selected company personnel. He agreed to the above, asking that we conduct our examination as quickly and in the least disruptive manner possible. He agreed that Ms. Collins and the purchasing department would not be notified of the examination until decided otherwise.

Mr. Steinberg has been with Bailey Books, Incorporated since 1988. Previously, he was Assistant Vice President for Financial Affairs from 1989 to 1996. He reports directly to Mr. Hal B. Marlow, President and CFO of the company.

As CFO, all operating divisions, including purchasing, report to him. It is his responsibility to establish and supervise the monitoring of internal controls within the operating divisions. In general, Bailey follows the policy of obtaining bids on as many purchases as possible. He pointed out that the competitive nature of the retail book industry required constantly obtaining the maximum product for the minimum cost. He has reiterated to managers on many occasions the necessity of cutting costs.

Guidelines for purchasing procedures are set forth in Mr. Steinberg's memorandum to all division heads and supervisors dated October 22, 2000. The memo calls for purchasers to obtain bids on all purchases of more than $50,000. However, purchases of more than $10,000 generally are expected to be bid unless a justifiable reason not to exists. A copy of the memo was provided by Mr. Steinberg, and is attached. The copy provided has been initialed and dated and is maintained in the evidence file, Room 874, Bailey Books.

(Page 4)

Bailey Books Incorporated

MEMORANDUM

TO: LINDA REED COLLINS, PURCHASING MANAGER
FROM: MARK W. STEINBERG, CHIEF FINANCIAL OFFICER
SUBJECT: PURCHASING GUIDELINES
DATE: OCTOBER 22, 2000

The purpose of this memo is to establish guidelines for major purchases.

Effective at once, purchasing will obtain at least three written bids for items of more than $50,000, in all cases. Bids also should be obtained for purchase amounts starting at $10,000, where practical.

These bids should be maintained in the file for documentation purposes.

If the lowest bid is not selected, a memo of justification should be prepared and approved by me before any purchase is made. You are to be especially concerned with miscellaneous and sundry items, because these items are not price competitive.

Any deviations from the above-stated policy must be approved by me.

(Page 5)

| Sample Report | Investigation Appendix |

Bailey Books Incorporated
MEMORANDUM

TO: FILE (02-4422)
FROM: LOREN D. BRIDGES, CFE
SUBJECT: REVIEW OF PERSONNEL FILES
DATE: FEBRUARY 4, 2002

Francis Morris, Personnel Manager, provided the personnel files of Linda Reed Collins, Mary Rodriguez De La Garza, and Roger McGuire for review. Pertinent data included:

Mary Rodriguez De La Garza:
Sept. 15, 1997	Mary Rodriguez De La Garza hired as secretary at annual salary of $20,000
Sept. 14, 1998	Merit salary increase to $22,000 annual
Sept. 17, 1999	Merit salary increase to $24,500 annual
Aug. 2, 2000	Transferred and promoted to purchasing agent at salary of $27,000
Aug. 4, 2001	Merit salary increase to $30,000 annual

Roger McGuire:
Feb. 20, 1999	Roger Donald McGuire hired as purchasing agent at salary of $28,000
Feb. 22, 2001	Merit salary increase to $31,000 annual

Linda Reed Collins:
June 1, 1997	Linda Reed Collins hired as purchasing agent at salary of $28,500
June 3, 1998	Merit salary increase to $31,250 plus participation in incentive plan
Nov. 8, 1999	Promoted to Purchasing Manager, salary increase to $36,000 annual, plus incentives
Nov. 10, 2000	Merit salary to $39,500 annual plus incentives
Nov. 11, 2001	Merit salary to $43,000 annual plus incentives

The personnel file reflected that Ms. Collins was consistently rated as "exceptional" by her supervisors in annual reviews. She has executed annual Conflict of Interest Questionnaires for 1997 through 2001 indicating that she and her spouse, Edward Collins, had no outside employment, investments or interests with companies doing business with Bailey Books.

The file did contain a copy of IRS form 668-W, Notice of Levy on Wages, Salary and Other Income, dated June 2, 1998, indicating that Ms. Collins and her spouse owed federal taxes of $53,219.09.

An IRS Release of Levy, indicating that the amount due had been paid in full, was filed December 8, 2000.

(Page 6)

Investigation Appendix   Sample Report

Bailey Books Incorporated
MEMORANDUM

TO: FILE (02-4422)
FROM: LOREN D. BRIDGES, CFE
SUBJECT: INTERVIEW OF ROGER DONALD MCGUIRE
DATE: FEBRUARY 4, 2002

Roger Donald McGuire, Purchasing Agent, Bailey Books, was interviewed at his office, Room 537, 6200 Bayshore, St. Augustine, Florida. After being advised of the identity of the interviewer and the nature of the inquiry, McGuire voluntarily provided the following information:

He has been employed by Bailey Books since 1999. He is a purchasing agent whose function is to purchase the book inventory. Purchasing policy guidelines require him to obtain bids for all purchases over $50,000. He said that bids are submitted in substantially all of his purchases of books, and that he estimates somewhere between 80 and 90 percent of his purchases are bid out.

Whenever he deviates from selecting the low bidder for a product, he writes a memo of justification to the file with approval from his manager. This does not happen on many occasions. The reasons for not obtaining bids for products include (1) emergency purchases; (2) sole source purchases; and (3) time pressures. McGuire is aware that the other purchases, made by Mary Rodriguez De La Garza and Linda Reed Collins, are made under the same guidelines.

He is not aware of favoritism regarding vendors. McGuire has received pressure from various vendors from time to time. Examples include "the hard sell" that many vendors try with purchasing agents; and occasional efforts by the vendors to get paid early so they can earn and collect their commissions. Every now and then, a vendor will attempt to give him a gratuity, such as a free case of liquor or a small gift. However, McGuire says he avoids any ties to the vendor, as such are prohibited by Bailey's employee guidelines.

He is unaware of any other purchasing employees making any exceptions to purchasing policy. McGuire thinks a great deal of his co-workers Mary Rodriguez De La Garza and Linda Reed Collins. He does not know whether they have accepted gifts or gratuities from vendors. McGuire thinks it is somewhat unusual that Ms. Collins reserves purchasing functions for herself, since hers is primarily a management function. He cannot explain why she has reserved this duty. He once volunteered to take over her accounts, but she said she would prefer to handle some of the purchasing function herself, to "keep her hand in the business."

(Page 7)

Bailey Books Incorporated

MEMORANDUM

TO: FILE (02-4422)
FROM: LOREN D. BRIDGES, CFE
SUBJECT: INTERVIEW OF MARY RODRIGUEZ DE LA GARZA
DATE: FEBRUARY 5, 2002

Ms. De La Garza was interviewed at her office in Room, 436, Bailey Building, 6200 Bayshore, St. Augustine, Florida. After being advised of the identity of the interviewer and the nature of the inquiry, Ms. De La Garza voluntarily provided the following information:

She has been employed at Bailey Books since 1997. In 2000, she was promoted and transferred to the purchasing department. Ms. De La Garza's function is to oversee the purchase of magazines and periodicals. She reports directly to Linda Reed Collins, the purchasing manager. The other employee in the department is Roger Donald McGuire.

Ms. De La Garza said that she is familiar with operating guidelines of the purchasing function. She is required to get bids for all purchases of more than $50,000, and, whenever possible, for purchases for less than that amount. As a rule, the purchases are bid for all items $10,000 and more.

In some instances it is not practical, or possible, to obtain bids; this is especially the case with sundry purchases. In addition, whenever shortages of merchandise occur and time is of the essence, bids are not sought. For approximately the last year, she has observed that Orion Corporation, a supplier of paper to Bailey Books, has received most, if not all, of the paper business. The salesman for Orion, Jim Nagel, seems to be very persuasive in dealing with Linda Reed Collins, Ms. De La Garza's boss.

When asked if there were any vendors who received preferential treatment, Ms. De La Garza hesitated. She finally said that something was bothering her, and she did not know how to discuss it.

When asked to explain, Ms. De La Garza said that she was concerned that any information she would offer might get back to Ms. Collins, and that she did not want to bring up false accusations. She said that there were several things that do not seem right.

(Page 8)

First, she said that Ms. Collins and her husband, Edward, had not been getting along for the past year or two. Edward has a charter boat business that has experienced serious financial problems, and she knew that Ms. Collins and he had been arguing over money.

She has seen Ms. Collins come to work several mornings in the last few months with her eyes reddened, and it appeared that she had been crying. On one or two occasions, when Ms. Collins has arrived upset, she had telephoned Nagel, and Ms. De La Garza thinks Nagel comforted her.

Ms. De La Garza does not know about any relationship between Nagel and Ms. Collins, but she does know that they are good friends. She is fairly certain that they have had lunch together on numerous occasions. Their friendship has been the subject of gossip and speculation; the office thinks that they are having an affair.

Ms. De La Garza knows that Nagel has received favored treatment as a vendor. Several months ago (exact date not recalled), she heard Ms. Collins call accounts payable and chew someone out who did not want to hand-cut a check for Nagel. She does not remember the exact circumstances, but she said that during the time she has worked at Bailey, Ms. Collins has never hurried up a payment for a vendor, with the exception of Nagel.

Ms. De La Garza does not believe Ms. Collins is doing anything illegal; she thinks, however, that Ms. Collins' judgment might be clouded by Mr. Nagel, whom she describes as a very good-looking and quite charming man.

When asked if anyone else had any knowledge of the business or personal relationship between Ms. Collins and Mr. Nagel, Ms. De La Garza replied that Sara Louise Dawson had worked on the Orion account before she left Bailey Books, within the last several months. She believes Ms. Dawson had a falling out with Ms. Collins, which prompted her to quit.

(Page 9)

Bailey Books Incorporated

MEMORANDUM

TO: FILE (02-4422)
FROM: LOREN D. BRIDGES, CFE
SUBJECT: INTERVIEW OF SARA LOUISE DAWSON
DATE: FEBRUARY 5, 2002

Sara Louise Dawson was interviewed at her residence, 2051 Wisconsin Ave., Apt. 16, St. Augustine, Florida, on a confidential basis. After being advised of the identity of the interviewer and the nature of the inquiry, she voluntarily provided the following information.

Ms. Dawson advised that she did not wish to answer any questions. She said that her employment at Bailey Books was a "closed chapter" in her life, which she did not wish to reopen. She described her relationship with Linda Reed Collins as "strained." She said that she wished she could be of assistance because "certain things at Bailey just weren't right," but she had "to get on with her life."

After further discussion with Ms. Dawson, in which the importance of her cooperation was emphasized, she agreed to speak to her brother-in-law, an attorney, about whether she should provide any information. She insisted that any communication with her, including this interview, be kept strictly confidential.

(Page 10)

Bailey Books Incorporated

MEMORANDUM

TO: FILE (02-4422)
FROM: LOREN D. BRIDGES, CFE
SUBJECT: TELEPHONE CONVERSATION WITH THOMAS C. GREEN, ATTORNEY
DATE: FEBRUARY 6, 2002

Thomas C. Green, an attorney with the law firm of Sharp, Green and Langfrom, 6600 Bayshore Parkway, St. Augustine, called me at my office at 10:00 a.m. on the above date.

Mr. Green said he had been contacted by Sara Louise Dawson, who had been referred by another attorney, regarding our request for an interview.

Mr. Green said he had interviewed Ms. Dawson and that her information would be "most helpful" to our inquiry. Mr. Green said he would not permit us to interview Ms. Dawson unless the company provided her with an indemnity against all claims arising out of her cooperation, and agreed to pay his attorney fees to attend the interviews.

Mr. Green would not provide any details about the nature of Ms. Dawson's information. He reiterated that we "would not be disappointed."

(Page 11)

Bailey Books Incorporated

MEMORANDUM

TO: FILE (02-4422)
FROM: LOREN D. BRIDGES, CFE
SUBJECT: MEETING WITH MARK W. STEINBERG, CFO AND LINCOLN S. WYZOKOWSKI, GENERAL COUNSEL
DATE: FEBRUARY 6, 2002

After discussing the facts, Mr. Steinberg and Mr. Wyzokowski agreed to provide an indemnity agreement to Sara Louise Dawson for her cooperation in the fraud examination regarding the purchasing function of Bailey Books Incorporated. Wyzokowski agreed to prepare the indemnity agreement, and to set up the interview of Ms. Dawson through her attorney.

(Page 12)

Bailey Books Incorporated

MEMORANDUM

TO: FILE (02-4422)
FROM: LOREN D. BRIDGES, CFE
TONYA VINCENT, CFE
SUBJECT: INTERVIEW OF SARA L. DAWSON
DATE: MARCH 3, 2002

Sara Louise Dawson was interviewed at the office of her attorney, Thomas C. Green, at Suite 400, 6600 Bayshore Parkway, St. Augustine. Mr. Green was present for the entire interview. After preliminary discussions about the nature of the inquiry, Ms. Dawson voluntarily provided the following information.

Ms. Dawson was employed at Bailey Books Incorporated in the Purchasing Department from February 1996 through July 2001. Her duties included the purchase of magazines and periodicals as well as sundries and paper products. In that capacity she worked for Linda Reed Collins from November 1999 until Ms. Dawson left the company.

After Ms. Collins' promotion, she began to favor Orion in paper purchases. Orion's prices were high and the quality of service was marginal. Deliveries often were late or incomplete, requiring Ms. Dawson to expend considerable time and effort in follow-up calls and correspondence.

On two occasions in the spring of 2001, Ms. Collins directed her to make substantial purchases from Orion and to authorize prepayment. The orders were not bid and prices quoted were higher than available from other, more reliable suppliers. Bailey Books also had a policy against prepayment of orders.

Ms. Dawson complained to Ms. Collins about Orion's past performance and suggested that other vendors be allowed to bid. Ms. Collins responded that the paper was needed now, that there was no time for bids and that the price differential was insignificant. Ms. Collins also said that prepayment was necessary so that Orion could rush the order.

Ms. Dawson said that, in fact, there was no urgent need for the paper, but that, based on past experience with Ms. Collins, she believed it was fruitless to resist, and she complied with her instructions.

(Page 13)

Shortly thereafter she checked with the receiving department and learned that the order had not been received. She advised Ms. Collins, who seemed unconcerned. Ms. Dawson then prepared a letter for Ms. Collins' signature requesting immediate shipment of the order. Ms. Collins declined to send the letter, saying it was not necessary, as Orion had assured her the shipment would be received shortly.

A few weeks later, Ms. Collins stopped by Ms. Dawson's office and closed the door. Ms. Collins told her that, because of Orion's "excellent service" and "loyalty" to Bailey Books that she wanted future purchases from them to be on a no-bid basis. Ms. Collins also instructed Ms. Dawson to prepay another order, in excess of $100,000 from Orion.

Ms. Dawson does not remember the exact dates or amounts, but suggested Becky Robinson in Accounts Payable might be able to provide more information.

Ms. Dawson knew that the previous Orion order had not yet been shipped and informed Ms. Collins. Ms. Collins became "nervous and jittery" and insisted she was mistaken. She again instructed Ms. Dawson to place the order; Ms. Dawson said she would need approval from higher up and an argument ensued. She did not place the order or talk to Ms. Collins again. At that time Ms. Dawson said she decided to look for new employment because her job had become too stressful.

Ms. Dawson also advised that other vendors, including Jerrico, had complained about being "squeezed" out by Bailey Books. Ms. Dawson thought that Jerrico's prices and service were superior to Orion's, but Ms. Collins would not take their product. Ms. Dawson, through Mr. Green, agreed to further interviews, as necessary.

(Page 14)

Investigation Appendix   Sample Report

Bailey Books Incorporated

MEMORANDUM

TO: FILE (02-4422)
FROM: LOREN D. BRIDGES, CFE
SUBJECT: INTERVIEW OF BECKY ROBINSON
DATE: APRIL 8, 2002

Becky Robinson, Accounts Payable Clerk, Bailey Books Incorporated, was interviewed at her office, Room 513, Bailey Building, 6200 Bayshore, St. Augustine, Florida. After being advised of the identity of the interviewer and the nature of the inquiry, she voluntarily provided the following information.

She has been employed by Bailey Books Incorporated since January 1999, and has always worked in the Accounts Payable Department. Her job is to review invoices for processing before payment. She checks the invoice mathematics and extensions, sees whether merchandise has been received, and verifies that the invoice has been approved for payment by the department head.

Ms. Robinson maintains the invoices. Canceled checks are maintained by Treasury, (she thinks in Ms. Deborah Roth's office). She provided copies of two invoices paid to Orion Corporation. The documents provided by her were initialed, dated, and secured in the evidence file maintained in Room 874, Bailey Books Corporation. Copies of the above-referenced documents are attached hereto.

A review of the invoices provided reflect a notation on invoices dated April 2, 2001 and April 21, 2001—in the amounts of $102,136, and $95,637, respectively—that payment was made before the merchandise was received. Ms. Robinson recalls that Ms. Collins called her on two occasions and said that Orion was experiencing cash flow problems, and to keep them as a vendor, it would be necessary to give them the money up front.

When Ms. Robinson told Linda Reed Collins that she was not supposed to approve payment before the merchandise had been received, Ms. Collins got agitated and told Ms. Robinson, "I am the senior purchasing official, and I am telling you to do what I say." Ms. Robinson did as she was instructed, but did not follow up to see if the paper had been received. Ms. Robinson did not report these incidents.

Ms. Robinson said that Ernie Quincy in Receiving would be able to tell whether the two shipments above had been received.

(Page 15)

ORION

Orion Corporation
2600 Industrial Drive
St. Augustine, Florida 32086

April 2, 2001

I N V O I C E

Bailey Books Incorporated
6200 Bayshore Drive
St. Augustine, FL 32082

    1,075 packages of 80 lb. standard
    white paper @ 95/m............... $102,136

TERMS: NET 30 DAYS

(Page 16)

ORION

Orion Corporation
2600 Industrial Drive
St. Augustine, Florida 32086

April 21, 2001

INVOICE

Bailey Books Incorporated
6200 Bayshore Drive
St. Augustine, FL 32082

    1006 packages of 80 lb. standard
    white paper @ 95/m.............. $95,637

TERMS: NET 30 DAYS

(Page 17)

Bailey Books Incorporated

MEMORANDUM

TO: FILE (02-4422)
FROM: LOREN D. BRIDGES, CFE
SUBJECT: INTERVIEW OF ERNIE QUINCY
DATE: APRIL 8, 2002

Mr. Ernie Quincy, Warehouse Manager of Bailey Books, was interviewed at his office, Room 114, Bailey Building, 6200 Bayshore, St. Augustine. After being advised of the identity of the interviewer and the nature of the inquiry, Mr. Quincy voluntarily furnished the following information:

A review of his outstanding invoices shows that Orion invoices—dated April 2 and April 21, 2001 have not been received in the warehouse. He remembers that shortly after receiving the invoices last year, he called Ms. Robinson, who referred him to Linda Reed Collins. Mr. Quincy then called Ms. Collins about not having received the paper, and she told him not to worry about it; that they had an understanding with the supplier that the paper would be delivered later.

Mr. Quincy thought that this situation was unusual, since no other shipments had been paid for in advance. He has been Bailey Books' Warehouse Foreman for 12 years.

(Page 18)

Bailey Books Incorporated

MEMORANDUM

TO: FILE (02-4422)
FROM: LOREN D. BRIDGES, CFE
SUBJECT: CHECKS PAYABLE TO ORION PAPER COMPANY
DATE: APRIL 9, 2002

Margaret O'Boyle, Treasurer's Office, Bailey Books Incorporated, provided copies of the checks described below. A review of Bailey Books Incorporated canceled checks, numbered 10106 and 10107, reflected the following:

    Check No. 10106
        Date: April 28, 2001
        Amount: $102,136
        Payment For: Orion Invoice dated April 2, 2001
        Endorsement: For Deposit to the Account of Orion Paper Company,
            Account No. 025269999 (stamped)
        Bank to which Deposited: Florida Marine National Bank, St.
            Augustine
        Date Deposited: April 30, 2001

    Check No. 10107
        Date: April 28, 2001
        Amount: $95,637
        Payment For: Orion Invoice dated April 27, 2001
        Endorsement: For Deposit to the Account of Orion Paper Company,
            Account No. 025269999 (stamped)
        Bank to which Deposited: Florida Marine National Bank, St.
            Augustine
        Date Deposited: April 30, 2001

Copies of the fronts and backs are attached, and they have been initialed and dated.

(Page 19)

Bailey Book Corporation
6200 Bayshore Drive
St. Augustine, FL 32085

Pay to the Order of ___Orion___

One hundred two thousand one hundred thirty six and no/100

April 28 20 01

10106

35-099
489

$ 102,136.00

Dollars

First National Bank
1001 Main Street
St. Augustine, FL132080

For ___Orion Invoice, 4/2/01___

Margaret O'Boyle

|:001355|: 114902722   10106 8967|:

FOR DEPOSIT ONLY
Orion Paper Company
Acct. No. 025269999

FLORIDA MARINE NATIONAL BANK
ST. AUGUSTINE

APR 3 0 2001

(Page 20)

Bailey Book Corporation
6200 Bayshore Drive
St. Augustine, FL 32085

10107

April 28, 20 01

35-099
489

Pay to the Order of ___Orion_____ $ 95,637.00

Ninety five thousand six hundred thirty seven and no/100 _____ Dollars

First National Bank
1001 Main Street
St. Augustine, FL 132080

For   Orion Invoice, 4/21/01   *Margaret O'Boyle*

|:001355|: 114902722   10107 8967|:

FOR DEPOSIT ONLY
Orion Paper Company
Acct. No. 025269999

FLORIDA MARINE NATIONAL BANK
ST. AUGUSTINE

APR 2 9 2001

(Page 21)

Bailey Books Incorporated

MEMORANDUM

TO: FILE (02-4422)
FROM: LOREN D. BRIDGES, CFE
SUBJECT: INTERVIEW OF DAVID LEVEY,
               JERRICO INTERNATIONAL PAPER COMPANY
DATE: APRIL 9, 2002

David Levey, Director of Sales, Jerrico International Paper Company, 2901 Island Ave., Philadelphia, PA 19530 was interviewed by telephone at his office. After being advised of the identity of the interviewer, he provided the following information on a voluntary basis:

Mr. Levey assumed his present position in 1996. At that time Bailey Books Incorporated was a major customer, with sales in excess of $500,000 annually. Since then the volume has consistently dwindled.

In January 2002, Mr. Levey met with Carl Sanderson, the owner of Jerrico, and discussed how to revive the Bailey Books account. Both Mr. Levey and Mr. Sanderson had heard "rumors" in the industry that Jim Nagel of Orion Corporation was "taking care of" Linda Reed Collins, Bailey's Purchasing Manager. Nagel has a very poor reputation in the industry and was caught "paying off" on another account several years ago. Mr. Levey declined to provide any further details or to identify the source of his information.

As a result of their meeting, Mr. Sanderson and Mr. Levey "decided to test the waters" at Bailey Books by submitting a bid at cost for a substantial quantity of Deluxe Bond and Standard White to see "if we could open the doors." The offer was made at the end of January 2002, and was not accepted. Since then Jerrico does not even bother to bid and expects no further significant sales to Bailey Books.

(Page 22)

Bailey Books Incorporated

MEMORANDUM

TO: FILE (02-4422)
FROM: LOREN D. BRIDGES, CFE
SUBJECT: INTERVIEW OF MARY RODRIGUEZ DE LA GARZA
DATE: APRIL 13, 2002

Ms. Mary Rodriguez De La Garza phoned and said that she had overheard a telephone conversation between Ms. Collins and apparently Mr. Nagel. She heard Ms. Collins arrange to meet Mr. Nagel for drinks this afternoon after work. Collins is supposed to meet Nagel at the bar at the Hotel Atlantic in St. Augustine. Accordingly, a physical surveillance was established, as set forth in the following log.

(Page 23)

Bailey Books Incorporated

MEMORANDUM

TO: FILE (02-4422)
FROM: LOREN D. BRIDGES, CFE
SUBJECT: SURVEILLANCE LOG
DATE: APRIL 13, 2002

On April 13, 2002, commencing at 4:50 p.m., a surveillance was established at the Hotel Atlantic, 6583 Bayshore, St. Augustine, Florida. The results of the surveillance are as follows:

Date/Time	Event
4:50 p.m.	Established surveillance in lounge.
5:55 p.m.	Linda Reed Collins and white male arrive at lounge and order drinks. Collins and unidentified male hold hands at table.
6:20 p.m.	Collins and unidentified male order another drink.
6:27 p.m.	Unidentified male and Collins kiss at the table.
6:40 p.m.	Break—surveillance terminated.
6:44 p.m.	Surveillance reinstituted. Twosome still at bar.
7:02 p.m.	Observed white male paying for drinks in cash. Twosome leaves, holding hands, and proceed to Room 652 at Hotel Atlantic. Both enter.
9:32 p.m.	Collins and male leave Room 652. Male gets into a late model Chevrolet, silver in color, Florida license MNX-782, and departs. Collins gets into a Nissan 300ZX, license NRC-130, and departs.
9:35 p.m.	Surveillance terminated.

(Page 24)

Bailey Books Incorporated

MEMORANDUM

TO: FILE (02-4422)
FROM: LOREN D. BRIDGES, CFE
SUBJECT: ANONYMOUS TELEPHONE CALL
DATE: APRIL 16, 2002

A telephone call was received advising Edward J. Collins and his wife, Linda Reed Collins, had the following balances with the below-named establishments as of March 14, 2002.

Account	Total Balance	Monthly Payments
St. Augustine Bank	$46,482	$2,361
Sears	$2,378	$281
Marine Savings	$110,232	$1,377
Bailey Credit Union	$14,826	$787
MasterCard	$10,041	$397
American Express	$5,990	Balance
Norwood Corporation	$3,892	$461
Bally Fashions	$1,436	$124
	Total Fixed Payments	$5,788

The caller advised that Edward J. and Linda Reed Collins had held a joint checking account since 1993 at Sunshine Federal Bank. The account had an average balance of less than $1,000, and was frequently overdrawn. No other accounts were located.

(Page 25)

Bailey Books Incorporated

MEMORANDUM

TO: FILE (02-4422)
FROM: LOREN D. BRIDGES, CFE
SUBJECT: REVIEW OF RECORDS
                ST. AUGUSTINE COUNTY COURTHOUSE
DATE: APRIL 17, 2002

Records of the St. Augustine County Courthouse reflected the following information regarding Edward J. Collins and Linda Reed Collins as of April 11, 2002.

1. Edward J. Collins is a defendant in three civil actions as follows:

    a. Bertram Yachts, Incorporated, vs. Edward J. Collins and Collins Marine Corporation, Case Number 00-4435. Bertram sued Collins individually and the corporation for nonpayment of $13,874 plus interest and attorney fees. The suit was filed April 23, 2000, and alleges that Collins took delivery of a marine winch on March 4, 1999, and that the amount is unpaid. The suit is still pending. Attorney for the Plaintiff is Sherry T. Marshall, Cummins and Marshall, Vero Beach, Florida.

    b. Bradford L. Jenkins vs. Edward J. Collins et al, Case Number 01-0964. This suit alleges that on June 27, 2001, Jenkins paid a deposit for Collins' charter boat, the Mistress, and canceled within the period provided by the contract. Collins check refunding the $3,500 was returned for insufficient funds. Collins did not make the check good.

    c. Bayview Bank vs. Edward J. Collins and Collins Marine Corporation, Case Number 01-5412. Collins was sued on April 21, 2001, for nonpayment of a working capital note with a current balance off $31,423. The note is unpaid.

(Page 26)

Bailey Books Incorporated

MEMORANDUM

TO: FILE (02-4422)
FROM: LOREN D. BRIDGES, CFE
SUBJECT: REVIEW OF RECORDS
SECRETARY OF STATE
DATE: APRIL 17, 2002

The Secretary of State's Office, Tallahassee, Florida, records reflects the following information about Collins Marine Corporation:

The Corporation was formed on July 23, 1993. Listed as incorporators are Edward J. Collins, James B. Vickers, and Linda Reed Collins. Officers are the same. Registered Agent is Frank R. Bledsoe, Attorney at Law, 764 Front Street, St. Augustine, Florida.

The Corporation's charter was suspended on February 15, 2001 for failure to pay $324 in franchise taxes to the state.

(Page 27)

Bailey Books Incorporated

MEMORANDUM

TO: FILE (02-4422)
FROM: LOREN D. BRIDGES, CFE
SUBJECT: REVIEW OF RECORDS
           CHATTEL MORTGAGES
DATE: APRIL 17, 2002

A review of Chattel Mortgages in St. Augustine County, Florida, reflect the following records concerning Linda Reed Collins and Edward Collins as of December 31, 2001:

Date Filed	Lien Holder	Property	Original Amount of Lien
3/12/00	St. Augustine Bank	1993 Mercedes 450SL	$55,000
9/12/00	Bailey Credit Union	1995 Nissan 300ZX	$21,505
8/17/01	Norwood Corporation	Stereo Equipment	$8,500

(Page 28)

Bailey Books Incorporated

MEMORANDUM

TO: FILE (02-4422)
FROM: LOREN D. BRIDGES, CFE
SUBJECT: REVIEW OF RECORDS
                DUN & BRADSTREET
DATE: APRIL 17, 2002

Records of Dun & Bradstreet reflect the following information about Collins Marine Corporation as of December 31, 2000:

	1998	1999	2000
Sales	302,000	257,000	193,000
Total Assets	157,000	146,000	118,000
Total Liabilities	104,000	161,000	183,000
Net Income	41,000	-13,000	-63,000

(Page 29)

Bailey Books Incorporated

MEMORANDUM

TO: FILE (02-4422)
FROM: LOREN D. BRIDGES, CFE
SUBJECT: REVIEW OF FINANCIAL CONDITION OF LINDA REED
           COLLINS
           AND EDWARD J. COLLINS FROM PUBLIC RECORDS
DATE: APRIL 18, 2002

A review of the financial condition of Linda Reed Collins and Edward Collins, assembled from public records, reflects the following for the year of 2001:

Income (net):

Linda Reed Collins	$35,400	
Edward J. Collins	————	
Total Income:		$35,400
Expenses:		
House Payments	16,524	
Automobile Payments		
'93 Mercedes	28,332	
'95 Nissan	9,444	
Stereo Equipment	5,532	
Food (estimated)	4,800	
Utilities (estimated)	2,400	
Total Expenses:		67,032
Unexplained Income:		$31,632

(Page 30)

Bailey Books Incorporated

MEMORANDUM

TO: FILE (02-4422)

FROM: LOREN D. BRIDGES, CFE
                   TONYA VINCENT, CFE

SUBJECT: INTERVIEW OF JAMES R. NAGEL

DATE: APRIL 19, 2002

James R. Nagel, Sales Representative, Orion Corporation, was interviewed at his office, Room 5214, 2600 Industrial Drive, St. Augustine, Florida. After being advised of the identity of the interviewers and of the nature of the inquiry, Mr. Nagel voluntarily provided the following information:

He has been a salesman for Orion since October 1992. He sells stationery and paper stock to a variety of business enterprises, including Bailey Books Incorporated. Bailey is not his largest account.

Mr. Nagel acknowledges that he knows Linda Reed Collins. He says their relationship is purely professional, and he has never socialized with her. He emphatically denies any improprieties of any kind, and says he has never offered any gratuities or kickbacks to Collins.

Mr. Nagel claims the prices he charges Bailey are competitive, and that if Bailey is paying higher prices, it is because they are getting better products. He was presented with two invoices, dated 4/2/01 and 4/21/01, which reflect the payments for products that were not received. Nagel claims he does not know anything about any missing products, and that Bailey's records were in error. He denies asking for payment in advance to help the cash flow of Orion Corporation.

Mr. Nagel denied our request to review Orion's books and records pertaining to the 4/2/01 and 4/21/01 invoices, saying the information was "none of your business" and "proprietary." He refused to answer any further questions without his attorney being present.

(Page 31)

Bailey Books Incorporated
MEMORANDUM

TO: FILE (02-4422)
FROM: LOREN D. BRIDGES, CFE
TONYA VINCENT, CFE
SUBJECT: INTERVIEW OF OWEN STETFORD
DATE: APRIL 21, 2002

Owen Stetford, Chief Financial Officer, Orion Corporation, was interviewed in his office at 2600 Industrial Drive, St. Augustine, Florida. Clifford Karchmer, Orion's General Counsel, also attended the meeting.

We advised Mr. Stetford and Mr. Karchmer of the nature of our inquiry and requested their cooperation. We had earlier asked Mr. Stetford to produce copies of Orion's records pertaining to sales to Bailey Books when we telephoned to set up the interview.

Mr. Stetford said that Orion Corporation was formed in 1970 by his grandfather and that the company is closely held. Mr. Stetford further stated that Orion is committed to the highest level of business integrity, that Bailey Books is a valued customer, and that he is anxious to cooperate as far as permitted by company counsel.

Regarding our request to review the Orion's records pertaining to sales to Bailey Books, and in particular the invoices dated April 2 and April 21, 2001, Mr. Stetford said that he would be unable to provide us with access to the original records on the advice of counsel. However, he said he personally reviewed the records and told us that Orion had no record of any receipt of payment for the above invoices, nor any record that such an order had been placed or shipped.

Mr. Stetford further advised, after reviewing our copies of the canceled Bailey Books checks payable to Orion for the above invoices, that Orion does not maintain any corporate accounts at Florida Marine National Bank. Furthermore, the correct corporate name is Orion Corporation, not Orion Paper Company, as the endorsements indicate.

Mr. Stetford emphatically stated that neither he nor any other corporate officer was aware of or condoned any improper activities regarding their sales. He said that he would direct Mr. Nagel to answer any questions regarding sales to Bailey Books Incorporated.

In this regard, we again asked for permission to examine Orion's records, particularly the account payable records for the period November 1999 through July 2001. Mr. Karchmer said that he would take our request under advisement.

(Page 32)

Investigation Appendix　　　　　　　　　　　　　　　　　　　　　　　　Sample Report

Bailey Books Incorporated

MEMORANDUM

TO: FILE (02-4422)
FROM: LOREN D. BRIDGES, CFE
            TONYA VINCENT, CFE
SUBJECT: INTERVIEW OF JAMES R. NAGEL
DATE: MAY 1, 2002

James R. Nagel was interviewed at the office of his attorney, Conrad Vance, of the law firm Vance, Selig and Reisman, Suite 1000, 1601 Harbor Drive, St. Augustine. At the conclusion of the interview Mr. Nagel voluntarily executed the attached statement. The original of this statement has been witnessed by Bridges and Vincent, and is maintained in the evidence file, Room 874, Bailey Books Corporation, 6200 Bayshore, St. Augustine, Florida 32082.

St. Augustine, Florida
May 1, 2002

I, James R. Nagel, furnish the following free and voluntary statement to Loren D. Bridges and Tonya Vincent of Bailey Books Incorporated. No threats or promises of any kind have been used to induce this statement.

Since 1992, I have been a sales representative employed by Orion Corporation. Since 1994, I have been responsible for paper sales to Bailey Books Incorporated.

In or about January 2000, Linda Reed Collins, Manager of Purchasing, told me that she would require a "commission" on all sales to Bailey Books by Orion. I advised my boss, Donald L. Marsh, Sales Manager, of Ms. Collins' demand. Mr. Marsh and I reluctantly agreed to make the payments because we believed that it would otherwise be impossible to make any sales to Bailey Books. No other person at Orion was informed of Ms. Collins' demand.

The payments to Ms. Collins began about February 2000. Ms. Collins told me that she would inflate the prices paid to Orion in order to cover the kickbacks. Thereafter, approximately $51,000 was paid to Ms. Collins by Orion Corporation checks, payable to Market Research, Inc. Ms. Collins told me that Market Research, Inc. was a company she had established. The checks were recorded on Orion's books as consulting fees, and were approved by Mr. Marsh and me.

In about March 2001, Ms. Collins told me that she would approve the payment of invoices to Orion for product that would not have to be delivered. Ms. Collins thereafter authorized the payment of two invoices in the amounts of $102,136 and $95,637, which were paid by Bailey Books Incorporated in April 2001. No product was shipped on these invoices. Ms. Collins and I established a bank account in the name of Orion Paper Company at Florida Marine National Bank and equally divided the proceeds of the above-mentioned invoices. Ms. Collins prepared my checks, which were then deposited to my personal checking account at Flagler National Bank in St. Augustine. I spent the proceeds on bills. Neither Mr. Marsh nor any other person at Orion was aware of the above activity.

I make this statement in order to express my regret for having engaged in the aforementioned conduct, and promise to make restitution to the extent possible. I knew my conduct was wrong, but I felt it was justifiable at the time. I will try to pay any losses that have occurred as a result of my activities.

I have read this statement, consisting of this page. I now sign my name below in the presence of the undersigned witnesses because the statement is true and correct to the best of my knowledge.

Witnesses:
Loren D. Bridges   _James R. Nagel_
                                                                          Signature

Tonya Vincent

(Page 34)

Bailey Books Incorporated

MEMORANDUM

TO: FILE (02-4422)
FROM: LOREN D. BRIDGES, CFE
               TONYA VINCENT, CFE
SUBJECT: INTERVIEW OF LINDA REED COLLINS
DATE: MAY 1, 2002

Ms. Linda Reed Collins was interviewed on May 1, 2002, by Loren D. Bridges and Tonya Vincent. She voluntarily provided the attached signed statement. The original of this statement has been witnessed by Bridges and Vincent, and is maintained in the evidence file, Room 874, Bailey Books Corporation, 6200 Bayshore, St. Augustine, Florida 32082.

(Page 35)

St. Augustine, Florida
May 1, 2002

I, Linda Reed Collins, furnish the following free and voluntary statement to Loren D. Bridges and Tonya Vincent of Bailey Books Incorporated. No threats or promises of any kind have been used to induce this statement.

I am Senior Purchasing Agent for Bailey Books Incorporated, and have been employed by Bailey Books since 1997. My job is to oversee the purchase of merchandise and other supplies for Bailey Books Incorporated. As part of my job, I am to ensure that Bailey Books Incorporated receives the highest quality products at the lowest possible cost.

Commencing in approximately February 2000, and continuing through the current time, I have accepted money from James Nagel, Sales Representative for Orion Corporation, St. Augustine, Florida. Nagel offered me money to ensure that his company received preferential treatment in supplying Bailey Books with stationery and paper products.

On those occasions that I accepted money, I was aware that Bailey Books Incorporated was not obtaining the best product at the lowest possible price. The price charged for products delivered during the time I accepted money was substantially higher than market value.

On two occasions in April 2001, I authorized the payment of invoices of $102,136 and $95,637, respectively. These invoices were paid without the receipt of any merchandise. Nagel and I subsequently split the proceeds of these invoices equally between us.

I estimate that I have received in excess of $150,000 in connection with Mr. Nagel. I am not sure that anyone at Orion Corporation knew of our arrangement. No one at Bailey Books had knowledge of, or participated in, my scheme.

I am aware that my conduct is illegal, and violated Bailey Books' policies. I participated in this scheme because my husband and I were having severe financial problems due to his business. My husband is not aware of this matter. I am truly sorry for my conduct, and I promise to repay any resulting damages.

I have read this statement consisting of this page. I now sign my name below because this statement is true and correct to the best of my knowledge.

Witnesses:

Witnesses:
 Loren D. Bridges   *Linda Reed Collins*
                                                Signature
 Tonya Vincent

(Page 36)

CONSENT TO SEARCH

_____
(Date)

_____
(Location)

I, _____, having been informed of my Constitutional right not to have a search made of the premises hereinafter mentioned without a search warrant and of my right to refuse to consent to such a search, hereby authorize _____, and _____ to conduct a complete search of my premises located at _____. The above mentioned individuals are authorized by me to take from my premises any letters, papers, materials or other property which they might desire.

This written permission is being given by me voluntarily and without threats or promises of any kind.

_____
(Signed)

WITNESSES:

_____

_____

This is to certify that on _____ at _____, the individuals described above, conducted a search of _____. I certify that nothing was removed from my custody.

_____
(Signed)

Witnessed:

_____

_____

CONSENT TO SEARCH

On (date) _____ item (s) listed below were:

                                     ___ Received From
                                     ___ Returned To
                                     ___ Released To

(Name) _____

(Street Address) _____

(City) _____

Description of
Item (s):   _____

              _____

              _____

              _____

              _____

              _____

              _____

              _____

              _____

              _____

Received by: _____

Received From: _____

Investigation Appendix   Sample Forms

TELEPHONE RECORDING CONSENT

_____
(Date)

_____
(Location)

I, _____,
             (Name)

_____ , hereby
             (Address)

authorize _____ and

_____, employees of

_____, to install a recording device on a telephone
    (Company Name)

located at _____
                    (Location)

for the purpose of recording any conversation I might have on that telephone with

_____ on or about _____.
  (Name of Subjects)   (Date)

I have given this written permission without threats or promises of any kind.

_____
(Signature)

Witnesses:

_____

_____

2005 Fraud Examiners Manual

CONSENT TO RECORD

_____
(Date)

_____
(Location)

I, _____,
(Name)

_____, hereby authorize
(Address)

_____ and _____,

representatives of _____, to place a Body Recorder on
(Company Name)

my person for the purpose of recording any conversation with _____

_____ which I might have on or _____
(Name of Subject (s))   (Date)

    I have given this written permission voluntarily and without threats or promises of any kind.

_____
(Signature)

Witnesses:

_____

_____

CUSTOMER CONSENT AND AUTHORIZATION FOR ACCESS TO FINANCIAL RECORDS

I, _____, having read the explanation of my rights which is
       (Name of Customer)

attached to this form, hereby authorize the _____
                                              (Name and Address of Financial Institution)

_____

to disclose these financial records:

to _____
              (Name of Person (s))

for the following purpose (s):

_____

_____.

I understand that this authorization can be revoked by me in writing at any time before my records, as described above, are disclosed, and that this authorization is valid for no more than three months from the date of my signature.

_____   _____
       (Date)   (Signature of Customer)

                                  _____

                                  _____
                                       (Address of Customer)

_____
       (Witness)

BAILEY BOOKS INCORPORATED

EVIDENCE CONTROL LOG

Bank Safe
Deposit Box: _____
(Name of Bank)

____ Evidence Control Center
Location _____

_____
(Address of Bank)

REPOSITORY
____ Office Safe/Vault   Other: _____
Location _____
(File Cabinet, etc.)

Location: _____

(1) Signature of person(s) placing evidence in or removing from repository. If entry to facility for other reasons, briefly state in column 2.	(2) Reasons	(3) File Case No.	ENTERED Time	ENTERED Date	DEPARTED Time	DEPARTED Date

FRAUD POLICY REVIEW PROPOSAL

[Date]

Mr./Ms. [   ]
[Department]
[Company Name]
[Address]
[City, State, Zip Code]

RE: [Fraud Detection and Deterrence Review]

Dear Mr./Ms. [   ]:

Pursuant to our discussion, XYZ & Associates ("XYZ") is pleased to present this proposal to the ABC Company (the "Company") to perform a review of the Company's policies and procedures to detect and deter fraud.

This review is designed to assist in determining ABC's procedures concerning adequate fraud detection and deterrence methods. This review cannot be relied upon to provide assurances that fraud does not or will not exist within the company. Rather, it is designed to highlight weaknesses, if any, in the existing system. A potential review of XYZ would also provide management with recommendations for a proactive fraud deterrence program.

The fee for these services will be $_____ plus expenses which include—but are not limited to— travel, telephone, photocopying and facsimile charges. One half of the fee is due upon signing this letter and the other half upon delivery of the report. All expenses will be billed at the conclusion of each month and are due upon receipt. Any invoice remaining outstanding for more than 30 days will be subject to a rebilling charge.

Please review this proposal. If *this proposal* meets with your approval, please sign and return one copy along with your check for $ _____ in the enclosed envelope. If you have any questions, please do not hesitate to call. Thank you.

Sincerely yours,

FRAUD EXAMINATION PROPOSAL

[Date]

[   ], Esq.
[Legal Department]
[Company Name]
[Address]
[City, State, Zip Code]

RE: [Fraud Examination]

Dear Mr./Ms. [   ]:

Pursuant to our discussion, XYZ & Associates ("XYZ") presents this proposal to the ABC Company (the "Company") to perform a fraud examination as a result of certain allegations which have come to the attention of the Company.

Our examination will be conducted in accordance with lawful fraud examination techniques which include, but are not limited to: examination of books and records; voluntary interviews of appropriate personnel; and other such evidence-gathering procedures as necessary under the circumstances. We cannot provide assurances that fraud, if it exists, will be uncovered as a result of our examination.

The fee for this examination will be $_____ per hour plus expenses which include, but are not limited to: travel, telephone, photocopying and facsimile charges. A retainer of $_____ is due upon signing this letter. All expenses will be billed at the conclusion of each month and are due upon receipt. Any invoice remaining outstanding for more than 30 days will be subject to a rebilling charge. The hourly rate will be applied against the retainer. Once the retainer reaches a fully applied status, an additional retainer of $_____ will be required. We estimate the entire engagement will not be more than $_____, excluding any testimonial requirements. Any depositions or court appearances will be billed at the rate of $_____ per hour. All outstanding invoices must be paid before any testimonial appearances.

Please review this proposal. If it meets with your approval, please sign and return one copy along with your check for $_____ in the enclosed envelope. If you have any questions, please do not hesitate to call. Thank you.

Sincerely yours,

FRAUD POLICY REVIEW OPINION

[Date]

Mr./Ms. [   ]
[Company Name]
[Address]
[City, State, Zip Code]

RE: [Fraud Detection and Deterrence Review]

Dear Mr./Ms. [   ]:

Pursuant to your request, XYZ & Associates ("XYZ") has performed a review of the policies and procedures of the ABC Company (the "Company") for the purpose of reviewing their adequacy to detect and deter fraud.

This review does not provide assurance that fraud does not or will not exist. Having completed the following steps, we have determined that in order to strengthen its fraud detection potential ABC's procedures need improvement in the areas outlined herein.

Part of the purpose of an internal control system is to assure that the assets of ABC are properly safeguarded from employee or outsider misapplication. In addition, an adequate system of internal control contains detection methods that if misappropriation takes place, the irregularity will come to the attention of those who can remedy the situation and take suitable action against it. An adequate system of internal control is not designed to prevent or detect a collusive fraud scheme among employees and/or management. Our review included some the following procedures:

[In this section, briefly describe the main procedures one followed. For example]:

a. We read ABC's policy and procedural manual.
b. Through interviews with personnel key to the operations at ABC, we determined if the existing policies and procedures were being followed.
c. We charted the current flow of business transactions as they are being recorded at ABC Company.
d. We compared the flow of transaction approval and recording with the policies and procedural manuals.

Page 2

The following discrepancies were noted in ABC's system of internal control:

[In this section, explain briefly the differences between the established internal controls and those procedures followed by the company's personnel.]

Based on our review, we recommend the following changes be instituted in ABC's internal accounting controls system:

[In this section, make your recommendations.]

In addition to the above recommendations, we suggest ABC consider the following proactive approach to fraud deterrence:

[In this section suggest proactive steps such as]:

>   An internal audit structure reporting to the board of directors
>   Active inquiry of fraudulent transactions
>   Hotlines
>   Annual conflict of interest statements
>   Annual review of employee expense accounts, etc.

This report is not intended for general circulation or publication, nor is it to be reproduced for any purpose other than that outlined above. XYZ does not assume any responsibility or liability for losses occasioned to one or others as a result of the circulation, publication, reproduction or use of our report contrary to the conditions of this paragraph. The validity of our report is predicated on the extent to which full, honest and complete disclosure was made by all parties.

We will be in contact with one soon to discuss its details of this report. In the meantime, if one have any questions, please feel free to call.

Sincerely yours,

FRAUD EXAMINATION OPINION
(EVIDENCE DOES NOT SUPPORT ALLEGATION)

[Date]

[   ], Esq.
[Law Department]
[Company Name]
[Address]
[City, State, Zip Code]

RE: [Fraud Examination]

Dear Mr./Ms. [   ]:

We have conducted a fraud examination concerning a possible [misappropriation of assets] of [Company Name]. This examination was predicated upon [information resulting from a routine audit of the company's books by the company's internal auditors].

Our fraud examination was conducted in accordance with lawful fraud examination techniques, which included [an examination of books and records; voluntary interviews of appropriate personnel; and other such evidence-gathering procedures as necessary under the circumstances].

Because of the nature of fraud, no assurances can be given that fraud does not exist. However, based on the results of our examination, we have found no evidence to support the conclusion that [the assets in question were misappropriated].

Sincerely,

FRAUD EXAMINATION OPINION
(EVIDENCE SUPPORTS ALLEGATION)

[Date]

[   ], Esq.
[Law Department]
[Company Name]
[Address]
[City, State, Zip Code]

RE: [Fraud Examination]

Dear Mr./Ms. [   ]:

We have conducted a fraud examination concerning a possible [misappropriation of assets] of [Company Name]. This examination was predicated upon [information resulting from a routine audit of the company's books by the company's internal auditors].

Our fraud examination was conducted in accordance with lawful fraud examination techniques, which included [an examination of books and records, voluntary interviews of appropriate witnesses/personnel, and other such evidence-gathering procedures as necessary under the circumstances].

Based on the results of our fraud examination, we find that there is sufficient evidence to support the conclusion that [assets in the amount of $ _____ were misappropriated from the company's bank account and that Mr./Ms. _____ appropriated these assets for his/her personal benefit].

Please call me to set up a meeting at your earliest convenience so we can present you with the details of the evidence we gathered during our fraud examination.

Sincerely,

FRAUD EXAMINATION OPINION
(INCONCLUSIVE EVIDENCE)

[Date]

[   ], Esq.
[Law Department]
[Company Name]
[Address]
[City, State, Zip Code]

RE: [Fraud Examination]

Dear Mr./Ms. [   ]:

We have conducted a fraud examination concerning a possible [misappropriation of assets] of [Company Name]. This examination was predicated upon [information resulting from a routine audit of the company's books by the company's internal auditors].

Our examination was conducted in accordance with lawful fraud examination techniques, which included [an examination of books and records; voluntary interviews of appropriate personnel; and other such evidence-gathering procedures as necessary under the circumstances].

The results of our examination are inconclusive. Because of the nature of fraud, no assurances can be given that fraud does not exist. However, based on our examination, there is currently insufficient evidence to support the conclusion that [the assets in question were misappropriated].

Sincerely,

Section 4
Criminology & Ethics

CRIMINOLOGY AND ETHICS

TABLE OF CONTENTS

INTRODUCTION TO CRIMINOLOGY/ UNDERSTANDING HUMAN BEHAVIOR

Applying Behavioral Theory to a Fraud Case	4.102
Fraud as an Act of Behavior	4.103
Behavioral Analysis and the Detection of Fraud	4.112
Operant Conditioning and the Deterrence of Fraud	4.113
Conclusion	4.120
Why People Obey the Law	4.121
Instrumental Perspective	4.121
Normative Perspective	4.122
Legitimacy	4.122
Voluntary Compliance	4.124
Measuring Legitimacy and Compliance	4.125
Legitimacy and Compliance	4.126
Implications of the Chicago Study	4.126
The Psychological Variables	4.127
Legitimacy and Experience	4.127
The Meaning of Procedural Justice	4.128
Influence of Control on the Meaning of Procedural Justice	4.130

THEORIES OF CRIME CAUSATION

Classical Criminology	4.201
Routine Activities Theory	4.202
Biological Theories	4.203
Psychological Theories	4.204
Cognitive Theories	4.204
Integrated Theories	4.204
Conditioning Theory	4.204
Social Structure Theories	4.205
Theory of Anomie	4.205
Social Process Theories	4.206
Social Learning Theories	4.206
Theory of Differential Association	4.206
Social Control Theory	4.208
Differential Reinforcement Theory	4.210

WHITE-COLLAR CRIME

What is White-Collar Crime?	4.301
Public Perceptions of White-Collar Crime	4.303
National Survey of Crime Severity Ratings: Selected Offense Stimuli	4.303

CRIMINOLOGY AND ETHICS

WHITE-COLLAR CRIME (CONT.)
Crimes of the Middle Classes—A Look at White-Collar Crime 4.305
    Profiles of Offenders 4.306
    Cressey Study 4.306
    Effect of Status 4.307
    Organizational Opportunity 4.307
    The Middle Class 4.308
    Methodology 4.308
    Offenders Ranked by Status, with Selected Demographic Information 4.309
    Cooperating Defendants 4.310
    Pleas by White-Collar Defendants 4.311
    Judgments 4.311
    Personal Suffering 4.312
    Imprisonment 4.312
    Contributing Factors 4.314
    Conclusion 4.314
Varieties of White-Collar Crime 4.315

ORGANIZATIONAL CRIME
Corporate Organization and Criminal Behavior 4.402
    The Image of the Corporation 4.402
    Clinard and Yeager 4.403
Types of Violations 4.405
Causes of Organizational Crimes 4.407
Opportunities for Unlawful Organizational Behavior 4.409
    Organizational Structure 4.410
    The Nature of Transactions 4.412
    Market Signaling 4.413
    The System Interface Problem 4.414
Criminogenic Organizational Structures 4.416
Corporate Executives and Criminal Liability 4.419
    Corporate Fraud Task Force 4.421
Management Behavior 4.422
Controlling Organizational Crime 4.423
    The Enforcement Effort: Preventing and Reducing Fraud 4.426
        Compliance 4.426
        Deterrence 4.426
        Increased Enforcement 4.427
    Fraud Prevention Programs 4.427

OCCUPATIONAL CRIME
Research in Occupational Fraud and Abuse 4.501
    Edwin H. Sutherland 4.501

CRIMINOLOGY AND ETHICS

OCCUPATIONAL CRIME (CONT.)

Donald R. Cressey	4.502
Cressey's Hypothesis	4.502
Non-shareable Financial Problems	4.503
The Importance of Solving the Problem in Secret	4.507
Perceived Opportunity	4.508
Rationalizations	4.509
Conjuncture of Events	4.513
Conclusions	4.513
Dr. Steve Albrecht	4.513
The Albrecht Study	4.513
The Fraud Scale	4.515
Richard C. Hollinger	4.517
The Hollinger - Clark Study	4.517
Hypotheses of Employee Theft	4.517
2004 Report to the Nation on Occupational Fraud and Abuse	4.524
Types of Organizations	4.526
Measuring the Cost of Occupational Fraud	4.527
How Occupational Fraud Is Committed	4.529
Detecting Occupational Fraud	4.534
Limiting Fraud Losses	4.539
The Perpetrators	4.542
Case Results	4.549

FRAUD PREVENTION PROGRAMS

Responsibility for Fraud Prevention	4.601
Vicarious or Imputed Liability	4.601
Responsibility (and Liability) of a Corporation's Directors and Officers	4.602
The Treadway Commission	4.603
COSO Recommendations	4.603
Control Environment	4.604
Risk Assessment	4.605
Control Activities	4.606
Information and Communication	4.606
Monitoring	4.607
Corporate Sentencing Guidelines	4.607
Fines	4.609
Calculating the Fine	4.609
Departures	4.612
Restitution	4.613
Remedial Orders	4.613
Probation	4.613

CRIMINOLOGY AND ETHICS

FRAUD PREVENTION PROGRAMS (CONT.)

Implementing an Effective Compliance Program Under the
    Corporate Sentencing Guidelines 4.614
        Establishing Standards 4.616
        Assigning Responsibility 4.616
            Audit Committees 4.617
        Don't Let the Wolves Guard the Hen House 4.617
        Communicating the Policy 4.617
            Training Employees 4.618
        Achieving Compliance 4.618
            Proactive Fraud Policies 4.619
            Management Oversight 4.620
            Monitoring Systems 4.622
        Disciplinary Action 4.624
        Appropriate Responses 4.625
        Relation of COSO and Corporate Sentencing Guidelines 4.625
        Sample Corporate Compliance Policy 4.626
Fraud Prevention Standards Under Sarbanes-Oxley 4.626
        Audit Committee Responsibilities 4.627
            Overseeing Audits 4.627
            Receiving Complaints 4.627
            Composition of the Audit Committee 4.627
        Management Responsibilities 4.628
            Management's Responsibility for Internal Controls 4.628
            Codes of Ethics for Senior Financial Officers 4.628
            Certification Obligations 4.629
        Whistleblower Protection 4.630
        Fraud Prevention Requirements for External Auditors 4.631
            Attesting to Internal Controls 4.631
            Restrictions on Non-Audit Activity 4.631
Fraud Prevention Policy 4.631
        Fraud Policy Objectives 4.631
        Selling Fraud Prevention to Management 4.632
            The Impact on the Bottom Line 4.633
            The Impact of Publicity 4.633
        Writing the Fraud Policy 4.633
            Policy Statement 4.633
            Scope of Policy 4.633
            Actions Constituting Fraud 4.634
            Nonfraud Irregularities 4.634
            Investigation Responsibilities 4.634
            Confidentiality 4.634
            Authorization for Investigation 4.634

CRIMINOLOGY AND ETHICS

FRAUD PREVENTION PROGRAMS (CONT.)

Reporting Procedures	4.634
Termination	4.635
Communicating the Fraud Policy	4.635
Orientation	4.635
Memoranda	4.635
Posters	4.635
Employee Morale	4.635
Legal Considerations	4.635
Ethics Programs	4.636
Origins of Ethics	4.637
Ethics' Current Place in Business	4.637
Ethics Program Development	4.637
Sample Corporate Compliance Program	4.639
Sample Fraud Policy	4.650
Fraud Policy Decision Matrix	4.654
Sample Code of Business Ethics and Conduct	4.655
Introduction	4.655
Competition and Antitrust	4.656
Fair Competition	4.656
Compliance with Laws and Regulatory Orders	4.657
Foreign Corrupt Practices Act	4.657
Conflicts of Interest	4.658
Gifts and Entertainment	4.658
Outside Employment	4.659
Relationships with Suppliers and Customers	4.660
Employment of Relatives	4.661
Confidential Information and Privacy of Communications	4.661
Confidential Information	4.661
Classified National Security Information	4.662
Company Assets	4.662
Cash and Bank Accounts	4.662
Company Assets and Transactions	4.663
Expense Reimbursement	4.663
Company Credit Card	4.663
Software and Computers	4.664
Political Contributions	4.664
Employee Conduct	4.665
Conduct on Company Business	4.665
Reporting Violations	4.665
Discipline	4.666
Compliance Letter and Conflict of Interest Questionnaire	4.667

CRIMINOLOGY AND ETHICS

PUNISHMENT AND THE CRIMINAL JUSTICE SYSTEM

The Police and Regulatory Inspectors	4.702
The Police	4.702
Regulatory Inspectors	4.704
Processing Offenders	4.706
Arraignment	4.706
Preliminary Hearing	4.707
Grand Jury	4.708
The Court System	4.708
Criminal Trials	4.709
Defense Lawyers	4.710
The Outcome of the Criminal Process	4.711
Sentencing Options	4.712
Pre-trial Diversion	4.713
Probation	4.714
Shaming	4.717
Corrections	4.718
Types of Sentences	4.719
Determinate Sentences	4.719
Indeterminate Sentences	4.720
Mandatory Sentences and Three-Strikes Law	4.720
Prisons	4.722
Rehabilitation	4.723
Jails	4.724
Community Corrections	4.724
Parole	4.725
Crime Statistics	4.725
Uniform Crime Reports	4.725
National Crime Survey	4.727
Self-Report Surveys	4.727
Crime Trends in the United States	4.727
Factors Bearing on Crime Rates	4.728
Age and Crime	4.729
Economics and Crime	4.729
Race and Crime	4.730
Gender and Crime	4.731
Career Criminals	4.731
Crime and the Media	4.732
Drugs	4.732
Public Attitudes Toward the Criminal Justice System	4.733
Americans View Crime and Justice Survey	4.733
Approval Ratings for Police	4.734

CRIMINOLOGY AND ETHICS

PUNISHMENT AND THE CRIMINAL JUSTICE SYSTEM (CONT.)
    The Courts 4.735
    USSC Survey on Fraud Crimes 4.736

ETHICS FOR FRAUD EXAMINERS
What is Ethics? 4.801
    An Ethical Decision Maker's Role 4.802
    Ethical Decisions 4.802
Morality, Ethics, and Legality 4.803
    The High Road 4.804
    Philosophy, Ethics, and Law 4.804
    Means and Ends 4.806
Values and Principles 4.806
    Values 4.807
    Principles 4.807
        The Imperative Principle 4.808
        The Utilitarian Principle 4.811
        The Generalization Principle 4.813
Some Concluding Remarks 4.817

ASSOCIATION OF CERTIFIED FRAUD EXAMINERS CODE OF PROFESSIONAL ETHICS
Commitment to Professionalism and Diligence 4.902
    Professionalism 4.902
    Specialized Knowledge and Formal Education 4.902
    Professional Admission Standards 4.903
    Social Recognition: A Reciprocal Relationship 4.903
    Standards of Conduct 4.904
    Individual Fraud Examiners 4.904
    Diligence 4.905
Legal and Ethical Conduct and Conflict of Interest 4.905
    Illegal Conduct 4.905
        Libel and Slander 4.905
        False Imprisonment 4.906
        Compounding a Felony 4.906
    Unethical Conduct 4.906
        Conflict of Interest and "Independence" Considerations 4.907
Integrity and Competence 4.908
    Integrity 4.909
    Professional Competence 4.909
        Programming 4.910
        Investigation 4.910
        Reporting 4.910

CRIMINOLOGY AND ETHICS

ASSOCIATION OF CERTIFIED FRAUD EXAMINERS CODE OF PROFESSIONAL ETHICS (CONT.)

Professional Skepticism	4.910
Court Orders and Testimony	4.911
Reasonable Evidential Basis for Opinions	4.912
Evidential Basis for Opinions	4.912
Guilt and Innocence	4.914
Confidential Information	4.915
Proper Authorization	4.917
Relation to Conflict of Interest	4.917
"Public" Information	4.917
"Blowing the Whistle"	4.917
Complete Reporting of Material Matters	4.917
Professional Improvement	4.917
Professional Standards and Practices	4.917
General Standards	4.917
Independence and Objectivity	4.917
Qualifications	4.917
Fraud Examinations	4.917
Confidentiality	4.917
Specific Standards	4.917
Independence and Objectivity	4.917
Qualifications	4.917
Fraud Examination	4.917
Confidentiality	4.917
Predication Standards	4.917
Bribery	4.917
Conflicts of Interest	4.917
Embezzlement	4.917
False Financial Statements	4.917
False Statements	4.917
Theft	4.917
Larceny	4.917

CFE CODE OF PROFESSIONAL STANDARDS

I. Preamble	4.1001
II. Applicability of Code	4.1001
III. Standards of Professional Conduct	4.1002
IV. Standards of Examination	4.1004
V. Standards of Reporting	4.1004

INTRODUCTION TO CRIMINOLOGY

In the criminology section, we will study the various reasons people commit crimes in general, and fraud crimes in particular. We will also examine the criminal justice system and how criminals are punished.

The procedure in this section will be to describe (1) behavior in general, (2) why people obey the law, (3) why people break the law, (4) what happens to lawbreakers, and (5) theories about crime and fraud deterrence.

The reader might find some of the following material confusing and contradictory. This is because humans, being what they are, can often be unpredictable and behave in ways that are difficult to control. We will therefore begin with a general understanding of behaviors that are common to us all.

UNDERSTANDING HUMAN BEHAVIOR

Much of the understanding of human behavior can be attributed to B.F. Skinner, described by many as one of the greatest social scientists of the twentieth century. Skinner promised that he would revolutionize not just psychology but all of human society with his theories of Behaviorism. Human behavior should be approached scientifically, Skinner said. Instead of worrying over men's souls or quibbling about what makes up the Self, behaviorists would deal with what people actually do. Analyzing people's actions, the behaviorist could then alter or direct any behavior for the greater good of all. Criminal behavior could be modified into productive action; rearing a family would cease to be a continual game of trial and error, the pitfalls replaced by basic behavioral principles.

Skinner's accomplishments may have fallen short of this lofty goal. And he's not as widely recognized as Sigmund Freud. But Skinner's influence permeates many areas, often without overtly being attributed to the methods Skinner proposed in *Walden Two* (1948) and *Science and Human Behavior* (1953). When lawyers argue the mitigating or exonerating circumstances of a client's case, they often use behaviorist ideas; entire theories of management rest on the assumption that *incentives* and *promotion* are not just the best way to sell something, they're the best way to ensure that employees work properly.

Many people recall Skinner's name from beginning psychology courses, where he is usually tagged with a note:

Reduced psychology to stimulus and response; denied free will.

But Skinner doesn't argue about a "personality" at work inside a person; he merely sets the idea aside in the interest of science. Behaviorists believe that it's impossible to observe a person's thoughts, or even desires—we see only the *results* of thought or desire. For example, we say someone *desires* something because of the way he responds to the thing desired.

Applying Behavioral Theory to a Fraud Case

Using an actual case[1] we can show how such theories work in general, and their applicability to fraud cases in particular:

A high school graduate and government employee once used her government credit card for personal purchases in an emergency. When no one detected her action, the employee charged another $4,500 in personal items to Uncle Sam.

The emergency is the *stimulus*, a situation that demanded a *response* from the woman. Call her Beth. In this case she responded by charging the money to her employer's credit card. As an act of behavior, the event was positively *reinforced* because the money solved the crisis, and there were no adverse effects whatsoever: Beth got exactly what she wanted. There is now a *conditioned response* in Beth's mind, linking the credit card and ready money.

That doesn't mean she will automatically charge money to the card every time she finds herself low in funds. Human beings are not pigeons in a laboratory automatically pecking red dots for food. Our environment and our choices are more numerous and so more complex.

In a scientific analysis of Beth's case, the association of a stimulus and a response has conditioned a behavior. Beth's personal history and her demonstrated predilections are important, but only as evidence of a pattern of behavior. We should simply note that the

---

[1] Case Study 2389 from the Association of Certified Fraud Examiners' *Report to the Nation on Occupational Fraud and Abuse* (1996).

card has worked for her before. This result will influence the next event when a stimulus (the lack of money) prompts a response.

In the example, the conditioning was obviously strong enough that Beth did make more charges, $4,500 more. Maybe she said to herself, "I'll pay back the money eventually. It's only temporary." That's what many career fraudsters say when they begin stealing.[2] But for behaviorists and fraud examiners, the intention to stop and make amends is a fiction; i.e., an intent is something that can't be observed or verified. What we know is what Beth did.

The fact of the matter is that people do take money, and do it repeatedly. The methods B.F. Skinner describes in his 1953 book *Science and Human Behavior* offer some reasons *why* Beth used the card again. Expanding our example in the next section we'll discuss fraud as an act of behavior, and then consider the implications of this analysis on the discovery and tracking of fraudulent acts. A final section addresses the ultimate issue: how behavior can be modified to prevent and deter fraud.

Fraud as an Act of Behavior

While Skinner's critics claim he shrank behavior down to stimulus and response, he explicitly asserts that the notion of a "simple reflex" is insufficient for thinking about how people actually behave. There are multiple factors involved in any behavioral event. Skinner calls the network of factors and effects *operant behavior*, emphasizing the variety of operations (as opposed to simple acts) which make up a moment like Beth's charging money to her employer's credit card.

Beth's fraud didn't happen as a reflex action, like a knee that jerks when it's tapped with a hammer. Given the lack of money (*deprivation*), Beth had several options available to her and chose to use the card. The decision itself was an act of behavior, whose consequences yielded the money. A scientific approach doesn't consider *Who Beth Is*, whether she's pleasant or irascible, or regard the decision as a private act determined by Beth in her mind or soul. We ask, (1) what were the circumstances that prompted the act, and (2) why did she act one way and not another?

Suppose, for example, that Beth's husband had lost his job, and they needed $750 for their house payment. This circumstance, where money is necessary and Beth is deprived of it,

---

[2] According to ACFE Chairman, Joseph T. Wells, in the video, *The Corporate Con*.

stimulates her to act. A strict chain of reasoning can even reveal a biological basis for this situation, since the money is directly linked to the house, which is necessary for shelter and the family's health. The *stimulus*, then, is clear. Still, the available *repertoire of response* in Beth's case must have been various. Maybe she could have approached her parents for the money, but didn't. Why not? Well, let's say she has borrowed money from them before, and they harassed her while she was paying it back. This behavior, then, has been conditioned with *aversive stimuli*—borrowing from her parents brings discomfort, not just a social pressure but perhaps a genuinely physical pain when Beth has to listen to the harangue.

Beth has other options. Her husband's unemployment checks will cover the payment, but they will not arrive until three weeks after the payment is due. Their friends aren't likely to have the money either, so perhaps the only thing to do is to request a forbearance from the bank. While the request is likely to be granted—supposing Beth has a good payment record—there are adverse effects to this act as well, since the bank will add a penalty amount to the loan and make a negative notation to Beth's credit record. So the forbearance option has also been conditioned adversely: if she doesn't have the money on time, Beth will face punishment, which she naturally wants to avoid. She won't ask her boss for an advance for the same reason: she fears that the request will place her in disfavor, and her experience has taught her that the boss's favor and her personal welfare are directly linked.

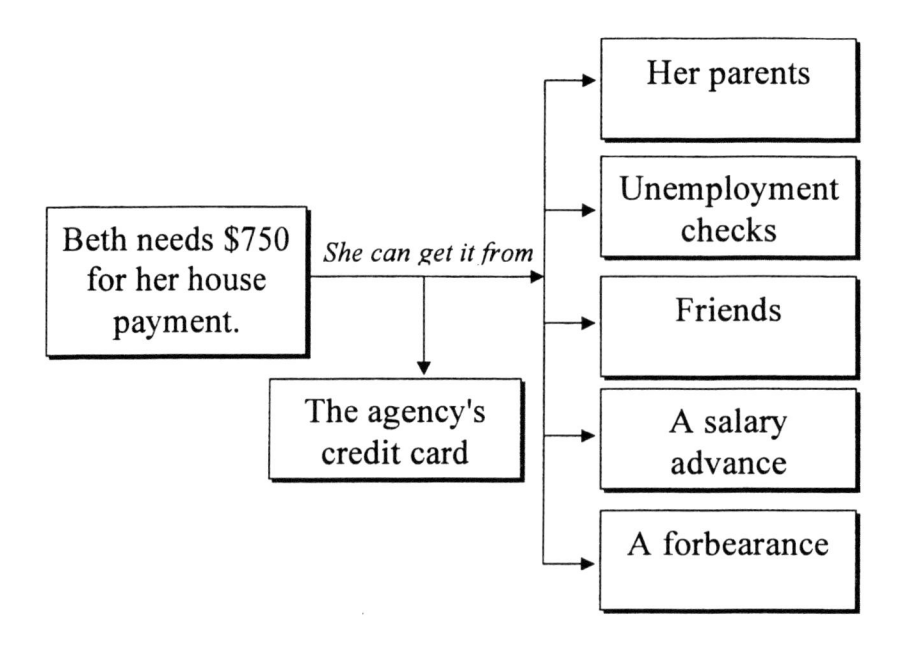

Beth's Fraud as Operant Behavior

So Beth turns toward the credit card. For several years, she's used it for business trips and supplies, and there's never been a question about her charges. Through the card, she can get the money she needs. She makes the charge, the bank is paid off, she promises to herself that she'll replace the money later. As we have seen, the credit card has now been conditioned as a source of ready money. Beth's moral status, her religious affiliations, her place as a respected employee around the office, are all irrelevant to a behavioral analysis. What matters is what she did and how she'll respond to similar circumstances in the future.

After her initial defalcation, Beth was again faced with a lack of money. Her kids needed shoes for school; a trip to her husband's home in Louisiana seemed just the thing to ameliorate the tension rising since his unemployment. To predict her action at this point, we would consider how she has behaved earlier. According to our supposition, Beth's decision to use the agency's card was occasioned by circumstances in which all her other available responses carried aversive consequences; the card, on the other hand, brought the necessary money with no concomitant negative effects.

But there was nothing forcing Beth to act as she did, only competing contingencies of circumstance. She might have found other ways to get the money she needed. She might have worked overtime, or she could have arranged a deal with her mother for the money which involved keeping the matter a secret from her haranguing father. Those venues notwithstanding, there were still other reasons not to use the card. Supposing that Beth was taught that stealing is wrong, using the card would have its own aversive effects in the form of guilt. If her guilt was sufficiently conditioned, she would turn to other options because they carried less aversion. She could have waited out the cash deprivation until her regular wages met the need. Or, she might have decided to go to the bank for a signature loan, even though the interest rate is abnormally high, since this would feel less aversive to her than the "pangs of guilt" associated with the card.

Given then that each point in her repertoire of behavior carries *some* aversive consequences, Beth's decisive act involves choosing the lesser, or more tolerable, of several discomforts. Because in this instance we know what her decision was, we can consider why, behaviorally, she acted as she did. No one had discovered and prosecuted her first charge, so she could feel reasonably sure of success the next time. The only deterrent, then, were her feelings of guilt.

For Skinner, these feelings don't arise as a private state within an individual, and guilt is not some instinct implanted by "human nature." Guilt, and in fact all ethical responses, are reactions people learn in their social training; the feeling accompanies acts which have been prohibited by a person's formative community. A man raised with strict teachings against sex as "sinful" and "depraved" will feel guilty about his sexual acts in ways that someone raised permissively will not. The fact that people who are guilty of atrocious acts often become paranoid, convinced that people know about their crime, demonstrates that the emotion is a socially generated condition. Like behavior in general, the emotions which accompany a particular act are conditioned by prior experience and knowledge.

A fraudster also overcomes feelings of guilt by explaining the act as something other than stealing.[3] When Orange County socialite Daniel Hernandez was convicted of taking $7.8 million from the precious metals company where he worked, he told the *L.A. Times*, "What I did was not wrong. That was my percentage that I stole.... . I was one hell of a good employee for my company." Perception equals reality in this instance: "stealing is wrong," the perpetrator says, "but I didn't steal; I just took what was mine." Any aversive consequences associated with the act can then be stepped gingerly around. The same sort of response is triggered in people who use the excuse "Everyone else was doing it." Hernandez averred, "[If] they hadn't given me a piece of the money for myself, it would have gone into someone else's pocket." Again, the comment ironically reveals the social nature of ethical mores: if everyone else is doing it, how can it be wrong? Either everyone is wrong, or the prohibition is a sham. Either way, the person who takes this route has relieved the aversive effects of guilt by deciding there was never anything to feel guilty about. If Beth used this excuse, she might have said, "I don't get paid enough for all the work I do. I'll just even up the deficit with this charge card." She's not stealing, just getting what she's due.

There is still another factor that Beth and people like her who commit fraud experience in an act of crime. What Skinner calls a *condition of strength* results from certain acts. In some situations, like when we command someone's attention, there are no immediate palpable rewards other than the person "paying attention": the phrase suggests that something is demanded and something given in the exchange. A person gains strength from someone's attention in many ways, from direct rewards (someone who pays you a lot of attention is more likely to give you things) to a general sense of safety and well-being (we "feel better about ourselves"). Money is a particularly rich source of behavioral strength, because, like

---

[3] See Wells, *The Corporate Con*.

the attention of others, it is tied positively to many different and desirable things. Money is so strongly conditioned with pleasant experiences that it can exert a power independent of the things it purchases: we say a miser "worships money for its own sake," but the miser is just as stimulated, behaviorally, as the man who is desperately saving up to buy a boat. The miser reacts to the feeling of strength he gains from the symbolic (and social) power which the money represents. His act of hoarding amounts to a reluctance to yield any of the symbolic strength he craves.

Beth arguably drew something like the miser's sense of strength from her clandestine charges. There was a literal power in being able to acquire goods and services with the card and she gained a symbolic power by (1) just knowing the money was there in case she needed it, and (2) by her impunity from detection and punishment. "Getting away with something" yields a sense of strength over others, and over our environment, so the strength acts to positively reinforce the clandestine act. Any guilt Beth felt was offset by the literal and symbolic strength she picked up from the money.

> **Avoiding the Aversion to Guilt**
>
> *•Treating the emotion as purely private: guilt is concealed along with the act itself, or borne as a noble act on behalf of others.*
>
> *• Defining the act as something other than a culpable one: not really stealing, just getting one's due; everyone else does the same thing.*
>
> *•Using the strength gained to offset the aversion: money and its symbolic power become ascendant.*

Thinking of Beth's fraud as *operant behavior*, we consider the network of acts involved in the crime. We ask not only why she did what she did, but why she didn't do any number of other things. We discover the *reinforcements*, positive and negative, which accompany actions.

If there were aversive stimuli associated with the behavior, we question how these were offset, ameliorated, or eliminated by other factors. Generally speaking, we work to assemble a complete picture of the behavior as an event, as a moment of conditioned responses which resulted in the act of behavior. Criminologists believe this understanding represents our best chance for modifying, or reconditioning, the way people behave—developing a method that reinforces the most worthy actions while discouraging destructive ones.

Criminology, like the discipline of Accounting, is not so much a body of knowledge as a way of organizing information. The accountant takes a folder of financial data and then arranges the material according to a method. Different values are listed in different places, and the whole is arranged—following a set of prearranged guidelines—into a statement. A fraud examiner who uses behavioral theories to analyze a fraud does something similar. The concepts of *operant conditioning* provide a method for making statements about a person's behavior.

Using another example,[4] we can recapitulate some of the key points of this method.

> *A buyer for a company convinced his superiors that business supplies purchased from three particular vendors were better than anything on the market. But the buyer's judgment was clouded by the fact that these vendors together had paid him $250,000 in kickbacks to buy their goods.*

A fraud examiner wishing to analyze the behavior of this buyer would begin by asking the following question:

1. *What were the various stimuli which produced the response, i.e. how can the operant behavior be described scientifically as a network of actions?*

To the untutored eye, the money itself would seem to be the stimulus. But in most instances, the money is actually the reward, or reinforcement, for the act of behavior.[5] In a famous set of experiments, Skinner conditioned pigeons to peck a red dot in order to receive food. The

---

[4] *Report to the Nation*, Case Study #2019.

[5] If the buyer were acting out of a miserly disposition, the money would be the stimulus, and the condition of strength would act as the reinforcement. However, let's assume our man is not a Scrooge, just a hapless perpetrator of fraud.

red dot was the stimulus, the behavior was pecking, and the food was the reinforcement. In the case study of the buyer, the act of behavior was rigging the bids, and the money was the reward, so we look elsewhere for the stimulus.

The Pigeon & the Fraudster

	Stimulus	Behavior	Reinforcement
Pigeon	*Red Dot*	*Pecking*	*Food*
Fraudster	*???*	*Rigging the bids*	*Money*

Most people would be attracted to an easy $250,000—we are conditioned to its uses and pleasures like the pigeon is conditioned to need food—but not everyone would commit fraud to get it. The circumstances surrounding the crime make the difference. There may have been some initial or ongoing hardship requiring cash, similar to Beth's emergency." Maybe the buyer thought he was underpaid and that he could remedy the deprivation with the money he obtained in the act. Even those factors, usually relegated to the realm of "feelings," can nevertheless influence the outcome of a behavioral event: the man may have rigged the bids because he felt unappreciated or disrespected at his company. The fraud is then an act that counters these negatives. Feeling deprived of appreciation or respect, he can gain these symbolically, as a condition of strength, in the act. In any of these instances, a condition of weakness—psychological or monetary—has been converted to a condition of strength. A negative stimulus, such as disrespect, is avoided by the act of acquiring money.

Any and all of these hypotheses would have to be verified through interviews, observation, and documentation. But the examiner approaches each possibility as part of the overall picture of operant behavior.

Closely related to the various stimuli which prompted the act are the factors which conditioned the response. The inquisitive examiner wonders,

2. *What were the reinforcements?*

We've already established the money itself as a primary reinforcer, since it makes possible so many other rewards. The relief and well-being money introduces into a situation of hardship reinforce the fraud as a positive source of alleviating aversion. But there may be other reinforcing consequences from the act. As with Beth, when the buyer "gets away" with the act, he gains a condition of strength; an impression of his impunity to laws, regulations, and his superiors' authority will reinforce the act of crime. The goodwill engendered among the vendors also reinforces the buyer, especially if there was a prior relationship. If, for example, the vendors were friends of the buyer from college, he would have been conditioned to do things that gain their approval. (Approval, like money, is tied to so many positive experiences that it can serve as a most powerful reinforcement.) Furthermore, the man may have gained a higher regard in his community by way of the cash. Perhaps he contributed some of it to charity (as Daniel Hernandez did in Orange County), and so enjoyed a prestige he hadn't known before. The prestige helps condition the act of fraud as a positive action.

Having established a pattern of stimuli and reinforcements in the man's behavior, there remains an especially vexing issue:

3. *Does it matter whether the act was initiated by the buyer or by the vendors?*

If the buyer was experiencing some immediate hardship, the act of behavior looks very much the same regardless of who initiated the fraudulent exchange. He is in either case stimulated primarily by the hardship, and has either seen the chance for fraud on his own, or been presented with it by his vendors. An exhaustive analysis would of course turn up subtle, and perhaps important differences, but the stimuli, response, and reinforcements remain the same. Motivated by the hardship, the buyer discovered the fraud as an available response, and was reinforced (at first anyway) by the results.

However, if there was no immediate hardship or deprivation at issue, the buyer is doing something very different when he approaches the vendors unaware. He looks to be stimulating himself outside the usual realm of circumstances. But for Skinner, thinking (the act of cognition) and directed-thinking, like planning a scheme, are behaviors and so they are subject to conditioning. Obviously, the analyst can't observe a person's thinking, but thoughts happen as "links in a chain of otherwise public events," and so have to be considered in a behavioral analysis. All of the buyer's former experience comes to bear on his act of planning the fraud. We should not stand aghast at the "deliberate" nature of the crime, but ask what about the man's prior conditioning led him to think, and so to behave, as he did?

There is no need for a high-sounding term for the behavioral question; the issue for the behaviorist and the layperson alike is "self-control." As a behavior, self-control is parallel to the techniques we all use to influence one another—establishing positive and negative effects that condition how a person acts. A father tells his teenaged son, "If you'll clean up this disaster area you call a room, I'll let you take the car on your date tonight." The father demands a clean room and reinforces the behavior with the use of the car. When the buyer considers and plans the act of fraud from initiation to completion, he is, in effect, playing a similar role in the conditioning of his own behavior.

This *is*, in fact, significantly different from a situation in which the vendors present an opportunity for fraud and the man seizes it. But the difference is not between a completely "free" decision and a conditioned behavior. In either case, the man was breaking the law; the fact that he hid the act suggests he "knew" what he was doing. The issue remains why, based on his prior conditioning, he participated in the fraud. Whether he planned the scheme himself or cooperated with others, we still have to evaluate the act as a behavior.

This doesn't mean that self-control has no place in a behaviorist analysis. In fact, fraud cases ultimately center around self-control. Legal charges very clearly state that the defendant "did knowingly commit" an act of fraud, and use words like *purposefully* in narrative accounts, to indicate that the social deterrents to the act were in place but the individual chose to ignore these. Behavioral theorists believe the only reliable way of controlling people's behavior is to condition their *self*-control. Punishment and continual supervision are not only expensive and arduous, they are poor tools in trying to change how people act.

So when we ask if the buyer initiated the rigged bids, it is a pertinent question, but only as part of a larger investigation into how the circumstances of the setting and the man's prior conditioning led him to act illegally. If we are appalled at the "deliberate" snubbing of the moral code, it's because the man has so starkly showed the inadequacy of the code in face of appropriately (though improperly) conditioned behavior. To understand his behavior, we have to control our outrage, and direct our energies at the same issues we bring to bear on any person's harmful action—why they did what they did, and how to prevent them, and others, from doing so again.

Behaviorism provides a method that examiners and investigators can use to make statements about people's actions. Instead of starting with certain premises about human nature or who someone is, the behaviorist collects information about the circumstances of an event. This information—organized according to the stimuli, repertoire of response, and reinforcements—reveals the network of actions that produced the behavior.[6] Like the scientist who collects evidence first and then analyzes the results, the behaviorist works to understand the event itself, as a unique convergence of influences.

Practically speaking, this approach is not as far removed from everyday life as it might seem. Common sense dictates that Beth's clandestine shopping spree was a categorically different act than Daniel Hernandez' multimillion dollar misappropriations. We know intuitively that Beth's behavior was a different animal than Hernandez'; behavioral analysis gives us a way of saying *how* different. If we are to detect, deter, and prevent fraudulent acts, we have to understand them *as acts*.

Understanding an act behaviorally, we treat a college kid filching dollars from his bursar's office with regard to the conditions of the act: *Why did he feel the "need" to take the money? What about his past experience influenced his theft? Based on the act and the kid's history, how likely is he to steal again?* On the other hand, we can consider the case of Charles Bazarian, a crooked financier charged with bilking investors for over $77 million in one year alone. Bazarian copped a standard plea that explained his crime as something besides a crime: federal regulators had interfered with and destroyed an otherwise legitimate business operation. But in an interview with the authors of *Inside Job*, an exposé of the 1980s S&L scandals, Bazarian declared, "I just borrowed tremendous amounts of money... [I] had an appetite that was absolutely incredible for, you know, money."[7]

The point is not just that Bazarian and the college kid committed drastically different acts. It's that we have to consider the different motivations, responses, and reinforcements that produced each act. Those are the factors which *make* the difference.

Behavioral Analysis and the Detection of Fraud

When a detective searches for a suspect's motive, the detective is using behaviorist methods of analysis. The suspect, it is assumed, was stimulated by some arrangement of factors. Many courses in criminology are built around the fundamental premise that crimes are particular sorts of behavior and best understood as the product of operant conditioning. Fraud examiners often use the same methods in approaching a case. When money is missing, the

---

[6] One strategy uses *induction*, the other *deduction*, in its logic. Induction begins with a principle and assembles evidence according to that principle; deduction gathers evidence and deduces a unifying principle.

[7] Pizzo, Stephen et al. *Inside Job. The Looting of America's Savings and Loans*. Harper-Perennial, 1991. p. 94.

examiner traces the known flow of funds and then asks, "Who had the opportunity and the motive to get at this money?" Even without being conscious of the fact, the examiner is performing a behaviorist analysis on the crime.

To conduct an investigation using the principles of behavior outlined above, the fraud examiner would assemble all the information possible to recreate the network of actions that produced the criminal behavior. This not only sheds light on likely suspects and the environmental factors which motivated them, but also assists in tracing the distribution of money. A thorough history of a suspect's activities and associates can point toward the most probable places to look for hidden funds.

Operant Conditioning and the Deterrence of Fraud

Ultimately, the question of fraud and behavior comes down to this—*what can we do about it?* We know that people commit these crimes, and at an alarming rate. Incidents range from the clerk who skims a few hundred dollars off a business' daily deposits, to multimillion-dollar scam artists who destroy entire organizations. There's a world of difference between the skimming clerk and the scamming S&L crook; so can we even analyze the two people within the same system of fraud?

A fraud examiner working with behaviorist principles knows that the difference between crimes lies in the different behaviors. The man who plays million-dollar games with other people's money is stimulated and reinforced by a distinctive set of factors, and so too is the clerk who builds a family nest egg from her three-figure thefts.[8] So when an examiner is asked to go beyond crime-solving and to consult on fraud's prevention, the job demands a thorough analysis of behavior.

Any economic exchange, from buying milk at the corner store to closing on a condominium, is an act of behavior. As we have seen, acts involving money are particularly charged because money is linked behaviorally to a myriad of experiences. Most parents teach the "value" of money to their children from the earliest stages, emphasizing that work, good behavior, and special efforts are all rewarded by cold hard cash. Employers are engaging in the same type of behavioral modification when they pay other people for labor. A weekly salary, for example, is what Skinner called a *fixed-interval reinforcement*—the worker gets a set amount of

---

[8] We call one a "major player" and the other "small-time," though the difference is actually categorical rather than comparative. The distinction is between different types of acts, with concomitantly different stimuli, responses, and reinforcements.

money for a set amount of time spent on the job. Wages are fixed hourly, or by the number of days, but in any case the money serves to reinforce the employee's working. To ensure continual performance between reinforcement cycles, employers hire supervisors to insist that workers work, or they dock workers' paychecks for missed days (conditioning missed time with aversive stimuli). Piecework or commission payments are examples of *fixed-ratio* reinforcements. For each part successfully manufactured, a company pays its machinist $50; for every $1,000 in sales, the salesperson gets $150. The ratio can be raised or lowered—according to demand, quality requirements, or the employee's ability—provided that the reinforcement is adequate to the task required. With either fixed-interval or fixed-ratio payment schedules, the aim remains the same: to reinforce, and so to perpetuate, the employee's productive behavior.

Thinking of employment as a system of behavior is important because so much fraud occurs in workplace environments, and because it highlights the connection between economics and people's actions. For both the crook and the dedicated worker, money exerts a powerful influence, and this is not likely to change. The resourceful employer, then, should consider the best way to establish a positive set of relations between employees and the funds flowing through the company. The more rigorously we understand how people behave, the better equipped we are to change the way they behave.

For example, what about Beth? She repeatedly made illegal charges to her agency's credit card. Once her crime was discovered, someone at the agency had to make a decision. Her supervisor—let's call him Barton—has one goal; he wants to make sure the fraud never happens again. His decision, then, (his act of behavior) will affect not only Beth herself, but the rest of the people working at the agency. Coming from a no-nonsense background, Barton's first impulse is to fire Beth. That way she's gone, and everyone else gets the message. He announces a policy of zero tolerance. The agency's staff is now on alert: unauthorized actions result in swift and irrevocable punishment. But this hasn't really solved Barton's problem.

Behavioral studies, such as those conducted by Skinner, show that punishment is the least effective method of changing behavior. Punishing brings "a temporary suppression of the behavior," but only with constant supervision and application. In repeated experiments, Skinner found that punishment—either applying a negative stimulus, or taking away a positive one—effectively extinguished a subject's behavior, but that the behavior returned "when the punishment was discontinued … and eventually all responses came out" again.

The subject would suppress the behavior as long as the punishment was applied directly and continually, but as soon as the punishment was withdrawn for a while, the behavior was attempted again; if there was no punishment following the attempt, the subject began to behave as before.

When Barton fired Beth, he punished her by taking away a positive stimulus, namely, her gainful employment. The agency may also have required her to pay back the funds she stole, and a court may have added charges for damages; the agency and court are depriving Beth of money, and also subjecting her to public disapproval. The behaviorist takes a long view of these proceedings, wondering if the punitive actions will reliably modify Beth's behavior. Punishment research suggests that as long as Beth feels the direct threat of suffering, she won't commit another fraud. However, if she sees a way to perpetrate a crime and has a reasonable chance of not getting caught, she'll likely act again. Barton may be rid of Beth, but another employer now has to deal with someone whose only motivation to avoid fraud is the present and direct threat of punishment.

Besides, Barton still has a staff to contend with, in an office environment that certainly allows, and perhaps even encourages, fraud. Several staff members have been tempted, as Beth was, by the easy money flowing through the office; some of them have even committed their own improprieties. When Barton institutes zero tolerance, he has conditioned the agency staff to fear the punishment of his authority, but this will require a constant emphasis in order to be effective. He has only moderately altered the conditions of his office through his punitive response. If he leaves everything else unchanged, he continues to operate in an environment vulnerable to fraud. Staff members have not so much learned to avoid committing fraud as they've learned to fear punishment. Their lesson is "Don't get caught."

Barton has another problem if he takes a simple punitive approach to the fraud. Punishment, according to Skinner, generates "emotions, including predispositions to escape or retaliate, and disabling anxieties." The fear of punishment is not only a poor way to change people's behavior, it can interfere with their normally productive actions. If Barton relies on handing down wrath as a way of managing his workers, he may find his solution creates more problems than it solves in the form of anxieties and nervous tension. He has good reason to remove Beth from the office environment—her continued presence might appear to sanction the illegal behavior. But the specter of punishment will only nominally bring him closer to stopping fraud, and he may disrupt the staff's performance in the process.

Behaviorally, reinforcement and punishment are distinguished by the ways that positive and negative forces are applied. A *positive reinforcement* presents a positive stimulus in exchange for the desired response. Fathers say to their sons, "You've cleaned your room. Good. Here's the key to the car." The behavior (cleaning) is given in return for the car. A *negative reinforcement*, on the other hand, withdraws a negative stimulus in exchange for the response. So the father says, "I'll stop hassling you if you clean this room." The negative (hassling) is withdrawn when the appropriate behavior is performed.

Reinforcing and Punishing

REINFORCEMENT	*Presents positive stimuli*	*Withdraws negative stimuli*
PUNISHMENT	*Presents negative stimuli*	*Withdraws positive stimuli*

In an act of *punishment*, the polarities, so to speak, are reversed. Faced with an undesired behavior, the punisher presents a negative stimulus. A father, hearing his son tell a particularly raunchy story, puts a bar of soap into the boy's mouth. Punishment may also be administered by withdrawing a positive stimulus. "Your room is still filthy," the father tells his languid child, "so you can't use the car." The boy suffers from thwarted desire.

Punishment fights a losing battle in manipulating behavior because it works by negative—administering unpleasantries and taking away desirables. A car or the thrill of a racy story doesn't become less attractive for its use in punishment; its power to stimulate is simply squelched. Reinforcement, on the other hand, proceeds like the old song, to "accentuate the positive." Skinner concludes that behavior is most effectively modified by managing and modifying desires through reinforcement; he wants to replace destructive behaviors with productive ones, instead of trying to punish an already existing impulse.

Behaviorism points toward a number of alternatives to punishment. Chief among these is to *modify the circumstances* surrounding the act. In Beth's case, the initial charges were occasioned by a financial hardship. Her supervisor may not have a direct way of averting this. But the employees' credit union might offer short-term loans at a moderate interest rate, thereby providing a route for alleviating members' financial difficulties which does not require a deceptive maneuver. In other instances, as we have seen in the case of the buyer rigging bids, employees engage in fraud because they feel underpaid or unappreciated.

Emotions, according to Skinner, are a predisposition for people's actions. Anger is not itself a behavior, but a state of being that predisposes people to do things like yell or fight. Obviously, anger is a part of a person's response, to the extent that an angry man is more likely to get in a shouting match with his friends. And since the emotional associations of any event are important factors in conditioning behavior, the associations can be manipulated in conditioning the behavior. That's why advertisers use cute babies to sell toilet tissue—the image associates the tissue with the emotions evoked by the baby. A company portrays its founder as a father figure for a similar reason. When managers are faced with disgruntled employees, they can modify these emotional circumstances, not just with "image" work, but with adequate compensation and by recognizing workers' accomplishments. Incentives programs and task-related bonuses follow this principle, assuming that employees who feel challenged and rewarded by their jobs will produce more work at a higher quality, and are less likely to violate the law.

Another nonpunitive approach drives the undesirable behavior into extinction by preventing the expected response. This is a specialized version of modifying the circumstances. Businesses perform an extinction strategy by implementing a system of internal controls. In requiring several signatures for a transaction, for example, a bank prevents any one employee from gaining access to money. This approach doesn't involve reinforcements or punitive measures; it simply modifies the structure in which acts take place. So if Barton, as Beth's supervisor, had conducted periodic reviews of Beth's agency credit account, or if her charges had required prior authorization, she would not have been able to use the card as she did. Limiting her access to funds would have severely curtailed the opportunity, and thus the likelihood, for fraud. The perception of internal controls provides a particularly strong deterrent to fraud because it obstructs the operant behavior which has heretofore been linked with positive reinforcement. We prevent the act by blocking the expected response. Criminal behavior is discouraged because crime doesn't pay.[9]

A related strategy overcomes improper behavior by encouraging the behavior's "opposite." Skinner says we can *condition incompatible behavior* that interferes with the person's usual acts. Instead of punishing a child's emotional tantrums, for example, the behaviorist rewards the child for controlling emotional outbursts; we drive the tantrums into extinction by not

---

[9] Lack of internal control is one of the most often cited deficiencies in organizations suffering from fraud. "Smaller organizations are the most vulnerable to occupational fraud and abuse because sophisticated internal controls, designed to deter occupational fraud, are less prevalent in smaller organizations." *Report to the Nation.* Association of Certified Fraud Examiners (1996) p. 35.

responding, and reinforce the stoical behavior. A destructive behavior is offset by an incompatible productive one. Since fraud involves dishonesty, secretiveness, and antagonistic behaviors, the astute manager finds ways to reward the opposite behaviors—honesty, openness, and cooperation. Barton could institute programs which elicit staff members' full participation in the agency's mission; he could make them aware of the issues affecting their work; he could find ways that people can work together in solving problems and advancing projects.

Of course it's easier to list these strategies in a few paragraphs than it is to implement them. Even the simplest seeming acts can become tangled as people and circumstances interact. A perfectly sound theoretical reinforcement—an employee incentives program, perhaps—may be viewed with suspicion by disgruntled workers. Behavioral modification is never easy, Skinner says; reinforcements "must be sensitive and complex" because people's lives are complicated and their behaviors sensitized. For example, people in groups often interact in alarming and unstable ways. Skinner demonstrates this tendency with the example of a whipping-boy game played by eighteenth-century sailors. The sailors tied up a group of young boys in a straight line, restraining each boy's left hand, and placing a whip in the right hand. The first boy in line was given a light blow on the back, and told to do the same to the person immediately in front of him. Each boy hit the next in line, and each one was hit in turn. As Skinner reports, "It was clearly in the interest of the group that all blows be gentle, [but] the inevitable result was a furious lashing."[10] Each boy in the line hit a little harder than he had been hit himself; so after a few cycles, the last blows would be, in fact, furious (especially since each swing was preceded by pain, creating an emotional disposition of anger and anxiety). Whipping sessions aren't a likely happening in most companies, but people often exhibit a similar bent for catalyzed reactions: whispering sessions gradually evolve into full-blown discussions that echo into the hallways; minor financial indiscretions grow toward large-scale larceny.[11]

Ideally, behavioral managers could anticipate this catalyzing and redirect the energies, but what if that's not an option? Though the dollar amounts (and the audacity) of some white-collar crimes boggle the average observer's mind, the crime remains an act of behavior and so should be approachable by the same method used to analyze a $4,500 credit card fraud.

---

[10] Skinner, B.F. *Science and Human Behavior*. Macmillan Publishing: New York, 1953. p. 309.

[11] Compare the excuse, "Everybody does it." It's often true that an impressive number of other people in the perpetrator's peer group were themselves breaking the law, a condition catalyzed by intense interaction and resulting in more serious crimes.

The perpetrator may be described as "obsessive" and "megalomaniacal," but he is still behaving in a network of actions, his behavior subject to operant conditioning.

The dollars are in fact misleading. Once the stakes reach a certain level, it's not even plausible to look for explanations involving a lack of respect or appreciation. Wheeler-dealers and armchair analysts often aver, "It's not really the money," and they're right. High-dollar criminals describe their machinations as a "kick" or thrill; they feel like they're playing a game, and it's the game of their lives. Behaviorists agree. Money is a "generalized reinforcer," linked with many positive factors directly, and often taking on a symbolic power of its own, yielding a condition of strength. Skinner says, "We are automatically reinforced, apart from any particular deprivation, when we successfully control the physical world."[12] So we need not be starving in order to act, especially with the sense of control—symbolic and literal—gained by acquiring money. Game-playing exerts something similar on its participants; someone who manipulates a chess board or a deck of cards successfully gains a sense of strength over external events. We can play the game "for its own sake" because it yields the impression of strength. Imagine, then, the behavioral stroke that happens when the game's power is combined with money's as a generalized reinforcer, and both of these factors are played out with real people and settings. The dealmaker is racing through a thicket of reinforcements, and the greater the risk—financial, legal, personal—the greater the thrill. The stimulus isn't the money as a thing in itself, anymore than money "for its own sake" prompts the miser. In either case, the condition of strength (we might even call it "power") feeds the behaving person; money just happens to be the reinforcer *par excellence* of our culture.

Dealing with high-stakes criminals will remain difficult, despite our understanding of their behavior. Not just because the amounts of money and the networks of action are so complex, but because the conditioning is so intense. How, for example, to replace the kick of "scoring" a $35-million-dollar take in a three-day scam? Can a career con be prompted to give up the deceitful practices which have marked his experience? Finding genuine and specific answers may be delayed for some time, but they will likely follow the same pattern we've discussed with other crimes:
- Modifying the circumstances of the behavior by, for example, making legitimate businesses a more opportune place for daring and innovative techniques;

---

[12] Skinner, p. 77.

- Extinguishing the criminal behavior by preventing its success, using regulation, controls, and supervision; and
- Encouraging behaviors incompatible with criminal activity, through educational practices and demonstrating "values" which call the criminal lifestyle, however flashy, into question.

The specific measures will be particular to the crime. The actions dictate the response. But whether we're dealing with a working mother's credit card fraud, or Michael Milken's palatial schemes, our methods can be behavioral. Fraud examiners may never eradicate crime completely, but approaching criminal acts scientifically, we can become more successful in anticipating and preventing the acts.

Conclusion

To successfully recognize, detect, and prevent fraud, the examiner has to take account of as many variables as possible, and has to learn a great deal about how human beings—as individuals and in groups—behave.

All the efforts of behavioral engineering notwithstanding, the question of behavior finally rests with the person who behaves. In *Walden Two*, the founder of Skinner's utopian community admits there is only so much that can be done by cultural design:

> *You can't foresee all future circumstances, and you can't specify adequate future conduct. You don't know what will be required. Instead you have to set up certain behavioral processes which will lead the individual to design his own "good" conduct when the time comes. We call that sort of thing "self-control."*[13]

No substitute exists for the conscious individual making a choice to act. And no science can predict or shape behavior with pure accuracy. There are just too many factors at work in the network of actions. However, self-control is a behavior, and so is guided by operant conditioning in the same way any other act would be.

It does little good, for example, to tell an alcoholic, "Stop drinking, control yourself." The command alone has little force, even if the alcoholic "wants" to stop drinking. Family members can suggest that the man simply throw away his bottles; "the principal problem,"

---

[13] *Id.* at p.96.

Skinner interjects, "is to get him to do it."[14] But the family can help condition the alcoholic's self-control by registering disapproval of drinking, by reinforcing the man's successful resistance to drink, and by encouraging the man to do things incompatible with a drinking life. They can't follow the man through every step of his life; he has to resist the impulse to sneak a sip on his own. But the behavior of resistance is strengthened by his family members' intervention. "Self-control," as a behavior, is shaped by "variables in the environment and the history of the individual."[15]

Understanding why people do certain things allows us to go beyond a simplistic insistence that criminals "control themselves." We will instead have to consider how this control can be conditioned, preventing the behavior directly when possible, but ultimately relying on each individual having adequately absorbed the principles of self-control.

Why People Obey the Law

Now that we have a general understanding of at least some of the reasons that humans behave the way they do, let us turn our discussion to why people obey (and contrarily break) the law. In his book *Why People Obey the Law*, Tom Tyler studies the two principal types of law-abiding peoples.[16]

Obviously, some people choose to obey the law while others flaunt it. Yet many otherwise law-abiding members of society evade taxes, occasionally use a controlled substance, commit fraud, or even drive under the influence. According to studies by Tyler, the instrumental and the normative perspectives attempt to explain why some follow the law to the letter while others obey selectively.

Instrumental Perspective

According to this theory, people obey the law because they fear punishment. When reviewing the incarceration rates in this country, it is not difficult to discern that this is the perspective most adhered to by policy makers.

---

[14] *Id.* at p. 240.

[15] *Ibid.* Family members in this type of situation often ask the alcoholic, "Don't you see what you're doing?" The answer may sometimes be "No," because self-knowledge is a discriminative behavior, an act of cognition that labels and organizes information. As a behavior, self-knowledge is of course influenced by conditioning; we recognize or "know" what we've been conditioned to know. Thus, treatment programs often encourage patients to reflect on their behavior in certain ways, conditioning a self-knowledge that will contribute to self-control.

[16] Tyler, Tom R. *Why People Obey the Law*. 1990. Yale University Press: New Haven.

A person of this belief might exceed the speed limit, thinking that the benefit of saved time outweighs the risk of the potential speeding ticket. These types are unlikely to rob a bank, though, considering that success is doubtful and the penalty steep. They weigh the pros and cons of compliance with the law and act accordingly.

Normative Perspective

The focus of this perspective is what one considers just and moral. When people believe compliance is their moral obligation, commitment to the law is voluntary, regardless of fear of punishment.

People of this belief may indulge in illegal drugs but refrain from stealing, one being morally acceptable in their view and the other not. Others may obey all laws out of the belief that the authorities are just. In any case, compliance is unforced and voluntary.

Naturally, the authorities prefer voluntary compliance. From their point of view, the normative is preferable to the instrumental perspective since the former does not require enforcement. If the public already believes in the government's moral right to govern, the authorities' job is made much easier.

Morality, however, can work against the government as it did with the U.S. public's moral indignation over Vietnam, for instance. Those who viewed the government's authority as legitimate supported the war, regardless of their own views as to its necessity. Others considered the on-going struggle useless and wrong and opposed it.

Another significant difference between the instrumental and the normative perspectives is whether one focuses on procedures rather than results. Those adhering to the normative point of view will, for example, be more concerned with being treated justly in court rather than with winning or losing their case. They will contentedly await judgment if dealt with fairly. People of this opinion are interested in neutrality, lack of bias, honesty, politeness, and respect for one's rights. The "due process," then, is most effective in promoting compliance to those of this view. The instrumentalist, on the other hand, focuses on the outcome of his case and is less concerned with procedures. In his mind, a procedure is fair if it is favorable.

Legitimacy

By definition, effective leadership must produce compliance with a leader's decisions. However, it is sometimes the case that when new legislation or policy is introduced, public support and compliance do not occur. Supreme Court decisions, notably on school prayer, do not necessarily produce general public acceptance of or adherence to policy. Likewise, if a company introduces a new policy that no employee may take a gift (no matter how small) from a potential vendor, many employees will continue to take small gifts anyway.

Altering citizens' behavior by manipulating access to valued resources or threatening to impose sanctions is known as *social control*. Once again, the concept is that reward and punishment are what cause people to obey the law. People maximize their personal gain and comply based on deterrence. Of course, life is more complicated than reward and punishment. Otherwise, the job of law enforcement would be easy. But social control appeals to authorities. The public understands deterrence, rewards, and punishment. In contrast, emphasizing the normative approach places power not in authorities, but in the people whose voluntary compliance is sought.

In studying general compliance with the law, sociologists have found that deterrence does not fully explain why people obey the law. Citizens choose to obey the law when the chances of being caught violating it are virtually zero, as when one might come upon a stop sign in a deserted street. Almost all Americans pay their income taxes in a voluntary system, even though chances of being caught shaving taxes owed are small. Yet citizens break the law when it is risky to do so, as when they buy illegal drugs or embezzle thousands of dollars from their company.

In a democracy, the legal system cannot function if it can influence people only by manipulating rewards and costs. The resources required to enforce such a regime are too high. Deterrence is expensive to enforce and does not guarantee an adequate level of obedience. Drunken driving is a good example. Studies show that an extremely high investment of resources is needed to convince people that the likelihood of being caught and punished for driving drunk is high. Public campaigns against drunk driving tend to temporarily reduce the number of DUIs or DWIs. As long as citizens think the chances of being caught are rising, the incidences of drunk driving remain lower. However, as soon as public perception of increased vigilance against drunk driving lessens, the number of arrests goes up again. Likewise, as is discussed later in the chapter on "Fraud Prevention Programs," increasing the perception of detection is a powerful anti-fraud program. If an employee thinks that his or her company is not paying attention to occupational fraud, then some employees are more likely to try and get away with it.

Consider the use of marijuana, an illegal yet still popular drug. If the reason people abstain from using this drug is that they believe in complying with the law, then obviously in their eyes the authorities have legitimacy. However, if they forgo marijuana use because it violates their moral values, then it is their convictions that are the deciding factor. If fear of legal punishment stops them, then deterrence carries greater weight with them. And if they refrain out of fear of social ostracism, then the social group's influence prevails.

A person's own normative values have "final say" about appropriate behavior. Unlike the reward and punishment approach, one's own values are in the end what produce compliance or noncompliance with the law. Psychologists refer to this as "internalized obligations," for which citizens take personal responsibility.

Voluntary Compliance
Voluntary compliance matters only to the extent to which it produces obedience that goes beyond self-interest, measured by most of us by reward and punishment. A normative speeder, for instance, will accept being a few minutes late to his appointment in order to obey the speed limit, thus making the roads safer for everyone. A normative employee will accept a salary freeze and not steal from the company to make up for the raise he was promised. In other words, these people will act against their own best interests if they feel compliance with the rule is of greater moral import.

Of course government authorities recognize that without the good will of the public, they could not function. Their aim must be to maximize compliance and minimize hostility toward laws, while gaining legitimacy in the eyes of the public. Any leader who wants to effectively govern must have legitimacy with his or her subordinates. The same is true for employers, managers, teachers, and army sergeants. Otherwise, compliance will not occur.

Due to its significant social impact, social scientists and politicians have found legitimacy to be an issue of major concern. It is seen as a reservoir of loyalty from which leaders can draw. Opinion polls on the public's attitude toward the law and the government are really about public confidence in the government's legitimacy. If the public does not have confidence in the legal system, obedience to laws is unlikely.

Studies show that both children and adults feel a strong obligation to obey the law. Whether we can attribute this to their normative values or the legitimacy of the authorities is the real question. Naturally, those who view the authorities as legitimate are more likely to comply.

This leads to the conclusion that normative support of the system leads to compliant behavior.

Measuring Legitimacy and Compliance

A study by Tyler (called "The Chicago Study") focused on six laws with which people deal on a daily basis: disturbing the peace, littering, driving while intoxicated, speeding, shoplifting, and parking illegally. Participants were asked how often they had broken these laws in the past year. Most admitted to parking illegally (51%) and speeding (62%), but very few admitted to shoplifting (3%). Twenty-seven percent confessed to disturbing the peace, 25% to littering, and 19% admitted to having driven while under the influence.

The second wave of interviews, in which participants were asked about a shorter time frame, produced similar results. To measure fear of punishment, respondents were asked how likely they thought it was that they would be arrested or issued a citation if they violated these six laws. Eighty-three percent thought it was likely they would be caught driving drunk; 78% thought the same for parking violations and shoplifting; 72% for speeding, 35% for disturbing the peace, and 31% for littering.

Participants were then gauged for peer approval. For shoplifting, 89% said that they thought that the five adults they know best would disapprove. Eighty-six percent said the same for drunk driving, as did 51% for littering, 52% for speeding, 44% for illegal parking, and 53% for disturbing the peace.

The next question was designed to measure respondents' morality. They were asked whether each offense was "wrong." Almost every one of the participants felt that any violations of the six laws were wrong. Speeding came out as the least immoral and shoplifting the most, with 99% of participants considering it morally objectionable.

One sees that citizens seem to view the breaking of laws as a violation of their personal morality. Interestingly, most believe the chances of getting caught are high. And since peer disapproval levels are relatively light, one can gather that the social group is the source of the least amount of pressure to obey laws.

More than four out of five participants felt a person should obey the law "even if it goes against what they think is right." Almost as many respondents felt that disobeying the law is seldom justified and that obedience and respect for authority are the most important virtues children should learn.

Legitimacy and Compliance

Legitimacy is regarded as the essential ingredient in what gives governments and leaders authority. The idea is that if the authorities have legitimacy, the public will obey the law. Tyler's Chicago Study, however, was designed to put this concept to the test.

The study did show that legitimacy is related to compliance. Participants who attributed greater legitimacy to authorities were more likely to obey the law, for instance. This does not prove a causal relationship, though. The results of the study were analyzed to account for demographic and sociological factors. This "regression analysis" suggests that legitimacy has a significant effect on compliance, regardless of the other factors.

Certainly legitimacy's impact on a person is influenced by his personal experiences with police and courts. A person who feels mistreated by the authorities is certainly less likely to have confidence in their legitimacy and therefore is less likely to obey laws. In such cases, peer approval seems to take on greater importance in those people's thinking. One more interesting result was that those participants who considered themselves politically liberal were more likely than those who regarded themselves as moderate to base compliant behavior on feelings of legitimacy.

Implications of the Chicago Study

Authorities do not take compliance with the law for granted. They often find that occasional noncompliance must be tolerated. Sometimes noncompliance is so widespread that it casts doubt upon the effectiveness and validity of the law itself. Prohibition, for example, was widely and often openly violated before its repeal. The results of the study suggest that normative values are more influential upon compliance than the reward and punishment approach. This is consistent with Skinner's behavioral theories discussed previously.

Again, the study shows that people have a high level of normative commitment to abide by the law. Most participants felt breaking the law was morally wrong and that laws should be obeyed even when one does not agree with them, the "my country, right or wrong" approach. Authorities who can tap into and encourage those views will of course inspire compliance. Employees who have a strong sense of loyalty to their employer will not violate company policies because such an act would be a betrayal to the company.

The Psychological Variables

The Chicago Study was designed to gauge the gap between citizens' concerns for favorable outcomes and procedural fairness. It also measures the extent to which fairness influences reactions to experience. The experience in question is of the everyday, average-citizen variety, the type of encounter most of us have with authorities over relatively minor matters. Participants reported calling the police for a number of reasons: accidents, disturbances, suspicious activities, and crimes against property or violent crimes. The majority of callers felt it was important for police to solve their problem, whether it was serious or not.

Police response time was satisfactory to most respondents. Only 15% felt that police did not respond quickly enough. Nearly 70% knew what actions the police had taken to solve the problem, and almost two thirds of those said the police settled the situation. The 43% who said the police failed to solve their problem admitted that they did do everything they could. All in all, 71% said they were satisfied with the outcome of their call. Most respondents also felt that they were treated quite well by the police. Eighty-six percent expressed overall satisfaction with their politeness, concern for their rights, propriety, attentiveness, honesty, and willingness to consider their opinions.

Respondents who were stopped by the police naturally had less magnanimous feelings toward them. Still, 73% of those who received tickets for minor offenses nevertheless considered the outcome fair, acknowledging that the ticket was deserved.

Satisfaction levels of participants who had to go to court were similarly high. Eighty percent considered their treatment fair. However, 36% stated they believed the judge could have reached a "better" outcome. Overall, though, participants were content with these elements of our justice system.

Legitimacy and Experience

People will accept unfavorable rulings if they believe they were dealt with fairly. Thus, fair procedures can cushion the blow of an outcome that is to one's disadvantage, without damaging the authorities' legitimacy. Of course, fair procedures can only go so far. If "fair" procedures consistently produce unfavorable results, the fairness of the procedures themselves will come into question.

People place importance on procedure for several reasons, first of which is simplicity. Often, the result itself is difficult to classify as fair or unfair. People therefore focus on the steps that lead up to the outcome. Another reason such emphasis is placed on procedures is that, with as much religious and ethnic diversity that the U.S. has, people do not always concur on what is fair. Although most people may not necessarily agree upon the outcome, they usually are of one mind as to the justice of the procedures.

The procedural aspects of the law, and how the public perceives them, must be of great importance to authorities. Of course, policy makers must have a good idea of what the public considers fair. If the public perceives a court's legal actions as just, they will support the outcome although it might not be to their advantage. Plea bargaining, for example, is often justified based on outcome. But if the inconsistency in plea agreements is seen as unfair, support for the legal system will weaken. Likewise, no-fault insurance may make sense in economic terms, but may dilute the basic principle underlying our legal system: that individuals are responsible for their own actions.

The same is true in the corporate environment. Employees will often accept unpopular company policies if the employees feel that the policy is applied "fairly." For instance, employees may be upset that the company provides only three paid sick days, but if the rule is applied to all employees in an equal manner, most employees will live with the policy. However, if some employees are allowed additional sick days and others are not, then employees begin to resent the policy and the company. In other words, these employees feel they are being treated unfairly.

The Meaning of Procedural Justice

An important issue left unaddressed until now is how people decide which procedures are fair and which are not. Previous efforts to study this question have focused on control. Two areas of control with which people are generally concerned are: *decision control* (control over the actual decisions made) and *process control* (control over the opportunity to state one's case).

To better illustrate, let us take the example of an attorney representing a client in court. While the client surrenders control of the case to his attorney, he may still seek to maintain as much control as he can through control of the process. According to the instrumental perspective, he will value the opportunity to testify only insofar as it helps to achieve a beneficial outcome to his case. Studies show, however, that most of us appreciate the chance to air our views, regardless of whether it influences the outcome or not. From this, one can conclude that process control has an independent impact on how one perceives fairness and whether one is satisfied with the outcome. (One's satisfaction with the outcome and one's opinion of fair procedures depends largely on one's degree of control.)

Again, one must ask what criteria people use to decide whether a procedure is fair. G.S. Leventhal proposed six standards for evaluating fairness of a procedure:

- Representativeness
- Consistency
- Suppression of bias
- Accuracy
- Correctability
- Ethicality

Representativeness relates to those parties whose concerns are affected throughout the allocation process. *Consistency* refers to the uniform and unbiased treatment of all of the affected parties. *Suppression of bias* guarantees that those involved with the outcome have no personal, vested interest in the case. This also prohibits a participant's reliance on previously formed opinions rather than just the evidence at hand, as when a juror convicts because he believes most defendants are guilty. *Accuracy* refers to objective high quality. *Correctability* involves the checks and balances provided in the system which allow unfair decisions to be corrected, such as the appeals process. *Ethicality* of course involves the degree to which procedures meet generally held ethical standards of fairness and morality. Torture, for instance, is a violation of ethicality, as it is a breach of basic moral codes.

Studies measuring the importance of Leventhal's six criteria show that people place the most importance on consistency. Accuracy, representativeness, and suppressing bias are also highly valued.

Based on Tyler's Chicago Study, the author's hypothesis is that in encounters with the police, people are more concerned with fairness than with the policeman's adherence to formal issues of rights, i.e., ethicality. In the courtroom, however, ethical standards and rights receive greater emphasis.

People's views on procedural fairness are affected by two factors: background characteristics and prior views. Race, education, income, sex, age, and political views are the most important background characteristics. Those who are liberal and better educated will place the most emphasis on ethicality when deciding if a procedure is just. Minorities are more likely to focus on consistency and suppression of bias, though. Prior views, formed perhaps from past experiences, carry more weight than background charac-teristics. Any background characteristic is certain to be overridden by one's prior views on a subject.

Influence of Control on the Meaning of Procedural Justice

The Chicago study assessed process control by questioning respondents about how much opportunity they had to state their case or present their problem. Decision control was measured by asking how much influence participants had over the determinations made by the third party in control. Most participants felt they had a high (43%) to moderate (20%) level of process control. In contrast, a number of participants felt they had little decision control (about half said "not much at all").

The Chicago Study thus leads one to conclude that process control judgments are the deciding factor when assessing procedural justice in terms of control. Process control judgments are also important in assessing how experience affects people's evaluation of procedural justice. Ergo, respondents are more concerned with their opportunities to speak out rather than their influence over the outcome. The belief of citizens that their views are being weighed and considered by the authorities and that the authorities are dealing fairly with them reinforces their belief in their own process and decision control.

In the employment context, the study tends to support the idea that employees should be involved in the development of policies and procedures. Instead of just distributing a fraud policy or an ethics policy, send out a questionnaire asking employees for their ideas on how fraud and corruption can be prevented in the company. If employees feel they have some control over the rules, they will be more likely to obey and follow them.

THEORIES OF CRIME CAUSATION

Understanding human behavior and why people obey the law helps explain some of the reasons people commit fraud. However, there have been a number of theorists who have attempted to explain specifically why people commit crimes. In more sophisticated sciences, such as chemistry and physics, theories build one upon another as new facts emerge from studies prompted by the reigning theories. In criminology (as in virtually all the social sciences) theories compete one with another for acceptance, with none of them adequately satisfying either practitioners or scholars in the field.

The reason for this jumble of interpretations of criminal activity in large part lies in the fact that human beings, unlike inanimate objects, think for themselves. You can push a rock in a certain direction and it will (all other things being equal) move in that direction. But you cannot predict as simple a matter as the direction in which a human being might decide to proceed when confronted with a choice. Perhaps you can guess that he will go to the right because you know that this is the direction in which the store he wants to go to lies. But any human being, for reasons that satisfy him, can decide on any given day that he prefers to go to the left, perhaps just to saunter or to get extra exercise, or for no particular reason that seems evident to him or to others.

Imagine how much more difficult it is to try to predict very complicated human behaviors, such as criminal acts.

The following sections summarize some of the better-known criminological theories, both past and present.

Classical Criminology

Classical criminology, based on the philosophical principle of *utilitarianism*, has its roots in the belief that human beings are rational and calculating creatures and therefore do things in order to avoid pain and produce pleasure. Some of the components of classical criminological theory are:
- People have free will which they can use to elect to engage in either criminal or noncriminal behavior
- Criminal behavior will be more attractive if the gains are estimated to be greater than the losses

- The more certain, severe, and swift the reaction to crime, the more likely it is that the penalties will control the behavior

Two theorists' names are associated with classical criminology — the Italian Cesare Beccaria and the Englishman Jeremy Bentham. Bentham, marvelously eccentric, willed that his body be preserved and placed in the entryway to the University of London and brought to the table when the faculty meets. It was and is: the body can be seen today by anyone visiting the school.

The policy implications of classical criminological thought, which are prominent today in theories grouped under the heading of "rational choice," are that penalties should be established that make the anticipated results of criminal behavior less appealing than the prospects of the losses, such as the loss of freedom. The theory also has a benevolent component in that it suggests that penalties that are too severe serve no purpose, since they are needlessly excessive for the deterrence they seek to achieve.

Utilitarianism remains a much-favored approach to crime, with its assumption that offenders will calculate potential gains and losses before they decide to disobey the law. The U.S. Sentencing Commission proposals are based almost totally on the idea of classical criminology, mandating that monetary penalties be calculated at a level that will induce companies to conclude that breaking the law is not fiscally appealing.

Several major difficulties inhere in the theory though. First, of course, many people do not stop and add up the gains and losses of lawbreaking before they engage in it. Second, the impact of penalties can be very different for different people: the thought of a week in prison may be awful to one person, a piece of cake to another. Third, it is very difficult to know whether the penalty will in fact result from the behavior: most offenders optimistically assume that they will not be caught.

Routine Activities Theory

Routine activities theory, a variation of classical theory, holds that both the motivation to commit crime and the supply of offenders is constant. There always will be a certain number of people motivated by greed, lust, and other forces inclining toward lawbreaking. The determining factor, particularly in predatory crimes such as those involving violence and theft, are the activities of potential victims. There are three important elements that influence crime:

- The availability of suitable targets, such as companies and individuals
- The absence of capable guardians, such as auditors and security personnel
- The presence of motivated offenders, such as unhappy or financially-challenged employees

Biological Theories

Biological theories maintain that criminal behavior is not the result of choice, that is, the calculation of benefits and potential losses, but rather is caused by the physical traits of those who commit crime. The foundations of biological theory were laid by Cesare Lombroso, an Italian doctor, who insisted that there were "born" criminals, people who were atavistic, that is throwbacks to more primitive human types. Lombroso spent his career measuring the bodies of offenders and concluded that they were marked by a high degree of asymmetry, with such things as sloping foreheads and other "anomalies." Later critics would point out that Lombroso used no control group—that is he did not measure people who were not criminals, and if he had done so he would have found that they shared equally in those kinds of traits that Lombroso presumed were indicative of criminal propensities.

Biological theory continues to flourish today, with theorists seeking to locate genetic distinctions between those who break the law and those who obey it. In a widely attended volume, *The Bell Curve*, Richard Herrnstein and Charles Murray argued that low intelligence and crime were intimately connected and that low intelligence (as measured by I.Q. scores) was genetically transmitted. Some scholars in the field savaged the Herrnstein-Murray position, but it received a good deal of media attention.

Biological theorists now take a much less deterministic position than Lombroso. They will point to this or that human characteristic and say that it, given certain environmental circumstances, is apt to produce illegal acts. Put another way, they report that they have found a large number of offenders with one or another specific biological trait, but that there are many more who have the trait who never get into any trouble with the law.

Psychological Theories

Theories rooted in psychology are based on the view that criminal behavior is the product of mental processes. The psychoanalytical ideas of Sigmund Freud focus on early childhood development and on unconscious motivations, that is, motivations of which the offender himself is not aware. Freud identified a three-part structure to human personality: the *id* (the drive for food, sex, and other life-sustaining things), the *superego* (the conscience which develops when learned values become incorporated into a person's behavior), and the *ego* (the "I" or the product of the interaction between what a person wants and what his conscience will allow him to do to achieve what he wants).

Cognitive Theories

Cognitive theories stress inadequate moral and intellectual development as lying at the root of criminal acts. There are also *personality theories*, which believe that traits such as extroversion are responsible for a significant amount of crime.

Integrated Theories

There are also *integrated theories* that draw from choice theory, biological theory, and psychological theory. One such argument is put forward by James Q. Wilson and Richard J. Herrnstein in their book *Crime and Human Nature*. Wilson and Herrnstein maintain that while criminal activity is a choice, this choice is heavily influenced by biological and psychological factors. They also explore social factors. The factors include family life, schools, and gang membership.

Conditioning Theory

H. J. Eysenck, working with what he calls *conditioning theory*, argues that the failure of a person to incorporate satisfactorily the dictates of society represents the major explanation for subsequent criminal behavior. Eysenck maintains that extroverted persons, both normal and neurotic, are more difficult to condition—that is, to train—than introverted persons, and that therefore extroverts get into more trouble than introverts.

Another psychological theme is that frustration is the precursor of aggression. The theory suggests that the expression of aggression, such as a fraud perpetrator "getting back" at his employer, will alleviate the frustration and allow the organism to return to a more satisfactory state.

Social Structure Theories

These theories concentrate on the kinds of societies that generate particular levels of crime. Why is crime so low in Japan and so high in the United States? Why do South American countries typically have high rates of homicide while England has such a relatively low level? There are various kinds of sociological theories, all based on similar premises but with differing kinds of emphases.

As a group, social structure theories suggest that forces operating in the lower-class areas of the environment push many of their residents into criminal behavior. Social structure theorists challenge those who would suggest that crime is an expression of psychological imbalance, biological traits, personal choice, etc. They argue that people living in equivalent social environments seem to behave in a similar, predictable fashion.

Theory of Anomie

Strain theories are a branch of the social structure theory. Strain theorists view crime as a direct result of the frustration and anger people experience over their inability to achieve the social and financial success they desire. The best-known strain theory is Robert Merton's *theory of anomie*. Robert Merton, a Columbia University sociologist, maintained that the discrepancy between what people are indoctrinated into desiring and the ways that are available to them to achieve such ends is the cornerstone for explanation of criminal behavior. More information about Merton is contained in the chapter on "Organizational Crime."

Merton's theory of anomie (that is, normlessless) was derived from the work of Emile Durkheim, a French sociologist who adopted the term in his effort to explain suicide rates among different social groups. For Merton, anomie in the United States was characterized by an almost overpowering emphasis on the acquisition of things and on the fact that social status and importance is usually measured in terms of money.

People can obtain money and material goods, Merton noted, by conforming, that is, by working at jobs and engaging in other legal enterprises that pay off. They also can withdraw from the fray, saying that they will not be driven by a desire for goods, but will opt out of the game that dominates the society. The most withdrawn often tend to be those who employ illegal drugs to provide their satisfactions. Then there are the *innovators*, those who refuse to play by the accepted rules of the game, but turn to outlawed methods in order to achieve what the society has told them that they must have to be acceptable members.

Social Process Theories

Not all sociologists believe that a person's social structure alone controls the direction of his or her values, attitudes, and behavior. After all, most people who reside in even the most deteriorated urban areas are law-abiding citizens. *Social process theories* hold that criminality is a function of individual socialization and the social-psychological interactions people have with the various organizations, institutions, and processes of society.

Though they differ in many respects, the various social process theories all share one basic concept: all people regardless of their race, class, or gender, have the potential to become delinquents or criminals.

Social Learning Theories

Social learning theories hold that criminal behavior is a function of the way people absorb information, viewpoints, and motivations from others, most notably from those to whom they are close, such as members of their peer group. Social learning theorists believe that all people have the potential to commit crime if they are exposed to certain kinds of circumstances. All people raised in France by French parents learn to speak that language; Poles learn to speak Polish. So too a person raised with attitudes that favor criminal acts will respond by committing such acts; the person raised and living in an environment where criminal activity would be unthinkable will avoid crime; indeed, it might not even occur to him as a solution to whatever problem is confronting him.

Theory of Differential Association

The theory of differential association is undoubtedly the best-known among all explanations offered in the United States to account for crime, though it too has been widely criticized on the grounds that it is just about impossible to test.

The theory first appeared as a systematic formulation in 1939 in the third edition of Edwin H. Sutherland's *Principles of Criminology*. Later, Sutherland would make his best-known contribution to criminology by coining the phrase *white-collar crime* and writing a monograph on the subject. Sutherland was particularly interested in fraud committed by the elite upper-world business executive, either against shareholders or the public. Sutherland said, "General Motors does not have an inferiority complex, United States Steel does not suffer from an unresolved Oedipus problem, and the DuPonts do not desire to return to the womb. The assumption that an offender may have such pathological distortion of the intellect or the emotions seems to me absurd, and if it is absurd regarding the crimes of businessmen, it is equally absurd regarding the crimes of persons in the economic lower classes."[1]

The theory of differential association begins by asserting that criminal behavior is learned. Explicating that idea, Sutherland specifies as a second point that criminal behavior is learned in interaction with other persons in a process of communication. If individuals acquiring criminal habits or propensities were exposed to situations, circumstances, and interactions totally of a criminal nature, it would be relatively easy to comprehend how this process of communication operates. In view of the enormous variation in standards and personalities to which any individual in our society is exposed, it becomes exceedingly difficult to discern those critical elements that induce criminal behavior without the intervention of some additional principle.

Sutherland's third point is that criminal behavior is acquired through participation within intimate personal groups. This particular stress suggests that the roots of crime must be sought in the socializing experiences of the individual. Unfortunately, the process of socialization is far from being adequately understood. Sutherland's fourth point indicates that the criminal learning process includes not only techniques of committing crime but also the shaping of motives, drives, rationalizations, and attitudes. Crime techniques often can involve a high degree of skill: picking pockets (and not getting caught at it) demands considerable adroitness. Being a successful prostitute demands knowing how to hustle customers, collect money, buy police protection, deal with a drunken or violent john, and a considerable number of other qualifications.

Fifth, Sutherland narrows his focus by indicating the kinds of pressures that move the learning process in the direction of acceptance of illegal pursuits. Careful to keep within the legal definitions of behavior, Sutherland stipulates that the specific direction of motives and drives is learned from definitions of the legal codes as favorable or unfavorable.

And sixth, he sets out his core point by establishing the principle of "differential association." According to this postulate, a person becomes criminal because of an excess of definitions favorable to violation of the law over definitions unfavorable to violation of the law. Then, as a means of demonstrating with greater clarity the character of associations that have a subsequent effect on behavior, Sutherland states his seventh point, that differential

---

[1] Quoted in Geis, Gilbert. *On White-collar Crime.* (Lexington: Lexington Books, 1982).

association may vary in frequency, duration, priority, and intensity. But there is no suggestion regarding which of these elements is apt to be more important than the others. Frequent contacts may promote feelings of boredom and indifference; one intense experience may overwhelm all prior learning or it may not. The axiom hardly helps us much in unraveling the causal contents of crime.

Sutherland's eighth point concerns the nature of learning and, again, is primarily a didactic statement of common behavioral science understanding rather than a contribution that moves the theory very far forward: learning criminal and delinquent behavior, Sutherland asserts, involves all the mechanisms that are involved in any other learning. The key problem is not that Sutherland is wrong; it is that he casts into the spotlight a theoretical problem that has plagued students of human behavior since time immemorial. If crime is to be understood as learned like anything else—say, basketball skills, cooking, patriotism, and flirting—then any theory that can unravel its ingredients will at the same time have to set before us an understanding of all human action. Sutherland's propositions can hardly pretend to approach so stunning an intellectual achievement and in this respect can be regarded as extraordinarily overambitious or, perhaps, simplistic.

As his next to last proposition Sutherland stresses that learning differs from pure imitation. His last point is a worthwhile reminder that while criminal behavior is an expression of general needs and values, it is not explained by these general needs and values because noncriminal behavior is an expression of the same needs and values. This injunction indicates that the generalizations sometimes employed to account for crime— such as the view that people steal because they crave "esteem" or are "greedy," or kill because they are "unhappy"—have little scientific merit. Persons, criminals and noncriminals, are motivated by much the same needs and values. They become or do not become criminals on the basis of their unique responses to common drives for prestige, happiness, success, power, wealth, and numberless other human aspirations. I may feel a pressing need for money and take an extra weekend job pumping gas, or try to borrow from a friend, or shrug my shoulders and figure that this time I'll do without. Another person, feeling the same need, may hold up a fast food outlet.

Social Control Theory

Travis Hirschi, in his 1969 book, *Causes of Delinquency*, first articulated the *social control theory*. A particularly important reason for the current dominance of control theory as the interpretative scheme for understanding crime and delinquency is that, unlike theories such as differential association, it offers a considerable number of testable propositions. Such propositions take the form of "if-then" statements: if something exists or is done, then it foretells that something will follow. Such formulations allow for experimental testing and rebuttal.

Control theory takes its cue from a classic of sociology, Emile Durkheim's *Suicide*, in which the French theoretician wrote:

> *The more weakened the groups to which [the individual belongs], the less he depends on them, the more he consequently depends on himself and recognizes no other rules of conduct than what are founded on his private interests (Durkheim, 1951, p. 209).*

Essentially, control theory argues that the institutions of the social system train and press those with whom they are in contact into patterns of conformity. Schools train for adjustment in society, peers press the ethos of success and conventional behavior, and parents strive to inculcate law-abiding habits in their youngsters even, Hirschi stresses, parents who themselves play fast and loose with the rules. The theory rests on the thesis that to the extent a person fails to become attached to the variety of control agencies of the society, his or her chances of violating the law are increased. This doctrine edges very close to being self-evident in its insistence that close affiliation with law-abiding people, groups, and organizations is predictive of law-abiding behavior, but it is notably rich with subordinate statements, some of them far from obvious.

Four aspects of affiliation are addressed by the theory:
- Attachment
- Commitment
- Involvement
- Belief

Attachment refers primarily to affectional ties with persons such as parents, teachers, and peers. *Commitment* refers to cost factors involved in criminal activity. People are committed to conventional behavior and probably have invested something—fiscally and emotionally—in their ultimate success, an investment that they are wary of risking by a criminal act. Commitment might involve things such as obtaining a better job or seeing one's children succeed. *Involvement* concerns matters such as time spent on the job, that is, participation in activities related to future goals and objectives. *Belief* refers to a conviction about the legitimacy of conventional values, such as the law in general and criminal justice prescriptions in particular.

Hirschi insists that there is no important relationship between social class and delinquency and crime; thus, a person in any class—lower, middle, or upper—who defaults on liaisons with the important formative agencies in our society will be more apt to find himself or herself on a path that ends in crime. Among important considerations, control theory stresses strongly "the bond of affection for conventional persons." "The stronger this bond, the more likely the person is to take it into account when and if he contemplates a criminal act" (Hirschi, 1969, p. 83). What happens essentially, the theory suggests, is that persons confronted with the possibility of behaving in a law-violative manner are likely to ask of themselves: "What will my wife—or my mother and father —think if they find out?" To the extent that persons believe that other people whose opinions are important to them will be disappointed or ashamed, and to the extent that they care deeply that these persons will feel so, they will be constrained from engaging in the sanctioned behavior.

Differential Reinforcement Theory

Differential reinforcement theory is another attempt to explain crime as a type of learned behavior. It is a revision of Sutherland's work that incorporates elements of psychological learning theory popularized by B. F. Skinner and the social learning theory discussed above. The theory was summarized by Ronald Akers in his 1977 work, *Deviant Behavior: A Social Learning Approach*.

According to these behavioral theorists, people learn social behavior by *operant conditioning*, behavior controlled by stimuli that follow the behavior. Behavior is reinforced when positive rewards are gained or punishment is avoided (negative reinforcement). It is weakened by negative stimuli (punishment) and loss of reward (negative punishment). Whether deviant or criminal behavior is begun or persists depends on the degree to which it has been rewarded or punished and the rewards or punishments attached to its alternatives. This is the theory of differential reinforcement.

WHITE-COLLAR CRIME

What is White-Collar Crime?

Since the term first was used there have been constant disputes regarding what is (or should be) the definition of white-collar crime. The designation was coined by Edwin H. Sutherland in December 1939 during his presidential address in Philadelphia to the American Sociological Society. Ten years later Sutherland published a monograph, *White-collar Crime,* in which he offered an arguable, vague definition of the concept in a footnote: White-collar crime was said to be: "Crime in the upper, white-collar class, which is composed of respectable, or at least respected, business, and professional men." These crimes were confined to acts performed by white-collar persons in occupational roles, thereby excluding "most of their cases of murder, adultery, and intoxication, since these are not customarily a part of their occupational procedures."[1]

A few pages after this definitional foray Sutherland illustrated white-collar crime by examples of thefts by chain store employees and overcharges by garage mechanics and watch repairers. There was little consistency between his definition and his illustrations of what might fall within it.

Nonetheless, the term *white-collar crime* has been widely incorporated into popular and scholarly language throughout the world, though the designation *economic crime* is sometimes used as well. The difficulty with *economic crime* is that so many illegal acts, including murder, often are committed in order to achieve economic gain. The United Nations, for its part, adopted the phrase "abuse of power" for those behaviors which correspond to white-collar crimes as defined by Sutherland. In addition, other designations, such as *upperworld crime, crimes by the powerful, avocational crime, crime in the suites,* and *organizational crime,* are sometimes employed to designate more or less the same phenomena as white-collar crime.

A major difficulty with the concept as formulated by Sutherland is that he is designating an offense category that has no equivalent in the law. Certain statute offenses can be identified as those that by and large will be committed by persons in the elite classes, offenses such as antitrust violations and insider trading, but what is to be done definitionally with, say, the proofreader, paid little more than minimum wage, who learns from information that he is working on of a merger between the company and one of its strong competitors. He buys

---

[1] Edwin H. Sutherland, White-collar Crime (New York: Dryden Press, 1949), p. 9.

stock and reaps a considerable profit, then is caught, and prosecuted as an inside trader. Is this person to be regarded as a white-collar criminal? Numerous further examples of situations which are definitionally ambiguous can be offered.

The *Dictionary of Criminal Justice Data Terminology*, published by the Federal Bureau of Justice Statistics, defines white-collar crime as "nonviolent crime for financial gain committed by means of deception by persons whose occupational status is entrepreneurial, professional or semi-professional and utilizing their special occupational skills and opportunities; also nonviolent crime for financial gain utilizing deception and committed by anyone having special technical and professional knowledge of business and government, irrespective of the person's occupation."

This definition certainly catches in its net a wide array of wrongdoers. But critics fault it for its explicit omission of violent offenses. What about a doctor who knowingly performs unnecessary surgery in order to collect a large fee and the patient dies? Or a surgeon who kills a patient because of his incompetence? Or how about the numerous deaths and injuries from toxic wastes, polluted air, and violations of health and safety regulations? Are such results not the product of white-collar crime?

Though there is no consensus within the scholarly community, one definition today of white-collar crime is that proposed by Albert J. Reiss, Jr. and Albert Biderman:

> *White-collar crime violations are those violations of law to which penalties are attached that involve the use of a violator's position of economic power, influence, or trust in the legitimate economic or political institutional order for the purpose of illegal gain, or to commit an illegal act for personal or organizational gain.*[2]

Opportunity is an important ingredient of white-collar crime. An unemployed youth needing funds might turn to armed robbery or burglary. He is in no position to violate the anti-trust laws, though doing so might well provide him with a great deal more funds and lesser likelihood of being caught. The bank president or the company chief executive, for their part, can deal with a personal cash shortage by a variety of illegal tactics that are tied to their business position. Criminals often will commit offenses in ways with which they are most familiar, ways which they can most easily accomplish, and those which have the lowest

---

[2] Albert J. Reiss, Jr., and Albert Biderman, Data Sources on White-Collar Law-Breaking (Washington, DC: National Institute of Justice, U.S. Department of Justice, 1980).

likelihood of dire consequences. An often-unheralded bonus of social status is access to opportunities for less dirty, "more decent" kinds of crime.

Public Perceptions of White-Collar Crime

Studies indicate that, at least in the abstract, white-collar offenses, particularly those that inflict physical harm, are seen by the public to be as serious if not more serious than more traditional kinds of crime, those offenses that, as one early criminologist noted, carry a "brimstone smell."

A poll by the National Survey of Crime Severity gathered the opinions of 60,000 respondents 18 years of age or older about a list of criminal acts. Each respondent was asked to rate the crimes listed. The results showed, among other things, that fraud by a grocer and a $10 embezzlement were perceived to be as serious as an obscene phone call. Acceptance of a bribe by a city politician and an armed robbery that netted $1,000 also were rated at about the same level. The following table presents the results of the study, showing the crimes in order of increasing seriousness and indicating the white-collar offenses in boldface type.

National Survey of Crime Severity Ratings: Selected Offense Stimuli

Ratings	Offense Stimuli
1.9	**An employee embezzles $10 from his employer.**
1.9	**A store owner knowingly puts "large" eggs into containers marked "extra large."**
1.9	A person makes an obscene phone call.
3.1	A person breaks into a home and steals $100.
3.2	**An employer illegally threatens to fire employees if they join a labor union.**
3.6	A person knowingly passes a bad check.
3.7	**A labor union official illegally threatens to organize a strike if an employer hires nonunion workers.**
5.4	**A real estate agent refuses to sell a house to a person because of that person's race.**
5.4	A person threatens to harm a victim unless the victim gives him money. The victim gives him $10 and is not harmed.
5.7	**A theater owner knowingly shows pornographic movies to a minor.**
6.1	**A person cheats on his federal income tax return and avoids paying $10,000 in taxes.**
6.1	A person runs a prostitution racket.

6.2	A person beats a victim with his fists. The victim requires treatment by a doctor but not hospitalization.
6.2	**An employee embezzles $1,000 from his employer.**
6.4	**An employer refuses to hire a qualified person because of that person's race.**
6.5	A person uses heroin.
6.9	**A factory knowingly gets rid of its waste in a way that pollutes the water supply of a city. As a result, one person becomes ill but does not require medical treatment.**
6.9	A person beats a victim with his fists. The victim requires hospitalization.
8.0	A person steals an unlocked car and sells it.
8.2	**Knowing that a shipment of cooking oil is bad, a store owner decides to sell it anyway. Only one bottle is sold and the purchaser is treated by a doctor but not hospitalized.**
8.6	A person performs an illegal abortion.
9.0	**A city official takes a bribe from a company for his help in getting a city building contract for the company.**
9.0	A person, armed with a lead pipe, robs a victim of $1,000.
9.2	**Several large companies illegally fix the retail prices of their products.**
9.4	A person robs a victim of $10 at gunpoint. No physical harm occurs.
9.4	**A public official takes $1,000 of public money for his own use.**
9.6	**A police officer knowingly makes a false arrest.**
9.6	A person breaks into a home and steals $1,000.
10.0	**A government official intentionally hinders the investigation of a criminal offense.**
10.9	A person steals property worth $10,000 from outside a building.
11.2	**A company pays a bribe to a legislator to vote for a law favoring the company.**
11.8	A man beats a stranger with his fists. The victim requires hospitalization.
12.0	**A police officer takes a bribe not to interfere with an illegal gambling operation.**
12.0	A person gives the floor plans of a bank to a bank robber.
13.3	A person, armed with a lead pipe, robs a victim of $10. The victim is injured and requires hospitalization.
13.5	**A doctor cheats on claims he makes to a federal health insurance plan for patient services. He gains $10,000.**
13.9	**A legislator takes a bribe from a company to vote for law favoring the company.**
14.6	A person, using force, robs a victim of $10. The victim is hurt and requires hospitalization.
15.5	A person breaks into a bank at night and steals $10,000.
15.7	**A county judge takes a bribe to give a light sentence in a criminal case.**

16.6	A person, using force, robs a victim of $1,000. The victim is hurt and requires treatment by a doctor but not hospitalization.
17.8	**Knowing that a shipment of cooking oil is bad, a store owner decides to sell it anyway. Only one bottle is sold and the purchaser dies.**
19.5	A person kills a victim by recklessly driving an automobile.
19.7	**A factory knowingly gets rid of its waste in a way that pollutes the water supply of a city. As a result, 20 people become ill but none require medical treatment.**
19.9	**A factory knowingly gets rid of its waste in a way that pollutes the water supply of a city. As a result, one person dies.**
20.1	A man forcibly rapes a woman. Her physical injuries require treatment by a doctor but not hospitalization.
33.8	A person runs a narcotics ring.
39.1	**A factory knowingly gets rid of its waste in a way that pollutes the water supply of a city. As a result, 20 people die.**
43.9	A person plants a bomb in a public building. The bomb explodes and one person is killed.
72.1	A person plants a bomb in a public building. The bomb explodes and 20 people are killed.

Source: The National Survey of Crime Severity by Marvin Wolfgang, Robert Figlio, Paul Tracy, and Simon Singer (1985). Washington, D.C.; U.S. Government Printing Office (Pp. vi-x).

Crimes of the Middle Classes—A Look at White-Collar Crime

Surveys carried out subsequently provide essentially the same result, that the public as a whole regards some white-collar offenses as serious matters. The difficulty with such surveys, however, is that they fail to convey in any effective manner the complexity of the white-collar offenses and the status of the offenders. It is one thing for a respondent to say that he regards toxic waste offenses that produce death as very serious violations, quite another for that person to regard the corporate executive responsible for such matters as an "evil" person. Because of this, white-collar offenders receive much less severe penalties than the street persons who commit the offenses that the public generally regards to be as serious as theirs.

The debate over just what constitutes a white-collar crime, and what drives the white-collar criminal, has been raging ever since Sutherland's seminal work. The authors of *Crimes of the Middle Classes*[3] offer a contribution that for the most part avoids theory-building, offering instead a statistical report of offenders convicted in federal court.

---

[3] Weisburd, David, et al. *Crimes of the Middle Classes. White-Collar Offenders in the Federal Courts.* New Haven: Yale UP, 1991

Using federal court records, and an unprecedented access to probation officers' presentencing investigation reports (PSIs), the authors determined that most people convicted of white-collar crimes are not upper class; that social status has only an indirect significance; and that, once a conviction is attained, higher status often means a stiffer sentence. The most important factor is "how personal situations and organizational opportunities combine" to make crime possible and attractive to average Americans.[4] White-collar crime does have a unique place in criminology, but the split is not between an underworld of the desperate poor and an elite universe of high-stakes shysters. White-collar crime has some relation to both of these mythological worlds but is largely the province of the middle classes, where organizational position is more important than pedigree and personal situations are more forceful than sociological trends.

Profiles of Offenders

The wide array of crimes called "white-collar"—from antitrust and securities violations to bank embezzlement and credit fraud—makes assembling a profile of the typical offender difficult, but not impossible. Most defendants are white males, with a moderate social status. They are slightly more likely than the general population to have a high school diploma (78 percent versus 69 percent), or a college degree (24.7 percent versus 19 percent for the general public). The majority, then, are not highly educated, and in at least one category—owning one's home—the offenders fall behind the average citizen: while 55 percent of Americans own their homes, only 45.3 percent of the offenders do. Social status is a factor in white-collar criminality, but as the authors point out, "The position conferred by status, rather than status itself, empowers the offender."[5] So a corporate manager, who was promoted from inside the company with only a ninth-grade education and who doesn't own his home is not as atypical an offender as might be supposed. The key is that, by his position in his company, he has the opportunity and means to commit a crime.

Cressey Study

Donald R. Cressey found in a 1953 study of embezzlers that most of those he examined "had lived beyond their means for some time before deciding to embezzle."[6] *Crimes* extends this statement more generally, remarking, "The most interesting fact about the white-collar offenders' aggregate financial status is not the value of their assets but the extent of their

---

[4] Weisburd, p. xiv.
[5] Weisburd, p. 61.
[6] Weisburd, p. 65n.

liabilities." Offenders often "have the material goods associated with successful people but may barely be holding their financial selves together."[7] These people have assembled a structure of respectability, but it is often built on the sands of debt. The Cressey Study is discussed in more detail in the chapter on "Occupational Crime."

Effect of Status

What is loosely called "class" or "social status" does have an effect on crimes. For example, one defendant used his position as chairman of a local bank board to set up loans for his ailing wood chip company. The loans would never have been approved without the chairman's influence, and he never reported them in his proxy statement to the bank's shareholders. Ultimately, the bank lost close to $6 million. In this case, the chairman's class standing made a difference. His ruse squares with the documented knowledge that officers and managers commit the business crimes with the widest impact (in terms of dollar amounts and victimization) while owners and workers generally commit narrower schemes.

Organizational Opportunity

Of all factors, organizational opportunity remains the determinant aspect of white-collar crime. Against Sutherland's emphasis on an elite group running high-class sting operations, *Crimes* shows that organization and complexity make a larger difference than the offender's social status. In a fascinating case, a church group used its daycare center to defraud the federal government of approximately $1 million. Their arrangement with the Department of Agriculture required the daycare's administrators to submit monthly vouchers reporting the number of meals they had served and the cost of food and labor. When auditors descended upon the scam, they found that for about $79,000 in actual expenses, the administrators had submitted almost $1 million in food costs, and $400,000 for labor. Teachers said they sometimes brought food to the center themselves because the children weren't being fed properly. There were also reports that "morning snacks were never served unless the government inspectors were expected, that the same children were run through serving lines twice when inspectors were present, and that some children were bused in from other daycare centers on inspection days."[8] The example shows, according to the authors, that a criminal's position in an organization, and the ability to organize the scam, have far more bearing on the crime than social status or class alone.

---

[7] Weisburd, p. 65.
[8] Weisburd, p. 94.

The Middle Class

People of moderate social standing are in fact more likely than members of the upper class to commit highly organized crimes from within a corporate structure.[9] Some offenders do fit the stereotype of "respectability and high social status" in white-collar crime, but most of them are solidly middle class. "They appear to represent the very broad middle of the society, much above the poverty line but for the most part far from elite social status," say the authors. Offenders "are mostly commonplace, not unlike the average American in most respects, though perhaps more often with personal lives that are in some state of disarray. The single quality that distinguishes them from other Americans is that they have been convicted of a federal crime." [10]

Methodology

All the conclusions in the *Crimes of the Middle Classes* are qualified. The authors and researchers drew from the federal court records of seven districts[11] and obtained access to the sentencing reports (PSIs) prepared by probation officers. PSIs had never been available to researchers before, and the close reading of these documents formed a central part of the project. Admittedly, the crimes and specific cases studied were selected, not drawn from a random sample. Eight crimes were targeted as "white-collar": securities violations, antitrust suits, bribery and influence-peddling, embezzlement, mail- or wire-fraud, tax fraud, false claims and statements (in official documents), and credit fraud. Certain violations—such as RICO charges against organized crime and breaking importation laws—were excluded, judged to lie outside the parameters of what most people think of as white-collar activity.

Even within their eight categories, the authors didn't examine every single case, deciding to focus on no more than 30 cases within each category in order to facilitate the close reading of PSIs. They warn that their findings were taken from studying people actually convicted, so the results don't take account of how often charges are actually filed and followed up by prosecution. By dealing with the convicted, they focused on the treatment of people already inside the federal system.

---

[9] The authors opine that "the individualism and independence" of professions like doctors or lawyers discourage their involvement in the organizational network that drives these crimes, though we are warned that "the growing participation of professionals in large private organizations" (such as HMOs) may change both the opportunity for and attitude toward criminal activity (89-91).

[10] Weisburd, p. 73.

[11] The districts and "central cities" were as follows: Central California (Los Angeles), Northern Georgia (Atlanta), Northern Illinois (Chicago), Maryland (Baltimore), Southern New York (Manhattan and the Bronx), Northern Texas (Dallas), and Western Washington (Seattle). A detailed discussion of the sampling process is included as Appendix 1.

Finally, the long-range nature of the project meant that the study's sample years—1976-78—were considerably past before the findings were published. New sentencing guidelines handed down in 1984 and adopted in 1987 may make the next version of this book look different, by the authors' own admission. The guidelines make some material which judges considered at their discretion (like the dollar amount of a crime) a *mandatory* element of sentencing. At the same time, the Sentencing Act systematically *excludes* judgments based on a defendant's "moral character," which had previously been a standard in assessments. Wheeler and company write that these developments will have to be accommodated in future studies, but they don't expect the new trends will seriously affect the general picture they present. "For example, we see no reason to believe that the role of organizational opportunity in white-collar crime ... is any different in substance in 1990 than it was in the late 1970s, although the particular organizations singled out for public inquiry and prosecution may well have changed."[12]

With these qualifications in mind, it remains useful to consider the findings of this report. The following chart summarizes the ranking of offenders by social status and in respect to certain demographic features.

Offenders Ranked by Status, with Selected Demographic Information

| **High**
•*Antitrust*
•*Securities*	These offenders committed the crimes with the largest dollar impact, and the widest geographic scope. They are overwhelmingly white (99%-plus) and male (99.1% for antitrust, 97.8% for securities). The groups are equally likely to hold a college degree (40.9% in either case), and their frauds were usually occupational in nature. There are revealing contrasts when these two types of offenders are compared: 1) Almost 97% of antitrust offenders had been steadily employed in the years preceding their crime, while only about 60% of the securities offenders had continually held a job. 2) The antitrusters had a median ratio of assets to liabilities of $200,000 (assets) to $40,000 (liabilities); the securities offenders medianly held $57,500 in assets with $54,000 in liabilities.

---

[12] Weisburd, p.xv.

	3) Antitrust violators were more likely to own their own homes (73.5% vs. 58.2%) and to be married (95.7% vs. 80.7%) than securities offenders.
Middle •*Tax fraud* •*Bribery*	These offenders are mainly white males, around 45 years old. Their crimes are not usually occupational—just 15% for tax fraud, less than 18% for bribery. Roughly 57% of offenders owned their own homes, and about 28% held a college degree. Their median assets ranged from $45,000–$49,500; median liabilities were between $19,000 and $23,500. The authors remark that although tax fraud is a typical white-collar crime, "two-thirds of the tax offenders work in the manufacturing or nonprofessional service sectors."
Low •*Credit fraud* •*Mail fraud* •*False claims*	This group was not as likely to be white—71.5% for credit fraud, 76.8% for mail fraud, 61.8% for false claims; or male—84.8% for credit fraud, 82.1% for mail fraud, 84.7% for false claims. They were generally younger than the other category offenders (less than 40 years old); less likely to be married (about 50%); and less likely to own their own home (roughly 34–45% across the three crime types). Their net worth, as the ratio of assets to liabilities, was remarkably low: $7,000/$7,000 for credit fraud; $2,000/$3,500 for mail fraud; $4,000/$5,000 for false claims.
Outside Hierarchy •*Bank embezzlement*	These offenders were placed outside the rankings because they were dramatically younger (a mean age of 31) and more likely to be female (44.8% female/55.2% male) than the other groups. While nearly 25% of the Low-status group was unemployed at the time of their crime, only 3% of embezzlers were without a job (just slightly above the 2.8% rate for High-status offenders). They are the group least likely to have a college degree (12.9%), or to own their own home (28.4%). Their median net worth was $2,000 in assets with $3,000 in liabilities. Male embezzlers were usually managers of a local banking operation, while females were most often tellers or clerical workers.

However difficult it may prove to sort out the demography of *Crimes*, the strength of the analysis lies in its tracing the path of criminals through the federal system. Following their core group from offense to conviction, the authors report on general trends in the treatment and sentencing of white-collar criminals. The most surprising conclusion states that people of higher social status, once convicted, are more likely than similar offenders to receive prison time and to be fined.

Cooperating Defendants

Some standard assumptions still apply. For example, informing on one's cohorts does help. Over 42 percent of cooperating defendants were charged with a single violation, while only

30 percent of noncooperating defendants were so lucky. Also, white-collar defendants receive bail rather easily: just one person in eight spends any time incarcerated before trial, and for the generally high-status antitrust defendants, the figure is fewer than one in 20. By comparison, in a control group of "common criminals"—i.e., people convicted of the "nonviolent economic crimes" of postal theft or postal fraud—at least 1/3 of the defendants spent time in jail before going to trial.[13]

Pleas by White-Collar Defendants

White-collar defendants are more likely to insist on a trial than other offenders. In at least 90 percent of federal cases, defendants will plead guilty, avoiding the expense and effort of a trial. But, over 18 percent of defendants in the *Crimes* sample (as opposed to the usual 10 percent) pled "Not Guilty." In cases like bank embezzlement, usually "simple cases with clear evidence," plea bargains are easily negotiated and "prosecutors may actively seek guilty pleas."[14] The decision on how to plead varies with the offender as much as the offense. For example, female bank tellers were especially prone to plead "Not Guilty," while many of the men embezzlers—generally "higher-level officials involved in more complex crimes"—proceeded to trial. Of all white-collar defendants, securities offenders are the ones most likely to insist on their day in court. Evidently, both the government and the defendants in these cases feel more strongly about their chances to win.

Judgments

Judgments against white-collar defendants often involve an assessment of personal suffering. It is widely held that, when convicted of a crime, these people suffer a greater blow personally and professionally than street criminals. Many observers think this suffering should be acknowledged in assessing a sentence. One federal judge is quoted as saying,

> *The white-collar criminal by virtue of his conviction has suffered a loss of position, usually loss of employment, sometimes status in his profession, other times the ability to ever find employment in anything requiring a fidelity bond or what have you. Whereas the common*

---

[13] Postal theft and postal forgery were selected as economic crimes without a direct link to violence. Other "common crimes" such as burglaries or larceny are state offenses, and so not appropriate to this study of the federal system. Postal theft involves acts like stealing government-issued checks, such as welfare payments; postal forgery involves the act of cashing these items. Clearly, the choice of these crimes (and not others) for comparison is debatable.

[14] Weisburd, p. 114.

street criminal hasn't had a career loss of a similar nature; indeed in some areas the conviction of a crime is some sort of a badge of maturity.[15]

Personal Suffering

Examining PSIs, the authors found that in about 65 percent of the cases overall, personal suffering was said to have played an overwhelming role in the defendant's case. Securities offenders and embezzlers topped the list, with 70 and 87 percent of these people (respectively) reporting some hardship. Of course, the reports involved statements by the defendants or their families, which could be self-serving.

And in actually looking at objective material—such as the loss of employment, marital separations and divorce, or mental health problems—the authors found the results "ambiguous." Credit fraud perpetrators, for example, seldom reported any suffering, but they had a 20 percent divorce rate during the time of their prosecution, the highest in the study. And there were often large gaps between different types of crimes. Compared to the securities offenders, with a 70 percent rate of suffering, only about 24 percent of antitrust offenders had similar complaints. The discrepancy may lie in how different crimes are viewed. "Antitrust violators, who steal *for* their companies and actually provide the services they say they do," aren't seen as harshly as "those who steal *from* their companies."[16] Securities offenders are stigmatized "because their crimes are often against their own clients," while bank embezzlers (with over 87 percent reported suffering) are judged with particular strictness "because they steal from their employers."[17]

In summary, the authors believe that the extra-legal suffering of white-collar defendants has some validity, but it's not always possible to be sure that prosecution alone caused the hardship. The contradictory images of these criminals as both exceptionally privileged and especially harassed "overstate their real experience in the legal system." Neither factor is as great as the standard rhetoric might suggest.

Imprisonment

Crimes does find that the highest status group—antitrust violators—were the least likely to receive prison time (about 1 in 5) and to draw the shortest sentence (1.8 months). Securities

---

[15] Weisburd, p. 116.
[16] Weisburd, p. 124.
[17] Weisburd, p. 125.

fraud led the group, with over 67 percent doing time, followed by tax fraud (58.9 percent) and mail fraud (55.1 percent). But in considering all offenders in all groups, the authors discovered that the higher an individual's status, the more likely the person was to be imprisoned: "All else being equal, doctors will have about a 30 percent greater likelihood of being imprisoned [for a white-collar crime] than truck drivers and almost a 13 percent greater likelihood than managers."[18] Judges seem to find persons of higher prestige more at fault, or in other words, more blameworthy, in the commission of their crimes.

One remarkable variable in determining the severity of punishment was where the case was tried. The districts of Maryland, Northern Illinois, and Northern Texas tended toward harsher sentences; Northern Georgia and Southern New York handed down the lightest.

More often than prison, the punishment of choice for white-collar criminals is the imposition of fines. Whereas six percent of the "common criminals" in the survey received fines, all of the antitrust violators did; embezzlers were the least likely group to be fined, but even so, their 15 percent rate far exceeded the norm. For fines as well as imprisonment, higher status usually meant a higher penalty. Analysis showed that "white defendants, those with more impeccable records, and those who have higher class positions are more likely to be fined."[19] But while the decision to fine seems based on status, the actual levies are often comparatively low. For antitrust suits, the mean fine was $9,808; for embezzlement, just $1,397. Even well-off offenders got off light: a man convicted of fixing the price of candy bars in an eastern state, with a net worth exceeding $190,000 was fined $3,500; another defendant, whose net worth approached $1.4 million, was fined $5,000 for credit fraud. Only 4 percent of offenders were ever given the statute's maximum penalty.

Obviously, most white-collar crimes don't even approach the billion-dollar levels of the stereotype. An accurate picture actually looks rather mundane. "For every truly complicated and rarified offense," according to Wheeler and his colleagues, "there are many others that are simple and could be carried out by almost anyone who can read, write, and give an outward appearance of stability."[20] More than anything else—more than status, or class position, or heritage—the white-collar criminal needs an opportunity and some sort of organization.

---

[18] Weisburd, p. 143.
[19] Weisburd, p. 157.
[20] Weisburd, p. 171.

Contributing Factors

The authors posit several factors which have contributed to the rising problem of economic crime:

- America's economy increasingly runs on credit, which often means rising personal debt. The offenders in the sample often showed serious discrepancies "between their resources and their commitments."[21]
- New information technologies mean that the opportunity for wrongdoing is growing, and many of the techniques are not widely comprehended by businesses or individuals.
- Government programs distributing large amounts of money make an enticing target for defalcations.
- The importance of credentials in a professionalized society may influence individuals "to inflate the credentials, or to make them up when they do not exist." This tendency involves everything from cheating on school entrance exams to falsifying credit applications.
- Most broadly, the authors observe an American culture based on affluence and ever-higher levels of success. "The continued pressure of a value system that rewards economic affluence or its visible by-products has its effects on the broad middle of American society."[22] Television, and advertising in general, promise that no one has to settle for second best, prompting those who find themselves running behind to fudge the difference, crossing ethical and sometimes legal lines.

Conclusion

Curbing this pernicious trend will not be easy, but there are ways. Since organizational opportunity determines so much criminal activity, the foremost deterrent is to pay heightened attention to "where the money is and how it flows" within any group. Obviously most businesses have some system of financial control, but the authors say "organizational intelligence" is often less than stellar. Offenders are not usually "the highly sophisticated swindlers" from the mass media, just "average people in a financial jam who see a way out through fraud."[23]

---

[21] Weisburd, p. 183.
[22] Weisburd, p. 184.
[23] Weisburd, p. 190.

Furthermore, like many analysts these days, the *Crimes* team believes it is far too easy to acquire money and goods on credit. Tightening the restrictions on credit cards and loans would directly address the role that debt plays in many schemes.

Finally, these authors center the problem of white-collar crime around values. As long as the places where citizens learn their priorities—schools, families, neighborhoods, mass media—emphasize high-pressure risk taking and material affluence over "honesty and moral integrity," many people will go for the gold, even if they have to steal it. It will never be easy, they acknowledge, to balance a market-based economy, which requires competition, with an equal insistence on forthrightness and fair play.

Varieties of White-Collar Crime

Criminologists offer an array of breakdowns of white-collar offenses, each one providing some analytical advantages, and each failing to meet the more rigorous scientific standards of precise categorization. One of the better known is that by Herbert Edelhertz, a onetime federal prosecutor. Edelhertz divides the offenses into four major types:

- *Ad hoc violations*: committed for personal profit on an episodic basis, for example tax cheating
- *Abuses of trust*: committed by people in organizations against organizations, for example, embezzlement, bribery, and kickbacks
- *Collateral business crime*: committed by organizations in furtherance of their business interests, for example, false weights and measures, antitrust violations, and environmental crimes
- *Confidence games*: offenses committed to cheat clients, for example, fraudulent land and bogus securities sales[24]

The last category illustrates the definitional dilemma surrounding the question of what is and what is not white-collar crime. Under the Reiss and Biderman definition, the category of confidence games would not be regarded as a white-collar crime since the perpetrators almost always intended from the outset to misrepresent their product and to cheat their customers. Of course, whether or not a behavior is regarded as a white-collar crime or not

---

[24]Herbert Edelhertz, The Nature, Impact and Prosecution of White-collar Crime (Washington, DC: National Institute of Law Enforcement and Criminal Justice, 1970).

has nothing to do either with the seriousness of the behavior or the manner in which the criminal justice system will handle it.

Most criminologists have adopted the distinction first made by Marshall B. Clinard (another recipient of the Association of Certified Fraud Examiners' Cressey Award) and Richard Quinney between *occupational crime* and *organizational crime*. Organizational crime is that committed by businesses, particularly corporations, and government. Occupational crime involves offenses against the law by individuals in the course of their occupation. An antitrust offense would be an organizational crime; accepting or offering bribes an occupational offense.

ORGANIZATIONAL CRIME

Organizational crime occurs in the context of complex relationships and expectations among boards of directors, executives, and managers on the one hand and among parent corporations, corporate divisions, and subsidiaries on the other. White-collar crime is distinguished from lower socioeconomic crimes in terms of the structure of the violation and the fact that administrative and civil penalties are more likely to be used as punishment than are criminal penalties.

While corporations cannot be jailed, they may be confined. Most corporate lawbreakers are handled by government regulatory agencies like the Federal Trade Commission, the Environmental Protection Agency, and the Food and Drug Administration. Enforcement measures might include warning letters, consent agreements or decrees not to repeat the violation; orders of regulatory agencies to compel compliance, seizure, or recall of goods; administrative or civil monetary penalties; and court injunctions to refrain from further violations.

Corporate crime is certainly not limited to the United States. Clinard and Yeager say it appears to be extensive in Europe, Japan, Australia and other areas. According to Delmas-Marty, French multinationals violate the law in many ways. They utilize both legal and illegal means in tax evasion. They may transfer profits from one subsidiary to another located in a country that has a more lenient tax system or presents a tax haven, like Switzerland. According to Cosson, French manufacturing corporations also falsify their bookkeeping to avoid payment of industrial and commercial taxes.

In Japan, the Diet (legislature) has passed a law for the punishment of crimes "relating to environmental pollution that adversely affects the health of persons." Under this law intentional or negligent emission by industries of a substance that causes danger to human life or health is to be punished with imprisonment or fines.

The Swiss banking system has often been accused of offering a hiding place for stolen or looted money, providing a screen for stock manipulations and shady promoters and helping tax evaders conceal both income and assets. Deposits in Swiss banks often are laundered to obscure their illegal origins, and then through new commercial transactions, the money is made legal and therefore concealed from tax authorities.

Corporate Organization and Criminal Behavior

Corporate offenses take place in a context of complex relationships and expectations in an organizational setting. It often is difficult to distinguish among the corporate participants which ones ought to be held personally responsible for the wrongdoing. Many offenses are the result of a myriad of decisions made by different persons and passing through a chain of command. Not uncommonly, when corporate acts are contrary to the law, upper level executives take pains to avoid learning what is going on so as to avoid responsibility if a scheme is uncovered. In some corporations, there is one executive, well-paid, who is only half in jest referred to as the "vice president in charge of going to jail."

In addition, of course, since the law largely treats corporations as persons they make more inviting prosecutory targets than individuals, most notably because they have deeper pockets and can be heavily fined to repay losses that have been inflicted on persons or on the society in general.

Government regulatory agencies such as the Federal Trade Commission (FTC), the Environmental Protection Agency (EPA), and the Food and Drug Administration (FDA) oversee corporate performance in areas assigned to them by Congressional mandate. Typically, the lawmakers enact a statute that is deliberately vague, allowing the enforcement agency to develop its own enforcement guidelines within the boundaries of the Congressional authorization. The agencies will sometimes seek to expand the reach of the law by selecting notably egregious cases for litigation and appeal, thereby anticipating a favorable ruling on what fundamentally is a somewhat novel interpretation of their mandate.

The Image of the Corporation

Large corporations have contributed significantly to industrial and commercial development throughout the world. Their size and resources enable them to organize and coordinate production and distribution. The capital resources of a large corporation provide it with the ability to develop, adopt, and alter technology on a mammoth scale. A considerable portion of the population has been accorded a high standard of living because of corporate activity.

At the same time, large corporations have the power to influence the manner in which laws are written and to commit acts that can inflict serious harm upon the population. They can hire lobbyists and lawyers who manipulate definitions of wrongdoing in the corporations' interests.

The very largeness and remoteness of the corporation from most of us is part of the reason that Americans traditionally have a love-hate attitude toward such organizations. We admire and desire their products, but we are uneasy about their power, a power that tends to be used single-mindedly in the pursuit of profits. Thomas Hobbes, a seventeenth century English political philosopher, stands out in the crowd that has been scornful of corporations. Hobbes' unsavory comparison was between corporations and ascarides, worms that eat at the entrails of what Hobbes called "natural man."[1] Centuries later, Robert Heilbroner, an economist, would castigate "the corporation with its wealth-seeking, its dehumanizing calculus of plus and minus, its careful inculcation of impulses and goals that should at most be tolerated."[2]

Corporations and their executives also often are the object of deprecatory humor. As far back as 1635, a satirist had a businessman proclaiming: "I love churches. I mean to rob my countrymen and build one."[3] In more recent times, a U.S. Senator told the story of a corporation officer who, when asked at a committee hearing if he were not ashamed of double-dealing persons who trusted him, was puzzled: "Who else can you cheat?" he wanted to know.[4] The putdowns of the business world are part of a common folklore, reflected in the belief that the expression "legitimate business" is an oxymoron.

According to William Kristol, public hostility toward big business dates back to the Populist movement of the late nineteenth century and suspicions of trusts that led to the 1890 Sherman Antitrust Act. People are suspicious as to whether goods produced by large corporations are of the highest quality or are available at the lowest possible price. In 1978, a survey by Seymour Lipset and Gordan Schneider concluded that major industries and corporations had dropped in public esteem greatly during the 1970s.

Clinard and Yeager

In a comprehensive study of corporate law-breaking, Marshall Clinard (a recipient of the Association's Donald Cressey Award) and Peter Yeager examined over a two-year period the records of 562 companies (477 of which where on the *Fortune 500* list) and found that 1,553 white-collar crime cases had been filed against them. Some 60 percent of the firms had at

---

[1] Thomas Hobbes, Leviathan (London: Andrew Crooke, 1651.
[2] Robert Heilbroner, In the Name of Profit (New York: Doubleday, 1973), p. 223.
[3] Christopher Hill, Society and Puritanism in Pre-Revolutionary England (Longon: Secker & Warburg, 1964) p. 267.
[4] John T. Noonan, Bribes (New York: Macmillan, 1984).

least one case against them; for those companies the average number of violations was 4.4. The oil, pharmaceutical, and motor vehicle industries were the most likely to be charged for wrongdoing, a matter that may be a function of enforcement priorities or a true reflection of their activities.

In a study by Irwin Ross, he analyzed 1,043 companies that at one time or another had appeared on the *Fortune* list of large industrial companies. Included in his study were five kinds of offenses: bribe-taking or bribe-giving by high-level executives, criminal fraud, illegal campaign contributions, tax evasion, and antitrust violations. One hundred seventeen, or 11 percent of the corporations, were violators.

The costs of corporate crimes not only include financial losses, but also injuries, deaths, and health hazards. Such crimes destroy public confidence in businesses and hurt the image of corporations. Clinard and Yeager say price-fixing offenses victimize the consumer and federal, state, and municipal governments while income tax crimes deprive the government and those dependent on it of needed revenue.

Clinard and Yeager believe that corporate violations are increasingly difficult to discover, investigate, or prosecute successfully because of their growing complexity and intricacy. This is particularly true, they believe, of antitrust cases, foreign payoffs, computer fraud, and illegal political contributions. In the last category, some corporations pay bonuses to their executives, with the understanding that part of that reward will be turned over to the coffers of a candidate that the corporation favors.[5]

Criminal activities involving corporations often are rooted in organizational subcultures and values, developed over time. A particularly comprehensive examination of how matters of life and death become embedded in routine decision-making and ultimately can lead to tragedy is provided in a book titled *The Challenger Space Shuttle Disaster* by Diane Vaughan, still another Cressey Award winner.[6]

Legal responses have been slow and ineffectual when dealing with economic organi-zational change. The law has emphasized the role of the individual actor in criminality, but has not examined the role of the organization in crime. Criminal activities often are rooted in

---

[5] Marshall B. Clinard and Peter C. Yeager, Corporate Crime (New York: Free Press, 1980).
[6] Diane Vaughan, The Challenger Launch Decision: Risky Technology, Culture, and Deviance at NASA. (Chicago: University of Chicago Press, 1996).

organizational subculture and attitudes developed over time and cannot be traced to individuals or groups within the organization. While individuals still carry out the criminal enterprise, their attitudes and characteristics are of little importance, as an organization will replace those employees unwilling to participate in a criminal activity.

Types of Violations

Clinard and Yeager found six main types of corporate illegal behavior:
- Administrative
- Environmental
- Financial
- Labor
- Manufacturing
- Unfair trade practices

Administrative violations involve noncompliance with the requirements of an agency or court and information violations such as refusal to produce information; failure to report information; and failure to file, secure certification, or acquire permits.

Environmental violations involve incidents of air and water pollution, including oil and water spills, such as the damage inflicted on the Alaska coastline by leakage from the *Exxon Valdez* which ran aground in Price William Sound during the night of March 23-24, 1989. The category also embraces violations concerning air and water permits that require capital outlays by corporations for the construction of pollution control equipment.

Financial violations include illegal payments or failure to disclose such violations, i.e., commercial domestic bribery, illegal domestic political contributions, payments to foreign officials, the conferring of illegal gratuities and benefits, and violations of foreign currency laws. Examples of securities-related violations are false and misleading proxy materials, misuse of nonpublic material information, and the issuance of false data.

Transaction violations involve the following: terms of sale (overcharging customers), exchange agreements (failure to apply increased prices equally to classes of purchasers, illegal changing of base lease conditions, illegal termination of base supplier-purchaser relationship, imposition of more stringent credit terms than those existing during the base period) and purchase conditions (failure to pay full price when due, insufficient funds checks, making preferential payments). Also included are *tax violations* involving fraudulent returns and deficiency in tax liability, *accounting malpractices* such as failure to record terms of transactions involving questionable pricing and promotional practices, and *false entries* such as recording fictitious sales and improper estimates such as misreporting of costs.

Clinard and Yeager classify *labor violations* into four major types: discrimination in employment, occupational safety and health hazards, unfair labor practices, and wage and hour violations. The four agencies responsible for bringing actions concerning these violations are, respectively, the Equal Employment Opportunity Commission, the Occupational Health and Safety Administration, the National Labor Relations Board, and the Wage and Hour Division of the Department of Labor.

Manufacturing violations involve three government agencies. The Consumer Product Safety Commission (CPSC) responds to violations of the Federal Hazardous Substances Act, the Poison Prevention Packaging Act, the Flammable Fabrics Act and the Consumer Product Safety Act. Violations dealt with in this arena include electric shock hazards, chemical and environmental hazards, and fire and thermal burn hazards.

The main categories of manufacturing violations of Food and Drug Administration (FDA) regulations are misbranding, mispackaging, mislabeling (such as packaging in incorrect or defective containers, lack of adequate or correct content or ingredient statements, lack of adequate or correct directions for use on labels), contamination or adulteration (such as lack of assurance of sterility or product prepared, held or stored under unsanitary conditions), lack of effectiveness of product (failure to meet USP standards, defect in product), inadequate testing procedures, and inadequate standards in blood or plasma collection and laboratory processing (improper procedures in choice and use of blood donors, lack of assurance of sterility).

Unfair trade practices involve abuses of competition (monopolization, price discrimi-nation, credit violations, misrepresentation), vertical combinations (tying agreements), and horizontal combinations (price fixing, bid rigging, illegal mergers, illegal interlocking directorships, and agreements among competitors to allocate markets, jobs, customers, accounts, sales, and patents).

Clinard and Yeager ranked violations as serious, moderate, or minor. The criteria they used to rank violations included:

- Repetition of the same violation
- Knowledge that the action involved violation of law (intent)
- Extent of the violation
- Size of monetary losses to customers, competitors, or government
- Unsafe products manufactured in large amount that were reaching the consumer
- Corporation's refusal to reinstate or rehire employees
- Corporation's refusal to recall defective products
- Corporation's refusal to honor agreements
- Corporation's threatening witnesses or employees
- Length of time the violation took place

They found that large corporations were far more likely to commit violations than small corporations and that large corporations bear a widely disproportionate share of sanctions for serious and moderate violations. The oil, pharmaceutical, and motor vehicle industries had the most violations.

Causes of Organizational Crimes

The sociologist Robert K. Merton first theorized that social structures provide motivation for misconduct. Merton focuses on competition, the importance of money in society and the erosion of norms that encourage legitimate money-making behavior. He also states that the interplay between cultural structure and social structure produces deviance. Two key elements of cultural structure are the goals that are deemed worthy for all members of society and the norms that spell out how they may be legitimately achieved. When the goals receive more emphasis than the norms, Merton states, the norms will lose their power to regulate behavior. This produces a state of "anomie," or normlessness—an important concept in sociology that is said to lead to lawlessness.

Merton also defines competitive economic activity—the production, exchange, distribution, and consumption of goods, with wealth assuming a "highly symbolic cast"—as "culturally-legitimated success-goals." This definition might not apply to many individuals with differing values, but fits closely to the behavior of most profit-seeking organizations. For a business, economic success means not only cultural approval, but survival. Regardless of the cultural emphasis on profits, an organization must seek profits, and profits will be a prime indicator of prestige within a society, as well as the key to social mobility within hierarchies of organizations. In short, money talks in the business world.

Economists don't necessarily buy into the notion that profit maximization is the prime goal for businesses. The uncertainties of life deprive managers of the information needed to form the expectations that are needed to make profits. Organizational complexities, including the division of labor, hierarchies, and imperfect information flow, limit the ability of large organizations to enforce management decisions aimed at profits. And managerial goals often tend in a direction other than profit, as when a company seeks growth, stability, a larger market share, or better perquisites for its own employees. These goals oriented away from money-making may result in companies that are pleased to settle for minimal profit levels so they can accomplish other important goals as well.

Merton states that to obtain financial success, individuals must compete, both for the means toward the goal and the goal itself. The availability of both the tools to compete and the profits themselves is limited by insufficient supply and demand. When these limits threaten a competitor with losses, innovation may result in the endless quest for strategic resources.

Diane Vaughan notes that organizations engage in intense competition for such resources as personnel, product development, land acquisition, advertising space, and sales territories. The ability to obtain these tools may be limited by scarcity, by the behavior of competing organizations, by consumer behavior, and by the ability of a business to take on new responsibilities. Thus, a company can fail to meet its goal either by failing to obtain the means for success or by entering the competition and not obtaining adequate resources, such as customers or government contracts. When the scarcity of strategic resources threatens a loss, unlawful conduct may follow.

Whether a company will cheat does not depend solely on competition for resources. Economic success is relative. One company may be pleased with a much smaller profit than its older competitor. Another company may be pleased by continuing improvement with respect to its competitors, while an industry giant may remain happy simply by maintaining market share. In other words, a company's goals may change over time and the only woe to be universally avoided is losing ground. Scarcity and the differing goals of different companies means access to needed resources can be blocked regardless of an organization's size, wealth, age, experience, or previous record.

Another variable in whether a company meets it goals is the response to success. If a company achieves a desired profit, it will often establish a new, higher standard, making financial success an infinitely moving target. This stokes pressures for success within even the most successful companies, creating new possibilities that blocked resources will lead to misconduct.

When illegal conduct succeeds in an organization, it tends to reinforce the bad behavior. While society frowns on the wrongdoing, the organization may come to think of the behavior as normal. The success then breeds further wrongdoing among individuals who are swayed into departing from rules they once regarded as legitimate. Without outside social controls—law enforcement, for example—a corrupt organization can affect the entire societal structure.

Complicating matters is the ability of organizations to lobby, sometimes after the fact, for legal norms that allow behaviors that society might not otherwise endorse. Statutes, rules, and regulations do not necessarily draw on bedrock values; they might even represent no one's core values in some cases. Instead, laws often represent compromises between legislators or regulators and those they regulate.

The ability of companies to get formerly unlawful behavior legitimized buttresses the ability and desire of other companies to embark on similar paths to success. At its worst, this produces a new norm that encourages illegitimate behavior that efficiently produces success. Such behavior might occur in some extreme cases even when legitimate means of obtaining success are available. It might even be deemed acceptable business practice within an organization.

The erosion of normative support for legitimate procedures, Vaughan writes, can produce such anticompetitive activities as price fixing, discriminatory price cutting, theft of trade secrets, false advertising, and bribery. These examples of misconduct can be viewed sociologically as the victimization of one organization by another to obtain resources that provide for upward mobility in the organizational pecking order.

Opportunities for Unlawful Organizational Behavior

Social structures alone do not explain an organization's use of illegal methods to go after scarce resources. Another necessary ingredient in the mix is opportunity. The opportunity to act unlawfully is present in some degree in all complex businesses because of their very presence in a legitimate economic order in which many transactions occur. The legitimate processes of business—for example, computer trades conducted in milli-seconds and in huge quantities—might provide the opportunity for wrongdoing and a minimal risk of detection. Knowing this, organizations might respond to the denial of resources by looking within their own boundaries for unlawful ways of obtaining them.

Much information on businesses, including product information, financial performance, and market size, is publicly available, but other organizational characteristics that set the stage for illegal behavior can be shrouded in secrecy. These include internal processes and structures that are not necessarily related to size or market clout. Vaughan hypo-thesizes that it is more than mere size that creates the opportunity for organizational misbehavior; the complexity of internal processes and structures of a business, regardless of its size, are what often set the stage.

Organizational Structure

Complex companies provide a structure that can foster misbehavior. They provide many settings where misconduct is possible. They isolate those settings in departments and in locations around a city, the country, or the world. The isolation, in turn, means that information about what one part of a company is doing may be unknown in another part. All this reduces the risk that misbehavior will be detected and punished. The larger a company grows, the more specialized its subunits tend to become. An internally diversified company may have few employees who fully understand the detailed workings.

Specialized departments in a large firm compete for resources not only with other firms, but with departments in their own firm. The need to outperform not only other businesses but other units within their own business can generate sufficient pressure to lead to misconduct. Vaughan notes that departments often have survival concerns that conflict with the larger interests of an organization. When given a chance to make decisions, she writes, lower-level managers will tend to act not in the interest of the firm, but in the interests of their departments.

Specialization also hides illegal activities, especially where a firm's tasks are kept separate and unrelated. Employees cannot garner knowledge about all the particulars of how a firm works. This protects a company from the effects of personnel turnover and leaks of information, because no one can offer much more than a piece of the jigsaw puzzle that paints the overall company picture. The same secrecy, however, raises the chances for misconduct.

Companies spell out rules in a common language to decide how tasks will be performed and to create common bonds that will facilitate decision-making. But a company's ability to coordinate all its activities varies considerably. Vaughan writes that organizational growth naturally leads to a progressive loss of control over departments. Executives cannot hope to keep track of all the units in a huge company and must rely on subordinates to carry out policy. Vaughan states that when the distance between top executives and subordinate units grows to a sufficient level "authority leakage" results. Such leakage means the company has become too unwieldy for an executive to enforce rules at all levels. "The organization, in short," Vaughan writes, "can diversify beyond the capability of those at the top to master it."

Such leakage allows subsidiaries, company researchers, accountants, or other departments to engage in misconduct without any assurance that internal controls will check the behavior. In some cases, as with computer crime, detecting misconduct might be beyond the ability of most employees. Conversely, authority leakage and specialization also can lead an organization to comply with societal rules even when the organizational pressures lean toward misconduct.

Does the existence of authority imply a loss of company control? While a company that cannot steer its employees' behavior might be viewed as irrational or incompetent, the ability to control information flow from top to bottom may not be possible. Research and theory suggest, to the contrary, that information is processed selectively through a company in ways that tend to protect the interests of departments and to promote efficiency.

Sometimes censorship of information promotes a company's interests. In other cases, "need to know" policies or ignorance of rules that are irrelevant to a department leads to inefficiencies. All these tendencies restrict information flows and create opportunities for one unit in a company to act outside the knowledge of other units. Censorship policies may originate in any part of a company and hide matters throughout the organization.

The tiered structure of most organizations obscures personal responsibility and tends to spread it throughout the company. Thus, determining where a decision to engage in misconduct originated can be difficult. The author John E. Conklin put it this way: "The delegation of responsibility and unwritten orders keep those at the top of the corporate structure remote from the consequences of their decisions and orders, much as the heads of organized crime families remain 'untouchable' by law."

The Nature of Transactions

Transactions between complex organizations can add to the potential for misconduct by offering legitimate means of pursuing scarce resources unlawfully and by providing an opportunity to hide the unlawful behavior. Vaughan writes that the transactions carry four distinguishing characteristics: formalization; complex processing and recording methods; reliance on trust; and general, rather than specific, monitoring procedures.

As organizations increase in complexity, the likelihood that they will engage in informal transactions diminishes. Exchanges between companies that are formal, complex, and impersonal are likely themselves to be formal, complex, and impersonal. Because large companies engage in large volumes of daily transactions, they have adopted rules aimed at making the exchanges routine. The same formalization that seeks to control behavior within an organization is applied to its dealings with outsiders.

An offshoot of this formal behavior is the growth of technological means for recording and carrying out business transactions. Computers and accounting systems use specialized languages that, in turn, can mask huge masses of information from an ordinary employee. Specialization means the rules and procedures governing the processing and recording of exchanges will vary among companies, as will the equipment and language used.

An organization usually will use the same computer languages, accounting procedures, and other recording techniques across its various departments, but that homogeneity will rarely exist when two complex organizations transact business. That creates problems for each company that wants to monitor an exchange. Indeed, it would be highly inefficient for a company to examine in detail every transaction it makes both before and after the fact.

Thus, companies presuppose a degree of trust when doing business with outsiders. Managers may supervise employees, and somewhat limit embezzlement, fraud and other illegal conduct, but doing that to an extreme will probably hamper business as well. Vaughan argues that limits on how much an organization can monitor its employees render trust a key to interorganizational exchanges almost by default. Efficient companies usually rely not on a "Big Brother approach" to monitoring employees, but on such techniques as spot checks, sampling, and checking of selected business indicators. These general oversight techniques will not always be sufficient for a company to learn of rules violations, but if they are known throughout the company, they may provide some general deterrence.

The four characteristics of transactions present separate opportunities for misbehavior, and become more potent factors when combined. A complex accounting system raises the potential for "creative accounting" and consequent fraud. Juggling of books has been made easier by the advent of computers and another layer of specialized knowledge needed to carry accounting systems on them. Computers have become pervasive in complex organizations, dominating daily operations. Their increased speed and efficiency also makes it possible to gain resources unlawfully with greater speed and efficiency.

The computer age has meant that a thief can steal resources without breaking and entering. Records, secret information, and money become available with the touch of the right buttons. Information, a prime asset, can be moved from one location to another. Huge amounts can be stolen in the blink of an eye, or with extraordinary gradualness and stealth over a long period. The offender need not be present to act, and programming can cause the occurrence and discovery of fraud and theft to occur in the future, leaving a temporal gap between the execution of a crime and its actual occurrence. Besides the susceptibility of technological recording procedures to misbehavior, trust and spot monitoring add to the likelihood that an exchange will involve unlawful behavior. In the risk-reward assessment by a potential offender, all the factors combine to make detection seem unlikely.

When formalization, recording procedures, trust, and general monitoring conspire to generate repeated violations within a company, the transaction system can be said to be at fault. The system might directly encourage misconduct by providing an easy shot at resources with little risk of detection. Michael Spence, in his book *Market Signaling* (Harvard University Press, 1974), illustrates this phenomenon.

Market Signaling

Spence's theory holds that the nature of transactions prevents an organization from discriminating in its decision making. Information is incomplete in the corporate world, and because the numbers of transactions are huge, it is impossible for a company to know the details of each individual purchase, agreement, order, contract or other transaction. The result: companies employ "signals" and "indexes" in making decisions on transactions involving uncertainties.

Spence cites the hiring of employees as an example. An employer must choose from among a pool of applicants when looking to fill a position. But the employer cannot gather complete information on each applicant. In assessing the potential competence of an employee, the employer might be able to obtain all relevant information, but in most cases such a search would cost more than it is worth to the employer. The organization, therefore, relies on readily observable characteristics in the applicant pool, some of which can be manipulated by the applicant and some of which cannot.

Signals are the observable, alterable characteristics, such as years of education, grades in school, or job skills. Sociologically speaking, these are achievements that an applicant has the ability to control and alter. *Indexes*, however, are observable, unalterable characteristics. These include race, ethnic group, and age. Applicants can make adjustments to make themselves desirable to potential employers in what is known as signaling. Fraud can result, if the signals are falsified, and an organization's monitoring procedures can allow the fraud to pass unnoticed.

Spence's model also applies to organizations. The key elements are a transaction between organizations; a decision maker and a pool of applicants; product uncertainty; and high observation costs that spur reliance on signals and indexes. One illustration of this model is the Medicaid system. Medicaid services are the product of a transaction among federal, state, or local governments and providers such as pharmacies, hospitals, nursing homes, and clinics. The providers submit applications to become qualified to participate. Some providers might manipulate the system improperly. And the ability to monitor the program is limited, spurring reliance on signals and indexes.

When legitimate access to resources such as Medicaid benefits appear to be uncertain, a business may falsify its signals to obtain what it wants. These market signaling situations can include such examples as defense contracts, merger negotiations, or processes for obtaining government approval of drugs. False signaling can occur on a regular basis in some organizations. A look at how much in resources an organization allocates to detection of the false signaling indicates the degree to which the organization believes that problem is chronic. Where such a focal organization, like Medicaid, becomes a repeated victim of fraud, factors associated with transactions are said, in sociological parlance, to create a "criminogenic transaction system," in which violations are produced regularly in the course of organizational exchanges.

The System Interface Problem

A system interface problem occurs when the language, rules, procedures, and recording systems of two organizations diverge to the point where the differences inhibit, rather than promote, a transaction. Exchange of resources stall in this situation, and deals become difficult to complete. One or both organizations may have to make adjustments and negotiations may founder. The problem can be short-lived or long-lived, depending on the nature of the relationship between the organizations. If one of the organizations is unwilling or unable to resolve the problem through legitimate means, the transaction system itself may become the avenue for illegal activity. In that case, the complicated nature of the transaction encourages the lawlessness, with perpetrators figuring, with some justification, that chances of detection are small.

Norms can be redefined during these failed exchanges as well, a phenomenon that has been noted in studies of organizations that are victimized by massive civil disturbances. As in the L.A. riots, some businesses were selectively looted by ghetto residents, while others in the same neighborhood were spared. The objective characteristics of businesses could not explain precisely the pattern of widespread looting. The most important factors appear not to be whether an attacked organization had any objectionable characteristics. Instead, the key consideration appears to be how organizations, especially classes of organizations, were perceived and defined by looters. Certain types of businesses—for example, a Korean-owned grocery store in an African-American neighborhood—came to symbolize economic exploitation, regardless of whether such exploitation existed. The studies suggest that the looters believed they could exploit an organization's resources because the organization itself was exploitative.

Vaughan suggests the interplay between such collective defining of perceived exploi-tation and redefinition of property rights provides insight into use of misconduct to resolve a system interface problem. System interface problems occur at least occasionally for all organizations which devote varying efforts to complete stalled transactions. But for some organizations, system interface problems may be the rule, raising a higher likelihood of fraud. In such cases, the transaction system is criminogenic.

The immensity, diffusion of responsibility, and the hierarchical structure of large corporations foster conditions conducive to organizational deviance. The large size of corporations, delegation of most responsibilities, and the degree of specialization of jobs allow for a degree of irresponsibility that might allow individuals in the corporation to remain largely unaccountable, often legally as well as morally. According to Conklin, executives at the higher levels of the corporation can absolve themselves of responsibility for crimes in stating that the illegal means used by their employees was done without the executives' knowledge, much the same way heads of organized crime families remain "untouchable" by the law by keeping themselves remote from the illegal activity.

Criminogenic Organizational Structures

Sociologist Edward Gross has asserted that all organizations are inherently criminogenic (that is, prone to committing crime), though not necessarily criminal.[7] Gross makes this assertion because of the reliance on "the bottom line." Without necessarily meaning to, organizations can invite fraud as a means of obtaining goals. Criminologist Oliver Williamson noted that because of a department's concern with reaching its goals, managers might well tend to maximize their department's own interests to the detriment of the organization.

Organizations also can be criminogenic because they encourage loyalty. According to Diane Vaughan, the reasons are that:

- The organization tends to recruit and attract similar individuals
- Rewards are given out to those who display characteristics of the "company man"
- Long-term loyalty is encouraged through company retirement and benefits
- Loyalty is encouraged through social interaction such as company parties and social functions
- Frequent transfers and long working hours encourage isolation from other groups
- Specialized job skills can discourage personnel from seeking employment elsewhere[8]

This in turn causes company personnel to sometimes perceive that the organization might be worth committing crime to maintain and further its goals. The use of formal and informal rewards and punishments, plus social activities and pressures to participate, link an employee's needs and goals to the success of the company. Society places value on the reputation of the company for which one works, reinforcing the link between an individual and corporate goals. When a company achieves its goals, its employees prosper. In short, the interests of an organization and its employees coincide, and that situation may set the stage for unlawful conduct by individuals on the organization's behalf.

---

[7]Edward Gross, "Organizational Structure and Organizational Crime." In Gilbert Geis and Ezra Stotland (Eds.), White-collar Crime: Theory and Research. Beverly Hills: Sage, 1980, pp. 53-76.
[8]Diane Vaughan, "Transaction Systems and Unlawful Organizational Behavior." Social Problems, 29:373-380.

Vaughan writes that organizational processes create "an internal moral and intellectual world" that causes individuals to identify with organizational goals. Company survival comes to mean individual survival, and when resources become scarce, the incentive to misbehave increases. Of course, not all agents will act unlawfully on a company's behalf, and how any employee behaves will be linked to factors that might not be related to the world of the organization.

When the structural pressure to commit fraud exists, a firm often cannot unite its agents in such activities. At least three factors prevent such unity. First, the pressure to commit fraud might not affect departments in a company equally. A sales department that must meet certain goals to generate profits will feel different competitive pressure than a product development department in the same company that is running smoothly. Some parts of companies might never experience pressure to cheat, and members of those departments will have no motivation to engage in misconduct on a firm's behalf.

Second, even in high-pressure departments, some employees will not have knowledge of the difficulty of obtaining needed resources. An employee will have no motivation to commit fraud unless he has full information about an organization's goals and how the department can achieve them. In other words, an employee usually needs a high degree of responsibility for a company's success, as well as the ability to bring about those goals, before a chance to engage in misbehavior can occur.

Third, outside societal behavior can produce values that conflict with those learned in an organizational environment. For example, fraternal or professional associations impart their own values to employees that may not coincide with a specific corporate code of honor. When faced with conflicting norms, Vaughan writes, employees will make their choices based on the rewards and punishments they perceive to accompany the alternatives. Where misbehavior is seen as too costly, it will not occur. Where an organization provides sufficient rewards to overcome the fear of punishment, misbehavior may occur despite competing norms. The amount of information an employee has will affect the decision on which way to go, as will an individual's financial and social dependence on the firm.

The mere fact that corporate and individual goals are often joined in organizations does not necessarily create a climate for illegal actions. As with any major decision, complexities often enter the picture. Temptations vary not only among departments, but within them. The availability of information and individual risk-reward assessments may generate lawful behavior that resists organizational pressures to violate the law, as well as unlawful behavior in the face of organizational pressures to comply. Put plainly, the likelihood that organizational processes will generate misbehavior is highly variable and cannot currently be measured with any degree of precision.

In explaining how employees are taught to make decisions that are correct from a corporation's standpoint, Drucker said a natural tendency exists in every large-scale organization to discourage initiative and encourage conformity. Madden and Margolis say corporations lead new managers through an initiation period designed to weaken their ties with external groups, including their own families, and encourage a feeling of dependence on and attachment to the corporation.

Geis found that quite often, individuals are trained in illegal behavior as part of the occupational role. Schrager and Short say criminal behavior stems more from the roles an employee is expected to fulfill than from individual pathology. Many executives know their behavior is illegal but tend to justify their behavior as simply common practice in the business world. Clinard and Yeager believed that in rationalizing their behavior, corporations follow a general tendency to obey laws selectively, i.e., obeying according to situational needs and determined by factors like social class and occupation.

Sutherland demonstrated that corporate executives are insulated from those who might disagree with their beliefs because they associate almost exclusively with people who are probusiness, politically conservative, and generally opposed to government regulation.

Silk and Vogel found that certain beliefs exist in the business world about government intervention in business and defend the corporation's acts to violate, such as "all legal measures proposed constitute government interference with the free enterprise system."

A problem common to many large corporations with intricate hierarchical structures tends to be a split between what the upper levels believe is going on below and the actual procedures being carried out. Clinard and Yeager say that the chief executive officer of a corporation often is isolated and messages transmitted down the line tend to become distorted. Clinard and Yeager found that all levels of the corporation might often agree to perpetuate the lack of full information, for the key to any successful conspiracy to violate the law probably lies in the fact that the higher-ups do not inquire about what is going on and the lower levels do not tell them.

Often in corporations, no single individual at the highest levels may make a decision alone to market a faulty product or take shortcuts on product testing, Clinard and Yeager say. Instead, decisions are made in small steps at each level possibly without any awareness of the illegal and potentially dangerous result.

McCaghy says profit pressure is "the single most compelling factor behind deviance by industry, whether it be price fixing, the destruction of competition or the misrepresentation of a product," such as making a shoddy product that will wear out and need to be replaced. Clinard and Yeager say certain industries, such as the drug and chemical businesses, have such severe competition and strong profit drives due to demands for continual development of new products that they may feel pressured to falsify test data, market new products before their full effects are known, or engage in unethical sales techniques that can have disastrous effects on human beings and the environment.

Corporate Executives and Criminal Liability

Many of the ethical and legal problems of a corporation result from the corporate structure that separates ownership from management. Typical large corporations are administered by a group of salaried managers where the board of directors exercise little direct power other than hiring or firing the managers, and so corporate managers have great autonomy over decisions regarding production, investment, pricing, and marketing.

Luthans and Hodgetts said that after performing a study with the American Management Society, 3,000 executives questioned "felt under pressure to compromise personal standards to meet company goals," but that they felt "that business ethics should still be a concern."

Executives tend to believe that their jobs are at risk if they cannot show a profit to higher management or the board of directors, and often they are. Clinard and Yeager hold that goals for managers are set too high, the employee then confronts a hard choice of risking being thought incompetent or taking unethical or even illegal shortcuts.

According to Clinard and Yeager, corporations often try to protect their executives from liability by agreeing to pay fines, court costs, and attorney's fees with corporate funds; bonuses or raises or liability insurance might offer protection to officers or directors. Generally, executive compensation and tenure remain untouched. There is much difficulty in criminal prosecution of executives because corporate violations are usually far more complex than conventional crimes. Also, the complexity of the legal proof required allows businessmen to test the limits of the law.

Businessmen might have sought legal advice on loopholes in the law before committing the offense, Clinard and Yeager say, which may be cited as evidence that the executives thought they were in legal compliance. Businessmen can hire highly skilled lawyers who present arguments as to the client's lack of previous convictions or unlikelihood of becoming a repeat offender as well as being able to cite numerous precedents where businessmen were charged but not imprisoned for similar violations.

Corporate offenders usually are not imprisoned with ordinary criminals, but usually are incarcerated in institutions designed for low-risk inmates with short sentences, presumably for the corporate offender's own physical safety. Justifications used in arguing against a prison sentence for corporate offenders include:

- Age and poor health
- Personal and family reasons
- Extent of punishment already suffered by virtue of being indicted
- Offense was not immoral
- Defendant has no prior record, is not a threat to society, and has been a prominent citizen active in community affairs
- Incarceration would accomplish nothing (no benefit to society)
- Defendant is repentant
- Victimization of corporate executives solely because of their position

Some corporate offenders are given community service as punishment, such as giving speeches about their offenses to businesses and civic groups, working in programs designed to aid the poor, or helping former ordinary criminal offenders secure job pledges from businesses.

Prior to 2001, corporate offenders generally received little, if any, public attention. Coverage of corporate scandals was often limited to business and trade publications. However, all of that changed with the Enron scandal. Suddenly, corporate offenders were front-page news, and prosecutors have increased their efforts in pursing corporate executives for wrongdoing in the corporate organization.

Corporate Fraud Task Force

In response to the high-profile corporate frauds of Enron, WorldCom, Global Crossing, and others, President George W. Bush created the Corporate Fraud Task Force in July 2002. The purpose of the task force is to provide direction and recommendations to the Department of Justice (DOJ) and other government agencies regarding the investigation and prosecution of corporate fraud.

One of the results of the task force was to revise the Department of Justice's guidelines for prosecuting business organizations. The main focus of the revisions was to increase the emphasis on and the scrutiny of the authenticity of a corporation's cooperation during an investigation. According to the DOJ, business organizations were often purporting to cooperate with the Justice Department, when in fact the corporation had taken steps to impede the quick and effective exposure of the complete scope of wrongdoing under investigation. The revisions made clear that such conduct should weigh in favor of corporate prosecution. The revisions also addressed the efficacy of the corporate governance mechanisms in place within a corporation to ensure that such mechanisms are truly effective, rather than mere paper programs.

The guidelines also emphasize the factors prosecutors should consider in making decisions regarding charging corporations with criminal conduct. These factors are:
1. The nature and seriousness of the offense, including the risk of harm to the public, and applicable policies and priorities, if any, governing the prosecution of corporations for particular categories of crime;
2. The pervasiveness of wrongdoing within the corporation, including the complicity in, or condonation of, the wrongdoing by corporate management;
3. The corporation's history of similar con-duct, including prior criminal, civil, and regulatory enforcement actions against it;
4. The corporation's timely and voluntary disclosure of wrongdoing and its willingness to cooperate in the investigation of its agents, including, if necessary, the waiver of corporate attorney-client and work product protection;
5. The existence and adequacy of the corporation's compliance program;
6. The corporation's remedial actions, including any efforts to implement an effective corporate compliance program or to improve an existing one, to replace responsible management, to discipline or terminate wrongdoers, to pay restitution, and to cooperate with the relevant government agencies;

7. Collateral consequences, including disproportionate harm to shareholders, pension holders and employees not proven personally culpable and impact on the public arising from the prosecution;
8. The adequacy of the prosecution of individuals responsible for the corporation's malfeasance;
9. The adequacy of remedies such as civil or regulatory enforcement actions.

The guidelines do not have the force of law and are advisory only, but they do set forth the DOJ's general framework of how prosecutors should analyze corporate criminal cases. A copy of the DOJ's revised principles is included at the end of this chapter.

Management Behavior

Brenner and Molander found that superiors are the primary influence in unethical decision making. Therefore, the use of sanctions to accomplish compliance with the law is but one of the various forces operating within a corporation encouraging or opposing violations of law. Stone found that the success of law enforcement "ultimately depends upon its consistency with and reinforcement of the organization's rules for advancement and reward, its customs, conventions and morals." He maintains that if the law is too much at odds with the corporation's "culture," employees will tend to cover up their tracks rather than to change their behavior.[9]

Corporations also argue "regulation is faulty because most government regulations are incomprehensible and too complex." Conklin found that antitrust laws are seen as inconsistent, hypocritical, poorly defined, and rarely enforced. Therefore, most regulations must be written in detail to cover as many contingencies as possible.

Silk and Vogel found several other actions used by business to rationalize conduct:
- Government regulations are unjustified because the additional costs of regulations and bureaucratic procedures cut heavy into profits
- Regulation is unnecessary because the matters being regulated are unimportant
- Although some corporate violations involve millions of dollars, the damage is so diffused among a large number of consumers that individually there is little loss

---

[9] Christopher Stone, Where the Law Ends: The Social Control of Corporate Behavior. New York: Harper & Row, 1975.

- Violations are caused by economic necessity; they aim to protect the value of stock, to ensure an adequate return for stockholders and to protect the job security of employees by ensuring the financial stability of the corporation

John Braithwaite is a researcher in white-collar crime at Australian National University in Canberra. He is also the recipient of the 1990 Cressey Award by the Association of Certified Fraud Examiners for his research in international white-collar crime issues. Braithwaite views white-collar crime as a product of the corporate subculture. In Braithwaite's view, corporations will turn to crime as a result of "blocked opportunities."

Because white-collar crime can exist only in secrecy, deviant subcultures develop (conspiracy among executives, for example), lines of communication are not allowed to develop, and people operate within spheres of responsibility.

Controlling Organizational Crime

Clinard and Yeager believe corporations that do violate and those that do not are distinguished by "corporate cultures" or ethical climates, which is the degree to which a corporation has made the choice to be unethical or not, to disregard the interests of the consumer and the public, and to disobey the laws that regulate its specific industry.

Efforts to control corporate crime follow three approaches: voluntary change in corporate attitudes and structure; strong intervention of the political state to force changes in corporate structure, accompanied by legal measures to deter or punish; or consumer action. Voluntary changes would involve the development of stronger business ethics and certain corporate organizational reforms; government controls might involve federal corporate chartering, deconcentration and divesture, larger and more effective enforce-ment staffs, stiffer penalties, wider use of publicity as a sanction, and possibly the nationalization of corporations; and consumer group pressures may be exerted through lobbying, selective buying, boycotts and the establishment of large consumer cooperatives.

Clinard and Yeager suggest that a wide, comprehensive industrial code of ethics, which many businessmen favor, would be of great help when a businessman wished to refuse an unethical request, would help define more clearly the limits of acceptable or ethical conduct, would improve the ethical climate of the industry, and would serve to reduce cutthroat practices where competition is intense. Greater stockholder involvement might enable greater corporate compliance with the law, but in actuality, it is the management staff that runs the company and makes the decisions and the stockholders are primarily concerned with stock growth and dividends.

In some cases, critical information dealing with possible law violations simply fails to reach the board of directors. New board members usually are nominated by the board and routinely approved by stockholders, making boards self-perpetuating. Board members are often drawn from management. Many corporations now employ outside directors and/or representatives of the public interest, much like the practice abroad of naming union representatives to boards. These public members represent the public and consumer concerns, ascertain whether the corporation is complying with the law, assist and maintain corporate public responsibility, help monitor the internal management system to discover faulty workmanship and report it to the board, serve as liaisons with government agencies with respect to legislation or standards, and serve as a hotline to receive information about deviance.

Clinard and Yeager found that mass media publicity about law violations probably represents the most feared consequence of sanctions imposed on a corporation. Publicity also can inform the public about the operation of regulatory controls and enable people to understand the purposes of the controls. Informal publicity ordinarily is carried as news items from the media while formal publicity is a requirement that a corporation must, as part of an enforcement action, publish an advertisement or some other statement acknow-ledging a violation and that corrective measures are being taken.

If illegal behavior consistently resulted in decreased patronage or even consumer boycotts, consumer pressure would be an effective tool in the control of illegal corporate behavior. However, say Clinard and Yeager, it appears not to be very effective. Consumers are often unaware when a corporation's products are unsafe or when it has been violating antitrust laws or polluting the environment. Without organized behavior, a consumer's withdrawal of individual patronage generally is ineffective.

Many corporations settle charges, without admitting or denying guilt, by consenting either to an administrative or a court-ordered decree banning future violations. In a consent agreement, the corporation reaches an understanding with the government agency not to violate the regulation again. In a decree, the agreement is ratified by the court.

Sporkin says consent decrees have enabled the appointment of special officers to investigate and pursue claims against erring managements and others on behalf of the corporation and its shareholders, the placement of people independent of management and not previously associated with the company on the board of directors, and the appointment of special review or audit committees. A problem with consent orders, however, is that they frequently are not followed up to find out whether the terms imposed are being met.

Violations of a consent order can be followed by an injunction, as can distribution of adulterated, contaminated, or mislabled products. Corporate violations of Securities and Exchange Act provisions can result in injunctions, as well as discriminatory labor practices, illegal economic actions, environmental pollution, and illegal political contributions.

Criminal fines and civil and administrative penalties against corporations are forms of monetary penalties. For completion, criminal cases average about one year from indictment to conviction, civil actions about two years, and administrative cases about four months. Criminal action against corporations is difficult to initiate because generally government agencies are dependent upon the records of the corporation and its ability or willingness to furnish needed information.

Not all experts agree that monetary penalties are appropriate. For example, a $25 million fine to a pauper would have no effect. One novel approach to punishing corporations was proposed by Coffee (1978). He advocates stock dilution or "equity fining." Under this approach, the convicted corporation would issue additional shares of stock to the state equal to the cash value of a fine. The state could collect the equity shares and sell them, trade them, or keep them for their earnings power. With respect to monetary penalties, some argue that these sanctions are limited to a person's own worth and therefore have limited utility. In 1992, Congress implemented the corporate sentencing guidelines, providing up to $290 million in fines for illegal corporate behavior. It is too early to determine the deterrent impact.

Some of the criteria considered when deciding to bring criminal action against a corporation are the degree of loss to the public, the duration of the violation, the level of complicity by high corporate managers, the frequency of the violation, evidence of intent to violate, evidence of extortion, the degree of notoriety endangered by the media, precedent in law, a history of serious violations by the corporation, deterrence potential, and the degree of cooperation demonstrated by the corporation.

Rules governing industry often have been initiated by parts of the industry itself. Kolko says a major achievement for corporations may have been the establishment of the Federal Trade Commission, which ruled out "unfair methods of competition" and served to stabilize the competitive game by making the biggest abuses of competition illegal.

Stone says as they age, almost all agencies show evidence of protecting the industries they are supposed to regulate rather than the public. Industries also gain influence over agencies by creating a business-oriented atmosphere between regulators and regulatees that may cause the regulators to feel unwarranted confidence in the possibility of voluntary compliance by corporations.

The Enforcement Effort: Preventing and Reducing Fraud

While the issues involved in the enforcement effort provide a context in which to assess the efforts to control white-collar crime, actual techniques of prevention need to be discussed. There are many theories about enforcement, sanctions, and punishments that are a part of controlling white-collar crime.

Compliance

Enforcement strategies include two main theories: compliance and deterrence. *Compliance* hopes to achieve conformity to the law without having to detect, process, or penalize violators. Compliance systems provide economic incentives for voluntary compliance to the laws and use administrative efforts to control violations before they occur. For example, the SEC has a host of administrative mechanisms to encourage voluntary compliance with its rules. The IRS also uses such measures in addition to criminal penalties. Most environmental crimes also are controlled by these means. In a compliance system, an offense is called a "technical violation."

Compliance strategies have been criticized by some criminologists. These experts believe that compliance has little effect, as sanctions are imposed after the infraction occurs. Since economic penalties are common punishments for violators, these penalties amount to little more than the proverbial "slap on the wrist" in the case of large, wealthy corporations.

Deterrence

As a strategy to control crime, *deterrence* is designed to detect law violations, determine who is responsible, and penalize offenders in order to deter future violations. Deterrence systems try to control the immediate behavior of individuals, not the long-term behaviors targeted by compliance systems.

Deterrence theory assumes that humans are rational in their behavior patterns. Humans seek profit and pleasure while they try to avoid pain. Deterrence assumes that an individual's propensity toward lawbreaking is in inverse proportion to the perceived probability of negative consequences.

Increased Enforcement
Formal levels of current enforcement in white-collar crime are, by all measures, extremely low. One view holds that increased enforcement can only come with a complete and total revision of the criminal justice system. Currently, people have little fear of detection because they know that the police and courts cannot keep up with the pace of criminal offenses. It is not necessary or even desirable to advocate longer prison sentences for offenders because we do not have the courts and jails to accommodate them. Perhaps a better plan would be to sacrifice the severity of punishment for certainty. Until potential offenders have the perception that they will be caught and punished, we cannot expect a reversal of the crime trend.

Fraud Prevention Programs
Although the government can provide incentives for organizations to prevent fraud, ultimately, it is up to management to institute prevention programs. The chapter on "Fraud Prevention Programs" describes methods whereby management can institute policies and procedures to help detect and prevent fraud.

U.S. Department of Justice

Office of the Deputy Attorney General

The Deputy Attorney General

Washington, D.C. 20530

January 20, 2003

MEMORANDUM

TO: Heads of Department Components
United States Attorneys

FROM: Larry D. Thompson
Deputy Attorney General

SUBJECT: Principles of Federal Prosecution of Business Organizations

As the Corporate Fraud Task Force has advanced in its mission, we have confronted certain issues in the principles for the federal prosecution of business organizations that require revision in order to enhance our efforts against corporate fraud. While it will be a minority of cases in which a corporation or partnership is itself subjected to criminal charges, prosecutors and investigators in every matter involving business crimes must assess the merits of seeking the conviction of the business entity itself.

Attached to this memorandum are a revised set of principles to guide Department prosecutors as they make the decision whether to seek charges against a business organization. These revisions draw heavily on the combined efforts of the Corporate Fraud Task Force and the Attorney General's Advisory Committee to put the results of more than three years of experience with the principles into practice.

The main focus of the revisions is increased emphasis on and scrutiny of the authenticity of a corporation's cooperation. Too often business organizations, while purporting to cooperate with a Department investigation, in fact take steps to impede the quick and effective exposure of the complete scope of wrongdoing under investigation. The revisions make clear that such conduct should weigh in favor of a corporate prosecution. The revisions also address the efficacy of the corporate governance mechanisms in place within a corporation, to ensure that these measures are truly effective rather than mere paper programs.

Further experience with these principles may lead to additional adjustments. I look forward to hearing comments about their operation in practice. Please forward any comments to Christopher Wray, the Principal Associate Deputy Attorney General, or to Andrew Hruska, my Senior Counsel.

Federal Prosecution of Business Organizations[1]

I. Charging a Corporation: General

A. General Principle: Corporations should not be treated leniently because of their artificial nature nor should they be subject to harsher treatment. Vigorous enforcement of the criminal laws against corporate wrongdoers, where appropriate results in great benefits for law enforcement and the public, particularly in the area of white collar crime. Indicting corporations for wrongdoing enables the government to address and be a force for positive change of corporate culture, alter corporate behavior, and prevent, discover, and punish white collar crime.

B. Comment: In all cases involving corporate wrongdoing, prosecutors should consider the factors discussed herein. First and foremost, prosecutors should be aware of the important public benefits that may flow from indicting a corporation in appropriate cases. For instance, corporations are likely to take immediate remedial steps when one is indicted for criminal conduct that is pervasive throughout a particular industry, and thus an indictment often provides a unique opportunity for deterrence on a massive scale. In addition, a corporate indictment may result in specific deterrence by changing the culture of the indicted corporation and the behavior of its employees. Finally, certain crimes that carry with them a substantial risk of great public harm, e.g., environmental crimes or financial frauds, are by their nature most likely to be committed by businesses, and there may, therefore, be a substantial federal interest in indicting the corporation.

Charging a corporation, however, does not mean that individual directors, officers, employees, or shareholders should not also be charged. Prosecution of a corporation is not a substitute for the prosecution of criminally culpable individuals within or without the corporation. Because a corporation can act only through individuals, imposition of individual criminal liability may provide the strongest deterrent against future corporate wrongdoing. Only rarely should provable individual culpability not be pursued, even in the face of offers of corporate guilty pleas.

Corporations are "legal persons," capable of suing and being sued, and capable of committing crimes. Under the doctrine of *respondeat superior*, a corporation may be held criminally liable for the illegal acts of its directors, officers, employees, and agents. To hold a corporation liable for these actions, the government must establish that the corporate agent's actions (i) were within the scope of his duties and (ii) were intended, at least in part, to benefit the corporation. In all cases involving wrongdoing by corporate agents, prosecutors should consider the corporation, as well as the responsible individuals, as potential criminal targets.

Agents, however, may act for mixed reasons -- both for self-aggrandizement (both direct and indirect) and for the benefit of the corporation, and a corporation may be held liable as long as one motivation of its agent is to benefit the corporation. In *United States v. Automated Medical Laboratories*, 770 F.2d 399 (4th Cir. 1985), the court affirmed the corporation's conviction for the actions of a subsidiary's employee despite its claim that the employee was acting for his own benefit, namely his "ambitious nature and his desire to ascend the corporate ladder." The court stated, "*Partucci* was clearly acting in part to benefit AML since his advancement within the corporation depended on AML's well-being and its lack of difficulties with the FDA." Similarly, in *United States v. Cincotta*, 689 F.2d 238, 241-42 (1st Cir. 1982), the court held, "criminal liability may be imposed on the corporation only where the agent is acting within the scope of his employment. That, in turn, requires that the agent be performing acts of the kind which he is authorized to perform, and those acts must be motivated -- at least in part -- by an intent to benefit the corporation." Applying this test, the court upheld the corporation's conviction, notwithstanding the substantial personal benefit reaped by its miscreant agents, because the fraudulent scheme required money to pass through the corporation's treasury and the fraudulently obtained goods were resold to the corporation's customers in the corporation's name. As the court concluded, "Mystic--not the individual defendants--was making money by selling oil that it had not paid for."

Moreover, the corporation need not even necessarily profit from its agent's actions for it to be held liable. In *Automated Medical Laboratories*, the Fourth Circuit stated:

[B]enefit is not a "touchstone of criminal corporate liability; benefit at best is an evidential, not an operative, fact." Thus, whether the agent's actions ultimately redounded to the benefit of the corporation is less significant than whether the agent acted with the intent to benefit the corporation. The basic purpose of requiring that an agent have acted with the intent to benefit the corporation, however, is to insulate the corporation from criminal liability for actions of its agents which be inimical to the interests of the corporation or which may have been undertaken solely to advance the interests of that agent or of a party other than the corporation.

770 F.2d at 407 (emphasis added; quoting *Old Monastery Co. v. United States*, 147 F.2d 905, 908 (4th Cir.), cert. denied, 326 U.S. 734 (1945)).

II. Charging a Corporation: Factors to Be Considered

A. General Principle: Generally, prosecutors should apply the same factors in determining whether to charge a corporation as they do with respect to individuals. *See* USAM § 9-27.220, *et seq.* Thus, the prosecutor should weigh all of the factors normally considered in the sound exercise of prosecutorial judgment: the sufficiency of the evidence; the likelihood of success at trial,; the probable deterrent, rehabilitative, and other consequences of conviction; and the adequacy of noncriminal approaches. *See* id. However, due to the nature of the corporate "person," some additional factors are present. In conducting an investigation, determining whether to bring charges, and negotiating plea agreements, prosecutors should consider the following factors in reaching a decision as to the proper treatment of a corporate target:

1. the nature and seriousness of the offense, including the risk of harm to the public, and applicable policies and priorities, if any, governing the prosecution of corporations for particular categories of crime (*see* section III, *infra*);

2. the pervasiveness of wrongdoing within the corporation, including the complicity in, or condonation of, the wrongdoing by corporate management (*see* section IV, *infra*);

3. the corporation's history of similar conduct, including prior criminal, civil, and regulatory enforcement actions against it (*see* section V, *infra*);

4. the corporation's timely and voluntary disclosure of wrongdoing and its willingness to cooperate in the investigation of its agents, including, if necessary, the waiver of corporate attorney-client and work product protection (*see* section VI, *infra*);

5. the existence and adequacy of the corporation's compliance program (*see* section VII, *infra*);

6. the corporation's remedial actions, including any efforts to implement an effective corporate compliance program or to improve an existing one, to replace responsible management, to discipline or terminate wrongdoers, to pay restitution, and to cooperate with the relevant government agencies (*see* section VIII, *infra*);

7. collateral consequences, including disproportionate harm to shareholders, pension holders and employees not proven personally culpable and impact on the public arising from the prosecution (*see* section IX, *infra*); and

8. the adequacy of the prosecution of individuals responsible for the corporation's malfeasance;

9. the adequacy of remedies such as civil or regulatory enforcement actions (*see section X, infra*).

B. Comment: As with the factors relevant to charging natural persons, the foregoing factors are intended to provide guidance rather than to mandate a particular result. The factors listed in this section are intended to be illustrative of those that should be considered and not a complete or exhaustive list. Some or all of these factors may or may not apply to specific cases, and in some cases one factor may override all others. The nature and seriousness of the offense may be such as to warrant prosecution regardless of the other factors. Further, national law enforcement policies in various enforcement areas may require that more or less weight be given to certain of these factors than to others.

In making a decision to charge a corporation, the prosecutor generally has wide latitude in determining when, whom, how, and even whether to prosecute for violations of Federal criminal law. In exercising that discretion, prosecutors should consider the following general statements of principles that summarize appropriate considerations to be weighed and desirable practices to be followed in discharging their prosecutorial responsibilities. In doing so, prosecutors should ensure that the general purposes of the criminal law -- assurance of warranted punishment, deterrence of further criminal conduct, protection of the public from dangerous and fraudulent conduct, rehabilitation of offenders, and restitution for victims and affected communities -- are adequately met, taking into account the special nature of the corporate "person."

III. Charging a Corporation: Special Policy Concerns

A. General Principle: The nature and seriousness of the crime, including the risk of harm to the public from the criminal conduct, are obviously primary factors in determining whether to charge a corporation. In addition, corporate conduct, particularly that of national and multi-national corporations, necessarily intersects with federal economic, taxation, and criminal law enforcement policies. In applying these principles, prosecutors must consider the practices and policies of the appropriate Division of the Department, and must comply with those policies to the extent required.

B. Comment: In determining whether to charge a corporation, prosecutors should take into account federal law enforcement priorities as discussed above. *See* USAM § 9-27-230. In addition, however, prosecutors must be aware of the specific policy goals and incentive programs established by the respective Divisions and regulatory agencies. Thus, whereas natural persons may be given incremental degrees of credit (ranging from immunity to lesser charges to sentencing considerations) for turning themselves in, making statements against their penal interest, and cooperating in the government's investigation of their own and others' wrongdoing, the same approach may not be appropriate in all circumstances with respect to corporations. As an example, it is entirely proper in many investigations for a prosecutor to consider the corporation's pre-indictment conduct, *e.g.*, voluntary disclosure, cooperation, remediation or restitution, in determining whether to seek an indictment. However, this would not necessarily be appropriate in an antitrust investigation, in which antitrust violations, by definition, go to the heart of the corporation's business and for which the Antitrust Division has therefore established a firm policy, understood in the business community, that credit should not be given at the charging stage for a compliance program and that amnesty is available only to the first corporation to make full disclosure to the government. As another example, the Tax Division has a strong preference for prosecuting responsible individuals, rather than entities, for corporate tax offenses. Thus, in determining whether or not to charge a corporation, prosecutors should consult with the Criminal, Antitrust, Tax, and Environmental and Natural Resources Divisions, if appropriate or required.

IV. Charging a Corporation: Pervasiveness of Wrongdoing Within the Corporation

A. General Principle: A corporation can only act through natural persons, and it is therefore held responsible for the acts of such persons fairly attributable to it. Charging a corporation for even minor misconduct may be appropriate where the wrongdoing was pervasive and was undertaken by a large number of employees or by all the employees in a particular role within the corporation, *e.g.*, salesmen or procurement officers, or was condoned by upper management. On the other hand, in certain limited circumstances, it may not be appropriate to impose liability upon a corporation, particularly one with a compliance program in place, under a strict *respondeat superior* theory for the single isolated act of a rogue employee. There is, of course, a wide spectrum between these two extremes, and a prosecutor should exercise sound discretion in evaluating the pervasiveness of wrongdoing within a corporation.

B. Comment: Of these factors, the most important is the role of management. Although acts of even low-level employees may result in criminal liability, a corporation is directed by its management and management is responsible for a corporate culture in which criminal conduct is either discouraged or tacitly encouraged. As stated in commentary to the Sentencing Guidelines:

Pervasiveness [is] case specific and [will] depend on the number, and degree of responsibility, of individuals [with] substantial authority ... who participated in, condoned, or were willfully ignorant of the offense. Fewer individuals need to be involved for a finding of pervasiveness if those individuals exercised a relatively high degree of authority. Pervasiveness can occur either within an organization as a whole or within a unit of an organization.

USSG §8C2.5, comment. (n. 4).

V. Charging a Corporation: The Corporation's Past History

A. General Principle: Prosecutors may consider a corporation's history of similar conduct, including prior criminal, civil, and regulatory enforcement actions against it, in determining whether to bring criminal charges.

B. Comment: A corporation, like a natural person, is expected to learn from its mistakes. A history of similar conduct may be probative of a corporate culture that encouraged, or at least condoned, such conduct, regardless of any compliance programs. Criminal prosecution of a corporation may be particularly appropriate where the corporation previously had been subject to non-criminal guidance, warnings, or sanctions, or previous criminal charges, and yet it either had not taken adequate action to prevent future unlawful conduct or had continued to engage in the conduct in spite of the warnings or enforcement actions taken against it. In making this determination, the corporate structure itself, *e.g.*, subsidiaries or operating divisions, should be ignored, and enforcement actions taken against the corporation or any of its divisions, subsidiaries, and affiliates should be considered. *See* USSG § 8C2.5(c) & comment. (n. 6).

VI. Charging a Corporation: Cooperation and Voluntary Disclosure

A. General Principle: In determining whether to charge a corporation, that corporation's timely and voluntary disclosure of wrongdoing and its willingness to cooperate with the government's investigation may be relevant factors. In gauging the extent of the corporation's cooperation, the prosecutor may consider the corporation's willingness to identify the culprits within the corporation, including senior executives; to make witnesses available; to disclose the complete results of its internal investigation; and to waive attorney-client and work product protection.

B. Comment: In investigating wrongdoing by or within a corporation, a prosecutor is likely to encounter several obstacles resulting from the nature of the corporation itself. It will often be difficult to determine which individual took which action on behalf of the corporation. Lines of authority and responsibility may be shared among operating divisions or departments, and records and personnel may be spread throughout the United States or even among several countries. Where the criminal conduct continued over an extended period of time, the culpable or knowledgeable personnel may have been promoted, transferred, or fired, or they may have quit or retired. Accordingly, a corporation's cooperation may be critical in identifying the culprits and locating relevant evidence.

In some circumstances, therefore, granting a corporation immunity or amnesty or pretrial diversion may be considered in the course of the government's investigation. In such circumstances, prosecutors should refer to the principles governing non-prosecution agreements generally. *See* USAM § 9-27.600-650. These principles permit a non prosecution agreement in exchange for cooperation when a corporation's "timely cooperation appears to be necessary to the public interest and other means of obtaining the desired cooperation are unavailable or would not be effective." Prosecutors should note that in the case of national or multi-national corporations, multi-district or global agreements may be necessary. Such agreements may only be entered into with the approval of each affected district or the appropriate Department official. *See* USAM §9-27.641.

In addition, the Department, in conjunction with regulatory agencies and other executive branch departments, encourages corporations, as part of their compliance programs, to conduct internal investigations and to disclose their findings to the appropriate authorities. Some agencies, such as the SEC and the EPA, as well as the Department's Environmental and Natural Resources Division, have formal voluntary disclosure programs in which self-reporting, coupled with remediation and additional criteria, may qualify the corporation for amnesty or reduced sanctions.[2] Even in the absence of a formal program, prosecutors may consider a corporation's timely and voluntary disclosure in evaluating the adequacy of the corporation's compliance program and its management's commitment to the compliance program. However, prosecution and economic policies specific to the industry or statute may require prosecution notwithstanding a corporation's willingness to cooperate. For example, the Antitrust Division offers amnesty only to the first corporation to agree to cooperate. This creates a strong incentive for corporations participating in anti-competitive conduct to be the first to cooperate. In addition, amnesty, immunity, or reduced sanctions may not be appropriate where the corporation's business is permeated with fraud or other crimes.

One factor the prosecutor may weigh in assessing the adequacy of a corporation's cooperation is the completeness of its disclosure including, if necessary, a waiver of the attorney-client and work product protections, both with respect to its internal investigation and with respect to communications between specific officers, directors and employees and counsel. Such waivers permit the government to obtain statements of possible witnesses, subjects, and targets, without having to negotiate individual cooperation or immunity agreements. In addition, they are often critical in enabling the government to evaluate the completeness of a corporation's voluntary disclosure and cooperation. Prosecutors may, therefore, request a waiver in appropriate circumstances.[3] The Department does not, however, consider waiver of a corporation's attorney-client and work product protection an absolute requirement, and prosecutors should consider the willingness of a corporation to waive such protection when necessary to provide timely and complete information as one factor in evaluating the corporation's cooperation.

Another factor to be weighed by the prosecutor is whether the corporation appears to be protecting its culpable employees and agents. Thus, while cases will differ depending on the circumstances, a corporation's promise of support to culpable employees and agents, either through the advancing of attorneys fees,[4] through retaining the employees without sanction for their misconduct, or through providing information to the employees about the government's investigation pursuant to a joint defense agreement, may be considered by the prosecutor in weighing the extent and value of a corporation's cooperation. By the same token, the prosecutor should be wary of attempts to shield corporate officers and employees from liability by a willingness of the corporation to plead guilty.

Another factor to be weighed by the prosecutor is whether the corporation, while purporting to cooperate, has engaged in conduct that impedes the investigation (whether or not rising to the level of criminal obstruction). Examples of such conduct include: overly broad assertions of corporate representation of employees or former employees; inappropriate directions to employees or their counsel, such as directions not to cooperate openly and fully with the investigation including, for example, the direction to decline to be interviewed; making presentations or submissions that contain misleading assertions or omissions; incomplete or delayed production of records; and failure to promptly disclose illegal conduct known to the corporation.

Finally, a corporation's offer of cooperation does not automatically entitle it to immunity from prosecution. A corporation should not be able to escape liability merely by offering up its directors, officers, employees, or agents as in lieu of its own prosecution. Thus, a corporation's willingness to cooperate is merely one relevant factor, that needs to be considered in conjunction with the other factors, particularly those relating to the corporation's past history and the role of management in the wrongdoing.

VII. Charging a Corporation: Corporate Compliance Programs

A. General Principle: Compliance programs are established by corporate management to prevent and to detect misconduct and to ensure that corporate activities are conducted in accordance with all applicable criminal and civil laws, regulations, and rules. The Department encourages such corporate self-policing, including voluntary disclosures to the government of any problems that a corporation discovers on its own. However, the existence of a compliance program is not sufficient, in and of itself, to justify not charging a corporation for criminal conduct undertaken by its officers, directors, employees, or agents. Indeed, the commission of such crimes in the face of a compliance program may suggest that the corporate management is not adequately enforcing its program. In addition, the nature of some crimes, *e.g.*, antitrust violations, may be such that national law enforcement policies mandate prosecutions of corporations notwithstanding the existence of a compliance program.

   B. Comment: A corporate compliance program, even one specifically prohibiting the very conduct in question, does not absolve the corporation from criminal liability under the doctrine of *respondeat superior*. See *United States v. Basic Construction Co.*, 711 F.2d 570 (4th Cir. 1983) ("a corporation may be held criminally responsible for antitrust violations committed by its employees if they were acting within the scope of their authority, or apparent authority, and for the benefit of the corporation, even if... such acts were against corporate policy or express instructions."). In *United States v. Hilton Hotels Corp.*, 467 F.2d 1000 (9th Cir. 1972), *cert. denied*, 409 U.S. 1125 (1973), the Ninth Circuit affirmed antitrust liability based upon a purchasing agent for a single hotel threatening a single supplier with a boycott unless it paid dues to a local marketing association, even though the agent's actions were contrary to corporate policy and directly against express instructions from his superiors. The court reasoned that Congress, in enacting the Sherman Antitrust Act, "intended to impose liability upon business entities for the acts of those to whom they choose to delegate the conduct of their affairs, thus stimulating a maximum effort by owners and managers to assure adherence by such agents to the requirements of the Act."[5] It concluded that "general policy statements" and even direct instructions from the agent's superiors were not sufficient; "Appellant could not gain exculpation by issuing general instructions without undertaking to enforce those instructions by means commensurate with the obvious risks." See also *United States v. Beusch*, 596 F.2d 871, 878 (9th Cir. 1979) ("[A] corporation may be liable for the acts of its employees done contrary to express instructions and policies, but ... the existence of such instructions and policies may be considered in determining whether the employee in fact acted to benefit the corporation."); *United States v. American Radiator & Standard Sanitary Corp.*, 433 F.2d 174 (3rd Cir. 1970) (affirming conviction of corporation based upon its officer's participation in price-fixing scheme, despite corporation's defense that officer's conduct violated its "rigid anti-fraternization policy" against any socialization (and exchange of price information) with its competitors; "When the act of the agent is within the scope of his employment or his apparent authority, the corporation is held legally responsible for it, although what he did may be contrary to his actual instructions and may be unlawful.").

   While the Department recognizes that no compliance program can ever prevent all criminal activity by a corporation's employees, the critical factors in evaluating any program are whether the program is adequately designed for maximum effectiveness in preventing and detecting wrongdoing by employees and whether corporate management is enforcing the program or is tacitly encouraging or pressuring employees to engage in misconduct to achieve business objectives. The Department has no formal guidelines for corporate compliance programs. The fundamental questions any prosecutor should ask are: "Is the corporation's compliance program well designed?" and "Does the corporation's compliance program work?" In answering these questions, the prosecutor should consider the comprehensiveness of the compliance program; the extent and pervasiveness of the criminal conduct; the number and level of the corporate employees involved; the seriousness, duration, and frequency of the misconduct; and any remedial actions taken by the corporation, including restitution, disciplinary action, and revisions to corporate compliance programs.[6] Prosecutors should also consider the promptness of any disclosure of wrongdoing to the government and the corporation's cooperation in the government's investigation. In evaluating compliance programs, prosecutors may consider whether the corporation has established corporate governance mechanisms that can effectively detect and prevent misconduct. For example, do the corporation's directors exercise independent review over proposed corporate actions rather than unquestioningly ratifying officers' recommendations; are the directors provided with information sufficient to enable the exercise of independent judgment, are internal audit functions conducted at a level sufficient to ensure their independence and accuracy and have the directors established an information and reporting system in the organization reasonable designed to provide management and the board of directors with timely and accurate information sufficient to allow them to reach an informed decision regarding the organization's compliance with the law. *In re: Caremark,* 698 A.2d 959 (Del. Ct. Chan. 1996).

Prosecutors should therefore attempt to determine whether a corporation's compliance program is merely a "paper program" or whether it was designed and implemented in an effective manner. In addition, prosecutors should determine whether the corporation has provided for a staff sufficient to audit, document, analyze, and utilize the results of the corporation's compliance efforts. In addition, prosecutors should determine whether the corporation's employees are adequately informed about the compliance program and are convinced of the corporation's commitment to it. This will enable the prosecutor to make an informed decision as to whether the corporation has adopted and implemented a truly effective compliance program that, when consistent with other federal law enforcement policies, may result in a decision to charge only the corporation's employees and agents.

Compliance programs should be designed to detect the particular types of misconduct most likely to occur in a particular corporation's line of business. Many corporations operate in complex regulatory environments outside the normal experience of criminal prosecutors. Accordingly, prosecutors should consult with relevant federal and state agencies with the expertise to evaluate the adequacy of a program's design and implementation. For instance, state and federal banking, insurance, and medical boards, the Department of Defense, the Department of Health and Human Services, the Environmental Protection Agency, and the Securities and Exchange Commission have considerable experience with compliance programs and can be very helpful to a prosecutor in evaluating such programs. In addition, the Fraud Section of the Criminal Division, the Commercial Litigation Branch of the Civil Division, and the Environmental Crimes Section of the Environment and Natural Resources Division can assist U.S. Attorneys' Offices in finding the appropriate agency office and in providing copies of compliance programs that were developed in previous cases.

VIII. Charging a Corporation: Restitution and Remediation

A. General Principle: Although neither a corporation nor an individual target may avoid prosecution merely by paying a sum of money, a prosecutor may consider the corporation's willingness to make restitution and steps already taken to do so. A prosecutor may also consider other remedial actions, such as implementing an effective corporate compliance program, improving an existing compliance program, and disciplining wrongdoers, in determining whether to charge the corporation.

B. Comment: In determining whether or not a corporation should be prosecuted, a prosecutor may consider whether meaningful remedial measures have been taken, including employee discipline and full restitution.[7] A corporation's response to misconduct says much about its willingness to ensure that such misconduct does not recur. Thus, corporations that fully recognize the seriousness of their misconduct and accept responsibility for it should be taking steps to implement the personnel, operational, and organizational changes necessary to establish an awareness among employees that criminal conduct will not be tolerated. Among the factors prosecutors should consider and weigh are whether the corporation appropriately disciplined the wrongdoers and disclosed information concerning their illegal conduct to the government.

Employee discipline is a difficult task for many corporations because of the human element involved and sometimes because of the seniority of the employees concerned. While corporations need to be fair to their employees, they must also be unequivocally committed, at all levels of the corporation, to the highest standards of legal and ethical behavior. Effective internal discipline can be a powerful deterrent against improper behavior by a corporation's employees. In evaluating a corporation's response to wrongdoing, prosecutors may evaluate the willingness of the corporation to discipline culpable employees of all ranks and the adequacy of the discipline imposed. The prosecutor should be satisfied that the corporation's focus is on the integrity and credibility of its remedial and disciplinary measures rather than on the protection of the wrongdoers.

In addition to employee discipline, two other factors used in evaluating a corporation's remedial efforts are restitution and reform. As with natural persons, the decision whether or not to prosecute should not depend upon the target's ability to pay restitution. A corporation's efforts to pay restitution even in advance of any court order is, however, evidence of its "acceptance of responsibility" and, consistent with the practices and policies of the appropriate Division of the Department entrusted with enforcing specific criminal laws, may be considered in determining whether to bring criminal charges. Similarly, although the inadequacy of a corporate compliance program is a factor to consider when deciding whether to charge a corporation, that corporation's quick recognition of the flaws in the program and its efforts to improve the program are also factors to consider.

IX. Charging a Corporation: Collateral Consequences

A. General Principle: Prosecutors may consider the collateral consequences of a corporate criminal conviction in determining whether to charge the corporation with a criminal offense.

B. Comment: One of the factors in determining whether to charge a natural person or a corporation is whether the likely punishment is appropriate given the nature and seriousness of the crime. In the corporate context, prosecutors may take into account the possibly substantial consequences to a corporation's officers, directors, employees, and shareholders, many of whom may, depending on the size and nature (e.g., publicly vs. closely held) of the corporation and their role in its operations, have played no role in the criminal conduct, have been completely unaware of it, or have been wholly unable to prevent it. Prosecutors should also be aware of non-penal sanctions that may accompany a criminal charge, such as potential suspension or debarment from eligibility for government contracts or federal funded programs such as health care. Whether or not such non-penal sanctions are appropriate or required in a particular case is the responsibility of the relevant agency, a decision that will be made based on the applicable statutes, regulations, and policies.

Virtually every conviction of a corporation, like virtually every conviction of an individual, will have an impact on innocent third parties, and the mere existence of such an effect is not sufficient to preclude prosecution of the corporation. Therefore, in evaluating the severity of collateral consequences, various factors already discussed, such as the pervasiveness of the criminal conduct and the adequacy of the corporation's compliance programs, should be considered in determining the weight to be given to this factor. For instance, the balance may tip in favor of prosecuting corporations in situations where the scope of the misconduct in a case is widespread and sustained within a corporate division (or spread throughout pockets of the corporate organization). In such cases, the possible unfairness of visiting punishment for the corporation's crimes upon shareholders may be of much less concern where those shareholders have substantially profited, even unknowingly, from widespread or pervasive criminal activity. Similarly, where the top layers of the corporation's management or the shareholders of a closely-held corporation were engaged in or aware of the wrongdoing and the conduct at issue was accepted as a way of doing business for an extended period, debarment may be deemed not collateral, but a direct and entirely appropriate consequence of the corporation's wrongdoing.

The appropriateness of considering such collateral consequences and the weight to be given them may depend on the special policy concerns discussed in section III, *supra*.

X. Charging a Corporation: Non-Criminal Alternatives

A. General Principle: Although non-criminal alternatives to prosecution often exist, prosecutors may consider whether such sanctions would adequately deter, punish, and rehabilitate a corporation that has engaged in wrongful conduct. In evaluating the adequacy of non-criminal alternatives to prosecution, *e.g.*, civil or regulatory enforcement actions, the prosecutor may consider all relevant factors, including:

1. the sanctions available under the alternative means of disposition;

2. the likelihood that an effective sanction will be imposed; and

3. the effect of non-criminal disposition on Federal law enforcement interests.

B. Comment: The primary goals of criminal law are deterrence, punishment, and rehabilitation. Non-criminal sanctions may not be an appropriate response to an egregious violation, a pattern of wrongdoing, or a history of non-criminal sanctions without proper remediation. In other cases, however, these goals may be satisfied without the necessity of instituting criminal proceedings. In determining whether federal criminal charges are appropriate, the prosecutor should consider the same factors (modified appropriately for the regulatory context) considered when determining whether to leave prosecution of a natural person to another jurisdiction or to seek non-criminal alternatives to prosecution. These factors include: the strength of the regulatory authority's interest; the regulatory authority's ability and willingness to take effective enforcement action; the probable sanction if the regulatory authority's enforcement action is upheld; and the effect of a non-criminal disposition on Federal law enforcement interests. *See* USAM §§ 9-27.240, 9-27.250.

XI. Charging a Corporation: Selecting Charges

A. General Principle: Once a prosecutor has decided to charge a corporation, the prosecutor should charge, or should recommend that the grand jury charge, the most serious offense that is consistent with the nature of the defendant's conduct and that is likely to result in a sustainable conviction.

B. Comment: Once the decision to charge is made, the same rules as govern charging natural persons apply. These rules require "a faithful and honest application of the Sentencing Guidelines" and an "individualized assessment of the extent to which particular charges fit the specific circumstances of the case, are consistent with the purposes of the Federal criminal code, and maximize the impact of Federal resources on crime." *See* USAM § 9-27.300. In making this determination, "it is appropriate that the attorney for the government consider, *inter alia*, such factors as the sentencing guideline range yielded by the charge, whether the penalty yielded by such sentencing range ... is proportional to the seriousness of the defendant's conduct, and whether the charge achieves such purposes of the criminal law as punishment, protection of the public, specific and general deterrence, and rehabilitation." *See* Attorney General's Memorandum, dated October 12, 1993.

XII. Plea Agreements with Corporations

A. General Principle: In negotiating plea agreements with corporations, prosecutors should seek a plea to the most serious, readily provable offense charged. In addition, the terms of the plea agreement should contain appropriate provisions to ensure punishment, deterrence, rehabilitation, and compliance with the plea agreement in the corporate context. Although special circumstances may mandate a different conclusion, prosecutors generally should not agree to accept a corporate guilty plea in exchange for non-prosecution or dismissal of charges against individual officers and employees.

B. Comment: Prosecutors may enter into plea agreements with corporations for the same reasons and under the same constraints as apply to plea agreements with natural persons. *See* USAM §§ 9-27.400-500. This means, *inter alia*, that the corporation should be required to plead guilty to the most serious, readily provable offense charged. As is the case with individuals, the attorney making this determination should do so "on the basis of an individualized assessment of the extent to which particular charges fit the specific circumstances of the case, are consistent with the purposes of the federal criminal code, and maximize the impact of federal resources on crime. In making this determination, the attorney for the government considers, inter alia, such factors as the sentencing guideline range yielded by the charge, whether the penalty yielded by such sentencing range ... is proportional to the seriousness of the defendant's conduct, and whether the charge achieves such purposes of the criminal law as punishment, protection of the public, specific and general deterrence, and rehabilitation." See Attorney General's Memorandum, dated October 12, 1993. In addition, any negotiated departures from the Sentencing Guidelines must be justifiable under the Guidelines and must be disclosed to the sentencing court. A corporation should be made to realize that pleading guilty to criminal charges constitutes an admission of guilt and not merely a resolution of an inconvenient distraction from its business. As with natural persons, pleas should be structured so that the corporation may not later "proclaim lack of culpability or even complete innocence." See USAM §§ 9-27.420(b)(4), 9-27.440, 9-27.500. Thus, for instance, there should be placed upon the record a sufficient factual basis for the plea to prevent later corporate assertions of innocence.

A corporate plea agreement should also contain provisions that recognize the nature of the corporate "person" and ensure that the principles of punishment, deterrence, and rehabilitation are met. In the corporate context, punishment and deterrence are generally accomplished by substantial fines, mandatory restitution, and institution of appropriate compliance measures, including, if necessary, continued judicial oversight or the use of special masters. See USSG §§ 8B1.1, 8C2.1, et seq. In addition, where the corporation is a government contractor, permanent or temporary debarment may be appropriate. Where the corporation was engaged in government contracting fraud, a prosecutor may not negotiate away an agency's right to debar or to list the corporate defendant.

In negotiating a plea agreement, prosecutors should also consider the deterrent value of prosecutions of individuals within the corporation. Therefore, one factor that a prosecutor may consider in determining whether to enter into a plea agreement is whether the corporation is seeking immunity for its employees and officers or whether the corporation is willing to cooperate in the investigation of culpable individuals. Prosecutors should rarely negotiate away individual criminal liability in a corporate plea.

Rehabilitation, of course, requires that the corporation undertake to be law-abiding in the future. It is, therefore, appropriate to require the corporation, as a condition of probation, to implement a compliance program or to reform an existing one. As discussed above, prosecutors may consult with the appropriate state and federal agencies and components of the Justice Department to ensure that a proposed compliance program is adequate and meets industry standards and best practices. See section VII, supra.

In plea agreements in which the corporation agrees to cooperate, the prosecutor should ensure that the cooperation is complete and truthful. To do so, the prosecutor may request that the corporation waive attorney-client and work product protection, make employees and agents available for debriefing, disclose the results of its internal investigation, file appropriate certified financial statements, agree to governmental or third-party audits, and take whatever other steps are necessary to ensure that the full scope of the corporate wrongdoing is disclosed and that the responsible culprits are identified and, if appropriate, prosecuted. See generally section VIII, supra.

Footnotes:

1. While these guidelines refer to corporations, they apply to the consideration of the prosecution of all types of business organizations, including partnerships, sole proprietorships, government entities, and unincorporated associations.

2. In addition, the Sentencing Guidelines reward voluntary disclosure and cooperation with a reduction in the corporation's offense level. See USSG §8C2.5)g).

3. This waiver should ordinarily be limited to the factual internal investigation and any contemporaneous advice given to the corporation concerning the conduct at issue. Except in unusual circumstances, prosecutors should not seek a waiver with respect to communications and work product related to advice concerning the government's criminal investigation.

4. Some states require corporations to pay the legal fees of officers under investigation prior to a formal determination of their guilt. Obviously, a corporation's compliance with governing law should not be considered a failure to cooperate.

5. Although this case and *Basic Construction* are both antitrust cases, their reasoning applies to other criminal violations. In the Hilton case, for instance, the Ninth Circuit noted that Sherman Act violations are commercial offenses "usually motivated by a desire to enhance profits," thus, bringing the case within the normal rule that a "purpose to benefit the corporation is necessary to bring the agent's acts within the scope of his employment." 467 F.2d at 1006 & n4. In addition, in *United States v. Automated Medical Laboratories*, 770 F.2d 399, 406 n.5 (4th Cir. 1985), the Fourth Circuit stated "that Basic Construction states a generally applicable rule on corporate criminal liability despite the fact that it addresses violations of the antitrust laws."

6. For a detailed review of these and other factors concerning corporate compliance programs, see United States Sentencing Commission, GUIDELINES MANUAL, §8A1.2, comment. (n.3(k)) (Nov. 1997). *See also* USSG §8C2.5(f)

7. For example, the Antitrust Division's amnesty policy requires that "[w]here possible, the corporation [make] restitution to injured parties...."

OCCUPATIONAL FRAUD

Occupational fraud is committed largely by individuals or small groups of individuals in connection with their occupation. It can include violations of law by businessmen, politicians, labor union leaders, lawyers, doctors, pharmacists, and employees who embezzle money from their employers or steal merchandise and tools.

Gary Green, in honing the white-collar crime concept, uses the term "occupational crime," which he defines as "any act punishable by law which is committed through opportunity created in the course of an occupation which is legal." Green further delineates occupational crime into four categories:

- Crimes for the benefit of an employing organization (organizational occupational crime)
- Crimes by officials through exercise of their state-based authority (state authority occupational crime)
- Crimes by professionals in their capacity as professionals (professional occupational crime)
- Crimes by individuals as individuals

Some scholars debate whether individuals should be held responsible for crimes committed on behalf of their organizations. Although some direct benefit accrues to the perpetrator, far more benefit accrues to the organization. Regardless of whether the organization is held liable, the fraud is a direct result of some human action or interaction. In the words of Parisi, "If [an organization] is like a gun, then there must be someone comparable to a triggerman."

Research in Occupational Fraud and Abuse

Edwin H. Sutherland

Relatively little research has been done on the subject of occupational fraud and abuse. Much of the current literature is based upon the early works of Edwin H. Sutherland. As previously discussed in the chapter on "Theories of Crime Causation," Sutherland believed that the learning of criminal behavior occurred with other persons in a process of communication. Therefore, he reasoned, criminality cannot occur without the assistance of other people. Sutherland further theorized that the learning of criminal activity usually occurred within intimate personal groups. This explains, in his view, how a dysfunctional parent is more likely to produce dysfunctional offspring. Sutherland believed that the learning process involved two specific areas: the techniques to commit the crime, and the attitudes, drives, rationalizations, and motives of the criminal mind. One can see how Sutherland's differential association theory fits with occupational offenders. Organizations that have dishonest employees will eventually infect a portion of honest ones. It also goes the other way: honest employees will eventually have an influence on some of those who are dishonest.

Donald R. Cressey

During the 1940s at Indiana University, one of Sutherland's brightest students was Donald R. Cressey (1919-1987). While much of Sutherland's research concentrated on upper-world criminality, Cressey took his own studies in a different direction. Working on his Ph.D. in criminology, he decided his dissertation would focus on embezzlers. To serve as a basis for his research, Cressey interviewed about 200 people who had been incarcerated for embezzling funds.

Cressey's Hypothesis

Cressey was intrigued by embezzlers, whom he called "trust violators." He was especially interested in the circumstances that led them to be overcome by temptation. For that reason, he excluded from his research those employees who took their jobs for the purpose of stealing—a relatively minor number of offenders at that time. Upon completion of his interviews, he developed what still remains as the classic model for the occupational offender. His research was published in *Other People's Money: A Study in the Social Psychology of Embezzlement*.

Cressey's final hypothesis was:

> *Trusted persons become trust violators when they conceive of themselves as having a financial problem which is non-shareable, are aware this problem can be secretly resolved by violation of the position of financial trust, and are able to apply to their own conduct in that situation verbalizations which enable them to adjust their conceptions of themselves as trusted persons with their conceptions of themselves as users of the entrusted funds or property.* [1]

---

[1] Donald R. Cressey, *Other People's Money* (Montclair: Patterson Smith, 1973) p. 30.

Over the years, the hypothesis has become more well known as the "fraud triangle." One leg of the triangle represents a *perceived non-shareable financial need*. The second leg represents *perceived opportunity*, and the final stands for *rationalization*. The role of the *non-shareable* problem is important. Cressey said, "When the trust violators were asked to explain why they refrained from violation of other positions of trust they might have held at previous times, or why they had not violated the subject position at an earlier time, those who had an opinion expressed the equivalent of one or more of the following quotations: (a) 'There was no need for it like there was this time.' (b) 'The idea never entered my head.' (c) 'I thought it was dishonest then, but this time it did not seem dishonest at first.'"[2]

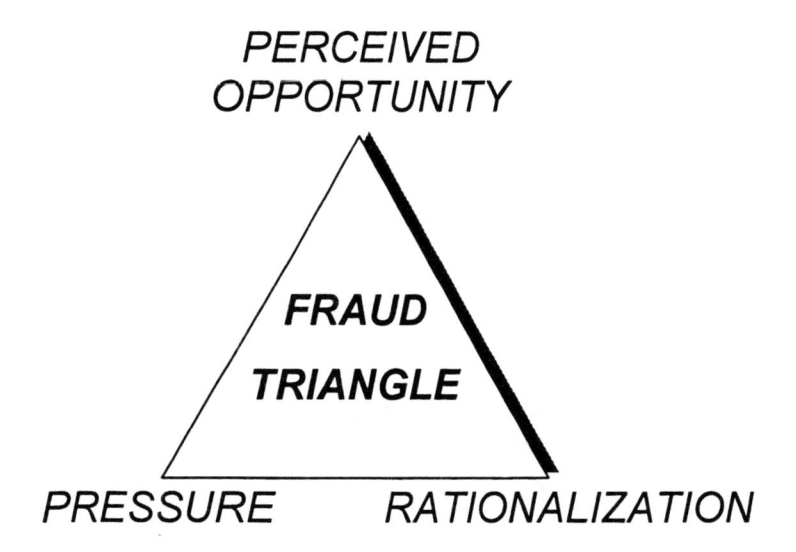

```
            PERCEIVED
           OPPORTUNITY
                /\
               /  \
              /    \
             / FRAUD\
            /        \
           / TRIANGLE \
          /_____\
     PRESSURE      RATIONALIZATION
```

"In all cases of trust violation encountered, the violator considered that a financial problem which confronted him could not be shared with persons who, from a more objective point of view, probably could have aided in the solution of the problem." [3]

Non-shareable Financial Problems

That which is considered "non-shareable" is wholly in the eyes of the potential occupational offender, Cressey said. "Thus a man could lose considerable money at the race track daily but the loss, even if it construed a problem for the individual, might not constitute a non-shareable problem for him. Another man might define the problem as one which must be kept secret and private, that is, as one which is non-shareable. Similarly, a failing bank or

---

[2] Cressey, p. 33.
[3] Cressey, p. 34.

business might be considered by one person as presenting problems which must be shared with business associates and members of the community, while another person might conceive these problems as non-shareable."[4]

In addition to being non-shareable, the problem that drives the fraudster is described as "financial" because these are problems that can generally be solved by the theft of cash or other assets. A person with large gambling debts, for instance, would need cash to pay those debts. Cressey did note, however, that there are some non-financial problems which could be solved by misappropriating funds through a violation of trust. For example, a person who embezzles in order to get revenge on her employer for perceived "unfair" treatment uses financial means to solve what is essentially a non-financial problem.

Through his research, Cressey also found that the non-shareable problems encountered by the people he interviewed arose from situations that could be divided into six basic categories: violation of ascribed obligations, problems resulting from personal failure, business reversals, physical isolation, status gaining, and employer-employee relations. All of these situations dealt in some way with status-seeking or status-maintaining activities by the subjects. In other words, the non-shareable problems threatened the status of the subjects, or threatened to prevent them from achieving a higher status than the one they occupied at the time of their violation.

VIOLATION OF ASCRIBED OBLIGATIONS

Violation of ascribed obligations has historically proved a strong motivator. "Financial problems incurred through non-financial violations of positions of trust often are considered as non-shareable by trusted persons since they represent a threat to the status which holding the position entails. Most individuals in positions of financial trust, and most employers of such individuals, consider that incumbency in such a position necessarily implies that, in addition to being honest, they should behave in certain ways and should refrain from participation in some other kinds of behavior."[5] In other words, a trusted position caries with it the implied duty to act in an acceptable manner. Persons in trusted positions may feel they are expected to avoid conduct such as gambling, drinking, drug use or other activities that are considered seamy and undignified.

---

[4] Cressey, p. 35.
[5] Cressey, p. 36.

When these persons fall into debt or incur large financial obligations as a result of some sort of "dishonorable" conduct, they feel unable to share the problem with their peers because this would require admitting that they have engaged in conduct that is 'beneath' them. By admitting that they had lost money through some disreputable act, they would be admitting – at least in their own minds – that they are unworthy to hold their trusted positions. So rather than seek help through legitimate means, they turn to fraud to solve the problem in secret.

PROBLEMS RESULTING FROM PERSONAL FAILURE

Problems resulting from personal failures, Cressey writes, are those that the trusted person feels he caused through bad judgment and therefore feels personally responsible for. Cressey cites one case in which an attorney lost his life's savings in a secret business venture. The business had been set up to compete with some of the attorney's clients, and though he thought his clients probably would have offered him help if they had known what dire straits he was in, he could not bring himself to tell them that he had secretly tried to compete with them. He also was unable to tell his wife that he'd squandered their savings. Instead, he sought to alleviate the problem by embezzling funds to cover his losses.[6]

"While some pressing financial problems may be considered as having resulted from 'economic conditions,' 'fate,' or some other impersonal force, others are considered to have been created by the misguided or poorly planned activities of the individual trusted person. Because he fears a loss of status, the individual is afraid to admit to anyone who could alleviate the situation the fact that he has a problem which is a consequence of his 'own bad judgment' or 'own fault' or 'own stupidity.'"[7] In short, pride goeth before the fall. If the potential offender has a choice between covering his poor investment choices through a violation of trust and admitting that he is an unsophisticated investor, it is easy to see how some prideful people's judgment could be clouded.

BUSINESS REVERSALS

Business reversals were the third type of situation Cressey identified as leading to the perception of non-shareable financial problems. This category differs from the class of "personal failures" described above because here the trust violators tend to see their problems as arising from conditions beyond their control: inflation, high interest rates,

---

[6] Cressey p. 42.
[7] Cressey, p. 48.

economic downturns, etc. In other words, these problems are not caused by the subject's own failings, but instead by outside forces.

Cressey quoted the remarks of one businessman who borrowed money from a bank using fictitious collateral. "There are very few people who are able to walk away from a failing business. When the bridge is falling, almost everyone will run for a piece of timber. In business there is this eternal optimism that things will get better tomorrow. We get to working on the business, keeping it going, and we almost get mesmerized by it . . . . Most of us don't know when to quit, when to say, 'This one has me licked. Here's one for the opposition.'" [8]

It is interesting to note that even in situations where the problem is perceived to be out of the trusted person's control, the issue of status still plays a big role in that person's decision to keep the problem a secret. The subject of the preceding case continued, "If I'd have walked away and let them all say, 'Well, he wasn't a success as a manager, he was a failure,' and took a job as a bookkeeper, or gone on the farm, I would have been all right. But I didn't want to do that."[9] The desire to maintain the appearance of success was a common theme in the cases involving business reversals.

PHYSICAL ISOLATION

The fourth category Cressey described was problems resulting from physical isolation. In these situations, the trusted person simply has no one to turn to. It's not that he is afraid to share his problem, it's that he has no one to share the problem with. He is in a situation where he does not have access to trusted friends or associates who would otherwise be able to help him. Cressey cited the case of one man who found himself in financial trouble after his wife had died. In her absence, he had no one to go to for help in dealing with his financial problems.[10]

STATUS GAINING

The fifth category involves problems relating to status gaining, which is a sort of extreme example of "keeping up with the Joneses" syndrome. In the previous categories the offenders were generally concerned with *maintaining* their status (i.e., not admitting to failure,

---

[8] Cressey, p. 47.
[9] Cressey, p. 48.
[10] Cressey, p. 52-53.

keeping up appearance of trustworthiness), but here the offenders are motivated by a desire to *improve* their status.

The motive for this type of conduct is often referred to as "living beyond one's means" or "lavish spending," but Cressey felt that these explanations did not get to the heart of the matter. The question was, What made the desire to improve one's status non-shareable? He noted, "…in this type of case a problem appears when the individual realizes that he does not have the financial means necessary for continued association with persons on a desired status level, and this problem becomes non-shareable when he feels that he can neither renounce his aspirations for membership in the desired group nor obtain prestige symbols necessary to such membership."[16] In other words, it is not the desire for a better lifestyle that creates the non-shareable problem (we all want a better lifestyle), rather it is the inability to obtain the finer things through legitimate means, and at the same time an unwillingness to settle for a lower status that creates the motivation for trust violation.

EMPLOYER-EMPLOYEE RELATIONS
Finally, Cressey described problems resulting from employer-employee relationships. The most common, he stated, was an employed person who resents his status within the organization in which he is trusted, and at the same time feels he has no choice but to continue working for the organization. The resentment can come from perceived economic inequities, such as low pay, or from the feeling of being overworked or underappreciated. Cressey said this problem becomes non-shareable when the individual believes that making suggestions to alleviate his perceived maltreatment will possibly threaten his status in the organization.[11] There is also a strong motivator for the perceived employee to want to "get even" when he feels ill-treated.

The Importance of Solving the Problem in Secret
Since Cressey's study was done in the early 1950s, the workforce was obviously different from today's. But the employee faced with an immediate, non-shareable financial need hasn't changed much over the years. That employee still must find a way to relieve the financial pressure that bears down upon him. Simply stealing money, however, is not enough; Cressey found it was crucial that the employee be able to resolve the financial problem in *secret*.

---

[11] Cressey, p. 57,

As we have seen, the non-shareable financial problems identified by Cressey all dealt in some way with questions of status; the trust violators were afraid of losing the approval of those around them and so were unable to tell others about their financial problems. If they could not share the fact that they were under financial pressure, it follows that they would not be able to share the fact that they were resorting to illegal means to relieve that pressure. To do so would be to admit the problems existed in the first place.

The interesting thing to note is that it is not the embezzlement itself which creates the need for secrecy in the perpetrator's mind, it is the circumstances that led to the embezzlement (a violation of ascribed obligation, a business reversal, etc.). Cressey said:

> "In all cases [in the study] there was a distinct feeling that, because of activity prior to the defalcation, the approval of groups important to the trusted person had been lost, or a distinct feeling that present group approval would be lost if certain activity were revealed [the non-shareable financial problem], with the result that the trusted person was effectively isolated from persons who could assist him in solving problems arising from that activity."

> Although the clear conception of a financial problem as non-shareable does not invariably result in trust violation, it does establish in trusted persons a desire for a specific kind of solution to their problems. The results desired in the cases encountered were uniform: the solution or partial solution of the problem by the use of funds which can be obtained in an independent, relatively secret, safe, and sure method in keeping with the 'rationalizations' available to the person at the time.[12] (emphasis added)

Perceived Opportunity

According to the fraud triangle model, the presence of a non-shareable financial problem, by itself, will not lead an employee to commit fraud. The key to understanding Cressey's theory is to remember that all three elements must be present for a trust violation to occur. The non-shareable financial problem creates the motive for the crime to be committed, but the employee must also perceive that she has an opportunity to commit the crime without being caught. This *perceived opportunity* constitutes the second element.

In Cressey's view, there were two components of the perceived opportunity to commit a trust violation: general information and technical skill. *General information* is simply the

---

[12] Cressey, p. 66-67.

knowledge that the employee's position of trust could be violated. This knowledge might come from hearing of other embezzlements, from seeing dishonest behavior by other employees, or just from generally being aware of the fact that the employee is in a position where he could take advantage of his employer's faith in him. *Technical skill* refers to the abilities needed to commit the violation. These are usually the same abilities that the employee needs to have to obtain and keep his position in the first place. Cressey noted that most embezzlers adhere to their occupational routines (and their job skills) in order to perpetrate their crimes.[13] In essence, the perpetrator's job will tend to define the type of fraud he will commit. "Accountants use checks which they have been entrusted to dispose of, sales clerks withhold receipts, bankers manipulate seldom-used accounts or withhold deposits, real estate men use deposits entrusted to them, and so on."[14]

Obviously, the general information and technical skill that Cressey identified are not unique to occupational offenders; most if not all employees have these same characteristics. But because trusted persons possess this information and skill, when they face a non-shareable financial problem they see it as something that they have the power to correct. They apply their understanding of the *possibility* for trust violation to the specific crises they are faced with. Cressey observed, "It is the next step which is significant to violation: the application of the general information to the specific situation, and conjointly, the perception of the fact that in addition to having general possibilities for violation, a specific position of trust can be used for the specific purpose of solving a non-shareable problem"[15]

Rationalizations

The third and final factor in the fraud triangle is the *rationalization*. Cressey pointed out that the rationalization is not an *ex post facto* means of justifying a theft that has already occurred. Significantly, the rationalization is a necessary component of the crime *before* it takes place; in fact, it is a part of the motivation for the crime. Because the embezzler does not view himself as a criminal, he must justify his misdeeds before he ever commits them. The rationalization is necessary so that the perpetrator can make his illegal behavior intelligible to himself and maintain his concept of himself as a trusted person.[16]

---

[13] Cressey p. 84.
[14] Cressey p. 84.
[15] Cressey p. 85
[16] Cressey pp. 94-95.

After the criminal act has taken place, the rationalization will often be abandoned. That is, of course, because of the nature of us all: the first time we do something contrary to our morals, it bothers us. As we repeat the act, it becomes easier. One hallmark of occupational fraud and abuse offenders is that once the line is crossed, the illegal acts become more or less continuous. So an occupational fraudster might begin stealing with the thought that "I'll pay the money back," but after the initial theft is successful, he will usually continue to steal past the point where there is any realistic possibility of repaying the stolen funds.

Cressey found that the embezzlers he studied generally rationalized their crimes by viewing them as: (1) essentially non-criminal, (2) justified, or (3) part of a general irresponsibility for which they were not completely accountable.[17] He also found that the rationalizations used by trust violators tended to be linked to their positions and to the manner in which they committed their violations. He examined this by dividing the subjects of his study into three categories: independent businessmen, long-term violators, and absconders. He discovered that each group had its own types of rationalizations.

INDEPENDENT BUSINESSMEN

The *independent businessmen* in Cressey's study were persons who were in business for themselves and who converted "deposits" which had been entrusted to them.[18] Perpetrators in this category tended to use one of two common excuses: (1) they were "borrowing" the money they converted, or (2) the funds entrusted to them were really theirs—you can't steal from yourself. Cressey found the "borrowing" rationalization was the most frequently used. These perpetrators also tended to espouse the idea that "everyone" in business misdirects deposits in some way, which therefore made their own misconduct less wrong than "stealing."[19] Also, the independent businessmen almost universally felt their illegal actions were predicated by an "unusual situation," which Cressey concluded was in reality a non-shareable financial problem.

LONG-TERM VIOLATORS

Cressey defined *long-term violators* as individuals who converted their employer's funds, or funds belonging to their employer's clients, by taking relatively small amounts over a period of time.[20] Similar to independent businessmen, the long-term violators generally preferred

---

[17] Cressey p. 93.
[18] Cressey, p. 101-102.
[19] Cressey, p. 102.
[20] Cressey, p. 102.

the "borrowing" rationalization. Other rationalizations of long-term violators were described, too, but they almost always were used in connection with the "borrowing" theme: (1) they were embezzling to keep their families from shame, disgrace, or poverty; (2) theirs was a case of "necessity"; their employers were cheating them financially; and (3) their employers were dishonest towards others and deserved to be fleeced. Some even pointed out that it was more difficult to return the funds than to steal them in the first place, and claimed they did not pay back their "borrowings" because they feared that would lead to detection of their thefts. A few in the study actually kept track of their thefts but most only did so at first. Later, as the embezzlements escalated, it is assumed that the offender would rather not know the extent of his "borrowings."

All of the long-term violators in the study expressed a feeling that they would like to eventually "clean the slate" and repay their debt. This feeling usually arose even before the perpetrators perceived that they might be caught. Cressey pointed out that at this point, whatever fear the perpetrators felt in relation to their crimes was related to losing their social status by the exposure of their non-shareable *problem*, not the exposure of the theft itself or the possibility of punishment or imprisonment. This is because their rationalizations still prevented them from perceiving their misconduct as criminal. "The trust violator cannot fear the treatment usually accorded criminals until he comes to look upon himself as a criminal."[21]

Eventually, most of the long-term violators finally realized they were "in too deep." It is at this point that the embezzler faces a crisis. While maintaining the borrowing rationalization (or other rationalizations, for that matter), the trust violator is able to maintain his self-image as a law-abiding citizen; but when the level of theft escalates to a certain point, the perpetrator is confronted with the idea that he is behaving in a criminal manner. This is contrary to his personal values and the values of the social groups to which he belongs. This conflict creates a great deal of anxiety for the perpetrator. A number of offenders described themselves as extremely nervous and upset, tense, and unhappy.[22]

Without the rationalization that they were borrowing, long-term offenders in the study found it difficult to reconcile converting money, while at the same time seeing themselves as honest and trustworthy. In this situation, they have two options: (1) they can readopt the

---

[21] Cressey, pp. 120-121.
[22] Cressey, p. 121.

attitudes of the (law-abiding) social group which with they identified before the thefts began; or (2) they can adopt the attitudes of the new category of persons (criminals) with whom they now identify.[23] From his study, Cressey was able to cite examples of each type of behavior. Those who sought to readopt the attitudes of their law-abiding social groups "may report their behavior to the police or to their employer, quit taking funds or resolve to quit taking funds, speculate or gamble wildly in order to regain the amounts taken, or 'leave the field' by absconding or committing suicide."[24] On the other hand, those who adopt the attitudes of the group of criminals to which they now belong, "may become reckless in their defalcations, taking larger amounts than formerly with less attempt to avoid detection and with no notion of repayment."[25]

ABSCONDERS
The third group of offenders Cressey discussed was *absconders* — people who take the money and run. Cressey found that the non-shareable problems for absconders usually resulted from physical isolation. He observed that these people, "usually are unmarried or separated from their spouses, live in hotels or rooming houses, have few primary group associations of any sort, and own little property. Only one of the absconders interviewed had held a higher status position of trust, such as an accountant, business executive, or bookkeeper."[26] He also found that the absconders tended to have lower occupational and socio-economic status than the members of the other two categories.

Because absconders tended to lack strong social ties, Cressey found that almost any financial problem could be defined as non-shareable for these persons, and also that rationalizations were easily adopted because the persons only had to sever a minimum of social ties when they absconded.[27] The absconders rationalized their conduct by noting that their attempts to live honest lives had been futile (hence their low status). They also adopted an attitude of not caring what happened to them, and a belief that they could not help themselves because they were predisposed to criminal behavior. The latter two rationalizations, which were adopted by every absconder in Cressey's study, allowed them to remove almost all personal accountability from their conduct.[28]

---

[23] Cressey, p. 122.
[24] Cressey, p. 121.
[25] Cressey, p. 122.
[26] Cressey, p. 128.
[27] Cressey, p. 129.
[28] Cressey, p. 128-129.

In the 1950s, when this data was gathered by Cressey, embezzlers were considered persons of higher socioeconomic status who took funds over a limited period of time because of some personal problem such as drinking or gambling, while "thieves" were considered persons of lower status who took whatever funds were at hand. Cressey noted, "Since most absconders identify with the lower status group, they look upon themselves as belonging to a special class of thieves rather than trust violators. Just as long-term violators and independent businessmen do not at first consider the possibility of absconding with the funds, absconders do not consider the possibility of taking relatively small amounts of money over a period of time."[29]

Conjuncture of Events

Perhaps the most important conclusion to be drawn from the Cressey study was that it took all three elements — perceived non-shareable financial problem, perceived opportunity, and the ability to rationalize — for the trust violation to occur.

> *"The three events make up the conditions under which trust violation occurs and the term 'cause' may be applied to their conjuncture since trust violation is dependent on that conjuncture. Whenever the conjuncture of events occurs, trust violation results, and if the conjuncture does not take place there is no trust violation."*[30]

Conclusions

Cressey's classic fraud triangle helps explain the nature of many—but not all—occupational offenders. For example, although academicians have tested his model, it has still not fully found its way into practice in terms of developing fraud prevention programs. Our sense tells us that one model—even Cressey's—will not fit all situations. Plus, the study is nearly half a century old. There has been considerable social change in the interim. And now, many anti-fraud professionals believe there is a new breed of occupational offender—one who simply lacks a conscience sufficient to overcome temptation.

Dr. Steve Albrecht

The Albrecht Study

Another pioneer researcher in occupational fraud and abuse is Dr. Steve Albrecht of Brigham Young University. Albrecht and two of his colleagues, Keith R. Howe and Marshall

---

[29] Cressey, p. 133.
[30] Cressey, p. 139.

B. Romney, conducted an analysis of 212 frauds in the early 1980s under a grant from the Institute of Internal Auditors Research Foundation, leading to their book entitled *Deterring Fraud: The Internal Auditor's Perspective*. The study's methodology involved obtaining demographics and background information on the frauds through the use of extensive questionnaires. The participants in the survey were internal auditors of companies who had experienced frauds.

Albrecht's research included an examination of comprehensive data sources to assemble a complete list of pressure, opportunity, and integrity variables, resulting in a set of 50 possible red flags or indicators of occupational fraud and abuse. These variables fell into two principle categories: perpetrator characteristics and organizational environment. The purpose of the study was to determine which of the red flags were most important to the commission (and therefore to the detection and prevention) of fraud. The red flags ranged from unusually high personal debts, to belief that one's job is in jeopardy; from no separation of asset custodial procedures, to not adequately checking a potential employee's background.[31]

The researchers gave participants both sets of 25 motivating factors and asked which factors were present in the frauds they had dealt with. Participants were asked to rank these factors on a seven-point scale indicating the degree to which each factor existed in their specific frauds. The ten most highly ranked factors from the list of personal characteristics, based on this study, were:

1. Living beyond their means
2. An overwhelming desire for personal gain
3. High personal debt
4. A close association with customers
5. Feeling pay was not commensurate with responsibility
6. A wheeler-dealer attitude
7. Strong challenge to beat the system
8. Excessive gambling habits
9. Undue family or peer pressure
10. No recognition for job performance[32]

---

[31] While such red flags may be present in many occupational fraud cases, one must re-emphasize Albrecht's caution that the perpetrators are hard to profile and fraud is difficult to predict. To underscore this point, Albrecht's research does not address—and no current research has been done to determine—if nonoffenders have many of the same characteristics. If so, then the list may not be discriminating enough to be useful. In short, while one should be mindful of potential red flags, they should not receive undue attention absent other compelling circumstances.

[32] Albrecht, p. 32.

These motivators are very similar to the non-shareable financial problems Cressey identified.

The ten most highly ranked factors from the list dealing with organizational environment were:
1. Placing too much trust in key employees
2. Lack of proper procedures for authorization of transactions
3. Inadequate disclosures of personal investments and incomes
4. No separation of authorization of transactions from the custody of related assets
5. Lack of independent checks on performance
6. Inadequate attention to details
7. No separation of custody of assets from the accounting for those assets
8. No separation of duties between accounting functions
9. Lack of clear lines of authority and responsibility
10. Department that is not frequently reviewed by internal auditors[33]

All of the factors on this list affect employees' opportunity to commit fraud without being caught. Opportunity, as you will recall, was the second factor identified in Cressey's fraud triangle. In many ways, the study by Albrecht, et al., supported Cressey's model. Like Cressey's study, the Albrecht study suggests there are three factors involved in occupational frauds: ". . . it appears that three elements must be present for a fraud to be committed: a situational pressure (non-shareable financial pressure), a perceived opportunity to commit and conceal the dishonest act (a way to secretly resolve the dishonest act or the lack of deterrence by management), and some way to rationalize (verbalize) the act as either being inconsistent with one's personal level of integrity or justifiable."[34]

The Fraud Scale[35]

To illustrate the concept, Albrecht developed the "Fraud Scale," which included the components of situational pressures, perceived opportunities, and personal integrity. When situational pressures and perceived opportunities are high and personal integrity is low, occupational fraud is much more likely to occur than when the opposite is true.[36]

---

[33] Albrecht, p. 39
[34] Albrecht, p. 5.
[35] Albrecht, et.al., p. 5.
[36] Albrecht, et.al., p. 6.

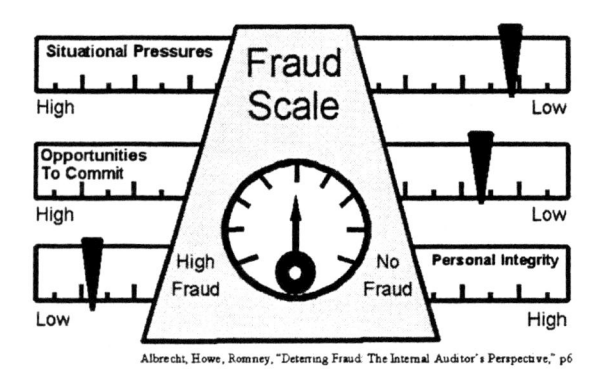

[Figure: Fraud Scale showing Situational Pressures (High–Low), Opportunities To Commit (High–Low), and Personal Integrity (Low–High), with a gauge indicating High Fraud to No Fraud.]

Albrecht, Howe, Romney, "Deterring Fraud: The Internal Auditor's Perspective," p6

Albrecht describes situational pressures as "the immediate problems individuals experience within their environments, the most overwhelming of which are probably high personal debts or financial losses."[37] Opportunities to commit fraud, Albrecht says, may be created by individuals, or by deficient or missing internal controls. Personal integrity "refers to the personal code of ethical behavior each person adopts. While this factor appears to be a straightforward determination of whether the person is honest or dishonest, moral development research indicates that the issue is more complex."[38]

In addition to its findings on motivating factors of occupational fraud, the Albrecht study also disclosed several interesting relationships between the perpetrators and the frauds they committed. For example, perpetrators of large frauds used the proceeds to purchase new homes and expensive automobiles, recreation property, expensive vacations, support extramarital relationships, and make speculative investments. Those committing small frauds did not.[39] Perpetrators who were interested primarily in "beating the system" committed larger frauds. However, perpetrators who believed their pay was not adequate committed primarily small frauds. Lack of segregation of responsibilities, placing undeserved trust in key employees, imposing unrealistic goals, and operating on a crisis basis were all pressures or weaknesses associated with large frauds. College graduates were less likely to spend the proceeds of their loot to take extravagant vacations, purchase recreational property, support extramarital relationships, and buy expensive automobiles. Finally, those with lower salaries were more likely to have a prior criminal record.[40]

---

[37] Albrecht, p. 5.
[38] Albrecht, p. 6.
[39] Albrecht, p. 42.
[40] Albrecht, p. xiv.

Richard C. Hollinger

The Hollinger - Clark Study

In 1983, Richard C. Hollinger of Purdue University and John P. Clark of the University of Minnesota published federally funded research involving surveys of nearly 10,000 American workers. Their book, *Theft by Employees*, reached a different conclusion than Cressey. They concluded that employees steal primarily as a result of workplace conditions, and that the true costs of the problem are vastly understated: "In sum, when we take into consideration the incalculable social costs ... the grand total paid for theft in the workplace is no doubt grossly underestimated by the available financial estimates."[41]

Hypotheses of Employee Theft

In reviewing the literature on employee theft, Hollinger and Clark concluded that experts had developed five separate but interrelated sets of hypotheses of employee theft. The first is external economic pressures, such as the "non-shareable financial problem" that Cressey described. The second hypothesis was that contemporary employees, specifically young ones, are not as hardworking and honest as those in past generations. The third theory, advocated primarily by those with years of experience in the security and investigative industry, is that every employee can be tempted to steal from his employer. The theory basically assumes that people are greedy and dishonest by nature. The fourth theory was that job dissatisfaction is the primary cause of employee theft, and the fifth, that theft occurs because of the broadly shared formal and informal structure of organizations. That is, over time, the group norms—good or bad—become the standard of conduct. The sum of their research generally concluded that the fourth hypothesis was correct.

EMPLOYEE DEVIANCE

Employee theft is at one extreme of employee deviance, which can be defined as conduct detrimental to the organization and to the employee. At the other extreme is counterproductive employee behavior such as goldbricking and abuse of sick leave. Hollinger and Clark defined two basic categories of employee deviant behavior: (1) acts by employees against property, and (2) violations of the norms regulating acceptable levels of production. The former includes misuse and theft of company property such as cash or inventory. The latter involves acts of employee deviance that affect productivity.

---

[41] Richard C. Hollinger and John P. Clark, *Theft by Employees* (Lexington: Lexingtion Books, 1983), p. 6.

Hollinger and Clark developed a written questionnaire which was sent to employees in three different sectors: retail, hospital, and manufacturing. The employees were presented with lists of category 1 and category 2 offenses and were asked which offenses they had been involved in, and with what frequency. The researchers eventually received 9,175 valid employee questionnaires, representing about 54% of those sampled. Below are the results of the questionnaires. The first table represents category 1 offenses—acts against property.[42] Hollinger and Clark found that approximately one-third of employees in each sector admitted to committing some form of property deviance.

Combined Phase I and Phase II Property-Deviance Items and Percentage of Reported Involvement, by Sector					
	Involvement				
Items	Almost Daily	About Once a Week	Four to Twelve Times a Year	One to Three Times a Year	Total
Retail Sector (N= 3,567)					
Misuse the discount privilege	0.6	2.4	11	14.9	28.9
Take store merchandise	0.2	0.5	1.3	4.6	6.6
Get paid for more hours than were worked	0.2	0.4	1.2	4	5.8
Purposely underring a purchase	0.1	0.3	1.1	1.7	3.2
Borrow or take money from employer without approval	0.1	0.1	0.5	2	2.7
Be reimbursed for more money than spent on business expenses	0.1	0.2	0.5	1.3	2.1
Damage merchandise to buy it on discount	0	0.1	0.2	1	1.3
Total involved in property deviance					35.1
Hospital Sector (N=4,111)					
Take hospital supplies (e.g. linens, bandages)	0.2	0.8	8.4	17.9	27.3
Take or use medication intended for patients	0.1	0.3	1.9	5.5	7.8
Get paid for more hours than were worked	0.2	0.5	1.6	3.8	6.1
Take hospital equipment or tools	0.1	0.1	0.4	4.1	4.7
Be reimbursed for more money than spent on business expenses	0.1	0	0.2	0.8	1.1
Total involved in property deviance					33.3
Manufacturing Sector (N=1,497)					
Take raw materials used in production	0.1	0.3	3.5	10.4	14.3
Get paid for more hours than were worked	0.2	0.5	2.9	5.6	9.2
Take company tools or equipment	0	0.1	1.1	7.5	8.7
Be reimbursed for more money than spent on business expenses	0.1	0.6	1.4	5.6	7.7
Take finished products	0	0	0.4	2.7	3.1
Take precious metals (e.g. platinum, gold)	0.1	0.1	0.5	1.1	1.8
Total involved in property deviance					28.4

Adapted from Richard C. Hollinger, John P. Clark, *Theft by Employees*, Lexington: Lexington Books, 1983. p42.

Following is a summary of the Hollinger and Clark research with respect to production deviance. Not surprisingly, they found that this form of employee misconduct was two to three times more common than property violations.[43]

---

[42] Hollinger and Clark, p. 6.
[43] Hollinger and Clark, p. 42.

Combined Phase I and Phase II Production-Deviance Items and Percentage of Reported Involvement, by Sector					
	Involvement				
Items	Almost Daily	About Once a Week	Four to Twelve Times a Year	One to Three Times a Year	Total
Retail Sector (N= 3,567)					
Take a long lunch or break without approval	6.9	13.3	15.5	20.3	56
Come to work late or leave early	0.9	3.4	10.8	17.2	32.3
Use sick leave when not sick	0.1	0.1	3.5	13.4	17.1
Do slow or sloppy work	0.3	1.5	4.1	9.8	15.7
Work under the influence of alcohol or drugs	0.5	0.8	1.6	4.6	7.5
Total involved in production deviance					65.4
Hospital Sector (N=4,111)					
Take a long lunch or break without approval	8.5	13.5	17.4	17.8	57.2
Come to work late or leave early	1	3.5	9.6	14.9	29
Use sick leave when not sick	0	0.2	5.7	26.9	32.8
Do slow or sloppy work	0.2	0.8	4.1	5.9	11
Work under the influence of alcohol or drugs	0.1	0.3	0.6	2.2	3.2
Total involved in production deviance					69.2
Manufacturing Sector (N=1,497)					
Take a long lunch or break without approval	18	23.5	22	8.5	72
Come to work late or leave early	1.9	9	19.4	13.8	44.1
Use sick leave when not sick	0	0.2	9.6	28.6	38.4
Do slow or sloppy work	0.5	1.3	5.7	5	12.5
Work under the influence of alcohol or drugs	1.1	1.3	3.1	7.3	12.8
Total involved in production deviance					82.2

Adapted from Richard C. Hollinger, John P. Clark, *Theft by Employees*, Lexington: Lexington Books, 1983. p45.

INCOME AND THEFT

In order to empirically test whether economics had an effect on the level of theft, the researchers sorted their data by household income, under the theory that lower levels of income might produce higher levels of theft. However, they were unable to confirm such a statistical relationship. This would tend to indicate—at least in this study—that real income is not a predictor of employee theft.

Despite this finding, Hollinger and Clark were able to confirm that there was a statistical relationship between employees' *concern* over their financial situation and the level of theft. They presented the employees with a list of eight major concerns, ranging from personal health to education issues to financial problems. They noted, "Being concerned about finances and being under financial pressure are not necessarily the same. However, if a respondent considered his or her finances as one of the most important issues, that concern could be partially due to 'unsharable (sic) economic problems,' or it could also be that current realities are not matching one's financial aspirations regardless of the income presently being realized."[44]

The researchers discovered that "in each industry, the results are significant, with higher theft individuals more likely to be concerned about their finances, particularly those who ranked finances as the first or second most important issue."[45]

AGE AND THEFT

Hollinger and Clark found in their research a direct correlation between age and the level of theft. "Few other variables ... have exhibited such a strong relationship to theft as the age of the employee."[46] The reason, they concluded, was that the younger employee generally has less tenure with his organization and therefore has a lower level of commitment to it than the typical older employee. In addition, there is a long history of connection between youth and many forms of crime. Sociologists have suggested that the central process of control is determined by a person's "commitment to conformity." Under this model — assuming employees are all subject to the same deviant motives and opportunities — the probability of deviant involvement depends on the stakes that one has in conformity. Since younger employees tend to be less committed to the idea of conforming to established social rules and structures, it follows that they would be more likely to engage in illegal conduct that runs contrary to organizational and societal expectations.

The researchers suggested that the policy implications arising from the commitment to conformity theory are that, rather than subjecting employees to draconian security measures, "companies should afford younger workers many of the same rights, fringes, and privileges of the tenured, older employees. In fact, by signaling to the younger employee that he or she is temporary or expendable, the organization inadvertently may be encouraging its own victimization by the very group of employees that is already least committed to the expressed goals and objectives of the owners and managers."[47] Although this may indeed affect the level of employee dissatisfaction, its policy implications may not be practical for non-fraud-related reasons.

---

[44] Hollinger and Clark, p. 67.
[45] Hollinger and Clark, p. 57.
[46] Hollinger and Clark, p. 57.
[47] Hollinger and Clark, p. 67.

POSITION AND THEFT

Hollinger and Clark were able to confirm a direct relationship between an employee's position and the level of the theft. As might be expected, theft levels were higher in jobs with greater access to the things of value in the organization. Although they found obvious connections between opportunity and theft (for example, retail cashiers with daily access to cash had the highest incidence), the researchers believed opportunity to be ". . . only a secondary factor that constrains the manner in which the deviance is manifested."[48] Their research indicated that job satisfaction was the primary motivator of employee theft; the employee's position only affects the method and amount of the theft *after* the decision to steal has already been made.

JOB SATISFACTION AND DEVIANCE

The research of Hollinger and Clark strongly suggests that employees who are dissatisfied with their jobs —across all age groups but especially younger workers— are the most likely to seek redress through counterproductive or illegal behavior in order to right the perceived "inequity." Other writers, notably anthropologist Gerald Mars and researcher David Altheide, have commented on this connection. Mars observed that among both hotel dining room employees and dock workers it was believed that pilferage was not theft, but was "seen as a morally justified addition to wages; indeed, as an entitlement due from exploiting employers."[49] Altheide also documented that theft is often perceived by employees as a "way of getting back at the boss or supervisor."[50] Jason Ditton documented a pattern in U.S. industries called "wages in kind," in which employees "situated in structurally disadvantaged parts [of the organization] receive large segments of their wages invisibly."[51]

ORGANIZATIONAL CONTROLS AND DEVIANCE

Hollinger and Clark were unable to document a strong relationship between control and deviance in their research. They examined five different control mechanisms: company policy, selection of personnel, inventory control, security, and punishment.

Company policy can be an effective control. Hollinger and Clark pointed out that companies with a strong policy against absenteeism have less of a problem with it. As a result, they would expect policies governing employee theft to have the same impact. Similarly, they

---

[48] Hollinger and Clark, p. 68.
[49] Hollinger and Clark, p. 77.
[50] Hollinger and Clark, p. 86.
[51] Hollinger and Clark, p. 86.

believed employee education as an organizational policy has a deterrent effect. Control through selection of personnel is exerted by hiring persons who will conform to organizational expectations. Inventory control is required not only for theft, but for procedures to detect errors, avoid waste, and ensure a proper amount of inventory is maintained. Security controls involve proactive and reactive measures, surveillance, internal investigations, and others. Control through punishment is designed to deter the specific individual, plus those who might be tempted to act illegally.

Hollinger and Clark interviewed numerous employees in an attempt to determine their attitudes toward control. Employees in the study perceived, in general, that computerized inventory records added security and made theft more difficult. With respect to security control, the researchers discovered that the employees regarded the purpose of a security division as taking care of outside—rather than inside—security. Few of the employees were aware that security departments investigate employee theft, and most such departments had a poor image among the workers. With respect to punishment, the employees interviewed felt theft would result in job termination in a worst-case scenario. They perceived that minor thefts would be handled by reprimands only.

Hollinger and Clark concluded that formal organizational controls provide both good and bad news. "The good news is that employee theft does seem to be susceptible to control efforts . . . . Our data also indicate, however, that the impact of organizational controls is neither uniform nor very strong. In sum, formal organizational controls do negatively influence theft prevalence, but these effects must be understood in combination with the other factors influencing this phenomenon."[52]

EMPLOYEE PERCEPTION OF CONTROL

The researchers also examined the perception—not necessarily the reality—of employees believing they would be caught if they committed theft. "We find that perceived certainty of detection is inversely related to employee theft for respondents in all three industry sectors—that is, the stronger the perception that theft would be detected, the less the likelihood that the employee would engage in deviant behavior."[53]

---

[52] Hollinger and Clark, p. 106.
[53] Hollinger and Clark, p. 117.

This finding is significant and consistent with other research. It suggests that increasing the perception of detection may be the best way to deter employee theft while increasing the sanctions that are imposed on occupational fraudsters will have a limited effect. Recall that under Cressey's model, embezzlers are motivated to commit illegal acts because they face some financial problem that they cannot share with others because it would threaten their status. It follows that the greatest threat to the perpetrator would be that he might be caught in the act of stealing because that would bring his non-shareable problem out into the open. The possibility of sanctions is only a secondary concern. The perpetrator engages in the illegal conduct only because he perceives there is an opportunity to fix his financial problem *without getting caught.* Therefore, if an organization can increase in its employees' minds the perception that illegal acts will be detected, it can significantly deter occupational fraud. Put simply, occupational fraudsters are not deterred by the threat of sanctions because they do not plan on getting caught.

Control in the workplace, according to Hollinger and Clark, consists of both formal and informal social controls. Formal controls can be described as external pressures that are applied through both positive and negative sanctions; informal controls consist of the internalization by the employee of the group norms of the organization. These researchers, along with a host of others, have concluded that—as a general proposition—informal social controls provide the best deterrent. "These data clearly indicate that the loss of respect among one's acquaintances was the single most effective variable in predicting future deviant involvement." Furthermore, ". . . in general, the probability of suffering informal sanction is far more important than fear of formal sanctions in deterring deviant activity."[54] Again, this supports the notion that the greatest deterrent to the fraudster is the idea that he will be caught, not the threat of punishment by his employer.

OTHER CONCLUSIONS

Hollinger and Clark reached several other conclusions based on their work. First, they found that "substantially increasing the internal security presence does not seem to be appropriate, given the prevalence of the problem. In fact, doing so may make things worse." Second, they concluded that the same kinds of employees who engage in other workplace deviance are also principally the ones who engage in employee theft. They found persuasive evidence that slow or sloppy workmanship, sick-leave abuses, long coffee breaks, alcohol and drug

---

[54] Hollinger and Clark, p. 121.

use at work, coming in late and/or leaving early were more likely to be present in the employee-thief.

Third, the researchers hypothesized that if efforts are made to reduce employee theft without reducing its underlying causes (e.g., employee dissatisfaction, lack of ethics), the result could create a "hydraulic effect." That is, tightening controls over property deviance may create more detrimental acts affecting the productivity of the organization—if we push down employee theft, that action may push up goldbricking. Fourth, they asserted that increased management sensitivity to its employees will reduce all forms of workplace deviance. Fifth, they concluded special attention should be afforded young employees, as these are the ones statistically the most likely to steal. However, it must be pointed out that although the incidence of theft is higher among younger employees, the losses associated with those thefts are typically lower than losses caused by more senior employees who have greater financial authority.

Hollinger and Clark asserted that management must pay attention to four aspects of policy development: (1) a clear understanding regarding theft behavior, (2) continuous dissemination of positive information reflective of the company's policies, (3) enforcement of sanctions, and (4) publicizing the sanctions.

The researchers summed up their observations by saying, "perhaps the most important overall policy implication that can be drawn . . . is that theft and workplace deviance are in large part a reflection of how management at all levels of the organization is perceived by the employee. Specifically, if the employee is permitted to conclude that his or her contribution to the workplace is not appreciated or that the organization does not seem to care about the theft of its property, we expect to find greater involvement. In conclusion, a lowered prevalence of employee theft may be one valuable consequence of a management team that is responsive to the current perceptions and attitudes of its workforce."[55]

2004 Report to the Nation on Occupational Fraud and Abuse

Occupational fraud and abuse is a widespread problem that affects practically every organization, regardless of size, location, or industry. The Association of Certified Fraud Examiners has made it a goal to better educate the public and anti-fraud professionals about this threat. In 1996, we released the first *Report to the Nation on Occupational Fraud and Abuse,*

---

[55] Hollinger and Clark, p. 144.

the largest known privately funded study on the subject. The stated goals of that report were to:
- Summarize the opinions of experts on the percentage and amount of organizational revenue lost to all forms of occupational fraud and abuse
- Examine the characteristics of the employees who commit occupational fraud and abuse
- Determine what kinds of organizations are victims of occupational fraud and abuse
- Categorize the ways in which serious fraud and abuse occurs

In 2002 we issued our second *Report to the Nation*. Like the first Report, the 2002 edition was also based on detailed case information supplied by CFEs, but this report expanded on the first. In 2002 we revised our survey instrument to gather more useful information on the specific methods used to commit occupational fraud. We also gathered information on the legal dispositions of the cases, which had not been included in the 1996 *Report*.

Like the fight against fraud, the task of gathering meaningful information about fraud is an arduous and ongoing process. With each successive edition of the *Report to the Nation*, it is our goal to provide, better, more accurate, and more useful information.

In the 2004 edition of the Report, we again expanded its scope. Our 2004 survey of CFEs was designed to gather the same key information that was present in the first two *Reports to the Nation*, but in this edition we added key questions on methods of detection and the effectiveness of anti-fraud controls in limiting fraud losses. We also added more demographic questions on the perpetrators and victims of occupational fraud to give us an even better picture of who commits fraud and who suffers from it.

The result of these changes is what we believe to be the most complete and useful edition of the *Report to the Nation* to date. The information contained in this Report should be of great value to anti-fraud practitioners everywhere. It also should offer stark lessons and valuable insights to any organization concerned with limiting its exposure to occupational fraud and abuse.

Copies of the entire *Report to the Nation* can be downloaded or viewed at no charge on the ACFE's website, www.CFEnet.com.

Types of Organizations

The following chart shows the distribution of frauds in our survey, based on the type of organization that was victimized. Most of the frauds occurred in privately held or publicly traded companies, although government agencies and not-for-profit organizations were well represented.

Privately held companies in our study suffered the largest median losses, followed by public companies and not-for-profit organizations. Government agencies had the lowest median losses by far, at $37,500 per scheme.

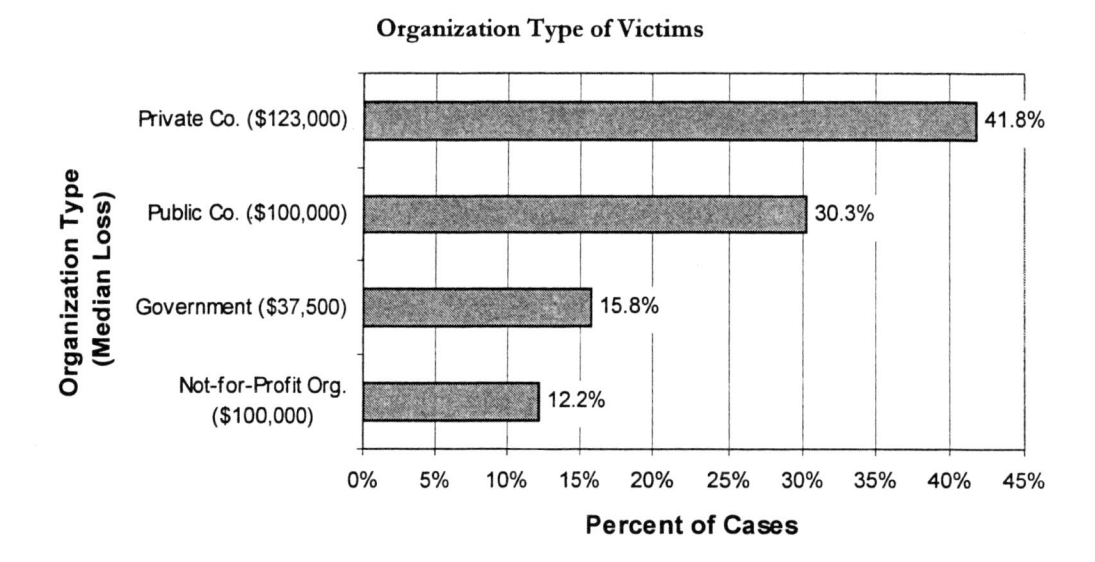

Organization Type of Victims

Organization Type (Median Loss)	Percent of Cases
Private Co. ($123,000)	41.8%
Public Co. ($100,000)	30.3%
Government ($37,500)	15.8%
Not-for-Profit Org. ($100,000)	12.2%

SMALL ORGANIZATIONS SUFFERED DISPROPORTIONATELY LARGE LOSSES

Approximately 46% of the frauds in our study attacked small businesses, which we define as organizations that employ fewer than 100 people. Given their relative size, the impact on small businesses from the occupational frauds in our survey was much greater than the impact on larger companies. The median loss in small companies was $98,000. Only the largest organizations – those with 10,000 or more employees – suffered greater losses.

Percent of Cases Based on Size of Victim Organization

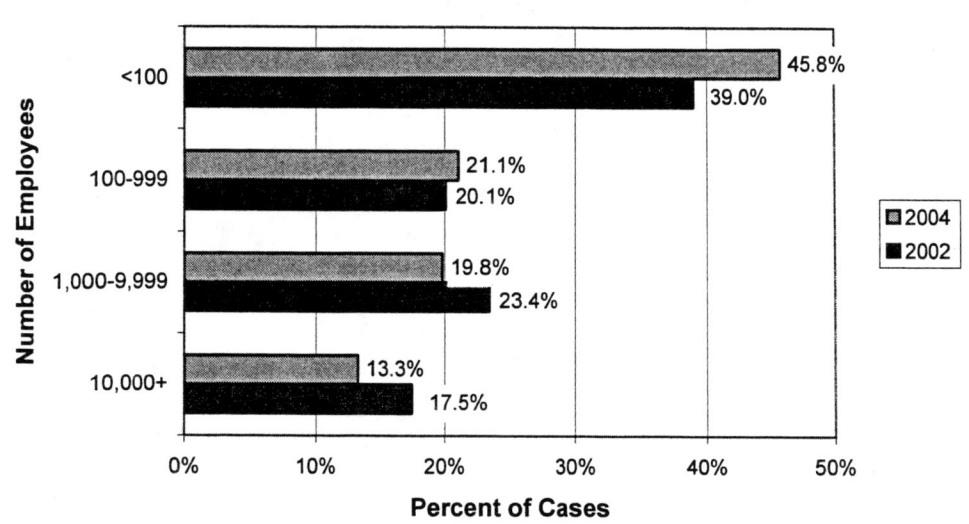

Number of Employees	2004	2002
<100	45.8%	39.0%
100-999	21.1%	20.1%
1,000-9,999	19.8%	23.4%
10,000+	13.3%	17.5%

Median Loss Based on Size of Victim Organization

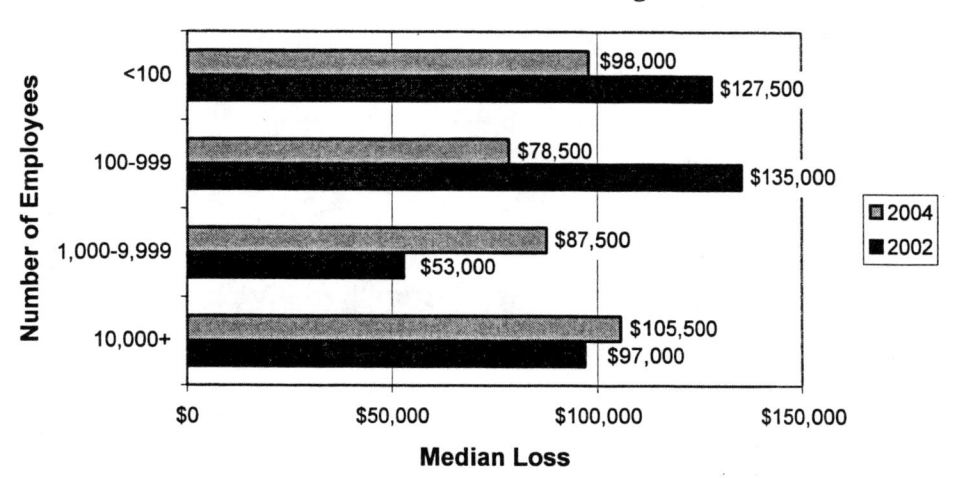

Number of Employees	2004	2002
<100	$98,000	$127,500
100-999	$78,500	$135,000
1,000-9,999	$87,500	$53,000
10,000+	$105,500	$97,000

Measuring the Cost of Occupational Fraud

Determining the true cost of occupational fraud and abuse is most likely an impossible task. Because fraud is a crime based on concealment, organizations often do not know when they are being victimized. Many frauds are never detected, or are only caught after they have gone on for several years. Furthermore, many frauds that are detected are never reported for a variety of reasons, and those frauds that are reported are often not prosecuted. Finally, there is no agency or organization that is specifically charged with gathering comprehensive fraud-related information. All of these factors combine to make any estimate of the total cost of occupational fraud just that – an estimate.

In our study we asked CFEs to give us their best estimate of the percent of revenues a typical organization in the U.S. loses in a given year as a result of occupational fraud (for government agencies, we asked what percent of the annual budget was lost). The answers to this question were based on the opinions of CFEs, not specific data from the cases they had reported. But keep in mind that our body of respondents was made up of experts in fraud prevention and detection, with 16 years' median experience in the field. Given the obstacles to developing meaningful data on the overall costs of fraud, this may be as reliable a source as is available.

The median response among the CFEs we surveyed was that the typical organization loses 6% of its annual revenues to occupational fraud, the same result we obtained from our studies in 1996 and 2002. This is a staggering figure. If multiplied by the U.S. Gross Domestic Product, which in 2003 totaled just under $11 trillion, it would translate into $660 billion in annual fraud losses.

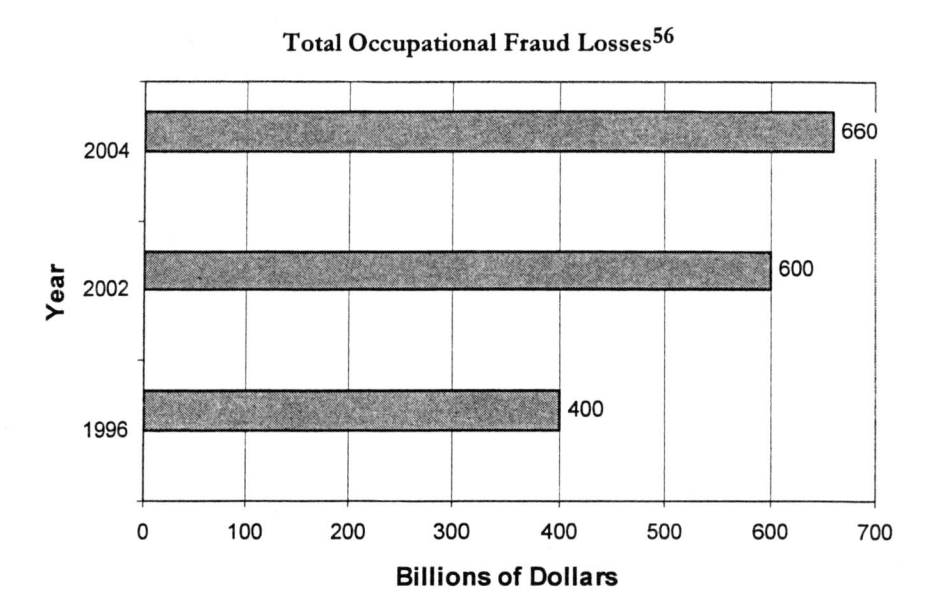

Total Occupational Fraud Losses[56]

Year	Billions of Dollars
2004	660
2002	600
1996	400

DISTRIBUTION OF DOLLAR LOSSES

There were 487 cases in our study in which the respondent was able to specify the amount of loss suffered by the victim organization. The median loss for all cases in the study was $100,000. As the following distribution shows, 15% of the frauds in our study caused losses

---

[56] Dollar figures are based on an estimated 6% loss of annual revenues to fraud, multiplied by Annual U.S. Gross Domestic Product.

of at least $1 million, while one in five cost at least $500,000. This distribution was very similar to the one in our 2002 Report.

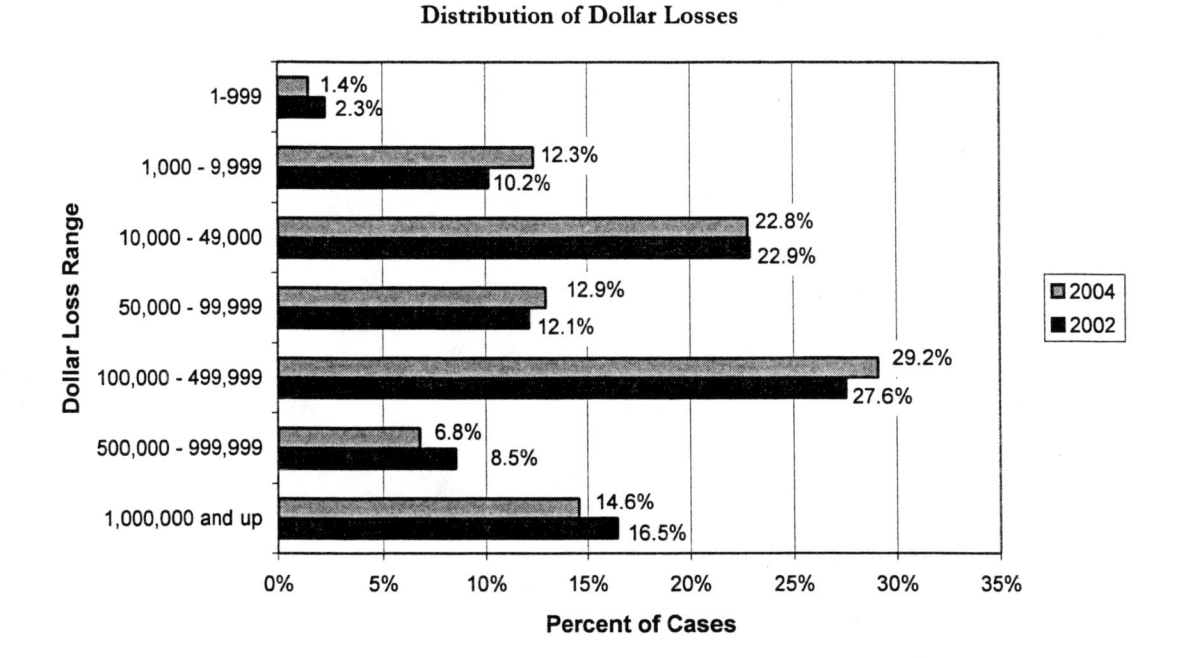

Distribution of Dollar Losses

Dollar Loss Range	2004	2002
1-999	1.4%	2.3%
1,000 - 9,999	12.3%	10.2%
10,000 - 49,000	22.8%	22.9%
50,000 - 99,999	12.9%	12.1%
100,000 - 499,999	29.2%	27.6%
500,000 - 999,999	6.8%	8.5%
1,000,000 and up	14.6%	16.5%

Percent of Cases

How Occupational Fraud Is Committed

One of the major goals of this Report was to classify each fraud according to the methods used by the perpetrator. This gives us a better understanding of how fraud is committed and the types of schemes that tend to produce the largest losses. Also, by breaking down occupational frauds into distinct categories, we are better able to study their common characteristics, which in turn assists in the development of better anti-fraud tools. Accordingly, every fraud in our study was classified according to the *Occupational Fraud Classification System* (commonly known as the Fraud Tree), which is discussed in the Financial Transactions section of this Manual.

As was first stated in the *1996 Report to the Nation*, all occupational frauds fall into one of three major categories:

- **Asset misappropriations**, which involve the theft or misuse of an organization's assets. (Common examples include skimming revenues, stealing inventory, and payroll fraud.)
- **Corruption**, in which fraudsters wrongfully use their influence in a business transaction in order to procure some benefit for themselves or another person, contrary to their duty to their employer or the rights of another. (Common examples include accepting kickbacks and engaging in conflicts of interest.)

- **Fraudulent statements**, which generally involve falsification of an organization's financial statements. (Common examples include overstating revenues and understating liabilities or expenses.)

Asset misappropriations were by far the most common of the three categories, occurring in over 90% of the cases we reviewed. However, these schemes had the lowest median loss, at $93,000. Conversely, fraudulent statements were the least commonly reported frauds (7.9%) but they had the highest median loss at $1,000,000. [57]

Methods of Fraud – All Occupational Frauds[58]

Category (Pct. Cases)	Median Loss
Fraud Stmt (7.9%)	$1,000,000
Corruption (30.1%)	$250,000
Asset Mis (92.7%)	$93,000

The median loss figure for fraudulent statements was much lower than we expected and was significantly lower than what was reported in our 2002 study. The reader must be cautioned that this does not necessarily indicate a declining trend in the costs associated with financial statement fraud. As indicated earlier, this report is based on a compilation of information from frauds investigated by CFEs. It was not intended to be a comprehensive study on financial statement frauds, and we were not necessarily working from a representative sample of those crimes. There were only 40 financial statement schemes reported in our survey, too few to draw a meaningful conclusion on the impact of all financial statement frauds. Furthermore, the losses caused by these schemes can vary wildly based on a number

---

[57] It should be noted that a number of cases involved aspects of more than one type of occupational fraud. For instance, several schemes involved both corruption and asset misappropriation. We were unable to subdivide the losses in cases where there were multiple schemes to show exactly how much of the loss was attributable to each of the component schemes. The same is true for the all charts in this report showing median loss based on scheme type.

[58] The sum of percentages in this chart exceeds 100% because a number of cases involved multiple schemes that fell into more than one category.

of factors related to the specific organization whose financials are falsified. Reports of recent scandals indicate that shareholders are still suffering massive losses due to financial statement fraud. While the median loss in our study was low, we still found that one in six financial statement fraud schemes cost its victims at least $10 million, with three cases generating at least $50 million in losses.

ASSET MISAPPROPRIATIONS – CASH VS. NON-CASH

As the previous chart illustrated, over 90% of the occupational fraud cases in our study involved the misappropriation of assets. Not surprisingly, the asset that was most frequently targeted was cash. Of 471 asset misappropriation cases we reviewed, 93% involved the misappropriation of cash, while only 22% involved misappropriation of non-cash assets. The median loss in the two categories was almost identical.

Breakdown of Asset Misappropriations[59]

Asset Targeted (Median Loss):
- Cash ($98,000): 93.4%
- Non-Cash ($100,000): 22.1%

Percent of Cases

CASH MISAPPROPRIATIONS

Out of 508 cases in our study, 440 cases (87%) involved some form of cash misappropriation. According to the Fraud Tree, cash frauds fall into one of three categories:

- **Fraudulent disbursements,** in which the perpetrator causes his organization to disburse funds through some trick or device. (Common examples include submitting false invoices or forging company checks.)
- **Skimming,** in which cash is stolen from an organization *before* it is recorded on the organization's books and records.

---

[59] The sum of percentages in this chart exceeds 100% because a number of cases involved the misappropriation of more than one type of asset.

- **Cash larceny**, in which cash is stolen from an organization *after* it has been recorded on the organization's books and records.

Approximately three-fourths of the cash frauds in our study involved some form of fraudulent disbursement, making this the most common category by far. Schemes that involved a fraudulent disbursement also had the highest median loss, at $125,000.

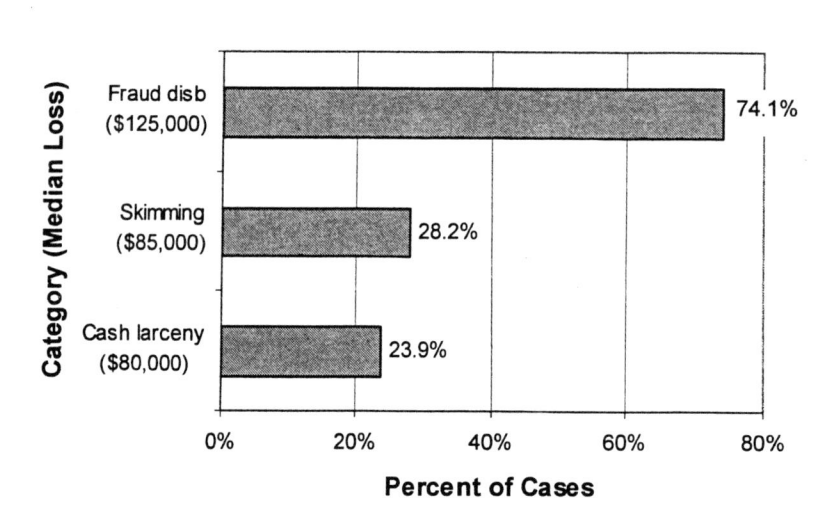

Breakdown of Cash Misappropriations[60]

Category (Median Loss)	Percent of Cases
Fraud disb ($125,000)	74.1%
Skimming ($85,000)	28.2%
Cash larceny ($80,000)	23.9%

FRAUDULENT DISBURSEMENTS

Approximately two-thirds of all the cases in our study (326 out of 508) involved some form of fraudulent disbursement. These schemes can generally be divided into five distinct subcategories:

- **Billing schemes**, in which a fraudster causes the victim organization to issue a payment by submitting invoices for fictitious goods or services, inflated invoices, or invoices for personal purchases.
- **Payroll schemes**, in which an employee causes the victim organization to issue a payment by making false claims for compensation.
- **Expense reimbursement schemes**, in which an employee makes a claim for reimbursement of fictitious or inflated business expenses.
- **Check tampering**, in which the perpetrator converts an organization's funds by forging or altering a check on one of the organization's bank accounts, or steals a check the organization has legitimately issued to another payee.

---

[60] The sum of percentages in this chart exceeds 100% because a number of cases involved multiple schemes that fell into more than one category.

- **Register disbursement schemes,** in which an employee makes false entries on a cash register to conceal the fraudulent removal of currency.

Just over half of the fraudulent disbursement cases in our study involved billing fraud, making this the most common type of fraudulent disbursement scheme. The highest median loss occurred in schemes involving check tampering.

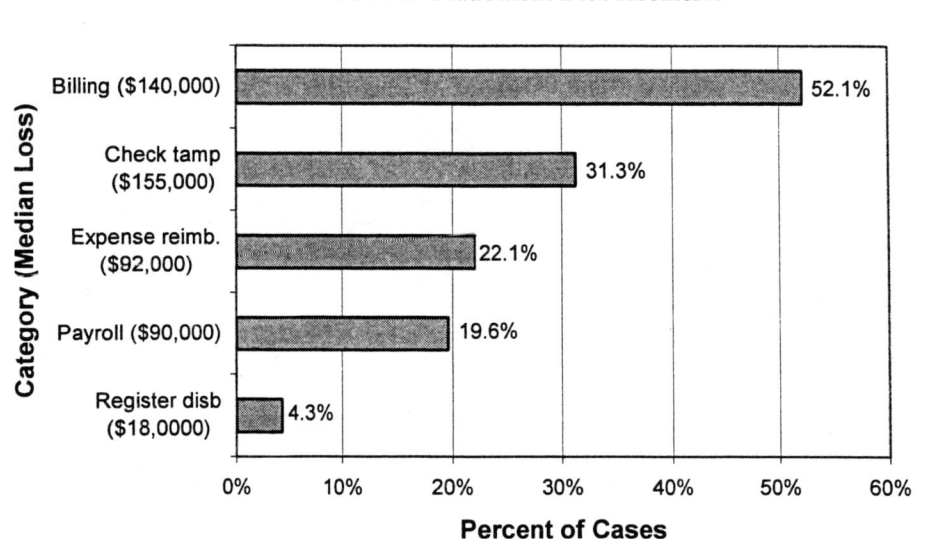

Breakdown of Fraudulent Disbursements[61]

Category (Median Loss)	Percent of Cases
Billing ($140,000)	52.1%
Check tamp ($155,000)	31.3%
Expense reimb. ($92,000)	22.1%
Payroll ($90,000)	19.6%
Register disb ($18,0000)	4.3%

COMPARISON OF ALL FRAUD CATEGORIES – 2002 AND 2004

The following table provides a comparison of the frequency and median loss data for all categories of occupational fraud in 2004 and 2002.

---

[61] The sum of percentages in this chart exceeds 100% because a number of cases involved multiple schemes that fell into more than one category.

Comparison of All Occupational Fraud Categories by 2004 and 2002 Data

Scheme Type	2004 Pct. Cases[62]	2004 Median Cost	2002 Pct. Cases	2002 Median Cost
Asset Misappropriations	**92.7**	**93,000**	**85.7**	**$80,000**
Cash Schemes	86.6	98,000	77.8	$80,000
Cash Larceny	20.7	80,000	6.9	$25,000
Skimming	24.4	85,000	24.7	$70,000
Fraudulent Disbursements	64.2	125,000	55.4	$100,000
Billing Schemes	33.5	140,000	25.2	$160,000
Payroll Schemes	12.6	90,000	9.8	$140,000
Expense Reimbursements	14.2	92,000	12.2	$60,000
Check Tampering	20.1	155,000	16.7	$140,000
Register Disbursements	2.8	18,000	1.7	$18,000
Non-Cash Misappropriations	20.5	100,000	9.0	$200,000
Corruption Schemes	**30.1**	**250,000**	**12.8**	**$530,000**
Fraudulent Statements	**7.9**	**1,000,000**	**5.1**	**$4,250,000**

Detecting Occupational Fraud

In any study of occupational fraud cases, perhaps the most important question that can be asked is, "How was the fraud detected?" After all, next to preventing fraud, the primary goal of any organization when it comes to this topic is to detect ongoing crimes as quickly as possible in order to minimize their negative impact. With this goal in mind, we sought to determine how the frauds in our study were initially detected by the organizations that were victimized. By studying how past frauds were identified, we hope to provide some guidance to organizations on how they can design their fraud detection efforts to catch future crimes.

Respondents were given a list of common means for detecting fraud, and were asked to identify how the frauds in their cases were initially discovered. As the following chart shows, the most common means of detection – by a wide margin – was through tips. The same was true in our 2002 study. We note that Section 301 of the Sarbanes-Oxley Act ("SOX") amends the Securities Exchange Act of 1934, requiring audit committees of publicly traded companies to establish procedures for "the confidential, anonymous submission by employees of the issuer of concerns regarding questionable accounting or auditing matters." This data, which suggests that tips are the most effective way to detect fraud, seems to support that mandate.

---

[62] Readers may note that the percentages in this column do not match the percentages in earlier charts. For instance, in this table skimming is shown to have occurred in 24.4% of cases in 2004, while in the chart entitled *Breakdown of Cash Misappropriations* skimming had a value of 28.2%. That is because this table shows percentages based on our entire pool of 508 schemes, whereas the other chart reflected the percentage of skimming schemes based on the pool of cash misappropriations.

Initial Detection of Occupational Frauds[63]

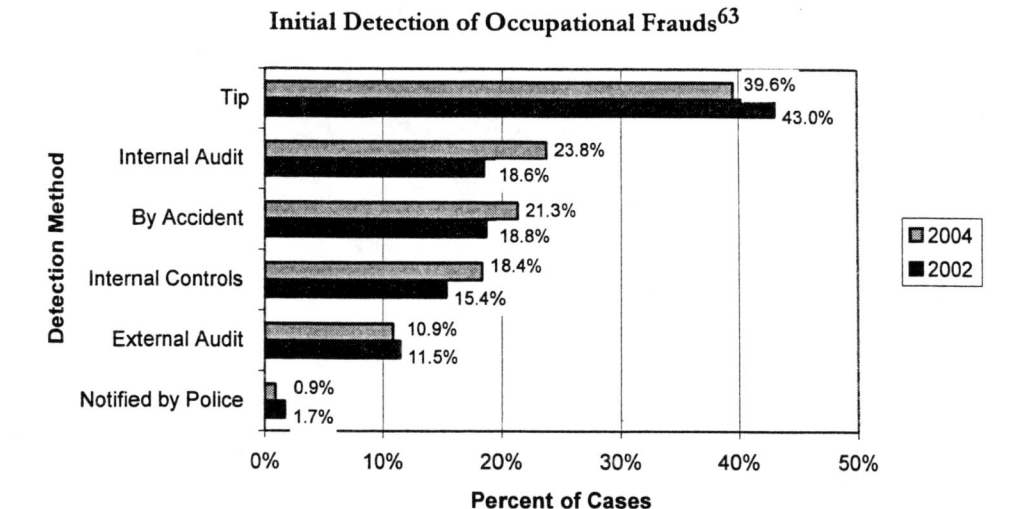

Detection Method	2004	2002
Tip	39.6%	43.0%
Internal Audit	23.8%	18.6%
By Accident	21.3%	18.8%
Internal Controls	18.4%	15.4%
External Audit	10.9%	11.5%
Notified by Police	0.9%	1.7%

The majority of tips in our study came from employees, but it is worth noting that tips from customers, vendors, and anonymous sources, were also common, each accounting for between 10 and 20% of all *tip* cases in 2004 and 2002.

Many organizations establish internal reporting mechanisms but fail to make these known or available to third parties such as customers and vendors who conduct business with the organization. It is often these third parties who are in the best position to see characteristics of occupational fraud. Although Section 301 of SOX only requires audit committees to establish procedures for confidential reporting by *employees*, our study clearly indicates that any effective reporting structure should be designed to reach out to customers, vendors, and other third party sources as well.

---

[63] The sum of percentages in this chart exceeds 100% because in some cases respondents identified more than one detection method.

Percent of Tips by Source[64]

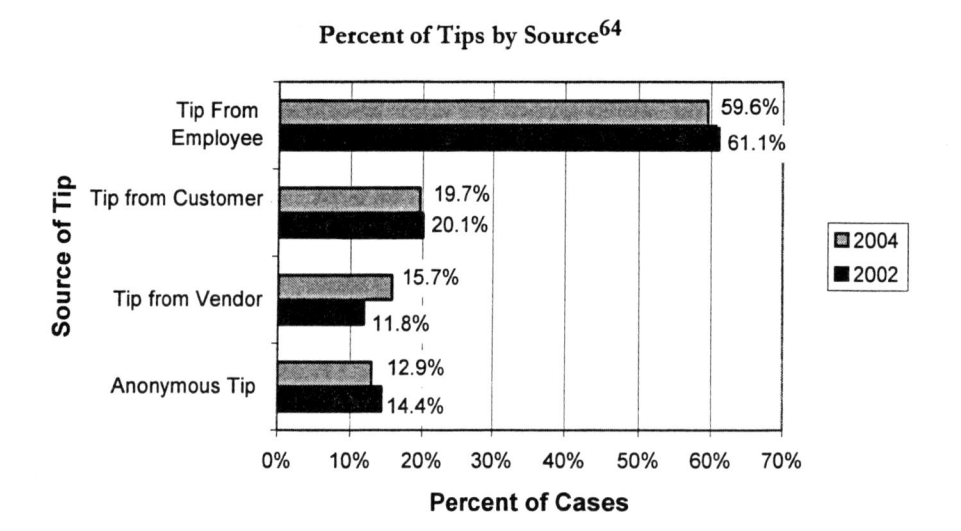

Source of Tip	2004	2002
Tip From Employee	59.6%	61.1%
Tip from Customer	19.7%	20.1%
Tip from Vendor	15.7%	11.8%
Anonymous Tip	12.9%	14.4%

Percent of Cases

DETECTING FRAUD BY OWNERS AND EXECUTIVES

Although the data from our survey strongly supports Sarbanes-Oxley's call for the establishment of anonymous reporting mechanisms, the information we gathered did not provide the same measure of support for the significant burden SOX (particularly Section 404) places on the function of internal controls as a fraud detection tool. Obviously, strong internal controls can have a significant impact on fraud and a well-designed control structure should be a priority in any comprehensive anti-fraud program. But as the chart showing *Initial Detection of Occupational Frauds* illustrates, internal controls placed fourth among the cases we reviewed – behind *accident* – in terms of the number of cases detected.

The limited effect of internal controls in detecting fraud was particularly evident when we measured the method of detection in cases committed by owners and executives. These schemes were the most costly in our study and they would be expected to be among the most difficult to detect, given the level of authority and the ability to override controls that owners and executives generally possess. Furthermore, under Section 302 of SOX, these cases must be disclosed to auditors and the audit committee regardless of whether they are material.

As the following chart shows, only 6% of the owner/executive cases were detected through internal controls, which was only one-third the rate for all cases. Of six detection methods that were tested, internal controls ranked fifth in owner/executive cases. On the other hand,

---

[64] The sum of percentages in this chart exceeds 100% because in some cases tips were received from more than one source.

over half of all owner/executive cases were initially discovered through a tip. This lends additional credence to SOX's mandate that audit committees establish internal reporting mechanisms such as hotlines.

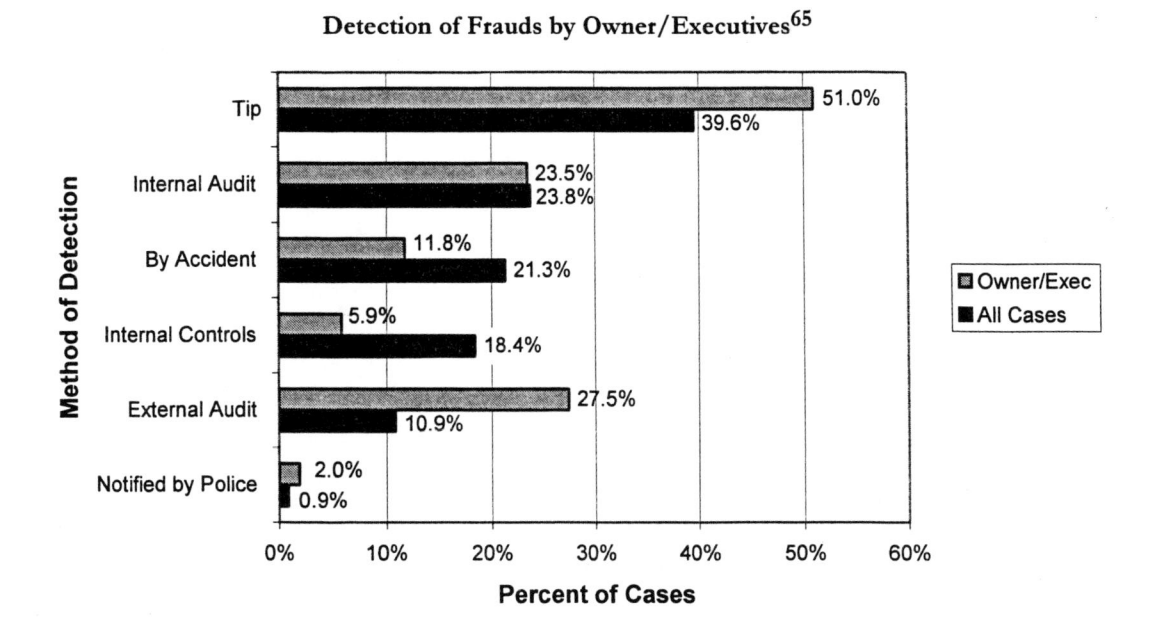

Detection of Frauds by Owner/Executives[65]

Method of Detection	Owner/Exec	All Cases
Tip	51.0%	39.6%
Internal Audit	23.5%	23.8%
By Accident	11.8%	21.3%
Internal Controls	5.9%	18.4%
External Audit	27.5%	10.9%
Notified by Police	2.0%	0.9%

DETECTING THE LARGEST FRAUDS

We also wanted to determine what methods of detection were most effective in high-dollar fraud cases. Limiting our review to the 71 cases in our study that caused losses of $1 million or more, we found that tips were again the most effective detection method, at 43%, which was slightly higher than the rate among all cases. Internal controls again faired poorly as a detection method, catching only 8% of the million-dollar cases in our study. External audits had a better rate of success among these high dollar frauds than among all cases, but they still only ranked fourth in terms of effectiveness, and they still lagged significantly behind internal audits in terms of catching high-dollar schemes.[66] External audits also trailed accidents in this category.

---

[65] The sum of percentages in this chart exceeds 100% because in some cases respondents identified more than one detection method.

[66] Of the 71 cases in our study exceeding $1 million in losses, we received 45 responses that specified the gross annual revenues of the victim organization at the time of the fraud. (This question only applied to commercial enterprises). Of these 45 cases, the loss caused by fraud appeared to exceed 5% of annual income (a common initial test for materiality) in 26 cases. Defining these frauds as "material", we found that only six of the 26 cases (23%) were detected by external audits. Narrowing this focus to "material" frauds that occurred in publicly traded companies, we encountered only five "material" fraud cases, none of which were identified by an external audit.

Detection Method for Million-Dollar Schemes[67]

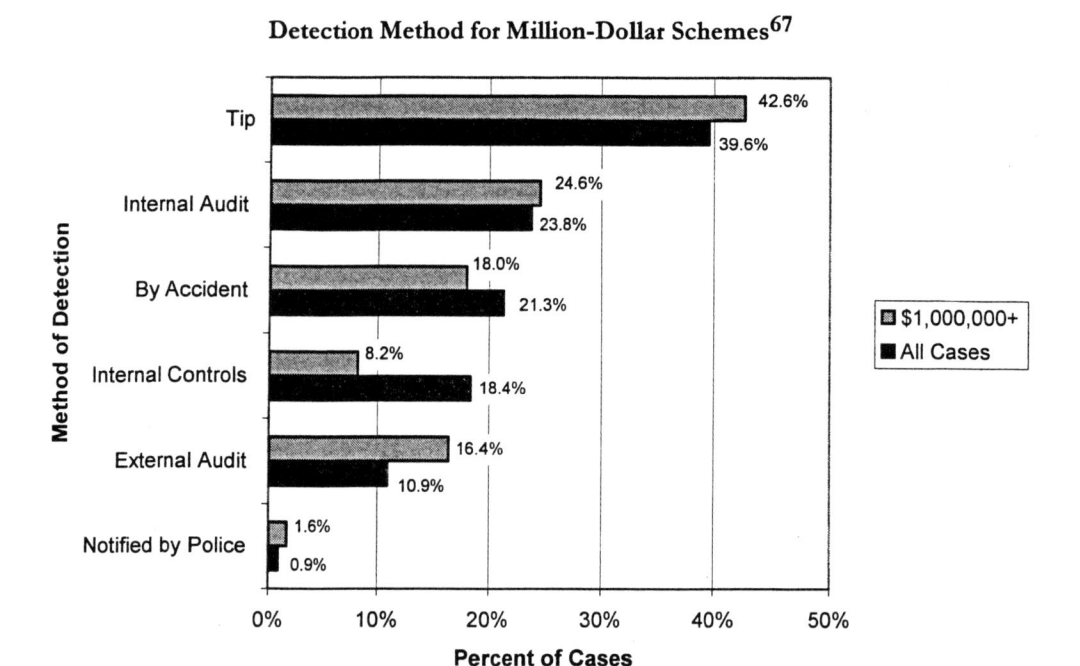

Method of Detection	$1,000,000+	All Cases
Tip	42.6%	39.6%
Internal Audit	24.6%	23.8%
By Accident	18.0%	21.3%
Internal Controls	8.2%	18.4%
External Audit	16.4%	10.9%
Notified by Police	1.6%	0.9%

Another way to measure the effectiveness of various detection methods in identifying large schemes is to measure the median loss in frauds based on how they were detected. When we ran this data, we found, to our surprise, that the median loss in schemes detected by *accident* was $140,000, which exceeded the median loss in all other categories. The fact that so many large frauds are detected by accident certainly implies that there is much more opportunity for organizations to reduce costs by proactively seeking out fraud and abuse.

The data in this chart also once again suggests that traditional internal controls do a poor job of catching large frauds. The median loss among schemes detected by internal controls was $40,000, which was less than half of the loss in the next-lowest category.

---

[67] The sum of percentages in this chart exceeds 100% because in some cases respondents identified more than one detection method.

Median Loss Based on Method of Detection

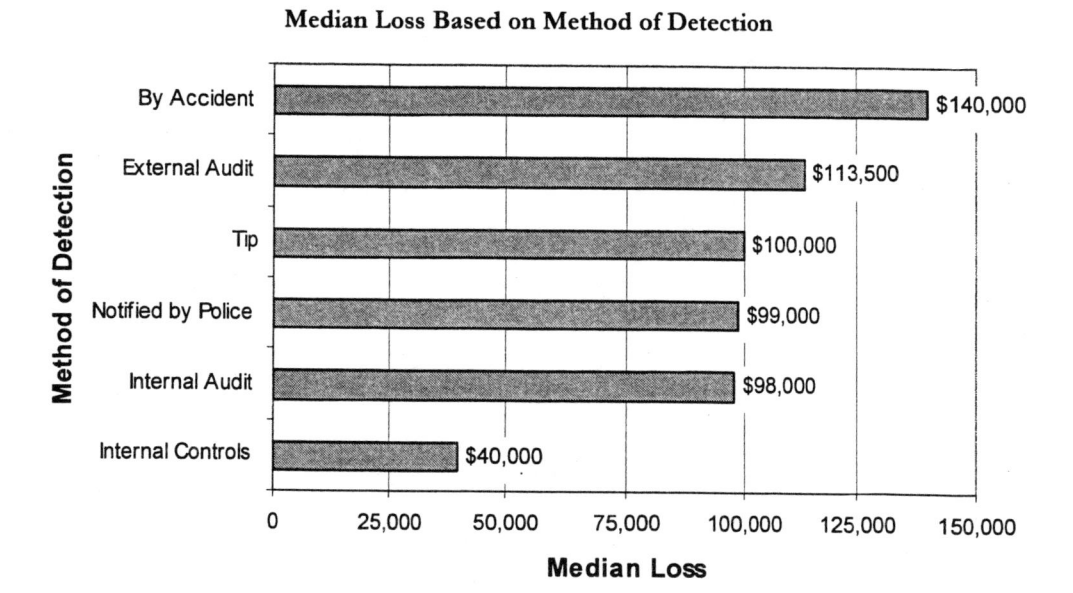

Method of Detection	Median Loss
By Accident	$140,000
External Audit	$113,500
Tip	$100,000
Notified by Police	$99,000
Internal Audit	$98,000
Internal Controls	$40,000

Limiting Fraud Losses

Respondents were asked whether the victim organizations in the cases they reviewed had certain anti-fraud measures in place at the time the frauds occurred. The three measures tested for were anonymous reporting mechanisms (typically hotlines), internal audit or fraud examination departments, and external audits. The following chart shows the percent of victim organizations that had adopted these measures at the time of their frauds. The numbers are very similar to the results from our 2002 survey.

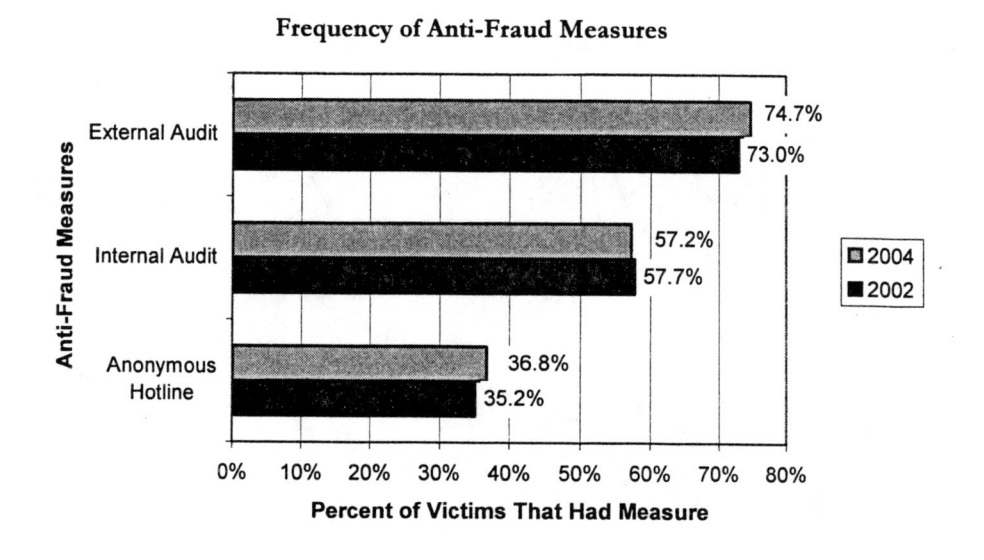

Frequency of Anti-Fraud Measures

Anti-Fraud Measures	2004	2002
External Audit	74.7%	73.0%
Internal Audit	57.2%	57.7%
Anonymous Hotline	36.8%	35.2%

ANONYMOUS FRAUD HOTLINES

In order to test the effectiveness of each anti-fraud control in limiting losses, we measured the median loss for organizations that had each control versus the median loss in organizations that did not. Using this test, we found that anonymous reporting mechanisms showed the greatest impact on fraud losses. Organizations that did not have reporting mechanisms suffered median losses that were over twice as high as organizations where anonymous reporting mechanisms had been established. This was consistent with the findings of our 2002 Report.

This result is also consistent with the data we gathered showing that the most common way for frauds to be discovered is through tips. Obviously, hotlines and other reporting mechanisms are designed to facilitate tips on wrongdoing. The fact that tips were the most common means of detection, combined with the fact that organizations which had reporting mechanisms showed the greatest reduction in fraud losses, indicates that this is an extremely valuable anti-fraud resource, and gives further support to Sarbanes-Oxley's mandate for confidential reporting mechanisms. As was discussed earlier, the effectiveness of these reporting mechanisms is significantly higher when they are made available to customers, vendors, and other third parties, not just employees. Organizations that rushed to implement employee hotlines to comply with Sarbanes-Oxley may not have incorporated those valuable additional sources of information.

Median Loss Based on Whether Organization Had Hotline

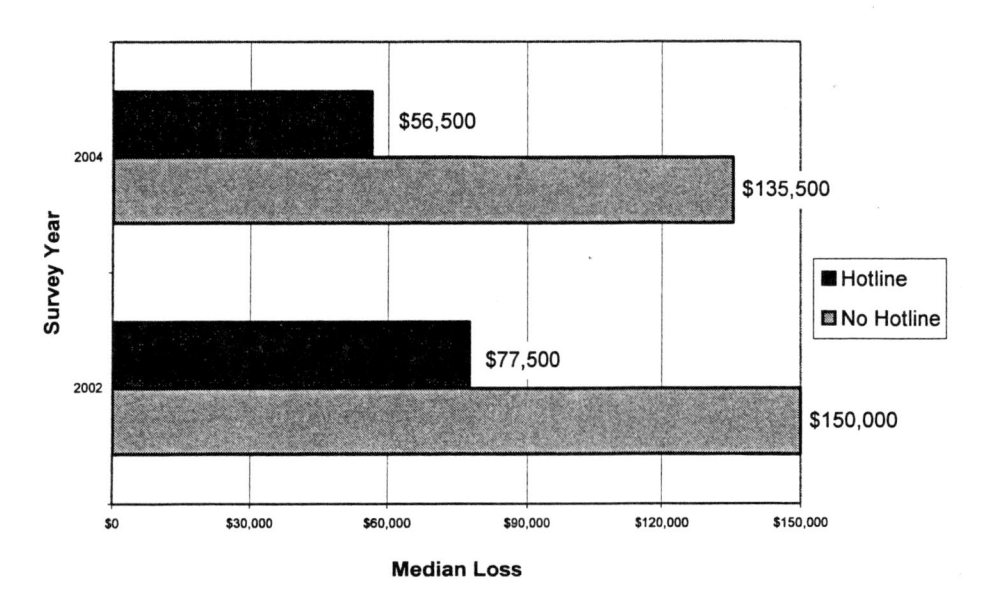

Survey Year	Hotline	No Hotline
2004	$56,500	$135,500
2002	$77,500	$150,000

Curiously, anonymous reporting mechanisms were the *least* common anti-fraud measure of the three we tested for. Only a little over one-third of victim organizations in our study had established anonymous reporting structures at the time they were victimized. Given the data from our study, we believe that anonymous hotlines and other reporting mechanisms provide real, measurable anti-fraud benefits, and given their relatively low cost compared to other anti-fraud controls, it would seem advisable for more organizations to implement them.

INTERNAL AUDITS

About 57% of the victim organizations in our study had internal audit or internal fraud examination departments. These organizations suffered a median loss of $80,000, compared with the median loss of $130,000 in organizations where there was no internal audit department.

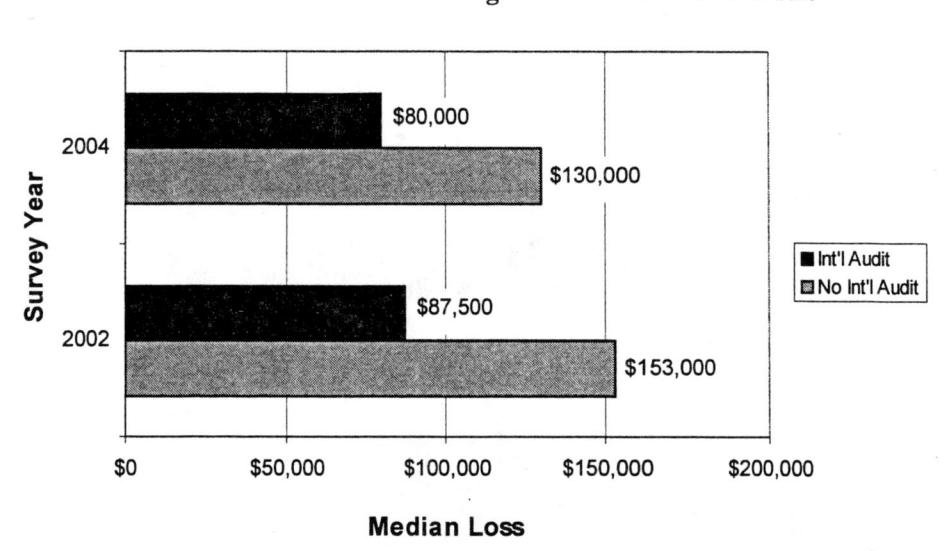

Median Loss Based on Whether Organization had Internal Audit

Survey Year	Int'l Audit	No Int'l Audit
2004	$80,000	$130,000
2002	$87,500	$153,000

The impact on fraud losses associated with internal audits was much greater than the impact associated with external audits (see below). Additionally, the data presented earlier on *Initial Detection of Occupational Frauds* shows that schemes were identified by internal audits at over twice the rate of external audits, despite the fact that victim organizations in our study were more likely to have external audits. The discrepancy between internal and external audits may be largely due to the fact that internal auditors generally are full-time employees of the victim organization, whereas external auditors spend a limited amount of time in a number of different organizations. In addition, external auditors are responsible only for detecting frauds that may have a material impact on the financial statements as a whole. Nevertheless, the discrepancies between the two disciplines suggest a need for greater fraud training for external auditors, particularly given the enhanced fraud detection responsibilities imposed on them by SAS No. 99.

EXTERNAL AUDITS

The most common anti-fraud measure among the victims in our study was the external audit. Seventy-five percent of victims employed outside auditors. However, the effectiveness of external audits in reducing fraud losses was not observable in our study. In fact, the median loss was actually *higher* in organizations that had external audits, as opposed to those that did not. Of course, there are several factors that contribute to the presence and size of fraud. But it was disappointing to find no trend indicating reduced losses as a result of external audits (such a trend did exist in 2002). The absence of a measurable impact as a result of external audits is consistent with the data we gathered on fraud detection, which showed that external audits generally ranked low – behind *accident* – as a means of catching fraud.

Median Loss Based on Whether Organization had External Audits

Survey Year	Ext'l Audit	No Ext'l Audit
2004	$100,000	$85,000
2002	$100,000	$140,000

The Perpetrators

The perpetrators of occupational fraud are those who use their positions within an organization for personal enrichment through the deliberate misuse or misapplication of the organization's resources or assets. In our survey, we asked respondents to provide detailed information about the perpetrators of the crimes they had investigated.[68] This data helps show how certain factors affect the nature of fraud and the size of losses inflicted upon victim organizations.

THE EFFECT OF THE PERPETRATOR'S POSITION

Generally speaking, the position a perpetrator holds within an organization will tend to have the most significant effect on the size of losses in a fraud scheme. As the level of authority for perpetrators rises, fraud losses rise correspondingly. This is borne out by the data in the following chart, which shows that the median loss in schemes involving owners and executives ($900,000) was more than six times as high as the median loss caused by managers, and more than 14 times as high as the median loss in schemes involving employees.

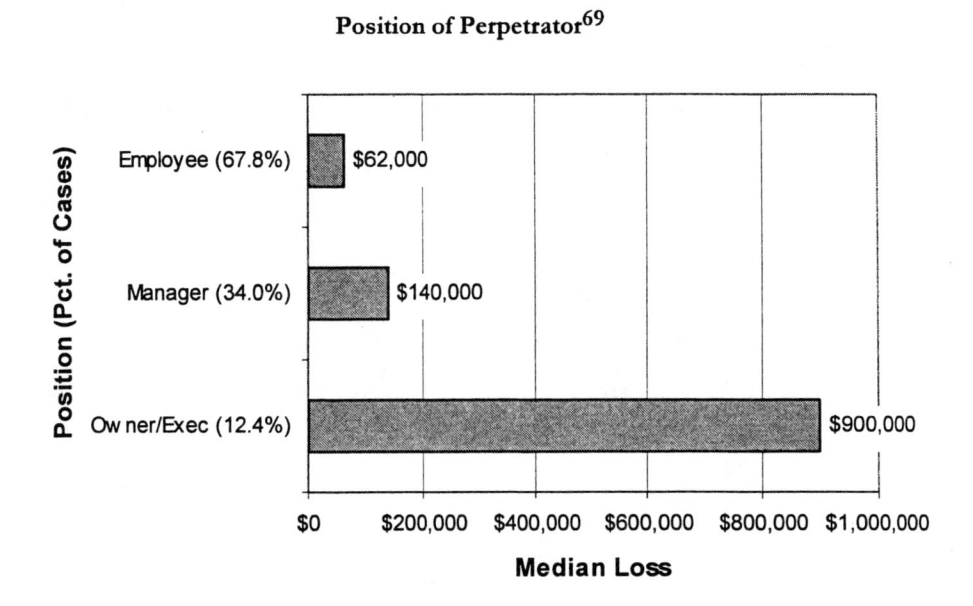

Position of Perpetrator[69]

Position (Pct. of Cases)	Median Loss
Employee (67.8%)	$62,000
Manager (34.0%)	$140,000
Owner/Exec (12.4%)	$900,000

THE PERPETRATOR'S ANNUAL INCOME

Similar to the data on position, the median loss in occupational fraud schemes generally increased as the perpetrator's annual income rose. Obviously, this information is influenced to a great deal by the perpetrator's position, since higher-level personnel would be expected to have higher salaries. There were very few cases in our study in which the perpetrator

---

[68] In cases where there was more than one perpetrator, respondents were asked to provide data on the "Principal Perpetrator," the person who was in charge of the scheme and in the respondent's view was the primary culprit.

[69] The sum of percentages in this chart exceeds 100% because some cases involved multiple perpetrators from more than one category.

earned more than $200,000 a year (just under 5%), but in these cases median losses exceeded $1,000,000.

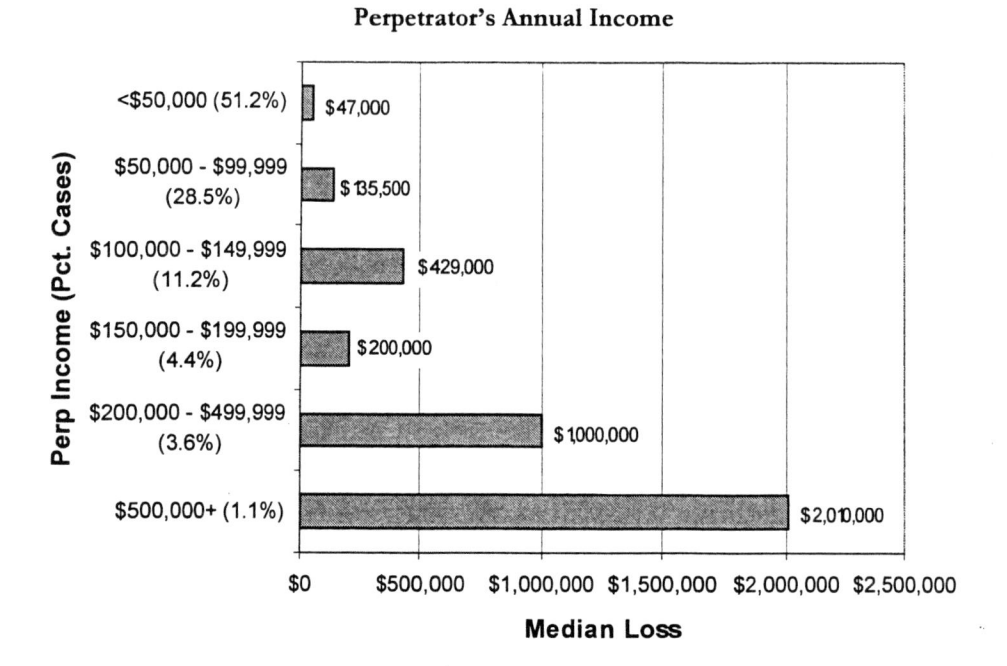

Perpetrator's Annual Income

Perp Income (Pct. Cases)	Median Loss
<$50,000 (51.2%)	$47,000
$50,000 - $99,999 (28.5%)	$135,500
$100,000 - $149,999 (11.2%)	$429,000
$150,000 - $199,999 (4.4%)	$200,000
$200,000 - $499,999 (3.6%)	$1,000,000
$500,000+ (1.1%)	$2,010,000

THE EFFECT OF TENURE

Similar to position, we found a direct correlation between the length of time a perpetrator had been employed with a victim organization and the size of the loss in the fraud scheme. This correlation most likely exists for two reasons: 1) the longer an employee works for an organization, the more likely he or she is to advance to higher levels of authority (see *position* data above); and 2) the longer an employee works for an organization, the greater degree of trust he or she will tend to engender from superiors and co-workers.

This second factor is significant because frauds are crimes that depend upon their victims' trust for success. The more reliance an organization places on an employee, the more autonomy and authority an employee receives, the greater the risk of fraud. This fact highlights the peculiar dichotomy of fraud: these crimes cannot succeed without trust, but neither can business. Employers must be able to delegate authority to employees and must be able to trust that their employees will act appropriately and in their organization's best interests, yet too much delegation, too much trust, creates an environment in which fraud can thrive. The key in any effective anti-fraud program is to strike the right balance between oversight and trust.

Tenure of Perpetrator

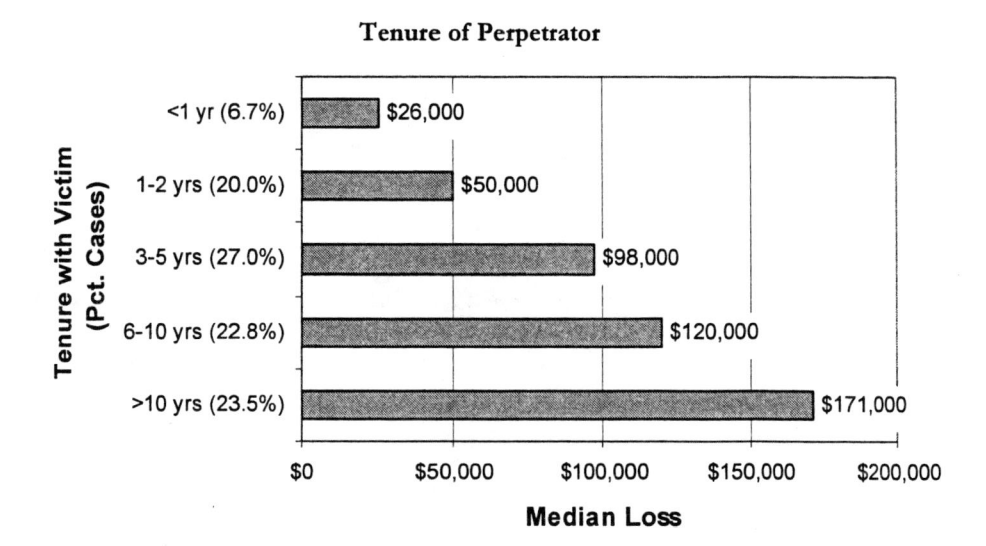

Tenure with Victim (Pct. Cases)	Median Loss
<1 yr (6.7%)	$26,000
1-2 yrs (20.0%)	$50,000
3-5 yrs (27.0%)	$98,000
6-10 yrs (22.8%)	$120,000
>10 yrs (23.5%)	$171,000

THE EFFECT OF GENDER

In our first occupational fraud study, conducted in 1996, men dominated the reported frauds, accounting for two thirds of the cases. Since then, that dominance has largely evaporated. In 2004 we found that the number of schemes was divided almost evenly between men and women, with only slightly more cases (52.9%) having been committed by men. Whatever strides women have made toward equality in the arena of occupational fraud were not evident when we compared median losses based on gender. Consistent with results from our earlier studies, the median loss in schemes committed by men remains significantly higher than the median loss in schemes committed by women, although the gap has narrowed somewhat from our 2002 results.

Because position appears to play such a strong role in determining the size of the loss in a fraud, we believe that the discrepancy in median loss for the two sexes most likely reflects the "glass ceiling" phenomenon, in which men tend to occupy more positions of high authority than women.

Gender of Perpetrator - Frequency

Gender	2004	2002
Male	52.9%	53.5%
Female	47.1%	46.5%

Gender of Perpetrator – Median Loss

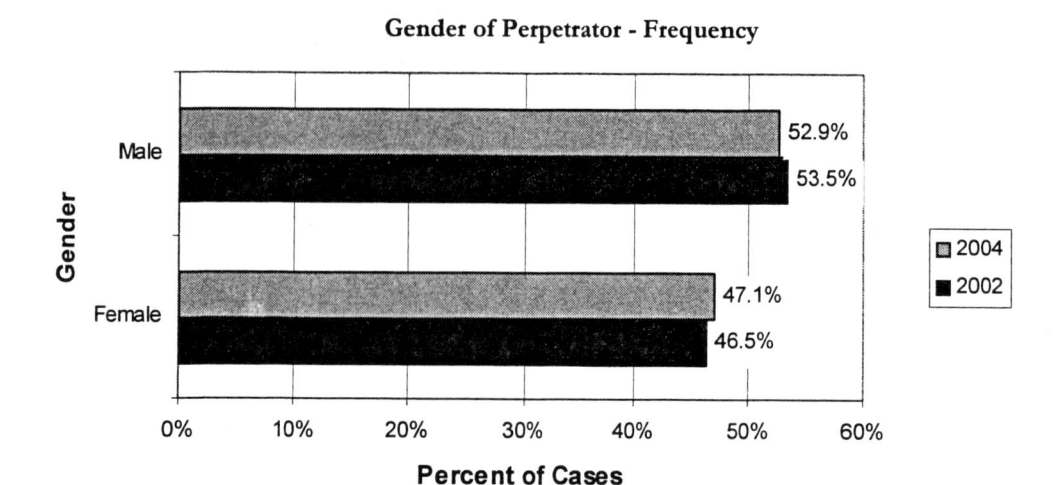

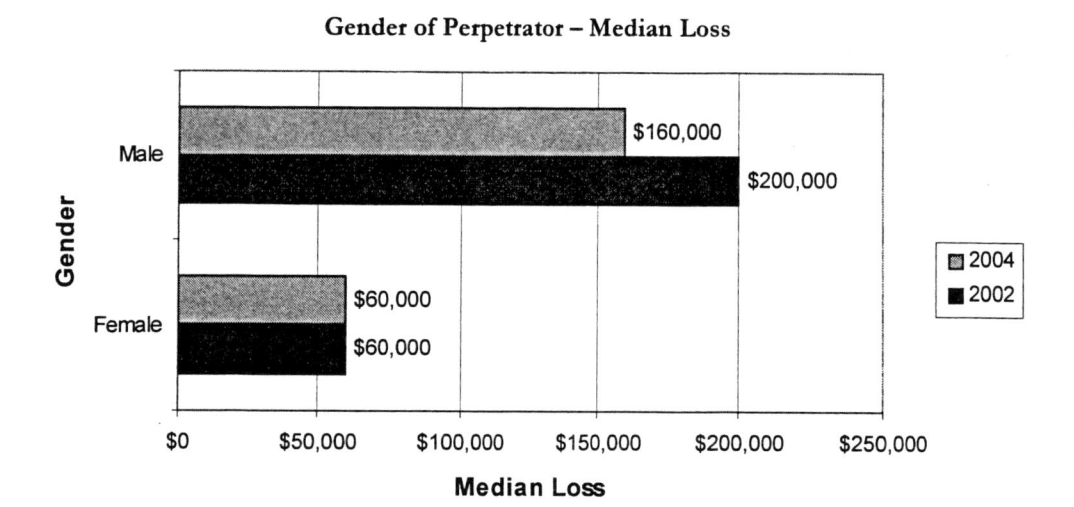

Gender	2004	2002
Male	$160,000	$200,000
Female	$60,000	$60,000

THE EFFECT OF AGE

There was a direct correlation in our study between the age of the perpetrator and the size of the median loss, a trend that was consistent with data from our 2002 Report. As with income, tenure, and gender, we believe age is most likely a secondary factor, typically reflective of the perpetrator's position in the organization. While there were only nine frauds in our study committed by persons over the age of 60, in those cases the median loss was $527,000, which was 29 times higher than the losses caused by the youngest perpetrators in our study.

Approximately half of the perpetrators in our study (49%) were over the age of 40, while only one in six (17%) were under the age of 30. This data runs counter to some studies that have suggested that younger employees are more likely to commit illegal acts.

Age of the Perpetrator - Frequency

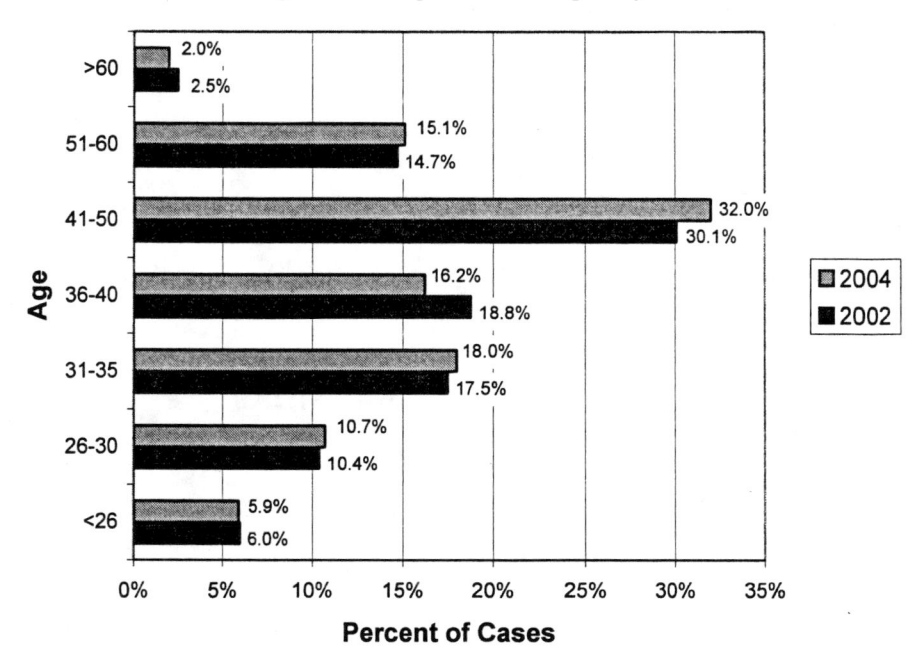

Age	2004	2002
>60	2.0%	2.5%
51-60	15.1%	14.7%
41-50	32.0%	30.1%
36-40	16.2%	18.8%
31-35	18.0%	17.5%
26-30	10.7%	10.4%
<26	5.9%	6.0%

Percent of Cases

Age of the Perpetrator – Median Loss

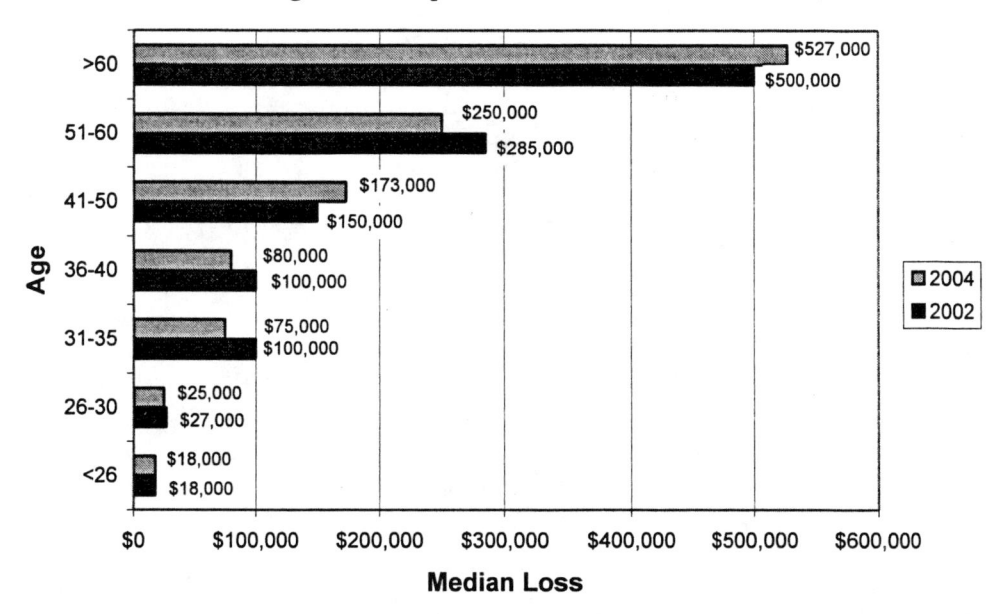

Age	2004	2002
>60	$527,000	$500,000
51-60	$250,000	$285,000
41-50	$173,000	$150,000
36-40	$80,000	$100,000
31-35	$75,000	$100,000
26-30	$25,000	$27,000
<26	$18,000	$18,000

Median Loss

THE EFFECT OF EDUCATION

Approximately half of the perpetrators in our study had no more than a high school education, while 42% had a bachelor's degree and 9% had a postgraduate degree. As the education level of the perpetrators rose, so did the losses they caused. The median loss in schemes committed by those with postgraduate degrees was $325,000, or 6.5 times larger than the median loss in schemes committed by those with a high school degree or less. This trend was to be expected given that those with higher levels of education tend to occupy higher positions and enjoy more authority within an organization. Curiously, this trend did not hold up in 2002, when we found that those with bachelor's degrees caused higher losses than those with postgraduate degrees.

Education of the Perpetrator - Frequency

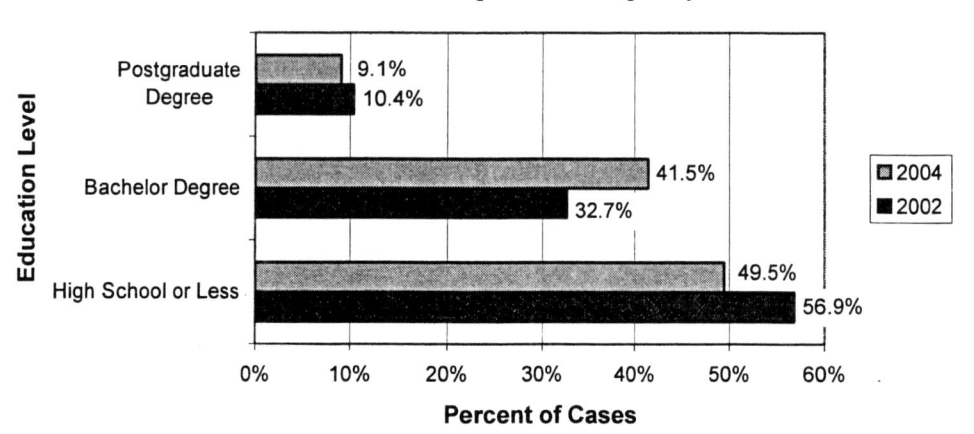

Education Level	2004	2002
Postgraduate Degree	9.1%	10.4%
Bachelor Degree	41.5%	32.7%
High School or Less	49.5%	56.9%

Education of the Perpetrator – Median Loss

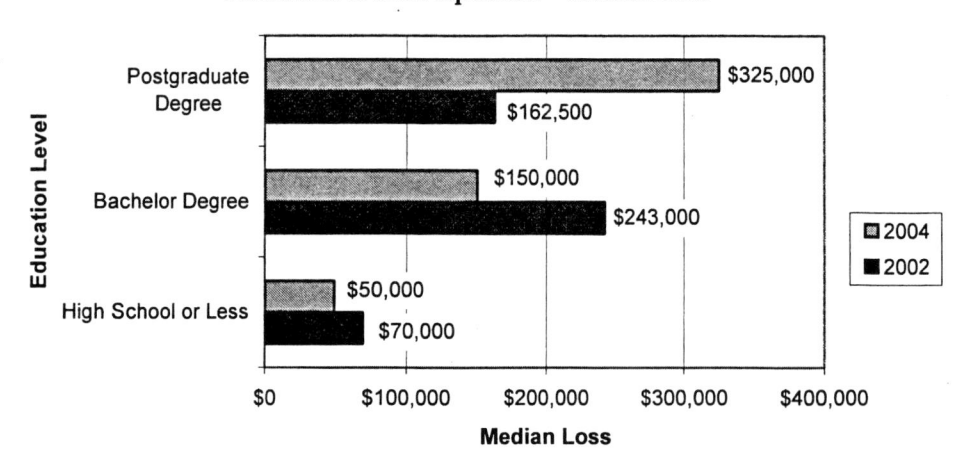

Education Level	2004	2002
Postgraduate Degree	$325,000	$162,500
Bachelor Degree	$150,000	$243,000
High School or Less	$50,000	$70,000

THE PERPETRATORS' CRIMINAL HISTORIES

As was the case in our previous studies, most of the perpetrators we encountered in this survey were first-time offenders. This finding is consistent with other studies, particularly the research of Dr. Donald Cressey, which suggests that most occupational fraudsters are not career criminals. There were 363 cases in which the respondent was able to provide information about the past criminal history of the perpetrator, and in 83% of those cases, the perpetrator had never been charged or convicted prior to the offense in question. This number actually reflected a slight decline from the results of our 2002 study. The number of perpetrators with prior convictions rose slightly, from 9% in 2002 to 12% in 2004.

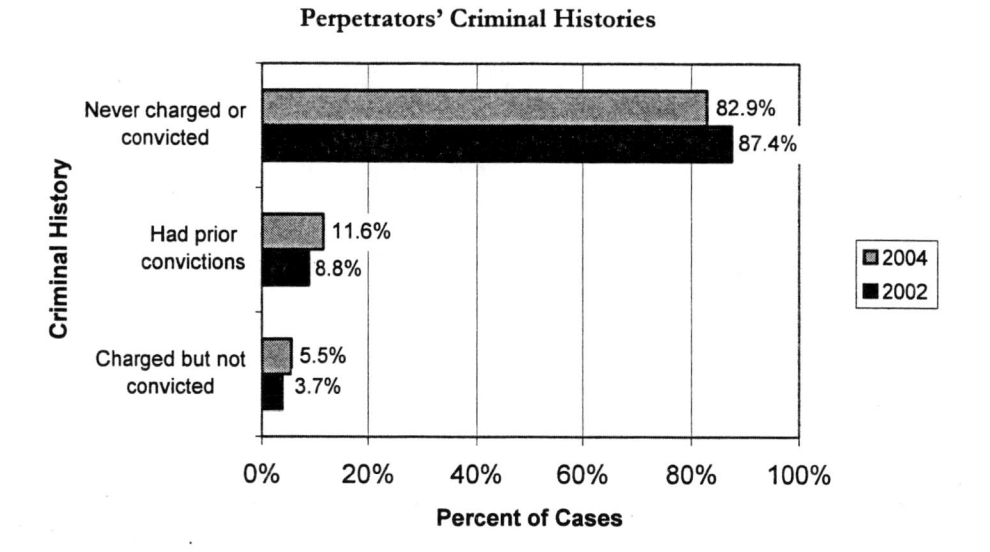

Perpetrators' Criminal Histories

Criminal History	2004	2002
Never charged or convicted	82.9%	87.4%
Had prior convictions	11.6%	8.8%
Charged but not convicted	5.5%	3.7%

Case Results

Respondents were asked to provide information on how the victim organizations dealt with perpetrators after they had caught them. There is a great deal of anecdotal evidence in the field suggesting that organizations are generally reluctant to prosecute fraud offenders; we sought to determine if that would be supported by the data in our study.

EMPLOYMENT ACTIONS TAKEN AGAINST FRAUDSTERS

When a person is caught defrauding his or her employer, the first and most immediate reaction by the victim organization will usually come in the form of an adverse employment action. We received 428 responses in which the CFE identified what adverse employment action was taken against the perpetrator. In 88% percent of cases, the victim organization fired the perpetrator.

This does not mean, however, that 12% of organizations retained the fraudsters. In many cases, the perpetrator quit or disappeared when it became apparent that his or her scheme was about to be discovered, before the victim organization had an opportunity to take action. Obviously, it would be very rare for an organization to retain an employee, manager, or officer after that person had defrauded the organization, although there are occasions where that occurs.

Adverse Employment Actions[70]

- Terminated: 87.9%
- Restitution: 22.9%
- No punish.: 6.5%
- Prob./susp.: 5.8%

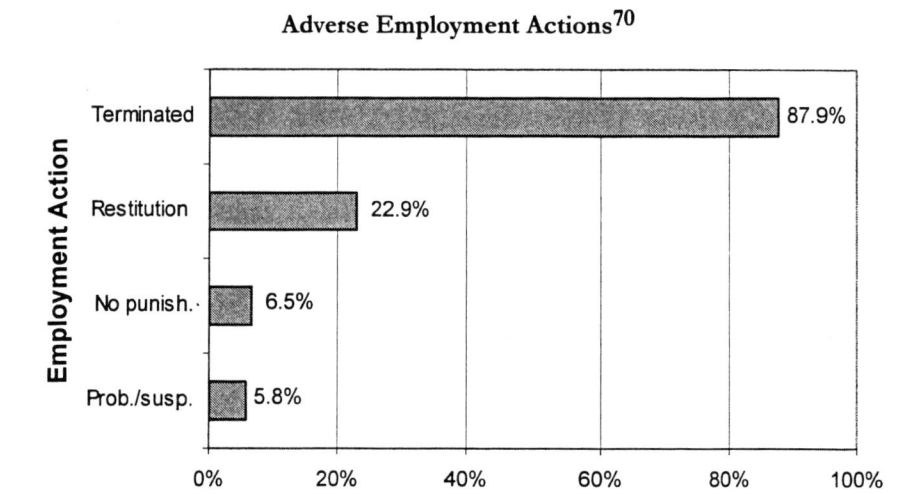

(Percent of Cases)

As the preceding chart shows, the victim organization entered into a restitution agreement with the perpetrator in 23% of the cases. When a private restitution agreement was reached, the victim company had a median recovery of 95% of its losses. By comparison, the median recovery in all cases was 20%. However, the "private restitution" cases tended to involve small frauds; the median loss in these cases was $59,000. It is often much more difficult to obtain a significant recovery in a larger fraud case.

CRIMINAL PROSECUTIONS

Despite frequent claims that organizations are hesitant to prosecute fraud offenders, our data showed that the majority of victim organizations referred their cases to law enforcement authorities. The rate of referral was slightly lower than in 2002, but at 69% it was still higher than anecdotal evidence frequently suggests.

---

[70] The sum of percentages in this chart exceeds 100% because in some cases the victim organization took more than one adverse action.

Cases Referred to Law Enforcement - Frequency

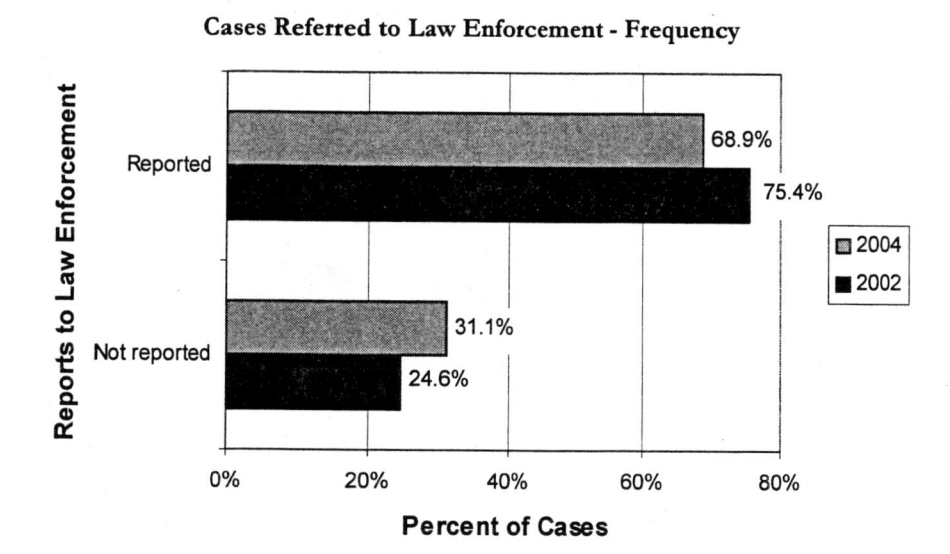

- Reported: 68.9% (2004), 75.4% (2002)
- Not reported: 31.1% (2004), 24.6% (2002)

Not surprisingly, the decision of whether to refer a case for prosecution seems to be strongly influenced by the size of the fraud. In cases that were referred to prosecutors, the median loss was $135,000. This was more than double the median loss in cases that were not referred.

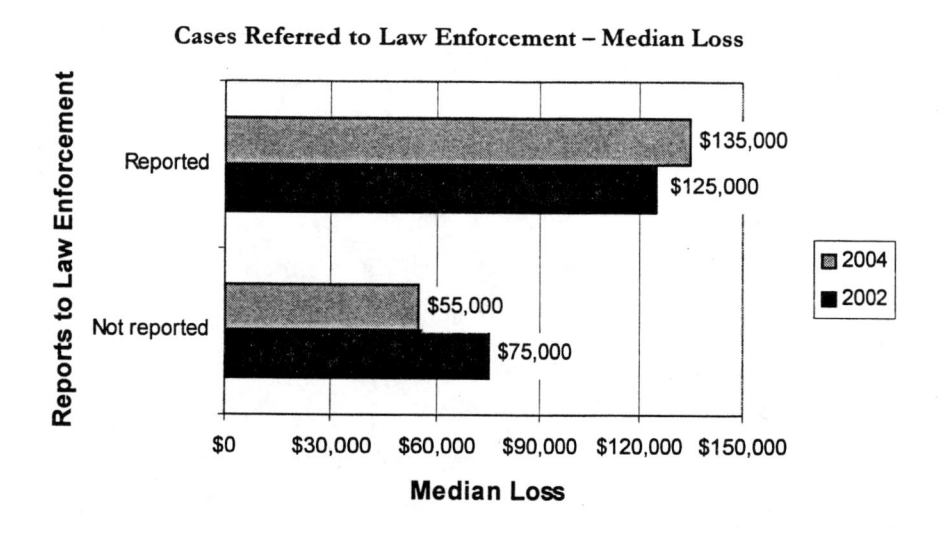

Cases Referred to Law Enforcement – Median Loss

- Reported: $135,000 (2004), $125,000 (2002)
- Not reported: $55,000 (2004), $75,000 (2002)

There were 339 frauds in our survey that were referred to law enforcement authorities. Among this group, we received 161 responses that specified the outcomes of the criminal actions, (over half of the criminal cases were still pending.) Among those cases in which the outcome was identified, we found that prosecutors were overwhelmingly successful in convicting fraudsters. Seventy-three percent of perpetrators pled guilty, and another nine percent were convicted at trial, while less than two percent were acquitted. These numbers were very similar to the results of our 2002 study.

Outcomes of Criminal Prosecutions

Criminal Case Outcome	2004	2002
Pled Guilty/No Contest	73.3%	70.5%
Declined to Prosecute	15.5%	13.1%
Convicted at Trial	9.3%	15.2%
Acquitted	1.9%	1.2%

CIVIL LAWSUITS

In addition to, or in place of, criminal prosecutions, organizations may also file civil lawsuits against perpetrators to recover stolen funds. In our study, civil actions were much less common than criminal referrals. This is not surprising, given that civil lawsuits can be very expensive and time consuming. Furthermore, it is common for fraudsters to have spent the proceeds of their crimes by the time they are detected, leaving them unable to satisfy a civil judgment even if the victim organization were to succeed in a lawsuit.

As a result of these factors, civil actions were typically only brought in very large cases. Less than one in five victim organizations filed a civil lawsuit against the perpetrator in their case, and in those cases the median loss was $470,000. Conversely, the median loss was only $60,000 in cases where no civil action was taken.

Cases in Which a Civil Suit was Filed - Frequency

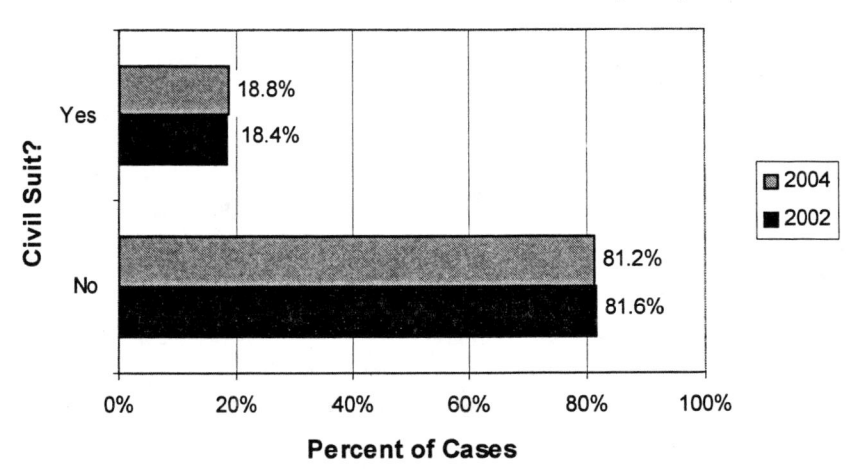

- Yes: 18.8% (2004), 18.4% (2002)
- No: 81.2% (2004), 81.6% (2002)

Cases in Which a Civil Suit was Filed – Median Loss

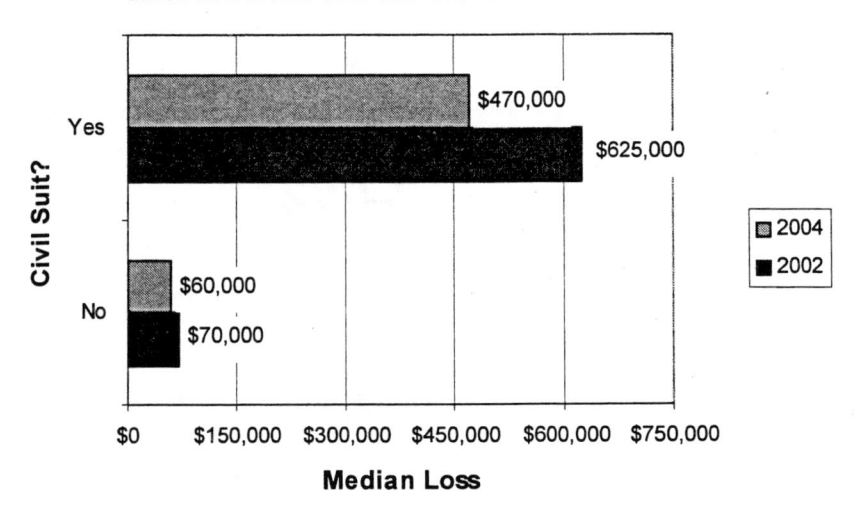

- Yes: $470,000 (2004), $625,000 (2002)
- No: $60,000 (2004), $70,000 (2002)

Of the 75 cases in our study that resulted in a civil lawsuit, 49 cases were still pending at the time of our survey. Among the remaining 26 cases, the victims were extremely successful. Twelve of those cases resulted in a judgment for the victim organization, while the remaining 14 were settled. There was not a single judgment in favor of a perpetrator. There were also no judgments in favor of perpetrators in 2002.

Outcomes of Civil Actions

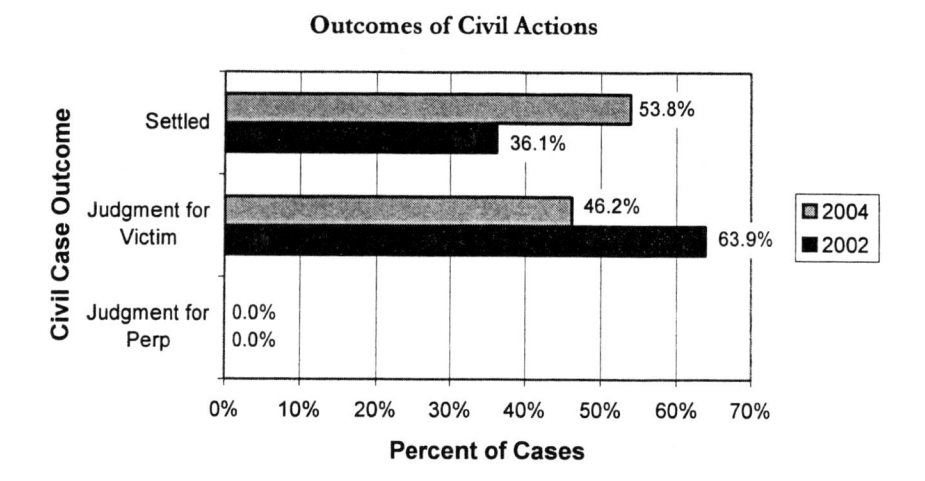

Civil Case Outcome	2004	2002
Settled	53.8%	36.1%
Judgment for Victim	46.2%	63.9%
Judgment for Perp	0.0%	0.0%

RECOVERING LOSSES CAUSED BY FRAUD

Even if organizations catch an occupational fraud scheme, they are not likely to recover their losses. As we stated earlier, the median recovery in all cases was only 20%. In over 37% of the cases we reviewed, the victim organization was unable to recover any of its losses, and 63% of the victims failed to recover more than half of what was stolen. About 22% of the victims managed to recover all of their losses (one-third of these did so through their insurance).

These statistics illustrate that the most cost-effective way to deal with fraud is to prevent it. Once fraud occurs, it is expensive and time consuming to try to recover what was stolen, and often those efforts prove futile.

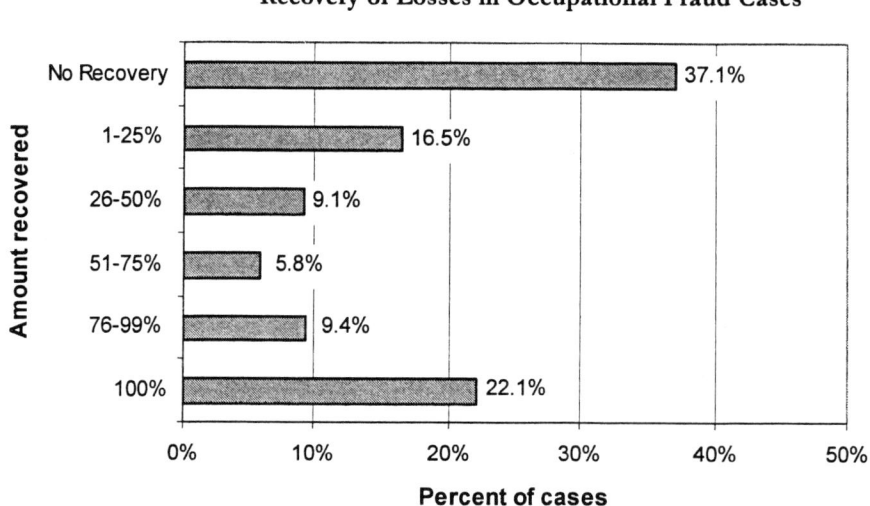

Recovery of Losses in Occupational Fraud Cases

Amount recovered	Percent of cases
No Recovery	37.1%
1-25%	16.5%
26-50%	9.1%
51-75%	5.8%
76-99%	9.4%
100%	22.1%

FRAUD PREVENTION PROGRAMS

Fraud prevention requires a system of rules, which, in their aggregate, minimize the likelihood of fraud occurring while maximizing the possibility of detecting any fraudulent activity that may transpire. The potential of being caught most often persuades likely perpetrators not to commit the fraud. Because of this principle, the existence of a thorough control system is essential to fraud prevention.

Responsibility for Fraud Prevention

Vicarious or Imputed Liability

Corporations and other organizations can be held liable for criminal acts committed as a matter of organizational policy. Fortunately, most organizations do not expressly set out to break the law. However, corporations and other organizations may also be held liable for the criminal acts of their employees if those acts are *done in the course and scope of their employment* and for the *ostensible purpose of benefiting the corporation*. An employee's acts are considered to be in the course and scope of employment if the employee has *actual authority* or *apparent authority* to engage in those acts. Apparent authority means that a third party would reasonably believe the employee is authorized to perform the act on behalf of the company. Therefore, an organization could be held liable for something an employee does on behalf of the organization even if the employee is not authorized to perform that act.

An organization will not be vicariously liable for the acts of an employee unless the employee acted for the ostensible purpose of benefiting the corporation. This does not mean the corporation has to receive an actual benefit from the illegal acts of its employee. All that is required is that the employee *intended* to benefit the corporation.

A company cannot seek to avoid vicarious liability for the acts of its employees by simply claiming that it did not know what was going on. Legally speaking, an organization is deemed to have knowledge of all facts known by its officers and employees. That is, if the government can prove that an officer or employee knew of conduct that raised a question as to the company's liability, and the government can show that the company willfully failed to act to correct the situation, then the company may be held liable, even if senior management had no knowledge or suspicion of the wrongdoing.

In addition, the evolving legal principle of "conscious avoidance" allows the government to prove the employer had "knowledge" of a particular fact which establishes liability by showing that the employer knew there was a high probability the fact existed and consciously avoided confirming the fact. Employers cannot simply turn a blind eye when there is reason to believe that there may be criminal conduct within the organization. If steps are not taken to deter the activity the company itself may be found liable.

The corporation can be held criminally responsible *even if those in management had no knowledge or participation* in the underlying criminal events and even if there were specific policies or instructions prohibiting the activity undertaken by the employees. The acts of any employee, from the lowest clerk on up to the CEO, can impute liability upon a corporation. In fact, a corporation can be criminally responsible for the *collective knowledge* of several of its employees even if no single employee intended to commit an offense. Thus, the combination of vicarious or imputed corporate criminal liability and the new Sentencing Guidelines for Organizations creates an extraordinary risk for corporations today.

Responsibility (and Liability) of a Corporation's Directors and Officers
Although many companies do not realize it, the current legal environment imposes a responsibility on companies to ferret out employee misconduct and to deal with any known or suspected instances of misconduct with efficient and decisive measures.

First, the doctrine of accountability suggests that officers and directors aware of potentially illegal conduct by senior employees may be liable for any recurrence of similar misconduct, and may have an obligation to halt and cure any continuing effects of the initial misconduct.

Second, the Corporate Sentencing Guidelines, which are discussed in more detail below, provide stiff penalties for corporations that fail to take voluntary action to redress apparent misconduct by senior employees.

Third, the Private Litigation Securities Reform Act of 1995 now requires, as a matter of statute, that independent auditors look for, and assess, management's response to indications of fraud or other potential illegality. Where the corporation does not have a history of responding to indications of wrongdoing, the auditors may not be able to reach a conclusion that the company took appropriate and prompt action in response to indications of fraud.

Fourth, the Delaware Court of Chancery in *In re Caremark International, Inc. Derivative Litigation*, 698 A.2d 959 (Del Ch. 1996), stated that, in its view, a director's duty of care includes a duty to attempt in good faith to assure corporate information and reporting systems exist. These systems must be reasonably designed to provide senior management and the board of directors timely, accurate information which would permit them to reach informed judgments concerning the corporation's compliance with law and its business performance.

The court in *Caremark* also stated that the failure to create an adequate compliance system, under some circumstances, could render a director liable for losses caused by non-compliance with applicable legal standards. Therefore, directors should make sure that their companies have a corporate compliance plan in place to detect misconduct and deal with it effectively. The directors should then monitor the company's adherence to the compliance program. Doing so will help the corporation avoid fines under the Sentencing Guidelines and help prevent individual liability on the part of the directors and officers.

The Treadway Commission

The National Commission on Fraudulent Financial Reporting (commonly known as the Treadway Commission) was established in 1987 with the purpose of defining the responsibility of the auditor in preventing and detecting fraud. The commission was formed by the major professional auditing organizations—the American Institute of CPAs, the Institute of Internal Auditors, and the National Association of Accountants. The Treadway Commission made several major recommendations that, in combination with other measures, are designed to reduce the probability of fraud in financial reports:

- A *mandatory independent audit committee* made up of outside directors.
- A *written charter* which sets forth the duties and responsibilities of the audit committee.
- The audit committee should have *adequate resources and authority* to carry out its responsibilities.
- The audit committee should be informed, vigilant, and effective.

COSO Recommendations

The Committee of Sponsoring Organizations was formed to support the implementation of the Treadway Commission. In 1992, the committee issued *Internal Control—Integrated Framework*. This report was a collaborative effort of the American Accounting Association, the American Institute of CPAs, the Financial Executives Institute, the Institute of Internal Auditors, and the Institute of Management Accountants. The report is meant to apply to all entities, public and private, regardless of size.

The COSO report complements Treadway's recommendation to the SEC that public companies' management reports include an *acknowledgment for responsibility* for internal controls and an assessment of effectiveness in meeting those responsibilities. The report provided the following definition:

> *Internal Control is a broadly defined process ... designed to provide reasonable assurance regarding the achievement of objectives in the following categories:*
> - *Reliability of financial reporting*
> - *Effectiveness and efficiency of operations*
> - *Compliance with applicable laws and regulations*

COSO also identified five interrelated components of internal control. The effectiveness of internal controls can be determined from an assessment of whether these five components are in place and functioning effectively. The five components are control environment, risk assessment, control activities, information and communication, and monitoring.

Control Environment

The control environment sets the moral tone of an organization, influencing the control consciousness of the organization and providing a foundation for all other control components. This component takes into account whether managers and employees within the organization exhibit integrity in their activities.

COSO envisions that upper management will be responsible for the control environment of organizations. Employees look to management for guidance in most business affairs, and organizational ethics are no different. It is important for upper management to operate in an ethical manner, and it is equally important for employees to view management in a positive light. Managers must set an appropriate moral tone for the operations of an organization.

In addition to merely setting a good example, however, COSO suggests that upper management take direct control of an organization's efforts at internal controls. This idea should be regularly reinforced within the organization. There are several actions that management can take to establish the proper control environment for an organization.

These include:
- *The establishment of a code of ethics for the organization.* The code should be disseminated to all employees and every new employee should be required to read and sign it. The code should also be disseminated to contractors who do work on behalf of the organization.

Under certain circumstances, companies may face liability due to the actions of independent contractors. It is therefore very important to explain the organization's standards to any outside party with whom the organization conducts business.

- *Careful screening of job applicants.* One of the easiest ways to establish a strong moral tone for an organization is to hire morally sound employees. Too often, the hiring process is conducted in a slipshod manner. Organizations should conduct thorough background checks on all new employees, especially managers. In addition, it is important to conduct thorough interviews with applicants to ensure that they have adequate skills to perform the duties that will be required of them.
- *Proper assignment of authority and responsibility.* In addition to hiring qualified, ethical employees, it is important to put these people in situations where they are able to thrive without resorting to unethical conduct. Organizations should provide employees with well-defined job descriptions and performance goals. Performance goals should be routinely reviewed to ensure that they do not set unrealistic standards. Training should be provided on a consistent basis to ensure that employees maintain the skills to perform effectively. Regular training on ethics will also help employees identify potential trouble spots and avoid getting caught in compromising situations. Finally, management should quickly determine where deficiencies in an employee's conduct exist and work with the employee to fix the problem.
- *Effective disciplinary measures.* No control environment will be effective unless there is consistent discipline for ethical violations. Consistent discipline requires a well-defined set of sanctions for violations, and strict adherence to the prescribed disciplinary measures. If one employee is punished for an act and another employee is not punished for a similar act, the moral force of the company's ethics policy will be diminished. The levels of discipline must be sufficient to deter violations. It may also be advisable to reward ethical conduct. This will reinforce the importance of organizational ethics in the eyes of employees.

Risk Assessment

Risk assessment involves an entity's identification and assessment of the risks involved in achieving organizational objectives. This component involves tailoring ethics policies or compliance programs to the nature of the organization's business. According to COSO, risk assessment is a three-step process:

- *Set objectives for the organization.* Management should establish mission statements or similar expressions of organizational objectives. These statements must take into account the nature of the organization's business, the industry in which the organization operates, and the political and economic environment in which it operates, as well as the organization's resources and goals. In stating its goals, the organization should establish measurable criteria so that progress can be measured. Goals should not be so lofty that they cannot be reached considering the organization's resources and environment. In setting objectives, input from all levels of management should be sought. Once an appropriate statement of objectives is established, it should be communicated to all employees.

- *Analyze potential risks of violations.* COSO divides risks into two categories: external risks and internal risks. External risks include things like increased competition, changes in technology, shifting economic conditions, and new legislation. Internal risks are factors such as personnel changes, availability of funds for organizational projects, new operating systems, and the development of new products.
- *Develop a strategy to manage risks.* Organizations should identify and be prepared to react to any external or internal risk. This means developing controls which are tailored to the inherent risks of the organization's business and establishing set policies for dealing with violations.

Control Activities

Control activities are the policies and procedures that enforce management's directives. Management should set forth policy and procedure guidelines in a manual that is issued to employees. A person or persons should be designated to keep statements of policies updated and to make sure they are properly disseminated. All control activities should be closely monitored by management, and changes should be made where control failures are identified. Consistent with the risk analysis component, when a control failure is identified the risk of additional failures should be considered in redesigning controls.

Information and Communication

This component relates to the exchange of information in a way that allows employees to carry out their responsibilities. Organizations should work to identify pertinent information and see that it is delivered to those who need it most. A proper information system will accomplish the following:

- *Assimilate important financial, operational, and compliance information.* This information should be drawn from both internal and external sources, meaning management may have to go outside the organizational structure to identify pertinent information. There should be a means of screening incoming information so that pertinent information is maintained but unnecessary information is not allowed to clog channels of communication.

Examples of pertinent information include facts on organizational performance, market conditions, competitor programs, economic changes, and legislative or regulatory changes.

- *Pass on pertinent information to those who need it.* Management should provide timely information to employees to help them carry out their duties more effectively. Important facts should be communicated in readily usable form. It is also important to communicate the importance of observing controls. Management should help employees understand their own roles in the internal control system and make it clear that internal controls have a high priority.
- *Provide for upstream communication.* Communication in an organization should flow in all directions. Employees should be provided with clear channels for reporting suspected control violations. Provisions should be made for employees to make anonymous reports in order to avoid fears of retaliation which can have a chilling effect on upstream communication. A similar reporting mechanism for customers and other external parties should be in place. Serious efforts should be made to follow up on these communications.

Monitoring

Monitoring is the process that assesses the quality of a control environment over time. This component should include regular evaluations of the entire control system. It also requires the ongoing monitoring of day-to-day activities by managers and employees. This may involve reviewing the accuracy of financial information, or verifying inventories, supplies, equipment and other organization assets. Finally, organizations should conduct independent evaluations of their internal control systems. An effective monitoring system should provide for the free flow of upstream communication as discussed under the information and communication component.

Corporate Sentencing Guidelines

Congress, in the Comprehensive Crime Control Act of 1984, mandated the uniform sentencing guidelines. The act also established the United States Sentencing Commission (USSC) which began studying sentences for *individuals* soon after the passage of the act. It was widely held in Congress that there was a great disparity of penalties for similar crimes committed by individuals. After three years of study, the USSC announced Sentencing Guidelines for Individuals. In November of 1987, these guidelines were applied in the 94 Federal Courts of the United States.

In 1988, the United States Sentencing Commission began a study of sanctions for corporate wrongdoing. After three years of study and hearings, on May 1, 1991, the USSC submitted its *Proposed Guidelines for Sentencing Organizations* to Congress. On November 1, 1991, the Guidelines automatically became law when Congress failed to take any action to amend or reject them. Among other things, the Corporate Sentencing Guidelines provide for the *substantial reduction of fines for corporations that have vigorous fraud prevention programs*. An effective program to detect and prevent violations of law, within the meaning set out in the Guidelines, is the only action that can be implemented by the corporation prior to the criminal acts that may later mitigate the organization's liability. Such a program, if properly structured and maintained, earns credit for a corporation which is taken into account at sentencing and reduces the sanctions that are imposed.

Guideline legislation is one of the most dramatic changes in criminal law in the history of this country. The guidelines not only seek to make punishments more uniform, they unquestionably and dramatically increase the severity of the punishment where certain aggravating factors are present. Conversely, the presence of an effective program to prevent and detect violations of the law is rewarded with a more lenient sentence. That reward can be worth several million dollars at the time of sentencing.

The purpose of the guidelines is to establish uniform, mandatory punishments for organizational crimes. The guidelines apply whenever an organization is sentenced for a felony or Class A misdemeanor.

The term *organization* includes the following entities:
- Corporations
- Partnerships
- Associations
- Joint-stock companies
- Unions
- Trusts
- Pension funds
- Unincorporated organizations
- Governments and political subdivisions thereof
- Nonprofit organizations

The introductory commentary to the guidelines clearly states that they are designed to provide incentives for organizations to maintain internal mechanisms for preventing, detecting, and reporting criminal conduct. Among other things, the guidelines provide for the substantial reduction of fines for organizations that have effective compliance programs.

If an organization is found liable for an offense, the guidelines provide for four types of remedies: fines, restitution, remedial orders, and probation.

Fines

Fines are based on two factors: the seriousness of the offense and the level of culpability by the organization. The seriousness of the offense determines the base fine to be imposed. This figure can be quite high. The organization's culpability is a measure of the actions taken by the organization which either mitigated or aggravated the situation. Depending on the culpability of the organization, the base fine can be increased by as much as 400% or reduced by as much as 95%.

Calculating the Fine

Under the guidelines, an organization's base fine is the highest of three numbers:
- The monetary loss suffered by the victim,
- The pecuniary gain received by the defendant, or
- An amount ranging from $5,000 to $72,500,000 as set forth in the Offense Level Scale Individual Guidelines. This is a table of preset penalties based on the seriousness of possible offenses.

FINE MULTIPLES

After the base fine is established, the next step in sentencing is to calculate the culpability multiplier of the organization. The calculation of this multiplier is a complicated process. Every organization begins with a preset score of 5 on a scale of 0 to 10. The organization's score is then increased or decreased based on the presence of aggravating or mitigating factors. Aggravating factors increase the score (and thus increase the fine for the organization) while mitigating factors decrease the score. The guidelines note four aggravating factors that can cause an organization's score to increase:

1. *Involvement in or tolerance of criminal activity.* Points will be added if high-level employees of the organization participated in, condoned, or were willfully ignorant of the offense. Points may also be added if there was pervasive tolerance of the offense by high-level

employees. Depending on the size of the organization, this can add from 1 to 5 points to an organization's culpability score.

2. *Prior history.* If that organization has previously been found criminally guilty of similar acts, or if the organization has been found guilty of a civil offense for similar acts on at least two occasions, points may be added to the culpability score. Depending on how long it has been since the previous offense, up to two points can be added to the organization's culpability score.

3. *Violation of a prior court order.* Points are added to the organization's culpability score if, in committing the offense at hand, the organization violated an injunction or other judicial order. Points are also added if the offense in question is similar to a prior offense for which the organization is already on probation, and if the commission of the current offense violated the probation order. This factor can add up to two points to the culpability score.

4. *Obstruction of justice.* Finally, points are added to the organization's culpability score if that organization interfered in any way with the investigation, prosecution, or sentencing of the offense in question. This does not always require an affirmative act by the organization. For instance, if the organization knew of an attempt by some party to obstruct an investigation, prosecution, or sentencing, and did nothing to prevent it, then the organization may be found to have obstructed justice. Simply stated, if the organization "turns a blind eye" to any form of obstruction, it faces the possibility of having its fine substantially increased under the guidelines. This factor can add up to three points.

FINE REDUCERS

The guidelines provide for an organization's fine to be increased if it acts "badly," but also provides for the reduction of fines if the company is "good." The guidelines set forth two mitigating factors which will reduce an organization's criminal fines:

1. *Self-reporting.* An organization's culpability score will be reduced if, within a reasonable amount of time after learning of the offense, the organization reports the offense to authorities, then cooperates in the investigation and accepts responsibility for its wrongdoing. There are three elements to the self-reporting mitigation credit: (1) reporting within a reasonable time, (2) cooperating in the investigation, and (3) accepting responsibility for the wrongdoing. The organization earns the most points (five) if it complies with all three elements. However, it can receive a smaller credit (two) even if it does not report the offense in a timely manner, as long as it cooperates in the investigation and admits its own wrongdoing. Even if the organization fails to cooperate, it can

nevertheless receive some credit (one) for accepting responsibility. This usually means pleading guilty to the offense prior to trial.

2. *An effective program to prevent and detect violations of the law.* The implementation of an effective compliance program is the only way an organization can mitigate potential fines before violations actually occur. It can knock up to three points (out of a possible 10) off of an organization's culpability score. The elements of an effective compliance program under the guidelines are discussed below.

Every organization begins with a culpability score of 5 under the guidelines. Each aggravating factor raises the culpability score, and each mitigating factor diminishes it. After all the factors have been considered, a final score is determined. Each score corresponds to a range of multipliers that determine how much the fine should be increased or decreased.

TABLE OF MINIMUM AND MAXIMUM MULTIPLIERS FROM THE GUIDELINES

The organization's fine is multiplied by the minimum and maximum multipliers for its culpability score to determine the possible range of fines.

Culpability Score	Multiplier Minimum	Maximum Multiplier
10 or more	2.00	4.00
9	1.80	3.60
8	1.60	3.20
7	1.40	2.80
6	1.20	2.40
5	1.00	2.00
4	.80	1.60
3	.60	1.20
2	.40	.80
1	.20	.40
0 or less	.05	.20

Assuming an organization had been fined $100,000, its culpability score could have a tremendous impact. If the organization's culpability score was 0 as a result of self-reporting and having an effective compliance program in place, that organization's fine range would be between $5,000 and $20,000. (Determined by multiplying $100,000 by .05 and .20, respectively.) On the other hand, if the presence of aggravating factors had left the organization with a culpability score of ten, its fine range would be $200,000 to $400,000.

Thus, in the case of a $100,000 base fine, there is a potential swing of $395,000 in the fine the organization will have to pay.

Departures

Courts are permitted to impose fines outside the range prescribed by the guidelines if there are special aggravating or mitigating circumstances in the case that would make a fine within the range inappropriate. Sentences that fall outside the guideline range are known as *departures*. The guidelines describe certain factors that would justify departures from the ordinary fine range, although the lists are not exhaustive.

UPWARD DEPARTURES

When a court imposes a fine that is greater than the maximum fine provided by the guidelines, this is known as an upward departure. The guidelines list the following as factors that could justify an upward departure:

- The offense involved a foreseeable risk of death or bodily injury.
- The offense constituted a threat to national security.
- The offense presented a threat to the environment.
- The offense presented a risk to the integrity or continued existence of a market.
- The offense involved official corruption.
- The organization's culpability score was reduced because it had an effective compliance program, but the program was only implemented because of a court order or administrative order. In cases such as this, the court can impose an upward departure to offset all or part of the reduction.
- The organization's culpability score is greater than 10.

DOWNWARD DEPARTURES

The guidelines list the following factors that could justify a downward departure:

- Substantial assistance to the authorities in the investigation or prosecution of another organization or individual.
- The organization is a public entity.
- Members or beneficiaries (other than shareholders) of the organization are direct victims of the offense. A downward departure in these cases may be warranted because a fine might increase the burden on the victims.
- The organization has agreed to pay remedial costs that greatly exceed the organization's gain from the offense.

- The organization has an exceptionally low culpability score because: there was no involvement by anyone with substantial authority in the organization; there was an effective compliance program in place; and the base fine was determined by some means other than the organization's gain from the offense.

Restitution

The guidelines require that, whenever possible, the organization must pay full restitution to the victims of the crime. Restitution is not viewed as a form of punishment in the guidelines, but rather as a means of remedying the harm caused by the offense.

Remedial Orders

The guidelines also provide for the imposition of remedial orders, which require an offending organization to fix a harm it has already caused (to the extent that the harm is not fixed by the payment of restitution) and prevent any future harms from occurring.

Probation

Finally, courts are required to impose probation on offending organizations under the following circumstances:

- To secure payment of restitution, enforcement of a remedial order, or to ensure completion of community service
- To safeguard the organization's ability to pay a monetary penalty that was not fully paid at the time of sentencing
- When an organization with at least 50 employees did not have an effective program to detect and prevent violations of law
- When the organization was adjudicated within the past five years to have committed misconduct similar to any part of the misconduct of the instant offense
- When a high-level employee was involved in the instant offense and was criminally convicted of similar conduct within the past five years
- When such an order is necessary to ensure changes are made to reduce the likelihood of future criminal conduct
- When the sentence does not include a fine
- When such an order is necessary in order to accomplish one or more purposes of sentencing set forth in 18, U.S.C., § 3553(a)(2)

When the offending organization has committed a felony, probation must run for at least one year. In no case may probation run for more than five years. The guidelines also recommend conditions for probation in various circumstances. These conditions include:
- Publicizing the nature of the offense, the organization's conviction, the punishment imposed, and the steps taken to prevent the recurrence of a similar offense
- Providing periodic reports to the court of the organization's financial condition and expenses
- Requiring the organization to submit to examinations of the organization's business records and to interviews of knowledgeable employees
- Requiring the organization to notify the court upon learning of a material adverse change to its financial condition or the commencement of any major legal proceedings, including bankruptcy, or any investigation by authorities
- Requiring periodic payments under the court's specifications, with priority in the order of restitution, fine, and any other monetary sanction
- Developing a program to avoid violations of law and a schedule to implement it
- Notifying the organization's employees and shareholders of its violation and its program to avoid and detect violations of law
- Reporting to the court on the organization's implementation of a program to avoid and detect violations of law and disclosing any investigation by authorities

If an offending organization violates its probation, this may result in:
- Resentencing
- The terms of probation being extended
- The imposition of more restrictive conditions

Implementing an Effective Compliance Program Under the Corporate Sentencing Guidelines

The United States Sentencing Commission recently promulgated modifications to the existing provisions of Chapter 8 dealing with effective compliance and ethics programs for business organizations that will become effective November 1, 2004. These new provisions narrowly tailor the criteria for compliance and ethics programs, thereby providing organizations with guidance in establishing and maintaining effective programs for detecting and preventing internal illegal activities, as well as mitigating sentencing culpability.

An effective compliance program is one that is reasonably designed, implemented, and enforced so that it generally will be effective in preventing and detecting criminal conduct. The guidelines encourage organizations to exercise due diligence in seeking to prevent and detect criminal conduct by their officers, directors, employees, and agents. Due diligence requires, at a minimum, the following seven steps:

- The organization must have established compliance standards and procedures to be followed by its employees and other agents that are reasonably capable of reducing the prospect of criminal conduct.
- Specific individual(s) within high-level personnel of the organization must have been knowledgeable about the content and operation of the compliance and ethics program and assigned overall responsibility to oversee compliance with such standards and procedures. Additionally, where the day-to-day operational responsibility has been delegated, the governing authority must have received, at minimum, annual reports regarding the implementation and effectiveness of such programs.
- The organization must have used reasonable efforts not to delegate substantial discretionary authority to individuals whom the organization knew, or should have known through the exercise of due diligence, had engaged in illegal activities or other conduct inconsistent with an effective compliance and ethics program.
- The organization must have periodically taken steps to communicate effectively its standards and procedures to all employees and other agents by requiring participation in training programs, and disseminating publications that explain in an appropriate manner, what is required of each individual, including high-level personnel and substantial authority personnel.
- The organization must have taken reasonable steps to achieve compliance with its standards by: 1) utilizing monitoring and auditing systems reasonably designed to detect criminal conduct by its employees and other agents; 2) periodically evaluating the program's effectiveness; and 3) having in place and publicizing a reporting system whereby employees and other agents could report, or seek guidance regarding, actual or potential criminal conduct by others within the organization while retaining anonymity or confidentiality, and without fear of retribution.
- The standards must have been consistently promoted and enforced through a) suitable incentives to perform in accordance with the organization's program, and b) appropriate disciplinary mechanisms, often including the discipline of individuals responsible for the failure to detect an offense. Adequate discipline of individuals responsible for an offense is a necessary component of enforcement; however, the form of discipline that will be appropriate will be case specific.

- After an offense has been detected, the organization must have taken all reasonable steps to respond appropriately and to prevent further similar offenses— including any necessary modifications to its program to prevent and detect violations of law.

Organizations must periodically assess the risk of illegal conduct and act appropriately to create, implement, or amend the above requirements as necessary.

Establishing Standards

The first step is to establish standards and procedures for agents and employees of the organization which are reasonably capable of reducing criminal conduct. One should start by producing a clear statement of management philosophy. This statement will serve as the backbone of all compliance procedures. This is similar to the COSO requirement that management must set the ethical tone for the organization.

Organizations should draft clear, concise compliance standards that are consistent with management's ethics policy and are relevant to business operations. A sample corporate compliance program is included later in this section. It should provide a framework from which fraud examiners can build compliance programs tailored to their own organizations.

Assigning Responsibility

The guidelines require the company to assign specific high-level personnel to oversee compliance with the standards. The comments to the guidelines state that overall responsibility for monitoring the compliance program should be vested with high-level personnel of the organization. High-level personnel are those who have "substantial control over the organization or who have a substantial role in the making of policy within the organization." Specific examples of high-level personnel include:

- Directors
- Executive officers
- Individuals in charge of major business or functional units of the organization
- Individuals with substantial ownership interests in the organization

Audit Committees

It is preferable for the board of directors or one of the board's committees to control the organization's compliance program. For instance, many companies place their compliance programs under the control of audit committees. There are three principal benefits to this practice:

- The involvement of the board of directors lends an air of authority to the compliance program. It clearly identifies the program as a matter of company policy.
- The involvement of a board committee provides oversight to the operation of the program by personnel who are not involved in the day-to-day operation of the program.
- Because of the procedures generally adhered to by board committees, the efforts made to implement an effective compliance program will probably be documented. This documentation can prove useful if the company ever has to defend its actions and seek mitigation of a criminal fine.

The compliance officer or compliance committee should have sufficient authority to ensure that standards are strictly adhered to. This person or persons will also serve to resolve questions about the program and to help measure its effectiveness.

Don't Let the Wolves Guard the Hen House

The guidelines require that the organization "use reasonable efforts not to include within the substantial authority personnel of the organization any individual whom the organization knew, or should have known through the exercise of due diligence, has engaged in illegal activities or other conduct inconsistent with an effective compliance and ethics program." Like COSO, the guidelines require that organizations hire ethical employees. This requires careful screening of applicants, thorough background checks on all applicants, and effective monitoring of the performance of current employees. Discipline or training should be provided to those employees who demonstrate a propensity to engage in illegal or unethical activities.

Communicating the Policy

The corporate compliance policy should be communicated to everyone who can potentially bind a corporation through their own misconduct. This includes the following:

- Executive officers and directors
- Managers and supervisors
- Low-level employees
- Independent contractors

Note in particular that organizations can be held liable for the acts of independent contractors if the contractor is acting for the benefit of the organization. It is therefore important to distribute copies of the compliance program to contractors as well as employees.

Training Employees

As required by the newly amended sentencing guidelines, organizations *must* conduct "effective training programs," as well as periodically and appropriately communicate the program's compliance requirements and procedures to all employees affected by the program, including upper-level personnel. These programs should be designed to inform employees about the company's stance on corporate compliance. They should also inform employees about what kinds of acts and omissions are prohibited by the law and by the organization. The training should be designed to help employees identify and avoid situations that could lead to criminal conduct. Common training techniques include:

- Lectures
- Training films
- Interactive workshops

Employees should be trained to understand the organization's ethical policy. They should also be trained to identify potentially compromising situations and learn how to avoid them. This training should be tailored to the nature of the organization's business, taking into account the external and internal risks that are inherent in that business. Training should also include a review of statutes and regulations that are particularly applicable to the organization.

Training should not be a one-time event. Simply handing out a copy of the company's compliance policy at the beginning of an employee's tenure is insufficient. Organizations should stress compliance by regularly emphasizing their standards to all personnel. For example, many companies disseminate a copy of their ethics policies every six months along with employee paychecks.

Achieving Compliance

An organization is required to take reasonable measures to ensure program compliance through monitoring, auditing, periodically evaluating the program's effectiveness, and having a publicized reporting system whereby employees and agents may retain anonymity or confidentiality when reporting, or seeking guidance regarding, actual or potential illegal conduct, and without fear of retribution. The following are examples of audit procedures that can be implemented into a compliance program that are specifically designed to detect and prevent fraud:

Proactive Fraud Policies

Proactive fraud policies are generated from the top of the operation. A proactive policy means that the organization will aggressively seek out possible fraudulent conduct, instead of waiting for instances to come to their attention. This can be accomplished by several means, including the use of analytical review, fraud assessment questioning, enforcement of mandatory vacations, job rotation, and surprise audits where possible.

USE OF ANALYTICAL REVIEW

Much internal fraud is discovered as a result of analytical review. To uncover such fraud and defalcations, they must materially impact the financial statements. Auditors should be especially mindful of the following trends:
- Increasing expenses
- Increasing cost of sales
- Increasing receivables/decreasing cash
- Increasing inventories
- Increasing sales/decreasing cash
- Increasing returns and allowances
- Increasing sales discounts.

FRAUD ASSESSMENT QUESTIONING

Fraud Assessment Questioning is a nonaccusatory interview technique used as a part of a normal audit. See the Investigation section for further details. It operates on the theory that employees' attitudes are a good indicator of potential problems, and that one of the most effective ways to deal with fraud is to ask about it.

Below are some suggested questions that can be asked as a part of the normal audit. Note that the questions here begin with the general and proceed to the specific.
- *Part of my duty as an auditor is to find fraud, waste, and abuse. Do you understand that?*
- *Do you think fraud is a problem for business in general?*
- *Do you think this company has any particular problem with fraud?*
- *Has anyone ever asked you to do anything that you felt was illegal or unethical?*
- *If you felt that there was a problem in the company with respect to fraud, what would you do?*
- *Do you have any indication that there is fraud occurring in the company now?*

ENFORCEMENT OF MANDATORY VACATIONS

Many internal frauds require manual intervention, and are therefore discovered when the perpetrator is away on vacation. The enforcement of mandatory vacations will aid in the prevention of some frauds.

JOB ROTATION

Some frauds are detected during sickness or unexpected absences of the perpetrator, because they require continuous, manual intervention.

EXAMPLE

A manager who embezzled $1.6 million from his company said, "If the company had coupled a two-week vacation with four weeks of rotation to another job function, my embezzlement would have been impossible to cover up." His fraud lasted three years.

SURPRISE AUDITS WHERE POSSIBLE

All too many fraud perpetrators know when auditors are coming, and therefore have time to alter, destroy, or misplace records and other evidence. A proactive fraud policy involves using the technique of surprise audits as much as possible. It might have a significant deterrent effect.

Management Oversight

It is most common for employees who steal to use the proceeds for lifestyle improvements. Some examples include more expensive cars, extravagant vacations, expensive clothing, new or remodeled homes, expensive recreational property, and outside investments. Managers should be educated to be observant to these signs.

EXAMPLE

Discovery of a $97,000 embezzlement that occurred over a two-year period resulted when an observant manager asked the internal auditors to examine the responsibilities of a seven-year veteran of the company. The manager noticed that this female employee had begun wearing designer clothes (and making a big deal about it), and was driving a new BMW. The manager was also aware of the fact that this employee had no outside income that might explain the upgrade in lifestyle.

INCREASING THE PERCEPTION OF DETECTION

Most experts agree that it is much easier to prevent than detect fraud. To prevent fraud, we should understand something about the mind of the potential perpetrator. Increasing the perception of detection might be the most effective fraud prevention method. Controls, for example, do little good in forestalling theft and fraud, if those at risk do not know of the presence of possible detection. In the audit profession, this means letting employees, managers, and executives know that auditors are actively seeking out information concerning internal theft. This can be accomplished in several ways.

EMPLOYEE EDUCATION

Each entity should have some policy for educating managers, executives, and employees about fraud. This can be done as a part of employee orientation, or it can be accomplished through memoranda, training programs, and other intercompany communication methods. The goal is to make others within the company your eyes and ears.

Any education effort should be positive and not accusatory. Illegal conduct in any form eventually costs everyone in the company through lost profits, adverse publicity, and decreased morale and productivity. These facts should be emphasized in training.

MINIMIZE EMPLOYEE PRESSURES

Pressures, such as financial hardship or family problems, can be especially difficult to detect on the part of the employees. Companies can take steps to assist an employee who might be having difficult times.

OPEN-DOOR POLICIES

If employees and others can speak freely, many managers will understand the pressures and might be able to eliminate them before they become acute.

EXAMPLE

The controller of a small fruit-packing company in California stole $112,000 from the company. When asked why, he said, "Nobody at the company ever talked to me, especially the owners. They were unfair. They talked down to me, and they were rude. They deserve everything they got."

EMPLOYEE SUPPORT PROGRAMS

Many progressive companies and agencies have realized the benefit of employee support programs. Some kinds of support programs include alcohol and drug assistance, and counseling for gambling, abortion, marital problems, and financial difficulties.

MANAGEMENT CLIMATE

If the style of management is conducted by objective measures rather than by subjective measures, then employees will not manufacture or imagine the performance criteria employed by management. In addition, it is obvious that management that is perceived to be dishonest will beget dishonest employees.

EXAMPLE

Jim, a loan officer for a mortgage bank, received his primary compensation based on the total volume of loans (measured by dollars) he was able to put on the books each year. Dollar volume was the only criteria for the compensation. In addition, the loan officers were all in competition with each other for the high volume award of the year. The pressure to earn more than his fellow officers became more acute each year.

When the mortgage company was closed down, most of Jim's loans were in default. Because Jim perceived that his job performance was based solely on volume, no attention was paid to the quality of the loans. In fact, it was discovered that on several occasions, Jim coerced the loan processing department to close loans, even though all the requirements had not been completed.

EXAMPLE

A large fast food chain lost $200,000 when one of its buyers got involved with a supplier. The company decided to notify all of its vendors of the company's policy prohibiting the giving of anything of value to influence a purchasing decision. Two vendors called in with complaints about competitors, resulting in the discovery of two other frauds totaling an additional $360,000.

Monitoring Systems

The guidelines specifically mention the importance of having a reporting system for employees and agents of the organization to report criminal conduct. Confidential hotlines are one of the best ways for an organization to monitor compliance.

REPORTING PROGRAMS

Each employee in the company should know where to report suspicious, unethical, or illegal behavior. A reporting program should emphasize that:

- Fraud, waste, and abuse occur in nearly all companies
- Such conduct costs the company jobs and profits
- The company actively encourages any employee with information to come forward
- The employee can come forward and provide information anonymously and without fear of recrimination for good-faith reporting
- There is an exact method for reporting, i.e., a telephone number, name, or other information
- The report need not be made to one's immediate superiors

HOTLINES

Hotlines have proved to be a very effective reporting mechanism. However, most hotline reports do not result in fraud cases. At the federal level, published reports indicate about five percent of hotline calls result in serious allegations. With careful screening of calls and proper handling, spurious complaints can be effectively weeded out. There are three general types of hotlines. The advantages and disadvantages of each are summarized below.

Part Time, In-House

These hotlines are assigned to an employee with other duties. An audit or security depart-ment usually staffs an in-house hotline. When the employee is out, a recorder takes calls. The main advantage is cost. The main disadvantage is that the hotline is not staffed full-time, which can discourage calls. Also, some people might be reluctant to report to the company.

Full Time, In-House

A full-time, in-house hotline may be feasible depending on the company size. The advantage is that people can make reports at any time, day or night, and talk to a person. The disadvantage is cost, and like the part-time line, some people might be reluctant to report directly to the company.

Third-Party

An outside company that specializes in services of this type most often staffs a third-party hotline. The advantages are cost, efficiency, and anonymity. A few are staffed around the clock, and will provide the information immediately to the client subscriber. They also provide anonymity to those who might be more comfortable with it. Their disadvantage is that the operation is beyond the company's control.

REWARDS

Some companies have a policy of rewarding information that leads to the recovery of merchandise, property, or money. Others offer rewards upon the criminal conviction of the person(s) involved. If a reward policy exists, strict criteria should establish reward payments, and such proposed policies should be reviewed and approved by counsel. The amount of reward paid by companies varies from fixed fees to a percentage of the recovery. Studies indicate that rewards should not exceed a few thousand dollars. *Crime Stoppers* recommends rewards not exceeding $1,000.

Disciplinary Action

Enforcing a compliance program means adhering to a system of disciplinary actions for rulebreakers. Employees must know that if they violate the company's compliance policy, they will be punished. The opportunity to commit fraud is psychologically more acceptable when employees believe fraud normally goes undetected and unprosecuted. New employees should be advised of the compliance program at the time of hire, and should sign an annual statement acknowledging their understanding of it. The range of possible punishments for violations of the policy should be spelled out. These may include:

- Reprimand
- Probation
- Suspension
- Reduction in salary
- Demotion
- Reimbursement of losses of damages
- Dismissal
- Referral for criminal prosecution or civil action
- A combination of the above

In addition, the guidelines recommend the discipline of individuals who are responsible for failing to detect offenses.

If a compliance program is not enforced, it is nothing more than a paper tiger. There are two purposes to any compliance program. The first is to prevent criminal conduct. The second is to mitigate any potential fines for criminal conduct by showing that the organization is dedicated to preventing illegal activity. If an organization does not enforce its compliance program, its chances of mitigating fines are nil. Therefore, organizations should adhere to well-defined procedures when investigating potential violations and when disciplining individuals for offenses. The organization's efforts should be documented so that it can prove that it made every effort to enforce compliance. For every allegation of an offense, the company should maintain:

- An account of the alleged offense
- A description of the steps taken to investigate the allegation
- A description of the actions taken by the organization in response to the violation.

Appropriate Responses

After detection of an offense, the organization must take all reasonable steps to appropriately respond to this offense and to prevent further similar offenses—including modifying its program and administering appropriate discipline for the individuals responsible for the offense and those who failed to detect it. When a control failure is identified, changes may be necessary. Both COSO and the guidelines require organizations to identify the weakness in the control system and make modifications to prevent similar failures in the future. The guidelines require that organizations explain the modifications they have made and demonstrate why they will be effective.

Relation of COSO and Corporate Sentencing Guidelines

The guidelines and COSO focus on the development of a stronger control system. The guidelines contain explicit requirements for an effective control program. COSO does not mandate specific actions. It only provides illustrations of what constitutes a strong control system. The seven minimum requirements of the guidelines are covered within the COSO system. The table below summarizes the relation between the components of the two pronouncements.

COMPONENTS	COSO	GUIDELINES
Control Environment		
Management	❑ Sets the ethical tone ❑ Leads by actions, such as rewarding ethical conduct while punishing unethical actions	❑ Sanctions for knowing, tolerating, or condoning improper conduct ❑ Rewards for cooperation and contrition ❑ "Due diligence" requirement ❑ Upper management oversight of compliance program
Integrity and Ethical Values	❑ Code of Ethics ❑ Mechanism to encourage employee reporting	❑ Code of Ethics ❑ Additional reporting mechanisms
Human Resources	❑ Hiring those who demonstrate integrity ❑ Consistent discipline	❑ Nondelegation of authority to those with criminal tendencies ❑ Consistent discipline
Risk Assessment	❑ Objectives related to operations, financial reporting, and compliance ❑ Identification and analysis of relevant risks ❑ A strategy to manage risks	❑ Incentives to maintain internal controls ❑ Identification of industry specific risks
Control Activities	❑ Policies and procedures to help ensure that management's directives are followed	❑ Standards and procedures capable of reducing the prospect of criminal conduct ❑ Determination of modifications needed to prevent future problems
Information and Communication	❑ The identification, capture, and communication of pertinent information in an appropriate format and time frame	❑ Effective communication of standards and procedures to all employees and other agents ❑ Required training *and* distribution of publications ❑ Establishment of additional reporting mechanisms (such as hotlines, helplines)
Monitoring	❑ Ongoing assessment of the internal control system	❑ Utilization of monitoring and auditing systems designed to detect criminal conduct. ❑ Periodic evaluation of program effectiveness

[Fiorelli, Rooney, COSO and the Federal Sentencing Guidelines, *INTERNAL AUDITOR*, April 1997]

Sample Corporate Compliance Policy

A sample corporate compliance policy is included at the end of this chapter.

Fraud Prevention Standards Under Sarbanes-Oxley

The Sarbanes-Oxley Act (SOA) set forth a number of preventative measures public companies must take to help reduce the threat of fraud. The Act as a whole is discussed in detail in the legal section of this manual. Here, we will cover only the portions of SOA that directly relate to fraud prevention.

Audit Committee Responsibilities

One of the keys to effective fraud prevention is assigning high-level personnel with responsibility for fraud prevention efforts. This signals to employees that fraud is a serious matter and it helps ensure that fraud prevention issues will receive consideration at the highest levels of the company. SOA mandates that audit committees for publicly traded companies be directly responsible for two key components of an effective fraud prevention program – outside audits and internal reporting mechanisms. It also establishes requirements for the composition of audit committees to ensure that they are capable of carrying out their duties.

Overseeing Audits

Section 301 of the Act requires the audit committee for every publicly traded company to be directly responsible for hiring, paying, and overseeing the work of the company's outside auditors. Auditors must report directly to the audit committee, and the committee is responsible for resolving disputes between auditors and the company's management.

Section 204 of SOA requires outside auditors to report certain information to the audit committee, including any alternative accounting treatments within GAAP that have been discussed with management, the effect of using those alternative treatments, and the treatment preferred by the auditors. This is designed to give the audit committee a warning in the event that management has used questionable or overly aggressive accounting in the preparation of the company's financial statements.

Receiving Complaints

Section 301 also specifies that audit committees must establish procedures for receiving and dealing with complaints and anonymous employee tips regarding irregularities in the company's accounting methods, internal controls, or auditing matters.

Composition of the Audit Committee

The Act also sets forth certain requirements regarding the composition of audit committees. Under Section 301, every member of the audit committee must also be a member of the company's board of directors, which ensures that the committee will have sufficient authority within the company to carry out its duties. Furthermore, section 407 of the Act requires every public company to disclose in its SEC reports whether or not at least one member of the audit committee is a "financial expert" and if not, to explain the reasons why. Financial experts are defined by SOA as persons who, through education and professional experience, possess the following: (1) an understanding of generally accepted accounting principles and financial statements; (2) experience in preparing or auditing financial statements of comparable companies and in accounting for estimates, accruals, and reserves in those companies; (3) experience with internal controls; and (4) an understanding of audit committee functions.

Finally, Section 301 expressly states that audit committees must be given sufficient authority and funding to hire attorneys and other advisors necessary to carry out their duties.

Management Responsibilities

Sarbanes-Oxley also places a number of requirements on management related to fraud prevention. It makes management directly responsible for internal controls, it requires companies to establish codes of ethics for their senior financial officers, and it requires CEOs and CFOs to personally certify their companies' financial reports.

Management's Responsibility for Internal Controls

Internal controls are among the most important aspects of any fraud prevention program. Section 404 of SOA requires each annual report filed with the SEC to contain an internal control report that: (1) states management's responsibility for establishing and maintaining an adequate internal control structure; and (2) contains an assessment of the effectiveness of the internal control structure and procedures of the company for financial reporting. Management's internal control assessment must be attested to and reported on by the company's outside auditors.

Codes of Ethics for Senior Financial Officers

In order to have an effective anti-fraud program, organizations must set clear standards for conduct; it is also critical to establish an ethical tone at the top of an organization to serve as a guide and example for employees. Sarbanes-Oxley addresses both of these issues by requiring publicly traded companies to disclose in their periodic reports whether they have adopted a code of ethics for their senior financial officers, and if not, to explain the reasons why. SOA also requires companies to make an immediate disclosure any time there is a change in the code of ethics or a waiver for a senior financial officer.

Certification Obligations

As part of an effort to eliminate financial statement fraud, Sarbanes-Oxley requires CEOs and CFOs of publicly traded companies to personally certify their companies' annual and quarterly SEC filings. There are two categories of officer certifications required by SOA: criminal certifications, which are contained in Section 906 of the Act, and civil certifications, which are contained in Section 302.

CRIMINAL CERTIFICATIONS

Under Section 906, all periodic filings with the SEC must be accompanied by a statement which certifies that the report fully complies with the SEC's reporting requirements and that the information in the report fairly presents, in all material respects, the financial condition and results of operation of the company. This statement must be signed by both the CEO and CFO. These certifications are known as "criminal certifications" because the Act imposes criminal penalties for violations of this section, including fines of up to $1 million and imprisonment of up to 10 years.

CIVIL CERTIFICATIONS

Section 302 requires that the CEO and CFO certify the following six items in every annual and quarterly report:

- They have personally reviewed the report.
- Based on their knowledge, the report does not contain any material misstatement that would render the financials misleading.
- Based on their knowledge, the financial information in the report *fairly presents* in all material respects the financial condition, results of operations, and cash flow of the company.
- They are responsible for designing, maintaining, and evaluating the company's internal controls, they have designed the controls to ensure that they receive material information about the company, they have evaluated the controls within *90 days prior to the report*, and they have presented their conclusions about the effectiveness of the controls in the report.
- They have disclosed to the auditors and the audit committee any material weaknesses in the controls and any fraud, *whether material or not*, that involves management or other employees who have a significant role in the company's internal controls.
- They have indicated in the report whether there have been significant changes in the company's internal controls, including any corrective actions with regard to significant deficiencies and material weaknesses.

IMPACT OF CERTIFICATION OBLIGATIONS

Sarbanes-Oxley requires CEOs and CFOs to take personal responsibility for their companies' financial statements; they cannot delegate their responsibilities to their subordinates and then claim ignorance when fraud is discovered. If the financials include fraudulent reporting, then the senior financial officers may be held individually civilly liable for the misstatements.

The "fairly presents" standard of item 3 is broader than what is required by GAAP. It essentially requires the CEO and CFO to certify that the company has selected appropriate accounting policies; has properly applied those accounting standards; and has disclosed financial information that reflects the underlying transactions of the company.

Item 4 requires senior financial officers to take an active role in the design and maintenance of their companies' internal controls. It not only requires the CEO and CFO to certify that they are responsible for controls, but also that they have evaluated their controls within 90 days prior to their quarterly or annual report. This effectively requires companies to continually re-evaluate their control structures. Item 5 requires the CEO and CFO to report any material weaknesses in their company's controls, along with any fraud involving management, whether it is material or not.

The overall effect of these certification requirements is to force CEOs and CFOs to take an active role in the anti-fraud efforts of their companies, making internal controls and fraud prevention a high priority.

Whistleblower Protection

A key to any fraud prevention program is the establishment of a mechanism by which fraud can be reported. As was stated above, Section 301 of Sarbanes-Oxley requires audit committees to establish mechanisms for receiving complaints about irregularities in a company's accounting, auditing, or internal control systems.

In order to protect those who make such reports, SOA established broad new protections for corporate whistleblowers. Section 806 of the Act creates civil liability for publicly traded companies that retaliate against employees who provide information or assist in the investigation of securities fraud. Penalties for violating this section include reinstatement, back pay with interest, and compensation for special damages such as litigation costs and attorneys fees.

Section 1107 makes it a crime to retaliate against a person for providing truthful information relating to the commission or possible commission of any Federal offense. This section offers much broader protection than the civil whistleblower protection afforded under Section 806. The whistleblower protections under § 1107 cover all individuals, not just employees of publicly traded companies. They also protect individuals who provide information about *any Federal offense,* not just securities fraud. Violations of § 1107 are punishable by fines of up to $250,000 and up to 10 years in prison for individuals. Corporations can be fined up to $500,000.

Fraud Prevention Requirements for External Auditors
Attesting to Internal Controls

As was stated above, § 404 of Sarbanes-Oxley requires a company's auditors to attest to and report on management's assessment of internal controls in each annual report filed with the SEC. In addition, each audit report must describe the scope of the auditor's testing of the company's internal control structure. The audit report must include an evaluation of whether the company's internal controls are acceptable and a description of material weaknesses in the control structure or any material noncompliance with controls.

Restrictions on Non-Audit Activity

In order to address concerns about potential conflicts of interest that can arise when public accounting firms receive consulting fees and other compensation for non-audit services from their audit clients, Sarbanes-Oxley established a list of activities that public accounting firms are now prohibited from performing on behalf of their audit clients. The list includes most consulting and expert services, although tax services are still permissible if they are approved in advance by the audit committee.

Fraud Prevention Policy

Another important element of an overall fraud prevention program is a written fraud policy that specifically spells out who in an organization handles varying fraud matters under differing circumstances.

Fraud Policy Objectives

A fraud prevention program will entail very similar objects as internal control. According to the Institute of Internal Auditors' Standards for the Professional Practice of Internal

Auditing, the primary objectives for management to achieve proper internal controls include reasonable assurance that:
- Financial and operating information is accurate and reliable
- Policies, procedures, plans, laws, and regulations are complied with
- Assets are safeguarded against loss and theft
- Resources are used economically and efficiently
- Established program/operating goals and objectives are met

A fraud prevention policy with the above-mentioned goals is the first step towards effective fraud deterrence.

Selling Fraud Prevention to Management

Management might not support fraud prevention for one of several reasons:
- Management's concerns often are elsewhere than audit or fraud. They don't typically understand that fraud is hidden and that losses go undetected without our knowledge. They also might refuse to believe that their own workers are capable of stealing even when studies suggest a third of us might do such a thing.
- Because of the hidden nature of fraud, managers are understandably reluctant to believe in the presence of fraud. And if one employee is caught committing fraud, management might too often claim that this is an isolated problem and not worth additional consideration. Management must understand that when instances of fraud are detected, it is too late to do anything about it.
- Management sometimes unreasonably feels that bringing up the issue will alienate the work force. This problem can be addressed by reminding management that the rank-and-file workers appreciate working for an honest company. It also is helpful to point out to management what the losses might be.

Many auditors complain that management does not adequately support fraud prevention efforts. That is largely for two reasons: either they believe that fraud is not really a problem in the company, or they believe that even addressing the subject has a negative impact. In either scenario, it is difficult for the auditor to break down management's built-in resistance to dealing with fraud prevention. Some of the following suggestions might be helpful in "selling" fraud prevention to management.

The Impact on the Bottom Line
One of the best ways to sell management on fraud prevention is by showing the impact on the bottom line. Fraud impacts net sales dollar for dollar. For example, if a company nets 20 percent on sales, they must sell five items at regular prices to recover losses from the theft of one item. Fraud can be very expensive.

The Impact of Publicity
Many corporate executives are more sensitive to adverse publicity than almost any other issue. Certainly, one way to convince management of the logic of fraud prevention is to point out that negative publicity, even in small cases, can have a devastating impact on the bottom line. This negative impact can be eliminated or reduced by a proactive fraud prevention program.

One of the more significant examples of adverse publicity can be demonstrated in the E. F. Hutton case. As one might recall, 20 or so executives of E.F. Hutton participated in a kiting scheme in the late 1980s. The fraud itself was insignificant to the bottom line, but its resulting impact was devastating to Hutton, which eventually sold out. This situation pointedly illustrates that insignificant fraud can have a very significant impact.

Writing the Fraud Policy
Companies often have an ethics policy that sets forth in detail what is expected in the ethical climate of the company. Still other companies have a fraud policy that specifically spells out who handles fraud matters under what circumstances. The components of a fraud policy will differ from company to company. Many fraud policies have some of the following elements.

Policy Statement
The policy statement sets forth that management is responsible for fraud, and each member of the management team should be familiar with the types of signals present within his scope of responsibilities. The policy statement also designates who is in charge of investigating suspected irregularities.

Scope of Policy
This area of the fraud policy statement covers what constitutes an irregularity and the fact that the policy covers everyone from management to worker.

Actions Constituting Fraud

This area sets forth in detail what actions constitute fraudulent conduct. This is important as it gives management the legal grounds to investigate and punish violators. The actions listed can include:

- Any dishonest or fraudulent act
- Forgery or alteration of documents
- Misapplication of funds or assets
- Impropriety with respect to reporting financial transactions
- Profiting on insider knowledge
- Disclosing securities transactions to others
- Accepting gifts from vendors
- Destruction or disappearance of records or assets
- Any similar or related irregularity

Nonfraud Irregularities

This section covers allegations of personal improprieties or irregularities and states that they should be resolved by management and not an auditor.

Investigation Responsibilities

This part deals with who will investigate suspected irregularities as well as to whom these irregularities will be reported: management, law enforcement, and legal counsel.

Confidentiality

Under this section, the confidential nature of the investigation is set forth. It states that the investigation will not be disclosed to outsiders except as required.

Authorization for Investigation

This delineates that whoever is in charge of the investigation has the authority to take control of and examine records.

Reporting Procedures

This part states that anyone suspecting fraud should report it and not attempt an investigation. It also states that management and others should not make statements regarding the alleged guilt of the perpetrator.

Termination
This section states that any recommendations to terminate employees should be reviewed by counsel and management.

Communicating the Fraud Policy
It obviously does little good to have a fraud or ethics policy if it is not communicated to the employees. This communication can be accomplished in several ways. Again, the communication of the policy should be presented in a positive, nonaccusatory manner.

Orientation
During initial employee orientation, the fraud policy should be discussed. This is the first opportunity the company has to make its point, and it should be made thoroughly.

Memoranda
An interoffice memorandum from the chief executive officer detailing the fraud policy is a good idea. Once again, the policy should concentrate on the positive aspects of working for an ethical company.

Posters
Some companies might wish to use posters displayed in common areas. However, this should be carefully considered as some employees might object to such tactics.

Employee Morale
If an employee is properly instructed, communication of a fraud policy can have a positive impact on morale. Honest workers want to work for an honest company. A fraud policy helps set the proper tone.

Legal Considerations
Many companies have learned that it is best to spell out specific unacceptable conduct. If the type of conduct that is considered unacceptable is not accurately detailed, there might be legal problems in discharging a dishonest employee. Check with your counsel regarding any legal considerations with respect to a fraud policy. One of the most important legal considerations is to ensure everyone and every allegation is handled in a uniform manner. A sample fraud policy is contained at the end of the chapter.

Ethics Programs

A written ethics policy is an excellent method by which management can objectively communicate its philosophy and develop a successful Ethics Program. The policy should be disseminated among employees, new and old. Additionally, some companies have found it effective to share the ethics policy with their vendors.

In most cultures, the majority of people share the same values. They agree on what is good and what is bad, what is right and wrong, and what is moral and immoral. Although all will not hold the same set of values, the social values of the majority will affect the beliefs and behaviors of all people.

The collection of a person's beliefs and morals makes up a set of principles known as *ethics*. Ethics are the judgments about right and wrong or, more specifically, a person's moral obligations to society that determine a person's actions. Determining ethical rights and wrongs is complicated by the fact that moral standards and generally accepted social behavior change with time. In addition, different groups in the same society may have conflicting ideas of right and wrong. These values and ethics of an individual are reflected in their actions as employees. There are four factors that generally affect the ethical decisions of employees:
- The law and other government regulations
- Industry and organizational ethical codes
- Social pressures
- Tension between personal standards and organizational needs

Employees' ethics, whatever they may be, influence a wide range of organizational decisions and actions.

A common fallacy in discussions about ethics is *If it's legal, it's ethical*. A common defense to charges of unethical behavior is to invoke the law. This legalistic approach to ethics mistakenly implies that actions that are not explicitly prohibited by the law are ethical. The main error in this approach is that legal standards do not establish ethical principles. Although abiding by the law is a part of ethical behavior, laws themselves do not describe how an ethical person should behave. One can be dishonest, unprincipled, untrustworthy, unfair, and uncaring without breaking the law. Ethical people measure their conduct by basic principles rather than rules. Thus, in making personal or occupational decisions, the law is only the minimum threshold in determining what is legally possible, and does not address how people should behave ethically.

Origins of Ethics

There are theories that state that by the time one becomes an adult and enters the workplace, a basic code of ethics is already in place. Ethical character is hardwired into the personality before or during adolescence. By this theory, if a person did not learn to be ethical in childhood, there is a slim chance that he or she will act ethically as an adult.

An opposing theory holds that operational values that guide behavior are not formed until early adulthood and, even after that, they are subject to change. Until one has to make serious, binding decisions, it is not necessary to act according to one's beliefs. By this theory, so long as individuals have the capacity to reflect and make value judgments, they can modify their personal ethics and change their behavior.

Business ethics programs rely on the validity of the latter theory. With the hope that adult behavior can be affected or modified, ethics programs are designed to steer employees in the right direction.

Ethics' Current Place in Business

The decline in public attitudes about business in recent years has reinforced the importance of ethics in the work place. Although there seems to be a further deterioration of public confidence, substantial endeavors have been made by organizations with respect to business ethics. These initiatives include adoption of codes of conduct, introduction of ethics into employee and management training, and the establishment of ethics and compliance offices.

Corporate ethics initiatives have accelerated over the last decade due in part to the impact of the U.S. Federal Sentencing Guidelines for Organizations. These guidelines can multiply or mitigate potentially devastating penalties for errant corporations, depending on their attempts to prevent such misconduct with effective compliance programs.

Ethics Program Development

Identifying key organizational characteristics and issues is a start to development of an ethics program. These items include:
- Understanding of why good people can commit unethical acts
- Defining current as well as desired organizational values

- Determining if organizational values have been properly communicated
- Producing written ethics policies, procedures, or structures
- Ascertaining how board members, stockholders, management, employees and any other pertinent members of the organization define success
- Determining if ethics is a leadership issue in the organization

With a good understanding of the above-mentioned issues, a more effective ethics program can be built. The following 12 components are necessary to develop, implement, and manage a comprehensive ethics program:

- Focus on ethical leadership
- Vision statement
- Values statement
- Code of ethics
- Designated ethics official
- Ethics task force or committee
- Ethics communication strategy
- Ethics training
- Ethics help and fraud report telephone line
- Ethical behavior rewards and sanctions
- Comprehensive system to monitor and track ethics data
- Periodic evaluation of ethics efforts and data

A sample of a typical Code of Business Ethics and an Annual Compliance Questionnaire are provided at the end of this chapter.

Sample Corporate Compliance Program[1]

I. SCOPE AND IMPLEMENTATION

This Corporate Compliance Program ("compliance program") applies to corporate headquarters and to all groups, operating divisions, and units of, and to all employees and agents of, *(company)* whose functions or responsibilities involve compliance with laws, regulations, or standards of conduct applicable to the operations or practices of the Corporation, in the United States or abroad.

II. STANDARDS OF CONDUCT

A. *(company)*'s standards of conduct for employee compliance with applicable laws and regulations are set forth in the Business Ethics Policy and the Employee Handbook for Nonexempt Employees ("Employee Handbook"), which may be revised and supplemented from time to time.

B. With the prior approval of *(company)* management, the Compliance Coordinator shall, as may appear necessary from time to time, revise and supplement the standards of conduct set forth in the Business Ethics Policy and the Employee Handbook.

C. The Compliance Coordinator shall, from time to time, distribute to relevant groups of employees materials incorporated by reference into the Business Ethics Policy, such as the HIMA Code of Ethics with respect to dealings with health care providers, professionals, and institutions.

III. ROLE OF THE COMPLIANCE COORDINATOR

A. The Compliance Coordinator shall have overall responsibility (1) to oversee compliance with the standards of conduct set forth in the Business Ethics Policy and the Employee Handbook, and with the compliance procedures established by or under the compliance program, and (2) to ensure the proper functioning of the compliance program.

B. The Compliance Coordinator shall confer generally with Management about matters relating to the compliance program, including all matters that, under the compliance program, the Compliance Coordinator is required to report to the Regulatory Affairs Committee of the Board of Directors under ¶ XI.B of the compliance program.

---

[1] Source: BNA/ACCA Compliance Manual: Prevention of Corporate Liability, pp. 1900:4-11. Published by The Bureau of National Affairs, Inc. (800-372-1033) <http://www.bna.com>

C. The Compliance Coordinator shall monitor developments relating to compliance with applicable laws, regulations, and standards of conduct, and, shall, from time to time, distribute to particular employees or groups of employees memoranda, news articles, or other informational materials that explain compliance requirements, report changes in requirements or industry standards, highlight the importance of compliance, or are otherwise relevant to their compliance responsibilities.

D. The Compliance Coordinator and/or the Corporate Compliance Audit Director shall review on a continuing basis the Corporation's internal procedures for preventing violations of law and shall create a compendium of such procedures, including:

   1. procedures for review of proposed product labeling, promotional materials, and advertising materials;

   2. procedures for obtaining opinions of counsel on proposed transactions or activities that may raise questions under the antitrust laws or other laws;

   3. procedures for review by regulatory affairs professionals of product testing, product modifications, introduction of new products and other matters that may raise regulatory issues;

   4. procedures for timely preparation and submission of disclosures and reports required by law; and

   5. internal and external programs.

E. The Compliance Coordinator shall (1) report to and meet with Management, as necessary and appropriate, with respect to any deficiencies identified or improvements needed in the compliance program, and (2) report to and meet with the Regulatory Affairs Committee of the Board of Directors as required by ¶ XI.B of this compliance program.

F. The Compliance Coordinator shall see to it that all reports of suspected misconduct or impropriety relating to *(company)* operations or practices are promptly, thoroughly, and properly investigated in accordance with a Standard Operating Procedure approved by Management; and that, where appropriate, disciplinary sanctions are imposed in accordance with ¶ IX of this compliance program.

G. The Compliance Coordinator shall discharge the responsibilities assigned to him or her by or under this compliance program.

H. The Compliance Coordinator shall take such other actions as are necessary and appropriate to implement and improve the compliance program.

I. _____ is designated as the Compliance Coordinator.

IV. DELEGATIONS OF AUTHORITY

    A. It is the policy of *(company)* that substantial discretionary authority shall not be delegated to individuals who the Corporation knows, or through the exercise of diligence could know, have a propensity to engage in illegal activities. In particular, substantial discretionary authority shall be delegated only to individuals who the Corporation is confident will not engage in illegal activities.

    B. The Compliance Coordinator shall, at least annually, review the delegations of discretionary authority within the Corporation, the checks, balances and controls applicable to such delegated discretionary authority, and the performance and background of the persons exercising such authority to determine whether any current delegation violates corporate policy. In conducting such review, the Compliance Coordinator may rely on information in personnel files, on the results of corporate audits, on the opinions of managers and supervisors, on consultation with the Corporation's independent outside auditors, on surveys of persons outside the Corporation who deal with the Corporation, and on other available information. At least annually, the Compliance Coordinator shall report in writing to the Chief Executive Officer the results of that review. The Compliance Coordinator shall recommend to Management any needed actions.

    C. The Compliance Coordinator and the Personnel Department shall from time to time jointly review the Corporation's procedures (including background and references checks) and criteria for filling (whether by new hiring or by promotion from within) positions involving substantial discretion, so as to ensure that only persons of integrity are selected for such positions. The Compliance Coordinator and the Personnel Department shall recommend to Management any needed actions.

V. COMMUNICATION OF STANDARDS AND PROCEDURES TO EMPLOYEES

    A. The Compliance Coordinator shall ensure, and, subject to ¶ B, at least annually shall certify in writing to the Chief Executive Officer, that:

        1. every officer and every key employee (as determined by the Compliance Coordinator) of the Corporation has, within the preceding twelve months, acknowledged to the Compliance Coordinator in writing that he or she has reviewed and understands the Business Ethics Policy;

        2. every employee of the Corporation whose function or responsibilities involve compliance with laws, regulations or standards of conduct applicable to the operations or practices of the Corporation (other than officers and key employees) has, within the preceding twelve months, acknowledged to the

Compliance Coordinator in writing that he or she has reviewed and understands the provisions of the Employee Handbook that relate to standards of conduct; and

3. every employee whose function or responsibilities involve compliance with laws, regulations or standards of conduct applicable to the operations or practices of the Corporation who was newly hired by *(company)* within the preceding twelve months has, within thirty days from the commencement of employment with *(company)* (a) received the Business Ethics Policy or Employee Handbook, as applicable, and (b) acknowledged to the Compliance Coordinator in writing that he or she has reviewed and understands the provisions of the Business Ethics Policy or Employee Handbook that relate to standards of conduct, as applicable.

B. If the Compliance Coordinator cannot truthfully make the certifications required by ¶A, he or she shall certify to the extent the facts permit, and shall identify the employees as to whom the required certification cannot be given, shall state the reasons (to the extent known) why the requirements of ¶A.1-3, as applicable, have not been satisfied with respect to those employees, and what measure will be taken promptly to satisfy those paragraphs, as applicable, with respect to those employees.

C. The Compliance Coordinator shall maintain records supporting the certifications called for by ¶A.

D. The Compliance Coordinator shall cause to be posted in prominent places accessible, in the aggregate, to all *(company)* employees whose functions and responsibilities involve compliance with laws, regulations or standards of conduct applicable to the operations or practices of the Corporation a Notice that:

1. states *(company)*'s commitment to comply with all applicable laws and regulations and the standards of conduct set forth in the Business Ethics Policy and the Employee Handbook;

2. designates the Compliance Coordinators (or a designee of the Compliance Coordinator) to receive any reports of misconduct or impropriety relating to *(company)*'s operations or practices of which any employees may have knowledge, whether committed by an employee of *(company)*, an employee of another company or organization, an employee of a governmental agency, or any other person;

3. states that no employee will suffer any penalty or retribution for good faith reporting of any suspected misconduct or impropriety;

4. states that reports of misconduct or impropriety may be anonymous;

5. states that reports of misconduct or impropriety may be made directly to a governmental agency;

6. states that _(company)_ will investigate all such reports, and that any _(company)_ employee found to have engaged in misconduct will receive prompt and appropriate discipline, up to and including dismissal; and

7. states that the Compliance Coordinator or designee (with telephone number) is available for consultation on any question a _(company)_ employee may have concerning the application to _(company)_'s operations or practices of any law, regulation, or standard of conduct or any other matter relating to _(company)_'s compliance program.

E. The Compliance Coordinator shall, in consultation and coordination with other units of the Corporation, arrange for compliance training sessions for all employees whose functions or responsibilities involve compliance with laws, regulations, or standards of conduct applicable to the operations or practices of the Corporation. Each such session shall include a presentation of some aspect or aspects of the laws, regulations, and standards of conduct applicable to the employees who attend the session. Every such employee shall attend at least one such session during each twelve months of employment with _(company)_. Special sessions shall be held, as necessary and convenient, for new employees. The Compliance Coordinator shall, at least annually, certify to the Chief Executive Officer that (1) every such employee has attended at least one such compliance training session within the preceding twelve months, or (2) that all but certain identified employees have attended at least one such session, the reasons why the identified employees have not attended one, and the measures that will be taken to ensure that those employees promptly attend such a session.

F. Each supervisor shall annually certify to the Compliance Coordinator in writing that he or she has personally:

1. discussed with each employee under his or her immediate supervision the standards of conduct set forth in the Business Ethics Policy or the Employee Handbook, as applicable;

2. informed each employee the strict compliance with such standards of conduct is a condition of employment; and

3. informed each such employee that _(company)_ will take disciplinary action, including dismissal as appropriate, for violation of such standards of conduct.

G. The Compliance Coordinator shall maintain a file of such certifications, and shall report, at least annually, to Management with respect to compliance with this provision of the compliance program.

H. The Compliance Coordinator and the Personnel Department shall jointly develop and implement tests or other methods to measure the effectiveness of the communications of standards and procedures to employees. The Compliance Coordinator and the Personnel Department shall report the results of such tests or measures to Management.

VI. MONITORING, AUDITING AND REPORTING

A. Monitoring

1. The Compliance Coordinator shall, by memorandum, at least annually, advise all employees with supervisory responsibility of their duty to monitor all activities of their subordinates in the course of their employment with *(company)* to ensure that those activities are conducted in compliance with all applicable laws, regulations, and standards of conduct.

2. Each supervisor shall sign a copy of the memorandum referred to in ¶ 1 and return it to the Compliance Coordinator, who shall maintain a file of such memoranda. The Compliance Coordinator shall, at least annually, report to Management with respect to compliance with this provision of the compliance program.

B. Auditing

1. The Corporate Compliance Audit Director shall be responsible for the conduct of internal non-financial audits to promote compliance with applicable laws, regulations and standards of conduct (other than those relating to financial matters).

2. The Chief Financial Officer of the Company shall be responsible for the conduct of internal financial audits to promote compliance with applicable laws, regulations and standards of conduct relating to financial matters.

3. Management shall arrange for the conduct of annual audits by independent outside auditors to promote compliance with applicable laws, regulations and standards of conduct, both financial and non-financial.

4. Copies of all internal and outside audits reports relating to compliance with laws, regulations, or standards of conduct (whether financial or non-financial) shall be provided to the Compliance Coordinator and to the Audit Committee or the Regulatory Affairs [Committee] of the Board, whichever is the appropriate recipient.

C. Reporting

   1. The Compliance Coordinator shall establish and oversee a reporting system, in which:

      a. any employee may report to the Compliance Coordinator (or a designee of the Compliance Coordinator) any suspected misconduct or impropriety relating to *(company)*'s operations or practices, whether committed by an employee of *(company)*, an employee of another company or organization, an employee of a governmental agency, or other person;

      b. no employee will suffer any penalty or retribution for good faith reporting of any suspected misconduct or impropriety; and

      c. any report of misconduct or impropriety may be anonymous.

   2. The Compliance Coordinator shall, at least annually, communicate to all *(company)* employees the policy of the Corporation that any employee who learns of an apparent violation of law or regulations or unethical conduct relating to the business or activities of the Corporation shall report such violation or conduct to the Compliance Coordinator (or a designee of the Compliance Coordinator), and may do so anonymously.

   3. At least annually, the Compliance Coordinator shall report to Management and to the Regulatory Affairs Committee of the Board on the functioning of the reporting system.

VII. DEBARRED INDIVIDUALS

   A. It is the policy of *(company)* that the Corporation shall not knowingly employ or retain as a consultant, with or without pay, any individual who is publicly listed by a federal agency as debarred, suspended, or otherwise ineligible for federal programs.

   B. To carry out its policy, the Corporation shall make reasonable inquiry into the status of any potential employee or consultant. Such reasonable inquiry shall include review of the General Services Administration's List of Parties Excluded from Federal Procurement Programs and *(information on debarments imposed by any other relevant federal agency)*.

   C. The Corporation's policy does not require the Corporation to terminate the employment or consultancy of individuals who become suspended, or are proposed for debarment during their employment or consultancy with the Corporation. The Corporation shall, however, remove such employees or consultants from responsibility for, or involvement with, governmental business until the resolution of such suspension or proposed debarment.

D. If such employee or consultant is debarred, his or her employment or consultancy with the Corporation shall be terminated.

VIII. BUSINESS DEALINGS WITH DEBARRED INDIVIDUALS AND ENTITIES, AND EMPLOYEES AND CONSULTANTS CHARGED WITH OR CONVICTED OF CRIMES

A. Debarred individuals and entities

1. It is the policy of *(company)* that it shall not knowingly form a contract with, purchase from, or enter into any business relationship with, any individual or business entity that is publicly listed by a federal agency as debarred, suspended, or proposed for debarment, other than (1) sales by the Corporation in the ordinary course of business and (2) purchases by the Corporation in the ordinary course of business of goods or services that are not specific to the Corporation's medical device operations regulated by the U.S. Food and Drug Administration, unless there is a compelling reason to do so.

2. The Corporation shall make reasonable inquiry as to the status of any potential business partner whose relationship to the Corporation would not be within the scope of ¶A(1) or ¶A(2). Such reasonable inquiry shall include review of the General Services Administration's List of Parties Excluded from Federal Procurement Programs and review of information on debarments imposed by *(any other relevant federal agency)*.

3. In the case of any decision to proceed with a business relationship not within the scope of ¶A(1) or A(2) and permissible under ¶A solely due to a compelling reason, the decision and the compelling reason shall be documented by the Compliance Coordinator.

B. Individuals Charged with or Convicted of Offenses Relating to Governmental Business

1. If any employee or consultant of the Corporation is charged by Indictment or Information with criminal offense, the Corporation shall remove that employee or consultant immediately from responsibility for, or involvement with, matters relating to the Corporation's business.

2. If the employee or consultant is convicted of an offense relating to the Company's business, his or her employment or consultancy with the Corporation shall be terminated.

3. With respect to any person convicted of a federal offense relating to the business or operations of *(company)*, the Corporation shall have and enforce the following policies:

   a. All business relations under the Corporation's control with such person shall be terminated, and such person shall not be re-employed or further retained by the Corporation in any capacity. This provision does not apply to any relationship involving the holding of any type of securities.

   b. No such person, nor any other person affiliated with such person, shall share any office space or storage space, or any building or computer system, with the Corporation.

   c. No such person shall be permitted to enter the premises of the Corporation, except as required by law.

IX. DISCIPLINE

A. It is the policy of *(company)* that the standards of conduct set forth in the Business Ethics Policy and in the Employee handbook shall be consistently enforced through appropriate disciplinary mechanisms. Disciplinary actions may be up to and including dismissal, and may extend, as appropriate, to individuals responsible for the failure to prevent, detect, or report an offense.

B. The Compliance Coordinator shall, in consultation with Management and supervisors as appropriate, establish and administer a company-wide disciplinary system, including written disciplinary cases. The system shall provide for the making of disciplinary decisions by appropriate company officials in consultation with the Compliance Coordinator.

C. The Compliance Coordinator shall maintain records of all disciplinary actions taken for violation of the standards of conduct set forth in the Business Ethics Policy and in the Employee Handbook.

D. The Compliance Coordinator shall, at least annually, report to Management in writing on the disciplinary system.

X. RESPONSE TO VIOLATIONS

A. It is a policy of *(company)* that, if a violation of any applicable law, regulation, or standard of conduct relating to the business of the Corporation is detected, the Corporation shall take all reasonable steps to respond appropriately to the violation and to prevent further similar violations, including any modifications to this compliance program. It is the policy of *(company)* that if *(company)* learns that any statement previously made by *(company)* to any governmental agency is false or incorrect in any material respect, *(company)* shall voluntarily and promptly (after appropriate preliminary investigation) report the matter to the governmental agency. It is also the policy of *(company)* that if *(company)* learns of a violation of any applicable law or regulation that is not known to the governmental agency but is likely to be of interest to that agency, *(company)* shall voluntarily and promptly (after appropriate investigation) report the matter to that agency.

B. Any employee of the Corporation who learns of a violation of the type referred to in ¶A shall report it to the Compliance Coordinator (or designee of the Compliance Coordinator). Although it is preferable that any such report be made by an employee who identifies himself or herself so that the matter may be investigated promptly and thoroughly, an employee may make such a report anonymously. Failure to report such a violation known to an employee may, itself, be a basis for disciplinary action.

C. Whenever the Compliance Coordinator receives information regarding a possible violation of any applicable law or regulation, the Compliance Coordinator shall take appropriate steps to examine information and conduct the investigation necessary to determine whether an actual violation has occurred. The Compliance Coordinator shall recommend to Management an appropriate course of action, and Management shall render a timely decision with respect to such recommendation. The Compliance Coordinator shall prepare a memorandum reflecting the information developed, the recommendation made, and the Management decision rendered, which memorandum shall promptly be furnished to the Audit Committee of the Board.

XI. ROLE OF THE REGULATORY AFFAIRS COMMITTEE OF THE BOARD OF DIRECTORS

　　A. The Regulatory Affairs Committee shall be responsible for reviewing and suggesting to Management any necessary improvements in:

　　　　1. the standards of conduct set forth in the Business Ethics Policy and the Employee Handbook; and

　　　　2. the compliance program generally.

　　B. The Regulatory Affairs Committee shall, at least annually:

　　　　1. receive a written report from, and meet with, the Compliance Coordinator with respect to the compliance program generally, including:

　　　　　　a. the Compliance Coordinator's review of delegations of authority within the Corporation;

　　　　　　b. the certifications required by ¶V.A of this program, and employee familiarity with the corporate standards of conduct generally;

       c. the certifications required by ¶V.D of his program, the compliance communications and training generally, including their effectiveness;

       d. the certifications required by ¶V.E of this program, the compliance by supervisors with ¶VI.A.2 of this program, and the participation of supervisors in this program generally;

       e. the results of internal and any external audits (whether financial or non-financial) relating to compliance with laws, regulations, or standards of conduct.

       f. the reporting system required by ¶VI.C of this program; and

       g. the disciplinary system required by ¶IX of this program;

  2. discuss with Management the compliance program and the report of the Compliance Coordinator; and

  3. report to the Board of Directors with respect to the report of the Compliance Coordinator and the Committee's meetings with the Compliance Coordinator and Management, and with respect to the compliance program generally.

C. At each meeting of the Regulatory Affairs Committee, the Compliance Coordinator shall report to the Committee any and all recommendations made by the Compliance Coordinator to Management, and decisions by Management, under ¶X.C of this program since last meeting of the Committee.

D. The Regulatory Affairs Committee shall adopt a standard operating procedure for the performance of its responsibilities under this compliance program.

Sample Fraud Policy

BACKGROUND

The corporate fraud policy is established to facilitate the development of controls that will aid in the detection and prevention of fraud against ABC Corporation. It is the intent of ABC Corporation to promote consistent organizational behavior by providing guidelines and assigning responsibility for the development of controls and conduct of investigations.

SCOPE OF POLICY

This policy applies to any irregularity, or suspected irregularity, involving employees as well as shareholders, consultants, vendors, contractors, outside agencies doing business with employees of such agencies, and/or any other parties with a business relationship with ABC Corporation (also called the Company).

Any investigative activity required will be conducted without regard to the suspected wrongdoer's length of service, position/title, or relationship to the Company.

POLICY

Management is responsible for the detection and prevention of fraud, misappropriations, and other irregularities. Fraud is defined as the intentional, false representation or concealment of a material fact for the purpose of inducing another to act upon it to his or her injury. Each member of the management team will be familiar with the types of improprieties that might occur within his or her area of responsibility, and be alert for any indication of irregularity.

Any irregularity that is detected or suspected must be reported immediately to the Director of _____, who coordinates all investigations with the Legal Department and other affected areas, both internal and external.

ACTIONS CONSTITUTING FRAUD

The terms defalcation, misappropriation, and other fiscal irregularities refer to, but are not limited to:

- Any dishonest or fraudulent act
- Misappropriation of funds, securities, supplies, or other assets
- Impropriety in the handling or reporting of money or financial transactions
- Profiteering as a result of insider knowledge of company activities
- Disclosing confidential and proprietary information to outside parties
- Disclosing to other persons securities activities engaged in or contemplated by the company
- Accepting or seeking anything of material value from contractors, vendors, or persons providing services/materials to the Company. Exception: Gifts less than $50 in value.
- Destruction, removal, or inappropriate use of records, furniture, fixtures, and equipment; and/or
- Any similar or related irregularity

OTHER IRREGULARITIES

Irregularities concerning an employee's moral, ethical, or behavioral conduct should by resolved by departmental management and the Employee Relations Unit of Human Resources rather than the _____ Unit.

If there is any question as to whether an action constitutes fraud, contact the Director of _____ for guidance.

INVESTIGATION RESPONSIBILITIES

The _____ Unit has the primary responsibility for the investigation of all suspected fraudulent acts as defined in the policy. If the investigation substantiates that fraudulent activities have occurred, the _____ Unit will issue reports to appropriate designated personnel and, if appropriate, to the Board of Directors through the Audit Committee.

Decisions to prosecute or refer the examination results to the appropriate law enforcement and/or regulatory agencies for independent investigation will be made in conjunction with legal counsel and senior management, as will final decisions on disposition of the case.

CONFIDENTIALITY	The _____ Unit treats all information received confidentially. Any employee who suspects dishonest or fraudulent activity will notify the _____ Unit immediately, and *should not attempt to personally conduct investigations or interviews/interrogations* related to any suspected fraudulent act (see **REPORTING PROCEDURE** section below). Investigation results *will not be disclosed or discussed* with anyone other than those who have a legitimate need to know. This is important in order to avoid damaging the reputations of persons suspected but subsequently found innocent of wrongful conduct and to protect the Company from potential civil liability.
AUTHORIZATION FOR INVESTIGATING SUSPECTED FRAUD	Members of the Investigation Unit will have: • Free and unrestricted access to all Company records and premises, whether owned or rented; and • The authority to examine, copy, and/or remove all or any portion of the contents of files, desks, cabinets, and other storage facilities on the premises without prior knowledge or consent of any individual who might use or have custody of any such items or facilities when it is within the scope of their investigation.
REPORTING PROCEDURES	Great care must be taken in the investigation of suspected improprieties or irregularities so as to avoid mistaken accusations or alerting suspected individuals that an investigation is under way. An employee who discovers or suspects fraudulent activity will *contact the _____ Unit immediately*. The employee or other complainant may remain anonymous. All inquiries concerning the activity under investigation from the suspected individual, his or her attorney or representative, or any other inquirer should be directed to the Investigations Unit or the Legal Department. No information concerning the status of an investigation will be given out. The proper response to any inquiries is: "I am not at liberty to discuss this matter." *Under no circumstances* should any reference be made to "the allegation," "the crime," "the fraud," "the forgery," "the misappropriation," or any other specific reference. The reporting individual should be informed of the following: • Do not contact the suspected individual in an effort to determine facts or demand restitution. • Do not discuss the case, facts, suspicions, or allegations with *anyone* unless specifically asked to do so by the Legal Department or _____ Unit.

TERMINATION   If an investigation results in a recommendation to terminate an individual, the recommendation will be reviewed for approval by the designated representatives from Human Resources and the Legal Department and, if necessary, by outside counsel, before any such action is taken. The _____ Unit does not have the authority to terminate an employee. The decision to terminate an employee is made by the employee's management. Should the _____ Unit believe the management decision inappropriate for the facts presented, the facts will be presented to executive level management for a decision.

ADMINISTRATION   The Director of _____ is responsible for the administration, revision, interpretation, and application of this policy. The policy will be reviewed annually and revised as needed.

APPROVAL

_____   _____
(CEO/Senior Vice President/Executive   Date

Fraud Policy Decision Matrix

Action Required	Investigation Unit	Internal Audit	Finance/ Accounting	Executive Mgmt	Line Mgmt	Risk Mgmt	Legal	Public Relations	Employee Relations
1. Controls to Prevent Fraud	S	S	S	SR	SR	S	S	S	S
2. Incident Reporting	P	S	S	S	S	S	S	S	S
3. Investigation of Fraud	P	S					S		S
4. Referrals to Law Enforcement	P						S		
5. Recovery of Monies due to Fraud	P								
6. Recommendations to Prevent Fraud	SR	SR	S	S	S	S	S	S	S
7. Internal Control Reviews		P							
8. Handle Cases of a Sensitive Nature	P	S		S		S	S		S
9. Publicity/Press Releases	S	S						P	
10. Civil Litigation	S	S					P		
11. Corrective Action/Recommendations To Prevent Recurrences	SR	SR		S	SR	S	S		
12. Monitor Recoveries	S		P						
13. Pro-active Fraud Auditing	S	P							
14. Fraud Education/Training	P	S			S			S	
15. Risk Analysis of Areas of Vulnerability						P			
16. Case Analysis	S	S							
17. Hotline	P	S							
18. EthicsLine	S	S					P		

P (Primary Responsibility) S (Secondary Responsibility) SR (Shared Responsibility)

Sample Code of Business Ethics and Conduct

Introduction

This section reaffirms the importance of high standards of business conduct. Adherence to this Code of Business Ethics and Conduct by all employees is the only sure way we can merit the confidence and support of the public.

Many of us came from a culture that provided answers or direction for almost every situation possible. Managing our business was not so complex, the dilemmas we faced were—for the most part—simple, making our choices relatively easy. We would probably all agree that managing in today's environment is not so simple.

This code has been prepared as a working guide and not as a technical legal document. Thus, emphasis is on brevity and readability rather than providing an all-inclusive answer to specific questions. For example, the term "employee" is used in its broadest sense and refers to every officer and employee of the company and its subsidiaries. The word "law" refers to laws, regulations, orders, etc.

In observance of this code, as in other business conduct, there is no substitute for common sense. Each employee should apply this code with common sense and the attitude of seeking full compliance with the letter and spirit of the rules presented.

It is incumbent upon you, as an employee of the company to perform satisfactorily and to follow our policies and comply with our rules as they are issued or modified from time to time.

These policies and rules are necessary to effectively manage the business and meet the ever-changing needs of the marketplace. Good performance and compliance with business rules lead to success. Both are crucial since our ability to provide you with career opportunities depends totally upon our success in the marketplace. Nonetheless, changes in our economy, our markets and our technology are inevitable. Indeed, career opportunities will vary between the individual companies. For these reasons, we cannot contract or even imply that your employment will continue for any particular period of time. While you might terminate your employment at any time, with or without cause, we reserve that same right. This relationship might not be modified, except in writing signed by an appropriate representative of the company.

This Code of Business Ethics and Conduct is a general guide to acceptable and appropriate behavior at the company and you are expected to comply with its contents; however, it does not contain all of the detailed information you will need during the course of your employment. Nothing contained in this code or, in other communications, creates or implies an employment contract or term of employment. We are committed to reviewing our policies continually. Thus, this code might be modified or revised from time to time.

You should familiarize yourself with this code so that you might readily distinguish any proposal or act that would constitute a violation. Each employee is responsible for his actions. Violations can result in disciplinary action, including dismissal and criminal prosecution. There will be no reprisal against an employee who in good faith reported a violation or suspected violation.

The absence of a specific guideline practice or instruction covering a particular situation does not relieve an employee from exercising the highest ethical standards applicable to the circumstances.

If any employee has doubts regarding a questionable situation that might arise, that employee should immediately consult his supervisor or higher level.

Competition and Antitrust
Fair Competition
The company supports competition based on quality, service and price. We will conduct our affairs honestly, directly and fairly. To comply with the antitrust laws and our policy of fair competition, employees:
- Must never discuss with competitors any matter directly involved in competition between us and the competitor (e.g. sales price, marketing strategies, market shares and sales policies).
- Must never agree with a competitor to restrict competition by fixing prices, allocating markets or other means.
- Must not arbitrarily refuse to deal with or purchase goods and services from others simply because they are competitors in other respects.
- Must not require others to buy from us before we will buy from them.

- Must not require customers to take from us a service they don't want just so they can get one they do want.
- Must never engage in industrial espionage or commercial bribery.
- Must be accurate and truthful in all dealings with customers and be careful to accurately represent the quality, features and availability of company products and services.

Compliance with Laws and Regulatory Orders

The applicable laws and regulatory orders of every jurisdiction in which the company operates must be followed. Each employee is charged with the responsibility of acquiring sufficient knowledge of the laws and orders relating to his duties in order to recognize potential dangers and to know when to seek legal advice.

In particular, when dealing with public officials, employees must adhere to the highest ethical standards of business conduct. When we seek the resolution of regulatory or political issues affecting the company's interests we must do so solely on the basis of merit and pursuant to proper procedures in dealing with such officials. Employees may not offer, provide or solicit, directly or indirectly, any special treatment or favor in return for anything of economic value or the promise or expectation of future value or gain. In addition, there shall be no entertaining of employees of the U.S. Government.

Foreign Corrupt Practices Act

No employee will engage in activity that might involve the employee or the company in a violation of the Foreign Corrupt Practices Act of 1977. The Foreign Corrupt Practices Act requires that the company's books and records accurately and fairly reflect all transactions and that we maintain a system of internal controls; transactions conform to management's authorizations; and the accounting records are accurate. No employee will falsely report transactions or fail to report the existence of false transactions in the accounting records. Employees certifying the correctness of records, including vouchers or bills, should have reasonable knowledge that the information is correct and proper.

Under the Act, it is also a federal crime for any U.S. business enterprise to offer a gift, payment or bribe, or anything else of value, whether directly or indirectly, to any foreign official, foreign political party or party official, or candidate for foreign political office for the purpose of influencing an official act or decision, or seeking influence with a foreign government in order to obtain, retain or direct business to the company or to any person.

Even if the payment is legal in the host country, it is forbidden by the Act and violates U.S. law.

Conflicts of Interest

There are several situations that could give rise to a conflict of interest. The most common are accepting gifts from suppliers, employment by another company, ownership of a significant part of another company or business, close or family relationships with outside suppliers and communications with competitors. A potential conflict of interest exists for employees who make decisions in their jobs that would allow them to give preference or favor to a customer in exchange for anything of personal benefit to themselves or their friends and families.

Such situations could interfere with an employee's ability to make judgments solely in the company's best interest.

Gifts and Entertainment

DEFINITION OF GIFTS

"Gifts" are items and services of value that are given to any outside parties, but do not include items described below.

- Normal business entertainment items such as meals and beverages are not to be considered "gifts."
- Items of minimal value, given in connection with sales campaigns and promotions or employee services, safety or retirement awards are not to be considered "gifts" for purposes of this code.
- Contributions or donations to recognized charitable and nonprofit organizations are not considered gifts.
- Items or services with a total value under $100 per year are excluded.

DEFINITION OF SUPPLIER

"Supplier" includes not only vendors providing services and material to the company, but also consultants, financial institutions, advisors, and any person or institution which does business with the company.

GIFTS

No employee or member of his immediate family shall solicit or accept from an actual or prospective customer or supplier any compensation, advance loans (except from established financial institutions on the same basis as other customers), gifts, entertainment, or other favors which are of more than token value or which the employee would not normally be in a position to reciprocate under normal expense account procedures.

Under no circumstances should a gift or entertainment be accepted which would influence the employee's judgment. In particular, employees must avoid any interest in or benefit from any supplier that could reasonably cause them to favor that supplier over others. It is a violation of the code for any employee to solicit or encourage a supplier to give any item or service to the employee regardless of its value, no matter how small. Our suppliers will retain their confidence in the objectivity and integrity of our company only if each employee strictly observes this guideline.

REPORTING GIFTS

An employee who receives, or whose family member receives, an unsolicited gift prohibited by these guidelines, should report it to his supervisor and either return it to the person making the gift or, in the case of perishable gift, give it to nonprofit charitable organization.

DISCOUNTS

An employee might accept discounts on a personal purchase of the supplier's or customer's products only if such discounts do not affect the company's purchase price and are generally offered to others having a similar business relationship with the supplier or customer.

BUSINESS MEETINGS

Entertainment and services offered by a supplier or customer may be accepted by an employee when they are associated with a business meeting and the supplier or customer provides them to others as a normal part of its business. Examples of such entertainment and services are transportation to and from the supplier's or customer's place of business, hospitality suites, golf outings, lodging at the supplier's or customer's place of business, and business lunches and dinners for business visitors to the supplier's or customer's location. The services should generally be of the type normally used by the company's employees and allowable under the applicable company's expense account.

Outside Employment

Employees must not be employed outside the company:
- In any business that competes with or provides services to the company or its subsidiaries, and/or

- In a manner which would affect their objectivity in carrying out their company responsibilities and/or
- Where the outside employment would conflict with scheduled hours, including overtime, or the performance of the company assignments. Employees must not use company time, materials, information or other assets in connection with outside employment.

Relationships with Suppliers and Customers

Business transactions must be entered into solely for the best interests of the company. No employee can, directly or indirectly, benefit from his position as an employee or from any sale, purchase or other activity of the company. Employees should avoid situations involving a conflict or the appearance of conflict between duty to the company and self-interest.

No employee who deals with individuals or organizations doing or seeking to do business with the company, or who makes recommendations with respect to such dealings, should:
- Serve as an officer, director, employee or consultant; or
- Own a substantial interest in any competitor of the company, or any organization doing or seeking to do business with the company. Substantial interest means an economic interest that might influence or reasonably be thought to influence judgment or action, but shall not include an investment representing less than 1% of a class of outstanding securities of a publicly held corporation. Every employee must complete the Conflict of Interest Questionnaire included with this book.

In addition, no employee who deals with individuals or organizations doing or seeking to do business with the company, or who makes recommendations with respect to such dealings, might:
- Have any other direct or indirect personal interest in any business transactions with the company (other than customary employee purchases of company products and services as consumers and transactions where the interest arises solely by reason of the employee relationship or that of a holder of securities);
- Provide telecommunications or information service or equipment, either directly or as a reseller in a manner that would place the objectivity or integrity of the company in question.

Our policy is that employees will not do business on behalf of the company with a close personal friend or relative; however, recognizing that these transactions do occur, they must be reported on the Conflict of Interest Questionnaire.

This policy is applicable equally to the members of the immediate family of each employee, which normally includes your spouse, children and their spouses, and the father, mother, sisters and brothers of yourself and your household.

Employment of Relatives

Relatives of employees will not be employed on a permanent or temporary basis by the company where the relative directly reports to the employee or the employee exercises any direct influence with respect to the relative's hiring, placement, promotions, evaluations or pay.

Confidential Information and Privacy of Communications
Confidential Information

Confidential information includes all information, whether technical, business, financial or otherwise concerning the company, which the company treats as confidential or secret and/or which is not available or is not made available publicly. It also includes any private information of, or relating to, customer records, fellow employees, other persons or other companies, and national security information obtained by virtue of the employee's position.

Company policy and various laws protect the integrity of the company's confidential information which must not be divulged except in strict accordance with established company policies and procedures. The obligation not to divulge confidential company information is in effect even though material might not be specifically identified as confidential and the obligation exists during and continues after employment with the company.

A few examples of prohibited conduct are:
- Selling or otherwise using, divulging or transmitting confidential company information;
- Using confidential company information to knowingly convert a company business opportunity for personal use;
- Using confidential company information to acquire real estate which the employee knows is of interest to the company;
- Using, divulging or transmitting confidential company information in the course of outside employment or other relationship or any succeeding employment or other relationship at any time; and
- Trading in the company stocks, or the stocks of any company, based on information which has not been disclosed to the public or divulging such information to others so

that they might trade in such stock. Insider trading is prohibited by company policy and federal and state law.

Employees shall not seek out, accept or use any confidential company information of or from a competitor of the company. In particular, should we hire an employee who previously worked for a competitor, we must neither accept nor solicit confidential information concerning that competitor from our employee.

Classified National Security Information

Only employees with proper government clearance and a need to know have access to classified national security information. Government regulations outlined in company instructions for safeguarding must be followed. Disclosing such information, without authorization, even after leaving employment, is a violation of law and this code.

Adverse information about employees having government clearance must be reported to the Security or Law Departments' representatives having responsibility for clearances.

Company Assets

Cash and Bank Accounts

All cash and bank account transactions must be handled so as to avoid any question or suspicion of impropriety. All cash transactions must be recorded in the company's books of account.

All accounts of company funds, except authorized imprest funds, shall be established and maintained in the name of the company or one of its subsidiaries and might be opened or closed only on the authority of the company's Board of Directors. Imprest funds must be maintained in the name of the custodian and the custodian is wholly responsible for these funds. All cash received shall be promptly recorded and deposited in a company or subsidiary bank account. No funds shall be maintained in the form of cash, except authorized petty cash, and no company shall maintain an anonymous (numbered) account at any bank. Payments into numbered bank accounts by the company might leave that company open to suspicion of participation in a possibly improper transaction. Therefore, no disbursements of any nature might be made into numbered bank accounts or other accounts not clearly identified to the company as to their ownership.

No payments can be made in cash (currency) other than regular, approved cash payrolls and normal disbursements from petty cash supported by signed receipts or other appropriate documentation. Further, corporate checks shall not be written to "cash," "bearer" or similar designations.

Company Assets and Transactions

Compliance with prescribed accounting procedures is required at all times. Employees having control over company assets and transactions are expected to handle them with the strictest integrity and ensure that all transactions are executed in accordance with management's authorization. All transactions shall be accurately and fairly recorded in reasonable detail in the company's accounting records.

Employees are personally accountable for company funds over which they have control. Employees who spend company funds should ensure the company receives good value in return and must maintain accurate records of such expenditures. Employees who approve or certify the correctness of a bill or voucher should know that the purchase and amount are proper and correct. Obtaining or creating "false" invoices or other misleading documentation or the invention or use of fictitious sales, purchases, services, loans, entities or other financial arrangements is prohibited.

Employees must pay for personal telephone calls and use, except to the extent that specifically defined benefit programs or allowances otherwise provide.

Expense Reimbursement

Expense actually incurred by an employee in performing company business must be documented on expense reports in accordance with company procedures. In preparing expense reports, employees should review these procedures for the documentation in order to be reimbursed for business expenses.

Company Credit Card

Company credit cards are provided to employees for convenience in conducting company business. No personal expenses can be charged on company credit cards except as specifically authorized by company procedures. Any charged personal expenses must be paid promptly by the employee. Company credit cards should not be used to avoid preparing documentation for direct payment to vendors. Where allowed by local law, charges on company credit cards for which a properly approved expense report has not been received at the time of an employee's termination of employment might be deducted from the employee's last paycheck. The company will pursue repayment by the employee of any amounts it has to pay on the employee's behalf.

Software and Computers
Computerized information and computer software appear intangible, but they are valuable assets of the company and must be protected from misuse, theft, fraud, loss and unauthorized use or disposal, just as any other company property.

Use of mainframe computers must be customer service or job related. Employees cannot access company records of any kind for their personal use. Misappropriation of computer space, time or software includes, but is not limited to, using a computer to create or run unauthorized jobs, operating a computer in an unauthorized mode or intentionally causing any kind of operational failure.

Personal computers can be used for company-sanctioned education programs as well as personal use incidental to company business use with the permission of your supervisor. However, personal use cannot be allowed for personal financial gain.

It is also understood that personal computers will occasionally be used at home with the permission of your supervisor.

Political Contributions
Federal law and many state laws prohibit contributions by corporations to political parties or candidates. The term "political contributions" includes, in addition to direct cash contributions, the donation of property or services, and the purchases of tickets to fundraising events. Employees can make direct contributions of their own money, but such contributions are not reimbursable. In addition, employees can make contributions to a company-sponsored Political Action Committee.

Where corporate political contributions are legal in connection with state, local or foreign elections, such contribution shall be made only from funds allocated for that purpose, and with the written approval of the president of the company making the contribution. The amounts of contributions made shall be subject to inter-company allocation.

It is improper for an employee to use his position within the company to solicit political contributions from another employee for the purpose of supporting a political candidate or influencing legislation. It is also improper for an employee to make a political contribution in the name of the company.

Employee Conduct
Conduct on Company Business
Dishonest or illegal activities on company premises or while on company business will not be condoned and can result in disciplinary action, including dismissal and criminal prosecution. The following illustrates activities that are against company policy, and which will not be tolerated on company premises, in company vehicles or while engaged in company business:

- Consumption and storage of alcoholic beverages, except where legally licensed or authorized by an officer of the company.
- The use of controlled substances, such as drugs or alcohol. The unlawful manufacture, distribution, dispensation, possession, transfer, sale, purchase or use of a controlled substance.
- Driving vehicles or operating company equipment while under the influence of alcohol or controlled substances.
- Illegal betting or gambling.
- Carrying weapons of any sort on company premises, in company vehicles or while on company business. Even employees with permits or licenses cannot carry weapons on company property or while on company business.

The company reserves the right to inspect any property that might be used by employees for the storage of their personal effects. This includes desks, lockers and vehicles owned by the company. It is a violation of company policy to store any contraband, illegal drugs, toxic materials or weapons on company property.

Reporting Violations
All employees are responsible for compliance with these rules, standards and principles. In the area of ethics, legality and propriety, each employee has an obligation to the company that transcends normal reporting relationships. Employees should be alert to possible violations of the code anywhere in the company and are encouraged to report such violations promptly. Reports should be made to the employee's supervisor, the appropriate security, audit, or legal department personnel, or elsewhere as the circumstance dictates.

Employees will also be expected to cooperate in an investigation of violations. In addition, any employee who is convicted of a felony, whether related to these rules or not, should also report that fact.

All cases of questionable activity involving the code or other potentially improper actions will be reviewed for appropriate action, discipline, or corrective steps. Whenever possible, the company will keep confidential the identity of employees about or against whom allegations of violations are brought, unless or until it has been determined that a violation has occurred. Similarly, whenever possible, the company will keep confidential the identity of anyone reporting a possible violation. Reprisal against any employee who has, in good faith, reported a violation or suspected violation is strictly prohibited.

All employees are required to notify the company within five (5) days of any conviction of any criminal statute violation occurring on the job. In addition, any employee who is convicted of a felony, whether related to these rules or not, should report that fact.

Discipline

Violation of this code can result in serious consequences for the company, its image, credibility and confidence of its customers and can include substantial fines and restrictions on future operations as well as the possibility of fines and prison sentences for individual employees. Therefore, it is necessary that the company ensure that there will be no violations. Employees should recognize that it is in their best interest, as well as the company's, to follow this code carefully.

The amount of any money involved in a violation might be immaterial in assessing the seriousness of a violation since, in some cases, heavy penalties might be assessed against the company for a violation involving a relatively small amount of money, or no money.

Disciplinary action should be coordinated with the appropriate Human Resources representatives. The overall seriousness of the matter will be considered in setting the disciplinary action to be taken against an individual employee. Such action, which might be reviewed with the appropriate Human Resources organization, might include:
- Reprimand
- Probation
- Suspension
- Reduction in salary

- Demotion
- Combination of the above
- Dismissal

In addition, individual cases might involve:
- Reimbursement of losses or damages
- Referral for criminal prosecution or civil action
- Combination of the above

Disciplinary action might also be taken against supervisors or executives who condone, permit or have knowledge of illegal or unethical conduct by those reporting to them and do not take corrective action. Disciplinary action might also be taken against employees who make false statements in connection with investigations of violations of this code.

The company in its sole discretion will determine the disciplinary action appropriate to a given matter. The listing of possible actions is informative only and does not bind the company to follow any particular disciplinary steps, process or procedure.

The company's rules and regulations regarding proper employee conduct will not be waived in any respect. Violation is cause for disciplinary action including dismissal. All employees will be held to the standards of conduct described in this booklet.

The company never has and never will authorize any employee to commit an act that violates this code or to direct a subordinate to do so. With that understood, it is not possible to justify commission of such an act by saying someone directed it in higher management.

Compliance Letter and Conflict of Interest Questionnaire

Annually, all officers of the company will represent in writing that there are no violations of this code known to the officer, after the exercise of reasonable diligence, or if such violations have been committed, to disclose such violations in a format to be specified.

Annually, each employee will review the Code of Business Ethics and Conduct, sign the code's Acknowledgment form and complete and sign the Conflict of Interest Questionnaire. If the employee's circumstances change at any time, a new Conflict of Interest Questionnaire or letter of explanation must be completed.

The Code of Business Ethics and Conduct Acknowledgment form should be signed and given to your supervisor for inclusion in your personnel file.

COMPANY NAME, INC.

Code of Conduct Compliance Questionnaire

Managerial employees are being asked to complete this Compliance Questionnaire. COMPANY NAME, Inc. and its subsidiaries are committed to providing a workplace where employees can and do act responsibly and ethically. The COMPANY NAME, Inc. Code of Conduct sets out specific standards of conduct which should govern our behavior towards our fellow employees, suppliers and customers. Please answer each of the following questions and, if necessary, provide an explanation. *For any "yes" response, please explain in the extra space provided on the last page.*

Conflict of Interest

1. During fiscal 2003, did you, or are you aware of anyone who received from any person or company doing business with your employer any loan, gift, trip, gratuity, or other payment which did or could cause prejudice toward or obligation to the giver, or could be perceived by others as creating an obligation to the giver? *(Note: Each item, or the total of items from a single vendor with a value of more than $50.00 must be reported, except that you do not need to report loans made by financial institutions on normal and customary terms, common stock dividends, or insurance policy payments).*

    ☐ Yes ☐ No

2. In fiscal 2003, did you, or are you aware of anyone who participated in or influenced any transaction between your employer and another entity in which they or any member of their family had a direct or indirect financial interest?

    ☐ Yes ☐ No

3. In fiscal 2003, did you, or are you aware of anyone who had a material financial interest in or held a position of influence with any business which furnishes goods or services to your employer? *(Note: The term "material financial interest" means someone who by virtue of their stock ownership or monetary interest in a company is able to direct or to influence business decisions, or a commissioned sales representative; "position of influence" means someone holding an influential position such as a sole proprietor, partner, member of a board of directors, an executive, or a manager.)*

    ☐ Yes ☐ No

4. For fiscal 2003, did you, or are you aware of anyone who used company assets or other resources (including funds, equipment, supplies, or personnel) for purposes other than company business or company-sponsored activities?

☐ Yes ☐ No

5. During fiscal 2003, did you, or are you aware of anyone who received gifts or entertainment from individuals or organizations having dealings with the Company, including but not necessarily limited to loans, any form of cash gratuities, private or personal discounts not sanctioned by the Company, or remuneration or service related to illegal activities?

☐ Yes ☐ No

6. During fiscal 2003, did you, or are you aware of anyone who accepted any consideration or special favors from suppliers or potential suppliers which in fact or appearance could be deemed a bribe, kickback or reward given to influence your business judgment?

☐ Yes ☐ No

7. Were you involved, or are you aware of any employee who was involved in a conflict of interest situation during fiscal year 2003?

☐ Yes ☐ No

8. I have read the attached Conflict of Interest Policy Statement which is set forth in the COMPANY NAME Inc. [and Subsidiaries] Code of Conduct and Compliance Program. Accordingly, I have listed below all relationships and outside activities which require disclosure under the policy. I have also listed names, addresses and the nature of the relationships of all persons or entities doing business with my employer from whom I or any member of my immediate family has received, directly or indirectly, cash or a gift of more than nominal value ($50.00) during the fiscal year ended May 31, 2003. *(If there are no persons or entities to be listed, so indicate by writing "NONE" in the first space provided below.)*

Name of Person / Entity	Nature of Relationship / Outside Activity

Political

9. In fiscal 2003, did you, or are you aware of anyone who received any payments from your employer for the purpose of making a contribution to any political party, candidate, or election committee?

   ☐ Yes ☐ No

Securities Trading

10. Did you, or are you aware of anyone who may have bought and/or sold stock based on confidential information, or communicated confidential information to influence COMPANY NAME, Inc. stock transactions?

    ☐ Yes ☐ No

Financial Integrity

11. Are you aware of any entries made in the books and records of your employer in fiscal 2003 that you believe are false or intentionally misleading?

    ☐ Yes ☐ No

12. Are you aware of any assets, liabilities, or transactions that you believe were improperly omitted from the books of your company in fiscal 2003?

    ☐ Yes ☐ No

13. In fiscal 2003, are you aware of anyone seeking to influence any governmental official (including foreign officials) or governmental employee, or individual doing business with your company, by offering money, goods, or services in return for some special consideration?

    ☐ Yes ☐ No

Other

14. Are you aware of any incident involving your employer which you feel constituted non-compliance with laws, regulations, policies, guidelines, procedures, or ethical principles, other than those matters referred to in other questions or incidents which have already been reported? *(Note: If you prefer to report an incident or violation anonymously, please answer this question "NO" and contact a member of the Ethics Committee or call the Confidential Ethics Hotline.)*

☐ Yes ☐ No

15. Please provide any explanations for "yes" responses.

    _____

    _____

    _____

16. In the space below, please provide any suggestions you may have for improving the Code of Conduct and Compliance Program.

    _____

    _____

    _____

_____

Printed Name

_____

Signature

_____

Date

COMPANY NAME, INC. AND SUBSIDIARIES

Employee	Company / Subsidiary	Location

Code of Conduct and Conflict of Interest Employee Certification

I have read the COMPANY NAME, Inc. and Subsidiaries Code of Conduct and Compliance Program.

- I understand that the standards and policies in that Code of Conduct represent the policies of COMPANY NAME, Inc. and its subsidiaries and that violating those standards and policies, or any legal and regulatory requirements applicable to my job, may result in penalties set forth in the Code of Conduct or other appropriate sanction.

- I understand that there are several sources within the company, including the Ethics Committee, that I can consult if I have questions concerning the meaning or application of the Code of Conduct or relevant legal and regulatory requirements.

- I understand that it is my responsibility to disclose to an Ethics Officer, a member of the COMPANY NAME, Inc. Operations Audit Department, a member of the Ethics Committee or the Company's Ethics Hotline any situation that might reasonably appear to be a violation of the Code of Conduct.

- I have read the attached Conflict of Interest Policy Statement which is set forth in the COMPANY NAME, Inc. and Subsidiaries Code of Conduct and Compliance Program. Accordingly, I have listed below all relationships and outside activities which require disclosure under the policy. I have also listed names, addresses and the nature of the relationships of all persons or entities doing business with my employer from whom I or any member of my immediate family has received, directly or indirectly, cash or a gift of more than nominal value ($50.00) during the fiscal year ended May 31, 2003. *(If there are no persons or entities to be listed, so indicate by writing "NONE" in the first space provided below.)*

Name of Person / Entity	Address	Nature of Business / Relationship

- I am not aware of any exceptions to standards and policies in the Code of Conduct except: *(if none, so indicate by writing "NONE".)*

_____

_____

Signature of Employee   **Date**

PUNISHMENT AND THE CRIMINAL JUSTICE SYSTEM

The criminal justice system involves people and agencies that apprehend and adjudicate presumed law-breakers and sanction those who either plead guilty or are convicted of violating the law. With white-collar crime, *nolo* pleas (*nolo contendere*: I do not choose to dispute the allegations) are also common. Almost invariably such pleas can reasonably be regarded as evidence of criminal guilt. They generally are resorted to in an attempt by the defendant to avoid the stigma of a criminal label and to undercut the strength of a possible civil suit.

The use of the word *system* in regard to criminal justice can be misleading since it implies that there exists an integrated network of cooperating organizations dedicated to a common overarching goal. In actual fact, this is far from true. The jurisdictional morass that marks the administration of criminal justice demonstrates that it is far from being a coherent system. The police typically are under local control. In most cities, they come under the jurisdiction of the mayor or the city manager, though, on rare occasions (such as in St. Louis) law enforcement falls under state jurisdiction. The trial courts generally are operated by the counties, who also employ prosecutors. The counties—there are slightly more than 3,000 of them in the United States—also are responsible for the running of the jails, which house persons awaiting trial who cannot raise or are not allowed bail, and those who are confined on misdemeanor charges. In addition, county personnel, in the form of sheriff's forces, are largely responsible for law enforcement in nonurban areas. In some cities, they serve as the local police under contractual arrangements. The state runs the appellate courts and the prisons where the more serious offenders are housed. In addition, more recently, private companies, such as the Corrections Corporation of America, have begun to take over the operation of some holding facilities—both jails and prisons—as part of a profit-making program that is legitimized by claims of greater efficiency and lower costs.

Criminal justice agencies in the United States process more than 2 million offenders each year and employ 1.4 million persons. The system costs taxpayers more than $55 billion annually, and that expense has been rising astronomically in the wake of laws that mandate tougher penalties. Because of the fear of such penalties there are fewer plea bargains and more trials. Longer sentences also have come with the three-strikes laws which have overtaxed existing penal facilities.

Calculated on a per capita basis, the operation of the criminal justice system in the United States costs each taxpayer somewhat more than $200 each year, an amount very similar to what is paid for transportation and health care.

Besides local, state, and county law enforcement there exists a very extensive federal criminal justice presence. The federal government forces primarily deal with offenses that cross state lines, though when public opinion is aroused the U.S. Congress has been known to pretend that a crime has interstate characteristics in order to bring it under the jurisdiction of agencies such as the Federal Bureau of Investigations which has considerably greater resources than most local constabularies. Thus, for instance, kidnapping was made a federal offense after the notorious Lindbergh case on the fictitious basis that child-stealers presumptively would carry their victim across a state boundary.

Most major prosecutions for white-collar offenses are generated by federal agencies, in part because the majority of laws which proscribe white-collar crime are federal statutes and rules of federal regulatory agencies. In part, also, most state and local authorities are more than willing to yield jurisdiction to police and prosecutors who have larger personnel pools that specialize in complex white-collar crime cases.

A closer look at some of the key players can provide a fuller understanding of how criminal justice operates.

The Police and Regulatory Inspectors

The Police

The police perform a variety of duties, most of them having little to do with the criminal law. They often are the first agency to whom people turn when they are confronted with vexing problems, such as a pet cat that cannot be lured back down from a tree or telephone pole. These duties are generally grouped under the heading of *order mainte-nance*. The police also are responsible for traffic control and accident investigations, matters that usually are far removed from law-breaking. They are the legal authorities with whom citizens are likely to have the greatest contact. In that regard, how a person feels about the criminal justice system often is a function of how that person was treated by a cop who may have stopped him for a speeding violation.

In terms of criminal justice, the function of the police is to investigate crimes, apprehend criminals, and turn them over to prosecutors for adjudication. There is considerable police frustration over what officers commonly regard as the leniency of the courts: it takes a certain detachment, almost stoicism, for a police officer to declare that his job is done when he has caught the person he believes is responsible for the offense, and that what happens afterwards is somebody else's business.

There are approximately 20,000 law enforcement agencies in the United States. The majority—about 13,600—are municipal police departments. Local jurisdictions also maintain more than 1,000 special police units, including park rangers, harbor police, transit police, and campus security forces. At the county level, there are some 3,000 sheriff's departments. In addition, almost every state maintains either a state police force or a highway patrol unit. Altogether, there are nearly one million persons employed in law enforcement—between 500,000 and 700,000 sworn officers or uniformed personnel and 150,000 civilian employees.

There are those who believe that the number of officers on patrol or in administrative positions has little relationship to the degree of crime control in a jurisdiction, and they parade statistics to seek to demonstrate their point. On the other hand, the striking decrease in the level of reported crime in the United States in the late 1990s has given law-and-order proponents considerable support in their continuing efforts to beef up the police presence, rewrite legal rules in order to make convictions easier to obtain, and increase the length of prison sentences.

Technological advances have aided the police immeasurably in solving crimes, but at the same time offenders themselves often utilize modern science to avoid detection. Sophisticated bank robbers will monitor the police radio system to make certain that they are not being sought by patrol cars. While security systems may seem to offer better protection against burglary, they also tip off offenders that the houses in which such devices are installed are likely to possess goods that are worth stealing.

Research indicates that arrests by the police are inversely related to the amount of time that has elapsed before officers arrive on the scene. This fundamentally depends on when they learn from others of the occurrence of a crime, since patrol efforts very infrequently result in the police coming upon a crime being perpetrated. If crimes are reported while they are in progress, there is a likelihood around 33 percent that the offender will be arrested. One minute later, that probability of arrest declines to 10 percent. If 15 minutes have passed before an officer arrives on the scene, the chance of arrest has dropped to 5 percent. The 911 emergency call system has significantly improved the ability of the police to respond more rapidly to reported criminal events.

Law enforcement in the United States differs in important regards from that in countries such as France and Great Britain. Most notably, European forces tend to be national, so that coordination amongst them is likely to be better than in America. There also is less likelihood of corruption. In Britain, for instance, officers generally are recruited from places other than where they will work, so that they will not bring to the job prior personal relationships that may hinder their effectiveness. In the United States, there has been a constant parade of corruption scandals that involve the police in the country's larger cities, often in connection with vice operations, matters such as numbers gambling, prostitution, and narcotics.

Regulatory Inspectors

There are some striking differences between local police personnel who rarely, if ever, will deal with fraud and white-collar crime and enforcement personnel whose sole responsibility is such matters. Perhaps most notable is the fact that regulatory inspectors have contact with what is regarded as a "better" class of people than the police generally handle. Inspectors often will have to confront company executives or professionals, such as physicians, who are suspected of violating criminals laws. These persons can be condescending, manipulative, and they can threaten political retaliation for any action taken against them. As a rule, regulatory offenders tend to be smarter than the average street offender. Their prestige and power alone can pose significant problems for a regulatory agent who earns one-tenth or one-twentieth of the income of the white-collar felon he is investigating. Ellen Hochstedler makes particular note of this enforcement problem:

> *Enforcement agents may be professionally intimidated by the superior training and expertise of the corporation's experts. The corporate violator and its human agents often enjoy more prestige, have access to greater resources, and have an advantage of superior information and knowledge compared with the enforcing agency and its agents.*[1]

Regulatory agents need to have command of technical information that can be extremely challenging. They often must have a first-rate science or accounting background to

---

[1] Ellen Hochstedler, Corporations as Criminals (Beverly Hills: Sage Publications, 1984), p. 105.

understand the violation or the ruse that is being perpetrated. These skills and talents do not come easily and it is noteworthy that successful regulatory inspectors often will be given attractive offers by the companies whose work they have to oversee, a situation hardly common for law enforcement officers who deal with street offenses.

In Britain, some claim regulators tend to be rather cozy with those they regulate. In part, this is because they assume that those being regulated are "gentlemen," that they want to do the correct thing.

Finally, the British enforcers assume that if they are on close terms with those they regulate, they will be told of problems (rather than having them hidden from them) and that together they and those they regulate can work expeditiously to solve such problems, such as industrial spillage, to the benefit of the public.[2]

American regulatory enforcers of white-collar crime statutes and rules generally adopt a more aggressive and confrontational stand. They tend to operate on the assumption that, unless watched closely and carefully, businesses, seeking to maximize profit, will not adhere to the law when they find that it is profitable and apparently risk-free to evade it.

On the other hand, the common adversarial and punitive policy in the United States is weakened by the fact that the laws often reflect a considerable input from those who are to be regulated and that businesses effectively discourage enforcement by using superior legal and technical resources to overwhelm it.

Take the case of controlling illegal hazardous waste disposal, which is governed by the Resource Conservation and Recovery Act (RCRA), adopted in 1976. It defines characteristics that make wastes hazardous, such as toxicity, reactivity, corrosivity, and flammability. The Environmental Protection Agency, which enforces the statute, has never shown what Peter Yeager sees as "real vigor" in seeing that the rules are obeyed.[3]

If federal enforcement is deemed lax, the approach of most states is even less forceful. The Environmental Law Institute reports that the typical approach to environmental protection

---

[2]Keith Hawkins, Environment and Enforcement: Regulation and the Social Definition of Pollution. (Oxford: Oxford University Press), 1984.
[3]Peter Yeager, "Industrial Water Pollution," in Michael Tonry and Albert J. Reiss, Jr., eds., Beyond the law: Crime in Complex Organizations. (Chicago: University of Chicago Press, 1993), pp. 142-176.

is through civil law and that only eight states have active criminal enforcement programs: California, Connecticut, Illinois, Maryland, New Jersey, New York, Ohio, and Pennsylvania.

Processing Offenders

A criminal case may result from a citizen complaint or from a law enforcement officer observing suspected criminal activity. The former is by far and away the most likely point of origin of a criminal charge. After this original notice, an investigation is launched if it is deemed appropriate. In the case of a burglary, an investigation might take relatively little time, particularly since the officers are well aware that they are not likely to resolve the offense with an arrest. White-collar crimes typically take much longer to investigate.

Once the investigation is complete, if the facts appear to so dictate, an arrest is made. An arrest warrant can be issued when the police provide a judge with evidence of probable cause, that is, a reasonable belief that the person being charged had committed the offense. Under certain conditions, arrests also can be carried out on police authority alone.

After arrest, the person is placed in custody. While in custody, he can be interrogated (with a lawyer present, if the defendant so chooses). For most offenses, those arrested can post bail and be released pending trial. The advantages of such release are considerable. For one thing, the person can arrange his defense under more satisfying conditions, and can later come to court with at least less of an appearance of a criminal who has spent time under lock and key.

Depending on the seriousness of the matter, a prosecutor may or may not become involved in the case at an early stage. For most street offenses, the prosecutor will see the evidence that has been gathered only after the police have finished their investigation. At this time, a decision will be reached regarding what charges will be filed. A complaint is used for misdemeanors; an information or indictment is employed for felony cases.

Arraignment

Because of due process considerations, the defendant has to be brought before the court shortly after his arrest. He enters a plea at this time in a proceeding that is called an *arraignment*. He will be given notice of the charges against him, be informed of his rights, and, if applicable, bail will be set. The bail is a bond to insure that he will show up for later proceedings; if he fails to do so the bail will be forfeited. Defendants charged with a capital or heinous offense or those who the court believes are likely to flee the jurisdiction may be denied bail.

A large majority of defendants released on bail return for trial. A study of eight state jurisdictions found that 15 percent jumped bail; in a federal study, this figure dropped to 10 percent. Those who jumped bail tended to:
- Be on bail for a longer period of time
- Have a serious prior record
- Be a drug user
- Have a poor work record
- Be disproportionately young, male, and nonwhite.

The federal Bail Reform Act of 1984 provides for the automatic release of defendants on their own recognizance (that is, without the posting of money or other security) unless circumstances seem to indicate that this is not a wise decision.

About 90 percent of the defendants will not go far beyond this point in the system, but instead will *plea bargain*. In the process, the defendant's attorney works out a deal with the prosecutor. Generally the charge is reduced in exchange for a guilty plea. Plea bargaining is endemic in American criminal justice, although it is not allowed in Alaska, where a state-operated court system and a relatively small number of cases permit the system to function without it.

Preliminary Hearing

A defendant is brought before a lower court judge for a preliminary hearing. At this hearing, the state is obliged to demonstrate that there exists "probable cause" to hold the defendant for trial. The state usually reveals the least amount of its case consistent with establishing this fact. The defendant may cross-examine witnesses and can obtain valuable insights or factual concessions. Particularly useful is the fact that witnesses will be obligated to stick with the story they tell during the preliminary hearing or else run the risk during the later trial of scathing cross-examination concentrating on their inconsistency and implying that they are liars.

The routine finding of probable cause is one of the objections to preliminary hearings (which have been abolished in England, where they originated) since no prosecutor will initiate proceedings unless he is certain that the evidence comes up to the "probable cause to hold for trial" standard, a standard that is not notably demanding. The time and expense involved in what typically is nothing more than a partial preview of the state's case are said to make preliminary hearings an outmoded affair.

Grand Jury

The Fifth Amendment mandates that "no person shall be held to answer for a capital or otherwise infamous charge unless on a present or indictment of a grand jury," but in most American jurisdictions today grand juries are by-passed in criminal proceedings.

Grand juries were intended to allow the defendant to avoid a public accusation and the trouble and expense of a public trial before establishing the likelihood of his having committed the crime. They also were intended to prevent hasty, oppressive, and malicious prosecutions.

The grand jury may initiate prosecutions on its own behalf by filing a presentment, or it may return indictments in cases called to its attention by the prosecutor. In such instances, it returns a "true bill." A grand jury hearing is conducted in secret and the defendant is not present.

Grand juries are particularly useful in uncovering or helping toward the prosecution of public officials, such as police officers or holders of electoral positions, because they help to relieve the prosecutor of the onus of the almost inevitable charge that he has "picked on" such persons for exclusively political reasons.

The Court System

There are approximately 25,000 court-related agencies in the United States. About 16,000 are criminal courts. Of those, about 13,000 try only misdemeanors, while more than 3,000 deal with felony cases. There are slightly more than 200 appellate courts.

The courts are supposed to provide an impartial forum for deciding conflicts between parties. For criminal courts the issue involves an allegation of a violation of a penal statute about which the accused can either admit guilt or can contest the charge in an open hearing before a judge, either with or without a jury. The courts hear about 1.5 million felony cases each year.

Criminal Trials

Parodied, exaggerated, and glamorized by the mass media, criminal trials represent in the public mind the intense jousting between defense attorneys, like the fictional Perry Mason and the real Johnnie Cochran, Jr., and dedicated prosecutors looking only for "justice," persons such as Marcia Clark and Christopher Darden.

Most critics, however, claim that a criminal trial is little better than a brawl. They attack the snares used by the attorneys to ambush witnesses. Trials are sometimes said to be settled only according to the preponderance of perjury.

The best-known essay on court procedures points out that particularly in the criminal courts there almost invariably develops a tacit understanding between the major players about the manner in which business is to be conducted. That understanding is not precisely in accord with the way most laypersons (schooled by television dramas and the O.J. Simpson trial) presume that criminal courts operate. What usually happens is that each player performs his or her role with full knowledge of the limits that will be tolerated. A public defender will not incessantly badger the court on behalf of a client; a prosecutor will not seek the toughest sentence that can be secured and drive the defendant to seek a jury trial rather than entering a plea. And this situation is encouraged by the judge, who sees that the players stay within the boundaries of their roles. The aim in the criminal court, as it is in many organizational settings, is to ease the work burden and the stress for each of the official participants who must work in the setting day in and day out.

Each officer of the court has the power to upset the routine, so that there are checks-and-balances that keep matters under control. The district attorney will not plea-bargain with an uncontrolled public defender or defense attorney. A constantly gung-ho prosecutor will make life much more difficult for the judge who, subtly or otherwise, can make the prosecutor's work more demanding and less successful. If a judge becomes altogether too active in challenging everything, he is making his own life more complicated; and few of us are willing to do that endlessly or unnecessarily.

Abraham Blumberg in a classic article observed how the criminal courts become sensitive to outside scrutiny because their officers are well aware that their practices, however necessary to get their job readily accomplished, are questionable on any number of grounds:

> *The hostile attitude toward "outsiders" is in large measure engendered by a defensiveness itself produced by the inherent deficiencies of assembly line justice, so characteristic of our major criminal courts. Intolerably large caseloads of defendants which must be disposed of in an organizational context of limited resources and personnel potentially subject the participants in the court community to harsh scrutiny from appellate courts, and other public and private sources of condemnation.*

As a consequence, an almost irreconcilable conflict is posed in terms of intense pressures to process large numbers of cases on the one hand, and the stringent ideological and legal requirements of "due process," on the other hand.

The method for working around this situational dilemma is to have each of the major role-players acquiesce to tactics that make their daily existence vocationally bearable:

> *A rather tenuous resolution of the dilemma has emerged in the shape of a large variety of bureaucratically ordained and controlled ... short cuts, deviations, and outright rule violations adopted as court practice in order to meet production norms. Fearfully anticipating criticism on ethical as well as legal grounds, all the significant participants in the court's social structure are bound into an organized system of complicity. This consists of a work arrangement in which the patterned, covert, informal breaches of "due proceszs" are institutionalized, but are, nevertheless, denied to exist.[4]*

Defense Lawyers

Much less well known than the role played by the attorneys who handle street crimes is that of the defense bar whose members specialize in white-collar crime cases. In a study of these attorneys, Kenneth Mann notes that two tactics mark their work: first, they seek to resolve the case as early as possible, to keep it from ballooning. Often this involves learning from their client about an active or pending investigation and meeting with the enforcement agents in an attempt to kill the case before any formal actions get underway.[5]

Mann conducted his study of white-collar crime defense lawyers in New York City, the locale where the most prominent of them usually work. He notes that his interviews shed

---

[4] Abraham S. Blumberg, "The Practice of Law as a Confidence Game," Law & Society Review, 15 (1967), p. 141.
[5] Kenneth Mann, Defending White-Collar Crime: A Portrait of Attorneys at Work. (New Haven: Yale University Press), 1985.

light on the fundamental qualities of the attorneys' function: "its commitment to helping the guilty go free [the lawyers almost invariably assume that their clients are guilty], its adversarial character, its tendency to operate on the margin of ethical, moral, and legal standards, and its reliance on the manipulation of people and organizations."[6]

Tactics employed by the white-collar crime defense lawyers are divided into two major types: first, *adversarial information control*, in which the lawyer argues in court or to an investigator that a subpoena for documents is improper. It might be claimed, for example, that the subpoena imposes a task too burdensome or too vague. The attorney also might insist that material already seized is inadmissible because of irregularities in the seizure.

Then there is what Mann labels *managerial information control*. It focuses on keeping inculpatory information from coming to the attention of the authorities. Typically, this strategy relies heavily on asserting an attorney-client privilege in order to inhibit the government from successfully locating incriminating materials. The aim of the attorney is to have the investigation stopped because those conducting it, given limited resources, are persuaded either that the material they need to be successful does not exist or that they will not be able to obtain it. "What is distinctive in white-collar crime cases is the centrality of information control strategies to defense work: they are fundamental modus operandi constituting a basic defense plan."[7]

The message for CFEs is clear: it indicates a compelling need to secure as much relevant data as possible before the iron curtain of concealment falls into place.

The Outcome of the Criminal Process

About a dozen offenders will be incarcerated in a prison or a jail for every 500 crimes that become known to the police. Of course, there probably are three to ten times as many crimes that occur that never come to police attention, in part because of the reluctance of a victim to complain, the fact that the victim (especially in a white-collar offense such as consumer fraud) is unaware that he has been ripped off, or perhaps because the victim is himself culpable, as when a drug dealer is robbed.

About 100 arrests result from the 500 crimes coming to police notice. Arrests tend to be considerably higher for crimes of violence, such as homicide and assault, than for property

---

[6] Ibid., p. 5.
[7] Ibid., p. 8.

offenses, such as burglary and auto theft. In crimes of violence, the victim often was known to the offender, while there typically is little identifying information for property crimes, since nobody actually laid eyes on the offender.

Ultimately, about one-third of those persons arrested will be sentenced. Of these, 80 percent are jailed while the remaining 20 percent are placed on probation or assigned to some form of community treatment.

Cases are dismissed for reasons such as:
- The matter is considered trivial.
- The prosecutor, perhaps because of limited resources, decides not to press charges. More often the decision is made because the prosecutor is not certain of a favorable verdict. Prosecutors, typically politically ambitious, seek to accumulate as high a success rate as possible, a matter helped along by not going forward with cases in which the outcome is doubtful.
- Not enough legally admissible evidence is available.
- It is deemed that the accused has been punished sufficiently. This judgment is particularly characteristic of cases involving white-collar offenders, who are believed to suffer greatly from the notoriety of charges against them and thereby to have learned their lesson without a need for further punishment.
- The complainant refuses to cooperate with the prosecutor, preferring to drop the matter.

Constitutional, statutory, and judicial due process protections mandate that the criminal justice system cannot transgress stipulated defendant rights. These include the right to be treated with fundamental fairness, to be notified in a timely fashion of the charges, to be present at the trial, to confront the prosecution's witnesses, and to have witnesses testify on his behalf. Furthermore, defendants have the right to an attorney, the right to a jury trial, as well as to a speedy trial. In more recent years, the issue of fair trial has expanded to include the right of both parties to be given before the trial information that has been secured by the other side, including interviews with witnesses, forensic information, and other investigatory materials.

Sentencing Options

There are a variety of sanctions available to the judge and, when they are charged with imposing sentences, the jury as well. Among others, there is pre-trial diversion, probation, and incapacitation or incarceration. If the sentence is imprisonment, it may be made under rules that dictate a determinate sentence (such as five years) or an indeterminate sentence (such as five to ten years). There are some offenses where the sentence is mandatory, dictated by a set of guidelines which typically allow for a decrease or increase of the stipulated amount of time to be served if certain other circumstances are present (for instance, whether the offender was armed).

Sentencing of white-collar offenders is often complicated by the fact that, while their behavior may have been notably harmful, this most likely will be their first criminal offense. They also typically come to court with an unblemished record of social accomplishments: church participation, seemingly strong family ties, and an array of civil achievements. These kinds of credentials work in their favor when it comes time to impose a sentence upon them. Studies of white-collar crime also point out that judges and defendants in such cases often share similar social and educational backgrounds, creating a certain empathy in the sentence. Note, for instance, the sentencing memorandum filed on behalf of a client who had committed an egregious income tax violation:

> *In short, the court must pass sentence upon a man with an unblemished record, whose character is one of the highest and whose achievements have been truly outstanding. It is submitted that nothing in this record suggests that [the defendant] needs prison rehabilitation or that he is ever likely again to break the law. In considering only this man as a human being, it is submitted that a prison sentence is unwarranted. The record for total good during a life span of 44 years weighs heavily against the isolated transgression of the evasions of taxes.*[8]

Pre-trial Diversion

While not truly a sentence, since it is not the consequence of a trial or a plea, diversion is often used at the local level for offenders who seem suited to what it has to offer. Under its terms, selected individuals, after they have been arrested but before further proceedings, will be placed into some form of treatment program. If it is assumed, for instance, that their troubles with the criminal law were fundamentally related to alcoholism, they may be ordered to attend Alcoholics Anonymous meetings a certain number of times each week for a specified period. Other offenders, particularly juveniles, might be diverted to different

---

[8] Ibid., p. 222.

kinds of counseling programs or placed in a remedial education group. Referrals to employment services might also be mandated.

In theory a person can be placed in a pre-trial diversion program almost indefinitely, though most judges will stipulate a time period. If the person successfully completes the program, a criminal record can be avoided. If the accused person fails in the diversion program, usually by nonparticipation, he can be tried for the crime that had earlier been charged against him. In practice, some judges demonstrate seemingly endless patience with such offenders, since they had originally determined that, given the situation, they did not want to imprison the alleged offender.

Probation

Many laypersons confuse *probation* with *parole*. Parole refers to the status of an offender after he has been released from prison or jail and is placed under supervision in the community. Probation typically is a sentence imposed prior to (and instead of) incar-ceration. Some judges, however, favor what is called "shock probation." They insist that the offender serve a brief time—perhaps only a week—in a penal institution in order to get a taste of what can be in store for them if they do not adhere to the law and to the probation conditions that are imposed upon them.

Probation laws vary from state to state, but the offender typically is placed under the control and guidance of a probation officer, who is to see to it that the conditions that are established are met. In practice, probation officers tend to be seriously overworked and usually provide only minimal supervision of their charges. Most of their contact with the probationer may be only by way of telephone calls to the person and the person's employer. Besides, probation officers are expected both to counsel and to control their roster of probations, roles that often are incompatible. Few probationers, for instance, will frankly discuss personal problems with a probation officer when they are aware that he can use what he learns as a basis for sending them to prison.

Most probation agencies are part of the state bureaucracy, though in larger areas they may be operated by the county. About 30 states combine the administration of probation and parole in a single agency.

After a person is convicted of a crime, the probation officer is charged with investigating his background in order to provide information that will be helpful to the judge in determining what punishment to impose. The judge almost invariably will follow the recommendation of the probation officer, though some judges, valuing their independence, insist on reports without any recommended disposition. Nonetheless, probation officers soon learn what matters influence particular judges. If they observe, for instance, that a judge will invariably be lenient with an offender who attends church regularly, they will highlight that element if it is their own judgment that the defendant deserves a break. They also can pinpoint items that they know will influence a given judge to impose a harsher sentence.

Probation implies a contract between the offender and the criminal justice system. Most probation rules require that the offender adhere to some or all of the following conditions:
- Maintain steady employment.
- Make restitution to the victim for losses or damages.
- Cooperate with the probation officer. This involves, among other matters, showing up for appointments, notifying the officer of change of address, intention to marry, a new job, or similar developments.
- Meet family responsibilities.
- Obey all laws. Many jurisdictions will incarcerate a probationer as a violator if they believe that he has committed another offense. They revoke his probation status, and thereby avoid the difficulties of a court proceeding. The probationer can fight this disposition, and request a hearing, but few are likely to do so successfully.

Rules specifically tailored to the particular offender also might be imposed. Probationers can be ordered to report for urinalysis or other forms of drug testing on a regular basis or they can be forbidden to drive or to go to places where alcoholic beverages are served. Until relatively recently, most jurisdictions forbade probationers from associating with persons who had a criminal record. But often these are the only friends a probationer might have and the rule has come to be regarded by many criminal justice personnel as unreasonable and unlikely to be obeyed. For probation officers, the rule often affords a basis to revoke the freedom of an offender when they believe that he is continuing to violate the law but they are unable to prove this.

Sentences of probation are for a fixed period of time, with the length generally determined by statute and in terms of the seriousness of the offense. Violent offenders often are not allowed by law to be put on probation.

There have been a number of recent innovative probation tactics, including house arrests and electronic monitoring.[9] Under electronic monitoring, the probationer wears equipment that allows the probation officer to establish his whereabouts at any time. House arrest usually involves confinement to the place where the person lives, typically with an exception made for working outside at a job.

Opponents of electronic monitoring see it as a "Big Brother" tactic that reminds them of the totalitarian regime depicted by George Orwell in his novel *1984*. They also find house arrest too similar to the kinds of tactics typically used in some foreign countries to deal with "political" criminals.

Given prison overcrowding problems, the lower cost of keeping persons on the streets offers an attractive alternative, though there always is the risk that the offender might commit a serious crime, thereby eliciting severe public criticism of the judicial and probation authorities. A desire to protect their reputation is a major consideration in decisions to impose a prison term on a person who arguably could do quite well in a controlled community setting.

White-collar crime offenders are usually regarded as prime candidates for probation. They are highly unlikely to reoffend, they usually have families to support, and they generally express remorse and say that they will never again fall into errant habits. Of course, they typically make a fine appearance in court: well-dressed, well-spoken, courteous, and contrite.

Besides, white-collar offenders tend to be older and, if imprisoned, might find the atmosphere intolerable, though there are a number of federal prisons, which outsiders scornfully call "country clubs," where the population is largely made up of "tame" white-collar offenders.

White-collar offenders also will receive lighter sentences if they cooperate with the authorities and bear witness against co-conspirators. In one study it was found that more than 42 percent of cooperating defendants were charged with a single offense compared to 30 percent of noncooperating defendants. White-collar offenders also are more readily granted bail: just one person in eight spends any time incarcerated before trial, and for the

---

[9] See Richard A. Ball, C. Ronald Huff, and J. Robert Lilly, House Arrest and Correctional Policy: Doing Time at Home. (Newbury Park, CA: Sage, 1988).

generally high-status offenders, the figure is fewer than one in 20. In a comparison group of "common criminals," at least one-third spent time in jail before their trial.[10]

Shaming

Criminologists lately have been paying a great deal of attention to the concept of *reintegrative shaming* as a punishment that might deter an offender from further wrongdoing. Put forward by an Australian, John Braithwaite, (who was the first winner of the Association of Certified Fraud Examiners' Cressey Award), shaming involves two subtle and delicate practices: first, pressure is put on the offender by those closest to him and those he respects and, sometimes, those he has victimized to acknowledge that what he did is wrong and to feel truly contrite about his deed. Second, the offender is reassured that those important to him continue to regard him with affection and welcome him, as a reformed person, back into the fold.

Critics believe that Braithwaite's ideas, modeled on Chinese and Japanese customs, might in theory be extremely effective, but that in cynical societies, such as the United States, they are not very likely to have much impact on hardened lawbreakers.

In America, shaming has tended to take a much harsher approach. The tactic was made famous by Nathaniel Hawthorne in *The Scarlet Letter*, in which an adulterer is forced to wear the letter "A" sewn into her cloak. Branding on the hand or forehead was used in seventeenth Century England for thieves and other offenders who were spared the more common punishment of death by hanging.

Today, a form of branding characterizes responses to certain criminal offenses. Some states require that when an offender is released from prison after serving time for sexual assault on a child, members of the community where he will live must be notified of his presence among them. Jurisdictions increasingly are resorting to such "shaming" approaches to isolate offenders and warn those they presumably might harm. In Pittsfield, Illinois, in 1996, as a condition of probation a farmer was required to place a large sign at the entrance to his driveway reading: "Warning: A Violent Felon Lives Here. Travel at Your Own Risk." The offender had bashed another farmer in the face with a fuel pump.

---

[10]David Weisburd, Stanton Wheeler, Elin Waring, and Nancy Bode, Crimes of the Middle Classes: White-Collar Offenders in the Federal Courts (New Haven: Yale University Press, 1991).

Similarly, persons convicted of drunk driving sometimes have to put special license plates on their cars. Shoplifters may be required to take out advertisements in their local papers showing their pictures and announcing their offense.

Opponents of such penalties point out that there is little scientific evidence of their value and that their legal justification is arguable. They say that the aim of justice is not vengeance and humiliation but to restore what was destroyed and to prevent an illegal act from recurring. They do not believe that the shaming approach that is becoming fashionable in the United States achieves such ends.

Corrections

The term *corrections* is one of those euphemistic words that increasingly are entering the language in order to soften the reality of a situation. Corrections is the general term for the process of administering punishment following a plea or a conviction in regard to a criminal offense. It most typically refers to imprisonment. Persons serve time in prisons most generally for felonies, while jails house persons convicted of misdemeanors or those awaiting trial who have been unable or are not permitted to raise bail to purchase some free time. Generally, sentences of a year or less are served in jail; those that are longer involve prison time.

The term *corrections* came into usage during a period in which the ruling philosophy was that confinement could reform a lawbreaker. Thus, prisons for young persons were rechristened as *reformatories*. The programs—at least in blueprint—focused on education, group therapy, skills training, and similar projects geared toward allowing a released inmate to live in a self-fulfilling manner after release. Nonetheless, the core of prison existence clearly was punitive and most observers regarded the "rehabilitative" programs as little more than window-dressing.

Today, the prevailing philosophy undergirding imprisonment is labeled "just deserts," that is, a person who has hurt others and undermined the wellbeing of the society has "earned" by his behavior the consequence of deprivation of liberty and the concomitant characteristics of imprisonment. There is no need, just desert advocates believe, to coat imprisonment with cozy descriptors: it is treatment that an offender deserves because of his self-interested illegal behavior.

Incapacitation is the ruling rationale of the just deserts approach. By definition, imprisonment reduces crime by removing the opportunity for the offender to violate the law. There is, of course, a considerable level of criminal activity within a correctional institution, primarily involving drug-taking and assaults, including sexual assaults. But, at least those outside the prison are protected from the depredations of those inside it. The key issue is that virtually all persons who are incapacitated in an institutional setting (including those sentenced under the three-strikes laws) will someday be released. If they are pushed further into crime by their prison experience it is possible that they may commit more and more serious offenses on their release than they would have if they were given a lesser or lighter sentence.

It is sometimes argued that white-collar criminals need not be imprisoned since because their violations most often are tied to the occupational positions they occupy, their patterns of offending can usually be eliminated by removing them from their business or professional positions. Doctors will no longer violate the laws governing medical benefit programs if their license to practice medicine is revoked, nor will inside traders have the chance to carry on their illegal activities if they are barred from trading either directly or by proxy.

The difficulty with this reasoning is that incapacitation involves questions of equity, that is, whether all those who violate the law are treated similarly, with no favoritism to the wealthy and wellplaced. There also is the matter of general as opposed to specific deterrence. *Specific deterrence* refers to keeping the individual who broke the law from doing so again. *General deterrence* involves demonstrating to others the consequences of law-breaking so that they will not succumb to the temptation of doing so. Those with philosophical inclinations might seek to puzzle out the justice of punishing one person in order to teach other people a lesson, but the criminal justice system, not concerned with such esoteric matters, seeks to serve the ends of both specific and general deterrence in its response to law violators.

Types of Sentences

Sentences that involve incapacitation can take several forms.

Determinate Sentences

A determinate sentence is one of a fixed number of years, usually set by the legislature, to be served upon conviction of a certain offense. In so-called "flat" determinate sentences, the offender must serve the entire time in prison, say five years for a fraud violation. More often (though decreasingly so in many jurisdictions) the flat sentence can be reduced, usually by as much as one-third, for "good behavior." This carrot is considered important by some prison administrators because it offers a reward for conforming to institutional rules beyond the avoidance of punishments meted out within the walls, such as solitary confinement.

A variation on the determinate sentencing approach is for the legislature to set a maximum term for any given offense and to allow the sentencing judge to exercise discretion to impose a time period up to that maximum. Often an accused person will enter a guilty plea during a bargaining session with the prosecution which will stipulate that the person will be recommended for a sentence less than the maximum (an agreement which judges almost invariably endorse) or that the person will be allowed to plead to a lesser offense than the more serious one in order to ensure that the sentence will not exceed a certain amount of time.

Indeterminate Sentences

Indeterminate sentences impose a range of time that can be served by the offender, say 5 to 20 years. This gap allows the correctional authorities to determine when to release the prisoner based upon his performance within the institution and an assessment of the likelihood that he will continue to pose a danger to the community. Once the most popular form of sentencing because it was believed that prison officials possessed the skill and wisdom to make accurate judgments about re-offending, indeterminate sentences have come into disrepute during the past decades. The objections largely have focused on the inequities involved—two persons committing the same offense often served vastly different prison terms. In addition, prison authorities were deemed to use the indeterminate sentence unfairly to take revenge on persons they did not like, as a punitive weapon rather than as a predictive device.[11]

Mandatory Sentences and Three-Strikes Law

Legislatures began adopting mandatory sentences for crimes out of a dissatisfaction with what they regarded as too-soft judges. The move has been led by the work of the U.S. Sentencing Commission. A typical mandatory sentence will disallow parole in the case of certain violent crimes or repeat offenses. Similarly, judges will not be permitted to place certain kinds of offenders on probation or to suspend their sentence. Most judges, of course, regard this inroad against their discretionary powers and autonomy unfavorably.

---

[11] See further James M. Byrne, Arthur J. Lurigio, and Joan Petersilia, eds., Smart Sentencing: The Emergence of Indeterminate Sentences. (Newbury Park, CA: Sage, 1992)

In one of its more controversial actions, the U.S. Sentencing Commission in November 1991 established rules for sentencing corporations for diverse white-collar offenses. The purpose of the rules was to "provide just punishment, adequate deterrence, and incentives for organizations to maintain internal mechanisms for preventing, detecting and reporting criminal conduct." The Commission's rules reflect the following principles:

First, that the Court must, whenever practicable, order the organization to remedy any harm caused by the offenses. The resources expended to remedy the harm should not be viewed as punishment, but rather as a means of making victims whole for the harm caused.

Second, if the organization operated primarily for a criminal purpose or primarily by criminal means, the fine should be set sufficiently high to divest the organization of all of its assets.

Third, the fine range for any organization should be based upon the seriousness of the offense and the culpability of the organization. The seriousness of the offense generally will be reflected by the highest of (a) the monetary gain, (b) the monetary loss, or (c) the amount noted in a guideline offense fine table. Culpability will generally be determined by the steps taken by the organization prior to the offense to prevent and detect criminal conduct, the level and extent of involvement in or tolerance of the offense by certain personnel, and the organization's actions since an offense has been committed.

The sentence schedule permits a court to place conditions on the way a business is run if the court believes that these changes are important to prevent further offending. Establishing more effective accounting procedures, hiring a waste control specialist, or expanding the board of directors beyond a group of intimates can be some of the conditions placed upon a corporation. On the other hand, if a company has established an internal regimen that seeks to control illegal actions it can receive credit from the court for this in regard to reduction of a fine or other stipulated penalties. The sentencing guidelines provide, however, that a corporation generally is not eligible for a fine mitigation if the crime was committed by a more senior employee with managerial authority.[12]

---

[12] For a thorough review of the U.S. Sentencing Commission's guidelines for organizational offenses see Henry J. Amoroso, "Organizational Ethos and Corporate Criminal Liability," Campbell Law Review, 17 (1995):47-70.

Prisons

William Penn is widely credited with beginning the practice of imprisonment in the United States. In England in Penn's time, capital punishment was the usual response to most crime, with more than 250 designated offenses carrying that penalty. Some mitigation had been introduced by the practice of transportation, whereby selected offenders were dispatched to the American colonies and, after America gained its freedom from British rule, to Australia.

Of the more than 500 prisons in the United States today, 150 are classified as maximum security, 225 as medium security, and 182 as minimum security. Since prison construction has not kept up with prison populations, overcrowding is a serious problem, and a large number of states are under federal court orders to reduce overcrowding and otherwise improve prison conditions.

More than four-fifths of prison inmates have a record of prior criminal offenses. Two-thirds are incarcerated for violent behavior, and more than half were using drugs at the time of their offense, with most of the drug use being on a daily basis. African Americans account for nearly half of the inmates in prisons, while 46 percent of all inmates are between the ages of 25 and 34. Prior to incarceration, the median income of inmates was lower than $10,000 a year.

Today, the growth in prison populations has been particularly pronounced. In 1985, there were 313 incarcerated persons in the U.S. per 100,000 population. That figure rose to 470 inmates per 100,000 persons in 2001. The growth largely was fueled by the imprisonment of drug offenders. At the end of June 1996, there were 1,630,940 people in federal and state prisons and local jails. This represents a rise of 4.4 percent over the previous year, though the rate of increase is a decline from the average 7.8 percent annual growth during the previous decade. There is something of a paradox in the rise in imprisonment since all reports indicate a falling off in the amount of crime since 1992. At the end of 2001, there were 1,962,220 people in federal and state prisons and local jails. By September 2004 this number jumped 1.9 percent to 2,147,947 people in federal and state prisons and local jails.

The total number of people in jail and prisons in the United States has tripled over the last twenty years as politicians have pressed for tougher sentencing laws and have built more prisons to seek to assuage public fears about violent crime.

Critics of prisons continue to argue that the rights of prisoners are too liberal. Prisoners have used the courts to seek to obtain greater privileges in regard to religion and speech, medical care, vocational and educational training, due process, and general living conditions.

At the same time, prisons have become increasingly violent, particularly as ethnic and racial groups clash. Interethnic and racial clashes have led to suggestions that prisoners ought to be segregated along racial and ethnic lines to reduce outbreaks of violence.

Federal prisons, which tend to be more richly funded, are regarded as superior to virtually all state institutions, and it is in them that most incarcerated white-collar offenders will do their time.

Rehabilitation

Intense debate in the area of corrections has centered about the question of whether prison and other programs can rehabilitate those exposed to them. A famous study by Robert Martinson reviewed more than 200 carefully designed research studies of diverse kinds of treatment programs for offenders and concluded that none of them showed much, if any, ability to turn persons away from a life of crime.[13] More recently, some scholars now maintain that Martinson's research was flawed and that his conclusion was inaccurate. They stress in particular that the error has been to look for improvement in all those who undergo one or another kind of treatment regimen; instead, the effort should be to determine what works for what kinds of persons and to concentrate on these conclusions when formulating treatment approaches.[14]

Certainly, some white-collar offenders have used the incarceration experience to redesign their lives, in a manner very much for the better. Charles W. Colson, a onetime special assistant to President Nixon, was described by Herbert Klein, Nixon's intimate friend, as "one of the meanest people I ever knew." Caught up in the Watergate scandal, Colson negotiated a guilty plea to one count of obstruction of justice in regard to his involvement in the burglary of the office of Daniel Ellsberg in an effort to defame Ellsberg, who had released the Pentagon Papers, which showed the falsity of government claims about the

---

[13] Robert Martinson, "What Works? - Questions and Answers About Prison Reform," Public Interest, 35 (1974):22-54.
[14] Francis T. Cullen and Paul Gendreau, "The Effectiveness of Correctional Treatment: Reconsidered the 'Nothing Works' Debate," in Lynne Goodstein and Doris Layton MacKenzie, eds., The American Prison: Issues in Research and Policy (New York: Plenum Press, 1989), pp. 24-30.

progress of the Vietnam war. Colson received a one-to-three year prison sentence and was fined $5,000.

During his time as an inmate at the Maxwell federal prison, Colson formed the Prison Fellowship, which sought to change the lives of convicts through a combination of "practical assistance and relentless evangelism."[15] So successful was Colson that two decades after his release he was awarded the Templeton Prize for Progress in Religion, a prize that carried a stipend of more than $1 million. "Twenty years later I see how God has used my life," Colson noted when receiving the award. "Sometimes the greatest adversities turn out to be the greatest blessings."

Not all white-collar offenders demonstrate so extraordinary a turnabout, but cynics are wont to say that if one of the problems involved in maintaining control in America's turbulent prison system has its basis in the lifestyles of many offenders, a "better class of prisoners," that is, more white-collar offenders, might help solve part of that problem.

Jails

There almost invariably is little in the way of treatment available in jails; they simply warehouse prisoners. Jails originated in France in the 1600s, and through the centuries they have been regarded as hellholes of pestilence and cruelty. In medieval England, a jail sentence was regarded as a sentence to death since conditions were so abominable. Today, more than 8 million people are placed in jails each year, some for several stays. The great majority are poorly educated, unemployed, impoverished, and drug-ridden.

Community Corrections

To ease overcrowding, community-based correctional facilities have become commonplace. While some persons might be sentenced directly to such programs, they typically house individuals who have completed some time inside institutional walls. Community-based programs emphasize the use of neighborhood residential centers, halfway houses, prerelease centers, and furlough programs.

---

[15] T. Carlson, "Deliver Us From Evil: Prison Fellowship's Saving Grace," Policy Review, 62 (1992):72-22; see Charles W. Colson, Born Again (Old Tappan, NJ: Chosen Books, 1976) Colson, Life Sentence (Minneapolis: World Wide, 1979).

Parole

Parole (from the French, and meaning "word" as in "word of honor") is the planned release and community supervision of offenders before the expiration of their sentence. Under most state laws, an offender is eligible for parole after serving one-third of his sentence. Parole decisions usually are made by a board or a commission, based on its members' conclusion regarding whether the offender will remain at liberty without violating the law. There is pressure on parole board members to be notably conservative in their actions, because any repetition of an offense by someone they release, particularly if the offense is heinous, will trigger community outrage against the board. On the other hand, overcrowded prison conditions dictate early release to make room for newcomers.

Parole is considered an act of grace, and once on parole the inmate is supposed to be closely supervised by a parole officer, though this rarely happens because of extraordinarily heavy caseloads.

A person may apply for a pardon that, if granted, releases him from further punishment and restores the civil rights that are forfeited upon conviction for a crime, including the right to vote, to serve on a jury, or to hold public office.

There are two types of pardons—(1) *full and absolute* and (2) *conditional*. Full and absolute pardons usually are granted only after conviction and upon a presumptive showing that the offender was actually innocent. The full and absolute pardon that Richard Nixon received from President Gerald Ford before possible criminal proceedings had begun was a rare exception to this rule.

A conditional pardon implies guilt and for this reason may be rejected by the person to whom it is offered. The grant of a pardon or other clemency is the prerogative of the Executive Branch (the President or state Governors) and may not be compelled by the petitioner or by the judiciary.

Crime Statistics

Uniform Crime Reports

The Federal Bureau of Investigation (FBI) compiles statistics on the extent of crime in the United States in a document called the Uniform Crime Report (UCR). The report is put together on the basis of information voluntarily submitted by more than 15,000 law enforcement departments. This includes virtually every significant public policing agency in the country.

The UCR divides crimes into Part I and Part II offenses. Part I offenses are murder and non-negligent manslaughter, forcible rape, robbery, aggravated assault, burglary, larceny, arson, and auto theft. While most persons would agree that these categories appear to incorporate most serious criminal behavior, the somewhat arbitrary nature of the categories should not be overlooked. In regard to rape, for instance, the category also embraces attempted rape, and studies have shown that men may be arrested for attempted rape for behaviors no more ominous (at least in comparison with forcible rape) than patting a female stranger on the behind in a rather menacing way. The police charge a serious crime in order to more readily persuade the offender to plead to a lesser offense.

The inclusion of arson on the list of major offenses illustrates that political concern enters into the compilations. It was added to the FBI Part I tables about a decade ago when legislators decided that the offense needed to be highlighted and mandated that the FBI upgrade it.

There are striking variations in the number of acts that fall into any of the Part I categories, so that a slight percentage shift in the number of auto thefts, for instance, can overwhelm important changes in homicides, since there are so many fewer of the latter. Let's say, as an example, that auto thefts increase 5 percent from 150,000 to 157,500. Meanwhile, homicides might have dropped 20 percent, from 20,000 to 16,000. Overall, presuming all the other Part I offenses stayed at their same level, the report would indicate that Part I offenses—that is, serious crime— had increased (from 170,000 to 173,500 for the two offenses being considered here).

Part II offenses include most other violations, though they omit traffic offenses and pay no heed to serious white-collar crime. When they do mention offenses that might fall into the white-collar category, often what they are tabulating as, say, forgery represents the passing of bad checks by drug addicts without bank accounts. When you add in theft of services, welfare fraud, petty confidence games, and credit card fraud you can account for virtually all of the crimes charged under possible white-collar crime headings.

The UCR figures are based on what is called "offenses known to the police." Data is also provided on arrests, though not on whether the case is resolved by a determination of guilt or not. Rates are reported per 100,000 population, a matter which skews the crime picture in some jurisdictions. In Las Vegas, for instance, the crime rate is higher per capita than it reasonably ought to be because the figures pay no heed to the very large tourist influx.

National Crime Survey

The National Crime Survey (NCS) is a statistical study carried out by the Bureau of the Census that annually conducts interviews with 136,000 individuals in 60,000 households about experiences of crime victimization. It shows UCR seriously underreporting; that is, the persons interviewed report a much greater amount of crime than that which figures in the UCR reports. About 55 percent of crimes of violence and one-quarter of thefts are found to be reported to the police. The NCS makes no attempt to measure any behaviors that would fit into the category of white-collar crime.

The UCR results show that crime victims and offenders share the same demographic characteristics. The average victim is young, male, uneducated, and poor. A somewhat counterintuitive result is that as wealth increases, the likelihood of being a victim of violence or burglary decreases. However, wealth is correlated positively with victimization by personal theft and larceny.

Self-Report Surveys

Self-report surveys typically involve a questionnaire on which a respondent indicates which offenses he has committed and how often he has done so within a specified period of time. They invariably are administered to juveniles because youngsters can more readily be located (in classrooms, for instance) and will be more likely to cooperate with the researcher, at least if they are persuaded by the guarantee of anonymity.

The surveys show that the most common juvenile offenses are truancy, alcohol use, and recourse to false identification, typically to gain entrance to a place out-of-bounds for underage persons or to buy liquor. Very few youngsters do not commit any offense at all that, if known and taken seriously, could not result in official action against them.

Crime Trends in the United States

Two facts dominate any review of American crime statistics:
- The United States demonstrates a strikingly high rate of crime compared to other countries which share most of its characteristics, that is, heavy urbanization, advanced technological development, and a relatively high standard of living.

- While American crime rates remain high in terms of international comparisons, there has been a dramatic decrease in the U.S. crime rate during the past six years.

The first point generally is regarded as a reflection of elements of American culture that press an unusually large number of the country's people to engage in crime. Other countries, such as Japan and Switzerland, which share many of our nation's characteristics, have very low crime rates, presumably because people do not regard law-breaking as an acceptable way to resolve real or imagined difficulties, such as personal animosities or the desire to get their hands on money.

The notable decrease in the American crime rate during the past half dozen years (from 1991 to 1996) poses intriguing questions. In this time period, reported crime, especially murder, has been dropping sharply, even though the economic conditions and disarray of poor slum families remain much as they always have been. The decline is the steepest recorded in a quarter of a century, and the homicide rate now has fallen to its lowest level since the 1960s, a period during which an explosion of violence marked the country's escalating crime problem. In New York City, for instance, the number of murders recently dropped from 1,995 in 1992, to 984 in 1996, to 572 in 2002.

Changes in crime rates typically are regarded as a function of the different percentages of the population in the most crime-prone age group, that is from 16 to 24. But the current decline seems to be above and beyond such demographic interpretation. Today, law enforcement and political forces claim credit for curbing crime, citing police strategies on guns, community policing, and efforts to improve the ambiance of slum neighborhoods by dealing with graffiti, loitering, and other indications of disorder.

Factors Bearing on Crime Rates

The emphases in its culture underlie to a very large extent the amount of crime that will be found in any given place. Some people in some places will not tolerate insults—they feel compelled to react violently; others have no trouble responding with calming words or departing from the situation as gracefully as possible. These are learned responses that are incorporated into the values that shape our lives. Some persons will return a wallet they find; others will empty it of cash and perhaps toss the wallet into the nearest mailbox. And these kinds of responses will vary, sometimes dramatically, between one country and another.

There are also certain factors that virtually everywhere correlate with levels of criminal activity. These are some of the major ones:

Age and Crime

The most obvious factor that plays into the amount of crime that will be manifest is the birth rate. The number of street crimes rises when a baby boom generation reaches adolescence, and it declines when that generation "ages out" of the early crime-prone years. Peaks and valleys in the number of people in different age groups will cause corresponding changes in crime rates. As America's population ages, however, it is anticipated that there will be a rise in white-collar crime because such offenses most often are committed by older persons who have worked themselves into positions of power and responsibility.

While youths from 15 to 18 make up only about 6 percent of the American population, they account for about 25 percent of all arrests for Part I offenses. The peak age for property crime is about 16 years, while for violent crime the high point is about 18 years.

Crime appears to decrease with age because people come to develop a long-term view of life and to learn to resist the need for immediate gratification. They also lose somewhat their belief in their own invulnerability. A decline in physical strength and agility (for instance, the ability to run rapidly from a crime scene) also may play a part.

Economics and Crime

The greatest amount of street crime is committed by persons in the lower socioeconomic strata in society. In two studies—one of active burglars and the second of robbers—Richard Wright and Scott Decker determined that offenders typically commit their crimes when they see themselves in immediate need of money, often for drugs and partying, sometimes for rent and food. To take a job offers no particular hope of resolving what for them has been allowed to become a pressing problem. Most of the offenders understand that they are likely to get caught sooner or later, but they regard that prospect resignedly as part of the price they must pay to get those things that are of immense importance to them at the time they want them.[16]

---

[16]Richard T. Wright and Scott H. Decker, Burglars on the Job: Street Life and Residential Burglary. (Boston: Northeastern University Press, 1994); Wright and decker, Robbers on Robbery. (Boston: Northeastern University Press, 1997).

Violent crimes, such as rape and homicide, also are concentrated, though by no means exclusively, in the lower socioeconomic class, and may in part be the result of rage at the frustrations of what can be a difficult existence. Rape is regarded as a crime of violence that is expressed by sexual aggression; often those who commit it are impotent. Rape of women by persons they know—acquaintance or date rape—is regarded as often particularly devastating to its victims because not only have they been sexually violated but they have had their trust in another human being destroyed, and they may come to be apprehensive about all men.

Race and Crime

Understanding the connection between race and crime rates can be a particularly sensitive subject. Nobody disputes that African Americans commit a very disproportionate amount of street crime in the United States. While they make up about 12 percent of the country's population, they commit almost half of the violent crimes known to the police and about one-third of the property offenses.

Most interpretations of the racial discrepancy in crime rates emphasize the economic deprivation suffered by African Americans, accompanied by familial social disorganization. Discrimination takes a heavy toll on the self-esteem and the well-being of black persons. Imagine, for instance, a commonplace circumstance. You are sitting in a restaurant and the waiter delays endlessly in bringing your order—and when it comes the food is cold. If you are white and presentable, you readily conclude that the restaurant provides unsatisfactory service. But if you are an African American you almost inevitably wonder whether the situation is a consequence of prejudice. These kinds of issues are daily occurrences for easily recognizable black people in a white society that remains unable to satisfactorily resolve its problems with race relations.

There are those who will insist that black crime (as well as some crime by whites) is the consequence of inferior intelligence that is genetically transmitted from one generation to the other. This position, heralded in the widely publicized book, *The Bell Curve*, has been very effectively demolished by a large number of studies and commentaries that point out the inept logic, selective citing of studies, and political bias (among a considerable array of other shortcomings) that characterize *The Bell Curve*.

Gender and Crime

It has been said that the solution to the crime problem in the United States, indeed, throughout the world, is really quite simple: just turn males into females, or at least get men to behave as women do. Women account for only one-quarter of arrests for property crimes (and these tend to be the less serious offenses, such as shoplifting) and but one-tenth of the arrests for violent crime. It has been maintained that as the feminist movement breaches the walls of patriarchy, the female crime rate would begin to approximate that of males, but this has not happened, at least not to date. There has been, however, some increase in the number of arrests of women for fraud as greater numbers of females move into the workplace.

The lower rate of female street crime might in part be a consequence of the lesser physical strength of women. The most common belief is that women are taught to conform socially much more effectively than men. Women are raised to be less aggressive and more nurturing. Probably because of this early training, women tend to feel deeper shame if caught in a criminal act.

Career Criminals

Researchers have found that offenders can roughly be divided into two major groups: those who occasionally commit crimes and a much smaller group made up of chronic offenders. A Philadelphia study determined that 52 percent of all street crimes were committed by 6 percent of the offenders. This group accounted for between 70 and 80 percent of all offenses in the area. Career criminals, the research suggests, have the following characteristics:

- They have been incarcerated for more than half of the two-year period preceding their most recent arrest
- They had a juvenile conviction prior to the age of 16
- They abused heroin or barbiturates during the two-year period prior to their current arrest, or had a pattern of such use as juveniles
- They had held a job for less than half of the two-year period preceding their arrest

Current American penal policy focuses heavily on career criminals and mandates incarceration for long periods. Approximately half of the states now have career criminal statutes, known as "three strikes, you're out" laws. Under such laws, a notably heavy sentence is mandated for the third conviction, regardless of the severity of the crime. Those favoring the laws believe that they will remove from the streets the most dangerous offenders. Opposition often focuses on the fact that the laws incarcerate persons—at heavy expense—until well beyond the age at which most of them represent a threat to the society. The laws also often catch in their web petty offenders, whose thefts of such things as a piece of pizza may be counted as part of the formula that dictates several decades of imprisonment on a third conviction.

Crime and the Media

Television thrives on the portrayal of violence, including the vivid depiction of actual events on news and feature programs, on children's shows, and as part of sitcoms. Newspapers follow suit, though what they write about and show in pictures becomes somewhat less immediate and gruesome than what television depicts. For criminologists the question is whether such public displays of criminal activity bear a relationship to the commission of crime.

Copy-cat offenders, who say that what they did was inspired by what they saw or read, are not uncommon, but it is difficult to ascertain the general impact of the mass media. Perhaps the most persuasive charge is that they desensitize people to horror, that is, they make bloodletting more commonplace and therefore more likely for persons who otherwise might be inhibited from such acts.

The media also are charged with inculcating desires for material possessions in people who have no realistic way of acquiring them except illegally, including very wealthy people who are prompted by advertising to obtain things that remain beyond their considerable means, things such as extremely expensive automobiles, jewelry, airplanes, and similar "baubles."

On the other hand, there are those who believe that watching television and being exposed to crime depictions might reduce potential criminal activity because they enable people to experience fantasies in a vicarious manner rather than acting them out.

Drugs

The effect of illegal drugs on criminal behavior has been hotly debated, particularly in the past few years when prominent conservatives, such as William Buckley, Jr., have joined in a crusade to refashion America's drug policy. The basis of their call is that the almost century-old "war on drugs" seems not to have produced a solution, but rather to have aggravated the problem. Of course, there is no way of knowing whether the drug problem that at this time dominates criminal behavior in the United States would have been even worse without the law enforcement efforts that have sought to deal with it.

Criminals may use heroin, cocaine, marijuana, methamphetamine (speed), among other drugs, to obtain pleasure or relaxation. These drugs typically reduce inhibitions and, for those that are expensive, they create a need to obtain money for their purchase.

Alcohol, another drug, though a legal one, also is closely tied to criminal behavior, particularly crimes of violence. Studies indicate that in as many as half of the homicides in the United States one or both parties had been drinking heavily right before the time of the killing.

Public Attitudes Toward the Criminal Justice System

Two recent surveys offer CFEs material to consider what the public thinks of law enforcement (all of us being enforcers in one way or another). The first treats how the public think about crime generally—what they think of the police, the courts, sentencing practices, etc. The U.S. Sentencing Commission study deals with fraud crimes in particular, ten of which are rated to compare the average sentence for a convicted felon (1) when the sentence is pronounced according to federal guidelines and (2) when the sentence is pronounced according to individual respondents, members of the general public.

Americans View Crime and Justice Survey

The authors of *Americans View Crime and Justice*[17] brought together data from public opinion polls conducted over the last 25 to 30 years along with the results of the 1995 National Opinion Survey on Crime and Justice (NOSCJ). The respondents were asked their attitudes toward crime, criminals, law enforcement, and the justice system. The responses state what the public *thinks* about these issues, which may not always add up to the facts. In some cases—*How high is the national crime rate for muggings? How vulnerable am I to crime?*—the respondents are simply wrong; people consistently overestimate the pervasiveness of crime, especially violent crime. These results do have the virtue, though, of letting us know what people are thinking, what they perceive as the problems, what they fear and support most. Whether the public is "right" or "wrong" on crime will remain a vexing question. The best response was made by Thomas Jefferson:

---

[17] *Americans View Crime and Justice. A National Public Opinion Survey.* Flanagan, Timothy J., and Dennis R. Longmire, eds. Thousand Oaks: Sage Publications, 1996.

I know of no sage depository of the ultimate powers of the society but the people themselves, and if we think them not enlightened enough to exert their control with wholesome discretion, the remedy is not to take it from them but to inform their discretion by education.

Approval Ratings for Police

For the last 30 years Americans have generally looked with favor on their police forces. From 70 to 80 percent of respondents consistently say the police are doing a good job. Wording makes a difference. The *New York Times* and CBS News asked respondents in 1991 whether they had "a great deal" or "quite a lot" of confidence in their local forces. Only about 55 percent said yes. But when they were asked if they had *some* confidence in their protectors, 86 percent of respondents said yes, they had *some* confidence.

So most people are on the side of law and order. This makes us feel good, but does it tell fraud examiners anything? When you consider a corollary of the main survey, it makes a good deal of difference. Bahram Haghighi and Jon Sorensen cite numerous studies showing that (1) people with low incomes and (2) whites with advanced schooling view police departments negatively. These two types of people go against the general grain in their disapproval of police. It's intriguing, then, to note that the people most likely to commit fraud in the workplace are white men with executive status and advanced college degrees.[18] This suggests that the willingness to commit fraud—like the willingness to hold up a Quicky Picky—has a great deal to do with the perpetrator's attitude toward the law. Simply put, those with the most negative attitudes about law enforcement are more likely to commit crimes. (This may seem axiomatic, but consider how useful this knowledge could be in evaluating and distinguishing among several suspects.)

One aspect of the approval question bears particular consideration by fraud examiners. In separate polls over the last 20 years, between 66 and 75 percent of respondents said they might "approve a policeman striking an adult male citizen." But less than 25 percent would approve of wiretapping. Citizens generally fear more for their privacy than for their persons when it comes to dealing with law enforcement. Examiners should consider this during their investigations and take care to avoid the appearance as well as the commission of improper surveillance.

---

[18] *Report to the Nation on Occupational Fraud and Abuse.* Association of Certified Fraud Examiners, 2002.

The Courts

American courts have not enjoyed much favor in the public eye during the past quarter-century. In a 1973 poll, 24 percent had "great confidence in the legal system." That number dropped to 18 percent in 1978, to 14 percent in 1988, and to 8 percent by 1993. Minorities, lower-income households, and urban dwellers look especially askance at how courts treat defendants. The dissatisfaction is general: several different studies found that more than 80 percent of the public thought the courts weren't tough enough on criminals. This is the familiar cry against liberalized courts determining legal, as opposed to actual, guilt.

Plea bargaining is seen as a major part of the problem. Just 25 percent said plea bargains were a good idea, with 67 percent opposed, and 8 percent neutral. College graduates are *least* likely to see plea bargaining as a problem, while those over age 30 and those with incomes between $15,000 and $30,000 find the practice most offensive.

Not surprisingly, 84 percent of respondents thought "expensive lawyers" were part of the courts' problem.

Sentencing practices stir up strong feelings, even among those who understand these practices very little. Generally speaking, "the public has only the vaguest notions of crime-related statistics and vastly overestimates victimization rates for violent and property crimes." Americans, fueled by demagogic politicians and "reality-based" television, think crime is more rampant than it really is.

Conventional wisdom holds that Americans are a punitive, "lock 'em up" society. This is especially true for "criminals who commit violent crimes": respondents favored punishment over rehabilitation for violent criminals 59 percent to 27 percent (the rest answering "both" or "neither"). But when asked a general question—"Should money be spent on social and economic problems or on police, prison, and judges?"—54 percent felt treating the social and economic issues was more important than building up the justice system. The authors of the National Opinion Survey on Crime and Justice assert that rehabilitation is more popular than the evening news makes it out to be. In typical crimes, respondents favor a lenient, rehabilitative sentence the more they learn:
- Details about the victim
- Details about the offender
- Details about sentencing options

USSC Survey on Fraud Crimes

While the National Opinion Survey on Crime and Justice surveys didn't deal directly with the question of fraud crimes, a report by the U.S. Sentencing Commission did. This study compared the sentencing for various crimes (violent and nonviolent) as prescribed by federal guidelines with the sentences suggested by individual citizens for the same crimes. The idea was to compare the guideline sentence, for forgery say, with what real people thought the sentence ought to be. In the aggregate, the USSC found no significant variation between guideline sentences and the respondents' sentences. On average federal guidelines gave a sentence of about 6 years, while respondents gave an average of 7 years.[19]

The close correlation between guideline sentencing and the sentences suggested by respondents holds true when all crimes are considered together. The guidelines give longer sentences for bank robbery (as a generalized category) but respondents give longer sentences for extortion and forgery. But there can be considerable variation when looking at individual crimes. The sentence for kidnapping, for example, is put by both the guidelines and respondents somewhere between 23 and 26 years. But for trafficking in crack cocaine, the guidelines are decidedly harsher than the public: the guidelines recommend a 22-year imprisonment while respondents only ask for 14 years. (If the respondents' median value, and not the overall average, is used, the difference is even greater: most people gave crack dealers only about 10 years, while mandatory minimum sentences kept the guidelines at 22 years.)[20]

Most literature on criminology has little to say about the crimes fraud examiners are charged to deal with, but the Commission's study treated white-collar crimes directly. The authors

---

[19] The details of the survey, available on the USSC web site (www.ussc.gov), distinguish between the "mean" values and "median" values of the sentences. The mean sentences average all responses together: for all crimes for example are 5.7 years for the guidelines and 7.2 years for respondents. The "median" sentences are adusted to accommodate the extreme variations of a large sampling. So the median sentence for all crimes is even closer: 2.5 years for the guidelines and 3 years for respondents. In this essay we report the mean value except as noted.

[20] The ramifications of any of these numbers have proven hard to trace. On the most basic level, for example, is the question of what prison sentences mean to the respondents, i.e., what do they think of imprisonment? Is it a punishment or focused on rehabilitation? What does the person think of as a "long" or "short" sentence. The authors point out that a year to one respondent may not mean the same thing as a year to someone else. "Perhaps respondents had different interpretations of prison time, some holding, for example, that a year in prison was a very severe sentence and others holding that a year was not very severe. This might lead some respondents to give longer sentences than others even though all wanted to impose sentences of the same severity... . In other words, one respondent may have a general tendency to give long sentences whereas another may be inclined to give generally short sentences."

define this type of offense as an illegal act "with predominantly pecuniary motives: the white-collar criminal offender is able to gain monetarily by exploiting through deceit either some feature of how money is loaned, stored, or transferred, or by conducting a false business transaction." Looking just at the fraud crimes in the study, it seems that individual citizens generally expect higher sentences for these convicts than the guidelines render. In the generalized category of Major Fraud (high dollar losses, institutional crimes), federal guidelines provide an average sentence of 3.5 years, while the public asks for 6.3 years. In the generalized category of Minor Fraud (lower dollar losses, individual crimes) the guidelines average 1.8 years, while the public says 4.4 years.

But crime is only generalizeable in abstractions. In the real world, people aren't tried for "major fraud," they're tried for embezzling money from an auto parts distributor. The USSC study accounted for this reality by giving respondents scenarios for different types of crime. The researchers called these specific descriptions of crime "vignettes." The difference can make a big difference. The sentence for "trafficking cocaine" is about 12 years from the guidelines, and about 14 years from respondents; remember, though, that the sentence for "trafficking *crack* cocaine" is 22 years according to the guidelines, while respondents asked for 14 or less.

For specific fraud crimes, as opposed to "major" or "minor" generalizations, respondents still asked for harsher sentences than those dictated by the guidelines. A broker selling worthless stocks and bonds draws 2.9 years from the guidelines, but respondents want 7.3 years. Using a stolen credit card gets 1.3 years from the guidelines, but 4.3 years from respondents.

Interestingly, the difference was slight for a bank officer causing a Savings and Loan to fail: 5.4 years (guidelines) to 6.1 years (respondents).[21] Apparently the public and the judiciary regard the financial officer's duty in a similar light. This departs from the usual disparities between the guidelines and respondents when fraud crimes are at issue. The one fraud vignette where respondents asked for *lower* sentences? Filing a false mortgage application with the intent to pay the money back: the guidelines say 3 years, respondents only asked for 2. The real key here was that the person making false statements to get the mortgage had to *intend* to pay the loan back. When the scenario was changed so the perpetrator was

---

[21] The difference actually tips the other direction with the median (as opposed to mean) numbers: the guidelines give the bank officer a median of 4 years, while the respondent sentences, when adjusted, ask for only 3.

making false claims and *did not* intend to pay back the money, the numbers changed: vagaries in the wording of the law make the average guideline sentence about 2 years, while respondents wanted to punish those who lied with no intention of repayment with almost 4 years imprisonment. It would seem that when people can understand, maybe even empathize, with a fraudster's motive, they're gentler in recommending jail time. (On the other hand, the guideline penalty for underreporting income for tax purposes is 2.5 years, almost 2 years less than the 4.4 years recommended by the public.)

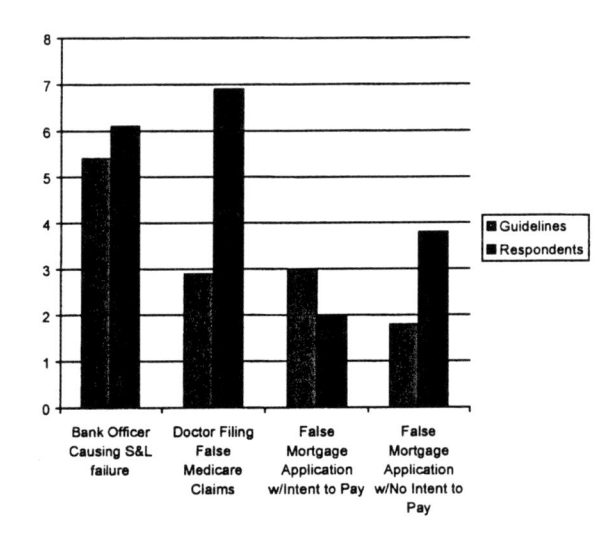

[Bar chart comparing Guidelines vs Respondents for: Bank Officer Causing S&L failure (~5.4 vs ~6.1), Doctor Filing False Medicare Claims (~2.9 vs ~6.9), False Mortgage Application w/Intent to Pay (~3.0 vs ~2.0), False Mortgage Application w/No Intent to Pay (~1.8 vs ~3.8)]

The Commission pointed out "generally speaking, fraud is punished far less severely" than street crimes by both the public and the guidelines. The exceptional instance, in which respondents asked for much harsher penalties, was selling defective helicopter parts. "It is the prospect of resulting injury or death that elicits long prison terms," say the authors. The violence, not the fraud, scares people into tougher sentences. (Another instance where respondents were tough enough to impress the Commission involved poisoning pain relievers in a drug store—again, the respondents presumably dealt more harshly because of the egregious endangerment.)

Looking specifically at the fraud crimes in the study, it would seem that respondents feel most strongly about those acts which affect the public, and by extension, individual citizens. Selling worthless stocks and bonds is going to burn a lot of mom-and-pop investors, so the respondents ask for longer sentences. But people are more tolerant of lying on an application because they see this in terms of an institution versus the individual. The USSC study ventures no answers in this direction. This is an opportunity for further research.

The Commission did find some intriguing results about various aspects of fraud crimes. With embezzlement, for example, the professional standing of the perpetrator made little difference to respondents: "the bank employee and the bank vice president both receive median prison terms of around two years." The guidelines, by contrast, do make a distinction, giving the employee a much shorter sentence.

The dollar amount of a crime had some bearing—sentences rose as the losses rose—but not on an even scale. After a certain point, respondents were not increasing the sentences in accord with the losses. For eight of the specific vignettes, respondents gave lighter additional punishments than the guidelines, which are calibrated to deal out longer sentences for larger dollar-amount losses. "In some sense," the Commission authors write, "respondents were allowing crime to pay."

It's not that people weren't considering the amount of money at all. Losses in the fraud vignettes ranged from $200 to $80 million, and respondents did give tougher sentences up the scale. What surprised researchers was the range of the scale, the huge amounts of money it took to make a difference in people's sense of "just punishment." Respondents made meaningful adjustments to their sentences only when the vignettes involved one of three ranges: (a) losses between $200 and $4,000; (b) losses between $40,000 and $3,000,000; and (c) losses between $17,000,000 and $80,000,000. Median sentences in the (a) range were about 2 years, in the (b) range about 4 years, and about 5 years for the (c) range. It clearly takes a lot of money to prompt people to adjust their sense of justice. For antitrust crimes, there was no significant difference in the respondent sentences, regardless of how much the perpetrators took. The authors lament, "It may be surprising to some that the difference between a public loss of $500,000 and $15 million has no demonstrable impact on median sentence!" For fraud crimes generally, "The median sentence increases far more slowly than the defendant's economic gain from the crime."

This survey also found that the criminal record for fraud defendants made little difference in respondents' minds. There was little or no difference between the sentences for someone with no criminal record charged with fraud and someone with two prior prison terms. (For both the median sentence is about three years.) The flat numbers here partially reflect the nature of white-collar crimes: someone with a lengthy prison record isn't likely to gain a position of fiduciary responsibility in a bank or large corporation. On the other hand, respondents may be considering each act of fraud as a discrete event, to be treated on its own terms.

Table 1 summarizes the average sentences for certain fraud crimes, as dictated by federal guidelines and according to respondents' answers. Table 2 treats selected crimes of a nonfraud nature.

TABLE 1
SENTENCES FOR FRAUD CRIMES, ACCORDING TO FEDERAL GUIDELINES AND SURVEY RESPONDENTS

TYPE OF FRAUD	Guidelines Sentence	Respondents Sentence
Major Fraud	3.5	6.3
Minor Fraud	1.8	4.4
Extortion	3.8	8.6
Money Laundering	3.8	5.0
Forgery/Counterfeit	2.4	6.3
Bribery	2.1	3.0
Larceny	1.7	4.9
Bank officer causing S&L failure	5.4	6.1
Selling defective helicopter parts to government	3.7	11.2
False mortgage application with intent to pay mortgage	3.0	2.0
Selling worthless stocks and bonds	2.9	7.3
Doctor filing false Medicare claims	2.9	6.9
Company official making use of inside information	2.9	4.3
Using stolen credit cards	1.7	4.2
Writing bad checks	1.6	4.6
Embezzlement: Bank officer stealing bank funds	1.3	4.3
Embezzlement: Bank employee taking bank funds	0.9	4.3
Forgery: Counterfeiting currency	4.7	7.6
Tax: Failure to file tax returns	2.5	4.4
Tax: Under-reporting income on tax	2.5	4.4
Bribery: Local official taking bribe	2.5	2.6
Money Laundering: coin dealer failing to file required forms	2.4	3.8
Money Laundering: Bank official failing to file proper forms	1.7	4.5
Soliciting funds for nonexisting charity	2.2	4.9
False mortgage application with no intent to pay back mortgage	1.8	3.8
Embezzlement: Postal worker taking postal funds	1.7	5.6

TABLE 2
SENTENCES FOR SELECTED NONFRAUD CRIMES, ACCORDING TO FEDERAL GUIDELINES AND SURVEY RESPONDENTS

CRIME	Guidelines Sentence	Respondents Sentence
Drug Trafficking: Cocaine	12.1	14.2
Drug Trafficking: Heroin	11.8	14.0
Drug Trafficking: Crack	21.8	14.2
Drug Trafficking: Marijuana	4.4	11.6
Bank Robbery: Weapon used with major injury to victim	17.5	17.9
Bank Robbery: Weapon used with minor injury to victim	14.1	14.4
Bank Robbery: Weapon fired with no harm to any victim	11.3	7.8
Bank Robbery: No weapon used	5.6	5.6
Drug Possession: Cocaine	0.5	2.8
Drug Possession: Marijuana	0.3	1.0

ETHICS FOR FRAUD EXAMINERS

In this section, we have discussed a number of behavioral and ethical principles applicable to both organizations and individuals. As a fraud examiner, the decisions you make will be extremely important to your client or company as well as to the individuals you may be called upon to investigate. Therefore, Certified Fraud Examiners are held to a very high ethical standard. The following material is designed to accomplish more than a mere recitation of rules of professional ethics for fraud examiners. It also contains discussion and explanation of many features of ethics in general. The first portion deals with principles of moral philosophy. These represent the "high road" in the study of ethics for fraud examiners. The latter portion deals more specifically with rules of behavior in situations that characterize fraud examiners' work. The applications of the Certified Fraud Examiner Code of Professional Ethics are discussed.

What is Ethics?

Wheelwright defined ethics as:

> *that branch of philosophy which is the systematic study of reflective choice, of the standards of right and wrong by which it is to be guided, and of the goods toward which it may ultimately be directed.*

This definition contains three key elements:
- Ethics involves questions requiring reflective choice (decision problems)
- Ethics involves guides of right and wrong (moral principles)
- Ethics is concerned with values (goods) inherent in ethical decisions

What is an ethical problem? A *problem situation* exists when you must make a choice among alternative actions and the right choice is not absolutely clear. An *ethical problem situation* is a problem situation in which the choice of alternative actions affects the well-being of other people, whether individually or collectively.

What is ethical behavior? You can find two standard philosophical answers to this question: (1) ethical behavior is that which produces the greatest good and (2) ethical behavior is that which conforms to moral rules and moral principles. The most difficult problem situations arise when two or more rules conflict or when a rule and the criterion of "greatest good" conflict. Some cases and discussions are given later in these materials to illustrate these difficulties.

Why does an individual or a group need a code of ethical conduct? While it has been said that a person should *be* upright and not be *kept* upright, a code serves a useful purpose as a reference and a benchmark. A code makes explicit some of the criteria for conduct peculiar to a profession, and in this way codes of professional ethics are able to provide some direct solutions that might not be available from general ethics theories.

Furthermore, an individual is better able to know what the profession expects. From the viewpoint of an organized profession, a code is a public declaration of principled conduct, and it is a means of facilitating enforcement of standards of conduct. Practical enforcement and profession-wide internal discipline would be much more difficult if members were not first put on notice of the standards.

An Ethical Decision Maker's Role

While one of the main purposes of ethics is to guide the actions of individual decision makers, the role of "decision maker" does not fully describe a professional person's entire obligation. Each person acts not only as an individual but also as a member of a profession and as a member of society. Hence, fraud examiners also are *spectators* (observing the decisions of colleagues), *advisors* (counseling with co-workers), *instructors* (teaching students or new employees on the job), *judges* (serving on disciplinary committees), and *critics* (commenting on the ethical decisions of others). All of these roles are important in the practice of professional ethics.

In considering general ethics, your primary goal is to arrive at a set of acceptable methods for making ethical decisions to fulfill all your roles. Consequently, an understanding of some of the general principles of ethics can serve as background for a detailed consideration of the behavior directed by the Certified Fraud Examiner Code of Professional Ethics.

Ethical Decisions

One of the key elements in ethics is *reflective choice*. Ethical problems almost always involve projecting yourself into a future in which you have to live with your decisions. Professional ethics decisions usually turn on these questions: "What written and unwritten rules govern my behavior?" and "What are the possible consequences of my choices?"

We could dispense with any discussion of ethical theories and rules if we were willing to accept a simple proposition: "Let conscience be your guide." Such a rule is appealing because it calls upon an individual's own judgment, which might be based on wisdom, insight, adherence to custom, or an authoritative code. However, it might also be based on caprice, immaturity, ignorance, stubbornness, or misunderstanding.

In a similar manner, reliance on the opinions of others or on the weight of opinion of a particular social group is not always enough. Another person or a group of people might perpetuate a custom or habit that is wrong. (Think about the signboard that proclaimed: "Wrong is wrong, even if everybody is doing it.") To adhere blindly to custom or to group habits is to abdicate individual responsibility. Titus and Keeton summarized this point succinctly: "Each person capable of making moral decisions is responsible for making his own decisions. The ultimate locus of moral responsibility is in the individual." Thus, the function of ethical principles and rules is not to provide a simple and sure answer to all your problems but to provide some guides for individual decisions and actions.

Morality, Ethics, and Legality

Is it all right to lie to catch a crook? Consider the following story about a fraud examination.

Abel, a fraud examiner, was hired by Megacorp, Inc. to discover the method stockroom employees were using to steal electronic parts from the inventory. Abel was given a cover identity known only to the president of Megacorp. His application was processed through the personnel department in the normal manner and he was hired as a stockroom clerk. On the job, Abel preserved his false identity, infiltrated the group responsible for the thefts, and produced sufficient evidence to have three people arrested and indicted.

While this story involves only one type of fraud (embezzlement) and one investigation method (undercover work), it can serve as a simple example of the moral, ethical, and legal issues facing fraud examiners. These issues involve principles of moral philosophy, rules of ethics, legal considerations, values, and—above all—the problem of distinguishing "right" from "wrong." One high executive, upon taking office, told his board that his would be an ethical administration, saying: "It is very simple. All it takes is knowing the difference between right and wrong." But knowing that difference is the hardest part!

The High Road

Most public and many private discussions of ethics quickly become philosophical—reaching toward lofty principles and broad generalizations about desirable behavior. People easily cite well-known guides and consider them ones that should never be violated. Such discussions often take place in a vacuum, apart from specific fact situations. People generally exhort themselves and others to observe the highest principles of moral behavior.

Such considerations—the "high road"—are necessary if we desire to lift the discussion above the nitty-gritty facts of everyday problems. However, the idealistic nature of this level of discussion often is not sufficient to help people cope with a problem immediately at hand. There are a variety of reasons for this deficiency and we will consider many of them later.

The high road is the realm of "moral philosophy" where philosophical principles guide the process of thinking about problems and distinguishing right from wrong. They are necessary in the process of everyday life. Even though an individual might not know them in all the twists and turns familiar to professional philosophers, their fundamental precepts are well understood in our concept of "common sense." We will explore three basic principles of moral philosophy in these materials.

Philosophy, Ethics, and Law

Moral philosophy exists at a global level, permeating all facets of the problems of distinguishing right from wrong. It deals with human judgments based on standards that identify "good" and "evil." These words have more impact than mere "right" and "wrong," but they convey essentially the same idea. You should know about two aspects of moral philosophy. The first is the human judgment process: it deals with ways of performing analyses (thinking) of problems. The second is the standards or values people can use to make moral principles useful. We will consider some values such as truth, honesty, faithfulness, and unselfishness.

"Ethics" can be distinguished from moral philosophy by its roots in society. People usually are more comfortable talking about "ethics" rather than "moral philosophy" because "ethics" seems more practical, while "moral philosophy" seems too intellectual and impractical. Indeed, "ethics" generally refers to a specific setting—a society, a culture, a nation, a profession, a small group. In this context, "ethics" refers to behavior that conforms to some societal norms or to a written code of ethics, such as the Certified Fraud Examiner Code of Professional Ethics.

When faced with an ethics-related problem, it is very appropriate to begin the analysis of a possible action by asking: "Is it legal?" Such analysis is at the most "practical" level. "Ethics" is somewhat less global and is connected to the setting. The law deals very specifically with actions that are permitted and actions that are prohibited. With all due respect to the law, it is nevertheless the lowest reference level for moral decisions. It happens, though not frequently, that a law might permit an action that is prohibited by a profession's code of ethics. Going one step further, a profession's code of ethics might permit actions that a moral philosopher would abhor. Likewise, laws and codes of ethics might prohibit actions that present no problem in moral philosophy.

For example, the American Institute of Certified Public Accountants (as well as such groups as the national associations of architects and attorneys) had rules of ethics that prohibited advertising, with the exception of broad-based institutional advertising. The professions believed that professional dignity and objectivity were enhanced by keeping practitioners out of the hurly-burly of this aspect of the commercial world. The U.S. Federal Trade Commission and the U.S. Department of Justice, however, reached a different conclusion. They decided that the prohibitions against advertising were against the laws barring restraint of trade. The government forced the professions to eliminate their rules against advertising. This example illustrates the triumph of one set of values (the government's belief that competition through advertising would benefit consumers) over another set (the professions' belief that professional dignity should be preserved).

All three areas—morality, ethics, and legality—are important for everyday decisions. It might not be enough to know that a contemplated action is legal. Nor may it be enough to know that an action is permitted or prohibited by a group's written code of ethics. It might not be helpful to know that reasoning based in moral philosophy seems to identify an action as right or wrong. The important thing is to know the distinctions among morality, ethics, and legality; to know the law; to know the rules; and to know the philosophy. Only with this knowledge can a fraud examiner know where he stands when deciding upon and justifying a course of action.

This course material observes one important limitation. It confines its consideration of ethics for fraud examiners to matters of moral philosophy, rules of ethics, and general values. It does not deal with detailed matters of the law or with questions about the legality or illegality of actions a fraud examiner might take. Matters of law are covered in the special section devoted to that subject. This is not to say that the law is unimportant. It is just beyond the scope of this part of the materials.

Means and Ends

Everyone knows some saying like: "The ends justify the means," or "Fight fire with fire." Fraud examiners can be particularly influenced by this idea because they need to deal with people who do not exercise moral reasoning, follow ethical rules, or keep within the law. These sayings have the purpose of justifying actions that otherwise could be considered immoral, unethical, or illegal. (After all, the American colonists openly defied British law, fomented a rebellion, and fought a war. We now regard them as heroes.)

Is it all right to lie? No, except ...

When a moral rule appears to be inflexible, people can always think of situations where they want to justify breaking the rule. Thus, some people would easily conclude that it is all right to lie to catch a crook. After all, if the moral rules were followed by everyone, then there would be no crooks (liars who steal inventory), so they brought it on them-selves, making it necessary for a fraud examiner to lie in return. The ends (catching crooks and upholding justice) justify the means (lying). Fight fire with fire!

The problem with means-ends analyses is that they are often superficial, ending with the needed justification but failing to consider other aspects and consequences of the actions. The justification of the undercover role of the fraud examiner must be carefully considered. The president of Megacorp must think about the moral-ethical-legal climate of the company once it becomes known that an undercover agent was employed. (How many more are around? What happened to trust?)

Values and Principles

There is a great difference between values and principles in moral thinking. *Principles* are the means of analysis—the ways of thinking about moral problems. In this regard a theory (principle) in ethics is "a theory about the nature and basis of morality and the standards for moral judgment, which arises out of the moral perplexities of everyday life." *Values*, on the other hand, are the criteria for "good" and "evil." To a certain extent, people can exercise moral thinking using a principled approach. In the end, however, values necessarily enter into the process.

Values

Many people assert that "you cannot teach ethics." In large part, they mean "you cannot teach values." Values are indeed personal and social criteria that are learned and internalized through a wide variety of influences—family, social status, peer groups, national origin, and the like. At any given time and place, some values are more widely held than others. Some values are more strongly held by people who are more religious than others, older, wealthier, poorer, more experienced, and so forth. Gordon Shea's management briefing—one of your primary reading list references—explains many of the influences that shape people's recognition and use of values in ethical thinking. (Shea, Gordon F., *Practical Ethics*, American Management Association, 1988)

This course material is not primarily concerned with values. Dealing with them too easily turns into sermons instead of instruction on the processes of moral and ethical thinking. Nevertheless, we cannot escape them.

Discussions about values often leads to "moral relativism," commonly translated: "When in Rome, do as the Romans do." Moral relativism denies the existence of absolute values that have not changed over time and among cultures. For example, slavery was apparently accepted as part of the social order in the Greek and Roman empires with little dissent. A moral relativist might say that slavery in ancient Greece was ethical because it was accepted, while a moral absolutist would say that slavery should never be considered morally right at any time in any place.

Thinking about values brings up the question of whether there are any natural values or whether all values are man-made by convention, that is by local general acceptance. Protagoras, one of Socrates' contemporaries, held thus: "Man is the measure of all things." This saying means that there is no natural morality, justice, or law; nothing in these realms is objectively true or false. Yet, people have continually sought some bedrock of absolute truth. Protagoras' epigram is said to be "widely scorned." Fraud examiners are no exception to the search for constant values that will help solve ethical problems.

Principles

A *principle*, as the term is used in these materials, is a method to analyze moral and ethical problems and to reach a decision. The three famous principles explained in the following pages are concerned with moral decisions made by following rules, considering consequences, and generalizing rules and consequences. As a method, each of them can be explained up to a point without reference to values. Ultimately, however, values need to be taken into account.

The three principles are the subjects of the major entries in the Certified Fraud Examiner reading list. They are "heavy-duty philosophy." The goal in making them the primary sources for the Certified Fraud Examiner Examination is to lift the discourse above the level of "current events." The daily newspapers are full of reports of ethics matters, and all of them invite analysis by one or more of these principles. Modern-day commentators speak and write about the ethical problems of the twentieth century. Their views and analyses might or might not stand the test of time.

These three principles have withstood time, scrutiny, criticism, scholarly commentary, and other forces that sink many lesser philosophical thoughts into obscurity. You will find that they also contain many elements generally considered "common sense," and elements to which your reaction might be: "Yes, I already understood that." So much the better: When logic, philosophy, and common sense are in accord, a person has comprehended a difficult task. We will proceed with some abbreviated explanations of these moral philosophies:

The Imperative Principle

The *imperative principle* directs a decision maker to act according to the requirements of an ethical rule. Strict versions of imperative ethics maintain that a decision should be made without trying to predict whether the action probably will create the greatest balance of good over evil. Ethics in the imperative sense is a function of moral rules and principles and does not involve calculation of consequences.

The philosopher Immanuel Kant (1724–1804) was the foremost advocate of the imperative school. Kant was unwilling to rely solely upon inclinations and values for decisions. He strongly preferred rules without exceptions. He maintained that *reason* and the strict *duty to be consistent* governed the formulation of his first law of conduct: "Act only according to that maxim by which you can at the same time will that it should become a universal law." (Act only as you are willing that everyone should act all the time.) This law of conduct is Kant's first formulation of his *categorical imperative*, meaning that it specifies an *unconditional obligation*. One such maxim (rule), for example, is: "Lying is wrong."

Suppose you believed it proper to lie in the course of a fraud investigation in order to induce employees to reveal information they would not otherwise disclose. The Kantian test of the morality of such a lie is: Can this maxim (lying is all right) be a moral rule which should be followed without exception by all people all the time? The specific actor involved (fraud examiner) and the specific circumstances (say, undercover investigation) are not especially relevant to test the universal morality of lying.

For all people to follow a rule, all people must know of it, and when everyone knows that the rule is that it is acceptable to lie when doing so is perceived to be necessary, then everyone faced by a questioner must be wary and distrustful. Even the fraud examiner must be wary and distrustful of the client who hired him, because it is conceivable that the client might have lied about the assignment in order to induce the examiner to follow a particular line of inquiry.

Since the nature of a universal rule is universal knowledge of it, any manner of lying is bound to fail the test of the categorical imperative because no one should believe that people should always lie all the time. Indeed, if lying were considered moral and ethical, and everyone lied all the time, nobody could be fooled by a particular lie. Thus, lying is wrong because, when made universal, the maxim (lying is all right) fails by its own contradiction. The liar cannot fool anyone.

Kant was content to rest his case on the duty to be consistent, but as practical people in an everyday world, we can insert some consideration of values into this discussion. Effective communication is valued by most people, but if lying were universally accepted as a maxim, all common communication would become impossible. Indeed, people who operate among liars find that the effects of double-cross and triple-cross, agents and double-agents, vastly complicate the task of knowing the truth. Hence, we can come full circle from Kant's philosophy of the categorical imperative—a method of analysis—to the necessity of truth—a time-tested value.

The Kantian imperative is indeed very strict. Elsewhere, Kant has said:

> *A lie is a lie, and is in itself intrinsically base whether it be told with good or bad intent. For formally a lie is always evil ... There are no lies which may not be the source of evil. A liar is a coward; he is a man who has recourse to lying because he is unable to help himself and gain his ends by any other means.*

However, before you conclude that Kant imposes impossible conditions for everyday life as a fraud examiner, consider the following excerpt where he admits that there can be justification for breaking a rule. Again, the example is based on truth-telling (lying).

> *But as men are malicious, it cannot be denied that to be punctiliously truthful is often dangerous. This has given rise to the conception of a white lie, the lie enforced upon us by necessity—a difficult point for moral philosophers. For if necessity is urged as an excuse it might be urged to justify stealing, cheating and killing, and the whole basis of morality goes by the board. Then, again, what is a case of necessity? Everyone will interpret it in his own way. And, as there is then no definite standard to judge by, the application of moral rules becomes uncertain. Consider, for example, the following case. A man who knows that I have money asks me: "Have you any money on you?" If I fail to reply, he will conclude that I have; if I reply in the affirmative he will take it from me; if I reply in the negative, I tell a lie. What am I to do? If force is used to extort a confession from me, if any confession is improperly used against me, and if I cannot save myself by maintaining silence, then my lie is a weapon of defense. The misuse of a declaration extorted by force justifies me in defending myself. For whether it is my money or a confession that is extorted makes no difference. The forcing of a statement from me under conditions which convince me that improper use would be made of it is the only case in which I can be justified in telling a white lie.*

The general objection to the imperative principle is the belief that so-called universal rules always turn out to have exceptions. The general response to this objection is that if the rule is stated properly to include the exceptional cases, then the principle is still valid. The problem with this response, however, is that human experience is complicated, and extremely complex universal rules would have to be constructed to try to cover all possible cases.

One value of the Kantian categorical imperative with its emphasis on universal, unconditional obligations is that it lets you know what to do when you are faced with an ethical decision problem. When only one rule derived from the categorical imperative is applicable, you might have no trouble following it. When two rules or two duties are in conflict, though, a serious problem can exist. Assume for the sake of illustration, another universal maxim is "Live up to all your professional duties." In the auditor/bank director illustration, these two rules ("Lying is wrong" and "Live up to all your professional duties") might be in conflict. Such conflicts of rules and duties create difficult problems because adherence to one of the rules means breaking the other.

Someone who is rule-bound might find himself or herself in a dilemma. This kind of dilemma is what prompts people to look for ways to weigh the consequences of actions. One way is described by the principle of utilitarianism discussed in the next section. Most professional codes of ethics have characteristics of the imperative type. Professionals are expected always to act in a manner in conformity with their self-imposed rules. However, critics frequently question not only the conduct but the rules on which conduct is based. Thus, a dogmatic imperative approach to ethical decisions might not be completely sufficient to maintain professional standards. A means of estimating the consequences of alternative actions might be useful.

The Utilitarian Principle

John Stuart Mill (1806–1873) is known as the apostle of the principle of *utilitarianism*, which was originated earlier by Jeremy Bentham. This principle maintains that the ultimate criterion of an ethical decision is the balance of good consequences (pleasure and avoidance of pain) over evil consequences (displeasure and pain) produced by an action. The emphasis in one form of utilitarianism, known as *act-utilitarianism*, is on the consequences of an action rather than on the logical consistency of following a rule. The criterion of producing the greater good is made an explicit part of the decision process. Consider these circumstances:

> *John lost his job, and his unemployment benefits are exhausted. He decided to conspire with a former co-worker at the plant to steal food from the commissary to feed his hungry family. A fraud examiner caught the pair.*

John's decision to steal can be said to be based on an act-utilitarian calculation that the "good" of feeding his hungry family outweighs the "evil" of stealing. Now the fraud examiner needs to decide whether the "evil" of failing to report John because he sympathizes with his condition is greater or less than the "good" of serving his employer as he promised. These moral choices are confined to a specific act in specific circumstances.

Mill perceived Kant's categorical imperative as an acknowledgment of the interest of mankind collectively instead of a matter of the intellectual willing of universal maxims. His major departure from Kant was to make explicit the idea that the desired end product of actions is the collective benefit. Mill said of Kant: "To give any meaning to Kant's principle, the sense put upon it must be that we ought to shape our conduct by a rule which all rational beings might adopt *with benefit to their collective interest.*" Sometimes the utility principle is called the "greatest happiness principle," but in this context "happiness" is not merely a frivolous emotion.

ACT-UTILITARIANISM

In *act-utilitarianism* analysis, the center of attention is placed on the individual act as it is affected by the specific circumstances of a situation. An act-utilitarian's ethical problem might be framed in this way: "What effect will my doing this act in this situation have on the general balance of good over evil?" This theory admits general guides, such as "Honesty is generally the best policy," and "Telling the truth is probably always for the greatest good." However, the emphasis is always on the specific situation, and the decision maker must determine whether he has sufficient grounds for thinking that it would be for the greatest general good to lie or steal in a particular case.

Utilitarianism demands consideration of values, although the principle can be expressed in terms of "good" and "evil" without explicit reference to values. Mill recognized that many forces influence a person's perceptions of values, particularly the social milieu in which that person lives. He also alludes to the verdict of competent people for determining suitable values—relying on the judgment of qualified people to rule on the identification of "the good." Ultimately responsibility for proper perceptions falls exactly where it belongs—on the individual decision maker. Nevertheless, Mill discoursed on matters of justice, from which certain values can be derived, among them these:

- Proper legal rights of people
- Moral rights of people
- Deserts—people deserve good for good and evil for evil
- Faithfulness
- Impartiality
- Equality

The difficulty with act-utilitarianism is that it seems to permit too many exceptions to well-established rules. By focusing attention on individual acts, the long-run effect of setting examples for other people is ignored. If John can justify stealing to feed his hungry family, then Jack can justify stealing to feed other hungry people, then Joe can steal for some other "good" cause, and before long everyone can justifying stealing on some ground. If an act-utilitarian decision is to break a moral rule, then the decision's success usually depends on everyone else's adherence to the rule. For example, to benefit from tax evasion for a good reason depends on other people not having an equally good reason for not paying their taxes.

RULE-UTILITARIANISM

Rule-utilitarianism, on the other hand, emphasizes the centrality of rules for ethical behavior while still maintaining the criterion of the greatest universal good. This kind of utilitarianism means that decision makers must first determine the rules that will promote the greatest general good for the largest number of people, irrespective of one's own position or condition. The initial question is not which action has the greatest utility, but which rule. Thus, the rule-utilitarian's ethical decision problem can be framed as follows: "What effect will everyone's doing this kind of act in this kind of situation have on the general balance of good over evil?" The principle of utility becomes operative not only in determining what particular action to take in a specific situation in which rules conflict but also in determining what the rules should be in the first place.

Mill responded to the critics of utilitarianism who charged that the principle encouraged selfish decisions to the detriment of people in general. His defense extended the principle beyond the confines of individuals (agents) and their singular acts:

> *I must again repeat what the assailants of utilitarianism seldom have the justice to acknowledge, that the happiness which forms the utilitarian standard of what is right in conduct is not the agent's own happiness but that of all concerned. As between his own happiness and that of others, utilitarianism requires him to be as strictly impartial as a disinterested and benevolent spectator. In the golden rule, we read the complete spirit of the ethics of utility. "To do as you would be done by," and "to love your neighbor as yourself," constitute the ideal perfection of utilitarian morality.*

The rule-utilitarian expression of "What effect will everyone's doing this kind of act in this kind of situation have on the general balance of good over evil?" can be given a very common sense expression: "What would happen if everybody did that?" In this form the question is known as *generalization*.

The Generalization Principle

Marcus G. Singer is a modern philosopher. His *Generalization in Ethics* deals with basic problems of moral philosophy. It sought to establish a rational basis for distinguishing between right and wrong, and thus to lay the groundwork for a rational and normative system of ethics.

Singer termed his logical construction the *generalization argument*, and here we will cast it in the framework of a principle for thinking about ethical problems. For all practical purposes, the generalization argument may be considered a judicious combination of the imperative and utilitarian principles. Stated succinctly, the argument is

> *If all relevantly similar persons acting under relevantly similar circumstances were to act in a certain way and the consequences would be undesirable, then no one ought to act in that way without a reason.*

A more everyday expression of the argument is the question: "What would happen if everyone acted in that certain way?" If the answer to the question is that the consequences would be undesirable, then your conclusion, according to the generalization test, is that the way of acting is unethical and ought not be done. Turning this form of the argument around, Singer also admits: "If the consequences of no one's acting in a certain way would be undesirable, then everyone ought to act in that way."

He gives an example of voting in a general election, asking: "What would happen if no one voted?" Presumably, the government would collapse and democracy would be repudiated. Even though political libertarians might applaud such a result, most Americans would consider this an undesirable outcome. Thus, since the consequences of no one voting would be undesirable, then everyone should vote. In Joseph Heller's novel *Catch-22*, Yossarian perverted the generalization argument when he refused to fly any more missions. Major Major countered: "Would you like to see our country lose the war?" Yossarian replied: "There are 10 million men in uniform who could replace me." Major Major: "But suppose everybody on our side felt that way." Yossarian: "Then I'd certainly be a damned fool to feel any other way. Wouldn't I?"

The key ideas in the generalization test are "similar people" and "similar circumstances." These features provide the needed flexibility to consider the many variations that arise in real problem situations. They also demand considerable judgment in determining whether people and circumstances are genuinely different or are just arbitrarily rationalized as different so that a preconceived preference can be "explained" as right. These keys give rise to Singer's expression of generalization as a principle:

What is right for one person must be right for any (relevantly) similar person in the (relevantly) same or similar circumstances.

Thus the generalization argument can be seen to have elements both of utilitarianism and imperative. It considers consequences in terms of their desirability, and it includes an imperative with the generalization of an "ought" to all similar people in similar circumstances. Nevertheless, the generalization argument can be difficult in some situations when it simply does not apply. These situations are known as *invertibility* and *reiterability*.

INVERTIBILITY

The generalization argument is invertible when (a) both doing something and not doing something would be undesirable, and (b) when both everyone and not everyone doing something would be undesirable. For example: "What if everyone were a full-time farmer?" The results would be undesirable in our society because all other social functions would disappear; our health would suffer for lack of doctors, our defense would disappear for lack of soldiers, and so forth. However, this cannot mean that no one should be a farmer because then we would all starve. "What if everyone were a fraud examiner?" (There would not be any work, and everyone would starve!) Singer's solution to the invertibility problem is to declare the generalization argument valid only when it cannot be inverted. He stated the exception as follows:

[When] the consequences of everyone's doing x [a particular action] would be undesirable, no one ought to do x," is valid only if it is not the case that the consequences of no one's doing x would also be undesirable.

Fraud examiners can become concerned about invertible-type considerations in a very practical way. Think about any extreme form of investigation method; for example, invigilation—the practice of intense scrutiny of an accounting activity for a short period of time to compare before-and-after conditions. If invigilation were performed all the time in a particular company, the method would lose its effectiveness because violators would adapt to its existence. If invigilation were never performed, it could never be effective. The generalization method of thinking, in this kind of situation, does not help solve the question of performing invigilation "all the time" or "none of the time." But when the question is framed in terms of performing invigilation some of the time at different companies, the generalization argument helps.

REITERABILITY

The generalization argument is reiterable when arbitrary times, places, or measures can be inserted in such a way as to make a decision appear to be nonsense. Singer illustrates reiterability with this example:

> *If everyone ate at six o'clock there would be no one to perform certain essential functions, things that must be attended to at all times, and so on, with the net result that no one would be able to eat at six or any other time, and with various other undesirable consequences.*

When an argument is reiterable, it also is invertible because the circumstances and the form of the argument are too particular; that is, the relevant circumstances are not general enough. The generality is lost in the imposition of particular details that are arbitrary and not essential to the description of the action, such as the time of day for eating. The generalization argument should not be made to depend on the details. Fraud examiners can get trapped in this illogical thinking when considering problems that can have nonessential details such as the time of day for conducting procedures, amounts of money involved in payments, places to conduct procedures, and the like. The problem of reiterability is a warning to beware of troublesome specifications of "relevant circumstances" in a generalization formulation of a decision problem.

Another case of reiterability involves a distinction made on the basis of a person belonging to a particular class of people, such as fraud examiners. If a particular action—for example, a false promise of leniency and confidentiality to an informant in order to extract information—can be justified to be not undesirable, then fraud examiners could be permitted to make such false promises. The test of reiterability is to be able to show that there are relevant differences distinguishing the class of persons (fraud examiners) from all other classes of persons and that there is a relevant difference in the particular circumstances (the fact situation in the investigation). If these differences cannot be convincingly demonstrated, then the argument is reiterable, and false promises are justified for everyone. In this example, however, notice that a serious consideration is the "desirability" conclusion about the false promise. The example of permitting false promises fails the test of desirability when one believes all promises must be kept by fraud examiners (that is, no false promises are permitted) because, like all other people in all other classes, a fraud examiner is only as good as his word.

Some Concluding Remarks

This review of principles in ethics provides some guide to the ways many people approach difficult decision problems. The greatest task is to take general principles of moral philosophy—the imperative, utilitarianism, or generalization—and apply them to a real decision. Their application through codes of professional ethics is where the challenge lies.

Codes of professional ethics and statutory law have two things in common. They are both based, more or less, on pervasive moral principles and values, and they both represent the aspects of behavior that a committee or legislature has chosen to put in writing. In both professional ethics and law, not every relevant guide for behavior has been written. Therefore, professional people, including fraud examiners, might find themselves "on their own" when they have to decide a proper course of conduct in a particular fact situation.

Two aspects of ethics operate in the professional environment—general ethics (the spirit) and professional ethics (the rules). Mautz and Sharaf (1961) have contributed the following thoughts to the association of general ethics and professional ethics:

> *The theory of ethics has been a subject of interest to philosophers since the beginnings of recorded thought. Because philosophers are concerned with the good of all mankind, their discussions have been concerned with what we might call general ethics rather than the ethics of small groups such as the members of a given profession. We cannot look, therefore, to their philosophical theories for direct solutions to our special problems. Nevertheless, their work with general ethics is of primary importance to the development of an appropriate concept in any special field. Ethical behavior in auditing or in any other activity is no more than a special application of the general notion of ethical conduct devised by philosophers for people generally. Ethical conduct in auditing draws its justification and basic nature from the general theory of ethics. Thus, we are well-advised to give some attention to the ideas and reasoning of some of the great philosophers on this subject.*

We have attended to the ideas and reasoning of philosophers, and now we turn to the Certified Fraud Examiner Code of Professional Ethics and its particular rules.

ASSOCIATION OF CERTIFIED FRAUD EXAMINERS
CODE OF PROFESSIONAL ETHICS

I. A Certified Fraud Examiner shall at all times demonstrate a commitment to professionalism and diligence in the performance of his or her duties.

II. A Certified Fraud Examiner shall not engage in any illegal or unethical conduct, or any activity which would constitute a conflict of interest.

III. A Certified Fraud Examiner shall, at all times, exhibit the highest level of integrity in the performance of all professional assignments, and will accept only assignments for which there is reasonable expectation that the assignment will be completed with professional competence.

IV. A Certified Fraud Examiner will comply with lawful orders of the courts, and will testify to matters truthfully and without bias or prejudice.

V. A Certified Fraud Examiner, in conducting examinations, will obtain evidence or other documentation to establish a reasonable basis for any opinion rendered. No opinion shall be expressed regarding the guilt or innocence of any person or party.

VI. A Certified Fraud Examiner shall not reveal any confidential information obtained during a professional engagement without proper authorization.

VII. A Certified Fraud Examiner shall reveal all material matters discovered during the course of an examination, which, if omitted, could cause a distortion of the facts.

VIII. A Certified Fraud Examiner shall continually strive to increase the competence and effectiveness of professional services performed under his or her direction.

The Certified Fraud Examiner Code of Professional Ethics was created by the Board of Regents of the Association of Certified Fraud Examiners and adopted January 1, 1989.

Commitment to Professionalism and Diligence

A Certified Fraud Examiner shall at all times demonstrate commitment to professionalism and diligence in the performance of his or her duties.

Professionalism

Professionalism is a quality desired by most people, but it is obtained at a price. Professionalism exists on two basic levels: (1) for the professional group as a whole and (2) for the individual Certified Fraud Examiner. Consider first the professional group as a whole.

People frequently refer to professions, to professional men and women, and to professional activities without defining the meaning of the concept "professionalism." Some fraud examiners say: "I might not know how to define it, but I know it when I see it." The U.S. Supreme Court once said the same thing about pornography. The five principal characteristics that help differentiate professional fields of endeavor from other vocations are:

- A body of specialized knowledge acquired by formal education
- Admission to the profession governed by standards of professional qualifications
- Recognition and acceptance by society of professional status, and concurrent recognition and acceptance of social responsibility by the professional
- Standards of conduct governing relationships of the professional with clients, colleagues, and the public
- A national organization devoted to the advancement of the obligations of the professional group

Specialized Knowledge and Formal Education

A fraud examiner's work involves specialized knowledge derived from several other fields—accounting, auditing, criminology, investigation, and law—to name a few. A profession might not have a body of knowledge truly unique unto itself, but it should have one that has a "mystique"—requiring study, comprehension, and practice, and be over and above the everyday abilities every other person might possess.

Continuing professional education is becoming a hallmark of professionalism. In recent years, ongoing efforts to increase competence and effectiveness has become required by some professions. The American Institute of Certified Public Accountants has led the way with the requirements for 120 hours of extra training every three years to maintain and increase professional competence. A majority of the state boards of accountancy now require continuing education as a prerequisite for renewing CPAs' licenses. The Association of Certified Fraud Examiners requires an average of 20 hours annually of continuing professional education, half of which must be directly related to fraud detection or deterrence.

Professional Admission Standards

The most highly esteemed professions, and some occupations that are merely regulated, govern admission to their ranks by qualifications contained in state law. If legal recognition is considered a requisite of a profession, then the number of "professions" is quite large, ranging from doctors of medicine to barbers. Some professions (e.g., Certified Internal Auditor, Certified Fraud Examiner) are not regulated by state or federal statutes. Many groups have the status of "profession" without the benefit of licensing laws, and the fraud examiner profession is one of these.

Certification examinations are offered in many professions—lawyers, doctors, real estate agents, insurance agents, financial analysts, management accountants, public accountants, internal auditors, and many others. The Uniform CFE Examination and certification is part of professional recognition for fraud examiners.

Experience is required for many, but not all, professional licenses and certifications. Experience of one or two years is required in most states for the CPA certificate. Experience is required to obtain the Certified Internal Auditor designation. Designation as a Certified Fraud Examiner requires at least two years experience in combination with other qualifications.

Social Recognition: A Reciprocal Relationship

No group of practitioners can become a "profession" merely by declaring itself to be one. Society must acknowledge the group as a professional body. At present, fraud examiners are at the stage of becoming a self-declared profession. Historically, other professions had the same starting point. Modern medicine overcame its roots in magic. Accountants rose from the level of bookkeepers. Internal auditors advanced social goals by presenting a responsible front to Congress and other public bodies. The list goes on.

Social recognition, however, is not necessarily permanent. Society will not continue to honor as professional any group that fails to serve a broad-based social and public interest. Thus the other side to the coin of recognition is: Certified Fraud Examiners must reciprocate and accept the social responsibility inherent in a professional status that serves the public interest.

Standards of Conduct

One way to achieve the social recognition that goes with professionalism is to adhere to the Certified Fraud Examiner Code of Professional Ethics. Other professions have such codes. They are the written versions of moral philosophy and values especially relevant to the group. Fraud examiners and other professionals must observe their codes with an awareness of the society around them. Care must be taken that rules are not created and followed in a self-serving manner, inimical to behavior expected by the public.

Possessing and following a set of behavior rules is one thing, possessing and following a set that meets public expectations is another. Other professions (law, architecture, and accounting, to name three) have found themselves under attack from the U.S. Federal Trade Commission and the U.S. Department of Justice when their rules were perceived to have introduced unwarranted restraints of trade. While the Certified Fraud Examiner Code of Professional Ethics might not seem to contain such rules, they might come under attack in some future, different setting. Certified Fraud Examiners must be prepared to experience change, when appropriate change is necessary.

Individual Fraud Examiners

When the focus of professionalism is turned to the individual Certified Fraud Examiner, its features for the group as a whole should not be forgotten. The individual member is presumed to possess a body of knowledge on his admission to the group and attainment of the Certified Fraud Examiner certificate. The individual is expected to adhere to the code of ethics and maintain membership in the national organization. Along with these features, the individual Certified Fraud Examiner exhibits professionalism by continually striving to honor the recognition granted by the public. In day-to-day life, this is accomplished by exercising diligence in performing Certified Fraud Examiner work.

Diligence

The "diligence in performing his or her duties" phrase in the rule refers to several activities that collectively define high-quality fraud examiner work. They include planning assignments and supervising assistants and colleagues, avoiding conflicts of interest, performing with competence, obtaining sufficient evidence to establish a basis for opinions, maintaining confidential relations, and avoiding distortion of facts. These activities are the subjects of other rules in the Certified Fraud Examiner Code of Professional Ethics, and they will be discussed in more detail later.

Legal and Ethical Conduct and Conflict of Interest

A Certified Fraud Examiner shall not engage in any illegal or unethical conduct, or any activity which would constitute a conflict of interest.

This rule is a composite of three prohibitions—illegal conduct, unethical conduct, and conflict of interest.

Illegal Conduct

The prohibition of illegal conduct seems straightforward. Some activities might be obviously illegal, but the legal status of others might not be so clear. A fraud examiner is always well advised to consult an attorney when questionable situations arise. At the same time, however, it might be difficult to know ahead of time whether such a consultation is necessary. Consider the following legal-related problems (but remember that this chapter on ethics is not intended to be your primary guide to legal matters).

Libel and Slander

Libel and slander can cause personal injury and subject a fraud examiner to a lawsuit for damages. Libel is a written defamation of someone else's character. Slander is a spoken defamation. The content of a libelous or slanderous message must:
- Contain words that injure another person's character or reputation or hold him up to ridicule
- Be communicated orally or in writing to other people
- Cause an actual damage to the person who is the subject of the communication

The risks involved in libel and slander are reasons for having the rule in the Certified Fraud Examiner code that prohibits expression of opinions on the guilt or innocence of people.

False Imprisonment

False imprisonment can mean more than putting a person behind bars. Courts have found many means of detainment to be false imprisonment, including locking an employee in a store, removing a distributor from a car, and detaining a witness by force. Even though drastic action might be essential, a fraud examiner must accomplish his task legally.

Compounding a Felony

The criminal act of compounding a felony can result from participating in a trade for restitution for agreeing to forgo prosecution. While plea bargains might be acceptable under the supervision of a court, Certified Fraud Examiners should be very careful and should obtain legal advice when negotiating private deals.

Some rules for professionals insert the word "knowingly" in relation to illegal activities, saying: "One should not *knowingly* be a party to an illegal activity." The Certified Fraud Examiner Code does not include this way out. Certified Fraud Examiners are generally not entitled to claim ignorance of the law. They are expected to know a considerable amount of law in connection with investigations, and they are expected to know when to consult a lawyer.

Unethical Conduct

The prohibition of unethical conduct is complicated. These materials have presented an array of issues in moral philosophy and ethical thinking—intertwining considerations of principles and values. This latter part is set forth in the Certified Fraud Examiner Code of Professional Ethics. Legitimate questions are: "What manner of unethical conduct is meant by this rule? Does it refer to general matters of moral philosophy and ethics, or is its applicability limited only to the rules in this code?"

A narrow focus on fraud examiners' professionalism would center attention only on the rules in the Certified Fraud Examiner Code of Professional Ethics. A broader social-responsibility focus would go beyond the code to the interaction of the fraud examiner with other people affected by his choices. The broader focus is more consistent with the concept of professionalism because the code itself is a limited set of rules. A fraud examiner must take personal responsibility for decisions, and be aware that other professionals often are criticized for adhering too rigidly to their codes. Lawyers face harsh criticisms when they seem to hide knowledge of criminal acts in their privileged communications. Doctors are often criticized for the things they tell their patients about terminal illnesses. Professions are criticized for having specialized rules that seem to permit their members to act contrary to social expectations.

Conflict of Interest and "Independence" Considerations

The term *conflict of interest* in the rule begs for definition. Try to enumerate the parties whose "interests" might conflict: The Certified Fraud Examiner, the Certified Fraud Examiner's clients (Client A with Client B with Client C), the Certified Fraud Examiner's employer, the public ("innocent bystanders"), and law enforcement agencies are the first to come to mind. These parties are involved in almost every investigation. The lines that connect these with each other and with the fraud examiner could look like a spaghetti bowl of multiple relationships. Deciding whether a conflict or a community of interests exists depends on the facts of each particular situation.

Nevertheless, some conflicts to avoid are clear enough. A Certified Fraud Examiner employed full-time by a company should not engage in other jobs that create a hardship or loss to the employer. A fraud examiner should not be a "double agent" employed by one company, but retained by another company or person to infiltrate the employer and transmit inside information (unless, of course, the employing company agrees to the arrangement in order to apprehend other parties employed by the company). A Certified Fraud Examiner should not accept engagements from both sides to a controversy—just like lawyers are prohibited from representing both parties in a transaction, lawsuit, or trial.

"Conflict of interest" and "independence" are related. The American Institute of Certified Public Accountants (AICPA) includes independence (and avoidance of conflict of interest) in its Code of Professional Conduct. Some particulars from the AICPA may be relevant, in part, for the Certified Fraud Examiner. Consider the following from the AICPA Code of Professional Conduct:

> *Independence will be considered to be impaired for audit engagements if an AICPA member had any of the following transactions, interests, or relationships:*
> – *Any direct or material indirect financial interest in the enterprise under audit*

> - *Any joint, closely held business investment with the enterprise under audit or with any officer, director, or principal stockholder thereof that was material in relation to the member's net worth to the net worth of the member's firm*
> - *Any loan to or from the enterprise under audit or any officer, director, or principal stockholder of the enterprise (except immaterial loans, home mortgages, and loans secured by property)*
> - *Any managerial-type connection with the enterprise under audit, such as a promoter, underwriter, or voting trustee, director or officer, or in any capacity equivalent to that of a member of management or of an employee.*

These rules for auditors exist specifically to convey to the public a perception of independence. Independence and conflict avoidance are enhanced by refraining from having financial and managerial interests in clients or in joint cooperation with clients' managers and directors. After all, they might be a suspect in an investigation. When a Certified Fraud Examiner works as an employee of a company, the prohibitions about employment are not relevant because the employer-employee relationship is known to the employer, who is the client and recipient of any reports. In such cases, independence and conflict should be considered in relation to all the other parties involved. Certainly, a mental condition of objectivity and honesty then governs the relation between the Certified Fraud Examiner and his employer. If the CFE does have a perceived conflict, it usually can be avoided through adequate disclosure.

Integrity and Competence

> *A Certified Fraud Examiner shall, at all times, exhibit the highest level of integrity in the performance of all professional assignments, and will accept only assignments for which there is reasonable expectation that the assignment will be completed with professional competence.*

This rule contains two parts. The first deals with integrity and the second with competence. Competence here is related to "diligence," as discussed previously in relation to the first rule in the Certified Fraud Examiner Code.

Integrity

If you were asked to name a desirable personal characteristic, "integrity" is one that would rank high on the scale, along with honesty, truthfulness, trustworthiness, and loyalty. Outside observers of Certified Fraud Examiners' activity will look for signs of integrity as a signal that trust is warranted. However, integrity hardly exists apart from other characteristics well-known in moral philosophy and recognized in the Certified Fraud Examiner Code of Professional Ethics.

Integrity requires honesty. It requires truthfulness. It requires trustworthiness. It requires confidentiality. It requires subordination of desires for personal gain to the interests of clients, employers, and the public. It requires independence of mental attitude and avoidance of conflicts of interest. "Integrity" is all these things wrapped up into one word.

In addition, integrity means that a Certified Fraud Examiner ought to have a well-developed sense of moral philosophy—an ability to analyze situations where no rules of the Certified Fraud Examiner Code are specifically applicable and to be able to distinguish right from wrong. It does not mean, however, that a Certified Fraud Examiner must be perfect in all technical matters, nor does it mean that Certified Fraud Examiners and others cannot have honest differences of opinion. In the course of a fraud examination, inadvertent errors, mistakes of judgment, and other problems might cause conflict. In such cases, a Certified Fraud Examiner can preserve integrity either by admitting error or by convincingly justifying a difference of perception or opinion.

Professional Competence

Professional competence refers to how well Certified Fraud Examiners do their job. Determination of competence always depends on the specific facts and circumstances of the assignment. Competence is best understood in the context of the *prudent practitioner*. The idea of a prudent professional practitioner is present in other social science theories, for example, the "economic man" of economic theory and the "reasonable man" of law. This concept can be summarized for fraud examiners as follows:

> *A prudent practitioner is assumed to have a knowledge of the philosophy and practice of fraud examinations, to have the degree of training, experience, and skill common to the average fraud examiner, to have the ability to recognize indications of frauds, and to keep abreast of developments in the perpetration and detection of fraud. Competence requires the CFE to be acquainted with the company, activity, function, or program under*

investigation; to review the methods of control in operation; to obtain sufficient evidence pertinent to the suspected fraud or illegal activity; to be responsive to unusual events and unfamiliar circumstances; to persist until any reasonable doubts about the evidence have been eliminated; and to exercise caution in instructing assistants and reviewing their work.

Professional competence also demands attention to three kinds of interference that can damage the independence and quality of a Certified Fraud Examiner's work. Fraud examiners who permit these conditions to interfere with the assignment demonstrate less than the desired level of professional competence. The three types of interference are programming, investigation, and reporting.

Programming

Fraud examiners must remain free from interference by managers who try to restrict, specify, or modify the procedures they need to perform, including any attempts to assign personnel or otherwise to control the examination work. Occasionally, client or employer managers try to limit access to information or to other personnel or to limit the amount of time available for the assignment.

Investigation

When appropriate, Certified Fraud Examiners must have free access to books, records, correspondence, and other evidence. They must have the cooperation of managers or other employees without any attempt to interpret or screen evidence.

Reporting

Client or employer managers should not be allowed to overrule the Certified Fraud Examiner's judgments on the appropriate content of a report. Integrity is destroyed and judgment is subordinated when the Certified Fraud Examiner is compelled to alter a report or to omit important information or to misstate facts. Certified Fraud Examiners must not let any feelings of misguided loyalty to the client, employer, or other sources of conflicts of interest interfere with their obligation to report fully and fairly.

Professional Skepticism

Fraud examiners must always perform their work with an attitude of skepticism, and begin with the belief that something is wrong or someone is committing a fraud (depending, of course, on the nature of the assignment and the preliminary information available). This attitude may make fraud examinations extensive and expensive. Relax-ation of this initial attitude of skepticism occurs only when the evidence shows no signs of fraudulent activity. At no time is a Certified Fraud Examiner entitled to "assume" a fraud problem does not exist. Professional skepticism can be dispelled only by evidence. As a result, opinions or attestations about a fraud-free environment are absolutely prohibited for Certified Fraud Examiners.

Court Orders and Testimony

A Certified Fraud Examiner will comply with lawful orders of the courts, and will testify to matters truthfully and without bias or prejudice.

The essence of this rule is truth-telling. The part about complying with lawful orders of the courts is a direction not to flee from a summons or subpoena issued by a court. Even though the rule specifies "courts," it is reasonable to extend it to other agencies that have the legal power to issue such orders (e.g., Congressional committees, grand juries, special prosecutors, quasi-judicial administrative agencies). Sometimes, legal counsel might devise stratagems to avoid immediate service of (or attention to) a summons. Fraud examiners can listen to such legal advice, but they also must weigh it against their own knowledge of proper and legal behavior. In some cases, a second legal opinion might be advisable. The fraud examiner could be on shaky grounds with a defense of "my lawyer told me to hide" when accused of obstruction of justice. (The lawyer might be in the cell next door.)

Truthful testimony often presents strategic problems. A fraud examiner, even one who is an attorney, should always be represented by counsel in a courtroom, deposition, or other testimony setting. The lawyers' own saying is: "An attorney who represents himself has a fool for a client." Counsel is invaluable for protecting a fraud examiner witness from improper questioning.

When testimony is sought in examination or cross-examination, a Certified Fraud Examiner always should respond to the questions that are asked—no more and no less. The attorney conducting the examination has the responsibility to ask the right questions, and the fraud examiner's counsel has the responsibility to object to misleading, improper, or irrelevant questions. The fraud examiner's counsel also has the obligation to correct any problems with the cross-examination. A "helpful" fraud examiner who tries to embellish the answers with additional material might offend the court or do unintentional harm to the case being made for one party or the other. Of course, a fraud examiner may invoke his own Constitutional rights, upon the advice of counsel.

Answers should always be delivered without bias or prejudice. It is the lawyer's job to be biased and prejudiced—in the context of the adversary judicial system—establishing the case for his own client or for the government. The greatest danger for delivering biased or prejudicial testimony exists when the broad question is: "Tell the court about your findings in your fraud examination." This is an open-ended invitation to spill the beans. If counsel does not object, the Certified Fraud Examiner is in the spotlight. However, responding to such an invitation amounts to delivering a report, and the next rule in the Certified Fraud Examiner Code of Professional Ethics can be used as a guide.

Reasonable Evidential Basis for Opinions

A fraud examiner, in conducting examinations, will obtain evidence or other documentation to establish a reasonable basis for any opinion rendered. No opinion shall be expressed regarding the guilt or innocence of any person or party.

Evidential Basis for Opinions

The accounting profession has similar rules, some of which are in its codes of ethics, some in their technical practice standards. Here is a sample of its provisions:

Sufficient competent evidential matter is to be obtained through inspection, observation, inquiries and confirmations to afford a reasonable basis for an opinion regarding the financial statements under examination. [AICPA Generally Accepted Auditing Standards]

Internal auditors should collect, analyze, interpret, and document information to support audit results. [The Institute of Internal Auditors, Inc. Standards for the Practice of Internal Auditing]

A member shall obtain sufficient relevant data to afford a reasonable basis for conclusions or recommendations in relation to any professional services performed. [AICPA Code of Professional Conduct]

A practitioner should obtain sufficient relevant data to afford a reasonable basis for conclusions or recommendations. [AICPA Management Advisory Services Standards]

Sufficient evidence shall be obtained to provide a reasonable basis for the conclusion that is expressed in the report. [AICPA Attestation Standards]

Sufficient competent evidence should be obtained to provide a reasonable basis for the examination report. [AICPA Standards for Examinations of Prospective Financial Information]

Clearly, the accounting profession considers "sufficient relevant data (evidence)" a compelling standard of practice, if not a matter of professional ethics. Evidence can be defined as all the information that influences a decision maker in reaching decisions that can take the form of a report, a set of recommendations, or similar products.

Evidence might be quantitative or qualitative; it may be objective or it may have subjective qualities; it may be absolutely compelling to a decision or it may be only mildly persuasive. The Certified Fraud Examiner's task is to collect and evaluate a sufficient amount of relevant evidence to afford a reasonable and logical basis for decisions.

Auditors sometimes say they gather evidence to show that financial statements are presented properly or that control procedures are operating effectively. They are following a time-tested method of investigation that consists of three parts:
- Recognize the problem or issue subject to investigation
- Gather sufficient relevant evidence about it
- Analyze the evidence and reach a conclusion about the problem or issue

Most auditors' propositions are expressed positively, such as: "The cash balance is accurately stated." However, an auditor actually will seek evidence to show that the cash balance is *not* properly stated. Imagine a cash balance that is the sum of 110 separate bank accounts. An audit team probably will sample these accounts instead of looking at all of them. The auditors look for evidence that some of these cash balances are misstated. If they fail to find any misstatements in a sufficiently large sample, they have not proved that the total is proper, but they have no reason to believe that it is materially misstated.

A literal report on this kind of work would be called "negative assurance," in which an auditor would say: "Nothing came to my attention to make me believe the cash balance is materially misstated." This statement of negative assurance is an accurate report of the audit process. As long as the "attention" consists of sufficient relevant evidence, the report is useful. Auditors might not know without any doubt that the balance is proper, but they are entitled to act as though it is because they have analyzed sufficient relevant evidence.

Some fraud examinations can take on this same character. Certified Fraud Examiners will be assigned to seek the truth about some business records or to try to determine whether some control procedures have failed. The Certified Fraud Examiner will seek evidence of misstatement or failure, and, if none is found, will report the positive results.

In other cases, a client or employer might already know that fraud, thefts, shortages, control failures, or other such events have occurred. The Certified Fraud Examiner's assignment then is to determine how the improper activity is being carried out, by whom, and to what extent. This kind of fraud investigation demands sufficient evidence, examples, and suitable documentation to prove the how/whom/extent findings. In these cases, the "negative assurance" type of conclusion is not appropriate. Certified Fraud Examiners must obtain the evidence to show the actual how/whom/extent conclusions.

Guilt and Innocence

The rule that prohibits opinions regarding the guilt or innocence of any person or party is a rule of prudence. The AICPA had a rule that prohibited CPAs from attesting that a company's financial forecast would be achieved. Most CPAs' reaction to the rule was: "Why would anyone want to do something so dumb?" The general answer was that without the explicit rule, someone might give an achievability attestation, the actual events would fall short, and the CPA (and all other CPAs) would suffer criticism. The rule was a rule of prudence. Clearly, it is prudent for a Certified Fraud Examiner to refrain from usurping the role of jury. In a courtroom, no good attorney would ask a Certified Fraud Examiner for such a conclusion, and no alert judge would allow such testimony.

The fraud examiner's job is to present the evidence in his report. Such evidence might constitute a convincing case pointing to the guilt or innocence of a person. But a clear line should be drawn between a report that essentially says "Here is the evidence" and one that steps over the line and says "He is the guilty (innocent) person." Nevertheless, there is a fine line between recommending action—forwarding the evidence to a law enforcement agency or filing a complaint or lawsuit—and giving an opinion on guilt or innocence. Certified Fraud Examiners may make such recommendations because they think the evidence is strong enough to support a case. They might even have a conclusion about guilt or innocence. The rule does not prohibit the Certified Fraud Examiner, under the proper circumstances, from accusing the person under investigation.

Confidential Information

A Certified Fraud Examiner shall not reveal any confidential information obtained during a professional engagement without proper authorization.

Confidential information rules in professional codes of ethics have the potential to create enormous conflicts—conflicts of principles and conflicts of values. Consider this possible exchange between a lawyer and client:

Client:
Because you have taken my case on this fraud charge, I think you should know more about my background.

Lawyer:
Go ahead.

Client:
Three years ago, I participated in an armed robbery and was never caught. My gun went off and killed the storekeeper. One of my buddies was accused and convicted. He's had all his appeals and is scheduled to be executed tomorrow. What can you do?

Lawyer:

Nothing.

"Nothing" may be oversimplifying the situation, but the point is that lawyers have a keen awareness of the privileged information rights of their clients. Most lawyers will stoutly defend their duty not to endanger this client, even at the cost of a life. Most laymen are shocked at this particular. One commentator responded to a lawyer defending the position with a sharp retort: "Do you mean you will sacrifice an innocent man to a rule?" This incredulity is well-aimed. It brings into sharp focus two conflicting values—the benefits of a long-standing rule of legal practice and the sanctity of life itself. Not all situations are this dramatic, but Certified Fraud Examiners can nevertheless get into similar conflicts.

Confidential information, for all practical purposes, is any and all information a Certified Fraud Examiner might obtain in the course of work, whether it be from the company or client for whom an investigation is performed or from any other source consulted during the work. The rules of confidential and privileged information are based on the belief that they facilitate a free flow of information between parties to the relationship. The nature of a fraud examination might make it necessary for Certified Fraud Examiners to have access to sensitive information. Clients and employers would be less likely to reveal such information or to provide access to sources if they could not trust a Certified Fraud Examiner to keep it confidential.

Privileged information is information that cannot be demanded, even by a court. Common law privilege exists for husband-wife and attorney-client relationships, and physician-patient and priest-penitent relationships have obtained the privilege through state statutes. The attorney-client privilege is statutory in some jurisdictions. Certified Fraud Examiners do not have any such privilege in common law or by statute. In all the recognized privilege relationships, the professional person is obligated to observe the privilege; it can be waived only by the client, patient, or penitent. (These people are said to be the holders of the privilege.) Likewise, a Certified Fraud Examiner's client or employer is the holder of the confidence. (The Law Section contains additional information on this subject.)

The Certified Fraud Examiner Code of Professional Ethics does not assume a privileged status for the fraud examiner-client/employer relationship. However, the examiner's client or employer holds the key known as "proper authorization" in the rule. If the client or employer consents to disclosure of information otherwise considered confidential, then the

Certified Fraud Examiner can transmit it to others. Sometimes consent is given when the consenter does not know exactly what information will be conveyed. Even with consent, therefore, a Certified Fraud Examiner should be careful to let the client/employer know what the consent covers. The best rule of prudence is to let the client/employer make the actual disclosure by transmitting the Certified Fraud Examiner's report, working papers, or other documentation. Then the client not only knows what is being disclosed but is the one making the disclosure.

Confidential information relationships do not die with the severance of the Certified Fraud Examiner-client or Certified Fraud Examiner-employer relationship. The confidentiality rule does not permit disclosure after the assignment is finished, or there is no clause permitting disclosure after a Certified Fraud Examiner is fired, resigns, or retires from an employing organization. Examiners who write "kiss and tell" memoirs about the inner secrets of an organization violate the confidentiality rule in the most blatant manner.

Proper Authorization

As just mentioned, one form of "proper authorization" is the consent given by a Certified Fraud Examiner's client or employer. Additional forms of authorization are possible. Other professions have exceptions that void the confidentiality or privilege rules. Lawyers can reveal client confidences if doing so is necessary to prevent a future crime. CPAs are not bound by confidentiality when responding to a court subpoena or summons, when participating in quality control reviews, or when initiating complaints to their disciplinary bodies.

Likewise, Certified Fraud Examiners are not bound by confidentiality when doing so would make them parties to a violation of the law. Care must be taken about remaining silent when silence could be construed as obstructing justice or engaging in a conspiracy. The advice of an attorney should be sought in such cases.

Questions may arise over information received from someone being investigated. Suppose an employee being questioned tells the Certified Fraud Examiner something "in confidence" concerning his role in a theft. Fraud examiners must remember that the confidentiality relationship runs first to the client or employer, and that this promise of confidentiality is understood to exist without being spoken. In the case of the employee- informant, the fraud examiner does not have an understood or unspoken promise of confidentiality and is not bound by the rule with respect to the informant. If the fraud examiner promises the employee-informant "confidentiality," the promise will probably turn out to be a lie, because the examiner has also promised the client/employer a report on all the relevant evidence. A Certified Fraud Examiner should not promise confidentiality or leniency to an informant for the purpose of extracting testimony. A Certified Fraud Examiner's reputation and effectiveness depends upon the integrity of the Certified Fraud Examiner's word.

Relation to Conflict of Interest

Another aspect of the confidentiality rule concerns the possibility that a fraud examiner might use information that is part of a conflict of interest with the client/employer. The Institute of Internal Auditors' Code of Ethics contains language that makes this relation very clear: "Members and Certified Internal Auditors shall be prudent in the use of information acquired in the course of their duties. They shall not use confidential information for any personal gain nor in any manner which would be contrary to law or detrimental to the welfare of their organization." Clearly, using information for personal gain or using information to the detriment of the client/employer is a close kin to lying and stealing. The lie comes from the Certified Fraud Examiner's breaking a pledge to maintain confidentiality, and the stealing comes from harming the client or employer.

When a Certified Fraud Examiner faces the potential for personal gain from confidential client information, a conflict of interest exists—the Certified Fraud Examiner's desire for wealth vs. the client/employer's desire for and trust in confidential services. One of the worst kind of ethical breaches would be to break the promise of confidentiality for personal gain. It is mere greed at work.

"Public" Information

It is tempting to consider confidential information to be "nonpublic information" instead of "all information" on the grounds that public information is available to everyone anyway. Such an interpretation is not appropriate. Public information might be hard to find and/or expensive to obtain and analyze. After all, the client or company paid the Certified Fraud Examiner a fee or salary to find and use public information, and a Certified Fraud Examiner's disclosure of it would give others a "free ride." When information is public, let others find it for themselves.

Some might argue that no confidence is abused if a Certified Fraud Examiner points others to public information that is published and widely distributed, for example, financial statements in annual reports or stories in national newspapers such as the *Wall Street Journal*.

The next step is to consider public information that is not published, for example, real estate deed restrictions, liens on property, and credit records. Defending a breach of confidence on the grounds "It was public anyway" is a weak excuse. Mere revelation of the source of information imparts signals of importance that are not public and that may guide others to information a client or employer believes is confidential.

"Blowing the Whistle"

Difficult problems arise over Certified Fraud Examiners' obligations to "blow the whistle" about clients' or employers' shady or illegal practices. The problem exists at two levels. The first is the managerial level, where the Certified Fraud Examiner might be employed or engaged by high-level managers who turn out to be involved in fraudulent practices. A Certified Fraud Examiner should always arrange to have a pipeline to levels of management above the operations under investigation. Thus, for example, evidence of managerial-level complicity can be reported to the board of directors and its audit committee without trampling on the confidentiality rule.

The other level—involvement by the directors or the highest level of management or ownership—presents the hard problems. In such cases, the only higher levels exist outside the organization, for example, the police or similar agencies, the U.S. Department of Justice, Department of Defense contract officers, and the like. These and other agencies are concerned with law or contract violations. A board of directors may withhold evidence of criminal acts, price fixing, or contract overcharges from them.

In general, examiners are not legally obligated to blow the whistle on clients or employers. However, circumstances might exist where they are morally and legally justified in making disclosures to appropriate outside parties. Such circumstances include those in which a client or employer has intentionally involved a Certified Fraud Examiner in its illegal or unethical conduct, or when a client or employer has distributed misleading reports based on the Certified Fraud Examiner's work. The confidentiality rule should not be viewed as a license or excuse for inaction where action may be appropriate to right a wrongful act committed or about to be committed by a client or employer. A Certified Fraud Examiner is under no obligation to go to jail with wrongdoers. When in doubt, consult legal counsel.

Complete Reporting of Material Matters

A Certified Fraud Examiner shall reveal all material matters discovered during the course of an examination which, if omitted, could cause a distortion of the facts.

In its simplicity, this rule demands full and fair reporting of the findings made in investigations. The two words—*material* and *distortion*—are key concepts.

Evidence and conclusions are material if knowledge of them would affect clients' decisions based on a Certified Fraud Examiner's report. *Materiality* is a user-oriented concept. If matters omitted from a report were known to the users, and their own perceptions and conclusions would be different in light of this knowledge, the omitted information is material. Certified Fraud Examiners are placed in the difficult position of determining not what they themselves consider important and material, but rather what they think users will consider important and material. They need to project a decision-making process onto the users instead of simply being introspective.

Therefore, it is very important for Certified Fraud Examiners to learn directly from clients and employers the type of information they consider important. Nothing is gained by playing a guessing game. A Certified Fraud Examiner should obtain as good an understanding as possible of the users' interests, the information desired, the level of detail needed, and other aspects of the users' needs.

The "distortion of facts" in the rule is cited in reference to omissions. "Distortion" is clearly related to the concept of materiality and users' decisions. It could likewise refer to the matters included in a report. A subtle stretching of the facts to make them look as if they support a preconceived conclusion would be a distortion that could cause users to undertake inappropriate actions. Sometimes the evidence to support a definitive con-clusion or recommendation is simply not obtainable—the evidence is missing or depends upon future events, for example. The Certified Fraud Examiner's obligation is to avoid rushing to judgment. When matters are not clear, the Certified Fraud Examiner's report should stress the tentative nature of the evidence and withhold judgment. To jump to conclusions could be considered a distortion of facts.

Professional Improvement

A Certified Fraud Examiner shall continually strive to increase the competence and effectiveness of professional services performed under his or her direction.

This rule contains both good advice and a specific directive for behavior. It is an admonition to progress toward greater expertise and thus better serve clients and employers.

The state of the "fraud arts" changes continually. Years ago, investigators needed to learn how to cope with computer fraud. Today, Certified Fraud Examiners are faced with a growing array of ways and means for perpetrating frauds. While many of these might not be new, or might be variations on old themes, it is still a challenge for Certified Fraud Examiners to know about all of them. A continuing learning process is necessary for Certified Fraud Examiners to increase their competence and effectiveness in conducting fraud examinations.

People who become Certified Fraud Examiners agree to complete 20 hours of continuing professional education each year. Course content is not specified in detail, but the requirement is that at least 10 hours will be spent on technical subjects that contribute directly to fraud examination expertise. Certified Fraud Examiners who also are CPAs, CIAs, or who hold other professional designations can double-count continuing education hours obtained in connection with the other certificates, as long as they meet the criteria for fraud examination continuing education. Further details about policies and procedures are available from the Association.

Professional ethics for Certified Fraud Examiners is not simply a matter covered by a few rules in a formal Code of Professional Ethics. Concepts of proper professional conduct permeate all areas of practice. Ethics are the foundation of Certified Fraud Examiners' self-regulatory efforts.

The principled approach to thoughtful decisions is important in fraud examination work in all settings—private practice, industrial, government and foreign employment, and other working arrangements. The ethics rules might appear to be restrictive, but they are for the benefit of the public as well as for the discipline, use, and protection of Certified Fraud Examiners.

Professional Standards and Practices

General Standards
Independence and Objectivity
Certified Fraud Examiners are responsible for maintaining independence in attitude and appearance, approaching and conducting fraud examinations in an objective and unbiased manner, and ensuring that examining organizations they direct are free from impairments to independence.

Qualifications
Certified Fraud Examiners must possess the skills, knowledge, abilities, and appearance needed to perform examinations proficiently and effectively. Certified Fraud Examiners who are responsible for directing fraud examinations must ensure they are performed by personnel who collectively possess the skills and knowledge necessary to complete examinations in accordance with these Standards. Certified Fraud Examiners must maintain their qualifications by fulfilling continuing education requirements and adhering to the Code of Ethics of the Association of Certified Fraud Examiners.

Fraud Examinations
Certified Fraud Examiners must conduct fraud examinations using due professional care, with adequate planning and supervision to provide assurance that the objectives are achieved within the framework of these standards. Evidence is to be obtained in an efficient, thorough, and legal manner. Reports of the results of fraud examinations must be accurate, objective, and thorough.

Confidentiality
Certified Fraud Examiners are responsible for ensuring that they and examining organizations they direct exercise due care to prevent improper disclosure of confidential or privileged information.

Specific Standards
Independence and Objectivity
ATTITUDE AND APPEARANCE
Independence of attitude requires impartiality and fairness in conducting examinations and in reaching resulting conclusions and judgments. Certified Fraud Examiners must also be sensitive to the appearance of independence so that conclusions and judgments will be

accepted as impartial by knowledgeable third parties. Certified Fraud Examiners who become aware of a situation or relationship that could be perceived to impair independence, whether or not actual impairments exist, should inform management immediately and take steps to eliminate the perceived impairment, including withdrawing from the examination if necessary.

OBJECTIVITY

To ensure objectivity in performing examinations, Certified Fraud Examiners must maintain an independent mental attitude, reach judgments on examination matters without undue influence from others, and avoid being placed in positions where they would be unable to work in an objective professional manner. All possible conflicts of interest should be disclosed.

ORGANIZATIONAL RELATIONSHIP

The Certified Fraud Examiner's reporting relationship should be such that the attitude and appearance of independence and objectivity are not jeopardized. Organizational independence is achieved when the Certified Fraud Examiner's function has a mandate to conduct independent examinations throughout the organization, or by a reporting relationship high enough in the organization to ensure independence of action.

Qualifications
SKILLS, KNOWLEDGE, ABILITIES, AND EXPERIENCE

Certified Fraud Examiners cannot be expected to have an expert level of skill and knowledge for every circumstance that might be encountered in a fraud examination. Nevertheless, Certified Fraud Examiners must have sufficient skill and knowledge to recognize when additional training or expert guidance is required. It is the responsibility of a Certified Fraud Examiner to ensure that necessary skills, knowledge, ability, and experience are acquired or available before going forward with a fraud examination.

Certified Fraud Examiners must be skilled in obtaining information from records, documents, and people; in analyzing and evaluating information and drawing sound conclusions; in communicating the results of fraud examinations, both orally and in writing; and in serving as an expert witness when appropriate.

Certified Fraud Examiners must be knowledgeable in investigative techniques, applicable laws and rules of evidence, fraud auditing, criminology, and ethics.

CONTINUING EDUCATION

Certified Fraud Examiners are required to fulfill continuing education requirements established by the Association of Certified Fraud Examiners. Additionally, Certified Fraud Examiners are responsible for securing other education necessary for specific fraud examination and related fields in which they are individually involved.

CODE OF ETHICS

Certified Fraud Examiners are to adhere to the Code of Professional Ethics of the Association of Certified Fraud Examiners.

Fraud Examination

DUE PROFESSIONAL CARE

Due professional care is defined as exercising the care and skill expected of a prudent professional in similar circumstances. Certified Fraud Examiners are responsible for ensuring that there is sufficient predication for beginning a fraud examination; that said examinations are conducted with diligence and thoroughness; that all applicable laws and regulations are observed; that appropriate methods and techniques are used; and that said examinations are conducted in accordance with these standards.

PLANNING AND SUPERVISION

Certified Fraud Examiners must plan and supervise fraud examinations in a manner to ensure that objectives are achieved within the framework of these standards.

EVIDENCE

Certified Fraud Examiners must collect evidence, whether exculpatory or incriminating, that supports fraud examination results and will be admissible in subsequent proceedings, by obtaining and documenting evidence in a manner to ensure that all necessary evidence is obtained, and the chain of custody is preserved.

REPORTING

Reports of the results of a fraud examination, whether written or verbal, must address all relevant aspects of the examination and be accurate, objective, and understandable.

In rendering reports to management, clients or others, Certified Fraud Examiners shall not express judgments on the guilt or innocence of any person or persons, regardless of the Certified Fraud Examiner's opinion of the preponderance of evidence. Certified Fraud

Examiners must exercise due professional care when expressing other opinions related to an examination, such as the likelihood that a fraud has or has not occurred, and whether or not internal controls are adequate.

Confidentiality

Certified Fraud Examiners, during fraud examinations, are often privy to highly sensitive and confidential information about organizations and individuals. Certified Fraud Examiners must exercise due care so as not to purposefully or inadvertently disclose such information except as necessary to conduct the examination as required by law.

Predication Standards

Knowing when to initiate an examination will largely be driven by the source of the information. Information can be derived from a number of sources—a complaint, an anonymous tip, by accident or through some proactive effort, such as an audit or survey. The value of the information has to be weighed and the creditability evaluated.

The purpose of a preliminary inquiry is to determine if there is some creditable information (red flags) that a fraudulent act has or will occur. If so, what is the examiner's responsibility?

Preliminary inquiries should be conducted expeditiously and not used as a means of holding in abeyance a decision of initiating a formal fraud examination. If a sufficient number of fraud indicators exists, a fraud examination should be initiated.

Because business activities/transactions are susceptible to fraudulent acts, all examinations should be approached with professional skepticism. That is, assume neither dishonesty nor unquestioned honesty of management/personnel.

Bribery

Bribery is the offering, giving, receiving, or soliciting of something of value for the purpose of influencing the action of an individual in the discharge of his duties. It can also include the securing of advantage over competitors by secret and corrupt dealing with employees or agents of prospective purchasers.

Any indication (through audit, tip, complaint, or accidental discovery) that such action (bribery) has occurred, may have occurred, or could occur should be investigated until the

Certified Fraud Examiner has established that it has occurred, or, within reasonable certainty, that it did not occur.

In the example given, the fact that there is a major control weakness is the only predication needed to investigate the situation further to determine whether there was fraud.

Conflicts of Interest

This generally refers to a clash between public or corporate interest and the private pecuniary interest of an individual or individuals. It arises when an officer or employee's personal or financial interest conflicts or appears to conflict with his official duties.

Any indication that there may be a conflict of interest or that there appears to be a conflict of interest should be reviewed/investigated. This is particularly important if the agency/company does not require employees to sign conflict of interest statements annually, and there is no active prevention program such as a computer cross check of employee phone numbers and addresses with those of contractors and vendors.

Embezzlement

Embezzlement is generally the fraudulent appropriation of property by one lawfully entrusted with its possession. It is the willful taking or conversion to one's own use, another's money or property of which the wrongdoer acquired possession lawfully by reason of some office, or employment, or position of trust.

Any indication that embezzlement has occurred or could be occurring should be investigated. If financial statements, inventory, or other documents appear out of order, no matter how innocuous or nonmaterial, a preliminary review should be made to determine if it is accidental or if a full scale investigation should be conducted. Again, the Certified Fraud Examiner should follow the situation until he is reasonably assured that there is no active fraud taking place.

False Financial Statements

This includes any false statement with regard to a corporation's financial condition. It means something more than merely untrue or erroneous information. It also implies that the statement is decidedly untrue and deceitful, and made with the intention to deceive a person to whom the false statement is made or exhibited.

Any indication that financial statements are not accurate requires further review to determine the reasons for their inaccuracy. While there may be legitimate reasons for the apparent inaccuracies, it is incumbent on the Certified Fraud Examiner to review the situation enough to determine those reasons and document his inquiry.

False Statements

False statements include oral or written statements made knowingly false, or made recklessly without honest belief in their truth, and with the purpose to mislead or deceive.

Any apparent inaccurate statements should be reviewed and the reasons for the inaccuracies documented, including the individuals responsible for the statements and the rationale behind them. If the inaccuracies seem more than minor discrepancies, or the reasons for the discrepancies appear unjustifiable, a full review may be necessary.

Theft

Theft is the taking of personal property belonging to another from his possession, or from the possession of some person holding the same for him without his consent, with the intent to deprive the owner of the value of the same, and appropriating it to the use and benefit of the person taking it.

Larceny

Larceny includes obtaining possession of property by fraud, trick, or device with a preconceived design or intent to appropriate, convert, or steal.

For larceny and theft, if there is any indication or pattern that property is missing, it is important that the Certified Fraud Examiner review the situation to determine if a full-scale investigation is warranted.

Association of Certified Fraud Examiners

CFE Code of Professional Standards

(Adopted by the Board of Regents, February 22, 2001)

[At the Board of Regents meeting in February 2001, the Board officially adopted the following CFE Code of Professional Standards. The standards expand on and provide further guidance for members on the ethical and professional duties listed in the CFE Code of Professional Ethics.

The standards were drafted by the Professional Standards and Practices Committee. The Committee will, in the future, provide additional comments to supplement these standards and will also develop practical scenarios to assist members in the application of the standards.]

I. Preamble

The Association of Certified Fraud Examiners is an association of professionals committed to performing at the highest level of ethical conduct. Members of the Association pledge themselves to act with integrity and to perform their work in a professional manner.

Members have a professional responsibility to their clients, to the public interest and each other; a responsibility that requires subordinating self-interest to the interests of those served.

These standards express basic principles of ethical behavior to guide members in the fulfilling of their duties and obligations. By following these standards, all Certified Fraud Examiners shall be expected, and all Associate members shall strive to demonstrate their commitment to excellence in service and professional conduct.

II. Applicability of Code

The CFE Code of Professional Standards shall apply to all members and all Associate members of the Association of Certified Fraud Examiners. The use of the word "member" or "members" in this Code shall refer to Associate members as well as regular members of the Association of Certified Fraud Examiners.

III. Standards of Professional Conduct

A. Integrity and Objectivity

1. Members shall conduct themselves with integrity, knowing that public trust is founded on integrity. Members shall not sacrifice integrity to serve the client, their employer or the public interest.

2. Prior to accepting the fraud examination, members shall investigate for potential conflicts of interest. Members shall disclose any potential conflicts of interest to prospective clients who retain them or their employer.

3. Members shall maintain objectivity in discharging their professional responsibilities within the scope of the engagement.

4. Members shall not commit discreditable acts, and shall always conduct themselves in the best interests of the reputation of the profession.

5. Members shall not knowingly make a false statement when testifying in a court of law or other dispute resolution forum. Members shall comply with lawful orders of the courts or other dispute resolution bodies. Members shall not commit criminal acts or knowingly induce others to do so.

B. Professional Competence

1. Members shall be competent and shall not accept assignments where this competence is lacking. In some circumstances, it may be possible to meet the requirement for professional competence by use of consultation or referral.

2. Members shall maintain the minimum program of continuing professional education required by the Association of Certified Fraud Examiners. A commitment to professionalism combining education and experience shall continue throughout the member's professional career. Members shall continually strive to increase the competence and effectiveness of their professional services.

C. Due Professional Care

1. Members shall exercise due professional care in the performance of their services. Due professional care requires diligence, critical analysis and professional skepticism in discharging professional responsibilities.

2. Conclusions shall be supported with evidence that is relevant, competent and sufficient.

3. Members' professional services shall be adequately planned. Planning controls the performance of a fraud examination from inception through completion and involves developing strategies and objectives for performing the services.

4. Work performed by assistants on a fraud examination shall be adequately supervised. The extent of supervision required varies depending on the complexities of the work and the qualifications of the assistants.

D. Understanding with Client or Employer

1. At the beginning of a fraud examination, members shall reach an understanding with those retaining them (client or employer) about the scope and limitations of the fraud examination and the responsibilities of all parties involved.

2. Whenever the scope or limitations of a fraud examination or the responsibilities of the parties change significantly, a new understanding shall be reached with the client or employer.

E. Communication with Client or Employer

1. Members shall communicate to those who retained them (client or employer) significant findings made during the normal course of the fraud examination.

F. Confidentiality

1. Members shall not disclose confidential or privileged information obtained during the course of the fraud examination without the express permission of proper authority or order of a court. This requirement does not preclude professional

practice or investigative body reviews as long as the reviewing organization agrees to abide by the confidentiality restrictions.

IV. Standards of Examination

A. Fraud Examinations

1. Fraud examinations shall be conducted in a legal, professional and thorough manner. The fraud examiner's objective shall be to obtain evidence and information that is complete, reliable and relevant.

2. Members shall establish predication and scope priorities at the outset of a fraud examination and continuously reevaluate them as the examination proceeds. Members shall strive for efficiency in their examination.

3. Members shall be alert to the possibility of conjecture, unsubstantiated opinion and bias of witnesses and others. Members shall consider both exculpatory and inculpatory evidence.

B. Evidence

1. Members shall endeavor to establish effective control and management procedures for documents. Members shall be cognizant of the chain of custody including origin, possession and disposition of relevant evidence and material. Members shall strive to preserve the integrity of relevant evidence and material.

2. Members' work product may vary with the circumstances of each fraud examination. The extent of documentation shall be subject to the needs and objectives of the client or employer.

V. Standards of Reporting

A. General

1. Members' reports may be oral or written, including fact witness and/or expert witness testimony, and may take many different forms. There is no single structure

or format that is prescribed for a member's report; however, the report should not be misleading.

B. Report Content

1. Members' reports shall contain only information based on data that are sufficient and relevant to support the facts, conclusions, opinions and/or recommendations related to the fraud examination. The report shall be confined to subject matter, principles and methodologies within the member's area of knowledge, skill, experience, training or education.

2. No opinion shall be expressed regarding the legal guilt or innocence of any person or party.

BIBLIOGRAPHY

Akst, Daniel. *Wonderboy Barry Minkow: The Kid Who Swindled Wall Street*. New York: Scribner's, 1990.

Albrecht, W. Steve. *Fraud Examination*. Mason, Ohio, Thomson South-Western, 2003.

Albrecht, W. Steve, Keith R. Howe, and Marshall B. Romney. *Deterring Fraud: The Internal Auditor's Perspective*. Altamonte Springs: The Institute of Internal Auditors Research Foundation, 1984.

Albrecht, W. Steve, Gerald W. Wernz, and Timothy L. Williams. *Fraud: Bringing Light to the Dark Side of Business*. New York, New York: Irwin Professional Publishing, 1995.

Albrecht, W. Steve, Marshal B. Romney, David J. Cherrington, I. Reed Payne, and Allan J. Roe. *How to Detect and Prevent Business Fraud*. Englewood Cliffs: Prentice-Hall, Inc., 1982.

American Accounting Association. *Accounting Education, Vol. 18, Number 2*. Sarasota, Florida, American Accounting Association, 2003.

American Accounting Association. *Accounting Horizons, Vol. 7, Number 4*. Sarasota, Florida, American Accounting Association, 2003.

American Accounting Association. *Auditing: A Journal of Practice & Theory, Vol. 22, Number 2*. Sarasota, Florida, American Accounting Association, 2003.

American Institute of Certified Public Accountants, Inc. *Accounting Standards, Original Pronouncements*.
— "The Auditor's Responsibility to Detect and Report Errors and Irregularities," SAS No. 53. New York, NY, 1990.
— "Illegal Acts by Clients," SAS No. 54. New York, NY, 1990.
— "Auditing Accounting Estimates," SAS No. 57. New York, NY, 1990.
— "Communication with Audit Committees," SAS No. 61. New York, NY, 1990.
— "Special Reports," SAS No. 62
— "Compliance Auditing Applicable to Governmental Entities and Other Recipients of Governmental Financial Assistance," SAS No. 63.
— "Consideration of Fraud in a Financial Statement Audit," SAS No. 82, 1996.
— "Consideration of Fraud in a Financial Statement Audit," SAS No. 99, 2002.

Androphy, Joel M. *White Collar Crime*. New York: McGraw-Hill, Inc., 1992.

Antle, Rick and Stanley J. Garstka. *Financial Accounting*. Cincinnati, OH: South-Western, 2002.

Arens, Alvin A., Randal J. Elder, and Mark S. Beasley. *Essential Auditing and Assurance Services: An Integrated Approach*. Upper Saddle River, New Jersey, Prentice Hall, 2003.

Arkins, Stanley S.; Barry A. Bohrer; Donald L. Cuneo; John F. Donohue; Jeffrey M. Kaplin; Robert Kasanof; Andrew J. Levander; and Sanford Sherizen. *Prevention and Prosecution of Computer and High Technology Crime*. Matthew Bender, 1988.

Associated Press. "Software Executive Pleads Guilty to Stock Fraud." *USA Today*. January 31, 1997.

Association of Certified Fraud Examiners, The. *2002 Report to the Nation: Occupational Fraud and Abuse*. ACFE, 2002.

Association of Certified Fraud Examiners, The. *2004 Report to the Nation: Occupational Fraud and Abuse*. ACFE, 2004.

Banks, David G. "Vendor Fraud: Finding Deals Gone Awry." *The White Paper*, Vol. 16, No. 5. September/October 2002.

BIBLIOGRAPHY

Barefoot, J. Kirk, CPP. *Employee Theft Investigation*. Stoneham, MA: Butterworth Publishers, 1979.

Beasley, M.S., J.V. Carcello, and D.R. Hermanson. *Fraudulent Financial Reporting: 1987-1997: An Analysis of U.S. Public Companies*. Committee of Sponsoring Organizations (COSO), 1999.

Beckett, Paul. "SEC, Publisher of On-Line Newsletter Settle Fraud Case Involving the Internet." *Wall Street Journal*, February 26, 1997.

Bintliff, Russell L. *White Collar Crime Detection and Prevention*. Englewood Cliffs, New Jersey: Prentice Hall, 1993.

Binstein, Michael and Charles Bowden. *Trust Me: Charles Keating and the Missing Millions*. New York: Random House, 1993.

Biegelman, Martin T. "Designing a Robust Fraud Prevention Program, Part One." *The White Paper*, Vol. 18, No. 1. January/February 2004.

Biegelman, Martin T. "Sarbanes-Oxley Act: Stopping U.S. Corporate Crooks from Cooking the Books." *The White Paper*, Vol. 17, No. 2. March/April 2003.

Bishop, Toby J.F. and Joseph T. Wells, CFE, CPA. "Breaking Tradition in the Auditing Profession." *The White Paper*, Vol. 17, No. 5. September/October 2003.

Black, Henry Campbell. *Black's Law Dictionary, Fifth Edition*. St. Paul, Minnesota: West Publishing Co., 1979.

Black's Law Dictionary. Sixth Edition. St. Paul, MN: West Publishing Co., 1990.

Blankenship, Michael B, ed., *Current Issues in Criminal Justice*. Vol. 3, *Understanding Corporate Criminality*. Garland Publishing, Inc., 1993.

Bliven, Bruce. "The Tempest Over Teapot." *American Heritage*. September-October, 1995.

BloomBecker, Buck. Spectacular Computer Crimes: What They Are and How They Cost American Business Half a Billion Dollars a Year! Homewood, IL: Dow Jones-Irwin, 1990.

Blount, Ernest C. *Occupational Crime: Deterrence, Investigation, and Reporting in Compliance with Federal Guidelines*. Boca Raton: CRC Press, 2003.

BNA/ACCA Compliance Manual: Prevention of Corporate Liability. Washington, D.C.: The Bureau of National Affairs, Inc., 1997.

Bologna, Jack. *Corporate Fraud: The Basics of Prevention and Detection*. Boston: Butterworth-Heinemann, 1984.

Bologna, Jack and Robert J. Lindquist. *Fraud Auditing and Forensic Accounting*. New York: John Wiley & Sons, 1987.

Bologna, Jack. *Handbook on Corporate Fraud*. Boston: Butterworth-Heinemann, 1993.

Bonner, S.E., Z.V. Palmrose, and S.M. Young. "Fraud Type and Auditor Litigation: An Analysis of SEC Accounting and Auditing Enforcement Releases," *The Accounting Review 73*. October, 1998.

Braithwaite, John. "An Exploratory Study of Used Car Fraud," in Paul R. Wilson and John Braithwaite (Eds.), *Two Faces of Deviance*. Brisbane: University of Queensland Press, 1978.

BIBLIOGRAPHY

Brian, Brad D. and Barry F. McNeil. *Internal Corporate Investigations, Second Edition.* Chicago: ABA Publishing, 2003.

Brickner, Daniel R. "SAS 99: Another Implement for the Fraud Examiner's Toolbox." *The White Paper*, Vol. 17, No. 3. May/June 2003.

Brown, William D. *Investigation and Prosecution of Insurance Fraud Prepared for the Federal Bureau of Investigation.* Dallas: Arter & Hadden, 1992.

Buckwalter, Art. *Investigative Methods.* Woburn, MA: Butterworth Publishers, 1984.

Caplan, Gerald M. *ABSCAM Ethics: Moral Issues & Deception in Law Enforcement.* Cambridge, Massachusetts: Ballinger, 1983.

Carozza, Dick. "Accounting Students Must Have Armor of Fraud Examination." *The White Paper*, Vol. 16, No. 1. January/February 2002.

Carr, James G. *1988 Criminal Procedure Handbook.* New York: Clark Boardman Company, Ltd., 1988.

Carroll, John M. *Confidential Information Sources: Public & Private.* Boston: Butterworth Publishers, 1975.

Cash, Lenhart and Defliese, *Montgomery's Auditing.* Eighth Edition. New York: Ronald Press Company, 1957.

Cissell, James C. *Federal Criminal Trials.* Charlottesville, VA: The Michie Company, 1983.

Cissell, James C. *Providing Federal Crimes.* U.S. Department of Justice, United States Attorney, Southern District of Ohio, May 1980.

Clarke, Michael. *Business Crime: Its Nature and Control.* New York: St. Martin's Press, 1990.

Clarkson, Kenneth W., Roger LeRoy Miller, and Gaylord A. Jentz. *West's Business Law: Text & Cases, Third Edition.* St. Paul: West Publishing Company, 1986.

Clinard, Marshall B., and Peter C. Yeager. *Corporate Crime.* New York: Macmillan Publishing Co., Inc., 1980.

Coderre, David G. *Fraud Detection: Using Data Analysis Techniques to Detect Fraud.* Vancouver: Global Audit Publications, 1999.

Coleman, James William. *The Criminal Elite: The Sociology of White Collar Crime.* Second Edition. New York: St. Martin's Press, Inc., 1989.

Comer, Michael J. *Corporate Fraud.* Aldershot: Network Security Management Ltd., 1998.

Comer, Michael J. *Investigating Corporate Fraud.* Aldershot: Gower Publishing Limited, 2003.

Computers at Risk: Safe Computing in the Information Age. National Research Council, Academy Press, 1991.

Comstock, Anthony. *Frauds Exposed; or, How the People are Deceived and Robbed, and Youth Corrupted.* Montclair, NJ: Patterson Smith, 1969.

Cressey, Donald R. *Other People's Money.* Montclair: Patterson Smith, 1953.

Davia, Howard R., Patrick C. Coggins, John C. Wideman, and Joseph T. Kastantin. *Accountant's Guide to Fraud Detection and Control, Second Edition.* New York, John Wiley & Sons, 2000.

BIBLIOGRAPHY

Davis, Robert C., Arthur J. Lurigio, and Wesley G. Skogan, ed. *Victims of Crime, Second Edition.* Thousand Oaks: Sage Publications, 1997.

Dean, Bruce A. "Wrap it Up: Packing Your Case for Prosecution." *The White Paper*, Vol. 16, No. 1. January/February 2002.

Department of the Treasury: Internal Revenue Service. *Financial Investigations: A Financial Approach to Detecting and Resolving Crimes.* Washington: U.S. Government Printing Office, 1993.

Dirks, Raymond L. and Leonard Gross. *The Great Wall Street Scandal.* New York: McGraw-Hill Book Company, 1974.

Domanick, Joe. *Faking It In America: Barry Minkow and the Great ZZZZ BEST Scam.* Chicago: Contemporary Books, 1989.

Drake, John D. *The Effective Interviewer: A Guide for Managers.* New York: AMACOM, 1989.

Early Detection: *Protecting Investors by Keeping Bad Brokers Out.* North American Securities Administrators, Fall 1997 Newsletter.

Edelhertz, Herbert, Project Director. *The Investigation of White-Collar Crime.* Washington, D.C.: U.S. Department of Justice Law Enforcement Assistance Administration., 1977.

Edelhertz, Herbert. *The Nature, Impact and Prosecution of White Collar Crime.* Washington, DC: National Institute of Law Enforcement and Criminal Justice, 1970.

Ekman, Paul. *Telling Lies.* New York: The Berkley Publishing Group, 1986

Elliott, Robert K., and John J. Willingham. *Management Fraud: Detection and Deterrence.* New York: NY, Petrocelli Books, Inc., 1980.

Elmer, Brian C., Richard L. Beizer, Peter J. Romatowski, Michael C. Eberhardt, and Henry S. Ruth. *Fraud in Government Contracts.* Washington, D.C.: Federal Publications, Inc., 1992.

Enforcement Issues Presented by the Internet. International Organization of Securities Commissions, September, 1997.

Entercept Security Technologies. *Attackers and Their Tools: How Entercept Protects Servers.* (www.entercept.com)

Ermann, M. David and Richard J. Lundman. *Corporate Deviance.* New York: Holt, Rhinehart and Winston, 1982.

False Identification: The Problem and Technological Options. Boulder, CO: Paladin Press, 1988.

Federal Bureau of Investigation. *Money Laundering: A Guide for Insurance Companies.* Washington, D.C.: U.S. Department of Justice, 1993.

Federal Deposit Insurance Corporation. 1991. *Insider Transactions.* FIL-43-91; Memorandum to Chief Executive Officer. Washington: April 15, 1991.

Flanagan, Timothy J., and Dennis R. Longmire, eds. *Americans View Crime and Justice. A National Public Opinion Survey* Thousand Oaks: Sage Publications, 1996.

BIBLIOGRAPHY

Flesher, Dale L., Paul J. Miranti and Gary John Previts. "The First Century of the CPA." *Journal of Accountancy*, October 1996.

Fridson, Martin S. *Financial Statement Analysis.* New York: John Wiley & Sons, Inc., 1991.

Fusaro, Peter C. and Ross M. Miller. *What Went Wrong at Enron.* Hoboken: John Wiley & Sons, Inc., 2002.

Gardner, Dale R. "Teapot Dome: Civil Legal Cases that Closed the Scandal." *Journal of the West.* October 1989.

Gaughan, Patrick A. *Measuring Business Interruption Losses and Other Commercial Damages.* Hoboken: John Wiley & Sons, 2004.

Geis, Gilbert, Ph.D. and Ezra Stotland (Eds.). *White Collar Crime: Theory and Research.* Beverly Hills: Sage, 1980.

Geis, Gilbert. *On White-Collar Crime.* Lexington, MA: Lexington Books, 1982.

Geis, Gilbert and Robert F. Meier. *White-Collar Crime: Offenses in Business, Politics, and the Professions.* Revised Edition. New York: The Free Press, A Division of Macmillan Publishing Co., Inc., 1977.

Georgiades, George. *Audit Procedures.* New York: Harcourt Brace Professional Publishing, 1995.

Government Accounting Office. *Guide for Incorporating Internal Control Evaluations Into GAO Work*, March 1987.

Government Accounting Office. *Standards and Policies for Evaluating and Reporting on Controls for Computer-Based Systems.*

Government Accounting Office. *Standards for Internal Controls in the Federal Government*, 1984.

Grau, Joseph J., Ph.D., ed., and Ben Jacobson, Investigative Consultant. *Criminal and Civil Investigation Handbook*, New York: McGraw-Hill Book Company, 1981.

Green, Scott. *Manager's Guide to the Sarbanes-Oxley Act: Improving Internal Controls to Prevent Fraud.* Hoboken, NJ: John Wiley & Sons, Inc., 2004.

Greene, Craig L. "Audit Those Vendors." *The White Paper*, Vol. 17, No. 3. May/June 2003.

Greene, Craig L. "When Employees Count too Much." *The White Paper*, Vol. 16, No. 6. November/December 2002.

Hafner, Katie, and John Markoff. *Cyberpunk: Outlaws and Hackers on the Computer Frontier.* New York: Simon & Shuster, 1991.

Hall, Jerome. *Theft, Law and Society.* 2nd Edition. 1960.

Hancock, William A., ed. *Corporate Counsel's Guide to Legal Audits and Investigations.* Chesterfield, OH: Business Laws, Inc., 1997.

Hawkins, Keith. *Environment and Enforcement: Regulation and the Social Definition of Pollution.* Oxford: Oxford University Press, 1984.

Hayes, Read. *Retail Security and Loss Prevention.* Stoneham, MA: Butterworth-Heinemann, 1991.

Heilbroner, Robert. *In the Name of Profit.* New York: Doubleday, 1973.

Henderson, M. Allen. *Flim Flam Man: How Con Games Work.* Boulder, CO: Paladin Press, 1985.

Hochstedler, Ellen. *Corporations as Criminals.* Beverly Hills: Sage Publications, 1984.

BIBLIOGRAPHY

Hollinger, Richard C. and John P. Clark, *Theft by Employees*. Lexington: Lexingtion Books, 1983.

Hough, Harold. *Satellite Surveillance*. Port Townsend, WA: Loompanics Unlimited, 1991.

Hubbard, Thomas D. and Johnny R. Johnson. *Auditing, 4th Edition*. Houston: Dame Publications, Inc., 1991.

Hylas, R.E. and R.H. Ashton. "Audit Detection of Financial Statement Errors," *The Accounting Review*. Vol. LVII, No. 4.

Inbau, Fred E., John E. Reid, and Joseph P. Buckley. *Criminal Interrogation and Confessions*. Baltimore: Wilkins, 1986.

Inciardi, James A. *Criminal Justice*. 3rd ed. San Diego: Harcourt Brace Jovanovich, 1990.

Ingram, Donna. "Revenue Inflation and Deflation." *The White Paper*, Vol. 16, No. 6. November/December 2002.

Inkeles, Alex. *National Character: A Psycho-Social Perspective*. New Brunswick: Transaction Publishers, 1997.

Institute of Internal Auditors. *Standards for the Professional Practices of Internal Auditing*. Altamonte Springs, 1978.

Investment Fraud and Abuse Travel to Cyberspace. Securities and Exchange Commission, June, 1997.

Jaspan, Norman. *Mind Your Own Business*. Englewood: Prentice-Hall, Inc., 1974.

Kant, Immanuel. *Foundations of the Metaphysics of Morals* (originally published in 1785), translated by Lewis W. Beck, Indianapolis, IN.: The Bobbs-Merrill Company, Inc., 1959.

Kant, Immanuel. *Lectures on Ethics*. New York: Harper & Row, 1963.

Kellogg, Irving. *How to Find Negligence and Misrepresentations in Financial Statements*. Colorado Springs, CO: Shepard's/McGraw-Hill, 1983.

Ketz, J. Edward. *Hidden Financial Risks: Understanding Off-Balance Sheet Accounting*. Hoboken: John Wiley & Sons, 2003.

Kimmel, Paul D., Jerry J. Weygandt, Donald E. Kieso. *Financial Accounting: Tools for Business Decision Making, 3rd Edition*. New York, John Wiley & Sons, 2004.

Koletar, Joseph W. *Fraud Exposed: What You Don't Know Could Cost Your Company Millions*. Hoboken: John Wiley & Sons, 2003.

Kramer, W. Michael. *Investigative Techniques in Complex Financial Crimes*. Washington, D.C.: National Institute on Economic Crime, 1988.

Langsted, Lars B., Peter Garde, and Vagn Greve, *Criminal Law Denmark, 2nd Ed.* Copenhagen: DJOF Publishing, 2004.

Lanza, Richard B. *Proactively Detecting Occupational Fraud Using Computer Audit Reports*. IIA Research Foundation, 2003.

Lundelius Jr., Charles R. *Financial Reporting Fraud: A Practical Guide to Detection and Internal Control*. New York: AICPA, Inc. 2003.

BIBLIOGRAPHY

MacInaugh, Edmond A. *Disguise Techniques: Fool All of the People Some of the Time*. Boulder, CO: Paladin Press, 1984.

Maggin, Donald L. *Bankers, Builders, Knaves, and Thieves: The $300 Million Scam at ESM*. Chicago: Contemporary Books, 1989.

Mancino, Jane. "The Auditor and Fraud." *Journal of Accountancy*. April 1997.

Mann, Kenneth. *Defending White-Collar Crime: A Portrait of Attorneys at Work*. New Haven: Yale University Press, 1985.

Marcella, Albert J., William J. Sampias and James K. Kincaid. *The Hunt for Fraud: Prevention and Detection Techniques*. Altamonte Springs: Institute of Internal Auditors, 1994.

Marshall, David H. and Wayne W. McManus. *Accounting: What the Numbers Mean, Third Edition*. Chicago: Irwin, 1996.

Mautz, R.K., and Hussein A. Sharaf. *The Philosophy of Auditing*. American Accounting Association monograph no. 6, especially Chapter 8, "Independence" and Chapter 9, "Ethical Conduct," Sarasota: American Accounting Association, 1961.

Mee, Charles L. Jr. *The Ohio Gang: The World of Warren G. Harding*. New York: M. Evans and Company, 1981.

Mill, John Stuart. *Utilitarianism*. Indianapolis: The Bobbs-Merrill Company, Inc., 1957.

Miller, Norman C. *The Great Salad Oil Swindle*. Baltimore: Penguin Books, 1965.

Moffit, Donald, ed. *Swindled! Classic Business Frauds of the Seventies*. New York: Dow Jones & Co, 1976.

Moran, William B. *Covert Surveillance & Electronic Penetration*. Port Townsend, WA: Loompanics Unlimited, 1983

Moritz, Scott. "Don't Get Burned by Smiling CEO Candidates." *The White Paper*, Vol. 16, No. 5. September/October 2002.

Mott Graham M. *How to Recognize and Avoid Scams, Swindles, and Rip-Offs*. Littleton, CO: Golden Shadows Press, 1992.

Murphy, T. Gregory. *Asset Forfeiture: Uncovering Assets Laundered Through a Business*. Washington, D.C.: U.S. Department of Justice, Bureau of Justice Assistance, 1992.

Naftalis, Gary P., ed. *White-Collar Crimes*. Philadelphia, PA: American Law Institute - American Bar Association, 1980.

Nash, Jay Robert. *Hustlers & Con Men: An Anecdotal History of the Confidence Man and His Games*. New York: Lippincott, 1976.

National Commission on Fraudulent Financial Reporting, 1987. *Report of the National Commission on Fraudulent Financial Reporting*. New York: American Institute of Certified Public Accountants, October.

Noonan, John T. Jr. *Bribes*. New York: Macmillan Publishing Company, 1984.

O'Brian, Keith. *Cut Your Losses!* Bellingham: International Self-Press Ltd., 1996.

O'Gara, John D. *Corporate Fraud: Case Studies in Detection and Prevention*. Hoboken, NJ: John Wiley & Sons, Inc., 2004.

BIBLIOGRAPHY

Olien, Rover M. And Diana Davids Olien. *Easy Money: Oil Promoters and Investors in the Jazz Age.* Chapel Hill: University of NC Press, 1990.

Patterson, James and Peter Kim. *The Day America Told the Truth.* New York: Prentice Hall Publishing, 1991.

Pizzo, Stephen et al. *Inside Job. The Looting of America's Savings and Loans.* New York: McGraw-Hill, 1991.

Powis, Robert E. *The Money Launderers: Lessons From the Drug Wars X How Billions of Illegal Dollars are Washed Through Banks and Businesses.* Chicago: Probus Publishing Company, 1992.

Poynter, Dan. *The Expert Witness Handbook.* Santa Barbara: Para Publishing, 1997.

Rabon, Don. *Investigative Discourse Analysis.* Durham: Carolina Academic Press, 1994.

Rakoff, Hon. Jed S., Linda R. Blumkin, and Richard A. Sauber. *Corporate Sentencing Guidelines: Compliance and Mitigation.* New York: Law Journal Press, 2002.

Rapp, Burt. *Check Fraud Investigation.* Port Townsend, WA: Loompanics Unlimited, 1991.

Rapp, Burt. *Credit Card Fraud.* Port Townsend, WA: Loompanics Unlimited, 1991.

Ramos, Michael J. *Consideration of Fraud in a Financial Statement Audit: The Auditor's Responsibilities Under New SAS No. 82.* New York: The American Institute of Certified Public Accountants, Inc., 1997.

Ramos, Michael J. *How to Comply with Sarbanes-Oxley Section 404: Assessing the Effectiveness of Internal Control.* Hoboken, NJ: John Wiley & Sons, Inc., 2004.

Reiss, Albert J., Jr. and Albert Biderman. *Data Sources on White-Collar Law-Breaking.* Washington, DC: National Institute of Justice, U.S. Department of Justice, 1980.

Report to the Nation on Occupational Fraud and Abuse. Austin, Texas: Association of Certified Fraud Examiners, 1996.

Rezaee, Zabiollah. *Financial Statement Fraud: Prevention and Detection.* New York: John Wiley & Sons, Inc. 2002.

Robertson, Jack C. *Auditing, Seventh Edition.* Boston: BPI Irwin, 1991.

Robertson, Jack C. *Fraud Examination for Managers and Auditors.* Austin: The Association of Certified Fraud Examiners, 1996.

Romney, Marshall B., W. Steve Albrecht, and D. J. Cherrington. "Red-flagging the White-Collar Criminal," *Management Accounting.* March, 1980.

Sarnoff, Susan K. *Paying For Crime.* Westport: Praeger, 1996.

Seidler, Lee J., Fredrick Andrews, and Marc J. Epstein. *The Equity Funding Papers: the Anatomy of a Fraud.* New York: John Wiley & Sons, 1997.

Scene of the Crime: U.S. Government Forensic Handbook. Boulder, CO: Paladin Press, 1992

Schulte, Fred. *Fleeced!* Amherst: Prometheus Books, 1995.

Sharp, Kathleen. *In Good Faith.* New York: St. Martin's Press, 1995.

Shea, Gordon. *Practical Ethics.* New York: American Management Association, 1988.

BIBLIOGRAPHY

Siegel, Larry J. *Criminology, 4th Edition.* New York: West Publishing Company, 1992.

Sifakis, Carl. *Hoaxes and Scams. A Compendium of Deceptions, Ruses and Swindles.* New York: Facts on File, 1993.

Silverstone, Howard and Michael Sheetz. *Forensic Accounting and Fraud Investigation for Non-Experts.* Hoboken, John Wiley & Sons, 2004.

Singer, Marcus G. *Generalization in Ethics.* New York: Atheneum, 1971

Skinner, B.F. *Science and Human Behavior.* . New York: Macmillan Publishing Co., 1953.

Snyder, Neil H., O. Whitfield, William J. Kehoe, James T. McIntyre, Jr., and Karen E. Blair. *Reducing Employee Theft: A Guide to Financial and Organizational Controls.* New York: Quorum Books, 1991.

Somers, Leigh Edward. *Economic Crimes: Investigative Principles and Techniques.* New York: Clark Boardman Company, Ltd., 1984.

Sophos: Anti-Virus for Business. *An Introduction to Computer Viruses.* (www.sophos.com)

Stone, Christopher. *Where the Law Ends: The Social Control of Corporate Behavior.* New York: Harper & Row, 1975.

Summerford, Ralph Q. and Robin E. Taylor. "Avoiding Embezzlement Embarrassment (and Worse)." *The White Paper*, Vol. 17, No. 6. November/December 2003.

Sutherland, Edwin H. *White-Collar Crime.* New York: Dryden Press, 1949.

Suthers, John W. And Gary L. Shupp. *Fraud & Deceit: How to Stop Being Ripped Off.* New York: Arco, 1982.

The Annals of the American Academy of Political and Social Science. *White-Collar Crime.* Vol. 525. Newbury Park, CA: Sage Periodicals Press, January 1993.

Thomas, William C. "The Rise and Fall of Enron." *Journal of Accountancy.* April 2002.

Thornhill, William T. Forensic Accounting: How to Investigate Financial Fraud. Burr Ridge, IL: Irwin Professional Publishing, 1995.

Titus, Harold T., and Morris Keeton, *Ethics for Today.* 4th ed., New York: America Book Stratford Press, Inc., 1966.

Tyler, Tom R. *Why People Obey the Law.* New Haven: Yale University Press, 1990.

United States General Accounting Office. *Government Auditing Standards.* rev. ed. Washington, D.C.: U.S. Government Printing Office, July, 1988.

United States General Accounting Office. *Financial Statement Restatements: Trends, Market Impacts, Regulatory Responses, and Remaining Challenges.* GAO-03-138, 2002.

Van Drunen, Guido. "Traveling the World in Style on the Company's Nickel." *The White Paper*, Vol. 16, No. 1. January/February 2002.

Vaughan, Diane. *Controlling Unlawful Organizational Behavior.* Chicago: The University of Chicago Press, 1983.

Vaughan, Diane. "Transaction Systems and Unlawful Organizational Behavior." *Social Problems*, 29:373-380.

BIBLIOGRAPHY

Vaughan, Diane. *The Challenger Launch Decision: Risky Technology, Culture, and Deviance at NASA.* Chicago: University of Chicago Press, 1996.

Villa, John K. *Banking Crimes: Fraud, Money Laundering, and Embezzlement.* Deerfield, Ill.: Clark, Boardman, Callaghan, 1991.

Walsh, Timothy J., CPP, and Richard J. Healy, CPP. *Protection of Assets Manual.* Santa Monica, CA: The Merrit Company, 1984.

Watson, Douglas M. "Whom Do You trust? Doing Business and Deterring Fraud in a Global e-Marketplace." *The White Paper*, Vol. 16, No. 2. March/April 2002.

Weisburd, David, et al. *Crimes of the Middle Classes. White-Collar Offenders in the Federal Courts.* New Haven: Yale UP, 1991.

Weisburd, David, Stanton Wheeler, Elin Waring, and Nancy Bode., *Crimes of the Middle Classes: White-Collar Offenders in the Federal Courts* New Haven: Yale University Press, 1991.

Wells, Joseph T. CFE, CPA. *Corporate Fraud Handbook.* Hoboken, NJ: John Wiley & Sons, 2004.

Wells, Joseph T., CFE, CPA. *The Encyclopedia of Fraud.* Austin, Texas: Obsidian Publishing Company, Inc.; 2002.

Wells, Joseph T., CFE, CPA. *Fraud Examination: Investigative and Audit Procedures.* New York: Quorum Books, 1992.

Wells, Joseph T., CFE, CPA. *Occupational Fraud and Abuse.* Austin, Texas: Obsidian Publishing Company, Inc, 1997.

Wells, Joseph T., CFE, CPA., Tedd A. Avey, BComm, CA, G. Jack Bologna, JD, CFE, BBA, and Robert J. Lindquist, CFE, FCA. *The Accountant's Handbook of Fraud and Commercial Crime.* Toronto: Canadian Institute of Chartered Accountants, 1992.

Wells, Joseph T., CFE, CPA. "A Fish Story — Or Not?" *Journal of Accountancy.* November, 2001.

Wells, Joseph T., CFE, CPA. "...And Nothing but the Truth: Uncovering Fraudulent Disclosures." *Journal of Accountancy.* July, 2001.

Wells, Joseph T., CFE, CPA. "...And One for Me." *Journal of Accountancy.* January, 2002.

Wells, Joseph T., CFE, CPA. "Accountancy and White-Collar Crime." *The Annals of the American Academy of Political and Social Science.* January 1993.

Wells, Joseph T., CFE, CPA. "Billing Schemes, Part 1: Shell Companies that Don't Deliver." *Journal of Accountancy.* July, 2002

Wells, Joseph T., CFE, CPA. "Billing Schemes, Part 2: Pass-Throughs." *Journal of Accountancy.* August, 2002.

Wells, Joseph T., CFE, CPA. "Billing Schemes, Part 3: Pay-and-Return Invoicing." *Journal of Accountancy.* September, 2002.

Wells, Joseph T., CFE, CPA. "Billing Schemes, Part 4: Personal Purchases." *Journal of Accountancy.* October, 2002.

Wells, Joseph T., CFE, CPA. "The Billion Dollar Paper Clip." *Internal Auditor.* October 1994.

BIBLIOGRAPHY

Wells, Joseph T., CFE, CPA. "Collaring Crime at Work." *Certified Accountant*. August 1996.

Wells, Joseph T., CFE, CPA. "Control Cash-Register Thievery." *Journal of Accountancy*. June, 2002.

Wells, Joseph T., CFE, CPA. "Corruption: Causes and Cures." *Journal of Accountancy*. April, 2003.

Wells, Joseph T., CFE, CPA. "Enemies Within." *Journal of Accountancy*. December, 2001.

Wells, Joseph T., CFE, CPA. "Follow Fraud to the Likely Perp." *Journal of Accountancy*. March, 2001.

Wells, Joseph T., CFE, CPA. "Fraud Assessment Questioning." *Internal Auditor*. August 1992.

Wells, Joseph T., CFE, CPA. "The Fraud Examiners." *Journal of Accountancy*. October, 2003.

Wells, Joseph T., CFE, CPA. "Follow the Greenback Road." *Journal of Accountancy*. November, 2003.

Wells, Joseph T., CFE, CPA. "Getting a Handle on a Hostile Interview." *Security Management*. July 1992.

Wells, Joseph T., CFE, CPA. "Ghost Goods: How to Spot Phantom Inventory," *Journal of Accountancy*. June, 2001.

Wells, Joseph T., CFE, CPA. "...Irrational Ratios." *Journal of Accountancy*. August, 2001.

Wells, Joseph T., CFE, CPA. "Keep Ghosts Off the Payroll." *Journal of Accountancy*. December, 2002.

Wells, Joseph T., CFE, CPA. "Lambs to Slaughter." *Internal Auditor*. June 2003.

Wells, Joseph T., CFE, CPA. "Lapping it Up." *Journal of Accountancy*. February, 2002.

Wells, Joseph T., CFE, CPA. "Let Them Know Someone's Watching," *Journal of Accountancy*. May, 2002.

Wells, Joseph T., CFE, CPA. "Money Laundering: Ring Around the Collar." *Journal of Accountancy*. June, 2003.

Wells, Joseph T., CFE, CPA. "Occupational Fraud: The Audit as Deterrent." *Journal of Accountancy*. April, 2002.

Wells, Joseph T., CFE, CPA. "The Padding that Hurts." *Journal of Accountancy*. February, 2003.

Wells, Joseph T., CFE, CPA. "Protect Small Business." *Journal of Accountancy*. March, 2003.

Wells, Joseph T., CFE, CPA. "The Rewards of Dishonesty." *The White Paper*, Vol. 17, No. 2. March/April 2003.

Wells, Joseph T., CFE, CPA. "Rules for the Written Record." *Journal of Accountancy*. December, 2003.

Wells, Joseph T., CFE, CPA. "Sherlock Holmes, CPA, Part 1." *Journal of Accountancy*. August, 2003.

Wells, Joseph T., CFE, CPA. "Sherlock Holmes, CPA, Part 2." *Journal of Accountancy*. September, 2003.

Wells, Joseph T., CFE, CPA. "Six Common Myths About Fraud." *Journal of Accountancy*. February 1990.

Wells, Joseph T., CFE, CPA. "So, You Want to be a Fraud Examiner." *Accounting Today*. December 16, 2002.

Wells, Joseph T., CFE, CPA. "Sons of Enron." *MWorld*, Volume 2, No. 1. Spring 2003.

Wells, Joseph T., CFE, CPA. "Ten Steps Into a Top-Notch Interview." *Journal of Accountancy*. November, 2002.

BIBLIOGRAPHY

Wells, Joseph T., CFE, CPA. "Timing is of the Essence." *Journal of Accountancy.* May, 2001.

Wells, Joseph T., CFE, CPA. "Why Ask? You Ask." *Journal of Accountancy.* September, 2001.

Wells, Joseph T., CFE, CPA. "Why Employees Commit Fraud." *Journal of Accountancy.* February, 2001.

Wells, Joseph T., CFE, CPA. "The World's Dumbest Fraudsters." *Journal of Accountancy.* May, 2003.

Welsch, Glenn A., D. Paul Newman, and Charles T. Zlatkovich. *Intermediate Accounting, Seventh Edition.* Homewood: Irwin, 1986.

Weston, Paul B., Kenneth M. Wells. *Criminal Investigation: Basic Perspectives*, 6th Ed. Englewood Cliffs, NJ: Prentice Hall, 1994.

Wheelwright, Phillip, *A Critical Introduction to Ethics*, 3rd ed., Indianapolis, IN.: Odyssey Press, 1959.

Whitlock, Charles R. *Easy Money.* New York: Kensington Books, 1994.

Wojcik, Lawrence A. "Sensational Cases and the Mundane—Lessons to be Learned." *The First Annual Conference on Fraud.* The American Institute of Certified Public Accountants, 1996.

Wold, Geoffrey H. and Robert F. Shriver. *Computer Crime: Techniques for Preventing and Detecting Crime in Financial Institutions.* Rolling Meadows, IL: Bankers Publishing Company, 1989.

Wolfgang, Marvin E., Robert Figlio, Paul Tracy, and Simon Singer. *The National Survey of Crime Severity.* Washington, DC: U.S. Government Printing Office, 1985.

Yeager, Peter. "Industrial Water Pollution," in Michael Tonry and Albert J. Reiss, Jr., eds., *Beyond the Law: Crime in Complex Organizations.* Chicago: University of Chicago Press, 1993.

Yount, Johnny. *Vanish: Disappearing through ID Acquisition.* Boulder, CO: Paladin Press, 1986.

Zack, Gerard M. *Fraud and Abuse in Nonprofit Organizations: A Guide to Prevention and Detection.* Hoboken, John Wiley & Sons, 2003.

Zalma, Barry. *Insurance Fraud and Weapons to Fight Fraud in California.* Culver City, CA: ClaimSchool, Inc., 1993